Selecting
Effective
Treatments

Includes *DSM-5*™ Chapter Update

Selecting Effective Treatments

A Comprehensive Systematic Guide to Treating Mental Disorders

Fourth Edition

LINDA SELIGMAN
LOURIE W. REICHENBERG

WILEY

For general information about our other products and services, please contact our Customer Care Department within the United States at (800) 762-2974, outside the United States at (317) 572-3993 or fax (317) 572-4002.

Wiley publishes in a variety of print and electronic formats and by print-on-demand. Some material included with standard print versions of this book may not be included in e-books or in print-on-demand. If this book refers to media such as a CD or DVD that is not included in the version you purchased, you may download this material at http://booksupport .wiley.com. For more information about Wiley products, visit www.wiley.com.

Library of Congress Cataloging-in-Publication Data:
Seligman, Linda.
Selecting Effective Treatments: A Comprehensive Systematic Guide to Treating Mental Disorders, Includes *DSM-5* Update Chapter/Linda Seligman and Lourie W. Reichenberg.—Fourth edition, DSM-5 update.
    p. ; cm.
  Includes bibliographical references and indexes.
  ISBN: 978-1-118-73801-6 (pbk.); ISBN: 978-1-118-73796-5 (ebk); ISBN: 978-1-118-73805-4 (ebk)
 I. Reichenberg, Lourie W., 1956- author. II. Title.
  [DNLM: 1. Diagnostic and statistical manual of mental disorders. 5th ed. 2. Mental Disorders–therapy.
3. Mental Disorders–classification. 4. Planning Techniques. 5. Treatment Outcome. WM 400]
  RC480
  616.89'14–dc23

                                           2013034129

Printed in the United States of America

10 9 8 7 6 5 4 3 2 1

This book is dedicated to Linda Seligman

Contents

Preface to the *DSM-5* Update Edition

A special welcome to professionals and students who are new to the *Selecting Effective Treatments* family. You will find within these pages a wealth of information that brings to life the diagnoses found in the new *DSM-5*, while at the same time cultivating a systematic, research-based approach to the assessment and treatment of mental disorders.

Returning readers will find a continuity within this text revision that allows them to pick up where the Fourth Edition left off. Great care has been taken to ensure that the new material remains true to the previous edition of *Selecting Effective Treatments* so that readers can seamlessly find the information they need in a format consistent with what they have come to expect.

Exclusive to this *DSM-5* Update Edition is a completely new chapter, Chapter 11. This new material bridges the gap between *DSM-IV* and *DSM-5*, which was published in May 2013. Criteria for new disorders are included—

hoarding, disruptive mood dysregulation disorder, and binge eating disorder, among others. The new spectrum approach to autism, schizophrenia, and other related disorders is discussed. Also included are two proposed disorders for further study—nonsuicidal self-injury (NSSI) and suicidal behavior disorder—to help practitioners assess and treat these emerging, and potentially life-threatening, disorders.

Welcome to all readers. It is my hope that you will find within these pages the information you need to conduct comprehensive assessments and create effective treatment plans for your clients. It has been my goal to streamline the process for you, to make diagnosis based on the new *DSM-5* more straightforward and understandable, and to provide you with a clinical tool you can rely on for years to come.

Lourie W. Reichenberg, MA, LPC
Falls Church, Virginia

Preface

Psychotherapy *is* effective in the treatment of mental disorders, and, in many cases, it is more effective than medication. The question now becomes which approaches to psychotherapy are effective in treating which mental disorders, under what conditions, and with which clients?

With the growing number of books published on the topic of evidence-based practice, it becomes increasingly difficult to keep abreast of the latest research. Many books have been published that focus on one particular disorder, espouse one preferred mode of treatment, or offer a compendium of articles by different authors, but few volumes have presented a systematic, research-based approach to the treatment of mental disorders.

As a result, approaches to treatment are often haphazard, with clinicians relying on familiar or comfortable models rather than on treatments that have demonstrated the greatest effectiveness. This may have been acceptable in the early years of psychotherapy, but with increasing focus on outcomes and evidence-based practice, clinicians must be able to defend their treatment choices—to an increasingly health-conscious consumer and to the managed care organizations (MCOs) that provide third-party reimbursements.

Selecting Effective Treatments, Fourth Edition, does not advocate for one particular theoretical model, nor does it restrict clinicians to a narrow range of approaches. Research does not support such a circumscribed view of therapy, and such an approach would not promote the optimal use of each therapist's special talents. Rather, this book seeks to increase clinicians' understanding of the symptoms and dynamics of mental disorders and to provide a range of treatment options for each disorder, allowing clinicians to blend their own therapeutic strengths and preferences with those approaches that have demonstrated effectiveness. Some information has been provided about the usefulness of medication for the various mental disorders; this information is included primarily to help clinicians determine when a referral for medication is in order and to assist them in anticipating the impact that medication is likely to have on their clients.

Selecting Effective Treatments should also help readers understand the impact of the clinician on treatment effectiveness. New outcomes research on the traits and characteristics of the therapist indicate that what the therapist does in session has more impact on treatment outcomes than the choice of therapeutic modality. As some have said, the therapeutic relationship is an evidence-based practice.

This book will help clinicians to select interventions that are likely to be effective, and explain their choice of treatment approach to their clients, to their supervisors and colleagues, and to the MCOs. This, in turn, should make it more likely that their clients will receive the type of counseling and psychotherapy they need.

Selecting Effective Treatments, Fourth Edition, is not a step-by-step treatment manual of how to provide therapy. It is a concise, reader-friendly synthesis of the latest empirical research, and it provides the background and information - clinicians need to be able to develop their own treatment plans for their clients that are evidence based, practical, and effective.

AUDIENCE

Most of the existing books on diagnosis and treatment of mental disorders have been written from a medical perspective, but most treatment of mental disorders is provided by psychologists, counselors, social workers, addictions counselors, and psychiatric nurses. Therefore, this book fills a gap in the literature by focusing on the needs of these nonmedical mental health practitioners and by recognizing the increasingly important part they play in treating mental disorders. This book is addressed to the students, interns, and practitioners in these fields who have a basic understanding of approaches to counseling and psychotherapy, and who need to know, without consulting multiple texts, what types of treatments work best for specific types of clients.

Clinicians, researchers, and educators in the mental health fields should all be able to use this book in their work. Clinicians, in particular, who read the book can expect to gain a deeper understanding of the complexities of diagnosis, as well as of the latest edition of the *Diagnostic and Statistical Manual of Mental Disorders (DMS-IV-TR)*. In addition, clinicians will be able to develop sound treatment plans and will gain greater confidence

and credibility, which should help them to be more effective in their practices.

ENHANCEMENTS TO THE *FOURTH EDITION*

Mental health professionals have a better understanding of the etiology, presentation, risk factors, prevalence, effective treatments, and prognosis for the major mental disorders. That knowledge continues to evolve to reflect the changing world in which we live. Hurricane Katrina, the tsunami in Japan, and other natural disasters, along with the events of September 11 and the wars in Iraq and Afghanistan, have provided us with new insights into the effects of trauma on adults and children. The evolution of the Internet and the explosion of social media, PDAs, and virtual reality have allowed the creation of innovative new delivery methods for psychotherapy. They have also raised ethical concerns that need to be addressed.

All sections of this book have been revised to reflect current information. Chapter revisions are particularly extensive in those areas where our knowledge has grown the most. The sections on diagnosis and treatment of childhood trauma, depression, bipolar disorders, borderline personality disorder, and the schizophrenia spectrum disorders have been expanded. In response to the recent wealth of research on the effect of the therapeutic alliance on treatment outcomes, the *Fourth Edition* includes an expansion of the preferred therapist characteristics section for each disorder.

Many enhancements have been made to the *Fourth Edition*, including expanded information on the spectrum concept of mental disorders in terms of autism spectrum disorders and schizophrenia. Information is expanded on exposure and response prevention, virtual reality, and EMDR for the treatment of adults and children with PTSD and other trauma-related disorders. Exciting new approaches to treatment included in this edition are transdiagnostic or unified approaches, mindfulness-based treatments, and several new interventions that are just beginning to show promise for their effectiveness in the treatment of specific mental disorders.

Also new to the *Fourth Edition* is an Appendix on suicide warning signs and risk factors. Suicide is associated with many of the disorders included in this book, and is a leading cause of death worldwide, especially for young adults, women in mid-life, and the elderly. Practitioners need to know the warning signs and risk factors to be able to assess and intervene effectively.

The goal of this Fourth Edition of *Selecting Effective Treatments* is to cite the most up-to-date and empirically based treatments for mental disorders while maintaining the format and integrity of previous editions.

ORGANIZATION

Chapter 1 provides information about diagnosis and treatment of mental disorders, new research on the importance of the therapeutic alliance, and introduces the "Do a Client Map" format that will be used throughout the book. The Client Map is a comprehensive model of treatment planning developed by Linda Seligman, which can be adapted to any diagnosis. This format has been retained from previous editions of this book and offers an effective, efficient, and easily adapted approach to diagnosis and treatment. The Client Map will be discussed in further detail in Chapter 1.

In Chapters 2 through 9, the mental disorders have been grouped into eight broad categories. Within each of these chapters, the material on each disorder generally has been organized into six sections:

1. Description of the disorder (including *DSM-IV-TR* criteria)
2. Typical client characteristics (symptoms, behaviors, characteristics, co-occurring disorders) that typify people with that disorder
3. Assessment tools available
4. Preferred therapist characteristics (empathy, directiveness, and other qualities of style and personality that typify clinicians likely to be successful in treating that particular disorder)
5. Research on effective treatment interventions
6. Prognosis

Each chapter begins with a case study and ends with a Client Map to facilitate treatment planning.

Chapter 10 identifies and discusses emerging trends in the ever-evolving fields of diagnosis and treatment of mental disorders.

ACKNOWLEDGMENTS

The most challenging part of writing this book was the loss of my colleague, co-author, and friend Linda Seligman. More than 20 years ago, Linda developed the DO A CLIENT MAP strategy to help her students with case conceptualization. She wrote the first and second editions of *Selecting Effective Treatments*, to consolidate the knowledge base of effective treatments into one concise book for nonmedical mental health practitioners.

When the opportunity to write the third edition of *Selecting Effective Treatments* presented itself, she asked if I would be interested in making the revisions. I was glad to have the chance to work with Linda. She was by then a well-respected professor, author, and lecturer around the world. This *Fourth Edition* is dedicated to Linda, for her commitment to education and research, to students and clients, and for the legacy she has left to the field of clinical psychology.

Of course, no project of this size could be accomplished without the help and support of others. I am deeply grateful to Rachel Livsey, senior editor at John Wiley & Sons, for her astute editorial direction and for shepherding this edition through the editorial process; and to Kate Lindsay at Wiley, who is truly an editor's editor; to my husband Neil, whose patience and forbearance make the writing of this, and other books, possible; and to the next generation—my grandchildren Izaak, Jaycee, and Orion. Their curiosity inspires me, their ability to live in the moment grounds me, and their innocence gives me hope for the future.

Lourie W. Reichenberg, MA, LPC

Introduction to Effective Treatment Planning

A usually quiet and withdrawn young woman became verbally abusive to her supervisor and warned him that if she were not promoted to a job commensurate with her outstanding abilities, she was going to "come back with a gun." A few weeks earlier, she had had a brief consultation with a psychiatrist, who diagnosed her as having a major depressive disorder and prescribed antidepressant medication.

A man who had been a capable and hardworking accountant was referred to an employee assistance counselor because of a sudden and extreme decline in his performance. After some brief and unsuccessful efforts were made to remotivate the man, he was fired from his job.

A woman had been treated with years of unsuccessful psychoanalysis, during which she had been told that her difficulty in concentration and her chaotic lifestyle reflected her efforts to avoid dealing with her early losses.

THE IMPORTANCE OF SYSTEMATIC AND EFFECTIVE TREATMENT PLANNING

Poor clinical understanding, inaccurate diagnosis, and inappropriate treatment contributed to all of the situations just described. The first woman had a history of both manic and depressive episodes; in fact, she had a bipolar disorder, and the antidepressant medication she was given contributed to the development of another manic episode. The man was suffering from a cognitive disorder resulting from a head injury incurred in a cycling accident. The second woman had attention-deficit/hyperactivity disorder and eventually responded well to a combination of behavior therapy and medication. These examples, based on actual clients, make clear the importance of accurate diagnosis and treatment planning.

The primary goal of diagnosis and treatment planning is to help psychotherapists from all disciplines—psychologists, counselors, social workers, psychiatrists, and psychiatric nurses—make sound therapeutic decisions so that they can help their clients ameliorate their difficulties, feel better about themselves and their lives, and achieve their goals.

A need for accountability as well as for treatment effectiveness mandates systematic treatment planning. As health-care costs have risen, the growth and impact of managed care have escalated, and third-party payers increasingly require mental health professionals to describe and justify their treatment plans. Case managers, who are usually mental health practitioners themselves, review treatment plans and determine whether they are appropriate. Clearly, the therapist's knowledge of treatment planning is an essential element of people's ability to receive the psychotherapy they need.

Requests for accountability also come from mental health agencies and clinics; from counseling centers at schools, hospitals, and residential facilities where therapy is done; and from funding agencies. Financial support is rarely adequate for mental health services in these settings, and therapists often must provide documentation of the services' effectiveness before they can obtain continued funding.

Unfortunately, treatment planning is sometimes viewed as a process that must be carried out for no better reason than to satisfy bureaucratic requirements. On the contrary, the fundamental reason for treatment planning is to facilitate effective delivery of mental health services. The purpose of this book, as the Preface has outlined, is to provide the most up-to-date information available on differential therapeutics—that is, the study of which treatment approaches are most likely to be effective in treating each of the mental disorders. This book seeks to facilitate the process of treatment planning by linking knowledge about treatments to information about diagnoses, usually made according to the guidelines in the *Diagnostic and Statistical Manual of Mental Disorders*, now in its fourth edition text revision, known as the *DSM-IV-TR* (American Psychiatric Association, 2000).

This book is not designed to present a rigid formula for treatment planning; the state of the art does not allow that, and, even if it were possible, it probably would not be desirable. Therapeutic effectiveness depends not only on the application of well-supported methods of intervention but also on such indefinable and complex ingredients as the therapist's style, the expertise and training of the therapist, the personalities of therapist and client, their demographic characteristics, and the alliance between the two of them. Therefore, this book presents information not just on the mental disorders and their appropriate treatment but also on the probable nature of the people suffering from each disorder, those characteristics of the therapist that are likely to contribute to effective treatment, and the prognosis for the treatment of each disorder.

In therapy, many roads can be taken to the same goal. This book seeks to point out which roads are likely to be smooth and rewarding and which are full of ruts and barriers. Plotting the actual course is up to the therapist and the client. Systematic treatment planning allows the clinician to map the therapeutic journey, revise the route as necessary, and repeat the trip with others if it turns out to be worthwhile, all without compromising the spontaneity of the traveler or the guide.

RESEARCH ON THE EFFECTIVENESS OF PSYCHOTHERAPY

The overall effectiveness of psychotherapy has long been established. As the meta-analytic review by Smith, Glass, and Miller (1980) concluded, "The average person who received therapy is better off at the end of it than 80% of those who do not" (p. 87). Lambert and Cattani-Thompson (1996) sum up the research by stating,

The research literature clearly shows that counseling is effective in relation to no-treatment and placebo conditions. The effects of counseling seem to be relatively lasting. These effects are attained in relatively brief time periods, with the percentage of clients who show substantial improvement increasing as the number of counseling sessions increases. (p. 601)

So the overall verdict on the outcome of psychotherapy is positive: For most people, therapy is more effective at ameliorating emotional disorders than is no treatment at all. These conclusions do not pertain only to the treatment of adults; effective intervention and prevention programs for children and adolescents have been documented as well (American Psychological Association Task Force on Evidence-Based Practice for Children and Adolescents, 2008).

As we learn more about the treatments that work particularly well with certain disorders, the next challenge is to disseminate that information to clinicians and the public, and to train therapists in effective techniques. In 1995, early in the movement toward evidence-based practice, the American Psychological Association identified 18 treatments shown to be empirically supported through randomized controlled trials for use with specific disorders—cognitive-behavioral therapy for bulimia, exposure therapy for specific phobia, and exposure and response prevention for obsessive-compulsive disorder (OCD), to name just a few. Since that time, publication of evidence-based interventions and therapies have been the focus of hundreds of articles and numerous books (Courtois & Ford, 2009; Huey & Polo, 2008; Kazdin, 2008; Magnavita, 2010; Norcross, Hogan, & Koocher, 2008). But the literature reminds us that clinical efficacy and clinical effectiveness are two different things. The efficacy of therapy relates to the results shown in the setting of a research trial, whereas clinical effectiveness is the outcome of the therapy in routine practice.

Comparative research is needed, and should explore both the relative advantages and disadvantages of alternative treatment strategies for people with different disorders and the therapeutically relevant qualities of the client, the therapist, and their interaction. Study of the therapeutic process contains many challenges, however, and even the best-defined therapy is difficult to reproduce because of its interactive nature. Other challenges inherent in the process of conducting research on therapy's effectiveness include the large number of client-related variables, variations in therapists' expertise, variations in the severity of disorders, participant and observer bias, the questionable ethics of establishing true control and placebo groups with people who have emotional disorders, and the difficulty of assessing how much progress has been made.

DETERMINANTS OF TREATMENT OUTCOME

Psychotherapy outcome is determined primarily by four clusters of variables:

1. Therapist-related variables, including the ability to inspire trust and hope; the facility for communicating empathy, caring, and positive regard; cultural competence, including spiritual and religious competency; and factors such as personality, age, gender, and ethnicity (Bachelor & Horvath, 2010; Barber et al., 2000; Diener, Hilsenroth, & Weinberger, 2007; Norcross & Wampold, 2011; Wampold & Brown, 2005). Therapist ability to form and maintain an alliance over the course of therapy has a particularly strong relationship to better therapeutic outcomes (Hersoug, Hoglend, Havik, von der Lippe, & Monsen, 2009; Muran & Barber, 2010; Norcross & Wampold, 2011).

2. Client-related variables, including demographic factors, diagnosis and symptoms, motivation for and expectations of treatment, history, support systems, ability to form relationships and collaborate with the therapist, personality, and the natural course of the client's disorder (Bohart & Tallman, 1999).

3. The therapeutic alliance, including the ability of the therapist and the client to agree on goals and treatment

procedures, the match between therapist- and client-related variables, and their collaboration and interaction (Greenberg & Watson, 2000; Norcross, 2011; Schnyder, 2009).

4. Treatment variables, including the theories that guide the treatment, the strategies used, medication, the treatment setting and context, the frequency and duration of treatment, and such adjuncts to treatment as self-help groups (Nathan & Gorman, 2007).

Maximization of the therapy's effectiveness should take account of all four clusters of variables.

This chapter presents an integrated model for treatment planning that will help therapists think systematically about that process and explore the factors to be considered in structuring treatment. These factors include, among others, the modality of treatment (group, individual, or family), the theoretical framework for treatment, the frequency and duration of treatment, and the treatment setting. This chapter goes on to summarize the available research on the first three clusters of variables related to outcome (therapist-related variables, client-related variables, and the therapeutic alliance).

The chapters that follow focus primarily on the fourth cluster of variables (treatment variables), to help therapists deepen their understanding of the mental disorders discussed in the *DSM-IV-TR* and their effective treatment. Because this book is designed to help clinicians move beyond the assumption that therapy is effective and on to an understanding of what works for whom, the large and growing body of literature on that subject is reviewed here. Some of the conclusions drawn from the literature are tentative, but they should provide a basis for future research into treatment planning, as well as for the development of effective treatment plans.

AN INTEGRATED MODEL FOR TREATMENT PLANNING

The integrated model presented here in skeleton form lists the five major elements (items I through V) that structure the information in the following eight chapters. When clinicians assess particular clients or disorders, they often do not have information about all the categories and subcategories in this outline, but effective use of the model does not depend on complete information. Indeed, gaps in the therapist's knowledge, as well as in the information available on a client, can actually be used to guide the development of a treatment plan and to indicate areas needing further research or investigation.

I. *Description of the Disorder.*
   A. *Diagnosis.* The *Diagnostic and Statistical Manual of Mental Disorders (DSM-IV-TR;* American Psychiatric Association, 2000) is the accepted system for classifying mental disorders in the United States, as well as in many other countries. Other diagnostic manuals are available, including the *Psychodynamic Diagnostic Manual* (PDM Task Force, 2006) and the *ICD-10 Classification of Mental and Behavioural Disorders* (World Health Organization, 2005). However, they have not attained widespread use and acceptance in the United States. [The American Psychiatric Association is in the process of revision and publication of the fifth edition of the *DSM. DSM-5,* as it will be titled, will conclude a decade-long process of research, assessment, writing, and editing. It is expected to be released in 2013; until that time, the *DSM-IV-TR* will continue as the standard used throughout this book.]

B. *Epidemiology*. Epidemiology includes both the incidence (number of new cases) and the prevalence (number of existing cases at a given time) of a disorder. Acute disorders tend to have a higher incidence; chronic disorders, a higher prevalence. Approximately 46.4% of Americans will have some type of mental disorder during their lifetimes (Kessler, Berglund, et al., 2005). In general, the more common the disorder and the better established the diagnosis, the more is known about its treatment, because of the greater opportunity for research on the disorder.

C. *Primary and secondary symptoms*. A mental disorder typically includes a cluster of symptoms, both primary and secondary (or underlying). The primary symptoms are those that must be present to meet the criteria for diagnosis according to the *DSM-IV-TR*, the major source of information on symptoms of mental disorders. Comparison of a disorder's criteria with a person's presenting symptoms is important in individualizing a treatment plan so that it meets the needs of that particular person. For example, two people may both be diagnosed with major depressive disorders. However, if one is suicidal and presents a danger to the self, whereas the other complains primarily of guilt and pr ... lems in eating, sleer... concentration, their ... will differ. Treat ... person will emp' ... second, cogniti' ... the guilt, and r ... to treat the ...

related to sleeping and eating may be the most important interventions.

D. *Typical onset, course, and duration of the disorder*. This information can be useful to clients as well as to the clinician who is engaged in treatment planning. Disorders vary widely in terms of their course. For example, some disorders, such as schizophrenia, are often chronic and need extended follow-up; others, such as major depressive disorder, tend to run a circumscribed course but frequently recur.

II. *Typical Client Characteristics*. The purpose of this section is to provide typical profiles of people with particular mental disorders. These profiles can facilitate diagnostic interviewing, alerting clinicians to client patterns that are likely to be present. By comparing these profiles with information gathered on individual clients, therapists can also identify areas that need exploration and can gain insight into clients' readiness for treatment, types of treatment that are most likely to be effective, adjunct and referral sources that may be useful, and pr... ... to ... ses. The following client c'... ...sing factors. among others, are ty'... ...ogies of men- treatment. ...assed. Many dis-
A. Gene'... ...ollow a genetic or ... ...s are often found in a cli- ...ily. Schizophrenia and bi- disorders ...orders are examples of cation of ...orders that are heritable. Identifi-cians to ...of these patterns enables clini-account ...to plan treatments that take ...of environmental or family

dynamics contributing to the development of a disorder. A family history of a disorder may also imply a biological element to its transmission, suggesting that medication may be especially useful. In addition, developmental patterns (such as the age at which a disorder is most likely to emerge) and predisposing factors (such as a precipitating incident or a background common to those who suffer from the disorder) also provide data useful in determining treatment plans. That information can also facilitate the formulation of plans to prevent relapse.

B. *Demographics.* Information about such variables as the typical socioeconomic environment, partner status, age, and family constellation of someone with a given disorder is included in this section. Information on background, including age, culture, ethnic identity, and other relevant factors, also is presented in this section.

C. *Source of referral and apparent motivation for treatment.* Clues to a person's probable response to treatment are often provided by the nature of the referral. For example, a person who ght therapy on the recom- of a career counselor wh has worked success- ment of their a greater moti- change al is someone planning. to treat-

D. *Treatment his* previous treatm orts

is important in determining what treatments are likely to be helpful. A long treatment history, especially one including numerous treatment failures, suggests a poor prognosis, but perhaps that outcome can be averted if a treatment is provided that takes previous treatment failures into account. Clinicians should familiarize themselves with the ways people have responded to treatment in the past, building on what was successful and avoiding what was ineffective.

E. *Personality profile.* Clients' personality profiles are obtained through psychological assessment, interviews, and observation by clinicians. Typical interpersonal and intrapsychic dynamics of clients with each mental disorder will be considered throughout this book, including such characteristics as cognitions, affect, behavior, defenses, and lifestyle.

F. *Developmental history.* A review of the client's background, including such areas as family relationships, work history, social and leisure activities, and medical conditions, usually provides valuable information on that person's strengths and areas of difficulty. If the client's successes and failures, support systems, and coping mechanisms are considered when treatment is planned, the treatment is likely to be more effective. Also, viewing people broadly and in context facilitates use of available resources, such as a supportive spiritual community, and helps clinicians avoid pitfalls to treatment, such as peers who encourage drug and alcohol use as well as antisocial behavior.

III. *Preferred Therapist Characteristics.* This section reviews the available information on therapist-related variables that are relevant to the treatment of a particular disorder or client. Such information may include the therapist's experience, theoretical orientation, and training; the therapist's personal and professional qualities; and the relationship between the client's and the clinician's personalities and backgrounds.

IV. *Intervention Strategies.* In this section, what is known about the effective treatment of a disorder is reviewed. Recommendations about treatment strategies are made, and areas where information is lacking are discussed.

A. *Approaches to psychotherapy and counseling.* This section contains a review of the literature on those approaches to therapy that seem to work best with the mental disorder under consideration. The following dimensions of the therapeutic process are important in treatment planning and, depending on the information available, are discussed in detail in subsequent chapters:

- Psychotherapeutic theories and strategies.
- Therapist's implementation of these theories and strategies (including level of directiveness, exploration, support, structure, and confrontation).
- Balance of focus—affective, behavioral, cognitive.
- Modality of treatment—individual, family, group.

B. *Medication.* This section considers the question of whether medication enhances treatment or is necessary in the treatment of a particular disorder. Although the focus of this book is the treatment of mental disorders by nonmedical clinicians who emphasize psychotherapy or counseling rather than drugs to effect change, a combination of medication and psychotherapy is typically more effective for some disorders than either one alone. Nonmedical therapists must be aware of these findings so that they can refer clients with such disorders for medical evaluation and provide treatment in collaboration with a psychiatrist or other medical specialist.

C. *Duration and pacing of treatment.* This section focuses on the typical length of treatment necessary for ameliorating symptoms of a disorder and on the swiftness of the therapeutic pace.

D. *Treatment setting.* Inpatient settings, partial hospitalization or day treatment, and outpatient settings all have their place in the treatment of mental disorders. Which setting is preferred or needed for each disorder will be discussed.

E. *Adjunct services.* These services include social and personal growth activities, support and self-help groups (such as Alcoholics Anonymous), leisure and exercise groups, professional and governmental services (such as legal aid and subsidized housing), and psychoeducational services (such as assertiveness training and education on effective parenting) that may enhance the effectiveness of psychotherapy.

V. *Prognosis.* This section provides information on how much change or improvement can be expected in a person experiencing the disorder under consideration, how rapidly progress is likely to occur, the likelihood of relapse, and the overall prognosis. Accurate assessment of prognosis depends on both the nature of the mental disorder and the motivation and resources of the person with the disorder. The severity of the client's disorder is relevant to outcome. In general, the more severe and long-standing the disorder, the poorer the prognosis. Disorders that are mild and short in duration and that have a clear precipitant tend to have better prognoses. For example, people with circumscribed, reactive, brief, situational problems, such as adjustment disorders and some mood and anxiety disorders, tend to have better treatment outcomes. In contrast, people with personality disorders, schizophrenia, and other disorders that are enduring and pervasive and that do not have an apparent precipitant typically respond to treatment more gradually and in more limited ways.

THE CLIENT MAP

The major elements of the treatment plan discussed in this chapter have been expanded and organized into a structured and systematic model for treatment planning called the Client Map. The steps of this treatment plan are represented by the acronym formed from the first letter in each of the 12 steps in this model: DO A CLIENT MAP. This acronym facilitates recall of the parts of the plan, reflects the plan's purpose, and guides its development. A clinician who supplies information about the following 12 items will have created the Client Map, a structured treatment plan for working with a particular client.

DO A CLIENT MAP

1. **D**iagnosis
2. **O**bjectives of treatment
3. **A**ssessments (for example, neurological tests, personality inventories, and symptom checklists)
4. **C**linician characteristics
5. **L**ocation of treatment
6. **I**nterventions to be used
7. **E**mphasis of treatment (for example, level of directiveness; level of supportiveness; cognitive, behavioral, or affective emphasis)
8. **N**umbers (that is, the number of people in treatment: individual, family, or group)
9. **T**iming (frequency, pacing, duration)
10. **M**edications needed, if any
11. **A**djunct services
12. **P**rognosis

The format represented by the DO A CLIENT MAP acronym is used throughout this book to illustrate the process of treatment planning for sample cases.

DIMENSIONS OF TREATMENT PLANNING

In general, treatment planning moves from the nature of the disorder through consideration of the client's characteristics and on to the treatment approach. That will be the sequence followed throughout most of this book. In the present section, however, the focus will be primarily on approaches to treatment and their impact on mental disorders. The parts of the Client Map considered here are diagnosis, objectives of treatment, assessments, clinician characteristics, location, interventions, emphasis, numbers, timing, medications, and adjunct services. Because information on diagnosis, assessments, interventions, and prognosis are specific to each disorder, they are discussed separately, and at length, in the chapters relating to each disorder.

Diagnosis (DO A CLIENT MAP)

Effective treatment planning begins with the development of an accurate multiaxial assessment, made according to the guidelines in the *DSM*. Such an assessment includes information on people's mental disorders, any relevant medical conditions, their stressors, and their overall levels of coping and adjustment as reflected by the Global Assessment of Functioning Scale. The diagnosis is the foundation for treatment planning. Once the diagnosis has been made, clinicians can move ahead to develop a complete and effective treatment plan.

Development of such a plan must take into consideration a number of variables. One of the most important considerations is to identify treatments that are likely to be effective in ameliorating the symptoms of the client's disorder. Ideally, clinicians should select treatment approaches that have received empirical support. That is not always possible, of course. Although empirically supported treatments have been identified for many disorders, especially the anxiety and mood disorders, eating disorders, and substance use disorders (Nathan & Gorman, 2007; Roth & Fonagy, 2005), a concise list of effective treatments for every disorder does not exist. In some cases, many diverse treatments have been found to be equally effective for a particular disorder; in other cases, no treatment approaches have received strong research support. We focus on what has been proven efficacious as well as what seems most likely to be effective in order to help clinicians achieve the best possible treatment options in the therapy they provide.

In 1995, the Division 12 Task Force of the American Psychological Association published guidelines for identifying empirically supported treatments (Task Force on Promotion and Dissemination of Psychological Procedures, 1995). As mentioned earlier, included with the criteria was a list of 18 treatments that the task force identified as having empirical support for use in treatment of particular diagnoses or specific populations. Each of the 18 treatments had been tested in randomized controlled trials and implemented using a treatment manual.

This research raised concerns about the applicability of these findings to people with diverse backgrounds and those with comorbid conditions. Questions also were raised about the use of manualized treatments and the impact and importance of the therapeutic alliance (Levant, 2005). A flurry of research since that time has focused on common factors that account for much of the variance across disorders, as well as the effect of the therapeutic alliance. Both of these important topics are discussed later in this chapter.

As research continues to explore the appropriate use of specific approaches to particular clients and disorders, the use of manualized therapy that provides clear and specific treatment guidelines and interventions has come under increased scrutiny. Although manual-based treatments can be an appropriate way to provide evidence-based therapy, therapist effects on outcome are often large and cannot be ignored (Anderson, Ogles, Patterson, Lambert, & Vermeersch, 2009; Malik, Beutler, Alimohamed, Gallagher-Thompson, & Thompson, 2003; Nielsen et al., 2011). The therapy relationship contributes as much to successful outcomes as the treatment selected and must be included as part of any evidence-based practice (Norcross, 2011). Without such attention, strict adherence to a treatment manual can lead to "ruptures in the alliance and, consequently, poorer outcomes" as well as thwart the therapist's ability to adapt treatment to the "attitudes, values, and culture of the client, a necessary aspect of multicultural counseling" (Ahn & Wampold, 2001, p. 255). Clinicians who are mindful of the alliance and use sound clinical judgment and flexibility, rather than rigid application of manuals seem most likely to have successful outcomes (Levant, 2005).

A growing number of studies, to be discussed in later chapters, assess the effectiveness of therapies for adults, children, and adolescents with particular disorders (Barlow & Durand, 2008; Mash & Barkley, 2006; Nathan & Gorman, 2007). Although some studies focus on only one or two approaches, others provide useful information on the effectiveness of various psychotherapies. In general, the desirable treatment approaches for a particular client or disorder are those that: demonstrate a high likelihood of addressing relevant problems, maximize the client's motivation, help the therapist and the client achieve the treatment goals, overcome obstacles, consolidate gains, and reduce the likelihood of a relapse (Beutler & Consoli, 1993). Unfortunately, evidence-based treatments are not available for all disorders. Despite more than 500 documented treatments available for children and adolescents, not all of the childhood disorders have evidence-based practices available (American Psychological Association Task Force on Evidence-Based Practice for Children and Adolescents, 2008; Schiffman, Becker, & Daleiden, 2006). Of those evidence-based practices that are identified, few have documentation manuals or videos that would allow them to be replicated (Chorpita, Becker, & Daleiden, 2007).

People with more than one diagnosis can be particularly challenging clients. People's cognitive and processing abilities, their premorbid functioning, and their access to resources all affect their response to treatment (Sachse & Elliott, 2001). Typically, a person who was at a lower level of functioning before therapy will still be at a lower level after therapy than a person who was at a higher level of functioning before therapy, even though both may have improved.

Also important in understanding psycho-pathology and treatment selection is the client's development and life stage. A growing number of studies discuss developmental processes, such as attachment, socialization, gender identity, and moral and emotional development. Understanding the client's stage of development is particularly important when treating children, adolescents, families, and older adults (Levant, 2005). Also important is knowing when a person developed a particular disorder and understanding the impact of that disorder on the person's development. People with long-standing disorders, for example, may well have failed to meet important developmental milestones, especially in self-direction and socialization.

Objectives of Treatment (DO A CLIENT MAP)

Decisions on treatment objectives or goals should be made in collaboration with the client. Using the best available information—considering costs, benefits, resources, and options—the therapist and the client work together to create a treatment plan. An active, involved client is crucial to the success of treatment (Levant, 2005). No matter how wisely the therapist selects an intervention strategy, and no matter how abundantly the therapist demonstrates the personal and professional qualities that are positively correlated with a good outcome, therapy is unlikely to be effective if the client is not ready or able to benefit from the therapeutic strategy and the therapist's positive qualities. In fact, such client-related variables as expectations of therapy, motivation for change, degree of participation, personality style, and severity of the disorder can improve or weaken treatment outcomes (Muran & Barber, 2010; Norcross, 2010; Prochaska & Norcross, 2010). Attention should be given, then, to those qualities in clients that are correlated with effective treatment, as well as to clinician characteristics and treatment approaches, discussed later.

Client's Readiness for Change Prochaska and Norcross (2010) address the importance of the person's readiness for change, which they describe as unfolding over five stages: (1) precontemplation, (2) contemplation, (3) preparation, (4) action, and (5) maintenance. Each stage represents a period of time characterized by discrete attitudes, behaviors, and language on the part of the client. The person must achieve certain tasks before moving on to the next stage. The stages are:

1. *Precontemplation.* People in this stage have no intention of changing their behavior. Although they might think about changing, or wish to change, they are unwilling to do anything that will promote change. In fact, they may be stuck in repetitive and ineffective thoughts and behaviors for years. To move beyond this stage, the person must recognize and admit there is a problem.
2. *Contemplation.* At this stage of change, the person is able to admit the problem, wants to change, and is willing to move beyond merely thinking about it. The task required to move to the next level of change is to take action—even a small first step—toward behavioral change.
3. *Preparation.* This is the stage in which behavior and intentions are aligned. The person is ready to make a change and begins to set goals and an action plan in preparation for moving on to the next stage.
4. *Action.* During this stage, people commit time and energy to modify their behavior and begin working to overcome their problems, to the point that their efforts become recognized by others.

The action stage may last from one day to six months. During this time the person is acquiring skills and strategies to help prevent relapse.

5. *Maintenance.* Maintaining and continuing behavioral change for longer than six months is the hallmark of the maintenance stage.

Clients with very low levels of readiness need therapists who can focus on consciousness raising, dramatic relief, and environmental evaluation. Supporting a client's readiness for change is the goal of motivational interviewing, a person-centered approach originally created by Miller and Rollnick (2002) for work with substance abuse. Resistance to treatment is not directly confronted by the therapist, rather it is reframed as ambivalence and the therapist, using his or her skills at creating the Rogerian conditions for change (empathy, congruence, and unconditional positive regard), sets up the conditions in which the client can explore both sides of the dynamic (Seligman & Reichenberg, 2010). Carl Rogers noted that "significant positive personality change does not occur except in a relationship" (Rogers, 1967, p. 73). Motivational interviewing helps the therapist to establish the conditions in which the client can choose to change.

Motivational interviewing is frequently used in the beginning of treatment for conditions that may be treatment refractory (for example, dually diagnosed disorders, eating disorders, gambling). Research shows that therapists who incorporate motivational interviewing into their interventions are more likely to achieve success with ambivalent clients (Stasiewicz, Herrman, Nochajski, & Dermen, 2006).

Client's Perceptions of Psychotherapy The research suggests that people who perceive their therapists as helping them, who have positive perceptions of their therapists' skills and facilitative attitudes, and who see themselves engaged in teamwork with their therapists are likely to show more benefits from therapy than people who do not share those perceptions. Conversely, therapists who were perceived by their clients as having lower levels of facilitative interpersonal skills or who communicated "subtle, disaffiliative messages" (Anderson et al., 2009, p. 757) were shown to result in worse clinical outcomes than when such messages were not perceived. Therefore, therapists should monitor their clients' perceptions of the therapeutic process, including their perceptions about the therapist, as part of ongoing treatment, so they can modify strategies, repair ruptures, and avoid early terminations (Hersoug et al., 2009; Lambert, 2010; Muran & Barber, 2010).

Client's Expectations for Treatment

People enter therapy with a broad range of expectations and attitudes. The well-known self-fulfilling prophecy seems to hold true: People who expect positive and realistic outcomes from therapy, and whose expectations are congruent with those of their therapists, are more likely to achieve those outcomes, whereas negative expectations lead people to abandon efforts to reach their goals. Therapists who instill hope and promote the client's positive expectations of treatment foster increased client participation in treatment and a reduction in symptoms. "Expectations of treatment effectiveness are powerful predictors of outcome in psychotherapy" (Meyer et al., 2002, p. 1051) and are an important part of building a positive therapeutic alliance.

Clients are also sensitive to the therapist's level of professional training, which, interestingly, had an inverse relationship on their rating of the therapeutic alliance (Hersoug et al., 2009). More research is needed to understand why more training is perceived as unhelpful by

clients. In the same study, the level of the alliance was stable from the beginning of treatment throughout the course of therapy. Distinctions must be made between the creation of the therapeutic alliance at the beginning of therapy and attending to the alliance during the middle and end phases of treatment (Horvath, Symonds, & Tapia, 2010). Directly attending to strains on the relationship before they become ruptures can help to solidify the relationship and provide a healthy way of interacting that clients can learn from and apply to their relationships outside of the session. Therapists who make assumptions, or use their intuition about the alliance, are frequently wrong. Successful therapists have learned to ask the client in session for their perceptions. To do otherwise is to risk harm to the alliance and may result in premature termination on the client's part (Norcross & Wampold, 2011).

At least some portion of the positive effect of therapy comes from what is known as the Hawthorne effect. Many people have been shown to improve simply as a result of having special attention paid to them (Prochaska & Norcross, 2010). The special attention paid to a client by a mental health professional can improve self-esteem, reduce anxiety, and promote improvement. Thus, empirical research is needed if one is to conclude that the effectiveness of any particular treatment methodology is more than just the result of person-to-person contact.

Assessments (DO A CLIENT MAP)

The development of a treatment plan for a given client begins with a thorough understanding of that person. Formats for intake interviews and mental status examinations are readily available elsewhere (Seligman, 2004) and are beyond the scope of this volume, but a brief and useful overview of relevant aspects of the client is provided by Strub and Black (2000).

They suggest gathering data on the following dimensions:

- Description of presenting concerns
- Demographic characteristics
- Mental status
- Cultural and religious background
- Physical characteristics and abilities, medical conditions
- Behavior
- Affect and mood
- Intelligence, thinking and learning style
- Family composition and family background
- Other relevant history and experiences
- Social behavior
- Lifestyle
- Educational and occupational history
- Family history of psychiatric illness
- Any other relevant areas

Clinicians also should collect and review any relevant records and prior assessment information (for example, psychological tests and medical evaluations). Most therapists seem to be making increased use of diagnostic interviews, inventories, and rating scales. In the preliminary stages of therapy, these help the clinician gather information on the client's diagnosis and dynamics. In the termination stages, they provide information on progress and outcome. The literature offers many objective and projective assessment tools developed in recent years that can play an important role in deepening understanding of clients (Antony & Barlow, 2010; Strub & Black, 2000). The following are some of the most useful:

- Structured diagnostic interviews, such as the NIMH Diagnostic Interview Schedule, the Schedule for Affective Disorders and Schizophrenia, the Brief Psychiatric Rating Scale, and the Symptom Checklist-90-R.
- General personality inventories, including the Minnesota Multiphasic Personality Inventory-2; the Millon Clinical Multiaxial Inventory-III; the Millon Adolescent Personality Inventory; the California Psychological Inventory; the Myers–Briggs Type Indicator; and the High School, Children's, and Early School Personality Questionnaire.
- Inventories for assessing specific symptoms, including the Beck Depression Inventory-II, the Beck Anxiety Inventory, the Hamilton Rating Scale for Depression, the State-Trait Anxiety Inventory, the Michigan Alcoholism Screening Test, the Conners' Rating Scale, the Behavior Assessment System for Children-2, and the Eating Disorders Inventory.

Inventories also may be used to assess other aspects of the person. These might include intelligence, aptitudes, achievement, interests, and values. Assessment is an important component of the treatment planning process and should be done with care. Effective treatment planning is unlikely unless the clinician has made an accurate diagnosis and has a good understanding of the client's development, concerns, strengths, and difficulties, acquired through a careful assessment.

Variables Related to the Client's Demographic and Personal Characteristics On the National Comorbidity Survey Replication, a structured interview administered to a national sample of people over the age of 18, nearly 50% of respondents reported at least one mental disorder during their lifetimes, and close to 30% had experienced such a disorder during the previous 12 months (Kessler et al., 2005). Of those who had experienced at least one disorder, half experienced symptoms by the age of 14, and three fourths by the age of 24. The most common disorders included anxiety, mood, impulse-control, and substance use disorders. People who experience symptoms commonly delay seeking treatment. On average, people with mood disorders wait 6 to 8 years before seeking treatment, and people with anxiety disorders wait 9 years to as long as 23 years before seeking treatment (Wang et al., 2005).

What distinguishes people who seek help for their concerns and who benefit in the process from people who do not? Those who do seek treatment are more likely to be female, college educated, and from the middle to upper classes, and they are more likely to have reasonable expectations for how therapy can help them. People who continue in therapy tend to be more dependable, more intelligent, better educated, less likely to have a history of antisocial behavior, and more anxious and dissatisfied with themselves than those who leave therapy prematurely (Garfield, 1986).

Those who leave treatment early are more likely to be ambivalent about change and seeking help. Principe, Marci, and Glick (2006) found that 40% of clients at community mental health centers and 20% seen in private practice terminated therapy in the first two visits. Because the therapeutic alliance forms early in treatment (Horvath and Laborsky [1993] found that it peaked at the third session), it is essential for clinicians to instill hope and the expectation of a positive therapeutic outcome early in treatment. Clients who have an expectation of a positive therapeutic outcome are more likely to enter into a positive therapeutic alliance and have a better outcome overall (Messer & Wolitsky, 2010).

Many personal characteristics in clients are correlated with outcomes. People who are friendly, open, in touch with their emotions, and able to express their thoughts and feelings in therapy are more likely to have positive treatment outcomes. Clients who are actively engaged in therapy, regardless of which therapeutic intervention is used, are more likely to improve. Clients who have good object relations, who demonstrate good ego strength, and who can take responsibility for problems rather than viewing them as external sources of difficulty are also more likely to have positive outcomes, as are those who are motivated to change. On the other hand, people who are too friendly, who have poor object relations, are hostile, or have Cluster A or B personality disorders are less likely to benefit from therapy (Sharpless, Muran, & Barber, 2010). Clients who have co-morbid disorders are also more likely to be resistant, have higher negative process, and have higher attrition rates.

Research on the relationship between outcomes and clients' personal characteristics is suggestive but not yet conclusive. Overall, however, indications are that therapy is particularly effective with White females who are intelligent, motivated, expressive, and not severely dysfunctional. Therapy can be helpful to people who do not fit this description, of course, but these findings point out some of psychotherapy's limitations, as well as the difficulty of adapting the therapeutic process to the needs of a particular client.

A "research–practice gap" seems to exist between the research on the most efficacious interventions and the interventions that practitioners actually use. In response to one survey, most clinicians said they do not always use empirically supported treatments (ESTs) in their practice. Many said they do not like working with treatment manuals. Schnyder (2009) notes that most psychotherapists are not trained in empirically supported treatment. Then, too, not all clients are looking for, or comfortable with, empirically supported therapies. One study found a 20% client dropout rate for empirically supported therapies (Schnyder, 2010).

Clinician Characteristics
(DO A CLIENT MAP)

Therapists' interpersonal skills influence the progress of therapy to such an extent that Anderson and colleagues (2009) state: "Many psychotherapies, as routinely practiced, are evidence-based when delivered by therapists who can offer high levels of interpersonal skills on a performance-based measure" (p. 767).

Indeed, individual differences between therapists strongly predict the alliance quality and treatment success (Muran, Safran, & Eubanks-Carter, 2010). Many therapist variables (e.g., gender, age, cultural background) have been found to have little influence on treatment outcomes. But therapists who rate higher on the Rogerian conditions (empathy, congruence, unconditional positive regard) develop better therapeutic alliances and continue to have more successful outcomes than those who rank lower. This was true regardless of the therapist's theoretical orientation (Zuroff, Kelly, Leybman, Blatt, & Wampold, 2010).

Fifty years of research underscores the importance of the effect of the therapist's interpersonal skills on treatment outcomes. The following characteristics, attitudes, and approaches on the part of therapists have been found to be correlated with therapists' effectiveness (Bowman, Scogin, Floyd, & McKendree-Smith, 2001; Greenberg, Watson, Elliott, & Bohart, 2001; Lambert & Barley, 2001; Lambert & Cattani-Thompson, 1996; Meyer et al., 2002; Muran & Barber, 2010; Orlinsky, Grawe, & Parks, 1994; Rimondini et al., 2010):

- Communicating empathy and understanding to clients.
- Having personal and psychological maturity and well-being.
- Manifesting high ethical standards.
- Being authoritative rather than authoritarian, and freeing rather than controlling of clients.

- Having strong interpersonal skills; communicating warmth, caring, respect, acceptance, and a helping, reassuring, and protecting attitude; affirming rather than blaming clients.
- Having appropriate emotion-handling skills, asking emotion-seeking queries, focusing emotion.
- Being nondefensive; having a capacity for self-criticism and an awareness of their own limitations, but not being easily discouraged; continuously searching for the best ways to help clients.
- Empowering clients and supporting their autonomy and their use of resources.
- Being tolerant of diversity, ambiguity, and complexity; being open-minded and flexible.
- Being self-actualized, self-fulfilled, creative, committed to self-development, responsible, and able to cope effectively with their own stress.
- Being authentic and genuine and having credibility.
- Focusing on people and processes, not on rules.
- Being optimistic and hopeful, having positive expectations for the treatment process, and being able to engender those feelings in clients.
- Being actively engaged with and receptive to clients, and giving some structure and focus to the treatment process.
- Establishing a positive alliance early on, and then attending to the alliance at every stage of treatment; addressing ruptures as they occur; managing negative processes effectively.

These findings suggest that the therapist who is emotionally healthy, active, optimistic, expressive, straightforward yet supportive, and who is able to temper that stance with encouragement of responsibility on the part of the client is the one most likely to achieve a positive outcome. More will be said on evidence-based therapy relationships later.

Therapists can also be aware of their own personality traits that have been shown to contribute to poor working alliances. Therapist defensiveness, over- or under-structuring sessions, excessive use of techniques, and being too demanding or critical can disrupt the development of a solid therapeutic alliance (Sharpless, Muran, & Barber, 2010).

Demographic Variables   Therapist demographic variables appear to be weaker predictors of outcome than client variables (Bowman, Scogin, Floyd, & McKendree-Smith, 2001). In a study comparing three treatment modalities—cognitive-behavioral therapy, interpersonal therapy, and medication—such therapist variables as age, gender, race, religion, and clinical experience were not found to be related to therapeutic effectiveness (Wampold & Brown, 2005).

In a meta-analysis on the effect of therapist gender on psychotherapy outcome, Bowman and colleagues (2001) looked at more than 60 studies and concluded that the gender of the therapist has little effect on outcomes. However, one study found that female clients prefer female therapists and that female therapists tend to form stronger therapeutic alliances with their clients than do male therapists (Wintersteen, Mensinger, & Diamond, 2005). Although the gender of the therapist may be important to some clients and is worth considering (especially in short-term counseling where rapid establishment of a positive therapeutic alliance is important), research has failed to demonstrate that gender matching leads to improved outcomes or reduced dropout rates (Cottone, Drucker, & Javier, 2003; Sterling, Gottheil, Weinstein, & Serota, 1998).

The literature also found no clear evidence that the therapist's age affects therapeutic outcomes, although one study found that age, when tied to a therapist's facilitative interpersonal skills (FIS) had a significant effect on treatment outcomes (Anderson et al., 2009). In general, clients seem to prefer clinicians who are mature enough to have had considerable experience in their field and who understand clients' age-related and developmental issues but who do not seem so old as to be out of touch with current developments in the profession.

Ethnic and Cultural Diversity   The ethnic and cultural match between client and therapist has also been the focus of much attention. Race appears to bear little relationship to therapeutic outcomes. Professional demeanor engenders stronger alliances. Therapists who are interested, alert, confident, and respectful; those who are courteous, trustworthy, and honest; and those who show warmth and are empathic, supportive, flexible, and down to earth are more likely to facilitate the trust that is necessary to work effectively with clients with any cultural background (Muran, Safran, & Eubanks-Carter, 2010).

Therapists who acknowledge and respect the diversity between collectivist and individualized cultures, who are aware that religion is important to religious people regardless of which religion it is, and who espouse the tenets of cultural competency are more likely to have successful therapeutic outcomes.

The client's degree of assimilation to the majority culture does seem to impact the relationship that develops between clients and their therapists. In their work with adolescents, Huey and Polo (2008) found that less acculturated teens had lower treatment effectiveness and higher dropout rates. Coleman, Wampold, and Casali (1995) conclude that clients who are not highly assimilated to the majority culture have more negative attitudes toward therapy and are more likely to prefer ethnically similar therapists. By contrast, clients who are highly assimilated to the majority culture sometimes feel stereotyped if they are automatically assigned to ethnically similar therapists (Sue, Ivey, & Pedersen, 1996).

In some cases, ethnic matching between client and therapist does seem to be indicated and may result in greater trust and understanding in the relationship. Overall, the research generally suggests that therapists who are culturally competent and attend to issues of culture as well as to their clients' wants and expectations in therapy are likely to be successful with both ethnically similar and ethnically different clients (Thompson, Bazile, & Akbar, 2004; Wong, Kim, Zane, Kim, & Huang, 2003).

In the few studies that have been conducted, the race of the therapist does not appear to affect therapeutic outcomes. However, Thompson, Bazile, and Akbar (2004) found that African American clients prefer to see African American therapists rather than European American therapists, and an earlier study (Lambert, 1982) noted that African American clients tend to leave therapy at higher than usual rates when they are working with European American therapists. These studies suggest that race may be a factor in determining length of treatment, if not therapeutic outcomes. Moreover, according to Hess and Street (1991), "Several studies have demonstrated that subjects express a greater preference for, engage in more self-exploration with, and are better understood by counselors of their same ethnic background than by those whose background differs from their own" (p. 71).

Experience and Professional Discipline Research on the link between therapist experience or expertise and outcome has yielded inconclusive results. Two earlier studies found that expertise was more important than theoretical orientation (Eells, Lombart, Kendjelic, Turner, & Lucas,

2005). However, two other studies that compared experienced clinicians to graduate students on their ability to conduct assessments of personality and psychopathology found no significant difference in their abilities. This was true regardless of whether the clinicians were conducting interviews, gathering biographical information, or administering and interpreting the Rorschach or the MMPI. Although these studies were conducted with clinical and counseling psychologists, Garb's research (1998), which focused on social workers and other mental health professionals, indicates similar results.

Beutler, Crago, and Arizmendi (1986) found no relationship between the therapist's professional discipline and therapeutic outcomes. In fact, Berman and Norton (1985) found that, overall, professionals and paraprofessionals were equally effective.

Nevertheless, Greenspan and Kulish's study (1985) of 273 clients who terminated treatment prematurely, but after at least six months, indicates that therapists with PhDs and personal experience of psychotherapy have lower rates of premature termination by clients than do therapists with MD or MSW degrees. Seligman (1995), however, reports that psychologists, psychiatrists, and social workers do not differ in their therapeutic effectiveness. So far, no clear and conclusive relationship has been found between the length of the therapist's training, the therapist's personal experience of psychotherapy, and the therapist's professional discipline, on the one hand, and therapeutic outcomes, on the other.

Location (DO A CLIENT MAP)

Research on selection of treatment settings is fairly limited. In general, the treatment location will be determined by the following seven considerations (Seligman, 2004):

1. Diagnosis, and the nature and severity of the symptoms.

2. Danger that clients present to themselves and others.
3. Objectives of treatment.
4. Cost of treatment, and the client's financial resources and insurance coverage.
5. Client's support systems, living situation, and ability to keep scheduled appointments.
6. Nature and effectiveness of previous treatments.
7. Preferences of the client and of significant others.

Therapists often take the following four variables into account when they are choosing among treatment options:

1. Finding the least restrictive setting.
2. Selecting a setting that provides the most optimal therapeutic care for the particular person and disorder.
3. Matching the person's needs with the specific treatment provided (settings without enough resources and those that are overly restrictive may be nontherapeutic).
4. Choosing the most cost-effective treatment (for example, if a day treatment program will suffice, inpatient or residential treatment should not be considered).

Often placement will be determined or limited by insurance providers or financial considerations. Clearly, decisions regarding the best placement for an adult, adolescent, or child will require weighing a variety of complicated and interrelated factors.

The decision about the treatment setting, like many of the other decisions that must be made as part of treatment planning, calls on clinical judgment because the literature gives only sketchy guidelines. Options typically include inpatient treatment (such as a hospital or residential treatment program), day treatment program, or outpatient treatment.

Residential Treatment   Residential treatment centers are the most restrictive environment for treating mental disorders. Placement is usually for an extended period of time, often a year or more, and most residential treatment centers are typically not located in the person's community; thus family and home visits are often not possible or are of limited duration. These programs provide a highly structured environment and may be appropriate for people with psychotic disorders, significant mental retardation, substance dependence, and other severe disorders. Residential treatment programs are sometimes necessary in the treatment of children with severe or profound mental retardation, conduct disorders, or psychotic disorders that do not respond to outpatient or pharmacological interventions. These children often exhibit chronic behavior problems, such as running away, substance use, and aggression (Jacobs et al., 2009; Johnson, Rasbury, & Siegel, 1997).

Inpatient Hospitalization   Inpatient hospitalization is considerably shorter than residential treatment. Hospital stays range from overnight to less than a month in most cases. Inpatient treatment programs are usually highly structured and oriented toward a rapid diagnosis and crisis stabilization. Inpatient hospitalization may be appropriate for people who pose a danger to themselves or to others and who have severe mental disorders. The following list provides examples of situations in which inpatient care might be considered:

- Suicide attempts or severe depression.
- Eating disorders in which a person cannot maintain body weight.
- Psychosis or irrational or bizarre thinking that makes a person a danger to self or others.
- Sexual abuse or neglect of a child, or a home environment that makes it unsafe for the child to remain in the home.

People with drug or alcohol problems who are physiologically dependent on harmful substances also may need a period of inpatient treatment. However, unless detoxification is needed, treatment of substance dependence can often be accomplished through day treatment or intensive outpatient programs, combined with the client's participation in self-help groups.

People are often discharged from a hospital to a less restrictive setting (generally an outpatient or day treatment program) as soon as warranted. Some studies indicate that a brief hospital stay followed by aftercare is more therapeutic than a longer stay. One study in the United Kingdom found that the longer the stay, the more gains were made in treatment for children and adolescents with conduct disorder (Jacobs et al., 2009). In general, the most efficient, least confining treatment setting should be used to reduce the stigma associated with treatment, maintain the client's independence and connection to the community, and reduce costs.

Partial Hospitalization   Day treatment and partial hospitalization programs permit people to live at home while attending a highly structured program focused specifically on their needs (such as schizophrenia, substance use, eating disorders, dual diagnosis, and others). Day treatment programs are less costly than inpatient hospitalization and often serve as transitions from inpatient or residential treatment settings to outpatient treatment. At the end of the day treatment program, stepped-down, half-day programs or weekly group meetings commonly are used to consolidate the gains that have been made. Day treatment has consistently been found to be beneficial in the treatment of psychosis, mood and anxiety disorders, and DSM Cluster B personality disorders (Lariviere, Desrosiers, Tousignant, & Boyer, 2010).

Outpatient Treatment   Far more people will be treated for mental disorders in outpatient

settings than will be seen in inpatient or day treatment settings. A wide variety of outpatient treatment programs are available including private practice, community mental health centers (which also usually offer inpatient treatment), and agencies focused on specific populations (for example, women, children, people from a particular cultural or ethnic background) or problems (for example, anxiety disorders, phobias, relationship conflicts, or career concerns).

Current Trends   Admissions to psychiatric hospitals have decreased substantially in the past 25 years and length of stay is much shorter (Butcher, Mineka, & Hooley, 2006). The trend toward shorter inpatient stays pertains to adults, adolescents, and children alike. Managed care and the development of medications that effectively control the symptoms of severe disorders have contributed to the reduction in hospitalization. The introduction of managed care has resulted in a shift away from inpatient services to outpatient, day treatment, and community-based services (Ross, 2001). In six states, psychiatric readmission rates were higher under managed care, leading the U.S. Department of Health and Human Services to conclude that "increased hospital readmission rates may indicate persons with severe mental illness are being released from inpatient care too quickly" (U.S. Department of Health and Human Services, Office of Inspector General, 2000, p. 1). At the same time, shorter hospital stays have prevented some unnecessary and costly treatments and have enabled some people to live their lives more fully.

Interventions (DO A CLIENT MAP)

Once the clinician has identified the treatment setting for a particular person, the next step probably will be to determine the specific approaches and strategies that will guide treatment. More than 400 psychotherapeutic approaches are available to clinicians (Stricker & Gold, 2006). However, few meaningful differences in outcomes seem to exist among therapies; on the contrary, therapies seem to have more similarities than differences. Earlier in this chapter, the overall effectiveness of psychotherapy was discussed. The research indicates that an overwhelming 75% to 80% of people benefit from therapy (Lambert & Ogles, 2004; Wampold, 2001).

Once it was established that most people benefit from psychotherapy, the fundamental question became, "What forms of psychotherapy are most effective, and what are the common ingredients of their greater effectiveness?" Although conclusive answers may never be found, a considerable body of research concludes that such common factors as the establishment of a healing process, a positive and collaborative therapeutic alliance, the client's hopefulness and belief that treatment can help, a credible treatment approach to address the client's symptoms, and the development of the client's self-efficacy and problem solving are key components of any successful therapy (Ahn & Wampold, 2001; Frank & Frank, 1991; Lambert & Bergin, 1994; Rogers, 1957; Rosenzweig, 1936; Wampold, 2001). A meta-analytic review of the literature concluded that as much as 70% of the outcome variance between different models of therapy was attributable to these common factors shared by all successful therapies (Wampold, 2001).

As we have seen, the differences in outcome are due more to the therapist, the client, and their alliance than to the particular theoretical model being used. In fact, the therapeutic alliance can account for as much as 30% of the variance in outcomes (Lambert & Ogles, 2004). Of course, the treatment approach and the strategies used do make an important contribution to outcome. The ability to maximize the effectiveness of psychotherapy, then, requires an understanding not only of therapeutic approaches and strategies but also of the client and clinician variables. More will

be said about this later. Now we look at the most common theoretical orientations in practice today. A brief description of each, as well as of its application and effectiveness, is provided.

Psychoanalysis Few studies are available on the effectiveness of classical psychoanalysis, partly because the lengthy and intense nature of the process means that each analyst can treat only a small number of clients. Therapists have generally been moving away from prolonged psychoanalysis and other treatments of long duration and toward the development of briefer psychotherapies. Nevertheless, a 30-year study on the effectiveness of psychoanalysis was conducted by the Menninger Foundation in the 1980s. A high percentage (63%) of those who had been selected for psychoanalysis had good or moderate outcomes. Readers are referred to the Psychotherapy Research Project (Wallerstein, 1986) for further details.

Psychodynamic Psychotherapy Psychodynamic psychotherapy has considerable empirical support and new evidence is emerging about its effectiveness for the treatment of a wide range of conditions and populations (Shedler, 2010). Meta-analytic reviews of treatment outcome studies and randomized controlled trials (RCTs) support its efficacy for mood and anxiety disorders, somatoform disorders, Cluster C personality disorders, schizophrenia, and substance-related disorders (Gottdiener, 2006; Leichsenring, 2005; Milrod et al., 2007; Shedler, 2010; Simon, 2009). One study of borderline personality disorder showed treatment benefits that were equal to, or exceeded, results with dialectical behavior therapy. These and other meta-analytic reviews also indicated long-term treatment benefits that lasted after therapy had been completed (Bateman & Fonagy, 2008; Levy et al., 2006). Readers who are interested in a more extensive review of psychodynamic treatment approaches and their effectiveness are referred to Leichsenring (2009).

Brief psychodynamic psychotherapy continues to grow in popularity. This approach to treatment borrows heavily from the psychoanalytic model, but treatment with this approach takes less time, is more directive, and incorporates other treatment techniques, such as cognitive therapy (Seligman & Reichenberg, 2010).

Ideal clients for brief psychodynamic psychotherapy are motivated to change; willing to make a commitment to therapy; psychologically minded; able to tolerate and discuss painful feelings; intelligent; in possession of good verbal skills, flexible and mature defenses, and a focal issue; and have had at least one meaningful childhood relationship (Messer, 2001; Messer & Kaplan, 2004; Messer & Warren, 1995).

Typical outcomes of brief psychodynamic therapy include symptom relief, improved relationships, better self-esteem, greater insight and self-awareness, better problem-solving ability, and a sense of accomplishment (Budman, 1981). The approach provides a corrective emotional experience for people who are not severely dysfunctional but who may be suffering from depressive disorders, anxiety disorders (especially posttraumatic stress disorder [PTSD]), adjustment disorder, stress, bereavement, and mild to moderate personality disorders (Goldfried, Greenberg, & Marmar, 1990).

Short-term psychodynamic psychotherapy (STPP) is also effective. A recent meta-analysis of 23 studies in which short-term psychodynamic therapy was used to treat a variety of somatic conditions showed positive results for decreasing somatic symptoms and improvement in psychiatric symptoms. It may be effective in a broad range of somatic and health-related symptoms (Abbass, Kisely, & Kroenke, 2009). It was also found to be effective in the treatment of adults with depression (Driessen & Hollon, 2010).

Interpersonal psychotherapy (IPT) is an empirically validated form of brief psychodynamic therapy that has proven as effective as medication and cognitive therapy in the treatment of depression (Bleiberg & Markowitz, 2008; Sinha & Rush, 2006). Based on the work of Harry Stack Sullivan, IPT was designed by Gerald Klerman and colleagues specifically for the treatment of depression. It is a focused, time-limited treatment approach that emphasizes social and interpersonal experiences (Seligman & Reichenberg, 2010). IPT has been successfully adapted for use with adolescents to decrease interpersonal problems and reduce substance use (Mufson, Dorta, Moreau, & Weissman, 2004). Readers are referred to Chapter 4 for a more complete examination of IPT.

Behavior Therapy Many studies over the past 30 years have substantiated the value of behavior therapy. For example, exposure and response prevention therapy has proven its effectiveness in the treatment of PTSD (Resick, Monson, & Rizvi, 2008). Exposure also is helpful in relieving symptoms of OCD. Systematic desensitization is helpful in treating symptoms of specific phobias and agoraphobia. Flooding or intense, prolonged exposure, along with medication, has been shown to effect significant improvement in agoraphobia, although this approach must be used with great caution.

Behavior therapy also is effective in the treatment of conduct disorder, behavioral difficulties associated with mental retardation, enuresis, substance-related disorders, and family conflicts. Other disorders likely to respond well to behavior therapy include: impulse-control disorders, sexual dysfunctions, oppositional defiant disorder, paraphilias, some sleep disorders, anxiety disorders, and mood disorders (Barlow & Durand, 2008; Nathan & Gorman, 2007; Roth & Fonagy, 2005).

People most likely to benefit from behavior therapy are those who are motivated to change, who follow through on homework tasks or self-help programs, and who have friends and family members who are supportive of their efforts to change. The literature contains many positive reports of behavior therapy's effectiveness. Nevertheless, assessment of the effectiveness of this treatment approach is complicated by its many strategies and variations.

Duration of treatment and specific techniques are critical variables in the determination of the effectiveness of behavior therapy. For example, one 2-hour session of in vivo exposure seems to be more effective than four half-hour sessions, and flooding can actually increase anxiety if it is not maintained long enough for the anxiety reaction to subside. Moreover, in the treatment of phobias, OCD, and sexual disorders, performance-based in vivo exposure methods are likely to be more effective than methods employing imaginal symbolic procedures. Support is better than confrontation in promoting clients' adherence to treatment plans in behavior therapy, but more research is needed before it can be determined exactly how this powerful treatment approach can best be used.

Behavioral activation therapy. The components of behavioral activation therapy (BAT) have been around for a long time, but only recently has this treatment modality gained momentum and empirical support as a stand-alone treatment for depression and co-occurring disorders (Martell, Dimidjian, & Herman-Dunn, 2010). The underlying premise in BAT is that emotions result in behaviors (rumination, avoidant behavior) that are repeated and over time cause people to feel stuck. By activating people with depression to perform different behaviors, planning and scheduling those behaviors, and reinforcing those behaviors, positive change results. BAT is easy to use and can be integrated into most theoretical orientations. A review of three meta-analyses and one RCT found that BAT was as effective as CBT and cognitive therapy in the treatment

of depression, and had lower dropout rates (Sturmey, 2009).

Cognitive and Cognitive-Behavioral Therapy Cognitive therapy, developed by Beck and his colleagues (Beck, Rush, Shaw, & Emery, 1979), is one of the most researched treatment modalities. Cognitive therapy assumes that people's thoughts are a dynamic representation of how they view themselves, their world, their past, and their future (in other words, their phenomenal field). Cognitive structures are viewed as the major determinants of people's affective states and behavioral patterns. Through cognitive therapy, people become aware of their cognitive distortions and correct their dysfunctional automatic thoughts and schemas, a correction that leads to overall improvement. The focus of treatment is on the present, and between-session tasks are important.

Cognitive therapy is often combined with behavior therapy, with the early rivalry between these two approaches having evolved into mutual appreciation and recognition of the value of their integration. Indeed, the efficacy of cognitive-behavioral therapy (CBT) has been well documented for the treatment of a large number of disorders including: unipolar depression, most types of anxiety disorders, childhood anxiety and depression, bulimia nervosa, substance use disorders, and transdiagnostic symptoms such as anger, impulsivity, and chronic pain (Butler, Chapman, Forman, & Beck, 2006; Epp, Dobson, & Cottraux, 2009; Hollon & Beck, 2004; White & Barlow, 2002; Wilson & Fairburn, 2007; Young, Rygh, Weinberger, & Beck, 2008).

Criticism of CBT has focused on concern that the therapy is a quick fix and does not involve insight or depth. Yet research indicates that CBT has lasting effectiveness, in some cases at least as long as seven years after the conclusion of therapy. CBT actually offers long-term advantages over medication in the reduction of relapse rates (Butler et al., 2006).

Dialectical behavior therapy (DBT), created by Linehan (1993) in her work with clients with borderline personality disorder (BPD), has also achieved some success. Based on cognitive-behavioral therapy, DBT integrates considerable support and insight-oriented therapy into treatment. Current research on the use of DBT with adolescents and others with suicidal ideation, depression, and self-harming behavior indicates that DBT is effective in reducing hospitalization rates, self-harming behaviors such as cutting, and depression (American Psychiatric Association, 2001; Linehan & Dexter-Mazza, 2008; Meyer & Pilkonis, 2006; Robins, Ivanoff, & Linehan, 2001). DBT has also been adapted for treating eating disorders, antisocial personality disorder, and substance use comorbid with BPD. A recent meta-analytic review of DBT found only moderate effect size and concluded that more RCTs are necessary (Öst, 2008). More information on DBT can be found in the discussion of borderline personality disorder in Chapter 8.

Acceptance and commitment therapy (Eifert & Forsyth, 2005) can be described by its acronym: Acceptance of thoughts, choosing goals that honor the client, and taking steps toward that action. In practice, ACT is based on relational frame theory and helps people to understand how they become entrapped in their thoughts. By using Eastern-influenced mindfulness exercises to accept their thoughts without judgment or rumination, clients are then able to move on to the action phase of treatment.

A meta-analytic review of 18 randomized controlled studies of ACT indicates that while ACT is more effective than no treatment at all for a variety of maladies, no conclusive evidence exists that ACT is superior to other treatments (Powers, Zum Vörde Sive Vörding & Emmelkamp, 2010). Randomized controlled trials are under way on the use of ACT in the treatment of depression, heroin addiction, pain disorders,

smoking, and stress in the workplace (Seligman & Reichenberg, 2010).

Humanistic/Experiential Therapy   Humanistic-experiential therapies, beginning with Carl Rogers's person-centered therapy (1951, 1965), emphasize the importance of client experience to effect change. Humanistic therapies assume that people value self-determination and the ability to reflect on a problem, make choices, and take positive action. Humanistic-experiential therapists facilitate the expression and processing of emotion. Enhancing their emotion processing skills helps people master and modulate their emotional arousal and ultimately expand their awareness and self-esteem (Gendlin, 1996; Greenberg & Watson, 2005).

Specific approaches that fall under the humanistic-experiential umbrella include: person-centered therapy, Gestalt therapy (Perls, 1969), process-experiential/emotion-focused therapy (PE-EFT), emotion-focused therapy for couples, relationship enhancement therapy for couples, and motivational interviewing.

Until recently, little controlled research was available on the effectiveness of humanistic therapies, but as the number of controlled outcome studies increases, evidence suggests that these treatment approaches are effective in reducing symptoms and improving functioning in a range of problems, including alcohol misuse, anxiety disorders, personality disorders, interpersonal relationships, depression, coping with cancer, trauma, marital difficulties, and sometimes even schizophrenia (Bozarth, Zimring, & Tausch, 2001; Cain & Seeman, 2001; Elliot, 2001; Gottman, Coan, Carrere, & Swanson, 1998; S. Johnson, 2004).

Three meta-analyses reached the same conclusion: Humanistic therapies are effective; they are more effective than no treatment; and post-treatment gains remain stable at 12-month follow-up (Elliott, 1995, 2001; Greenberg,

Elliott, & Lietaer, 1994). CBT showed a modest superiority to person-centered therapy and non-directive supportive treatments, but that more process-directive therapies, such as Gestalt therapy, emotion-focused therapy for couples, and process-experiential therapies are at least as effective as CBT (Elliott, 2001). Elliott concludes that with specific problems or with particular groups of people, person-centered therapies can be as effective, if not more effective, than CBT.

As discussed earlier, motivational interviewing (MI) helps people resolve their ambivalence about change and commitment to treatment. MI is most often added to the beginning of treatment for disorders that can be treatment refractory such as depression, alcohol and substance-related disorders, gambling, and eating disorders. MI increases retention rates during treatment and decreases relapse at 3-month follow-up (Connors, Walitzer, & Dermen, 2002).

Other Approaches to Psychotherapy Although most of the empirical research on psychotherapy's effectiveness has focused on the psychodynamic, behavioral, humanistic, and cognitive approaches, research is growing in other areas. Lack of empirical research does not mean that a particular therapy is ineffective. On the contrary, research consistently indicates that no one theoretical orientation is significantly more effective than another overall. Other approaches that may also be effective include:

Adlerian approaches, which have recently grown in popularity, are particularly useful in treating behavioral disorders of children, family and other interpersonal conflicts, mild depression and anxiety, and concerns focused on goals and direction.

Existential psychotherapy is best suited to relatively well-functioning people with mild depression, mild anxiety, or situational concerns that raise questions about the meaning and direction of their lives. It is often useful for people coping with life-threatening illnesses, issues of grief and loss, and life transitions.

Mindfulness-based therapies. More than 30 years ago, Jon Kabat-Zinn (1990) developed mindfulness-based stress reduction (MBSR) for the treatment of pain and chronic illnesses. MBSR, with its focus on present-moment awareness, meditation, and relaxation techniques, has helped people reduce pain related to physical illness, decrease stress, improve self-regulation of emotions and thoughts, and reduce unwanted behaviors such as smoking, binge eating, insomnia, and alcohol and substance-related disorders (Seligman & Reichenberg, 2010; Walsh & Shapiro, 2006). Many therapies now incorporate Eastern ideas, such as mindfulness (Linehan, 1993); acceptance (Brach, 2004; Eifert & Forsyth, 2005); emotional transformation (Goleman, 2003); and focusing, altruism, and service (Walsh, 2000). Asian therapies are second only to behavior therapies in the amount of empirical research on their effectiveness, and many clinicians view meditation and yoga as integral to stress reduction and incorporate them into their treatment plans or offer them in their practice as part of a holistic approach to treatment. Interested readers will find additional discussion of mindfulness-based stress reduction in Chapter 3.

Integrated approaches. An integrative approach is one that combines treatment approaches and strategies in a logical, systematic way to maximize the chances of a positive therapeutic impact. This is different from a cookbook approach that specifies the use of certain types of therapy for certain disorders and is different from an eclectic approach that employs a fairly random and unsystematic array of interventions. Surveys of practice reflect a shift toward integrated or eclectic treatment. Nearly 34% of psychologists, 23% of counselors, and 26% of social workers describe their primary theoretical orientation as integrated or eclectic (Prochaska & Norcross, 2010).

Transdiagnostic approaches that address common symptoms found across a variety of disorders have become a growing trend. This could be especially helpful in treatment refractory disorders such as eating disorders and alcohol and substance use disorders. Anger, emotional dysfunction, and impulsivity are just three of the symptoms that are found frequently in many different disorders that would benefit from focused clinical attention. More will be said about transdiagnostic treatment approaches in Chapter 10.

Again, because no one therapeutic orientation has been found to be more effective than others, clinicians with a solid background in one primary theoretical orientation can draw from other theories and interventions to create treatment plans that seem most helpful for the current needs of a particular client (Seligman & Reichenberg, 2010), or they can combine two complementary approaches into a new integrated treatment—for example, the blending of behavior therapy with experiential therapy in the creation of acceptance and commitment therapy (Eifert & Forsyth, 2005).

As we have seen, the existence of so many common factors in therapy suggests that there are not really hundreds of discrete approaches to psychotherapy but instead are many variations on a far smaller number of well-established themes. The existence of so many commonalities among therapeutic approaches raises an interesting issue: Are the differences among therapies genuine, and do these therapies have differential effectiveness? Or is any apparent differential effectiveness among therapies due more to particular therapists' effectiveness, if not to the chemistry of particular therapeutic relationships? Let's turn now to look in more detail at a very powerful factor in the success of therapy—the therapeutic alliance.

The Therapeutic Alliance   Discussion of interventions is not complete without discussion of the therapeutic alliance. The therapeutic alliance is the collaborative working relationship that develops synergistically between the client and the therapist. While not an intervention itself, the working alliance contributes significantly to the outcome of treatment. In fact, it is safe to say that if there is no alliance, there is no positive outcome of treatment. Developing, maintaining, and repairing this alliance across the course of treatment, then, becomes an important, even essential, focus of the clinician's attention.

In recent years, the therapeutic alliance has become one of the most researched variables in psychotherapy. Recently, two task forces of the American Psychological Association joined forces to review more than 20 meta-analyses of the research related to the therapeutic alliance to determine the specific variables that contribute to effective outcomes in treatment. Interested readers are referred to *Psychotherapy Relationships That Work, 2nd ed.* (Norcross, 2011) for the complete results. Following is a synopsis of some of the research-supported conclusions:

- The therapeutic alliance is part of evidence-based practice.
- The therapeutic alliance is effective across all treatment modalities (e.g., psychodynamic, humanistic, cognitive-behavioral) and types of interventions (individual, group, couples).
- The alliance works in conjunction with variables (such as therapist and client characteristics, and the selection of interventions) to create effective therapy.
- Therapist behaviors that enhance the alliance should be included in practice and treatment guidelines.
- Tailoring the relationship to the needs of the client enhances treatment effectiveness.

Empathy. An overall effect size of .30 was found between therapist empathy and client success (Norcross & Lambert, 2011). Empathy also predicted better outcomes for newer therapists. Not just rote repetition of a client's words, true empathy involves compassion and an attitude of profound interest—almost as if the therapist were stepping into the other person's psychological shoes. In *A Way of Being*, Rogers (1980) wrote about empathy: "It means entering the private perceptual world of the other . . . being sensitive, moment by moment, to the changing felt meanings which flow in this other person" (p. 142). When clients truly feel heard, they are more likely to be comfortable exploring their feelings on a deeper level. With appropriate empathy, therapists are able to choose interventions that are appropriate for the client's needs at that time. Greenberg, Watson, Elliott, and Bohart (2001, p. 382) identify four ways in which empathy contributes to outcome:

1. Feeling understood increases client satisfaction and thereby increases self-disclosure, compliance with the therapist's suggestions, and feelings of safety.
2. Empathy provides a corrective emotional experience.
3. Empathy promotes exploration and the creation of meaning, facilitating emotional reprocessing.
4. Empathy contributes to the client's capacity for self-healing.

Effective therapists model congruence and genuineness. The therapist is authentic, real, and does not put up a false professional front or facade (Rogers, 1957). Congruence is evident among the therapist's thoughts, emotions, and behaviors. The assumption behind this is that the therapist has developed a great deal of self-insight, has come to terms with their own issues, and does not harbor any anger or contempt. The genuine

and congruent therapist is likely to provide an environment in which the client can explore emotions and look to the therapist as a role model.

The therapist provides warmth and positive regard. The therapist's regard for the client remains constant and positive. It is unconditional, nonjudgmental, and not based on anything the client might do or say, but rather reflects appreciation and caring for another human being. The therapist shows this regard for a client through the use of empathy and understanding.

Collaboration and goal consensus is an active and ongoing process that enhances client well-being. Successful therapists respect and solicit clients' feedback, do not promote their own agendas, and do not begin problem solving until treatment goals have been determined.

Exactly how the therapeutic alliance contributes to successful outcomes in therapy remains a mystery, confounded by definitions of variables, theoretical definitions, and research methodology. Research studies rate the alliance as responsible for anywhere from less than 10% to as much as 30% of the variance in therapeutic outcome (Horvath & Laborsky, 1993; Lambert & Barley, 2001; Martin, Garske, & Davis, 2000). Martin and colleagues conducted a meta-analytic review of 79 studies of the therapeutic alliance and found that although the alliance had only a modest effect on outcomes (0.22), the effect is consistent across large numbers of studies and is not linked to many other variables. The authors validate the hypothesis that "the alliance may be therapeutic in and of itself" (p. 446).

In other words, if a good alliance is formed between client and therapist, the client will experience the relationship as therapeutic regardless of which treatment approach is used. Krupnick and colleagues (1996) found that even when the primary intervention is medication, the therapeutic alliance is still important to outcomes. Medical professionals, especially doctors and psychiatric nurses, are paying more attention to the importance of a positive therapeutic alliance (Prochaska & Norcross, 2010).

Establishing an alliance. Therapists can facilitate the development of a solid working alliance by:

- Role induction that helps clients learn how to be clients and to make good use of the therapy session.
- Open disclosure of the therapist's background and procedures.
- The therapist's and the client's agreement on realistic goals and tasks.
- The therapist's asking the client for feedback.

Role induction also seems helpful in the development of attitudes in clients that are conducive to a positive outcome. In role induction, clients are oriented to the therapeutic process and are given clear information on what is expected of them, what the therapist can offer, and what therapy will probably be like. The client's engagement in the therapeutic process is a variable that is correlated with a positive therapeutic outcome. Duncan, Miller, Wampold, and Hubble (2010) emphasize the importance of the qualities of the therapist as a person, and the positive effect of the therapist on treatment. Clients who have a positive perception of the therapist, who believe that the focus is on their own goals and expectations, and who are comfortable with the pace of treatment are more likely to succeed. Also important is the ability of the client and the therapist to view themselves as engaged in a common endeavor.

A successful therapeutic alliance makes it possible for the client to accept and follow the treatment faithfully and bridges the gap between process and outcome. The conditions conducive to a positive therapeutic alliance have been discussed earlier in this chapter, but therapists should not limit their attention to those conditions; they should also attend to clients' preferences.

Bordin (1979) suggests three important aspects of the therapeutic alliance:

1. An affective bond between the client and therapist.
2. Agreement between client and therapist about the goals of treatment.
3. A sense of working collaboratively on the problem.

The alliance across various therapies and modalities. Fifty years of research consistently indicates the importance of the therapeutic alliance in achieving good outcomes across all treatment methodologies and modalities (Norcross, 2011). Matching therapy to specific disorders and to the entire person is often effective (Norcross, 2011). Any matching or tailoring of treatment should also include the therapeutic relationship. But effective therapy is complicated and involves a host of variables that have more of a synergistic relationship than simply matching people with appropriate treatment.

Repairing ruptures to the alliance. Because clients who rate the alliance as positive are more likely to stay in therapy, to have positive outcomes, and to rate therapy as helpful, therapists should routinely monitor their client's responses to therapy. Such monitoring provides the opportunity to repair any ruptures as they come up. This process that has been found to actually strengthen the therapeutic alliance (Greenberg & Watson, 2000; Safran, Muran, & Eubanks-Carter, 2011).

Effective therapists manage the countertransference. The therapist's countertransferential reaction to the client must be managed if therapy is to be effective (Hayes, Gelso, & Hummel, 2011). Therapists can protect themselves from these feelings by using empathy, having insight into their own feelings, and seeking therapy or supervision.

The Alliance with Families. Forming a therapeutic alliance when working with families requires different skills from when working with individuals, and often involves establishing multiple alliances across a multigenerational system. Beck, Friedlander, and Escudero (2006) note that no single alliance should be considered in isolation because "a therapist's alliance with each family member affects and is affected by the alliance with all other family members" (p. 355).

Multiple studies on the alliance between therapist and families have found that a strong alliance was more likely to occur if the following conditions were met:

- The family agreed with the therapist on goals, had confidence that treatment would bring about positive change, and developed a good emotional connection with the therapist.
- The therapist promoted rapport and exhibited warmth.
- The therapist was optimistic and had a sense of humor.
- The therapist was active in sessions (Beck, Friedlander, & Escudero, 2006).

The client's perception of the alliance, rather than the therapist's perception, is the best predictor of treatment outcome (Quinn, Dotson, & Jordan, 1997). However, in their study of family research, Quinn and colleagues found that the woman's perception of the alliance was more important than the man's perception in predicting outcome.

Conversely, a weak alliance between the family system and the therapist was found when a family member had distrust of the counseling process or when there was disagreement over goals. Robbins, Turner, and Alexander (2003) showed that much like that in individual therapy, the therapeutic alliance in family therapy is

also created early on—in the first three or four sessions—and is also predictive of outcome.

No Treatment   Sometimes the best intervention is no intervention at all. Despite the demonstrated effectiveness of therapy, an estimated 5% to 10% of people who receive psychotherapy deteriorate during treatment (Lambert & Ogles, 2004). Although little research is available on the negative effects of psychotherapy, no treatment may be the best recommendation for the following people:

- People at risk for a negative response to treatment (for example, people with severe narcissistic, borderline, obsessive-compulsive, self-destructive, or oppositional personality patterns).
- People with a history of treatment failures.
- People who want to support a lawsuit or a disability claim and thus may have an investment in failing to make progress.
- People at risk for no response (for example, people who are poorly motivated and not incapacitated, people with malingering or factitious disorder, and those who seem likely to regress as a result of the therapeutic process).
- People likely to show spontaneous improvement (for example, healthy people in crisis or with minor concerns).
- People likely to benefit from strategic use of the no-treatment recommendation (for example, people with oppositional patterns who are refusing treatment, and people whose adaptive defenses would be supported by a recommendation of no treatment).

The no-treatment recommendation is intended to protect clients from harm, prevent clients and therapists from wasting their time, delay therapy until clients are more receptive to it, support prior gains, and give people the message that they can survive without therapy. Although this option may make theoretical sense, clinicians do not seem to use it with any frequency, at least partly because of the great difficulty of predicting who will not benefit from therapy and the risk involved in discouraging people from beginning therapy when they may really be able to make good use of it. Nevertheless, therapists may want to give more consideration to this recommendation, especially in light of the current emphasis on short-term productive treatment.

Emphasis (DO A CLIENT MAP)

The multitude of approaches to psychotherapy reflects only one aspect of the diversity that exists in treatment interventions. Variation in the implementation of therapies also greatly increases the diversity of approaches. Clinicians adapt models of psychotherapy to their own personal styles and individualize treatments to meet the needs of particular clients. Therefore, the application of an approach to psychotherapy differs from one therapeutic relationship to another. The dimensions discussed in this section reflect some of the ways to adapt treatment to an individual.

Directive Versus Evocative   The directive approach can be viewed as encompassing cognitive and behavior therapies and such techniques as systematic desensitization, flooding, positive reinforcement (including token economies, contingency contracting, and extinction), strategic techniques (such as suggestion, paradox, and metaphor), humor, homework tasks, and bibliotherapy (Malik et al., 2003). In all these approaches the therapist assumes an authoritative stance, clearly defines target concerns, and designs a specific program to change overt and covert symptoms.

A study by Malik and colleagues (2003) found that psychodynamic therapy was the least directive of eight therapies examined. Psychoanalysis is characterized by a therapist who is clearly an authority figure, but such psychoanalytic techniques as free association are evocative or experiential. The process-experiential therapies, such as humanistic, Gestalt, or person-centered models, were also low on directiveness and high on evocativeness, focusing on the therapist-client interaction and encouraging clients to choose their own topics or modes of processing. Those approaches emphasize such processes as catharsis and abreaction; genuineness, empathy, and reflection of feeling; support; affection; praise; authenticity; and unconditional positive regard.

Two clients are used here to illustrate how treatment emphasis differs, depending on the client. Both Anne and Bettie have similar presenting problems. Each is a woman in her early twenties who has sought counseling after a broken engagement, but their circumstances and their views of therapy are very different and thus warrant different levels of directiveness.

Anne is in her second month of an unplanned pregnancy. She is receiving little help from her family or from her former fiancé. She is unemployed and is living with a single friend who has two children. Anne is not sure what she wants to do about her pregnancy and has been using alcohol as a way to avoid thinking about her difficulties. She has not had previous therapy and is uncertain of why the nurse with whom she spoke at an abortion clinic has referred her to a counselor, although she is motivated to get some help.

Bettie's situation is quite different. Although she too is depressed that her former fiancé ended their engagement, she views this as a time to review her goals. She believes that she focused too much of her time and energy on her fiancé and has neglected her career and her education. She is interested in returning to college, learning more about some of her aptitudes and preferences, and establishing a better balance between her social life and her career. At the same time, she is angry that she feels a need for therapy, and her disappointment in her former fiancé has led her to feel mistrustful of others.

Anne does not have the leisure or the sense of direction for an evocative approach. She needs a directive therapist, not to tell her what to do about her pregnancy, but to give her a structure for expediting her decision making and helping her gain some control of her life. In addition, her use of alcohol is endangering her unborn child and creates urgency in this situation. Bettie, by contrast, would be more amenable to experiential or person-centered therapy, which would afford her the opportunity to engage in self-examination and goal setting.

In general, a directive approach has been correlated with a focus on goal attainment and with lower than average levels of therapeutic alliance (Hersoug et al., 2009; Malik et al., 2003; Muran & Barber, 2010). Alternatively, an evocative approach seems more likely to be successful with people who are self-directed and more able to participate in a sound alliance between client and therapist (Malik et al., 2003; Sharpless et al., 2010).

Exploration versus Support   This is another dimension that has received little but theoretical examination in the literature. Nevertheless, it is often cited as an important aspect of treatment (Rockland, 2003; Wallerstein, 1986).

The dimension of exploration versus support, like the dimension of directiveness versus evocativeness, exists on a continuum. Approaches that emphasize exploration typically are probing, interpretive, and analytical, stressing the importance of insight, growth, and an understanding of past influences and patterns. By contrast, approaches that emphasize support tend to be present-oriented, symptom-focused, and more action-oriented. Psychoanalysis and psychodynamic psychotherapy, using such techniques as free association, analysis of transference, examination of dreams, and interpretation, emphasize exploration. The other end of the continuum is represented by the behavioral model, with its focus on the present, on circumscribed and measurable changes, and on reinforcement of positive coping mechanisms. Person-centered counseling, although less action-oriented, also reflects a supportive approach in which client strengths and self-direction are reinforced.

Models at each end of the continuum, of course, as well as those in the middle, inevitably include both exploration and support. They are distinguished by the balance between exploration and support rather than by the absence of one or the other. Rockland (2003), for example, outlines a psychodynamic approach to supportive therapy that provides both supportive and exploratory interventions. By tailoring the appropriate levels of support to the client's needs, Rockland focuses on improving ego functioning, reality testing, and clarity of thought, rather than attempting to resolve unconscious conflicts.

One of the few studies of this dimension of therapy was conducted by Wallerstein (1986), who concluded that insight is not always necessary for change. In 45% of the cases he examined, changes that were achieved seemed to go beyond the amount of insight that was attained, whereas insight surpassed discerned change in only 7% of these cases. Overall, Wallerstein concluded, supportive therapy was more effective in these cases than had been expected, and it did not seem to be less effective than exploratory therapy. Schnyder (2009) notes that 70% of therapy is supportive therapy with or without medication, despite the lack of empirical support for this treatment modality.

Bettie and Anne, the clients discussed earlier, need different levels of exploration. Bettie, a strong client who is interested in personal growth and introspection, is a good candidate for an approach that is at least moderately probing in nature, such as brief psychodynamic therapy. Anne, by contrast, needs a supportive approach that will help reduce the stress she is experiencing and enable her to draw on her existing strengths to cope with her situation.

Other Aspects of Emphasis   Other aspects of emphasis include the balance of treatment focus on past, present, and future and the relative attention paid to developing the therapeutic alliance, among others. Emphasis also entails considering how to adapt a treatment approach to a specific person. For example, a clinician may use CBT with many clients but will apply that approach differently for each one. When considering emphasis in developing treatment plans, then, clinicians should also give some thought to what elements of the chosen theoretical orientation will be emphasized and which will be downplayed as treatment progresses. For example, CBT with Anne might focus primarily on behavior, whereas CBT with Bettie probably would pay more attention to thoughts.

Although most therapists probably make intuitive judgments of whether their clients will benefit from high or low levels of exploration and high or low levels of support, and of which aspects of treatment to stress, more research on these dimensions would facilitate effective treatment planning.

Numbers (DO A CLIENT MAP)

The therapist must also decide who will be treated. Some disorders, such as OCD, are best resolved with individual therapy; others, such as oppositional defiant disorder or substance use disorders, are best treated with a family therapy component. Group treatment is another consideration.

Individual Psychotherapy   Individual psychotherapy certainly has demonstrated its effectiveness. Individual therapy seems to be the modality of choice for people whose intrapsychic difficulties cause them repetitive life problems, for people in crisis or with urgent concerns, for people with problems that might cause them distress or embarrassment in a group setting, and for people who are vulnerable, passive, and low in self-esteem (Clarkin, Frances, & Perry, 1992). Although individual therapy is generally a safe choice, it does have certain limitations. It does not offer the client the opportunity to receive feedback from anyone but the therapist, it gives the therapist only one source of information about the client, it encourages transference reactions, it affords little chance to address family dynamics, and it offers only a limited opportunity to try out new interpersonal behaviors in therapy sessions.

Group Psychotherapy   Group therapy seems to be effective from both cost and outcome standpoints. In general, studies find its impact to be comparable to that of individual therapy. Group therapy has been shown to be effective for a variety of different problems and conditions including substance-related disorders, eating disorders, borderline personality disorder, and bereavement (Reichenberg, 2010). Group psychotherapy usually is the treatment of choice for interpersonal problems, including loneliness, competitiveness, shyness, aggressiveness, and withdrawal, as well as for people who have problems with intimacy and authority (Fenster, 1993). Group therapy offers an environment more like everyday life and therefore provides an arena for interaction and learning from others. Group therapy can promote self-esteem, reduce resistance, and diffuse feelings of differentness and shame.

In deciding whether a particular person is likely to benefit from group psychotherapy, therapists need to consider not only the impact of the group on the client but also the impact of the client on the group. Ideal clients for group therapy seem to be those who are motivated, aware of their interpersonal difficulties, capable of taking some responsibility for their concerns, and able to give and accept feedback. People who are extremely aggressive, confused, self-centered, or fearful of others may have a harmful impact on group interaction and are unlikely to derive much benefit from that process. If group therapy is used at all with clients like these, it probably should be deferred until they have made noticeable progress in individual or family psychotherapy.

Therapy groups may be either heterogeneous (composed of people with different problems) or homogeneous (composed of people with similar problems). People with similar disorders and problems can often learn coping skills from each other, benefit from feedback and modeling, and receive support and validation. Heterogeneous groups often focus on group interaction and help people build interpersonal skills.

Couples and Family Therapy   Research has demonstrated that couples therapy and family therapy are effective in general and may be superior to alternative treatment modalities for some problems and disorders. Empirically supported interventions for couples include behavioral couples therapy (BCT) for the treatment of substance abuse (Ruff, McComb, Coker, & Sprenkle, 2010); emotion-focused couples therapy (Greenberg & Johnson, 1988; S. Johnson, 2004); and relationship enhancement therapy (Guerney, 1977, 1994). Integrated behavioral couples therapy that incorporates elements of mindfulness and acceptance also shows promise for the treatment of distressed couples (Christensen, Wheeler, & Jacobson, 2008).

Family therapy is often indicated for problems that stem from, are affected by, and have an impact on the family system. Empirical research has found specific types of family therapy to be an integral part of the successful treatment of many disorders, including schizophrenia, major depressive disorder (Barlow & Durand, 2008), and anorexia nervosa (Wilson & Fairburn, 2007). Children and adolescents seen for therapy will usually have family therapy as a component of their treatment, especially for conduct disorder, oppositional defiant disorder, and ADHD (Kazdin, 2008). People with disorders that seem to have a genetic or familial component, such as substance-related disorders, bipolar disorders, and OCD, are also likely to benefit from family therapy (Finney, Wilbourne, & Moos, 2007; Miklowitz & Craighead, 2007; Sachs, 2004). Additional information on each of these disorders and the integration of family therapy into treatment planning is delineated in the relevant chapters of this book.

Research continues on the appropriate uses of these treatment modalities, but most of the information in the literature about the respective strengths and benefits of the three primary modalities of therapy—individual, group, and family—is inferential. The following list summarizes this information, showing the client groups for which each of the modalities is recommended:

Individual Counseling	Group Therapy	Family Therapy
Highly anxious, withdrawn, isolated, or introverted clients; people who have difficulty with ambiguity; people seeking help with intrapsychic concerns; extremely	Anxious clients with authority concerns; people with pervasive personality dysfunction who have made progress in individual therapy; people with interpersonal	People who have problems with family structure and dynamics; people with intergenerational or other family conflicts; families with communication problems; families
		(continued)

(continued)

Individual Counseling	Group Therapy	Family Therapy
suspicious, guarded, hostile, paranoid, or destructive people who have difficulty with trust; people seeking independence and individuation; people with very intimate or idiosyncratic concerns; people with concerns of very long duration in which improvement rather than maintenance is sought; people in crisis	concerns; people who may feel stigmatized or scapegoated as a result of individual therapy (such as the identified patient in a family); people who are likely to give the therapist excessive power; people who need reality testing and group feedback; people with specific behavioral concerns (such as eating disorders or alcohol dependence) that are shared with other group members; people with limited financial resources; people who have been through traumatic experiences that also have been experienced by others in their treatment group	needing consolidation; acting-out adolescents; families with limited resources, when more than one family member needs help; families with no severe pathology; children; families with a member who has a chronic or recurrent mental disorder

Timing (DO A CLIENT MAP)

The typical client is seen once a week for a session of 45 to 50 minutes in length, but the frequency of therapy sessions can vary. One session every other week is often used in supportive therapy, particularly toward the end of treatment, whereas clients in psychoanalysis commonly have five sessions per week. The duration of therapy also varies widely, of course, and is often difficult to predict, but research indicates that most of the therapeutic effect will take place within the first 10 to 20 sessions (Schnyder, 2009).

The limited research comparing long-term treatment with short-term treatment is specific to one treatment modality and one disorder (such as dialectical behavior therapy for borderline personality disorder) or combines many studies across a broad range of disorders. For example, Hansen and Lambert (2003) looked at nearly 5,000 people in various outpatient settings and found that half achieved significant change in 15 to 19 sessions. A similar study of 75 people estimated that 11 sessions was the average number for 50% of the people to achieve significant change (Anderson & Lambert, 2001).

A recent report on therapy attendance at an outpatient clinic indicated that 23% of clients did not return after the first session. Of those, 4% cancelled; 8.7% were no shows; 5.7% rescheduled; and in another 5.7% of cases, the therapist missed or rescheduled the session. Follow-up phone calls to the clients revealed that 85 to 90% expressed satisfaction with the quality of the counseling they had received (Carlstedt, 2011). The largest group (24%) attended an average of 1 to 4 sessions; and only 2.15% attended 10 sessions. The short-term nature of the clinic setting has implications for how therapy is conducted. Rather than spending the first three sessions conducting intake for diagnosis and assessment, the time would be better served providing crisis counseling and focusing on the alliance.

Orlinsky and Howard (1986) conducted meta-analyses of studies that looked at the relationship between length of therapy and therapeutic outcome. They concluded that the total number of sessions—and, to a lesser extent, duration of treatment—are positively correlated with therapeutic benefit. Not all studies show the same relationship, however, and a small number show a curvilinear relationship between outcome and number of sessions. More empirical research is necessary to determine the most effective length of treatment for people with specific disorders. Typically, short-term therapy is not just less long-term therapy; the goals, the treatment interventions, the disorders, and the clients themselves are likely to differ. Therefore, research must consider presenting problems, diagnoses, client profiles, and other variables when the research question is one of determining outcomes on the basis of therapy's duration.

Today's emphasis on short-term therapy has increased the importance of studying approaches to brief treatment and determining the people for whom they are suitable. Many studies have demonstrated that short-term treatment can have a significant and lasting positive impact, but that is only the case for some clients and some disorders. Roberts (2002), for example, found that brief therapy is indicated in the immediate aftermath of a crisis, such as a suicide attempt, trauma, or national disaster such as occurred on September 11.

Short-term cognitive therapy seems to be appropriate when problems are related to stress, dysfunctional behaviors, academic problems, interpersonal difficulties, and career concerns (Littrell, Malia, & Vanderwood, 1995), and brief psychodynamic psychotherapy is suitable for both chronic and nonchronic depression (Luborsky et al., 1996).

A thorough assessment at the beginning of treatment is essential to determine if brief therapy will be appropriate. The following criteria should be considered:

- The nature and severity of the disorder.
- The client's readiness to change.
- The client's ego strength.
- The client's motivation for an enduring therapeutic relationship.
- The client's ability to relate to the therapist (Lambert & Anderson, 1996).

Typically, people who are motivated, who do not have personality disorders, and who have a focal concern or crisis, a positive history, good ego functioning, and a sound ability to relate well to others and express their emotions make good clients for short-term therapy. In general, clients with fewer symptoms and better pretreatment functioning achieve better results faster than those with more serious disorders.

People for whom short-term therapy usually is not indicated are those who are very hostile, paranoid, or psychotic or who have long-standing, severe problems. Eating disorders, bipolar disorders, dysthymic disorder, borderline personality disorder, and antisocial personality disorder are examples of disorders that generally do not respond well to short-term therapy.

In general, short-term therapy seems likely to be effective with a substantial percentage of clients (approximately 75%). In fact, time-limited treatment can encourage people to be more focused and to make more rapid progress. Again, however, candidates for this approach to treatment must be carefully selected.

Medication (DO A CLIENT MAP)

Medication, combined with therapy, seems particularly useful for disorders involving debilitating anxiety, endogenous (melancholic) depression, mania, or psychosis. Therapy alone may be all that is needed in treating problems involving adjustment, behavior, relationships, mild to moderate anxiety, reactive depression, and some personality disorders. Many disorders in the second group, however, such as eating disorders, some personality disorders, and impulse-control disorders, are often accompanied by underlying depression. Medication is increasingly being used along with therapy to enhance the impact of psychotherapy on the primary diagnosis by alleviating the underlying symptoms.

Sometimes psychotherapy and medication can have a synergistic relationship, especially in the treatment of major depressive disorder. The medication acts first and, by energizing clients and promoting some optimism, enables them to make better use of psychotherapy; the impact of the therapy in turn promotes compliance with the recommended drug treatment. Antidepressant medications are particularly helpful in reducing vegetative symptoms, while the psychotherapy aids with many facets of adjustment and coping. Although the effects of the therapy may take longer to appear than the effects of the medication, the effects of the therapy are likely to last longer.

As already mentioned, this book is directed primarily toward nonmedical clinicians who do not themselves prescribe medication as part of the treatment they provide. Nevertheless, nonmedical clinicians who understand the role that medication can play in the treatment of mental disorders can determine when a client's progress might be accelerated by a referral for a medication evaluation and collaboration with a physician, usually a psychiatrist. For clients who are taking medication for mental disorders, ongoing assessment of medication compliance often is an important part of psychotherapy and reflects a holistic approach to treatment (Pratt & Mueser, 2002).

Psychotropic medications can be divided into five different groups (antipsychotics, antidepressants, mood stabilizers, anxiolytics, and other medication). Following is a brief overview of five of the psychotropic medications clients might be prescribed:

1. *Antipsychotic medications.* These drugs are primarily for the treatment of schizophrenia and other disorders involving delusions and hallucinations. People with Tourette's disorder, pervasive developmental disorders, and severe cognitive disorders also can benefit from these drugs. This category includes the phenothiazines (such as Thorazine, Prolixin, Mellaril, and Stelazine); such antipsychotic drugs as clozapine (Clozaril), haloperidol (Haldol), and risperidone (Risperdal, Invega, Invega Sustenna); and newer atypical antipsychotic medications with better tolerability and fewer extrapyramidal symptoms, including ziprasidone (Geodon), olanzapine (Zyprexa), quetiapine (Seroquel), and aripiprazole (Abilify).

2. *Antidepressant medications.* These drugs fall into the following groups:
   a. Tricyclic and heterocyclic antidepressants, which facilitate the treatment of moderate to severe major depressive disorder (especially with melancholia); enuresis; trichotillomania; panic attacks; bipolar depression; and eating, sleep, and obsessive-compulsive disorders. Examples of this type of drug include imipramine (Tofranil), doxepin (Sinequan), clomipramine (Anafranil), and amitriptyline (Elavil).
   b. Monoamine oxidase inhibitors (MAOIs), such as phenelzine (Nardil) and tranylcypromine (Parnate), which are often effective for atypical depression, severe phobias, anxiety disorders, panic disorder, obsessional thinking, hypochondriasis, and depersonalization disorder. They are also used to treat disorders that have not responded to other antidepressant medication.
   c. Selective serotonin reuptake inhibitors (SSRIs) are effective in the treatment of depression, as well as of such disorders as eating and somatoform disorders that are accompanied by underlying depression. They may

also be effective in reducing anxiety, especially when it is combined with depression. This category includes fluoxetine (Prozac), sertraline (Zoloft), citalopram (Celexa), fluvoxamine (Luvox), and paroxetine (Paxil).

    d. Serotonin and norepinephrine reuptake inhibitors (SNRIs) affect levels of both serotonin and norepinephrine. SNRIs include venlafaxine (Effexor), duloxetine (Cymbalta), and mirtazapine (Remeron). SNRIs may be more effective than SSRIs in the treatment of severe depression (Preston, O'Neal, & Talaga, 2010).

    e. Bupropion (Wellbutrin) is an atypical antidepressant that is frequently used alone or in combination with an SSRI.

3. *Mood stabilizers.* Lithium, the best-known mood stabilizer, is effective in reducing symptoms of mania, depression, and mood instability. Newer mood stabilizers include topiramate (Topamax), divalproex (Depakote), valproic acid (Depakene), and lamotrigine (Lamictal). They are used for treatment of bipolar disorders, cyclothymic disorder, and schizoaffective disorder.

4. *Benzodiazepine/antianxiety drugs.* These medications are used for reduction of anxiety, panic attacks, and insomnia. They also can facilitate withdrawal from drugs or alcohol and can enhance the impact of antipsychotic medication. Examples of these drugs are alprazolam (Xanax), lorazepam (Ativan), diazepam (Valium), and clonazepam (Klonopin). Some of these drugs are highly addictive and dangerous and so must be prescribed and used with great care.

5. *Other drugs.* Additional drugs helpful in the treatment of ADHD include methylphenidate (Ritalin, Concerta), atomoxetine (Strattera), and amphetamine mixed salts (Adderall). In 2007 the FDA approved dimesylate (Vyvanse) to treat ADHD in children age 6 to 12.

    Naltrexone (ReVia) and Methadone for prevention of misuse of alcohol and narcotics, respectively. Benzodiazepines are sometimes helpful in the treatment of irritability and agitation associated with withdrawal from substances. If withdrawal is accompanied by psychosis or paranoia, antipsychotic medications may also be helpful.

    Some medications are also prescribed "off label" for the treatment of psychiatric disorders. For example, beta-blockers, which are commonly prescribed for the treatment of high blood pressure, may also be prescribed to relieve the physical symptoms of anxiety disorders (Preston et al., 2010).

Electroconvulsive therapy (ECT) also deserves mentioning because of its beneficial use in the treatment of severe depression, particularly when psychotherapy and medication have failed, and especially when the depression is characterized by melancholia or accompanied by psychotic features. Although ECT has some worrisome side effects, these have been reduced over the years, and this treatment can bring benefit to people with treatment-resistant depression.

Adjunct Services (DO A CLIENT MAP)

Adjunct services can provide additional sources of support, education, and training. Parent skills training, for example, can be a useful adjunct to treatment for conduct disorder and reinforces what the child learns in therapy. Nutrition counseling can help people with eating disorders develop realistic goals that are appropriate to their weight and type of disordered eating. A person who has lost a family member to suicide might benefit by attending a peer support group with people with similar losses.

And 12-step programs such as Narcotics Anonymous or Alcoholics Anonymous can help people with substance-related disorders during the recovery process.

Adjunct services can also be suggested for family members. For example, families coping with a diagnosis of autism or a schizophrenia spectrum disorder might benefit from receiving psychoeducation about the disorder and attending caregiver support groups. Couples counseling or family counseling often helps family members understand the client better. For example, a woman with dependent personality disorder might benefit by participating in concurrent individual and couples counseling, to help her husband understand and support the changes she is trying to make.

All adjunct services should reinforce the goals the client is working on. Whether it is an exercise program, volunteer activities to improve socialization, mindfulness and stress-reduction workshops, or biofeedback to help people recognize bodily sensations, the types of services suggested should reinforce progress that a client is making in individual therapy. Between-session assignments can help clients get the most out of their sessions. For example, those who are technologically savvy might use computerized logs and journals to chart progress or participate in Internet support groups between therapy sessions to help them stay on task. The Internet has become one of the leading providers of health-care information, and clients can reinforce their efforts through special forums, support groups, and online resources relating to their areas of concern.

Near the conclusion of treatment, therapists might want to refer clients to adjunct services to begin work on secondary issues that have been raised in therapy but were not the central focus of attention. Referrals for marital counseling, family therapy, biofeedback, or career counseling might be appropriate at this time, depending on the person's goals.

Myriad types of adjunct services are available to suit the distinct needs of each client and the timing of treatment. Less well-functioning clients might need assistance in obtaining government services, such as legal aid or housing assistance, or referrals might be needed for inpatient hospitalization or day treatment. Therapists who creatively and diligently stay abreast of the available community resources will be able to refer clients to the appropriate services as needs arise.

Prognosis (DO A CLIENT MAP)

Prognosis refers to the likelihood that clients will achieve their objectives when treated according to the plan that has been developed to help them. Prognosis depends largely on two variables: the nature and severity of the disorders and problems and the client's motivations to make positive changes.

EXAMPLES OF TREATMENT PLANNING: ANNE AND BETTIE

Application of the preceding information on treatment planning to the cases of Bettie and Anne (discussed earlier in this chapter) should clarify the type of treatment likely to benefit each of them. This format, with examples of Client Maps for specific disorders, will be followed in subsequent chapters of the book.

Client Maps of Anne and Bettie

Although both women are coping with broken engagements, Anne is also dealing with an unplanned pregnancy, and she has used alcohol and avoidance as coping mechanisms. Bettie, by contrast, has more self-confidence and more personal resources, and she is able to view her unexpected change in plans as an opportunity for personal growth.

Both women probably would benefit from short-term therapy. Bettie should be seen weekly; she has significant concerns but is in no danger. Anne should be seen more frequently, until she has resolved her immediate crisis and dealt successfully with her alcohol use. Bettie is more self-directed. Although she does evidence some cognitive dysfunction, resistance, and mild depression, Bettie may respond well to a modified form of person-centered therapy that encourages her to develop her self-confidence and her self-awareness and to establish goals and direction, as well as interpersonal skills. Anne, by contrast, is less motivated toward self-exploration and is primarily interested in resolving her immediate concerns. Her therapy will probably focus more on cognitive-behavioral areas, emphasizing decision making and behavioral change.

Anne seems likely to respond best to individual therapy because she is in crisis, must make a rapid decision about her pregnancy, and is not currently interested in personal growth and development. Bettie, however, would probably benefit from either individual or group psychotherapy, or from a combination of the two—perhaps short-term individual therapy followed by participation in a personal growth group for women or a psychotherapy group for young adults.

Neither Anne nor Bettie seems to need medication, although Anne's therapist should make sure that Anne is receiving any necessary medical care and is aware of the risks of her alcohol use. Both Anne and Bettie are capable of self-regulation and are in touch with reality. An outpatient treatment setting, such as a community mental health center or a private practice, seems an appropriate location for treatment. Adjunct services, such as Alcoholics Anonymous and even inpatient treatment, may be considered for Anne if her alcohol misuse is severe enough.

After their immediate concerns have been resolved, both Bettie and Anne may decide to continue treatment, but their goals are likely to differ. Bettie will probably seek to improve her relationship skills, clarify her goals and direction, and enhance her self-esteem. Anne will probably need to develop better coping mechanisms and greater independence and may need to look at past issues to understand and change her poor choices.

The research on therapeutic variables does not yield definitive descriptions of the exact types of psychotherapy that would be best for each of these women. Nevertheless, it does offer guidelines for designing a treatment plan likely to be effective for each of them. Following are Client Maps for Anne and Bettie.

CLIENT MAP OF ANNE

Diagnosis

Axis I: 296.23 Major depressive disorder, single episode, severe, without psychotic features
305.00 Alcohol abuse
Axis II: Dependent personality traits
Axis III: No known physical disorders or conditions, but pregnancy reported
Axis IV: End of engagement, unplanned pregnancy, housing problems, unemployed
Axis V: Global assessment of functioning (GAF Scale): current GAF = 45

Objectives of Treatment

Establish and maintain abstinence from alcohol
Provide direction and structure so client can determine best outcome of pregnancy
Reduce stress
Stabilize living situation
Locate suitable employment
Improve coping skills

Assessments

Thorough medical evaluation to determine impact of alcohol use on pregnancy

Michigan Alcohol Screening Test

Clinician Characteristics

Knowledgeable about the development and symptoms of alcohol abuse

Structured and directive

Skilled at setting goals and direction

Able to promote motivation, independence, and optimism

Location of Treatment

Outpatient

Consider inpatient treatment if alcohol abuse worsens

Interventions to Be Used

Motivational therapy at the start, to enhance compliance with treatment plan

Cognitive-behavioral therapy

Emphasis of Treatment

Initial directive and supportive emphasis

Emphasis on cognitions and behavior

Numbers

Primarily individual therapy

Timing

Rapid pace

Longer duration (more than six months) to address issues of relapse prevention and dependence

Twice weekly sessions until client is out of crisis and more stable

Medications Needed

None

Adjunct Services

Support group to develop social and coping skills and provide support

Homework assignments

Twelve-step program such as Alcoholics Anonymous or Women for Sobriety

Prognosis

Good (after client gets past crisis), assuming she is motivated to stop drinking and find adequate coping skills
for dealing with her problems

Relapse common

CLIENT MAP OF BETTIE

Client Map of Bettie

Diagnosis

Axis I: 309.0 Adjustment disorder with depressed mood

Axis II: V71.09 No diagnosis on Axis II

Axis III: None reported

Axis IV: Problems with primary support group: end of engagement

Axis V: Global assessment of functioning (GAF Scale): current GAF = 77

Objectives of Treatment

Reduce stress and reinforce positive coping skills
Explore and determine goals and future direction
Develop relationship skills

Assessments

Myers-Briggs Type Indicator
Strong Interest Inventory

Clinician Characteristics

Supportive and exploratory
Skilled at fostering resilience
Able to promote exploration of long-term objectives

Location of Treatment

Outpatient

Interventions to Be Used

Initially cognitive-behavioral therapy
Process-experiential therapy

Emphasis of Treatment

Initial supportive emphasis
Emphasis on emotions and values

Numbers

Primarily individual therapy

Timing

Rapid pace
Short duration (less than six months)
Weekly sessions

Medications Needed

None

Adjunct Services

Career counseling
Referral to support group for women

Prognosis

Excellent

This chapter has presented an outline for a comprehensive treatment plan, the DO A CLIENT MAP. It has also reviewed the literature on the dimensions of effective therapy and on the contributions that the qualities of the therapist, the qualities of the client, and the interaction between therapist and client can make to therapeutic outcomes. The next eight chapters describe the various mental disorders and report on research of treatment approaches that have been found to be effective with those disorders. That information, in combination with the information presented in this chapter, should help clinicians maximize the success of their efforts to help clients in psychotherapy.

2

Mental Disorders in Infants, Children, and Adolescents

Shannon's first arrest occurred when she was 9 years old and was caught stealing a videotape from a local store, but her parents had been receiving complaints about her since kindergarten. She frequently pushed and hit younger children and took their toys. She tore up flowers and bushes in the neighbors' gardens and threw eggs at their houses. When the neighbors complained to her parents, Shannon and some friends retaliated by stealing the neighbors' mailbox and breaking bottles in their driveway.

At school, Shannon had trouble staying in her seat. She frequently interrupted other children and the teacher. She rarely completed her schoolwork independently, and she often lost her assignments.

Shannon's parents were concerned, but they both had experienced similar problems in school, and both had left high school without graduating. Both were employed to support the family (Shannon and two older children), the mother as a schoolbus driver and the father as a mechanic. Parental supervision was limited; the oldest child, age 16, watched Shannon and her brother after school.

Shannon's history reflects symptoms of disruptive behavior and attention deficit. These are common symptoms of mental disorders among children and adolescents.

OVERVIEW OF MENTAL DISORDERS IN INFANTS, CHILDREN, AND ADOLESCENTS

The need for mental health services for the nation's youth is evident in the following statistics:

- 1.5 million children ages 12 to 17 meet the criteria for admission to an alcohol treatment center (Substance Abuse and Mental Health Services Administration [SAMHSA], 2003).
- An estimated 12% of the 63 million children in the United States have a mental disorder (Oltmanns & Emery, 2007).
- In 2001, 23% of all victims of violent crime were children ages 12 to 17.
- Homicide and suicide are the second and third leading causes of death among young people ages 15 to 19. (Accidental death is the first.)
- Firearms were the cause of death in more than 80% of teen homicides and about half of teen suicides (Centers for Disease Control and Prevention, 2003). One study found that more than 90% of children and adolescents who committed suicide had a mental disorder (Shaffer & Craft, 1999).

Research repeatedly indicates that the best way to reduce the incidence and severity of mental disorders is prevention. Therefore, early identification of both symptoms and strengths and effective treatment of emotional problems in young people are critical in reducing the overall prevalence and severity of mental disorders.

Unlike the mental disorders discussed in other chapters of this book, which are related to one another by their similarity of symptoms, those discussed in this chapter are linked by their early age of onset. This chapter addresses the 13 major categories of disorders usually first diagnosed in infancy, childhood, or adolescence, as listed in the *Diagnostic and Statistical Manual of Mental Disorders (DSM-IV-TR)* (American Psychiatric Association, 2000). The chapter also briefly reviews childhood presentations of some disorders discussed elsewhere in the book. Although most of the disorders discussed in this chapter usually begin in childhood, many often continue into adulthood. It is estimated that 20% of children with chronic disorders will continue to have problems throughout their lives. Therefore, the information in this chapter is relevant to all therapists.

Etiology of Mental Disorders in Young People

Many theories have been advanced about the etiology of childhood mental disorders. Psychodynamic theorists typically describe these disorders as developmental fixations or regressions and attribute them to early childhood conflicts, experiences, or problems in attachment. Medical models look for neurological or genetic causes. Behavior theory posits that these disorders are the result of learned experiences. Ecological and social learning theorists consider the impact of environmental factors on the child. Developmental theorists look at age-related patterns and deviations from those patterns.

All these theories are relevant to an understanding of the full spectrum of mental disorders found in young people. For example, mental retardation reflects a deviation from age-appropriate levels of cognitive development, and some of the pervasive developmental disorders are characterized by a regression in language and social development. Other disorders, such as Rett's disorder, have neurological, biological, or genetic determinants. Conduct disorder often is linked to chaotic and antisocial family patterns.

Attachment also has an impact on child development. Bowlby (1969/1982) describes attachment as a process: A child produces behaviors in reaction to stress; these behaviors, in turn, elicit other behaviors from the caregiver that ideally provide a sense of security for the child, usually through physical closeness or proximity (Ainsworth, Blehar, Waters, & Wall, 1978). Bowlby's theory suggests that the quality of all subsequent interpersonal relationships is affected by the nature of attachment relationships formed during infancy. Findings suggest that insecure attachment during the early years can affect children's cognitive and social development, their relationships across the lifespan, and even their skills in parenting the next generation (Zeanah & Boris, 2000).

Children typically are referred for psychotherapy when their behaviors or symptoms interfere with their daily functioning or with the functioning of their families. Problems in school, such as inattention, misbehavior, or academic deficits, often prompt teachers or school counselors to suggest therapy. Academic problems often coexist with social–emotional problems, such as insecure attachment, inappropriate peer relationships, aggression, social isolation, low self-esteem, and lack of motivation. The family members of children with difficulties like these frequently experience considerable stress and anxiety themselves and may be struggling with their own mental disorders. Therefore, the therapist working with a child usually has targets of intervention in addition to the child—namely, the school, the family, and the environment. The therapist needs to be knowledgeable about social, educational, and community resources for children and families. The therapist also needs to be an excellent diagnostician because comorbidity and confusing presentations (such as a depressive disorder masked by anger or a bipolar disorder that looks like hyperactivity) are common in childhood mental disorders.

Prevalence and Client Characteristics

As many as 20% of adolescents and children may have a mental disorder (U.S. Department of Health and Human Services [DHHS], 2006). This translates into 7.7 million to 12.8 million children. Less than a third of those children are believed to be receiving the type of treatment they need (DHHS, 2006). An epidemiological study conducted by the National Institute of Mental Health (NIMH, 2005) estimates that half of all mental disorders begin by the age of 14. The National Comorbidity Survey Replication (Kessler, Berglund, et al., 2005) found that anxiety disorders have the highest lifetime prevalence rate (28.8%), followed by disruptive behavior and attentional disorders, including ADHD, conduct disorder, and oppositional defiant disorder (24.8%). Mood disorders (20.8%) and substance abuse disorders (14.6%) also are prevalent across the lifespan (Kessler, Berglund, et al., 2005).

In 2005, 16% of school-age children (4 to 17 years old) had parents who had talked to a health-care provider or school personnel about their child's emotional or behavioral difficulties in the previous 12 months. However, only about 6% of these children received any mental health treatment (NIMH, 2005). Boys have more emotional difficulties than girls in this age group. Seven percent of boys received some type of mental health treatment or help with emotional concerns other than medication, compared to 3% of girls. Boys were also more likely to be prescribed medication for behavioral and emotional difficulties (NIMH, 2005).

Mental disorders appear to be "the chronic diseases of the young" (NIMH, 2005), beginning in childhood and adolescence and affecting the core areas of life, including educational achievement, relationships, and occupational success (Kessler, Berglund, et al., 2005). Failure to recognize and diagnose these disorders, as well as delays in treatment, can exacerbate the situation, leading to mental illness that is more severe and more resistant to treatment, as well as to the development of co-occurring (or comorbid) disorders as the adolescent moves into young adulthood. Left untreated, early-onset mental disorders can lead to school failure, long-standing mood disorders, substance misuse, instability, and violence (Kessler, Berglund et al., 2005).

By definition, mental disorders in youth have an onset prior to the age of 18. Unlike adults, who usually come to therapists without a diagnosis, children often initially receive diagnoses in medical or educational settings. Their diagnoses usually address their major symptoms but may overlook comorbid disorders, so the therapist should be alert to additional symptoms or disorders that may require complex treatment planning.

Children with mental disorders vary in appearance. Some, for example, have obvious physical anomalies. Children with some disorders of neurobiological etiology, such as Rett's disorder or some types of mental retardation, typically have associated physical characteristics, such as microcephaly (small head), short stature, or atypical facial structure. By contrast, children with disorders of a psychosocial etiology, such as conduct or separation anxiety disorders, usually evidence no external physical symptoms.

Because children present differently in different settings, therapists should collect information from multiple sources in order to make accurate diagnoses. The collection of information should almost always include input from teachers and parents. A variety of checklists are available to assess behaviors. These inventories, including the Conners' Teacher and Parent Rating Scales (Conners, 1997), the Achenbach Child Behavior Checklist (Achenbach, 1991), and the Behavior Assessment System for Children, 2nd edition (BASC) (Reynolds & Kamphaus, 2002), are usually used to facilitate the collection and organization of information. Each assesses such characteristics as anxiety, depressive symptoms, hyperactivity, inattention, impulsivity, atypical thoughts, aggressive or delinquent behaviors, and somatic complaints.

Therapy with children usually involves contact with their families because a disorder and its concomitant behaviors will both affect and be affected by family life. The impact of financial and emotional stressors, transitions, and family relationships on a child's emotional health should all be assessed. Additional services may be required to provide treatment, support, and resources to siblings and parents, who may have their own emotional difficulties.

Preferred Therapist Characteristics

Therapists working with children should have a broad range of professional and personal skills. They must be patient and calm. They should have a clear understanding of their own values and of their own childhood and parenting experiences. As neutral adults, therapists typically are the focus of children's negative and positive reactions. Children may refuse to talk, make insulting and disparaging statements to their therapists, or even attack their therapists physically. Children may also relate to therapists in seductive or manipulative ways or look to the

therapist to save them. Countertransference reactions to these behaviors may interfere with treatment unless therapists carefully monitor and understand their feelings and use them only in ways that are therapeutic. Therapists may also need to manage their own rage in response to child maltreatment and their need to save children from their caregivers.

In addition to basic psychotherapy skills, therapists who work with children must have sound knowledge of human development over the lifespan. One of the therapist's most important tasks will be to distinguish between age-appropriate and atypical behaviors: Some of the disorders discussed in this chapter are characterized by behaviors that may be developmentally appropriate at some ages but clinically significant at others. In diagnosing attention-deficit/hyperactivity disorder (ADHD), for example, one task of the clinician is to determine how much activity is typical for the client's chronological age.

Collaboration with other professionals is another important task for therapists working with children. Young people who come for therapy may also have been seen by physicians, psychiatrists, school counselors, social workers, speech therapists, and family therapists. Ongoing consultation and collaboration with other professionals will be crucial to providing the most effective and efficient treatment. At the same time, however, too many helpers can fragment the treatment, so therapists may need to assume a case management role in order to coordinate services for children and their families and in order to ensure that all the treatment providers have shared and congruent goals.

Working with children and adolescents pose special challenges to the development of the therapeutic alliance. In family therapy, for example, developmental differences between children, adolescents, and adults require flexibility in communication skills on the part of the therapist.

Therapists may also need to finesse the dynamics of the parent–child–therapist alliance building. Engaging children in conversation one-on-one is a different dynamic when parents are in the room. Connecting with children without alienating parents may require finesse on the part of the therapist.

Cultural considerations must also be taken into account in family therapy. Multiple expectations, backgrounds, and hopes for the future may be combined in the room.

Different, and sometimes clashing, cultural values can cause friction between family members, and between therapist and family members. Especially with regard to cultural mores about age and gender, the therapist who uses respect and consideration with regard to traditional roles is more likely to gain respect and cooperation. Tension between first-generation immigrants and their more bicultural children can also impact the alliance. Therapists who are able to bridge the generational and the cultural divide will be found to be more credible and trustworthy. In such cases, therapists must not only be culturally aware, but also aware of how alliances between family members on cultural issues may evolve, and how their own cultural biases may unintentionally split the alliance (Escudero, Heatherington, & Friedlander, 2010; McGoldrick, Giordano, & Garcia-Preto, 2005).

Improving the alliance with adolescents can be difficult. Only by truly being there for the adolescent, as a good listener and as an ally, and by helping the child find personally meaningful goals, can the therapist work to improve the alliance (Escudero et al., 2010). Therapists who present themselves as allies are the most likely to improve the alliance with their adolescent clients.

Pacing of the alliance building is also different when working with adolescents than with adults. Most children are not self-referred, and may take a while to warm up to therapy and to realize how it can benefit them. Working with the adolescent on their concerns and promoting self-efficacy may be best, especially in the beginning of treatment. Pushing for strong feelings and emotions early on, before the alliance has a chance to form, may be premature. Helping parents to see their child's vulnerability and helping them to soften their feelings toward the child may result in the first steps toward positive change. Some initial success may be needed before therapy is viewed as valuable in the eyes of the adolescent (Escudero et al., 2010).

Parenting a child with a mental disorder can evoke feelings of failure, frustration, sadness, anger, and helplessness. The child's needs may also overwhelm the family, impairing its functioning and family relationships. Therefore, therapists working with children must give empathy and support to families as well as guidance about parenting, information about the particular disorders involved, and referrals for family therapy and other ancillary services.

Intervention Strategies

Treatment planning for children is a complex task; individual psychotherapy is rarely the sole treatment modality. Children experience at least two systems—the family and the school—that affect their behavior and emotional well-being. A therapist may be seeing a child for individual therapy while the child also is involved in special education, family therapy, medical treatment, and the juvenile justice system. Treatment of the child will usually require contact and cooperation with all the agencies and professionals concerned.

Interventions that take into account the child's stage of development, level and stage of change, demographic factors (for example, race, ethnicity, and socioeconomic status), and such personality traits as impulsivity and coping style have been found to improve treatment outcomes and reduce dropout rates (Prochaska & Norcross, 2010). Cultural variables should also be taken into account when diagnosing mental disorders and developing treatment plans for children (Paniagua, 2001).

Direct intervention strategies may include individual, group, and family therapy or consultation, as discussed in the following paragraphs. Other sections of this chapter discuss in greater detail the treatment modalities effective for specific disorders.

Individual Therapy   The structure of individual therapy—regularly scheduled sessions of fixed length and frequency that are conducted at a stable location—is in itself an important intervention. This kind of structure can give children a positive experience with clear limits and boundaries, as well as an environment in which trust and safety can readily be established.

Because adolescents are usually able to participate in traditional talk therapy, individual therapy for adolescents is similar to therapy for adults. Cognitive-behavioral, psychodynamic, person-centered, integrative, and other approaches can be used with adolescents who have sufficient ego strength and cognitive functioning to benefit from these methods of intervention. If the adolescent has significant expressive language disorders or mental retardation, however, some accommodations may be necessary so that accessible interventions can be provided.

Play Therapy   Not only is play therapy often the most developmentally appropriate way to connect with a child, research indicates it works (Baggerly, Ray, & Bratton, 2010; Elkind, 2007; White & Wynne, 2009). A meta-analysis of 93 play-therapy and filial studies conducted over a 50-year period revealed a large treatment effect (Bratton, Ray, Rhine, & Jones, 2005). Specifically, filial therapy conducted by parents was more effective than therapist-led play therapy;

nondirective humanistic approaches were more effective than directive approaches; and overall, play therapy was found to be a statistically viable intervention (Bratton et al., 2005).

Play therapy can be used to help children express themselves and modify their behaviors. Play therapy can be conducted in either group or individual treatment settings. Play therapists have an assortment of toys, games, and art supplies and assume that children will seek out the toys and activities that are relevant to their emotional needs. In the same way that physical, cognitive, and social–emotional development follow predictable patterns, play progresses through developmental stages. An understanding of the stages of play can provide therapists with a useful frame of reference for understanding children.

The process of play therapy varies and will depend on the theoretical orientation of the therapist. In person-centered play therapy, for example, children are allowed free expression in their play, and therapists reflect feelings, assuming that this process will be therapeutic in itself and that children have the ability to solve their own problems (Baggerly, Ray, & Bratton, 2010). In psychodynamic play therapy, therapists interpret the symbolism in the play; the assumption here is that unconscious material is brought into consciousness so that the child's ego is able to resolve unconscious psychic conflicts. Social learning theorists view play therapy as an opportunity for therapists to teach prosocial play behaviors and for children to practice appropriate social interactions. Cognitive-behavioral play therapy provides a more directive approach that incorporates cognitive and behavioral theories into traditional play therapy (Baggerly, 2010).

Group Therapy   Published outcome studies indicate that group therapy is the most frequently offered treatment modality for children and adolescents (Weisz & Hawley, 2002). Elementary school-age children tend to profit most from homogeneous groups that address a specific problem, whereas adolescents can benefit from groups that focus on a variety of issues (Thompson, Rudolph, & Henderson, 2003). A number of empirically supported treatments have been delivered in group format, including treatments for depression, anger, and anxiety disorders such as posttraumatic stress disorder. Group therapy can address behavioral difficulties, educational and social problems, and intrapsychic issues. The group format usually involves shared discussion about the personal issues of group members, an exchange of feedback, and opportunities for peer support, modeling, and behavioral rehearsal.

Many approaches to group therapy have been developed based on different theoretical models, as well as based on children's varying needs. For example, person-centered group therapy may be effective for children with adjustment disorders following natural disasters (Shen, 2010). Children with severe disruptive behavior disorders, however, typically require groups that have more structure and emphasize behavioral change. Other types of structured groups are those established with the purpose of helping members work toward a common goal. For example, groups to teach adolescents to cope with depression would include a carefully sequenced set of lessons. Impulse control, anger management, and problem solving are other areas in which structured therapeutic groups can benefit young clients. Training in these areas, based on cognitive-behavioral theory, teaches such skills as recognizing and labeling affect, managing stress, using relaxation techniques, understanding appropriate interpersonal distance, starting and stopping conversations, identifying problems, and evaluating alternative solutions.

Not all children should be involved in group therapy, however. Yalom (1995) recommends screening children for group readiness, and Dishion, McCord, and Poulin (1999) suggest that the problem behaviors of adolescents with conduct disorder may actually increase with exposure to others who have similar problems. Moreover, children who are actively experiencing psychotic thoughts are usually not appropriate candidates for group therapy.

Family Interventions On the assumption that a child's or an adolescent's behavior is shaped by the family, therapists often involve families in treatment. The goal of this kind of intervention is to change those interactions among family members that may be contributing to or sustaining a troubled child's difficulties. Structural family therapy, for example, seeks to develop appropriate boundaries between family members and subsystems. Another therapeutic goal in this model of therapy is the empowering of adults to take on the responsibilities of parenting. Interactional models focus on improving communication skills among family members. The parents, the troubled child, and the siblings may be guided in making "I" statements and in rephrasing content or expressing emotions in constructive ways; modeling and role playing are often used to achieve this goal. The particular approach to family therapy will be determined by the nature of the family's dynamics and difficulties and the child's disorder.

Clinical research supports family involvement for a variety of childhood problems, including autism, conduct disorder, oppositional defiant disorder, ADHD, eating disorders, and substance use disorders (Carr, 2009; Nathan & Gorman, 2007; Weisz & Kazdin, 2010). Younger children also fare better with increased family or parental involvement. Of individual, group, and family modalities, family therapy is the most underused and has a higher dropout rate. Therapists who implement family therapy should address the issue of participation up front and discuss barriers that may preclude parent and family participation. Family patterns of dysfunction may need to be addressed through couples counseling or individual counseling.

Parental psychoeducation may also be used to complement a child's treatment. In this approach, information is presented to the parents about their child's disorder, and methods are suggested for creating positive change. Psychoeducation often involves a prescribed curriculum, presented over a series of sessions.

The issue of confidentiality with children is complicated because the family is an integral part of the treatment, if only in a supportive way (for example, in family members' provision of transportation or payment). Therapists need to clarify the boundaries and limits of confidentiality with the child as well as with the other family members before therapy begins. What information will be communicated to parents, as well as how that communication will occur, should be agreed on during the planning phase of treatment. These negotiations will be especially important when the child is a mature adolescent.

Transdiagnostic Approach   A transdiagnostic or unified approach to treatment focuses on specific symptoms or behaviors regardless of diagnosis. For example, impulsive behavior is found in many childhood disorders—ADHD, childhood bipolar disorder, and conduct disorder to name a few. A transdiagnostic approach would be to treat the symptom of impulsivity regardless of the specific diagnosis. Many new programs are sprouting up that provide symptom-focused treatment for young children, school-age children, and adolescents. Affect dysregulation is a common feature of anxiety and mood disorders, PTSD, and disruptive behavior disorders such as ODD and conduct disorder (Paula, 2009). Children who become distressed quickly and have difficulty regulating their emotions would benefit from therapy that helps them recognize and label their emotions, and connect them to triggering events. Play therapy for affect regulation combines a cognitive-behavioral approach with play to help these children develop a range of coping strategies and tools they can use to regulate their emotions before they erupt into explosive or unpredictable behavior.

Other Treatment Modalities   Behavioral change programs for use at home or in school are frequently an integral part of psychotherapy with children. Filial therapy, in which trained play therapists instruct parents or teachers to be therapeutic agents at home or in the classroom, has been shown to increase caregiver empathy and reduce children's behavior problems. Through didactic instruction, supportive supervision, and play therapy simulations in session, at home, or in the classroom, parents and teachers reinforce the learning that is taking place in session (Landreth & Bratton, 2006). Symptoms that may benefit from this type of intervention include repetitive or habitual behaviors, impulsive or off-task behaviors that interfere with the completion of schoolwork, and PTSD symptoms resulting from trauma and domestic violence. Filial therapy requires carefully planned collaboration and is rarely effective without the support and involvement of the adults in a child's daily life. Treatment manuals can be helpful when conducting filial therapy with children and their families (see Bratton, Landreth, Kellam, & Blackard, 2006).

Psychotropic medication is increasingly used with children; psychostimulants for ADHD are particularly common. The positive effect of stimulant medication has been documented repeatedly, but its use continues to be a source of debate among physicians and psychotherapists. Antidepressant medication is often prescribed for children with mood disorders, including bipolar disorder, although recent research indicates that placebo works just as well in 50% to 60% of children (Bridge et al., 2007). Given the risk that selective serotonin reuptake inhibitors (SSRIs) pose for children, medication should not be used until several attempts at psychotherapy have failed, or in the most treatment refractory cases (Dulcan, 2009). Other medications used to treat childhood mental disorders include neuroleptics, such as haloperidol (Haldol) for tic or psychotic disorders, and atypical antipsychotics. Therapists working with children should be aware of the potential drug therapies and their side effects.

Residential or day treatment programs and hospitalization are interventions for severe disorders in young clients. These may be necessary for children who pose a danger to themselves or to others. Residential treatment programs are sometimes used in the treatment of children with severe or profound mental retardation, conduct disorder, severe eating disorders, substance use disorders, or psychotic disorders that do not respond to outpatient or pharmacological interventions.

Prognosis

Outcome research for mental disorders in children and adolescents is limited and rarely encompasses the full range of treatments available or accounts for comorbid disorders. Most research provides information only on short-term outcomes; additional longitudinal research is needed. Further information will be provided throughout this chapter on effective treatments for specific mental disorders in young people.

One weakness of outcome research is that it tends to focus on behavioral or cognitive-behavioral interventions (Weisz & Hawley, 2002); there has been little research on nonbehavioral approaches. Readers should keep this limitation in mind when outcome research is discussed. We now turn to the mental disorders of childhood.

MENTAL RETARDATION

The criteria for diagnosis of mental retardation includes onset prior to age 18, below-average intellectual functioning (IQ below 70), and impaired adaptive functioning in at least two important areas, such as communication, social skills, and work (American Psychiatric Association, 2000). Mental retardation has a pervasive impact on cognitive, emotional, and social development. The prognosis for improvement in functioning is significantly correlated with the degree of intellectual impairment.

Description of the Disorder

Historically, mental retardation has been diagnosed from results of individual intelligence tests, such as the Wechsler intelligence scales (2001) and the Stanford-Binet Intelligence Scales; level of social functioning has also been incorporated into the diagnosis. Performance on standardized IQ tests determines the subcategory of retardation. An inventoried IQ score in the range of 50–55 to 70, two to three standard deviations below the mean, reflects *mild* mental retardation. An IQ score in the range of 35–40 to 50–55, or three to four standard deviations below the mean, reflects *moderate* mental retardation. An IQ score in the range of 20–25 to 35–40, or 4–5 standard deviations below the mean, reflects *severe* mental retardation. An IQ score below the range of 20–25 reflects *profound* mental retardation. Because of the many physical anomalies that may be associated with severe and profound levels of retardation, children with those low levels of functioning usually can be identified during infancy. In contrast, mild to moderate levels of retardation may not be diagnosed until children begin school.

Recent estimates suggest that approximately 1% to 3% of the general population can be diagnosed with mental retardation (Bebko, Weiss, Demark, & Gomez, 2006). Approximately 40% to 60% of people with mental retardation have identifiable biological causes for the disorder, such as genetic and chromosomal abnormalities, prenatal and perinatal difficulties, or acquired childhood diseases (Handen & Gilchrist, 2006). Boys are 3 times more likely than girls to be diagnosed with mental retardation, which may in part be accounted for by fragile X syndrome—the most common cause of inherited mental retardation (Mash & Wolfe, 2010). Down syndrome is the most widely known genetic type of mild or moderate retardation. Severe and profound retardation commonly have neurological origins and may be associated with more than 200 physical disorders, including cerebral palsy, epilepsy, and sensory disorders.

Mild and moderate mental retardation are also more common among children of low socioeconomic status (SES) and children from minority groups (Mash & Wolfe, 2010). This correlation with SES has led to questions about the validity of these diagnoses. The issue is confounded by the fact that children with mild retardation often demonstrate age-appropriate behaviors at home but developmentally inappropriate behaviors at school. Brooks-Gunn, Klebanov, Smith, Duncan, and Lee (2003) undertook a study of IQ and SES and found that differences between African American and white children were reduced by 71% when SES was accounted for. As the population of the United States becomes increasingly diverse, therapists will need to exercise caution in diagnosing mental retardation. The therapist should make a thorough examination of clients' cultural and socioeconomic contexts and of their non-academic functioning. The therapist will also have to determine whether the assessment tools being used are culturally biased.

Typical Client Characteristics

The American Association on Mental Retardation (AAMR, 2002) developed a multifaceted diagnostic approach that takes into account a person's ability and level of support needed rather than IQ when defining mental retardation. The largest classification, comprising 85% of people with this disorder, are people with mild mental retardation. Children with mild levels of retardation may not exhibit atypical behaviors in all environments. They often master self-care, as well as social and job skills. Children with mild levels of retardation may demonstrate highly adaptive behaviors in nonacademic settings. Their cognitive deficits may become apparent only when they are placed in situations that require higher order reasoning skills, such as reading, writing, or mathematics. To learn these skills, the children usually require special education, which adapts the curriculum to their learning needs.

People with moderate mental retardation comprise approximately 10% of those with mental retardation. Children diagnosed with moderate mental retardation may achieve intellectual levels as adults of the average 4- to 7-year-old child (Butcher, Mineka, & Hooley, 2006). Even though their rate of learning is slow, they may learn to read and write, obtain a full understanding of spoken language, and be partially responsible for self-care. However, due to poor motor skills, lack of coordination, bodily deformities, and sometimes an angry or hostile temperament, they may not be able to achieve complete independence.

A child with a severe level of retardation will frequently exhibit significant motor deficiencies in addition to cognitive impairment. The child may require a wheelchair for mobility and may require assistance with feeding, toileting, and self-care. Speech and language deficiencies may necessitate a facilitated communication device, such as a picture board or word cards. People with severe mental retardation comprise 3% to 4% of those with mental retardation. They are generally diagnosed at a very young age because of developmental delays and physical anomalies (Mash & Wolfe, 2010).

Profound mental retardation is rare, comprising only 1% to 2% of people with mental retardation. Because of severe cognitive impairments, these individuals are capable of learning only basic self-care behaviors and are likely to need lifelong care. Epilepsy, congenital heart defects, and other medical conditions are likely to co-occur in this population.

Comorbid psychological and physical disorders are common among people with mental retardation. Thirty percent to 50% of children with mental retardation experience serious emotional difficulties in addition to their disorder (Handen & Gilchrist, 2006). Most common are ADHD, oppositional defiant disorder, conduct disorder, anxiety disorders, and depression. Johnson (2002) notes that these disorders may be the most common reasons why children are placed in special educational settings.

In recent years, fetal alcohol syndrome has received increasing attention from the medical and research communities. Children with this medical condition often develop mild mental retardation. Co-occurring disorders and symptoms include ADHD, decreased impulse control, and diverse learning problems. Despite public education programs about the dangers of alcohol use during pregnancy, the incidence of fetal alcohol syndrome is 5 to 20 cases per 10,000 births (Weber, Floyd, Riley, & Snider, 2002).

Preferred Therapist Characteristics

Therapists working with people diagnosed with mental retardation must be able to establish realistic goals and accept limited progress. They must be knowledgeable about human development

and the correlation between intellectual level and development in thinking, communication, and social and motor skills. They should exhibit patience and genuineness in their interactions with people with mental retardation.

Therapists must also have excellent collaborative skills because often multiple services are provided by a variety of agencies. Harbin, McWilliam, and Gallagher (2000) identify four key elements in creating interventions for people with mental retardation: early intervention to reduce dysfunction, a family-centered approach, integration of therapy into the child's environment, and inclusion of the child within the academic and social environment.

People with mental retardation probably will need treatment into adulthood to help them achieve as much independence as possible. Therefore, therapists may serve as long-term case managers, coordinating a variety of services and playing a role as advocates for these clients. Therapists must work closely with the families of people with mental retardation to facilitate the ongoing treatment of this population.

Intervention Strategies

Early intervention is essential to the effective treatment of children with mental retardation. Special education, home health care, language stimulation, and social skills training at an early age can have a great impact on treatment outcomes. A developmental approach, which takes account of children's cognitive age rather than their chronological age and sets goals based on individual abilities and needs, is crucial to working with children with mental retardation.

Many people with mild or moderate levels of retardation have the potential to function in socially appropriate ways if they are provided with adequate training. Handen and Gilchrist (2006) suggest that parent training, community-based treatment, and individual psychotherapy can all be effective in promoting these clients' positive self-regard and improving their social and occupational skills.

The value of community-based treatment resources, such as occupational therapy, group support, and recreational facilities, are also substantiated by empirical evidence that documents the benefits of these programs for children diagnosed with mental retardation (Handen & Gilchrist, 2006).

Most children with severe and profound levels of retardation will ultimately reside in public institutions. Therapists involved in their treatment can contribute to their quality of life by helping them develop recreational interests and interpersonal relationships.

Behavior modification has long been viewed as the treatment modality of choice for mental retardation and has been especially helpful in decreasing self-injurious behaviors (SIBs). Kahng, Iwata, and Lewin (2002) report that SIBs generally respond well to behavioral treatment, with a success rate of 80%. The effectiveness of behavioral interventions increases when the treatment is designed to meet the specific needs of the individual.

Family counseling may be indicated, to improve parent–child interactions and educate families about services available in the community. Families of children with mental retardation could benefit from supportive therapy, particularly when the initial diagnosis is made and at times when changes or adaptations for the child are required. Marital problems are common among parents of children with mental retardation and may also require intervention, as may issues of loss and grief that are similar to those experienced by parents during bereavement.

Psychopharmacology plays an increasingly important role in the control of such symptoms as aggression, agitation, and hyperactivity associated with mental retardation. Lithium and antipsychotic medications have been used to reduce aggressive behaviors and SIB in children with mental retardation. Psychostimulants for ADHD (which affects 9% to 16% of children with mental retardation) are often prescribed to control hyperactivity and improve concentration.

As mentioned earlier, case management for people with mental retardation is often an important part of treatment planning, particularly for adolescents and young adults. Advocacy with schools, agencies, and families and facilitation of appropriate job placement are tasks that can be included in a treatment plan, as can coordination of a multimodal treatment team.

Prognosis

Mental retardation has implications for a person's entire lifespan. Adults with a mild level of retardation often live independently and maintain jobs with minimal supervision. People with a moderate level of retardation may ultimately be able to live independently in group-home settings and gain employment in sheltered workshops. Social skills training, career counseling, and development of self-awareness skills may all facilitate these clients' efforts at being independent. Therapists working with children and adults who have severe and profound levels of mental retardation may be able to effect many positive changes. For example, behavioral techniques to reduce SIB have been proven effective. Regardless of the degree of retardation, therapists can make a difference in improving the lives of people diagnosed with mental retardation.

LEARNING, MOTOR SKILLS, AND COMMUNICATION DISORDERS

The *DSM-IV-TR* estimates that the prevalence of learning disorders ranges from 2% to 10%, with approximately 5% of students in public schools having a learning disorder. Children with language and learning disorders account for 75% of all public school special education services (Woo & Keatinge, 2008). Approximately 4% to 6% of children have motor skills deficits.

Description of the Disorders

According to the *DSM-IV-TR*, a determination that a child's level of functioning is significantly below expectations is made if the child's score on achievement tests is more than two standard deviations below the child's IQ. Functioning is measured with such standardized assessments as the Woodcock Johnson-III Tests of Achievement (Woodcock & Johnson, 2001) or the Wechsler Individual Achievement Test, 2nd edition (Wechsler, 2001).

Deficiencies of vision or hearing should be ruled out as causes of impairment before learning disorders are diagnosed. The category of learning disorders not otherwise specified describes academic deficits that do not meet the criteria for specific learning disorders. This diagnosis may be used when a child exhibits deficits in more than one academic area, when the deficits do not reach the required degree of significance (2 standard deviations below age- and ability-based expectations) or in a learning area not specifically named in the *DSM*.

Learning, motor skills, and communication disorders currently are thought to be related to genetics, brain function, and environmental risk factors (Mash & Wolfe, 2010). Family patterns of learning disabilities have long been recognized. Approximately 35% to 45% of boys with learning disorders have at least one parent who had similar learning problems. Environmental factors associated with learning disorders include low SES, poor self-esteem, depression, and perceptual deficiencies (Silver, 2006). As a result of these concomitant problems, differential diagnosis may be difficult, and treatment may require both educational and psychological interventions.

Typical Client Characteristics

Reading disorders are found in approximately 4% of school-age children, making it the most common learning disability (Kamphaus, 2000); of that group, 60% to 80% are boys. Children with reading disorders may have difficulty decoding unknown words, memorizing vocabulary lists, and comprehending written passages. There is a growing body of research that indicates that early interventions can successfully improve reading, math, and writing skills (Lyon, Fletcher, Fuchs, & Chhabra, 2006). Conversely, lack of interventions can lead to continued problems throughout adolescence and into adulthood.

Approximately 1% of school-age children can be diagnosed with mathematics disorders (American Psychiatric Association, 2000). Children with mathematics-related deficiencies may have procedural, semantic memory, and visual-spatial problems that contribute to learning disabilities in mathematics (Geary, 2003). Frequent procedural errors can result from poor understanding of the concepts, the use of procedures more commonly employed by younger children, and difficulties in sequencing. Semantic memory problems can include memory deficits and difficulty retrieving facts. Problems with visual-spatial relations can cause children to misinterpret or misunderstand spatially represented information. Any combination of these problems, in addition to the child's own lowered expectations, can contribute to mathematics disorders (Geary, 2003).

Disorders of written expression are rarely found in isolation; another learning disorder is also present in most cases (American Psychiatric Association, 2000). The difficulties associated with disorders of written expression are typically reflected in multiple areas, which include handwriting, spelling, grammar, and the creation of prose.

Preferred Therapist Characteristics

Therapists working with children who have learning disorders must be able to take a broad view of their clients, determining and assessing a range of possible contributing factors and coexisting mental disorders. Therapists should be able to evaluate children's perceptual and cognitive processes, as well as their emotional functioning. Children with significant language deficits may require nonverbal approaches to therapy, such as play therapy or activity–group therapy. Therapists should be able to work effectively as part of a treatment team that includes school; family; and occupational, physical, or language therapists.

Intervention Strategies

The primary interventions for children with learning disorders will occur at school. The major goal will be the remediation of learning and skill deficits. A child who demonstrates significant underachievement (more than two standard deviations below measured ability) may be eligible for special education. The Individuals with Disabilities Education Act of 1997 and the Reauthorized IDEA of 2004 spell out services to all children with disabilities (Yell, 2011). Initially implemented in 1975 as Public Law 94–142, the Education for All Handicapped Children Act was renamed in 1990 as the Individuals with Disabilities Education Act and requires an individualized education plan, developed by the school according to the child's individual needs, as well as the provision that all children with learning disabilities must be educated in the least restrictive environment.

The IDEA 2004 includes a responsiveness to intervention approach to provide earlier identification of students with learning disabilities and a systematic, research-based approach to interventions.

Children with learning disorders frequently come for counseling because of problems with their interpersonal skills. The same perceptual difficulties that impair academic learning can interfere with a child's comprehension of social information and may result in inappropriate social behaviors (Silver, 2006). Based on cognitive-behavioral models, social skills training programs teach behaviors associated with making a personal approach, attending and communication skills, and understanding the nature of social interactions and personal space (Lyon et al., 2006). The lessons are primarily didactic but are typically given in small-group settings to facilitate practice and feedback.

Therapists are especially likely to see children with learning or related disorders if there is a coexisting psychological disorder. Treatment plans should take into account not just the coexisting mental disorder but also the academic, interpersonal, family, and self-esteem issues that typically accompany learning problems.

Prognosis

Although some early learning deficits are related to developmental delays and can improve with maturation, many such deficits continue to have a negative impact on functioning throughout adolescence and adulthood. Learning disorders and related disorders, left undiagnosed and untreated, can lead to extreme frustration, loss of self-esteem, inadequate education, under-employment, and more serious disorders in adulthood. Proactive interventions, including psychotherapy and social skills training, can have a significant positive impact on children with these disorders.

PERVASIVE DEVELOPMENTAL DISORDERS

Pervasive development disorders are also known as autism spectrum disorders (ASDs) in recognition of the underlying similarities in diagnosis and the hierarchical nature of the disorders. The two terms are used interchangeably.

Description of the Disorders

DSM-IV-TR describes five pervasive developmental disorders (PDDs). All five have a great impact on neurological, emotional, linguistic, and sometimes physical development. The following five disorders are differentiated by age, pattern of onset, and nature of symptoms.

1. Autistic disorder
2. Pervasive developmental disorder not otherwise specified (PDD-NOS)
3. Asperger's disorder
4. Childhood disintegrative disorder
5. Rett's disorder

The first three disorders, autistic disorder, Asperger's disorder, and PDD-NOS, are considered to be a hierarchy of symptoms commonly referred to as the autism spectrum. These autism spectrum disorders (ASDs) are heterogeneous, and yet each typically have deficits in socialization, communication, and behavior (American Psychiatric Association, 2000; Baird et al., 2001; NIMH, 2004). Rett's disorder and childhood disintegrative disorder (CDD) are more serious (and rare) disorders. Children with Rett's or CDD tend to regress over time, whereas those with ASDs may improve. Because of the complex array of symptoms associated with pervasive developmental disorders, an accurate differential diagnosis is crucial to aid in the development of early interventions and appropriate treatment plans.

The most recent findings from the Centers for Disease Control and Prevention indicate that 1 in 150 children are affected by autism spectrum disorders (CDC, 2007). The rate increases to 1 in 94 for male children. That is more than a 10-fold increase since the early 1990s (CDC, 2007), making autism more frequent than pediatric AIDS, diabetes, and cancer combined. Various explanations for the dramatic increase include broader diagnostic criteria, increasing awareness of autism, children being diagnosed at a younger age, and methodological differences in prevalence research, among others (Dawson & Faja, 2008).

The underlying cause(s) of autism remains unknown. A genetic susceptibility in conjunction with environmental factors may lead to disruptions in brain development at a critical point in the child's development. Researchers believe individual differences result in multiple developmental pathways that result in abnormal neural circuitry and the development of autistic symptoms.

ASDs tend to occur more frequently in family members than in the general population. Research shows that when a family has one child with autism, the risk of having a second child with the same disorder is greater than in the general population, particularly if the mother conceives within 12 months of giving birth to another child. Fragile X syndrome (a chromosomal disorder more common in males) has been found in as many as 25% of cases of autistic disorder (Kabot, Masi, & Segal, 2003). To date, more than 100 genes have been tested in the search for an autism susceptibility gene (Dawson & Faja, 2008). Although results are promising, research continues to point to the interaction of multiple genes as providing a genetic susceptibility that is then exacerbated by environmental influences.

The types of these early environmental risk factors are legion. Childhood vaccinations that contained mercury had once been considered the culprit but extensive research and epidemiological studies have failed to find a link (Wilson, Mills, Ross, McGowan, & Jadad, 2003).

Many infants show symptoms of ASDs as early as 6 months. These early symptoms include lower incidence of smiling and spontaneous vocalizations, less face-gazing behaviors, and fewer attempts to seek physical contact (Maestro et al., 2002). Symptoms tend to increase between 6 to 12 months of age, with most 1-year-olds on the autism spectrum exhibiting core symptoms.

As children get older, decreased social interest, poor social skills, and a limited capacity for empathy become apparent. Speech is often limited or atypical, and children with ASDs often have difficulty sustaining a conversation. Most exhibit rigid, stereotyped, repetitive behaviors, such as rocking, flapping, or head banging. Children diagnosed with ASDs tend to under- or overreact to sensory stimuli and have difficulty with change and variations from their regular routines. Many children with ASDs can also be diagnosed with mental retardation, although some high-functioning children have cognitive abilities in the average or superior range which is frequently the case in Asperger's disorder (Baird et al., 2001). Moreover, a variety of general medical conditions, including chromosomal abnormalities and chronic infections, often can be found in children with ASDs.

Such conditions as ADHD, obsessive-compulsive disorder (OCD), mental retardation, and learning disorders frequently are comorbid with ASDs. These and other co-occurring disorders make differential diagnosis difficult, especially in young children and in children with severe disability or superior intelligence. Interested readers are referred to Gallo (2010) for complete information on differential diagnosis of autism spectrum disorders across the lifespan.

The autism spectrum disorders have many similarities, but each is diagnosed based on distinguishing characteristics. Discussion of these follows.

Autistic Disorder Autistic disorder is characterized by significant deficits in socialization, communication, and behavior (American Psychiatric Association, 2000). Social difficulties are reflected by limited initiation of social interaction or conversation, lack of interest in other people, dysfunctional emotions, poor skills in imitating affective expressions, and limited empathy. Children with autistic disorder are often found to have social motivation impairments that inhibit their response to social and environmental input (Dawson & Faja, 2008).

Autistic disorder is 4 to 5 times more prevalent in males than in females and has been found throughout the world and in families of all ethnic, racial, and socioeconomic backgrounds (American Psychiatric Association, 2000).

The degree of impairment in communication skills varies widely among people with autistic disorder. Some may be largely or totally mute, whereas others do eventually develop age-appropriate language skills; nearly all, however, have problems with the use of narrative language and with comprehension, and they tend to show abnormalities in spoken language. These problems further impair their socialization.

Children with autistic disorder rarely engage in make-believe play that mimics human activity. Their play more often exhibits repetitive, stereotyped interactions with inanimate objects—for example, lining toys up in a row rather than engaging in imaginative play. As these children grow older, this play activity may evolve into obsessional interest in mechanical objects, time schedules, or factual data. In as many as 30% of cases, children with autistic disorder may also exhibit tics and stereotypical movements and vocalizations (Baron-Cohen, Allen, & Gillberg, 1992). Fascination with moving things (such as ceiling fans and light switches), aggressive and hyperactive behavior, abnormalities in sleeping and eating, and a preoccupation with some narrow interest (dinosaurs, trains, meteorology) are also likely.

Another characteristic of autistic disorder is onset before the age of 3. Infants with autistic disorder can often be distinguished from other children by such symptoms as deficits in pointing ability, reluctance to look at others, and inability to orient to their names (Kabot et al., 2003). Sleeping and eating disorders are also common. Although it is not included in the *DSM-IV-TR* diagnostic criteria, some studies indicate that a period of normal language and behavioral development in infants can be followed by a period of regression around the age of 15 to 19 months in as many as 40% of cases (Kabot et al., 2003). Mental retardation accompanies this diagnosis in 75% to 80% of children (NIMH, 2004). Nearly a third of children develop seizures, with the incidence of seizures being more common in females, in children with lower IQs, and in children with less language and motor skills abilities. The CARS was not significantly different between those with ASD who had seizures and those who did not (Hartley-McAndrew & Weinstock, 2010). Tuberous sclerosis is also common (NIMH, 2004).

Children with autistic disorder are particularly likely to have relatives who have affective disorders. Anxiety is common (R. L. Koegel, Koegel, Vernon, & Brookman-Frazee, 2010), and bipolar or major depression is found in about one third of the families of people with autism (DeLong, 1994; Kabot et al., 2003).

Pervasive Developmental Disorder Not Otherwise Specified (PDD-NOS)

PDD-NOS is most frequently used as the diagnosis for pervasive developmental disorders that do not fit into any of the other categories because of insufficient symptoms, age of onset criteria, or improvements that make the diagnosis of autism no longer valid. At least two pathways result in a PDD-NOS diagnosis. The first is to meet the criteria for the pattern of symptoms for a PDD, but of lesser severity. The second diagnostic pathway involves meeting the criteria for PDD in only one or two domains. Adults who present with autism but in whom onset before age 3 cannot be verified would also fall into this category. Atypical autism would also be coded as PDD-NOS.

Asperger's Disorder

Like autism, Asperger's disorder is typified by impaired social skills and repetitive or stereotypical behaviors. Unlike autistic disorder, however, Asperger's disorder typically does not involve significant delays or impairment in the development of language, oral communication, or cognitive functioning (American Psychiatric Association, 2000). Children with this disorder also often develop age-appropriate self-help skills. Although children with Asperger's disorder have limited skills in social interaction, they may seek out interpersonal situations. This is one of the characteristics that sets Asperger's disorder apart from the other PDDs (Smith-Myles & Simpson, 2002).

Asperger's disorder is estimated to affect about 48 in every 10,000 children (Smith-Myles & Simpson, 2002). The disorder is at least 5 times more common in males, and onset is somewhat later than autism (American Psychiatric Association, 2000). There also appears to be elevated incidence of Asperger's disorder among family members.

Other Pervasive Developmental Disorders

Rett's disorder and childhood disintegrative disorder are more rare forms of PDDs. In these disorders, the child begins to regress after a period of relatively normal development, and profound disabilities result.

Rett's Disorder   Rett's disorder was first identified in 1966 by Dr. Andreas Rett. This neuro-developmental disorder is characterized by a period of normal development during the first 5 to 48 months of life. This period is followed by progressive loss of abilities and ultimately by severe or profound retardation. Recent research has traced the cause of Rett's disorder to a genetic mutation of the MeCP2 gene located on the X chromosome (Colvin et al., 2003). This disorder is rare, and is estimated to affect one to four in 10,000 females (Newsom & Hovanitz, 2006). Males have not been found to have Rett's disorder.

Children with this disorder exhibit deceleration of head growth, stereotypical hand movements (usually hand wringing or hand washing), lack of social involvement, poorly coordinated gait or trunk movements, mental retardation, and severely impaired receptive and expressive language development (American Psychiatric Association, 2000). Other symptoms, such as seizures, delays in physical growth, and scoliosis, vary with the individual and with age. Forty percent of people with Rett's disorder never develop clear nonverbal communication, whereas others are able to use eye movements and body language to communicate (Colvin et al., 2003). People with this disorder remain severely functionally dependent. Because of the increasing evidence of the biological basis of Rett's disorder, it may be eliminated from the next edition of the *DSM*, or coded as a medical condition on Axis III.

Childhood Disintegrative Disorder   Children diagnosed with childhood disintegrative disorder manifest apparently normal development until at least the age of 2. At some point between the ages of 2 and 10, however, they exhibit

significant regression of functioning in at least two of the following areas:

- Language
- Social skills
- Elimination
- Play
- Motor skills

Children with this extremely rare disorder eventually exhibit social, communication, and behavioral deficits that are similar to those of children with ASDs. Severe mental retardation also usually accompanies childhood disintegrative disorder. This disorder is more common among males (American Psychiatric Association, 2000). Childhood disintegrative disorder is considered to be quite rare (1.1 to 6.4 per 100,000) and without adequate research specifying the timing and symptoms of regression. The *DSM-5* is expected to address whether childhood disintegrative disorder is different from autistic regression, and how CDD fits into the autism spectrum.

Typical Client Characteristics

Children with autism spectrum disorders have multiple deficits in the areas of language and behavior but social deficits are considered the hallmark of the disorder (Koegel et al., 2010). By the age of 2, children with ASDs exhibit abnormal eye gaze, frequently avoid eye contact, and fail to establish mutual gaze with their caregivers (White, Koenig, & Scahill, 2007). These types of social deficits are noticeable across all PDDs, including high-functioning autism and Asperger's disorder.

Children with ASDs do not demonstrate the social behaviors that one expects in children of their age. They typically do not seek parental attention, hugs, or social cues and do not engage in imitative or interactive play (Woo &

Keatinge, 2008). Their social skills may improve with age or circumstances although the quality of their interactions continues to be weak. Other characteristics of people with PDDs vary and depend on the specific disorder; most of the available research focuses on autism and Asperger's disorder.

Autistic speech usually reflects such atypical features as echolalia or rote repetition of what others have said. Older children with autism may develop fairly complex speech, but participating in conversational language remains a challenge for them because they miss social and conversational cues. Children with autistic disorder and Asperger's disorder often have difficulty with changes in routine or when transitioning from one activity to another and may engage in repetitive stereotyped patterns of behavior at these, and other times of stress. Stereotypes may involve spinning, rocking, arm flapping, hand clapping or other repetitive gestures that serve a self-regulating function when the child becomes overly stimulated. These stereotypes are commonly referred to as *self-stims* or merely *stims* (Gallo, 2010).

Repetitive behaviors are manifested differently in children with autism and those with Asperger's disorder. A person with autism tends to exhibit repetitive motor behaviors related to an object—for example, banging a drum repeatedly. Alternatively, a person with Asperger's disorder is more likely to be preoccupied with one subject, becoming an expert in a particular area of interest, such as dinosaurs or the solar system (Smith-Myles & Simpson, 2002).

Good verbal abilities, average to above-average intelligence, and less severe symptoms may actually mask the extent of social dysfunction found in people with Asperger's disorder (Mayes & Calhoun, 2004). Like children with autistic disorder, children with Asperger's have difficulty reading social cues. People with Asperger's disorder tend to be self-centered and are often loners. These traits interfere with their ability to form meaningful relationships and may be confused with schizoid personality disorder, although people with Asperger's disorder are more likely to desire and even seek out social contact. Even so, they do not know how to participate in the usual give-and-take of communication once that contact has been made (McConnaughy, 2005; Smith-Myles & Simpson, 2002).

Children with ASDs do not participate in make-believe or symbolic play. Rather, their play is more likely to involve repetitive motor behaviors or lining up objects in a row. Children often demonstrate uneven cognitive abilities with relative strengths in visual and spatial skills. In general, the lower the child's IQ, the more severe the autistic symptoms will be. Self-injurious behaviors are also found in most children with ASDs, although these behaviors commonly are serving a communication function (e.g., to alert the caregiver of pain or illness that warrants attention). Disorders of eating and sleeping are common in most autistic children. Having a first-degree relative with a PDD typically has a profound impact on the family. Nearly all parents of children with autistic disorder were found to have clinically significant levels of stress related to the challenges of having a child with a severe disability (Koegel, 2000; Koegel et al., 2010). Siblings often have peer problems, feel lonely, and are concerned about their brother or sister who has the disorder (Bagenholm & Gillberg, 1991). Marital difficulties commonly develop as the parents of the child focus their energies on the often fruitless search for a remedy.

Assessment

A diagnosis of a pervasive developmental disorder can be facilitated by the use of screening instruments and more in-depth behavioral assessments. The child's cognitive and linguistic abilities will determine the nature of the assessment techniques and measures used (Woo & Keatinge, 2008). Parental reports of the child's developmental and behavioral progress can improve the effectiveness of the rating scales (Kabot, Masi, & Segal, 2003). A number of screening tools are available that distinguish children with autism and other PDDs from the general population. The Pervasive Development Disorders Screening Test II, the Social Communication Questionnaire (formerly called the Autism Screening Questionnaire), and the Pervasive Developmental Disorders Questionnaire have all been found to be effective (Baird et al., 2001; Kabot et al., 2003).

The Checklist for Autism in Toddlers (CHAT; Baron-Cohen, Allen, & Gillberg, 1992) identifies early signs of the disorder by assessing imaginative play, social interest, social play, indication of interest through pointing, and following of another's gaze. The CHAT had a positive predictive value of 83% for autism and other PDDs in one study in which it was part of a two-stage screening process (the first stage identified children with profound sensory and motor impairment). The M-CHAT, a version of the screening tool, has recently been developed to discriminate between PDDs and development and language delays. The M-CHAT has not yet been evaluated as a general population screening tool (Baird et al., 2001).

The Pervasive Developmental Disorder Screening Test II (PDDST-II) was developed by Siegel (1999) to screen for autism spectrum disorders in primary care and other settings. The PDDST-II is not available in printed form. It consists of a parental report measure that the parents complete in the clinician's office (Eaves & Ho, 2004). Another instrument currently being developed for early screening is the Screening Tool for Autism in Two-Year-Olds (STAT; Stone, Coonrod, Turner, & Pozdol, 2004). The STAT is designed to differentiate between children with autism and those with other developmental disorders.

After a child has been screened for PDDs, a more extensive assessment is needed. The National Research Council (NRC, 2001) recommends a "multidisciplinary evaluation of social behavior, language, and nonverbal communication, adaptive behavior, motor skills, atypical behaviors, and cognitive status by a team of professionals experienced with autism spectrum disorders" (p. 214). A variety of assessment instruments have been created that measure degree and severity of autism symptoms in children. For example, the Childhood Autism Rating Scale (CARS; Schopler, Reichler, De Vellis, & Daly, 1991) is the most widely used (Kabot et al., 2003). It assesses children's performance in 15 different domains, relating to people, imitation, emotional response, body use, object use, adaptation to change, visual response, listening response, sensory response, fear or nervousness, verbal communication, nonverbal communication, activity level, intellectual functioning, and general impressions. The CARS severity rating also can be used to assess longitudinal progress.

The Autism Diagnostic Observation Schedule (ADOS) and the Autism Diagnostic Interview–Revised (ADI-R) provide a more detailed assessment after a screening tool has determined that more in-depth assessment is needed. According to Gallo (2010, p. 25), the ADOS "is the gold standard used in autism research." It is a structured interactive tool for use with the child and parent and can be helpful when the diagnosis is not clear or if the child's history is not available to support the diagnosis. The ADI-R (Lord, Rutter, & Couteur, 1994) demonstrates reliability and validity with preschool children. It requires considerable time to administer the five-part questionnaire. The Autism Behavior Checklist (ABC) is one of the oldest rating scales, but according to Kabot it lacks "sensitivity and specificity" and is considered to have limited usefulness (Kabot et al., 2003, p. 29).

Separate scales have been developed to measure symptom severity in school-age children with Asperger's disorder. The Gilliam Asperger's Disorder Scale (GADS; Gilliam, 2001) has been shown to be both reliable and valid (Kabot et al., 2003). A population screen was developed by Ehlers and Gillberg (Ehlers, Gillberg, & Wing, 1999), and other scales, such as the Asperger's Syndrome Diagnostic Scale (Myles, Bock, & Simpson, 2001), and the Autism Spectrum Quotient, are available, although they are relatively new and have not been systematically evaluated (Baird et al., 2001). At present, none of these scales are able to distinguish credibly between Asperger's disorder, PDD-NOS, and high-functioning autism (Woo & Keatinge, 2008).

Preferred Therapist Characteristics

Given the growing number of young children who are being diagnosed with ASDs, therapists working with children must be familiar with the range of symptoms associated with these disorders and be able to make appropriate referrals for assessment, intervention, and educational planning. Therapists can play an important role as part of a multidisciplinary team, through the screening and assessment process and helping develop behavioral interventions that suit the child's particular needs and learning style (Kabot et al., 2003). The major concerns for most families remain early assessment and intervention, accessing appropriate services and funding for those services, and finding an educational placement in the least restrictive setting. Therapists can provide support to families throughout this complicated process. Their referrals and advocacy can be invaluable in helping parents obtain knowledge about their legal rights and provisions under applicable federal and state laws.

Intervention Strategies

Early intervention and intensive, behaviorally based treatment are key to developing positive outcomes in autism and PDDs (Dawson & Faja, 2008; Smith, 2010). Although there is no single best treatment option, Kabot and colleagues (2003) conducted an analysis of the peer-reviewed literature and found agreement among the professionals that highly structured, specialized programs work best. They also found the following components to be important in early interventions for autism spectrum disorders:

- Screening should be conducted at the earliest age possible.
- Interventions must be intensive.
- Programs should include parent training and support.
- Interventions should focus on improving social and communication skills.
- Individual goals and objectives should be set.
- Training should emphasize generalizability to other areas.

A proliferation of programs have developed that include home-, center-, and school-based interventions for children with autism and PDDs (Dawson & Osterling, 1997; Handleman & Harris, 2001; Harris, Handleman, & Jennett, 2005). Some of the programs for autism focus on core deficit areas and accept children who have Asperger's, PDD-NOS, and other PDD diagnoses. Choosing among the many programs available can be a daunting task, especially given the lack of research available. Each family will need to determine whether to enroll their child in a school-based program, keep the child in a home-based setting, or consider one of the few centers, which often provide the most up-to-date treatments but may not be convenient or affordable. Many of these programs are affiliated with a university and often have long waiting lists. Because of the pervasive nature of the symptoms, treatment is multifaceted and usually requires collaboration by many health-care providers. Children with autism and PDDs are usually involved in special education, speech and language therapy, and physical therapy. Those with Rett's disorder or childhood disintegrative disorder may also be under the care of physicians, neurologists, or other medical specialists. Consultation with other service providers, as well as case management of this broad spectrum of services, may fall to the therapist.

Autistic Disorder The number of programs specializing in behavioral interventions for autism are increasing at an exponential rate. An exciting finding is that earlier interventions (before age 3) have resulted in greater treatment gains in language and social skills, and a reduction in behaviors that prevent learning from taking place such as self-injurious, self-stimulating, and isolating behaviors (Koegel et al., 2010; Smith, 2010). The most effective interventions for children with autism disorder are structured and are based on the child's interests, teach tasks as a series of simple steps, engage the child's attention, and provide positive reinforcement for behavior (NIMH, 2004). Parental involvement plays a major role in treatment outcomes.

One model home-based program, the UCLA Early and Intensive Behavioral Intervention (EIBI) program, provides one-to-one behavior modification for children under age 3 for a period of 3 years (Smith, 2010). The program enrolls children ages 3 and under and begins with 20 hours a week and accelerates to 40 hours per week as the child adapts to the program. Goals of the program include improving communication and academic skills, teaching self-help skills, improving motor skills, and engaging in play. Research shows the program

has yielded a significant and substantial effect size (Reichow & Wolery, 2009).

Another home-based behavioral intervention is pivotal response training. Ten years ago Koegel (2000) reported that when pivotal response interventions (PRI) for autism targeted two key areas of the child's functioning—motivation and child initiations—upward of 85% of children under age 5 who were diagnosed with autistic disorder learned to use verbal language as their primary mode of communication. Over the years, modifications to the program and earlier interventions with children younger than age 3 has increased the success rate to 95% (Koegel, Camarata, Koegel, Ben-Tall, & Smith, 2008). PRI have also been found to improve academic performance and reduce aggressive, self-stimulating, and self-injurious behaviors. In this approach, parents are trained as interventionists who work with the child throughout the day. Such parent education programs have been found to be effective in increasing communication skills, decreasing disruptive behaviors, and increasing generalizability of treatment gains (Koegel et al., 2010). In addition, such programs have also been shown to reduce parental anxiety and increase parental feelings of empowerment.

Other approaches with demonstrated effectiveness are available, but once a child approaches school age, the most effective interventions are those that involve an individualized education plan (IEP) to address not only the child's academic concerns but also the social and emotional challenges they will encounter (Dunn, 2005; Dunn & Honigsfeld, 2009). Under the federal Individuals with Disabilities Education Act (IDEA), children with PDDs are entitled to public education that is free and appropriate to their needs. But not all states offer intensive early intervention programs, and those that do are frequently underfunded and not able to offer high-quality evidence-based interventions. The bulk of the financial burden often falls to the families of young children diagnosed with ASDs.

Asperger's Disorder   Because of their intelligence, language skills, and level of independent functioning, children with Asperger's disorder often are not diagnosed until they enter school (Tsatsanis, Foley, & Donehower, 2004). Parents rarely report concerns about their child's early development. If anything, children with Asperger's are more likely to be described as precocious, savants, or *little professors*.

Treatment interventions include individualized behavior therapy, group therapy in which children can practice their skills with peers, psychoeducation, and social skills training. Children with Asperger's are mainstreamed with other children as much as possible.

Assessment of social skills can help determine specific areas that require individualized attention. The social skills inventory developed by Taylor and Jasper (Maurice, Green, & Foxx, 1996) rates abilities on such traits as establishing eye contact, taking turns with toys, initiating greetings, and answering social questions. Displaying empathy, asking questions, and relating to peers are included in advanced skills assessment.

Adolescence is a difficult time for many children, and children with Asperger's are particularly vulnerable. Social skills training that incorporates script fading, social stories, and role-playing new situations can be effective methods to help the adolescent develop conversation skills, understand appropriate social behavior, and reduce anxiety associated with social situations (Adams, Gouvousis, VanLue, & Waldron, 2004; Sarokoff, Taylor, & Poulson, 2001; Tsatsanis et al., 2004). At school, peer modeling and peer buddies for all students can help reduce social pressure and improve relationships with peers (Dawson & Faja, 2008). Parents of children with Asperger's disorder may need to educate

teachers about their child's particular needs at various stages of development or to intervene if their child becomes the object of bullying or other aggressive behavior from their peers.

Overall Treatment Recommendations

In addition to behavioral treatment, people with autism and PDDs typically require a variety of adjunct services, which may include speech and language training, social skills training, and the creation of an IEP. Medication is sometimes also helpful, particularly if SIBs, tantrums, and severe aggression are not responsive to behavior modification. The medications used are those used to treat similar symptoms in other disorders— SSRIs for the treatment of anxiety, depression, or OCD; stimulants for hyperactivity and inattention; neuroleptics to treat aggressive and self-injurious behaviors; and anticonvulsants for the one in four children with ASDs who also have seizures (NIMH, 2004).

A variety of other innovative treatments have been suggested, such as vitamins, gluten-free diets, sensory integration, and facilitated communication. To date, the value of these treatments has not been conclusively demonstrated.

"Parents are the point people who ensure continuity across the lifespan of the child" (Kabot et al., 2003, p. 30). As such, parents need education, advocacy training, and support. In addition to parents' primary role in the assessment of autism and PDDs, parental involvement includes training to become cotherapists (Lovaas & Smith, 2003), attending meetings to assist in the development of individual treatment plans, and belonging to support groups. Family consultation, as well as supportive therapy for parents and siblings, should usually be included. Therapists work with parents to serve as advocates, coordinate services, and reduce family stress. Couples or sibling therapy can be beneficial as a means of providing emotional support and as a source for useful information about the disorder. Families should also be referred to networking resources such as the Autism Society of America, the Rett's Syndrome Association, and the Online Asperger Syndrome Information and Support (OASIS). Most of these groups have online resources and local chapters throughout the country.

Prognosis

Due to the heterogeneity of autism and the pervasive developmental disorders, prognosis varies widely. Early intervention appears to be the most important factor related to a positive outcome (Baird et al., 2001; Lovaas & Smith, 2003; NIMH, 2004); however, there is no cure for these disorders. Treatment for children and their families requires a lifespan developmental approach (Dawson & Faja, 2008). The prognosis for people with Asperger's disorder is excellent; many live independent lives. Prognoses for PDDs are not as good. Residential treatment is probable for those with Rett's disorder and childhood disintegrative disorder because of the progressive nature of these disorders.

ATTENTION-DEFICIT DISORDER

Attention-deficit/hyperactivity disorder (ADHD) is a neurobiological disorder that cannot be prevented and currently has no cure. To be effective, early diagnosis and treatment interventions should focus on symptom management, address comorbid diagnoses, and continue as long as symptoms are present.

The *DSM-IV-TR* divides this disorder into three subtypes:

1. Predominantly hyperactive–impulsive type
2. Predominantly inattentive type
3. Combined type

Future refinement of the subtypes, or the addition of degrees such as mild, moderate, and severe, may be helpful in diagnosis and treatment.

Overview of the Disorder

The Centers for Disease Control and Prevention estimate that 5.4 million children in the United States have attention-deficit/hyperactivity disorder (Visser, 2010). Attention-deficit/hyperactivity disorder is found in as many as 50% of the children seen for psychotherapy and many children with this disorder have concomitant learning disorders, antisocial difficulties, low self-esteem, and depression. Thirty-seven percent may continue to exhibit myriad psychosocial difficulties across the lifespan (Anastopoulos & Farley, 2003) with as many as 5% to 10% developing more serious mental disorders, and 10% to 25% developing substance-related problems (Barkley, 2006).

As many as 4% to 8% of school-age children have been diagnosed with ADHD, making it the most prevalent neurological disorder of childhood (AACAP, 2007a; Polanczyk & Rohde, 2007). Boys are more likely to develop the disorder than girls, by a 2.5:1 ratio (Polanczyk, de Lima, Horta, Biederman, & Rohde, 2007). This ratio declines to 1.6:1 in adulthood (Kessler, Adler, et al., 2005). ADHD has been identified in almost every country in which it has been studied, including Japan, China, Turkey, South America, and the Middle East (Mash & Wolfe, 2010). A review of 102 studies resulted in a worldwide prevalence rate of 5.3% (Polanczyk et al., 2007). The rates appear to be highest in South America and Africa, and lowest in the Middle East (Nigg & Nikolas, 2008). Interestingly, in the United States, ADHD occurs less frequently in Hispanic American children than in non-Hispanic Black children or non-Hispanic White children (Pastor & Reuben, 2008).

The current research indicates that ADHD is a neurobiological disorder that negatively impacts the functioning of the brain's neural circuits, which are instrumental in attention, cognitive control, and decision making. Irregular metabolism of brain chemistry contributes directly to ADHD behavioral patterns. Premotor and superior prefrontal lobe regions of the brain, areas that are responsible for directing executive functioning and impulse control, appear to be much less active in people with ADHD (Smith, Barkley, & Shapiro, 2006). Recent research on the link between time perception and behavioral control indicates that the cerebellum, the area of the brain that controls the mind's internal clock, may also be involved (Nigg & Nikolas, 2008). The disorder has a strong genetic component, often appearing in several members of a family. In twin studies, as much as 70% to 80% of the variance can be attributed to heredity (Nigg & Nikolas, 2008).

By definition, ADHD has an onset prior to age 7; is present in two or more settings (such as at home and in school); and interferes with social, academic, or occupational functioning. The person with this disorder also exhibits six or more symptoms of inattentiveness or hyperactivity-impulsivity that have persisted for at least six months (American Psychiatric Association, 2000). Symptoms of inattention include failure to give close attention to details, difficulty with focused or selective attention, poor follow-through on instructions, failure to finish work, difficulty organizing tasks, misplacement of things, distraction by extraneous stimuli, and forgetfulness. Hyperactive–impulsive characteristics are more visible, so the hyperactive–impulsive type of ADHD is usually identified at a younger age. Hyperactive–impulsive behaviors include fidgeting, running about, difficulty playing quietly, acting as if driven by a motor, talking excessively, blurting answers, and interrupting. Overall, people with ADHD have more impulsivity and novelty-seeking behavior and poorer inhibitory control than other people (Smith et al., 2006).

ADHD may have a bi-directional cause. In other words, the child's behavior can interrupt the child–parent relationship early in the child's life (Murray & Johnston, 2006). The influence of a child's temperament, developmental maturity, language and communication skills, and early caregiver ability to teach self-regulating behavior interact synergistically in this crucial period. The result may be increased vulnerability to ADHD or the development of successful behavioral control. Preschool children who exhibit ADHD-like symptoms of impulsiveness and defiance, for more than a year, are more likely to continue to have problems in middle childhood and adolescence (Mash & Wolfe, 2010). Even so, many toddlers who would seem to be at risk for developing ADHD do not, in fact, develop the disorder, and some toddlers who successfully navigate this developmental stage may show symptoms, such as inattention, later on when they enter school (Nigg & Nikolas, 2008). Diagnostic prediction remains uncertain and until definitive research is available, identification of ADHD in preschool children will remain controversial.

Typical Client Characteristics

As mentioned earlier, the current prevalence rates for ADHD range from 3% to 7% of all children (American Psychiatric Association, 2000). Gender differences have shown that males with ADHD present with more aggressive and oppositional behavior than females, who are more likely to have symptoms of the inattentive type of ADHD. Research on the effect of gender on the development and course of ADHD indicates that girls and boys tend to exhibit comparable levels of impairment in academic and social functioning (Gaub & Carlson, 1997); have similar patterns of impairment in executive functioning and cognitive control (Hinshaw, Klein, & Abikoff, 2007); and exhibit similar familial patterns of neuropsychological problems (Doyle, Biederman, Seidman, Rske-Nielsen, & Faraone, 2005). Girls, in general, are less likely to exhibit disruptive behaviors than boys, and it is possible that some girls with ADHD are missed when the current criteria are applied. Future research may address this as well as the effects of other gender-specific variations such as hormones, differences in levels of maturity, and externalizing versus internalizing symptoms.

The Multimodal Treatment Study of ADHD (MTA; MTA Cooperative Group, 1999, 2004) is the largest study ever undertaken of one specific disorder. The MTA study indicates that 50% of children with ADHD have a co-occurring *DSM-IV* diagnosis, with oppositional defiant disorder being the most frequent, followed by anxiety disorders and conduct disorder. Mood and tic disorders often coexist with ADHD as well, although the nature of the relationship is less clear.

Often the comorbid disorders are masked by the ADHD, but they may be persistent and have deleterious effects. For example, 30% to 50% of those with ADHD have co-occurring depression or anxiety. These disorders increase the risk of substance misuse or suicidal ideation or even death via suicide (Mash & Wolfe, 2010). The effects of co-occurring conditions should not be underestimated, as they may persist after treatment for ADHD, as part of a cluster (sequelae) of difficulties the individual experiences.

Symptomatic behaviors vary and depend on the age at presentation and the type of ADHD. The symptoms of ADHD prior to age 3 may include behaviors that disrupt family life and are not conducive to preschool attendance. Such symptoms include increased motor activity, excessive climbing, aggression, and destructiveness. The common feature in elementary school-age children with ADHD is difficulty in sustaining attention, particularly during long, monotonous, repetitive tasks. (These children can usually focus their attention on tasks that include small instructional units or fast-paced multisensory presentations.) Other common symptoms include poor impulse control, restlessness, and overactivity. Children may also exhibit noncompliant and antisocial behaviors related to their impulsivity.

Impulsive behaviors typically impair functioning in many areas. They can result in poor interpersonal relationships and academic difficulties. Barkley (2006) reports that 25% to 40% of children with ADHD have comorbid learning disorders. Children with ADHD also are at greater risk for accidental injury and may experience significant sleep problems. As a result of all these difficulties, children with ADHD commonly manifest poor social skills and low self-esteem. Family conflict and discomfort at school also often accompany these children's behaviors, resulting in continued academic difficulties, with as many as 30% to 50% of children with ADHD being retained at least one grade in school and 25% to 36% never graduating from high school (Barkley, 2006).

Current research suggests that those who have ADHD by age 6 are more likely to have depression and suicidal thoughts in adolescence (CDC, 2007). The symptoms of ADHD can persist across the lifespan. As many as 30% to 50% of children with ADHD will be symptomatic through adolescence and adulthood (Barkley, 2006). The symptoms of the disorder typically change, however. Hyperactivity is unusual among adolescents with ADHD; restlessness, poorly organized schoolwork, failure to complete independent work, and high-risk behaviors are more common indicators of this disorder in teenagers (Cantwell, 1996).

Difficulties that follow adolescents with ADHD into adulthood often result in underemployment in relation to their intelligence, education, and family backgrounds. They tend to change jobs frequently, have difficulty creating and maintaining stable relationships, and are more likely to be cited for traffic violations and motor vehicle accidents (Barkley, 2006). Adult symptoms can include restlessness, impulsivity, inability to concentrate, and short attention span, among others. Although many adults who have ADHD were never formally diagnosed in childhood, treatment for adults has been found to be effective in addressing these cognitive and behavioral symptoms. Depending on the frequency and severity of symptoms and the results of behavioral checklists, medication may be prescribed to accompany psychotherapy.

Hallowell and Ratey (1994) list the following 20 diagnostic criteria for a diagnosis of adult ADHD, with the presence of 15 or more considered to be significant: a sense of not meeting one's goals, difficulty getting organized, chronic procrastination, multiple ongoing simultaneous projects, blurting out inappropriate comments, frequent searches for high stimulation, intolerance of boredom, distractibility, creativity, trouble following proper procedures, low frustration tolerance, impulsive behaviors, a tendency to worry, a sense of insecurity, mood swings, restlessness, a tendency toward addictive behavior, chronic problems with self-esteem, inaccurate self-observation, and a family history of ADHD or bipolar disorders (pp. 73–74).

Research has shown compelling evidence of a greater prevalence of ADHD among members of the same family. Smith and colleagues (2006) report that between 10% and 35% of first-degree relatives of children diagnosed with ADHD also exhibit characteristics of that disorder, and studies of twins confirm a genetic component of ADHD. First-degree relatives have also been found to have an elevated incidence of depression, alcohol misuse, conduct-related problems, and antisocial disorders (Doyle

et al., 2005) Thus, a child with ADHD often has a parent or sibling with the disorder, which may lead to a chaotic home environment and make it difficult for the parents to establish the clear guidelines needed by a child with ADHD. In addition, more severe behavioral problems create disruptions in the relationship between parent and child and strain family functioning). A more stable family environment, earlier assessment and treatment, and parent training have been shown to have ameliorating effects on the long-term outcome of the disorder.

Assessment

ADHD is one of the most researched disorders of childhood. In an effort to provide responsible treatment interventions, several professional organizations including the American Academy of Child and Adolescent Psychiatry (AACAP; 2007a), American Medical Association (Goldman, Genel, Bezman, & Slanetz, 1998), and the American Academy of Pediatrics (2001) have published policy statements as a guideline for clinicians. Considerable consensus exists among the groups, including the following recommendations for assessment:

- Assessment and diagnosis should include a medical/neurological exam.
- The developmental history should screen for a family history of ADHD and explore the nature of marital and parent-child relationships, and the mental and physical health of caregivers.
- Parent and teacher reports (including interviews, grades, and behavior reports) and standardized rating scales should be gathered.
- *DSM-IV-TR* criteria should be followed, including assessment for comorbid conditions.

The assessment should also include clinician observation of the child's behavior.

The process of diagnosing ADHD should include comprehensive behavioral, psychological, educational, and medical evaluations to rule out or identify physical, chemical, or environmental contributing factors (Barkley, 2006). Cognitive and achievement assessments, as well as parents' and teachers' input on behavior rating scales, are important for providing information from a variety of settings. The inclusion of a continuous performance test (CPT), a computerized test in which a child is asked to press a button when a specific letter follows another, can provide a measure of the person's ability to sustain attention and control impulsivity over time. A variety of CPTs, such as the Test of Variables of Attention (TOVA), help clinicians distinguish between the three subgroups of ADHD (combined type, predominantly inattentive type, and predominantly hyperactive–impulsive type).

Behavior checklists also provide an assessment of attentional patterns. The Conners' Rating Scales-Revised (Conners, 1997) offer long and short versions of child and adolescent, teacher, and parent rating scales for ADHD. The most commonly used rating scales for ADHD are the Achenbach Child Behavior Checklist (CBCL); Parent, Teacher, and Youth Self-Report forms (Achenbach, 1991); and the Behavior Assessment System for Children, 2nd Edition (BASC-2; Reynolds & Kamphaus, 2002). All use a 4-point Likert-type scale to assess a range of behaviors. The Adult ADHD Self-Report Scale is a six-item self-report questionnaire developed by the World Health Organization to screen for adult ADHD (Kessler, Adler, et al., 2005). A version of the Conners' Rating Scale is also available for adults. The Conners instrument is frequently used by physicians to monitor the effects of medication. The CBCL and the BASC-2 evaluate a broader spectrum of comorbid symptoms, such as depression, anxiety, atypical thoughts, and delinquent and withdrawn behaviors. The BASC-2 includes a scale that allows the therapist to check the validity of responses and facilitates assessment of the predominantly inattentive type of ADHD.

Although not offering conclusive diagnoses, magnetic resonance imaging (MRI) and positron emission tomography (PET) technology have been used to study neurological activity in people with ADHD. Preliminary results suggest that the appearance of significant brain abnormalities may ultimately allow the diagnosis of ADHD to be based on direct assessment of brain functioning. At this time, however, these procedures are being used solely for research purposes.

One difficulty with the diagnosis of ADHD is its reliance on a history derived from teachers' and parents' reports. Negative relationships between the child and these adults may skew these assessments. Moreover, the *DSM* requirement that the identified behaviors be more frequent and more severe than those found in children at comparable developmental levels is sufficiently vague to create diagnostic problems, particularly in children of preschool age. In recent years a dramatic increase in the diagnosis of ADHD in preschoolers has been reported, raising questions about what constitutes normal developmental behavior.

Preferred Therapist Characteristics

Hyperactive behavior typically affects the therapeutic relationship, just as it affects a person's daily life. The therapist needs to present a calm and patient demeanor to avoid escalating the excitable behaviors of a person with ADHD. Many transference and countertransference issues can arise as a result of the emotional volatility in a person with this disorder. To be effective, therapists must be clear about their own emotional issues and able to distinguish them from those of the client.

Children with ADHD frequently experience negative interactions with others, particularly adults, as a result of their impulsive and sometimes noncompliant behaviors. Consequently, the development of a trusting, accepting relationship with the therapist is a critical element of treatment. Therapy can be enhanced by the provision of a structured setting where boundaries of time and safety are clearly established by the therapist.

Therapists who work with people with ADHD need to have a working knowledge of the neurological and genetic components of the disorder. Therapists need to be able to educate parent and child about ADHD and to work collaboratively with others involved in the child's treatment, such as teachers, physicians, and family members. Therapists should be comfortable with using behavior management strategies and setting and enforcing limits yet also be flexible enough to tailor treatment to meet the individual needs of the child. They also need a clear developmental yardstick against which to measure problems and improvements in the child's behavior.

Intervention Strategies

A multimodal treatment strategy that combines stimulant therapy (medication), parent training and counseling, and behavioral-targeted classroom interventions is the most effective treatment for ADHD (AACAP, 2007a). Family counseling, individual counseling for the child focusing on social skills training or other specific needs, and support groups for parents are helpful adjunctive treatments that can be individualized to meet the family's needs. Each part of the multimodal treatment strategy is discussed briefly below. Additional information on these

interventions can be found in the following section on disruptive behavior disorders, and in the resources listed at the end of this chapter.

Therapists working with children with ADHD rely primarily on behavioral interventions to reduce behavioral problems and emotional difficulties. Behavioral treatments for children with ADHD are based on operant conditioning, the shaping of behavior through the use of positive reinforcers. ADHD is seen as a disorder of performance, rather than of knowledge or skills. Therefore, treatment most often is designed to improve attention and enhance motivation for these children to display their knowledge. To be effective, these interventions must be used across all environments (home, classroom, and therapy) and for months or even years (Smith et al., 2006). They are demanding of time and resources; they involve teaching, practice, encouragement, reinforcement, and monitoring; and they require cooperation on the part of teachers and parents.

Parent Management Training   Negative behavior traits found in children with ADHD can disrupt the entire family system. Therefore, treatment should include a parent management-training component to help reduce parent-child conflict. Parent training reduces parental stress, increases parental sense of control and self-esteem, and is effective as a preventive intervention in preventing escalation of ADHD symptoms along the developmental pathway to such comorbid disorders as ODD or CD (Anastopoulos & Farley, 2003; Smith et al., 2006). There are a variety of PT approaches, with most of them ranging from 8 to 12 sessions and suitable for children between the ages of 4 and 12.

Although many different PT treatments exist, they all help educate parents about ADHD, promote awareness and encouragement of socially competent behavior, teach self-evaluation strategies, model good communication skills, and provide consistent rewards and consequences (Anastopoulos & Farley, 2003; Barkley, 2006; Smith et al., 2006).

One promising approach for children has been developed by Barkley (Smith et al., 2006). This approach educates parents on what and how to communicate with the child to best address the child's deficit in executive functioning. The program also includes a component that recognizes that many children with ADHD develop ODD. Barkley includes a training program for parents on contingency management techniques in an effort to prevent the development of ODD.

Due to their developmental stage, many adolescents do not respond well to parent management training. Clinicians might consider alternative treatments, such as problem-solving or parent–child interaction training for older children with this disorder (Zisser & Eyberg, 2010).

School-Based Interventions Consistent and regular communication among parents, teachers, school counselors, and therapists is an integral part of multimodal treatment, so that desirable behaviors will be reinforced in multiple settings. Many children with ADHD qualify for additional resources at school, and the therapist can be instrumental in working collaboratively with the school and family in this process. Children with ADHD often exhibit disruptive behavior in classroom settings in which they are required to sit quietly or be attentive for extended periods of time. Classroom interventions usually consist of behavioral techniques that promote teachers' use of selective attending, ignoring of inappropriate behavior, the establishment of clear rules, rewards for success, daily progress notes, increased transition times, and matching of academic materials to the attention span and ability level of the child (Barkley, 2006). A meta-analysis on the effectiveness of 70 separate school intervention programs found that classroom behavioral and academic interventions can improve performance and behavior of children with ADHD, with the greatest improvements occurring with contingency management procedures and peer tutoring approaches (Smith et al., 2006). Effective contingency management strategies included token rewards, as well as group rewards for the entire class.

Individual Therapy Individual therapy can be instrumental in helping a child cope with academic, social, and family stressors. Counselors can model such traits as self-confidence, empathy, flexibility, resilience, and being nonjudgmental, which can become a part of the child's repertoire of coping skills. Treatment plans can address the individual needs of the child and address issues of low self-esteem, losses and disappointment, stress, or comorbid anxiety and mood disorders.

Individual therapy that focuses on improving communication skills, recognition of nonverbal messages, and appropriate approach behaviors has promoted social skill development in children with ADHD.

Due to deficits in executive functioning, children and adolescents with ADHD benefit from learning skills that help improve their daily functioning, such as time management, anger management, impulse control, and replacing negative messages with positive self-talk. However, research on social skills training has produced mixed results (Smith et al., 2006). Such variables as type of ADHD, co-occurring conditions, parent versus teacher ratings, and the presence of ODD have produced inconsistent results. Smith and colleagues note there may actually be an increase in negative and antisocial behaviors when children with ADHD, ODD, or CD are placed together in groups. Therefore, group therapy for children with ADHD is not recommended.

Medication Management Despite the growing number of children who are currently on prescription medication for ADHD, medication alone cannot resolve the problem, and may be contraindicated in certain children. Research indicates that when pharmacological treatment or behavioral treatment is removed, symptoms of ADHD return to pretreatment levels (Greenhill & Ford, 2002). Because it increases anxiety, stimulant medication is inappropriate in the treatment of some co-occurring disorders, such as anxiety or childhood bipolar disorder and must be recommended with care.

The use of psychostimulant medication for treatment of ADHD has increased fivefold since 1989 (Greenhill & Ford, 2002) and has been the focus of considerable research. Smith and colleagues (2006) report that stimulant medications are "the most studied and the most effective treatment for the symptomatic management of ADHD" (p. 88). Recent research stresses the improved effectiveness of combining intensive behavior therapy with psychostimulant medication.

The MTA Study, along with the 1998 NIH Consensus Development Conference on ADHD and the publication of the *McMaster Evidence Based Review of ADHD Treatments*, provides convincing research for the effectiveness of stimulant treatments for the symptoms of ADHD (Greenhill & Ford, 2002). In nearly 200 studies of psychostimulants (methylphenidate, amphetamines, or pemoline), 70% of children responded well to the medication, compared with 13% to placebo (Greenhill & Ford, 2002).

Effective drugs are thought to stimulate the production of the neurochemicals that facilitate brain functioning. Contrary to the popular misconception that these children are hypersensitive or hyperattentive, neurodevelopmental research suggests that ADHD is actually a problem of underarousal. Methylphenidate (Ritalin) is prescribed in more than 85% of the cases in which medication is recommended (Greenhill & Ford, 2002), with dextroamphetamine (Dexedrine) second, and pemoline (Cylert) third. Approximately 80% of children with ADHD will respond positively to one of these medications (Greenhill & Ford, 2002). Atomoxetine (Strattera) was approved by the FDA in 2003 for use in children and adults with ADHD (Smith et al., 2006). Strattera is not a stimulant and therefore has no abuse potential. Other nonstimulant medications sometimes used in the treatment of ADHD include tricyclic antidepressants, buspirone (BuSpar), bupropion (Wellbutrin), and the antihypertensive drugs clonidine (Catapres) and guanfacine (Tenex). Safety and efficacy issues with regard to use of these medications in children have not been fully addressed.

Therapists may become involved in monitoring clients' reactions to medication and should be in contact with prescribing physicians. Additional research is needed on desired outcomes, as there is currently no standard of success. Some look for a 25% reduction of ADHD symptoms, whereas others continue the dosage until the child's behavior in the classroom is not disruptive. The Abbreviated Conners' Teacher Rating Scale can be used to determine when a child's behavior has sufficiently improved.

Stimulant medications have been well researched and judged safe; however, no research has looked at the long-term impact of these medications on children after the 24-month mark (Rapport & Moffitt, 2002). The most common side effects of stimulant medication for treating ADHD are decreased appetite and insomnia. Less common side effects include abdominal pain, headaches, and dizziness (Smith et al., 2006). Suppression of growth, particularly in older children, occurs rarely and generally remits when the medication is discontinued (Greenhill & Ford, 2002). In less than 1% of children, vocal or motor tics may develop.

Medication for ADHD may be contraindicated when there is a history of tic disorders. Stimulants have similar efficacy from childhood through adolescence (Smith et al., 2006). Unfortunately, there is limited research available at this time on the effect of treating toddlers and preschoolers with psychostimulants and controversy continues about treating the very young child for what may very well be developmentally appropriate behavior.

Not all children respond well to medication, and there has been some indication that those with coexisting anxiety are less likely to respond to methylphenidate (Ritalin) and experience more side effects. Greenhill and Ford (2002) suggest that characteristics of young age, low rates of anxiety, low severity of the disorder, and high IQ may predict good response. The decision to treat a child with medication should be based on the severity of the symptoms; on the preferences of the parents and the child; on the ability of the child, the parents, and the school to cope with the disorder; and on the success or failure of alternative treatment.

Other Interventions Additional therapies that may be included as part of a multimodal treatment strategy include social skills training, family therapy, and group support. None of these therapies has received empirical support as stand-alone treatments for ADHD, but can be an important part of a multimodal treatment plan and allow therapy to meet the specific needs of each child and family situation.

Social skills training. Social skills training programs teach behaviors that can improve interpersonal relationships. Such skills as identifying personal space, starting and maintaining a conversation, setting boundaries, and accepting and giving compliments are all addressed in these programs. The research on social skills training is mixed, but it seems to be a helpful part of

a multimodal treatment approach (AACAP, 2007a).

Group support for families. Numerous online support groups, such as Children with Attention Deficit Disorders (www.chadd.org) and the Attention Deficit Disorder Association (ADDA; www.add.org), provide information and family support.

Prognosis

An integrated approach continues to be the accepted treatment for children with ADHD (AACAP, 2007a; Barkley, 2006; Hinshaw et al., 2007). Studies cited earlier support the benefits of psychostimulant medication as part of a multimodal treatment approach that includes parent training and teacher training components (Carr, 2009; Hinshaw et al., 2007).

Future research on ADHD needs to focus on the underlying biological, psychological, and environmental contributors to this disorder. In the absence of a cure, early interventions that focus on prevention, foster resilience, and train parents and teachers to help children reduce their impulsivity, decrease oppositional behaviors, and become more aware of social cues from their environment, have been shown to help alter the developmental course of the disorder so that fewer children proceed along the pathway to the development of a disruptive behavior disorder, which we turn to next.

DISRUPTIVE BEHAVIOR DISORDERS

The *DSM-IV-TR* (American Psychiatric Association, 2000) describes two disruptive behavior disorders: oppositional defiant disorder (ODD) and conduct disorder (CD). Research suggests that ODD, CD, and antisocial personality disorder (discussed further in Chapter 8) represent a continuum of behaviors. In other words, early onset and greater severity of symptoms of ODD increase the potential for a child to develop CD, and the diagnosis of CD increases the likelihood of the symptoms progressing into antisocial personality disorder. Biopsychosocial differences determine the pathway, with earlier onset of symptoms indicating a more severe course (McMahon, Wells, & Kotler, 2006).

Throughout the course of this book we have seen many examples of how genetics, in combination with the environment, work together to create many disorders seen in children and adults. The disruptive behavior disorders are no exception. A meta-analytic review of twin and adoption studies found that genetics accounts for 41% of the variance in behaviors associated with antisocial personality disorder in general, and increases to 50% when looking at conduct disorder symptoms in particular (Rhee & Waldman, 2002). The authors found that 39% of the responsibility for conduct disorder were environmental experiences that the twins did not share, such as an experience of being sexually abused. The remaining 11% of the variance in conduct disorder is attributed to environmental factors the twins had in common, such as family financial resources. Temperament and ODD characteristics were also found to have a genetic link, and the presence of these traits in childhood is also predictive of the development of later conduct problems (Saudino, Ronald, & Plomin, 2005).

As discussed in the section on ADHD, comorbidity of ADHD and either ODD or CD is found in nearly 50% of children under the age of 12 who meet the criteria for ADHD (Pliszka, Carlson, & Swanson, 2001). Mash (2006) warns that, "when ADHD is present, the onset of conduct disorder is earlier, the developmental progression from less serious to more serious antisocial behavior is more rapid, and the risk of psychopathy may be greater" (p. 20) than if the child had had CD without ADHD. If ADHD is present, its treatment is essential to the successful treatment of both ODD and CD.

ODD often co-occurs with CD. In some instances, symptoms overlap and treatment will be the same for each. In other cases, as in co-occurring CD and anxiety, both disorders may require treatment. Not only do disruptive behavior disorders cause difficulties in childhood, they can set the trajectory for lifelong problems including the development of antisocial personality disorder and other serious mental disorders in adolescence and adulthood. Even so, most adolescents with ODD or CD do not develop antisocial personality disorder as adults (Lahey, 2008).

Description of the Disorders

Much overlap exists between the current *DSM-IV-TR* diagnostic criteria for ODD and CD. Rather than viewing the two disorders as distinct entities, clinicians should be aware of the hierarchical nature of the disorders and consider both diagnoses when conducting assessments. Lahey (2008) writes, "Youth do not suddenly shift from normality to abnormality when they engage in their fourth ODD symptom or their third CD symptom. Rather, the more symptoms of ODD or CD that a youth exhibits, the more serious the consequences" (p. 336). Rather than distinguishing between the two disorders, the International Classification of Diseases (ICD-10; World Health Organization, 2005) considers the entire number of ODD *and* CD symptoms in the diagnosis of these disorders. It is hoped that this gap in the assessment of disruptive behavior disorders will be resolved in future revisions to the *DSM*.

Oppositional Defiant Disorder According to the *DSM-IV-TR*, oppositional defiant disorder (ODD) is described as "a pattern of negativistic, defiant, disobedient, and hostile behavior toward authority figures that persists for at least six months" (American Psychiatric Association, 2000, p. 100). Characteristic behaviors include:

- Anger and hostility
- Resistance to authority figures
- Being deliberately annoying others and being easily annoyed by others
- Resentful and vindictive behavior

Children with ODD also tend to blame others for their own negative behavior. At younger ages, children may manifest ODD through temper tantrums, kicking, power struggles with parents, disobedience, spitefulness, and low tolerance for frustration. Common complaints from the parents of older children with this disorder are that their children argue, threaten, show disrespect for adults, destroy property in a rage, refuse to cooperate, and are stubborn.

These symptoms often appear to be an exacerbation of typical childhood misbehaviors. The diagnosis of ODD is made when these behaviors are of greater frequency, duration, and intensity than would be expected for the child's age and when they cause social, occupational, and academic impairment (American Psychiatric Association, 2000). Often these children come to the attention of school counselors and therapists when the oppositional behaviors interfere with functioning at school. Until then, parents may not recognize the behaviors as being unusual. Oppositional behaviors are sometimes reinforced: When a child acts inappropriately, an adult reacts with hostility or frustration, and the child responds by escalating the negative behaviors.

ODD is one of the most common disorders of childhood and early adolescence. Estimates of the prevalence of ODD vary greatly from 3% to 6% of children worldwide (Rey, Walter, & Soutullo, 2007), to 2% to 16% of children in the United States (American Psychiatric Association, 2000), to upwards of 35% of children in low-income families (Webster-Stratton, Reid, & Murrihy, 2010).

Many causes and risk factors have been identified that contribute to the creation of ODD: harsh or ineffective parenting, family history of mental illness, the temperament or genetic makeup of the child, parental peer and environmental risk factors, developmental risk factors such as delayed language or learning disabilities (Webster-Stratton et al., 2010). In preschool boys, ODD is related to lower verbal IQ, insecure attachment to parents, and more conflicted family interactions (Speltz, McClellan, DeKlyen, & Jones, 1999). ODD is also positively correlated with physical abuse, low SES, delinquent friends, and being raised in an urban location (Mash & Wolfe, 2010). ODD usually begins by age 8, with peak prevalence occurring between the ages of 8 and 11 (American Psychiatric Association, 2000). Before puberty, boys diagnosed with ODD outnumber girls, but the rates seem to equalize after age 12. Early onset of ODD predicts a more difficult course, with greater risk of developing ADHD, conduct disorder, and antisocial personality disorder (Lahey, 2008).

Conduct Disorder   Conduct disorder (CD) is one of the most frequently encountered diagnoses in settings that provide therapy to young people: one third to one half of the children seen for treatment in mental health clinics present with symptoms of CD (Kazdin, 2008). Estimates of the prevalence of CD vary and depend on the population sampled. It has been estimated that between 1 and 4 million children and adolescents in the United States exhibit symptoms of CD (Chamberlain & Smith, 2003). The disorder is found among boys at a 3 to 4 times higher rate than among girls (Kazdin, 2008), though the gender ratio evens out in adolescence.

A diagnosis of CD is based not just on the presence of conduct-disordered behavior; as with all mental disorders, the disturbance must cause clinically significant impairment in social, academic, or occupational functioning. Diagnosis requires the presence of repetitive and persistent violations of the basic rights of others or violations of major age-appropriate societal norms or rules. The *DSM-IV-TR* lists 15 behaviors that characterize conduct disorder, divided into the following four main groups:

1. Aggression against people and animals
2. Destruction of property
3. Deceitfulness or theft
4. Serious violations of rules

For a diagnosis of this disorder, three or more incidents reflecting these symptoms must have been present during the previous 12 months, with at least one during the previous 6 months.

Substantial research has identified numerous factors that increase a child's risk of developing CD, including child temperament, parenting factors, socioeconomic factors, prenatal complications, exposure to violence, and association with antisocial peers (Kazdin, 2008; McMahon et al., 2006). Noncompliant behavior—that is, a disregard for adults—is a key ingredient of the development of severe conduct problems at home, at school, and with peers. Research indicates that when treatment interventions address issues of noncompliance, improvement is made in all areas of behavior (McMahon et al., 2006).

CD is divided into childhood-onset and adolescent-onset types. A diagnosis of childhood-onset type is made when at least one manifestation of this disorder occurred prior to the child's reaching the age of 10. Adolescent-onset type is diagnosed if the characteristics of the disorder did not appear before age 10. The prognosis for the childhood-onset type is worse than for the adolescent-onset type; early-onset conduct disorder is frequently a precursor to serious illegal and harmful behaviors in adolescence and adulthood, including substance misuse, property crimes, and violence. Children with early-onset CD are also at increased risk for abuse by their parents, depression, dropping out of school, and other disorders (Webster-Stratton et al., 2010). By the time a child reaches the age of 18, CD has often evolved into the more serious and enduring diagnosis of antisocial personality disorder, particularly if the CD began early and continued throughout adolescence.

Comorbidity with other disorders often occurs and complicates the diagnosis of CD. Kazdin (2008) reports that diagnoses involving disruptive or externalizing behaviors, such as CD, ODD, and ADHD, often occur together. Between 45% and 70% of children with CD have ADHD; 84% to 96% of children with CD have also met the criteria for ODD; and CD is frequently comorbid with anxiety and mood disorders. The high rate of comorbidity of depression and CD increases the risk of serious outcomes, such as substance misuse and suicide. The suicide risk increases if the conduct-disordered person is female or has experienced a recent stressor, such as legal or disciplinary problems, school problems, or is not in a school or work situation (Evans et al., 2005; McMahon et al., 2006).

Co-occurring anxiety appears to have an ameliorating effect on aggression. One study (Hinshaw & Lee, 2003) reports that boys with co-occurring anxiety based on inhibition and fear are less aggressive than boys with CD alone. CD is also strongly associated with symptoms of mania (Evans et al., 2005), which often presents in childhood as irritable mood and includes symptoms of physical restlessness and poor judgment.

Academic difficulties and deficits, including grade failure, increased dropout rates, low verbal intelligence, poor reading skills, and other learning disorders also are commonly found in children with CD. Clinicians should assess and treat all comorbid disorders, as treatment of all coexisting disorders is likely to improve prognosis of conduct disorder (Evans et al., 2005).

Some researchers draw on attachment theory (Bowlby, 1969/1982) and social learning theory in understanding childhood disorders. Insecure attachment between parent and child has been linked to aggressive behavior, low self-esteem, poor coping skills, low socialization skills, and poor interpersonal relationships in the child as well as increased maternal stress, child abuse, and neglect (Brinkmeyer & Eyberg, 2003). This perspective has had an impact on treatment models, as will be seen in the section on interventions.

Typical Client Characteristics

Although ODD and conduct disorder lie on a continuum of behavioral problems, most children with ODD do not subsequently develop conduct disorder. Even so, it is helpful to remember that most children with conduct disorder started with a preexisting or co-occurring ODD and continued along the developmental pathway.

Oppositional Defiant Disorder   Young people diagnosed with ODD have low tolerance for frustration or delayed gratification. They expect their demands to be granted immediately. Many children with ODD exhibit aggressive behaviors. These children are at risk for substandard academic performance and school suspension and expulsion, and have higher dropout rates. Communication and learning disorders also are common in children with ODD. Impulsive behaviors typical of children with ADHD and often seen in ODD may intensify oppositional behaviors and contribute to poor social judgment and faulty decision making.

Conduct Disorder   As discussed earlier, genetic influences contribute to such traits as difficult temperament, impulsivity, problems with executive functioning, and hyperactivity. These negative, hostile behaviors of children with CD often keep others away or evoke equally hostile responses, and a negative pattern often is perpetuated. Age-inappropriate stubbornness, hostility, defiance, and other oppositional behaviors may be noticeable as early as preschool (Mash & Wolfe, 2010) and cause difficulty in parent–child and teacher–student relationships. Inappropriate behaviors can be categorized as either overt or covert. Overt behaviors, such as theft, assault, and the setting of fires, have a direct impact on others. These behaviors are more often exhibited by males (American Psychiatric Association, 2000). Covert, or nonconfrontational, behaviors, exemplified by verbal fights, gossip, lying, shoplifting, or truancy, are more often exhibited by females with CD.

Children and adolescents with CD have difficulty developing satisfactory interpersonal relationships. They typically lack empathy, are hostile toward adults, dominate other children, and, as adolescents, are likely to have numerous sexual partners. These relationship deficits are thought to have a connection with early problems in attachment as well as an environmental component. For example, around the age of 10, children with behavior problems are typically rejected by their better functioning peers and so gravitate toward associations with acting-out peers (Greenberg, Lengua, Coie, Pinderhughes, & Conduct Problems Prevention Research Group, 1999; McMahon et al., 2006).

Due to the high incidence of family risk factors, a multidimensional assessment that includes careful analysis of the family, environment, peer group, and skills of those with CD is necessary to the development of appropriate treatment plans. Parents of young people with CD tend to have a high incidence of psychopathology themselves.

Depression, antisocial personality disorder, criminal behavior, and alcohol misuse are often found in the parents of children with conduct disorder. These families also exhibit an increased incidence of marital discord and unemployment (Lahey, 2008).

Parent modeling of problem behavior also contributes. Harsh parenting as well as inconsistent use of punishment is often found, as well as poor supervision and child monitoring (McMahon et al., 2006). Family relationships are often strained and lacking in affection. Families may include a parent or an older sibling with antisocial behavior. Mothers are particularly likely to exhibit symptoms of depression, anger, and feelings of isolation. These parental characteristics are correlated with premature termination of the children's treatment and with increased likelihood that the children's disruptive behaviors will return after treatment has ended.

Modeling of poor behavior by parents, such as marital violence, paternal pet abuse, and paternal drinking are positively related to the symptom of fire setting; exposure to marital violence and harsh paternal and maternal parenting are associated with animal cruelty (Becker, Stuewig, Herrera, & McCloskey, 2004). Those who engage in fire setting are at 3 to 4 times increased risk for later arrest for a violent crime. Fire setting, cruelty to animals, and other dangerous and physically harmful behaviors are also predictors of poor long-term outcomes.

Children with CD often come from large families, live in substandard housing in areas with high crime rates, and attend school in disadvantaged settings (Kazdin, 2008). In school settings, children who meet the criteria for CD typically have both academic and behavioral problems. Language-processing deficits are also common and may interfere with comprehension and with the processing of social information.

Aggression in childhood is viewed as part of a syndrome that typically continues on to norm-violating behaviors in adolescence (Kazdin, 2008). Children who begin to exhibit such behavior in childhood rather than adolescence are most likely to exhibit severe antisocial symptoms. Researchers have begun to organize clinically meaningful subgroups of aggressive children based on a continuum of types of behaviors. The continuum ranges from starting rumors, arguing, using slang, bullying, engaging in threatening behavior, and striking back in anger, to physical fighting (Lochman et al., 2010).

Bullying is a form of aggression that has been the subject of increasing attention and research. Bullying occurs primarily in school settings, and nearly 75% of children experience at least one bullying incident in any given year. Episodes of bullying occur alarmingly early in a child's experience, with 50% of children in kindergarten having experienced some form of bullying behavior by another child (McMahon et al., 2006). Bullying behavior peaks during the adolescent years and decreases during high school.

Assessment for Disruptive Behavior Disorders

The multiplicity of problems and contributing factors that are involved in these disorders, particularly in CD, makes their assessment and treatment extremely complex. Due to the high incidence of family risk factors, a multidimensional assessment that includes careful analysis of the family, environment, peer group, and skills of those with CD is necessary to the development of appropriate treatment plans. Multiple systems and settings may be included in the assessment process. The assessment of children with CD, for example, may involve professionals from other agencies, such as law enforcement, the judicial system, and social services, as well as consultation with teachers and others in the school system. In almost all cases, a family interview is indicated.

Information regarding behaviors and attitudes observed at school should also be considered. Low self-esteem related to poor academic performance may exacerbate problems. The Conners' Teacher Rating Scale (Conners, 1997) and the teacher versions of the CBCL (Achenbach, 1991) and BASC (Reynolds & Kamphaus, 2002) enable teachers to provide information about children's aggressive behaviors, as well as any hyperactive, inattentive, somatic, depressive, and other behaviors. The importance of including reports from multiple informants in the diagnostic assessment of ODD and CD is highlighted by Hart and colleagues (1994), who found that reports from teachers have the strongest correlation with criterion behaviors observed in 177 boys between the ages of 7 and 12 in a clinic setting; reports from parents and other children were less valid.

The first step in devising a treatment plan for children with ODD or CD is to assess the degree of danger the children pose to themselves or others and to evaluate the impact that the environment may be having on their continued development. Such behavior checklists as the Achenbach Child Behavior Checklist (CBCL; Achenbach, 1991) or the Behavior Assessment System for Children (BASC) (Reynolds & Kamphaus, 2002) are useful in identifying the parents' perceptions and the severity of the child's behaviors. If the client has a clear suicide plan or intends to harm others, parents or appropriate authorities must be notified, and residential treatment should be considered. The psychological status of the parents and the parents' perceptions of the child's behaviors may also be so impaired that the home is not an appropriate setting for the child. Alternative placement may be necessary if the child's relationship to the parent is aggressive or if the child is abused.

The therapist should also identify any co-occurring disorders that may contribute to or compound the effects of the primary disorder. The possibility of ADHD, learning disorders, depression, thought disorders, a history of abuse, substance use, neurological difficulties, and other medical conditions should always be considered. Psychological testing is recommended and should include assessment of cognitive, perceptual, and social–emotional functioning. A neurologist can be consulted to rule out seizure activity, and a psychiatrist may be consulted regarding the advisability of medication. This lengthy diagnostic process can provide invaluable guidance in treatment.

Assessments for these disorders must be developmentally, culturally, and contextually sensitive (McMahon et al., 2006). Any assessment should take the child's age, developmental pathways, cultural and socioeconomic background, as well as family and peer influences, into account.

Preferred Therapist Characteristics

Working with a child with a disruptive behavior disorder can be challenging. Therapists should have a solid understanding of the multiple causal factors that lead to the development of these disorders and should have the ability to assess and treat comorbid disorders. Successful interventions usually will involve multiple professionals and community agencies working together toward an integrated treatment that includes the home, school, and community (McMahon et al., 2006).

Clients with ODD typically transfer their negative feelings toward authority, as well as their perceptions of hostility in the environment, to their therapists. Therapists working with young clients diagnosed with ODD must have great patience and be cognizant of their own feelings about control, anger, defiance, and misbehavior. Therapists must also recognize their own countertransference issues to prevent them from having a negative impact on treatment (Hanna & Hunt, 1999).

Clients with conduct disorder may be involved in legal proceedings, and may be court-ordered into treatment. Good collaboration skills to work with other agencies, social workers, probation officers, and others in the legal system may be required.

Therapists may be called on to develop behavioral strategies for changing negative behaviors and provide training in social skills and problem solving. Therefore, knowledge of behavior therapies, family therapy, and psychoeducation is needed. If long-term treatment is indicated, therapists must be able to provide a consistently supportive relationship.

Therapists who work with children and adolescents with disruptive behavior disorders will need to work collaboratively with parents, teachers, and others on the development of appropriate behavioral interventions. The therapist should have the ability to assess such family processes as the affective bond between the caregiver and child, parental discipline strategies, and the ability of the parents to apply and maintain consistent structure and discipline (Henggeler & Schaeffer, 2010). Therapists may be called on to provide behavior therapy, anger management, social skills training, and parent education.

Adolescents who have co-occurring ADHD and CD have the highest level of callousness and lack of emotion of any clinic-referred clients (Lahey, 2008). They often misperceive other people's intentions and respond in an overly harsh or hostile manner. They may seem mistrustful, with no empathy for other people. Helping clients to resurrect empathy that has been quashed since childhood or never learned, may be an important goal of therapy. Boys with childhood onset CD with the lowest

levels of guilt tend to be interpersonally exploitative. They also have a reduced physiological reaction to other people's distress cues, and may be moving forward on the continuum toward antisocial personality disorder (Cimbora & McIntosh, 2003). Therapists who work with defiant, aggressive adolescents should take care to establish a respectful, empathic therapeutic relationship. Hanna and Hunt (1999) point to the importance of respect, humor, genuineness, and the use of concise language by therapists working with this population. The client's disruptive, angry, callous, provocative, or intimidating behaviors may stir up unresolved conflicts or negative feelings from the therapist's own youth. Therapists should not engage in win–lose battles, should not trust the adolescents' portrayal of their own behavior, should not fear manipulation, and should not become intimidated when working with aggressive adolescents. Therapists may need to work with the legal system or with court-ordered services and so must have knowledge of those systems. Therapists' expertise appears to be an important predictor of successful treatment outcomes for clients with CD (Kazdin, 1993).

Intervention Strategies

Early intervention for young children who begin to display conduct problems can protect them from moving along the developmental pathway to ODD, CD, and APD. Ongoing interventions should occur as needed throughout childhood to help families and children cope with environmental and familial stressors, academic and school-related problems, and emotion dysregulation. More than 1,500 controlled outcome studies exist on the treatment of ODD and CD. Because the intervention and treatment strategies for these two disorders are quite similar, they have been combined here.

Early Intervention Programs   Early interventions for children with conduct problems are more effective, easier, and have a protective element for children who might otherwise escalate into increased problem behavior, peer rejection, self-esteem deficits, conduct disorder, and academic failure (Mash & Wolfe, 2010).

High-risk children who exhibit disruptive and aggressive behaviors at home and in school are likely to benefit from early intervention programs. The trend is to match the needs of the child and family with the amount and type of intervention (Webster-Stratton et al., 2010). By working with parents and teachers of children as young as 2 to 8, adults can learn effective discipline, communication and coping skills, and ways to strengthen social supports. Early studies found that such interventions reduced behavioral problems in more than two thirds of the children whose parents were involved. The younger the child was when treatment was started, the more positive the behavioral adjustment at home and school (Mash, 2006; Webster-Stratton et al., 2010).

Transdiagnostic Approaches   As discussed earlier in this chapter, commonalities of symptoms across diagnoses has led increasingly to the use of transdiagnostic treatment approaches that work to alleviate one, or a cluster, of symptoms. Commonalities in disruptive childhood behavior disorders include emotion dysregulation, impulsivity, anger management, learning deficits, and deficits in social skills. Interventions that reach across diagnoses to help children at age-appropriate levels foster prosocial skills. The overall and long-term benefits of these programs need further study.

Anger management training is one cognitive approach that has received some support in the treatment of behavior problems. Lochman and colleagues (2010), for example, describe the Anger Coping and Coping Power programs, which teach elementary school-age children to use cognitive-behavioral strategies for coping with anger. Skills are taught such as emotional awareness, relaxation techniques, perspective taking, social problem solving, and dealing with peer pressure. Goal setting was identified as an important determinant of treatment effectiveness. In two different samples, the program was shown to reduce levels of delinquent behavior and substance use, decrease anger, and improve prosocial behavior. These gains were maintained at 1-year follow up (Lochman et al., 2009).

Parent management training, multisystemic training, and problem-solving skills training (PSST) have all been found to work well with conduct-disordered children. Behavioral interventions generally yield outcomes that are more positive than those for nonbehavioral treatments, and adolescent girls demonstrate better outcomes than those for children in any other age or gender group (Kazdin, 2008). Children with multiple risk factors, earlier onset of symptoms, severely aggressive behavior, and family adversity will have poorer treatment outcomes. It seems that for many childhood disorders, the synergistic effect of multiple risk factors portends a poorer prognosis.

Parent Management Training (PMT)   PMT is the most studied treatment for CD and provides clinical evidence that changing family interaction processes positively alters child behavior (Kazdin, 2010). PMT, developed by Patterson in 1982, is the model for many current training programs for parents. PMT is a cognitive-behavioral approach that teaches such skills as monitoring children's behaviors, maintaining discipline, and providing rewards. Outcome studies find that PMT reduces children's aggression, oppositional and antisocial behaviors, and increases their prosocial behaviors (Webster-Stratton et al., 2010). These behaviors, once learned, can be generalized to school settings. Improvements in siblings' behavior and decreased maternal stress and depression are beneficial side effects of PMT (Kazdin, 2010). Longitudinal studies indicate that PMT has continuing effectiveness 10 to 15 years after the original training (Webster-Stratton et al., 2010).

The Incredible Years is a PMT-style program that uses videotaped vignettes, role playing, a discussion group for parents, and peer support. In the basic curriculum, parents learn to play with and praise their children, to set limits, and to reduce harsh discipline. The advanced curriculum teaches such concepts as time-outs, problem solving, anger management, and communication skills. The goals of the Incredible Years program are to increase parent–child bonding, increase positive parenting strategies (i.e., ignoring, logical consequences, redirecting attention, monitoring, and problem-solving skills), to improve the parent's support network, and improve school readiness. Webster-Stratton and colleagues (2010) report improvements in parent–child bonding, parent confidence and teaching strategies, and increased family support. Parents also showed improvement in their own communication and anger management skills. Clinically significant improvement at 3-year follow-up was found in two thirds of the children rated. A later version was developed for teacher training in schools.

Treatment manuals and parent training materials are often a part of PMT. Additional research indicates that video-based treatment, when combined with therapist-led discussion groups, leads to improvements that can still be measured at 1- and 3-year post-treatment intervals (Kazdin, 2010).

Problem-Solving Skills Training (PSST)
It is clear that cognitive-behavioral approaches that teach problem-solving techniques decrease aggressive behaviors, but the effects are greatest in children who have achieved formal operational cognitive levels (generally by age 11) and in adolescents with strong ego functioning (Durlak, Fuhrman, & Lampman, 1991; Kazdin, 1993, 2008). Webster-Stratton and Reid (2010) found that the most effective parent interventions included training in communication and problem solving.

PSST teaches children to define a problem, identify goals, generate options, choose the best option, and evaluate the outcome. Techniques from social learning theory, such as modeling, role playing, reinforcement, and shaping of behaviors, enhance clients' ability to make decisions. PSST leads to significant reductions in parents' and teachers' ratings of children's aggressive behaviors, both immediately after treatment and 1 year later. Adding a parent-training component further improves treatment outcomes (Kazdin, 2010). Kazdin (2008) studied the effectiveness of PSST in an elementary school classroom, and found that those who received the training exhibited less disruptive behavior and more prosocial behavior. The beneficial impact was still noticeable 2 years later and points to a school intervention that can be easily implemented and improves outcomes.

One study that focused on high-risk children between ages 11 and 14, evaluated a variety of intervention models that included the use of groups for parents, groups for teenagers, combined parent and teen groups, and self-directed workbooks. All of these therapeutic interventions were effective, but those that featured parents' involvement demonstrated the most positive results (Dishion & Andrews, 1995).

Functional Family Therapy
Functional family therapy, developed by Alexander and Parsons in 1982, is derived from parent management training as well as from communication training and behavioral, structural, and systems theories of family therapy. At its core, this therapy

attempts to identify faulty or dysfunctional inter-actions in the family and replace them with more functional responses and behaviors. Func-tional family therapy attempts to reduce defen-siveness and blame and increase positive interactions among family members. It has been implemented among adolescents with CD whose behaviors have resulted in court involve-ment. Outcomes include improved family communications and the clients' decreased in-volvement with the courts up to two-and-one-half years after treatment (Kazdin, 1997).

Functional family therapy has also been shown to alter conduct problems of varying severity and to lower recidivism rates for young people who break the law (Kazdin, 2008). This treatment modality, used with young people with ODD or CD, has been found superior to psychodynamic or person-centered treatment in controlled studies. Treatment outcomes include increased family communication and a lower incidence of contact with the court system.

Multisystemic Therapy (MST)

MST is a family- and community-based treatment for adolescents who present with such serious clini-cal problems as substance misuse, sexual disor-ders, chronic antisocial behavior, serious mental health issues, and family dysfunction. MST addresses the multiple contexts in which CD is manifested. Therapists introduce individual, peer, and school interventions that involve some of the techniques already mentioned. Eight pub-lished outcome studies indicated that this ap-proach, used with adolescents exhibiting violent criminal behaviors, has shown promise in the treatment of criminal behavior, substance abuse, sexual disorders, and emotional disturbance. More than 30 states and 10 countries currently run licensed MST programs, and 1% of adoles-cent offenders at risk of incarceration in the United States have been treated with MST (Henggeler & Schaeffer, 2010).

Individual and Group Psychotherapy

Indi-vidual psychotherapy nearly always will be a part of the treatment plan for a young person di-agnosed with CD or ODD. Milder forms of dis-ruptive behavior disorders often respond well to individual therapy that includes consultation with parents and school. In these cases, treat-ment planning should include a prevention component. In addition to PSST (discussed ear-lier), anger management training and reality therapy have been shown to be effective with people with CD or ODD.

Reality therapy can provide a framework for challenging the distorted environmental perceptions often held by adolescents involved in or at risk for problem behavior. This ap-proach, developed by Glasser (1990), is fre-quently used in day treatment or hospital settings. The therapeutic relationship and such techniques as contracting and the use of re-wards and consequences help clients meet their needs in healthy, positive ways. Insight often improves after behavior has changed (Hanna & Hunt, 1999).

The use of group therapy to treat CD and ODD has demonstrated mixed results. Social skills training groups like those developed by Kazdin (2003) have been successful in decreasing the oppositional behaviors and increasing the prosocial behaviors of children with ODD. Therapy groups for adolescents with CD have been less successful. Treatment in hospitals, schools, and correctional facilities often include a group therapy component in which peers come together to talk about their problems. Kazdin (2003) warns that placing adolescents with CD together in groups could impede im-provement because of the tendency for the group to bond and reinforce deviant behavior. To minimize contagion of acting-out behaviors, Lochman and colleagues (2003, p. 279) recom-mend the following course of action in anger control training:

- Use two group leaders in a small (four- to six-person) group environment.
- Set clear expectations.
- Develop consequences for negative behavior during group.
- Include positive feedback.
- Establish groupwide contingencies for positive reinforcement.
- Encourage prosocial activities outside of the group.

Medication   Medication alone is ineffective in treating CD or ODD (AACAP, 2007d; Kazdin, 2008). However, pharmacotherapy has been found to be beneficial in the treatment of specific symptoms, such as aggression, and of such comorbid conditions as ADHD, mood disorders (depression and bipolar disorder), anxiety, and paranoid ideation with aggressiveness. McMahon and colleagues (2006) note that lithium, clonidine, anticonvulsants, antidepressants, and psychostimulants such as Ritalin are commonly used in the treatment of people with disruptive behavior disorders.

Hospitalization and Day Treatment Programs   Sometimes a young person's behavior becomes sufficiently dangerous or uncontrollable, or the family dysfunction so severe, as to warrant the child's placement in a group home, hospital, or residential setting. The *DSM-IV-TR* criteria for CD are not often sufficient for hospitalization. However, additional symptoms, such as a substance-related disorder, self-destructive or suicidal behavior, or homicidal or aggressive behavior, may make hospitalization necessary, as might severe symptoms of comorbid depressive disorder, bipolar disorder, psychosis, or intermittent explosive disorder (AACAP, 2007b).

Inpatient, partial hospitalization, and residential treatment programs should provide detoxification from drugs or alcohol, as well as time and resources both for in-depth evaluation and for stabilization on medication. A therapeutic milieu that includes behavior modification, family therapy, parent training, and individual and group therapy should also be included for young people diagnosed with disruptive behavior disorders who are receiving intensive treatment.

Day treatment programs offer similar benefits to those available in hospital or residential settings, but they allow the young person to return home at night and are usually less costly than hospitalization. Day treatment programs typically are intensive, running from 5 to 8 hours a day, 5 days per week. In addition to individual, group, and family therapy, these programs often include special education and behavioral consultation as part of individualized intervention plans. Day treatment programs have been found to reduce behaviors associated with CD and to improve social skills and family functioning (McMahon et al., 2006).

Prognosis

Many factors are associated with successful treatment of disruptive behavior disorders. The most effective treatment approaches start early, involve both parents and children, and are behavior focused (Kazdin, 2008). In a meta-analytic review of treatment outcomes for disruptive behavior disorders, Carr (2009) found outcome to be related to parent involvement with training. Children who participated in individual therapy were half as likely to improve as children whose parents actively participated in behavioral parent training.

Risk factors at onset of CD, such as early onset, severely aggressive behavior, and family adversity, can result in a poor long-term prognosis and influence responsiveness to treatment (Kazdin, 2010) but early intervention can preclude the development of more severely disruptive behavior. In CD with late or adolescent onset, children can draw on a history of appropriate behaviors. In general, family-based therapy is better for younger children, whereas older children do better with multicomponent interventions.

Often these disorders are thought of as having poor prognoses and being costly to society because such a large number of these children remain involved with mental health agencies or the criminal justice system throughout the lifespan (Webster-Stratton et al., 2010). However, young people diagnosed with ODD or CD certainly can show a positive response to treatment. The most critical element of successful treatment for this population appears to be parents' participation in ongoing support and periodic retraining. Prevention, both for high-risk children who have not yet met the criteria for ODD or CD and for those who have had these disorders but have improved through therapy, is also essential in reducing the incidence and severity of these disorders.

FEEDING AND EATING DISORDERS OF INFANCY OR EARLY CHILDHOOD

The *DSM-IV-TR* category of feeding and eating disorders of infancy or early childhood includes three disorders that interfere to a significant degree with a child's development, social functioning, or nutritional health: pica, rumination disorder, and feeding disorder of infancy or early childhood. The first two can also be diagnosed in adults but are much more common in children. We will look at each of these disorders in more detail below.

Description of the Disorders

Pica Pica is characterized by the consumption of nonnutritive substances for at least one month. The substances that are eaten vary across the lifespan. Infants and preschool children with this disorder typically eat such items as paint, paper, hair, or cloth. Older children typically eat insects, plants, clay, pebbles, or animal droppings. Soil, ice, clay, and hair are the most common substances eaten by adults who have pica (American Psychiatric Association, 2000; Roberts-Harewood & Davies, 2001). The diagnosis of pica should not be made if the eating habits are consistent with the cultural values and beliefs of the person and that person's family.

Pica often coexists with mental retardation or another disorder (often a neurological one). It becomes the focus of treatment only if it interferes with the person's functioning to a significant extent. Children with pica usually do not present for treatment until a medical complication has resulted. Lead poisoning is a common complication of eating paint chips. Other resulting medical problems include obstructed bowels, intestinal perforations, or infections. Although rare, repeated ingestion of hair (known as trichobezoar or Rapunzel syndrome) may result in the development of an intestinal hairball that must be surgically removed (Memon, Mandhan, Qureshi, & Shairani, 2003).

Pica is rare and is most often found in preschool children and among children with severe emotional disturbances. Onset is usually between the ages of 12 and 24 months. Prevalence of pica is significantly greater among children with mental retardation (as high as 30% in that population) or autistic disorder (as high as 60%). Its prevalence is also higher among children with behavior disorders and children from families with low SES (Kronenberger & Meyer, 2001). The disorder may also occur in pregnant women. One study of pregnant women found that 33% of the women with pica had a history of childhood pica, and 56% had a positive family history of the disorder, suggesting that the disorder may have a learned component (Roberts-Harewood & Davies, 2001).

Rumination Disorder Rumination disorder is found primarily in infants, with a typical age of onset of 3 to 12 months. This rare disorder is also found in older children and adults diagnosed with mental retardation (American Psychiatric Association, 2000). The symptoms include repeated regurgitation and remastication of food. The disorder develops after a period of normal eating and digesting and is not due to a general medical condition. Children with rumination disorder typically exhibit straining postures and sucking movements that facilitate the regurgitation. They appear to derive satisfaction from this activity, although they also are often irritable and hungry (American Psychiatric Association, 2000). Most children recover spontaneously from this disorder, but it should be taken seriously when it occurs, because death from malnutrition results in as many as 25% of cases (American Psychiatric Association, 2000).

Two subtypes of rumination disorder have been distinguished. The psychogenic subtype is reserved for those children who show no evidence of mental retardation. The etiology of psychogenic rumination is thought to be related to negative interactions between infants and caregivers, especially around feeding issues. The self-stimulating subtype is most likely to be found in children with mental retardation, whose ruminative behaviors are linked to cognitive rather than social deficits (Kronenberger & Meyer, 2001).

Feeding Disorder of Infancy or Early Childhood This disorder is diagnosed when a child exhibits persistent failure to eat adequately and has not gained age-appropriate weight or has lost a significant amount of weight over a period of at least one month. The symptoms must not be related to a general medical condition or to a lack of available food. Onset must be before the age of 6 years and usually occurs during the first year of life (American Psychiatric Association, 2000). This disorder can lead to a dangerous medical condition: nonorganic failure to thrive. Families of children with feeding disorder of infancy or early childhood often (but not always) exhibit such psychosocial contributory factors as low SES, emotional disorders in the parents, high environmental stress, and abuse and neglect of the child (Wilson, 2001). Feeding disorder of infancy or early childhood may be found in children who also have reactive attachment disorder that is linked to conflicts occurring in connection with feeding (Kronenberger & Meyer, 2001). Recent research notes a link between childhood failure to thrive and mothers who have eating disorders (Blissett, Meyer, & Haycraft, 2007). In general, eating problems and disordered eating are commonly found in the mothers of children with childhood feeding disorders (Mash & Wolfe, 2010).

Accurate data about the prevalence of feeding disorders of infancy or early childhood is sparse because these disorders typically occur in conjunction with mental retardation, pervasive developmental disorders, or other mental disorders, and may not be coded separately. They are listed on Axis I only if they are prominent enough to require separate treatment. In recognition that disordered eating and avoidant and restricted food intake occurs at all ages, the *DSM-5* may reclassify feeding disorders of early childhood as eating disorders.

Typical Client Characteristics

Children with feeding disorder of infancy or early childhood may be irritable and difficult to console. They may exhibit slowed growth patterns or sleep–wake cycle disturbances. Psychosocial problems, such as parental psychopathology, poor parent–child interactions, poverty, and neglect, are significant correlates of this disorder (Mash & Wolfe, 2010). Insecure attachment and a high incidence of negative interactions and emotions, including anger, sadness, and frustration, have been reported among children with the diagnosis of nonorganic failure to thrive related to feeding and eating disorders (Lyons-Ruth, Zeanah, & Benoit, 1996). An estimated 1% to 5% of pediatric hospital admissions are for failure to thrive. The *DSM-IV-TR* reports that up to one half of these admissions may reflect feeding disturbances unrelated to a medical condition (American Psychiatric Association, 2000).

Preferred Therapist Characteristics

Children with feeding and eating disorders usually first present in medical settings when physical conditions have developed from their impaired eating. Therefore, therapists affiliated with hospitals are most likely to see children with these disorders, although the parents of these children may be seen in any treatment setting.

Therapists working with this population must be at ease with potentially life-threatening situations. Therapists must also be good collaborators, able to consult with and contribute to a team of medical professionals. Training in family systems and cognitive-behavioral approaches can help therapists deal with the familial correlates of these disorders, as well as with parents' resistance and with their anger about feeling blamed for their children's symptoms.

The treatment of anorexia nervosa and bulimia nervosa is addressed in Chapter 6, but Wilson and Fairburn (2007) and others have identified children younger than 10 who are restricting their diets because of concern about body fat. Therefore, therapists working with children who have eating problems should be knowledgeable about anorexia nervosa and bulimia nervosa.

Intervention Strategies

In addition to medical monitoring, the primary treatment modality for children with feeding and eating disorders is work with the family. Cognitive-behavioral and educational approaches are useful in addressing issues related to parenting. Provision of information on children's developmental and eating patterns is commonly the first step toward a positive outcome. Linscheid (1992) suggests providing the child with a parent substitute who can offer a warm, nurturing feeding environment while the parents receive counseling to address any issues that are interfering with their nurturing of the child.

Pica is often addressed through parent training in behavior management strategies. This kind of training promotes closer monitoring of the child's eating, as well as the use of behavioral rewards or consequences. Charts for recording the ingestion of appropriate foods can be developed and can be used with stickers or other rewards for the child's eating of appropriate nutritive substances. This approach is usually adequate for discouraging children from eating inappropriate substances (Kronenberger & Meyer, 2001).

A limited number of research studies have been conducted on the effect of vitamin and mineral supplements in the treatment of children with pica. Three promising studies indicate a reduction in symptoms of pica in children who were given a daily multivitamin or iron supplements (Pace & Toyer, 2000). More research is needed on the relationship between pica and nutrition.

When feeding disorder of infancy or early childhood is accompanied by failure to thrive, the treatment is similar to that for reactive attachment disorder. If the disorder involves the child's refusal of food, then behavioral techniques can be helpful and may include positive reinforcement for eating, the modeling of positive eating behaviors, control of between-meal eating, and reduction of mealtime distractions (Kronenberger & Meyer, 2001).

Prognosis

In the majority of cases, feeding and eating disorders in young children remit after a few months of appropriate intervention. However, early feeding problems may contribute to the later development of eating disorders. Jacobi, Hayward, de Zwaan, Kraemer, and Agras (2004) conducted a meta-analysis of risk factors associated with eating disorders and reported one longitudinal study which indicated that pica and early digestive problems were related to later onset of bulimia (Marchi & Cohen, 1990); however, a second longitudinal study indicated that early feeding problems were unrelated to the development of either anorexia or bulimia nervosa in adolescence or childhood (Kotler, Cohen, Davies, Pine, & Walsh, 2001). Clearly, additional research is needed on the relationship between early childhood eating problems and later disordered or binge eating. Pica may persist for years, especially if it is present in conjunction with mental retardation.

TIC DISORDERS

The disorders discussed in this section are typified by "sudden, rapid, recurrent, nonrhythmic, stereotyped motor movement or vocalization" (American Psychiatric Association, 2000, p. 108). These symptoms typically worsen under stress and are less noticeable during sleep, or when the child is involved in an engrossing activity.

Description of the Disorders

Tics may be simple or complex, and affect movements or vocalizations. Examples of simple motor tics are eye blinking, neck jerking, facial grimacing, shrugging, or coughing. Simple vocal tics include clearing one's throat, grunting, sniffing, or barking. Complex motor and vocal tics incorporate complete actions or words that are repeated involuntarily and in rapid, staccato fashion. Complex motor tics include jumping, grooming, or smelling an object. A child with complex vocal tics may repeat sentences or phrases out of context. Other types of complex vocal tics include palilalia (repetition of one's own sounds or words) and echolalia (repetition of the sound, word, or phrase last heard). Despite its overuse in the media to represent Tourette's disorder, coprolalia (the use of socially unacceptable or obscene words) is found in only 10% to 20% of people with tics. Tic disorders are more common in boys.

A diagnosis of a tic disorder is appropriate only if the onset of the disorder occurs prior to age 18, if the symptoms are not the result of drugs or a medical condition (such as Huntington's disease), and if the symptoms cause significant distress or impairment (American Psychiatric Association, 2000). Towbin and Cohen (1996) report that tic disorders vary according to five properties:

1. Frequency (the number of tics that occur over a given period).
2. Complexity (the nature of the tic itself).
3. Intensity (the forcefulness of the tic; some tics are subtle, whereas others seem almost explosive or violent).
4. Location (the parts of the body affected by the tic).
5. Duration (the length of time that tics persist in each episode).

Assessment according to these properties can be helpful in determining what type of disorder is involved, the exacerbating factors, and the appropriate treatment and its impact.

Tic disorders have a higher incidence in children with certain coexisting disorders that have a neuropsychiatric component, including ADHD, learning disorders, pervasive developmental disorders, anxiety disorders, OCD, disruptive behavior disorders, and mood disorders (Storch et al., 2005). Motor tics can sometimes be a side effect of the psychostimulants used in the treatment of other disorders; therefore, many clinicians do not prescribe stimulant medication for children who have concurrent Tourette's disorder. The spectrum of tic disorders includes the following disorders.

Tourette's Disorder Tourette's disorder, named after Gilles de la Tourette, who first identified it, is diagnosed on the basis of tics that occur many times a day and that combine multiple motor tics with one or more vocal tics. The motor and vocal tics need not occur simultaneously in order for this diagnosis to be made. The severity and the location of the tics may change over time, but the diagnostic criteria require that the symptoms occur for a period of at least one year, with no more than a three-month tic-free period (American Psychiatric Association, 2000). As many as 1% of children have Tourette's disorder, with boys outnumbering girls by a 4:1 to 6:1 ratio (Kadesjo & Gillberg, 2000). People with this disorder usually also have relatives with the disorder.

Tourette's disorder often begins with intermittent, simple eye blinking. Tics initially may present only a few times each week or may be almost constant. Over time, the tic behaviors usually become persistent (of higher frequency or longer duration) and occur at multiple sites on the body. These involuntary movements have been reported to occur as frequently as 100 or more times per minute (Berardelli, Curr, Fabbrini, Gillio, & Manfredi, 2003). The tics often interfere with academic or work performance as well as with social relationships. By the age of

10, children with Tourette's disorder may be aware of urges that forewarn them of impending tics; a tic itself may be described as an itch or a tickle. Because of these premonitions, adolescents and adults may perceive their tics as at least partly voluntary. Some report the ability to suppress their tics during the school day or while at work and then "release" their tics when they come home (Jankovic, 2001). Usually by adolescence or early adulthood, spontaneous remission of tics has resulted in a 50% reduction in tics (Leckman, 2002) but cases of disabling Tourette's disorder have been found in adults.

Chronic Tic Disorder Chronic tic disorder resembles Tourette's disorder except that it involves single or complex motor or vocal tics (not both). The symptoms are also of lesser intensity and frequency than in Tourette's disorder and are usually confined to the eyes, face, head, neck, and upper extremities. This disorder sometimes is comorbid with ADHD and is exacerbated by stress, excitement, boredom, fatigue, and exposure to heat (Jankovic, 2001). Chronic tic disorder has a duration of more than 12 months.

Transient Tic Disorder Transient tic disorder resembles chronic tic disorder except for its duration: It lasts at least four weeks but no longer than one year. Emotional tension is often the cause of simple forms of transient tic disorder.

The prevalence of chronic tic disorder and transient tic disorder is not known. Many children with these disorders never come to the attention of the medical or mental health communities. Estimates suggest that the prevalence of Tourette's disorder is about 0.7% in school-age children, but estimates can range as high as 4.2% when all types of tic disorders are included (Jankovic, 2001). Research on the course of tic severity over the first two decades of life indicates that after a mean tic onset of 5.6 years of age, maximum tic severity usually peaks between 8 and 12 years of age and is frequently followed by a decline in symptoms (Leckman et al., 1998). The prevalence of tic disorder in early adulthood is half the rate in children. The research has implications for treatment, especially during the adolescent years when short periods of remission, from a few weeks to a year, may occur (American Psychiatric Association, 2000).

Typical Client Characteristics

In most children, tic disorders have an intermittent course—increasing in frequency and then waning at various intervals. Anxiety, stress, and fatigue are known to worsen all tic disorders (Bagheri, Kerbeshian, & Burd, 1999). Leckman and Cohen (1994) report cases of families who chastised children for tic-related behaviors and thereby increased stress, which in turn led to increased frequency and severity of tics; severe cases of Tourette's disorder may be related to this pattern of family dynamics. Tic disorders often have an impact on self-image and functioning. Social withdrawal may result from interactions with others who focus on and criticize the tic-related behaviors.

Tic disorders often co-occur with ADHD (50% of children with Tourette's have ADHD), learning disabilities (25% to 30%), and OCD (25% to 40%). Other behavior problems associated with Tourette's disorder include poor impulse control, anxiety and depression, inability to control anger, sleep problems, emotional outbursts, and self-injury (Bagheri et al., 1999; Jankovic, 2001).

Preferred Therapist Characteristics

Therapists working with children who have severe tic disorders need skills in establishing positive and supportive working relationships with younger clients and with their parents.

Tourette's disorder in particular introduces stressors into family dynamics, and these stressors may in turn exacerbate the condition. Tourette's disorder is often a lifelong disorder that requires ongoing support and advocacy from the therapist.

Therapists should be adept at individualizing treatment for the child; have a working knowledge of behavioral techniques, including habit reversal training; and be capable of working with professionals in the educational and medical arenas.

Intervention Strategies

The treatments of choice for tic disorders currently include habit reversal behavioral training, stress reduction techniques, psychoeducation of children and families about the disorder, advocacy with education professionals, and medication management, when appropriate (Porta et al., 2009).

Choosing among these interventions to formulate an effective treatment plan requires careful analysis of the type of disorder that is involved, as well as analysis of any underlying stressors that may be exacerbating the disorder. Noninvasive transcranial magnetic stimulation has been tried, but was not found to be effective in reducing tics (Orth et al., 2004). Recently, a more invasive medical procedure, which involves implanting electrodes into specific areas of the brain, has shown promise for people whose tics are treatment refractory (Porta et al., 2009).

The initial goal of treatment is not to eliminate all tics completely, but to educate the child and the parents about the nature of the disorder and the influence that stress, anxiety, and fatigue can have on symptoms. Children should be helped to achieve a degree of control over tics that allows them to function as normally as possible.

After establishing a positive working relationship and having made efforts to educate the family about the disorder and the role that stress plays in exacerbating symptoms, the therapist should facilitate the collection of baseline data about the frequency of the tics. Sometimes the act of collecting the data is therapeutic in itself, and the frequency of the tics may diminish (Bagheri et al., 1999). Baseline data guide the behavioral and environmental interventions, which constitute the next step in treatment.

Therapists or school counselors can suggest classroom modifications to reduce stress. These may include development of clear expectations, a low student-teacher ratio, predictable schedules, and contracts specifying rewards for behavioral control. Flexibility is important; perhaps the child can be allowed to leave the classroom when a tic occurs, or maybe academic requirements can be adjusted. School curricula that accommodate a variety of learning styles can allow children with Tourette's disorder to use learning strategies that make use of their strengths.

Behavioral techniques are often used to diminish tic-related behaviors. Self-monitoring, for example, involves children in recording the occurrence and frequency of tics (Kronenberger & Meyer, 2001). This approach is particularly helpful in children with multiple developmental problems and can be used to document the amount of progress that has been made (Bagheri et al., 1999). In relaxation training, children are taught to use such methods as progressive relaxation of muscle groups, deep breathing, or imagery before or during episodes of tics. Habit-reversal training uses reinforcement and other behavioral techniques to enable people with tic disorders to recognize premonitory urges, become aware of the presence of tics, monitor their own behaviors during stress-inducing situations, use relaxation techniques, and perform competing behaviors that are incompatible with the performance of the tic-related behavior

(Piacentini & Chang, 2005). This approach has achieved significant success in the treatment of Tourette's disorder and in the treatment of chronic motor or vocal tic disorders, but care should be taken, as some children who undergo behavior modification to directly target symptoms of Tourette's disorder may have an increase of tic symptoms (Bagheri et al., 1999).

Tourette's disorder often has a negative impact on peer relationships, especially among children and adolescents. Children with Tourette's disorder typically benefit from participation in social skills training groups, similar to those used for children with learning disorders, which can help them develop skills in relaxation and play and can teach them appropriate behaviors for approaching others. An adjunct to treatment that should be considered for the family is the Tourette's Syndrome Association, which provides many types of information, as well as family support networks all around the country (www.tsa-usa.org).

Pharmacological treatment usually is reserved for those people who do not respond well to behavioral and environmental interventions. Dopamine antagonist drugs (Haldol, Orap) and the atypical neuroleptic risperidone (Risperdal) are the most effective in terms of tic reduction, but serious side effects may include tardive dyskinesia, sedation, and tremors. For mild-to-moderate tics, or for those clients who want to avoid neuroleptic side effects, clonidine (Catapres) or guanfacine (Tenex) have been prescribed. Both are reported to reduce irritability and impulsivity and may reduce symptoms of ADHD as well (Porta et al., 2009). Especially in children, the use of multiple drugs should be avoided, if at all possible, to eliminate the risk of potential drug interactions and serious side effects.

Comorbid disorders must also be taken into account when treating children with tic disorders. The behaviors associated with comorbid

ADHD, OCD, and anxiety and mood disorders make the treatment more challenging, and should be addressed through behavior therapy whenever possible.

Prognosis

After achieving a peak period in adolescence, 50% of tics will spontaneously disappear. For those whose tics continue, a growing body of research indicates that habit-reversal training (HRT) is effective in reducing tics. Deckersbach, Rauch, Bulhmann, and Wilhelm (2006) showed reduced tic severity, improvements in life satisfaction, and improvement in psychosocial functioning during HRT therapy. In some cases, behavioral interventions can result in a reduction of medication by as much as 50% (Bagheri et al., 1999). For people with Tourette's syndrome whose tics are severe or who cannot tolerate the side effects of medication, deep brain stimulation (DBS) may be a promising treatment for the future.

ENCOPRESIS

Encopresis is one of two elimination disorders listed in the DSM. Enuresis, the passage of urine, will be discussed next.

Description of the Disorder

Encopresis is defined by the *DSM-IV-TR* as "repeated passage of feces into inappropriate places, whether intentional or involuntary" (American Psychiatric Association, 2000, p. 118). This diagnosis is applicable only if the person has a chronological or developmental level equivalent to at least 4 years of age and if the symptoms were present at least once a month for a minimum of three months. The symptoms must not be due to a general medical condition or to a reaction to medications. In order to establish an appropriate treatment plan, the therapist should determine whether the child has ever had an extended period of continence before the onset of encopresis.

Most children are developmentally, cognitively, and psychologically ready to achieve toilet training between 24 and 30 months of age (Kuhn, Marcus, & Pitner, 1999), and nearly all children in the United States are fully toilet trained by the age of 5 years. The *DSM-IV-TR* states the prevalence of encopresis among 5-year-olds as 1%. Encopresis is more common in boys, and the disorder is rare beyond the age of 16.

The *DSM-IV-TR* (American Psychiatric Association, 2000) distinguishes between encopresis with constipation and overflow incontinence and encopresis without these symptoms. These distinctions usually reflect differences in etiology and subsequent treatment. Kuhn et al. (1999) suggest that children diagnosed with encopresis without constipation can be divided into four subgroups: those who fail to obtain initial bowel training, those who exhibit fear of the toilet, those who use soiling to manipulate, and those with chronic diarrhea or irritable bowel syndrome.

Encopresis with constipation often develops after an occurrence of severe constipation resulting from an illness or a change in the diet. The resulting impaction of fecal material can cause painful bowel movements, and anal fissures or irritations have also been reported as contributing factors (Cox, Sutphen, Borowitz, Kovatchev, & Ling, 1998). Children develop a fear response and withhold feces in order to avoid painful bowel movements. The child avoids using the toilet, parents respond with requests for more frequent toileting, and a parent-child conflict develops. The resistance and fecal soiling continue. This scenario accounts for the majority of cases of encopresis.

Encopresis without constipation seems better understood as the result of operant conditioning, in which the child receives reinforcement (usually increased attention from the parents) for soiling. Significant emotional problems are reported in approximately 20% of children with the disorder (Peterson, Reach, & Grube, 2003).

Typical Client Characteristics

Five percent to 20% of children exhibit encopresis without constipation. These children often have other significant mental disorders, such as mental retardation, conduct disorder, or oppositional defiant disorder. Their behavior is usually manipulative and they receive secondary gains from the soiling.

Children with both types of encopresis may feel shame and low self-esteem related to their symptoms. Parental anger and rejection, as well as children's avoidance of social situations in which they may be embarrassed (such as overnight visits with friends), may further contribute to their distress and impairment. Smearing of feces (usually to hide the evidence) is sometimes present and can exacerbate negative family reactions. Twenty percent of children with encopresis experience more emotional and behavior problems, bullying, and antisocial behaviors than those who do not soil (Joinson, Heron, Butler, & von Gontard, 2006).

Preferred Therapist Characteristics

The therapist will need good skills in establishing rapport with both the child and the parents and in collaborating with physicians. The child must feel secure with the therapist in order for the treatment to be successful. Similarly, the relationship with the parents must enable them to feel support, as well as some relief from the guilt that parents of children with encopresis often experience.

Intervention Strategies

The effectiveness of encopresis treatment programs varies substantially by type. Cox and colleagues (2003) report the importance of identifying symptoms to determine whether a behavioral problem is present or whether the child's problems are "bowel-specific" (p. 376), as the latter may be more easily treated. The Virginia Encopresis Constipation Apperception Test (VECAT; Cox et al., 2003) shows promise as a tool to help determine symptoms and diagnose encopresis with and without constipation. Biofeedback, behavioral interventions, medical management, play therapy, and family-focused approaches have all been used in the treatment of encopresis.

Successful treatment of this disorder requires collaboration among parents, the child, the therapist, and the physician. Enhanced toilet training (ETT), which combines behavioral treatment (reinforcements, instructions and modeling, parent education) with medical management, has shown promise. A recent outcome study showed that ETT resulted in fewer symptoms compared with medical management alone, required fewer doses of laxatives, and resulted in longer intervals without symptoms (Ritterband et al., 2003).

An innovative Internet version of ETT was created by the University of Virginia and Vanderbilt University. The Web site (www.ucanpooptoo.com) provides a wide range of treatment modules for encopresis, allowing children to select the modules most relevant to their needs. An animated guide walks children through the tutorials, modules, and follow-up pages, with an audio accompaniment to the text. The site is easily accessible to parents and children in the privacy of their homes, provides effective learning tools, and reduces barriers to treatment (visits to doctors, transportation, time away from work and school, fees). Ritterband et al. (2003) report a 70% cure rate (the number of children without any accidents postassessment) for the Web-based group versus 45% for the control group after 3 weeks of treatment.

The authors of the study note that this is one of the first studies to empirically evaluate the use of an Internet program to help treat a medical condition. Internet treatments have significant potential benefits including increased accessibility, detailed information, privacy, and low-cost delivery. Finally, an animated, entertaining system may enhance compliance by children and be a positive adjunct to therapy.

Some children with encopresis are resistant to treatment. In cases like these, a behavioral assessment should be made to determine whether co-occurring aggression, oppositional behavior, or temper tantrums are hindering toilet training. In these cases, psychodynamic approaches may be useful. Cuddy-Casey (1997) used psychodynamic play therapy with a child who was both enuretic and encopretic and achieved resolution of the elimination disorders in 13 sessions. She suggests that persistent elimination problems may reflect the child's power struggles with the parents or a history of toileting-associated trauma that may need intervention.

Prognosis

Encopresis may continue for some time, but it is rarely chronic. When symptoms are long lasting, as many as one in five children may develop psychological problems, but this is believed to be a result of encopresis, rather than the cause of it (Peterson et al., 2003). Optimal treatment for encopresis involves a combination of medical intervention and behavior modification. Positive reinforcement involving rewards for appropriate toilet use are likely to enhance any type of treatment chosen. To succeed, the overall treatment plan must be one to which the parents will subscribe and lend their support. In a review of 42 studies, such multimodal treatments were found to be effective in 43% to 75% of cases (McGrath, Mellon, & Murphy, 2000). Early

intervention and treatment clearly are key to a good prognosis.

ENURESIS

Enuresis is the repeated voiding of urine into the bed or clothes and is considered clinically significant if it occurs at least twice per week during three consecutive months or if it interferes with the child's social or interpersonal functioning. In order for this diagnosis to be appropriate, the child must have both chronological and mental ages of at least 5 years, and the disorder must not be caused by a general medical condition.

Description of the Disorder

Diurnal enuresis occurs during the daytime and is considered to be related to poor toilet training, social anxiety, or preoccupation with other activities (American Psychiatric Association, 2000). Nocturnal enuresis is more common. It usually occurs during the first one third of the night, occasionally during the REM stage of sleep, and may occur during deep sleep that prevents awareness of the need to urinate. Children with nocturnal enuresis may also experience episodes of sleepwalking, encopresis, and nightmares and may report dreams about urinating (Rapoport & Ismond, 1996).

Early incidents of nocturnal enuresis are often the result of the child's sleeping deeply, having a small bladder, and other symptoms the child will outgrow in the course of development. However, Kazdin (2000) notes that enuresis in middle and later childhood is a risk factor for the development of other emotional disorders and that parents ought to intervene if the situation has not remitted by then.

Secondary enuresis, which follows a period of appropriate bladder control, is most likely to develop between the ages of 5 and 8 (American Psychiatric Association, 2000). The prevalence of the disorder decreases with age, with 15% experiencing spontaneous remission each year. Thus, nocturnal enuresis is found in 15% to 25% of 5-year-old boys and girls; 8% of 12-year-old boys; and only 1% to 3% of all adolescents (Thiedke, 2003). Only 1% of cases continue into adulthood.

Diurnal enuresis is more common among girls and is rarely seen after the age of 9 (American Psychiatric Association, 2000). Contextual factors should be considered in cases of diurnal enuresis because it is often related to anxiety around missing school activities or to a reluctance to use school toilets (Rapoport & Ismond, 1996).

Typical Client Characteristics

Seven to 10 million children in the United States wet the bed at night on a regular basis. Nocturnal enuresis can lead to anxiety for the child and may cause embarrassment, particularly around the overnight visits to friends and family members. Children may also experience lowered self-esteem as a result of this disorder. Parental anger may contribute to these negative emotions. Miller found that 23% to 36% of parents had used punishment as the primary method of addressing their children's enuresis (Thiedke, 2003). Needless to say, punishment and shame are contraindicated and only serve to lower the child's self-esteem.

A family history of enuresis is a predictor for this disorder to occur in children. The likelihood of having enuresis is 5 to 7 times greater in children with one parent who also had the disorder. According to Houts (2010), 85% of the children with this disorder are monosymptomatic. They have no underlying medical problem, only lose bladder control at night, and never have been dry at night for a 6-month

period of time. These children respond well to behavioral treatment.

The current research indicates that three variables are necessary for nighttime control of bladder functioning: normal bladder capacity, effective arousal from sleep when the bladder is full, and a decrease in nighttime urine production. An imbalance in any of these areas, which often occurs in children, is currently thought to be the cause of nocturnal enuresis (Houts, 2010). Research is also beginning to look at a chromosomal link to nocturnal enuresis. Additional studies will help determine treatments of the future.

Preferred Therapist Characteristics

The therapist should have a solid foundation in family dynamics and techniques of behavioral treatment. Much of the family's associated emotional distress can be alleviated if education about the disorder is provided, guilt is relieved, and symptoms are rapidly addressed with behavioral techniques that reduce the frequency of wetting. A thorough assessment which includes assessment for any co-occurring disorders such as conduct disorder, ODD, ADHD, or problem areas in the family such as recent separation or divorce, increased arguments, or other disruptions that may interfere with the parents committing to the full length of treatment should be addressed before behavior therapy for enuresis begins (Houts, 2010). Ninety percent of the children with nocturnal enuresis do not have any underlying medical problem.

Intervention Strategies

The initial phase of treatment for enuresis involves establishing rapport with the family and the child. Education about enuresis and its treatment can diminish anxieties related to the disorder. The collection of baseline data may effect some change in the enuretic behaviors and will provide necessary information for measuring progress. Children are often asked to keep a voiding diary in which they log both daytime and nighttime urination patterns for 1 week. Following a medical checkup to rule out problems with bladder function, most children respond well to behavioral approaches to enuresis.

The enuresis alarm or some variation on it has been found to be the most effective and least expensive form of therapy (Houts, 2010; Lyon & Schnall, 2005; Thiedke, 2003). A popular version of this system involves an alarm worn on the body: A sensor is attached to a pad that is placed inside the child's pants, and the alarm is placed on the child's wrist or in a pocket. If the pad becomes wet, a sensor in the pad triggers the alarm and increases awareness of the need to urinate. This system may need to be used for up to 15 weeks and can be useful both day and night. This system reportedly has a cure rate of 75% (Houts, 2010).

A variation on this system, called dry-bed training, was developed by Azrin, Sneed, and Foxx (1973). This version adds retention training (in which the children are taught to hold their urine for as long as possible during daytime hours) to the alarm-and-pad system. To date, it has been more successful than any other treatment modality. However, there is no evidence to show a remission benefit for dry-bed training without the alarm, indicating the key role for alarm therapy (Lyon & Schnall, 2005). Relapse is common, but repetition of the treatment usually brings about successful resolution of any relapse.

There is a 10% to 30% dropout rate in treatment of enuresis with alarms. Thiedke (2003) cites acting-out behavior on the part of the child, high levels of anxiety in the mother, a lack of concern about the condition on the part of the parents and the child, and other familial traits, such as low parental education level, high SES, and an unstable family situation, as contributing to poor compliance with behavioral alarms.

Full-spectrum home training (FSHT; Houts, 2010) has evolved over nearly 30 years of research. This behavioral approach can be started with children as young as 6; it combines basic urine alarm treatment, cleanliness training, retention control training, and overlearning to prevent relapse after 14 consecutive dry nights. Due to the commitment of time and the importance of arousing a child each time the alarm goes off in the middle of the night for the first 4 weeks, parents and children are asked to sign a contract (Houts, 2010). FSHT has been taught in group and individual formats with comparable outcomes. Separate groups should be formed for children 12 and older to reduce the embarrassment of being with younger children. Based on five outcome studies, 75% of children stopped bedwetting at the end of the average 12-week training. At 1-year follow-up, 6 out of every 10 children remained permanently dry.

Continued wetting is a failure to learn how to be dry. The urine alarm works by training the child to make an inhibitory pelvic floor response during sleep that stops the flow of urine. Alternatively, the child may get up and use the bathroom. Although frequently prescribed and used, medication for nocturnal enuresis is not recommended because it does not train the child to change behavior. Neither does the recent trend toward overnight diapers or pant liners, which actually have the effect of habituating the child to being wet at night.

Drugs, including antidiuretics, tricyclic antidepressants, and anticholinergic medications that may increase bladder capacity, have been used to treat enuresis, but none has been shown to have enduring effects. A meta-analysis of desmopressin (DDAVP), the most frequently prescribed medication for nocturnal enuresis, showed the medication to reduce symptoms by one to two nights a week compared with a placebo (Lyon

& Schnall, 2005). However, when treatment was discontinued, relapse rates ranged from 80% to 100% (Thiedke, 2003). The Cochrane Incontinence Group Trials compared DDAVP to alarms and found that the medication was more effective the first week. After 3 months, however, alarms were responsible for 1.4 fewer wet nights a week than medication (Lyon & Schnall, 2005).

Clearly a behavioral component is necessary for successful treatment of nocturnal enuresis. This is confirmed by several studies on combined treatment with desmopressin and conditioning alarms. Although the children initially improved during treatment using both methodologies, the use of alarms alone yielded higher improvement rates once the treatment stopped. Desmopressin may be a good choice, however, for situational use, such as for sleepovers, camping, and vacations (Lyon & Schnall, 2005).

Imipramine (Tofranil), an antidepressant, was found to reduce wetting frequency in 85% of children treated, but the symptoms returned within three months after the medication was discontinued (Lyon & Schnall, 2005). Given the potential side effects of this medication, it should be considered only after other options have been exhausted.

Alternative approaches to treatment have not been studied as extensively, but the following have been found to have a positive effect: acupuncture, retention control, biofeedback, caffeine restriction, hypnosis, and elimination diet. Children who continue to experience nocturnal enuresis, or those who are noncompliant with the alarm-and-pad treatment, may have behavioral problems or an underlying medical condition that needs to be addressed.

Prognosis

Spontaneous remission occurs in many children with enuresis. For those who do receive

treatment, the classical conditioning method, represented by the enuresis alarm and dry-bed training or FSHT, has been found superior to no treatment at all, to psychodynamic psychotherapy, and to medication. A systematic review and meta-analysis of 53 randomized controlled trials found that enuresis alarm programs with family intervention are an effective treatment for nocturnal enuresis (Glazener, Evans, & Paro, 2003). According to Houts (2010), such programs are effective in more than 70% of cases. A logical approach would be to combine behavior modification techniques with the alarm system, reserving the use of DDAVP for sleepovers or other appropriate occasions. Houts (2010) notes that children who wet more than one time per night may have an underlying condition that prevents them from achieving success. Whatever the treatment plan, relapse prevention, follow-up, support, and encouragement are important components to reduce anxiety and improve self-esteem in the child.

SEPARATION ANXIETY DISORDER

Separation anxiety disorder is one of the most common anxiety disorders found in children. An estimated 4% to 10% of all children experience the symptoms of separation anxiety at some point in their development (Mash & Wolfe, 2010). Approximately one third of the cases will persist into adulthood (Shear, Jin, Ruscio, Walters, & Kessler, 2006).

Description of the Disorder

The essential characteristic of this disorder is excessive distress upon separation from home or primary attachment figures. Manifestations of the distress may include worry about caretakers being harmed, reluctance or refusal to go to school or be separated from caregivers, fear about being alone, and frequent somatic complaints, such as headaches, stomachaches, and nausea and vomiting. Children with separation anxiety disorder often have difficulty at bedtime. They may express fear of going to sleep, request someone stay with them until they do, experience frequent nightmares, and attempt to sleep in their parents' bed. For diagnosis, *DSM-IV-TR* requires evidence of three or more of these symptoms for at least four weeks, with an onset prior to 18 years of age.

In public, children with separation anxiety disorder may cling to their parents. They often visit the school health clinic with minor physical complaints, or they ask to call home and have their parents come to take them home (Popper & Gherardi, 1996). As these children mature, the symptoms may change, with absenteeism and somatic complaints being particularly prominent. Children with separation anxiety disorder frequently present with symptoms of other anxiety disorders and often report many specific fears, as well as feelings of sadness and of not being loved. Mood disorders, conduct disorder, impulse control disorders, and ADHD also frequently coexist with separation anxiety disorder (Shear et al., 2006). The fear of getting lost is particularly common in these children (Albano, Chorpita, & Barlow, 2003). Communication disorders and reluctance to go to school are also common.

The etiology of separation anxiety disorder varies. In some cases it is precipitated by a stressful event, such as a significant loss, separation from loved ones, or exposure to danger. This disorder may also stem from an insecure attachment to the primary caregiver, or it may occur in families in which a parent is overly involved (Hudson & Rapee, 2001). Separation anxiety disorder has been associated with enmeshed family relationships. As with many of the other disorders seen in childhood, a careful analysis of contextual and interpersonal factors is important in making a diagnosis and developing treatment plans. Kendall, Aschenbrand, and Hudson (2003) suggest separate structured interviews with family members to rate the severity and onset of the distress.

Females seem more likely to present with this disorder than males, although some studies have found no gender differences. In older children, this disorder can be a contributing factor in refusal to go to school (Albano et al., 2003). This disorder is frequently seen in adults as well as children. Relevant adult avoidance situations, such as work, would most likely be added to the criteria.

Typical Client Characteristics

Popper and Gherardi (1996) report that the peak prevalence of this disorder occurs before adolescence and seems to be related to issues surrounding increasing independence and resultant changes in family relationships. Albano and colleagues (2003) suggest that many children begin to exhibit these symptoms around the ages of 5 or 6, when they enter school for the first time. Its onset is often subtle, with the child making innocent requests for physical closeness to the parent because of a physical complaint or a nightmare. The parent may unwittingly reinforce the fearful behavior by allowing the child to stay nearby. Stress may exacerbate the symptoms, and separation anxiety disorder can have a chronic course if not treated early. Children with separation anxiety disorder are at increased risk of developing other anxiety disorders in adolescence (Aschenbrand, Kendall, Webb, Safford, & Flannery-Schroeder, 2003). Early onset of separation anxiety disorder also appears to be predictive of adult panic disorders.

Children with this disorder sometimes have academic and social problems related to their absenteeism, as well as discomfort with other children. Their fears may preclude their participation in social activities including sleepovers, and their lack of participation interferes with their peer relationships.

Mothers of children with separation anxiety disorder have a high prevalence of anxiety or depressive disorders. Lower SES and lower levels of parental education also have been associated with greater prevalence of separation anxiety disorder. It also appears to be more common among white families (Albano et al., 2003), although Paniagua (2001) notes that internalizing disorders are often overlooked or misdiagnosed in children of color due to lack of understanding of cultural context or clinician bias.

Assessment

When treating anxiety disorders in childhood, therapists must assess the degree to which significant people in the child's life exacerbate or reduce the child's anxiety. Careful assessment of anxiety and avoidance behavior in daily life, as well as observations of the child interacting with the parents, is necessary. The Separation Anxiety Disorder Subscale on the Spence Children's Anxiety Scale (Spence, 1997, 1998; Spence, Barrett, & Turner, 2003) is a 44-item assessment that differentiates separation anxiety from generalized anxiety disorder, social anxiety disorder, OCD, panic disorder, and fear of physical injury.

Care should also be taken to distinguish separation anxiety disorder from school refusal. As many as 75% to 80% of those who refuse to go to school also experience separation anxiety, yet the two groups have distinguishing characteristics (Coleman & Webber, 2002). Children with separation anxiety disorder are more likely to be female, prepubescent, and from families with lower SES. School refusers are more likely to be adolescent, male, and from families with higher SES. In addition, for separation anxiety disorder to be the diagnosis, the child must experience significant fear on separation from the attachment figure. For school refusal, the child is more likely to have anxiety or fear about a specific situation within the school setting (Coleman & Webber, 2002).

Preferred Therapist Characteristics

Therapists working with children who have separation anxiety should work to establish trust and build rapport, accepting the child where he or she is and remaining flexible enough to tailor the treatment program to fit the child's individual needs. The therapist should model appropriate social skills, self-talk, and behavior. The therapist will also be responsible for assigning homework, creating practice situations in session, and developing in vivo experiences. Therapists must also be adept at family counseling and capable of providing training and feedback to the parents, who may be overly anxious themselves.

In general, the literature supports the inclusion of parents in the treatment of children with mental disorders, as parental involvement generally increases treatment efficacy (Kendall et al., 2003). However, a relationship has been found between anxiety and overly involved parents. More research is needed to determine the degree to which parental involvement can improve or hinder treatment of separation anxiety disorder (Barrett & Shortt, 2003; Hudson & Rapee, 2001). Therefore, an integral part of the therapist's role is to determine if the parents are enmeshed with the child. The therapist is often the primary facilitator of the child's separation from the parent and must be confident and clear in that role. If the therapist presents any insecurity or uncertainty, the child and the parent may not receive the emotional support required for them to effect separation.

Intervention Strategies

Separation anxiety disorder can be classified as a phobic response, usually surrounding the fear of leaving the primary caregiver, but occasionally it is related to fear of social and school situations. Fears and phobias are acquired through classical conditioning. Such fears can be unlearned through the use of the behavioral technique of exposure therapy, in which the child systematically confronts the feared situation through graded exposure. The research shows this type of therapy to be highly effective in the treatment of phobias (Evans et al., 2005). Little research is available on treatment effectiveness specific to separation anxiety disorder, but growing empirical evidence indicates that cognitive-behavioral therapy is the treatment of choice for childhood anxiety. Consequently, the course of treatment for separation anxiety disorder almost always includes a cognitive-behavioral approach.

One treatment program that has been shown to be effective in as many as two thirds of cases is the Coping Cat model, a manualized treatment developed by Kendall (Podell, Martin, & Kendall, 2008; Podell et al., 2010). The treatment program also has a beneficial effect on some comorbid conditions in addition to separation anxiety disorder. Coping Cat is a multifaceted treatment program that includes education as well as cognitive, affective, sociological, parent and family, and behavioral elements. This cognitive-behavioral method builds on the therapist–child relationship and also provides psychoeducation on the physiological signs of excessive anxiety, normal anxiety, self-talk associated with anxiety, the use of relaxation to reduce anxiety, and behavioral skills. A key component is the hierarchical use of exposure tasks to provide real experiences with arousal and management of anxious distress. Generally, the first half of treatment is the educational phase and the second half is the exposure phase.

Therapists teach their young clients that having some anxiety is reasonable. Children learn to identify the cognitive process involved and develop coping skills so that they can meet their fears head-on, thereby making avoidance unnecessary. By first practicing in session and then rehearsing outside of session, the child develops confidence that the coping skills are working.

If school attendance is an issue and the symptoms are of brief duration, a return to school may be sufficient treatment. Children with chronic features of the disorder, however, such as a long history of absenteeism, many visits to the school clinic, or significant problems at school, may require additional treatment. School counselors may become involved in the development and implementation of a plan for returning the child to school or shaping attendance behaviors by rewarding progressive approximations (bringing the child to the perimeter of the school property, to the front door, and finally to the classroom, and gradually extending the time that the child remains at school). After the child's return to school, individual and family psychotherapy, in addition to ongoing school consultation, can be implemented to address any underlying anxieties that may continue and that may shift to another manifestation or to another child in the family.

Family therapy as part of the treatment plan is particularly important when enmeshment is contributing to the disorder or when maternal or paternal anxiety or depression contribute to the child's anxious behavior. Parents of children with separation anxiety disorder may be dependent on their children or may be emotionally immature themselves. The goal of therapy in these cases would be to reestablish appropriate hierarchies and boundaries between the family subgroups.

In 1996, the first randomized control studies on the effect of CBT plus parent involvement were conducted with anxious children. Family anxiety management training includes teaching parents coping skills to help them manage their own anxiety, training parents in contingency management, and providing parents with problem-solving and communication skills (Barrett & Shortt, 2003). After treatment, 88% of children were free of anxiety, and the positive effect of treatment was still found five to seven years later. Age and gender did appear to play a significant role in the treatment. Researchers found that CBT plus parental involvement was more effective in younger children (age 7 to 10) and girls. Older children and boys were as likely to benefit from individual therapy to reduce their anxiety as they were from family anxiety management training. In severe cases, hospitalization may be required in order to force the separation that parent and child may be unable to accomplish.

Such strategies as relaxation techniques and contracting for progressive improvement have also been used successfully in the treatment of separation anxiety disorder. Group work may also be indicated in the treatment of anxiety disorders, but has not been researched specifically for treatment of separation anxiety disorder.

Medication has been used in the treatment of separation anxiety disorder, although few studies are available on the effectiveness of medication for anxiety disorders in children. At this writing, studies are under way to compare Coping Cat treatment (CBT) with sertraline (Zoloft), the combination of the two, and a placebo pill. The study will include combined data from six different locations (Kendall et al., 2003).

Prognosis

Kendall and colleagues (2003) report that 65% to 75% of children treated with the Coping Cat program recovered from their symptoms and remained symptom free for a substantial period of time. The remaining 25% to 35% were typically older children who had more complicated cases and co-occurring disorders.

A significant number of adults with multiple anxieties report having had a history of childhood separation anxiety disorder, a finding which suggests that separation anxiety disorder is a precursor of later anxiety disorders, especially agoraphobia and panic disorders (Evans et al., 2005). Children with separation anxiety disorder are also at risk for developing mood disorders in adulthood (Evans et al., 2005), as well as for substance-related disorders (Kendall et al., 2003). Childhood separation anxiety frequently continues into adulthood and affects the person across the lifespan (NIMH, 2005).

SELECTIVE MUTISM

The term *elective mutism* was first included in the *DSM-III* in 1980. The name was changed to *selective mutism* in the *DSM-IV* to more accurately reflect the child's choice, or selection, of contexts in which he or she remains silent.

Description of the Disorder

Selective mutism is characterized by a person's consistently not speaking in some social contexts, such as school, although the person does speak in other contexts, usually at home (American Psychiatric Association, 2000). Symptoms are not due to unfamiliarity or discomfort with the language, nor are the symptoms the result of embarrassment over stuttering or another communication disorder. The minimum duration required for diagnosis of this disorder is 1 month. Black and Uhde (1995) found that 97% of people diagnosed with selective mutism also had comorbid symptoms of social phobias, and 30% had specific phobias. Developmental disorders, anxiety, and nocturnal enuresis are also commonly found in children with selective mutism.

Kronenberger and Meyer (2001) describe children with four subtypes of selective mutism:

1.   Children who are shy and fearful, with significant stranger anxiety.
2.   Children who are noncompliant and hostile.
3.   Children whose mutism is the result of a traumatic or upsetting event or experience.
4.   Children who have a symbiotic relationship with the primary caregiver and who are manipulative and controlling, although they sometimes seem shy.

Each of these subtypes presents a different clinical picture and may respond to different methods of intervention.

Selective mutism occurs in approximately 0.5% of all children (Bergman, Piacentini, & McCracken, 2002). Girls are slightly more likely to present with this disorder than boys. It usually begins before the age of 5. Because their symptoms occur only in social situations, at school, or among strangers, children with selective mutism may frequently be misdiagnosed, or their symptoms may not interfere with the child's functioning until the start of preschool or elementary school. Although many parents report that their children function normally at home, these children often have academic and social difficulties at school, and teasing by peers is particularly common.

Typical Client Characteristics

In a study of Norwegian children, Kristensen (2000) found selective mutism to be comorbid with developmental disorders or delays nearly as frequently as with anxiety disorders. Many children with selective mutism met the criteria for an anxiety disorder (74% of those with selective mutism), developmental disorder or delay (68%), and an elimination disorder (31%).

Anxiety disorders tend to run in families, whether as a result of genetics, environment, or a combination of both. Various studies have found that parents of children with selective mutism score higher on assessments of social phobia, avoidant personality disorder (Black & Uhde, 1995), schizotypy in mothers, and anxiety in fathers (Kristensen & Torgersen, 2001), indicating that social anxiety in children with selective mutism usually is a family phenomenon. Rettew (2000) suggests that symptoms of shyness, social anxiety, and avoidant personality disorder lie on a continuum.

Assessment

Early diagnosis and treatment of selective mutism are important. Assessment of selective mutism should include a complete family history of the child, including a multigenerational history of social anxiety and phobias as well as the chronology of the child's linguistic abilities as observed in a variety of settings (home, school, and social situations, such as parties and visits with extended family). Schwartz and Shipon-Blum (2005) suggest that a videotape of the child playing spontaneously at home with a parent or sibling can be helpful in ruling out a pervasive developmental disorder or language delay. A complete assessment should determine what, if any, precipitating factors led to the child's mutism, the role of anxiety or defiance in the child's behavior, the nature of the attachment to the primary caregiver, and whether the child's behavior reflects extreme shyness.

Childhood assessments of anxiety, such as the Multidimensional Anxiety Scale for Children or the Hamilton Anxiety Scale, can be helpful in determining the level of the child's anxiety (Morris & March, 2004; Schwartz &

Shipon-Blum, 2005). The Beck Anxiety Inventory for Children may be helpful to establish a baseline or assess progress in ongoing therapy.

Preferred Therapist Characteristics

The therapist treating a child for selective mutism should be confident, consistent, calming, reassuring, and supportive. This stance is helpful to the parents, who are likely to be insecure and anxious themselves, and it will also help the child develop trust and feel comfortable speaking in novel settings. The therapist may coordinate an assessment with a speech and language specialist, as many children have co-occurring developmental delays. The therapist may need to serve as an advocate for the child, facilitating the establishment of a special education plan or initiating an evaluation of the child's school functioning, and so must be comfortable working collaboratively.

Intervention Strategies

Appropriate treatment for this disorder should initially emphasize reducing the child's level of anxiety, increasing the child's self-esteem, and improving behaviors in social settings (Cohan, Chavira, & Stein, 2006). Teaching social and other skills can help reduce the child's feelings of fear and shyness and help the child learn to express needs more directly. As the child becomes less anxious, treatment will emphasize behavior therapy aimed at improving the child's comfort level in social environments.

Several approaches have been used in encouraging children diagnosed with selective mutism to talk. Stimulus fading, a method similar to systematic desensitization, has had success with children who speak in some situations. In this approach, a person with whom the child does speak (often the mother) accompanies the child to the site where the child is mute. The child is gradually introduced to the feared situation while the parent withdraws. The child may also be rewarded for increasing communication and social interaction. These behaviors can then be generalized through shaping and reinforcement techniques.

Play therapy can also be useful in treating this disorder, especially if the child will not speak to the therapist. The symbolic nature of play allows the child a nonverbal modality in which to safely process uncomfortable feelings and upsetting experiences that may be at the heart of selective mutism.

Cognitive-behavioral therapy has been found to be effective in treating selective mutism (Morris & March, 2004) by helping children reduce their anxious fears and develop positive thoughts. Given the role that families play in the perpetuation of this disorder, intervention with the family is usually indicated. Structural family therapy is a logical choice because of its goal of restructuring family roles and relationships. This approach can engage and empower the nonenmeshed parent (usually the father) and establish appropriate boundaries and family hierarchies, with the parents in charge of the family (Kronenberger & Meyer, 2001). In some cases marital therapy or individual therapy for one parent is indicated so that issues in the parental relationship to the child can be addressed.

School intervention is an important aspect of helping the child with selective mutism become comfortable speaking across settings. Cunningham has developed a school-based 10-stage program that teaches professionals, parents, and teachers to encourage the child to talk to teachers and peers. Resources are available for professionals, parents, and educators who wish to work collaboratively (McHolm, Cunningham, & Vanier, 2005).

Psychopharmacological strategies are also being used in the treatment of selective mutism. Morris and Marsh (2004) report strong evidence for the effectiveness of SSRIs in the treatment of childhood anxiety, but studies on the use of SSRIs to treat selective mutism are limited. One study indicated that when flu-oxetine (Prozac) has been used, parents have reported improvement, but teachers and clini-cians working with the children have not (Black & Uhde, 1994). Such strategies as relaxa-tion and desensitization, used in treating anxiety disorders, have also been used with selective mutism (see Chapter 5 for more information on relaxation techniques). However, family-based psychotherapy remains the most often used ap-proach to treatment for selective mutism (Butcher et al., 2006).

Prognosis

Popper and Gherardi (1996) report that approx-imately half the children with selective mutism are able, after treatment, to talk in public by the age of 10. For young children with this disorder, then, the prognosis is relatively good; the prog-nosis is less optimistic for those who still exhibit symptoms beyond age 12 (Livingston, 1991). Family therapy, behavior modification, and pharmacotherapy with SSRIs are the most fre-quently used treatments for selective mutism. Early diagnosis and intervention are key to pre-venting long-term effects of this condition.

REACTIVE ATTACHMENT DISORDER

An understanding of attachment theory is a neces-sary precursor to any discussion of reactive attachment disorder. The work of Bowlby (1969/ 1982) and Ainsworth (Ainsworth et al., 1978) demonstrate the critical role of attachment in the normal socialization and biological development of children. Bowlby defined attachment theory as

a way of conceptualizing the propensity of human beings to make strong

affectional bonds to particular others and of explaining the many forms of emotional distress and personality dis-turbance, including anxiety, anger, de-pression, and emotional detachment, to which unwilling separation and loss give rise. (1969, p. 127)

Attachment, then, is the emotional bond that exists between infant and caregiver. Biological maturation is strongly related to early attachment bonds. Development of the ability to modulate emotional arousal and self-soothe is dependent on having had a "safe base" or secure attachment with a primary caregiver. The way in which secure and insecure attachment patterns evolve and affect children's development is the focus of many studies that offer compelling evidence about the relationship between secure attachment and the development of security, self-image, and intimate relationships throughout the lifespan. Ainsworth's research on the Strange Situation (Ainsworth et al., 1978) further contributed to at-tachment theory. Both Bowlby and Ainsworth believed attachment to be a lifespan concept.

Description of the Disorder

Reactive attachment disorder (RAD) is an uncommon disorder that begins before the age of 5, in which children manifest severe distur-bance in social relatedness. Children with RAD are those whose attachment to their primary caregivers has been disrupted so that future rela-tionships are also impaired. These children have experienced extremely poor care involving persistent disregard of their basic emotional or physical needs or disruptions in primary care-givers, and it is this pathogenic care that has caused the disturbance in social functioning (American Psychiatric Association, 2000).

The *DSM-IV-TR* delineates two subtypes of RAD. The inhibited type characterizes children who seem extremely withdrawn, unresponsive, or hypervigilant. The disinhibited type characterizes children who demonstrate no preferential attachment to any caregiver but instead are excessively social and seek comfort indiscriminately (Zeanah, 2009). Children with this type of RAD may even follow or seek solace from strangers.

The disinhibited type of RAD has often been found in children who have been institutionalized or maltreated. A study of children adopted out of institutions indicates that indiscriminate sociability is one of the most persistent social abnormalities (Zeanah et al., 2004) and may persist for years, even when children subsequently attach to new caregivers. The inhibited subtype is characterized by a failure to respond to or initiate social interactions in a developmentally appropriate way.

Children placed in foster care or institutional care settings are at increased risk for developing RAD (Wilson, 2001; Zeanah & Boris, 2000), as are children who experience severe trauma before the age of 5 (Sheperis, Renfro-Michel, & Doggett, 2003). However, the diagnosis does not apply to all children who may not have formed a secure attachment. Wilson (2001) describes the disorder as lying on a continuum of attachment problems with symptoms of increasing severity found in insecurely attached children.

Studies have considered the relationship of early attachment experiences to behaviors among preschool children. In many cases, children identified as hostile and aggressive have also manifested disordered attachment behaviors with their mothers (Speltz, McClellan, DeKlyen, & Jones, 1999). Therefore, RAD may reflect the roots of oppositional defiant disorder and conduct disorder (Lyons-Ruth et al., 1996), and early identification and treatment of RAD may prevent the later development of ODD and CD.

Typical Client Characteristics

Evidence that a child has problems with emotional attachment can appear before the first birthday and includes such symptoms as detached or unresponsive behavior, difficulty being comforted, severe colic, or feeding difficulties and failure to thrive. Little information is available on the prevalence of RAD, although Richters and Volkmar (1994) suggest it might be less than 1%. To date, most studies have focused on high-risk populations. For example, one study found that 38% of children who entered foster care before the age of 4 had signs of RAD (Zeanah et al., 2004).

Many symptoms, such as somatic complaints, disruptive behavior, and poor social relatedness, pose a challenge in diagnosis, as many symptoms of RAD are similar to the disruptive behavior disorders and pervasive developmental disorders, and can also be confused with symptoms of childhood bipolar disorder, anxiety, PTSD, and dissociative disorder (Hall & Geher, 2003; Hanson & Spratt, 2002; Sheperis, Renfro-Michel, & Doggett, 2003). *DSM-IV-TR* criteria exclude children with pervasive developmental disorders from also having a diagnosis of RAD. Strong links with later psychopathology have been found for infants who exhibit disorganized attachment (Green & Goldwyn, 2002).

Children with RAD are also at risk for language delays, difficulties in emotion regulation, and developmental delays, symptoms that can be mistaken for ADHD, especially in the school setting (Zeanah, 2009). Hall and Geher (2003) found that such behaviors as indiscriminate affection toward strangers, compulsive lying and stealing, and sexual behaviors differentiate RAD from ADHD. The symptoms of a child with RAD usually improve when that child is in a more favorable environment. Despite the overlap of symptoms, there is little empirical research on RAD and its comorbid disorders.

Assessment

No comprehensive and reliable test is available for the diagnosis of RAD. Rather, assessment is made based on semistructured interviews, global assessment scales, attachment-specific scales, and behavioral observations (Sheperis et al., 2003). The Child Behavior Checklist (Achenbach, 1991), the Behavior Assessment System for Children (BASC; Reynolds & Kamphaus, 2002), the Eyberg Child Behavior Inventory (ECBI; Eyberg & Pinkus, 1999), and the Sutter-Eyberg Student Behavior Inventory-Revised (SESBI-R; Eyberg & Pinkus, 1999) are among the most useful. Two scales directly related to RAD, the Reactive Attachment Disorder Questionnaire and the Randolph Attachment Disorder Questionnaire (Randolph, 1996), show potential but should not be used as the sole diagnostic instrument, as the first questionnaire was normed in Europe and the second does not measure the insecure attachment subtype (Sheperis et al., 2003).

The growing interest in examining attachment in older children and adults led to the creation of the Adult Attachment Interview (AAI) by George, Kaplan, and Main (1984). The instrument employs a 60- to 90-minute interview to assess adult attachment and provides information on how attachment experiences affected the person's development as an adult and parent.

Preferred Therapist Characteristics

Therapists working with children who have attachment disorder should understand the dynamics of the attachment process. Rebuilding a relationship between the child and the parents will be the primary goal of treatment. A psychodynamic or family systems conceptual framework for analyzing family dynamics is helpful in understanding this disorder and its treatment. One of the greatest challenges for therapists dealing with RAD is managing their own negative feelings toward the caregivers and remaining supportive and empathic while still establishing appropriate guidelines and boundaries for child care. The therapist must also be able to consult with and contribute to a team of medical professionals.

Intervention Strategies

The goal of treatment for children with RAD is to improve the relationship between the child and the primary caregiver. The caregiver-child relationship forms both the basis for assessment of symptoms and the nexus for treatment of RAD (AACAP, 2005). Three modalities can help children with RAD and their caregivers develop more effective, positive interactions: working through the caregiver, working with the dyad (caregiver and child), or working with the child alone.

Of utmost importance is to ensure that the child has a caregiver who is emotionally available, sensitive, and responsive, and to whom attachment can develop (Robinson, 2002). The next step in treating children with RAD is to address those behaviors that interfere with the development of adequate and secure attachments (Hansen & Spratt, 2002; Hart & Thomas, 2000). Initially, psychoeducation for the caregivers will focus on parenting skills and on the nature of positive attachment behaviors.

Psychoeducation may be accompanied by parent-child dyad therapy, in which the therapist models positive interactions and facilitates parent-child play. At least two dyadic interactive therapy programs have been shown to be effective. Infant-parent psychotherapy seeks to improve the emotional communication between the child and caregiver (Lieberman, Silverman, & Pawl, 2000). The second program, interaction guidance, focuses on behavior and involves videotaping and shaping (McDonough, 2000). Both incorporate suggestion and positive reinforcement and highlight parenting strengths as observed in the session. Dyadic therapy may later be widened to include other family members. In accordance with attachment theory and the goal of improving the relationship between the child and the primary caregiver, individual therapy with the child should be considered only as an adjunct to dyadic therapy, especially with younger children (AACAP, 2005).

Additional treatment goals address the assessment and development of attachment behaviors in the parents. Caregiver characteristics that have been shown to be risk factors include depression, poverty, a history of abuse in the parent's own childhood, and lack of social support (Wilson, 2001). Any abusive or neglectful behaviors certainly must be modified, and quickly. Marital or individual psychotherapy may also be in order. An assessment of the parents' relationships to their individual families of origin can provide the therapist with a baseline assessment of the parents' levels and styles of attachment. Research using the Adult Attachment Interview (Cowan, Cohn, Cowan, & Pearson, 1996) shows significant links between parental attachment and a child's externalizing and internalizing behaviors. This kind of information can stimulate therapeutic discussions with the parents. A cognitive-behavioral framework can be used to identify inappropriate thoughts and actions in the parenting process, and psychodynamic therapy can address unresolved issues from childhood that are interfering with the ability to parent.

In aggressive or violent children, evidence-based treatments such as multisystemic therapy or parent training, which were discussed extensively in the previous sections on ODD and CD, may be considered. No data are available on the use of pharmacotherapy to treat RAD. Caution should be used in the consideration of such interventions, particularly in preschool-age children.

Interventions that involve physical restraint, "rebirthing," holding therapy, or regression therapy to create reattachment have not been empirically validated and have been associated with serious harm, including death. Both the American Psychiatric Association (2002) and AACAP (2003) have issued policy statements opposing coercion therapies for children with serious disturbances such as RAD.

Therapists must carefully monitor the family situations of children diagnosed with RAD. In some cases, where no gains or changes have been made to improve the quality of child care, or in cases where the children are so aggressive that they are unmanageable in the home, protective removal of the child may be warranted (AACAP, 2005); the options include placing the child in foster care, with a relative, or in respite care. Establishing a consistent, safe environment that provides positive care and nurturing is essential to the child's safety and the alleviation of this disorder.

Prognosis

Research has demonstrated a connection between insecure attachment and subsequent behavior and impulse-control problems, low self-esteem, poor peer relationships, psychiatric syndromes, criminal behavior, and substance abuse (Sheperis et al., 2003; Wilson, 2001; Zeanah & Emde, 1994). Clearly, early and effective intervention is indicated for RAD. Interventions based on attachment theory are relatively new; however, so only limited evaluation data are available. Nevertheless, the treatment of RAD offers many possibilities for future research and holds promise as a way to prevent later behavior disorders.

STEREOTYPIC MOVEMENT DISORDER

Stereotypic movement disorder is rarely the primary focus of assessment and treatment. It usually accompanies more severe disorders.

Description of the Disorder

Stereotypic movement disorder, according to the *DSM-IV-TR*, is characterized by repetitive, apparently intentional, driven, nonfunctional, and often self-injurious behaviors, such as hand waving, rocking, head banging, or self-biting. These behaviors persist for at least four weeks and interfere with normal activities.

Comorbidity with mental retardation and pervasive developmental disorders is common (American Psychiatric Association, 2000). Stereotypic movement disorder has also been identified in children diagnosed with anxiety disorders and mood disorders. As is true of most secondary disorders, stereotypic movement disorder should be diagnosed only if it is so severe as to warrant separate treatment.

Typical Client Characteristics

Children with stereotypic movement disorder exhibit the repetitive behaviors just described and may present with bruises, bite marks, cuts, and scratches (American Psychiatric Association, 2000). These behaviors are voluntary, although the children may report that they cannot stop them. The behaviors, sometimes manifested by children who have inadequate social stimulation, often begin after a stressful event and may continue despite chastisement from family members and teasing by peers (Rapoport & Ismond, 1996). The family histories of children with stereotypic movement disorder often include compulsive or other stereotypic behaviors.

The *DSM-IV-TR* reports that self-injurious behavior occurs at all ages and in both genders. Head banging is more prevalent in males at a ratio of 3:1; self-biting occurs more frequently in females.

Preferred Therapist Characteristics

Therapists working with children with stereotypic movement disorder should be aware of common comorbid disorders and their treatments. For example, childhood stereotypes (repetitive movements) may indicate an underlying disorder, such as autism or other pervasive developmental disorders or Tourette's syndrome. An adolescent or adult onset, however, might be an indication of stimulant abuse. Treatment should take into account the severity and cause of the disorder, and the age of the person.

Behavioral strategies are typically the first line of treatment, so therapists need a working knowledge of the basic elements of behavior change therapies. Skill in cognitive-behavioral and psychodynamic play therapy may also be helpful, as may family counseling and collaboration with physicians and educators. Therapists need to be calm and empathic with these clients, particularly if underlying anxiety or depression is present.

Intervention Strategies

Treatment for stereotypic movement disorder is similar to that used for behaviors associated with autism, tic disorders, and OCD. Applied behavior analysis has been shown to be clinically effective in reducing problem behavior and increasing appropriate skills for people with mental retardation, autism, and stereotypic behavior. Forty years of literature and three meta-analyses have concluded that treatments such as this, based on operant principles of learning, were effective in reducing problem behavior, including stereotypic behavior and self-injurious behavior, and in a variety of settings including homes, schools, and hospitals (Hagopian & Boelter, 2005).

In applied behavior analysis, baseline data are collected, to determine the initial frequency and timing of the targeted behaviors and later to evaluate progress. Then a behavioral plan is developed for modifying behaviors. The plan may follow a classical model or a model based on operant conditioning.

The classical paradigm for conditioning pairs the stereotypic behavior with some aversive stimulus or competing behavior. This type of aversion or competition is intended to decrease the frequency of the targeted behavior. For example, a rubber band may be placed around a child's wrist, and the child is given instructions to pluck the band each time the stereotypic behavior begins. As another example, tape may be placed over the thumb of a child in order to interfere with the automatic nature of chronic thumb sucking.

Operant conditioning uses both positive and negative reinforcers to change a targeted behavior. In the case of stereotypic movements, a chart may be developed and particular time periods may be delineated, with the child being rewarded with a sticker for each time period in which the behavior is not manifested; at the end of a week, the stickers can be redeemed for prizes. Therapists facilitate the development of these plans, but special education teachers often oversee their execution. Therefore, consultation between therapists and teachers may contribute to the effectiveness of the treatment.

If the stereotypic movements are related to a mood disorder or an anxiety disorder, play therapy may be the treatment of choice. These treatments can help children identify the sources of their discomfort. When their distress is alleviated, the children may not need to manifest behavioral expressions of their distress.

Prognosis

Little information is available about the prognosis for stereotypic movement disorder, perhaps because it is rarely the primary focus of treatment and usually accompanies more severe disorders. One study of behavior modification in autistic preschoolers showed a reduction in stereotypic behaviors at ages 3 and 4, but not among 2-year-olds, leading researchers to surmise that early and consistent intervention improves outcomes. Successful reduction of targeted behaviors via behavior modification is likely, although this disorder may persist for years, sometimes with changes in its nature. This outcome is especially likely in people with severe or profound levels of mental retardation (American Psychiatric Association, 2000).

ADDITIONAL MENTAL DISORDERS DIAGNOSED IN CHILDREN AND ADOLESCENTS

Many of the mental disorders considered in later chapters of this book are found in young clients, although they are far more prevalent in adults. The remainder of this chapter discusses differences in the diagnosis and treatment of some of those disorders when they are found in children and adolescents. Discussion of some disorders does not follow the usual format of this book if information of particular relevance to children is unavailable in certain areas. Readers should also review later sections of this book to obtain a complete picture of these disorders.

Depression

The development of depression in children can result from a variety of environmental, genetic, and socioeconomic factors. In any case, early assessment and treatment is important to the development of good emotional health across the lifespan.

Description of the Disorder   Symptoms of depression in childhood can include behavioral and emotional dysregulation, somatic complaints, lack of energy and interest, and isolation or school refusal. Children generally cannot identify the specific causes of their complaints, but tend to act out their distress.

Typical Client Characteristics School-age children experiencing depression are likely to be irritable and to present somatic complaints such as headaches, stomachaches, and fatigue (Field & Seligman, 2004). In young children, separation anxiety disorder often is characterized by features of depression, including crying, sulkiness, irritability, and a sad appearance. Clinicians should be sure that separation anxiety disorder is not misdiagnosed as a depressive disorder.

Adolescents' symptoms of depression are similar to those of adults and include sad feelings, social withdrawal, and, in about 10% of cases, mood-congruent hallucinations. Adolescents are less likely than younger children to complain of physical problems and to cry, but irritability continues to be a characteristic complaint along with problems in relationships, impaired school performance, and substance misuse.

Early onset in the childhood years of either depression or dysthymia are generally considered to be indicative of a more severe course across the lifetime. Early recognition, assessment, and intervention are imperative so that these children can learn how to regulate their emotions, develop coping skills, and ameliorate some of the risks associated with untreated depression.

Assessment A complete assessment for mood disorders in children should include taking careful medical, developmental, and social histories along with a history of the presenting problem. Assessing the range of symptoms, degree of severity, and whether psychotic features accompany the mood disorder is important to accurate diagnosis and treatment. The Child Depression Inventory (Kovacs, 1983) is the most widely used assessment of depression in children ages 7 to 17 (Silverman & Rabian, 1999). It has been extensively studied and is reported to have high stability and internal consistency. Other assessment tools for children include the Child Assessment Schedule (CAS), the Interview Schedule for Children (ISC), the Diagnostic Interview for Children and Adolescents (DICA), the Diagnostic Interview Schedule for Children (DISC), and the Children's Depression Rating Scale-Revised (CDRS-R).

A comprehensive family medical history should also be taken to determine any genetic predisposition to mood disorders. Depression in mothers is often found to be a contributing factor to childhood depression so early identification and treatment of mothers with depression is an important concern. Even so, research has shown that ameliorating maternal depression is not enough. Both mother and child must receive treatment in order for treatment of childhood depression to be effective (Luby, 2009; Luby, Belden, & Tandon, 2010). The Beck Depression Inventory (Beck, Steer, & Brown, 1996) and the Parenting Stress Index (Haskett, Nears, Ward, & McPherson, 2006) are helpful in diagnosing adult depression.

Preferred Therapist Characteristics The diagnosis of depression in childhood requires a therapist with a good understanding of child development and of age-related differences in presentations of this disorder. Such traits on the part of the therapist as empathy and the ability to work collaboratively with parents are important. Skillful recognition of suicidal ideation, good listening skills, and a nonjudgmental attitude are also important (Mackinaw-Koons & Fristad, 2004). As mentioned earlier, issues related to confidentiality become more difficult when working with adolescents and their parents. Confidentiality of the adolescent must be maintained in order to develop an effective therapeutic alliance, and for the youth to believe that the therapist is an ally and an advocate. But therapists must not shy away from confronting behavior that threatens harm to the child's safety. Many therapists tell the parents in the initial session that they will provide an overview of what the child says, but not specific details. However, therapists must draw the line at threats to the safety of the child such as suicidal behavior, unprotected sex, dangerous driving, and other behaviors that may put them in harm's way.

Intervention Strategies Recommended treatment for children with mood disorders is similar to that for adults (see Chapter 4), but some programs and guidelines are especially pertinent to young clients with these disorders. As with all mood disorders, safety comes first and any suicidal ideation or attempts must be addressed, a safety plan developed, and the client stabilized before psychosocial treatments for depression can begin.

Limited research is available on specific interventions for pediatric depression. Weisz and colleagues (1995) conducted a meta-analysis of outcome studies and found that children with depression who received psychotherapy were 77% more likely than controls to show improvement on posttreatment assessments and continued to be better off than 69% of the controls on follow-up assessments. Goodyer and colleagues (2007) note that 30% to 50% responded well to brief nonspecific treatment. From the limited information on research available, Birmaher and Brent (2010) deduced that nonspecific, supportive interventions and psychoeducation might be fine for a first line approach to childhood depression. If improvement does not occur, clinicians should choose a more structured approach such as CBT or interpersonal therapy, which have some RCTs to indicate their effectiveness with depressed youth (Weisz & Kazdin, 2010) and seem to be more effective than family behavior therapy. Only after monotherapy has

failed, or in severe or treatment refractory cases, should combination therapy consisting of CBT and medication be considered (Birmaher & Brent, 2010).

Other psychosocial treatment options include cognitive-behavioral play therapy, psychoeducation, and lifestyle modifications, although little evidence is available on treatment effectiveness for these modalities. Research indicates that children who actively participate during therapy are more likely to stay in therapy and therefore, more likely to benefit from the interventions. Cognitive behavioral play therapy integrates psychoeducation and play into a treatment program to help children learn to regulate their affect, a common feature of childhood depression (Paula, 2009).

Clarke and colleagues (2002) designed the STEADY intervention model for adolescents with depression. This psychoeducational group training includes workbooks, readings, and quizzes to help adolescents track mood and activities, understand and comply with medication, set goals, and develop alternatives to negative thinking. The training takes place over six to nine sessions followed up with monthly phone calls and up to six additional optional sessions as needed.

Lifestyle modifications such as regular exercise, developing good sleep hygiene, implementing coping skills to reduce stress, and participation in fun and interesting activities can also be effective treatment of adolescent depression.

Although medications are being used effectively in the treatment of mood disorders in adults, little research is available on their effectiveness in children. When medication is used to treat mood disorders in children and adolescents, the child must be well monitored in order to prevent serious side effects. Adequate monitoring may not be possible if the child has a very disorganized home life. SSRIs in particular have been shown to increase the risk of suicidal idea-tion and behavior in children and adolescents, especially during the early months of treatment (Handen & Gilchrist, 2006). Since 2004, these medications have been required by the U.S. Food and Drug Administration to carry a black box warning label. Certainly, more research is needed in this area of pharmacology.

Medication should never be the first line treatment for childhood depression. Random-ized controlled trials found that 50% to 60% of children respond positively to placebo (Bridge et al., 2007). Therefore, evidence of effectiveness is lacking. Unless the child has severe symptoms, is homicidal or suicidal, or several courses of psy-chotherapy have been ineffective, the risk of prescribing SSRIs seems to outweigh the bene-fits at this time (Birmaher & Brent, 2010). For a complete discussion of treatment interventions for childhood mood disorders see American Academy of Child and Adolescent Psychiatry (2007c) practice parameters for the treatment of children and adolescents with depressive disorders.

Prognosis Even with successful interventions, risk of relapse of depression in children and adolescents was found to be as high as 40% to 60% (Field & Seligman, 2004). The risk of re-currence continues into adulthood. Comorbid disorders, such as ADHD, conduct disorder, personality disorders, and co-occurring sub-stance-related disorders, can further complicate treatment of mood disorders in childhood and adolescence.

Bipolar Disorder

Nearly a third of children between the ages of 6 and 12 who are diagnosed with major depres-sion will go on to develop bipolar disorder (AACAP, 2007b). Thus, it is important for cli-nicians to know the signs and symptoms of childhood affective disorders and to be able to differentiate between disorders that share similar symptoms.

Description of the Disorder Although the incidence of adult bipolar disorder is lower than unipolar depression, both conditions can have childhood or adolescent onset. Research conducted by the National Institute of Mental Health (2002) suggests that bipolar disorder affects 2% of the general population, 15% of whom manifest symptoms in childhood or adolescence.

Recent attention has focused on studies that are finding a large rate of increase in diag-noses of bipolar disorder in children (Blader & Carlson, 2007). Several different reasons for this increase have been hypothesized including: improved diagnostic measures, a loose rather than a strict interpretation of *DSM-IV-TR* criteria, changes in the diagnosis of ADHD which have resulted in some children and ado-lescents being reclassified, increased numbers of children who are being seen by doctors for se-vere emotion dysregulation and behavioral problems (and are being prescribed antipsy-chotic medications), doctors are more aware of pediatric cases of bipolar disorder now and are correctly diagnosing children who were mis-diagnosed in the past, and, an actual increase in the number of children developing the disorder (Blader & Carlson, 2007; Carlson, 1998; Gellar & Luby, 1997; Moreno et al., 2007). The sud-den increase also raises questions about possible misdiagnosis and the potential for overprescrib-ing medications.

Using *DSM-IV-TR* criteria, 1% of children would meet the criteria for bipolar disorder (McLellan, Kowatch, & Findling, 2007). This number increases to 13% if a broader set of criteria (i.e., the presence of four rather than five manic symptoms) is used (Blader & Carlson, 2007).

Controversy has risen between experts, and this is borne out in the research, as some authors use a more expansive interpretation of the *DSM-IV-TR* criteria in the symptoms they include. This, of course, increases the diagnosis of bipolar disorder and inflates prevalence rates. It is hoped that the *DSM-5* will address issues of diagnosis related to bipolar disorder in children and adolescents. Until then, our discussion will continue to follow *DSM-IV-TR* criteria.

Current understanding points to a combination of biological, psychological, and environmental factors weaved together in the development of bipolar disorder. A genetic predisposition interacts with temperament to create vulnerability and then a stressful or even traumatic life event occurs that triggers the disorder.

Symptoms of bipolar disorder frequently overlap with ADHD, ODD, and conduct disorder Family history, age of onset, and symptoms such as reduced need for sleep and hypersexuality may be more apparent in bipolar disorder than the other childhood disorders. Emotion dysregulation, while frequently present, is not pathognomonic for bipolar disorder. Rather, mood swings are characteristic of most adolescents and are often mistaken for a bipolar disorder.

As mentioned earlier, prevalence rates vary widely, depending on whether a strict adherence to the *DSM-IV-TR* or a broader set of criteria are used.

Adults diagnosed with bipolar disorder were found to have had difficult temperaments and sleep problems even as infants. This differed significantly from children with ADHD.

Antecedents to the development of bipolar disorder in childhood can include birth complications, prenatal maternal alcohol or substance abuse, loss or trauma in childhood, and negative parenting style (Garno et al., 2005; Neria, Bromet, Carlson, & Naz, 2005; Pavuluri, Birmaher, & Naylor, 2005).

Environmental influences such as families in which parents exhibit a high degree of criticism, negativity, and emotional overinvolvement increases the risk of severity (Miklowitz & Cicchetti, 2010). The parent–child interaction is a bidirectional process. Thus, the parent's high expressed emotion hinders the child's ability to self-regulate emotions. Misbehavior results including acting out on the part of the child, which proves the parent's right in their negative beliefs about their child and the criticism again escalates into a cycle of worsening pathology.

Therapists may find it helpful to differentiate between euphoric symptoms of mania (grandiosity, pressured speech, and hypersexual behavior) and symptoms that are dysphoric in nature, such as irritability, anger, and aggression.

Typical Client Characteristics   Children and adolescents who are diagnosed with bipolar disorder differ from their adult counterparts in two very important ways. What constitutes a manic episode in children is often very different from adult mania, and the length of manic episodes is rarely clearcut, nor does it meet the 1-week-duration requirement of the *DSM-IV-TR*. As a result, most cases of childhood bipolar disorder are diagnosed as bipolar disorder-NOS. Mania in children is often found in a mixed state, and mood shifts may last days or even hours (Leibenluft, Charney, Towbin, Bhangoo, & Pine, 2003). Mixed episodes may be more frequent than manic episodes in children, adolescents, and adults (Youngstrom, Birmaher, & Findling, 2008). Chronic behavioral and mood instability is also more likely in children as mania can be characterized by irritability, temper tantrums, and other dysfunctional behavior (Biederman, Mick, Faraone, & Wozniak, 2004).

Preschool. Manic symptoms can be identified as early as the preschool years. Luby and Beldon (2006) found that the constellation of hypersexuality, elation, grandiosity, hypertalkativeness, and flight of ideas in preschoolers differentiated bipolar disorder from ADHD, ODD, or conduct disorder 92% of the time.

Childhood. Children with bipolar disorder may exhibit emotional, cognitive, and behavioral symptoms. Bipolar rages or emotional storms that may last longer than 30 minutes are a common symptom of mania (DuVal, 2005; NIMH, 2002). Grandiosity, flight of ideas, hypersexuality, and decreased need for sleep are highly specific to bipolar disorder and can often differentiate bipolar disorder from ADHD.

Future research in this area will help clarify the issue. Until then, clinicians are wise to keep this controversy in mind when assessing children with symptoms of bipolar mania.

Early recognition and accurate diagnosis of bipolar disorder is important because the disorder can become an extremely debilitating condition and is associated with high rates of substance abuse and suicide, the third leading cause of death in adolescents (National Center for Health Statistics, 2003). It is also important to have an accurate diagnosis so that the appropriate treatment recommendations can be made.

Adolescents. The *DSM-IV-TR* indicates that adolescents with bipolar disorder are more likely to exhibit psychotic features, to have difficulties in school, to misuse substances, and to manifest antisocial behavior. ADHD, ODD, and conduct disorder frequently co-occur with bipolar disorder in children and adolescents. Therapists should be aware that substance misuse and certain prescription drugs including antidepressants, stimulants used in the treatment of comorbid ADHD, and steroids may precipitate a manic episode (Miklowitz & Cicchetti, 2010).

Substance abuse is the most common disorder co-occurring with adolescent bipolar disorder. A substance abuse history, in turn, increases the likelihood of suicide or self-injury (Goldstein et al., 2005).

Assessment A psychometric measurement has not been designed specifically for the diagnosis of bipolar disorder in children and adolescents. The Washington University Schedule for Affective Disorders and Schizophrenia for School-Age Children (K-SADS) has been used as a diagnostic tool and has a mania rating scale (K-SADS MRS) that provides good concurrent validity (Hunt et al., 2005; Pavuluri, Brimaher, & Naylor, 2005). Findling and colleagues (2005) reported that the Young Mania Rating Scale (YMRS) has been validated and is useful in distinguishing between bipolar disorder and other disorders, although Hunt and colleagues (2005) found it to be a helpful list of symptoms but not useful in distinguishing between diagnoses.

Preferred Therapist Characteristics To understand and treat bipolar disorder in children and adolescents, one needs a solid understanding of symptoms and treatment of adult bipolar disorder. Considering the potentially life-threatening nature of the illness, therapist competence in the treatment of bipolar disorder in this young population is imperative. Mental health providers must be willing to refer to a more experienced provider when necessary.

As mentioned earlier, a negative communication cycle between parent and child may have existed for years and contributes to the child's inability to be able to regulate emotions. Parents who are critical, negative, and overly involved tend to perpetuate a cycle in which the child responds in the same manner, becomes depressed, and ultimately acts out with inappropriate behaviors, reinforcing the parents' behavior of criticalness, negativity, and over involvement. Therapists who are able to identify this family dynamic and work with parent and child to improve their interactions, may reduce the negative communication cycle (Miklowitz & Ciccetti, 2010). In one study, parents of children with bipolar disorder said they often felt blamed, criticized, and responsible for their children's illnesses (Mackinaw-Koons & Fristad, 2004). In the same study, parents reported that symptoms of hypersexuality posed particular difficulties, for even in the absence of any allegations or basis for suspicion of abuse, therapists frequently assumed sexual abuse had occurred because the child was exhibiting sexually provocative behavior. Certainly, all suspected child abuse must be reported, but hypersexuality is a frequent symptom of bipolar disorder and care must be taken to distinguish bipolar symptoms from those of abuse (Mackinaw-Koons & Fristad, 2004).

Intervention Strategies Randomized controlled trials are lacking specific to treatment of bipolar disorder in children. Combination therapy seems to be the best approach. Family-focused therapy, family-focused CBT, and psychoeducation have all been shown to be helpful. Family education is also an important component of treatment of bipolar disorder in children and can enhance medication compliance and relapse prevention.

Family-Focused Therapy. Miklowitz and Goldstein (1997) developed a manual-based version of family-focused therapy (FFT) for adolescents with bipolar disorder. The goal of family-focused therapy is to reduce symptoms, provide the child with coping tools, decrease the level of expressed emotion from relatives, and improve family problem-solving skills. This therapy also helps the adolescent understand and accept the diagnosis of bipolar disorder, comply with medications, manage stress, reduce family tensions, and self-monitor symptoms to help prevent relapse (Pavuluri et al., 2004). A small open trial of FFT for adolescents demonstrated that when used in conjunction with medication, mania and depression was reduced, and parents noticed a reduction in behavior problems over a

two-year period (Miklowitz, Biuckians, & Richards, 2006). Similar results were found for school-aged children (Pavuluri et al., 2004).

Child- and Family-Focused Cognitive-Behavioral Therapy (CFF-CBT). Pavuluri and colleagues (2004) combine CBT and interpersonal psychotherapy to address the needs of the child and the family. CFF-CBT is presented as the RAINBOW program, representing the rainbow of moods the child experiences along with an easy-to-remember acronym of skills that are taught during therapy sessions (Routine; Affect regulation; I can do it; No negative thoughts; Be a good friend; Oh, how can we solve the problem?; and Ways to get support). Preliminary research shows that CFF-CBT decreased symptom severity and increased functioning in children. Parent satisfaction was also rated as high.

Psychoeducation. Multifamily psychoeducation groups have also been found to be helpful in the treatment of childhood bipolar disorder. Material about the disorder is taught and skills are practiced in weekly groups that include parents and children. Following the psychoeducation component, the parents and children break into subgroups to provide support and guidance. Children reported greater mood stability and their parents benefited as well (Miklowitz, 2008b).

Dialectical Behavior Therapy. Dialectical behavior therapy (DBT) has also been supported for the treatment of this disorder (Goldstein, Axelson, Birmaher, & Brent, 2007). Teaching children and their parents how to regulate emotions and avoid mood swings is an appropriate treatment.

Medications. Children of all ages are being prescribed lithium, anticonvulsants, antipsychotics, and electroconvulsive therapy for the treatment of this disorder, but only lithium has been approved by the FDA for the treatment of bipolar disorder in adolescents 12 years of age or older (Weller, Danielyan, & Weller, 2004). However, these medications are prescribed based on their use in adults with bipolar disorder even though little evidence exists to support their use in younger populations. Until additional research is available, caution is advised in the use of psychotropic drugs as they can have serious side effects. Continuing concerns about the side effects of SSRIs in people under the age of 21 also need to be addressed.

Miklowitz and Cicchetti (2010) warn that bipolar disorder is more than just emotional reactivity to environmental cues. He reminds us that children with emotion dysregulation or those with borderline personality disorder have chronic emotional lability, whereas children with bipolar disorder cannot help themselves when they are experiencing mania or a mixed state. These children will also have periods of time without affective dysregulation, unlike others for whom it is a permanent state.

Prognosis As illustrated here, bipolar disorder is a complicated disorder and its diagnosis and treatment in children adds even more complexity. Adolescent onset bipolar disorder seems to predict a more serious course, with increased potential for multiple hospitalizations, co-occurring substance use disorders, suicidal ideation, and completed suicides (Lewinsohn, Seeley, & Klein, 2003). The risk for more severe outcomes increases when psychosis, mixed episodes, and low SES are involved (Birmaher et al., 2006).

Diagnosis and treatment of bipolar disorder in the preschool and elementary school years remains controversial. Longitudinal studies are needed to determine if early detection and treatment, perhaps as early as the preschool years, does prevent later development of more serious symptoms and high-risk behaviors such as substance abuse and suicidal ideation, or, if such early detection actually causes harm from treatment with medications. New research and longitudinal studies specific to children are needed to address this issue.

Childhood-Onset Schizophrenia

The diagnosis of schizophrenia in childhood is rare. When it does occur, it is often linked to childhood trauma or sexual abuse.

Description of the Disorder Childhood-onset schizophrenia occurs in fewer than one child in ten thousand, with boys being twice as likely as girls to develop the disorder (Asarnow & Kernan, 2008). The *DSM-IV-TR* criteria for children are the same as those used for adults, with primary symptoms including hallucinations, delusions, loose associations, and illogical thinking (American Psychiatric Association, 2000). Prodromal symptoms may begin about two to six years before the onset of psychosis (Evans et al., 2005). Onset before the age of 6 is extremely rare; nevertheless, when onset of schizophrenia does occur in childhood, the symptoms are likely to persist through adolescence and into adulthood (Mash & Wolfe, 2010). Histories of adults diagnosed with schizophrenia often reveal the presence of unusual personality styles as well as language or motor problems in childhood (Evans et al., 2005).

Considerable evidence links childhood trauma, particularly sexual abuse, with the development of psychotic symptoms as an adult. In one study, 70% of adults with auditory hallucinations reported a childhood history of sexual or physical abuse (Read, van Ohs, Morrison, & Ross, 2005). The positive symptoms of schizophrenia (hallucinations, delusions, and thought disorder) were more likely to occur if childhood trauma (emotional, physical, psychological, or sexual abuse) occurred before the age of 16 (Spauwen, Krabbendam, Lieb, Wittchen, & van Ohs, 2006).

The frequency of schizophrenia increases dramatically with the beginning of adolescence, with onset of the disorder occurring about five years later for females than males (Kopelowicz, Liberman, & Zarate, 2007). Use of marijuana, alcohol, and stimulants (cocaine and amphetamines) have been found to increase the incidence of psychosis. These drugs are well documented to increase psychotic symptoms in vulnerable individuals (Kopelowicz et al., 2007).

More than 68% of people with childhood-onset schizophrenia have a comorbid disorder. The most common are developmental disorders, ODD, CD, anxiety, PTSD, and depression.

Typical Client Characteristics Symptoms are insidious in young children, rather than chronic, and may include illogical conversation or thought patterns, as well as magical thinking. Auditory hallucinations occur in more than 80% of children with schizophrenia; delusions are found in as many as 63%, although these delusions may not be well formed (Asarnow & Kernan, 2008). The difficulty in applying this diagnosis to children is that loose associations and illogical thinking are not unusual before the age of 7. With older children, however, these symptoms should be taken quite seriously. In general, school performance, peer relationships, language, and motor development lag behind their peers. Negative symptoms (e.g., cognitive slippage, decrease in executive functioning, flat affect) occur before positive symptoms (delusions and hallucinations). Prodromal symptoms most likely to appear in adolescence include social withdrawal, a decline in academic functioning, odd behavior, and magical beliefs (Kopelowicz et al., 2008). Irritability; lack of concern for appearance; sleep problems; mood

changes; inappropriate emotion; and decreased motivation, energy, and concentration are also common (Evans et al., 2005).

Research continues on brain development and schizophrenia in children, as does the search for a genetic component to psychosis. Adolescence is a time of tremendous brain development, and cannabis use increases the risk of developing psychotic symptoms. Fully 10% of psychosis can be traced back to cannabis use (Fergusson et al., 2006). Further, a study by Caton and colleagues (2007) found that 25% of people who were diagnosed with a drug-induced psychosis later developed a non-drug-related psychosis.

Preferred Therapist Characteristics Training and experience are similar to those required for working with adults with psychotic disorders. Therapists should also be well versed in the treatment of the comorbid childhood disorders mentioned earlier. In particular, the symptoms of PTSD and childhood psychosis can look very similar. Schizophrenia tends to be familial, and therapists need to be alert to the possibility that other family members are likely to have elevated rates of thought disorders or more subtle neurocognitive impairments. Disorders on the schizophrenia spectrum, such as schizoaffective disorder or schizoid, paranoid, or avoidant personality disorder may also be present (Asarnow & Kernan, 2008). A difficult aspect of the work with a family that has a child with schizophrenia is helping the family members with the uncertain prognosis.

Intervention Strategies One of the most effective interventions for early episode psychosis is family intervention combined with medication (Pitschel-Walz, Leucht, Bauml, Kissling, & Engel, 2001). Family climate is one of the most powerful predictors of relapse in schizophrenia (Kopelowicz et al., 2007). Structured education and family interventions that reduce anxiety and stress, teach family members to be less critical and negative, and reduce excessive emotional involvement of family members are important to the creation of a low-stress environment in which the child can effectively reside. As is the case for adults, childhood-onset schizophrenia requires multiple treatment modalities. In addition to family therapy, treatment for children and adolescents will most certainly include cognitive-behavioral training, cognitive restructuring, social skills training, interpersonal psychotherapy, compliance therapy, and pharmacological management.

Therapists may become involved in the development of educational plans, which should incorporate social and emotional goals. Social skills training involving the teaching of approach behaviors, interpersonal interaction, playing with peers, and effective communication should be included. Stress management interventions may also be useful to young people diagnosed with schizophrenia, given that high levels of stress have been found to increase dysfunctional thought patterns and the likelihood of psychotic episodes. Modification of the home environment, promotion of a positive attitude on the part of the parents, and training of the parents in effective coping strategies are all likely to be helpful. Additional useful psychoeducational family interventions could include teaching communication and problem-solving skills and providing specific factual information about the disorder and its treatment.

As in adults, psychotic symptoms in children usually respond to antipsychotic medication, although the side effects of these medications are not as well tolerated. Atypical antipsychotics are used most frequently to reduce the positive symptoms (e.g., delusions and hallucinations). Executive functioning and cognitive symptoms take longer to resolve.

Prognosis Early diagnosis and appropriate treatment can improve long-term outcomes in children with schizophrenia (French, Smith, Shiers, Reed, & Rayne, 2010). Bellack and Mueser (1993) found that children who received family interventions in addition to medication had a relapse rate of only 17%, in comparison with a relapse rate of 83% among a control group in which children received medication only. Advances are being made in terms of research on genetic and environmental factors that contribute to schizophrenia. Recent research implicates dopamine levels in the brain as a key factor in the onset of psychotic symptoms. Childhood trauma and substance misuse in adolescence are also related. Future research will focus on preventive measures that reduce the symptoms or delay or defer the onset of this debilitating disorder.

Anxiety Disorders

The prevalence rates in community samples of anxiety disorders among children ranges from 2.4% to 17%, making them the third most common psychiatric disorders of childhood and adolescence, behind ADHD and ODD (Podell, Martin, & Kendall, 2008). More than half of these children will go on to experience a major depressive episode as part of their anxiety syndrome. The principal risk factor for the onset of a childhood anxiety disorder is having a parent with an anxiety or mood disorder (Morris & March, 2004). Among adolescents, anxiety disorders pose a major threat to academic competency, with half of adolescents with anxiety disorders leaving school prematurely (Woo & Keatinge, 2008).

Children experience the same anxiety disorders commonly found in adults, although the symptoms are more developmentally and age appropriate. For example, social phobia generally has an onset in elementary school-age children and may present as performance anxiety, hesitancy to speak to adults, read aloud in class, or write on the chalkboard. Obsessive-compulsive disorder, panic disorder, and other anxiety disorders generally begin later in adolescence or early adulthood, although affected individuals often report symptoms first began in childhood (Steketee & Pigott, 2006). Assessment of childhood anxiety disorders can begin with such tools as the Child Behavior Checklist (CBCL; Achenbach & Rescorla, 2001), the Multidimensional Anxiety Scale for Children, the Children's Yale-Brown Obsessive-Compulsive Scale, or the Revised Children's Manifest Anxiety Scale (Barrett, Duffy, Dadds, & Rapee, 2001; Morris & March, 2004; Reynolds & Richmond, 1985; Silverman & Rabian, 1999).

Substantial empirical support exists for exposure and response prevention therapy in the treatment of anxiety disorders in children. Additional treatment strategies include cognitive restructuring to correct distortions in thinking, behavior therapy, psychoeducation, social skills training, and medication. Typically, homework and office-based modeling techniques are used. Family interventions also play a critical role in the treatment of children.

Most anxiety disorders with childhood onset will be treated with the same interventions used to help adults: cognitive-behavioral therapy, systematic desensitization, exposure therapy, social skills training, and, in some cases, EMDR. Childhood-onset anxiety disorders are resistant to traditional insight-oriented therapy.

Increasing evidence indicates that the effects of childhood trauma can result in lifelong problems. Symptoms of trauma frequently go undiagnosed and untreated and may ultimately result in disruptive behaviors, violence or suicidal ideation, sleeplessness, substance abuse, and other externalizing behaviors (Hoch, 2009). Following is a closer look at trauma and childhood-onset PTSD. Treatment of other anxiety disorders of childhood is the same as treatment recommendations for adults. Readers will find additional information on symptoms, assessment, and treatment in Chapter 5.

Posttraumatic Stress Disorder

Posttraumatic stress disorder (PTSD) is common in children exposed to a variety of childhood traumas including physical and emotional abuse. Trauma and stress negatively alter the neural networks in the brain that mediate the stress response and can have lasting impact throughout childhood and into adulthood (Perry, 2008). The Adverse Childhood Experiences Study, an epidemiological study of 17,000 adults, has been reporting myriad emotional, physical, behavioral, and social problems following trauma and abuse in childhood (Anda et al., 2006). The effects of trauma are strongly correlated to degree of exposure, thus the more abuse and trauma a child experiences, the higher the risk for additional affective symptoms and behavioral problems, including dissociation, memory problems, poor impulse control, and emotion dysregulation (Perry, 2008).

The criteria for PTSD in children are the same as for adults. Children's distress may be manifested in slightly different ways, however, because of their different level of cognitive and emotional functioning. Nightmares are common among children with PTSD, although they may not be able to remember the content of the dreams. Avoidance of any event or place associated with the trauma, difficulty falling or staying asleep, irritability, exaggerated startle responses, and withdrawal behaviors are also typical of children with PTSD (Evans et al., 2005).

In childhood, the most damaging types of trauma include physical and sexual abuse, emotional abuse and neglect, and exposure to domestic violence (Hoch, 2009). Nearly one million substantiated cases of child maltreatment in the United States were reported in 2004 (U.S. Department of Health and Human Services, 2006). Children raised in such chaotic environments are frequently subjected to abuse or neglect on more than one occasion, which can result in disruptions to appropriate developmental needs. Problems with attachment, emotion and behavioral regulation, dissociation, and the development of biological, cognitive, and psychosocial systems can ensue. Cook and colleagues (2003) found that early childhood trauma creates a biological vulnerability and increases the risk of developing disorders such as autism, learning disabilities, and externalizing behaviors. During middle childhood and adolescence, these children are susceptible to disorders of self-regulation including eating disorders, substance use disorders, and conduct disorders, as well as major depression. Trauma has also been linked to deficits in executive functioning, and self-injury, suicidal behavior, substance use disorders, and criminal activity (Anda et al., 2006; Beers & DeBellis, 2002). Exposure to community violence, car accidents, traumatic grief and loss, and life-threatening medical illness have also been found to produce symptoms of PTSD in children.

Longitudinal studies of PTSD in childhood suggest it can become a chronic psychological disorder for some children, persisting well into adulthood and sometimes lasting a lifetime. The earlier in life the trauma occurs, the greater the impact (Adler-Tapia & Settle, 2009a; Perry, 2008). Effective treatment of PTSD in children is important to halt the potential development of dysfunction, pathology, adult antisocial behavior, and an intergenerational cycle of abuse and revictimization.

Typical Client Characteristics Children who are exposed to family violence may become fearful, passive, and withdrawn, or they may identify with the attacker and exhibit externalizing behaviors (Tyndall-Linn, 2010). Age, proximity to the attack, duration and frequency of domestic disputes, and previous coping mechanisms will all impact how the child responds. Some children seem more vulnerable than others to extremely stressful events. Boys seem to be more protected from the effects of trauma. In one study, the 6-month prevalence rate of PTSD was 3.7% of boys and 6.3% of girls ages 12 to 17 (Kilpatrick et al., 2003).

Evans et al. (2005) reported on a survey of adolescents which found that 23% had been both a victim of violence and had witnessed a violent crime. Children who experienced such traumas commonly exhibited detachment, sadness, restricted affect, and dissociative episodes. Children exposed to repeated or chronic traumas, such as abuse, exhibited even more troubled behaviors.

Adolescents exposed to severe trauma frequently experience difficulties with academic performance; increased sexual activity; substance misuse; and an increase in aggressive, reckless, or avoidant behavior. Depression and substance-related disorders were found to co-occur in nearly 75% of the adolescents diagnosed with PTSD (Kilpatrick et al., 2003).

Preferred Therapist Characteristics Therapists who work with traumatized children should have appropriate skills to develop a strong therapeutic alliance with these children and their caregivers. Clinicians may be called on to provide parenting skills training to caregivers, psychoeducation and safety skills training to children and adolescents, and develop positive coping strategies to help both groups develop appropriate affect expression and regulation, relaxation, and communication skills.

Because of the difficult nature of working with childhood trauma, the clinician must also make active self-care a priority. Maintaining a balanced lifestyle, setting realistic boundaries and expectations, focusing on positive results, taking care of one's health, establishing connections to family and friends, and keeping work in perspective can help clinicians avoid burnout and vicarious traumatization (Norcross & Drewes, 2009). Supervision while working with traumatized children and their families is essential.

Assessments   When working with children who have experienced trauma, abuse, violence and potentially life-threatening conditions, assessments should be made for symptoms of PTSD such as depression, shame, and behavior problems. A self-report measure, the Trauma Symptom Checklist for Children (TSCC), helps identify trauma-related symptoms (Briere, 2005), and the Beck Depression Inventory-II (BDI-II, Beck, Steer, & Brown, 1996) measures depressive symptoms. Achenbach's Child Behavior Checklist (CBCL; Achenbach & Rescorla, 2001) or the BASC (Behavior Assessment Scale) will help to evaluate behavior problems. The Child's Reaction to Traumatic Events Scale-Revised (CRTES-R) is a 23-item self-report measure designed to assess the effect of stressful life events on the child (Jones, Fletcher & Ribb, 2002).

Assessment of traumatic symptoms in children may result in suspicions of physical or sexual abuse. Clinicians are required to report such findings to Child Protective Services or to the appropriate agency under the mandated reporting laws that exist in each state.

Intervention Strategies   Many different types of treatments are available for children who have been the victims of trauma. Whether the treatment is cognitive-behavioral, emotion-focused, or includes a component of play therapy, any effective therapy of childhood PTSD will include the following essential components:

- Risk screening and triage
- Assessment, case conceptualization, and treatment planning

- Psychoeducation
- Confronting stress reactions
- Narration of the trauma
- Emotion regulation
- Adaptive coping
- Parental skills training
- Addressing grief and loss
- Developing safety skills and relapse prevention (National Child Traumatic Stress Network; www.nctsn.org)

Five randomized controlled trials have demonstrated the effectiveness of trauma-focused cognitive-behavioral therapy (TF-CBT) with sexually abused children (Cohen, Mannarino, & Deblinger, 2006; Rubin, 2009). TF-CBT is a family-focused, components-based treatment approach for children who have been traumatized by sexual abuse or grief and loss (Hoch, 2009). TF-CBT is an adaptable and flexible approach which values the therapeutic alliance and respects cultural values. Training, including web-based training programs, assist the therapist to work with these traumatized children (www.musc.edu/tfcbt). In one 5-year study, TF-CBT was found to be more effective than person-focused therapy in the treatment of children who had experienced sexual abuse (Cohen, Deblinger, Mannarino, & Steer, 2004). Much evidence supports the use of EMDR in the treatment of adults with PTSD, and the treatment has been adapted and expanded for use with children as well. Research is limited, but three outcomes studies are available on the use of EMDR for trauma resulting from a specific incident. EMDR alleviated PTSD symptoms of children exposed to a hurricane (Chemtob, Nkashima, & Carlson, 2002; Rubin, 2009); EMDR was found to be effective in the treatment of Iranian girls who had been sexually abused (Jaberghaderi, Greenwald, Rubin, Dolatabadim, & Zand, 2004); and among children ages 8 to 12, who had reported one or more traumas (Jeffres, 2004). EMDR has also been shown to help children foster resiliency (Zaghrout-Hodali, Alissa, & Dodgson, 2008). When using EMDR with children, therapists need to adapt the intervention to match the developmental level and language abilities of the child (Adler-Tapia & Settle, 2009a, b).

A meta-analytic review of 50 years of outcome studies on play therapy determined that play therapy interventions improve self-concepts of children, decrease internalizing behaviors (including anxiety), lessen externalizing behaviors, and increase social adjustment (Ray, 2006). Research specific to play therapy interventions with children who have experienced trauma is sparse, but intensive child-centered play therapy has been shown to be helpful in reducing traumatic symptoms following incidents of domestic violence, helping children and their families cope with the effects of a chronic illness, and reducing physiological symptoms of PTSD such as anxiety, hypersensitivity, and worry in school-aged Chinese children in the wake of a devastating earthquake (Shen, 2010; Tyndall-Linn, 2010). These studies support previous findings that small group, child-centered play therapy can significantly reduce symptoms of PTSD in children. Cognitive-behavioral play therapy may also be an effective tool, but more research is needed.

Prognosis Increasing knowledge about the effects of childhood trauma leads us to the conclusion that early intervention and treatment is imperative in the aftermath of a traumatic event, sexual or physical abuse, violence, or traumatic grief and loss. An increasing number of assessment tools and treatment interventions are available specifically for this population. Additional research is needed to identify the most effective interventions for children and adolescents. Due to the effect of early childhood trauma across the lifespan, it is hoped that future research will provide additional criteria for the diagnosis of PTSD in very young children.

TREATMENT RECOMMENDATIONS: CLIENT MAP

This chapter has focused on disorders that usually begin before the age of 18, as well as disorders that typically begin later but sometimes manifest earlier. Beyond their early age of onset, these disorders vary widely, although most are reflected by behavioral difficulties. The following general treatment recommendations, organized according to the format of the Client Map, are provided for the disorders discussed in this chapter.

CLIENT MAP

Diagnosis
Disorders usually first diagnosed during infancy, childhood, or adolescence

Objectives of Treatment
Eliminate dysfunctional behavior
Improve academic functioning
Improve socialization and peer-group involvement
Promote family understanding of the disorder
Improve parenting and family functioning

Assessments
Assessment of intelligence, attention, and learning abilities
Assessment of behaviors, fears, mood, and other relevant symptoms

Clinician Characteristics

Skilled at providing support and building rapport while setting limits and overcoming resistance

Knowledgeable about developmental patterns and issues in children

Able to collaborate with family members, teachers, school counselors, and physicians

Location of Treatment

Usually outpatient

Day treatment centers increasingly available for troubled children

Interventions to Be Used

Behavior therapy, especially reality therapy, emphasizing strategies for behavior change

Cognitive therapy

Establishment of a baseline

Setting of realistic goals

Modification and tracking of behavior

Use of reinforcements and logical consequences

Education on the disorder for the child and the family

Training in communication and other skills

Play therapy (for young children)

Emphasis of Treatment

Structured but supportive

Primarily oriented toward the present

Numbers

Individual and family therapy

Peer-group counseling and play therapy possibly helpful

Timing

Usually medium-term therapy, with a rapid pace

Medications Needed

Usually recommended for ADHD, Tourette's disorder, OCD, psychotic disorders, and severe forms of other disorders

Adjunct Services

Parent education

Rewarding activities for children

Prognosis

Varies according to the disorder

CLIENT MAP OF SHANNON

This chapter began with a description of Shannon, a 9-year-old girl who, for several years, had been displaying a broad range of behavioral and academic problems. As is common among children with attention-deficit and disruptive behavior disorders, the parents had manifested similar symptoms as youngsters. Consequently, they had difficulty appreciating the severity of Shannon's symptoms and helping her modify her behavior. The following Client Map outlines the treatment recommended for Shannon.

Diagnosis

Axis I: 312.8 Conduct disorder, childhood-onset type, moderate
314.01 Attention-deficit/hyperactivity disorder, predominantly hyperactive–impulsive type, moderate
Axis II: V71.09 No diagnosis on Axis II
Axis III: None reported
Axis IV: Arrest, academic problems, lack of adequate supervision
Axis V: Global assessment of functioning (GAF Scale): current GAF = 50

Objectives of Treatment

Eliminate conduct-disordered behavior
Improve attention, academic skills, and grades

Assessments

Assessment of intelligence and learning abilities
Conners' rating scales

Clinician Characteristics

Skilled at building rapport, overcoming resistance, setting limits, using family interventions

Location of Treatment

Community mental health center

Interventions to Be Used

Reality therapy, emphasizing strategies for behavior change (to help client recognize the self-destructive nature of her behavior)
Contract for behavioral change
Help in recognizing triggers for impulsive behavior and substituting alternative behaviors
Training in healthy ways to meet her needs
Setting of realistic goals in family and school meetings (for help in improving attention and academic achievement)
Reinforcement for positive behaviors

Emphasis of Treatment

Structured but supportive, primarily present-oriented

Numbers

Individual therapy with family involvement
Counseling group at school (to help in improving social skills and reinforcing positive changes)
Consultation with school counselor, teachers, and representatives of the legal system (to provide the experience of consequences for theft but also an avenue for demonstrating sincere efforts to change)

Timing

Medium- or long-term treatment, weekly sessions, rapid pace

Medications Needed

Referral to a child psychiatrist for determination of whether medication is indicated for reducing symptoms of ADHD

Adjunct Services

Parent education
Involvement in some interesting, action-oriented pursuit likely to provide a success experience
Possible involvement in a Big Sister program

Prognosis

Good, with parental cooperation; otherwise, fair

RECOMMENDED READING

Journals, including *Adolescence, Child Abuse and Neglect, Child Development, Developmental Psychology, Elementary School Guidance and Counseling, Journal of Abnormal Child Psychology, Journal of the American Academy of Child and Adolescent Psychiatry*, and *Journal of Clinical Child Psychiatry*.

American Academy of Child and Adolescent Psychiatry. (2007). AACAP official action: Practice parameter for the assessment and treatment of children and adolescents with attention deficit/hyperactivity disorder. *Journal of the American Academy of Child & Adolescent Psychiatry, 46*, 894–921.

Baggerly, J. N., Ray, D. C., & Bratton, S. C. (Eds.). (2010). *Child-centered play therapy research: The evidence base for effective practice*. Hoboken, NJ: Wiley.

Barkley, R. A. (2006). *Attention-deficit hyperactivity disorder: A handbook for diagnosis and treatment* (3rd ed.). New York, NY: Guilford Press.

Barkley, R. A., & Murphy, K. R. (2006). *Attention deficit hyperactivity disorder: A clinical workbook* (3rd ed.). New York, NY: Guilford Press.

Mash, E. J., & Barkley, R. A. (Eds.). (2010). *Assessment of childhood disorders* (4th ed.). New York, NY: Guilford Press.

Miklowitz, D. J., & Cicchetti, D. (Eds.). (2010). *Understanding bipolar disorder: A developmental psychopathology perspective*. New York, NY: Guilford Press.

Rubin, A., & Springer, D. W. (Eds.). (2009). *Treatment of traumatized adults and children: Clinician's guide to evidence-based practice*. Hoboken, NJ: John Wiley & Sons.

Beth H., a 47-year-old divorced Jewish woman, sought counseling 2 weeks after a biopsy revealed that she had breast cancer. She reported that she had been consumed by fear and grief since her diagnosis and had been unable to make decisions about her treatment. The physicians had told her that she could choose either a mastectomy or a combination of removal of the tumor and the surrounding tissue along with 30 radiation treatments. Beth was terrified that the radiation itself would cause secondary cancers, and she viewed the mastectomy as the safer option. However, that choice was also frightening and confusing to her because she was apprehensive about the extensive surgery and the resulting physical changes. Beth had explored the possibility of reconstructive surgery concurrent with her mastectomy. Once again, however, she had been confronted with an array of choices, all of them with risks and drawbacks. Beth's physicians cautioned her that putting the surgery off too long might worsen her prognosis, but her anxiety and her sorrow were preventing her from making a decision. Despite these worries, Beth continued to fulfill all her personal and professional responsibilities satisfactorily.

Beth reported that her life had been difficult over the past year but that she had been managing to keep it all under control. She and her husband had divorced a year before, and Beth had just begun to socialize as a single person. She had a successful career as a benefits manager for a county government. She also had a 12-year-old daughter, Amanda, whom she described as the greatest joy in her life. She had several close women friends and maintained positive relationships with her father and her younger sister. She reported great enjoyment of outdoor activities, especially hiking, camping, and bird-watching.

Beth's diagnosis of cancer raised several powerful fears that were linked to her symptoms. Her mother had died of breast cancer at the age of 50, and Beth feared that she too would die and not see her daughter grow up. She was also apprehensive that even if she did survive, the diagnosis and the subsequent surgery would prevent her from developing close intimate relationships and marrying again. She was terrified that her disease was hereditary and that her daughter would inherit this legacy. Finally, she was fearful that she would need chemotherapy after the surgery. Beth reported that she had successfully coped with many problems over the course of her life but had never before felt so hopeless and worried.

Beth is an emotionally healthy woman who has functioned well throughout her life. She has good relationships with family and friends, rewarding interests, and a usually optimistic view of her life and of herself. The diagnosis of breast cancer, however, especially coming not long after her divorce, raised many fears about her future and left her feeling anxious and discouraged. Beth was experiencing an adjustment disorder with mixed anxiety and depressed mood.

This chapter focuses on adjustment disorder and other conditions that may be a focus of clinical attention (formerly known as the V-code conditions). These typically are the mildest categories of symptoms described in the fourth edition text revision of the *Diagnostic and Statistical Manual of Mental Disorders*, or *DSM-IV-TR* (American Psychiatric Association, 2000).

OVERVIEW OF SITUATIONALLY PRECIPITATED DISORDERS AND CONDITIONS

Common life events such as the loss of a job, diagnosis of a serious medical condition, divorce, or the death of a loved one can trigger stressful emotions that may disrupt the normal course of life. Adjustment disorders, as well as other conditions that may be the focus of clinical attention (referred to in this chapter as conditions), usually have an identifiable precipitant or cause and are often relatively mild and transient, especially if the person has no other mental disorders.

Description of the Disorders and Conditions

Helping people address the precipitant and its impact on their lifestyle and adjustment are usually the primary focus of treatment; any emotion dysregulation and dysfunctional behavior resulting from the precipitant receive secondary attention. In treating these disorders and conditions, clinicians commonly help clients to do one of three things: eliminate the precipitant that is causing the stress,

adapt to and manage the changes it has produced, or gain a realistic view of the precipitant and reframe their thoughts about it. Any dysfunctional symptoms accompanying the stressful life change will correspondingly be alleviated, if not eliminated.

Sometimes clinicians have difficulty determining whether a person is experiencing a condition or an adjustment disorder. Adjustment disorders by definition result in noticeable impairment or dysfunction and/or marked distress beyond what would be expected in reaction to the stressor (American Psychiatric Association, 2000). Conditions are normal or expectable reactions to life events and are therefore not viewed as mental disorders, although the conditions are associated with some upset or dysfunction that may be alleviated by psychotherapy and may be associated with comorbid mental disorders. Beth, for example, was immobilized by symptoms of apprehension and depression, which reflected an adjustment disorder. Had she been saddened and worried by the diagnosis of cancer but nevertheless in control and able to make appropriate medical decisions, she would have been described as experiencing a condition, probably a phase-of-life problem.

Adjustment disorders and conditions tend to be relatively brief in duration. If there is a long-standing cause or precipitant, however (such as abuse, a long-standing and worsening medical illness, or treatment via neuroleptic medications), the adjustment disorder or condition may be enduring.

Following is a helpful five-level taxonomic structure (Strain, Klipstein, & Newcorn, 2011) clarifying the relative levels of severity of these two categories:

1. Normal state
2. Problem-level (for example, the conditions)
3. Adjustment disorder

4. Minor disorder or not otherwise specified diagnosis
5. Major disorder

In other words, the conditions represent more dysfunction than what is considered normal, but not enough for a diagnosis of a mental disorder, whereas an adjustment disorder is viewed as the mildest type of mental disorder listed in the *DSM-IV-TR*.

Typical Client Characteristics

Nearly everyone has experienced either an adjustment disorder or a condition or both. They occur at all levels of mental health, intelligence, affluence, and psychological sophistication. Their symptoms may be triggered by a broad range of transitions and changes, such as mistreatment and abuse, diagnosis of a life-threatening illness, or divorce, and may reflect and be related to common problems of living, such as occupational dissatisfaction, relationship conflict, or caregiving of an ill or elderly parent. Although few people go through life without experiencing a disturbing loss or life change, some people—especially those who have effective coping mechanisms and ways of handling stress, those who have support systems and confidants, those who have a record of successfully coping with previous stressors, and those whose overall functioning is good—are less likely to be troubled by these problems. People are also typically more successful at handling stressful life circumstances if those events are not severely disruptive and if there are not multiple stressors. The impact of stressors seems to be additive, to the point in which stressor pile up occurs. In other words, a major stressor (such as diagnosis of a life-threatening illness) accompanied by several minor stressors (such as relocation and a new job) are probably going to have a much greater impact than an isolated major stressor.

Preferred Therapist Characteristics

People with adjustment disorders or conditions typically work best with therapists who are supportive, affirming, collaborative, and empathic and who provide the stimulus, direction, and decision-making and other skills needed for the clients to mobilize themselves and use their resources more effectively. Treatment is typically short term and focused on helping people cope more effectively with their stressful changes or circumstances. Therapists should be comfortable with brief, structured interventions that may involve psychoeducation and referral to outside sources of help and information but that are unlikely to involve extended exploration. Therapists should also be comfortable dealing with persons in crisis who may be feeling overwhelmed, discouraged, and even suicidal. Because adjustment disorders and other conditions may stand alone or be accompanied by a broad range of other disorders, therapists need to be skilled diagnosticians so that they can determine quickly whether coexisting mental disorders are present that may interfere with the client's efforts to cope.

Intervention Strategies

Treatment for adjustment disorders and conditions varies and depends on the nature of the associated crisis or life circumstance and on the presence of any coexisting disorders. In general, however, treatment will be designed to help people achieve a clear understanding of what is going on in their lives, of their reactions to those situations, and of their options. People's current resources and coping mechanisms provide the foundation for treatment, and efforts will be made to increase clients' awareness of their existing strengths, to build on those strengths, and to help them develop new coping skills if those are needed. For example, people with a condition called *partner relational problem* might be taught how to improve their communication skills, clarify their expectations of their partners, seek a mutually agreed-on and rewarding relationship, and enhance their other relationships. People who have experienced the death of a loved one will usually need help in expressing and managing their grief; in dealing with the impact the loss has on their lives; and in establishing new and realistic goals, directions, friends, and activities.

Therapists will typically seek to build rapport quickly so that they can function as collaborators, helping people to mobilize their resources, gather information, make informed decisions about their future, and cope effectively with any anxiety or depressed mood that may result. Normalizing people's troubled reactions, if that is warranted, can be helpful. A support group composed of others who are dealing with similar life circumstances can reduce feelings of aloneness and can help people accept and understand their responses to what triggered the stress, obtain information about it, learn more effective ways of coping, and foster resilience in the face of future stressors. Support groups for people coping with cancer, for people who have experienced the death of a loved one, for people going through marital separation or divorce, and many others are widely available and can greatly enhance the process of therapy.

Prognosis

The prognosis is excellent for returning people with adjustment disorders and conditions to their previous levels of functioning. In fact, some people seem to function even better afterward because they have gained self-confidence from handling their situation effectively and because they developed or improved their coping skills

over the course of therapy. Therefore, treatment of adjustment disorders and conditions is often a growth-promoting experience for clients. However, if a stressor is unremitting, if the person is unsuccessful in coping with the stressor, or if the person has preexisting emotional difficulties, the symptoms may not abate or may even evolve into a more significant mental disorder.

ADJUSTMENT DISORDERS

According to the *DSM-IV-TR*, "The essential feature of an adjustment disorder is a psychological response to an identifiable stressor or stressors that results in the development of clinically significant emotional or behavioral symptoms. The symptoms must develop within three months after the onset of the stressor(s)" (American Psychiatric Association, 2000, p. 679). Precipitating stressors may be of any severity and may be chronic.

Description of the Disorders

Adjustment disorders are one of the few *DSM* diagnoses that are by definition time limited. This diagnosis can be maintained for a maximum of six months after the termination of the precipitating stressor. If symptoms persist beyond this period, the diagnosis must be changed. However, because many precipitants (such as a disabling medical condition or a dangerous environment) are chronic and enduring, this diagnosis may be maintained for many months or even years. An adjustment disorder that remits within six months is described as acute; one that lasts longer is classified as chronic.

The category of adjustment disorders is sometimes thought of as a residual category, one that is not used if the symptoms also meet the criteria for another mental disorder. The diagnosis of adjustment disorder typically stands alone on Axis I of a multiaxial assessment, but it can be used along with the diagnosis of another mental disorder if the development of the adjustment disorder is separate from the development of the other mental disorder. For example, a person with a preexisting somatization disorder might develop symptoms of an adjustment disorder after a marital separation. In that case, both diagnoses would be listed.

A wide variety of stressors can precipitate an adjustment disorder. Stressors may be single events (such as the end of a relationship or the loss of a job) or multiple events (such as diagnosis of an illness and concurrent partner relational conflict). The stressors may be circumscribed events, recurrent events (such as relapses of an illness), or continuous circumstances (such as financial problems or death of a spouse). The most common stressors for adults are partner relational difficulties, divorce or separation, financial problems, and relocation; for adolescents the most common stressors are school-related problems, relationship problems, and parental divorce or conflict. Because the impact of stressors tends to be additive, assessment should look beyond the presenting concern to determine what other circumstances may be affecting a person.

The reaction to the stressor, rather than the presence of the stressor itself, is what determines whether a person has an adjustment disorder. A significant stressor (such as the loss of one's home in a flood) may have little impact on one person, whereas a relatively minor stressor (such as the end of a brief dating relationship in adolescence) may evoke a very strong reaction in another person. An adjustment disorder seems particularly likely to develop when a stressor touches on an area of vulnerability for the client and leads to an adverse reaction.

Adjustment disorders differ from conditions in being characterized by impaired functioning or reactions exceeding those that would normally be expected—in other words, by a strong negative psychological response to a stressor. A condition, by contrast, refers to a context, a problem, or a situation rather than to excessive reactions and symptoms.

The *DSM-IV-TR* specifies six types of adjustment disorders. When this diagnosis is made, the clinician should specify whether the type is adjustment disorder with depressed mood, with anxiety, with mixed anxiety and depressed mood, with disturbance of conduct, with mixed disturbance of emotions and conduct, or unspecified. Examples of the unspecified type include adjustment problems characterized by work inhibition or mild physical symptoms without an apparent medical cause. Depression and anxiety are the most common accompaniments of adjustment disorders in adults, whereas disturbances of conduct are particularly common among adolescents with adjustment disorders (Benton & Lynch, 2006). Such behaviors as vandalism, fighting, truancy, reckless driving, and other self-destructive acts are typical of youth with adjustment disorders, and this kind of disorder may be confused with conduct disorder if a careful history is not taken.

No randomized controlled trials or other research has been conducted on adjustment disorders. Short-term therapy seems appropriate, although longer lengths of treatment may be considered if stressors are chronic or repetitive.

Adjustment disorder is the most frequently occurring diagnosis in an outpatient setting. Estimates range from 2% to 8% of the general population (American Psychiatric Association, 2000) to as high as 18% in outpatient treatment (Pelkonen, Marttunen, Henriksson, & Lonnqvist, 2005). Adjustment disorder with depressed mood is the most common subtype (11.6%), followed by adjustment disorder with anxious mood. Because many people with an adjustment disorder do not seek treatment and experience spontaneous remission of symptoms, its incidence is difficult to assess and may be considerably higher than these estimates. The prevalence and severity of this type of disorder are typically greater in adolescents, with as many as one third experiencing an adjustment disorder. Disappointment in relationships was found to be the most frequent stressor cited in adolescent adjustment disorder (Benton & Lynch, 2006). Adjustment disorders occur equally between males and females, and across all cultures (American Psychiatric Association, 2000; Benton & Lynch, 2006). Cultural differences in the expected reaction to specific stressors, (grief or job loss for example), and in expression of emotion must be carefully attended to by the clinician (Casey, 2009).

Increased Suicidal Risk

Despite the fact that adjustment disorder is often considered a residual disorder, the rate of suicide among people with adjustment disorder is similar to that for depression, schizophrenia, and other more chronic disorders, and needs to be addressed (Pelkonen et al., 2005).

Adolescents tend to have fewer coping skills, less experience dealing with life's disappointments, and more impulsive behavior. Those who have not learned to regulate their emotions or who do not have supportive families or other outlets for their stress, often turn to alcohol or drugs, acting out behaviors, or self-harm. In this population, suicidal ideation and self-harming behaviors were found to be as high as 25% (Pelkonen et al., 2005). Adolescent males with this diagnosis seem to have the highest likelihood of dying by suicide, especially if ADHD, depression, conduct disorder, or the use of drugs or alcohol co-occur with adjustment disorder.

Portzky, Audenaert, and van Heeringen (2005) found that the suicidal process was shorter and without prior indication of emotional problems in adolescents with adjustment disorder compared to those with major depression.

Alcohol or substance use increased the risk. Adjustment disorder is the most frequently occurring diagnosis among people who engage in deliberate self-harm (Casey, 2009). Self-poisoning was the most frequent self-harm behavior in the 15- to 19-year age group (this includes self-poisoning with prescription drugs). Among those who engaged in deliberate self-harm, 31% were given a diagnosis of adjustment disorder on admittance to the hospital. Even so, suicidal thoughts were admitted to in only 11% of adolescents with adjustment disorder.

Clearly it is important to assess all people with adjustment disorders for suicidal ideation and plans, but this is especially important in adolescents who may rapidly and impulsively become suicidal. Two demographic categories are at increased risk: (1) adolescent males who have experienced a recent interpersonal loss or conflict, especially those with impulsive temperaments and those who use alcohol and other substances; and (2) females between the ages of 45 and 64 who have access to prescription drugs and other means of poisoning. (See Appendix for more information on suicide assessment and prevention strategies.)

Background and support make a difference in a person's resilience and ability to cope with life's problems. In a group of people with adjustment disorders who had attempted suicide, more than 50% came from unstable homes, were orphaned, or had experienced some type of emotional deprivation in childhood (Polyakova, Knobler, Ambrumova, & Lerner, 1998).

Typical Client Characteristics

Adjustment disorders occur in all cultures and age groups but seem to be diagnosed more frequently in those with above-average incomes (Benton & Lynch, 2006; Casey, 2009). Adjustment disorders also are particularly common among people who have little experience in dealing effectively with previous stressful events, have multiple stressors, or are coping with life-threatening illnesses. One study identified adjustment disorder as the most commonly diagnosed mental disorder in the oncology setting (Akechi et al., 2004). A separate study in Japan found that 35% of people who had a recurrence of cancer met the criteria for an adjustment disorder (Okamura et al., 2002). Similarly, a high incidence of adjustment disorder was found among a sample of older adults anticipating cardiac surgery; 50.7% had an adjustment disorder related to their medical condition and its treatment.

Especially among older workers, involuntary job loss often results in a cascade of stressful life events that have a negative effect on psychological well-being and physical health. This is compounded by the fact that at a time when a person is experiencing extreme stress and could benefit from treatment, they are the least able to afford it, and often their insurance ended with their employment. The person may also be unable to afford prescriptions or other necessary services (Arehart-Treichel, 2009). Unemployment has also been related to an increase in anxiety and hopelessness about the future (Arehart-Treichel, 2009; Bartley & Ferrie, 2010). In as many as half of all mental-illness-related deaths, job loss predated the development of depression and the subsequent suicide (Blakely, Collings, & Atkinson, 2003). So, even though job loss may not be a direct cause of suicidal risk, it remains related through a number of indirect pathways (Blakely et al., 2003).

Although overall downward trends in the economy, including economic recessions, do not seem to increase the overall rate of mental disorders, unemployment, especially when unemployment occurs in conjunction with debt or the loss of a home, does increase the occurrence of adjustment disorders and increases suicidal risk

(AAS, 2006; Brand, Levy, & Gallo, 2008; Burgard, Brand, & House, 2007).

Other factors that seem to predispose people to develop an adjustment disorder include financial difficulties, a history of mood disorders or alcohol-related disorders, family conflict, poorly controlled physical pain, and feelings of loss of control. Precipitating life events for women include crisis or loss of a relationship which may lead to increased depression or use of prescription drugs or alcohol. One European study found that women in mid-life who are single, widowed, or divorced also have a higher rate of depressive symptoms and an increased risk of suicide (Bernal et al., 2007).

Echoing the European research, the American Foundation for Suicide Prevention reported a 57% increase in poisoning deaths by women who completed suicide—the biggest increase in suicide statistics between 1999 and 2005 (American Foundation for Suicide Prevention, 2005; Hu, Wilcox, Wissow, & Baker, 2008). More research is needed to determine why women in middle age have the fastest growing rate of suicide, increasing by nearly 4% each year since 1999 ("U.S. Suicide Rate Increasing," 2008).

No evidence exists to tie adjustment disorders to underlying organic or biological factors. Rather, the common link in the development of these disorders seems to be stress (Benton & Lynch, 2006). Many disorders co-occur with adjustment disorder, with major depressive disorder occurring the most frequently at 46% (Casey, 2009). Distinguishing between an anxiety disorder and an adjustment disorder with anxiety may be difficult, but adjustment disorders must occur within three months of a stressor and do not last more than six months after the stressor has ended (American Psychiatric Association, 2002). With the exception of PTSD, anxiety disorders do not have any time limits or requirements for symptom presentation. Substance use disorders are also frequently seen in adjustment disorders as people attempt to reduce their stress by turning to drugs and alcohol. A detailed intake interview that assesses for alcohol and substance use is imperative. One study found that 59% of people diagnosed as having an adjustment disorder were later rediagnosed with a substance use disorder (Greenberg, Rosenfeld, & Ortega, 1995).

In children, adjustment disorders are most likely to co-occur with conduct or behavioral problems.

Assessment

Despite being one of the most commonly occurring disorders in clinical practice, no specific assessment tools exist for the diagnosis of adjustment disorders (Casey, 2009), nor do any of the structured interviews available to clinicians, except the SCID (First, Spitzer, Gibbon, & Williams, 2002), apply to adjustment disorders.

Clinicians must be able to distinguish between normal reactions to stressful life events (e.g. sadness following a miscarriage) and reactions that are pathological (attempted suicide after a miscarriage). Nothing can take the place of a good clinical assessment that considers context and longitudinal course (Casey, 2009). Clinicians can gain a better understanding of intensity and severity of symptoms by using instruments designed to assess levels of stress, mild anxiety, or depression. Checklists can also be helpful in assessing client attitudes and progress, especially in employment-related issues. Tools that promote self-awareness and help clients clarify options can be useful—for example, developing a chronology of important life events and taking inventories of interests or marital satisfaction. The Myers-Briggs Type Indicator (Myers & McCauley, 1985) and the Lifestyle Assessment Questionnaire (National Wellness Institute, 1983) can also help people understand why they are having difficulty with

particular situations, what resources they may be able to draw on, and what options they have.

Preferred Therapist Characteristics

Most people with adjustment disorders have a relatively high level of previous functioning. They probably are capable of handling the stressors themselves but are daunted by the stressors' suddenness or by their perceived lack of resources and coping skills. Therapists should communicate confidence that with some support and direction, these people will be able to resolve their problems themselves. This optimistic attitude should strengthen people's coping mechanisms and encourage them to face the stressors with a hopeful outlook. Therapists should be culturally competent and understand cultural differences in expressions of emotions. They should also be able to consider personal circumstances and the context of the stressor; if the response is proportional to the triggering event; understand cultural norms for emotion expression; and be able to distinguish between pathological behavior and behavior that is culturally acceptable.

Intervention Strategies

Little research is available on the best treatment interventions for adjustment disorders. There are no randomized controlled trials, nor is adjustment disorder included in the major national studies or the National Comorbidity Survey conducted by the NIMH (Casey, 2009). Short-term therapy seems appropriate, although longer lengths of treatment may be considered if stressors are chronic or repetitive.

Most adjustment disorders improve spontaneously without treatment when stressors are removed, attenuated, or accommodated, but therapy can facilitate recovery. It can hasten improvement, provide coping skills and adaptive mechanisms to avert future crises, and minimize poor choices and self-destructive behaviors that may have adverse consequences. As necessary, therapy also can address long-standing maladaptive thought processes, emotional expressions, and behavioral patterns.

Goals of treatment are to help clients develop problem-solving techniques to reduce or remove the stressor; to provide psychoeducation to help the client cognitively reframe when the stressor cannot be removed; or to alter response to the stressor through the use of relaxation and mindfulness-based techniques.

A flexible crisis-intervention model probably best characterizes the type of therapy most suited for the treatment of adjustment disorders. This model of therapy focuses both on relieving the acute symptoms that clients are experiencing and on promoting clients' adaptation to and ability to cope with the stressors. Therapy would also support the clients' strengths, paying little attention to past problems unless these problems suggest patterns that should be addressed in an effort to promote effective coping with current stressors. Education and information are usually part of the treatment and are intended to help people take a realistic look at their situations and become aware of options and resources that may be useful. Helping people develop the skills and attitudes they need to cope with future stressors also is an important element in treatment. The following are five typical steps in short-term crisis intervention used to treat adjustment disorders (Butcher et al., 2006):

1. Clarifying and promoting understanding of the problem.
2. Identifying and reinforcing the client's strengths and coping skills and teaching new coping skills if needed.
3. Collaborating with the client to develop a plan of action that will mobilize and empower the client.
4. Providing information and support to promote affective, cognitive, and behavioral improvement in the client.
5. Terminating treatment, making appropriate referrals, and following up.

The overriding goal of this brief, problem-focused orientation to treatment is to return people to previous or higher levels of functioning and to change some of their self-destructive behaviors and reactions so that the chances of a recurrence are reduced with the next life change.

A wide variety of interventions have been suggested for treatment of adjustment disorders. The specific interventions employed depend on the symptoms associated with the particular adjustment disorder as well as on the nature of the stressors, the strengths and challenges of the client, and the theoretical orientation of the therapist. For example, to cite just a few of the diverse approaches that can be used, people with depressive symptoms probably will respond to techniques borrowed from cognitive and interpersonal therapy (see Chapter 4), people experiencing anxiety probably will benefit from learning how to use relaxation techniques (see Chapter 5), and those with problems of conduct are likely to respond to behavior therapy (see Chapters 2 and 6). Because approximately one third of people with adjustment disorders, particularly adolescents, have suicidal thoughts, preventing suicide must of course be a priority of treatment (see Appendix). Dialectical behavior therapy has achieved much success in the treatment of self-harming behaviors and suicidal behaviors. Interventions such as relaxation, bibliotherapy, assertiveness training, and visual imagery are often combined with cognitive interventions in the treatment of this disorder so that behaviors as well as beliefs can be changed.

An example of a cognitive-behavioral approach to treatment is suggested by Meichenbaum and Deffenbacher (1988), who developed stress inoculation training (SIT) in the late 1980s. SIT includes the following three overlapping phases:

1. Conceptualization: developing a warm, collaborative relationship through which the problem can be assessed and reconceptualized.
2. Skill acquisition and rehearsal: developing coping strategies (for example, relaxation, communication skills, and decision making).
3. Application and follow-through: applying coping strategies to current problems and taking steps to prevent relapse.

Guidelines recently developed in the Netherlands for managing adjustment disorders in occupational and primary health care confirm the use of stress inoculation training and gradual exposure to increasing stress as a method to enhance the person's problem-solving capacity in relation to the work environment (van der Klink and van Dijk, 2003).

Brief psychodynamic psychotherapy also seems to be a useful approach in treating adjustment disorders. This approach does involve interpretation and the use of positive transference, two techniques that are usually associated with long-term treatment. However, because brief psychodynamic psychotherapy typically focuses on a single concern presented by the client, treatment can be both crisis-oriented (involving environmental manipulation and crisis resolution) and insight-oriented (promoting understanding of the connection between the impact of the crisis and the client's personality dynamics).

The therapist using brief psychodynamic psychotherapy typically is supportive, active, flexible, and goal-directed, working in a time-limited context (nearly always fewer than 25 sessions) to restore the client's previous level of equilibrium. This model seems particularly well suited to problems of acute onset experienced by people with positive prior adjustment and a good ability to relate to others and engage in a therapeutic relationship. Ideally, such clients are also verbal, psychologically minded, and highly motivated to benefit from treatment.

According to Bloom (2002), studies of treatment in which brief psychodynamic psychotherapy was used with children and adolescents experiencing adjustment disorders show that client improvement is superior to no intervention at all and that such therapies are as effective as time-unlimited interventions. Several advantages of brief psychodynamic psychotherapy seem to be a reduction in the use of defense mechanisms and an increase in coping skills. Both of these changes serve to quicken the pace of people's ability to deal with disconcerting life changes and in effecting immediate improvement (Kramer, Despland, Michel, Drapeau, & de Roten, 2010).

Solution-focused therapy is another brief approach that is likely to be effective in the treatment of adjustment disorders. Developed by de Shazer (1991) and others, this approach emphasizes health, positive reframing, and rapid resolution of problems. Its hallmark is de Shazer's Miracle Question (p. 113):

> Suppose that one night there is a miracle and while you were sleeping the problem that brought you to therapy is solved. How would you know? What would be different? What will you notice different the next morning that will tell you that there has been a miracle?

This question helps people focus on goals that are likely to lead to the resolution of the precipitants of their difficulties and to improvement in coping and feelings of empowerment.

Dialectical behavioral therapy can be particularly helpful in teaching clients how to regulate the stress and the emotional distress that result from significant life changes. Through exercises that help people become more mindful of their feelings, able to express both positive and negative emotions in an appropriate manner, and tolerate their emotions, the therapist can help clients proactively work through their anger. Being able to recognize, express, tolerate, and regulate emotions is a valuable coping skill for clients who are going through a crisis or life transition (Dimidjian & Linehan, 2008; Linehan et al., 2006; van Dijk, 2011).

The therapist's understanding of the specific nature of the crisis that led to the development of an adjustment disorder can guide the selection of appropriate treatment interventions. Relaxation training and mindfulness-based stress reduction can teach people to reduce their levels of stress and result in improved sleep, reduced symptoms of anxiety, and reduced pain and anxiety associated with medical conditions or procedures (Ferguson & Sgambati, 2008; Kabat-Zinn, 1990; Mackenzie, Carlson, Munoz, & Speca, 2007). A randomized controlled trial of mindfulness-based stress reduction for survivors of breast cancer showed significant improvements in mental health (reduced depression and anxiety about cancer recurrence) and quality of life than those who did not use MBSR (Lengacher et al., 2009).

Parent management training can reduce child and adolescent behavior problems (Kazdin, 2003, 2007). Problem-solving therapy can help people define the problem, generate alternative solutions, overcome avoidance and procrastination, and implement the solution. Evidence-based applications of problem-solving therapy include: marriage and relationship issues, suicidal ideation, behavior disorders in children, and reducing negative affect and improving quality of life in people with medical conditions (Nezu, Nezu, & McMurran, 2008).

Environmental manipulation that is acceptable to the client, such as a change of residence, a job transfer, hired help for a new baby, or reorganization of shared duties at home or at work can be useful.

Bibliotherapy—the assignment of books written by others who have knowledge about concerns similar to the client's—also can provide useful information and a clearer perspective. For example, excellent books are available on such specific stressors as cancer (Seligman, 1996), divorce (Margulies, 2001; Trafford, 1992; Viorst, 1998), and career changes (Bolles, 2006).

Group therapy can be a useful addition to treatment. It can provide a support system, teach and reinforce coping mechanisms, improve self-esteem, and promote reality testing through group members' sharing their perceptions of the client's situation. Groups composed of people going through similar life circumstances (cancer, marital separation or divorce, or bereavement, for example) can be particularly helpful. Group therapy typically does not provide crisis intervention, however, so it may not be a sufficient response to the urgency of a client's situation. A combination of group and individual therapy can be particularly useful to people with adjustment disorders: The individual therapy addresses the immediate crisis, and the group therapy provides support and an arena for testing new ideas and behaviors.

If a stressor directly or indirectly involves the client's family, at least a few sessions of family therapy may be useful in solidifying the support that the person is receiving, ensuring that the person's efforts to cope with the stressor are not being undermined by the family, and addressing any family circumstances that may be related to the stressful situation. Any problems involving secondary gains from the extra attention that people may be receiving when they are in crisis can also be identified and addressed in family therapy. The family can benefit from seeing that adjustment disorders occur when a psychosocial stressor challenges a person's capacity to cope. This may enable them to provide appropriate support and practical help to the person with the adjustment disorder.

Medication is usually not necessary in the treatment of adjustment disorders, although in some cases medication may help people manage anxiety or depression. Any use of medication should be time-limited and symptom-focused, and it should be perceived as secondary to the therapy, which promotes development of coping skills and seeks to prevent future emotional disorders.

People with adjustment disorders usually can be encouraged to resume their former lifestyle, to expect a return to normal functioning in a relatively short time, and to deal with the stressor as expeditiously as possible. Typically, the longer a person avoids dealing with a stressful situation, the more difficult it will be for the person to handle the situation effectively. Therefore, timing is an important variable in treatment. Early detection and treatment of adjustment disorders seem to enhance the prognosis, so it is unfortunate that many people with these relatively mild disorders do not seek treatment for their symptoms.

Prognosis

Of all the disorders, the prognosis for treatment of adjustment disorders is one of the most positive and is particularly good for adults. Those who are able to minimize disruptions to life roles, regulate emotional distress, and remain actively involved in aspects of life that hold meaning and importance to them will generally do well. A meta-analysis of people who developed adjustment disorders in response to a diagnosis of cancer, for example, showed that those who received problem-focused cognitive-behavioral therapy experienced significant positive changes in coping with cancer, developing a fighting spirit, reducing anxiety, and clarifying their perceptions of their problems, both at the

conclusion of the 8-week intervention and at 4-month follow-up (Meyer & Mark, 1995).

Although the overall prognosis for treatment of adjustment disorders is excellent, the prognosis is not as good for males and for people with behavioral symptoms or comorbid disorders. The literature suggests that adolescents with adjustment disorders frequently develop other, more severe, disorders (Benton & Lynch, 2006). Adolescent males in particular have been found to have increased suicidal ideation shortly after the occurrence of the relevant stressor (Portzky et al., 2005). This should be kept in mind during treatment.

People with adjustment disorders tend to seek subsequent psychotherapy. Whether this pattern reflects an incomplete recovery from the adjustment disorder, a subsequent adjustment disorder, the onset of another disorder, or simply a wish for more personal growth is not clear from the literature, but it does highlight the importance of including a preventive component in the treatment of adjustment disorders.

OTHER CONDITIONS THAT MAY BE A FOCUS OF CLINICAL ATTENTION

The various conditions discussed here encompass concerns that may well be amenable to psychotherapy but that are not in themselves mental disorders. To differentiate between a condition that may be focus of clinical attention and an adjustment disorder, consider two factors: a precipitant, and the presence of marked distress beyond what would be expected as well as dysfunction in social or occupational (academic) functioning.

Description of the Conditions

People with these conditions may not have any mental disorders; they may have coexisting mental disorders that are unrelated to the condition; or they may have mental disorders that are related to the condition, but the condition is listed on the multiaxial assessment because it is severe and important enough to warrant separate attention.

These three possibilities can be illustrated by three hypothetical clients who seek counseling after losing a job. Each of these clients would be described as having an occupational problem (a condition). The first client is a well-functioning person with no coexisting mental disorders who lost her job because the company went out of business; now she needs help in locating new employment. She is coping well, but would benefit from some help in planning her job search and developing her job-seeking skills. The second person lost his job for the same reason and has no mental disorders related to his unemployment, but he reports that he cannot seek employment requiring outdoor work because of his extreme fear of snakes; he would be described as having an occupational problem and a coexisting but relatively unrelated mental disorder, specific phobia. The third person lost her job because her use of alcohol led to frequent absences; she would have a coexisting and related diagnosis of alcohol dependence.

Not all current stressors are listed as conditions on Axis I of a multiaxial assessment; Axis IV is the usual place to list the stressors. Axis I should be reserved for circumstances that have a significant or pervasive impact on a person's life and so merit special clinical attention.

The *DSM-IV-TR* groups the conditions as follows.

Psychological Factors Affecting Medical Condition

In this condition, psychological symptoms, maladaptive behaviors, a mental disorder, or other psychological factors are having a negative impact on a person's medically verified physical illness (specified on Axis III). The psychological factor may be increasing the risk of complications. It may also be contributing to an exacerbation of the medical condition or a poor outcome of treatment for that condition. When this condition is listed, both the psychological factor and the medical condition are named. For example, if a person with lung cancer (coded on Axis III as neoplasm, malignant, lung, primary) continues smoking against medical advice, that person's multiaxial assessment would also include, on Axis I, maladaptive health behaviors affecting malignant lung neoplasm. The condition, of psychological factors affecting medical condition, often reflects a negative cycle in which a medical condition causes stress, physical discomfort, and worry, which in turn lead to emotions and behaviors that worsen the person's physical disorder.

Medication-Induced Movement Disorders

This category includes neuroleptic-induced Parkinsonism, neuroleptic malignant syndrome, neuroleptic-induced acute dystonia, neuroleptic-induced acute akathisia, neuroleptic-induced tardive dyskinesia, medication-induced postural tremor, and medication-induced movement disorder not otherwise specified. All these conditions describe symptoms that manifest themselves physiologically and are side effects of medication (usually neuroleptic drugs). Consequently, many people with these conditions have a comorbid diagnosis of a psychotic disorder. These movement disorders include a considerable array of symptoms, among them rigid muscle tone, a pill-rolling tremor, a masklike facial appearance (Parkinsonism), muscle contractions causing abnormal movements and postures (dystonia), restlessness and anxiety (akathisia), and involuntary movements of the face, tongue, or limbs (tardive dyskinesia). Many of these symptoms are irreversible.

Adverse Effects of Medication Not Otherwise Specified This condition is similarly caused by medication. However, it encompasses symptoms other than movement, such as hypotension and sexual dysfunction.

Relational Problems This broad category includes the following five conditions: (1) relational problems related to a mental disorder or general medical condition (such as an adolescent daughter's withdrawal from her mother who is coping with breast cancer), (2) parent-child relational problem, (3) partner relational problem, (4) sibling relational problem, and (5) relational problem not otherwise specified (such as problems with colleagues, friends, or in-laws). These descriptors are used to label interpersonal difficulties significant enough to warrant clinical attention. Such difficulties may be related to poor communication skills, weak parenting skills (such as difficulty in maintaining discipline), over- or underinvestment in relationships, lack of empathy and caring for others, or family changes and role conflicts.

Problems Related to Abuse or Neglect Conditions in this category include physical abuse of child, sexual abuse of child, neglect of child, physical abuse of adult, and sexual abuse of adult. These descriptors are used both for the survivors and the perpetrators of abuse; different code numbers indicate the distinction. These conditions are often accompanied by coexisting and related mental disorders, such as antisocial personality disorder or alcohol abuse for the perpetrator and posttraumatic stress disorder or borderline personality disorder for the survivor. Nearly 30% of people who have been abused will become abusers themselves, so a person may have more than one condition from this section (Butcher et al., 2006).

Almost 3 million cases of child abuse and neglect are reported each year in the United States. In 2004, 872,000 children were officially found to have been abused or neglected (U.S. Department of Health and Human Services, 2006). Birth parents or other parental figures (stepparents, adoptive parents) are the main perpetrators of childhood abuse and neglect (Azar & Wolfe, 2006). Mothers are more likely to neglect their children, whereas fathers are more likely to abuse. Eighty-nine percent of sexual abuse, 58% of physical abuse, and 67% of emotional abuse is committed by males (Sedlak & Broadhurst, 1996).

People who have been abused manifest a broad range of reactions; no consistent pattern of postabuse adjustment has been identified. Some may emerge from the experience without significant emotional difficulties, but more commonly symptoms of depression, self-destructive behavior, hypervigilance and anxiety, withdrawal, repressed anger, substance misuse, dysfunctional and abusive relationships, shame, and low self-esteem are present.

The child's safety must be the first priority for therapists who work with children. With adolescents and older adults, establishing trust, providing support, and using more active therapeutic interventions have been shown to make a difference in restoring or preserving the emotional health of people who have been abused. Clearly, abuse and neglect are conditions that merit intensive treatment, both for the survivors and for the perpetrators.

Additional Conditions That May Be a Focus of Clinical Attention This broad and diverse group includes 12 conditions:

1. *Noncompliance with treatment* is refusal to follow treatment recommendations for either a mental disorder or a medical problem. Many factors may contribute to the development of this condition. For example, the original medical or

mental disorder may have been misdiagnosed or not fully explained to the person, so he or she may have little motivation to comply with treatment, or a mental disorder (perhaps even the one being treated) may be interfering with the person's interest in treatment. As another example, people with bipolar disorders sometimes enjoy their manic or hypomanic episodes and so resist treatment. The appeal of secondary gains may also counteract the benefits of successful treatment. A thorough evaluation of people with this condition, as well as a thorough evaluation of their families and their occupational and environmental contexts, is important to a full understanding of the dynamics of this condition.

2. *Malingering* is defined as the deliberate production of symptoms for the purpose of gaining some external benefit, such as a military discharge or disability payments. This condition sometimes accompanies a diagnosis of antisocial personality disorder. People with this condition are often involved in lawsuits or have other legal problems. They may be uncooperative and withholding in treatment in an effort to avoid full disclosure that might jeopardize external benefits. With malingering, as with many of the other conditions, a thorough understanding of the context is important, as is corroborative information from other sources if it can be obtained. The Structured Interview of Reported Symptoms (Rogers, Kropp, Bagby, & Dickens, 1992) is a useful tool for detecting feigned symptoms, as is the use of open-ended questions to elicit information. Clinicians seem skilled at detecting malingering, but this

descriptor should still be used with caution.

3. *Adult, childhood, or adolescent antisocial behavior* is used to label both isolated acts and repeated patterns of antisocial behavior not due to a mental disorder. Patterns of antisocial behavior associated with this condition generally begin in adulthood and are accompanied by a relatively stable lifestyle, so that the person does not meet the criteria for antisocial personality disorder. Clinicians should be careful to rule out not only antisocial personality disorder but also conduct disorder, substance use disorders, or another impulse-control disorder before concluding that this condition is present. People with this condition often have accompanying financial, occupational, and relationship problems and tend to misuse drugs and alcohol.

4. *Borderline intellectual functioning* is coded on Axis II and reflects an IQ in the 71–84 range, below normal but above the criteria for mental retardation. Interpersonal difficulties, adjustment difficulties, and other behavioral difficulties are often found in people with this condition, just as they are in people diagnosed with mental retardation.

5. *Age-related cognitive decline* is characterized by cognitive impairment and decline that are within normal limits. The decline is significant enough to cause distress but not significant enough to meet the criteria for dementia or another cognitive mental disorder. People with this condition may have difficulty remembering other people's names, keeping appointments, or solving complex problems, but they do not forget such information as their own names

and addresses. Fears that they are developing dementia may lead them to seek assessment and treatment. Neurological and psychological evaluations, including assessment of memory and verbal fluency, can help determine whether this condition or a more serious disorder is present.

6. *Bereavement* is a response to the death of a loved one. Common symptoms include sadness, regret about actions taken around the time of the death, anxiety, mild somatic symptoms, loss of appetite, and difficulty sleeping. These symptoms may subsequently be diagnosed as a major depressive disorder if they are longstanding (usually more than two months), if they cause severe impairment, and if they include such signs of a major depression as strong feelings of guilt and worthlessness, suicidal ideation and preoccupation with death, psychomotor retardation, or loss of contact with reality (other than fleeting moments of seeing or hearing the deceased). People with few support systems and those with coexisting medical problems are at particularly high risk for severe reactions to a death (Reichenberg, 2010). Responses to death vary widely among cultures, so a client's background, ethnicity, and religious beliefs should be considered when a diagnosis related to bereavement is made.

7. *Academic problem* reflects difficulties in scholastic achievement that are not due to a mental disorder (such as a learning disorder, a communication disorder, or mental retardation). Children and adolescents, of course, are most likely to present with this condition, which may involve such issues as poor study skills, little interest in school subjects or achievement, or a poor image of their own academic abilities.

8. *Occupational problem* includes such concerns as career choice and dissatisfaction, job loss or change, demotion, or difficulty fulfilling the requirements of a job. High stress, reduced self-esteem, insecurity, anger, resentment, and fears about the future may accompany this condition (Seligman, 1996). Career counseling and assessment can be helpful both in clarifying the concerns of people with this condition and helping them resolve those concerns.

9. *Identity problem* encompasses a variety of doubts about self-image or direction and involves such issues as sexual orientation, morals and values, friendships, group loyalties, and long-term goals. These concerns are most likely to emerge during middle and late adolescence, but also are common in adults going through a sort of midlife reevaluation. People with an external locus of control, as well as those experiencing a life change, a family breakup, a loss, a challenging developmental task, or a values conflict with others, are especially prone to identity problems.

10. *Religious or spiritual problem* reflects issues related to a loss of faith, questions about religious beliefs or affiliation, problems associated with conversion to another faith, or other spiritual concerns. Consultation with a spiritual or religious adviser as well as with a psychotherapist may help people cope more successfully with these concerns (Cujé, 2010). Religious and spiritual beliefs can be very important in helping people find meaning and direction in their lives and

maintain good self-esteem and interpersonal relationships.

11. *Acculturation problem* focuses on issues related to a move from one culture to another. It may entail such concerns as balancing loyalty to one's culture of origin with an interest in adopting one's current culture, feeling alienated and isolated in the new culture, longing for one's former home or culture, or conflicts among family members who acculturate differently after immigration.

12. *Phase of life problem* includes such circumstances as illness, divorce, retirement, graduation, marriage, the birth of a baby, a relocation, or other life change. It is distinguished from an adjustment disorder in terms of the nature and severity of the person's reaction to the change; adjustment disorder reflects more difficulty and emotional dysfunction in response to the change.

The conditions just listed are problems in living that are experienced by most people. Often reactions to these conditions go untreated, and people manage to deal with them with varying degrees of success. People with these conditions who do not have coexisting mental disorders are typically in good contact with reality, and their reactions usually are consistent with the stressors or life circumstances they are experiencing. Nevertheless, they may be experiencing considerable unhappiness and dissatisfaction with their lives and may benefit from therapy.

Typical Client Characteristics

Across the course of a lifetime, every person will experience a loss, a life transition, a spiritual or identity concern, or other condition that may be the focus of attention. Those who seek therapy are likely to have fewer support systems and less effective coping skills, or to be more proactive in seeking help to work through life's problems.

Preferred Therapist Characteristics

Therapist variables indicated for treatment of conditions vary little from those indicated for treatment of adjustment disorders. People probably will respond best to therapists who are supportive and flexible and yet who challenge them to grow and develop. Therapists should encourage these clients to take responsibility for their own treatment when that is possible, but should also provide direction, resources, and information as needed. The therapist should maintain an attitude that is optimistic and that anticipates rapid progress. With the conditions, as with adjustment disorders, clinicians must be astute diagnosticians so that they can ascertain quickly whether coexisting mental disorders are present; that factor will determine the specific nature of a particular client's treatment.

Intervention Strategies

Treatment for the conditions usually is similar to treatment for adjustment disorders. The major difference is that less attention probably will be paid to the client's emotional, social, and occupational dysfunction, and more attention will be paid to the presenting concerns and the person's existing strengths and coping abilities, especially if no coexisting mental disorders have been identified. People can benefit from support and from the reassurance of having their reactions normalized. People experiencing conditions typically need education and information about their situation and about the options available to them. Environmental changes can be useful, as can the inclusion in therapy of others who are involved in the problem (for example, family members, friends, or business colleagues). Brief approaches to treatment are emphasized.

No controlled studies have been located on the treatment of the conditions generally, but suggestions can be inferred from studies of treatment for specific types of conditions and from information on the treatment of related disorders. Specific approaches to therapy have been developed or adapted to ameliorate some of the conditions. For example, a large body of literature is available on theories and strategies of career counseling that can guide therapy for people coping with occupational problems. Career counseling typically promotes values clarification, information seeking, and decision making; teaches such skills as interviewing and résumé writing; and promotes self-awareness and career maturity (Seligman, 1994). Bibliotherapy (especially reading about occupations) and informational interviewing for the purpose of learning about job roles can accelerate the progress of therapy.

Relational problems. Family therapy is likely to be useful for most people coping with relationship problems and family change and conflict. Many books are available to familiarize therapists and clients with patterns of family communication and effective ways of dealing with those patterns. Among these are *Families and Change* (McKenry & Price, 2005), *Spiritual Resources in Family Therapy* (Walsh, 2009), and *The Seven Principles for Making Marriage Work* (Gottman & Silver, 2000).

Bereavement. Many books also are available to help people work through the process of loss and bereavement. The field has evolved considerably since Kübler-Ross first laid the foundation with her work on death and dying (1997, 2001; Kübler-Ross & Kessler, 2001). Individual and group therapy both have their place in helping people through loss, but therapists should not assume that the grieving process, nor grief therapy, takes a one-size-fits-all approach. On the contrary, grieving can be affected by multiple variables including: the cause of death (homicide, suicide, heart attack), stage of life

(child, adult, elderly), whether there was time to say good-bye (car accident versus at the end of a long illness), the relationship with the deceased (parent, spouse, child, brother, coworker), and internal variables of the mourner.

Grieving the death of a person by suicide is an example of how all of these variables interplay to create a unique grieving experience for each person. A loss caused by suicide makes the grieving process more difficult, as mourners do not always receive the support they need. The death may be shrouded in stigma, questions, and guilt which prevent the bereaved from receiving the compassion they need. Complicated grief can result. Complicated grief sometimes occurs when extenuating factors make grieving difficult, for example, after multiple losses in a short period of time, or after the suicide of a family member (Begley & Quayle, 2007).

Clinicians who work with grieving clients generally help them to achieve the following four tasks: accept the loss, work through the pain, adjust to life without the person, and reinvest in life. Therapists who take into account underlying attachment issues, who are culturally competent, who recognize the variables that modulate the mourning process, who are compassionate, and who are aware of the effects of vicarious traumatization, are more likely to be successful in their ministrations and may find grief work to be rewarding and enriching (Reichenberg, 2010).

Acculturation. Stress-related health problems abound in first-generation immigrants and the risk of poor health is 5 times higher for women. A strong association exists between ethnicity and poor self-reported health. This effect is mediated by socioeconomic status, poor acculturation, and discrimination (Wiking, Johansson, & Sundquist, 2004). For Hispanic, Asian, and Arabic men, acculturation has also been linked to substance abuse (Arfken, Kubiak, & Farrag, 2009). Eating disorders are more likely to occur in women. Interventions that take into account the effect of acculturation, and promote healthy lifestyles, seem most appropriate for this population.

Phase-of-life problem. A major life change such as retirement or the birth of a baby requires time to adjust. Those who require more help could benefit from psychoeducation to help them understand and accept the transition, support groups to provide coping strategies and help normalize their feelings, and individual therapy to help regulate emotions and improve decision making. Workshops for separation and divorce, new mother play groups, and retirement coaching can all help people master their current life transition. People experiencing phase of life problems should also be encouraged to marshal their resources and enlist the support of family and friends.

Identity problems. Adolescents and adults who develop identity problems may have their situations exacerbated by social stigma, bullying, and name-calling, both online and in person. The American Academy of Child and Adolescent Psychiatry (AACAP) estimates that as many as 50% of school-age children have been bullied at one time or another. Being the target of bullying behavior can have negative effects on academic, social, emotional, and behavioral functioning. Those who are bullied need additional support and may seek professional counseling to help them manage their anger in more productive ways.

People who are victims of bullying behavior should involve parents, educators, principals, and other authority figures. Left unchallenged, bullying can result in increased stress and anxiety, and leave a lifelong scar. Early recognition and treatment seem to be the key to minimizing the long-term effects of bullying behavior.

Borderline intellectual functioning. An approach to both group and individual therapy that is cognitive-behavioral in nature and is geared to the developmental level of the client has been found effective in helping people with borderline intellectual functioning (Paxon, 1995). Multimodal therapy has also demonstrated effectiveness with these clients, as well as with people who have experienced abuse and neglect.

Psychological factors affecting a medical condition. Strategies that address the mind-body connection, such as biofeedback, relaxation, and encouragement of a healthy lifestyle, can help people with psychological factors affecting a medical condition (Seligman, 1996). Collaborative treatment, in which therapist and physician work together, is indicated for these clients, as well as for people coping with medication-induced movement disorders. Mindfulness-based stress reduction has proven its effectiveness in helping to reduce stress, pain, and anxiety in people with medical conditions.

Antisocial behavior. People with long-standing antisocial behavior typically benefit from counseling in a homogeneous group setting. That environment can facilitate their receiving feedback and learning and practicing new ways to meet their goals and cope with stress.

Support groups can be particularly helpful to people coping with the conditions listed in the *DSM-IV-TR*; sometimes these groups provide all the treatment that is needed. Therapy or self-help groups composed of people with similar life circumstances (such as bereavement, retirement, a recent divorce, a serious illness, or abuse) can be particularly useful in offering information and modeling coping mechanisms as well as in providing feedback and support.

Courses designed to develop such skills as parenting, assertiveness, and anger management also can be useful to people with these conditions. The group environment of the classes can also offer support and encouragement while normalizing concerns.

Many people coping with these conditions will have coexisting mental disorders, of course, particularly people who are perpetrators or survivors of abuse or neglect. Treatments for coexisting mental disorders should become part of the help that is provided to these people (see relevant chapters of this book for treatment options).

Prognosis

The prognosis for treatment of most of these conditions, if they stand alone, is quite good, although the diversity of conditions and of people manifesting these conditions mandates caution in generalizing. Typically, people who benefit the most from treatment are those who have the highest pretreatment levels of functioning and self-concept and are motivated to receive treatment. Borderline intellectual functioning, medication-induced movement disorder, and age-related cognitive decline are not likely to improve much in response to therapy, but treatment of these conditions may well have a positive impact on the outlook and coping abilities of people with these conditions. People with long-standing antisocial behavior also tend not to have a positive response to treatment. Nevertheless, most conditions that are short term and that have developed in response to specific precipitants (such as a death or a relocation) are likely to have an excellent prognosis, especially if they are not accompanied by other mental disorders.

TREATMENT RECOMMENDATIONS: CLIENT MAP

The following list organizes the recommendations made in this chapter for the treatment of situationally precipitated disorders (adjustment disorders and other conditions) according to the Client Map format.

CLIENT MAP

Diagnoses
Adjustment disorders
Other conditions that may be a focus of clinical attention

Objectives of Treatment
Increase knowledge and understanding of the situation
Promote information gathering
Enhance strengths
Improve coping, problem solving, and decision making
Relieve symptoms
Promote use of support
Restore at least prior level of functioning

Assessments
Measures of transient anxiety, depression, and stress
Problem checklists

Clinician Characteristics
Flexible yet structured
Present-oriented

Optimistic

Skilled in diagnosis and treatment of a broad range of disorders

Location of Treatment

Outpatient

Interventions to Be Used

Empowerment of client

Crisis intervention

Bibliotherapy

Brief psychodynamic psychotherapy

Cognitive-behavioral therapy

Brief solution-focused therapy

Emotion-focused therapy

Stress management

Strengthening and development of coping skills, such as assertiveness, decision making, communication, relaxation, reframing, and others

Other short-term or active approaches

Emphasis of Treatment

Moderate emphasis on support

Probing only when relevant to current concerns

Focus to be determined by specific precipitant and response

Numbers

Usually individual therapy

Concurrent or later group therapy sometimes indicated

Family sessions sometimes indicated

Timing

Usually brief duration and rapid pace

Timing may need modification in the presence of coexisting mental disorders

Medications Needed

Usually none

Adjunct Services

Inventories to clarify goals and direction

Education and information

Peer support groups composed of people with similar concerns

Possibly environmental manipulation

Prognosis

Excellent if cause or precipitant can be changed, especially if no underlying mental disorder is present and person has good premorbid functioning and self-esteem

CLIENT MAP OF BETH H.

This chapter began with the case of Beth H., a 47-year-old woman who had been diagnosed with breast cancer. Short-term counseling helped Beth decide to have a mastectomy, with immediate reconstruction, to facilitate her rapid return to work and help her maintain her positive body image. Fortunately, chemotherapy was not needed. Beth became involved with a support group that helped normalize her feelings and provided information, role models, and encouragement.

After the immediate medical crisis was over, Beth continued to receive therapy to help her establish rewarding goals and directions for herself and implement health- and lifestyle-related goals. Like most people with adjustment disorders, Beth needed only some short-term counseling to help her mobilize her resources, make decisions, and establish a rewarding direction for herself. The self-awareness, support systems, and coping strategies she gained from the therapeutic process should enable her to cope more effectively with future life transitions. This chapter concludes with a Client Map of Beth.

Diagnosis

Axis I: 309.28 Adjustment disorder with mixed anxiety and depressed mood
Axis II: V71.09 No diagnosis on Axis II
Axis III: 174.9 Neoplasm (malignant, breast)
Axis IV: Diagnosis and treatment of breast cancer, divorce
Axis V: Global assessment of functioning (GAF Scale): current GAF = 72

Objectives of Treatment

Reduce anxiety and depression related to cancer diagnosis
Help client make sound decisions about her medical treatment
Promote establishment of healthy patterns of eating, sleeping, exercise, and self-care
Continue client's efforts to cope with her divorce and develop a rewarding lifestyle
Help client resume previous level of functioning and maintain self-esteem

Assessments

Measure of Adjustment to Cancer Scale
Profile of Mood States

Clinician Characteristics

Supportive and accepting yet action-oriented
Knowledgeable about cancer and the mind-body-spirit connection

Location of Treatment

Outpatient

Interventions to Be Used

Cognitive-behavioral therapy, designed to promote a fighting spirit, normalize reactions, and empower the client
Bibliotherapy on treatment options and reactions to cancer
Mindfulness-based stress reduction
Use of information-gathering and decision-making strategies
Identification and mobilization of previously successful coping mechanisms
Visual imagery and relaxation
Planning to improve wellness, socialization

Emphasis of Treatment

High emphasis on supportiveness

Moderate emphasis on directiveness

Focus on the present, with exploration of cognitions, behaviors, and affect, especially fears and coping skills

Numbers

Primarily individual therapy, with a few counseling sessions including client and her daughter

Timing

Short term

Weekly sessions

Rapid to moderate pace

Medications Needed

None

Adjunct Services

Support group for women coping with breast cancer

Prognosis

Excellent

RECOMMENDED READING

Boss, P. (2006). *Loss, trauma, and resilience: Therapeutic work with ambiguous loss.* New York, NY: Norton.

Brach, T. (2004). *Radical acceptance.* New York, NY: Bantam Dell.

Bridges, W. (2001). *The way of transition: Embracing life's most difficult moments.* Cambridge, MA: Perseus Press.

Crosson-Tower, C. (2005). *Understanding child abuse and neglect* (6th ed.). Boston, MA: Allyn & Bacon.

Cujé, B. B. (2010). *Become the person you were meant to be: The choice cube method, step-by-step to choice and change.* Arlington, VA: Booksurge.

Dalai Lama, & Cutler, H. C. (1998). *The art of happiness: A handbook for living.* New York, NY: Riverhead Books.

Jackson-Cherry, L., & Erford, B. T. (2010). *Crisis intervention and prevention.* Upper Saddle River, NJ: Pearson.

Kabat-Zinn, J. (1990). *Full catastrophe living: Using the wisdom of your body and mind to face stress, pain, and illness.* New York, NY: Dell.

Kushner, H. S. (2004). *When bad things happen to good people.* New York, NY: Anchor Books.

O'Donohue, W. T., & Fisher, J. E. (Eds.). (2008). *Cognitive behavior therapy: Applying empirically supported techniques to your practice.* Hoboken, NJ: Wiley.

Seligman, L. (1998). *Promoting a fighting spirit: Psychotherapy for cancer patients, survivors, and their families.* San Francisco, CA: Jossey-Bass.

Trafford, A. (1992). *Crazy time: Surviving divorce and building a new life* (Rev. ed.). New York, NY: HarperCollins.

van Dijk, S. (2011). *Don't let your emotions run your life: Dialectical behavior therapy skills for helping teens.* Oakland, CA: New Harbinger Books.

Viorst, J. (1998). *Necessary losses.* New York, NY: Free Press.

Walsh, F. (2009). *Spiritual resources in family therapy* (2nd ed.). New York, NY: Guilford Press.

Mood Disorders

Karen C., a 30-year-old married African American woman, was brought to a therapist by her mother. Karen reported feeling severe depression and hopelessness. She was barely able to care for her 5-year-old child or her home, and she had not gone to her part-time job as an aide at her child's school for over two weeks. Her accompanying symptoms included significant weight gain, excessive fatigue and sleeping, and severe guilt.

Karen and her husband had been married for 8 years. Karen's husband was in the military, which meant that he was frequently away from home. Karen had always found his absences difficult and had encouraged her husband to leave the service. He complained that she was too dependent on him, and he urged her to develop her own interests.

Apart from her work at their child's school, Karen had few outside activities, and she had few supports other than her mother, who had been widowed shortly after the birth of Karen, her only child. Karen's mother had not remarried. She told Karen that she had been so devastated by the death of Karen's father that she would never get involved with another man. The mother seemed to have experienced episodes of severe depression, although she had never received treatment for them.

Conflict had been increasing in Karen's marriage and had reached a peak about three weeks before, when Karen's husband left for an overseas tour of duty in what both viewed as a safe part of the world. Karen was fearful that he would become involved with another woman and never return home, even though her husband's behavior gave her no justification for her concerns. She berated herself for not being a good wife and stated that life was not worth living without her husband. The only bright spot for Karen over the past few weeks had come when she received a handwritten letter from him. She read it again and again and did feel better for a few hours, but her depression soon returned.

Karen's developmental history was unremarkable except for her having been ill quite often. After her graduation from high school, she had worked as a secretary and lived with her mother until her marriage. She had dated little before her marriage, but she did remember having felt very depressed at least once before in her life, when a young man she had dated a few times became engaged to another woman.

Karen is suffering from a severe depression that has impaired her level of functioning. A precipitant can be identified for Karen's current episode of depression, but her symptoms do not suggest either an adjustment disorder or a condition; her reactions show too much dysfunction to be reflective of either one. Instead, Karen is experiencing a mood disorder characterized by depression.

OVERVIEW OF MOOD DISORDERS

This chapter provides information on the diagnosis and treatment of the various types of mood disorders—major depressive disorder, dysthymic disorder, depressive disorder not otherwise specified, bipolar I disorder, bipolar II disorder, and cyclothymic disorder, all of which typically include significant depression. Although three of these disorders (bipolar I and II and cyclothymic disorder) also include inordinately elevated moods (mania or hypomania), the primary focus of the first section of the chapter will be depression, the common ingredient of all these disorders.

Description of the Disorders

Primary symptoms of depression are feelings of discouragement and hopelessness, a dysphoric mood, a loss of energy, and a sense of worthlessness and excessive guilt. Physiological (or vegetative) symptoms are common and typically include changes in appetite and sleep, with insomnia and loss of appetite the most common manifestations.

In the 1970s, the professional literature commonly distinguished between exogenous or reactive depression, linked to an external event or situation, and endogenous, melancholic, or biochemical depression, having a physiological basis. Endogenous depressions are less common than reactive ones. With the third edition of the *DSM*, both forms of depression were encompassed by major depressive disorder. However, episode subtypes include: with melancholic features, with atypical features, or with catatonic features; therefore an understanding of the different types of depression is important.

With melancholic features. Melancholia, or an absence of pleasure or interest, typically accompanies endogenous depression. Endogenous depressions seem to be more biologically driven, have a later age of onset, and are more likely to report a family history of depression. They are also far more likely than atypical (or reactive) depressions to involve delusions or hallucinations, psychomotor retardation or agitation, extreme guilt, and worsening in the morning. Melancholic features include vegetative symptoms of reduced eating and sleeping. This type of depression tends to respond less well to SSRIs.

With atypical features. Atypical depression differs considerably from melancholic depression. Reverse vegetative symptoms (overeating and oversleeping) are characteristic of atypical depression (Matza, Revicki, Davidson, & Stewart, 2003). Despite its name, atypical depression was found in 36.4% of the depressed sample in the National Comorbidity Survey (Matza et al., 2003). The disorder is characterized by earlier age of onset and greater chronicity and is found in a high number of depressed women (70% of subjects in a study reported by Agosti and Stewart, 2001). Higher rates of paternal depression, childhood neglect, sexual abuse, suicidal thoughts and attempts, disability, and co-occurring disorders such as substance misuse, panic, and anxiety are seen in people with atypical depression. This disorder does not always respond to selective serotonin reuptake inhibitors (SSRIs) or tricyclic antidepressants. Rather, MAOIs have been found to be more effective. Research is currently being conducted on a patch delivery method of MAOIs that would reduce the unpleasant side effects.

With catatonic features. This subtype is appropriate if two or more of the following *DSM-IV-TR* criteria are present in the current episode: catalepsy (motor immobility), purposeless and excessive motor activity, extreme negativity to instructions, posturing as a statute, echolalia, or echopraxia (American Psychiatric Association, 2000). Catatonic symptoms can wax and wane, may range from stupor to excitement, and are estimated to be present in 13% to 31% of mood disorders (most frequently in bipolar disorder). Catatonic features are also seen in other disorders such as schizophrenia, dementia, and conversion disorder, and can be a symptom of an underlying medical condition. People with catatonic symptoms should always be referred for a medical examination (Penland, Weder, & Tampi, 2006). Catatonia may respond well to electroconvulsive therapy or to benzodiazepines (Hung & Huang, 2006).

With postpartum onset. The *DSM* also identifies another type of major depressive disorder, postpartum depression, beginning within four weeks of giving birth. Women are at increased risk of developing this disorder if they have a history of premenstrual depression, negative life events during pregnancy, partner relational problems, or inadequate social support after giving birth (Saxena & Sharan, 2006). Rapid intervention and follow-up preventive treatment are needed so that the depressed mother does not pose a danger to the child or to the parent-child relationship. Somerset and colleagues (2006) estimate the occurrence of postpartum depression to be in the range of 8% to 22%.

Seasonal recurrence. Depression can also be seasonal. Many people experience reduced energy and other symptoms of seasonal affective disorder (SAD) when the days grow shorter in the fall, with remission of symptoms in the spring. This type of depression can also occur during summer months. SAD is related to the amount of available natural light and linked to such biological phenomena as light sensitivity and problems in melatonin secretion. This seasonal pattern is present in 4% of the population of the United States, and is particularly common in women and young people, as well as in people living in northern climates (American Psychological Association, 2000). Additional symptoms include loss of interest in activities that were previously considered

pleasurable, withdrawal from friends and family, carbohydrate craving, headaches, fatigue, and daytime hypersomnia (Quinn, 2007). Remission is sometimes followed by a period of elevated mood.

Suicidal ideation is a common symptom in depression, one that obviously requires attention. People with depression are at 30 times higher risk of suicide than people who are not depressed (Haley, 2004; Ohayon & Schatzberg, 2002; Schatzberg, 2005). Among the elderly, depression is associated with increased suicide rates as well as increased mortality from a variety of other medical causes (Penninx, 2006). Readers are referred to the Appendix for a comprehensive review of the steps for evaluating suicidality.

Psychotic features are reported in nearly 19% of people who meet the criteria for major depression, most often in people who are severely depressed and meet eight or nine of the *DSM-IV-TR* criteria for the disorder (Ohayon & Schatzberg, 2002). Even those who do not have hallucinations or delusions may have impaired reality testing. They typically feel guilty and worthless and believe that those who care about them are undermining them or would be better off without them. By definition, psychotic depression requires hallucinations or delusions to co-occur with depression (Swartz, 2010). Often the psychotic features are so severe (or disturbing) that symptoms of depression are missed and an erroneous diagnosis of schizophrenia is made (Swartz, 2010). Accurate differential diagnosis is important to reduce medication errors, improve treatment, and return the client to his or her previous level of functioning as quickly as possible.

Typical Onset, Course, and Duration of Depression
A first episode of depression generally occurs during young or middle adulthood but may occur at any age, as can a recurrence.

The initial episode of depression tends to occur earlier in women than in men; men are more likely to have an initial episode in midlife. Depression may be primary or secondary to a preexisting chronic mental or physical disorder (such as alcohol dependence). Depression often coexists with a personality disorder (most often borderline, histrionic, or dependent personality disorders). Depression may also begin in childhood. In this case, it is often characterized by agitation rather than by overt sadness. Depression has been associated with abuse in childhood (Schatzberg, 2005) and may co-occur with ADHD and disruptive behavior disorders. An earlier age of onset is associated with a worse prognosis and greater symptom severity.

Relevant Predisposing Factors Depression can have many possible origins, dynamics, and precipitants. Familiarity with these and an ability to understand the determinants of a particular person's depression are essential to the formulation of an effective treatment plan. From a biopsychosocial perspective, a genetic predisposition toward depression, combined with negative life experiences and a pessimistic temperament, can contribute to depression. Beck and other cognitive theorists view depression as a result of faulty logic and misinterpretation, involving a negative cognitive set and core cognition. Behavioral theorists hypothesize that people who become depressed have poor interpersonal skills and therefore receive little positive social reinforcement. The interpersonal model explains depression as stemming from undue dependence on others as well as from conflict and poor communication in relationships. Biological approaches view depression as resulting from a dysregulation of serotonin and other neurotransmitters in the brain. Decreased prefrontal activity in the brains of people who are depressed has been well documented with PET scans (Schatzberg,

2005). Developmental models suggest that people who experience depression are more likely to have had difficult childhoods, early traumatic experiences, an inappropriate level of maternal care, low cohesion or adaptability in the family, and controlling or rejecting parents (Marecek, 2006).

The onset of depression often follows one or more traumatic or otherwise stressful life events, which frequently involve interpersonal loss. Stressors involving loss are strongly correlated to depression, whereas stressors involving threat or danger are more likely to precipitate anxiety (Kessler, 2006a). Depression can be defined as a "maladaptive, exaggerated response to stress" (Korszun, Altemus, & Young, 2006, p. 41). Stressors may include problematic interpersonal relationships, career disappointments, and others (Whisman, Weinstock, & Tolejko, 2006). Indeed, the anticipation of an impending loss can trigger a return of unresolved feelings about an earlier loss and can precipitate depression. This pattern is particularly likely in people who have experienced a high number of significant negative life events (shame and humiliation, violence, trauma, and abuse).

According to Pettit and Joiner (2006), interpersonal factors are among the strongest predictors of depression chronicity. Perceived criticism, hostile communications, and interpersonal problems can be powerful predictors of relapse as well as of a poor response to treatment. Several authors (Coyne, 1976; Joiner, 2000) have identified another sort of self-propagatory process as contributing to depression. They found that people who were depressed emphasized negative self-evaluations and sought out confirmation from others to verify their own negative self-view. Not only does this process reinforce negative thoughts and exacerbate depressive symptoms, but the process itself may promote rejection and criticism from others. Weinstock and Whisman (2004) found that the seeking of negative feedback was directly correlated with depressive symptoms.

Depression often has a genetic or familial component, particularly for those whose mothers were depressed (Goodman & Tully, 2006), although Kessler (2006a) notes that a family history of anxiety, substance misuse, or other psychological disorder is just as likely to predict depression.

Women are much more likely to experience depression than men, but whether this difference suggests a causative factor that is hormonal or environmental and social is unclear. Depression occurs in as many as 15% of women during pregnancy and postpartum, and the increasing rate of depression in women of childbearing years is cause for concern.

A growing body of literature on maternal depression shows adverse outcomes for children, beginning in the womb. Deficits in cognitive functioning, vulnerability to developing psychopathology, and early symptoms of depression have been found in children exposed prenatally to their mother's depression. These children also have an increased risk of having dysregulated neuroregulatory systems and frontal brain activity (Wadhwa et al., 2002).

Babies born to depressed mothers also will probably experience the negative effects of having a depressed parent. When compared to nondepressed mothers, depressed mothers display less positive affect, increased sadness or irritability, and negative and intrusive behavior toward their children. Rather than being consistent disciplinarians, depressed mothers are likely to alternate between lax and harsh discipline (Goodman & Tully, 2006).

Children of depressed parents typically have greater levels of depression themselves at every stage of development—infant, toddler, child, adolescent, and adult (Goodman & Tully, 2006). Earlier age of onset of depression, greater functional impairment, and recurrence are also correlated with parental depression.

Epidemiology Ten million Americans and more than 100 million people worldwide will experience depression in a given year. Although only 20% to 25% of those who experience clinical depression will actually receive treatment, a large percentage of the people who are seen by therapists are treated for mood disorders. The prevalence of clinical depression seems to be increasing, and its onset is occurring at an earlier age (Somerset, Newport, Ragan, & Stowe, 2006).

Depression has a broad range of severity. Most people with depression are able to carry on with their lives and may even succeed in concealing their symptoms from others. In some people, depression may be present for many years at a subclinical level, becoming a deeply ingrained part of the personality. People with severe depression, however, typically manifest significantly impaired functioning.

Depression accounts for 75% of psychiatric hospitalizations. The exact number of hospitalizations for suicide attempts or suicidal ideation is unknown, but young people with the combination of a mood disorder and a substance-related disorder have particularly elevated suicide rates, as do people with concurrent diagnoses of a mood disorder and borderline personality disorder, or with depression accompanied by delusions, panic, or anxiety disorders (see Appendix for a more detailed discussion of suicide assessment).

Typical Client Characteristics

Extensive research supports the theory that pessimism increases depressive symptoms (Girgus & Nolen-Hoeksema, 2006). Seligman (1990) has written about the importance of what he calls *learned helplessness* in the dynamics of depression. He theorizes that many people who are depressed have long-standing motivational, interpersonal, cognitive, and affective deficits, as well as low self-esteem, resulting from a long series of uncontrollable and painful events that seem to make them depression-prone. They tend to set unrealistic goals, have little sense of competence, and view others as more powerful and capable than themselves.

People suffering from depression frequently experience discord with their spouse or partner. One negative outcome of living with a depressed person is an increased burden on the partner caused by the depressed person's emotional strain, lack of energy, and fear of future relapse (Benazon & Coyne, 2000). Wives of depressed men reported taking on more household responsibilities than did husbands of depressed women. Spouses of depressed women tend to rate their wives more negatively on measures of depression, dependence, and detachment (Whisman et al., 2006). Couples, overall, exhibit more negative behavior and decreased problem-solving ability when one person is depressed. Interestingly, negative ratings continue even when depression remits. Spouses of depressed people are more negative and critical, which creates a negative feedback loop that ultimately increases relapse rates for depression (Whisman et al., 2006). Therefore, couples therapy may be an effective adjunct to individual therapy, especially for women who are depressed. Preventing relationship distress and divorce can be an effective prophylactic measure in warding off depression.

Girgus and Nolen-Hoeksema (2006) looked at cognitive variables in the development of depression, including thoughts about body image, self-esteem, and perceived self-efficacy. High self-esteem has an ameliorating effect on stress and depression. Self-efficacy is also believed to buffer stress. When stress is high, people with low self-esteem have more depression.

Women have a greater interpersonal orientation than do men. Many women experience sociotropy—heightened concern about what others think; this increases dependence on the approval of others and correlates with incidence of depressive episodes. Stressors in the interpersonal realm are associated with increased depression in women, as is going along with what other people think without expressing an opposing opinion. Girgus and Nolen-Hoeksema (2006) found that both of these traits occur more frequently in women than in men.

Assessment

The Beck Depression Inventory (BDI; Beck, Steer, & Brown, 1996), Hamilton Rating Scale for depression, and the Structured Clinical Interview for DSM (SCID; First, Spitzer, Gibbon, & Williams, 2002) are frequently used to assess depression. Co-occurring disorders should also be assessed, as well as the quality and stability of the client's strengths, support system, and relationships with others. In addition, people with depression often have a history of early developmental difficulties. Therefore, history taking should include questions about any possible familial background of depression and about childhood development. Information that reveals a family history of depression and a history of early developmental problems may help both the therapist and the client understand the nature and dynamics of the disorder. Specific assessments for bipolar disorder and mania are presented in the bipolar section.

Preferred Therapist Characteristics

The Treatment of Depression Collaborative Research Program (Krupnick et al., 1996) of the National Institute of Mental Health indicates that the therapeutic alliance seems far more important than the intervention strategy in determining outcomes of treatment for depression. Even people in the placebo and clinical management conditions of that study demonstrated significant alleviation of depression, apparently because of the power of a positive therapeutic alliance. The quality of the alliance was important both early and late in treatment and for all groups, including those receiving psychotherapy and those receiving medication. Krupnick speculates that medication alone as a treatment for depression may not be effective because it often is not provided in the context of an ongoing positive therapeutic alliance.

Ideally, a therapist working with a person who is depressed should strongly communicate the Rogerian conditions of genuineness, caring, acceptance, and empathy; should be able to provide support, structure, reality testing, optimism, and reinforcement; and should be a strong role model. The therapist needs to be knowledgeable about suicidal risk and intervene actively if suicide is threatened (refer to Appendix).

Therapy should be moderately high in directiveness, at least in the early stages of treatment. Therapists should gradually decrease directiveness over the course of treatment, however, to prevent clients from becoming too dependent and to increase client self-esteem. Supportiveness will also need to be fairly high initially; people who are depressed are in considerable pain, and a probing approach runs the risk of opening new painful areas. Clients also need considerable acceptance and positive regard at the start of treatment because of the fragility of their self-concepts.

The focus of the initial stages of treatment usually will be on cognitive and behavioral areas of concern rather than on affective areas. Affect certainly should receive some attention, but extensive discussion of depression tends to entrench its symptoms and contributes to the client's sense of discouragement and hopelessness; a focus on the cognitive or the behavioral area is more likely to mobilize the client.

Therapists who encourage clients' active involvement in goal setting and treatment will help them to develop a sense of mastery, better reality testing, clearer interpersonal boundaries, and a repertoire of problem-solving skills and coping mechanisms.

Intervention Strategies

Depression takes many forms, and diagnosis of the particular form is crucial in determining the best treatment. In general, individual psychotherapy without medication is appropriate for treatment of mild to moderate depression that is uncomplicated by a bipolar pattern, by coexisting psychosis, by cognitive impairment, by mental retardation, or by misuse of substances (Young, Rygh, Weinberger, & Beck, 2008). For severe or complex forms of depression, the combination of medication and psychotherapy is almost always recommended.

Treatment of depression will typically be provided one to two times a week in an outpatient setting and will be paced fairly rapidly, but not so rapidly as to threaten or discourage the client. Such inventories as the Beck Depression Inventory, as well as concrete, mutually agreed-on assignments, can give the client optimism and a sense of progress and direction. Therapy for depression tends to be short term (12 to 20 sessions over a period of three to six months) and usually does not exceed a year. The treatment of depression can also be enhanced by adjunct services to help people establish a sense of direction and become involved in rewarding activities (such as social groups and sports) likely to increase their sense of competence and confidence.

Couples therapy and family therapy can enhance treatment by providing support to the family as well as by ameliorating any family conflict that may be contributing to the depression. Group therapy can be a helpful adjunct to individual therapy for people who are mildly depressed. However, it would not be appropriate as the primary mode of treatment for people with severe depression; their hopelessness and lack of energy make it difficult for them to engage actively in that process.

Empirical research suggests the efficacy of behavioral, cognitive-behavioral, and interpersonal therapy for the treatment of depression.

Prognosis

The prognosis for a positive response to treatment for depression is excellent; a high percentage of people improve regardless of which treatment is used. Prognosis is correlated with many factors, which include the severity of the depression, the existence of intact partner relationships, high learned resourcefulness, absence of dysfunctional social relationships, and the presence of any Axis II disorders (Craighead, Sheets, Brosse, & Ilardi, 2007).

Severe depression tends to be a self-limiting disorder and rarely lasts longer than 6 to 12 months, but depression has a high rate of relapse, up to 90% in one study, especially during the first few months after treatment. An important part of any treatment for depression should include a relapse prevention component which usually involves follow-up sessions, perhaps at monthly intervals, to maintain progress and facilitate rapid treatment for relapses.

We will now consider the nature and treatment of the following mood disorders as defined by the fourth edition text revision of the *Diagnostic and Statistical Manual of Mental Disorders*, or *DSM-IV-TR* (American Psychiatric Association, 2000):

- Major depressive disorder
- Dysthymic disorder
- Depressive disorder not otherwise specified (NOS)

- Bipolar I and II disorders
- Cyclothymic disorder

All these disorders typically have depression as a prominent feature, but the depression varies in its intensity, duration, and pattern of onset. Bipolar disorders and cyclothymic disorder are also characterized by unpredictable shifts in mood, as well as by elevated moods.

The mood disorders section of the *DSM-IV-TR* also includes bipolar disorder not otherwise specified (NOS), mood disorder due to a general medical condition, substance-induced mood disorder, and mood disorder NOS. Nearly all the major sections of the *DSM-IV-TR* include substance-induced disorders, medical disorders due to a general medical condition, and NOS variations. Substance-induced disorders will be discussed in Chapter 6, and impulse-control disorders and mental disorders due to a general medical condition will be discussed in Chapter 7; little attention will be paid in this book to the NOS disorders because of their variability and the lack of standard definitions.

MAJOR DEPRESSIVE DISORDER

In the United States alone, major depressive disorder affects nearly 15 million adults, or 6.7% of the population. It is one of the leading causes of disability, and contributes to job loss, substance abuse, and increased suicides.

Description of the Disorder

According to the *DSM-IV-TR*, a major depressive episode is manifested by the presence of a depressed mood (dysphoria) or loss of enjoyment or interest in almost everything (anhedonia) and the presence of at least four of the following seven symptoms nearly every day for at least two weeks:

1. Significant weight or appetite change (found in over 70% of people with this disorder)
2. Insomnia or hypersomnia (found in nearly 90%)
3. Psychomotor retardation or agitation
4. Fatigue or loss of energy (found in 78%)
5. Feelings of guilt or worthlessness
6. Reduced ability to think or concentrate
7. Recurrent thoughts of death or suicide

These symptoms are accompanied by significant distress or impairment in functioning. Although depression usually is not difficult to identify, irritability sometimes masks depression in children and adolescents. Somatic complaints also may deflect attention from depression but are frequently associated with depression, as are sexual difficulties, excessive worry and ruminating, and problems of substance use.

A major depressive disorder consists of one or more major depressive episodes. In diagnosing a major depressive disorder, clinicians must make determinations related to the following eight factors:

1. *Severity:* Mild, moderate, severe, in partial remission, or in full remission (no symptoms for two months or longer).
2. *Presence of psychotic features:* Mood-congruent (consistent with the depressive attitudes), mood-incongruent, or none. (Psychotic features are found in 10% to 35% of people with major depressive disorder, at equal rates in men and women; Wilhelm, 2006.)
3. *Chronicity:* Persistent depression for at least two years.
4. *Presence of melancholic features:* Depression of endogenous or biochemical origin suggested by loss of interest or pleasure, lack of reactivity to pleasurable events, and at least three of the following symptoms: (1) characteristically different quality of depression from that associated with a bereavement, (2) worsening of symptoms in the morning, (3) awakening typically at least two hours before usual time, (4) experience of psychomotor retardation or agitation, (5) significant weight loss or loss of appetite, (6) unwarranted guilt, (7) flat rather than reactive mood, (8) good response to medication, (9) lack of a clear precipitant, and (10) absence of a personality disorder. Depression with melancholic features has a stronger genetic link than other forms of depression.
5. *Presence of atypical features:* Atypical depression improves in response to actual or anticipated positive events and is accompanied by at least two of the following characteristics: (1) weight gain or increase in appetite, (2) sleeping at least 10 hours a day, (3) heavy feelings in arms or legs, and (4) a prolonged pattern of sensitivity to rejection that is severe enough to cause impairment.
6. *Presence of postpartum onset:* Begins within four weeks of giving birth. Postpartum depression is often accompanied by high anxiety, mood lability, and an increased rate of obsessional thoughts, often focused on the baby's well-being (Somerset et al., 2006). The illness has a 30% to 50% likelihood of recurrence with subsequent births (American Psychiatric Association, 2000).
7. *Presence of full interepisode recovery:* Greater likelihood of recurrence and less likelihood of good response to

treatment are associated with the absence of complete recovery between multiple depressive episodes. The pattern of multiple depressive episodes without full interepisode recovery often reflects an underlying dysthymic disorder, discussed later in this chapter.

8. *Presence of seasonal pattern:* Characterized by depression, usually of moderate severity, that begins at the same time each year for at least two years. Episodes of this nature outnumber any other type of depression the person has experienced.

Typical Client Characteristics

Symptoms of a major depressive disorder usually begin with dysphoria and anxiety and develop over several days or weeks, although the onset may be sudden and may closely follow a loss or other stressor. Without treatment, this disorder typically runs its course in about six months to one year, but residual symptoms can be present for two years or more, reflecting a chronic disorder. Overall impairment during episodes is typical and may be so severe as to prevent even minimal functioning. Constant feelings of lethargy and hopelessness may be present, and people typically have to struggle to perform daily routines or even to get dressed in the morning. Recurrence is a strong possibility with this disorder, and its likelihood increases with each subsequent recurrence.

Women have a 1.5 to 3 times higher prevalence rate of depression than men (Kessler, 2006). The rate of depression in women is so high that the World Health Organization estimates that major depression is the leading cause of disease-related disability among women internationally. It is also the leading cause of disability in the U.S. for men and women age 14 to 44 (Üstün, Ayuso-Mateos, Chatterji, Mathers, & Murray, 2004).

People with major depressive disorder typically have other emotional and family problems, including a family history of depression and alcohol misuse (Wilhelm, 2006). This relationship seems to hold true for women more than for men. At least 25% of people with major depressive disorder have a preexisting dysthymic disorder (a long-standing mild to moderate depression), a combination that is sometimes referred to as double depression. They also frequently have coexisting disorders, notably substance-related disorders, eating disorders, anxiety disorders, and personality disorders. Children with major depressive disorder are particularly likely to have a coexisting mental disorder. Overlap of depression and medical conditions is also high, as in Parkinson's disease, multiple sclerosis, epilepsy, dementia, cancer, metabolic illnesses, and other physical conditions (Dozois & Dobson, 2002). Clients beginning treatment for depression should also be referred for a physical examination. (Additional information on depression in children and adolescents is provided in Chapter 2.)

Several studies have found an association among cognitive thought patterns, stressful life events, and incidence of major depressive disorder and suggest that the combination of a stressor and a depression-prone personality has a high correlation with the onset of a major depressive disorder. Stressors involving an interpersonal loss are particularly likely to trigger a major depressive episode. Clinicians should bear in mind that drugs (both prescribed and street drugs) and alcohol also can precipitate depressive symptoms.

Girgus and Nolen-Hoeksema (2006) report that women who experience major depressive episodes have a sense of hopelessness, pessimism, and failure, and tend to be self- critical and vulnerable. Seligman (1990) and others have found that people experiencing depression are more likely to attribute their symptoms to negative life events rather than to their own internal cognitions. People who ruminate about their own behavior have more depressive symptoms. Indeed, reflection and brooding tend to increase depression because rumination is more likely to be focused on negative thoughts. People with depression also tend to be less successful at problem solving, to have distorted negative interpretations of events, and to amplify their negative emotions. Many studies confirm a connection between severe depression and a preexisting personality pattern that includes dependence, need for approval, anxiety, dysfunctional thinking, neuroticism, and a weak self-image (Widiger, Mullins-Sweatt, & Anderson, 2006).

Trauma has also been found to contribute to a vulnerability to depression across the life span. Traumatic events occurring early in life can alter neurobiological stress responses and increase susceptibility to major depressive disorder (Penza, Heim, & Nemeroff, 2006). Physical, sexual, and emotional abuse; accidents; physical illness; surgery; parental loss or separation; an unstable family life; inadequate parental care (perhaps due to the parent's own mental or physical illness); family violence; rejecting or inconsistent parenting; lack of family warmth; and insecure attachment can all contribute to the development of major depressive disorder. Substance misuse, comorbid mental disorders, and suicide attempts have also been shown to increase as a result of these factors.

Preferred Therapist Characteristics

As discussed in depth earlier, therapists most likely to be effective in treating people with major depressive disorder are those who are structured, focused on the present, and able to attend to interpersonal issues and deficits. They can establish clear and realistic goals with clients and encourage optimism and a higher level of activity.

Intervention Strategies

Several approaches to treatment have been found to improve prognosis for depression. Clinicians often begin treating depression with psychotherapy alone, with the addition of medication if improvement is not noted after several months of psychotherapeutic treatment. Although medication seems to act more quickly on symptoms than psychotherapy does, it still may require three to five weeks for a therapeutic response, and the effects of the medication are generally not as enduring unless it is continued. Clients also tend not to be as accepting of medication as they are of psychotherapy. Given the low rate of medication compliance, one goal of psychotherapy may be to address problems related to medication compliance. Future research should focus on which types of treatment will work best with particular clients and their specific symptoms and needs.

Psychotherapy   Many studies, including two meta-analytic reviews, have demonstrated that cognitive-behavioral therapy and interpersonal therapy are likely to have a significant and relatively rapid impact on the symptoms of major depressive disorder (Craighead et al., 2007). Treatment of both initial and residual symptoms through CBT, either alone or in combination with medication, has been associated with a reduced rate of recurrence (Craighead et al., 2007). Those with a low level of social dysfunction responded better to interpersonal psychotherapy than to other treatments. Poor response to IPT is seen in people with co-occurring panic disorder, cognitive dysfunction, and personality disorders.

Cognitive-behavioral therapy has demonstrated a slight but not usually significant superiority to interpersonal therapy in the treatment of major depressive disorder, and both approaches have demonstrated a slight superiority over treatment by medication alone. Good results have been obtained in as few as eight sessions, but at least 16 sessions seem indicated for the treatment of severe depression.

Cognitive and Cognitive-Behavioral Therapy. Cognitive-behavioral therapy and cognitive therapy are the most extensively evaluated forms of psychotherapy for depression. It remains unclear whether cognitive therapy alone is sufficient in the treatment of depression. However, some studies have found the combination of medication and CBT to be more effective than either intervention alone (Young et al., 2008). In addition, the medication-only group had a higher dropout rate. Cognitive therapy may be more successful with some types of clients than with others. Cognitive-behavioral therapy was found to be particularly effective with young people, with 70% responding well (Kaslow & Thompson, 1998; Reinecke, Ryan, & DuBois, 1998).

A meta-analysis of all the clinical trials for depression conducted between 1977 and 1996 concluded that cognitive therapy was superior to antidepressant medication and a variety of other psychotherapies in the treatment of mild or moderate depression (Gloaguen, Cottraux, Cucherat, & Blackburn, 1998). CBT was found to be about equal to behavior therapy. Cognitive-behavioral therapy also appears to provide some protective effect against depression recurrence, as CBT's maintenance effects at 1-year posttreatment were equal to or superior to 1 year of antidepressant medication and clearly superior to short-term (16-week) medication treatment (Craighead et al., 2007). CBT has been shown to reduce both symptoms of depression and relapse rates, after medication management has ended (Young et al., 2008).

Interpersonal Psychotherapy. Interpersonal psychotherapy (IPT), based on the work of Harry Stack Sullivan and the psychodynamic therapists, and developed by Klerman, Weissman, Rounsaville, and Chevron (1984), has been empirically validated as effective in the treatment of severe depression as well as its milder forms (Craighead et al., 2007). Klerman and his colleagues describe IPT as "a focused, short-term, time-limited therapy that emphasizes the current interpersonal relations of the depressed patient while recognizing the role of genetic, biochemical, developmental, and personality factors in causation and vulnerability to depression" (p. 5).

In the IPT model, depression is viewed as having three components: symptom function, social and interpersonal relations, and personality and character problems (Mufson, Dorta, Moreau, & Weissman, 2004). IPT focuses on the first two components while taking account of the third in the formulation of interventions. Proponents of IPT hold that four problem areas play key roles in depression: abnormal grief, nonreciprocal role expectations in significant relationships, role transitions (such as retirement or divorce), and interpersonal deficits (Bleiberg & Markowitz, 2008).

The IPT model has developed strategies for dealing with each of these focal problem areas and matches treatment to clients' concerns. In general, IPT concentrates on the clients' history of significant relationships, the quality and patterns of the clients' interactions, the clients' cognitions about themselves and their relationships, and the associated emotions. Clients are helped to increase optimism and acceptance, develop strengths and coping mechanisms, obtain relevant information on depression, and enhance their competence. IPT differs from the cognitive-behavioral approaches in that it uses little homework and places less emphasis on planning actions and assessing progress; it places more emphasis on insight, relationships, and clarification of patterns. Through the use of genuine process comments and countertransference, the therapist helps the client to have a corrective emotional experience (Teyber & McClure, 2011).

Research indicates that IPT is as effective as antidepressant medication in the reduction of acute depression in women, whereas other psychodynamic therapies have not been found to be as effective (Hollon, 2000; Sinha & Rush, 2006). In recent years, IPT has been tailored for treatment of subpopulations of people with mood disorders including: postpartum depression, dysthymia, bipolar depression, depressed adolescents, and the elderly (Bleiberg & Markowitz, 2008; Teyber & McClure, 2011). Interested readers are referred to Weissman, Markowitz, and Klerman (2000) and Teyber and McClure (2011), for a more extensive review of IPT.

Emerging Therapies in the Treatment of Depression A number of other treatments for depression show promise. Following are a few of these new treatment approaches:

> *Behavioral activation therapy.* This brief, structured treatment is an outgrowth of cognitive-behavioral therapy, although behavioral activation focuses specifically on behavior activation without requiring cognitive change. By focusing on problem solving, long-term change, and completion of goals, behavioral activation helps people with depression to overcome the urge to escape or engage in avoidance behaviors such as alcohol use or other behaviors that help them forget about their problems. Scheduling daily activities and engaging in pleasurable behaviors also helps to improve self-esteem, increase activity level, and reduce rumination.
>
> Behavior activation therapy has received empirical support for the treatment of

depression (Dimidjian, Martell, Addis, & Herman-Dunn, 2008; Manos, Kanter, & Busch, 2010). One study indicates that behavior activation therapy is as effective as medication and slightly better than cognitive therapy in relieving moderate to severe depression. Other studies show the effects of behavior activation treatment to be as enduring as CBT and more enduring than medication (Dimidjian et al., 2006; Dobson et al., 2008; Hollon, Stewart & Strunk, 2006). Results of a meta-analysis conclude that behavioral activation "may be considered a well-established and advantageous alternative to other treatments for depression" (Mazzucchelli, Kane, & Rees, 2009, p. 383).

> *Mindfulness.* Mindfulness-based cognitive therapy is based on the work of Jon Kabat-Zinn (1990) who developed mindfulness-based stress-reduction (MBSR) for chronically ill patients. This intervention is designed to prevent future recurrence of depression in people who have recovered from an episode of depression. Rather than asking people to change their cognitions, mindfulness-based therapy helps people become aware of their thoughts, feelings, and bodily sensations and learn to accept them without judgment. By viewing thoughts as merely thoughts, and not some directive that needs to be acted on or a faulty cognition that needs to be changed, people can become mindful of the thought in the moment and then let it pass. Segal, Williams, and Teasdale (2002) developed a detailed treatment manual for mindfulness-based cognitive therapy. Initial research shows promise for the use of mindfulness therapy in the prevention of recurrent

depressive episodes, but more empirical validation is needed (Carmody, Baer, Lykins, & Olendzki, 2009; Godfrin & van Heeringen, 2010; Ma & Teasdale, 2004; Teasdale et al., 2000).

Medication   Medication, of course, is often used for severe or treatment-resistant depression, although 30% to 50% of people with non-psychotic major depression do not respond to antidepressant medication (Keitner et al., 2009). Moreover, problems associated with medication include clients' reluctance to take medication, potential suicidal ideation when antidepressant treatment is first implemented, side effects, incomplete remission of symptoms, and high rates of recurrence when the medication is discontinued (Ohayon & Schatzberg, 2002). Seventy-five percent of people in the United States who are treated for depression receive antidepressant medication (Kluger, 2003). However, nearly one third of the people who are prescribed medication take it for less than 30 days (Marecek, 2006). Therefore, the clinician should carefully consider whether a client should be referred for medication and, if so, should closely monitor its impact.

A combination of psychotherapy and medication could be preferable to either treatment method alone in the treatment of outpatients with major depressive disorder, although studies are lacking on combined treatment. While medication and therapy both have a place in the treatment of depression, psychotherapy has been found to provide protection against relapse that medication alone cannot provide (Imel, Malterer, McKay, & Wampold, 2008; Maina, Rosso, & Bogetto, 2009).

The particular nature of the depression, however, and its accompanying symptoms suggest whether medication is likely to be helpful and, if so, which medication. The SSRIs—fluoxetine (Prozac), paroxetine (Paxil),

sertraline (Zoloft), citalopram (Celexa), escatilopram (Lexapro), and fluvoxamine (Luvox)—work by blocking the reuptake of serotonin. Each SSRI has its own profile and side effects, which may include nervousness, sexual dysfunction, weight gain, nausea, diarrhea, and insomnia. Newer atypical antidepressants, such as venlafaxine (Effexor), have been found to be more effective in cases of treatment-resistant depression and the endogenous or melancholic subtype of major depressive disorder (Nemeroff & Schatzberg, 2007).

Differences of efficacy, tolerability of side effects, exclusion of women of childbearing years from clinical trials (even though they have the highest rate of unipolar depression), and lack of information on comorbid medical disorders have all muddied the waters in research on the effectiveness of psychopharmacology for the treatment of mood disorders.

Medication is generally indicated if depression is severe, recurrent, or chronic; if psychosis is present; and if psychotherapy alone has not helped (Dozois & Dobson, 2002; Nemeroff & Schatzberg, 2007).

Since the 1970s, the practice of polypharmacy—the concurrent use of multiple psychotropic medications—for the treatment of unipolar depression has increased from 3.3% in the 1970s to 43.8% in the early 1990s (Glezer, Byatt, Cook, & Rothschild, 2009). The increasing availability of psychotropic drugs has increased the number of medication options for people with depression. However, efficacy of polypharmacy for unipolar depression has not been well established, and the potential for increased risks, including a greater number of drug-drug interactions, decreased treatment compliance, and increased side effects, have been found (Glezer et al., 2009). The American Psychiatric Association guidelines recommend monotherapy for unipolar depression beginning with an SSRI for a full treatment trial before switching to another antidepressant or a more complicated treatment regimen. To date, no studies have shown clear benefits of atypical antipsychotic use in the treatment of nonpsychotic depression and the growing practice is not without controversy. In addition to the potential for serious side effects, including tardive dyskinesia, metabolic syndrome, and severe weight gain, no long-term safety or efficacy data is available (Keitner et al., 2009). The risk benefit ratio must be considered. To date, aripiprazole (Abilify) is the only atypical antipsychotic with FDA approval for this type of use (Philip, Carpenter, Tyrka, & Price, 2009).

Day Treatment Programs Although the hospital may sometimes be the initial setting for treating people with severe depression, outpatient day treatment programs and residential crisis centers are more cost effective, and seem to achieve slightly better short- and long-term outcomes for people whose depressions warrant close supervision, usually because they are suicidal, psychotic, or immobilized by depression (Sledge et al., 1996).

Electroconvulsive Therapy Electroconvulsive therapy (ECT) is sometimes used to treat severe symptoms of major depressive disorder, particularly in those who present with psychosis or immediate suicide risk (Yatham, Kusumakar, & Kutcher, 2002). The efficacy rate of ECT is reported to range from 50% to 100% in these cases. A meta-analysis of 15 controlled studies that compared ECT with other treatments for depression found that a full course of ECT was more effective than medication or simulated ECT (Kho, van Vresswijk, Simpson, & Zwinderman, 2003). ECT has been found to be equally effective in the treatment of unipolar and bipolar depression (Bailine et al., 2010; Medda et al., 2009).

Criteria for the use of ECT include a need for rapid symptom reduction, a history of good response to ECT, the client's preference for ECT, and the inappropriateness or ineffectiveness of medication or other treatment approaches. Although ECT has been greatly improved in recent years, both ECT and antidepressant medication have side effects, and their risks need to be weighed against their possible benefits.

Other Treatments for Depression A growing number of alternative forms of treatment have been found to provide some benefit in the treatment of depression. Exercise, in particular, has received much positive press in recent years and the latest research upholds its positive effects on mood. Similarly, light therapy, transcranial magnetic stimulation, and vagus nerve stimulation have been proposed for the treatment of mood disorders. Empirical research is limited, so readers should obtain more information and be cautious before proceeding with these treatment options.

Exercise therapy. Exercise therapy holds much promise in the treatment of this disorder, specifically in improving mood, reducing symptoms of depression, and possibly leading to remission of major depression in older adults (Blumenthal et al., 2007; Barbour, Edenfield, & Blumenthal, 2007). Much research has revealed the beneficial effects of exercise in the treatment of depression that occurs in conjunction with chronic health problems such as hypertension, diabetes, and cardiovascular disease.

The health benefits of exercise can contribute to resilience and may protect individuals who are at greater genetic risk for developing major depressive disorder (Matta, Thompson, & Gotlib, 2010). Although the evidence of the positive effect of exercise on depression is growing, its clinical use as an adjunct to established treatment approaches such as psychotherapy and psychopharmacology is still in its infancy. More research is needed on the optimal type, amount, and intensity of exercise that could be beneficial for people with major depressive disorder.

Light therapy. Daily light therapy for at least four weeks has been shown to significantly reduce symptoms in seasonally related major depressive disorder, although some people with winter recurrences of depression benefit more from a combination of light therapy and medication or cognitive therapy (Rosenthal, 2006). Bright light therapy has recently been shown to be effective in treating nonseasonal depression, as well as seasonal affective disorder (Golden et al., 2005).

Transcranial magnetic stimulation (TMS), a noninvasive procedure that generates short magnetic pulses through a person's scalp, has shown some promise in treating medication-resistant depression. The outpatient procedure lasts 30 to 40 minutes and is usually repeated daily for four to six weeks. It does not require anesthesia or sedation and has been marketed as a treatment option for those who cannot tolerate medication or its side effects, and as an alternative to electroconvulsive therapy. Studies on the effectiveness of repetitive TMS are limited (Janicak et al., 2008). TMS received clearance from the FDA in 2008.

Vagus nerve stimulation (VNS therapy) also has been approved by the FDA as an intervention for people who suffer from severe, treatment-resistant depression. In VNS, a device implanted into the chest sends electrical pulses to the vagus nerve in the neck, which in turn activates areas of the brain that lead to an improvement in mood. Treatment effectiveness has varied in initial studies, and more empirical data is needed (Feder, 2006).

Prognosis

The prognosis for rapid symptom relief of major depressive disorder through medication, psychotherapy, or both is good: Nearly 70% of people treated for major depressive disorder experience remission of their symptoms within one year (Young et al., 2008). A good prognosis has been found to be positively associated with the number and supportiveness of social resources, with mild to moderate depression, with increased learned resourcefulness, and for those with intact partner relationships (Young et al., 2008).

For many people, recurrence of depression continues to be a problem. Indeed, as many as 50% will experience a relapse within 10 years. Those who experience two episodes will have a 90% chance of having a third episode (Young et al., 2008). Those treated with psychotherapy seem to do far better in terms of relapse than those treated with medication alone. Rates of recurrence are highest during the first four to six months after recovery and have a negative correlation with response to treatment. In other words, those people who have had a rapid and complete response to treatment are the ones least likely to have a recurrence.

Overall, then, the prognosis for recovery from a given episode of a major depressive disorder is good, but many factors contribute to a high likelihood of relapse. A poorer long-term prognosis exists for those whose depression is accompanied by psychotic features. A recurrence of depression for these people is likely to also include psychosis. The prognosis is generally also worse for people with accompanying pervasive maladjustment. The prognosis for major depressive disorder is worsened by the presence of a coexisting general medical condition, by substance misuse, or by the presence of long-standing depression prior to treatment. Those with co-occurring personality disorders tend to have poor treatment responses to every treatment intervention except CBT (Craighead et al., 2007). The elderly also have a particularly high rate of relapse.

Extended treatment and follow-up can improve prognosis. For example, treatment may comprise 6 to 18 weeks of intensive psychotherapy, 4 to 9 months of less intensive relapse prevention, and maintenance and follow-up that may continue for years. Teaching people to recognize the early symptoms of depression, to reduce and manage stress, to increase the level of mastery and pleasure in their lives, and to make good use of support systems is also likely to reduce rates of recurrence.

DYSTHYMIC DISORDER

People with dysthymic disorder may experience mild to moderate impairment or limitations that are due to their depression but overall tend to maintain an acceptable level of social and occupational functioning. Sometimes people with this disorder grow so accustomed to their symptoms that they assume that the way they are feeling is normal; consequently, only a small percentage of people with this disorder seek treatment.

Description of the Disorder

Dysthymic disorder is characterized by the presence of chronic depression, usually mild to moderate in severity, on most days for at least two years. (In children and adolescents, a minimum duration of one year is required for diagnosis, and the primary manifestation of the disorder may be irritability rather than depression.) According to the *DSM-IV-TR*, at least two of the following six symptoms also are present:

1. Poor appetite or overeating
2. Insomnia or hypersomnia
3. Low energy or fatigue
4. Low self-esteem

5. Difficulty in concentrating or decision making
6. A sense of hopelessness

Other common symptoms of dysthymic disorder include reduced activity and accomplishment, guilt and self-doubts, withdrawal from social and other activities, and vegetative symptoms (disturbances in eating, sleeping, and weight). Suicidal ideation and thoughts of death may be present but are less common in people with dysthymic disorder than in those with major depressive disorder.

People diagnosed with dysthymic disorder have not had manic or hypomanic episodes, and their symptoms are not due to substance use. They do manifest some distress or impairment as a result of their symptoms, but typically not as much as people diagnosed with major depressive disorder.

In establishing the diagnosis, the clinician also makes the following determinations about the disorder:

- *Age of onset:* Most common periods of onset include late adolescence or early adulthood, with 50% having an onset before age 21 (Butcher et al., 2006).
- *Presence of atypical features:* Described in the section on major depressive disorder.

Pettit and Joiner (2006) report that the average length of a dysthymic episode is 10 years, but it can persist for 20 years or more. People often only seek treatment for relief of related symptoms, such as a change in weight or a failure to achieve success in their careers. The possibility has been raised that dysthymic disorder is really a personality disorder rather than a mood disorder and is a pervasive, enduring, and potentially lifelong way of dealing with the world.

Dysthymic disorder is common, particularly among females. Lifetime prevalence rates are between 2.5% and 6% (Kessler, Berglund, et al., 2005). Among people 60 years of age and older, approximately 18% have been found to meet the criteria for this disorder, and in this group, the disorder is more common in men than in women by a 2:1 ratio (Kessler, 2006a). Even among those who seem to recover from dysthymic disorder, nearly half may relapse within two years.

Typical Client Characteristics

Some researchers theorize that an episode of depression leaves a person vulnerable to future episodes, due to pessimism, negativity, lack of resilience, and chronic environmental stressors. One study showed that negative cognitive patterns are easily activated, and depression may be erosive. Men with dysthymic disorder are particularly likely to present with accompanying situational problems, usually in the areas of work or family.

Prior, comorbid, or familial mental disorders are common in people with dysthymic disorder. A coexisting or previous childhood mental disorder (such as conduct disorder, ADHD, or learning disorder) is often reported, as is a family history of depression. Dysthymic disorder frequently is accompanied by a personality disorder or by another physical or mental disorder. Anxiety, eating, and substance use disorders are particularly common. People with dysthymic disorder are also at considerably elevated risk for development of a subsequent major depressive disorder, and therapists should be alert to that possibility.

Personality patterns of people with dysthymic disorder tend to be similar to those of people with major depressive disorder. They typically are low in self-esteem and low in extroversion; they feel helpless and vulnerable, ruminate on interpersonal relations, and have difficulty handling stressful events or social

disappointments (Pettit & Joiner, 2006). Underlying hostility and conflict avoidance may be present, as well as dependence and a low tolerance for frustration. People with dysthymic disorder may have a long-standing pattern of avoiding their difficulties by fleeing into overwork or excessive activity. Pettit and Joiner note that avoidance of conflict gradually results in losses of self-esteem, self-efficacy, and the possibility of obtaining relationships or jobs. People with dysthymic disorder are often divorced or separated and likely to come from lower socioeconomic groups. Somatic and physiological complaints (such as eating and sleeping problems) are common and may be the presenting problem when treatment is sought. Children with this disorder, like those with major depressive disorder, often are irritable and complaining.

In some ways, people with dysthymic disorder present more of a challenge to the therapist than do people with major depressive disorder. People with dysthymic disorder have been depressed for so long that they may not know how to be anything but depressed, and they may be resistant to and apprehensive about change. Secondary gains associated with their depression, such as attention and reduced demands, may reinforce their sad, helpless stance, and they may hesitate to relinquish those gains without the assurance of continuing rewards and attention. These clients also present some suicide risk. Although their depression is not as severe as in a major depressive disorder, they do have the resourcefulness and the energy to make a suicide attempt, whereas a severely depressed client may be too incapacitated to attempt suicide.

Preferred Therapist Characteristics

The type of therapist recommended for people diagnosed with dysthymic disorder is quite similar to the type of therapist recommended for people with major depressive disorder. The establishment and maintenance of a strong working alliance are important in motivating people to continue to comply with treatment. The therapist working with a person who has dysthymic disorder can be somewhat less supportive and more confrontational, however, and can expect clients to complete more extra-therapeutic tasks because these people generally are less impaired and more resilient than those with major depressive or bipolar disorders.

Intervention Strategies

The psychotherapeutic approaches to treating major depressive disorder discussed earlier in this chapter also are recommended for the treatment of dysthymic disorder. These include cognitive, cognitive-behavioral, and interpersonal therapy, particularly in combination with the teaching of social skills and such related skills as assertiveness and decision making. Promoting the development of coping skills to address the client's sense of hopelessness and helplessness can also make a positive difference.

Although research specific to the treatment of dysthymic disorder is sparse, some information on its treatment is available. In a 3-year follow-up study of people with dysthymia, Rhebergen and colleagues (2010) found chronicity and length of the disorder were related to slower progress and continuation of some symptoms after recovery had been achieved. Chronic dysthymia was also found to be related to poorer social and physical functioning 3 years after recovery from dysthymia. Thus, any treatment for this chronic disorder will need to address thought processes and negative thinking that persists. Cognitive therapy, such as schema therapy, to address the underlying dysfunctional schemas that people live by may be an appropriate treatment for dysthymia (Young et al., 2008).

Seligman's positive psychology has been shown to reduce depression in people who are mildly depressed (Seligman, Steen, Park, & Peterson, 2005). Through positive interventions such as gratitude visits, keeping a positive journal, and identifying signature strengths and applying them in new ways, clients showed reduced scores on the Beck Depression Inventory and increased scores on the Steen Happiness Index (SHI). Although positive psychology has been shown to be effective in a limited sampling of mildly depressed people, additional research is necessary to determine the effectiveness of positive interventions on more serious depressive disorders. Nevertheless, therapists should assess a client's strengths and coping skills and incorporate these strengths into counseling objectives and treatment goals as part of overall strength-based interventions (Smith, 2006).

Gillies (2001) indicates that interpersonal therapy (IPT) is as effective for dysthymia as for major depressive disorder. IPT has also been shown to be effective in treating double depression (the combination of major depressive disorder and dysthymic disorder). Supportive therapy, positive psychology, and group therapy seem to play a greater role in the treatment of dysthymic disorder than in major depressive disorder. People with dysthymic disorder have more energy and a better level of functioning, so they are more able to engage and participate in group therapy and make use of supportive interventions. For older adults, interventions that focus on problems and solutions are more likely to be accepted than insight-oriented therapies (Karel, Ogland-Hand, & Gatz, 2002).

People who are depressed often have difficulties in their relationships. Craighead and colleagues (2007) report that behavioral marital therapy (BMT) can be as effective as CBT in relieving symptoms of depression and marital distress. Similarly, behavior therapy has empirical validation in the treatment of severe depressive disorders. People who are depressed often have partners with emotional disorders, a finding that raises the question of whether difficult marriages contribute to the incidence of depression or whether people who are depressed select partners with similar traits. Regardless of the answer, family counseling in combination with individual therapy is indicated for many people with dysthymic disorder, as well as for people with other forms of depression.

Although people with dysthymic disorder have milder symptoms than people with major depressive disorder, successful treatment of dysthymic disorder often takes longer than treatment of shorter and more severe depressive disorders. People with dysthymic disorder have been depressed for so long that their impaired functioning may have had a profound impact on many areas of their lives, including work, relationships, and leisure activities, so they may need to restructure and repair their lives in these areas. Moreover, their long-standing depression probably has become so deeply entrenched that they lack the coping skills to overcome it on their own. Beck (2005) found that going over treatment goals and prioritizing them can often help when clients get stuck or fail to make progress. When therapists give clients the choice of whether to discuss skill development in session or to work on it outside of session, clients often report a greater sense of control and investment in the process. Some basic education and development may need to take place before the symptoms of the depression will remit.

Medication is often used in treatment of dysthymic disorder, as it is in treatment of major depressive disorder. However, the risk is high that clients will discontinue antidepressant treatment early on (Olfson, Marcus, Tedeschi, & Wan, 2006). One advantage of combining psychotherapy and medication is to afford an opportunity to educate clients on the importance of medication compliance and to provide continued encouragement toward that end. Current research is investigating the place of medication in the treatment of dysthymic disorder. SSRIs, in particular, have demonstrated effectiveness in the treatment of this disorder (Nemeroff & Schatzberg, 2007). For example, sertraline (Zoloft) has shown effectiveness in reducing symptoms, and one study showed paroxetine (Paxil) to be more effective than problem-solving psychotherapy in treating dysthymia (Williams, Barrett, & Oxman, 2000).

Despite the recent increased use of pharmacotherapy in combination with psychotherapy to treat dysthymic disorder, psychotherapy is still central because of the importance of improving overall functioning, promoting social and coping skills, and establishing a rewarding lifestyle. Especially given the research that shows that most people stop antidepressant medication in the first 30 days and that fewer than 30% continue medication beyond 90 days, combining talk therapy with pharmacotherapy seems to be prudent (Olfson et al., 2006).

Therapists working with people with dysthymic disorder seem to have a broader range of therapeutic options from which to choose than do therapists working with more severely depressed people. In general, psychotherapy aimed at treating dysthymic disorder is most effective if it is moderately supportive, moderately structured and directive, focused on cognitions and behavior more than on affect, and composed of an array of educational and psychotherapeutic interventions designed to modify cognitions, increase activity, and improve self-esteem and interpersonal skills. Treatment will also probably pay some attention to the past, in an effort to elucidate repetitive and self-destructive patterns and clarify the dynamics that are perpetuating the depression.

Prognosis

The spontaneous remission rate from dysthymia is less than 10% per year (American Psychiatric Association, 2000). The remission rate improves with treatment. Viable goals for treatment of dysthymic disorder include relief of depression and associated anxiety, amelioration of somatic and physiological symptoms, increased optimism and sense of control, and improved social and occupational functioning. Without treatment, the prognosis for dysthymic disorder is poor. In general, people with dysthymic disorder who can recall a healthier way of functioning, who have some good interpersonal skills and support systems, who have maintained a reasonably rewarding lifestyle, and whose depression is not deeply entrenched are likely to respond well to treatment. For people who do not meet those criteria, for those who have had untreated dysthymia for an extended period of time, and for those with dysthymia in conjunction with depression (double depression), therapy may be long and difficult and perhaps unsuccessful. Setting limited goals and focusing on gains may help promote optimism in both the client and the therapist, even if a full recovery cannot be obtained.

DEPRESSIVE DISORDER NOT OTHERWISE SPECIFIED

As is true of most other categories of mental disorder listed in the *DSM-IV-TR*, a not otherwise specified (NOS) category is included at the end of the section on depression. This particular NOS category, however, unlike most others, is used often by clinicians because many manifestations of depression are not encompassed by the depressive disorders listed in the *DSM*. According to *DSM-IV-TR*, depressive disorder NOS is defined as a disorder with depressive features that do not meet the criteria for any other specific depressive disorder or adjustment disorder. This category can be used, for example, to describe a recurrent depression with episodes briefer than two weeks, premenstrual dysphoric disorder (depression associated with the menstrual cycle), depression occurring in the residual phase of a psychotic disorder, or a depression that is not severe enough to meet the criteria for major depressive disorder but is too brief for a diagnosis of dysthymic disorder. Treatment recommendations for the other types of depression provide the basis for determining the treatment of depressive disorder NOS, with treatment adapted to meet the needs of the particular client.

BIPOLAR DISORDERS

We now take a look at the bipolar disorders. Four types of bipolar disorder have been identified in the *DSM-IV-TR*:

1. Bipolar I disorder
2. Bipolar II disorder
3. Cyclothymic disorder (considered separately later in this chapter)
4. Bipolar disorder NOS

Each disorder will be considered individually.

Description of the Disorders

Bipolar disorders are highly complex mood disorders that are distinguished by episodes of dysfunctional mood, potentially including major depressive episodes, mild to moderate depressive episodes, manic episodes, hypomanic episodes, and mixed episodes, often separated by periods of relatively normal mood. Because of the complexity of bipolar disorders and the high incidence of co-occurring disorders, bipolar disorders are often misdiagnosed, although one study reports that people are much more likely than in the past to be diagnosed accurately (Jefferson, 2003). Greater awareness of this disorder and its many manifestations across a lifetime has improved diagnostic accuracy (Johnson & Fristad, 2008).

Bipolar I disorder, by definition, must include at least one manic episode reflecting an extremely elevated mood. It also may include episodes of major depression and of hypomania (an elevated mood that is less severe than a manic episode). Bipolar I disorder typically includes disturbances of mood, cognition, and behavior, and may include psychotic symptoms, although the disorder is not the result of a psychotic disorder, nor is it superimposed on a psychotic disorder. The nature of a person's first episode tends to reflect the nature of the person's dominant type of episode for the illness; that is, a person who has an initial episode of depression as part of a bipolar I disorder has a 90% likelihood of subsequent episodes of depression. In men, the first episode of this disorder is usually a manic one; in women, it is more likely to be a depressive episode (American Psychiatric Association, 2000).

Bipolar II disorder differs from bipolar I disorder primarily in its lack of any manic episodes. It includes at least one hypomanic episode of at least four day's duration, and at least one depressive episode and, like bipolar I disorder, causes considerable distress or impairment in functioning. Psychotic features are not often found in bipolar II disorder. Symptoms of bipolar II disorder can be confused with histrionic and borderline personality disorders; all three disorders include symptoms of irritation, affective instability, aggressiveness, and rage. But bipolar II is a mood disorder with hypomanic symptoms that last days. Care must be taken to distinguish between a mood disorder and a more chronic, persistent pattern of responses to environmental

cues which distinguishes a personality disorder. Additional discussion of differential diagnosis between bipolar disorder and borderline personality disorder is included in the discussion of personality disorders in Chapter 8.

Perugi, Ghaemi, and Akiskal (2006) estimate that as many as 90% of people being treated for bipolar disorders have the bipolar II subtype. Comorbidity between a bipolar disorder and borderline personality disorder is only 9%, the same as with other personality disorders (Paris, 2007).

Accurate diagnosis between the bipolar disorders is imperative so that appropriate treatment can be established. Distinguishing between bipolar I and bipolar II can present some problems for the clinician. In general, bipolar II is characterized by a shorter period of excitement and a longer depressive phase. A study by Judd and colleagues (2003) found that people with bipolar II disorder are depressed 93% of the time. The depressive episode of bipolar II disorder is more likely to include mixed states with agitation, irritability, and racing thoughts, which are particularly dangerous as these symptoms are the "main diagnositic substrate for occurrence of suicide" (Akiskal & Benazzi, 2006, p. 49). Additional distinctions between the two disorders include milder, if any, psychotic symptoms, fewer hospitalizations, increased episode frequency, and more frequent incidents of rapid cycling in people with bipolar II (Quinn, 2007). Some evidence suggests that bipolar II disorder is more debilitating than bipolar I and results in more family dysfunction and increased rates of suicide.

Risk of misdiagnosing either disorder as unipolar depression is high, especially if the first presentation is during the depressive phase of the disorder. Bipolar II disorder also has an increased frequency of co-occurring disorders which can alter the diagnostic landscape (Skeppar & Adolfson, 2006). Following is a brief description of manic, hypomanic, depressive, and mixed episodes.

Manic Episodes (Found Only in Bipolar I)

According to the *DSM*, a manic episode is a period of "abnormally and persistently elevated, expansive, or irritable mood" lasting at least one week (American Psychiatric Association, 2000, p. 357). At least three of the following seven symptoms accompany the elevated mood:

1. Grandiosity
2. Reduced need for sleep
3. Increased talkativeness
4. Racing thoughts
5. Distractibility
6. Increased activity
7. Excessive pleasure seeking, to a potentially self-destructive extent (for example, hypersexuality, excessive spending, or gambling)

dramatic emotions. Anger and aggression that occur when other people set limits are also common. Manic episodes frequently result in hypersexuality or promiscuous behavior, excessive spending or schemes that result in severe financial consequences, or delusions about the person's importance that may result in contacting public officials or in conflicts with the police. The judgment and impulse control of people experiencing a manic episode are poor, and they typically are hyperactive and distractible. Their speech tends to be loud, pressured, and intrusive. People experiencing manic episodes often have delusions or hallucinations (usually of a grandiose type), which may lead clinicians to misdiagnose them as having schizophrenia. The following is a description of one person whose experience typifies the manic phase of bipolar I disorder.

Evelyn R. is a 27-year-old White woman with a stable marriage and work history. During a manic episode, she slept little, staying up most of the night to make plans for her future, which was to include the purchase of several houses, and love affairs with many of her coworkers and acquaintances. When her startled husband objected, she informed him that she was in the prime of her life and that he should stay out of her way. A brief period of hospitalization was required to prevent Evelyn from destroying her marriage and spending all the couple's resources.

A manic episode, like an episode of major depression, is typically quite severe and causes impairment in social and occupational functioning. People experiencing this phase of bipolar I disorder tend to have grandiose thoughts and feel they are powerful and destined for great success. They have little insight into the potential risks of their behavior or into the feelings of others, and they may become hostile and threatening if challenged. Symptoms of mania include changes in thinking, appearance, behavior, and energy level, as well as impaired judgment and the expression of

Hypomanic Episodes

Hypomania, or partial mania, is similar to the symptoms of mania but without loss of reality testing, without psychosis (hallucinations and delusions), and without significantly impaired functioning (Oakley, 2005). These episodes resemble mild versions of manic episodes in terms of symptoms and accompanying mood. The symptoms of hypomania include increased energy, racing thoughts, less need for sleep, and more goal-directed behavior. Hypomanic episodes have a minimum duration of four days. Recognizing a hypomanic episode—which is, by definition, part of bipolar II disorder, and is also found in bipolar I—can be a challenge. Hypomania may not always present as a good mood, but may include anger and irritability. The therapist meeting initially with a person who is having a hypomanic episode may mistakenly think that the person is simply in a very good or very bad mood, but the mood's unremitting nature, its usual lack of a precipitant, the person's history of dysfunctional mood episodes, and engaging in behaviors that have negative consequences will distinguish a hypomanic episode from a normal mood.

Depression   Over the lifespan, people with bipolar disorder spend nearly half of their lives depressed, compared with only 10% of the time manic or hypomanic (Judd et al., 2003). The persistence of bipolar depression is worth noting, as it can be debilitating. The depressive phase of a bipolar disorder closely resembles the depression associated with a major depressive disorder, but with some differences. The depression associated with a bipolar disorder often entails less anger and somatizing and more oversleeping and psychomotor retardation. Episodes of bipolar depression also result in increased rates of suicide compared to major depressive disorder, an important distinction to note. Bipolar depression may include psychotic features, such as delusions and hallucinations.

Clinicians should be aware that bipolar and unipolar mood disorders with psychotic features are the most frequently occurring psychotic disorders, and are frequently misdiagnosed as schizophrenia (Baldessarini & Tondo, 2003).

The American Psychiatric Association guidelines on the management of bipolar disorders note that people with a bipolar I or II disorder who are experiencing a depressed mood are frequently misdiagnosed as having a unipolar major depressive disorder. As a result, they may receive inappropriate treatment (American Psychiatric Association, 2004a).

Episodes of mild to moderate depression are associated with cyclothymic disorder but not with bipolar I or bipolar II disorders. These episodes are discussed further in the section on cyclothymic disorder.

Mixed Episodes   Forty percent of people with bipolar disorders experience mixed episodes (Miklowitz, 2008a). In these episodes, the criteria for both a major depressive episode and a manic episode are met nearly every day for at least one week. During a depressive episode, talkativeness, distractedness, and racing thoughts can be considered to be symptoms of a mixed state. Depression with heightened sexual arousal can also occur in a mixed state (Quinn, 2007). Somatic agitation is often associated with increased suicide risk (Balázs et al., 2006).

Duration of Episodes   The average duration of an episode of dysfunctional mood is two and a half to four months, but may be as short as a few days. The depressive phase tends to be the longest, with an average duration of six to nine months. The manic phase has an average duration of two to six weeks. An average of 33 months elapses between episodes of dysfunctional mood, but five years or more may elapse between the first and the second episode, with the time between episodes becoming shorter and the episodes themselves becoming longer as they recur. Typically, the pattern of the episodes' duration and frequency stabilizes by the fourth or fifth episode. Episodes tend to end abruptly. Without treatment, people with bipolar disorders typically have 10 or more episodes over the course of their lives; the frequency of the episodes varies from 3 per year to one every 10 years.

Specifiers   In diagnosing bipolar I or II disorders, the clinician should indicate the nature and severity of the current episode and should list the appropriate specifiers, including:

- *For all four types of episodes.* Presence or absence of a seasonal pattern, psychosis, catatonic features, postpartum onset, rapid cycling, and interepisode recovery.
- *For depressive episodes.* Specify presence of melancholic features or atypical features (both discussed earlier).

An additional course descriptor for bipolar I and II disorders is determination of the presence of rapid cycling. Rapid cycling, or switching between depression and mania, is found in 13% to 20% of people with bipolar disorder (Miklowitz, 2006a) and is more frequent in females. Rapid cycling, by definition, includes four or more discrete episodes of depression, mania, hypomania, or a mixture of depression and mania (mixed episode) in a single year. Determining when one episode ends and another begins usually is difficult. Coryell (2002) notes that rapid cycling appears to be a transient state. Even so, this pattern is linked to increased dysfunction and to a poorer prognosis.

Prevalence   Lifetime prevalence rates for bipolar I and bipolar II disorders are 0.8% and 0.5%, respectively (American Psychiatric Association, 2000). Figures in the National Comorbidity Survey Replication (Kessler, Chiu, et al., 2005) indicate that 2.6% of the U.S. population has a bipolar disorder in a given year. Untreated, bipolar disorders carry a considerable risk of relapse and mortality. Statistics on the number of suicide attempts and completions indicate that as many as 50% of people with bipolar disorder attempt suicide, and nearly 20% complete it (Leahy, 2004). Although people with bipolar disorders are even more likely than people with major depressive disorder to require

hospitalization, or to die by suicide, fewer than one third ever receive treatment (Miklowitz & Craighead, 2007).

Both genders are equally represented among people with bipolar I disorder, but women are more likely than men to develop bipolar II disorder. Onset of a bipolar I disorder is usually earlier than for major depressive disorder, with more than half experiencing onset before the age of 30 (American Psychiatric Association, 2000). Onset may occur any time after age 5, although the incidence of bipolar I disorder peaks in the late teens and early twenties, and a first episode is unlikely before the age of 12 or after the age of 50.

Typical Client Characteristics

Bipolar I disorder is a highly heritable illness, more so than bipolar II or major depressive disorder (unipolar depression). Twin studies indicate a 65% to 75% concordance rate for monozygotic twins in comparison to 14% for dizygotic twins (Barnett & Smoller, 2009). Lifetime prevalence of mood disorders among family members of people with bipolar I disorder are 8 to 10 times higher than in the general population. Similarly, 50% of people with bipolar I disorder have at least one parent with a mood disorder (Sachs, 2004).

Both bipolar I and bipolar II disorders can be exacerbated or triggered by a stressful life event. Stressful family interaction patterns can exacerbate a preexisting biological predisposition toward bipolar disorder and lead to emotional dysregulation. Several studies have found that overactivity following positive life events and goal attainment can also lead to a manic episode (S. L. Johnson, 2004). Researchers theorize that the brains of people with bipolar disorder do not deactivate after an event, but instead continue on into euphoria and manic symptoms.

While experiencing hypomania, people typically are more goal-focused, productive, and cheerful, and have expansive moods. Such enthusiasm, however, is generally out of proportion to the event, and racing thoughts and flight of ideas that accompany hypomania can disrupt concentration. People in a hypomanic episode might be described as not being able to talk fast enough to keep up with their own thoughts. Irritability, being quick to find fault, and high energy may also be present. Hypomanic episodes often are missed in diagnosis, as many people who experience mild euphoria, greater productivity, and expansive moods are not likely to be troubled by them. However, as with mania, a greater risk of self-harm through injury or accident accompanies a hypomanic episode.

Kessler and colleagues (1999) found that bipolar I disorder was comorbid with at least one other disorder 100% of the time. Other commonly co-occurring disorders include impulse-control disorders, personality disorders, anxiety disorders, and other disorders related to affect regulation (Miklowitz, 2006a). Diagnosis of bipolar disorders can be complicated by the presence of comorbid disorders and is frequently misdiagnosed as a personality disorder. However, Miklowitz and others estimate that fewer than 28% of people with bipolar disorder meet the criteria for an Axis II personality disorder when they are in remission.

Bipolar disorder is the most likely of any Axis I disorder to be accompanied by a co-occurring substance-related disorder. Bipolar I co-occurs with substance abuse or dependence in 60% of cases; bipolar II, in 48% (Zarate & Tohen, 2002). Treatment of dual disorders often provides a challenge for clinicians, as people with the combination of the two disorders tend to have worse outcomes, higher rates of mixed mood episodes, greater suicidality, a shorter time to relapse, and a larger number of psychosocial difficulties. Dual diagnosis is addressed later in this chapter.

Zarate and Tohen (2002) note a 13% to 23% comorbidity rate of bipolar disorders and impulse-control disorders (pathological gambling, intermittent explosive disorder, kleptomania, pyromania, and trichotillomania), and these disorders often precede the onset of a bipolar disorder. People with bipolar disorder are also more likely to have other comorbid mood disorders, most often dysthymic, cyclothymic, or schizoaffective disorder. Many people later diagnosed with bipolar I disorder had premorbid cyclothymic disorder involving unstable but less severe mood changes. Not only do these co-occurring disorders complicate the diagnosis of bipolar disorder, but their treatment often exacerbates the symptoms of bipolar disorder. For example, stimulants used to treat ADHD can trigger a manic episode, or anxiolytics used to treat panic disorder can decrease inhibitions and increase impulsivity.

Adolescents with bipolar disorders tend to have interpersonal and academic problems and can be misdiagnosed as having the more common conduct disorder or ADHD. In a study of adolescents with bipolar I symptoms, as many as 57% had co-occurring ADHD. The overlap of symptoms of ADHD and bipolar disorder—such as racing thoughts, impulsivity, distractibility, poor insight, impaired judgment, excessive activity, and impaired attention—also make differential diagnosis difficult. Bipolar disorders and ADHD differ in that ADHD generally has an early onset (before age 7), is chronic rather than episodic, and does not involve elevated moods or psychotic features (Altman, 2004). ADHD, as well as conduct disorder and psychotic disorders, are all more likely to be comorbid with bipolar disorder than with unipolar depression. For a more complete discussion of differential diagnosis of childhood bipolar disorder, refer to Chapter 2.

One in three people with bipolar disorder has significant employment-related losses. Deficits in work-related functioning can continue 1 or even 2 years after a hospitalization due to a bipolar disorder (Miklowitz & Craighead, 2007). In fact, only 20% of people with bipolar disorder are able to continue to work at expected levels in the first 6 months following an episode, and more than 50% have employment-related difficulty for the following 5 years. Bipolar disorder is one of the top three disabilities in the United States, along with chronic pain disorder and back problems (Druss et al., 2009).

The disorder also takes a toll on partner and family relationships. Results of the National Comorbidity Survey Replication showed that 44.6% of people with bipolar disorder report having severe impairment in their relationships at home, and 50% have problems related to their social life as a result of their disorder (Druss et al., 2009). Criticism, high-expressed emotion, overprotectiveness, lack of problem-solving skills, and problems with intimacy are often present in families of people with bipolar disorders. Marital distress is reported at a higher rate in people with bipolar disorder than in the general population (Miklowitz & Craighead, 2007).

Medication nonadherence is an important issue for many people with bipolar disorder. Despite the risk of relapse and serious symptoms, as many as 50% of those in treatment discontinue their medications over time (Johnson & Fulford, 2008). Stigma, financial costs of the medication, debilitating and sometimes toxic side effects, and a nonbiological attribution of the disorder are the reasons most frequently given for medication noncompliance.

Assessment

Sachs (2004) discusses the importance of the therapist establishing a collaborative relationship with both clients and their psychiatrists to ensure that treatment goals include medication compliance. Medication compliance should be a goal of therapy for clients with bipolar disorder. Therapists should also be prepared to provide psychoeducation and family therapy or couples counseling as needed.

The Treatment Attitudes Questionnaire (TAQ; Johnson & Fulford, 2008) is a 44-item self-report measure of symptom awareness and attitudes toward treatment for bipolar disorder. Limited research is available on its value as a predictive measure for who will remain compliant, but the questionnaire can help clinicians address areas of concern and develop treatment plans.

Even though considerable progress has been made over the years in the diagnosis and treatment of bipolar disorders, accurate diagnosis is not always made on the first presentation, especially if the person presents with depression. Unless a history of manic episodes can be identified, the disorder probably will be misdiagnosed as a major depressive disorder rather than a bipolar disorder. The Structured Clinical Interview for the *DSM-IV* (SCID-I/P; First, Spitzer, Gibbon, & Williams, 2002) can be used to confirm a diagnosis of bipolar disorder.

Bipolar disorders are most easily diagnosed when people present with a sudden onset of severe mania lasting weeks or months (Oakley, 2005). When symptoms of mania are severe enough to induce psychosis, however, bipolar I disorder is frequently mistaken for schizophrenia. In general, psychosis that accompanies bipolar I disorder is mood-congruent. For example, a grandiose and expansive mood might be accompanied by grandiose hallucinations or delusions.

Sometimes accurate differential diagnosis can only be done longitudinally, after careful consideration of family history, chronology of symptoms, response to treatment, and functioning between episodes. A useful self-assessment tool is to develop a life chart that includes major life events overlaid with episodes of depression, mania, and psychosis. The chart can help clients to see the long-term impact of the disorder on their career, relationships, and social functioning (Gruber & Persons, 2010).

Hypomanic symptoms are not easily recognized, so the Hypomania Checklist 32 (HCL-32) may be given to clients to assess their symptoms, although the inventory requires more validation to determine whether it can accurately discriminate between subtypes of bipolar disorder. The need for assessment and management of suicide risk remains constant throughout treatment for bipolar disorder. Therapists must remain vigilant and familiarize themselves with the risk factors for suicide mentioned earlier in this chapter.

Preferred Therapist Characteristics

Keeping people with bipolar disorder engaged in treatment is a challenge. The therapeutic alliance plays an important role in the successful treatment of people with this disorder, just as it does in the treatment of those with depressive disorders.

Because of the chronic nature and frequent recurrence of symptoms, the primary role of the therapist who works with people with bipolar disorder is to "use the alliance as a mood stabilizer" (Havens & Ghaemi, 2005, p. 138) to provide one solid supportive relationship in which the person can trust and turn to, during manic times and during depression, with confidence and for support.

Research suggests that the quality of the alliance predicts better success in managing symptoms of mania (Strauss & Johnson, 2006). The strength of the alliance can help clients through the moments of clinical despair as well. Bipolar depression can result in a complete loss of hope

in the world, what Havens and Ghaemi call "an expected reaction that grows out of the experience of suffering for years from bipolar illness" (p. 138), and from the medications necessary for its treatment.

Intervention Strategies

STEP-BD, the largest overall clinical research of bipolar disorder was conducted between 1998 and 2005 and the resulting database has spawned more than 30 publications and 100s of articles on new research and treatment recommendations for bipolar disorder (Miklowitz, 2008a; Parikh, LeBlanc, & Ovanessian, 2010). STEP-BD included data from three major randomized controlled trials of medication, psychosocial interventions, and a combination of the two. The overall findings are legion and beyond the scope of this book. However, the following treatment intervention strategies are informed by what was learned from STEP-BD.

Medication management is the first line of treatment for bipolar disorders (American Psychiatric Association, 2004a). Mood stabilizers, however, work best for the treatment of mania, while psychotherapy seems to have a bigger impact on depression. Combination treatment, which combines psychotherapy and medication, seems to be more beneficial than medication alone in the treatment of bipolar disorder (Jones, 2004; Miklowitz, Otto, et al., 2007; Sachs, 2004, 2008).

The nature and severity of the episode of dysfunctional mood, as well as the accompanying impairment, will guide the specific choice of treatment. Co-occurring substance abuse is common and has a negative impact on treatment outcomes. A collaborative care model in which psychiatrist, therapist, and family interact to ensure the client's safety, provide assessment information, and begin treatment seems to be the best approach (Sachs, 2004). Miklowitz (2006a) describes three distinct phases of treatment for bipolar disorder—acute, stabilization, and maintenance:

1. *Acute phase.* This phase begins when the person meets the criteria for an episode (mania, hypomania, depression, or mixed) and treatment begins (Sachs, 2004). Bipolar symptoms, particularly those that are present during the manic phase, are sometimes so severe and so self-destructive that hospitalization is needed. The period of hospitalization is typically brief, lasting only until medication has had an opportunity to stabilize the client's mood.

   Providing therapy during the acute phase is likely to be very difficult, especially when symptoms of euphoria and grandiosity increase resistance to the idea that treatment is necessary. The flight of ideas and high activity levels of people in a manic episode make analysis and clarification of concerns all but impossible. If therapy is attempted during the manic phase, it will probably have to be very structured and concrete, involving short, frequent sessions focusing more on behavior and milieu than on introspection and exploration of affect.

2. *Stabilization phase.* A relapse prevention plan should be created when the client is stabilized. Timing is of utmost importance, as people who are experiencing a manic or hypomanic mood will have difficulty recognizing their crisis or moderating their euphoric and upbeat behavior. Miklowitz notes two predictors of rehospitalization for people with bipolar disorder: medication non-compliance and failure to recognize early signs of relapse. When clients are stabilized, work should begin on

helping them identify prodromal symptoms, list preventive measures, and create a written plan or contract that details the procedures to follow if relapse occurs. Indeed, because of the difficulty of treating people during the manic phase of a bipolar disorder, several authors have suggested that collaborative care contracts be created and signed when the person is between episodes. These contracts can be used to authorize treatment if the person develops manic symptoms at some future date. Such contracts identify behaviors that might indicate relapse, specify constructive behaviors, and give a family member (or therapist) permission to seek treatment on the client's behalf should such previous efforts fail (Sachs, 2004).

Much in the literature focuses on the importance of educating family members about bipolar disorder (Miklowitz, 2008a; Sachs, 2004). Especially when there is an acute onset, family members can be a stabilizing force in the person's life, overseeing medication compliance and monitoring safety plans. Separate education programs for family and partners of people with bipolar disorder can increase knowledge of resources and social supports, improve medication compliance, decrease family stress, and improve coping strategies.

During this phase, individual psychotherapy and family therapy can often help people maintain medication compliance, recover from the symptoms of their disorder, restore a normal mood, and start to establish a framework of structure and support. In communication enhancement therapy, family members learn active listening, positive expression of feelings, making positive requests for behavior change, and giving negative feedback. Other issues such as family or couples conflict, and high expressed emotion are also addressed in this phase of treatment (Miklowitz, 2008a). The stabilization phase ends when the client has recovered from the acute episode.

3. *Maintenance phase.* After people with bipolar disorders have moved into the maintenance phase of treatment, the focus turns to maintaining recovery and preventing another episode from occurring. Adjunct treatment to address family and relationship issues, as well as career and employment-related concerns, can begin. Sachs (2004) suggests that maintenance therapy should continue for at least one year following the first manic episode (and any subsequent episode). A history of three or more episodes would be an indication that long-term maintenance of bipolar disorder is needed.

Treatment during the normal or depressive phases of bipolar disorders generally can be very helpful if the guidelines discussed earlier for the treatment of depression are followed. Treatment usually will be more supportive and less confrontational than therapy for major depressive disorder, however, because medication is really the primary mode of treatment for bipolar I and II disorders. The relatively high level of functioning experienced by many people between episodes of a bipolar disorder suggests that less emphasis is needed on social skills, although educating people about the nature of their disorder and tools to prevent relapse is an important element of the treatment (Lam et al., 2003).

Now we turn to the specific components of combination treatment for bipolar disorder—

medication and psychosocial interventions. Other treatment options follow.

Medication   As mentioned earlier, medication is the primary mode of treatment for bipolar I and II disorders. Lithium has long been the standard treatment for bipolar disorders, and the response rates range from 60% to 80% (Delgado & Gelenberg, 2001). Lithium acts primarily on manic symptoms. However, lithium alone fails to produce a sustained remission (at least three years in duration) in approximately 75% of people with bipolar disorders, and the compliance rate for people with bipolar disorder who take lithium is worse than any other group of people taking any other drug (D. Sue, Sue, & Sue, 2006).

Twenty years ago, lithium was the only medication option for people with bipolar disorder. Fortunately, positive results have been found with other classes of drugs, including anticonvulsants such as lamotrigine (Lamictal), divalproex sodium (Depakote), and others; atypical antipsychotics such as olanzapine (Zyprexa), clozapine (Clozaril), risperidone (Risperdal), quetiapine (Seroquel), aripiprazole (Abilify), and ziprasidone (Geodon). At least one study has indicated that some of these medications reduce recurrence rates of mania when compared with placebo or with lithium or valproate treatment alone (Yatham & Kusumakar, 2002). However, additional research needs to be conducted on the long-term side effects of these newer drugs, as well as their usefulness in maintenance and relapse prevention.

The choice of medication depends on whether rapid cycling, psychotic features, depression, or severe mania are present and also varies according to the phase of treatment—acute, stabilization, or maintenance—(Aubry, Ferrero, & Schaad, 2007; Miklowitz, 2008a).

Medication adherence should be built into the treatment plan and nonadherence should be addressed. Clients' feelings about having moods curtailed by medication, missing the high or euphoric periods, and medication side effects, such as weight gain, sweating, and sexual dysfunction, can all contribute to ambivalence about maintaining the medication regimen. Self-stigma can also prevent people from accepting their disorder and making a concerted effort to follow treatment recommendations. An important goal of therapy then, is to provide education about medication and its side effects, as well as to enhance motivation to stay compliant.

A complete discussion of medication is beyond the scope of this book. Interested readers are referred to the American Psychiatric Association's *Practice Guideline for the Treatment of Patients with Bipolar Disorder* (2004a) or the three-part World Federation of Societies of Biological Psychiatry (WFSBP) *Pharmacotherapy of Bipolar Disorders* (2007).

Sometimes antidepressant medication or other activating drugs prescribed for unipolar depression can bring about mania, hypomania, or akathesia, a mixed state in which a person is agitated and depressed at the same time. Akathesia increases the risk of suicide. Such a state would not be diagnosed as a bipolar disorder, but would be considered a substance-induced mood disorder, unless symptoms lasted longer than a month after the medication is stopped or there is a prior history of manic symptoms (Miklowitz, 2008a). Early recognition of akathesia or mixed states, and consultation with the prescribing physician is necessary to avoid any untoward consequences.

Treating insomnia is also an important element of treatment for bipolar disorder since lack of sleep can sometimes trigger mania. Melatonin and medications such as benzodiazepines are sometimes used to enhance sleep.

Clear-cut, evidence-based data does not exist for the treatment of bipolar II with medication. Most treatment guidelines generally express treating bipolar II in the same manner as bipolar I (Quinn, 2007). However, treatment differs if rapid-cycling, mixed states, or psychosis are present.

Combination Therapies After clients become stabilized, psychotherapy can begin. Goals for individual therapy include medication and treatment compliance; alleviating acute symptoms; remedying any occupational, interpersonal, or other lifestyle problems that have resulted from the disorder; and preventing or minimizing future episodes.

Three types of psychotherapy have received empirical support as an adjunct to medication in the treatment of bipolar disorder: family-focused psychoeducational treatment (FFT; Miklowitz, 2008b), IPT with social rhythm therapy (Frank et al., 2005), and cognitive behavioral therapy (Miklowitz et al., 2007). Recent research indicates adjunctive therapies may be particularly helpful in improving adherence to medication (Sachs, 2008). A brief discussion of each modality will be discussed next.

Family-focused therapy. Three randomized controlled trials on family-focused therapy found that medication and FFT led to lower relapses rates and longer periods between relapse; FFT was associated with improvement in both manic and depressive symptoms; and rates of rehospitalization were lower (12%) than for the group receiving individual therapy (60%). FFT in combination with medication appears to ameliorate tension in the family. Miklowitz (2008b) published a family-focused treatment manual for bipolar disorder in which he recommends educating the family and the client that bipolar disorder is an illness that probably will recur, helping them recognize the biopsychosocial causes (for example, stress, poor sleep hygiene, family criticism), accept that medication will be necessary, and identify prodromal symptoms of mania and depression so that they can recognize and address these symptoms proactively. FFT also helps the person to separate his or her personality from the disorder, and to reestablish relationships that had been disrupted due to an episode. This combination therapy was adapted for treatment with adolescents and their families and also found to be helpful (Miklowitz, 2008a).

Interpersonal therapy and social rhythm therapy. IPT (discussed in more detail in the section on unipolar depression), in conjunction with medication, has been shown to reduce the amount of time bipolar clients spend in the depressive phase of the disorder (Frank et al., 2005). Also, people who stayed in IPT had fewer recurrences than those who switched from one mode of treatment to another. As in other areas of bipolar disorder, establishing routines and consistency seems to provide a protective factor. Social rhythm therapy combines IPT with a focus on the person's circadian rhythms in an effort to help the client understand the effects of the sleep–wake cycle on moods and to plan ahead for situations that might normally be disruptive (Frank, 2005; Frank & Swartz, 2004). Behavioral techniques that encourage people to chart the precipitants, nature, duration, frequency, and seasonality of their mood episodes can be effective in raising awareness about what might trigger future episodes. Maintaining a stable, balanced, and healthy lifestyle and proactively coping with stressors can also help.

Cognitive-behavioral therapy. Randomized controlled trials showed the benefits of cognitive-behavioral therapy as an adjunct therapy to improve medication compliance, reduce bipolar symptoms, and reduce relapse (Scott et al., 2006). Mania inoculation training is a type of therapy that builds on CBT and helps clients work on cognitive distortions that frequently occur with manic symptoms of grandiosity and narcissism. In mania inoculation training, clients learn that they are not all-powerful,

nor are they completely powerless. Rather, they learn to see the normative middle (Leahy, 2004).

Other Treatments   Many different treatment options are available. Those that have been found to improve treatment outcomes are listed next.

Day treatment. Day treatment or partial hospitalization programs should be considered for people who are not yet stable on their medication, are having difficulty in multiple areas of their lives, or who need more structure and support than can be provided in an outpatient setting (Quinn, 2007).

Group therapy. Group therapy has been found to enhance medication and other treatment compliance and may be useful during the recovery phase (Colom et al., 2005). Couples therapy has also been associated with improved medication compliance and a better overall course for the disorder (Roth & Fonagy, 2005). Group or couples therapy is usually not indicated for people experiencing a severe episode of a bipolar disorder, because the nature of their symptoms makes it difficult for them to engage in the group process.

Self-help groups. Such self-help groups as the Depression and Bipolar Support Alliance (DBSalliance.org) and the Family-to-Family program of the National Alliance for the Mentally Ill (www.nami.org) can be sources of support and information.

Electroconvulsive therapy. ECT occasionally can play an important role in the treatment of bipolar disorders, especially for people who are actively suicidal or are agitated, who have psychotic depression, or for whom other treatments have failed (Yatham et al., 2002). The efficacy rate of ECT is reported to range from 50% to 100% in these cases.

Vagus nerve stimulation. As mentioned earlier, vagus nerve stimulation (VNS therapy) also has been approved by the FDA for treatment of depression. To date, no studies have been conducted specific to VNS therapy for bipolar depression (Quinn, 2007).

Alternative treatments. Many alternative treatments for bipolar disorder have been proposed including: transcranial magnetic stimulation (TMS), light therapy, omega-3 fatty acids, vitamin and nutritional approaches, exercise, yoga, and qigong (Quinn, 2007). None of the alternative forms of therapy for bipolar disorder listed here have been found to be effective and TMS has been reported to trigger mania in some cases (Sakkas, 2003). Randomized controlled trials are lacking, and these approaches should not be viewed as alternatives to medication for people with bipolar disorder. At best, some may serve as adjunctive therapy to medication and psychotherapy.

Addressing Dual Diagnosis

People with bipolar disorders have the highest co-occurrence of a substance use disorder of any Axis I disorder (Goldstein & Levitt, 2006). Substance use (even a small amount), especially when it co-occurs with psychosis, dramatically increases the risk of relapse and hospitalization, for people with bipolar disorder. Substance misuse can also increase violence, aggression, and suicide risk in this population (Wilcox, Conner, & Caine, 2004). Thus, early detection and treatment not only of bipolar disorder but of co-occurring substance use disorders are cornerstones of effective treatment.

The lifetime prevalence rate of alcohol use for people with bipolar I disorder is 58%, and 37.5% for substance use and dependence (Grant et al., 2005). Cocaine and stimulant abuse was found to be as high as 38% in one study of people who have bipolar disorder (Camacho & Akiskal, 2005). Therapists should make suicide assessment and substance use discussions a part of every phase of treatment, not only at intake, for people with bipolar disorders (Sachs, 2004).

Because most clients are not likely to bring up their problems of substance use, standardized self-report questionnaires can be useful. Self-report measures such as RAPS, CAGE, AUDIT, and SASSI have been found to be more accurate than personal interviews (Noordsy, McQuade, & Mueser, 2003; Quinn, 2007). Interested readers are referred to Chapter 6 on behavior and impulse control disorders for a more detailed look at these instruments for detecting alcohol misuse.

Many people with substance use and bipolar disorders are referred to rehabilitation programs that do not provide treatment for their bipolar disorder. In addition, many people with bipolar disorder are refused treatment at rehabilitation centers because of their mental disorder. According to Sachs, no empirical evidence exists to indicate that separate interventions are effective. The substance use disorder and the bipolar disorder should be treated simultaneously. People dually diagnosed with bipolar disorder and a substance use disorder should participate in integrated treatment consisting of relapse prevention, group therapy, psychoeducation on symptoms of bipolar disorder and triggers for substance misuse, encouragement and monitoring of medication compliance, urine screenings for drug use, and discussion of issues relevant to both disorders, such as recognizing signs of relapse, stress management and relaxation techniques, and cognitive-behavioral therapy to improve resistance to misusing substances (Sachs, 2004).

Prognosis

Over the course of a lifetime, bipolar disorder has a 90% recurrence rate, with most recurrences happening within two years of an initial episode, even when treatment recommendations are followed (Perlis et al., 2006). Although most people have a positive response to initial treatment for the disorder, the risk of re-currence is highest in the first year after diagno-sis. Recurrence rates fall over the next two years and then range from 20% to 30% each year thereafter (Coryell, 2002). Continued maintenance treatment is recommended for those who have recovered from an episode of bipolar I disorder.

As we have discussed, medication manage-ment, psychotherapy, stabilization, and long-term maintenance for people with bipolar disorder are complicated by a variety of factors, including co-occurring disorders, family situa-tion, and medication compliance. Decisions about long-term maintenance of medication should be based on many factors, including se-verity of manic episodes, level of insight during episodes, side effects of the medication, acute-ness of onset, and the person's ability to handle the risk of relapse and its effects on his or her life. As we have already seen, a large cause of treatment failure in people with bipolar dis-order is nonadherence to medication regimens (Jefferson, 2003).

Prognosis is worse if the person with bipolar disorder has had multiple prior episodes or has a co-occurring substance use disorder, rapid cycling, or a negative family affective style (Miklowitz, 2008b). The primary goal of treat-ment should be to ensure that mood regulation is maintained while also treating the symptoms of the disorder. Clearly, more research is needed on treatment recommendations for people du-ally diagnosed with bipolar disorder and sub-stance use or other disorders.

Despite these findings, the prognosis for controlling a bipolar disorder with consistent medication and psychotherapy is fairly good. This means that people may need to be on med-ication for many years. Monitoring of progress, blood tests to assess the effects of the medication, and follow-up are important in obtaining treat-ment compliance. Although six to nine months

of lithium treatment may suffice for a first epi-sode, extended maintenance on lithium or other medication is strongly recommended for most people who have had recurrent episodes, to re-duce the likelihood of future recurrences.

Preventive use of therapy is also recom-mended, although its efficacy has not yet been well documented. Interpersonal and social rhythm therapy, family-focused therapy, and CBT may play an important role in follow-up treatment of people with bipolar disorders. Even though medication will be provided by a psychi-atrist or other physician, a nonmedical therapist can monitor progress, encourage appropriate use of the medication, and facilitate the adjustment of people with a history of bipolar disorder. Treatment approaches that combine various medications (such as mood stabilizers with atyp-ical antipsychotics) in an effort to provide tar-geted, individualized treatment is common (Quinn, 2007).

CYCLOTHYMIC DISORDER

Cyclothymic disorder is, in a sense, a longer but milder version of bipolar I and II disorders, just as dysthymic disorder can be thought of as a longer and milder version of major depressive disorder (although any biological relationship between the pairs is unclear).

Description of the Disorder

Cyclothymic disorder entails a period of at least two years (one year for children and adolescents) during which a person experiences numerous episodes of hypomania and mild-to-moderate depression (with symptom-free periods lasting no longer than two months). The *DSM-IV-TR* (American Psychiatric Association, 2000, p. 398) describes these depressive episodes as being, "of insufficient number, severity, pervasiveness, or duration to meet full criteria for a major depressive episode." Similarly, the hypomanic episodes do not meet the criteria for a manic episode. The mood changes tend to be abrupt and unpredictable and to have no apparent cause.

People with cyclothymic disorder have continual mood cycles that are usually briefer (days or weeks rather than months) and less severe than those characteristic of bipolar I or II disorders. The instability and moodiness associated with cyclothymic disorder, however, tend to make people difficult coworkers and companions, so some social and occupational dysfunction typically results. This disorder sometimes resembles and can be confused with a borderline or histrionic personality disorder. Interested readers are referred to Hatchett (2010) for a complete review of differential diagnosis.

Cyclothymia affects approximately 0.6% of the population (Regeer et al., 2004), but the disorder is probably underdiagnosed because the long-standing behavior becomes so familiar that it is viewed as normal. Cyclothymic disorder, like other mood disorders, usually begins in late adolescence or early adulthood and, without treatment, tends to have a chronic course, with no significant symptom-free periods. This disorder appears to be equally common in males and females.

Typical Client Characteristics

In addition to mood swings, people with cyclothymia often report sleeplessness, increased libido, racing thoughts, having more creative wordplay (e.g., puns), being optimistic, and participating in risk-taking behaviors. Mild hypomania, in which a person feels more energetic, confident, and alert, is not likely to be viewed as a problem by people experiencing this symptom. In particular, increased creativity is often found in people with cyclothymia and also in family members. This trait is sometimes viewed as adaptive as people report greater productivity, creativity, and energy (Akiskal, 2005). Depressive symptoms, when they occur, tend to be more troublesome and frequently include hypersomnia and other features of atypical depression. Thus, people who seek treatment usually do so at the insistence of family or friends who grow tired of their inconsistent moods.

Sleep disturbance and disruption of daily circadian and social rhythms are central features of cyclothymia, as of all bipolar disorders (Totterdell & Kellett, 2008). Extreme fluctuations in mood can result from disruptions in circadian rhythms, evolving into faulty cognitions that cause people to have difficulty controlling their moods, or to control them counterproductively (Jones, 2001; Mansell, 2007). This disorder sometimes is accompanied by substance-related, personality, somatoform, and sleep disorders and, in about one third of cases, is a precursor to another mood disorder, most often bipolar II disorder. The risk that a cyclothymic disorder will eventually develop into bipolar I or II ranges from 15% to 50%, and is related to early age of onset and family history for bipolar disorder, although it is difficult to predict who will subsequently develop a full manic episode (American Psychiatric Association, 2000; Maina, Salvi, Rosso, & Bogetto, 2010; Miklowitz, 2008b). Bipolar symptoms tend to worsen premenstrually and postpartum, so these may be times of increased incidence of hypomania for women (Quinn, 2007).

First-degree relatives of people with cyclothymic disorder have an increased incidence of bipolar disorders. Some researchers note a common childhood history of being hypersensitive, hyperactive, and moody. If interventions are not begun early, the difficult personality may evolve into a more serious disorder. Miklowitz (2008b) notes that children with parents who have bipolar disorders are more likely to exhibit cyclothymic disorder compared with other children.

Preferred Therapist Characteristics

Symptoms of mania and hypomania are generally unrecognized and underdiagnosed by clinicians (Forty et al., 2010). The Hypomania Checklist (HCL-32) is a 32-item self-report checklist that can help to distinguish between unipolar depression and depression with hypomanic symptoms (Angst et al., 2005). A shortened version (HCL-16) can be used as a screening tool with people who initially present with depression (Forty et al., 2010).

Price (2004) reports other roadblocks to diagnosis and ultimately treatment of cyclothymia include stigma about having a mental illness, having relatives who have bipolar disorders so in comparison their own symptoms are "not that bad," and being unaware that cyclothymia is a treatable disorder. Therapists should keep in mind that clients with cyclothymic disorder are often misdiagnosed as having borderline or histrionic personality disorders. Therapists who can help these clients develop insight into their mood fluctuations, identify triggers, and assist them in changing their cyclothymic temperament are more likely to be successful. Asking about family history of mood disorders and onset of mood disorder symptoms is an important part of the assessment.

Intervention Strategies

Little research is available specifically on the treatment of cyclothymic disorder; but treatments that help people regulate sleep, circadian rhythms, and social rhythm have been shown to be effective in treating bipolar disorders in general (Frank et al., 2005). Interpersonal and social rhythm therapy (IPSRT), family-focused therapy (FFT), and cognitive behavior therapy that incorporates circadian mood regulation (Totterdell & Kellet, 2008) seem to be helpful, especially when used in conjunction with medication to help stabilize mood

(Miklowitz, 2006b; Rizvi & Zaretsky, 2007). Mood-stabilizing medications are better for alleviating manic rather than depressive symptoms, whereas psychotherapy appears to be better at helping to alleviate depression. Caution should be used when prescribing antidepressants because they may trigger a manic episode in this population.

The depressive cycles of this disorder also tend to produce more dysfunction than do the hypomanic episodes. In addition, although hypomania that presents as irritability and anger, or episodes during which little sleep results in racing thoughts and reckless decisions, can certainly cause problems, people rarely seek treatment for periods during which they experience elevated mood, increased energy and activity levels, and greater self-esteem (S. L. Johnson, 2004).

Family therapy is indicated, as it is for most of the disorders discussed in this chapter, because the unpredictable mood shifts experienced by people with this disorder may well have damaged their family relationships. Educating the family that cyclothymic disorder is a mood disorder rather than willful behavior can help rebuild those relationships. Miklowitz's family-focused therapy (Miklowitz, 2008b) is one approach to family counseling that seems likely to help people with cyclothymic disorder. In that treatment model, the clinician guides the family through three focused modules that include psychoeducation, communication enhancement training, and problem-solving skills training. Goals of family-focused therapy are to reduce stress, help family members develop a nonblaming stance, increase medication compliance, improve communication skills, provide psychoeducation about the disorder, and help the family develop problem-solving strategies.

Career counseling and interpersonal skill development will usually be helpful supplements to the treatment of people with cyclothymic disorder. Their mood changes will probably have made it difficult for them to negotiate a smooth career path and develop a repertoire of positive social skills and coping mechanisms.

Group therapy may also be useful. People with cyclothymic disorder are generally healthy enough to interact with other group members and may benefit from the opportunity to try out new ways of relating, receive feedback, and make use of the role models provided by others.

In general, then, psychotherapy for people with cyclothymic disorder will be multifaceted. Treatment will include individual psychotherapy and may also include group therapy, family therapy, career counseling, and education. If medication is indicated, the treatment will usually include a mood stabilizer. Therapy should be structured and relatively directive to keep clients focused. It generally combines supportive and exploratory elements, to help clients understand their patterns of interaction, and will emphasize cognitive and behavioral strategies.

Prognosis

The combination of psychotherapy and medication has a good likelihood of reducing symptoms and effecting overall improvement in people with cyclothymic disorder. Nevertheless, the longstanding nature of this disorder and the chronicity of related disorders suggest that complete recovery may be difficult. Due to the risk that cyclothymia may evolve into bipolar disorder, long-term treatment is usually indicated for this disorder.

TREATMENT RECOMMENDATIONS: CLIENT MAP

Types of mood disorders discussed in this chapter include major depressive disorder, dysthymic disorder, depressive disorder NOS, bipolar I and II disorders, and cyclothymic disorder. The information presented in this chapter about these disorders is summarized here according to the 12 elements in the Client Map format.

CLIENT MAP

Diagnosis

Mood disorders (major depressive disorder, dysthymic disorder, depressive disorder NOS, bipolar I and II disorders, cyclothymic disorder)

Objectives of Treatment

Stabilize mood
Alleviate depression, mania, and hypomania
Teach relapse prevention strategies and prevent relapse
Improve coping mechanisms, family and other relationships, career, and overall adjustment
Establish a consistent and healthy lifestyle

Assessments

Measures of depression and suicidal ideation, such as the Beck Depression Inventory and the Schedule of Affective Disorders and Schizophrenia (Seligman & Moore, 1995)
Measures of hypomania, including the Hypomania Checklist-32
Medical examination for physical symptoms
Broad-based inventory of mental disorders, such as the Minnesota Multiphasic Personality Inventory, to identify comorbid disorders
Self-assessments of alcohol and substance use, such as the RAP, CAGE, MAST, AUDIT, and SASSI

Clinician Characteristics

High in Rogerian conditions of empathy, genuineness, caring, and others
Comfortable with client's dependence and discouragement
Resilient
Able to promote motivation, independence, and optimism
Structured and present-oriented as well as capable of addressing long-standing patterns of difficulty and dysfunction

Location of Treatment

Usually outpatient setting, but inpatient setting if symptoms are severe, if risk of suicide is high, or if there is loss of contact with reality

Interventions to Be Used

Cognitive-behavioral, interpersonal and social rhythm therapy, STEP-BD models of treatment
Family-focused therapy
Education about disorder
Relapse prevention

Emphasis of Treatment

Emphasis on cognitions and behavior
Initially directive and supportive
Later on, less directive and more exploratory

Numbers

Primarily individual therapy
Family or couples therapy often indicated
Group therapy useful after symptoms have abated

Timing

Medium duration (at least three to six months)
Moderate pace (one to two sessions per week)
Maintenance and extended follow-up phases common

Medications Needed

Mood stabilizers often indicated in combination with psychotherapy, especially for manic symptoms or severe depression

Adjunct Services

Increased activity
Homework assignments
Career counseling
Development of social and coping skills
Homogeneous support groups

Prognosis

Good for recovery from each episode
Fair for complete remission
Relapses common

CLIENT MAP OF KAREN C.

This chapter began with a description of Karen C., a 30-year-old woman who began experiencing severe depression after her husband's departure for a tour of duty. Karen's case reflects many of the characteristics of people suffering from depression. Karen's mother had episodes of depression, a disorder that often has a familial component. Karen herself had suffered an early loss with the death of her father, was dependent and low in self-esteem, had few resources and interests, and looked to others for structure and support. Her current depression seemed to be a reactive one, triggered by her perception that her marriage was at risk. Her symptoms were typical of major depressive disorder and included both emotional features (hopelessness, guilt) and somatic features (sleep and appetite disturbances, fatigue). The following Client Map outlines the treatment for Karen.

Diagnosis

Axis I: 296.23 Major depressive disorder, single episode, severe, without psychotic features, with atypical features
Axis II: Dependent personality traits
Axis III: No known physical disorders or conditions, but weight change reported
Axis IV: Separation from husband due to his tour of duty, marital conflict
Axis V: Global assessment of functioning (GAF Scale): current GAF = 45

Objectives of Treatment

Reduce level of depression
Eliminate physiological symptoms
Improve social and occupational functioning
Increase self-esteem, sense of independence, and activity level
Improve communication and differentiation in marital relationship
Reduce marital stress and conflict
Reduce cognitive distortions and unwarranted assumptions

Assessments

Beck Depression Inventory, to be used at the start of each session
Assessment of suicidality, as needed
SASSI, CAGE, or other self-report measure of alcohol or substance use
Physical examination

Clinician Characteristics

Supportive and patient, yet structured
Able to model and teach effective interpersonal functioning
Able to build a working alliance rapidly with a discouraged and potentially suicidal client
Possibly female (and thereby able to serve as a role model)

Location of Treatment

Outpatient setting
Period of inpatient treatment possible if client does not respond to treatment quickly and remains relatively
    immobilized by depression

Interventions to Be Used

Interpersonal therapy to explore patterns in client's significant relationships (effects of early loss of her father,
    dependent and enmeshed relationship with her mother, extended conflict with her husband)

Encouragement of social interactions

Analysis and modification of client's thoughts about herself and her roles and relationships through cognitive therapy

Exploration of her associated emotions

Primary focus on client's present relationship with her husband and her lack of self-direction (interpersonal role disputes and interpersonal deficits)

Attention to helping client clarify and communicate her expectations and wishes to her husband and re-negotiate their relationship

Encouragement for client to review strengths and weaknesses of her past and present relationships and to try out improved ways of relating, both at home and in therapy sessions

Encouragement of increased activity and regular exercise to increase client's energy level

Use of such strategies as role playing, examination of logic and belief systems, teaching of communication skills, and modeling

Emphasis of Treatment

High level of directiveness, given client's near-immobilization by her depression

Provision of guidance and structure by the therapist, in view of client's lack of a sense of how to help herself

Reduction of guidance and structure over time, to promote an increase in client's own sense of mastery and competence and to help her take responsibility for her life

High degree of support at the outset, given client's lack of friends and confidants

Shift of focus to include more exploration and education as client's symptoms abate and as she begins to develop some additional outside support systems (but support to remain relatively high)

Attention to both cognitive dysfunction (inappropriate generalizations, self-blame) and behavioral deficits (lack of activities, poor social and interpersonal skills, dependence on others)

Primary emphasis of treatment to be on client's relationships, even though affective symptoms are prominent (focusing on her feelings of depression would probably only further entrench her sense of hopelessness, and the precipitant of her present depression seems to be interpersonal)

Numbers

Individual therapy as the initial approach to treatment

Marital counseling once client's husband returns home

Client's mother may also be invited to attend several sessions if this idea is acceptable to client

Timing

Two sessions per week initially (to facilitate reduction of client's depression and suicidal ideation and improve her functioning)

One session per week after she is able to return to work

Relatively gradual and supportive pace at first (but as fast as client's fragile condition will allow)

Anticipated duration of three to nine months

Possible extension of treatment beyond symptom abatement (for preventive impact, given long history of dependent personality traits, and for possible value in averting recurrences)

Medications Needed

Referral to a psychiatrist for determination of whether medication may be indicated (given client's severe depression and hopelessness, even though hers seems to be a reactive rather than an endogenous depression, and given that medication combined with psychotherapy seems particularly effective in treating major depressive disorder)

Adjunct Services

Suggestion of some nondemanding tasks (such as reading about assertiveness, and increasing and listing pleasurable activities, particularly those involving socialization)

Physical exercise

Participation in a women's support group after depression has been reduced

Prognosis

Very good for symptom reduction in major depressive disorder, single episode

Less optimistic for significant modification of underlying dependent personality traits

About a 50% probability of another major depressive episode (possibility should be discussed with client and
her family and addressed through extended treatment, follow-up, or both)

RECOMMENDED READING

Beck, J. (2005). *Cognitive therapy for challenging problems.* New York, NY: Guilford Press.

Evans, K., & Sullivan, J. M. (2001). *Dual diagnosis: Counseling the mentally ill substance abuser* (2nd ed.). New York, NY: Guilford Press.

Frank, E. (2005). *Treating bipolar disorder: A clinician's guide to interpersonal and social rhythm therapy.* New York, NY: Guilford Press.

Keyes, C.L.M., & Goodman, S. H. (Eds.). (2006). *Women and depression.* New York, NY: Cambridge University Press.

Martell, C. R., Dimidjian, S., & Herman-Dunn, R. (2010). *Behavioral activation for depression: A clinician's guide.* New York, NY: Guilford Press.

Miklowitz, D. J. (2008). *Bipolar disorder: A family focused treatment approach* (2nd ed.). New York, NY: Guilford Press.

Miklowitz, D. J. (2011). *The bipolar survival guide* (2nd ed.). New York, NY: Guilford Press.

Quinn, B. (2007). *Bipolar disorder.* Hoboken, NJ: Wiley.

Rosenthal, N. E. (2006). *Winter blues: Everything you need to know to beat seasonal affective disorder* (2nd ed.). New York, NY: Guilford Press.

Sachs, G. S. (2004). *Managing bipolar affective disorder.* London, England: Science Press.

Teyber, E., & McClure, F. H. (2011). *Interpersonal process in therapy: An integrative model* (6th ed.) Belmont, CA: Brooks/Cole.

Williams, M., Teasdale, J., Segal, Z., & Kabat-Zinn, J. (2007). *The mindful way through depression.* New York, NY: Guilford Press.

Anxiety Disorders

Roberto M., a 27-year-old Latino man, sought therapy at the insistence of his fiancée, Luisa. For the past 4 months, Roberto had been experiencing nightmares and intrusive memories of having been sexually abused during his childhood by his family's housekeeper. Roberto had withdrawn from Luisa as well as from his other friends. He no longer engaged in running and other exercise, which had been a daily activity for him in the past. He refused to visit his parents, who still lived in the house where the abuse had occurred.

Luisa reported that Roberto appeared anxious and irritable. When she encouraged him to get out of the house and do something enjoyable, he became angry and told her that she just did not understand.

The change in Roberto had been triggered by a visit to the dentist. Roberto, who needed extensive dental work, apparently became emotionally and physically uncomfortable during the process. When he sought to leave the dental chair in the middle of the procedure, the authoritarian dentist told Roberto that he would just have to "put up with it." The powerlessness of the situation, the attitude of the dentist, and the reclining position of the chair brought back memories that Roberto had long tried to push out of his mind.

During the time of the abuse, the housekeeper had told Roberto that she would harm his baby sister if he told anyone, so he had kept it to himself. As an adult, he felt ashamed of his experiences and had continued to keep them secret. Although he had never forgotten his mistreatment by the housekeeper, Roberto had done his best to act as if the abuse had never happened, and he had built a rewarding life for himself. Now, however, those experiences could no longer be pushed aside.

Roberto was experiencing an anxiety disorder—posttraumatic stress disorder (PTSD)—typified by both emotional and physiological sensations of tension and apprehension, as well as by a reexperiencing of the trauma and by withdrawal. Although the condition sexual abuse of child (discussed in Chapter 3) would also probably be used to describe Roberto's childhood experiences, the diagnosis of PTSD is used as well, to convey the emotional distress and impairment that he was experiencing. His symptoms cannot accurately be classified as an adjustment disorder because the precipitant happened so long ago and because the nature and severity of Roberto's symptoms do not fit the profile for an adjustment disorder. Roberto did have some underlying depression, but his overriding emotion was anxiety.

OVERVIEW OF ANXIETY DISORDERS

This chapter reviews the diagnosis and treatment of five categories of anxiety disorder:

1. Phobias (including agoraphobia, specific phobia, and social phobia)
2. Panic disorder
3. Obsessive-compulsive disorder
4. Trauma-related stress disorders (post-traumatic stress disorder and acute stress disorder)
5. Generalized anxiety disorder

Although these disorders differ in terms of duration, precipitants, secondary symptoms, and impact, they are all characterized primarily by anxiety.

Description of the Disorders

Anxiety disorders represent one of the most prevalent mental health problems in the United States, with more than 18% of the population (40 million adults) experiencing an anxiety disorder in any given year (Kessler, Chiu, et al., 2005). People with anxiety are more likely to consult physicians than psychotherapists for treatment of anxiety symptoms. In fact, more people consult physicians due to stress-related anxiety than due to bad colds and bronchitis (Barlow, 2002). Social phobia is the most commonly reported anxiety disorder.

Many explanations have been advanced for the causes of anxiety. These explanations differ, but all are valid for some types of anxiety and for some people. In biological terms, anxiety disorders are likely to involve an inherited vulnerability that is activated by stressful life events. The person's ability to cope is then negatively impacted by a negative or distorted cognitive style.

Other theories conceptualize the cause of anxiety in different ways. Psychoanalytic theorists, for example, suggest that anxiety is the product of experiences in which internal impulses, previously punished and repressed, evoke distress that signals danger of further punishment if the impulses are expressed. To restate this theory in cognitive-behavioral terms, a stressor is believed to produce the perception of a threat, and this perception in turn is thought to produce a dysfunctional emotional reaction (anxiety). We learn to view a particular stimulus as frightening, either through our own experiences (conditioning) or through the experiences of others (social learning), so threats of that stimulus evoke apprehension and avoidance behavior. Existential theory explains free-floating or generalized anxiety as reflecting discomfort with the inherent meaninglessness of life.

Anxiety is a common and useful response inherent in everyday experiences. It plays an adaptive role, warning people of potential hazards and risky choices and providing a stimulus for effective action. For example, higher initial levels of distress in response to a diagnosis of cancer have been found to enhance coping (Fawzy et al., 1993). Anxiety becomes a disorder, however, when it is characterized by great intensity or duration and when it causes significant distress and impairment. Anxiety may become problematic at any age, but nearly three quarters of people have their first episode by age 21 (Kessler, Berglund, et al., 2005).

Anxiety, like depression, takes many forms, but anxiety usually is not severely debilitating, nor is it usually accompanied by loss of contact with reality. Anxiety may be free-floating and without obvious cause, or it may be what is called *signal anxiety*, occurring in response to a fear-inducing stimulus (such as recollection of an accident or pictures of snakes). Levels of anxiety fall on a continuum from mild to severe. Most people with anxiety try to manage or conceal their symptoms and go about their lives, often avoiding situations that increase their anxiety. The tendency to avoid anxiety has a circular effect, however, and often contributes to the development or worsening of fears.

Anxiety is characterized by both emotional and physiological symptoms. Fear and apprehension are the primary emotional symptoms but are often accompanied by others, including confusion, impaired concentration, selective attention, avoidance, and, especially in children and adolescents, behavioral problems. Anxiety-related symptoms contribute to suicidal ideation and behaviors as often as depressive symptoms do (Barlow, 2002). Common physiological symptoms of anxiety include dizziness, heart palpitations, changes in bowel and bladder functioning, perspiration, muscle tension, restlessness, insomnia, irritability, headaches, and queasiness. Children and adolescents who experience anxiety show an "attentional bias for threat" (Evans et al., 2005, p. 173) just as adults do. In other words, they are hypervigilant for signs of possible danger. They are also likely to present somatic manifestations of their anxiety and are prone to depression later in life.

Some symptoms of anxiety, such as heart palpitations and shortness of breath, are in themselves frightening and may lead the person who has them to believe that a heart attack is in progress or that some other serious physical ailment exists. Thus, anxiety often breeds further anxiety. Because many medical conditions can be the cause of anxiety-like symptoms, any unexplained physiological symptoms that accompany anxiety warrant a referral for medical evaluation.

Typical Client Characteristics

People who are prone to anxiety tend to see themselves as powerless and may view the world as a source of harm and threat. These people typically have few effective support systems and usually have not had a history of successfully coping with stressors. They characteristically have a high level of underlying stress (called *trait anxiety*), are pessimistic, have a need to overprotect and overcontrol, and react with elevated stress (called *state anxiety*) to even minor disturbances. Stress has been linked to a pattern of distorted self-evaluation, inability to control negative thoughts, selective attending to critical statements, and hypervigilance for threat or danger (Barlow, 2002). Like depression, anxiety tends to run in families through a combination of genetic predisposition, neurochemical process, and environmental factors (Evans et al., 2005).

More females than males seek treatment for anxiety disorders. Barlow (2002) suggests that the combination of negative life events, external locus of control, and attributional style may account for the increase in anxiety disorders in women. Others have suggested that men who are anxious may turn to alcohol rather than to therapy.

Anxiety is often accompanied by secondary symptoms and disorders. When depression is also present, the result may be what has been termed an *agitated depression*. As many as half of those with an anxiety disorder also have a personality disorder, particularly dependent or avoidant personality disorder (Woo & Keatinge, 2008). Substance misuse and dependence on others are also common and may represent efforts to control the symptoms through self-medication and overreliance on support systems. Unfortunately, those behaviors seem more likely to worsen the anxiety than to alleviate it.

Assessment

Diagnosis of an anxiety disorder can be facilitated by the use of a brief inventory of anxiety symptoms. Probably the one most widely used is the Beck Anxiety Inventory, which assesses four categories of anxiety symptoms—neurophysiological, subjective, panic related, and autonomic (Beck & Steer, 1990).

When assessing clients with anxiety disorders, clinicians should be aware of any relevant cultural factors. Ethnic identity, gender roles within the family, and level of acculturation play important roles in clinical presentation, assessment, and treatment. Eye contact, verbal and nonverbal communication, personal space, and verbal cues, such as tone and volume, may vary from culture to culture. Coping styles may also vary. For example, African Americans tend to use such coping strategies as gratitude and religiosity more than European Americans (White & Barlow, 2002). Some symptoms may also occur more frequently in specific cultural groups. For example, nearly 60% of African Americans with panic disorder experience occasional sleep paralysis compared with less than 8% of European Americans (White & Barlow, 2002). Some disorders may occur frequently in certain cultures but be nearly nonexistent in others. For instance, Cambodian populations experience "sore neck syndrome," and some Hispanic populations experience *ataque de nervios* (uncontrollable behaviors such as physical or verbal aggression, crying, and shouting) following the death of a loved one or other stressful life events (Paniagua, 2001; White & Barlow, 2002, p. 335).

Two commonly used semistructured interviews for the assessment of anxiety disorders are: the Anxiety Disorders Interview Schedule for the *DSM-IV* (ADIS-IV; Brown, Di Nardo, & Barlow, 1994) and the Structured Clinical Interview for *DSM-IV* Axis I Disorders (SCID-I; First, Spitzer, Gibbon, & Williams, 2002). Many self-report measures are also available, but the therapist should keep in mind that responses on these measures are not always accurate. Men, in particular, are more likely to underreport fear (McCabe & Antony, 2002). For a complete discussion of assessments for anxiety, the reader is referred to *The Practitioner's Guide to Empirically Based Measures of Anxiety* (Antony, Orsillo, & Roemer, 2001).

Preferred Therapist Characteristics

Although little research is available on the optimal therapist for the anxious client, that therapist is probably one who is stable and calm, untroubled by anxiety, and able to exert a relaxing and reassuring effect on the client. Beck and Emery (1985) suggest that the therapist be a model of patience and persistence, encouraging rather than forcing change.

The therapist treating anxiety, like the therapist treating depression, will probably begin with a moderate level of directiveness and a high level of supportiveness. A person who is anxious typically feels fragile and apprehensive and needs support and encouragement to engage in therapy. Although some directiveness on the part of the therapist is needed to give structure to the sessions, the anxious client is in emotional pain and therefore will usually be eager to collaborate with the therapist in relieving the symptoms. Once the debilitating anxiety has been reduced, the therapist can assume a more probing stance. Most people with anxiety have had a period of relatively healthy functioning before the onset of symptoms and should be able to respond to and grow from some exploration.

The therapist working with an anxious client should be comfortable enough with the client's pain and tension to refrain from taking complete control of the therapeutic process. Nevertheless, the therapist should also have enough concern and compassion to keep searching for an approach that will have a beneficial impact on the client. The therapist should be flexible and able to draw from a variety of therapeutic approaches in finding an optimal combination of techniques.

Intervention Strategies

Cognitive and behavioral treatments for anxiety disorders have the broadest research base and empirical support in the treatment of anxiety disorders. Several innovative and yet comprehensive models of psychotherapy that are gaining in practice as well as in empirical research of their effectiveness include mindfulness-based practice. Medication, too, seems to have a place in the treatment of some anxiety disorders.

Common Strategies Treatments for most anxiety disorders will usually include the following eight elements:

1. *Establishment of a strong therapeutic alliance* that promotes the client's motivation and feelings of safety.
2. *Assessment of the manifestations of anxiety* and of the stimuli for fears. Although treatment of anxiety disorders usually does not emphasize psychodynamic interventions, an anxiety disorder related to a trauma may require considerable processing of affect, as well as exploration of past experiences and patterns.
3. *Referral for medical evaluation* to determine any contributing physical disorders, as well as the need for medication.
4. *The teaching of relaxation skills* and incorporation of regular relaxation into the person's lifestyle. Effective approaches to relaxation include meditation, physical exercise, mindfulness-based strategies, progressive muscle relaxation, visual imagery, and breathing retraining, among others.
5. *Analysis of dysfunctional cognitions* that are contributing to anxiety and substitution of empowering, positive, more accurate cognitions.
6. *Exposure to feared objects*, which can be accomplished in many ways, including in vivo or imaginal desensitization, eye movement desensitization and reprocessing, and flooding.
7. *Homework*, to track and increase the client's progress and to promote the client's responsibility.
8. *Solidification of efforts to cope* with anxiety and prevent a relapse.

Cognitive-Behavioral Therapy Optimal treatment of anxiety disorders involves multiple components, usually emphasizing cognitive-behavioral therapy (Barlow, Allen, & Basden, 2007; Evans et al., 2005; Stewart & Chambless, 2009). Cognitive-behavioral therapy is not one specific treatment approach; rather it is the generic name given to the combination of cognitive therapy with behavior therapy. Because anxiety disorders vary considerably, treatment must be tailored to the specific nature of the disorder. Exposure-based treatment (developed by Wolpe, 1958), called *systematic desensitization*, involves teaching clients to relax while exposing them to the feared object or situation. This type of cognitive- behavioral approach can be particularly effective in the treatment of panic or specific phobia. Also effective is stress inoculation training (SIT), in which people learn to develop skills (muscle relaxation, thought stopping, breath control, guided self-dialogue, covert modeling, and role playing) to help them cope with anxiety. SIT includes three phases: (1) conceptualization of the problem and building of rapport, (2) skill acquisition and rehearsal, and (3) application and follow-through (Meichenbaum, 2008). Depending on the particular client and disorder, such techniques as imaginal and in vivo desensitization, relaxation, and hypnotherapy, which are designed to reduce fear and anxiety, may also be appropriate.

Acceptance-Based Therapies In Eastern traditions, acceptance is considered a positive and desired state that helps relieve overall suffering. When added to behavior therapy or cognitive behavior therapy, acceptance can become a tool of change.

Specific clinical interventions that are consistent with and foster psychological acceptance include interoceptive exposure in the treatment of panic attacks (Barlow, Craske, Cerny, & Klosko, 1989; O'Donohue & Fisher, 2008), mindfulness meditation (Kabat-Zinn, 1990), which is found in mindfulness-based stress reduction (MBST; Kabat-Zinn, 1990), dialectical behavior therapy (Linehan, 1993), and acceptance and commitment therapy (Hayes, Strosahl, & Wilson, 2005; Walser & Westrup, 2008). In these models, clients are taught to integrate mindfulness into their daily lives. As they become aware of their metacognitions or "thinking about their thinking," they are more likely to change their dysfunctional thoughts and modify their actions and behaviors as a result.

These types of therapies are different from traditional CBT in which thoughts are specifically targeted and challenged for elimination. In acceptance therapies, metacognitions are recognized and accepted for what they are—merely thoughts that are going through the mind—without analyzing or ruminating on them (Wells, 2009).

Group Therapy

Group therapy is often used along with or in lieu of individual therapy in the treatment of anxiety. People with similar anxiety-related symptoms and experiences (for example, PTSD after a rape or social anxiety in interpersonal situations) can provide each other with a powerful source of encouragement, role models, and reinforcement. Group therapy is generally contraindicated in the treatment of OCD.

Family Therapy

Family counseling can also be a useful adjunct to treatment. A highly anxious and constricted person may have a strong impact on the life of the family. Family members may benefit from help in understanding the disorder and in learning how to respond supportively and helpfully and without providing the secondary gains that may reinforce the symptoms. In some cases, as in the treatment of agoraphobia, partners may be trained as cotherapists, to encourage and motivate continued change at home.

Medication

Collaboration with a physician is important in treating some people with anxiety disorders because, as previously mentioned, anxiety-like symptoms can be caused by many medical conditions, such as those in the following list:

- Cardiopulmonary disorders (mitral valve prolapse, angina pectoris, and cardiac arrhythmia)
- Endocrine disturbances (hyperthyroidism, hypoglycemia)
- Neurological disorders
- Inflammatory disorders (rheumatoid arthritis, lupus erythematosus)
- Biochemical changes due to substances (diet or cold medications, amphetamines, caffeine, nicotine, or cocaine)

The therapist and the physician must determine whether a physical symptom is causing a psychological symptom or vice versa.

Medication sometimes can accelerate the treatment of certain anxiety disorders, among them panic disorder and obsessive-compulsive disorder, but hospitalization is rarely necessary. Outpatient psychotherapy of medium duration (months rather than weeks or years), combining cognitive and behavioral interventions with between-session practice, will usually be the best approach to treating anxiety disorders.

Prognosis

Two thirds to as many as 95% of people with anxiety disorders show significant improvement after CBT, and some studies indicate that these improvements generally are maintained at 7-year follow-up (Evans et al., 2005). Prognosis for the treatment of specific anxiety disorders varies according to the disorder. Some anxiety disorders, such as phobias, usually respond very well to treatment; others, such as obsessive-compulsive disorder, are sometimes treatment resistant. Recurrences of anxiety disorders, like recurrences of mood disorders, are common. The setting of goals that focus on measurable behavioral and affective change is integral to treatment, and procedures for assessing progress toward goals (such as observation and the use of checklists, diaries, questionnaires, inventories, and even videotapes) often play a role in the monitoring of change. The next sections of this chapter focus on specific anxiety disorders and provide more information on their treatment and prognoses.

PANIC DISORDER

According to the *DSM-IV-TR* (American Psychiatric Association, 2000), a panic disorder is characterized by at least two unexpected panic attacks, neither of which can be explained by medical conditions or substance use, with one or more followed by at least a month of persistent fear of another attack, worry about the implications of the attack, and/or behavioral change (usually designed to avert future attacks) in response to the attack.

The *DSM-IV-TR* recognizes a connection between panic disorder and phobic avoidance by establishing two subtypes of panic disorder: panic disorder without agoraphobia and panic disorder with agoraphobia. (A subsequent section of this chapter discusses agoraphobia itself, with or without panic disorder.) About half of all people with panic disorder will fall into each of the two groups. People who have panic

disorder with agoraphobia typically associate their panic attacks with where they have occurred and avoid those places in an effort to prevent future attacks. They also are likely to misinterpret the attacks as imminent heart attacks or other catastrophes. As the panic attacks occur in more and more places, people with this disorder tend to restrict their activities until, in severe cases, they refuse to leave home; unfortunately, this safety-seeking behavior tends to maintain these people's inaccurate cognitions. Agoraphobia generally occurs within the first year of onset of panic attacks. People who have panic disorder without agoraphobia experience similar physical feelings of dizziness, rapid pulse, and fear of losing control or going crazy, but they tend not to associate those feelings with a particular place. They do, however, develop fear of having another attack, and frequently fear they may have a serious medical condition. They often seek medical treatment to allay their fears of an underlying terminal illness.

Description of the Disorder

The hallmark of panic disorder, as the name suggests, is attacks of panic that are unexpected. A panic attack is a circumscribed period of intense fear or discomfort that develops suddenly, usually beginning with cardiac symptoms and difficulty in breathing. A full panic attack is accompanied by at least four physiological symptoms, which may include sweating, nausea, and trembling in addition to rapid heartbeat, chest pain, and difficulty in breathing. Panic attacks typically peak within 10 minutes, sometimes in as little as 2 minutes, and rarely last longer than 30 minutes (Eifert & Forsyth, 2005).

Three types of panic attacks have been identified: unexpected or uncued attacks (with no apparent trigger), situationally bound or cued attacks (in anticipation of specific stimuli, such as hearing that a thunderstorm is predicted), and situationally predisposed attacks (usually associated with specific fear-inducing triggers, such as the actual experience of a thunderstorm). By definition, at least some of the panic attacks that accompany panic disorder are unexpected, but people with this disorder may have all three types of attacks.

Panic attacks are common; up to 50% of adults will experience at least one panic attack in their lifetime, with only 10% developing recurrent attacks and panic disorder (Roy-Byrne & Cowley, 2007). A given person may have infrequent panic attacks, with little impact, or may have many attacks each week, resulting in considerable distress and impairment.

Even a small number of panic attacks can be upsetting. The degree of upset depends on the person's interpretation of the symptoms, the person's underlying fears, and the extent of the person's anticipatory anxiety. People sometimes believe that their panic symptoms are indications of having a heart attack, losing control, or going crazy. They often experience a strong urge to escape.

A physiological explanation of an initial panic attack focuses on the pivotal role of the amygdala and an overreaction of the autonomic nervous system to stressful life events (Roy-Byrne & Cowley, 2007). Thus, a biological predisposition to stress causes an amplification of body sensations and anxious experiences in response to stressful triggers. In a sense, panic disorder can be viewed as a phobia of bodily sensations. The feelings of panic are caused by fear and stress, those bodily sensations are then misinterpreted, and the outcome is both increased fear and greater likelihood of additional panic attacks, in a self-perpetuating cycle.

Estimates suggest that as many as half of all people with panic disorder have other disorders as well. Substance-related disorders (especially alcohol, used as self-medication in an effort to control panic attacks) is a frequent concomitant of panic disorder. Mood disorders, especially depression, occur in 25% to 65% of people with panic disorder (Barlow, 2002). Personality disorders (most commonly avoidant, dependent, or histrionic) are found in 40% to 65% of those with panic disorder (Baker, Patterson, & Barlow, 2002). Other kinds of anxiety disorders are also common.

Panic disorder typically has a sudden onset, beginning with a severe panic attack. Approximately 1% to 3.5% of the population of the United States will experience a panic disorder at some time in their lives (American Psychiatric Association, 2000). The approximate 2:1 female-to-male ratio has been consistently found in studies conducted around the world (Barlow, 2002). Onset for panic disorder peaks between the ages of 15 and 24, and again between the ages of 45 and 54, although young children and older adults may also experience initial panic attacks (Baker et al., 2002). Identifiable stressors typically accompany the initial attack, but the panic attacks tend to recur even after the stressor is resolved (Roy-Byrne & Cowley, 2007). In women, panic symptoms may be influenced by hormonal changes postpartum or by the female reproductive cycle (White & Barlow, 2002).

Panic disorder can become chronic and debilitating. It ranks as one of the five mental disorders that cause the most days lost from work and result in decreased quality of life (Goodwin et al., 2005). Nocturnal panic, in which people awake from sleep in a state of panic, is a common feature of this disorder, found in as many as 70% of cases (Craske & Barlow, 2008).

Typical Client Characteristics

Both panic disorder and its close relative, agoraphobia, seem to run in families, yet the results of genetic studies have not been conclusive. Roy-Byrne and Cowley (2007) report that most recent theories of the etiology of panic disorder focus on a genetic predisposition that is then triggered by one or more stressful life events, causing the person to "amplify body sensations and an anxious experience via catastrophic and other cognitive distortions" (p. 338). The risk of developing panic disorder is particularly high for female relatives of people with this disorder, whereas the male relatives of people with panic disorder are at particular risk for problems related to alcohol use (often, as mentioned, a mechanism for coping with anxiety). Panic disorder has also been linked to later-onset depression, temperament, over-protective or rejecting parents, and somatic conditions such as respiratory illness (Evans et al., 2005; Goodwin et al., 2005).

Assessment

White and Barlow (2002) endorse a comprehensive multimodal approach to the assessment of panic disorder with or without agoraphobia, including a clinical interview, behavioral assessment, self-report, and medical evaluation. Symptoms should be assessed before, during, and following treatment to determine how therapy is progressing. Such self-monitoring tools as panic diaries, self-report scales, and daily records are important for obtaining an accurate assessment and diagnosis as well as for treatment planning. Although not a formal assessment, establishing a fear and avoidance hierarchy can be helpful. The client is asked to create a list of feared situations. After the list is completed, the client is asked to rate both fear and avoidance for each item, with 0 representing no anxiety/panic or avoidance, and 8 representing a full range of anxiety and avoidance. This fear and avoidance hierarchy and the ADIS-IV (Brown et al., 1994) mentioned earlier can provide useful measurements of avoidance, severity of

panic, and panic-related symptoms, and can help determine the goals and priorities of therapy.

Preferred Therapist Characteristics

The first session with clients experiencing panic disorder is critical in establishing a successful therapeutic alliance. People with this disorder typically have a history of unsuccessful personal and professional efforts to ameliorate their anxiety and may feel demoralized as well as ashamed at not having been successful. These people also may feel angry at having been referred to a psychotherapist for what they believe is a medical or physical problem. Normalizing these reactions, as well as reassuring clients that effective treatments for this disorder are available, can contribute greatly to their motivation to engage in yet another treatment.

Psychoeducation about the symptoms and treatment of panic disorder often is a necessary component of working with clients. The therapist may need to be directive about the importance of monitoring and assessment of the panic disorder. The recommendations in the preceding section about the ideal therapist to treat anxiety disorders are also pertinent here.

Intervention Strategies

Cognitive therapy in combination with some form of behavioral therapy has become the treatment of choice for panic disorder. Family therapy, medication, and stress-reduction and mindfulness-based therapies also have their place, as will be discussed.

Cognitive-Behavioral Therapy Many controlled clinical trials support the efficacy of various types of cognitive-behavioral therapy in the treatment of panic disorder (White & Barlow,

2002). Cognitive therapy, enhanced by behavioral interventions and sometimes combined with medication, has been found to be more effective than other interventions, no treatment, or treatment with medication alone (Baker et al., 2002; Evans et al., 2005). White and Barlow (2002) report a meta-analysis that included 43 controlled studies of treatment for panic with agoraphobia. The results showed that CBT was associated with the largest effect size compared to approaches that combined drug treatment with psychological interventions. These findings make sense, because the disorder stems primarily from misinterpretations of physical symptoms. The cognitive interventions seek to change people's catastrophic and distorted thinking, and such behavioral techniques as distraction, comforting rituals, meditation, and relaxation contribute to the physiological reduction of anxiety that contributes to panic attacks.

Cognitive therapy has a strong positive impact on both the frequency of attacks and the fear of future attacks. Between 80% and 100% of people with panic disorder were panic-free after treatment, and treatment gains were maintained for up to two years (Craske & Barlow, 2008).

Panic control therapy is a multifaceted cognitive-behavioral treatment program for panic disorder seeks to address the mistaken beliefs people have about the meaning of physical sensations (Craske & Barlow, 2008; White & Barlow, 2002). PCT emphasizes psychoeducation, relaxation training, cognitive restructuring, and interoceptive exposure, which involves progressive evocation of the somatic sensations of panic attacks. Interoceptive exposure exercises are introduced that simulate the feelings evoked by a panic attack. For example, spinning in a chair until dizzy, running up and down stairs until out of breath, or breathing into a paper bag are exercises that serve to evoke the fear of a panic attack. Treatment interventions help people recognize that these sensations are not life threatening, and help clients confront their mistaken beliefs about the meaning of physical sensations so their fears can be extinguished. Such behavioral techniques as breathing retraining and relaxation enhance people's recovery from the disorder. Inventories and logs are used to assess the severity of the disorder and to track progress. PCT has been shown to reduce panic with 85% to 87% of people being free of panic attacks at the end of treatment (Forsyth, Fuse, & Acheson, 2008). Treatment gains with PCT were also maintained at 2-year follow-up, whereas gains made with medication were lost (Barlow, Craske, Cerny, & Klosko, 1989).

New Treatment Modalities Several new therapies that have not been empirically validated, but show promise in the treatment of panic disorder include acceptance and commitment therapy (ACT) and sensation-focused intensive treatment (SFIT). SFIT combines treatments for panic and avoidance in an intensive self-study format over 8 consecutive days. Treatment involves intentional exposure to the most feared situations without teaching techniques for reducing the anxiety. Findings of a pilot study showed that SFIT reduced panic symptoms and that a large portion of the gains made were maintained. The results show promise, but further research is needed (Bitran, Morissette, Spiegel, & Barlow, 2008). As discussed earlier, ACT combines acceptance, compassion, and commitment to goals with interventions drawn from CBT. Clients learn to identify their thoughts and feelings and practice mindful acceptance when fear arises. Because ACT is relatively new, no long-term measures of efficacy are available at this time (Eifert & Forsyth, 2005). ACT is described in more detail in the section on generalized anxiety disorder.

Family and Group Therapy Both family and group therapy have also received some support in treatment of this disorder. Family interventions, combined with specific treatments for panic attacks, can help ameliorate the impact that this disorder has on family functioning and relationships. Group therapy using cognitive-behavioral interventions has demonstrated high levels of effectiveness.

Medication Medication is sometimes part of the treatment plan for panic disorder, but fast-acting beta-blockers and benzodiazepines can actually contribute to relapse of social anxiety disorder (Turk, Heimberg, & Magee, 2008) by artificially promoting relaxation and limiting people's ability to self-soothe and credit themselves with overcoming the disorder. Consequently, a referral for medication probably should be made only if psychotherapy alone clearly is not effective or if a person is having many severe panic attacks each week. Selective serotonin reuptake inhibitors (SSRIs) are the preferred pharmacological treatment for panic disorder because they have few side effects, no dietary restrictions, and absence of tolerance or withdrawal symptoms. To date, three SSRIs, paroxetine (Paxil), sertraline (Zoloft), and fluoxetine (Prozac), have been approved by the FDA for the treatment of panic (Roy-Byrne & Cowley, 2007). Tricyclic antidepressant medications, notably clomipramine (Anafranil) and imipramine (Tofranil), have also contributed to the amelioration of panic disorder, as have monoamine oxidase inhibitors (MAOIs) and benzodiazepines. Two benzodiazepines, alprazolam (Xanax) and clonazepam (Klonopin), have been approved by the FDA. Both have been found to be more effective than a placebo (Evans et al., 2005). Although frequently prescribed by physicians for the treatment of panic disorder, benzodiazepines involve the risk of developing physical dependence and withdrawal symptoms and have been shown to be ineffective in the treatment of comorbid depression (Roy-Byrne & Cowley, 2007). Antidepressant medication has been found to suppress panic attacks but not to diminish anticipatory anxiety, whereas anxiolytics have been found to reduce overall anxiety but not to affect panic attacks. Thus, medication should almost never be the sole modality of treatment for panic disorder. Roy-Byrne and Cowley (2007) report that the combination of psychotherapy and medication may enhance efficacy in treating panic attacks, but relapse often occurs when the medication is discontinued.

Whether a person with panic disorder is referred for medication, the person almost always should be referred for an overall medical evaluation so that the therapist can be sure that the symptoms are indeed of psychological origin. Because people with panic disorder frequently believe their symptoms to be physiological in origin, they are likely to be receptive to the suggestion of a physical examination.

Prognosis

The prognosis for successful treatment of panic disorder, primarily through relatively short-term cognitive-behavioral therapy, is excellent, especially if treatment is sought early in the course of the disorder. One study (Craske & Barlow, 2008) found that 80% to 100% of the people treated were panic free after approximately 15 sessions of treatment, and 50% to 80% of that number were viewed as having been cured of the disorder. More recent research is not quite as optimistic, but indicates a 75% to 95% success rate at the end of 8 to 14 weeks of treatment for panic disorder, with gains maintained 1 to 2 years later (Barlow, 2002). A multicenter study of the efficacy of medication therapy and CBT found that, early on, there was no difference in effectiveness between combined therapy and either CBT or medication alone. However, after treatment ended, CBT alone was found to be superior to medication alone or combined treatment (Evans et al., 2005). This finding is consistent with other studies that have shown a relapse rate of 30% to 90% following discontinuation of medication (Roy-Byrne & Cowley, 2007). Treatment of panic disorder without agoraphobia has a slightly higher rate of success than the rate for panic disorder with agoraphobia (Roth & Fonagy, 2005). Likelihood of relapse is strongly related to the presence of comorbid Axis I and II disorders.

PHOBIAS

The *DSM-IV-TR* describes three categories of phobia: agoraphobia, specific phobia (formerly known as simple phobia), and social phobia. Specific phobia and social phobia are the most common.

Description of the Disorders

Phobias are characterized by two ingredients: a persistent, unwarranted, and disproportionate fear of an actual or anticipated environmental stimulus (for example, certain animals or insects, heights, being alone, enclosed places), and a dysfunctional way of coping with that fear, with resulting impairment in social or occupational functioning (such as refusal to leave one's home). People with phobias often experience either limited-symptom or full panic attacks when they are confronted with or expect to encounter the objects of their fear. Unlike attacks associated with panic disorder, panic attacks associated with phobias are usually cued attacks in which triggers can be identified. Anticipatory anxiety often accompanies an established phobia and may be associated with long-standing underlying apprehension and with avoidance behavior. People often react to these exaggerated and disabling fears with self-protective primal reactions (fight, flight, freeze, or faint). People with phobias typically are aware that their reactions are unreasonable yet feel powerless to change them.

The *DSM* reports a lifetime prevalence of 3.5% for agoraphobia with or without panic disorder (American Psychiatric Association, 2000). Agoraphobia is more common in females, perhaps as much as twice as common as in males.

The incidence of new phobias is highest in childhood and then decreases with maturity, although many phobias have a chronic course. The median age of onset of specific phobia is 7 years (Sadock, 2007). Myriad studies have shown that anxiety in childhood and adolescence often leads to depression later (Barlow, 2002). Most phobias develop suddenly, with the exception of agoraphobia, which tends to have a gradual onset. Phobias, particularly agoraphobia, social phobia, and phobias of the animal type, seem to run in families, but whether this phenomenon is due to learning or to genetics is unclear. People with phobias usually reduce their anxiety by avoiding feared stimuli but simultaneously reinforce their fears through this phobic avoidance. As a result, phobias that have been present for longer than one year are unlikely to remit spontaneously (Antony & Barlow, 2002).

Typical Client Characteristics

The strongest symptoms experienced by people with phobias are racing heart, muscle tension, the urge to run, rapid breathing, an impending feeling of doom, feeling fidgety, shortness of breath, cold hands or feet, trembling, and pounding in the chest (McCabe & Antony, 2002). These symptoms may appear to a greater or lesser extent and in different order of occurrence in the various types of phobias. People with blood and injection phobia may also experience fainting, whereas those with other phobias do not (Antony & Barlow, 2002). Most people encountering a phobic item or situation describe a rush of fear followed by symptoms of arousal. The extent to which the person is sensitive to this physiological response plays a key role in the development of anxiety disorders.

Genetics and biology influence who develops a phobia. Antony and Barlow (2002) conclude that what is most likely inherited is a "low threshold for alarm reactions or vasovagal responses which then interact with environmental influences to set the stage for the development of phobia" (p. 405). Thus, the interaction of anxiety sensitivity and expected anxiety leads to avoidant behavior in an attempt to reduce the fear. Complicating the situation, people with specific phobias tend to hold distorted beliefs about the situations and objects they fear.

People with phobias may be apprehensive and tentative, fearing failure and exposure, at the thought of the feared object or situation or when they are approaching new experiences (McCabe & Antony, 2002). They often feel vulnerable and have deficits in social skills and coping mechanisms. The particular nature of their phobias may limit their social and occupational opportunities and cause conflicts in their relationships. One client, for example, a successful lawyer, had a phobia related to driving. His job was accessible via public transportation, but when he and his wife began to discuss buying a house in the suburbs, he told her that she would have to arrange her work hours so that she could drive him to and from work. The resulting marital conflict led this client to seek therapy.

Assessment

In assessing clients for phobias, clinicians must be able to distinguish between phobias and delusional fears (Antony & Barlow, 2002). Assessment instruments, interview questionnaires, and self-reports are helpful for assessing phobias and are discussed in more detail in the section on specific phobias.

Preferred Therapist Characteristics

Exposure therapy is the most frequently used therapy for the treatment of phobias and may sometimes result in the therapist's treating the phobia where it occurs—at the client's home, for example, or other places (such as elevators or dentists' offices) that evoke fear. The therapist needs to be comfortable taking charge of the therapy and providing structure, direction, and suggested assignments while developing a positive working relationship with the client. Butcher, Mineka, and Hooley (2006) report that encouragement, instruction, suggestion, exhortation, support, and modeling on the part of the therapist can all contribute to the client's improvement.

Intervention Strategies

Exposure-based interventions are the most empirically validated treatments for phobias. The determination of which exposure approach is likely to be the most successful, as well as how that approach should be implemented, depends on the nature and severity of the phobia and on the particular client. For example, massed-exposure sessions and spaced-exposure sessions can both be effective, but some people prefer not to participate in massed-exposure sessions, and their preference should be respected. The following information on exposure-based therapies will be referred to again for the treatment of other anxiety-related disorders.

Exposure-Based Therapies

Exposure-based treatments that present people with feared

objects or situations have been found to be the most effective and empirically supported treatments of phobia (Barlow, 2002; Evans et al., 2005; Head & Gross, 2008; McCabe & Antony, 2002). Exposure-based therapy may occur in vivo or through imaginal desensitization, which occurs in the therapist's office and may include visualization or pictures of the feared object. Various types of pacing may be used (intensive, spaced, or graduated). Regardless of the location or pacing, all exposure-based treatments share the following five common features:

1. Development of anxiety hierarchies.
2. Imaginal or in vivo systematic desensitization, possibly through modeling.
3. Cognitive restructuring.
4. Encouragement of expressions of feeling, a sense of responsibility, and self-confidence.
5. Attention to any family-related issues that may be impinging on the phobia or affected by it and, frequently, inclusion of a partner or significant other in the desensitization process and in communication skills training (especially for the treatment of agoraphobia).

Other components that are frequently added to exposure-based treatment, such as relaxation training, breathing retraining, and paradoxical intention, have been found to be no more effective than the aforementioned combination of interventions alone (Barlow, 2002; Ferguson & Sgambati, 2008; Levis, 2008).

Unless the therapist has reason to believe that a person's phobia is linked to a more complex problem (such as a history of abuse), treatment will usually focus primarily on the symptom itself. A range of techniques has been designed to gradually introduce the person into the feared situation and teach fear-reducing techniques while the anxiety is being experienced. Most approaches to treating phobias are structured and directive and include procedures for quantifying and measuring the severity of the presenting problem and monitoring the client's progress. For example, progress in the treatment of agoraphobia can be reflected by the distance from home that a person becomes willing to travel and by the person's degree of anxiety while away from home.

Most theorists advocate exposing people to feared situations long enough for their fears to be aroused and reduced within a single session. Some studies, however, have also substantiated the value of allowing people to leave frightening situations when their anxiety becomes too uncomfortable, as long as they rapidly return to those situations. Encouraging people to focus on their anxiety and control it through coping self-statements, thought stopping, and relaxation techniques is preferable to encouraging the reduction of fear through distraction.

Flooding. Flooding or implosion involves prolonged and intensive exposure (usually 30 minutes to 8 hours) to the feared object until satiation and anxiety reduction are achieved. Teaching people to use coping self-statements enhances the impact of this exposure because it forces the person to reevaluate the actual threat. Flooding can cause overwhelming initial anxiety, however. If not properly implemented, it can ultimately worsen fears and related physical and emotional conditions, and it is often unappealing to clients. Therefore, it is not often used, but it is sometimes helpful if the feared situation can easily be recreated without causing any danger and when the client can be closely monitored—for example, treating a man with a balloon phobia by having him spend two 45-minute sessions in a room filled with balloons. By contrast, flooding would not be recommended for a driving phobia because that approach clearly could create danger.

Graduated exposure. Graduated exposure involves having a person confront the object of a phobia for a very brief time and then increasing the duration of exposure until the person can remain reasonably calm in the presence of the feared object or situation for approximately 1 hour. This approach could be effective, for example, with a person who is able to look at cars and ride in cars while others are driving, but who has the specific fear of driving a car. Initially, the person could be encouraged to drive the car in the driveway or on his or her own street for a few minutes. The driving time would then gradually be increased as the person became more comfortable with driving.

Systematic desensitization. Systematic desensitization begins by setting up an anxiety hierarchy—a list of the person's fears, organized according to severity. The therapist begins with the least frightening presentation of the feared object (often a picture or other image) and uses relaxation techniques to help the person become comfortable with that level of exposure. Presentations of the feared object gradually move up the hierarchy, with the person becoming acclimated to each successive level. For example, a person with a phobia of snakes might be shown a picture of one snake. After becoming comfortable with that level of exposure, a picture of several snakes might be shown in the next session, and so on, until the person reaches the top level of the hierarchy— the ability to look at a live snake. Systematic desensitization can be imaginal (conducted in the imagination), in vivo (conducted in context), or a combination of the two. More complex fears, as well as fears that are not amenable to treatment via in vivo exposure, can often be successfully treated through imaginal systematic desensitization.

Virtual reality. Technological advances in virtual reality applications over the past 15 years have widened the delivery options for exposure therapy (Riva, 2009). Virtual reality has been used to simulate in vivo exposure for specific phobias including fear of flying, acrophobia, MRI claustrophobia, fear of driving, fear of cockroaches, spiders, and dogs, and many others (Andrews, 2005). More controlled studies are needed on the use of virtual reality to treat phobias. In early studies, virtual reality was found to be equally as effective as in vivo or imaginal therapy (Antony & Barlow, 2002). Despite the great potential of virtual reality-assisted therapy, Rothbaum (2005) warns that incorporating the virtual experience into psychotherapy requires sensitivity to ethical considerations, and that VR should be approached as a tool, not as a substitute for therapy. Therapists must remain mindful of the therapist–client dynamic, and, as with all types of therapy, be qualified to provide VR therapy.

Pacing of exposure. A variety of effective options are also available when it comes to determining the pacing of exposure-based treatments. These include intensive therapy that occurs in one extended 2- to 3-hour session, treatment spaced out over weeks, and graduated treatment that slowly moves up the hierarchy of anxiety. For example, using graduated treatment, a client with a fear of elevators would move slowly up the fear hierarchy by first approaching an elevator, then standing in an elevator, then using the elevator to go up one floor, and finally taking the elevator to the top of the building. This would occur gradually over the course of several sessions, as the client's anxiety level decreased. In contrast, intensive exposure that occurs in one session would require the client to move through the same hierarchy in one intensive 2- to 3-hour session. For many phobias (such as animals, blood, dental procedures), one 2- to 3-hour session of in vivo exposure results in clinically significant improvement in 90% of cases (McCabe & Antony, 2002).

Cognitive restructuring. Although cognitive therapy can be an important adjunct to exposure therapy, it has not been shown to be effective alone in the treatment of phobias. However, cognitive-behavioral interventions can accelerate the treatment of phobias. For example, Socratic questions are designed by therapists to elucidate clients' cognitive distortions and encourage the testing of their validity, helping clients to understand, normalize, and manage their fears. CBT views inordinate fears as being maintained by mistaken or dysfunctional appraisals of situations. Sessions are structured, directive, and problem-oriented. Manageable homework assignments are another central feature of the treatment and are designed to help people face their fears and test and modify their cognitions. These assignments include such experiences as undergoing gradual exposure to feared stimuli, telling others about fears in order to reduce shame, and assessing the validity of beliefs. CBT stresses the principle of overcoming fears by confronting, rather than avoiding, them.

Prognosis

As already mentioned, childhood phobias often remit without treatment, but phobias that have been present for at least one year are unlikely to do so. Most people with phobias do not seek treatment for their symptoms, however, but tend simply to modify their lifestyles so as to tolerate their phobias. This tendency is unfortunate because specific phobias are among the most effectively treated disorders, and several controlled studies have found that up to 90% of people have significant symptom reduction after just 2 to 3 hours of therapy (Evans et al., 2005). Barlow and colleagues (2002) report a positive and enduring response to treatment in 60% to 70% of people who received exposure-based therapy for phobias. The literature indicates that exposure-based gains are lasting, even when treatment consists of a single 3-hour session. In studies of children and adolescents, CBT produces treatment gains even at 1-year follow-up (Evans et al., 2005).

No information is available on the effectiveness of medication alone in treating specific phobias. When phobias are not accompanied by severe depression or panic attacks, they generally do not require referral for medication. This point is expanded on in later sections of this chapter, which deal with the three types of phobias.

Complete remission of a phobia is unusual, and people do tend to retain mild symptoms after treatment, although functioning is much improved. The presence of agoraphobia and personality disorders are frequently associated with relapse.

Let us turn now to an examination of the three types of phobias described in the *DSM-IV-TR:* agoraphobia, specific phobia, and social phobia.

AGORAPHOBIA

Agoraphobia, especially in association with panic disorder, is the most common phobia presented by people seeking treatment. The *DSM-IV-TR* reports that 95% of people who seek treatment for agoraphobia also have panic disorder (which was discussed earlier). Agoraphobia is defined by the *DSM-IV-TR* as "anxiety about being in places or situations from which escape might be difficult (or embarrassing) or in which help might not be available in the event of having an unexpected or situationally predisposed panic attack or panic-like symptom" (American Psychiatric Association, 2000, p. 396). The name of this disorder means "fear of the marketplace" (*marketplace* being the translation of the Greek term *agora*).

Description of the Disorder

People with agoraphobia generally experience fear of losing control and having a limited-symptom panic attack (that is, developing one or a few specific symptoms—for example, loss of bladder control, chest pains, or fainting). As a result of this fear, the individuals restrict their travel and may refuse to enter certain situations without a companion. Places from which escape is difficult (such as cars, tunnels and bridges, supermarket checkout lines, and crowds) are particularly frightening. Exposure to phobic situations typically triggers intense emotional and somatic anxiety, including such symptoms as dizziness, faintness, weakness in the limbs, shortness of breath, and ringing in the ears. People with agoraphobia tend to avoid situations they perceive as dangerous and seek situations where they feel safe. Symptoms can lead to mild to severe restrictions in lifestyle. In severe cases of agoraphobia, people may define a "safe zone" (usually their homes) and be unable to go outside the perimeters (White & Barlow, 2002). This disorder typically begins in the person's twenties or thirties, later than most other phobias.

Typical Client Characteristics

People with agoraphobia tend to be anxious, apprehensive, low in self-esteem, socially uncomfortable, vigilant, concerned about their health, and occasionally obsessive. Depression, anticipatory anxiety, and passivity are common as well; these symptoms not only exacerbate this disorder but are also reactions to the circumscribed lives of the people who suffer from it. Medical problems are often presented, and people with this disorder may view those problems as the reasons for their limited mobility.

People with agoraphobia may avoid caffeine, exercise, and sexual and other activity that produces somatic sensations resembling those associated with panic. White and Barlow term this "interoceptive avoidance" (2002, p. 330). They may also develop substance use problems in an effort to reduce their anxiety, with men more likely than women to self-medicate (Eifert & Forsyth, 2005). Accompanying disorders, particularly avoidant, dependent, and histrionic personality disorders, as well as a history of generalized anxiety disorder, separation anxiety disorder, and social isolation in childhood, are often reported, along with a family history of agoraphobia (Meyer & Deitsch, 1996).

Sometimes a person with agoraphobia feels simultaneously dominated by and dependent on a significant person. This is often the "safe person," the one with whom the person who has agoraphobia feels most comfortable, yet who also often contributes to the dynamics of the disorder. For example, a man's safe person may be his wife, but she may be covertly reinforcing his fears so as to maintain his need for her. Marital difficulties may trigger or exacerbate agoraphobia; the disorder can provide the secondary gain of cementing a marital relationship.

Assessment

The triggering role of stress is common in all anxiety disorders (White & Barlow, 2002). Symptoms can be particularly severe for some women in association with premenstrual dysphoric disorder (White & Barlow, 2002) and are often worsened by caffeine consumption. Such inventories as the Beck Anxiety Inventory (Beck & Steer, 1990), the Mobility Inventory for Agoraphobia (Chambless, Caputo, Gracely, Jasin, & Williams, 1985), and the Agoraphobic Cognitions Questionnaire (Chambless, Caputo, Bright, & Gallagher, 1984) can be useful in assessing symptoms. Suicide risk should also be assessed, as people with agoraphobia often have significant impairment in functioning and quality of life and have an increased rate of suicidal ideation (Baker et al., 2002).

Preferred Therapist Characteristics

Providing support, compassion, acceptance, and empathy is essential in the treatment of all anxiety disorders (Eifert & Forsyth, 2005). This is especially true for agoraphobia. Encouragement and reinforcement can also help the client take risks. The therapist's comfort with providing structure and contextual therapy, as well as with the client's initial dependence, is particularly important. As is true with all phobias, therapist modeling can have a positive effect.

Intervention Strategies

According to White and Barlow (2002), agoraphobia that is seen for treatment is usually a part of panic disorder. If the panic disorder is treated, the agoraphobia often improves, as do any co-occurring mood and personality disorders. The effectiveness of panic-control therapy (PCT) in the treatment of panic disorder with agoraphobia has been well documented in numerous studies and one meta-analysis (Goldstein, de Beurs, Chambless, & Wilson, 2000). White and Barlow (2002) report that more than 25 controlled clinical trials support the effectiveness of PCT for the treatment of panic disorder with agoraphobia. A meta-analysis of treatment outcomes in 43 controlled studies showed that PCT yielded the largest effect size (0.88) in comparison to cognitive therapy or medication alone (Barlow et al., 2002). Approximately 75% of the people treated for agoraphobia achieved significant improvement in symptoms and functioning, and 65% maintained gains at 2-year follow-up (Barlow et al., 2002).

Several new approaches show promise, but more research is needed to determine if they are as effective as PCT. Sensation-focused intensive treatment (SFIT) combines treatments for panic and avoidance in a CBT self-study format that takes place over 8 consecutive days (White & Barlow, 2002). Acceptance and commitment therapy (ACT), as explained earlier, is another treatment methodology that shows promise. Clearly, additional studies need to be conducted on the effectiveness of these treatments.

If the agoraphobia is not accompanied by panic attacks, then behavioral methods in combination with cognitive therapy are generally the treatment of choice (White & Barlow, 2002). Not surprisingly, exposure to frightening situations—in sessions and through homework assignments—is the key element of most approaches to treating agoraphobia, and many variations on this strategy have been developed. The client should remain in the exposure situation long enough, and should repeat the exposure frequently enough, for the anxiety to be diminished. This procedure is called *habituation*. Fear of habituation may precipitate clients' noncompliance with treatment and their premature termination; therefore, a carefully paced and supportive approach is indicated.

One study indicates that clients treated with 12 sessions of graduated, self-paced exposure showed an 87% improvement, with 96% remaining in remission after 2 years and 77% at 5 years. The most important predictor of relapse was "residual agoraphobia," suggesting the need to ensure that treatment continues until all symptoms are eliminated (White & Barlow, 2002).

Other behavioral interventions shown to reduce symptoms of agoraphobia include training in relaxation and assertiveness. Cognitive therapy—using thought stopping, restructuring of negative thoughts, and training in positive self-statements about coping abilities—has also contributed to symptom relief, especially in combination with exposure (Goldstein et al., 2000; White & Barlow, 2002). Logs of symptoms and of exposure activities are helpful adjuncts to treatment and can be used to assess and reinforce progress. Skills training has also been shown to be a useful adjunct to CBT.

Both family and group therapy can also enhance the treatment of agoraphobia; indeed, several studies suggest that family dynamics should receive attention in the treatment of people with agoraphobia because the disorder affects the entire family system. White and Barlow (2002) report an uncontrolled clinical trial which indicated that training spouses as cotherapists effected a 90% improvement rate in the person with agoraphobia. Other studies showed continuing improvement at 4- and 9-year follow-up. Partner involvement, either as coaches or as participants in family therapy, improves communication, educates spouses or significant others about the manner in which their role as a safe person actually reinforces agoraphobic behavior, improves the modification of behavior, and helps maintain continued success after treatment has ended. Husbands who were supportive and involved in their wives' recoveries reported concurrent marital improvement. As for group therapy, treatment in a group setting can help reduce dependence on the safe person and can offer models and support, as well as motivation for remaining in the group and practicing behaviors between sessions and after treatment ends (White & Barlow, 2002).

Although little research is available, some movement has been made in the area of self-directed treatments for agoraphobia. Several studies have compared therapist instruction with computer-assisted instruction and text instruction in treatment delivery. No difference in outcomes was found; however, in severe cases of agoraphobia, text instruction was not shown to be effective (White & Barlow, 2002). More research is needed on alternative methods of delivering mental health treatment in general.

Medication, particularly drugs designed to reduce anxiety, is sometimes combined with psychotherapy in the treatment of agoraphobia. Research indicates that although such combination treatment is effective in the short term, high relapse rates occur when the medications are discontinued. Over the long term, medication shows no advantage over cognitive-behavioral therapy alone (White & Barlow, 2002). Such medications as anxiolytics and benzodiazepines may actually reduce the effectiveness of CBT, as they decrease the anxiety necessary for exposure therapy to work. Moreover, withdrawal from medication sometimes triggers a relapse. Medication does have a role in the treatment of agoraphobia, especially when it accompanies panic disorder, but medication alone clearly is inferior to exposure treatment, and, even as an adjunct to psychotherapy, medication should be used with great caution, perhaps only for severe and treatment-resistant cases.

Prognosis

Although many people with agoraphobia continue to have underlying fears, there is no doubt that treatment dramatically improves their quality of life. Effective treatment has also been shown to have a positive impact on co-occurring anxiety and depression and, in one study, was also shown to reduce alcohol misuse (White & Barlow, 2002). Although relapse is not unusual, a relapse seems easier to treat than the original disorder.

SPECIFIC PHOBIAS

The *DSM-IV-TR* defines a specific phobia as "a marked and persistent fear that is excessive or unreasonable, cued by the presence or anticipation of a specific object or situation" (American Psychiatric Association, 2000, p. 449).

Phobias are classified into five groups:

1. Animal type
2. Natural environment type (such as heights or thunderstorms)
3. Blood-injection-injury type
4. Situational type (such as flying, escalators, bridges, public speaking)
5. Other type (such as fear of choking or contracting an illness)

Description of the Disorders

Common specific phobias include fear of dogs, snakes, heights, thunderstorms, flying, injections, and the sight of blood, but they may also involve unusual objects or situations, such as balloons or stairs with openings between the treads.

The situational type, which usually begins in the middle twenties, is most common in adults; the animal type and the blood-injection-injury type are most common in children. Females are more likely to develop phobias, particularly of the animal type. Men are more likely to fear spiders, deep water, and heights. Antony and Barlow suggest that differences in phobia rates between genders may be related to the fact that men tend to underreport their fears. Women are more likely to have learned fearful behavior through modeling. Women, in general, seek treatment at higher rates than men. One study of men and women

found that the most frequently feared objects and situations (in descending order) are heights, snakes, closed spaces, spiders, injuries, flying, darkness, and dentists (Antony & Barlow, 2002).

Adults with specific phobias typically recognize the excessive or unreasonable nature of their reactions, but the phobias still may interfere with activities and relationships and may cause considerable distress. Exposure to feared stimuli typically results in high anxiety and perhaps even in a situationally related or cued panic attack. Tantrums and clinging may be manifested by children in frightening situations. A minimum duration of six months is required for the diagnosis of a specific phobia in a person under the age of 18.

Phobias in children are relatively common and seem to be of sources of natural danger such as snakes, the dark, heights, and blood. Most remit spontaneously; if a phobia persists into adulthood, however, it is unlikely to remit without treatment. A phobia may stem from a childhood fear that has not been outgrown and has been entrenched by avoidance, or the phobia may have begun in adulthood. Researchers disagree on the exact role that experience, vicarious acquisition, and information learning have on the development of phobias. Genetics and environment both seem to play a role in the development of specific phobias, but the extent that either plays and the differences in their role in causing phobias are yet to be resolved (Antony & Barlow, 2002). Some people present with multiple phobias, but these often involve a common underlying fear that can become the focus of treatment.

Specific phobias are quite common, with a lifetime prevalence rate ranging from 7% to 11% (McCabe & Antony, 2002). Nearly 50% of the population has a lifetime fear of one sort or another (Antony & Barlow, 2002). However, only a small percentage of people develop a disabling phobia that interferes with daily life, and even fewer will seek treatment for their phobias; instead, the usual responses are modifications in lifestyle and accommodation to avoid episodic anxiety.

Typical Client Characteristics

Very little information is available about common personality patterns in people with specific phobias, probably because the disorder is so pervasive and diverse and tends to be linked more to experiences than to personality traits. Nevertheless, people with specific phobias do have a disproportionate number of first-degree relatives who have similar phobias and who may share a common genetic predisposition toward fear and/or may have communicated these phobias to other family members (Antony & Barlow, 2002).

Anxiety in response to physical sensations may play a role in the development of specific phobias, especially claustrophobia (McCabe & Antony, 2002). When anticipating or confronting feared objects or situations, people with specific phobias typically become agitated and tearful and may experience physical symptoms of anxiety, such as shortness of breath, fear of doom, desire to run, and heart palpitations. People with phobias of the blood-injection-injury type sometimes faint in the presence of the feared stimulus. A medical examination may be a useful safeguard with fragile or highly anxious clients, to ensure that they can handle the temporarily increased stress caused by treatment.

Phobias are often accompanied by other anxiety, mood, and substance-related disorders and may have been preceded by traumatic or very frightening experiences (McCabe & Antony, 2002). The therapist should elicit information on antecedent events, comorbid disorders, and secondary gains that may complicate treatment of the disorder.

Assessment

Assessments that measure phobic reactions to spiders and snakes are available. For example, the Spider Questionnaire (SPQ; Klorman, Hastings, Weerts, Melamed, & Lang, 1974) and the Snake Questionnaire (SNAQ; Klorman et al., 1974) are both 30-item self-report scales. No published assessments for fears of other animals, such as cats, birds, or rodents are currently available. However, a questionnaire for dog phobia is in development. Other assessments for specific phobias include the Medical Fear Survey, a 50-item self-report scale that measures fear of injections, blood drawing, sharp objects, and medical examination, and the Dental Anxiety Inventory, which measures fear of dental procedures. A more complete discussion of assessment tools for specific phobias can be found in McCabe and Antony (2002).

Preferred Therapist Characteristics

Treatment of specific phobias is often anxiety provoking for clients, and a therapist who models nonfearful behavior can be an important part of treatment. However, Antony and Barlow (2002) report that observational learning is not enough to effect significant change. A therapist who is supportive and optimistic about the outcome of treatment and who can communicate acceptance and empathy while still encouraging people to experience frightening situations is ideal. Creativity and flexibility can be useful in planning exposure and related treatments. When working with clients who are averse to in vivo exposure, especially in phobias related to heights, therapists may need to accompany the client to the location.

Intervention Strategies

Specific phobias are the most treatable of all anxiety disorders. Exposure, typically involving prolonged contact with feared objects or situations, is the empirically supported treatment of choice for this disorder. In this approach, a list (usually including about 10 feared stimuli) is developed. To facilitate the establishment of a hierarchy, each of the listed stimuli is then rated on a scale of 1 to 100 for the level of fear and avoidance it provokes. In vivo or imaginal desensitization is then used to lessen fear. This approach to treatment involves relaxation and exposure to one item at a time until the anxiety connected to that item is reduced to a manageable level. In vivo treatment is usually preferable, but imaginal exposure involving visualization and pictures can also be effective, especially if it is combined with carefully planned actual contact with feared stimuli outside the treatment sessions. Most children, however, are not developmentally capable of benefiting from imaginal exposure (Head & Gross, 2008). Some use is being made of virtual reality techniques to provide exposure treatment for fear of flying and other specific phobias. One extended session (2 to 3 hours) may lead to extremely significant improvement in 90% of cases of specific phobia (McCabe & Antony, 2002).

Combining exposure treatment with encouragement to develop a sense of mastery usually contributes to the effectiveness of treatment for specific phobias. Exposure treatment can also be enhanced by the following techniques:

- Imaginal flooding (used carefully)
- Use of positive coping statements
- Paradoxical intention (focusing on anticipatory anxiety)
- Thought stopping
- Thought switching
- Success rehearsal
- Assertiveness training
- Hypnosis
- Cognitive restructuring

- Increased exposure to and awareness of internal cues of anxiety
- Modeling by the therapist or another
- Reinforced practice
- Supportive and family therapy

Cognitive strategies can be integrated into an exposure-based treatment program to enhance treatment effectiveness. However, cognitive approaches alone are usually ineffective in the treatment of specific phobias. One study indicated that cognitive restructuring alone was better than either education or being placed on a wait-list and not receiving treatment for dental phobia. In general, however, exposure-based treatment combined with cognitive restructuring is the most effective treatment approach (Antony & Barlow, 2002).

Massed exposure, which takes place in a single 2- to 3-hour session, seems to lead to significant fear reduction (Antony & Barlow, 2002), particularly for circumscribed phobias, such as dental phobias or phobias of the animal type. More complex phobias, as well as the blood-injection-injury type (which may cause fainting), usually need somewhat longer and more gradually paced treatment.

Medication is rarely indicated in the treatment of specific phobias, and may actually interfere with the person's ability to benefit from the effects of exposure-based treatments. Benzodiazepines, in particular, tend to reduce anxiety and prevent the person's fear from reaching the level necessary for the client to benefit from exposure-based treatment (Antony & Barlow, 2002). Short-term treatment with benzodiazepines (for example, taking alprazolam during an airplane flight or 30 minutes before dental treatment) was found to be effective for reducing anxiety connected to a specific event. However, in both cases, greater fear was experienced with the next occurrence of the feared situation. In contrast, cognitive-behavioral therapy was associated with fear reduction and further improvements (Antony & Barlow, 2002).

Few studies have looked at the effectiveness of group therapy for specific phobias. One study using exposure and modeling to treat spider phobia yielded significant improvement (Öst, 1996). Groups of three or four were found to be more effective than groups of seven or eight.

Prognosis

The prognosis for treatment of specific phobias is generally excellent, with most people (70% to 85%) showing significant improvement. Often, however, some residual apprehension associated with feared stimuli remains or returns years later. If noncompliance is impeding treatment, the presence of secondary gains should be investigated.

SOCIAL PHOBIA

Social phobia is defined by the *DSM-IV-TR* as "a marked and persistent fear of one or more social or performance situations in which the person is exposed to unfamiliar situations or to possible scrutiny by others" (American Psychiatric Association, 2000, p. 456). Underlying the situational fear is worry that the person will do or say something that will be humiliating or embarrassing (Hofmann & Barlow, 2002). Social phobia, also called *social anxiety disorder*, is very common. The National Comorbidity Survey Replication indicates a 12% lifetime prevalence rate (Kessler, Berglund, et al., 2005).

Description of the Disorder

Social phobias often focus on one or more specific situations, such as public speaking, eating in public, taking tests, attending parties, interacting with authority figures, and being interviewed. For men, urinating in a public restroom may cause undue anxiety.

Situations involving evaluation are likely to be particularly threatening. Actual or threatened exposure to such situations typically produces an immediate anxiety response that may involve noticeable physical symptoms, such as blushing, perspiration, hoarseness, and tremor (Markway & Markway, 2003). These symptoms can contribute to worsening of the original fear by exacerbating embarrassment. Typically, people with social phobia avoid anxiety-provoking social or occupational situations. Continued avoidance behaviors associated with social phobia can sometimes lead to social isolation.

People who fear most social situations are described as having a generalized type of social anxiety disorder. One client who was typical of people with social phobia, generalized type, had married the daughter of a family friend and secured stable employment, but his life was still shaped by his phobia. He sought treatment at the age of 35 because he saw himself as harming his family; he had turned down several promotions because they involved leading meetings, and he refused to attend events at his child's school because of his fear of meeting new people. He and his wife had little social life outside their immediate families.

Considerable impairment can be evident in people with social phobia. Staying in their comfort zones and avoiding anxiety-producing experiences tend to reduce personal and professional opportunities. People with this disorder are frequently underemployed, have a relatively low rate of marriage, and may have panic attacks and suicidal thoughts related to the phobia. As is true with specific phobias, adolescents and adults typically recognize the excessive nature of their fears. Nevertheless, social phobia is unlikely to remit without treatment.

Children with this disorder often exhibit selective mutism, school refusal, separation anxiety, and excessive shyness. Duration of at least six months is required for the diagnosis of this disorder in a person under the age of 18.

Several explanations have been offered for social phobia, including deficits in social skills, conditioned responses to painful experiences, emotional blocks, deficits in perceptual or cognitive processing, and oversensitivity to anxiety. The onset of social phobia may immediately follow a humiliating incident, or it may be insidious (Markway & Markway, 2003). Males and females are equally likely to seek treatment for social phobia, but the disorder seems to be more common in women, at a ratio of 3:2 (Kessler, Berglund, et al., 2005). For both men and women, however, social phobia tends to begin in childhood or adolescence; it rarely begins after the age of 25 and, without treatment, usually has a chronic course (Turk et al., 2008).

Typical Client Characteristics

People with social phobia tend to fear their own emotional reactions to new situations. In social interactions, they rate themselves negatively; exhibit "socially pleasing behaviors," such as smiling, agreeing, apologizing, and making excuses; and typically manifest submissive and avoidant behavior (Hofmann & Barlow, 2002). Because they expect they will not measure up in social situations, they are often hypervigilant for any reactions that reinforce their negative expectations (Markway & Markway, 2003). This excessive focus on their own reactions siphons their attentional resources away from performance of the task at hand, and results in decreased performance on tests, in social interactions, and in interpersonal skills. The outcome is increased anxiety and a vicious loop that includes avoidance of the feared situation and impaired performance.

In addition to exhibiting low self-esteem, people with social phobia may be fragile and easily hurt; sensitive to anger, criticism, or other means of social disapproval; and weak in social skills (Hofmann & Barlow, 2002). These deficits can take many forms. For example, some people with this disorder mask their anxiety with aggression; others seem shy and insecure; and still others participate in avoidant behaviors, such as drinking alcohol before a social event, limiting the time they remain at a social event, or avoiding eye contact (Markway & Markway, 2003).

Both genetic and social factors play a role in the development of social phobia. Twin studies show a 24% concordance rate of social phobia in identical twins, suggesting a genetic component. Hofmann and Barlow (2002) report that social phobia occurs at a rate 3 times higher for relatives of people with the disorder. Inherited temperament characteristics of shyness, timidity, or fearfulness when meeting new people can contribute to the disorder. Behavioral inhibition in childhood is frequently associated with the development of social phobia in adolescence (Hofmann & Barlow, 2002). Social skills, like many others, are learned through family interactions and practice. Thirteen percent of people with social phobia have reported that observational learning was an important part of the development of their disorder (Markway & Markway, 2003).

Social phobia is also associated with accompanying disorders 70% to 80% of the time. In most cases, social anxiety disorder preceded the development of these other conditions. Fifty percent of people with social phobia also have a depressive disorder, as many as one third also misuse alcohol, a dangerous combination that results in increased suicidal risk (Kessler, Chiu, et al., 2005; Turk et al., 2008). Other anxiety disorders, avoidant personality disorder, and substance-related disorders commonly co-occur. Educational, marital, occupational, financial, and interpersonal difficulties are also likely to be seen in people with social phobia.

Assessment

Behavioral assessment tests, interview-rated scales, and self-report scales such as the Fear of Negative Evaluation Scale and the Social Interaction Anxiety Scales (SIAS; Mattick & Clarke, 1998) can be very helpful in assessing social anxiety. Journals, logs, and other self-monitoring forms can also be used to assess symptoms and monitor progress. Because of the high incidence of co-occurring disorders, clients should also be assessed for other anxiety disorders, depression, and substance-related disorders in particular.

Preferred Therapist Characteristics

Clients with social phobia typically bring their interpersonal discomfort into the therapy room and are fearful of possible rejection or disapproval by the therapist. An important role for the therapist, then, is to help clients manage the initial anxiety well enough that they do not flee therapy before the process can begin. The development of trust can be a slow process. This is especially true for people with intense social fears and those who have co-occurring avoidant personality disorder (Markway & Markway, 2003). The client with social phobia may not be ready for exposure therapy or may be unable to complete homework assignments due to sensitivity to perceived criticism. Therapists working with such clients must take care not to be rejecting, angry, or critical. They should examine their own beliefs about the process of change, recognize the need to slow down the process, and praise attempts at progress, rather than looking for immediate results or perfection.

Intervention Strategies

The treatment of social phobia is more complex than the treatment of a specific phobia because the impact of social phobia is usually broader and greater. Although the repertoire of useful behavioral interventions is the same for all phobic disorders, the treatment plan for social phobia is typically multifaceted and is aimed both at reducing fear and at improving socialization and social skills. Cognitive interventions are almost always integrated with behavioral ones.

A review of five meta-analyses of treatment for social anxiety disorder concluded that all types of cognitive-behavioral therapies studied (exposure alone, cognitive restructuring alone, exposure combined with cognitive restructuring, social skills training, and applied relaxation) showed moderate to large effect compared to wait list controls for adults with the disorder (Rodebaugh, Holaway, & Heimberg, 2004). The same results occurred regardless of whether treatment was provided to the individual or in a group setting. Interestingly, exposure interventions in the treatment of social phobia, even without cognitive restructuring techniques, achieved the same results as exposure therapy with cognitive restructuring, or exposure therapy alone (Rodebaugh et al., 2004). Even so, cognitive therapy with exposure is the most commonly recommended treatment option for social anxiety disorder. Treatment manuals provide a step-by-step discussion of exposure-based therapy alone (Heimberg & Becker, 2002), and integrated exposure and cognitive restructuring for social anxiety disorder (Turk et al., 2008).

Some form of self-monitoring is also a valuable aspect of the treatment and may involve soliciting feedback from others, role playing, rehearsal with videotaping or audiotaping, self-ratings, and ratings by others. Homework assignments, to facilitate the application of in-session learning, are almost always part of the treatment. Social skills training may focus on communication skills, tone of voice, posture, eye contact, and other aspects of socialization, according to the needs of the individual client.

Relaxation techniques, such as abdominal breathing, visualization, and progressive muscle relaxation, can also be helpful in reducing the anxiety associated with social phobia (Berstein, Borkovec, & Hazlett-Stephens, 2000; Markway & Markway, 2003). Cognitive-behavioral group therapy (CBGT), developed by Heimberg and colleagues (1998) for treatment of social phobia, is included in a list of empirically supported treatments by the American Psychological Association (Hofmann & Barlow, 2002). CBGT is usually conducted in weekly 2.5-hour sessions over a 12-week period. Clients reported less anxiety posttreatment, which was maintained at 6-month follow-up. CBGT (like CBT) is based on the assumption that changes in cognitions are necessary for treatment progress to occur. Group therapy is valuable for people who are not too incapacitated by social phobia. The group interaction gives people the opportunity to learn new skills from others, experiment in a safe setting with new ways of relating, and receive feedback from peers.

Other treatments such as mindfulness, attention training, self-efficacy interventions such as guided mastery, and interpersonal therapy also show promise in the treatment of social phobia (Rowa & Antony, 2005; Scott & Cervone, 2008). Additional research is necessary to determine if they are effective. Medication does not cure social phobia, but it is sometimes used in combination with psychotherapy, especially to reduce performance anxiety and improve people's ability to participate in therapy. To date, only three SSRIs—fluvoxamine (Luvox CR), paroxetine (Paxil), and sertraline (Zoloft)—and the serotonin-norepinephrine reuptake inhibitor venlafaxine (Effexor XR) have received FDA approval for the treatment of social anxiety disorder. Other medications, such as MAOIs, beta-blockers, and benzodiazepines, have also been used with some success. Limited studies have been conducted on the effectiveness of benzodiazepines—clonazepam (Klonopin) and alprazolam (Xanax)—on social phobia. Both were found to be more effective than placebo at reducing social anxiety symptoms; however, benzodiazepines can lead to physical dependence and a high rate of relapse after discontinuation. They are also contraindicated in people who use alcohol or who have co-occurring depression. Hofmann and Barlow (2002) report that most people returned to pretreatment levels 2 months after discontinuing medications and that relapse rates are higher when medication is used than in the use of cognitive-behavioral therapy alone.

Prognosis

Behavioral, cognitive, and combined cognitive-behavioral interventions have been found to be successful in the treatment of social phobia (Evans et al., 2005; Rodebaugh et al., 2004; Turk et al., 2008). Direct comparison has not indicated greater efficacy of any one of these and probably CBT should generally be the treatment of choice. Evans and colleagues note that a variety of medications have been reported to be helpful in 40% to 55% of cases, but these clients still retained clinically significant symptoms. A combination of medication management and CBT showed a slightly greater efficacy than either treatment alone.

OBSESSIVE-COMPULSIVE DISORDER

Great strides have been made over the past 30 years in understanding and successfully treating obsessive-compulsive disorder (OCD). According to the *DSM-IV-TR*, people diagnosed with OCD have obsessions (recurrent intrusive thoughts, images, or impulses) or compulsions (repetitive, purposeful, driven behaviors or mental acts designed to reduce anxiety or avoid a feared circumstance) or a combination of the two (American Psychiatric Association, 2000). These thoughts and behaviors are distressing and interfere with daily activities and social and occupational functioning. People with OCD typically realize that their thoughts or behaviors are excessive and unreasonable yet are unable to get rid of them. In adolescents or adults who do not see the excessive or unreasonable nature of their thoughts or actions, the disorder is described as "with poor insight." The course of this often chronic disorder is typically static or gets worse without treatment.

Description of the Disorder

Specific obsessions and compulsions are the hallmarks of this disorder and distinguish it from the similarly named but unrelated obsessive-compulsive personality disorder (OCPD), in which obsessions and compulsions are not present; rather, a perfectionistic or compulsive lifestyle characterizes people with OCPD (see Chapter 8). In OCD, obsessions typically have some content that is unacceptable to the client (because it is immoral, illegal, disgusting, or embarrassing) and that creates considerable anxiety. The client may also engage in magical thinking and believe that having a thought is tantamount to acting on that thought, or fear that their thoughts may bring about harm to themselves or others.

Compulsions, as already mentioned, are behavioral or mental acts, often ritualized, that must be carried out to prevent anxiety, discomfort, or unwanted thoughts and events. People with OCD usually have both obsessions and compulsions, and these are yoked in some way. For example, a woman who had obsessions about accidentally shutting her cat in the refrigerator also had the compulsion of emptying out and replacing the contents of her refrigerator several times a day, to be sure that the cat was not in there.

Four patterns are particularly common in OCD and are listed here in descending order of prevalence (Steketee & Barlow, 2002):

1. Obsessions focused on contamination are accompanied by excessive washing and avoidance of objects viewed as carriers of germs and disease. Anxiety, shame, disgust, and extremely involved rituals are common in people with these symptoms.
2. Obsessive doubts lead to time-consuming and sometimes ritualized counting, repeating, and checking (for example, of appliances or of door and window locks). Guilt and worry about forgetting something important usually characterize these people.
3. Obsessions without compulsions sometimes occur (usually thoughts of a religious nature, or of sexual or violent acts that are horrifying to the person).
4. A powerful need for symmetry or precision can cause the person to perform even routine activities (such as eating and dressing) with extreme slowness.

Common compulsions in addition to those just listed include counting, hoarding, repeating, organizing, asking for reassurance, and touching in some ritualistic fashion. Many people with OCD exhibit multiple symptoms that often overlap, such as checking and contamination-related symptoms (Steketee & Barlow, 2002). Symptoms of OCD tend to wax and wane over time, based on life stress (Franklin & Foa, 2007).

It is estimated that 3 million Americans have OCD at any given time (Steketee & Pigott, 2006). The chronic nature of the disorder and its debilitating effects have resulted in OCD being the 10th leading cause of medical disability in the industrialized nations (Murray & Lopez,

1996). OCD seems equally common in both genders, but it begins earlier in males. The disorder can begin as early as the age of 2, but it most often begins in the late teens for males and in the early twenties for females. It rarely begins after age 50 (Steketee & Barlow, 2002). The disorder frequently has a sudden onset, which often follows a stressful or traumatic life event. In 40% of cases, however, no precipitant is found.

Current research primarily supports a biological (genetic) cause in the development of OCD, along with the formation of dysfunctional beliefs through verbal instructions, observational learning, or modeling (Taylor, Thordarson, & Sochting, 2002). The symptoms of OCD—intrusive thoughts and compulsive actions—are found in mild versions in up to 90% of the general population; however, these thoughts may occur 10 times a month or less, whereas people with full-blown OCD find it difficult to avoid obsessing and may spend hours a day performing compulsive rituals.

Typical Client Characteristics

Many characteristic personality patterns have been identified in people with OCD. People with OCD tend to have rigid consciences and strong feelings of guilt and remorse. They feel driven and pressured, ruminate excessively, doubt themselves, are concerned with control, have a high need for reassurance, and tend to be indecisive and perfectionistic. Both memory factors and emotional factors may lie at the heart of OCD. They typically conceal their symptoms for years before seeking help, and they feel shame and guilt about their symptoms. They sometimes are aggressive and avoid intimacy and affectionate feelings. Compulsive hoarding is found in as many as 30% of people with OCD (Steketee & Frost, 2004).

Co-occurring disorders are common. About one third of people with OCD have a coexisting major depressive disorder or dysthymic disorder; 39% have another anxiety disorder, such as social phobia, generalized anxiety disorder, PTSD, or panic disorder (Kessler, Berglund, et al., 2005). Body dysmorphic disorder co-occurs in 12% of people with OCD (Butcher et al., 2006). Cluster C personality disorders (especially dependent and avoidant personality disorders) occur in as many as 50% of people with OCD, although co-occurring OCPD is rare (Steketee & Pigott, 2006). Eating disorders (particularly bulimia) are found concurrently in nearly 10% of people with OCD. More than any other anxiety disorder, alcohol and substance use may become a problem for people with OCD as they turn to substances to reduce their anxiety. Tourette's disorder seems to be genetically linked with OCD, and research is ongoing in this area. As many as 63% of people with Tourette's disorder have OCD, but only 17% of people with OCD have Tourette's disorder (Franklin & Foa, 2008).

OCD exists on a continuum of severity. The amount of time spent on compulsions can be excessive and many people with this disorder have difficulties in their relationships and in employment as a result. Insight also must be measured as some people with OCD are unaware that their behavior is excessive. Lack of insight is a specifier for the disorder and is associated with poorer treatment outcomes, as is co-occurring depression which may reduce the client's hope about therapy being successful (Franklin & Foa, 2008). Imaginative, dissociative, and schizotypal processes have also been found to be related to the development of OCD symptoms. Specifically, an overreliance on imagination during reasoning can result in inferential thinking that is inconsistent with reality (Aardema & Wu, 2011).

Assessment

Assessment tools for OCD generally involve a clinical interview, as well as self-report and behavioral assessment instruments. Steketee and Barlow consider the Yale-Brown Obsessive Compulsive Scale (Y-BOCS; Steketee, Frost, & Bogart, 1996) as "one of the most useful measures of OCD symptoms from a clinical standpoint" (2002, p. 536). Observations during the interview can further inform assessment of OCD. For example, clients may avoid touching doorknobs, check and recheck items, or continually ask for reassurance. Indecisiveness, perfectionism, and a need for constant reassurance are symptoms of OCD that may hinder the assessment process. Taylor and colleagues (2002) recommend that therapists be gentle but persistent, remind clients of time constraints of the session, and ask more closed rather than open-ended questions. In the course of the interview, thought-action fusion—the belief that a thought will actually happen—can reduce the client's desire to disclose obsessions.

A self-report measure, the Obsessive-Compulsive Inventory-Revised (OCI-R; Foa et al., 2002) is an 18-item report that yields results on six separate subscales: washing, checking, ordering, obsessing, hoarding, and neutralizing. The OCI-R has good internal consistency and test-retest reliability. Resistance is especially likely to impede treatment of OCD in people who are depressed and who have poor insight, overvalued ideations, and difficulty seeing the unreasonable nature of their thoughts and behaviors (Franklin, Ledley, & Foa, 2008). In planning treatment for OCD, it is important to assess for symptoms associated with any co-occurring disorders (Taylor et al., 2002).

Preferred Therapist Characteristics

People with OCD tend to drop out of treatment prematurely, but those who stay in treatment are likely to have relatively high success rates (Watson, Anderson, & Rees, 2010). Therapists who work with this population should be capable of developing and implementing structured exposure and response-prevention treatment protocols that may require both the therapist and the client to tolerate emotional distress. Prompting the client to cooperate with treatment may require the therapist to remind the client that exposure therapy is the client's choice, to reassure the client about treatment efficacy, and to assure the client that the therapist will work with him or her through the process (Zoellner, Abramowitz, Moore, & Slagle, 2008). A delicate balance between support and pressure should be maintained by the therapist working with a client who has OCD. The shame, guilt, anxiety, and reluctance to self-disclose that are common in people with this disorder require a therapist who is respectful, encouraging, and flexible. At the same time, the therapist needs to be structured, firm, specific, and able to plan ahead.

Intervention Strategies

The literature on the treatment of OCD is consistent in recommending exposure and response prevention therapy as the first-line treatment of choice for OCD. Prolonged exposure to obsessional cues, and strict prevention of rituals, have been found to be more efficacious than relaxation, anxiety management training, or placebo medication. A review of 12 outcome studies found a treatment response rate of 83% and much of the gains were maintained at long-term follow up (Franklin & Foa, 2008; McCabe & Antony, 2002; S. Taylor et al., 2002). The first step in applying this treatment usually involves obtaining a clear idea of the nature, frequency, and severity of the obsessions, compulsions, and anxiety.

Both the exposure and the response prevention need to be carefully planned and controlled.

The exposure typically is graduated, beginning with situations that evoke low anxiety and then moving on to higher levels of anxiety-provoking stimuli as clients become habituated to the lower levels. Franklin and Foa (2008) emphasize the importance of not terminating the exposure while the person's level of distress is still high; thus exposure sessions should last from 45 minutes to 2 hours, to allow ample time for anxiety to rise and then fall. Once clients have developed some comfort and familiarity with this procedure, they are encouraged to continue the exposure and response prevention at home, often with the help of friends or family members. Keeping a written diary of these experiences helps the client track and solidify progress.

Although exposure and response prevention are the essential ingredients of treatment for OCD, up to 25% of clients refuse this treatment approach (Woo & Keatinge, 2008). Other treatment approaches and interventions that have been found to be effective include cognitive approaches designed to help people challenge their errors in thinking. This can provide results that are similar to exposure and response prevention therapy (Abramowitz, 1997; Head & Gross, 2008). Family involvement in treatment improves outcomes for children and adolescents, although higher rates of family dysfunction reduce treatment effect (Franklin & Foa, 2008).

Acceptance and commitment therapy (ACT) was initially used in the treatment of substance addiction. It has since been adapted for use with anxiety and depression. The resulting effect is a paradoxical decrease in distressing thoughts and an increase in metacognitive awareness (Wells, 2009). A randomized controlled trial of ACT for OCD versus progressive relaxation training for pain showed similar results with both treatments. Further research is indicated (Twohig et al., 2010).

Therapy for OCD is typically of relatively brief duration (sometimes fewer than 10 sessions). Between-session assignments, however, as well as relapse prevention training, are essential in effecting and maintaining improvement (Franklin & Foa, 2008).

Medication has been proven effective in the treatment of OCD. The drugs most commonly used include SSRIs such as fluoxetine (Prozac), sertraline, paroxetine, and fluvoxamine, as well as the tricyclic antidepressant clomipramine (Steketee & Barlow, 2002). It may be 6 to 10 weeks before these medications have a demonstrable impact on the symptoms of OCD, but they can reduce symptoms by as much as 60% (Franklin & Foa, 2008). Treatment gains are lost, however, when medication is stopped. Other medications, such as clonazepam (Klonopin) and buspirone (BuSpar), may also be used to augment exposure and response prevention and SSRI treatment, especially if severe depression or anxiety is present.

Prognosis

Therapists should try to set realistic goals for the treatment of OCD. Although a high percentage of people completing treatment do experience significant improvement, incomplete improvement is far more likely than full recovery. However, even a 50% reduction in symptoms is likely to make a considerable difference in people's lives.

Factors associated with a positive prognosis include the presence of compulsions, low anxiety and depression, brief duration of the disorder before help is sought, the client's insight into the unrealistic nature of the thoughts and actions, the client's positive social and environmental adjustment, and the presence of an identified precipitant for the onset of the disorder (Franklin & Foa, 2008; McCabe & Antony, 2002; Steketee & Barlow, 2002; Taylor, Thordason, et al.,

2002). Compulsions and checking symptoms seem to respond particularly well to treatment. People with early onset, low social functioning, excessive ruminations, persistent symptoms in the years immediately following diagnosis, and co-occurring hoarding behaviors or schizotypal personality disorder are more likely to have worse outcomes (Steketee & Barlow, 2002).

POSTTRAUMATIC STRESS DISORDER AND ACUTE STRESS DISORDER

Trauma, and its aftermath, has been the focus of considerable clinical attention in recent years. Both posttraumatic stress disorder (PTSD) and acute stress disorder involve a reaction to an extreme traumatic stressor that has caused or threatened death or severe injury. Extreme stressors include sexual assault, military combat, automobile accidents, violence or threatened violence, and natural disasters, among others. A person's contact with the stressor may involve direct experience, observation (as in the case of a firefighter or a witness to an accident), or vicarious experience (as when a friend, family member, or close associate experiences the stressor). Simply put, PTSD is an understandable response to an extremely stressful situation that results in chronic anxiety (Golier, Legge, & Yehuda, 2007).

Description of the Disorders

The *DSM-IV-TR* includes the following criteria as relevant to the diagnosis of posttraumatic stress disorder and acute stress disorder:

- Great fear and helplessness in response to the traumatic event.
- Persistent reexperiencing of the event (for example, through dreams, upsetting recollections, or intense distress on exposure to reminders of the event).
- Loss of general responsiveness, and at least three indications of avoiding reminders of the trauma (for example, feeling detached from others, believing that one's life is foreshortened, and dissociating from or being unable to recall major aspects of the traumatic experience).
- At least two persistent symptoms of arousal and anxiety (such as sleep disturbances, anger or irritability, hypervigilance for threats, severe startle responses, and difficulty concentrating) that are apparently due to the stressor and are severe enough to cause significant distress or impairment.

Common additional symptoms include shame, survivor guilt or self-blame, lack of interest in usual activities (particularly sexual relationships), alexithymia (inability to identify or articulate emotions), mistrust of others, withdrawal from close relationships, difficulty in self-soothing, fear of losing control or going crazy, and psychosomatic symptoms. Sleep disturbances or nightmares are also a common response to experiencing a traumatic event (Davis, Newman, & Pruiksma, 2009). People often believe that their previous ways of coping and making sense of the world no longer work, and they are left feeling confused and without direction. Trauma-related disorders involve symptoms of anxiety in all systems—physical, affective, cognitive, and behavioral—but they always reflect the three major characteristics of these disorders: reexperiencing, avoidance and numbing, and increased arousal (Litz, Miller, Ruef, & McTeague, 2002).

The primary differences between PTSD and acute stress disorder are time of onset and duration. Acute stress disorder begins within four weeks of exposure to a traumatic stressor and lasts at least two days but no longer than four weeks; it sometimes develops into PTSD. The symptoms of PTSD, by definition, persist for more than one month. Approximately 80% of survivors with ASD will develop PTSD six months later; and 70% will still have the diagnosis of PTSD after two years (Bryant & Harvey, 2000). PTSD is described as acute if it lasts for less than three months and as chronic if the symptoms last longer. The disorder is termed *PTSD with delayed onset* if the symptoms begin more than six months after exposure to the stressor.

The estimated lifetime prevalence rate of PTSD in the general population is approximately 5% to 14%, reflecting the high prevalence of life-threatening events in this society (Golier et al., 2007). Recent studies show that 61% of men and 51% of women in the United States have been exposed to at least one traumatic event over the course of their lives. Not everyone who is exposed to trauma will develop PTSD. It is generally believed that between 20% and 30% of people exposed to a traumatic experience actually go on to develop the disorder (Najavits, 2007). More than one third of people who have been raped or assaulted, 20% to 30% of U.S. war veterans, as many as 16% of survivors of natural disasters, 17% of victims of crime, and up to 75% of people who survived concentration camps have developed PTSD (Litz et al., 2002; Golier et al., 2007).

Adolescents are twice as likely as adults to be victims of serious violent crime (Evans et al., 2005) and a national survey reports that 20% of adolescents meet the criteria for PTSD (Kilpatrick et al., 2003). In adolescence, typical traumas involve serious automobile accidents, traumatic exposure to homicide or suicide, life-threatening medical illness, and physical and sexual abuse.

The interaction of biopsychosocial elements may explain why some people develop the disorder while others do not. A generalized biological vulnerability may underlie the condition with some people being more vulnerable to negative affect and anxiety (Keane & Barlow, 2002). Research verifies that there is a greater occurrence of PTSD in children born of mothers who were pregnant and who escaped from the World Trade Center on September 11, suggesting biological sensitivities. Research on the 14% of Pentagon workers who had developed PTSD 7 months after the attack of September 11 found that women were 5 times more likely than men to meet the criteria for the disorder. Those who experienced more intense emotional reactions and who felt less safe prior to the attack were at increased risk for developing PTSD (Grieger, Fullerton, & Ursano, 2003).

Typical Client Characteristics

As mentioned earlier, three clusters of symptoms are most likely to occur in people who develop PTSD after a traumatic experience: reexperiencing traumatic distress, avoidance of traumatic reminders, and increased arousal.

Reexperiencing of the traumatic event may include ruminating thoughts, recurrent dreams, flashbacks, or disassociative episodes in which the person feels as if he or she is literally reliving the troubling scene (e.g., car accident, shooting, natural disaster). Sometimes auditory hallucinations may occur such as hearing victims of the trauma calling out for help or visualizing graphic images as if they were happening again in real time. Recurrent dreams can be particularly troubling as the person relives the horror he or she is trying to forget, night after night. Some may startle awake or wake up with a panic attack.

The second cluster of symptoms relate to attempts on the part of the person to avoid or escape from these feelings. People may avoid people, places, or social situations that serve to remind them of the trauma. Disassociation or emotional numbing may rob them of their humor, joie de vivre, and hope for the future.

A flat or restricted range of affect may blunt their pleasure in life and leaving them feeling as if they are not the person they used to be.

Hyperarousal to danger, the third cluster of symptoms, may result in the person being easily startled by noises or people, misreading social cues, or a heightened state of alertness, that prevents the person from being able to relax or stand down. Insomnia may result.

The impact of a trauma seems to be particularly severe and long-lasting when it has a human cause. For example, a rape is likely to be more disturbing than a tornado. The impact also seems to be worse if an event is sudden and unexpected, if the person who experiences it has had no prior experience of dealing with such an event and therefore has poor coping skills (Litz et al., 2002), and if people involved in the event are perceived by some as having deserved their fate (for example, if an accident has occurred as a result of engaging in high-risk behavior). If a trauma involves others who did not survive (as in a war or an accident), the survivor often experiences guilt along with the other symptoms of PTSD. Suicidal ideation, depression, somatization, increased impulsivity, substance-related disorders, and other anxiety disorders often develop along with PTSD. Future stressors become inordinately troubling, and people sometimes feel permanently damaged, with little control over their lives.

Although people who have been through traumas initially may seem to have recovered, they are often left with residual and underlying symptoms (such as mistrust, avoidance of close relationships, and psychic numbing). These symptoms can last for many years and may be maintained at a low level by the use of drugs or alcohol, denial, and withdrawal. Reminders of a trauma, however, as well as other stressors or negative life events, can trigger a reexperiencing of the trauma, and the residual symptoms can develop into full-blown PTSD months or even many years after the original trauma (Keane & Barlow, 2002).

Environment, and the degree of trauma experienced, can also play a role in the development of this disorder. A history of exposure to trauma in childhood has been linked to the development of several different disorders including PTSD. The degree or severity of the trauma can also have an impact.

Most people who develop PTSD have other co-occurring disorders such as other anxiety disorders, substance use disorders, and depression (Najavits, 2007). Suicidal and parasuicidal behaviors, weak social support, family and marital problems, sexual dysfunction, somatic complaints, and poor communication skills are often present. People who have experienced multiple traumas across the life span are at increased risk for developing PTSD and may also exhibit poor self-care, difficulty regulating affect, and perceptual distortions (Litz et al., 2002). Effective coping skills should be developed through treatment, as such skills can help people work through a trauma when it happens and also ward off symptoms of PTSD.

Other factors that predispose a person to develop PTSD include recent stressful life changes or circumstances, and having an external locus of control. Family history of mental illness, especially of anxiety, mood, or psychotic disorders, is also correlated with the development of PTSD.

A study of residents of Manhattan, conducted three to six months after the 2001 attacks on the World Trade Center, found that 56% had one or more symptoms of distress related to the attacks. Why one person developed PTSD while another did not was found to be related to the person's prior history, loss of family or friends, job loss, displacement, and female gender (Resnick, Galea, Kilpatrick, & Vlahov, 2004).

Childhood Trauma   Onset of trauma-related disorders may occur at any age, although children often do not recognize the sources of their symptoms. In children, repetitive themes during play and persistent nightmares reflect the trauma; agitation and confusion reflect their distress. Childhood traumas are often associated with subsequent delays in academic achievement and social and moral development, as well as disruptions in relationships with family and peers. Trauma in adolescence has been correlated with reckless actions, high-risk sexual behavior, substance abuse and dependence, and aggressiveness (Evans et al., 2005).

Children who are sexually abused sometimes manifest no symptoms or awareness of the experience in childhood; such prominent symptoms as nightmares, reexperiencing of the trauma, and increased arousal may surface only in adulthood, when they encounter upsetting sexual or interpersonal situations. However, these people's self-images and socialization have probably been adversely affected for many years by the abuse.

Combat Veterans More than 2 million American men and women have served in Operation Enduring Freedom in Afghanistan and Operation Iraqi Freedom. Of these, 81% came under fire; 79% know someone who was seriously wounded or killed; 73% witnessed or experienced an accident that involved serious injury or death; 72% were ambushed or assaulted; and 58% were exposed to dead bodies or body parts (Grieger et al., 2006). More than 300,000 veterans are estimated to have developed PTSD or another anxiety or mood disorder (Tanielian & Jaycox, 2008).

One in five returning U.S. military personnel report symptoms of PTSD. Active duty veterans younger than 25 have higher rates than those over 40. Greater combat exposure is also associated with increased risk (Hoge et al., 2004; Seal et al., 2009). Care must be taken to provide adequate assessment of depression, panic,

substance use, and suicidal ideation in this vulnerable population. Readers are referred to the Appendix for additional information on suicide assessment and prevention.

The Committee on Treatment of Posttraumatic Stress Disorder (Institute of Medicine, 2008) suggests that there may be differences in treatment between civilian populations and veteran populations with PTSD. Additionally, veterans with PTSD returning from Iraq and Afghanistan may be different enough from veterans of previous wars that the studies of former conflicts (particularly Vietnam) may not be relevant to the current veteran population. One specific difference between combat veterans and civilians who experience a traumatic event is their training. Combat veterans are trained to fight rather than to flee a dangerous situation. Scaling down this hypervigilance after they return home is necessary to their successful reentry into society. Recognizing the emotional truths of war is imperative for the therapist working with soldiers and veterans who develop PTSD (Lighthall, 2010).

Assessment

Before treatment for PTSD can begin, the first priority is to ensure that the client is in a safe environment, has access to basic survival resources, and is not currently being abused or victimized. Clients who are currently in the midst of a crisis, clients who are actively suicidal or homicidal, and clients who have significant depressive symptoms will need to be referred for hospitalization or case management to address these issues first before they can participate in outpatient treatment for PTSD (Davis et al., 2009; Rubin, 2009).

The assessment process can be particularly painful for people with PTSD. Therapists should be sensitive to physiological symptoms that arise as a result of talking about the trauma experience. Hypervigilence, rageful outbursts, or self-harming behaviors may all be part of the client's reaction. Keeping safety in mind, therapists should inquire about the recency of the trauma, the client's behaviors and reactions to it, the level of threat he or she poses, and the conditions in which the behaviors tend to increase.

In some cases, the therapist will determine that any substance abuse, suicidal ideation, or explosive anger must be addressed separately, before treatment for PTSD can begin. In less severe cases, monitoring dangerous behaviors and increasing safety may be incorporated into trauma-focused therapy (Zayfert & Becker, 2007).

The goal of assessment in PTSD is not just to diagnose and measure PTSD symptoms, but also to measure the client's current level of functioning and to assess support, coping skills, cognitive style, and the client's strengths and resilience. The Clinician-Administered PTSD Scale (CAPS; Blake et al., 1990) and the PTSD Checklist (Blanchard, Jones-Alexander, Buckley, & Forneris, 1996) are just a few examples of a number of assessment tools specific to PTSD that have flourished in the past 20 years. Checklists, scales, diagnostic interviews, and psychophysiological assessments are also available.

Assessment scales for children include the PTSD section of the K-SADS (Chambers et al., 1985) and the Child Behavior Checklist (Achenbach, 1991), which have both been discussed earlier. Other assessments for children are available that measure trauma symptoms, dissociation, depression, and behavior problems. Children, and their parents and caregivers, should also be observed to see the interaction between them. Additional assessments for parents are also available to measure stress, parenting practices, and the parents' own PTSD symptoms resulting from their child's trauma (Rubin, 2009).

Of course, exploration of the client's pre-trauma history, the presence of any co-occurring disorders, and any trauma specific beliefs about safety, self-blame, trust, randomness, control, and benevolence of the world may also be an important part of the assessment process, especially if cognitive-behavioral treatment approaches will be used. The Posttraumatic Cognitions Inventory (PTCI; Foa, Ehlers, Clark, Tolin, & Orsillo, 1999) and the Personal Beliefs and Reactions Scale (PBRS; Resick, Schnicke, & Markway, 1991) are just two of the many assessment tools available for this purpose. A comprehensive discussion of assessment tools is beyond the scope of this book. Readers are referred to Barlow's *Anxiety and Its Disorders* (2002) for a complete review, or Davis, Newman, & Pruiksa (2009) for a look at specific instruments in the assessment of trauma and related cognitions.

Preferred Therapist Characteristics

Therapists who work with adults or children with PTSD must do more than just establish the Rogerian conditions of warmth, positive regard, empathy, and consistency in building the client's trust. They must also provide a safe and secure therapeutic environment in which the person can regain a sense of control and empowerment. Clients should not be forced to discuss a traumatic event until they feel safe enough and secure enough in the relationship to do so.

Validation of the client's experience is an important part of empowerment. Therapists must walk a thin line that carefully balances an acknowledgment of the client's vulnerability and fear on the one side, with comments on their resilience and strength to have endured, on the other side. Providing some psychoeducation about common reactions to trauma can help to normalize a client's reactions and feelings.

If the trauma occurred many years before treatment, therapy may be a slow process of gradually building trust and helping the person access the troubling memories. Establishing a collaborative relationship in which the client feels safe, is able to discuss sensitive topics, and has input into goals and pacing of the treatment can go a long way toward restoring a client's sense of control and empowerment, creating commitment to the treatment process, and improving the likelihood of treatment success as a result (Rubin, 2009).

Reluctance to engage productively in treatment—manifested particularly by mistrust of the therapist, noncompliance with treatment recommendations, and missed appointments—is common in people with PTSD or acute stress disorder. To maximize the development of trust, the client's preferences should be elicited and respected. For example, women who have been raped may have a strong preference for a female therapist. Similarly, returning war veterans may prefer a therapist who has experienced active duty.

Secondary or vicarious trauma can occur in the therapist working with a client who has experienced a trauma. Indications of secondary or vicarious trauma might be shifts in the therapist's sense of safety, view of the world, and feelings of vulnerability. The therapist whose caseload emphasizes trauma-related work is especially prone to these reactions. Awareness of the possibility of these reactions, balance in the therapist's life and caseload, supervision, and peer consultation can help the therapist deal with secondary trauma.

Intervention Strategies

Treatment for acute stress disorder and PTSD should begin as soon as possible after the trauma, and preventive treatment is recommended even before symptoms emerge. In general, effective treatments of trauma-related disorders are designed to promote the accessing and processing of the trauma, the expression of feelings, increased coping with and control over memories (to dilute pain), reduction of cognitive distortions and self-blame, and restoration of self-concept and previous level of functioning.

Our knowledge about treatments for PTSD has improved dramatically over the last 10 years. Exposure-based therapies have the most empirical evidence of efficacy in the treatment of PTSD (Keane & Barlow, 2002; Rauch et al., 2009; Thomas et al., 2010). Most exposure-based treatments, however, also include a CBT component, such as cognitive restructuring, anxiety management training (AMT), or coping skills training. A combination approach that is designed to meet the specific client's unique circumstances seems to be the most useful. For people with severe symptoms, or for those who are very distraught or impaired, interventions designed to rebuild a sense of safety and control should precede exposure to the trauma. Internet-based treatments have been shown to reduce anxiety and help to build a strong therapeutic alliance (Knaevelsrud, & Maercker, 2010; Wagner, Knaevelsrud, & Maercker, 2007).

Prolonged Exposure Therapy   As mentioned earlier, exposure therapy is a behavioral intervention that involves exposure to the feared stimuli until the client's anxiety is extinguished. Extended exposure to the trauma memory itself seems to be the best method for the treatment of PTSD (Foa, Keane, Friedman, & Cohen, 2009; Resick & Calhoun, 2001). Flooding, or prolonged exposure, requires the client to recall or imagine the feared situation in vivo, through visual imagery, or with the assistance of virtual reality. In work with Operation Iraqi Freedom veterans, virtual reality exposure therapy was conducted using a virtual Iraq (Gerardi, Rothbaum, Ressler, Heekin, & Rizzo, 2008; Zoellner et al., 2008).

A fear hierarchy is then created of major stimuli that are feared and avoided, and the client is requested to focus on feared cues for 45 minutes daily. The client begins with a moderately feared stimuli hierarchical list. In nine biweekly therapy sessions, the client is asked to describe the trauma scene in the present tense. Several descriptions are conducted in each session, leaving time at the end of each 90-minute session to ensure the client's anxiety is decreased. The client progresses through the hierarchy until the fear is extinguished.

The purpose of exposure therapy is to activate the fear memory and to provide new information that is incompatible with the fear so that new learning can take place. Other models of exposure therapy may use fewer or shorter sessions, include audiotaping, have therapists visit feared locations with the client, or other variations.

Cognitive Processing Therapy Cognitive-processing therapy (CPT), developed in 1992 by Resick and Schnicke, combines elements of exposure therapy, anxiety management training, and cognitive restructuring. It has been found to be as effective as exposure therapy in the treatment of rape-related PTSD (Keane & Barlow, 2002). Similar combination treatments have been found to be effective for PTSD related to motor vehicle accidents.

Designed especially for survivors of sexual assault, CPT is a 12-session structured model in which exposure is combined with cognitive restructuring to change people's disrupted cognitions. Exposure is accomplished through information about the trauma, recollection of responses, and discussion of the trauma's meaning. Exposure must be handled carefully to ensure that people are not retraumatized. It should include frequent reminders of safety and survival, be conducted in pieces, and continue until anxiety diminishes.

Development of coping skills, changes in maladaptive beliefs, and identification of a safe setting all are essential to appropriate processing of the traumatic memories. Writing about the traumatic event is used in CPT but is always paired with training in coping skills. Written recollections of the traumatic event are first read to the therapist, who facilitates understanding, exploration of responses, and expression of emotions. People then are instructed to read their accounts to themselves daily, to habituate themselves to the experience and increase their understanding of the traumatic events and of their reactions.

Anxiety Management Training Other approaches have also demonstrated effectiveness in treating people with trauma-related disorders. Anxiety management training (AMT), for example, typically combines prolonged activation of traumatic memories with such strategies as relaxation, cognitive restructuring, and biofeedback, designed to modify these memories and the associated fears (Keane & Barlow, 2002). A study of Vietnam combat veterans with PTSD found AMT to be as effective as exposure-based treatment in decreasing the frequency and intensity of intrusive war memories and avoidance of stimuli reminiscent of war (Pantalon & Motta, 1998).

Other Treatments for PTSD Other interventions are sometimes used in the treatment of posttraumatic stress disorder, even though their clinical efficacy has not been clearly established. EMDR, group and family therapy, stress inoculation training, and medication are other treatment options that have not been empirically validated but may be beneficial in the treatment of PTSD.

Eye movement desensitization and reprocessing. Eye movement desensitization and reprocessing (EMDR; Shapiro, 1989) pairs visual stimulation (eye movements), kinesthetic stimulation (taps), or auditory stimulation (tones) with a focus on traumatic memories and associated negative beliefs. Reports of the effectiveness of EMDR with Vietnam veterans with PTSD have been encouraging, although EMDR has not been found to be superior to AMT or CBT (Keane & Barlow, 2002; van der Kolk et al., 2007). The American Psychiatric Association notes EMDR can be effective in treating symptoms of PTSD. Research suggests that there is rapid relief of symptoms when EMDR is used in conjunction with other therapeutic interventions.

Group and family therapy. Development of support systems is another important ingredient of treatment for acute stress disorder and PTSD. Peer support and therapy groups involving others who have had similar experiences can be particularly helpful in reducing a person's feelings of being stigmatized and alone; for example, group therapy seems to have become the primary mode of treatment for Vietnam veterans. Although a group made up of people who have survived traumas can provide considerable help, it can also contribute to an exacerbation of the trauma; therefore, if group therapy is to be conducted, the therapist should screen participants carefully and should closely control disclosure of and exposure to descriptions of traumatic experiences.

If symptoms of PTSD have been present for an extended period, the disorder has probably had a negative impact on social and occupational pursuits and on family relationships. Therapy with people in this situation should usually take a broad focus. Iraq war veterans with PTSD, for example, had problems with alcohol abuse, anger, relationships, and overall psychosocial functioning following deployment (Maguen et al., 2010). Therefore, therapy with troubled veterans has to go beyond the exploration of their traumatic wartime experiences and must promote improvement in communication skills, socialization, and trust of others. Similarly, people who were abused as children have a higher than average likelihood of experiencing abuse as adults, and this vulnerability may have to be addressed in therapy (Messman & Long, 1996). Moreover, because the initial abuse often came at the hands of a father or a stepfather, it probably has contributed to family difficulties.

Stress inoculation training. Stress inoculation training (SIT) has also been used successfully to treat PTSD. SIT includes education and training in six coping skills (muscle relaxation, thought stopping, breath control, guided self-dialogue, covert modeling, and role playing).

Other useful ingredients of treatment include education about the nature of trauma-related stress disorders, encouragement for assertiveness and mastery experiences, anger management, stress management, grounding, containment of anxiety, affirmations, and expressive therapies (involving art and movement). Hypnotherapy is often used to help people retrieve and deal with dissociated memories.

Medication   The FDA has approved the SSRIs paroxetine (Paxil) and sertraline (Zoloft) for the treatment of PTSD. Other SSRIs may also be effective. Atypical antipsychotics, benzodiazepines, and beta-blockers have been used to treat symptoms of PTSD, but to date, no one medication has been found that addresses the complex sequelae of symptoms of PTSD. Nevertheless, many different medications have been effective in the treatment of symptoms related to PTSD, such as anxiety, sleeplessness, and depression.

Prognosis

Two thirds of people exposed to a serious trauma do not develop PTSD (Eifert &

Forsyth 2005), and many others have symptoms that quickly remit spontaneously after a trauma. With treatment, the prognosis usually is also good for recovery for those who have developed PTSD, especially for people whose functioning was positive before exposure to trauma, whose onset of symptoms was rapid, whose symptoms have lasted less than six months, whose social supports are strong, and who have received early treatment (Keane & Barlow, 2002). The prognosis for treatment of delayed-onset PTSD does not seem to be as good, at least in part because that type of PTSD is often accompanied by another psychological disorder (Roth & Fonagy, 2005). Although people's vivid memories of their traumatic experiences cannot be erased through therapy, most people can be helped to resume or even improve on their former levels of functioning. Foa, Davidson, and Rothbaum (1995), for example, report a 91% rate of significant improvement after treatment that combined exposure and stress inoculation training. Relapses are not uncommon, especially under stress, but they may be averted through extended follow-up treatment. The Committee on Treatment of Posttraumatic Stress Disorder (2008) suggests that future research should investigate whether earlier interventions might reduce chronicity, whether group therapy is efficacious, if treatment efficacy varies by population (e.g., combat veteran, male), and the optimal length of treatment duration for psychotherapy and medication management.

GENERALIZED ANXIETY DISORDER

The last type of anxiety disorder we will discuss is generalized anxiety disorder. According to *DSM-IV-TR*, people diagnosed with GAD have "excessive anxiety and worry" about at least two life circumstances for most days during a period of at least six months (American Psychiatric Association, 2000, p. 476). The worry is difficult to control, causes appreciable distress or impairment, and is accompanied by at least three of the following physiological symptoms (at least one in children):

- Edginess or restlessness
- Tiring easily
- Difficulty in concentrating
- Irritability
- Muscle tension
- Difficulty in sleeping

Description of the Disorder

Generalized anxiety disorder (GAD) is a pervasive disorder in which biological and psychological vulnerabilities combine to create "a diathesis of chronic anxiety" (Barlow et al., 2002, p. 323). Stress related to negative life events triggers neurobiological reactions. The focus of attention can shift from the negative event to a self-evaluative focus that ultimately creates a negative feedback loop.

The most common affective and somatic symptoms of GAD (in descending order of frequency) include: inability to relax, tension, fright, jumpiness, unsteadiness, apprehension, and uncontrollable worry. Such somatic symptoms as dry mouth, intestinal discomfort, tension-related headache, and cold hands are also common. The most prevalent cognitive and behavioral symptoms include difficulty in concentrating, apprehension about losing control, fear of being rejected, inability to control thinking, confusion, high negative affect, overarousal, and tendency to anticipate the worst (Campbell & Brown, 2002). For the diagnosis to be made, the symptoms should not be substance induced or due to a medical condition.

Anticipatory anxiety is a central manifestation of GAD. This symptom is more likely to be found in people who are homemakers, retirees, or disabled—primarily people who do not work outside the home. According to Barlow (2002), anticipatory anxiety is a future-oriented perspective in which people are in a constant state of hypervigilance and overarousal in expectation of threat-related stimuli. The term *generalized anxiety disorder* is clearly not a misnomer; the anxiety expresses itself through a multitude of pervasive symptoms that typically are without obvious immediate precipitants and that leave people feeling frightened and overwhelmed.

Approximately 80% to 90% of people with GAD have had another disorder, most frequently major depressive disorder, social phobia, specific phobia, dysthymic disorder, or panic disorder (Roy-Byrne & Cowley, 2007). Substance-related disorders are also frequent companions of GAD. Worry and anxious apprehension are central features of both anxiety and depression. It is not surprising to find that people who have GAD also experience a 62% rate of major depressive disorder and a 39% rate of dysthymia over their lifetimes (Campbell & Brown, 2002).

GAD often begins in childhood or adolescence. In early-onset GAD, the client usually cannot identify a precipitant for the disorder or report exactly when it started. Early-onset GAD is associated with a childhood history of fears, avoidant behavior, academic and social difficulties, and a disturbed home environment. People usually seek treatment when they are in their twenties, and the disorder tends to have a chronic course and a poorer treatment outcome (Barlow et al., 2002). Some theorists view GAD as similar to a personality disorder because of its early and insidious onset and its often chronic nature.

Typical Client Characteristics

GAD tends to be associated with selective attending to information that is threatening, as well as difficulty handling ambiguity. In ambiguous situations, a person with GAD is likely to interpret the outcomes in the most negative way.

GAD seems to be especially prevalent among young adults with long-standing feelings of nervousness and a history of physical disease or alcohol or prescription drug misuse (Butcher et al., 2006). Feelings of tension, vulnerability, and early experiences of lack of control over their environments are common in people with GAD, as are insecure attachments to early caregivers (Campbell & Brown, 2002). Some research suggests people with GAD have a pattern of disrupted family life and periods of adjustment involving dependence and low self-esteem.

In general, anxiety disorders rarely begin in older adults. However, GAD is one of the most likely anxiety disorders to be present in older adults, occurring at a rate of 0.7% to 7.1% in older adults, usually after a precipitating event (Roemer, Orsillo, & Barlow, 2002). Lifetime prevalence of GAD is approximately 5% of the population (Kessler, Berglund, et al., 2005). GAD is far more common in primary care settings; among low-income, African American women; and among those who seek medical care (Roemer et al., 2002). As with most of the other anxiety disorders, females are twice as likely as males to experience GAD.

Both men and women with GAD are likely to have had one or more negative, important, and unexpected life events associated with the onset of the disorder. For men, the number of such events is also correlated with the likelihood of developing GAD. Many people with GAD report being worried their entire lives.

Assessment

The intake interview for a person believed to have GAD should gather data about the following areas (Barbaree & Marshall, 1985):

- Relevant cognitions (as reflected by self-statements, expectations, fears, attributions, evaluations)
- Somatic and physiological complaints
- Relevant behaviors
- Severity and generalizability of the disorder
- Antecedents and precipitants
- Consequences for relationships and for responses from others
- Family and individual history of emotional disorders
- Previous attempts to manage anxiety
- Overall lifestyle

A comprehensive interview can provide important information about the dynamics of the disorder, and this information can in turn dispel some of the client's fears about the symptoms. Such inventories as the Beck Anxiety Inventory (Beck & Steer, 1990), the Penn State Worry Questionnaire (Meyer, Miller, Metzger, & Borkovec, 1990), and the Anxiety Disorders Interview Schedule (Brown et al., 1994) are also helpful in diagnosing GAD. A key diagnostic question for GAD is, "Do you worry excessively about minor matters?" (Brown, O'Leary, & Barlow, 1993, p. 140).

Preferred Therapist Characteristics

Information in earlier sections dealing with the ideal therapist for a client with an anxiety disorder is also relevant here. Providing psychoeducation about the disorder can sometimes normalize the symptoms and provide relief from anxiety. The therapist should have a wide repertoire of anxiety management techniques so that those approaches most likely to work with a given client can be selected. If exposure techniques will be used, therapists should provide advance explanation of precisely what will happen and explain the benefits for this type of intervention. Therapists who relay a sense of confidence are more likely to be successful. People diagnosed with GAD are sometimes reluctant to engage in treatment, primarily because of the ego-syntonic nature of their symptoms or because of their attribution of the symptoms to medical causes. They are often likely to seek medical treatment for their somatic complaints rather than to seek out therapy. Therefore, a collaborative stance and good reasoning abilities on the part of the therapist will also be helpful. Such nonspecific therapeutic qualities as warmth, empathy, acceptance, and the ability to encourage trust and collaboration are important in promoting clients' involvement in treatment.

Intervention Strategies

Cognitive-behavioral therapy is the most frequently used approach in the treatment of GAD. The two targets of intervention are excessive, uncontrollable worry and the persistent overarousal that accompanies it. Treatment approaches that work tend to be active and multifaceted and to include cognitive restructuring, relaxation techniques, training in anxiety management, exposure techniques, and problem-solving skills (Nezu, Nezu, & McMurran, 2008). Several of these elements will be discussed in more detail. Many other effective approaches are also available for reducing the symptoms of GAD. The cognitive and behavioral approaches can facilitate the development of individualized, multifaceted interventions for treatment of GAD that take into account the clients' and therapists' preferences, clients' life-styles, and the nature of the disorder.

Cognitive Therapy   The cognitive restructuring techniques suggested by Beck and Emery in (1985) form the basis of many of the treatments in use today. They include the use of logic and educational (Ericksonian) stories, systematic testing and rational restructuring of beliefs, eliciting and examination of automatic thoughts via free association and behavioral tasks, use of the active voice, emphasis on how rather than why in inquiry, reattribution, decatastrophizing, and induction and modification of visual images. This approach is active, logical, and organized, emphasizing good therapist–client rapport and collaboration, as well as specific interventions.

Beck and Emery (1985) describe a brief, time-limited approach (5 to 20 sessions) for treating GAD. This approach emphasizes an inductive/Socratic method of teaching (questions are the primary form of intervention), and homework is an important component. Four stages of treatment are described:

1. Relieving the client's symptoms
2. Helping the client recognize distorted automatic thoughts
3. Teaching the client logic and reason
4. Helping the client modify long-held dysfunctional assumptions underlying major concerns

Behavior Therapy   The primary goal of behavior therapy for GAD is stress management. The following approaches are some of those available for helping control stress:

- Progressive muscle relaxation
- Autogenic training (calming the body and mind)
- Guided imagery
- Yoga

- Self-monitoring through logs of anxiety levels and self-calming activities
- Diaphragmatic breathing
- Meditation
- Biofeedback
- Exercise
- Expressive therapy
- Systematic desensitization

Affective Therapy   Cognitive and behavioral approaches have been shown to be the most effective and are emphasized over affective treatment strategies in the treatment of GAD. Nevertheless, some attention should also be paid to affect, so as to facilitate the decrease of anxiety. Beck and Emery (1985) propose a five-step process, based on the acronym AWARE, for dealing with the affective component of an anxiety disorder:

A: *Accept feelings*. Normalize, identify, and express them. People are encouraged to go on with life despite their anxiety and to learn such strategies as self-talk to develop some mastery of their anxiety.

W: *Watch the anxiety*. Seek objectivity and distance. People are encouraged to use diaries and ratings to demonstrate that the anxiety is situational, time-limited, and controllable.

A: *Act with the anxiety rather than fight it in dysfunctional ways*. People are encouraged to act against their inclinations by confronting fears rather than avoiding them, and to deliberately seek out anxiety-provoking situations in order to inoculate themselves against anxiety.

R: *Repeat the steps*. People are taught that doing so will establish learning and facilitate the process.

E: *Expect the best*. People are encouraged to maintain an optimistic outlook.

Cognitive-Behavioral Therapy In the past 20 years, cognitive-behavioral therapy for the treatment of GAD has been validated in more than 13 controlled studies. CBT successfully reduces symptoms of GAD and results in robust changes (Borkovec & Ruscio, 2001). A review of 16 meta-analyses yielded the following results: combined cognitive and behavioral treatments were more effective than cognitive, behavioral, or relaxation treatments alone; group interventions were comparable to individual interventions and had lower dropout rates (11%); treatment gains were maintained at 6-month follow-up; and treatment that is designed to meet the needs of the individual can increase effectiveness (Butler, Chapman, Forman, & Beck, 2006).

A combined cognitive and behavioral approach described by Brown and colleagues (1993) involves both exposure to worry and prevention of worry-related behavior. CBT was used in both group and individual therapy and typically included 12 to 15 sessions. Clients were encouraged to focus on their worries for 30 minutes without using distraction or any of the other dysfunctional means of avoidance that tend to increase worrying in the long run. The following techniques were used to help people become habituated to their troubling thoughts and reduce anxiety:

- Self-monitoring of mood levels
- Analysis and modification of catastrophizing and other cognitive distortions
- Relaxation training, including cue-controlled relaxation
- Problem solving
- Cognitive countering
- Time management

Stress Management Training Mercer (2008) provides an outline of stress management interventions for the treatment of GAD and other anxiety disorders. People who used these techniques reported improvement on measures of health, ability to complete daily responsibilities at home and work, and more confidence about their coping skills. Typical stress management interventions can be conducted in group or individual sessions, and usually last for 6 to 19 sessions. Following an assessment phase, most stress management interventions involve didactic education about anxiety, relaxation, distraction, cognitive restructuring, and exposure. Clients were also encouraged to identify their strengths and to engage in pleasurable activities.

Acceptance and Commitment Therapy (ACT) As discussed earlier, acceptance and commitment therapy (ACT) seems to be well-suited to the treatment of anxiety disorders. ACT focuses on helping people create a meaningful life, rather than emphasizing anxiety reduction. One of the core skills learned in ACT is how to recognize and stop self-perpetuating and self-defeating emotional, cognitive, and behavioral avoidance routines. A 12-week ACT program outlined by Eifert and Forsyth (2005) included:

- Psychoeducation about the purpose of anxiety, its benefits, and how it becomes disordered.
- Evaluation of clients' strategies for coping with anxiety.
- Focus on value-driven behavior as an alternative to anxiety.
- In-session experiential exposure exercises that encourage clients to practice mindful observation, acceptance, and cognitive diffusion.
- Commitment to engage in actions that are more consistent with clients' values.

With its focus on acceptance, rather than avoidance, ACT techniques can be appropriately integrated into other cognitive-behavioral therapies (Eifert & Forsyth, 2005). Roemer, Orsillo, and Salters-Pedneault (2008) found that treatment with ACT resulted in clinically significant reduction in worry. At posttreatment follow-up, 78% of study participants no longer met the criteria for GAD.

One randomized controlled trial of ACT and cognitive therapy indicated that people who received the mindfulness component experienced more awareness and were less likely to avoid their anxieties than those who received cognitive therapy only (Forman, Herbert, Moitra, Yeomans, & Geller, 2007). More research is under way on this promising new treatment.

Medication   Medication is not often necessary in the treatment of GAD. In cases where it is indicated, benzodiazepines such as alprazolam (Xanax) show short-term efficacy in 75% of cases (Evans et al., 2005), but usually should be avoided for ongoing, long-term treatment. Buspirone (Buspar) has also been determined to be effective in controlled studies and does not have a sedating side effect. Antidepressants are typically preferred over benzodiazepines. Venlafaxine (Effexor) was the first antidepressant to receive FDA approval for the treatment of GAD (Roy-Byrne & Cowley, 2007).

Despite its frequent use in treating anxiety disorders, medication has been found to have a negative effect on the maintenance of improvement after psychotherapy is discontinued. In addition, people who take medication during therapy do not have a full opportunity to experience and deal with their anxiety and so are typically less tolerant of and less able to cope with any return of the anxiety. Therefore, medication for clients experiencing GAD should be used with considerable caution and should be monitored carefully; the inherent risks may not be worth the temporary relief of anxiety. Cognitive-behavioral approaches to anxiety reduction may be safer and have shown to be more effective, and in many cases result in discontinuation of medication (Evans et al., 2005; Gosselin, Ladouceur, Morin, Dugas, & Baillargeon, 2004).

Prognosis

Spontaneous remission of GAD is uncommon, but most people who receive cognitive-behavioral therapy for GAD show significant and consistent improvement. In fact, approximately 71% maintain their improvement at 6-month follow-up (Evans et al., 2005), although many will not be entirely free of symptoms (as is also the case with most of the other anxiety disorders). Treatment design should take account of the fact that this disorder usually does not remit fully. Indeed, Evans and colleagues report that early trials indicate that only one third of people treated for GAD achieve full remission, and those who rely solely on medication for treatment experience an 80% relapse rate following discontinuation of drugs. Therefore, treatment should include training in the use of preventive and coping mechanisms as well as in the signs of relapse so that clients can be helped to continue managing anxiety and stress effectively on their own.

TREATMENT RECOMMENDATIONS: CLIENT MAP

Treatment recommendations for the anxiety disorders discussed in this chapter are summarized here according to the framework of the Client Map.

CLIENT MAP

Diagnoses

Anxiety disorders (panic disorder, agoraphobia, specific phobia, social phobia, obsessive-compulsive disorder, acute stress disorder, posttraumatic stress disorder, and generalized anxiety disorder)

Objectives of Treatment

Reduce anxiety and related behavioral, cognitive, and somatic symptoms of the disorder

Improve stress management, social and occupational functioning, sense of mastery

Assessments

Often will include physical examination to rule out medical disorder

Measures of anxiety or fear

Checklists, interview, and scales specific to each disorder

Clinician Characteristics

Patient

Encouraging

Supportive yet firm and flexible

Concerned but not controlling

Calming and reassuring

Comfortable with a broad range of behavioral and cognitive interventions

Location of Treatment

Generally outpatient, sometimes contextual

Interventions to Be Used

Cognitive-behavioral and behavior therapy, especially modification and replacement of distorted cognitions, in vivo and imaginal desensitization, exposure, and response prevention

Acceptance and commitment therapy

Eye movement desensitization and reprocessing

Training in anxiety management

Stress inoculation

Problem solving

Relaxation

Assertiveness training

Self-monitoring of progress

Homework assignments

Emphasis of Treatment

Usually present-oriented

Moderately directive

Supportive

Usually cognitive and behavioral

Numbers

Individual or group therapy, according to the nature of the disorder

Ancillary family therapy as needed, particularly for heritable disorders and those that have affected family functioning

Timing

Usually weekly treatment of brief to moderate duration (8 to 20 sessions)

Moderate pacing

Possibly flexible scheduling, as necessitated by contextual treatment

Medications Needed

Usually not needed unless anxiety is disabling

May supplement treatment in some forms of anxiety disorders, especially obsessive-compulsive disorder

Adjunct Services

Hypnotherapy

Biofeedback

Meditation and mindfulness

Exercise

Other approaches to stress management

Planned pleasurable activities

Prognosis

Variable according to the specific disorder

Generally good for amelioration of symptoms

Fair for complete elimination of signs of the disorder

CLIENT MAP OF ROBERTO M.

This chapter began with a description of Roberto M., a 27-year-old man who developed symptoms of strong anxiety after a visit to the dentist reactivated memories of childhood sexual abuse. Roberto's diagnosis and treatment plan are presented here according to the format of the Client Map.

Diagnosis

Axis I: 309.81 Posttraumatic stress disorder, delayed onset

Axis II: V 71.09 No diagnosis on Axis II

Axis III: Fatigue, difficulty sleeping, other physical complaints reported, but no general medical condition diagnosed

Axis IV: Other psychosocial and environmental problems: childhood abuse; Problems with primary support group: conflict with fiancée

Axis V: Global assessment of functioning (GAF Scale): current GAF = 55

Objectives of Treatment

Reduce level of anxiety and accompanying somatic symptoms

Increase level of self-confidence

Reduce guilt and shame

Increase productivity at work

Improve relationship with fiancée

Help client cope effectively with his history of abuse

Assessments

Referral to a physician for medical examination

Beck Anxiety Inventory

Clinician Characteristics

Male (at client's request)

Supportive and encouraging

Skilled at empowerment

Location of Treatment

Outpatient

Interventions to Be Used

Encouragement for retrieval and discussion of memories at a gradual pace and in a safe fashion

Cognitive restructuring for feelings of guilt, shame, and self-blame

Training in coping skills, including progressive relaxation

Encouragement for resumption of exercise program

Eye movement desensitization and reprocessing

Writing about abuse (after some improvement in therapy) and reading account aloud to the therapist, with use of coping skills to combat anxiety created by this process

Goal setting and realistic planning for resumption of previous lifestyle

Acceptance and commitment therapy to help client focus on creating a lifestyle consistent with his values

Emphasis of Treatment

Moderately directive, to mobilize client's energy and give structure to the treatment in view of client's feeling confused, overwhelmed, and hopeless at the start

Moderately supportive, to bolster self-esteem and avoid adding the experience of even more threat

With abatement of symptoms, increasingly collaborative emphasis

Emphasis on exploration of the past (to help client cope with the abuse), but also on current successes

Numbers

Individual therapy as initial mode of treatment

With lessening of client's anxiety, several joint sessions with him and his fiancée, to help her understand what he was experiencing, encourage her to provide support, and help them both resume their previously close, positive relationship

Timing

Twice a week initially, for rapid reduction of anxiety, and then weekly sessions for at least three to six months

Moderately rapid pace, in view of client's previous high level of functioning and the fact that client was in considerable emotional pain

Medications Needed

None

Adjunct Services

Information about the prevalence and impact of abuse, especially for males

Prognosis

Good for significant reduction of symptoms

Optimistic but less positive for elimination of long-standing mild anxiety

RECOMMENDED READING

Barlow, D. H. (2007). *Clinical handbook of psychological disorders: A step-by-step treatment manual* (4th ed.). New York, NY: Guilford Press.

Bourne, E. J. (2005). *The anxiety and phobia workbook* (4th ed.). New York, NY: Harbinger.

Craske, M. G., Antony, M. M., & Barlow, D. H. (2006). *Mastering your fears and phobias: Therapist guide* (2nd ed.). New York, NY: Oxford University Press.

Hayes, S. C., & Strosahl, K. D. (2010). *A practical guide to acceptance and commitment therapy.* New York, NY: Springer Press.

Kabat-Zinn, J. (1990). *Full catastrophe living: Using the wisdom of your body and mind to face stress, pain, and illness.* New York, NY: Delacorte Press.

O'Donohue, W. T., & Fisher, J. E. (Eds.). (2008). *Cognitive behavior therapy: Applying empirically supported techniques in your practice* (2nd ed.). Hoboken, NJ: Wiley.

Rubin, A., & Springer, D. W. (Eds.). (2009). *Treatment of traumatized adults and children: Clinician's guide to evidence-based practice.* Hoboken, NJ: Wiley.

Stahl, B., & Goldstein, E. (2010). *Mindfulness based stress reduction workbook.* Oakland, CA: New Harbinger.

CHAPTER

6 Disorders of Behavior and Impulse Control

George W., a 36-year-old White male, was referred for therapy by the courts. After his third conviction for driving while intoxicated, George was sentenced to a 6-month stay in a work-release program. Therapy was a required part of his participation in that program.

George had begun misusing alcohol when he was 14 years old and had been drinking excessively ever since. His father, his maternal grandfather, and two of his three brothers also used alcohol in harmful ways.

George had been married to his second wife for 2 years, and they had a 1-year-old child. His first marriage had ended in divorce 4 years before, partly because his wife would no longer tolerate George's drinking. George had maintained contact with his two children from that marriage.

George was employed as a supervisor for a construction firm. He had been with the same company for more than 10 years, despite frequent absences. He consumed little alcohol during the day, but would begin drinking beer as soon as he returned home from work. George reported frequent weekend episodes of binge drinking, as well as occasional blackouts. He had repeatedly tried to stop using alcohol on his own and had been alcohol-free for 6 months at the time of his marriage to his second wife, but he stated that financial difficulties associated with the birth of their child had led him to resume drinking. George said that his wife was unhappy about his drinking and had expressed disappointment that they never went out socially, but he believed that their lack of a social life really mattered little to her because she was so absorbed in caring for their baby.

George reported some mild depression and stated that he was shy and uncomfortable around people. He reported that alcohol had helped him feel more self-confident and establish friendships with a group of men who apparently also drank to excess.

George had been suffering for more than 20 years from alcohol dependence, a disorder of behavior and impulse control. As is common among people with this disorder, George reported a family history of alcohol misuse. As is also typical of people with disorders of behavior and impulse control, George's mental disorder affected most, if not all, areas of his life; he presented with impairment in interpersonal, occupational, and other areas.

The possible diagnosis of an underlying avoidant personality disorder was considered. George's problems otherwise seemed related to his alcohol dependence, which became the focus of treatment.

OVERVIEW OF DISORDERS OF BEHAVIOR AND IMPULSE CONTROL

The following five categories of disorders of behavior and impulse control are discussed in this chapter:

1. Substance-related disorders
2. Eating disorders (anorexia nervosa, bulimia nervosa, and EDNOS/binge eating disorder)
3. Sexual and gender identity disorders (sexual dysfunctions, paraphilias, and gender identity disorders)
4. Impulse-control disorders not elsewhere classified (pathological gambling, intermittent explosive disorder, pyromania, kleptomania, and trichotillomania)
5. Sleep disorders

This section of the chapter provides an overview of diagnosis and treatment of the entire group of disorders of behavior and impulse control. Subsequent sections of the chapter focus individually on the five categories of disorders.

Description of the Disorders

Disorders of behavior and impulse control are characterized primarily by behavioral concerns, behaviors that are engaged in to excess (as in alcohol dependence, bulimia nervosa, and pathological gambling), behaviors that are engaged in too little (as in anorexia nervosa), behaviors that are inappropriate (as in the paraphilias and kleptomania), behaviors that are unrewarding (as in the sexual dysfunctions), and sleep disorders (which can involve sleeping too much, sleeping too little, or unrewarding sleep patterns). All these disorders can cause impairment in social and occupational functioning, and many are life threatening.

The prevalence of the behavioral disorders varies considerably. Some of these disorders (such as pyromania and transvestic fetishism) are rarely encountered by most therapists; others, such as the alcohol use disorders, are frequently seen in therapy. The primary symptom of all the disorders discussed in this chapter is undesirable behavior. However, because many of these disorders typically begin in adolescence, persisting and often worsening without treatment, people commonly also have serious developmental, occupational, social, and other deficits. Rather than benefiting from the normal developmental experiences of adolescence and early adulthood, people with behavioral disorders sometimes focus their lives around their dysfunctional behavior. When they finally do seek help to change their behavior, their failure to have developed age-appropriate maturity, self-confidence, and life skills complicates the treatment process and becomes an important secondary focus of treatment.

Typical Client Characteristics

Some of these disorders, such as the alcohol use disorders, have a strong genetic or familial component; others, such as anorexia nervosa, are often related to a characteristic pattern of family interactions and expectations that predispose a person to develop a particular set of symptoms. Many people who present with disorders of behavior and impulse control come from families in which neither positive relationships nor problem-solving skills were modeled.

Most impulse-control disorders begin with a complex interaction of biology and environment. Genetic vulnerability, a neurological basis for many of the symptoms of dependence, and a chronic course that includes relapse underscore the biological bases of misuse. Researchers have mapped the biological effect of many behaviors on the reward centers in the brain. Activation of these reward centers has been linked to pleasurable behaviors, cravings for drugs or alcohol, tolerance, loss of control, and impaired functioning. Certain activities, such as use of cocaine or heroin, sex, gambling, and eating produce the greatest impact on the brain's reward system. Characteristics of the user, such as clinical depression, low self-esteem, anxiety, or phobias, are initially alleviated by the use of substances or indulging in these pleasurable activities, but the activity frequently causes more symptoms with continued use. Genetic variations in the person's metabolism and neurological response are important contributors to how the drug or activity will affect that person, as well as to the risk of dependence. Finally, the role of such environmental factors as familial history of substance use, peer pressure, availability of substances, and living in an environment that triggers cravings are important contributors to relapse after treatment. All three contributing factors (impulsive behavior, biological components of the user, and environmental factors) must be considered when developing effective treatment and relapse prevention programs. Therapists should also take into account the continuum of symptoms, from occasional use with little or no impact on functioning on one end, to severe dependence and resultant impairment of social, employment, and other functioning on the opposite end.

More than half of those who have one behavior disorder have a coexisting disorder. A second impulse-control disorder or a substance use disorder is most common, but other disorders that frequently co-occur include personality disorders (especially antisocial personality disorder), mood disorders, anxiety or panic disorder, social phobias, and psychotic disorders. The coexisting disorders may be preexisting or may be initiated or worsened by the behavior disorder. Still, nearly half of all people with behavioral disorders do not have other underlying personality or other emotional disorder. Some

may have preexisting conditions that have contributed to the development of their behavioral disorders, and some, as in the bidirectional relationship between sleep disorder and depression, may develop emotional disorders secondary to their behavioral problems, but many do not have additional diagnoses. This is particularly true of people diagnosed with sexual dysfunctions, gender identity disorder, or sleep disorders. Specific information on the particular personality patterns that characterize people with the various impulse-control disorders is provided in later sections.

Assessment

The following information on assessments relates to all impulse-control disorders. Specific assessment tools for individual disorders will be addressed in the appropriate sections.

Assessment for impulse-control disorders should consider the symptom severity as well as the impact of the symptoms on quality of life. A careful assessment of any impulse-control disorder should include questions about impulsivity and aggression, repetitive behaviors the person feels compelled to do but later regrets, mood, substance use, and suicidal and homicidal ideation, as well as an inquiry into the client's history of nonsuicidal self injurious behaviors (such as skin picking, hair pulling, cutting). Impulse-control disorders frequently co-occur with other impulse-control disorders; thus, the full range of behavior may not be evident without a complete assessment.

Stress and trauma play a key role in the development and continuation of impulse-control disorders. Assessment should include level of stress and its impact on quality of life. Support, including family and peer groups, should also be determined. If there is any indication of childhood abuse, the Childhood Trauma Questionnaire (Bernstein et al., 1994) can help assess the nature and severity of the abuse and the Child's Reaction to Traumatic Events Scale-Revised (CRTES-R; Jones, Fletcher. & Ribb, 2002) can help assess any symptoms that may have resulted. When treating traumatized youth, dissociative symptoms should also be assessed using any of the multiple tools available including the Children's Dissociative Experiences Scale and Post-Traumatic Symptom Inventory (Stolbach, 1997) or the Adolescent Dissociative Experiences Scale (Armstrong, Carlson, & Putnam, 1997).

Several useful standardized rating scales are available to assess symptoms of impulse-control disorders including the Minnesota Impulsivity Interview and the Structured Clinical Interview for Diagnosis of Obsessive-Compulsive Spectrum Disorders (Stein, Harvey, Seedat, & Hollander, 2006, p. 311). Symptoms of aggression and impulsivity also can be evaluated with the Barratt Impulsiveness Scale Version 11 (BIS-11). Hollander and colleagues (2006) report that the BIS-11 is one of the most frequently used measures of impulsivity, is easy to administer, and takes 10 to 15 minutes to complete the 30 questions. Such self-report measures as the Spielberger State-Trait Anger Expression Inventory (STAEI) can be useful in evaluating impulsive aggression. The Overt Aggression Scale-Modified (OAS-M) is a semistructured interview that also is useful in measuring the frequency and severity of aggressive behavior (Coccaro, Harvey, Kupsaw-Lawrence, Herbert, & Bernstein, 1991).

A complete assessment for an impulse control disorder should also include questions about the history of the disorder, such as when did symptoms first appear, its severity and duration, history of previous treatment and other efforts to stop the behavior, the last period of abstinence, and any triggers that might precede engaging in the behavior. Coping skills that can be a positive support in treatment should also be determined, including any family support, spirituality, and positive habits such as exercise and hobbies.

Preferred Therapist Characteristics

In their work, therapists are called on to treat a variety of people with diverse symptoms. Miller and Carroll (2006) found that clients' ratings of their working relationships with their clinicians is predictive of treatment outcome. Clinicians who rate higher in warmth and empathy have clients who show greater gains in therapy. Nowhere is the therapeutic alliance more important than in the work therapists do with people who have impulse-control disorders.

Therapists working with this population need to have not only expertise in relationship building and strategies of psychotherapy but also need to pay particular attention to developing and maintaining a positive therapeutic alliance. Any potential ruptures to the alliance must be addressed.

Therapists also should have a good understanding of the nature of their clients' disorders, because education is typically an important component in the treatment of behavioral disorders. Therapists should have a treatment style that is directive and structured and involves goal setting and follow-up but that is also supportive and empathic.

Many therapists originally trained in abstinence-only programs are beginning to accept the utility of adopting a warm turkey approach to alcohol, substance abuse, gambling, and other impulse control disorders. Therapists who are able to work with clients where they are, who help them set realistic treatment goals, and who work collaboratively toward achieving those goals one step at a time, are the most likely to be effective in the treatment of these types of disorders.

Skill in conducting group and family sessions as well as individual therapy sessions may also be required. Therapists should be comfortable incorporating self-help groups into treatment plans, and collaborating with other professions (psychiatrists, physical therapists, dietitians) and paraprofessionals such as peer counselors. Coordination of a multifaceted treatment plan is typically part of the therapist's role in treating behavioral disorders.

Intervention Strategies

Beginning with an effective assessment screening and continuing through treatment planning, interventions for people with behavior problems should focus on options that offer a continuum of care. Selection of appropriate levels of service is especially important when working with people who have a substance abuse problem or severe eating disorder and should be based on such factors as type of disorder, severity, physiological and emotional distress, related biopsychosocial problems, co-occurring disorders, and the person's age and motivation for treatment. Integrating assessment into interventions ensures that people will get individualized attention that focuses on their specific needs. Treatment should be tailored for each person rather than follow a one-size-fits-all approach.

The basic tenet of mental health professionals is the same as it is for the medical community: "First, do no harm." Therefore, before delving into the empirically supported treatment interventions, we turn first to the research on what does not work in treating this population.

What Doesn't Work For treatments that truly are not effective, generally there is no research base to support that fact. Norcross, Koocher, and Garafalo (2006) conducted a Delphi Poll of 290 mental health professionals and 225 addictions experts and compiled the following list of what is probably not effective in the treatment of mental/behavioral disorders.

The list includes thought field therapy, aromatherapy, healing touch techniques, equine therapy for eating disorders, neurolinguistic programming, psychosynthesis, Scared Straight or DARE programs for substance abuse or dependence, emotional freedom technique, bioenergetics therapy, insight-oriented therapies for sex offenders, acupuncture, and psychosocial therapies for pedophilia, among others.

The results of the Delphi Poll are fairly consistent with several books and articles on the subject (Hunsley, Crabb, & Mash, 2004; Lilienfeld, Lynn, & Lohr, 2003) and reinforce the President's New Freedom Commission on Mental Health (2003; www.mentalhealthcommission.gov) call for the increased use of empirically supported treatments and the decreased reliance on treatments for which little empirical evidence exists. For a broader look at evidence-based practice, readers are referred to the American Psychological Association's Presidential Task Force on Evidence-Based Practice (2005).

When selecting treatments that are effective, one need only turn to the growing number of evidence-based practices. But we must remember that lack of proof of efficacy does not mean a treatment is not effective. Some treatments have not been the subject of research, or are so new that there is not enough research available. We now turn to an overview of empirically supported treatment interventions. A more detailed discussion of treatment methodologies will be included later, in the sections on specific disorders.

Motivational Interviewing Motivation can be a problem for many people who have behavior disorders, especially those who are court ordered into treatment following a sexual assault, DWI, or other criminal acts. Motivational interviewing helps people resolve their ambivalence and recognize and verbalize their internal motivations to change. Through the use of open-ended questions, reflective listening, and affirmations and summarization about behavior change, the therapist skillfully evokes "change talk" that helps people take charge of their desire to change (Levensky, Kersh, Cavasos, & Brooks, 2008; Rollnick, Miller, & Butler, 2008). Using the motivational interviewing approach, therapists express empathy for people who have behavior problems, help them accept their ambivalence about treatment by normalizing commonly expressed feelings, identify discrepancies between people's words and behavior, and create self-efficacy (Springer, McNeece, & Arnold, 2003). Such techniques have been found to increase treatment compliance rates and improve motivation for beginning behavior change (Stasiewicz, Herrman, Nochajski, & Dermen, 2006). Motivational interviewing can become an important part of treatment for behavior and impulse-control disorders, especially with reluctant, treatment-resistant, and well-defined clients.

Several assessments are available to measure people's readiness and motivation to change. Most are based on the Transtheoretical Model of Change (Prochaska & Norcross, 2010). For those who are not yet in a substance treatment program, the Readiness to Change Questionnaire (RTCQ; Rollnick, Heather, Gold, & Hall, 1992) can be effective. SOCRATES (Stages of Change Readiness and Treatment Eagerness Scale; Miller & Tonigan, 1996) assesses the clients' insights into their own drug, alcohol, or substance use and assigns a level of change readiness based on the Prochaska model. URICA (University of Rhode Island Change Assessment; McConnaughy, Prochaska, & Velicer, 1983) provides a similar assessment for people who misuse drugs.

Setting Treatment Goals

Early assessment and treatment efforts should focus on reducing high-risk behaviors, such as driving while intoxicated, intravenous drug use, polysubstance use, violent and suicidal behavior, and unprotected sex. Intervening to reduce behaviors that pose a risk to self and others takes first priority over other goals, even the immediate goal of abstinence (Tucker, Vuchinich, & Murphy, 2002).

The setting of goals should be a collaborative effort between the client and clinician. Many different pathways can be effective avenues of change. Although complete abstinence is the goal of 75% of treatment programs, harm reduction approaches that focus on reducing problem drinking to non-problem drinking could be beneficial for people with mild to moderate alcohol misuse (Blume & Marlatt, 2008; Bowen, Chawla, & Marlatt, 2010; Tucker et al., 2002). Those who fail at a trial of reasonable reduction are more likely to be receptive to a subsequent goal of abstinence.

The philosophy of harm reduction can be applied to any high-risk behavior (Cusick, 2005). In contrast to programs that take an abstinence only approach, the harm reduction approach values any behavioral change that results in a reduction of the harm or the risk of harm (Marlatt, 1998). For example, marijuana may be used as a "reverse gateway drug" to help people reduce their use of more harmful substances (for example, cocaine, or hypnotics). Harm reduction models focus on positive changes in behavior and lifestyle, such as substituting methadone maintenance for heroin, or on interventions aimed at stopping high-risk drinking and driving.

Behavioral Therapy

Not surprisingly, the treatment of disorders of behavior and impulse control emphasizes behavioral interventions including: behavioral counts, logs, and checklists; goal setting; learning, practicing, and mastering new behaviors; reducing or eliminating dysfunctional behaviors; reinforcement, motivation enhancement, and consequences; and between-session tasks. Exercise, relaxation, mindfulness, desensitization, role playing, and other techniques may also be incorporated into the treatment plan. Information and education are usually a part of treatment as people are taught about the negative impact of their behaviors on their quality of life and as they learn new and more effective behaviors to replace the old ones.

Cognitive-Behavioral Therapy A great number of empirical studies have indicated that cognitive-behavioral therapy is effective in the treatment of a large number of behavioral and impulse-control disorders. Smoking, eating disorders, and gambling all seem to respond well. Psychotherapy also helps to ameliorate any co-occurring depression or anxiety.

Family Therapy Family therapy, too, is a salient component of treatment for these disorders. Behavioral concerns typically have had an adverse impact on family relationships, and help may be needed in that arena. Families usually also benefit from education about the nature of the disorder and about how best to help their loved ones maintain desired behavioral changes. Moreover, family members themselves (for example, the enabling wife of a husband who misuses alcohol or the overwhelmed mother who does not know how to cope with her daughter's eating disorder) are often participants in patterns that contribute to the perpetuation of the behavioral disorder. When family members are helped to change patterns that maintain, reinforce, and provide secondary gains, the likelihood of improvement is increased, and the families benefit as well. Multifamily therapy groups, as well as therapy for an individual family or family member may be appropriate.

Adjunct Treatments People with eating disorders, substance use disorders, and pathological gambling will usually benefit from receiving therapy together with others who have experienced similar difficulties. Group therapy allows people to learn from others' successes and failures and to receive feedback and encouragement from other group members. Group therapy also enables people to increase their social interest and involvement and to develop and practice their social skills. It facilitates reality testing and the challenging of defenses, offers points of comparison, promotes self-understanding and self-acceptance, and is often less threatening than individual therapy. Group therapy is particularly useful in the early stages of treatment when motivation may be uncertain, but it usually is not indicated for people who are fragile or disturbed. Self-help peer groups, such as Rational Recovery, Alcoholics Anonymous, moderatedrinking.com, Narcotics Anonymous, and Gamblers Anonymous, can be another important component of treatment.

Medication Medication is usually not the primary mode of treatment for behavioral disorders, with the exception of male sexual dysfunction and several of the sleep disorders, but it sometimes can contribute to the treatment process. For example, antidepressant medication may reduce hopelessness and inertia in people with bulimia nervosa so that they are able to benefit from psychotherapy, and naltrexone (ReVia) may be used to help jumpstart recovery from alcohol dependence.

Many behavioral disorders, including the substance-related disorders and the eating disorders, are physically harmful and even life threatening. Other disorders that have behavioral manifestations, such as the sexual dysfunctions, intermittent explosive disorder, and hypersomnia, sometimes have a physiological cause. For both reasons, many of the disorders discussed in this chapter warrant clients' referral to physicians for evaluation. Medical information can be useful in determining the most appropriate treatment plan for a particular individual.

Professional Interventions Refusal to seek treatment and denial of the severity of their symptoms is common among people with impulse-control disorders. If a person clearly needs treatment for a gambling, eating, or substance use disorder but is reluctant to obtain help, a therapist often will assist friends and family members in organizing what is called an intervention.

Developed by Vernon Johnson (1986), founder of the Johnson Institute, this approach involves having two or more people concerned about someone's substance use meet with that person, usually along with a therapist, to present information on the negative impact of the behavior and encourage the person to accept help. Typically, treatment is prearranged, and consequences (such as loss of a job or a relationship) if the person does not agree to treatment are clearly stated. Interventions have been shown to be successful both at involving a person in treatment and at leading to a positive outcome (Schuckit, 2010).

A less formal type of intervention, known as ARISE, has also been found to be effective. The ARISE model provides an intervention continuum that starts with the first call from families or concerned others and goes through five or six sessions in which family members and friends are encouraged to take steps toward ending the cycle of addiction. Rather than a single confrontation, the intervention matches the family's pressure to the person's resistance. Whether the person enters treatment, the support needs of the family network are addressed, and the family develops hope that their efforts will make a difference. The ARISE model takes into account that intervention is rarely successful the first time; rather, multiple interventions may

be necessary over the course of treatment (Garrett, Landau-Stanton, Stanton, Stellato-Kabat, & Stellato-Kabat, 1997).

Relapse Prevention Relapse rates have often been used to judge treatment outcomes. Marlatt (1998) suggests that after an initial lapse following treatment, one of two outcomes is possible. The client either goes back to using substances and is said to have relapsed, or gets back on track in the direction of positive change (prolapse). Lapses are common in any of the impulse-control disorders and are to be expected whenever anyone attempts to change behavior. Therefore, an important piece of any substance use treatment program should be educating people about relapse and fine-tuning their relapse prevention skills. Aftercare programs should also be established to monitor and encourage long-term success (Tucker et al., 2002; Witkiewitz & Marlatt, 2004).

Regardless of the substance used, three quarters of all relapses are associated with three contributing factors: negative emotional states, interpersonal conflict, and social pressure (Marlatt, 1998). To a lesser extent, positive emotions can also trigger a relapse, especially when combined with socializing. Other conditions that are likely to trigger a relapse are physical pain, urges, and cravings. Therapists can use this list to help clients develop plans to resist relapse and develop coping mechanisms so that they are better prepared to deal with future stress.

Research has shown that a wide range of treatments, in different combinations, across a variety of settings and treatment modalities, can be effective in the treatment of behavioral disorders (Tucker et al., 2002). Abstinence may not always be the initial goal, nor the end result, but a growing body of research over the past 20 years indicates that the majority of people can and do make significant modifications in their behavior; significant enough so that they no longer meet the criteria for a *DSM-IV-TR* disorder.

Prognosis

The prognosis for treatment of the behavioral disorders varies according to the nature of the particular disorder and the motivation and lifestyle of the client. Perhaps the greatest barrier to treatment is the inherently gratifying nature of many of these disorders. For example, even though the eating disorders and substance-related disorders often cause physical, social, and possibly occupational difficulties for the people diagnosed with them, the rewards of being thin or being intoxicated are very powerful and are difficult to counteract in therapy. Relapses are common. The basic course of treatment may be relatively brief, but extended aftercare and follow-up are indicated (through self-help groups, intermittent psychotherapy appointments, drug testing, medical examinations, homework assignments, and family or individual therapy) for consolidation of gains, prevention of relapse, facilitation of adjustment, and assistance in coping effectively if a relapse does occur. With appropriate treatment and follow-up, and with motivation on the part of the client, the prognosis is good for significant improvement if not for complete remission of most behavioral disorders.

Now we move on to a discussion of specific impulse-control disorders, beginning with the substance-related disorders. Eating disorders, sexual disorders, and sleep disorders follow.

SUBSTANCE-RELATED DISORDERS

The category of substance-related disorders, as listed in the *Diagnostic and Statistical Manual of Mental Disorders (DSM-IV-TR)*, includes two substance use disorders—substance abuse and substance dependence—and a wide variety of substance-induced disorders.

Description of the Disorders

The substance use disorders describe maladaptive behavioral patterns of using drugs and alcohol; the substance-induced disorders label such symptoms as intoxication, mood changes, and sleep-related problems that stem directly from maladaptive patterns of using drugs or alcohol. Consequently, a substance use disorder often will be accompanied by the diagnosis of one or more substance-induced disorders.

Substance Abuse The *DSM-IV-TR* diagnosis of substance abuse involves recurrent and self-destructive use of drugs or alcohol leading to significant impairment or distress. This disorder is characterized by at least one of the following four substance-related symptoms:

1. Impairment in primary roles (for example, employee, parent, partner, student).
2. Recurrent use of drugs or alcohol in hazardous situations (such as while driving or operating machinery).
3. Recurrent substance-related legal problems (such as arrests for driving while intoxicated).
4. Continued use of a substance despite the awareness that it is having a negative impact.

Substance abuse is often characterized by sporadic use of substances (for example, weekend rather than daily use) and entails fewer physiological effects and less consumption of drugs or alcohol than substance dependence. Nevertheless, substance abuse can also have a profound impact on a person's lifestyle and is often a precursor of substance dependence. Substance abuse can be diagnosed only in people who have never met the criteria for substance dependence related to the particular substance in question.

Substance Dependence The *DSM-IV-TR* describes substance dependence as "a maladaptive pattern of substance use, leading to clinically significant impairment or distress" (American Psychiatric Association, 2000, p. 197). According to the *DSM*, at least three of the following seven symptoms will be manifested at any time in the same 12-month period:

1. Signs of tolerance, such as needing more of the substance to obtain the same effect.
2. Symptoms of withdrawal.
3. Use of more of a substance than was planned.
4. Enduring desire or unsuccessful efforts to reduce use of the substance.
5. Extensive devotion of time to substance-related activities or to recovering from the effects of the substance.
6. Minimal or reduced involvement in career and social activities.
7. Continued use of a substance despite the awareness that it is having a negative impact.

Substance dependence can be described as being with or without physiological dependence; in a controlled environment (such as a hospital, prison, or halfway house); on agonist therapy (such as Methadone); in early (first 12 months) or sustained (longer than 12 months) remission; and in partial (one or more criteria for dependence have been met but not enough for the diagnosis) or full (no criteria have been met) remission. The development of tolerance and physical or psychological symptoms of withdrawal that occur when the person stops using the substance, may indicate substance dependence, but are not necessary for a diagnosis, according to the *DSM-IV-TR* criteria. The *DSM-IV-TR* specifies 11 classes of psychoactive substances that are used in maladaptive ways:

1. Alcohol
2. Amphetamines and amphetamine-like substances

3. Caffeine
4. Cannabis
5. Cocaine
6. Hallucinogens
7. Inhalants
8. Nicotine
9. Opioids
10. Phencyclidine (PCP) or phencyclidine-like substances
11. Sedatives, hypnotics, and anxiolytics

The *DSM-IV-TR* also includes other or unknown substance use disorders (such as anabolic steroids, prescription and over-the-counter medications that do not fall into the above categories, amyl or butyl nitrate, and nitrous oxide) and polysubstance dependence, which involves the use of three or more categories of substances (not including caffeine or nicotine), with no one substance predominating during a 12-month period. In diagnosing a substance use disorder, the clinician specifies the substance and whether the symptoms meet the criteria for abuse or dependence.

Substance use disorders do not necessarily entail long-standing and pervasive impairment; in fact, most people who misuse drugs or alcohol are employed and have families. Nevertheless, substance use disorders typically have a powerful negative impact on the users, as well as on the people who are close to them.

Substance-induced disorders vary from substance to substance; their manifestations depend on the impact of the specific substances. This category includes the following disorders:

- Substance intoxication
- Substance withdrawal
- Substance-induced delirium
- Substance-induced persisting dementia
- Substance-induced persisting amnestic disorder
- Substance-induced psychotic disorder

- Substance-induced mood disorder
- Substance-induced anxiety disorder
- Substance-induced sexual dysfunction
- Substance-induced sleep disorder
- Hallucinogen persisting perception disorder (flashbacks)

More than 9% of Americans (22.2 million people) meet the criteria for substance abuse or dependence (SAMHSA, 2006). Studies of people in treatment for mental disorders found polysubstance use rates of 40% to 60% (Mueser, Drake, Turner, & McGovern, 2006). The combination of substance use and a co-occurring personality, mood, or anxiety disorder is also high. This pattern of dual disorders is difficult to treat because it becomes a vicious cycle: the substance use worsens the coexisting disorder, which in turn increases the person's tendency to use drugs or alcohol to self-medicate. Often, moreover, the substance use masks the symptoms of the underlying disorder, further complicating the treatment picture.

The co-occurrence of ADHD and substance use disorders is just one example. One recent study found a 44% prevalence rate of ADHD in people who entered a residential treatment program for substance abuse (McAweeney, Rogers, Huddleston, Moore, & Gentile, 2010). This is consistent with ADHD rates of 15% to 35% in adults seeking treatment for substance use disorders, and is 10 times the prevalence rate of 4.5% found in the general adult population (Faraone & Biederman, 2005; Kessler, 2006b). Adults with ADHD are more likely to have significant difficulties in personal and occupational functioning, as well as executive functioning deficits that make them more vulnerable to developing a substance use disorder. Indeed, as many as 50% of people who have been diagnosed with ADHD in childhood go on to develop a substance use disorder. A separate study found a reduction in substance use disorders in people who

had received treatment for ADHD. Screening for ADHD prior to admission into a substance abuse program, and integration of treatment for both disorders could improve treatment outcomes.

The bottom line is that dual diagnosis of a substance use disorder and another mental disorder results in a more severe course of illness, increases the need for integrated treatment of both disorders, and results in lower rates of abstinence and increased rates of relapse (Levin & Hennessy, 2004; Mueser et al., 2006; Wilens & Upadhyaya, 2007). Clearly, diagnosis and treatment of co-occuring disorders is fundamental to the development of successful treatment interventions for alcohol and other substance use disorders.

Suicide and suicidal ideation are also common in people with substance use disorders, eating disorders, and gambling, and seem to increase as substance use increases (Evans et al., 2005). While depression frequently underlies suicidal ideation, impulse control disorders in combination with the use of substances significantly predicts the transition from suicidal thoughts to the development of a plan and making a suicide attempt (Nock, Hwang, Sampson, & Kessler, 2010). This is particularly worrisome because people who misuse substances have an available lethal weapon—drugs or alcohol—and the combination of intoxication and impulsivity may lead a binge to become a suicide attempt. With the use of multiple drugs becoming increasingly common, suicide becomes even easier through the use of a mixture of drugs, such as alcohol and tranquilizers. As many as 25% of people entering treatment for substance use have made a previous suicide attempt (Chamberlain & Jew, 2005). Readers can find additional information on risk factors and warning signs of suicide in the Appendix to this book.

The next two sections of this chapter—on disorders related to alcohol and drugs, respectively—provide an overview of the nature and treatment of some of the specific substance use disorders. In each section, the primary focus will be on the use disorders (abuse and dependence) rather than on the induced disorders, which can vary widely and often require medical intervention. Nevertheless, the therapist must always determine whether a substance use disorder is accompanied by one or more induced disorders, and treatment must take account of the combination of disorders that are present.

ALCOHOL-RELATED DISORDERS

Twenty-five percent of all people seeking treatment for mental health or medical issues are likely to have an alcohol use disorder (McCrady, 2006). Assessment, diagnosis and treatment of alcohol-related disorders is crucial to the successful treatment of any co-occurring disorders.

Description of the Disorders

Alcohol-related disorders represent a large and costly health problem in the United States: 15.4 million people have an alcohol use disorder alone, with another 3.3 million having both drug and alcohol disorders (SAMHSA, 2006).

Approximately 200,000 deaths each year are directly attributable to alcohol use, a total that includes 25% of all suicides and 50% of homicides as well as a large percentage of automobile and other types of accidents. On a positive note, alcohol use has declined or remained stable for most age groups for the past 25 years.

Alcohol is the most widely used substance during the adolescent years (Evans et al., 2005). By their senior year of high school, 85% of students report having used alcohol and those who start drinking before the age of 14 are at increased risk for developing alcohol dependence

later in life. Of adolescents who misuse alcohol, 30% to 50% have co-occurring diagnoses of ADHD or conduct disorder (Flory, Milich, Lynam, Leukefeld, & Clayton, 2003). Researchers point to possible common traits that underlie these disorders including poor impulse control, common genetic factors, and similar environmental factors. These factors are not simply additive; they combine synergistically to result in the development of more adverse outcomes and impaired functioning in later life. Research has shown that an earlier age of first use of alcohol is associated with the development of a variety of problems including more serious substance-related use, social problems, co-occurring disorders, criminal activity, and the development of psychopathy (Carroll & Ball, 2007).

People between the ages of 20 and 35 are most likely to misuse alcohol. People rarely begin drinking after the age of 45, and those who began drinking earlier sometimes remit spontaneously in midlife. Men and women typically have different patterns of alcohol use. Women who consume alcohol to excess are more likely to drink alone; to feel guilty and attempt to conceal their drinking; to combine alcohol with other drugs; and to suffer from depression, anxiety, and insomnia. Alcohol problems seem to start later and progress faster in women and are more closely linked to stressful life circumstances (Sullivan, Fama, Rosenbloom, & Pfefferbaum, 2002).

Some ethnic groups have a higher prevalence of alcohol problems than others. People from Hispanic, American Indian, or Eskimo cultures, for example, are overrepresented among those with alcohol problems. Alcohol use rates are also significantly higher among Caucasian adolescents than African American or Asian American youth. In some cases, alcohol consumption could be the result of biological factors. For example, being of Asian heritage may be protective against the development of an alcohol use disorder. Fifty percent of people of Chinese, Korean, or Japanese heritage possess the ALDH2*2 allele, which results in unpleasant physical symptoms such as nausea, flushing, and increased heart rate, whenever alcohol is consumed. People with one ALDH2*2 allele have a fivefold decrease in alcohol dependence; people with two ALDH2*2 alleles have a ninefold decrease. They are also less likely to use other substances, or to smoke tobacco (Eng, Luczak, & Wall, 2007).

Typical Client Characteristics

People who misuse alcohol often seek treatment for concerns other than alcohol, such as interpersonal, occupational, and legal difficulties; cognitive impairment; and physical problems. Many have co-occurring personality disorders or underlying personality traits that make them more susceptible to alcohol misuse. For example, people who misuse alcohol tend to score high on obsessive-compulsive, depressive, and sociopathic factors on the Minnesota Multiphasic Personality Inventory (Chamberlain & Jew, 2005). They also tend to score higher in imagination, intellectual ability, extroversion, passivity, instability, anxiety, and interpersonal undependability on the California Psychological Inventory (Meyer, 1983).

People with alcohol-related disorders often have underlying anxiety and depression. As they do with other substances, people sometimes use alcohol to reduce their anxiety, and to feel more comfortable in social situations. Alcohol is also used to alleviate dysphoria or depression, although this is likely to backfire, as alcohol is a depressant and frequently leads to worsening of depressive symptoms. Similarly, people with bipolar disorder often turn to alcohol to lessen the severity of a manic or psychotic episode (Laudet, Magura, Vogel, & Knight, 2004).

Up to 50% of males in treatment have co-occurring antisocial personality disorder; 25% to 30% of females are likely to have developed a depressive disorder prior to developing an alcohol use disorder (McCrady, 2006).

For adolescents, alcohol use and abuse are frequently correlated to peer group behavior. Most adolescents who are enrolled in treatment programs do not believe that they have a problem. Eighty percent of adolescents in treatment have been court ordered through the juvenile justice system, the remainder have been urged by parents or school officials to get treatment. Adolescents may be quite ambivalent about treatment, because they have many reasons to continue their behavior and, unlike older people with an alcohol problem, have not experienced many of the physical and economic consequences of their behavior. This lack of motivation for treatment must be addressed early on if treatment is to be successful with this population (Godley, Smith, Meyers, & Godley, 2009).

Similar to adults, 70% of adolescents in treatment have co-occurring disorders, most frequently conduct disorder, ADHD, depression, anxiety, and PTSD. As many as one fourth of this population also have thought about or attempted suicide. Before treatment can begin, a large number of adolescents must first be referred for psychiatric evaluation or for treatment of underlying trauma (Godley et al., 2009).

Women and alcohol. Problems with alcohol use affect about 4.6 million women in the United States (Sullivan et al., 2002). These women typically have special issues that need to be addressed, such as relationship and parenting concerns, partner abuse, a history of trauma, and barriers to treatment (such as finances, transportation, and child care). They often have difficulty in intimate relationships, as well as drinking patterns that are linked to those of significant others in their lives. Women develop drinking problems later in life than men do, frequently in response to a stressful life event, such as divorce or the death of a family member. Women who misuse alcohol are more likely than men who misuse this substance to be single; to have lower self-esteem; to have more severely disturbed personalities; and to be increased risk for liver disease, depression, physical or emotional abuse, and cognitive deficits resulting from alcohol use (Hommer, Momenan, Kaiser, & Rawlings, 2001). These women have a high incidence of trauma in their backgrounds, including rape, incest, and abuse, and are more likely than men to attempt suicide. Unfortunately, they also are less likely to seek treatment. Some evidence indicates that women are better at concealing their disorder, and thus avoid or delay getting help (Sullivan et al., 2002). Family responsibilities, a lack of empowerment, and the stigma associated with women who misuse alcohol can all be barriers to their seeking treatment.

Women metabolize alcohol differently than men do and tend to be more susceptible to its toxic effects (Lieber, 2000). Research shows that although women consume less alcohol than men and for shorter periods of time, death rates among females who misuse alcohol are 50% to 100% greater than their male counterparts. These serious biological, sociological, and behavioral differences between males and females indicate that therapists should tailor treatment to the particular needs of women and should expect slower recovery, greater cognitive impairment, and increased presence of comorbid disorders (Sullivan et al., 2002). Because women do better in programs that focus on female issues, whenever possible they should be directed toward women's meetings in such support groups as Alcoholics Anonymous and Women for Recovery.

Assessment

People who misuse alcohol often present with concerns other than alcohol, so a multidimensional assessment should be conducted to determine whether alcohol is the central difficulty, typically the one that must be addressed before the others can be ameliorated. The first consideration in treating alcohol use disorders is to assess the extent and severity of the problem, the person's motivation to change, and social and other factors maintaining the current pattern of use.

Screening measures should be brief and easily administered, and should accurately establish the presence (or absence) of alcohol misuse (Tucker et al., 2002). Four verbal self-reports that meet these criteria and screen for alcohol problems include the Rapid Alcohol Problems Screen (RAPS4; Cherpitel, 2000), the Michigan Alcoholism Screening Test (MAST; Selzer, 1971), the CAGE Screening for Alcohol Abuse (Buchsbaum, Buchanan, Centor, Schnoll, & Lawton, 1991; Mayfield, McLeod, & Hall, 1974), and the Alcohol Use Disorders Identification Test (AUDIT; Saunders, Aasland, Babor, DeLaFuente, & Grant, 1993). An Internet-based version of the AUDIT was found to have good reliability overall, but to have lower reliability on the subscale of alcohol dependence (E. T. Miller et al., 2002).

Motivation should also be assessed, as it is an important component in behavioral change. Prochaska and colleagues (2010) developed a five-stage model (discussed in more detail in Chapter 1) in which each stage represents a different level of motivational readiness: precontemplation, contemplation, preparation, action, and maintenance. Taking the stage of readiness for change into account can assist the therapist in matching the treatment plan to the client's motivational level and determine whether motivational enhancement is a necessary part of the treatment process. Weaving motivational enhancement approaches into the treatment process has been associated with more positive outcomes (McCrady, 2006). Adolescents and others who did not seek treatment voluntarily may need additional prompting in the areas of values clarification, goal-setting, and choice theory before they can actively engage in treatment as being part of enlightened self interest (Glasser, 1990; Sampson, Stephens, & Velasquez, 2009).

Other self-report measures of antecedents to drinking (AWARE; Miller & Harris, 2000), and the Desires for Alcohol Questionnaire (DAQ; Love, James, & Willner, 1998) can also help anticipate the intention, desire, and relief from negative affect that a person experiences when contemplating alcohol use. Interested readers will find a comprehensive discussion of screening and diagnostic instruments for alcohol problems in Donovan (2007).

Preferred Therapist Characteristics

As in the treatment of all substance use disorders, therapists working with people who misuse alcohol should adopt a strengths-based approach, be positive, and focus on improving the patient's overall health and well-being rather than focus on disease or addiction (Donovan, 2007). Clinician behavior, and the development of the clinician-client relationship, can result in better compliance with treatment and better treatment outcomes. Clinicians who are empathic, who develop a collaborative approach to goal setting and treatment, and who are flexible are more likely to have clients who achieve positive results than those who set the client's goals and demand treatment compliance (Epstein & McCrady, 2009). Therapists should promote optimism, commitment, and a sense of responsibility. Therapists who are honest and direct as well as compassionate and empathic seem to work best with this population. Confrontation and self-disclosure on the part of the therapist should be used judiciously but can sometimes facilitate progress and reduce resistance to treatment.

Therapists should be careful, however, not to impose their own experiences on their clients.

Knowing when to validate the client's experience and when to in-validate the experience are also important skills (Koerner & Linehan, 2008). Validating the difficulty the client is having in changing behavior or remaining abstinent is a positive, empathic, and supportive intervention that can instill self-esteem and improve the therapeutic alliance. But knowing when to invalidate the client's experience is more challenging. Koerner and Linehan note that when client's willpower is flagging and they develop what Ellis refers to as "can't-stand-it-itis," the therapist must respond with an intervention that reinforces "Yes, you can!" By drawing on the client's resilience and past successes, and strengthening responses that are consistent with therapeutic goals, therapists can help clients modify their dysfunctional feelings and overcome challenges to their stated goals.

Therapists should be prepared for clients to engage in some alcohol use while in treatment and should not be discouraged if it occurs. At the same time, a therapy session should not be held if a client arrives intoxicated.

Intervention Strategies

It should be readily apparent that to be successful, treatment for alcohol use disorders requires multiple components that can motivate people for change, address the alcohol addiction, alleviate co-occurring problems, mend family and social disruptions, and adequately educate people about relapse. Treatment approaches that have consistently demonstrated positive outcomes in controlled trials and those that provide enough flexibility so that treatments can be tailored to address individual needs seem likely to work best (Donohue, Allen, & LaPota, 2009).

The *DSM-IV-TR* distinguishes between alcohol abuse and alcohol dependence. Most people who drink in a harmful or even hazardous way do not meet the criteria for alcohol dependence, therefore careful assessment must be made to distinguish between the two.

People who abuse alcohol, but have not reached the stage of dependence, can be helped by brief, focused interventions rather than abstinence-based or long-term treatment. Moderation, or controlled drinking, rather than complete abstinence, seems to be a reasonable first goal for people with mild to moderate alcohol problems (Donovan, 2007; Epstein & McCrady, 2009; Hester, Delaney, & Campbell, 2011).

DiClemente (2003) notes that achieving abstinence after one has become dependent is best viewed as a long-term goal. A study by King and Tucker (2000) of people who met the criteria for alcohol dependence and who spontaneously resolved their drinking problems without treatment found that those who stopped drinking excessively and drank moderately made an average of five attempts at change, whereas those who ultimately became abstinent had made an average of 41 attempts at moderation. Clearly, moderate drinking does not work for everyone. Sanchez-Craig and colleagues (1995) report that most people eventually use alcohol in moderation and that people find the idea of controlled drinking more acceptable than abstinence.

Determining the goal of treatment—abstinence or maintained self-regulation—is an important first step. A recent report of the screening stage of an RCT in the United Kingdom found that the strongest predictors of goal preference were gender, drinking pattern, recent detoxification, and level of social support for drinking. Specifically, 54% of participants indicated a preference for abstinence and 45.7% preferred nonabstinence as a treatment goal. Those more likely to prefer abstinence included women, the unemployed, those with more serious medical and psychological disorders, who

reported drinking heavily, reported less social support for their drinking, with greater confidence in their ability to quit drinking, and those who had more concerns about their future (Heather et al., 2010).

Differences in treatment outcomes in an RCT underscored that clients' stated intentions and treatment goals (abstinence versus nonproblem drinking) were predictive of treatment outcome (Adamson, Heather, Morton, & Raistrick, 2010). In other words, study participants who set a goal of abstinence were more likely to achieve that goal and maintain it at 3-month follow-up and less so at 12-month follow up. Those who set a goal of nonproblem drinking were less likely to achieve abstinence. Client intent is an important, if understudied, predictor of treatment outcome and should be considered in the development of treatment goals (Adamson et al., 2010). The authors also recommend that goal intent should be a part of the assessment process and should be a basis for collaboration between client and therapist.

If abstinence is the goal, contracts can be useful in affirming the goal and in specifying the steps that people can take when they feel the desire for drugs or alcohol. Motivation, readiness to change, self-efficacy (people's belief in their ability to control their substance use), and controlling urges and cravings are critical elements that should be addressed in a treatment program (Marlatt & Witkiewitz, 2007; Tucker et al., 2002).

Therapy with people who have alcohol use disorders typically follows a series of eight stages:

1. Identifying the problem.
2. Taking a detailed history.
3. Determining treatment setting.
4. Helping motivate people toward change.
5. Setting goals.
6. Providing education and interventions to develop coping mechanisms.

7. Offering concurrent involvement in family therapy and self-help groups.
8. Maintaining change through follow-up and relapse prevention.

Interventions for alcohol dependence have shifted away from intensive residential and rehabilitative programs toward brief, multifaceted interventions or lower-intensity treatment spread out over a longer time period (Finney, Wilbourne, & Moos, 2007). There is a lack of evidence to support residential program effectiveness, and growing concerns that they might actually be ineffective (Norcross, Koocher, & Garofalo, 2006), as well as costly in the eyes of managed care. Nevertheless, more intensive programs sometimes are indicated for people with long-standing misuse of alcohol, especially if they have a history of treatment failures. Withdrawal can be dangerous if alcohol consumption is high, and hospitalization may need to be the first step in treatment. Even if hospitalization is not indicated, a medical examination almost always is, because of the damaging effects of alcohol.

Combined Behavior Intervention   Hundreds of different approaches to alcohol use disorders are available. Hester and Miller (2003) reviewed 47 different treatment modalities and found the highest probability of success among motivation enhancement, cognitive therapy, and social skills training. The least effective treatments were educational tapes, videos, or films; confrontational counseling; and relaxation techniques or 12-step programs as a frontline treatment (Springer, 2009).

Research has shown that a wide range of treatments, in different combinations, across a variety of settings and treatment modalities, can be effective in the treatment of alcohol dependence. Such interventions are cost-effective in that they reduce substance-related problems and the expenses associated with them. COMBINE, a federally funded study, found that motivational enhancement therapy combined with cognitive behavior therapy and active participation in self-help groups used in conjunction with medication management using naltrexone for the treatment of alcohol dependence nearly doubled the rate of positive outcomes (Anton et al., 2006). Such combinations of interventions more effectively meet the specific needs of the individual, and help to reduce lapses, as well as relapses, in the treatment of alcohol-related disorders (Donovan & Marlatt, 2008).

There are a vast number of treatment programs and combinations available. Readers are invited to review Springer and Rubin (2009), McCrady (2006), and other newer texts for a comprehensive review of alcohol treatment. What follows is a look at the different components that are frequently combined to create an effective alcohol treatment program.

Cognitive and Behavioral Therapy   Cognitive and behavioral therapies have been found to be an effective component of treatment for alcohol and other substance use disorders. A recent meta-analysis of 53 controlled trials of cognitive behavior therapy for adults with alcohol or other substance use disorders found CBT to be effective across a variety of types of CBT, varied substances, and diverse study participants. The effect size was largest with women, cannabis users, and when CBT was compared to no treatment (Magill & Ray, 2009).

Moderation Training   Rotgers (2008) outlines a cognitive-behavioral approach to moderation that has received empirical support. Behavioral self-control training (BSCT) is available in four manual-based treatment approaches as well as a computerized version. Those who fail at this initial trial are then more likely to consider abstinence. A moderation method allows for incremental steps toward self-care, and people may feel empowered to choose what works for them. Safe alcohol use guidelines are available, as is research on client preference, and predictors of moderation outcomes (Dawson et al., 2005; Heather, Adamson, Raistrick, & Slegg, 2010; Saladin & Santa Ana, 2004; Sanchez-Craig, Wilkinson, & Davila, 1995). Moderation training has been around for decades and offers an important, and empirically based, alternative to abstinence only programs.

Behavioral Group Therapy   Behavior therapy usually is conducted in a group setting so that participants can reinforce and confront each other as appropriate and serve as role models and sources of support and information. Behavioral group therapy may include relaxation training, assertiveness training, role playing, stress management, development of other sources of gratification, and enhancement of coping skills. Cognitive therapy, including cognitive restructuring, is almost always a part of a comprehensive program.

Motivational Interviewing   A brief focus on motivational interviewing at the beginning of substance use interventions produces abstinence rates twice that of controls (Burke, Arkowitz, & Menchola, 2003). Motivational interviewing is especially helpful at reducing anger and hostility with court-ordered clients, and is more effective than coping or social skills training at reducing resistance to the therapist (Project MATCH Research Group, 1998). In cases where domestic abuse co-occurs with alcohol use, motivational interviewing can reduce anger and enhance readiness for behavioral change (Murphy & Maiuro, 2009).

Social Skills Training   Many people, especially adolescents, who misuse alcohol will also benefit from problem solving and social skills training. Compared to their peers, substance-abusing adolescents have at their disposal less mature mechanisms for solving their problems, most of which are related to interpersonal relationships. Adolescent substance users tend to use impulsive, careless, and avoidant problem solving skills (Jaffe & D'Zurilla, 2003). Social skills training focuses on improving communication and assertiveness skills by helping people recognize and label thoughts and feelings, initiate social interactions, and respond appropriately to criticism. The training frequently takes place in a group setting to foster interaction, role plays, and feedback from other group members (Wagner & Austin, 2009).

Guided Adolescent Problem Solving (GAPS) is a brief, five-session, manualized treatment program for individuals with alcohol and other drug related problems (Wagner & Austin, 2009). GAPS incorporates components of motivational interviewing, psychoeducation, cognitive behavior therapy, and assertiveness/communication skills training into an effective program that helps adolescents recognize and avoid triggers, cope with stress, navigate challenging social situations, and learn to set goals for the future. GAPS, is just one example of an empirically supported, problem-solving intervention for alcohol and other drug-related problems (Bender, Springer, & Kim, 2006).

Medication   To date, only three medications have been approved by the FDA for the treatment of alcohol use disorders in the United States—naltrexone, disulfiram, and acamprosate (Sewell & Petrakis, 2011). Naltrexone (ReVia) was approved by the FDA in 1995 as a safe and effective adjunct to treatments for alcohol use disorders. Research indicates that naltrexone reduces alcohol cravings and alcohol-seeking behavior, and helps those who take it to maintain control over their drinking. Naltrexone, used in conjunction with short-term psychotherapy and participation in self-help groups, has been found to help reduce the frequency and severity of relapse (Donovan et al., 2008). Vivitrol, an injectable form of Naltrexone, which is delivered monthly, was approved by the FDA in 2006. To date, usage remains low, but results seem promising and more outcome studies are expected in the future as this option becomes integrated into the treatment of alcohol use disorders (Abraham & Roman, 2010).

Disulfiram (Antabuse) has sometimes been a part of the treatment of alcohol use disorders, particularly for people who have a long history of alcohol problems and who have failed at efforts to maintain sobriety in the past. Antabuse is an alcohol antagonist. If taken regularly, it acts as an emetic when combined with alcohol. Although it has been in use for more than 40 years, evidence of its effectiveness is limited. In one study, 46% of participants dropped out of treatment.

Noncompliance, poor relapse prevention, and the risk of severe reactions associated with the medication suggest that Antabuse should be used cautiously, particularly with people who are depressed or who have heart disease, hypertension, or other serious health problems (Williams, 2005).

Acamprosate (Campral) is the third medication to be approved by the FDA for alcohol dependence. It first became available in the United States in 2005, but has not achieved the success it enjoyed in Europe. One study showed acamprosate was no better than placebo for reducing the unpleasant physical and psychological symptoms associated with withdrawal (Kranzler, 2006). Acamprosate is intended to be used as part of a comprehensive relapse prevention plan for those who have already achieved abstinence from alcohol.

Although a variety of medications, such as benzodiazepines, antipsychotics, and antidepressants, have been shown to alleviate specific symptoms related to alcohol use (such as anxiety, depression, mood swings, psychosis, and

cravings), no medication has been found to be sufficient on its own to effect recovery from alcohol misuse.

Relapse Prevention Relapse prevention is an important part of any successful behavioral change. Tools that help clients recognize and overcome cravings for alcohol should be built into the treatment plan. Urge surfing, a cognitively based technique that incorporates mindfulness and acceptance, can help people recognize, cope with, and replace cravings for alcohol before they have a lapse (Lloyd, 2008).

Marlatt and Gordon (1985) and Witkiewitz and Marlatt (2004) have developed a comprehensive cognitive-behavioral relapse prevention model that helps people reduce their risk of relapse by identifying high-risk situations, improving coping skills, developing self-efficacy, maintaining motivation, reducing negative affect, and creating life balance. The success of relapse prevention programs can be enhanced with other tools at the therapist's disposal such as use of mobile phones or computer technology to meet the recovery needs of clients (Gustafson et al., 2010) or the addition of mindfulness meditation as a coping skill (Brewer, Bowen, Smith, Marlatt, & Potenza, 2010).

For some people, especially those dually diagnosed with an alcohol use disorder and a mental disorder, control of their drinking may take longer to achieve. For them, dual diagnosis meetings of AA or NA or a harm reduction support group may be better suited to their needs.

Environment and Aftercare Environment plays an important role in who will succeed in their goals. As with most forms of substance use disorders, treatment of alcohol abuse or dependence should go beyond use of the substance and focus on areas that have been harmed or thwarted as a result of the person's alcohol misuse. Women who misuse alcohol often need help with parenting skills, past physical and sexual abuse, social support systems, career counseling, and feelings of low self-esteem. Treatment should encourage development of those skills that are needed to establish a rewarding and alcohol-free lifestyle. People seem to go through a particularly difficult phase during the early months of abstinence, when they are struggling to adjust to sobriety. Halfway houses, day treatment programs, and other follow-up or aftercare programs can facilitate the transition from severe alcohol use to self-sufficiency and abstinence.

Family Therapy   Families in which alcohol is misused typically have more than one person who has a strong need for therapy. The children may be suffering the impact of the parents' inconsistent and negative behavior and may manifest emotional and behavioral disorders and early alcohol use themselves, as well as low self-esteem and confused goals and aspirations. Spouses or partners of those who misuse alcohol are sometimes enabling, indirectly encouraging the alcohol use because of their own dependence needs. Therefore, therapy should also address the needs of family members, both to treat their immediate problems and to help them avoid the continuation of patterns that promote alcohol use disorders. Involving the family in the therapy can also increase the accuracy of the available information on the client's drinking.

12-Step Programs   For maximum effectiveness, peer support groups should be part of a multifaceted treatment plan. Participation in a 12-step program in conjunction with formal treatment is correlated with greater treatment success (Anton et al., 2006; Spiegel & Fewell, 2004). Alcoholics Anonymous (AA) is the most widespread 12-step program. Its primary tenets are that alcoholism is a progressive disease and that once someone has become an "alcoholic," he or she will always be an alcoholic and cannot

stop drinking without help. Alcoholics Anonymous currently has more than 50,000 groups in the United States. Each AA group has its own focus and personality. It is important for people to attend meetings in which they feel most comfortable.

Other Programs   Some people are uncomfortable with 12-step programs because of their strong spiritual component, and addressing this issue beforehand in therapy may facilitate people's involvement with the program or decision to participate in an alternative self-help program. Rational Recovery is a self-help group based on Ellis's rational emotive behavior therapy (Ellis & Tafrate, 1997). Other groups, such as Smart Recovery, LifeRing, Secular Organization for Sobriety (SOS), Moderation Management, ModerateDrinking.com, and Women for Recovery, provide alternatives to Alcoholics Anonymous that deemphasize religious and spiritual elements and do not insist on abstinence as a goal.

Prognosis

Long-term outcome for treatment of alcohol use disorders is related primarily to the person's motivation, goals for abstinence or controlled drinking, coping skills, social support, and level of stress (Adamson et al., 2009; Oltmanns & Emery, 2007). These factors appear to be more important than the type of treatment provided (inpatient or outpatient, individual or group, self-help or professional). Other factors related to a positive outcome include increased length of treatment, discovery of substitutes for alcohol (such as pleasurable activities, jobs, new relationships, or involvement in spiritual or self-help groups), and frequency of attendance at self-help meetings.

Even so, therapists are reminded that success in any impulse control disorder is a process. The likelihood of a relapse after treatment is high. Of people who have been treated for alcohol use, 70% to 90% relapse within the first year after treatment. Therefore, relapse prevention is an essential element of treatment. Therapists should not give the message that treatment failure is inevitable. However, therapists and clients must recognize that many people will not maintain long-term abstinence after their initial treatment and may need additional treatment, particularly during the first year, in addition to long-term follow-up. This is especially true for those who are dually diagnosed. Thus, the prognosis is good for improvement of alcohol use disorders but fair at best for total abstinence, although approximately 20% do achieve long-term sobriety, some even without treatment (American Psychiatric Association, 2000; Schuckit, 2010).

DRUG-RELATED DISORDERS

In addition to alcohol, the *DSM-IV-TR* specifies 10 classes of psychoactive substances that are used in maladaptive ways:

1. Amphetamines and amphetamine-like substances
2. Caffeine
3. Cannabis
4. Cocaine
5. Hallucinogens
6. Inhalants
7. Nicotine
8. Opioids
9. Phencyclidine (PCP) or phencyclidine-like substances
10. Sedatives, hypnotics, and anxiolytics

The *DSM-IV-TR* also includes other or unknown substance use disorders (such as anabolic steroids, prescription and over-the-counter medications that do not fall into the above categories, amyl or butyl nitrate, and nitrous oxide)

and polysubstance dependence, which involves the use of three or more categories of substances (not including caffeine or nicotine), with no one substance predominating during a 12-month period. Now we look at each of these disorders in further detail, before a discussion of typical client and therapist characteristics, intervention strategies, and prognosis.

Description of the Disorders

More than 5% of the U.S. population will meet the criteria for a drug-related disorder at some time in their lives (Finney, Wilbourne, & Moos, 2007). That number goes up for certain occupations. For example, medical professionals have an elevated incidence of substance use disorders, perhaps because of their easy access to drugs. Although most people who misuse drugs have a drug of choice, studies have noted an increasing tendency for people to misuse more than one drug. This complicates the treatment picture and makes accidental overdoses more likely. People with comorbid substance use disorders also have a particularly high incidence of suicidal and homicidal behavior.

An important difference between people who misuse drugs and those who misuse alcohol is the illegality of many drugs. People who misuse alcohol may also have legal difficulties, typically due to their having driven while intoxicated, but those who misuse other substances are often involved in felonies and devote extensive time and energy to obtaining the funds needed to purchase drugs. Many people with problems of drug use (and some of those with alcohol problems) come to therapy involuntarily, having been ordered into treatment by the courts, and may be suspicious, guarded, and resentful. With these clients, therapists need to address issues of criminality and anger as well as those of substance use.

Like people with alcohol use disorders, people who misuse drugs have a broad range of physical and emotional symptoms and often present with social and occupational impairment. Many people who misuse drugs have difficulty with impulse control, handling negative emotions, low self-esteem, and stress. Indeed, stress and negative emotion are frequently the cause of lapses and relapses in treatment.

Drug use most often begins in adolescence, peaks in early adulthood, and then decreases with age (Tucker et al., 2002). Substance misuse begins as part of a syndrome of adolescent problem behaviors (for example, risky sex, truancy, theft, lying, dangerous driving) that are both maladaptive and adaptive. They serve adolescent developmental needs of individuating from parents, bonding with peers, and coping with failure, boredom, social rejection, and low self-esteem, but can prevent young people from developing healthy social, academic, and adjustment skills. Adults who use drugs or alcohol in maladaptive ways may have learned to cope through dishonesty, manipulation, placating, or abusing others, and these patterns may be carried into their therapy (Jessor, Donovan, & Costa, 1991).

More than 50% of people who misuse drugs meet the criteria for an additional psychiatric disorder (Tucker et al., 2002), with a lifetime possibility of developing a major depressive disorder 3 times that of people who do not use substances. Drug use is also strongly associated with ADHD, conduct disorder, and antisocial personality disorder.

Drug abuse and dependence are also familial disorders; people with these disorders often were first exposed to drug use in the home. Families of people who misuse drugs seem to have a high incidence of impulse-control problems and interpersonal conflict. Antisocial behavior, as well as alcohol use and other substance use disorders, are often found in these families, as are high levels of marital disruption, disciplinary inconsistency, emotional disorders, and lack of child monitoring. Being raised in a chaotic home environment is a predictor of poor school performance, conduct disorder, and future illicit drug use (Tarter, Sambrano, & Dunn, 2002).

Minority groups may be at higher risk for illness and death resulting from substance use disorders, and may be underserved in treatment services. Cultural differences may also affect assessment outcomes for substance use disorders due to racial bias, language translation difficulties, and cultural test-bias (Blume, Morera, & de la Cruz, 2007). Assessing acculturation and enculturation are important concepts for therapy in general, and may be helpful in determining risk for the development of addictive behaviors.

The following sections discuss the categories of drugs included in the *DSM-IV-TR* in its description of the substance use disorders. Some information on treatment of each of these categories of drugs is included here in order to link that information to the category of drugs.

Amphetamines   More than 34 million people worldwide abuse amphetamine and methamphetamine, making it second only to cannabis in frequency of abuse (United Nations, 2010). The effect of amphetamines are almost instantaneous—5 minutes after snorting or 20 minutes after swallowing, abusers feel an increase in energy and performance, sex drive, self-confidence, euphoria, and suppressed appetite. Negative side effects include stomach cramps, agitation and irritability, confusion, an inability to sleep, paranoia, violent behavior, and hallucinations (Rawson, Sodano, & Hillhouse, 2007). The growing number of young people treated for ADHD with methylphenidate (Ritalin), amphetamine combinations (Adderall), or pemoline (Cylert) has increased the availability and misuse of amphetamine-like drugs among college students. The Monitoring the Future survey (2009) found 5-year declines in the use of amphetamines among 10th and 12th grade students, but a higher rate of use among college students than their same-age peers who did not attend college. More than 7 million people are estimated to have misused stimulant drugs intended to treat ADHD (Kroutil et al., 2006). The drugs are used recreationally to stay awake, boost academic performance, and lose weight. However, as many as 75,000 people show signs of dependence (Kroutil et al., 2006). Abuse of these stimulants is about equally divided between males and females, and many reported using stimulants in conjunction with alcohol or other substances. Amphetamines can be swallowed or crushed and snorted. Stimulants cause a buildup of dopamine in the brain which improves mood and increases energy. Prolonged use can cause irregular heartbeat, insomnia, weight loss, mood disturbances, as well as anxiety and paranoia. Over time, increased amounts of the medication are required to achieve the same effect, and withdrawal of the drug can result in severe depression-like symptoms including fatigue, insomnia, and loss of interest in daily activities. Mood swings may continue for months. Amphetamines are the most likely of any drug to produce symptoms that mimic those of mental disorders, such as panic attacks, obsessive-compulsive states, and clinical depression. Continued use may lead to paranoid delusions, hallucinations, suicidal ideation, and violence (Ockert, Baier, & Coons, 2004). Treatment should include individual counseling emphasizing behavioral and cognitive approaches and relapse prevention.

Caffeine Caffeine increases energy, enhances mental concentration, and produces feelings of well-being in people who consume moderate amounts. Although no caffeine use disorders per se are included in the *DSM*, caffeine-induced disorders are listed and are characterized by anxiety, restlessness, and sleep disturbances. A cycle

can evolve in which a person does not get restful sleep because of caffeine but perpetuates the problem by using caffeine to stay awake during the day.

As many as 96% of adults have used caffeinated beverages. The average daily intake is 200 to 400 milligrams (roughly the equivalent of three to four 8-ounce cups of brewed coffee). Caffeine use is higher in people who are dependent on other drugs and in those who have a history of mental disorders. Recent published case reports identify excessive use of caffeinated coffee as leading to anxiety, hostility, and psychotic syndrome in susceptible individuals (Winston, Hardrick, & Jaberi, 2005). Symptoms of caffeine intoxication include nervousness, rapid heartbeat, anxiety, tremors, insomnia, and in very high doses, fatality. There is also a correlation between the amount of caffeine ingested and the use of benzodiazepines and other anti-anxiety medication (Schuckit, 2010).

Generally, consumption of caffeine begins in childhood, with the use of caffeinated sodas. Use of brewed beverages, including coffee and tea, typically begins in early to late teens. Caffeine usage appears to peak in the twenties and thirties, after which use stabilizes and then declines.

The current popularity of caffeine-infused energy drinks is not without concern. Energy drinks are considered dietary supplements and therefore the level of caffeine is not regulated by the FDA. Children and others who drink large amounts of these drinks are at risk for developing rapid heart rate, increased systolic blood pressure, and caffeine intoxication (Hedges, Woon, & Hoopes, 2009).

Approximately 40% of people who use caffeine have attempted to quit, citing such health reasons as anxiety, insomnia, gastrointestinal problems, heart arrhythmia, and fibrocystic disease of the breast (Schuckit, 2010). Because of caffeine's addictive quality, effects of a sudden withdrawal can include headaches, fatigue, irritability, mild depression, mild anxiety, difficulty concentrating, nausea, and muscle pain. Withdrawal symptoms can range from mild to severe, with as many as 13% of people developing symptoms that interfere with work or daily activities (Reid, 2005). Tapering off the use of caffeine over 7 to 14 days is recommended for people who make heavy use of caffeine.

Cannabis People who use cannabis (including marijuana and hashish) typically value the relaxation, increased sensory awareness, and elevated mood it provides. However, when used in high doses, over a long period of time, or by particularly susceptible first-time users, marijuana can cause severe anxiety, paranoid thinking, and perceptual distortions similar to those produced by hallucinogens. People with underlying schizophrenia, depression, or another mood disorder are particularly vulnerable to these adverse effects (Evans et al., 2005). One study found that 10% of all psychosis can be traced back to cannabis use (Fergusson et al., 2006). Cannabis often is used along with other substances, especially nicotine, alcohol, and cocaine (American Psychiatric Association, 2000). Cannabis probably is the most commonly used illegal drug, and its use is particularly prevalent in young adult males.

The potency of marijuana has increased in recent years due to plant breeding and improved growing techniques. Whereas the typical marijuana cigarette in the 1960s contained 10 mg of tetrahydrocannabinol (THC, the psychoactive ingredient in marijuana), current THC content is 150 to 200 mg. The biological effects of higher doses of THC are unknown; most research on marijuana is based on the lower doses found many years ago. Current studies are investigating the toxic effects of marijuana smoke across the life span, including immune system impairment and cardiovascular and pulmonary

problems. Marijuana smoke contains 50% to 70% more carcinogenogenic hydrocarbons than tobacco smoke (National Institute on Drug Abuse [NIDA], 2009). Because those who smoke cannabis tend to hold their breaths while smoking, marijuana may be more detrimental to the lungs than cigarettes.

The effects of long-term cannabis use are beginning to show in the aging population. Recent research indicates that although marijuana use has declined among teenagers, there was a 300% increase between 1991 and 2001 in marijuana use among adults ages 45 to 64 (NIDA, 2004) and a 22% increase in marijuana use disorders during the same time period (Compton, Grant, Colliver, Glantz, & Stinson, 2004). Marijuana has been shown to quadruple the user's risk of a heart attack within the first hour of smoking (NIDA, 2009) and to increase the risk of head and neck cancer.

Long-term use of cannabis can cause neurological impairment, including reduction in memory and learning that can last for weeks after the effects of the drug has worn off. As a result, chronic use has been related to reduced career status, increased absences from work, accidents, and more sick days due to lung problems than tobacco smokers. Problems in fertility, sexual functioning, and low-birth-weight babies born to pregnant women who smoked marijuana have also been reported (McGrath et al., 2010; Pape, 2004).

Beginning use of marijuana during adolescence may have serious effects, including patterns of use that are similar to addiction (Evans et al., 2005). Longitudinal studies of cannabis use from adolescence through adulthood indicate that weekly usage in adolescents predicts an increased risk of substance dependence as an adult. Early users are also at increased risk of moving on to other illicit drugs, of suicidal ideation, of suicide attempts, of violence, and of developing schizophrenia (Moore et al., 2007).

According to the National Institute on Drug Abuse (2009), about 16% of all admissions to substance use treatment facilities in the United States are for marijuana, and most admissions for cannabis use are male (73%), white (51%), and young (36% under 20 years old). Marijuana was the third most commonly misused drug mentioned in drug-related hospital emergency room visits in 2002, the latest year for which figures are available.

Significant cannabis withdrawal symptoms have been documented; they include restlessness and irritability, chills, nausea, decreased appetite, and headaches. Most symptoms will go away in a day or two, but sleep and mood disturbances that accompany withdrawal can last for weeks. The desire to alleviate these withdrawal symptoms can lead to continued use of cannabis and frequent relapse.

No medication is known to reduce cannabis use. Treatment is similar to that for misuse of other substances. One study found that a 14-session cognitive-behavioral group treatment program for marijuana had the same effectiveness as a two-session individual treatment program that included motivational interviewing and advice on ways in which to reduce marijuana use (Stephens, Roffman, & Curtain, 2000). Both treatments educated clients on triggers and helped them develop avoidance strategies. Thirty percent of participants were found to be abstinent after one year.

Cocaine Cocaine seems initially to boost self-esteem and optimism, increase mental and physical abilities, and convey feelings of power. These symptoms last only as long as brain cocaine levels are rising; within minutes, declining levels promote cravings, cocaine-seeking behavior, depression, and irritability (Evans et al., 2005). Because this drug is highly addictive, use can quickly progress to abuse and then to dependence in a short period of time (American Psychiatric Association, 2000). Extended use of cocaine leads to many negative symptoms, including anxiety, depression, suicidal ideation, weight loss, aggressiveness, sexual dysfunction, sleeping problems, paranoid delusions, and hallucinations. The Substance Abuse and Mental Health Services Administration (2010) estimates 2.1 million people currently use cocaine; including 610,000 who abuse crack.

Compared to people who abuse alcohol, cocaine users tend to be younger, and are less likely to be married or employed (Hambley, Arbour, Sivagnanasundaram, 2010). Cognitive impairment can result from chronic cocaine use and may negatively impact motivation and ability to change, as well as overall executive functioning. To improve the effectiveness of treatment, clinicians should integrate cognitive assessments into the design and implementation of treatment plans for chronic cocaine users (Severtson, von Thomsen, Hedden, & Latimer, 2010). Death rates are higher for cocaine use than for any other drug, as cocaine increases the risk of death from heart arrhythmia, stroke, and respiratory failure, as well as the risk of accidents, suicide, and homicide (Smith & Capps, 2005). More than 80% of those who use cocaine combine the drug with alcohol, creating a potentially deadly level of cocaethyline in the liver. This combination enhances cocaine's euphoric effect, but also increases the risk of sudden death.

When making an assessment, care should be taken to distinguish between cocaine-induced psychosis, which will remit in several days to a week, and delusions and hallucinations that last for weeks and may signal an underlying psychotic state (schizophrenia spectrum disorder or bipolar disorder). Polysubstance dependence involving benzodiazepines, antidepressants, and other substances should also be considered, along with any co-occurring Axis I or Axis II disorders.

Treatment should include referral to an outpatient drug treatment program if the misuse is recurrent and severe. If individual therapy is indicated, cognitive-behavioral approaches with a relapse intervention component have been shown to be most effective. Contingency management, also called motivational incentives (MI) is showing promising results in helping people stay in treatment. MI uses a rewards-based system, similar to a token economy, in which people can earn points for abstaining from drug use and then exchange points earned for items such as a movie or gym pass. No medication has currently been approved by the FDA for the treatment of cocaine dependence (NIDA, 2009). Twelve-step and community-based programs can be an important part of relapse prevention. Additional services such as vocational counseling, marital counseling, or housing assistance may be necessary depending on the person's treatment needs.

Prognosis is particularly poor for people who use cocaine in combination with other substances. In a 6-month follow up of residential treatment for alcohol and substance use disorders, cocaine poly-drug users had the lowest levels of post-treatment reduction in substance use (Hambley et al., 2010).

Hallucinogens   Hallucinogens, such as lysergic acid diethylamide (LSD) and methylenedioxy-methamphetamine (MDMA or ecstasy), can alter perceptions and promote insight, introspection, and feelings of euphoria, but the negative effects of hallucinogens include psychosis, mood changes, illusions (not usually hallucinations), and cognitive impairment. People who misuse hallucinogens often have accompanying interpersonal, academic, and occupational problems. Symptoms of depression, anxiety, and mood swings can last for weeks or months following discontinuation of these substances (Smith & Capps, 2005). Side effects can be long-term. Twenty-five percent of people who were diagnosed with a drug-induced psychosis later developed a non-drug-related

psychosis (Canton et al., 2007). Hallucinogen persisting perception disorder—that is, flashbacks, which can occur intermittently for years—is a particularly distressing consequence of hallucinogen use. Hallucinogens have historically been the realm of young white males and party or club settings, but MDMA usage later expanded to nonwhite groups and non-club settings (Maxwell, 2005). Use of LSD has declined in recent years, most likely the result of lack of availability and increased use of ecstacy and other so-called club drugs (Johnston, O'Malley, Bachman, & Schulenberg, 2011). The increased usage of MDMA is associated with polysubstance use, negative health consequences, and sometimes permanent brain damage or death (Wu et al., 2009).

Inhalants   Two million teenagers currently report having sniffed or inhaled substances, such as marking pens, correction fluid, glue, nail polish remover, gasoline, spray paint, lighter fluid, and anesthetic gases (Wu, Pilowsky, & Schlenger, 2004). Unlike other substances, misuse of inhalants tends to begin early, typically between the ages of 7 and 12, and reduces with age (Johnston et al., 2011). These substances, which are readily available in most homes, produce euphoria and an out-of-body sensation. They also have many short- and long-term side effects ranging from headaches and nausea to irreversible brain damage and death. Inhalant use has been tied to a cluster of adolescent behaviors including antisocial acts, use of other drugs, and emotional difficulties. The use of inhalants is often associated with family, social, and school-related difficulties as well as with depression, anxiety, hostility, suicide attempts, and physiological damage to nerves, organs, and muscles. Inhalant abuse is particularly common in adolescents and preadolescents, in rural areas, and among Native Americans or people of multi-ethnic heritage. Smith and Capps (2005) indicate that 17% of all teenagers have used inhalants at least once in their lives—girls as often as boys, an unusual finding in drug use statistics (Wu et al., 2004). People typically use inhalants only briefly during adolescence before moving on to other substances.

Nicotine Nicotine can increase learning and attention, improve mood, and promote relaxation. It is also highly addictive and is associated with 25% of all deaths in the United States. The health benefits of smoking cessation have been well established and each year 20 million Americans attempt to quit smoking. Unfortunately, only about 6% will achieve long-term success. Nearly 24% of men and 17.9% of women in the United States smoke tobacco (National Health Interview Survey, 2008). Lifetime prevalence of nicotine dependence is approximately 20%. Increasing education about the dangers of smoking has resulted in a substantial decrease in adolescent and teen smoking. Adolescents and women are more vulnerable to becoming dependent on nicotine. Nicotine use is twice the rate among people with mental disorders than it is in the general population and often coexists with alcohol dependence, schizophrenia, mood disorders, and anxiety disorders (Selby, Voci, Zawertailo, George, & Brands, 2010).

The most effective treatment for smoking cessation combines nicotine replacement therapy (NRT) with a psychosocial program. The common withdrawal symptoms include irritability, impatience, depressed mood, restlessness, increased appetite, and weight gain (Evans et al., 2005). Five types of NRT have been approved by the FDA (nicotine gums, patches, nasal sprays, inhalers, and lozenges) to help relieve some of the symptoms of nicotine withdrawal. When used in combination with behavior therapy, transdermal patches have produced abstinence rates of approximately 60% (Syad, 2003).

The FDA has also approved bupropion (Zyban) and varenicline (Chantix) for the treatment of nicotine dependence. Varenicline works by interfering with nicotine receptors in the brain. The medication lessens the pleasurable effects of smoking while reducing the uncomfortable symptoms of nicotine withdrawal. As with NRT, these medications are most effective when combined with psychotherapy.

Published case reports indicate hallucinations, mania, agitation, anger, irritability, suicidal thoughts, and death may be rare but potential side effects of varenicline use (Radoo & Kutscher, 2009). Both varenicline and bupropion carry the FDA's black box warning label—the agency's strongest safety warning—over possible adverse neuropsychiatric side effects. Given that people with mental disorders have an incidence of nicotine dependence 2 times higher than the average population, clinicians should carefully watch for side effects when these medications are prescribed for people with co-occuring mental disorders. More research is needed especially regarding use of these medications in adolescents and pregnant women.

Smoking cessation is difficult, and relapse is common. The American Cancer Society (2006) reports that 25% to 33% of people use medication or NRT for smoking cessation and about 5% to 16% of people quit smoking on their own, without treatment. As mentioned earlier, combining NRT with psychosocial treatment increases the success rate even more.

Clinical practice guidelines for the treatment of tobacco use and dependence have been developed and disseminated by the U.S. Surgeon General. In keeping with current research on effective practice, these guidelines recommend combining counseling and medication for a more robust treatment approach. The guidelines cite the positive relationship between number of sessions of counseling and providing support during the long and difficult process of breaking the addiction. Three types of therapy seem to be the most helpful in smoking cessation: problem solving, skills training, and securing outside social support to encourage and retain treatment gains. Motivational interviewing techniques are also recommended for people who are ambivalent about quitting smoking (Fiore et al., 2008). A reference guide outlining these treatment recommendations for tobacco use and dependence is available from the U.S. Public Health Service at www.ahrq.gov/clinic/tobacco/tobaqrg.htm.

A Delphi panel of 37 international experts created an algorithm for pharmacotherapy for smoking cessation that divides treatment into stages and aids the clinician in recommending medication or a combination of medications based on the client's specific needs (Bader, McDonald, & Selby, 2009). The Delphi algorithm is limited to pharmacotherapy. However, most experts agree counseling is an important and necessary component of successful treatment and relapse prevention. Interested readers are referred to counseling algorithms by Hughes (2008), LeFoll and George (2007), and Selby (2007).

The prognosis for overcoming nicotine addiction is about equal for men and women, and equal among white, black, and Hispanic populations. Treatment is as effective for people with severe mental illnesses (schizophrenia spectrum disorders, bipolar disorder) as the general population (Banham & Gilbody, 2010). New research indicates that people who are able to quit smoking may actually have a genetic advantage over people who are not successful in their attempts. A so-called *quitter gene* makes it easier to quit smoking. Future research will be needed to determine what types of treatment work best with each person's particular DNA combination. These new findings also have implications for people who are dependent on other substances, including methamphetamine, cannabis, and cocaine (Drgon et al., 2009).

Opioids Opioids, including heroin, morphine, and prescription pain relievers with opioid-like action, produce a rapid sense of intense euphoria. Opioid use typically is preceded by use of other drugs. Twenty-two percent of first-time users become dependent. Opioid tolerance develops rapidly, and use of this substance often leads to theft, prostitution, and other illegal behaviors as means of paying for the substance. Use of opioids can lead to a wide range of negative symptoms, which include psychosis, sleep and sexual difficulties, depression, mania, and such medical conditions as hepatitis, skin infections, and damage to the heart and lungs.

Opioid users are a heterogeneous group. Twenty years ago, people who misused opioids were likely to come from lower socioeconomic urban settings, but greater availability of heroin in the suburbs and even rural areas has resulted in increased use across all age groups (Evans et al., 2005).

Most people dependent on heroin have poor motivation to change. Denial is an inherent part of opioid dependence and must be addressed if treatment is to be effective. People who misuse opioids tend to lose sight of daily activities in search of the next fix (O'Brien & McKay, 2007).

The percentage of young adults (aged 17 to 28) who report having used heroin at least once in their lifetime was 1.6% in 2009. This was a 0.3% decrease from the previous year (Johnston et al., 2010). Worldwide, it is estimated that 15.9 million people are intravenous drug users. Of that number, approximately 3 million are also seropositive for human immunodeficiency virus (Mathers et al., 2008). Due to needle sharing and unsafe sexual practices, they are also at increased risk for hepatitis B and C. Most people dependent on opioids have at least one co-existing mental disorder, most often major depressive disorder, an alcohol use disorder, antisocial personality disorder, or an anxiety disorder (especially posttraumatic stress disorder). Coexisting disorders should be treated with appropriate medication and psychotherapy.

Detoxification and treatment of withdrawal symptoms are the first steps in a long-term treatment approach to opioid dependence. Methadone, used as a less harmful but still addictive opioid, has been used to treat heroin dependence for more than 30 years, with success rates that range between 60% and 70% in some treatment centers (O'Brien & McKay, 2007).

Misuse of prescription painkillers has also increased markedly in recent years. One in 10 high school seniors reported nonmedical use of Vicodin (hydrocodone) in the past year, and 1 in 20 used oxycodone (NIDA, 2009). Approximately 1.2 million adolescents currently misuse opioid-related pain relievers and other analgesic medications, such as codeine, fentanyl (Sublimaze), hydrocodone (Vicodin, Lortab), methadone (Dolphine), morphine (Kadian, Avinza), oxycodone (OxyContin, Percocet, Percodan), and others. A newer medication, tramadol (Ultram), has many pain-control properties of the opioids but has a lower risk of dependence.

Other medications found to be effective in the treatment of opioid dependence include levo-alpha-acetylmethadol (LAAM), buprenorphine (Subutex), and naltrexone (ReVia). LAAM has opiate effects similar to methadone, but is longer lasting and needs to be administered only every 72 hours. Buprenorphine produces effects similar to heroin, but there is a limit, so that higher doses do not produce greater effects, and overdose is not possible. Naltrexone works by blocking opiate receptors in the brain and is effective only after a person has gone through detoxification. All three of these treatment options have been shown to be effective. O'Brien and McKay (2007) provide a detailed comparison of studies of treatment effectiveness and treatment length for each of these pharmacological treatments. However, additional research is necessary to determine if there is a single most effective course of treatment.

Therapeutic communities are another avenue to treatment, particularly for those with a long history of opioid use. Therapeutic communities are drug-free residential settings that use a hierarchical model with treatment stages that confer increasing levels of freedom and responsibility. They encourage responsibility, insist on honesty and self-examination, and use peer counselors, mediation, and group process to effect change. Longer stays (more than two months) are associated with improved success in therapeutic communities.

The prognosis for recovery for men and women who use opioids is poor in the short term, with nearly a 90% recidivism rate in the first 6 months following treatment; long-term prognosis is better, with more than a third achieving abstinence. Traits that improve prognosis are three years or more of abstinence, stable employment, being married, engaging in few antisocial activities, little or no dependence on other substances, and fewer problems with the criminal justice system. Like that of cocaine, the mortality rate among those who use heroin is high, with almost 2% per year dying from suicide, homicide, accidents, and such diseases as AIDS, tuberculosis, and other infections (Schuckit, 2010).

Phencyclidines (PCP)   Use of phencyclidines (PCP), ketamine, and related substances can produce euphoria and feelings of detachment and dissociation. These drugs also cause many severe psychological problems, however, including rage, disinhibition, panic, mania, unpredictability, psychosis, and flashbacks, as well as such physical problems as seizures, confusion, delirium, coma, and even death from respiratory arrest (Evans et al., 2005). Aggressive behavior and poor judgment are particularly likely consequences of PCP use. Ketamine is odorless and tasteless and is sometimes slipped into drinks and used during sexual assaults and date rape. It produces amnesia and a period of impaired awareness (Evans et al., 2005). Ketamine use is on the rise among late teens and young adults, especially in urban areas, and at dance clubs and all-night raves (NIDA, 2009).

Sedatives, Hypnotics, and Anxiolytics Sedatives, hypnotics, and anxiolytics, including barbiturates, benzodiazepines (such as Ativan, Klonopin, Xanax, and Valium), and other prescription sleeping and antianxiety medications are among the most frequently prescribed psychoactive drugs. One-year usage is nearly 13% of the U.S. population, with 2% taking a prescribed sedative on any given day. About 6% of the population report illicit use. Those who began nonmedical use of prescription drugs prior to the age of 13 are more likely to develop prescription drug abuse and dependence compared to those who began using after 21 (McCabe, West, Morales, Cranford, & Boyd, 2007). The *DSM-IV-TR* notes that sedative use is often associated with dependence on other substances and may be used to reduce the ill effects of alcohol, cannabis, cocaine, heroin, methadone, and amphetamines (American Psychiatric Association, 2000). These substances have often been prescribed for the people who ultimately misuse them, the sense of well-being and relaxation provided by the drugs having led people to persist in their use. Many of these substances are highly addictive brain depressants. They cause a range of symptoms, among them delirium, psychosis, and amnesia. These substances are potentially lethal, especially in combination with alcohol.

Polysubstance Dependence According to the Community Epidemiology Work Group (CEWG; NIDA, 2003), polysubstance dependence is increasing at a fast pace with the proliferation of "an ever-growing array of illicit and licit substances" (p. 4) contributing to an increase in health problems and deaths. Polysubstance dependence is defined as the use of at least three types of substances (not including nicotine and caffeine) within a 12-month period in which the criteria for substance dependence are not met by any one substance but are met by the group of drugs as a whole. The majority of drug-related deaths involve more than one drug, including cocaine (83%), heroin (89%), and methamphetamine (92%). A recent study of oxycodone-related deaths indicated that 97% also involved other drugs, such as benzodiazepines, alcohol, cocaine, other opioids, marijuana, or antidepressants (NIDA, 2003). People who abuse MDMA have a higher incidence of polysubstance use including alcohol, marijuana, prescription opioids, cocaine, and inhalants (Wu et al., 2009). Health-related concerns include possible drug interactions as well as potential functional deficits and structural changes to the brain from continued use of multiple substances over time. Cross-tolerance may result, as the person requires higher doses of different drugs, or uses cannabis or alcohol to tamp down the effects of stimulants.

Other (or Unknown) Substance-Related Disorders The *DSM-IV-TR* (American Psychiatric Association, 2000) includes this category for substance-related disorders not included in the 11 specific drug categories previously mentioned. Other (or unknown) substance-related disorders refer to misuse of prescription and over-the-counter drugs not previously mentioned, anabolic steroids, and to situations in which the substance is unknown.

During 2006, there were nearly 2 million drug-related visits to emergency rooms nationwide, and nearly one third of those visits were the result of misuse or abuse of prescription or over-the-counter medications (NIDA, 2009). Nonmedical use of pharmaceuticals or dietary supplements has reached an all-time high, with 15.2 million people age 12 and older reporting taking a prescription pain reliever, tranquilizer, stimulant, or sedative for nonmedical purposes at least once in the year prior to the survey (SAMSHA, 2010).

Most people who misuse anabolic steroids are males who want to enhance sports performance or improve physical appearance by increasing muscle mass. Steroids can be injected or taken orally. The immediate effects of steroids are a sense of well-being and a feeling of being invincible. According to the Monitoring the Future survey, anabolic steroid use increases as boys enter high school, with the number of 12th graders abusing anabolic steroids reported to be 1.5% as of 2010 (Johnston et al., 2011). Rates are higher among athletes and college students, especially men who also use alcohol and other substances. Signs of steroid use include increase in muscle mass over a short period of time, severe acne, hair growth, development of breasts in men, and lowered voice. Misuse of steroids can result in mood swings, manic-like symptoms, paranoid jealousy, and even violence (NIDA, 2009). When the drug is stopped, withdrawal symptoms can include severe depression, which sometimes leads to suicide.

Amyl or butyl nitrite causes a slight euphoria and may slow down time perception as well as dilate the blood vessels. The most common side effects are nausea, dizziness, and anxiety. Use is relatively high among homosexual men (Schuckit, 2010).

Assessment

Treatment for all substance-related disorders should include medical and psychological assessments. Treatment plans can only be developed after a comprehensive assessment has been made, because issues of dependence, motivation, and history of usage will help determine level of treatment.

Assessment is an important aspect of diagnosis and treatment planning for substance use disorders. Clinicians will not only assess for substance use, abuse, and dependence, but also for prior history, coping skills, and a variety of biological, psychological, and social factors that contribute to the development of the substance use disorder.

Because of the prevalence of dual diagnoses in people with drug use disorders, careful assessment and diagnosis are essential before treatment is planned. The *DSM-IV-TR* (American Psychiatric Association, 2000) warns against diagnosing a mental disorder based on symptoms observed while a person is withdrawing from substances. Even severe symptoms (such as delirium, dementia, or hallucinations) that have developed as a result of drug use will normally abate within a period of several days to four to six weeks after the substance has been discontinued (Stevens & Smith, 2005). Distinguishing between independent and substance-induced symptoms and disorders requires a careful history taking that includes symptoms, duration, age of onset, relationship to times of substance use, behavior during periods of abstinence from drugs, and close observation to determine if symptoms diminish with continued abstinence.

The Addiction Severity Index (McLellan et al., 1992) is the most widely used standardized test for assessing substance use disorders. It is easy to administer and can be used with diverse populations to assess multiple substances in a variety of treatment settings. The ASI can also be used to chart progress over time (Rawson et al., 2007). Medical tests, including a urinalysis and other laboratory-analyzed tests, a medical examination, and an EEG to look at general brain function can provide further information on the nature of a person's substance use and its physiological impact.

These screening procedures can help determine whether detoxification, a residential treatment program, or a partial hospitalization program is needed or whether outpatient treatment is sufficient. People who are having toxic reactions to a substance, are delusional or having hallucinations without insight into their cause, or are in danger of harming themselves or others probably require hospitalization for protection and safety (Schuckit, 2010). Those who are physiologically dependent on a substance also may require inpatient treatment to detoxify, prior to beginning outpatient treatment for substance use.

Some people seem to deteriorate after detoxification. Memory problems and other mild cognitive deficits emerge, and people may develop anxiety and feelings of being out of control. If these symptoms are not dealt with through education and therapy, they can frighten people into a relapse. The early stages of recovery are tenuous, and close monitoring and support are needed.

Preferred Therapist Characteristics

Therapist characteristics may have a stronger impact on treatment outcome than the type of treatment provided (Finney, Wilbourne, & Moos, 2007). In general, therapists who are more empathic, less confrontational, and more interpersonally skilled fare better with clients with substance use disorders, possibly due to the creation of better therapeutic alliances. Some judicious sharing of the therapist's own experiences with substances can promote rapport and straightforwardness in the therapeutic relationship. However, the focus should be kept on the client's concerns, and therapists should not assume that what has been personally helpful to them will necessarily be helpful to others.

Therapists working with this population need a solid understanding of drugs, their current nicknames, their symptoms and prevalence, and the environments that promote their use, as well as an understanding of the legal and medical issues pertinent to people who misuse drugs.

Because many people with drug use disorders are referred for treatment from criminal justice sources, these clients may be less cooperative and less likely to be motivated to change. Therapists who use motivational interviewing strategies probably will be more effective and more apt to create sustained, long-term change (Rollnick et al., 2008; Sampson et al., 2009; Stasiewicz et al., 2006).

A considerable challenge therapists face is developing appropriate ways of handling their own reactions to clients' reluctance to change so that they can continue communicating respect, empathy, optimism, and acceptance to even the most frustrating clients.

Intervention Strategies

Treatment goals for people who misuse drugs include abstinence or moderation management, improved well-being (physical, emotional, social, and occupational), and, as necessary, improved family and overall functioning. Treatment for people who misuse drugs is similar to treatment for people with alcohol use disorders and usually includes the following components: detoxification and, if necessary, treatment for symptoms of withdrawal; motivation enhancement therapy to assess and improve motivation to change; drug education; individual and group behavior therapy with motivational incentives as needed; psychotherapy to address coping skills; any co-occurring disorders; or issues related to trauma or grief and loss; adjunct services including family therapy, self-help groups, and 12-step programs; life skills training to address problems in relationships and employment; and pharmacotherapy as needed.

Treatment should be individualized to meet the needs of the particular person and incorporate a strong relapse prevention component.

Relapse, especially within the first year after treatment, is common for people who have been treated for substance use disorders. People implementing any type of behavioral change are confronted by cravings, thoughts, and environmental stimuli that remind them of the behaviors they are trying to change. Witkiewitz and Marlatt (2004) describe relapse and relapse prevention as dynamic processes that are complex and unpredictable. Nevertheless, approximately one third of people who participate in treatment for substance use disorders do remain abstinent, and another third are significantly improved after treatment.

Cognitive-behavioral coping skills therapy (CBCST) is a highly structured substance abuse treatment program that employs cognitive restructuring and coping skills training to help people overcome alcohol and drug dependence. CBCST not only focuses on treatment of substance abuse, but addresses any life issues that are related to the person's substance use or relapse (Parrish, 2009). Project MATCH, discussed earlier in this chapter, is relevant as well. Treatment manuals for this evidence-based intervention are available from the National Institute of Health and NIDA, which are listed in the resources at the end of this chapter (www.drugabuse.gov/txmanuals/cbt/cbt4.html).

Family behavior therapy has been found to be one of the most effective drug treatment programs available for adults and adolescents with drug abuse and dependence disorders (Springer, 2009). In addition to decreased marijuana use, the program is effective for "hard" substances such as cocaine, heroin, and PCP. Family behavior therapy has more than 20 different interventions and has also been shown to reduce depression, anxiety, and negative emotions (Bender et al., 2006; Dutra et al., 2008; McIntyre, 2004). FBT is a skill-based therapy, therefore, therapists set behavioral goals and use a contingency management system to track and reinforce positive change. The program usually lasts 6 months and includes pretreatment, postreatment relapse prevention, and follow-up. In addition to issues of child management and parenting, family functioning, life satisfaction, and co-occurring disorders are addressed with protocol plans in place for each (Donohue et al., 2009).

Although behavior therapy has been the most common approach to treating problems of drug use, supportive therapy (promoting impulse control and environmental change) and dialectical behavior therapy (focusing on mindfulness), in combination with behavior therapy, have also been used with some success.

Improving interpersonal skills to promote development of a peer group that does not misuse drugs can be an important treatment ingredient for people who may not know how to relate to others without using drugs. Developing leisure activities to fill time previously spent in drug-related activities can also be helpful. People with the typical personality patterns (shyness, anxiety) of those who misuse prescription drugs are particularly likely to benefit from relaxation and assertiveness training.

Involvement in self-help groups is often part of the treatment plan. Cocaine Anonymous and Narcotics Anonymous are among the most familiar. Dual Recovery Anonymous (DRA; www.draonline.org) is a 12-step program specifically for people with chemical dependency and a co-occurring mental disorder. Participation in structured smoking-cessation programs like those offered by the American Cancer Society has also been effective in helping a substantial number of people stop smoking.

Treatment for people with co-occurring drug use and a significant mental disorder should take into account the fact that these people have more than just two illnesses; they tend to have multiple impairments that permeate all areas of their lives. A dual diagnosis is likely to result in more negative outcomes (hospitalization, suicide attempts, violence, incarceration, homelessness, and serious illnesses such as HIV and hepatitis), and requires integrated long-term treatment that includes staged interventions, outreach, education, motivational interviewing, CBT, skill development, and social support (Drake et al., 2001). In looking at evidence-based practices, Drake and colleagues found that substance use treatment programs that do not address comorbid disorders are not effective. Integrated services must address both substance use disorders and any comorbid mental disorders concurrently. (See Chapter 9 for additional interventions for dual diagnosis.)

Medication can enhance the treatment of substance use disorders in two ways. First, it can help alleviate the symptoms of comorbid disorders like schizophrenia or a bipolar disorder, which may be contributing to people's dysfunctional use of substances (for example, if they are using substances as self-medication), and which may also be impairing people's judgment. Second, medication is sometimes used to help in directly modifying a person's use of substances. For example, methadone is used to modify use of heroin, and nicotine patches are effective in helping people stop smoking cigarettes. Although pharmacotherapy does have a place in the treatment of substance use disorders, drugs must be used judiciously with people who already are prone to misuse substances. Moreover, medication as the primary mode of treatment may interfere with people's ability to learn the skills they need in order to remain abstinent and improve their lives.

Education is another important component of most drug and alcohol treatment programs. Understanding the negative effects of drugs and alcohol, as well as recognizing in themselves the triggers and patterns of misuse, can contribute to people's motivation and enable them to deal more effectively with the challenges of abstinence.

For many people, substance use is reinforced by peer groups, and group counseling as well as self-help programs can counteract that influence. Self-help groups like Alcoholics Anonymous, Rational Recovery, Women for Sobriety, and Narcotics Anonymous are almost always part of the treatment plan for problems of substance use and become a central ingredient of most aftercare programs. Self-help programs also have groups for family members (for example, Al-Anon, Alateen, and Adult Children of Alcoholics) that are useful in helping them deal with another family member's maladaptive substance use and encourage that family member's recovery.

People who misuse drugs seem to respond strongly to life crises, especially those involving arguments and losses (Najavits, 2009). Negative emotions often precipitate a relapse, so therapy should help people who misuse drugs find effective ways of coping with negative events (Witkiewitz & Marlatt, 2004). Extended aftercare, as well as monitoring and building on people's coping mechanisms, are useful in preventing relapses. Periodic blood or urine testing can also be helpful in motivating people to remain drug free and in keeping therapists informed of relapses. Environmental change is yet another intervention that improves relapse prevention, especially for people whose families and peer groups encourage their drug use. It takes several years of abstinence for recovery to be well established; this suggests the need for an equivalent period of aftercare, follow-up, and attendance at meetings of self-help groups.

Although not much research is available on the effectiveness of rehabilitation programs, they, too, have their place in the treatment of substance misuse. Schuckit (2010) delineates the following 11 treatment procedures and characteristics found in most rehabilitation programs:

1. Establish goals that improve physical and mental health, enhance motivation toward abstinence, help the person create a life without substance use, and teach techniques for avoiding and minimizing the duration of relapses when they occur.
2. Assess the best treatment setting and determine if detoxification is necessary. Inpatient care should be reserved for those who are a danger to themselves or others, have not succeeded in outpatient settings, have co-occurring mental disorders, are physiologically dependent on substances, or have chaotic lives that require inpatient treatment.
3. Do not include medication as an integral part of the treatment of substance use unless specifically needed for co-occurring disorders, severe symptoms of withdrawal, or treatment of opioid or nicotine dependence.
4. Use group therapy as an important component of alcohol and substance use programs.
5. Include self-help groups, such as Alcoholics Anonymous, Narcotics Anonymous, and Cocaine Anonymous, to provide inexpensive, helpful peer support.
6. Incorporate a psychotherapy component that includes life skills training.
7. Address issues of family involvement and peer relationships.
8. Improve social support and life situations.
9. Include paraprofessionals in the treatment approach.
10. Build relapse prevention procedures into the treatment and aftercare phases.
11. Maintain follow-up aftercare for at least 6 to 12 months following treatment.

Marlatt (1998) found that fewer than 25% of people who misuse substances seek treatment programs. Those with relatively mild substance use disorders frequently make positive changes on their own, including reduction in substance use, switching to a less addictive substance, abstinence, and modified usage.

Prognosis

High relapse rates, often more than 50%, are reported for problems of drug use. The people with the best prognosis are those with stable family backgrounds, intact marriages, jobs, minimal or no criminal activity, less use of drugs and alcohol, and less severe coexisting emotional difficulties (Schuckit, 2010). A positive prognosis is also associated with people who comply with treatment; who can see the positive consequences of abstaining from drugs and alcohol; and who rate high on measures of self-efficacy, motivation to change, and coping skills (Witkiewitz & Marlatt, 2004).

The prognosis is less optimistic for people with coexisting emotional disorders; in fact, the more severe the accompanying diagnosis, the worse the prognosis. Several studies have found that the main contributing factor to relapse is negative affect. Thus, effective regulation of emotions is a necessary component in any treatment or relapse prevention program (Witkiewitz & Marlatt, 2004). The overall emotional health of the client, then, is usually a better predictor of outcome than is the severity of the addiction.

People who misuse nicotine, in particular, are known to relapse even after years of abstinence. Use of many drugs, such as the opioids, declines with age whether or not treatment is provided. Therefore, middle adulthood may be a time when people who misuse drugs are especially receptive to treatment.

This ends the discussion of alcohol and substance use disorders. We now turn to the other disorders of behavior and impulse control: eating disorders, sexual dysfunction and gender identity disorder, and impulse control disorders not otherwise specified.

EATING DISORDERS

Two eating disorders are listed in this section of the *DSM-IV-TR*: anorexia nervosa (AN) and bulimia nervosa (BN), along with the residual diagnosis of eating disorder not otherwise specified. A third disorder, binge eating disorder (BED), is included in the *DSM* appendix and is currently categorized under eating disorder not otherwise specified (EDNOS).

This section focuses on eating disorders most likely to be found in adolescents and adults. Other eating disorders, found primarily in children, were described in Chapter 2.

Description of the Disorders

Eating disorders are among the most prevalent mental disorders for women and girls. Overall prevalence rates of 0.5% to 3.7% have been reported for anorexia nervosa; rates of 1% to 4.2% have been reported for bulimia nervosa (American Psychiatric Association, 2000). The incidence of BED ranges from 0.7% to 4%. As many as 25 million people have met the criteria for BED at some point in their lifetimes.

These disorders often are chronic, include marked functional impairment and distress, are associated with increased suicidal ideation, involve repeated and multiple relapses, and may result in severe medical problems and even death (Rivas-Vazquez, Rice, & Kalman, 2003; Stice, Burton, & Shaw, 2004). Approximately 10% of

people with anorexia nervosa die as a result of the disorder, the highest mortality rate of any mental disorder, including major depressive disorder (Costin, 2007).

Since 1960, the incidence of eating disorders has been increasing, and the age of onset is getting younger. The onset of anorexia nervosa is typically between the ages of 10 to 30; for 85% of people with this disorder, onset comes between the ages of 13 and 20, but children as young as 9 have been affected (Costin, 2007). Bulimia nervosa typically has a somewhat later onset and is often preceded by anorexia nervosa, which then evolves into bulimia nervosa in as many as 50% of the cases. BED most frequently occurs in young to middle adulthood and has an estimated prevalence rate of 3% in adults. About 8% of people who meet the criteria for obesity also have BED (Grilo, Sinha, & O'Malley, 2002).

Both anorexia nervosa and bulimia nervosa are most common in young women. Anorexia nervosa is 10 times more frequent in women than men (Grilo & Mitchell, 2009), although these disorders also are being reported with increasing frequency in men and older women. Binge eating is found equally as often in men as women, but men may not meet the diagnostic criteria of distress following a binge eating episode (Hudson, Hiripi, Pope, & Kessler, 2007). Men are also more likely to use overexercise as a compensatory behavior (Anderson & Bulik, 2003). The *DSM-IV-TR* reports BED as occurring 5 times more often in women as men (American Psychiatric Association, 2000). Men with eating disorders tend to have a different pattern than women; they tend not to seek treatment and are more likely to dismiss or ignore symptoms. Friends and family of these men may also attribute symptoms to other causes (such as drug use or excessive exercise to achieve muscle definition) rather than to an eating disorder (Woodside, 2004).

Anorexia nervosa appears to be more prevalent in American women of European descent than in African American women (Hoek et al., 2005; Striegel-Moore et al., 2003) while BED is found equally in both groups (Taylor, Caldwell, Baser, Faison, & Jackson, 2007).

Negative affect and depressive symptoms in adolescence may be associated with increased risk for the onset of all types of eating problems, including disordered eating, dietary restriction, purging, and recurrent fluctuations in body weight (Johnson, Cohen, Kotler, Kasen, & Brook, 2002). Other early predictors of eating disorders include pica in childhood (predictive of bulimia nervosa), picky eating and eating conflicts around mealtime (predictive of anorexia nervosa), sexual abuse or physical neglect, low social support, low self-esteem, and an avoidant style of coping with stressful events (Jacobi et al., 2004). Many people with eating disorders have a history of anxiety, depression, and maladaptive personality traits (Johnson et al., 2002).

In a review of 320 longitudinal and cross-sectional studies of eating disorders, Jacobi and colleagues (2004) found the following factors predictive of anorexia nervosa: OCD, perfectionism, and negative self-evaluation. The same research found that onset of bulimia nervosa was related to childhood obesity, parental problems including alcoholism and obesity, family criticism about weight and body image, and negative self-evaluation. Family heredity and modeled behavior are important factors in the development of eating disorders. Mothers who have eating disorders themselves tend to deal with children's eating in unhealthy ways by developing odd feeding schedules, using food for rewards and punishment, using food to provide comfort, and being overly concerned about their daughters' weight (Agras, Hammer, & McNicholas, 1999). Some parents are controlling and restrict their children's food intake; research has shown these children are more likely to eat when they are not hungry, to seek out prohibited foods, and to

develop a full-blown eating disorder when they are older (Birch, Fisher, & Davison, 2003). Eating disorders that begin in childhood can be especially difficult to treat.

Anorexia Nervosa Anorexia nervosa, according to the *DSM-IV-TR*, involves a person's refusal to maintain normal body weight. As a result, body weight is 85% or less of what would be expected for the person's age and height. Other symptoms of the disorder include great fear of becoming fat (even though underweight), a disturbed body image (seeing themselves as overweight even though they are underweight), dread of loss of control, and, in females, amenorrhea (absence of at least three consecutive expected menstrual cycles). Anorexia nervosa tends to be found in families with eating disorders (Keel & Striegel-Moore, 2009). Twin studies suggest a genetic component for anorexia, possibly as high as 56% (Bulik et al., 2006). People with a mother or sister with anorexia nervosa are 12 times more likely to develop the disorder themselves and 4 times more likely to develop bulimia nervosa. New research points to a genetic predisposition for such traits as anxiety, perfectionism, and obsessive-compulsive thoughts and behaviors. People with this underlying genetic predisposition also may be more susceptible to anorexia nervosa. Neurological research indicates that women who develop anorexia nervosa have excess activity in the brain's dopamine receptors, which regulate pleasure (Kaye et al., 2005).

In addition to emaciation, common physiological symptoms of anorexia nervosa include cold intolerance, dry skin, an increase in fine body hair, low blood pressure, and edema (Costin, 2007). Metabolic changes, potassium loss, and cardiac damage can result from this disorder and can be lethal. OCD-like compulsions regarding food are often seen and include ritualized behavior surrounding binges. People with AN may also dread and avoid eating in public for fear of being judged.

Two types of anorexia nervosa have been identified. People with the restricting type of the disorder (the more common type) do not engage in binge eating or purging but do maintain low weight by severely limiting their intake of food. People with the binge eating/ purging type habitually engage in binge eating and compensatory behaviors (such as self-induced vomiting or inappropriate use of laxatives, diuretics, or enemas) and, despite their binge eating, meet the low-weight criterion for anorexia.

Co-occuring disorders often include depression and anxiety. Nonsuicidal self-injurious behavior is also frequently seen in people with anorexia nervosa.

Bulimia Nervosa   While the prevalence of anorexia nervosa appears to be holding steady, bulimia nervosa has been on the rise in the past 20 years (Stice & Bullick, 2008). People with bulimia nervosa engage in behaviors similar to those of people with anorexia nervosa, binge eating/purging type, but do not meet the full criteria for that disorder, usually because their weight is more than 85% of normal body weight. Bulimia nervosa, according to the *DSM-IV-TR*, involves an average of at least two binges per week, usually accompanied by compensatory behavior (such as self-induced vomiting, fasting, laxative use, or extreme involvement in exercise) for at least three months, as well as a sense of being out of control during these episodes. Binges may last anywhere from a few minutes to a few hours during which the person consumes on average, approximately 1,500 calories (Craighead, 2002). People give many reasons for their binges, including (in descending order) tension and anxiety, food cravings, unhappiness, inability to control appetite, hunger, and insomnia. Eating disorders are often

considered to be a coping mechanism people use to regulate negative emotions.

People who binge have many ways of controlling their weight, including purging. Purging behavior is often learned from friends and seems to have some support among adolescent girls as an acceptable way to control weight. In fact, dieting is often a precursor to the development of bulimia nervosa. The self-induced vomiting seems to increase feelings of self-control and to reduce anxiety, and these secondary gains often make it a difficult behavior to extinguish. In addition to purging, people with bulimia nervosa use many other compensatory behaviors, including fasting, exercising excessively, spitting out food, and using diuretics, laxatives, and diet pills, or a combination of these behaviors.

Physical signs usually accompany the self-induced vomiting often associated with binge eating. These signs include swelling of the parotid glands, which produces a chipmunk-like appearance; scars on the back of the hand (from the hand's contact with the teeth while vomiting is being induced); chronic hoarseness; and dryness of the mouth. Physiological reactions to purging include dental cavities and enamel loss, electrolyte imbalance, cardiac and renal problems, and esophageal tears. Long-term effects of frequent binge eating and purging can include amenorrhea, anemia, dehydration, and acute heart dysrhythmia. Impaired nutrition can also increase the risk for osteoporosis, reproductive problems, diabetes, and high cholesterol (Sagar, 2005).

Binge Eating Disorder (BED)   Binge eating disorder consists of a pattern of binge eating episodes on an average of two days per week over a period of at least six months, without the persistent use of compensatory behavior required for a diagnosis of bulimia nervosa (American Psychiatric Association, 2000). People with BED may consume large quantities of food in a short period, eat until they are uncomfortably full, feel out of control when eating, feel guilt and embarrassment over the quantity of food they eat, eat alone frequently, and eat even when they are not physically hungry. BED may be the most common eating disorder, and it can lead to obesity and the concomitant health risks associated with being overweight. Overeating has been shown to be influenced by both genetic and environmental variables, with heredity being responsible for 45% (Adan & Kaye, 2011). Loss of control over eating is the primary distinguishing feature of BED. But those who overeat and do not report feelings of lack of control over their eating would not fit the criteria for BED (Craighead, 2002).

Research shows that most binges typically begin with a mood change. People report feeling anxious or tense before a binge, relief of anxiety during the binge eating episode, and absence of anxiety at the conclusion. Several researchers have written about how such affective dysregulation has a bipolar quality (McElroy & Kotwal, 2006). Binge eating may occur on a continuum with normal eating, with "passive overeating" (p. 120) being the least severe form, impulsive or compulsive overeating representing an intermediate form, and recurrent binge eating being the most severe (McElroy & Kotwal, 2006).

EDNOS　 A preponderance of eating disorders are classified in the current *DSM* as eating disorders not otherwise specified (EDNOS; Adan & Kaye, 2011). The diagnosis is used for every eating disorder except anorexia and bulimia nervosa (Fairburn, 2007). For example, purging disorder (without compensatory bingeing or other behaviors) and night eating syndrome are both under consideration for inclusion in the *DSM-5*, and would currently be classified as EDNOS. Male eating disorder, binge eating disorder, and subclinical cases of bulimia and anorexia are also categorized under EDNOS. More than 50% of people who seek treatment for eating disorders are classified as EDNOS (Fairburn, 2007).

Typical Client Characteristics

That eating pathology is rooted in efforts to regulate negative mood states has been known for quite some time (Stice et al., 2004). Eating has been reported to provide comfort and distraction from negative feelings. However, as with most impulse-control disorders, after the behavior has been completed, it actually leads to more negative affect, assuming a continuing course. Depressive symptoms have been found to be predictive of onset of binge eating. Conversely, feelings of shame, guilt, and negative affect following a binge eating or binge and purging episode increase the risk for depression (Fairburn, 2007).

Disturbances in early attachment have also been hypothesized to contribute to the development of eating disorders. A child or infant who is insecurely attached may not be able to process emotions in a healthy way and may use food as a coping method. Self-regulation problems may ensue such as anorexia, bulimia, compulsive overeating, anxiety, or depression (Zerbe, 2008).

Anorexia Nervosa　 Low self-esteem, denial, shame, depression, and problems related to socialization, sleeping, and sexual desire are commonly found in people with anorexia nervosa, as are obsessive-compulsive features, especially related to a preoccupation with food (Costin, 2007). People with anorexia nervosa often cook for their families but refuse to eat what they have prepared because of their intense fear of gaining weight. They tend to be resistant to treatment because their disorder is ego-syntonic, and they typically do not want to change their eating behavior.

People with the restricting type of anorexia nervosa commonly are dependent, introverted, compulsive, stubborn, perfectionistic, asexual, and shy. They have low self-esteem and feel ineffectual. They tend to come from affluent homes where food had an important role. They also tend to have been well-behaved children and often played an important part in holding the family together. Many have been parentified children in enmeshed families and were overprotected, constricted, and overregulated. They lack autonomy and a clear sense of their own identity. They had eating problems as children or had one or more family members who displayed some type of disordered eating themselves (Bulik et al., 2006).

Bulimia Nervosa   Most people with bulimic symptoms report problems with interpersonal relationships. They tend to be anxious, depressed, demoralized, self-critical, and secretive about their eating behaviors. People who binge and purge typically feel shame, guilt, powerlessness, and a sense of being out of control. Because of these feelings, people with bulimia nervosa wait an average of six years before seeking treatment (Fairburn & Harrison, 2003). Although they usually are sexually active, they tend to have sexual difficulties, as well as conflicted feelings about intimate relationships. They tend to be more extroverted, more emotional, less rigid, more anxious, more guilty, and more depressed than those people with eating disorders who do not habitually binge (Costin, 2007). One study found that multi-impulsivity (defined by three of the following: heavy alcohol use, a suicide attempt, self-mutilation, repeated shoplifting, and sexual disinhibition) was more common in people diagnosed with bulimia (18%) than in those with anorexia (2%) and people without eating disorders (2%) (Nagata, Kawarada, Kirike, & Iketani, 2000). Fischer, Smith, and Anderson (2003) found that people with bulimia had increased scores on impulsive urgency and tended to act rashly in the face of negative emotion.

Bulimic behavior, unlike restriction of food intake, tends to be ego-dystonic, and people with this symptom experience considerable hunger and disappointment in connection with their need to binge and purge. As a result, they are more likely to seek treatment than are those with anorexia nervosa, restricting type.

People with bulimic symptoms are also particularly likely to have first-degree relatives with mood disorders, substance use disorders, and obesity (Jacobi et al., 2004). People with bulimia nervosa tend to see their families as low in cohesiveness and as discouraging of intellectual and recreational activities, independence, assertiveness, and open expression of feelings. These families tend to be highly critical, especially of body image and weight, and have high levels of conflict. Lilenfeld et al. (1997) suggested that some people with bulimia nervosa may have a familial vulnerability for impulsivity and affective instability.

Binge Eating Disorder   People with BED tend to have higher rates of depression and reduced self-esteem related to body image. They also report greater impairments in quality of life, especially regarding work life and sexual life (Hudson et al., 2007; Wildes & Marcus, 2009). Medical complications frequently result from obesity including greater incidence of diabetes mellitus and other health problems. Impulsive behavior traits are also seen in people with BED who may lack deliberation and fail to consider consequences before acting (McElroy & Kotwal, 2006).

EDNOS   Much diagnostic variety exists in this category. Atypical anorexia or bulimia that is subthreshold for current DSM-IV-TR diagnostic criteria would be classified as EDNOS, as would purging disorder in which self-induced vomiting, use of laxatives or diuretics or other compensatory behaviors are present without binge eating. People with purging disorder are afraid of becoming fat and are overly concerned with body shape or weight (Keel & Striegel-Moore, 2009).

Night eating syndrome which affects nearly 6 million Americans, including more than 33% of those who are morbidly obese, would also be diagnosed as EDNOS. Symptoms include lack of hunger in the morning, consuming more than half of one's total daily caloric intake after dinner time, and disrupted sleep or insomnia.

Other mental disorders are highly likely to accompany anorexia nervosa, bulimia nervosa, and BED. Most people with these disorders have also experienced a major depressive disorder, and many have met the diagnostic criteria for anxiety disorders and substance use disorders (Johnson et al., 2002; Stice et al., 2004). Perfectionistic traits and obsessive-compulsive disorder are unusually likely to occur in people with anorexia nervosa (Jacobi et al., 2004). More than half of people with eating disorders have accompanying personality disorders (Rosenvinge et al., 2000). People with eating disorders, particularly those with a coexisting diagnosis of borderline personality disorder, have a higher than average prevalence of childhood sexual abuse, ranging from 40% to 70% of women and 10% of men (Costin, 2007; Woodside, 2004; Woodside et al., 2001). Women with bulimia nervosa also tend to have rates of anxiety, antisocial personality disorder, and familial substance misuse that are higher than in the general population (Grilo et al., 2002).

Assessment

Anorexia nervosa, bulimia nervosa, and BED are physically damaging and potentially lethal disorders. Therefore, the first step in treatment is to assess the client's eating behaviors and any physiological damage by taking a careful history and referring the client for examination by a physician. Craighead (2002) recommends that therapists ask the following

questions as part of the initial assessment of eating-disordered clients:

- To what extent is the client motivated for treatment at this point?
- Is the client willing to self-monitor?
- For clients who are binge eating only, is the client willing to focus on reducing binge eating before addressing weight loss? Is the client interested in nondieting interventions?
- Does the client have other mental health problems that might influence the choice of treatment or expected length of treatment?
- What are the functions of the binge eating, the purging, or the eating restriction?

Such inventories as the Questionnaire on Eating and Weight Patterns-Revised (QEWP-R; Yanovski, 1993) and the Eating Disorder Examination Questionnaire, 12th edition (EDEQ; Fairburn & Cooper, 1993) can be useful in obtaining an accurate assessment of the disorder's severity. These self-reports screen for the presence of specific eating disorders, provide useful information about the frequency of problem eating and dieting behaviors and attitudes, and are found to be effective tools in the identification of people with possible eating disorders or problems (Craighead, 2002; Grilo et al., 2002). A life chart can be helpful in determining onset of symptoms, as well as in establishing the relationship between stressful life events and symptoms. Suggested areas to include are a chronology of the client's memories of significant life events throughout the life span, mood and self-esteem, interpersonal relationships, and changes in weight (including any compensatory behaviors). Past treatment should also be included. Documenting eating problems over time can be helpful in pointing out patterns and identifying the usually chronic and fluctuating course of the disorder.

Other useful tools in the assessment of eating disorders include self-reports of eating behavior, assessments of cognitive processing, self-efficacy scales, and body image assessments. Due to the high percentage of people with concomitant eating and personality disorders, care should be taken to assess for relevant personality traits and disorders.

Preferred Therapist Characteristics

The therapeutic alliance can have a greater effect on client success than any other type of intervention for eating disorders (Maine, McGilley, & Bunnell, 2010). People with eating disorders typically are very sensitive to disapproval or interpersonal rejection. Consequently, they need considerable support and approval in therapy to help them disclose symptoms that typically seem shameful to them. The following clinician attributes are critical to establishing a positive therapeutic alliance with people who meet the criteria for eating disorders:

- Sustaining empathy
- Practicing patience and a long-term perspective
- Limiting battles for control
- Making behavioral agreements and contracts
- Challenging cognitive distortions
- Balancing nurturing with authoritativeness

An excellent and comprehensive discussion of each dimension of the therapeutic alliance and its impact on clients with eating disorders can be found in McGilley and Szablewski (2010). Costin (2007) reports that early on she tells her clients that the battle will be between the client and the eating disorder, not between the therapist and client. Therapists will need to handle these clients' strong dependence needs by gently encouraging self-control, independence, and active involvement in treatment. At the same time, therapists will also need to be structured, to provide stability and constancy, and to set limits to protect these clients, even hospitalizing them if that becomes necessary.

Therapists should assume a collaborative approach when working with people diagnosed with eating disorders. People are more motivated to change if they believe a goal can be attained. Having positive expectations has been shown to be predictive of positive treatment outcome (Arnkoff, Glass, & Shapiro, 2002). Thus, early in treatment, therapists should attempt to assess, discuss, and foster clients' expectations of improvement, as part of the development of a positive therapeutic alliance (Constantino, Arnow, Blasey, & Agras, 2005).

Therapy for people with eating disorders should address readiness to change and motivational issues (Geller, Brown, Zaitsoff, Goodrich, & Hastings, 2003). For a detailed discussion of motivational interviewing and Prochaska's readiness to change theory, refer to the previous section on the treatment of substance use disorders.

Because of the high likelihood that people with eating disorders will have at least one other mental disorder, therapists treating these clients need to be knowledgeable not only about eating disorders but also about the many other disorders that may also be present. Assessment of co-occurring disorders will be necessary to planning effective treatments.

Intervention Strategies

Less than one third of people with eating disorders ever enter into treatment. Of those who do receive treatment, symptom remission occurs in only 40% to 60% of cases (Stice et al., 2004).

Effective interventions for eating disorders should focus on developing an effective therapeutic alliance, reducing negative affect, modifying eating behaviors, identifying situations that trigger behavior, and continuing motivation to change (Maine, Davis, & Shure, 2008; McGilley & Szablewski, 2010; Stice et al., 2004). Relapse prevention is an important part of any program for disordered eating and should be integrated into treatment.

Multidisciplinary Approach A multidisciplinary approach seems best for working with people with severe anorexia nervosa or bulimia nervosa. A treatment team consisting of a physician, a nutritionist, and a mental health professional can monitor the impact of the disorder on the person's health. Exposure and response prevention are important components of treatment for people who binge and purge. Presenting people with both prebingeing and purging cues in multiple settings while preventing or delaying those behaviors can enhance treatment, although this approach should also be combined with other treatment interventions.

Cognitive-Behavioral Therapy Cognitive-behavioral therapy has demonstrated efficacy for the treatment of eating disorders (Wilson, Grilo, & Vitousek, 2007). In the past 10 years, refinements have been made to CBT treatment to include techniques for improving metacognition, and reduce the overvaluation of weight and body shape. Research has found that treatment refractory patients are helped by individualization of the treatment approach to address variables that are maintaining the disorder. For instance, problems of low self-esteem, perfectionism, interpersonal difficulties, and affect dysregulation may need to be addressed specifically along with the course of CBT treatment (Fairburn, Cooper, Shafran, & Wilson, 2008). Grilo and Mitchell (2009) suggest a model of

CBT treatment for eating disorders that includes three phases. The first phase involves psychoeducation about the eating disorder and expectations for treatment, including homework, self-monitoring, and a gradual approach to normalized eating. The second phase includes the use of cognitive restructuring to identify, challenge, and change maladaptive thinking. The final stage includes relapse prevention and problem-solving skills to help clients cope with stress and apply their newly found skills to other areas of their lives.

Dialectical Behavior Therapy (DBT) Dialectical behavior therapy has been adapted for use with BED and may prove useful in treating people with chronic eating disorders who are resistant to treatment and those who also have borderline features, such as nonsuicidal self-injurious behaviors and dissociative episodes (Craighead, 2002). Since DBT aims at reducing negative emotions and improving emotion-regulation skills, it may be especially helpful for those with high negative affect, impulsivity, and those who use eating to help them regulate their emotions.

In one controlled study, DBT adapted for BED (DBT-BED) was found to be more effective than the untreated control group. A later randomized controlled trial compared DBT for BED to Active Comparison Group Therapy (ACGT). Both were found to be effective, with a 64% post-treatment abstinence rate for DBT-BED versus 36% for ACGT. The study also found that reduction in binges and abstinence was achieved more quickly with DBT-BED than with ACGT, and that DBT-BED had a lower dropout rate (Safer, Robinson, & Jo, 2010). One model described by Craighead (2002) for the treatment of BED and bulimia nervosa helps clients identify maladaptive cycles, such as emotional eating, eating when not hungry, restrictive eating, ignoring satiety clues, and planned binges. This information is then used to tailor treatment to the client's specific problems. For example, if a frequent trigger is skipping meals and getting too hungry, people would be advised on how to plan more frequent, low-calorie snacks.

Manualized Treatment In 1985, Fairburn developed a structured manual that describes a cognitive-behavioral approach to treating eating disorders. That manual, last revised in 2007, has been widely adopted; since that time, manual-based CBT has become the preferred treatment for bulimia nervosa (Fairburn, 2007). The approach it describes consists of 19 sessions of individual therapy that span approximately 20 weeks. The approach emphasizes problem solving and is both present- and future-oriented. The treatment is divided into three stages. The first stage includes information on the treatment approach, on eating disorders, and on nutrition. Self-monitoring is begun, and techniques to modify behavior are taught, in an effort to restore healthy patterns of eating. Cognitive interventions are emphasized in the second stage, during which people are helped to identify and modify their dysfunctional thoughts about eating, weight, and body size. The third stage emphasizes the maintenance of gains and the prevention of relapses. The treatment program developed by Fairburn is typical of those used to treat eating disorders. The program combines cognitive and behavioral interventions, with some attention to affect, into a structured format that can be used either with individuals or with groups.

The past decade has seen a proliferation of manual-based treatment specific to each of the eating disorders. Manuals cover the gamut of treatment options: in-patient treatment, self-help, family-based, individual, adolescent body image distortion, and so on. A survey of patient attitudes about manual-based treatment approaches conducted by Krautter and

Lock (2004) reported that patients found it a highly effective and acceptable form of treatment, however, one-quarter of respondents thought more individual and family therapy could be helpful.

Interpersonal Psychotherapy (IPT) Interpersonal psychotherapy also has been shown to be effective in treating eating disorders, but is less effective than cognitive-behavioral therapy, particularly in the treatment of bulimia nervosa and binge eating disorder (Wilson, Grilo, & Vitousek, 2007). The main emphasis of IPT is on helping people identify and modify current interpersonal issues (e.g., losses and communication problems).

Group Therapy Although research has not established the superiority of group over individual therapy in the treatment of people with eating disorders, group therapy for these clients offers many benefits. These include mutual support, reduction of shame, diffusion of power struggles, feedback from multiple sources, role models, and the opportunity to practice interpersonal skills. At the same time, group therapists must ensure that group members have sufficient empathy to participate successfully in the group and that the group does not encourage competitive weight loss.

A Transdiagnostic Approach Using a dimensional model to look at eating disorder behaviors across the lifetime provides a wealth of information and new possibilities for treatment interventions. Such eating disorder behavior as binge eating, vomiting, laxative and diuretic misuse, fasting, low body weight or BMI (body mass index), are all potential behaviors found in people with disordered eating, regardless of their specific eating disorder diagnosis (Fairburn et al., 2008; Fairburn et al., 2009). Enhanced cognitive behavioral therapy (CBT-E) was developed by

Fairburn et al. (2008) and pares down traditional CBT to focus more on behavior than thought records and logs. At the same time, CBT-E focuses on society's overvaluation of the thin ideal, dietary restraint and restriction, and recognizing changes in mood or environment that trigger changes in eating behavior. By offering two forms— focused and broad—treatment interventions can be tailored to the eating disorder specifically or to other issues such as self-esteem, emotion regulation, perfectionism, or other issues with which the person may be struggling. While research is still ongoing, one randomized controlled trial of CBT-E for bulimia and EDNOS found both the focused and the broad treatments to be effective, with focused being the most likely to be used and the broad version reserved for people who have additional problems that need to be addressed along with the eating disorder (Fairburn et al., 2009).

Family Therapy   Family therapy may be a useful adjunct in the treatment of eating disorders, particularly for adolescents with anorexia nervosa, whose family dynamics often contribute to the development of the disorder (Wilson & Fairburn, 2007). Family members of people with eating disorders commonly are coping with their own emotional difficulties, and family therapy may help them, in addition to improving the overall functioning of the family. People with eating disorders also often have issues related to separation and individuation from their families of origin, and these too can be addressed through family therapy.

Hospitalization   Hospitalization sometimes is needed for people with eating disorders. The primary goal of hospitalization for the severely underweight person with anorexia is to implement refeeding and weight gain. For the person diagnosed with binge eating or bulimia, it may be necessary to establish control over excessive bingeing and purging (Costin, 2007). Hospitalization may also be necessary to ensure the person's safety in the case of suicide attempts, ideation, or threats, or if severe anxiety or symptoms of depression are interfering with the person's normal ability to function. If the client does not seem to be in immediate danger, however, outpatient treatment may be adequate as long as steps are taken to restore normal weight and to curtail other self-damaging behaviors.

Internet Delivery Methods   The use of the Internet for delivery of treatment interventions for eating disorders is still in its infancy, so few studies exist that document its effectiveness. Yager (2001) used case examples to show how e-mail could serve as an effective adjunct to face-to-face therapy for anorexia nervosa. Clients who communicated via e-mail with their therapists several times a week had increased levels of treatment compliance and reported higher satisfaction with treatment. Luce, Winzelberg, Zabinski, and Osborne (2003) found Internet delivery methods can be used for education, prevention, interventions, and maintenance of therapeutic change. Internet groups often fulfill the same purposes as face-to-face support groups, providing a venue for self-disclosure, giving information, and offering direct emotional support. Internet groups have also been found to be effective in reducing levels of social isolation. However, the Internet must be used cautiously. Some sites promote disordered eating and can worsen symptoms.

Medication   At present, no medication has been approved specifically for the treatment of eating disorders. Research is needed on the effect on symptoms of a variety of medications. For example, atypical antipsychotics such as olanzapine (Zyprexa) have been shown to decrease symptoms of agitation and anxiety and increase weight gain in people with anorexia. Some limited studies have shown that antidepressants can treat underlying serotonin dysregulation and obsessive-compulsive and depressive symptoms (Rivas-Vazquez et al., 2003). In one study, fluoxetine (Prozac) was found to reduce relapse frequency (Kaye et al., 2005).

Antidepressant medication, the anticonvulsant topiramate (Topamax), and opioid antagonists, such as naltrexone (ReVia), have been found to reduce binge eating associated with bulimia nervosa and BED, but relapse is highly likely when medication is withdrawn (Grilo et al., 2002; Rivas-Vazquez et al., 2003). Several studies and meta-analyses of treatment for bulimia nervosa indicate that a combination of medication and psychotherapy produces "more robust effects" (Rivas-Vazquez et al., 2003, p. 565) than either modality alone. Given the high rate of relapse when medication is withdrawn, cognitive-behavioral therapy is recommended to help effect behavioral change (Mitchell, Agras, & Wonderlich, 2007).

Pharmacotherapy may be considered as one component of a more comprehensive treatment strategy for eating disorders. However, until more definitive research is available, medication should be used with care and should not be routinely recommended for people with eating disorders.

Maintaining a dual focus on the eating disorder and other problems the client is facing seems to be an effective way to proceed in therapy. Duration seems to be an important variable in the treatment of eating disorders. Longer treatments, typically lasting at least four to six months, are usually more successful. People with severe eating disorders may need treatment of at least a year in duration.

Prognosis

Improvement of eating disorders has been reported in terms of reductions in binge eating and purging and in terms of the cessation of all disordered eating patterns. Treatment that follows recommended guidelines is likely to have a considerable impact on eating patterns, typically reducing binge eating and purging by a rate of at least 75%. The prognosis is less favorable for complete remission of an eating disorder. Statistics for each disorder are listed below.

Anorexia nervosa has a variable course with those who achieve remission early being the most likely to recover from the disorder completely (Grilo & Mitchell, 2009; Keel & Striegel-Moore, 2009). In general, 44% of people with anorexia nervosa recover completely through treatment, 28% are significantly improved, 24% are unimproved or significantly impaired, and 10% die prematurely from the effect of starvation or suicide. Over time, the majority of people with anorexia nervosa go on to develop bulimia nervosa, with a concomitant increase in weight.

The prognosis for treatment of bulimia nervosa is somewhat better. Sagar (2005) reports a study in which 5 to 10 years after diagnosis of bulimia, approximately 50% of women had recovered completely, 20% continued to meet the criteria for the disorder, and about 30% had relapsed.

Fairburn and colleagues (2000) report higher recovery rates for BED than for bulimia in a 5-year follow-up; 51% of the bulimia group continued to have a clinical eating disorder, compared with only 18% of the BED group.

According to Wilson and Fairburn (2007), early response to treatment is the best predictor of a positive prognosis for treatment of an eating disorder. Good prognosis is also associated with the following factors:

- Good premorbid functioning
- A positive family environment
- The client's acknowledgment of hunger
- Greater maturity (including psychosexual maturity) and self-esteem

- High educational level
- Early age of onset
- Less weight loss
- Shorter duration of the disorder
- Less denial of the disorder
- Overactivity
- Absence of coexisting mental disorders

As with most of the other impulse-control disorders, relapses of eating disorders are common and are often triggered by stressful life events. Moreover, even if people no longer meet the full criteria for an eating disorder, many continue to experience dysphoric moods and to engage in unhealthy eating. Treatment should be extended through follow-up or support groups to prevent and address setbacks. Follow-up treatment should also be helpful in reducing family, social, and occupational difficulties that often persist after the eating disorder has been eliminated.

SEXUAL AND GENDER IDENTITY DISORDERS

Most sexual disorders, just like substance- related disorders and eating disorders, involve behavioral patterns that are dysfunctional or self-destructive. Unlike eating disorders or substance use disorders, however, sexual disorders are usually not physically self-injurious, nor do they usually cause pervasive dysfunction. Nevertheless, they are often closely linked to people's satisfaction with their relationships, and these disorders may both reflect and cause impairment in relationships. Some paraphilias may also lead people to break the law in an effort to find sexual gratification.

The *DSM-IV-TR* divides sexual and gender identity disorders into three categories: sexual dysfunctions, paraphilias, and gender identity disorder. In a sense, all three are disorders of behavior involving dysfunctional and inappropriate responses to stimuli, but the people with these three disorders tend to be very different in terms of lifestyle and personality patterns, motivation for treatment, and interactions with their therapists. Their disorders also differ in terms of duration, severity, and impact. The treatments for all three categories have some common ingredients (the primary one being the facilitation of expressions of normal, healthy sexuality), but the three will be discussed separately here because of the important differences among them. Sexual difficulties do not always cause distress. As a result, prevalence rates can sometimes be distorted.

Sexual Dysfunctions

This category of disorders involves disturbances in sexual desire or functioning that cause significant distress and interpersonal difficulties. Sexual dysfunctions are highly prevalent in our society, and the prevalence rates increase with age (DeRogatis & Burnett, 2008). The *DSM-IV-TR* includes the following sexual dysfunction disorders:

- Sexual desire disorders
- Sexual arousal disorders
- Orgasmic disorders
- Sexual pain disorders
- Sexual dysfunctions due to a general medical condition
- Substance-induced sexual dysfunction

Description of the Disorders   Assessment and treatment of sexual disorders is complicated; not all people who experience a loss of sexual desire or lack of sexual arousal are concerned about the loss. Typically, people who seek treatment for these disorders want to have healthy and rewarding sexual relationships but have encountered difficulties in doing so. The *DSM-IV-TR* organizes this category according to stages in the sexual response cycle and lists the following disorders.

Sexual desire disorders: Sexual desire disorders include hypoactive (deficient) sexual desire disorder and sexual aversion disorder. Loss of desire is the most common sexual disorder among women (Basson, 2007). These disorders are experienced by as many as 50% of the population at some point in their lives. Problems with sexual desire result in lack of sexual thoughts or fantasy, no sexual desire, and lack of interest in sex (McCabe, 2005). Prevalence rates vary from 0% to 7% in males to 5% to 46% in females. Sexual desire disorders tend to increase with age. Postmenopausal women have the highest incidence of sexual desire disorders (Wiegel, Wincze, & Barlow, 2002).

Sexual arousal disorders: There are two sexual arousal disorders: female sexual arousal disorder and male erectile disorder. Both reflect a lack of physiological arousal and sexual excitement. Sexual arousal disorders are very common, affecting approximately one third of all women and 10% to 20% of men. Age increases the risk of male erectile problems, with the incidence of the disorder increasing with each decade of life (DeRogatis & Burnett, 2008). Fully one half of all men 40 to 70 years old report erectile difficulties (Wiegel et al., 2002). Male erectile disorder is almost always a disorder of the acquired type rather than of the lifelong type. In middle age, interest in sexual activity is greater for men than for women. However, it is positively correlated with health in middle age for both genders (Lindau & Gavrilova, 2010).

Orgasmic disorders: The *DSM-IV-TR* orgasmic disorders include female orgasmic disorder, male orgasmic disorder, and premature ejaculation. Female orgasmic disorder is more common than male orgasmic disorder and affects approximately 30% of women. Premature ejaculation also is very prevalent, affecting up to 29% of men, and 60% of men over the age of 60

(Wiegel et al., 2002; Wincze, Bach, & Barlow, 2008). Together, premature ejaculation and male erectile disorder comprise nearly all the sexual dysfunctions treated in men.

Sexual pain disorders: Sexual pain disorders include dyspareunia (genital pain, usually diagnosed in females) and vaginismus (involuntary vaginal contractions). In one study, vaginismus was found in 3% to 25% of women (ter Kuile, Weigenborg, Beekman, Bulte, & Melles, 2009). It often has a biological basis and may be a conditioned response to previous pain related to sexual relations. Fear and avoidance behavior seem to play a role in this disorder, and it is sometimes associated with previous sexual abuse (ter Kuile et al., 2009).

Sexual dysfunctions due to a general medical condition: Approximately 50% of sexual dysfunctions in men are caused by medical conditions or substances. Diabetes, endocrine disorders, vascular disease, hypertension, and injuries are some of the more common medical causes of these dysfunctions (DeRogatis & Burnett, 2008). Gynecological surgery, vaginitis, and menopause are some of the medical conditions that can cause sexual dysfunctions in women.

Substance-induced sexual dysfunction: Many substances, including alcohol, opioids, anxiolytics, and some medications for hypertension, can cause sexual dysfunction. Most of the antidepressants, with the exception of bupropion (Wellbutrin) and mintazapine (Remeron), are known to cause sexual dysfunction. Benzodiazepines have been found to delay orgasm, and some antipsychotic medications have been found to decrease libido and cause erectile difficulties (Segraves & Althof, 2002).

To warrant a diagnosis of a sexual dysfunction, symptoms must be recurrent and persistent and must cause considerable distress and interpersonal difficulty. The symptoms are not attributable to another Axis I disorder (such as PTSD). In making the diagnosis, the clinician specifies the disorder and indicates whether it is of the lifelong or acquired type, of the generalized or situational type, and due to psychological factors or due to combined factors (psychological and physiological).

Most sexual dysfunctions begin in early adulthood, although some, particularly male erectile disorder, tend to begin later (Segraves & Althof, 2002). Treatment for sexual dysfunctions typically is not sought until people are in their late 20s or early 30s.

The course of these disorders is quite variable. Some are situationally related, precipitated by stress or relationship difficulties, and remit spontaneously once the situation has improved. Others are chronic or progressive, worsening as anxiety about the disorder increases.

Sexual dysfunctions have many possible determinants including lifestyle factors such as obesity, smoking, and lack of exercise (Wincze, Bach, & Barlow, 2008). Relationship factors affect sexual dysfunction for both men and women, with women who experience the most relationship problems also having the lowest level of sexual desire (McCabe, 2005). Substances or medical conditions should be investigated first. Therapists should also explore the client's cultural and family background, knowledge about sexuality, sexual and relationship history, potential history of sexual abuse, self-image, and the possibility that the client has a coexisting mental disorder. Wiegel and colleagues (2002) report that the sexual dysfunctions are likely to be associated with negative attitudes toward sex on the part of clients and their parents, clients' dissatisfaction with and instability in their intimate relationships, and clients' discomfort with their sexual identities. A history of abuse in childhood and a dysfunctional family background also contribute to the development of these disorders (Segraves & Althof, 2002). Other factors associated with sexual dysfunction include fear of rejection and abandonment, difficulty sharing control and trusting others, poor communication skills, anger and hostility, guilt about sexual thoughts and behaviors, impaired self-esteem, anxiety (especially about sexual performance), depression, and inaccurate information about sexual functioning. These symptoms may be either causes or consequences of sexual dysfunctions.

Typical Client Characteristics A clear association has not been found between particular personality traits or backgrounds and sexual dysfunctions. However, anxiety is almost always a component of these disorders. Negative attitudes toward sex have been found to be linked to sexual dysfunction in both men and women (Wiegel et al., 2002). Many people with one sexual dysfunction have symptoms of other sexual dysfunctions. For example, in one study, 40% of those diagnosed with hypoactive sexual desire disorders also met the criteria for arousal or orgasmic disorders (Segraves & Althof, 2002). Once a sexual dysfunction develops it is more likely to continue and to permeate all phases of sexual functioning, negatively impacting desire, arousal, and orgasm. People may experience a problem in one phase that progresses to a problem in another phase. For example, male premature ejaculation may lead to erectile dysfunction. Concern about performance can also impact sexual functioning (McCabe, 2005).

Recent research indicates that relationship intimacy and attachment anxiety moderate the association between sexual function and dysfunction in women (Stephenson & Meston, 2010). Many women experiencing decreased sexual desire share the characteristics of being married, having a psychological disorder, being perimenopausal, and being a cigarette smoker (Kingsberg, 2004). Nappi and Lachowsky (2009) cite declining estrogen levels as having deleterious effects on women's sexual desire and responsiveness.

Age also plays a role in sexual functioning. A national study of 3,005 adults age 57 to 85 yielded the following information (Lindau et al., 2007):

- The prevalence of sexual activity declines with age.
- At all ages, women are less likely to report being sexually active.
- Among those who are sexually active, nearly half experience some sort of sexual problem—low desire (43%) and anorgasmia (34%) for women, and erectile dysfunction (37%) for men.

Only 50% of women who reported having a sexual dysfunction also endorsed being distressed about it (DeRogatis & Burnett, 2008). Causal factors may also include interpersonal issues, boring sexual routine, and other co-occurring disorders such as depression or substance use disorders. Satisfaction in sexual functioning is correlated with all aspects of body image, including weight, physical condition, feeling physically attractive, and being sexually attracted to one's partner (Kingsberg, 2002; Pujois, Meston, & Seal, 2010). Being the victim or perpetrator of sexual trauma increases the likelihood of developing a sexual dysfunction. Traumatic sexual experiences have been found to have a profound effect on sexual functioning for many years after the traumatic event, resulting in arousal disorders in women and erectile dysfunction in men (Lauman, Paik, & Rosen, 1999).

Assessment   A variety of assessment tools are available to assist in the diagnosis of sexual dysfunction. Scales and inventories that measure attitudes toward sexuality can be helpful. Although it does not assess for *DSM-IV-TR* criteria specifically, the DeRogatis Interview for Sexual Functioning (DISF; DeRogatis, 1997) provides a semistructured interview across five domains: sexual fantasy and cognition, sexual behavior and experiences, orgasm, sexual drive, and sexual arousal.

The Sexual Interest and Desire Inventory— Female (SIDI-F) is a brief, 17-item rating scale that assesses sexual desire disorder (Sills et al., 2005).

Because attitudes toward sex have been found to be linked to sexual dysfunction in both men and women, measuring specific attitudes that may adversely affect treatment is helpful. The Sexual Opinion Survey (SOS; White, Fisher, Byrne, & Kingma, 1977) measures responses to sexual stimuli on a range of negative to positive. The survey includes 21 items on a 6-point Likert scale. Norms have been established for the SOS based on gender, age groups, countries, and religions. Discrepancies between husbands' and wives' scores on the SOS have been associated with lower sexual satisfaction rates (Wiegel et al., 2002).

Numerous other assessments, such as the Sexual Dysfunction Scale (McCabe, 1998), the Female Sexual Function Index (Rosen et al., 2000), the Sexual Desire Inventory (Spector, Carey, & Steinberg, 1996), and the International Index of Erectile Functioning (IIEF; Rosen, Cappelleri, & Gendrano, 2002), are reviewed in greater detail by Wiegel and colleagues (2002); all provide valid measures of different sexual dysfunctions.

The Early Sexual Experiences Checklist (ESEC; Miller, Johnson, & Johnson, 1991) is a quick, 9-item questionnaire used to detect unwanted sexual experiences that occurred before the age of 16. One section asks detailed questions about the most distressing event. Information on the time, duration, frequency, and degree of distress experienced, as well as the amount of coercion involved, is explored. The test can be completed in less than 5 minutes, and it avoids pejorative labels. The ESEC provides the client with an opportunity to report childhood sexual abuse without having to do so in a face-to-face interview (Wiegel et al., 2002).

Preferred Therapist Characteristics Treating sexual dysfunctions can be challenging to therapists because they must have expertise in the specific techniques of sex therapy and must also be skilled at providing support and encouragement, communicating empathy, and establishing a relationship with a client who is likely to feel uncomfortable, embarrassed, and exposed. Many people have never talked openly about their sexual attitudes and behaviors before seeking therapy and will have difficulty doing so with a therapist. The client may avoid specific details, minimize the problem, and display unfamiliarity with terminology. The therapist must be sure to conduct a detailed inquiry in terms that are comprehensible to the client and that reduce threat and anxiety as much as possible. Maintaining a nonjudgmental stance is particularly important. Orienting the client quickly to the nature of the treatment may also be useful because the client may be apprehensive about what will be required.

Transference reactions, sometimes of an erotic nature, are frequent in the treatment of sexual dysfunctions because of the intimate nature of the discussions. The therapist should be aware of the development of transference; addressing, discussing, normalizing, interpreting, and diffusing the transference will usually prevent it from undermining psychotherapy. Therapists should be experienced in working with couples. Even if the individual is the only one seeking treatment, therapists must recognize that sexual dysfunction disorders affect the couple as a whole and plan interventions accordingly.

Intervention Strategies The first step in treating a sexual dysfunction is to determine the cause of the difficulty by taking a comprehensive medical, sexual, and psychosocial history and referring the client for examination by a physician. People who experience low sexual desire may benefit from interventions that target specific aspects of body image (Pujois, Meston, & Seal, 2010). Although most sexual dysfunctions are psychological in origin, many do have a physiological basis. Prescription medications, for example, as well as other drugs and alcohol, are common physiological causes of sexual dysfunction. Whatever the cause, psychotherapy may be indicated, but medical treatment may also need to be part of the plan.

Interventions should focus on the client's attitude toward sex, their relationship, and any performance anxiety (McCabe, 2005). People often experience sexual difficulties for years before seeking treatment. By the time a client seeks help, the disorder may have been exacerbated by multiple disappointing sexual experiences, avoidance of sexual contact, and long-standing self-blame, all of which may complicate treatment.

A repertoire of techniques for treating these disorders has been developed by Masters and Johnson (1970), Kaplan (1995), Leiblum (2007), Wincze and Carey (2001), Marnach & Casey (2008), and others. Discussion of the specific techniques designed for particular disorders is beyond the scope of this book—the reader is referred to these authors for that information—but some elements are common to most treatment of sexual dysfunctions, and these elements will be reviewed here.

Treatment of these disorders tends to be primarily behavioral. Nevertheless, cognitive and psychodynamic interventions can also be useful in modifying self-damaging thoughts and resolving such long-standing problems as abuse, family dysfunction, and mistrust.

Psychoeducation. Sexual dysfunctions are often exacerbated by inadequate or incorrect information about the process of sexual arousal and about what is considered normal sexual functioning. For example, attitudes about the inappropriateness of sexual activity for older people, or erroneous beliefs about differences between types of female orgasm, can inhibit sexual functioning and cause people to feel uncomfortable with healthy feelings and behaviors. Educating people about sexuality and sexual functioning can help dispel some of their self-blame and modify unrealistic expectations.

Couples Therapy. If the person with a sexual dysfunction has a consistent sexual partner, that partner should almost always be involved in the therapy. Sexual dysfunctions grow out of relationships and affect relationships, so they must be considered in context. Information should be gathered on the couple's interpersonal and sexual relationship to determine whether any difficulties in their interaction have a bearing on the sexual dysfunction. Data should be gathered from the partners while they are together and while they are apart, because they will often have discrepant perceptions of their sexual relationship. In most cases, some couples therapy is helpful, focusing on communication (both verbal and nonverbal), expectations, assertiveness, and sexual desires and behaviors.

Many people develop or exacerbate sexual dysfunctions because of what Masters and Johnson refer to as "spectatoring"—the process of watching and monitoring their own sexual performance as well as their partners' responses during sexual relations. Typically, the tension and anxiety associated with this self-monitoring prevent relaxation and comfortable involvement in sexual behaviors, worsening the sexual dysfunction and leading to a vicious cycle in which the sexual dysfunction promotes spectatoring, which in turn increases the severity of the sexual dysfunction.

The first step in the behavioral treatment of a sexual dysfunction, then, is reduction of spectatoring and its accompanying anxiety. To accomplish this step, the couple may be taught nonthreatening relaxation techniques (such as progressive relaxation or nonsexual massage) and may be asked to refrain temporarily from overt sexual activity. Increasing the focus on pleasure can help people gradually resume a more rewarding sexual relationship and apply specific techniques, taught in therapy, that can improve sexual functioning.

Sensate focusing is a common technique used early in treatment although some studies indicate that focusing on specific techniques like sensate focusing can actually increase performance anxiety and have opposite of the intended effect. Sensate focusing is designed to help the couple enjoy closeness and intimacy without intercourse, in order to reduce pressure and demands. Other specific techniques that may play a role in the treatment of sexual dysfunction include systematic desensitization, masturbation for women with inhibited orgasm, bridging (making the transition from masturbation or manual stimulation to intercourse), the squeeze technique (to teach control for men with premature ejaculation), and imagery and fantasy to enhance sexual arousal.

Wiegel and colleagues (2002) suggest helping clients create a broader goal of creating pleasurable sexual experiences with their partner, rather than just restoring functioning. Medications can be used to enhance pleasure-focused therapy, but should not be the sole treatment. Effective therapy for sexual dysfunctions should include the following:

- Sensate focus: experiential/sensory awareness exercises.
- Stimulus control and scheduling.
- Cognitive restructuring, to increase flexibility in attitudes and promote commitment to change.
- Communication skills training to address interpersonal concerns as well as promote education on healthy sexuality.

Five factors have been found to improve therapeutic outcomes: quality of the couple's relationship, motivation (particularly of male partner) for treatment, absence of severe mental disorders, physical attraction between partners, and early compliance with assigned homework.

Therapy for sexual dysfunctions tends to be relatively brief, although a history of sexual trauma, medical conditions, and medication may necessitate longer treatment. Masters and Johnson often conducted their therapy sessions on an intensive daily basis, but weekly therapy has been shown to be equally effective (Segraves & Althof, 2002).

Vaginismus, in which anxiety and fear result in avoidant behavior, has been treated with exposure therapy and case studies seem promising. Exposure therapy includes psychoeducation, relaxation exercises, gradual exposure, cognitive training focused on changing dysfunctional beliefs about sex in general and penetration in particular, and sensate focused exercises and physical therapy (ter Kuile et al., 2009; Rosenbaum, 2007). For orgasmic disorder, medication can help create or delay orgasm but cannot resolve problems within the relationship. Couples or individual psychotherapy is necessary (Althof, 2007).

Group Therapy. Some sexual dysfunctions also seem to benefit from group therapy that is designed to provide support as well as education, role models, and reduction of guilt and anxiety. Group treatment was found to decrease cost, increase motivation, normalize problems, and provide peer support and comfort in discussing private sexual problems (Segraves & Althof, 2002). The downside to group therapy for sexual dysfunctions is the limitation on providing extensive individual attention to specific problems.

Therapy groups have been used for women with orgasmic disorders and for men with erectile disorders. Groups for couples have also been used successfully. Minimal differences in treatment effectiveness for groups versus individual treatment have been found (Segraves & Althof, 2002).

Medication. Medication is generally the first-line treatment for male erectile dysfunction but has not been found to ameliorate female sexual dysfunction (Ashton, 2007). FDA approval of sildenafil citrate (Viagra) in 1998 revolutionized the treatment of male erectile dysfunction. Similar medications, tadalafil (Cialis) and vardenafil (Levitra), were approved by the FDA in 2003. All three have been proved to be effective in treating erectile dysfunction. Penile implants, transurethral or vacuum therapy, and intracavernosal injection therapy are other medical treatments that are viable options for men who, for health reasons, cannot take sildenafil citrate, tadalafil, or vardenafil for problems of erectile dysfunction.

Since 2002, when a large clinical trial revealed the health risks of hormone replacement therapy for women, long-term hormone therapy is no longer routinely recommended for menopausal symptoms, but some women use it for short-term relief. Localized estrogen therapy is also available in the form of a vaginal ring, cream, or tablet. Testosterone deficiency may contribute to hypoactive sexual desire disorder, especially in women who have experienced menopause post-surgery. One study showed greater sexual satisfaction in women receiving testosterone versus placebo. Additional safety trials are needed (Kingsberg, Simon, & Goldstein, 2008). Both men and women may recieve testosterone replacement therapy, although testosterone supplementation therapy for women has not been approved by the FDA.

One study indicated that bupropion (Wellbutrin) can be effective in increasing female libido. Most people with sexual dysfunctions will be referred for a medical examination, and in those cases where medication seems likely to enhance treatment, the possibility can be raised when the referral is made. Alternative treatments such as yoga, herbal supplements, and relaxation techniques may help improve sexual functioning in women. Mindfulness and acupuncture also show promise. Among these, only yoga has been empirically examined and found effective for use with men suffering from premature ejaculation (Brotto, Krychman, & Jacobson, 2008).

Therapists also need to be aware of co-occurring disorders that impact a client's sexual functioning. For example, people with binge eating disorder also report decreased sexual functioning, which is associated with concerns about their body shape (Castellini et al., 2010). The therapist needs to determine the best combination of interventions for treating a person who has both a sexual dysfunction and another mental disorder or emotional difficulty.

Prognosis Prognosis is particularly good for treatment of vaginismus but fair to poor for treatment of sexual desire disorders. Approximately half of all sexual dysfunctions show improvement in response to treatment, but these gains tend not to be fully maintained. Fifty percent to 70% of men and women with sexual desire disorders achieved modest gains following psychotherapy. Those gains were not maintained at 3-year follow-up; however, those who had received treatment reported that they had improved their level of satisfaction with their relationship despite their lack of desire (Segraves & Althof, 2002).

All studies with long-term follow-up showed a high incidence of relapses. Better treatment gains are related to improvements in the quality of the relationship between partners. Therapists working with people who have sexual dysfunctions should communicate realistic expectations (improvement rather than cure; likelihood of setbacks) and should plan for follow-up visits and relapse prevention. New epidemiological studies on women's sexual dysfunction have increased in recent years and recommendations have been made to the committees overseeing the *DSM-5*. More information is needed on the etiology, assessment, and treatment of these disorders. Problems related to sexual functioning involve a complicated integration of biological, social, relational, and psychological events. Differing patterns of dysfunction across age, gender, and demographic groups make it clear that further research is needed (Brotto et al., 2008). Effective interventions will require an appreciation of the complexity of these influences (Segraves & Althof, 2002).

Paraphilias

The *DSM-IV-TR* describes the essential features of a paraphilia as "recurrent, intense, sexually arousing fantasies, sexual urges, or behaviors generally involving (1) nonhuman objects, (2) the suffering or humiliation of oneself or one's partner, or (3) children or other nonconsenting persons" (American Psychiatric Association, 2000, p. 566). These urges or behaviors persist for at least six months and typically lead to impairment in social and sexual relationships and in other important areas of functioning, as well as to considerable distress. The *DSM-IV-TR*'s extensive list includes the following paraphilias:

- Exhibitionism (exposing one's genitals to an unsuspecting stranger).
- Fetishism (sexual activity focused on objects).
- Frotteurism (touching and rubbing against others without their consent).
- Pedophilia (sexual activity with children).

- Sexual masochism (enjoyment of humiliation or suffering during sexual activity).
- Sexual sadism (deriving pleasure from causing others to suffer).
- Transvestic fetishism (cross-dressing).
- Voyeurism (covert observation of people who are disrobed or engaged in sexual activity).
- Paraphilia not otherwise specified, including such behaviors as telephone scatologia (lewd telephone calls), necrophilia (sexual interest in corpses), partialism (a focus on part of the body, such as feet), zoophilia (sexual behavior involving animals), coprophilia (sexual behavior involving feces), klismaphilia (sexual behavior involving enemas), and urophilia (sexual behavior involving urine).

Specific criteria are provided in the *DSM-IV-TR* for each of the paraphilias, but discussion of these criteria is beyond the scope of this book. Here, the paraphilias will be considered as an entire class of disorders.

Description of the Disorders   Paraphilias are believed to be more prevalent than the statistics would indicate, largely because only a small percentage of people with these disorders seek help. In general, people with paraphilias do not see themselves as having emotional disorders and tend not to seek treatment on their own initiative; rather, they come into treatment at the urging of a friend or family member (usually the spouse or partner) or because actions associated with their paraphilia have led to their arrest.

People with paraphilias typically commit large numbers of paraphilic acts and, by the time they are identified, may have committed hundreds of sexual offenses, leaving many victims (Seligman & Hardenburg, 2000). These patterns have led to difficulty in estimating the prevalence of these disorders.

People with paraphilias come from all ethnic and socioeconomic backgrounds. Their sexual orientation may be heterosexual, homosexual, or bisexual.

Paraphilias vary widely in terms of severity. Many disorders of a hypersexual nature lie below the diagnostic line and cannot be classified as a true paraphilia. Such "paraphilia-related disorders" as termed by Kafka (2007, p. 446) may include compulsive masturbation, telephone sex, dependence on pornography, cybersex, and protracted promiscuity, among others. Such behaviors may co-occur with other sexual disorders, or with other Axis I disorders, particularly substance abuse, anxiety or mood disorders, and disorders of impulse control. Paraphilia-related disorders should be accurately identified, assessed, and diagnosed, as they may contribute to partner relationship problems, other sexual-related disorders, and confound or prolong treatment of co-occurring Axis I disorders (Kafka, 2007).

Mild versions of paraphilias may include only disturbing fantasies, perhaps accompanied by masturbation (Seligman & Hardenburg, 2000). The person's ability to control the thoughts, urges, and behavior, and whether the activity or fantasy is required for sexual arousal to occur, are two ways in which severity can be determined. Severe cases of paraphilia may involve the use of threats or force, injury to others, victimization of children, or even murder.

For example, one client, a successful 32-year-old lawyer, had rewarding intimate relationships with women but fantasized a great deal about causing women to suffer. He bought pornographic magazines with sadistic themes and enjoyed films in which women were injured, raped, or killed. He had never hurt a woman, but he sought therapy because he was afraid he would lose control of his fantasies and would injure someone. This client had a mild paraphilia.

By contrast, another client, an accountant, had a severe paraphilia: pedophilia. His only sexual experiences had been with young boys. He had been arrested three times and had received treatment while in prison. Although he, like the other client, also had a professional career, he had lost his job because of his imprisonment, and he feared that his prison record would prevent him from locating future employment in his field.

Expression of paraphilic impulses often follows a cycle that is also common in other disorders of impulse control. Tension builds in the person until it is relieved by a paraphilic act; guilt and regret ensue, with the person often promising a change in behavior. In time, however, tension builds up again, and it is once again released through the undesirable behavior. People with paraphilias may develop a tolerance for their behaviors and require increased frequency or intensity to satisfy their cravings.

Some believe paraphilias may have a biological cause (Kafka, 2007). Paraphilias often develop in adolescence and early adulthood, peaking between ages 20 and 30 and then remitting in later adulthood (Allen & Hollander, 2006). The most common paraphilias are pedophilia, exhibitionism, and voyeurism (American Psychiatric Association, 2000). Paraphilias are seen less often in females; sexual masochism and sexual sadism, for example, are estimated to be found at a 20:1 ratio in males compared to females (Allen & Hollander, 2006). The diagnosis of two or more paraphilias in one person is not unusual.

Typical Client Characteristics Although about half of all people with paraphilias are married, most have some impairment in their capacity for intimate relationships (American Psychiatric Association, 2000). Their sexual activities tend to be ritualized and unspontaneous.

Most experience some distress and anxiety connected to their disorder, as well as interpersonal difficulties and social rejection. Kafka and Hennen (2002) found that the typical person in outpatient therapy for paraphilia is a 37-year-old, middle-class, White male with some college education and a job. Many of these men had been abused as children (30%); had problems in school (41%); and had been in a psychiatric hospital (25%). Paraphilias sometimes can be directly attributed to childhood sexual or physical abuse.

Pedophilia, often taking the form of incest, is one of the most common paraphilias treated by psychotherapists. Men who are attracted to young girls typically have marital difficulties, are anxious and immature, and have problems with impulse control. Men who molest young boys tend to avoid any adult sexual experiences and are attracted only to children. Their paraphilia is especially likely to be chronic.

The most commonly co-occurring disorders in people with paraphilias are depressive disorders, substance use disorders, ADHD, social phobia, and other anxiety disorders (Allen & Hollander, 2006). Other impulse-control disorders, OCD, and reckless driving are also found more frequently in people with paraphilias than in the average population.

Assessment Because of the range of presentations of paraphilias, therapists should conduct a careful assessment to determine the nature and severity of the disorder, other areas of concern, and strengths of the person with a paraphilia. Questions concerning the nature, onset, duration, frequency, and progression of symptoms are important, as is a detailed outline of any arrests, presentence reports, or information from probation or parole officers, as many people with paraphilias have arrest records (Seligman & Hardenburg, 2000). Co-occurring disorders, especially substance-related disorders, other impulse-control disorders, personality disorders, ADHD, and mood and anxiety disorders, should be assessed prior to developing an effective treatment plan (Kafka, 2007).

Preferred Therapist Characteristics Therapists will have to deal with the reluctance of many people diagnosed with paraphilias to engage in treatment. People with paraphilias, like those with drug and alcohol problems, generally enjoy the behaviors involved in their disorder. Typically the negative consequences rather than the behaviors themselves lead people with paraphilias to accept treatment. As a result, they may be ambivalent toward or resistant to treatment and, especially if their treatment is court ordered, may be guarded and suspicious. Thus, it may be difficult to establish a positive therapeutic relationship with these clients.

Some therapists find that they have strong countertransference reactions to people with paraphilias, particularly paraphilias that involve children. One of the challenges for therapists is to manage their own feelings so that these do not undermine the therapeutic relationship and increase clients' guilt and distress.

Therapists should be aware that many paraphilia-like behaviors are often found in people experiencing psychosis, mania, and substance use disorders. People diagnosed with mental retardation, antisocial personality disorder, and dementia may also engage in unusual sexual behaviors. Behaviors in these cases, and in situations in which symptoms begin in adulthood, are infrequent, and are ego-dystonic. Consequently, a diagnosis of paraphilia may not be appropriate.

Intervention Strategies Psychodynamic or insight-oriented treatment has been shown to be ineffective in treating paraphilias. And cognitive-behavioral therapy has limited

effectiveness with these treatment-resistant disorders. Although treatments for specific paraphilias vary to some extent, the therapeutic principles and strategies used to modify erotic responses and associated behaviors are generally the same for all paraphilias and typically include:

- Identification of triggers and substitution of alternative responses and behaviors.
- Stress reduction.
- Aversion therapy that pairs paraphilic urges and fantasies with negative experiences, such as undesirable images, electric shocks, or noxious odors.
- Covert sensitization, which uses negative images (such as images of imprisonment or humiliation) to discourage paraphilic behavior.
- Covert extinction, in which the paraphilic behavior is imagined, but without the anticipated reinforcement or positive feeling.
- Orgasmic reconditioning.
- Thought stopping.
- Cognitive restructuring.
- Encouragement of empathy for the victim.
- Overall improvement of coping skills and lifestyle.

Some people with paraphilias engage in sexual activities with children, animals, or objects because they are afraid of rejection if they seek sexual relationships with adults. Improvement of social and assertiveness skills and education about sexuality can encourage people to engage in sexual activities involving peers. Increasing awareness of the effect of one's behaviors on the victims, promoting empathy for the victims through role playing, and exposure to victims' experiences can also be effective in promoting healthier interpersonal behaviors and responses (Allen & Hollander, 2006; Maletzky, 2002).

Antiandrogenic medication, such as medroxyprogesterone acetate (Depo-Provera), which lowers testosterone, has also been used, particularly in the treatment of people who are sexually attracted to children and who are hypersexual. This medication reduces sexual urges and behavior by reducing testosterone levels. To date, there have been no large controlled trials of such medication, but case reports indicate that antiandrogenic medication is effective in reducing sexual fantasies, thoughts, and behavior, and reducing recidivism in sex offenders (Allen & Hollander, 2006). Surgical interventions, including brain surgery and removal of the testes, have also been used, but their use is still experimental, as well as controversial. Of course, these interventions are only used with the consent of the person diagnosed with a paraphilia.

Selective serotonin reuptake inhibitors (SSRIs) may also be prescribed for paraphilias. SSRIs have been shown to be effective largely due to their antiobsessional effects on thoughts and behavior (Laws & O'Donohue, 2008). Given that depression and anxiety frequently occur along with paraphilias, SSRIs may be effective in enhancing treatment of both a paraphilia and a comorbid disorder.

Group therapy can be an appropriate vehicle for treating paraphilias if it is individualized to address issues specific to each person. Individual sessions should supplement group work and consider the unique set of biological, social, historical, and familial variables that contribute to each person's behavior (LaSasso, 2008). People with paraphilias can help one another modify their behaviors, learn and practice better interpersonal skills, and prevent relapse. As with other disorders of impulse control, people with what are often called *sexual addictions* can benefit from participation in 12-step programs modeled after Alcoholics Anonymous, such as Sex Addicts Anonymous, Sexual Compulsives Anonymous, and Sex and Love Addicts. Family therapy also can be helpful, especially if the paraphilic behaviors have damaged current family relationships or if sexual abuse has occurred in the family of origin.

An important component of any treatment program for paraphilia is the inclusion of relapse prevention techniques. Individual cognitive-behavioral treatment with an emphasis on harm reduction that focuses on the replacement of criminal sexual behavior with more healthy and legal behaviors seems most appropriate (Marshall, Fernandez, & Serran, 2006).

Prognosis   Paraphilias tend to be treatment resistant, and behaviors tend to increase when the person is under stress. Relapses are also common, so short-term improvement does not provide any assurance of continuing change (Allen & Hollander, 2006; Maletzky, 2002). Long-term treatment and supervision may be needed for these clients. The prognosis seems better for people with good ego strength and flexibility, intrinsic motivation for treatment, and normal adult sexual experiences. The prognosis is worse for people with coexisting mental disorders, early onset and high frequency of paraphilic behaviors, substance misuse, and lack of remorse for their behavior (Seligman & Hardenburg, 2000).

Gender Identity Disorder

Information in this section is based on the current edition of the *DSM-IV-TR* and the majority of the professional literature on gender identity disorder (GID). Readers should keep in mind that GID is a controversial diagnosis and many people believe that GID should not be categorized as a mental disorder. At some point in the future, GID, like homosexuality, may be removed from the *DSM* and be viewed as simply an uncommon but not unhealthy pattern.

Description of the Disorder   Gender identity disorder (GID), according to the *DSM-IV-TR*, is characterized by a strong and enduring cross-gender identification, along with discomfort about one's assigned gender. These symptoms are not due to a physical condition. They are of sufficient severity to cause considerable distress or impairment in functioning. The age of the client determines whether the diagnosis is gender identity disorder in children or gender identity disorder in adolescents or adults.

Two theories have been advanced to explain GID, also known as gender *dysphoria*, *transsexualism*, or being *transgendered*. Some believe GID has a biological basis that has not yet been identified; others view GID as a conditioned response. Each of these theories may explain the disorder in some people.

No biological marker has been found for GID at present. However, evidence exists that certain behavioral traits linked to biological processes may be involved. For example, there is evidence that prenatal hormonal variations can affect masculine or feminine behavior. Two case studies of monozygotic twins in which gender differences emerged early on in one child but not the other, seem to endorse the hormonal variations hypothesis (Segal, 2006). Continued research on this topic will undoubtedly reveal additional relationships among genetic, prenatal, perinatal, and sociological factors in the development of GID.

GID is relatively rare. Carroll (2007) reports two studies in the Netherlands and Scotland that show a consistent prevalence of 1 in every 11,000 males and 1 female out of 30,000. Internalizing disorders (anxiety and depression) commonly co-occur with GID. What remains to be determined is whether these feelings contribute to or result from gender dysphoria.

Typical Client Characteristics   People with GID typically prefer activities, occupations, and dress associated with the gender other than their biologically assigned gender. The age of onset of cross-gender behaviors in children with GID is typically during the preschool years. Children with GID often prefer playmates of the opposite sex, and in fantasy play will often take on the role of the other gender. In conjunction with the child's expressed dislike of his or her biological gender and sexual anatomy, these characteristics point to the child's strong cross-gender identification.

Gender identity and gender role are typically viewed as developing before the emergence of sexual orientation. Most people with GID do not view themselves as homosexual. Transgendered people may be heterosexual, homosexual, bisexual, or asexual, just like the rest of the population (Langer & Martin, 2004).

Carroll (2007) notes that gender dysphoria is much more common in children than in adults. Basically, people with GID do not show a greater tendency toward psychopathology than the population at large. In fact, they are generally otherwise emotionally healthy people who have the strong belief that they are in the wrong-gendered body.

Considerable social and occupational impairment is associated with GID, at least in part because of societal attitudes and reactions. Egan and Perry (2001) report that the greatest problem for adolescents with GID is the effect of peer pressure for gender conformity and the message they receive that they must avoid cross-gender-type behavior or activities. Peer pressure to conform bears a direct negative relationship to self-esteem, peer relationships, and self-efficacy. Social pressure to behave heterosexually begins in elementary school. This pressure appears to be more intense for boys, whereas nonconforming gender behavior among girls is more socially acceptable (Langer & Martin, 2004). Internalizing behaviors, such as depression, anxiety, and social withdrawal, are sometimes presented by people with this disorder (especially by boys). Adolescents often manifest adjustment, self-esteem, and peer relationship difficulties, along with acting-out behavior.

People with GID are more likely to present for treatment because of these associated symptoms than because of their gender discomfort. They also may seek psychotherapy as a condition of being accepted for sex-reassignment surgery.

Assessment   Gender identity is a fluid concept that encompasses four dimensions: social role, gender identification, sexuality, and the body (Carroll, 2007). As with other disorders listed in the *DSM-IV-TR* (American Psychiatric Association, 2000), GID is only a disorder if it causes distress in one or more areas of functioning. Following a medical evaluation, a psychological assessment for gender dysphoria will be similar to other comprehensive psychological assessments, with the additional focus on a complete sexual and gender history. For a more in-depth look at assessing GID, refer to Carroll (2007).

Preferred Therapist Characteristics   Research has shown that therapists' comfort levels and attitudes can affect the client's disclosure of sexual issues and the appropriate handling of sexual topics. Therapists who are not familiar with or not comfortable working with transgendered people should refer them to a qualified therapist with experience in this area.

People with GID typically focus on making the body correspond to the self-image they have in their brains rather than the reverse. They typically are not interested in changing their feelings about their gender. An emphasis on relieving any depression and anxiety and exploring options is usually more successful than focusing treatment on changing the gender dysphoria.

Treatment may be complicated if clients have come as a requirement for gender-reassignment surgery. In this case, therapists may find themselves in the role of "gatekeeper" (Carroll, 2007, p. 505), in determining readiness and referral of transgendered clients for hormones, surgery, or other medical treatment. Therapists need to be aware of and deal with their own countertransference reactions and any discomfort they may have with these clients and with the surgery clients may be seeking. Whether therapists agree with their client's choices, they must respect that the decision of how to resolve gender dysphoria lies within the client.

Intervention Strategies   Treatment for children with GID is controversial. Some suggest early intervention in the hopes of changing GID behavior. However, others believe that gender identification is determined by the age of 2 or 3 and has an underlying biological component, so, rather than focusing on the gender issues, therapists should focus on treating the symptoms of depression, anxiety, impaired self-esteem, and social discomfort that frequently result from social ostracism and inappropriate peer relationships.

Children with GID are often brought to therapy to help them with their unhappiness about their biological gender and to work on relationships with family and peers. It seems prudent to focus on alleviating children's current distress rather than on problems the children may encounter in adulthood. Involving children in activities that are not strongly associated with either gender, such as board games, can offer them new and rewarding social opportunities that will not elicit ridicule. Play therapy can be a useful vehicle for introducing children to new activities and role models. The intensity of discomfort with his or her gender varies from person to person, and many children who manifest symptoms of GID in childhood have a lessening of those symptoms with age. For others, however, the development of secondary sex characteristics such as breasts or facial hair during adolescence is a physical reminder of their gender-related unhappiness and leads to a worsening of symptoms.

It is unclear how frequently gender dysphoria continues into adolescence and adulthood. Green (1987) conducted a longitudinal study of 66 boys who had received treatment for gender dysphoria in childhood. Only one of the boys continued to express the same feelings in adulthood; however, 75% of the boys had developed a clear preference for homosexuality, leading later researchers to conclude that there may be a link between early cross-gender behavior and homosexuality.

If gender dysphoria persists into adolescence and adulthood, the likelihood of changing gender-related attitudes and identifications is low. Therefore, goals should focus on choosing ways to improve adjustment and life satisfaction. Setting realistic goals is essential to the effective treatment of GID. Promoting adjustment or helping people make decisions about biological treatment are usually more viable goals than eliminating the symptoms of GID. In making choices, people should be encouraged to reflect not only on their own preferences but also on the reactions of family members, colleagues, friends, and society at large, and on the clients' own responses to those reactions.

Lifestyle and relationship changes, which may involve clients' living in their preferred gender roles, are one avenue to improved adjustment and satisfaction. Other avenues include hormone therapy and gender-reassignment surgery. In hormone therapy, biological males take estrogen, and biological females take testosterone. These hormones not only effect physiological changes that are gratifying to some people with GID but also improve their sense of well-being. Gender reassignment is a controversial, complex, and multifaceted process that involves hormone treatments, trial cross-gender living, and eventual surgery. Only a small percentage of people with GID pursue this treatment option. Standards of care guidelines that require consultation between mental health professionals and medical professions prior to gender reassignment surgery have been developed by the Harry Benjamin International Gender Dysphoria Association (HBIGDA, 2001). The guidelines can be followed by practitioners to outline the process of assessment and treatment for GID (Carroll, 2007).

Prognosis Few controlled studies have been conducted on the treatment of GID. Not all transgendered adolescents have gender dysphoria or seek sex reassignment. In a longitudinal study of adolescent girls with GID, approximately 50% developed a homosexual orientation, and 35% to 45% persisted in their desire to become the opposite sex. It is not known how many eventually had sex reassignment surgery (Butcher, Mineka, & Hooley, 2006). More research, including longitudinal studies, clearly is needed in this important area.

Some outcome research has focused on the results of gender-reassignment surgery. Many express satisfaction with the results of the surgery, reduced levels of depression and anxiety, and no problems in their new gender (Oltmanns & Emery, 2007). However, some continue to have significant problems of adjustment, and 2% of those who undergo this surgery commit suicide. The likelihood of a negative treatment outcome is greatest in people who have coexisting psychological disorders such as severe depression or personality disorders.

IMPULSE-CONTROL DISORDERS NOT ELSEWHERE CLASSIFIED

Substance-related disorders, eating disorders, and paraphilias have already been discussed in this chapter. The remaining impulse-control disorders listed in the *DSM-IV-TR* are included in the present section. This group of disorders includes the following:

- Intermittent explosive disorder
- Kleptomania
- Pyromania
- Pathological gambling
- Trichotillomania

Description of the Disorders

All impulse-control disorders are characterized by repeated failure to resist an impulse to perform a behavior that is harmful. These disorders typically are characterized by increasing tension or arousal before the harmful behavior is performed, and by feelings of release or pleasure after the act has been completed. Although it may be followed by feelings of guilt and remorse, the behavior itself is usually ego-syntonic.

Although the behaviors associated with the disorders in this section vary considerably, most are found in adolescents and adults and result in significant morbidity and mortality (Grant & Portenza, 2007). Most impulse-control disorders follow a chronic course, but may be episodic and get worse under stress. These disorders are also strongly associated with comorbid diagnoses of OCD, substance-related disorders, and mood disorders (Hollander & Stein, 2006).

Some believe that impulse-control disorders have a common underlying dynamic or cause. Possible explanations for these disorders include a biological cause (neurological predisposition) combined with psychosocial causes (such as dysfunctional role models), exacerbated by environmental stress (Hollander, Baker, Kahn, & Stein, 2006). All these possibilities should be considered in seeking to understand a particular person's impulsive behavior.

Intermittent Explosive Disorder
According to the *DSM-IV-TR*, this disorder involves "discrete episodes of failure to resist aggressive impulses that result in serious assaultive acts or destruction of property" (American Psychiatric Association, 2000, p. 663). The symptoms are not caused by another mental disorder, a medical condition, or drug or alcohol use, although use of disinhibiting substances such as alcohol often accompany the aggressive episodes.

Intermittent explosive disorder may affect as many as 6.3% of the population and is believed to be more common in males than in females, although one study found the ratio of males to females to be 1:1 (Coccaro, Posternak, & Zimmerman, 2005; Coccaro & Danehy, 2006). Mean age of onset of this disorder is 16 years of age; it tends to peak in early adulthood and then abates in midlife. Intermittent explosive disorder is also found in as many as one third of first-degree relatives of people with this disorder (Coccaro & Danehy, 2006).

An episode of intermittent explosive disorder tends to occur rapidly, lasts less than 30 minutes, and frequently involves property destruction and verbal or physical assault (Coccaro & Danehy, 2006). Provocation, if any, seems to be minor and is frequently from a person familiar to the person with the disorder.

Forty-four percent of people with intermittent explosive disorder also have other impulse-control disorders (McElroy, Soutullo, Beckman, Taylor, & Keck, 1998). Mood disorders, including bipolar and cyclothymic disorders; anxiety; and substance use are also common in this population. Clinicians should be particularly careful to differentiate between intermittent explosive disorder and bipolar disorder, which may have similar symptoms; the two disorders call for different treatments. As with most of the impulse-control disorders, intermittent explosive disorder appears to have a neurological basis and is often triggered by a stressful life event. People with this disorder often have a history of job loss, relationship conflict, legal difficulties, and injuries resulting from fights or accidents. They may be self-destructive as well as harmful to others and may experience suicidal ideation. A history of reckless behavior often is also present.

Kleptomania A dramatic increase in the amount of research on kleptomania has occurred in the past decade. This disorder is characterized by unplanned, solitary, recurrent theft of unneeded objects. The person's goal is the act of stealing, not the objects that are taken.

Although rare, kleptomania is fairly common in psychiatric in-patients. More than 60% of persons with kleptomania are women. Kleptomania is distinguished from shoplifting because the goal is relief from symptoms rather than monetary gain (Grant, 2006). The disorder often begins in late adolescence, and the mean age at the time of evaluation is mid to late 30s for women, and in middle age for men. It is often diagnosed in middle-aged women who are mildly depressed and experiencing interpersonal losses and who feel a sense of injustice and deprivation in their lives (Grant, 2006). Anxiety, shame, and guilt are common in people with kleptomania, with nearly 100% reporting they have had depression at one point in their lives. One theory holds that the person with kleptomania is trying to relieve negative affect and depression by participating in high-risk behaviors such as shoplifting (Grant, 2006). Some report pleasure and tension in the beginning of this disorder, which can become a habit as the behaviors become routine.

Many persons with kleptomania have concomitant eating disorders (especially bulimia nervosa), OCD, mood disorders, substance-related disorders, and personality disorders—especially paranoid and histrionic personality disorder. Other impulse-control disorders are also common. Thirty-two percent have attempted suicide. There is also a high rate of extroversion and of hoarding behavior among people who have kleptomania (Grant & Kim, 2002).

Kleptomania is distinguished from shoplifting because the person does not take the items for monetary value or out of anger or vengeance, but due to an inability to resist the impulse to steal (Blanco et al., 2008). Shoplifting, especially among adolescents and young adults, is common, with a lifetime prevalence rate of 11.2%. However, fewer than 5% of people who shoplift can accurately be diagnosed as having kleptomania. Conduct disorder or antisocial personality disorder are more common diagnoses for people who frequently steal. Most people with this disorder report waiting 10 years before seeking treatment, largely due to embarrassment and shame (Grant, 2006). Some enter treatment only because of a court order or arrest. More research on etiology and treatment interventions is needed on this debilitating disorder.

Pyromania This disorder describes a small percentage of people who engage in the harmful setting of fires, specifically those who repeatedly set fires for the purposes of pleasure and tension relief rather than for financial gain or revenge. People with this disorder not only set fires but have an interest in anything associated with fires. They set off false fire alarms and associate themselves with fire departments, sometimes becoming firefighters themselves.

Fire setting, which usually begins in childhood, accounted for 65 thousand fires in the United States in 1997, and juvenile fire setting accounts for 55% of all arson arrests (Hardesty & Gayton, 2002). Separate from pyromania, childhood fire setting is most often associated with conduct disorder, ADHD, or adjustment disorder (Lejoyeux, McLoughlin, & Ades, 2006). Adolescents who set fires were found to lack parental monitoring, to have suicidal ideation, and to be aggressive but also shy and rejected by their peers (Lindberg, Holi, Tani, & Virkkunen,

2005; MacKay, Paglia-Boak, Henderson, Marton, & Adlaf, 2009).

Fire-setting recidivism rates vary widely in the literature, ranging from 4% to 60%. Those with co-occurring substance use disorders, personality disorders, mental retardation, or psychosis were most likely to repeat fire-setting behaviors. Although 27% of adolescents report having set at least one fire, most fire setting is not related to pyromania. Ritchie and Huff (1999) found only 3 cases of pyromania in 283 cases of arson. The incidence of pyromania is rare.

Elliott (2002) divides people who set fires into four groups that can be labeled curious, crisis, delinquent, and pathological. It is only the fourth category in which the multiple fire setting reflects pyromania. These people set fires to fulfill a need and reduce tension. Their involvement with fire can provide a sense of power and social prestige.

Pyromania can occur at any age, from childhood through adulthood. Lejoyeux and colleagues (2006) report that the average age of people diagnosed with pyromania is 20. Pyromania is often associated with a dysfunctional family background (especially characterized by an absent father and misuse of alcohol), poor social skills, interpersonal difficulties, low self-esteem, alcohol intoxication, enuresis, sexual dysfunction, depression, antisocial behaviors, cruelty to animals, and a history of childhood mental disorders (such as ADHD, conduct disorder, learning disorders, and mild mental retardation). Fifty-four percent of people with pyromania can be diagnosed with alcohol dependence.

Behavior therapy should direct people with pyromania away from their interest in seeing fires and replace these behaviors with more socially acceptable forms of tension reduction and ways of meeting their needs for power, self-esteem, and belonging. Co-occurring disorders, such as mental retardation, psychosis, and alcohol abuse and dependence, must be addressed if treatment is to be effective.

Pathological Gambling   The primary feature of this disorder is persistent preoccupation with self-destructive gambling. This relatively common disorder is found in 2.5 million adults, with an additional 5.3 million at risk for developing the disorder (Ladd & Petry, 2003). Nearly 40% of people who seek treatment for problems with gambling are women (Ladd & Petry, 2003; Stinchfield & Winters, 2001). They tend to be depressed, and frequently use gambling to reduce negative affect and dissociate from their problems (Pallanti, Rossi, & Hollander, 2006). Gambling affects 3% of the population and usually begins in adolescence for males but later for females.

Pathological gambling is sometimes accompanied by other mental disorders, notably substance-related disorders, ADHD, other impulse-control disorders, anxiety disorders, mood disorders (especially bipolar disorder), and personality disorders (Kessler et al., 2008; Pallanti et al., 2006). More than half of people who engage in pathological gambling have been diagnosed with an alcohol or substance use disorder. Several studies have also noted greater incidence of hostility, obsessive-compulsive traits, and paranoia in people who both gamble and misuse substances (Ladd & Petry, 2003; Ledgerwood, Steinberg, Wu, & Potenza, 2005; Petry, 2000).

Seventy-one percent of people who engage in pathological gambling reported experiencing depression at some time in their lives, and 20% to 40% reported they had attempted suicide. The severity of the gambling problem, younger age of onset, criminal activity related to gambling, and impulse-control disorders of family members were correlated with increased suicide risk. Several studies note that the suicide rate in cities where gambling is legal is 4 times higher than in cities without legalized gambling (Ledgerwood et al., 2005; Pallanti et al., 2006).

Clearly, an important part of any treatment of pathological gambling will include assessment of suicide risk and the development of an appropriate safety plan.

Similar to those of people with other impulse-control disorders, characteristics of people who gamble include preoccupation with the harmful behavior, loss of control, tolerance, withdrawal-like symptoms, and cycles of abstinence and relapse (American Psychiatric Association, 2000; Ladd & Petry, 2003). People who gamble excessively also tend to be intelligent, overconfident, energetic, extroverted, competitive, restless, and prone to take risks (Pallanti et al., 2006). Gambling, compulsive eating, and alcohol misuse all involve a level of detachment, and Jacobs (1988) suggests that transient dissociative states are likely to occur during these types of addictive activities. Family, financial, occupational, and legal problems are common in people with pathological gambling, as is difficulty in sustaining intimate, emotionally expressive relationships (Ladd & Petry, 2003).

The families of origin of people with this disorder commonly manifest dysfunctional substance use, mood disorders, antisocial behavior, gambling, and an emphasis on material gain. Often people diagnosed with pathological gambling have as children experienced harsh and inappropriate discipline and significant losses. They are also more likely to have co-occurring depression or another mood disorder (Kennedy et al., 2010).

Pathological gambling typically has three phases (Butcher et al., 2006):

1. Introductory phase, during which winning promotes overconfidence and further involvement in gambling.
2. Losing, in which undue risks are taken and financial resources are depleted.
3. Desperation, in which gambling becomes frenzied and people borrow or embezzle large sums of money, write bad checks, and engage in other kinds of nonviolent criminal behavior.

These phases may extend over as many as 15 years. Chronicity is usually determined by the amount and frequency of the gambling behavior (Pallanti et al., 2006). Involvement in the 12-step program Gamblers Anonymous is a valuable adjunct to cognitive-behavioral therapy for people with this disorder because it can offer extensive involvement in self-help and emphasize the need for ongoing self-monitoring and use of coping skills

Trichotillomania   This disorder is characterized by recurrent plucking of hair from one's own head and body. Hair may be pulled out in clumps, or individually. The practice results in perceptible hair loss, usually from one location (most generally the scalp), but it is common to see the number of locations increase with age (Duke, Keeley, Geffken, & Storch, 2010). Mouthing or eating the hairs is a common feature of the disorder, this can result in the development of hairballs and may precipitate medical complications. Trichotillomania is more common in females and tends to be linked to negative affective states (depression, negative self-evaluation) and hypoarousal (boredom, fatigue, sedentary activities), which serve as cues for hair-pulling behavior (Franklin, Tolin, & Diefenbach, 2006). The hair pulling typically provides feelings of tension release and gratification and perhaps also of stimulation. This disorder typically begins within five years of puberty and often is chronic, although its severity changes, usually in response to changes in stressors. The actual numbers of people with trichotillomania is unknown as people with the disorder tend to be secretive. Many women hide their hair loss with scarves or wigs or claim that they have alopecia to distract friends and family members from recognizing they have a problem. Men are more likely to shave their heads which provides a socially acceptable way of hiding their disorder. A study of a sample of college students found that 3.4% of females and 1.5% of males had engaged in clinically significant hair pulling at some point in their lives (Christenson, Mackenzie, & Mitchell, 1991). Other physically self-damaging behavior is common in people with this disorder, as are substance use, mood, and anxiety disorders. Although trichotillomania is not often presented in treatment, it may be found in as many as 6 to 8 million people (3% to 15% of the population). People with trichotillomania often experience significant levels of distress and impairment in social functioning, including loss of intimacy, decreased contact with friends and family, and avoidance of leisure pursuits, such as athletics, swimming, and dating, in part due to embarrassment about their behavior and appearance (Franklin et al., 2006; Stemberger, Thomas, Mansueto, & Carter, 2003). Most people diagnosed with trichotillomania also have at least one concurrent mental disorder, most often mood or anxiety disorders, although substance-related disorders, OCD, eating disorders, and personality disorders (most often borderline personality disorder) are also common.

It is likely that there is a biological basis for the disorder. Trichotillomania is associated with increased rates of OCD in first-degree relatives (Bienvenu et al., 2000). To date, little empirical research is available on treatment interventions for this disorder, although preliminary findings indicate that CBT is the treatment of choice for adults and children with trichotillomania (Flessner et al., 2010; Franklin et al., 2006; Woods, Wetterneck, & Flessner, 2006).

Typical Client Characteristics

In addition to the information already provided about the common characteristics of people with these disorders, overall, impulse-control disorders are typically associated with other mental disorders, including PTSD, Cluster B (dramatic, emotional, or erratic) personality disorders, depressive disorders, anxiety disorders, eating disorders, and substance-related disorders. Suicidal ideation is common, especially among people with pathological gambling. Alcohol and benzodiazepines may be used to reduce self-control and allow people to act on destructive impulses. The impulsive behavior itself is typically used to relieve anxiety and depression.

Although some people with impulse-control disorders may not be severely troubled by their symptoms, others experience considerable shame, embarrassment, and guilt. They recognize that other people find their behaviors unacceptable, so they frequently take steps to conceal their actions. These disorders commonly have a negative impact on interpersonal relationships and occupational functioning and are associated with increased carelessness, morbidity, and mortality (Hollander et al., 2006). People with these disorders typically have limited, conflicted, or unrewarding patterns of socialization. Many also tend to be passive and have difficulty expressing their feelings. People with impulse-control disorders often share three key characteristics: failure to defer gratification, distractibility, and disinhibition or impulsiveness. A history of neglect and abuse is often seen in people with impulse-control disorders, as well as a family history of substance misuse, mood disorders, and anxiety.

Preferred Therapist Characteristics

Establishing a therapeutic alliance will be easier with some people with impulse-control disorders than with others, depending on the disorder. For example, people with kleptomania sometimes welcome the opportunity to obtain help with their underlying anger and depression and so are willing clients. However, people with paraphilias are typically reluctant to enter treatment because they do not want to give up their gratifying behaviors. People with these disorders may seek therapy only as a result of a court order or because of pressure from friends and family members. Stein et al. (2006) suggest that an initial period of negotiating the framework for the therapeutic relationship may be necessary when working with clients with impulse-control disorders. During this time, therapist and client build rapport, work together to establish boundaries, determine client responsibilities, set limits for the relationship, define a structure, and decide whether abstinence versus control will be the treatment goal.

People with impulse-control disorders tend to be defensive, to engage in denial and avoidance, and to resist taking responsibility for the consequences of their behavior. They may perceive others as forcing them to act as they have, and they may view themselves as blameless. In most cases their insight is limited, so engaging them in therapy is likely to present quite a challenge to therapists.

Therapists may view some of the behaviors of people with impulse-control disorders (such as fire setting, paraphilias, or physical abuse of their partners) as distasteful and reprehensible. Another challenge to therapists, then, is managing their own feelings about these clients' behaviors and remaining objective while communicating acceptance and support.

Intervention Strategies

Little research is available on the treatment of many of these impulse-control disorders, so treatment recommendations are tentative and based primarily on theory and on what has been effective in treating individual cases and similar disorders. Developing an appropriate treatment plan involves exploring the behavioral, cognitive, and affective components of the disorder, as well as the impact of the disorder on the person's lifestyle.

Behavioral techniques usually will form the core of treatment for people with impulse-control disorders. Such techniques as stress management, impulse control, distraction, relaxation training, systematic desensitization, contingency contracting, habit reversal training, and aversive conditioning commonly are used to discourage impulsive behavior. Overcorrection through public confession and restitution has been part of the treatment of these clients. People also need help in finding better ways to meet the needs that had been addressed by the impulsive behaviors.

Many other types of interventions can contribute to effective treatment of impulse-control disorders. Because these disorders typically worsen under stress, raising awareness of stressful triggers (such as anniversary dates and family visits) is important, as is an accompanying effort to assist in stress reduction. Reinforcement with praise and tangible rewards can also help modify dysfunctional behaviors and reduce stress. Assertiveness training and improvement of communication skills can help alleviate interpersonal difficulties and increase people's sense of control and power. If an impulsive behavior has reached addictive proportions, people may experience symptoms of withdrawal after its cessation. This withdrawal will also require attention so that a relapse can be prevented.

The specific choice of interventions depends on the nature of the disorder, of course. For example, relaxation training to promote anger management has been effective in treating people with problems involving angry driving (Deffenbacher, Filetti, Lynch, Dahlen, & Oetting, 2002). Improvements in anger and impulsivity scores have also been seen in people with borderline personality disorder as a result of dialectical behavior therapy (Linehan, 1993).

This could have implications for people with intermittent explosive disorder. DBT in combination with duloxetine (Cymbalta) showed promise in one case study for kleptomania (Rudel, Hubert, Juckel, & Edel, 2009).

In treatment of trichotillomania, cognitive-behavioral therapy has been shown to be superior to both medication and placebo in two studies. At present, and based on a limited number of studies, habit reversal training, awareness training, and stimulus control seem to form the core cognitive-behavioral intervention strategies for trichotillomania (Franklin et al., 2006). Although limited research is available, a recent article on treatment practices indicated CBT and medication are the standard treatments for both adults and children with trichotillomania (Flessner et al., 2010).

Treatment for pathological gambling generally follows the model developed to treat substance-related disorders. A meta-analytic review and look at 25 studies found that cognitive-behavioral therapy, motivational interviewing, and imaginal desensitization were effective treatments for pathological gambling (Gooding & Tarrier, 2009). Effect size was greatest at 3 months, but also was high at 6 and 12 months.

Other treatment interventions that might be added to CBT include inpatient treatment and rehabilitation programs, family therapy, psychoeducation, and participation in self-help groups. Medication may also be helpful in reducing gambling addiction. Separate studies, including one case report, show promise for lithium, the opioid agonist nalmefene, and disulfiram. Each of these medications reduced the study participant's desire to gamble and helped them gain control over their behavior (Hollander & Stein, 2006; Mutschler et al., 2010). Additional research is needed. People who engage in pathological gambling and other impulse-control disorders usually need help in coping with their high need for stimulation. Like most impulse-

control disorders, the negative behavior is inherently gratifying, so it reinforces itself and makes treatment difficult. It seems likely that the treatments most likely to succeed will be those that combine behavioral therapy with medication management.

Group therapy with other people who share the same problems can often reduce the attraction of an impulse by providing peer confrontation and support. This approach to treatment is particularly useful for people who engage in pathological gambling and for those who have been diagnosed with intermittent explosive disorder.

Gamblers Anonymous, modeled after Alcoholics Anonymous, offers an important avenue to peer support and is often helpful as an adjunct to therapy. However, Gamblers Anonymous has not been found to be helpful when used as the only form of treatment. Dropout rates have been shown to be as high as 70% within the first year, and one study indicated that only 8% remained abstinent at 1-year follow-up (Pallanti et al., 2006).

Many recovered gamblers have achieved recovery not by remaining abstinent, but by reducing gambling behavior and eliminating habits that were problematic (Slutske, Piasecki, Blaszczynski, & Martin, 2010). Slutske and colleagues predict the number of pathological gamblers seeking treatment would probably increase if a "warm turkey approach" (p. 2173) was available that allowed people to reduce their gambling rather than totally abstain. In one study, only 10% of participants achieved total abstinence from gambling after one year, even though most remained asymptomatic and no longer met the *DSM-IV-TR* criteria for pathological gambling. Some research indicates that most people who initially endorse a reduction in their gambling behavior eventually work toward a goal of abstinence (Ladouceur, Lachance, & Fournier, 2009).

Although no randomized controlled studies of treatment effectiveness for kleptomania exist, case reports indicate some success with behavior therapy that includes covert sensitization combined with exposure and response prevention for people diagnosed with this disorder. Grant (2006) describes several case reports in which people with kleptomania used covert sensitization to visualize negative consequences of their stealing behavior. For example, one woman who imagined increased nausea and eventual vomiting whenever she had the urge to steal had only one relapse in 19 months following four sessions of covert sensitization over an 8-week treatment period. Behavioral techniques, such as imaginal desensitization, learning to substitute alternative sources of satisfaction and excitement, and aversive breath-holding followed by journaling, were also found to be effective in individual case studies (Grant, 2006). Other promising treatments for this disorder include medication management (SSRIs, mood stabilizers, anti-epileptics, and opioid agonists), cognitive behavior therapy in combination with medication management, and the use of naltrexone to reduce the urge to steal (Grant, 2006; Grant & Kim, 2002; Grant & Odlaug, 2008).

Limit setting is an important component of treatment for impulse-control disorders. Impulsive symptoms often offer short-term positive reinforcement. People must learn to deal with the long-term negative consequences of their behavior, whether these consequences are legal or interpersonal. Family therapy is often indicated as well, particularly for people with pathological gambling or kleptomania, those who abuse family members, and adolescents engaged in pyromania. Often families must be brought into the loop and educated about how their own behaviors may be enabling those of their loved one. For example, bailing people out of trouble seems to reinforce and perpetuate the behavior. Family members may also be called on to help reinforce limits, such as requiring people who engage in pathological gambling to take their mood stabilizing medication or setting curfews for adolescents engaged in fire setting.

Exploration of cognitions can help clients and therapists understand the thinking that promotes these disorders—thoughts like "Setting fires will show people I'm not really a weakling" or "If I can gamble only a little longer, I'm sure I'll get that big win." An understanding of the adverse consequences of their behavior can also help people with impulse-control disorders modify their actions. A 1-day Trauma Burn Outreach Prevention Program that focused on the medical, financial, legal, and societal impact of fire-setting behavior resulted in a recidivism rate of less than 1%, compared to 36% recidivism in the control group (Franklin et al., 2002). Underlying depression and anxiety, as well as other coexisting symptoms, also need to be relieved, typically through cognitive therapy, as the impulsive behavior is often a way to manage those feelings.

Some people with impulse-control disorders benefit from psychodynamic treatment designed to help them deal with childhood losses and abuse and to help them gain an understanding of the underlying reasons for their behavior. People who are high in insight and motivation are particularly likely to benefit from therapy with a psychodynamic component. Clients with alexithymia (inability to identify or articulate emotions) and those with high degrees of dissociative behavior, often found in conjunction with trichotillomania and pathological gambling, may benefit from awareness training to help them be more conscious of their behavior and develop insight into stressors and emotional precursors to their maladaptive behavior.

Emotion-focused therapy (Greenberg, 2002) can help people recognize, label, tolerate, and regulate negative affect. Therapists work as emotion coaches to help people use their emotions in healthy ways, rather than dissociating or acting out in an attempt to reduce anxiety and negative affect. Similarly, in acceptance and commitment therapy (Eifert & Forsyth, 2005; Herbert, Forman, & England, 2008), therapists help clients "ACT": *a*ccept thoughts and feelings, *c*hoose direction, and *t*ake action.

Therapy also needs to attend to the correlates of the disorders, including legal, financial, occupational, and family difficulties. Development of leisure activities and increased involvement with career responsibilities and family members can help replace impulsive behavior.

Medication is sometimes useful in the treatment of impulse-control disorders. Impulsive behaviors sometimes have a neurological component that can be modified by such drugs as mood stabilizers, anticonvulsant medication, or antidepressants. SSRIs, including fluoxetine (Prozac), sertraline (Zoloft), and paroxetine (Paxil), have been shown to reduce impulsivity and have been helpful to people with intermittent explosive disorder, pathological gambling, kleptomania, and trichotillomania (Flessner et al., 2010; Stein et al., 2006). Mood stabilizers and anticonvulsants such as lithium, valproate, and topiramate have been shown to reduce impulsivity, especially when bipolar disorder is also present. Atypical antipsychotics have also shown promise in the treatment of impulse-control disorders. These medications reduce aggressive symptoms and, although they may not be the first-line treatment, have been beneficial in treating trichotillomania (Stein et al., 2006). Antidepressants and other medications can also have an indirect beneficial impact on impulse-control disorders by alleviating accompanying depression and other symptoms. Some classes of medications, such as the benzodiazepines, tend to reduce inhibitions and would therefore not be appropriate for the treatment of impulse-control disorders.

Prognosis

As with the prognoses for most other impulse-control disorders, the prognosis for the disorders reviewed here is uncertain. Relapse is common, especially at times of stress, loss, or disappointment, and it should be addressed in treatment. Few figures are available on success rates for treatment of these disorders, although research suggests that children treated for pyromania have a good prognosis and that people with late-onset trichotillomania have a poor prognosis (Franklin et al., 2006). Like people with substance use, people with pathological gambling often go through repetitive cycles of abstinence and relapse (Ladd & Petry, 2003). Several of the disorders, however, including intermittent explosive disorder, tend to diminish spontaneously over time. The good news is that in recent years we have learned more about these disorders and have a broader array of evidence-based interventions from which to choose in the treatment of impulse-control disorders.

SLEEP DISORDERS

Sleep disorders are a very different type of behavioral disorder from the disorders discussed previously in this chapter. Unlike most of the others, sleep disorders provide few secondary gains and rewards, and people clearly want to be free of their symptoms.

The *DSM-IV-TR* includes four major subgroups of sleep disorders, distinguished by whether or not they result from another disorder or difficulty:

1. Primary sleep disorders (not caused by a medical condition, a substance, or another mental disorder). These are primary insomnia; primary hypersomnia; narcolepsy; breathing-related sleep disorder; circadian rhythm sleep disorder;

and the parasomnias, which are nightmare disorder, sleep terror disorder, and sleep walking disorder.

2. Sleep disorder related to another mental disorder.
3. Sleep disorder due to a general medical condition.
4. Substance-induced sleep disorder.

Description of the Disorders

Sleep disorders are reflected by disturbances in the restorativeness and continuity of sleep and involve too much sleep, too little sleep, or dysfunctional sleep (American Psychiatric Association, 2000).

A review of the specific disorders encompassed by the category of primary sleep disorders will provide familiarity with the major clusters of symptoms included among all the sleep disorders.

Primary Insomnia This disorder is described by the *DSM-IV-TR* as "difficulty initiating or maintaining sleep or of nonrestorative sleep that lasts for at least one month and causes clinically significant distress or impairment" (American Psychiatric Association, 2000, p. 599). This fairly common disorder is more prevalent in later life, among women, and in people with personality traits that predispose them to worry and anxiety (Nowell, Buysse, Morin, Reynolds, & Kupfer, 2002). Insomnia has been linked to a constant state of hyperarousal typically reflected by increased metabolic rate, and an overall increase in adrenocorticotropic hormone (ACTH) and cortisol levels (Mahowald & Schenck, 2005). Difficulty falling asleep is its most common manifestation. Secondary symptoms, including mild anxiety, depression, irritability, difficulty concentrating, and fatigue, may interfere with daytime functioning. However, many people with insomnia report less daytime fatigue than people without insomnia, again pointing to a 24-hour cycle of hyperarousal.

Primary Hypersomnia This disorder is characterized by prolonged sleep (typically 9 to 12 hours per night), excessive daytime sleepiness (despite adequate sleep), or sometimes both, for more than one month. It is more common in men than in women, tends to begin in young adulthood, and, without treatment, usually has a chronic course. The tiredness, as well as the napping and the lengthy periods of sleep that characterize the disorder, can have an adverse impact on a person's social or occupational activities. People with this disorder tend to have a first-degree relative who also has primary hypersomnia.

Narcolepsy This disorder is characterized by at least three months of daily irresistible attacks of sleeping that typically last 10 to 20 minutes. Upon awakening, the person is refreshed but may have another attack in 2 to 3 hours. Cataplexy, or loss of muscle tone, occurs in about 70% of people with this disorder and may cause them to fall or collapse. Cataplexy is often precipitated by an intense emotion such as surprise, anger, or laughter (American Psychiatric Association, 2000). Sleep paralysis, the inability to move, is another troubling symptom of this disorder and most often occurs on waking. Hypnogogic hallucinations occur in 20% to 40% of those with narcolepsy but are not pathognomonic for narcolepsy. These hallucinations indicate that REM sleep is intruding on the waking state, and they are often the first symptom of this disorder. Sleep paralysis and hypnogogic hallucinations have recently been linked to depression (Szklo-Coxe, Young, Finn, & Mignot, 2007). In one third of cases, this disorder has a hereditary component, as does breathing-related sleep disorder (Ohayon & Okun, 2006). Narcolepsy is relatively rare, affecting only 1 in 10,000 to

20,000 people. Slightly more men than women have been diagnosed with this disorder. It usually begins in puberty and rarely has a first occurrence after the age of 40. This chronic disorder can contribute to accidents, depression, and work problems. Co-occurring disorders (primarily mood disorders, substance-related disorders, and generalized anxiety disorder) are found in 40% of people with narcolepsy (Savard & Morin, 2002).

Breathing-Related Sleep Disorder Abnormal respiration during sleep can lead to the excessive daytime sleepiness that is often the presenting problem for this disorder. Loud snoring and gasping during sleep are other clues to the presence of this disorder, although shallow breathing may be present instead. Breathing-related sleep disorder occurs in up to 10% of adults, a rate that is even higher in the elderly (American Psychiatric Association, 2000). Linked to obstructive sleep apnea, this is not only a condition of middle-aged, obese men, in whom it is especially prevalent; it also can be seen in thin individuals, postmenopausal women, and 3% of children (Mahowald & Schenck, 2005; Savard & Morin, 2002). Typically, people with this disorder have as many as 300 episodes a night in which air flow ceases for 10 seconds or longer and is restarted with accompanying arousal. People with this disorder may be unaware of their repeated awakenings, but their bed partners can describe the characteristic breathing and snoring patterns. If left untreated, this disorder can contribute to the development of hypertension and heart failure. This disorder is often hereditary. Breathing-related sleep disorder has increased in children since routine removal of children's tonsils and adenoids was discontinued.

Circadian Rhythm Sleep Disorder This disorder results from a mismatch between people's natural biological clocks and the demands of their lifestyles. Subtypes—including delayed sleep phase type, in which people have preferred times for sleeping and waking that are significantly later than those of most people and that usually begins in adolescence; jet lag type; and shift work type—reflect common examples of such mismatches. Difficulty falling asleep at prescribed times leads to sleepiness at other times, which in turn often leads to irregular sleeping patterns and use of caffeine and other stimulants, which then exacerbate the disorder.

Parasomnias Parasomnias are characterized by undesirable physical happenings during sleep and include nightmare disorder, sleep terror disorder, and sleepwalking disorder. All three disorders are particularly common in children. The first two involve upsetting dreams but are distinguished by the point in the sleep cycle when they occur and by people's reactions upon awakening. Sleep terror disorder, which usually begins between the ages of 4 and 12, is characterized by repeated awakening from dreams with a loud scream or cry and accompanying disorientation. People with nightmare disorder, by contrast, are alert upon awakening and can clearly report details of their frightening dreams. Sleepwalking affects 1% to 5% of children, with onset typically between the ages of 6 and 12 and elimination of sleepwalking typically by the age of 15; nearly 4% of adults also experience sleepwalking (American Psychiatric Association, 2000). Most parasomnias occur during the transition in the wake-sleep cycle.

A sleep disorder can also be related to another mental disorder (most often a mood or anxiety disorder). In the case of insomnia, the relationship between insomnia and other disorders such as depression or substance use is bidirectional—that is, the other disorder may cause insomnia, and insomnia may contribute to the emotional disorder. Insomnia may also be secondary to a medical condition (such as pain, restless leg syndrome, fever, or a neurological disorder). Substance-induced sleep disorders can be caused by alcohol, caffeine, nicotine, amphetamines, and other substances.

A diagnostic sleep laboratory that can provide polysomnographic studies of sleep patterns is invaluable in diagnosing most of these sleep disorders, especially breathing-related sleep disorder, primary insomnia, and narcolepsy. These studies should be conducted before a diagnosis of these disorders is finalized. A sleep diary kept by the client can also provide useful information on sleeping patterns. Sleep disorders in childhood, such as sleepwalking and night terrors, are considered age appropriate and normative. They usually do not require treatment unless self-injury or danger requires the implementation of measures to protect the child from physical harm (LaSasso, 2008).

Typical Client Characteristics

Sleep disorders are quite varied, as are the people who experience them. The *DSM-IV-TR* reports that 30% to 45% of adults complain of insomnia in any given 1-year period. People with sleep disorders are more likely to be female; older; and experiencing health problems, a recent loss, or considerable stress (Savard & Morin, 2002). Sleep problems may be related to environmental cues, as many people with insomnia can sleep well in new surroundings, whereas those without insomnia are more likely to have difficulty sleeping in new environments (Nowell et al., 2002).

People with insomnia report greater muscle tension, greater arousal, and increased incidence of stress-related illnesses (such as headaches and gastrointestinal problems). Problems during the day include poor concentration and reduced energy. Chronic insomnia can lead to increased risk of panic disorder, depression, development of another mental disorder within one year of onset, and alcohol misuse (Nowell et al., 2002). Driving while drowsy has been estimated to be the cause of more than 100,000 motor vehicle accidents annually in the United States (National Highway Traffic Safety Administration [NHTSA], 2003).

People with a sleep disorder related to another mental disorder typically have difficulty expressing their feelings directly and tend to channel their emotional concerns into somatic symptoms. In some cultures (Southeast Asian, for example), sleep complaints may be viewed as more acceptable than mental disorders and presentation of insomnia or hypersomnia may be a way to seek help for underlying concerns that people are reluctant to acknowledge (Paniagua, 2001).

Assessment

The following assessments should be part of a thorough evaluation of sleep disorders:

- Semistructured clinical interview
- Use of a sleep diary for at least a week
- Self-report measures
- Laboratory polysomnography if symptoms warrant

The clinical interview should evaluate the type of sleep disorder, symptom severity, frequency, and duration, as well as any daytime symptoms. Sleep habits, contributing factors to the sleep disturbance, family or personal history of sleep problems, triggers (for example, recent loss, divorce, work difficulties), as well as late-night eating and relaxation routines should be included. Dysfunctional cognitions that the person has developed in response to the sleep problem, as well as past treatment, should also be discussed.

Detailed interviewing is particularly indicated with people who present with circadian rhythm sleep disorders, because their lifestyles and their work schedules often contribute to the disorder. Another reason for thorough interviewing is the finding that up to 30% of those who complain of difficulty falling or remaining asleep actually do sleep well (Mahowald & Schenck, 2005).

Several assessment measures are available, including the Insomnia Interview Schedule (Morin, 1993), a semistructured interview; the Structured Interview for Sleep Disorders (SIS-D; Schramm et al., 1993), which has a 90% concordance rate with a polysomnographic assessment; and the Sleep-EVAL, a computerized assessment that takes upwards of an hour to complete and is consistent with *DSM-IV-TR* criteria (Ohayon et al., 1997). Self-reports, such as the Sleep Hygiene Practice Scale (SHPS), a 30-question self report of sleep habits (Yang & Ebben, 2008), or a sleep diary that can be maintained for one or two weeks prior to treatment, provide reliable and cost-effective baseline data on symptoms and severity and are less subject to exaggeration of sleep difficulties than an informal self-report (LaSasso, 2008).

An important measure of sleep-related cognitions can be found in the Dysfunctional Beliefs and Attitudes about Sleep Scale (DBAS; Morin & Espie, 2003). This 30-item self-report scale asks for responses to such statements as "I am concerned that chronic insomnia may have serious consequences for my physical health" in an effort to assess how realistic a person's sleep expectations are. The DBAS is a useful tool for focusing cognitive therapy aimed at debunking sleep myths and negative thoughts (Savard & Morin, 2002).

Laboratory polysomnography, an all-night assessment in a sleep lab, is often warranted, particularly for organic causes such as sleep apnea or when leg movements interfere with sleep. The American Academy of Sleep Medicine (AASM) has developed practice guidelines for the use of polysomnography in the evaluation of sleep disorders, as not all sleep problems will require such an extensive assessment (Kushida et al., 2005).

Preferred Therapist Characteristics

Complaints of insomnia and other sleep disorders are often trivialized or ignored by practitioners (Savard & Morin, 2002). Therapists treating people with sleep disorders seem to be most successful if they take sleep disorders seriously and take a directive yet supportive stance. People with these disorders often have deferred seeking help until the problems felt overwhelming, and they need reassurance and active intervention to modify the symptoms quickly. People with sleep disorders are sometimes reluctant to engage in exploration of their lifestyles and possible underlying concerns, and this reluctance must be addressed and reduced by therapists as part of a comprehensive assessment.

Intervention Strategies

Insomnia and hypersomnia are often related to or caused by other disorders or situations that require attention, such as depression, stress reactions substance-related disorders, and restless leg syndrome (Moul, Morin, Buysse, Reynolds, & Kupfer, 2007). People with sleep disorders also may have life circumstances—such as a recent loss, a stressful life event, or environmental factors, such as a noisy or an uncomfortable living situation—that interfere with their ability to get a good night's sleep. Therefore, when a person presents with symptoms of a sleep disorder, a careful assessment interview is necessary to ascertain the dynamics of the disorder.

Insomnia and depression may be bidirectional. In other words, depression may cause insomnia and having insomnia may eventually lead to depression. In one study, 14% of people with insomnia met the criteria for depression (Yang & Ebben, 2008). People who present with insomnia are more likely to develop MDD within four years (Szklo-Coxe, Young, Peppard, Finn, & Benca, 2010). If a disorder such as major depressive disorder or a substance-related disorder seems to be causing the sleep disorder, focusing on the underlying disorder usually will take priority. Nearly 40% of people with insomnia had another mental disorder. Successful treatment of that disorder may automatically relieve the sleep disorder. However, therapists often will have difficulty shifting the client's focus from the sleeping difficulties to the concerns that underlie them.

Research on the use of psychotherapy to treat sleep disorders is limited. Most of the relevant research has been done by medical researchers working in sleep laboratories. Nevertheless, the literature does provide some guidelines for using psychotherapy to treat sleep disorders once medical causes have been ruled out. If it has been determined that the focus of treatment will be on the sleep disorder, the first steps usually will be to ensure that the person has a sleeping environment conducive to restful sleep and to ensure good sleep hygiene (Kushida et al., 2005). The sleep schedule should be stabilized as much as possible, eliminating naps and caffeine and establishing healthy patterns of eating, drinking, and exercising.

As a general rule, people who clearly are not getting enough sleep, typically people with insomnia or circadian rhythm sleep disorder, can be treated primarily via behavior therapy. Many behavioral techniques have been shown empirically to be effective. Stimulus control therapy and progressive muscle relaxation have the most empirical support in the treatment of insomnia. Sleep restriction, CBT, followed by multicomponent therapy without CBT, biofeedback, paradoxical intention requiring the person to stay awake, and limiting the time available to sleep are other effective treatments (Kushida

et al., 2005). Bright light therapy can be helpful for disorders related to circadian rhythm. People who are sleeping too much, however, or who are exhausted even though they seem to have had enough sleep (typically people with narcolepsy, breathing-related sleep disorder, and hypersomnia), usually require medication or medical treatment. People with parasomnias, especially children, require primarily reassurance and help in reducing any stress and anxiety that may be contributing to the disorder.

Generally, behavioral treatments are more effective than medication when long-term outcome for treatment of insomnia is considered (Yang & Ebben, 2008). Stimulus control therapy consists of a set of instructions to be followed at bedtime to reduce behaviors that are incompatible with sleep and to address circadian factors. Such a list might include the following instructions:

- Go to bed when tired.
- Use the bedroom only for sleep-related activity and sex. Do not eat, watch television, work, or read in the bedroom during the day or night.
- Do not take a nap during the day.
- If unable to sleep after trying for 15 to 20 minutes, get up and go to another room. Return to bed only when tired again.
- Wake up in the morning at the same time regardless of the amount of sleep the night before.

Relaxation therapy, including progressive muscle relaxation, biofeedback, and cognitive thought-stopping techniques, has been consistently found to be effective in the treatment of insomnia. Sleep hygiene education, although the least effective of the behavior therapies when used on its own, includes health-related practices such as diet, exercise, and control of substance use, and helps people regulate their environment (light, noise, and temperature) so that it is conducive to sleep.

Cognitive-behavioral treatment addresses the maladaptive cognitions that tend to perpetuate insomnia: The difficulty in sleeping causes worry about not sleeping, and the worry in turn exacerbates the difficulty in sleeping. Breaking the cycle is important in reducing the symptoms. Meditation, use of positive imagery, and light therapy are other sleep-enhancing techniques.

Sedative-hypnotic medications are among the most commonly used treatments for insomnia; there were 42 million prescriptions filled in 2005 (della Cava, 2006). In 2007, the FDA requested product warning labels and brochures be distributed along with prescriptions for sedative-hypnotic sleeping aids including ramelteon (Rozerem), zolpidem (Ambien), zaleplon (Sonata), and 10 others. These drugs have been linked with such rare complex sleep-related behaviors as driving and eating while asleep (Saul, 2007).

Some people have found melatonin and other over-the-counter remedies to help them fall asleep. Mellatonin has also been found to be useful in overcoming the symptoms of jet lag (Bonnet & Arand, 2008), but the long-term impact of these substances has not been fully documented, so these remedies should be used with great care, if at all.

Circadian rhythm sleep disorder, jet lag type and shift work type, are best treated through lifestyle modification that stabilizes sleeping patterns. Chronotherapy, or resetting of the biological clock, is another approach to treatment of this disorder (Mahowald & Schenck, 2005). The delayed sleep phase type of this disorder, for example, can be treated through phase advancing, which systematically, gradually, and progressively schedules earlier bedtimes for people with this disorder. Phototherapy (light therapy), stress management, relaxation, avoidance of

alcohol and caffeine, and improved sleep habits can enhance treatment (Yang & Ebben, 2008).

Unlike insomnia, excessive sleeping or fatigue usually results from an underlying medical disorder such as sleep apnea (Mahowald & Schenck, 2005). Consequently, treatment of these symptoms should always include a medical evaluation. Medical treatments vary according to the disorder. For example, primary hypersomnia and narcolepsy can be treated successfully with stimulant medication, such as amphetamines. Narcolepsy also benefits from two or three scheduled daily naps of 20 to 30 minutes each. Antidepressant medications can relieve the cataplexy that often accompanies narcolepsy. Breathing-related sleep disorders can be treated with weight loss, nasal continuous positive airway pressure (via CPAP machines) that regulates breathing, and, if all else fails, sometimes by surgery. People with fatigue and chronic sleepiness also can benefit from the establishment of a regular sleeping schedule and healthy eating and exercise. Psychotherapy, addressing both underlying stressors and the stress introduced by the sleepiness, is often indicated.

The parasomnias are usually due to difficulties in the transition from sleep to wakefulness. Rather than having a psychological origin, parasomnias, like sleepwalking, support the concept that wake and sleep are not mutually exclusive states (Mahowald & Schenck, 2005). In children, the parasomnias usually do not reflect underlying pathology and are generally outgrown without any intervention.

Parasomnias may be triggered in adults by alcohol, sleep deprivation, physical activity, emotional stress, or medication. Recurrent frightening or upsetting dreams may also reflect the surfacing of painful memories, which may require therapeutic attention.

In addition to specific treatments for the sleep disorders, people with these disorders also usually benefit from education and attention to any underlying conflicts or sources of excessive arousal. Education as part of treatment can provide people with needed reassurance and dispel myths and cognitive distortions. If the sleep disorder has been long-standing and chronic, it may have damaged a person's career and relationships, caused psychological distress, or resulted in the formation of an Axis I disorder (Zahedi, Kamath, & Winokur, 2008). These issues, too, may need to be addressed in therapy.

Prognosis

The prognosis for reducing sleep disorders is quite good, but an accurate assessment of etiology is critical in determining outcome. Those with a medically or physiologically caused sleep disorder usually respond well to medical treatment or to alleviation of the cause. Those with a psychologically determined sleep disorder are likely to respond well to behavioral psychotherapy as long as any underlying disorders are also addressed. The parasomnias have a high probability of spontaneous remission.

Breathing-related sleep disorders and narcolepsy may need lifelong treatment, but usually can be well controlled through that treatment. The prognosis for both primary insomnia and circadian rhythm sleep disorder is uncertain and depends primarily on lifestyle and the ability to reduce stress and change behavior.

TREATMENT RECOMMENDATIONS: CLIENT MAP

This chapter has focused on the diagnosis and treatment of five groups of disorders of behavior and impulse control: substance-related disorders, eating disorders, sexual and gender identity disorders, impulse-control disorders not elsewhere classified, and sleep disorders. Although the symptoms of these disorders vary widely, they do have an underlying commonality: behavioral dysfunction. The following general treatment recommendations, organized according to the format of the Client Map, are provided for disorders of behavior and impulse control.

CLIENT MAP

Diagnosis

Disorders of behavior and impulse control: substance-related disorders, eating disorders (anorexia nervosa, bulimia nervosa, and binge eating disorder), sexual and gender identity disorders (sexual dysfunctions, paraphilias, and gender identity disorder), impulse-control disorders not elsewhere classified (pathological gambling, intermittent explosive disorder, pyromania, kleptomania, and trichotillomania), sleep disorders

Objectives of Treatment

Increased knowledge of the disorder
Reduction of dysfunctional behaviors
Acquisition of new and more positive behaviors
Improved ability to meet own needs
Stress reduction
Lifestyle improvement
Relapse prevention

Assessments

Physical examination (especially important for sleep disorders, sexual disorders, bulimia nervosa, and anorexia nervosa)

Symptom inventories

Establishment of baseline severity of symptoms

Determination of presence of coexisting mental disorders

Clinician Characteristics

Knowledgeable about individual, group, and family therapy

Well informed about specific disorder

Able to be structured and directive yet supportive

Able to manage potential negative feelings about client's behavior

Able to work effectively with client's reluctance, limited motivation, and hostility

Location of Treatment

Usually outpatient setting

Short-term inpatient treatment possible for severe cases of substance-related disorders and eating disorders

Therapeutic communities, day treatment programs, online support also possible

Interventions to Be Used

Multifaceted program emphasizing behavior therapy and cognitive-behavioral therapy

Measurements of change

Education

Improvement of communication and relationship skills

Stress management

Impulse-control strategies

Emphasis of Treatment

Highly directive

Moderately supportive

Primary focus on current behaviors and coping mechanisms

Some attention to past patterns and history

Numbers

Group therapy particularly important when motivation for change is low

Individual and family therapy also important

Timing

Rapid pace

Short to medium duration, with extended aftercare focused on relapse prevention

Medications Needed

Usually not the primary mode of treatment, except in male erectile dysfunction

Medication can accelerate progress in some cases, especially in helping curtail drug and alcohol use, address some sleep disorders, and alleviate underlying depression

Adjunct Services

Peer support groups such as Alcoholics Anonymous, Narcotics Anonymous, Overeaters Anonymous, Gamblers Anonymous, Rational Recovery

Prognosis

Good prognosis for significant improvement if client is (or becomes) motivated to change

Relapse common

CLIENT MAP OF GEORGE W.

This chapter began with a description of George W., a 36-year-old male with a 22-year history of maladaptive alcohol use. George was also experiencing legal, interpersonal, occupational, and marital problems. He reported some underlying depression and social discomfort. George was seen in therapy after his arrest for driving while intoxicated. The following Client Map outlines the treatment provided to George, a course of treatment typical of what is recommended for people who misuse alcohol or have other disorders of behavior and impulse control.

Diagnosis

Axis I: 303.90 Alcohol dependence, severe
Axis II: 799.90 Diagnosis deferred on Axis II. Rule out avoidant personality disorder or avoidant personality traits
Axis III: High blood pressure, intestinal discomfort reported
Axis IV: Incarceration for third DWI conviction, marital conflict, occupational problems
Axis V: Global assessment of functioning (GAF Scale): current GAF = 50

Objectives of Treatment

Establish and maintain abstinence from alcohol
Improve marital relationship
Improve social skills
Improve occupational functioning
Build coping and life skills, as well as enjoyment of life
Obtain diagnosis and treatment for medical complaints

Assessments

Thorough medical evaluation to determine impact of alcohol use on client's physical condition and obtain
    treatment for physical complaints
Michigan Alcoholism Screening Test

Clinician Characteristics

Knowledgeable about the development and symptoms of alcohol dependence
Structured and directive
Skilled at setting limits

Location of Treatment

Outpatient setting (rather than inpatient setting with concurrent medical evaluation and supervision), given
    that client had been alcohol free for several weeks as a result of incarceration

Interventions to Be Used

Group behavior therapy as primary approach
Individual therapy, later family therapy and marital therapy as needed
Cognitive-behavioral therapy
Motivation enhancement therapy to encourage readiness for change
Encouragement for abstinence
Education about stress management, problem solving, communication skills, impact of alcohol, and mal-
    adaptive patterns of alcohol use
Development of leisure and social activities not focused on drinking
Build relapse prevention into treatment plan

Emphasis of Treatment

Directive
Focused on current behavior
Elements of both support and exploration

Numbers

Individual, group, family, and couples therapy

Timing

Rapid pace
Medium duration
Extended follow-up and participation in 12-step program

Medications Needed

None
Naltrexone (ReVia) to be considered in case of early relapse

Adjunct Services

Alcoholics Anonymous (at least three meetings per week)
Later participation in Adult Children of Alcoholics
Al-Anon for client's wife

Prognosis

Fair (client internally and externally motivated, acknowledges need to reduce or eliminate drinking, aware that
    job and marriage are in jeopardy, but reluctant to make the commitment to long-term abstinence)
Better with long-term follow-up and continued participation in Alcoholics Anonymous
Relapse common

RECOMMENDED READING

Agency for Healthcare Research and Quality. (2006). *Management of eating disorders.* AHRQ Publication No. 06-E010. Research Triangle Park, NC: RTI-UNC Evidence-Based Practice Center.

Bowen, S., Chawla, N., & Marlatt, G. A. (2010). *Mindfulness-based relapse prevention for addictive behaviors: A clinician's guide.* New York: Guilford Press.

Hollander, E., & Stein, D. J. (Eds.). (2006). *Clinical manual of impulse-control disorders.* Arlington, VA: American Psychiatric Publishing.

Leiblum, S. R. (2007). *Principles and practices of sex therapy* (4th ed.). New York, NY: Guilford Press.

Maine, M., McGilley, B. H., & Bunnell, D. (Eds.). (2010). *Treatment of eating disorders: Bridging the research-practice gap.* Burlington, MA: Elsevier.

NIDA. *A cognitive behavioral approach: Treating cocaine addiction.* Available: www.drugabuse.gov/txmanuals/cbt/cbt4.html

Pandi-Perumal, S. R., Verster, J. C., Monti, J. M., Lader, M., & Langer, S. Z. (Eds.). (2008). *Sleep disorders: Diagnostics and therapeutics.* New York, NY: Informa Healthcare.

Rollnick, S., Miller, W. R., & Butler, C. C. (2008). *Motivational interviewing in health care: Helping patients change behavior.* New York, NY: Guilford Press.

Springer, D. W., & Rubin, A. (Eds.). (2009). *Substance abuse treatment for adolescents and adults: Clinician's guide to evidence-based practice.* Hoboken, NJ: Wiley.

CHAPTER

7

Disorders in Which Physical and Psychological Factors Combine

Dr. Martin C., a 62-year-old African American male, was referred for therapy by his physician. Martin had sought medical help for intestinal discomfort. He believed that he had cancer of the small intestine. His father had died of that form of cancer in his sixties when Martin was a teenager.

Over the past year, Martin had consulted three physicians (including an oncologist), had had a thorough medical evaluation, and was found to have nothing more than frequent indigestion and constipation due to poor eating habits. Because Martin had difficulty accepting this diagnosis, his physician referred him for therapy.

Martin had been a history professor for almost 35 years. He had been promoted to associate professor about 25 years ago, after the publication of an influential book he had written on the history of war, but he had never been able to equal that accomplishment. His efforts to achieve promotion to full professor had been unsuccessful.

Martin was also experiencing stress at home. He had been divorced from his first wife 15 years ago and had been married for 8 years to a woman 20 years younger than he. Martin felt that she was disappointed in him because of his lack of professional success, and he was worried about the future of their marriage. He coped with this worry by working long hours and taking a great

deal of nonprescription medication for his gastric symptoms. He was rarely home, had few friends and leisure activities, and had considerable difficulty verbalizing his feelings.

Martin initially sought help for a physical problem—intestinal discomfort and gastric distress—but his physician believed that Martin's complaints had an emotional cause. Martin was experiencing a disorder called *hypochondriasis*, which is included in one of four broad groups of disorders considered in this chapter. In these disorders, physical complaints are intertwined with emotional difficulties, and attention must be paid to both groups of symptoms.

OVERVIEW OF DISORDERS IN WHICH PHYSICAL AND PSYCHOLOGICAL FACTORS COMBINE

This chapter begins with an overview of disorders involving an interrelationship of physical and psychological concerns. It goes on to provide information on the diagnosis and treatment of the four groups of disorders that fit this description:

1. Somatoform disorders (somatization disorder, undifferentiated somatoform

319

disorder, conversion disorder, pain disorder, hypochondriasis, and body dysmorphic disorder)
2. Factitious disorders
3. Delirium, dementia, and amnestic and other cognitive disorders
4. Mental disorders due to a general medical condition

Description of the Disorders

People with these disorders typically present for treatment with concerns about a physical or medical complaint. They sometimes seek therapy after referral from a physician who has not been able to find a medical cause for their complaints or who believes that the clients' emotional difficulties would be helped by psychotherapy even though they may stem from a medical condition. These clients may or may not be aware of the dynamics of their disorders. Heightened concerns about physical issues can serve a purpose. Instead of feeling the pain associated with certain emotions, the feelings are translated into physical symptoms. People often are unaware of how or why their emotions are transferred onto physical experiences. Nevertheless, anxiety and other difficult emotions are kept out of conscious awareness and are directed instead to the physical realm of the body. In addition, people may derive benefit from the attention and sympathy their physical symptoms elicit from others. Because clients focus primarily on their physical concerns, they may be surprised by and resistant to the suggestion that they would benefit from psychotherapy.

Typical Client Characteristics

People with disorders in which physical and psychological factors combine typically have difficulty expressing emotions directly and so may channel concerns into the physiological realm.

Often the combination of psychological and biological difficulties began in childhood and persisted into adulthood. It is not uncommon for somatoform disorders also to be found in other family members. Modeled behavior can play a role in symptom development. The exact cause of somatoform disorders remains unknown. But a complex interaction between biological, psychological, and environmental factors seems to be at the root of most of these disorders. Comorbid conditions are almost always present, particularly anxiety, depression, and personality disorders.

People with one of the disorders discussed in this chapter typically have trouble managing environmental stress and tend not to be insightful or psychologically minded. Sometimes people with these disorders have strong dependence needs and want others to take care of them. They frequently have impairment in both the interpersonal and the occupational aspects of their lives, and are often reluctant to discuss their psychological difficulties with others.

Disturbances in perception and expression of affect were found in people with somatoform disorders. Normal physical sensations are perceived more strongly by these people, amplified, and then cognitively misinterpreted as signs of physical illness. The body then becomes the focus of attention, rather than being aware of moods, stress, or their own emotions. People with somatoform disorders also tend to amplify their own pain, and have little tolerance for physical symptoms.

A history of trauma and family dysfunction is commonly found in the backgrounds of people who develop somatoform disorders. These include physical or sexual abuse, emotional neglect, loss of a parent early in life, and trauma. Childhood experiences of chronically ill family members are also common (Nickel & Egle, 2006). Issues of attachment may underlie the development of somatoform disorders. Insecure attachment style has been associated with higher levels of depression, greater catastrophizing, physical complaints, pain, and more frequent trips to the doctor (Nickel, Ademmer, & Egle, 2010).

The cluster of symptoms commonly seen in somatoform disorders—depression, anxiety, and somatic complaints—may be related to serotonin levels in the brain. A similar pattern is found in children who experience headaches and stomachaches and early school refusal.

Assessment

Effective management of these disorders is dependent on accurate and comprehensive psychological and medical assessments. Special attention should be paid to the development of the therapeutic relationship as well as the following factors: reason for referral, if any; the symptoms and concerns the client identifies; the ability of the therapist to take these symptoms seriously; developing an effective treatment plan that focuses on symptom reduction rather than cure; and effective coordination with medical providers to rule out actual physical causes and to treat any co-occurring disorders.

The Anxiety Disorders Interview Schedule for *DSM-IV*-Lifetime Version (ADIS-IV-L; DiNardo, Brown, & Barlow, 1994) is a semi-structured diagnostic interview tool for anxiety disorders and accompanying somatoform disorders and mood states. The ADIS-IV-L can be helpful in differential diagnosis, in determining the frequency and severity of symptoms, and in identifying the presence of suicidal ideation and alcohol and substance misuse (Allen, McHugh, & Barlow, 2008).

Part of a comprehensive assessment should also include taking a complete family history, assessing congruence of symptoms and known illnesses over time, inquiring about trauma and stressors, and documenting resilience, support,

and coping skills. Suicidal ideation and risk should also be assessed, particularly in people with pain disorder, body dysmorphic disorder, and factitious disorder.

Distinguishing among somatoform disorders, factitious disorders, and malingering can present a challenge for the clinician. In all three cases, the client may present with the same symptoms; the key variable is intentionality of the client's behavior. Eisendrath (2001) suggests therapists consider the behavior to lie on a continuum from unconscious and unintentional production of symptoms (somatoform disorders), to intentional production of symptoms for possibly unconscious motives (factitious disorders), to intentional fabrication of symptoms for secondary gain (malingering). The most commonly fabricated symptoms are command hallucinations, dissociative identity disorder, and posttraumatic stress disorder (Woo & Keatinge, 2008).

Preferred Therapist Characteristics

Most patients who receive a referral from a primary care physician for mental health therapy do not follow through (Craven & Bland, 2006). Therapists, therefore, need to be skilled at developing rapport and communicating support and interest so that a helpful therapeutic relationship is established fairly rapidly with those who do make an appointment. Providing a supportive environment in which these clients feel safe and in which negative feelings can gradually be explored, may result, over time, in improved coping mechanisms, increased self-esteem, and symptom relief. Therapists who proceed too quickly, however, or are harshly confrontational, or unsympathetic will find these clients terminating treatment prematurely. Therefore, the therapist must carefully control discussion of the presenting complaints. Therapy is most likely to be successful if the therapist is understanding of the symptoms and worries that clients have because of their physical complaints, but also uses concrete and structured interventions that are flexible and empowering while involving little in-depth analysis. Attempting to distinguish between symptoms that are "real" and those that are "merely psychological" is a potentially harmful and futile exercise that goes against current neurological findings about the connection between pain and the body. All complaints of physical symptoms have both a physical and a psychological origin. It is safe to say that the client is distressed by physical symptoms, even though some of those physical symptoms may be exacerbated by psychological factors. Most somatoform disorders probably involve a complex process of "psychophysiological hyperreactivity, exaggerated sensitivity to somatic sensation, exaggerated illness fears, and mood disturbance" (Nathan & Gorman, 2002, p. 450). Therapists treating people with these disorders also benefit from having information on medical conditions and should be comfortable collaborating with physicians.

Intervention Strategies

Few controlled studies exist on the treatment of the disorders covered in this chapter. Nevertheless, case studies and theoretical articles provide a good indication of effective approaches to treatment. Research that is available on a particular disorder will be listed in the specific section.

The first step in treating people who present with interrelated physical and psychological complaints is to obtain a medical consultation (or to confer with physicians whom the client has already consulted) to determine whether a physical disorder really is present. An early assessment of mental status and cognitive functioning also is important. If a medical condition is present, the therapist should become familiar with the impact of the condition on the client

and should ensure that appropriate medical treatment is provided if it is needed. Clients should be kept informed about their medical condition and should be involved in decisions about treatment whenever that is possible. Clients who feel that their medical symptoms are being ignored may manifest an increase in somatization.

A long-term, helpful therapeutic relationship based on trust and collaboration and free of medical evaluations, tests, and measurement of symptoms may be the best approach. Therapy is usually integrative and multifaceted, focusing on affective, cognitive, and behavioral areas to build up the person's coping skills, reduce accompanying depression and anxiety, modify negative cognitions that promote hopelessness and dependence, and help people meet their needs more effectively.

Most somatoform disorders occur in conjunction with an anxiety or mood disorder, so behavior therapy, cognitive behavior therapy, stress management, and hypnotherapy also are useful in helping people integrate the physical and emotional aspects of themselves and maximize their strengths. If the client is experiencing significant impairment, either cognitive or physical, psychotherapy will need to take that impairment into account. Therapy for people with interrelated physical and psychological complaints generally de-emphasizes interpretation and analysis, because of the resistance and discomfort those approaches may provoke. Throughout the treatment process, great care should be taken to establish and nurture a positive therapeutic alliance. These clients may be receptive to nonverbal therapies, such as meditation, biofeedback, massage, and other relaxation techniques that do not require them to verbalize their feelings, although there is little empirical research on the effectiveness of these treatments with the disorders covered in this chapter. Leisure and career counseling can advance treatment, and marital or family counseling can be useful to repair any damage to relationships that may have resulted from the disorder. Particularly when working with children and adolescents, parental education and training may be necessary to prevent reinforcement of secondary gains (such as time off from school, and extra attention that the clients receive when they feel ill).

Prognosis

The prognosis for treating disorders in which physical and psychological factors combine varies greatly according to the specific disorder, the nature and dynamics of the client's temperament, the strength of the alliance created between the therapist and the client, and the treatment of any co-occurring disorders. If clients can acknowledge having emotional concerns that could benefit from therapy, they may well derive considerable benefit from their treatment. Therapy cannot only reduce people's focus on their perceived physical complaints but also increase their self-confidence and self-esteem and improve the quality of their lives. Nevertheless, the presence of cognitive impairment or a medical illness, as well as clients' continued emphasis on medical rather than psychological concerns, may limit the progress of therapy.

SOMATOFORM DISORDERS

Somatoform disorders are among the most difficult mental disorders to treat. First, a physician must investigate symptoms to rule out any underlying physical disorder. When none is found, the person is referred to a mental health professional who must determine whether the somatic symptoms are part of a somatoform

disorder or belong to another anxiety or mood disorder. The therapist must also be aware of the broader family history and cultural context of the client.

Somatoform disorders are the most frequent psychological disorders to appear in nonpsychological settings, comprising nearly one third of patients who seek medical care and accounting for an average of $265 billion a year in medical care costs (Barsky, Orav, & Bates, 2005; Nickel, Ademmer, & Egle, 2010).

Description of the Disorders

Somatoform disorders are characterized by physical complaints or symptoms that are not fully explained by a medical condition or by another mental disorder and are believed to be caused (at least in part) by psychological factors. People who have these disorders, however, genuinely believe that they are afflicted with the symptoms and physical illnesses they are presenting. They are not deliberately producing these symptoms, so they are typically very distressed about their physical complaints and about the failure of the medical community to find and address a medical cause for their symptoms. The fourth edition text revision of the *Diagnostic and Statistical Manual of Mental Disorders* (*DSM-IV-TR*) lists the following six types of somatoform disorders (American Psychiatric Association, 2000).

Somatization Disorder This disorder, also known as Briquet's syndrome, is one of the most severe of the somatoform disorders (Bond, 2006). In one study, as many as 10% of those with somatization disorder were confined to wheelchairs and spent, on average, seven days a month in bed. Somatization disorder is characterized by multiple medically unexplained physical complaints, beginning before the age of 30 and lasting for at least several years, for which a person seeks medical treatment and makes modifications in lifestyle. Over the course of the disorder, by definition, the person has experienced at least four pain symptoms, two gastrointestinal symptoms (usually nausea and bloating), one symptom related to sexual or reproductive activity, and one neurological or conversion symptom. Common symptoms of this disorder include shortness of breath, menstrual complaints, nausea and vomiting, burning sensations in the genitals, limb pain, amnesia, and a sensation of having a lump in the throat (Escobar, 2004). Emotional lability, a susceptibility to anxiety and depression, and overly dramatic and manipulative behavior have all been noted in people with somatization disorder. The combination of multiple physical symptoms and affective dysregulation often results in "disruptive and disrupting lifestyles" (Bond, 2006, p. 262).

More than half of people with somatization disorder were exposed, as children, to illness or physical disease in one or both parents (Bond, 2006). The clients take on the chronic illness behavior they have observed, and secondary gains typically result. This disorder, which often goes unrecognized and untreated (Phillips, 2001), causes considerable distress as well as social and occupational impairment. Somatization disorder is associated with increased absences from work, increased time spent in bed, and reduced life satisfaction (Stuart & Noyes, 1999).

This relatively rare disorder is present in 0.2% to 2.0% of women and less than 0.2% of men (American Psychiatric Association, 2000). Although it is far more common in women than in men in the United States, increased incidence of the disorder in men in countries such as Greece and Puerto Rico suggest that cultural factors may influence gender ratio (Holder-Perkins & Wise, 2001). Somatization disorder often is accompanied by anxiety, mood, and personality disorders as well as by alcohol use disorders and attentional difficulties.

Somatization disorder usually follows a chronic course, beginning in adolescence, although symptoms may wax and wane. This disorder has a familial component, with as many as 10% to 20% of female relatives of those with this disorder also experiencing somatization disorder. Male relatives have been found to have increased rates of antisocial personality disorder and alcohol use disorders (Holder-Perkins & Wise, 2001).

Undifferentiated Somatoform Disorder

This disorder involves the presence, for at least six months, of one or more somatic symptoms, not attributable to a medical condition, that cause significant upset or dysfunction. Common complaints include persistent fatigue, loss of appetite, gastrointestinal symptoms, and genito-urinary symptoms (American Psychiatric Association, 2000). The diagnosis of undifferentiated somatoform disorder is generally used to describe multiple physical symptoms that resemble but do not meet the full criteria for somatization disorder (American Psychiatric Association, 2000). People with undifferentiated somatoform disorder tend to present in physician's offices with symptoms such as heart palpitations, chronic fatigue, dizziness, noncardiac chest pain, and unexplained pelvic pain (Nathan & Gorman, 2002). Somatization complaints are often a symptom of major depressive disorder, and many people with anxiety disorders overly focus on bodily issues, so it is not surprising that co-occurrence of mood and anxiety disorders is usually found in more than 50% of the people presenting with physical complaints (Simon, 2002).

Conversion Disorder

This disorder was well known in Freud's time but is relatively rare today. Prevalence rates vary from 11 to 500 per 100,000 people, and it appears to be more frequent in women than men at a ratio estimated to range from 2:1 to 10:1 (American Psychiatric Association, 2000). Conversion disorder involves a loss or change in motor or sensory functioning, and it results in such symptoms as blindness; tingling, numbness, or paralysis of a limb; impaired balance; inability to speak; and seizures or pseudoseizures. The physical symptom typically has no medical cause but is associated with and symbolic of a conflict, a stressor, or a psychological difficulty that lies outside the person's awareness. For example, a woman who witnessed the killing of her husband and child subsequently developed a conversion disorder in which she became unable to see. Emotional stress, loss of a parent or other close relationship, and divorce often precipitate the development of a conversion disorder (Bond, 2006).

Diagnosing conversion disorder requires great care and consultation with physicians. The literature describes many cases in which this diagnosis was made in error because a medical disorder was overlooked. Thirty percent of people initially diagnosed with conversion disorder were found to have an underlying neurological illness (such as head injury, EEG abnormality, multiple sclerosis, tumors, or petit mal seizures) or were eventually diagnosed with an illness that explained their symptoms (Holder-Perkins & Wise, 2001).

Among people manifesting pseudoseizures, a common symptom of conversion disorder, 70% had a coexisting neurological disorder, and the majority had an IQ below 80. The *DSM-IV-TR* identifies the following subtypes of conversion disorder:

- With motor symptom or deficit (such as impaired balance, difficulty swallowing, paralysis)
- With sensory symptom or deficit (for instance, inability to feel pain or blindness)
- With seizures or convulsions
- With mixed presentation (if more than one category is appropriate)

Pain Disorder   This disorder entails either an excessive reaction to an existing physical pain (pain disorder associated with both psychological factors and a general medical condition) or preoccupation with a pain that is not shown to have any medical origin (pain disorder associated with psychological factors only). According to Bond (2006), in pain disorder associated with both psychological factors and a general medical condition, the level of pain should be "markedly in excess" of what is expected (p. 263). When a pain disorder is suspected, clients should be referred for a complete physical examination, and the therapist should conduct a thorough mental status exam; a diagnosis of pain disorder can be made only in the absence of physical illness or injury that fully explains the symptoms. Bond notes that pain disorder frequently occurs after a minor injury or illness that caused pain and has since improved; nevertheless, the client still reports chronic, severe, disabling pain. This exaggerated pain response is more likely in the presence of secondary gains, including attention from family members or freedom from work or unpleasant experiences or responsibilities. Depression and anxiety sometimes accompany this relatively common disorder, as does impairment in functioning. Pain disorder is most often diagnosed in adolescence and young adulthood. Women with pain disorders are more likely than men to experience certain types of chronic pain, such as severe and persistent headaches and musculoskeletal pain. Pain of a sexual nature (for example, genital pain) is often reported by women who were sexually abused in childhood (Stoeter et al., 2007; Stuart & Noyes, 1999).

This disorder typically begins abruptly and worsens over time. When pain disorder is associated with a medically diagnosed physical condition, it can be exacerbated by physicians' minimization or inadequate treatment of pain. People whose pain is associated with a terminal illness or severe depression are at increased risk of suicide (American Psychiatric Association, 2000).

Hypochondriasis   This is probably the best-known variant of somatoform disorder. It is characterized by the belief that minor physical complaints (such as chest pain or a headache) are symptoms of serious conditions, such as a heart attack or a brain tumor. This fear of having a serious medical condition lasts for at least six months, typically begins in early adulthood, and causes marked distress or dysfunction, although the belief is not of sufficient intensity to be described as delusional. Men and women are equally affected by this disorder, which is often accompanied by depressive and anxiety disorders. Hypochondriasis is fairly common and is believed to affect 4% to 9% of people who seek medical treatment in outpatient settings (Simon, 2002).

Body Dysmorphic Disorder   This disorder involves preoccupation with an imagined or slight flaw in physical appearance. Facial flaws such as acne or the perception of a larger than average nose are most likely to concern people with this disorder, but they typically have more than one concern; genitalia, hair, and breasts are other common areas of focus. People with this disorder are not delusional and can acknowledge that they may be exaggerating, but they do not have a realistic image of themselves. (A delusional form of this disorder is coded under delusional disorder, somatic type.) This disorder typically causes marked distress or dysfunction.

Body dysmorphic disorder has high comorbidity with other mental disorders, including mood disorders, anxiety disorders, substance abuse or dependence, and psychotic disorders. Personality disorders have been found to co-occur in 70% to 100% of people with body dysmorphic disorders (Veale & Neziroglu, 2010). Men are also more likely to have avoidant personality disorders, alcohol use disorders, and bipolar disorders (Phillips, 2001). Suicidal ideation is also common. People with this disorder are more likely to seek help initially from dermatologists and surgeons than from therapists and to request therapy only after a physician referral. This disorder is often overlooked in assessment because people may be embarrassed or ashamed to discuss their preoccupations about their physical features. Veale and Neziroglu (2010) recommend asking clients during intake assessment: "Do you worry a lot about the way you look and wish you could think about it less?" (p. 6) as a simple screening tool for body dysmorphic disorder.

Typical Client Characteristics

The etiology of somatoform disorders remains unknown but an interplay among biological, environmental, and psychological components are thought to underlie their development. Because a large percentage of people with somatoform disorders have first-degree relatives who also have the disorder, a familial pattern of focusing on bodily symptoms and problems may be a contributing factor. Research indicates a relationship between somatoform disorders, mood and anxiety disorders, and antisocial personality disorder, but the underlying connection between these disorders is not clear. More research is necessary to find the connection between these disorders.

Biologically, heightened physiological arousal in these individuals results in amplification of bodily experiences. A biological predisposition to a low pain threshold may result in these clients misreading or being overly attentive to bodily cues. This combined with a higher vulnerability to stress, and fewer coping skills or reduced recognition or acceptance of emotional expressions, may result in psychological stress that manifests as hysical complaints.

Many people with somatoform disorders report a family history of illness, and clients' symptoms may mirror those experienced by family members when the clients were children. The clients themselves may have been sickly when they were younger and may have learned that, in their families, physical illness gained more attention than verbal expressions of emotional discomfort.

A look at all the somatoform disorders indicates that they typically begin in adolescence or young adulthood and follow a chronic but often inconsistent course. Most types of somatoform disorder are more common in women and in people who live in rural areas, are not well educated, have below-average intellectual functioning and socioeconomic status, are not psychologically minded or insightful, and have difficulty identifying and expressing their feelings.

People with these disorders tend to become preoccupied with their illnesses and medical histories and de-emphasize other areas of their lives, often experiencing social and occupational impairment as a result. In some cases their physical complaints become a way to relate to others and gain sympathy and attention. Use of both prescription and nonprescription medication to relieve symptoms is common. As many as 30% of people with somatization pain disorder become dependent on analgesics.

Somatization disorder seems to have a familial component. The families of origin of people with somatization disorder have a prevalence of mental disorders, ranging from 44% in one study to 70% in another (Stuart & Noyes, 1999). The authors found that behavior modeling by the parents, child temperament, and genetic influences all contribute to the development of somatization disorders.

Somatization Disorder   People with somatization disorder usually restrict their activities, movement, and levels of stimulation in the belief that if they protect themselves in this way, they may prevent a worsening of their pain or other symptoms (Phillips, 2001). Their preoccupation with their body often leads to a de-emphasis on other areas of their lives as they focus instead on medication schedules, medical appointments, and tests. Social isolation and depression frequently result, which in turn may precipitate an intensification of the symptoms, reduced energy, low self-esteem, and problematic sleeping and eating patterns (K. A. Phillips, 2009).

Stuart and Noyes (1999) found that nearly 20% of people with somatization disorder reported experiencing a chronic illness before the age of 16. Alexithymia, the inability to identify or articulate emotions, sometimes contributes to and coexists with somatoform disorders, especially with hypochondriasis and somatization disorder (Holder-Perkins & Wise, 2001).

As adults, people with somatization disorder often have major depressive disorder, suicidal ideation, substance misuse, and neurological disorders, and may be dependent, overly emotional, exhibitionistic, narcissistic, disorganized, dependent, and self-centered. Co-occurring personality disorders often include borderline, histrionic, or avoidant personality disorders (Holder-Perkins & Wise, 2001; Stuart & Noyes, 1999).

Pain Disorder   Somatoform pain disorder is chronic pain that cannot be explained, even after invasive diagnostic and therapeutic procedures have been completed. It is more common in women (34%) than men (22%) (Fröhlich, Jacobi, & Wittchen, 2006). People with pain disorder have often had early exposure to people experiencing pain. Children's reactions of pain tend to mirror their parents' reactions and are more often governed by the parents' affect than by the illness itself (Stuart & Noyes, 1999). As adults, their experience of pain is often connected to a threatened loss or unresolved conflict that raises negative feelings, which are then expressed through somatization (Bond, 2006). Pain disorder often reflects masked depression. Families of people with this disorder also have a high incidence of chronic pain, dysfunctional alcohol use, and depression.

Conversion Disorder   People with conversion disorder are usually willing to discuss their symptoms, often at great length and in specific detail. This contrasts sharply with people who are deliberately feigning symptoms and tend to become defensive, evasive, and suspicious when symptoms or inconsistencies in their behavior are pointed out. Pain is unusual in conversion disorder. Clients frequently report symptoms occurring on the left side of their bodies.

Conversion disorder is most common in adolescents and women who are not medically or psychologically sophisticated and who may have limited education and intellectual ability. Sexual abuse is frequently found in the histories of these women.

Conversion disorder is often associated with major depressive disorder, with approximately 85% of people with conversion disorder meeting the criteria for major depression at some point in their lives (Holder-Perkins & Wise, 2001). Other commonly co-occurring disorders include somatization disorder, anxiety disorders, alcohol use disorders, dissociative disorders, and personality disorders.

Hypochondriasis   People with hypochondriasis are particularly likely to have symptoms similar to people with obsessive-compulsive disorder (OCD), especially obsessive thoughts about illness and the compulsive need to check the Internet for medical information and health sites (Fallon & Feinstein, 2001). Hypochondriasis is often associated with an early bereavement, a history of illness in the family, and overprotective parents.

Hypochondriasis commonly is accompanied by anxiety, depression, mistrust, underlying anger and hostility, obsessive-compulsive traits, fear of disease, a low pain threshold, and disturbed early relationships. Personality disorders are present in as many as 61% of people with hypochondriasis, with avoidant, paranoid, and obsessive-compulsive personality disorders being the most common (Stuart & Noyes, 1999). Hypochondriasis can be situational or chronic, typically worsening during times of stress or emotional arousal (Fallon & Feinstein, 2001).

Body Dysmorphic Disorder   Similar to hypochondriasis, people with body dysmorphic disorder are likely to have obsessive thoughts about their bodies, especially any perceived flaws. People's self-consciousness can lead them to engage in prolonged grooming and staring into mirrors, to dress in concealing garments, and to seek repeated surgeries for perceived flaws (K. A. Phillips, 2009). Others become preoccupied with avoidance behaviors such as drinking, cannabis use, and bingeing and purging, in frantic efforts to control their anxiety. Still others may avoid public situations, to the point of becoming housebound (Veale & Neziroglu, 2010).

Men with body dysmorphic disorder tend to be preoccupied with body build, genitals, thinning hair, and height, whereas women are more likely to focus on hips and weight and have increased incidence of bulimia nervosa and anxiety disorders. For men, dissatisfaction with their physique or musculature may lead to the use of anabolic steroids or overexercising.

Assessment

Up to 50% of people with somatization disorder will also meet *DSM* criteria for lifetime depression. Similarly, most people who have depression will identify at least one unexplained bodily symptom (Woolfolk & Allen, 2007). Depression and anxiety disorders co-occur with somatoform disorders to such an extent that both anxiety and depression should be assessed and treated first as an effective treatment for these disorders. Other disorders may also be present and their symptoms need to be identified in order for appropriate treatment plans to be developed. Specific assessment tools for anxiety and mood disorders can be found in Chapters 4 and 5.

Preferred Therapist Characteristics

Therapists generally should assume a warm, positive, optimistic stance in treating people with somatoform disorders. These clients need a stable relationship that inspires confidence and provides acceptance, approval, and empathy. This requirement may present a challenge because some people with somatoform disorders are frustrated and angry with the medical community's inability to resolve their physical complaints. They may be resentful of a referral for psychotherapy, viewing the referral as a statement that others think their complaints are "all in their minds." These negative feelings are often displaced onto the therapist, who may bear the brunt of these clients' discouragement and unhappiness.

One of the most helpful interventions for the therapist working with a client with somatoform disorder is the development of an accepting and collaborative relationship. Some therapists experience annoyance and even anger with these clients if the clients refuse to let go of the belief that they have serious physical disorders or if the clients view therapists and physicians as adversaries who are refusing to find physical causes for the symptoms. Therapists need to be aware of their own reactions to these clients' behaviors and attitudes so that they can build a positive therapeutic alliance and prevent countertransference reactions from harming the therapeutic relationship.

The therapist should gradually shift the focus off the physical illness and encourage stress management, increased activities and socialization, and positive verbalization. Reinforcement should be used when the client does not dwell on the bodily symptoms but instead takes an active role in self-help.

Intervention Strategies

As with all the disorders in this chapter, a team approach to treatment of somatoform disorders is indicated, with the physician and the therapist working together. The therapist can even be presented as a consultant who will help alleviate the impact of stress on the client's physical complaints while the physician focuses on the medical aspects of those complaints. This stance reassures clients that their physical complaints are being taken seriously and treated appropriately. A collaborative approach also allows the therapist to monitor the client's medical care and discourage unnecessary tests or medical consultations while making sure that the physician does indeed take the client seriously. Bond (2006) reports that it is not the severity of the symptoms that are troublesome, but the person's dramatic and persistent complaints about them. Presenting both the physiological and the psychological component of treatment as an integrated package can promote treatment compliance and increase the chances of a successful outcome.

Overall treatment goals should focus on improving functioning rather than on reducing physical symptoms; if functioning is improved, in most cases, the symptoms will spontaneously decrease. Somatically focused anxiety is a common characteristic of these disorders. Bond (2006) suggests that it is best understood as a cognitive distortion. Thus, clients' tendencies toward amplification (their selective perception and exaggeration of physiological symptoms), as well as their withdrawal from relationships and activities, can be reduced through cognitive-behavioral therapy. The focus of therapy should be on the present rather than on the past and should seek to increase skills in stress management and coping, facilitate verbal expression of feelings, promote empowerment, and encourage healthy cognitions as well as increased activity and socialization. Confrontation and emphasis on insight, if used at all, should be reserved for later phases of treatment with these clients.

Medical complaints should be de-emphasized. The therapist should avoid taking a position on the veracity of the medical complaints and certainly should not engage in arguments with the client. People with somatoform disorders genuinely experience and believe in the symptoms they present, and therapists should treat those beliefs gently. Understanding and addressing the social context of people with this disorder is essential because context typically reinforces and explains the presence of the symptoms.

Although information on somatoform disorders is increasing, the empirical research on effective treatment of somatoform disorders is limited. Many approaches and techniques have been suggested and have demonstrated success, such as the following three-stage treatment process:

1. In Stage 1, therapy begins with a concrete focus on physical symptoms, teaching people strategies for reducing them. Techniques like biofeedback and relaxation training are usually well received because of their emphasis on the body.
2. Stage 2 emphasizes supportive discussion of symptoms and lifestyle and helps the client make connections between the two, raising awareness of difficulties that may be experienced in the interpersonal, occupational, and leisure areas as well as in self-expression.
3. Stage 3 employs cognitive and emotive approaches, enabling people to gain deeper awareness of their cognitive distortions; become better able to identify and express their emotions; and make changes in thoughts, feelings, behaviors, relationships, and lifestyle.

Following is a brief look at available treatments for each of the specific somatoform disorders.

Somatization Disorder New research is emerging on the treatment of somatization disorder. One randomized controlled trial of affective cognitive-behavioral therapy (ACBT) for the treatment of somatization disorder consisted of weekly 60-minute sessions spread across a 10-week period. Sessions focused on symptom assessment, teaching relaxation and stress-reduction, sleep hygiene, and distraction techniques, and the use of cognitive restructuring interventions. The spouse or significant other was invited to attend two sessions with the goal of improving family support and reducing behaviors that might be reinforcing the disorder. At the end of the 10-week period, 40% of participants said they were much improved or very much improved. Treatment gains remained constant at 6- and 12-month follow up (Allen et al., 2006). Findings of this study were consistent with other clinical trials reviewed by Kroenke (2007).

Affective cognitive-behavioral therapy begins with a focus on the client. Therapists are empathic, nonjudgmental, and ask questions that reflect their interest in the client's well-being. Most people who present with somatoform disorders are not likely to be very psychologically minded, so treatment is framed in terms of stress management and focuses on a reduction in bodily symptoms. Relaxation techniques, sleep hygiene, and positive coping skills such as distraction, assertiveness, and self-esteem are taught. As with any other behavioral therapy, homework is assigned and symptom monitoring forms are a part of each weekly session. A manualized version of ACBT, along with appropriate assessment tools and symptom logs is included as an appendix to Woolfolk and Allen (2007).

Conversion Disorder Case reports from the literature indicate that acute and less severe conversion reactions respond well to support and therapy to address precipitating stressors, reassurance that not all physical symptoms have an underlying cause, and hope and expectation that clients will get better soon. More chronic cases may require longer term treatment and more intensive behavioral approaches (Simon, 2002). Antidepressant or antianxiety medication and hypnosis have also been shown to play a positive role in the treatment of conversion disorder.

Pain Disorder Major depression accompanies chronic pain in 57% to 72% of the cases. Suicidal thoughts tend to increase as a result of the degree and intensity of pain, so these issues must be addressed in people with somatoform pain disorder so that treatment can be effective. Interpersonal therapy, cognitive-behavioral therapy, and mindfulness-based stress reduction have all shown promise in the treatment of this disabling disorder.

Interpersonal therapy. IPT-P for depression and pain is a brief, 8-session adaptation of the evidence-based IPT (discussed earlier in Chapter 4). The therapist begins by listening to and accepting the client's pain story, and providing psychoeducation about the relationship between pain and depression. In subsequent sessions, IPT strategies are interspersed with pain management strategies. Pain intensity is evaluated at the beginning and end of each session, self-care strategies are provided, and successes are reinforced. Any barriers to treatment are addressed as they occur. During the final session, the client is asked to anticipate problems that may arise and brainstorm how to use IPT-P strategies effectively. Participants in an uncontrolled pilot study of 17 women with gynecological pain and comorbid depression indicated high satisfaction with the intervention, decreased severity of depression, and better adherence to treatment (Poleshuck et al., 2010). IPT-P shows promise, but additional research is necessary to determine if the intervention provides an effective adjunct to traditional medical treatment for pain management.

Cognitive-behavioral therapy. Results of two meta-analyses of cognitive-behavioral therapy (CBT) used for pain management and relapse prevention indicate that CBT and behavior therapy are both effective interventions to help people with pain disorder reduce pain and improve mood. Both types of treatment were also found to be effective when integrated into rehabilitation programs (Bond, 2006).

An informal 1 to 10 rating scale of pain's severity can be useful in assessing progress that has been made in the treatment of pain disorder. Simon (2002) notes that pain symptoms can be reduced by combining strategies to promote pain management (such as imagery and relaxation training) with techniques designed to reduce negative self-talk and increase physical activity. In this manner, nonpain behaviors are reinforced and cognitive restructuring occurs.

Medication management. Seventy-five placebo-controlled trials tested the efficacy of antidepressant medication on pain disorder. Most studies found medication more effective than a placebo (Simon, 2002), and a slightly improved outcome when medication is combined with psychotherapy.

Group therapy. Group therapy is another appropriate intervention for the management of somatoform pain disorder. A meta-analysis of the effectiveness of group psychotherapy for this population found that outpatients improve more than inpatients, homogeneous groups have better outcomes, and groups that included males and females had better outcomes than single-gender groups (Burlingame, Fuhriman, & Mosier, 2003). A manualized version of interpersonal psychodynamic therapy for the treatment of somatoform pain disorders has been developed for groups (Nickel, Ademmer, & Egle, 2010). After the initial assessment interview, the heterogeneous group meets for 90 minutes twice weekly for the first 30 sessions, with the final 10 sessions being held weekly. In addition, several individual sessions are held intermittently. A portion of each group focuses on psychoeducation about acute and chronic pain, the connection between stress and early adverse experiences on current perception of pain, the biopsychosocial model, and modifying client's cognitions. The balance of the time is spent in group interaction. A relationship-focused treatment approach is used which enables patients to access their own emotions and correct distortions in attribution. The treatment shows promise, and a randomized clinical trial is currently underway that compares interpersonal psychodynamic group therapy with another theoretical orientation, and an untreated control group.

Mindfulness-based stress reduction. As mentioned earlier, more than 250 mindfulness-based stress reduction programs are offered in major cities across the country. Many of these programs are offered in conjunction with treatment for specific illnesses such as cancer or heart disease. Others are generic or focused specifically on decreasing anxiety or reducing chronic pain (Kabat-Zinn, 2003; Miller, Fletcher, & Kabat-Zinn, 1995; Kabat-Zinn, Chapman, & Salmon, 1997).

Some hospitals have pain treatment units that facilitate the treatment of people with pain disorder. These programs typically aim at decreasing people's experience of pain as well as their reliance on medication, while increasing their activity levels, their cognitive control over the pain, and their effective use of coping mechanisms (Simon, 2002). Such programs usually offer a multidisciplinary approach to treatment and typically include the following elements:

- Detoxification from medication (if needed)
- Physical, occupational, and recreational therapy
- Acupuncture
- Trigger-point injections
- Transcutaneous electrical nerve stimulation (TENS)
- Group, individual, and family therapy
- Various forms of relaxation

Hypnosis, biofeedback, and relaxation have also contributed to the treatment of hypochondriasis and of pain disorder. One meta-analysis of hypnotic analgesia found that hypnosis produced substantial pain relief for 75% of the people studied (Price, 2006).

Hypochondriasis Hypochondriasis is a fear or anxiety of having a medical illness. As in the treatment of anxiety disorders, cognitive-behavioral therapy can help in a variety of ways: by reducing obsessive thinking about bodily concerns, correcting misinformation, and addressing cognitive distortions (e.g., catastrophizing, selection perception, and misattribution) that serve to maintain these fears. Fallon and Feinstein (2001) suggest a comprehensive approach to treating hypochondriasis that has application to the other types of somatoform disorders as well. Therapy begins with the establishment of a trusting relationship that validates the client's experience. Therapists should remain tolerant and sympathetic despite the client's resistance to psychotherapy. Following a careful history taking, the therapist can focus on helping the client understand how stress can aggravate symptoms. The client is asked to keep a self-report log of stressors so that a connection can be made between precipitating events and development and exacerbation of symptoms.

Once that goal has been accomplished, therapy typically includes the following five steps:

1. Exploration of the client's attitudes toward illness.
2. Presentation of information on the client's medical condition.
3. Perceptual retraining to help the client focus more on external information and less on internal cues.
4. Ericksonian suggestions that the client's symptoms will be reduced.
5. Encouragement of self-talk and internal dialogue to reduce stress and anxiety.

A number of case studies show the effectiveness of antidepressant medication in the treatment of hypochondriasis. Reported response rates were between 60% and 80% (Simon, 2002).

Body Dysmorphic Disorder Randomized controlled studies for CBT or behavioral therapy are lacking. Several meta-analyses of cognitive-behavioral therapy for body dysmorphic disorder favored CBT over wait list controls. Exposure and response prevention alone may be as effective in combined treatment with cognitive therapy in reducing symptoms. Habit reversal training (HRT) for psychogenic

excoriation (skin scratching and picking) was also found to be effective in one study (Adams, Adams, & Miltenberger, 2008; Teng, Woods, & Twohig, 2006). Most of the research on body dysmorphic disorder had a small sample size and should be considered with caution (Neziroglu & Khemlani-Patel, 2002; Veale & Neziroglu, 2010).

Obsessive features in people with body dysmorphic disorder or hypochondriasis have responded well to behavior therapy—both habit reversal and exposure and response prevention seem to have their place in the treatment of specific symptoms of this disorder. Cognitive therapy, too, can be helpful, especially in addressing any overvalued ideals of body image or rigid thinking (K. A. Phillips, 2009). People with body dysmorphic disorder tend to value themselves according to an idealized version of how they think they should look, and hold on to these beliefs very rigidly. A cognitive-behavioral treatment model has been proposed by Veale and Neziroglu (2010).

Phillips (2001) suggests the following treatment strategies for body dysmorphic disorder:

- Target body dysmorphic symptoms in the treatment (do not focus exclusively on depression or anxiety).
- Use medication such as SSRIs as a first-line approach for those with severe disorders. Often medication can make cognitive-behavioral therapy possible by reducing depressive and physical symptoms enough so that the person can benefit from therapy.
- For milder forms of the disorder that are not accompanied by co-occurring disorders, use intensive CBT without medication. Schedule frequent sessions with accompanying homework. The cognitive component should include exposure and response prevention.

- Add CBT booster sessions to prevent relapse.
- Include psychoeducation about body image that encourages acceptance and discourages surgery or other medical interventions.

Treatment of any accompanying depression and anxiety can also be helpful in the treatment of this disorder. Two randomized controlled trials provide some evidence for the effectiveness of selective serotonin reuptake inhibitors (SSRIs) in the treatment of adults with body dysmorphic disorder. Additional research is needed on the treatment of adolescents and adults with accompanying psychosis.

Group Therapy Group therapy also is an important component of treatment for somatoform disorders, particularly for hypochondriasis, pain disorder, and body dysmorphic disorder (Simon, 2002). It can promote socialization, provide support, and facilitate direct expression of emotions. For those with body dysmorphic disorder, realistic feedback from peers about clients' appearance can be more powerful than feedback from a therapist (Simon, 2002). Group therapy can also change people's expression of symptoms, reduce depression, modify avoidance behaviors, help people assume responsibility for their symptoms, enhance their ability to enjoy life, provide information and support as well as reinforcement, and teach relaxation and other positive behaviors.

Family Therapy Family members usually should be involved in the treatment of somatoform disorders. They can learn to reinforce positive behavior and, as appropriate, to ignore or de-emphasize the client's physical complaints. People diagnosed with somatoform disorders should learn to get attention and affection through means other than physical illness; for

most people, this learning is best gained and reinforced in the family environment. People with somatoform disorders tend to be more receptive to therapy when it is endorsed not only by a professional whose opinion is valued but also by a friend or a family member—yet another reason for involving the client's close friends or family members in treatment. If the client has a history of conflicted and dysfunctional family relationships or is still troubled by the illness or death of a family member, therapy may need to pay some attention to those issues in an effort to reduce their present impact.

Adjunct Treatment Because many people with somatoform disorders have neglected the social and occupational areas of their lives, those areas should receive attention through therapy. People will often need to build support systems, develop leisure activities that may have been avoided before, and establish and work toward realistic and rewarding career goals. Environmental modifications, such as walking to work with a neighbor, may encourage some of these lifestyle changes by reducing secondary gains of physical complaints and altering patterns of activity.

Medication Increasingly, medication has been used to treat somatoform disorders. Although analgesic medication usually does not reduce the pain associated with these disorders, antidepressant medication is often recommended to alleviate the underlying depression and often leads to reduction in the somatic symptoms. Although medication generally is not indicated for the treatment of hypochondriasis, several clinical trials have shown improvement ranging from 77% to 80% in patients treated with Prozac (Phillips, 2001). Fluoxetine has also been shown to be beneficial for clients with hypochondriasis that is treatment-resistant (Fallon & Feinstein, 2001).

Pain disorders, too, show significant improvement in response to antidepressant medication. However, the medication does not teach people to develop coping skills and rebuild their lives. Thus, even if medication is helpful, psychotherapy also seems essential to effecting and maintaining a positive response to treatment. Whatever approach to the treatment of somatoform disorders is used, what should be encouraged is healthy, independent, responsible behavior.

Prognosis

Somatoform disorders tend to be persistent and resistant to treatment. Factors associated with a good prognosis are the presence of a stressful precipitant for the symptoms, brief and circumscribed symptoms, the ability to form stable relationships, the capacity to feel and express emotions directly, the ability to form a therapeutic alliance, and the ability to be introspective. A negative prognosis is most likely when people fail to recognize that their concerns are probably excessive.

Prognosis varies according to the specific disorder, the individual client, and treatment methodology. One study conducted at Harvard University found improvement in somatoform disorder after brief, intensive therapy (Holder-Perkins & Wise, 2001). The gains were maintained 1 year after treatment ended. Conversion disorder almost always spontaneously disappears within a few days or weeks but may recur under stress and tends to be difficult to treat once it becomes entrenched. Conversion symptoms of blindness, aphonia, and paralysis usually respond well to treatment, but pseudoseizures and tremors are less likely to remit (Maldonado & Spiegel, 2001). Pain symptoms can be chronic and disabling, but pain treatment centers report a 60% to 80% rate of significant improvement among people with pain disorder, and that

improvement is well maintained after discharge. Hypochondriasis can be a chronic and fluctuating disorder, although most people with this disorder do improve significantly.

Body dysmorphic disorder tends to be a chronic and stable disorder that is often difficult to treat, although recent research shows promise for the effectiveness of cognitive-behavioral therapy that focuses on exposure treatment and response prevention (Phillips, 2001; Veale & Neziroglu, 2010). As is the case with other somatoform disorders, insight-oriented therapy does not appear to be effective for body dysmorphic disorder; neither does surgery nor nonpsychological medical treatment. Pharmacotherapy with SSRIs appears to help, but relapse often occurs when the medication is discontinued. Somatoform disorders can be challenging to treat, but most clients do benefit considerably from therapy, sometimes in combination with medication.

FACTITIOUS DISORDERS

Factitious disorders are "characterized by physical or psychological symptoms that are intentionally produced or feigned in order to assume the sick role" (American Psychiatric Association, 2000, p. 513). Unlike people with somatoform disorders, who genuinely experience and believe in their physical complaints, people with factitious disorders purposely simulate symptoms in order to be treated as though they are ill. They are not feigning the symptoms in order to escape work or other obligations; rather, their primary goal is to assume the role of patient and to receive care, nurturance, and attention.

Description of the Disorders

Factitious disorders, also known as Munchausen's syndrome, are among the most difficult disorders to diagnose because of the person's untruthfulness and hidden agendas, as well as the degree to which they will inflict self-harm to substantiate their claims of illnesses (Feldman, Hamilton, & Deemer, 2001). People with this disorder typically feign severe physical or psychological symptoms (for example, psychosis or abnormal bleeding). Their affect tends to be incongruent with these symptoms, often reflecting indifference or lack of concern. They are eager to undergo invasive medical procedures but generally will not allow communication with previous physicians. They avoid accurate diagnosis through changes of residence, physicians, and symptoms.

The onset of a factitious disorder is usually in early adulthood, but the disorder may begin in childhood, often following a medically verified physical illness that places these people in a rewarding patient role in which they are nurtured and receive attention. Sometimes people with factitious disorders have worked in medical settings or are otherwise familiar with medical personnel and illnesses, and this familiarity facilitates their simulation of the symptoms of illness. Alternatively, people with factitious disorder sometimes research their feigned disorders so that they can present a convincing story. This disorder is more common in males (American Psychiatric Association, 2000) and is severe in that it typically prevents people's involvement in normal social and occupational activities. Due to the lack of research and people's unwillingness to admit to this disorder, prevalence rates of factitious disorder are unknown, although it seems to be relatively rare (Feldman et al., 2001).

In a variation on this disorder, factitious disorder by proxy (otherwise known as Munchausen's disorder by proxy and diagnosed as factitious disorder not otherwise specified), parents or caregivers deliberately create or exaggerate physical or psychological symptoms in people under their care (such as children or people who are elderly or disabled). Infants and young children are the most likely victims. Caregivers may coach people in their care to confirm or present signs of the illness, or they may harm the people in their care so that they will appear ill. The symptoms bring attention, support, and sympathy to the caregivers.

People with factitious disorder by proxy sometimes cause the deaths of people in their care through suffocation, poisoning, or other means. The estimated death rate for children involved in this pattern ranges from 10% to 60% (Schreier, 2002; Sheridan, 2003; Stirling, 2007). Many others are disfigured or impaired, as a result either of harm from their caregivers or of harm from unnecessary medical procedures. In a meta-analysis of published cases, Schreier indicates that these children had as many as "40 to 100 operations for nonexistent conditions" (p. 985) and that 75% of the children who died as a result of this disorder died in hospitals.

The American Professional Society on the Abuse of Children recently recommended that a child who is the victim of this abuse be diagnosed with pediatric condition falsification (PCF) and that factitious disorder by proxy be reserved for the perpetrator of the abuse (Shaw, Dayal, Hartman, & DeMaso, 2008).

Typical Client Characteristics

People with factitious disorders tend to be immature, dramatic, grandiose, and demanding; they insist on attention while often refusing to comply with prescribed treatments. In addition to what is usually the primary motivator, the wish for attention and nurturing (Feldman et al., 2001), common underlying motivators are self-punishment, the desire to obtain compensation for past suffering and perceived wrongs, and the desire to obtain drugs. Their behavior may be learned, as people with factitious disorders typically had parents who were normally harsh and demanding but who became caring and loving when their children were ill, thus reinforcing a dysfunctional pattern of behavior. People with this disorder also may have developed positive early relationships with physicians, thereby further reinforcing their symptoms.

Males with factitious disorders tend to be unstable and egocentric, often exaggerating their accomplishments, whereas females tend to be younger, more stable, and more likely to be in the medical field (Schreier, 2002). Factitious disorder has been seen in children and teenagers who induce or claim illness to receive medical attention.

People with factitious disorders typically have other somatoform disorders and have a high incidence of anxiety, mood, and substance use disorders. Men are more likely to have comorbid bipolar disorders; borderline personality disorder more commonly co-occurs in women (Feldman et al., 2001). First-degree relatives of those with factitious disorders also often have mental disorders, chronic medical problems, and poor coping skills. People with factitious disorders may have undergone many surgical procedures and other medical tests and treatments that produced genuine physical complaints that now complicate the treatment picture.

Schreier (2002) notes that people with factitious disorder by proxy usually are young mothers who on the surface appear devoted to their children but are actually hurting their children to meet the mothers' own self-serving needs (such as to gain access to or attention from the medical community). Their backgrounds often include a history of family dysfunction and abuse. Medical settings may be familiar and comfortable to them because of their own illnesses or work experiences. The recidivism rate for these mothers is high and underscores the need to obtain a swift and accurate diagnosis before the child, or other children, are injured or made sick again. Symptoms on the part of the caregiver include falsification of medical conditions, direct harm induction, inappropriate affect (one mother was reported to be "gleeful" when describing her son's acute life-threatening events), and a wide variety of other symptom presentations (Schreier, 2002). Some commonly used mechanisms to falsify the child's presentation include suffocation and poisoning, falsification of laboratory tests, withholding nutrition, manipulation of catheters and intravenous fluids, and coaching the child on which symptoms to report (Shaw et al., 2008).

Most of the children involved are younger than 5 years of age, with a mean of 7 to 15 months between the onset of symptoms and diagnosis (Schreier, 2004). Presentation in older children is similar, with older children being more likely to be coached by, and collude with, their parents. As many as 55% of these children may have an actual co-occurring illness (Levin & Sheriden, 1995).

Factitious disorder by proxy is rare, with approximately 600 new cases being reported annually in the United States (Shaw et al., 2008). More than 75% of the people with this disorder are mothers; fathers represent nearly 7%, and grandparents and other child-care providers can also be at fault. A prior history of depression, suicide attempts, or trauma is commonly found in the backgrounds of these people. Many have co-occurring personality disorders (e.g., narcissistic or antisocial personality disorder), and as many as 22% have a history of childhood abuse or abuse in their current relationship (Rand & Feldman, 2001; Sheridan, 2003). However, no consistent patterns of behavior have been found in parents and other caregivers who exaggerate or actually cause medical symptoms in the children in their care (Kozlowska, Foley, & Crittenden, 2006).

Assessment

Myriad somatic, cognitive, and behavioral difficulties may be presented by the client with factitious disorder. According to Simon (2002), these
symptoms may often be "clearly inconsistent
with any known disease" (p. 455). Because the
client's goal is frequently to maintain the sick
role, accurate assessment of symptoms can be
exceedingly difficult. Neither has an assessment
tool been found to help with diagnosis of factitious disorder by proxy. These people may seem
fine on the surface, and actually appear to be
concerned with obtaining medical care for their
child.

Preferred Therapist Characteristics

Establishing a therapeutic alliance with a person
diagnosed with a factitious disorder will usually
be extremely difficult. The therapist should be
supportive and empathic but should also gently
confront the deception. Strong confrontation
should be avoided because typically that will be
met with denial and hostility. Schreier (2002)
suggests that consulting with the client's physician can be especially effective in working with
these clients. Consultation with the physician
can confirm whether there is a medical basis for
the client's complaints, a past history of repeated
unexplained illnesses, or, as often happens, a history of the client's changing doctors frequently.
Therapists should avoid power struggles, open
conflict, and humiliation of people with factitious disorders and must manage their own feelings of anger and frustration in dealing with the
clients' deceptions and manipulations. Viewing
the symptoms as a cry for help rather than as
hostile or manipulative behavior can be helpful
to both therapist and client.

In the case of factitious disorder by proxy,
active measures must be taken to confirm the
diagnosis, because of concerns about the well-
being of the child. The diagnosis should be
made by a multidisciplinary team consisting of
at minimum a physician, a mental health
professional, a nurse, a legal consultant, and child
protective services. Because of the rare nature of
the disorder and the likelihood that diagnosis
will occur in a hospital setting, clinicians most
likely will not be involved. For a complete
discussion of psychiatric assessment, legal, and
procedural matters, readers are referred to Shaw
and colleagues (2008).

Intervention Strategies

People with factitious disorders are rarely seen
for psychotherapy because they typically are not
motivated to address their disorder, but they
may appear in treatment as a result of pressure
from a family member or as part of court-
ordered treatment to retain custody of their children. Some may remain in treatment if attention
is paid to their feigned complaints and if the
treatment meets some of their dependence
needs, although most will leave treatment once
they realize that they have been found out.
While in treatment, people with factitious disorders are likely to be hostile and to resist the formation of a positive therapeutic relationship.

Therapists should try to establish realistic
treatment goals with these clients. Personality
reconstruction through therapy is unlikely;
however, improvement in coping skills, reduction in self-injurious behavior and dangerous
medical procedures, and symptom reduction are
all realistic goals. Feldman and colleagues (2001)
found that those diagnosed in the early stages of
factitious disorder are more amendable to psychotherapeutic interventions, but no interventions are now known to be consistently effective
in treating factitious disorders, so treatment recommendations are based on theory rather than
on empirical data. Many people with factitious
disorders who are reluctant to engage in psychotherapy may be more willing to participate in

therapeutic stress management and so this may serve as a way to engage them in treatment. These interventions can help those with factitious disorders abandon the sick role and construct a healthier self-image. Ironically, treatment of clients who have factitious disorder may require therapists to be deceptive themselves. Eisendrath (2001) suggests a double-bind approach to treatment in which clients are offered a benign medical intervention (such as biofeedback) and are told that failure of the treatment will confirm a diagnosis of a factitious disorder. This apparently leads some people to choose recovery. One reason for the success of this approach is that it allows people to give up factitious behaviors without embarrassment—an important element of treatment. However, therapists may be uncomfortable with the apparently misleading nature of this intervention.

In factitious disorder by proxy, early detection is essential to prevent injury or death of the child or other target of the harmful behavior. Children whose caregivers can be diagnosed with factitious disorder by proxy may need to be hospitalized or removed from the home for their own protection. The available information on the treatment of this disorder is nearly all anecdotal or theoretical. Because the condition is rare, has no predetermined cause or pattern, and because of parents' and caregivers' capacity for deceit and adamant denials of malicious intent, it is extremely difficult to form an effective intervention for factitious disorder by proxy. A complete discussion of symptoms, assessment protocols, and legal considerations for this disorder can be found in Shaw and colleagues (2008).

Prognosis

In some cases, a factitious disorder that develops in response to environmental stress will remit spontaneously when the stressor has passed.

Once a factitious disorder becomes chronic and part of a person's lifestyle, however, the prognosis for spontaneous recovery is poor. Factors associated with responsiveness to treatment include coexisting Axis I mental disorders (such as depression, anxiety, or substance use), obsessive-compulsive or histrionic personality traits, and the ability to establish a therapeutic alliance. The presence of severe personality disorders reduces the likelihood of a successful treatment outcome (Feldman et al., 2001). Factitious disorder by proxy is difficult to treat, as these caregivers commonly deny any responsibility for producing symptoms in those under their care. Despite treatment efforts, relapse rates remain as high as 50% (Simon, 2002).

DELIRIUM, DEMENTIA, AND AMNESTIC AND OTHER COGNITIVE DISORDERS

The *DSM-IV-TR* defines three categories of cognitive disorders: delirium, dementia, and amnestic disorder, as well as cognitive disorders not otherwise specified. The cognitive disorders are a heterogeneous group with diverse symptoms and origins, although all of these disorders have a genuine physical cause. Common causes include Alzheimer's disease, a systemic illness, a head injury, or deleterious exposure to a psychoactive or toxic substance (such as alcohol).

Description of the Disorders

According to the *DSM-IV-TR*, all of the cognitive disorders are characterized by "a clinically significant deficit in cognition that represents a significant change from a previous level of functioning" (American Psychiatric Association, 2000, p. 125). Common symptoms of cognitive disorders include not only impairment in memory (especially of recent memory) but also impairments in:

- Abstract thinking
- Perception
- Language
- Ability to concentrate and perform new tasks
- Overall intellectual performance
- Judgment
- Attention
- Spatiotemporal orientation
- Calculating ability
- Ability to grasp meaning and recognize or identify objects
- Perceptions of body and environment

The symptoms of a cognitive disorder can encompass many of the symptoms associated with other mental disorders, such as depression, anxiety, personality change, paranoia, and confusion. Consequently, other mental disorders may be mistaken for the cognitive disorders that they resemble, and cognitive disorders also can be mistaken for other mental disorders (for example, some people diagnosed as having Alzheimer's disease actually have pseudodementia, a form of depression that has similar symptoms). This error is unfortunate, because effective treatments are available for depression, but an effective treatment for Alzheimer's disease has yet to be found. (However, considerable progress has been made in finding ways to slow disease progression.)

In light of the diagnostic challenge presented by the cognitive disorders, their diagnosis must take account of symptoms as well as of possible causes. The clinician should obtain a psychiatric or neurological evaluation when one of these disorders is suspected. EEGs and other medical tests, as well as such psychological tests as the Wechsler Intelligence Scales and the Halstead-Reitan Neuropsychologic Battery, can help determine the likelihood of cognitive disorders being present. The therapist may also find the Mini–Mental State Exam useful in making a preliminary diagnosis of a cognitive disorder.

Cognitive disorders are present in approximately 1% of the adult population and are expected to increase in prevalence with the lengthening of the life span (D. Sue, Sue, & Sue, et al., 2006). Discussion of specific etiologies and related presentations of these disorders is beyond the scope of this book; clinicians treating people with cognitive disorders will want to consult the *DSM* for the detailed descriptions and diagnostic criteria provided there.

Delirium This disorder is typified by abrupt onset and clouded consciousness, as well as by impairment of recent memory and attention, with accompanying disorientation. Hallucinations and delusions are common (Butcher et al., 2006). Emotional, perceptual, and psychomotor disturbances, as well as changes in the sleep–wake cycle often accompany this disorder, which can occur at any age but is most common in children and the elderly. Delirium can be caused by a medical condition, by substance use, or by multiple etiologies. Possible specific causes of delirium include central nervous system disease (such as epilepsy), cardiac failure, electrolyte imbalance, head injury, infection, and postoperative states. Butcher and colleagues (2006) report that the most common cause of delirium is drug intoxication or withdrawal. Toxicity from medication may also contribute, as does anesthesia. Postoperative delirium is common in the elderly following surgery. This disorder typically has an inconsistent course and a positive response to appropriate treatment, although it is associated with increased mortality in the hospitalized elderly and those who have an underlying medical illness (American Psychiatric Association, 2000).

Dementia This disorder is more likely to have an insidious onset and a progressive and pervasive course. It is characterized by multiple cognitive deficits, including memory impairment. Common symptoms of this disorder are decline in language functioning; difficulty in recognizing even familiar people and objects; and impairment in abstract thinking, judgment, and insight. An overall decline in social and occupational functioning nearly always accompanies this disorder. Delusions, especially those of persecution, often are symptoms of this disorder and may lead to aggressive and destructive behavior. Hallucinations and depression also often accompany dementia. Level of consciousness and alertness may be unaffected. The most common causes of dementia are Alzheimer's disease and vascular disease, but many other causes exist as well, including traumatic brain injury, brain tumors, HIV, substances (such as alcohol, inhalants, and sedatives), neurological and endocrine conditions, and vitamin deficiencies. This disorder is most prevalent among people over the age of 85. As many as 25% of people in this age group have severe dementia (American Psychiatric Association, 2000).

Amnestic Disorder

This disorder is characterized by memory impairment, especially learning and recall of new information, without other significant accompanying cognitive deficits. This disorder, too, has multiple possible etiologies, including head trauma, encephalitis, alcohol use with accompanying vitamin B$_1$ (thiamine) deficiency, sedative misuse, and brain tumors. Age at onset of amnestic disorder varies, as does the progression of the disorder and length of illness. Transient amnesia may last from several hours to a few days, whereas amnesia caused by head trauma may continue over a period of years.

Typical Client Characteristics

Few generalizations can be drawn about people with cognitive disorders because the causes and symptoms of these disorders vary so greatly. Most people with cognitive disorders will be past midlife, and many will have coexisting medical or substance use disorders. Additional client characteristics are linked to specific disorders.

Dementia is one of the most common cognitive disorders, found in about 5% to 7% of people over the age of 65 (Sue et al., 2006). Dementia of the Alzheimer's type affects 2% to 4% of people over the age of 65 and encompasses nearly 80% of people with dementia (Butcher et al., 2006). That disorder has a genetic component, with approximately 50% of people with a family history of the disease developing Alzheimer's in their eighties and nineties (Sue et al., 2006). Protective factors, such as higher educational and occupational achievement, use of nonsteroidal antiinflammatory drugs or estrogen replacement therapy, and vitamin E, have been found to delay the onset of Alzheimer's disease (Sue et al., 2006). Vascular dementia is more common in men than women and among people with a history of diabetes and hypertension. It often coexists with depression (Butcher et al., 2006).

Many forms of cognitive disorders have an external cause, such as excessive use of drugs or alcohol, a blow to the head, or exposure to a toxic substance, and will often be associated with habits or lifestyle. For example, substance-induced cognitive disorders usually will be accompanied by concurrent diagnosis of a substance use disorder.

Assessment

Clients presenting with symptoms of dementia or other cognitive-related disorders should first be referred for a comprehensive medical and neurological assessment. Therapists should work closely with medical personnel when establishing and implementing treatment plans.

Preferred Therapist Characteristics

Therapists treating people with cognitive disorders should either have training in the physiological and neurological aspects of these disorders or collaborate with someone who does have that training. The therapeutic relationship that is established with a person who has a cognitive disorder will depend to a large extent on the person's level of functioning. In general, a therapist working with a person who has cognitive deficits will have to be directive, supportive, and reassuring. The therapist may have to take charge of the treatment and determine what psychological and medical interventions are necessary, although client autonomy should be maintained as much as possible. Promoting awareness of reality usually will be an important part of the therapist's role, as will provision of information. Family consultation, education, and intervention, as well as assistance in obtaining adjunct services, such as family support groups, residential treatment facilities, respite care, and medical care may also be necessary. Therapists will also need to deal with their own feelings about treating people whose disorders may have a poor prognosis and limited prospects for improvement.

Intervention Strategies

The goal of treatment of cognitive disorders is to delay the onset of symptoms and slow the progression of the disease while also alleviating symptoms, modifying risk factors, and reducing mortality (Sue et al., 2006). Such treatment involves a multifaceted approach in which psychotherapy is combined with medical and neurological treatment, including drugs or surgery, needed to assess and arrest or reduce the cognitive impairment. Medication may target such symptoms as depression, anxiety, psychosis, and aggressiveness, and it may address the disorder itself. Medications, such as donepezil (Aricept) and rivastigmine (Exelon), are being used

to treat dementia of the Alzheimer's type as well as other cognitive disorders. Although studies show that those who received the medications do better cognitively and in overall global functioning compared to those who receive a placebo, participants still manifest considerable decline over the course of the illness (Black et al., 2007). Two relatively new medications approved for the treatment of Alzheimer's disease—galantamine (Razadyne) and memantine (Namenda)—appear to provide some positive cognitive benefits as well (Forchetti, 2005; Reisberg et al., 2003).

Environmental manipulation may be indicated to help people cope more effectively with their living situation despite their impairment and maintain some form of employment as long as possible. Change in routine, stress, and external stimuli should be reduced so as not to exacerbate symptoms. A person in the advanced stages of one of these disorders may need to be placed in a supervised living situation.

A comprehensive approach to intervention should include support for caregivers, who are at increased risk of depression, stress symptoms, and isolation (Butcher et al., 2006). Support groups, relaxation techniques, and coping skills can help reduce depression, worry, guilt, and the difficulty of caring for family members who have progressive or chronic cognitive disorders. Counseling, information, support, and help with making decisions, expressing feelings, and setting goals can enable family members to cope more effectively with the challenges of caring for someone with a cognitive disorder. Family members may also benefit from help in identifying and making use of community resources, such as respite care and in-home help that are available to them. Peer support groups are often available in the community and can help share information, normalize feelings, and provide support and a safe and understanding place for caregivers to express themselves.

Although psychotherapy typically plays a secondary role in direct treatment of most cognitive disorders, it can be an important complementary part of the medical treatment. Therapy seems particularly helpful to people in the early or mild stages of dementia of the Alzheimer's type and of vascular dementia. Therapy probably will be most useful if it emphasizes behavioral interventions, encouraging people to remain as active and independent as possible and helping them compensate for changes in their capacities by building on any coping mechanisms that are still accessible to them. Behaviorally oriented therapy can also help these people control their destructive impulses and their emotional lability. Attention should be paid to keeping people appropriately informed about the nature of their disorders, helping them express their feelings about the changes they are experiencing, and maximizing their contact with reality via family pictures, clocks, and other visual and verbal reminders. These therapeutic interventions can help reduce such secondary symptoms as social withdrawal, depression, denial, fear, confusion, impulsive behaviors, and negative feelings about themselves, which are common in people in the early stages of cognitive disorders (Sue et al., 2006).

People with cognitive disorders caused by psychoactive substances often will have a coexisting diagnosis of a substance use disorder. Psychotherapy will play an important role in these people's treatment, helping them eliminate their self-destructive use of drugs or alcohol, a modification that in turn will probably ameliorate the accompanying cognitive disorder and greatly reduce the chances of a recurrence.

Prognosis

The prognosis for recovery from a cognitive disorder is as variable as the disorders themselves and is usually determined by the cause of the disorder. Those disorders stemming from psychoactive substances, metabolic abnormalities, and systemic illnesses tend to be time limited and usually are followed by full recovery or significant improvement. Dementia of the Alzheimer's type, however, currently has no known cure. Death usually occurs within five years of onset of the disease, which is the fourth leading cause of death in the United States (Sue et al., 2006).

MENTAL DISORDERS DUE TO A GENERAL MEDICAL CONDITION

According to the *DSM-IV-TR*, a "mental disorder due to a general medical condition is characterized by the presence of mental symptoms that are judged to be the direct physiological consequence of a medical condition" (American Psychiatric Association, 2000, p. 181). In other words, these disorders are caused by a medical condition; they do not reflect people's upset in response to the diagnosis of a medical condition but rather result from the physiological impact of the medical condition. The causative medical condition should be listed on Axis III of the multiaxial assessment.

Nonpsychiatric medical conditions can be direct or physiological causes of a broad range of mental disorders, including psychotic disorders, mood disorders, anxiety disorders, sexual dysfunction, and sleep disorders. Specific diagnoses cited in this section of the *DSM* include catatonic disorder due to a general medical condition (such as neurological and metabolic abnormalities), personality change due to a general medical condition (such as endocrine and autoimmune conditions), and mental disorder not otherwise specified due to a general medical condition. Diagnosis of disorders such as these is usually made by a psychiatrist or a neurologist. Psychotherapists may well collaborate in the treatment of people with these disorders, as well as in the treatment of their family members, but treatment that targets the medical condition will generally be the primary intervention. Because of the scope and diversity of these disorders and their etiologies, further discussion of their diagnosis and treatment will not be provided here. Nevertheless, clinicians should keep these disorders in mind when making diagnoses.

TREATMENT RECOMMENDATIONS: CLIENT MAP

This chapter has discussed the category of disorders in which physical and psychological factors combine. The following summary of treatment recommendations is organized according to the format of the Client Map.

CLIENT MAP

Diagnoses

Disorders in which physical and psychological factors combine (somatoform disorders; factitious disorders; delirium, dementia, and amnestic and other cognitive disorders; mental disorders due to a general medical condition)

Objectives of Treatment

Reduce somatization

Promote more constructive expression of feelings

Maximize functioning and coping skills

Improve socialization and use of leisure time

Assessments

Physical examination

Assessments of anxiety, depression, personality, and intellectual functioning as indicated

Clinician Characteristics

Knowledgeable about physical disorders

Willing to collaborate with physicians

Skilled at handling reluctant clients

Structured and concrete

Warm and optimistic

High in tolerance of frustration

Location of Treatment

Usually outpatient setting

Interventions to Be Used

Team approach to treatment involving both medical and mental health professionals

Empathy and reflection of feelings to promote awareness of and ability to verbalize emotions

Holistic approach

Teaching of stress management and coping skills

Encouragement of positive ways to request attention and support

Use of relaxation techniques

Improvement in socialization

Behavioral change strategies to improve functioning

Gentle confrontation as needed

Emphasis of Treatment

Supportive emphasis

Moderately directive emphasis

Some attention to history, with primary orientation toward the present

Integrated focus on cognitive, behavioral, and affective areas (with behavioral interventions usually predominating)

Numbers

Primarily individual therapy

Family therapy to reduce secondary gains and help family members understand and cope with the disorder

Group therapy, as functioning permits, to promote socialization

Timing

Geared to readiness of client

May need to be gradual and long term

Medications Needed

As indicated by the physical disorders and specific emotional symptoms; antidepressant medication often helpful

Adjunct Services

Leisure and career counseling

Prognosis

Fair in general, but widely variable according to disorder

CLIENT MAP OF DR. MARTIN C.

This chapter began with a description of Dr. Martin C., a 62-year-old male who was referred for psychotherapy by his physician after seeking medical help for what Martin was convinced was cancer.

Diagnosis

Axis I: 300.7 Hypochondriasis, moderate, with poor insight

Axis II: V71.09 No diagnosis on Axis II

Axis III: No known physical disorders or conditions, but client reported symptoms of gastric distress

Axis IV: Occupational and financial difficulties, marital conflict, physical concerns

Axis V: Global assessment of functioning (GAF Scale): current GAF = 60

Objectives of Treatment

Improve skills related to stress management and coping

Improve marital relationship and communication

Facilitate development of realistic occupational and financial goals

Improve medical condition

Improve ability to identify and express feelings

Enhance self-esteem and client's enjoyment of life

Assessments

Physical evaluation

Broad-based personality inventory, such as the Minnesota Multiphasic Personality Inventory

Clinician Characteristics

Warm, optimistic

Skilled at handling reluctant clients

Knowledgeable about medical concerns

Mature and experienced

Supportive and accepting throughout, yet directive and structured

Location of Treatment

Outpatient setting

Interventions to Be Used

Multifaceted collaboration between therapist and physician, with therapist and client as primary engineers of treatment (to ensure compatibility of physical and psychological treatments and give client a sense of control missing from other areas of his life)

Education about the impact of stress on gastric functioning

Education about dietary approaches to reducing gastrointestinal discomfort

Supportive and reflective counseling designed to promote awareness of feelings and ability to verbalize them

Techniques of stress management, including progressive relaxation and expansion of leisure activities

Exploration of career-related attitudes, abilities, and opportunities, with goal of establishing more realistic and rewarding career goals

Discussion of partial retirement combined with consulting and half-time teaching (to reduce stress and stabilize client's financial situation)

Marital therapy (to improve communication between client and his wife, help them understand each other's feelings, and define a realistic and mutually acceptable lifestyle)

Emphasis of Treatment

Structured, relatively directive, but encouraging

Client to take appropriate responsibility for his own treatment and his lifestyle

Numbers

Individual and couples therapy

Timing

Weekly sessions

Rapid pace

Medium duration

Medications Needed

Carefully monitored medication as needed for gastrointestinal distress

Adjunct Services

Financial and retirement planning

Leisure counseling

Prognosis

Fair to good

RECOMMENDED READING

Forchetti, C. M. (2005). Treating patients with moderate to severe Alzheimer's disease. *The Primary Care Companion to the Journal of Clinical Psychiatry, 7,* 155–161.

Mittelman, M. S., Roth, D. L., Coon, D. W., & Haley, W. E. (2004). Sustained benefit of supportive intervention for depressive symptoms in the caregivers of patients with Alzheimer's disease. *American Journal of Psychiatry, 161,* 850–856.

Shaw, R. J., Dayal, S., Hartman, J. K., & DeMaso, D. R. (2008). Factitious disorder by proxy: Pediatric condition falsification. *Harvard Review of Psychiatry, 16,* 215–224.

Veale, D., & Neziroglu, F. (2010). *Body dysmorphic disorder: A treatment manual.* Hoboken, NJ: John Wiley & Sons.

Woolfolk, R. L., & Allen, L. A. (2007). *Treating somatization: A cognitive behavioral approach.* New York, NY: Guilford Press.

Personality Disorders

Emily L., a 25-year-old White woman, was referred to a psychotherapist by the hospital where she had been treated after her eighth suicide attempt. The therapist to whom she was referred would be her fourth one; nevertheless, Emily responded with initial optimism to the new therapist and provided an extensive narration of her long-standing difficulties.

Emily was the fourth and last child born to her parents within the first six years of their marriage. Her father abandoned the family a year after Emily's birth, and she had had no contact with him since that time. Emily's mother remarried about five years later, and she and her children had moved into a three-bedroom apartment with her new husband and his two teenage sons.

The older boy, age 15, soon began to sexually abuse Emily. He won her silence and cooperation by telling her that he loved her best and by threatening to harm her pets if she did not do what he wanted. The first time Emily balked at complying with his demands, he proved the seriousness of his threats by killing her canary.

After about a year, Emily's stepfather found her undressed in her stepbrother's room. The stepfather became enraged with Emily, now 7 years old, and accused her of trying to ruin his family. He also blamed Emily's mother and became increasingly abusive, both emotionally and physically, toward Emily and her mother.

When Emily was 10 years old, her mother committed suicide. Emily and her siblings were separated and put in foster homes. Emily remained in her foster home until she dropped out of high school and married at 17.

At the time she provided this information, Emily was married to her second husband. Her first husband had been physically abusive, particularly when he was intoxicated. Her current husband was also physically abusive. ("At least he doesn't drink" was Emily's comment on the situation.)

Emily herself presented with many difficulties. She reported having been depressed for as long as she could remember, with frequent episodes of suicidal ideation and behavior. She often plucked out her eyebrows and eyelashes, as well as the hair on her head, and reportedly spent a great deal of time each day putting on makeup and styling her hair to disguise the hair loss. She was nearly 100 pounds overweight and often consumed alcohol to excess, a behavior that she blamed on her first husband. She had little contact with her siblings and had no close women friends, but she had engaged in several brief but intense extramarital relationships, one with her husband's brother. She had a spotty employment history, with some computer skills and intermittent work for temporary agencies, but she reported that her depression made it difficult for her to get to work consistently and on time. Emily's principal diagnosis was borderline personality disorder.

OVERVIEW OF PERSONALITY DISORDERS

Personality disorders are a long-standing and deeply ingrained pathology that permeates a person's entire being. People with personality disorders generally lack resilience, especially under stress; are inflexible when it comes to change; and engage in vicious cycles of repetitive self-defeating behaviors. Most people with personality disorders have trouble accepting appropriate responsibility for their difficulties; they usually blame others for their problems, but sometimes they blame themselves too much.

People with personality disorders also have poor coping mechanisms and relationship skills. Because their disorders are so enduring and deeply entrenched, and because people with personality disorders typically have little insight and tend to externalize their difficulties, their disorders are difficult to treat (Beck, Freeman, Davis, & Associates, 2004).

Description of the Disorders

Personality disorders are life-long characterological disorders. They are characterized by maladaptive attitudes and behaviors that show up in at least two of the following areas:

- Perceptions and understanding of oneself and one's environment.
- Expression, nature, range, and appropriateness of emotions.
- Interpersonal skills and relationships.
- Impulse control.

The attitudes and behaviors of people with personality disorders typically are rigid and inflexible, causing distress and/or impairment in important areas of their lives (American Psychiatric Association, 2000).

Presenting concerns generally focus on symptoms of depression or anxiety, typically reflecting an additional disorder listed on Axis I of a *DSM-IV-TR* multiaxial assessment. (Personality disorders are listed on Axis II.) These clients typically have little awareness of their underlying dysfunctional personality patterns. Their personality styles generally are ego-syntonic and acceptable to these clients, who are rarely able to grasp the effect of their personalities on others. Even for people whose personality disorders are ego-dystonic or in conflict with their self-image, change is difficult because typically they have never manifested healthy personality patterns and do not have good coping or adjustment skills.

In the past, personality disorders were explained almost exclusively from a psychodynamic perspective, but they are now viewed as resulting from a combination of biological and psychosocial factors (Beauchaine & Hinshaw, 2008; Livesley, 2003, 2007). Although genetic factors predispose a person to certain traits of temperament, environmental factors can have a favorable or unfavorable impact on those traits. Such psychosocial factors as family dysfunction, physical or sexual abuse in childhood, an invalidating environment, adversity, attachment-related issues, difficulties in early learning, and sociocultural influences can all exacerbate a biological predisposition toward a personality disorder (Beck et al., 2004; Livesley, 2003; Millon, Grossman, Millon, Meagher, & Ramnath, 2004; Paris, 2003). Childhood anxiety and depression are often precursors to adult development of personality disorders (Paris, 2003).

Personality disorders are evident by adolescence or early adulthood, if not earlier, and tend to continue throughout life. Diagnosis of a personality disorder in a person under the age of

18 is made only if symptoms have been present for at least one year. The only exception is antisocial personality disorder, which, by definition, cannot be diagnosed before the age of 18 (American Psychiatric Association, 2000).

Personality disorders vary considerably in terms of degree of impairment. Researchers have viewed the borderline, paranoid, and schizotypal personality disorders as the most dysfunctional (Millon & Grossman, 2007; Sperry, 2006; Van Luyn, Akhtar, & Livesley, 2007). These disorders are characterized by poor social skills, hostility, and fragility. The obsessive-compulsive, dependent, histrionic, narcissistic, and avoidant personality disorders typically involve the least dysfunction. People with these disorders are able to seek out and deal with others in a relatively coherent fashion and can adapt to or control their environments in meaningful ways. Although all personality disorders tend to wax and wane in severity according to life circumstances and stressors, some (for example, obsessive-compulsive, histrionic, narcissistic, and schizotypal personality disorders) worsen with age, whereas others (such as borderline and antisocial personality disorders) tend to improve (American Psychiatric Association, 2000).

Personality disorders are prevalent, although they are often overlooked in clinical settings. No comprehensive figures exist for the total prevalence of personality disorders in the population (Crits-Christoph & Barber, 2007). However, the 2001–2002 National Epidemiologic Survey on Alcohol and Related Conditions reported that 30.8 million adults in the United States (14.8%) meet the diagnostic criteria for at least one of seven personality disorders. Three personality disorders—borderline, narcissistic, and schizotypal—were not included in the study. More than 43,000 people participated in the survey, which was conducted by the National Institute on Alcohol Abuse and Alcoholism (National Institutes of Health and the National Institute on Alcohol Abuse and Alcoholism [NIH & NIAAA], 2004).

Gender distribution varies from one personality disorder to another. Women are more likely to be diagnosed with borderline personality disorder (75% female). Eighty percent of the people diagnosed with antisocial personality disorder are male (Millon et al., 2004). It is unclear whether such gender differences are, at least in part, biases in making the diagnosis or actual variations in gender distribution.

Similar concerns arise in relation to culture and personality disorders. Asians, for example, are more likely to exhibit signs of shyness and collectivism, whereas North Americans and Europeans are more assertive and individualistic (D. Sue, Sue, & Sue, 2006). These cultural differences are reflected in the types of personality disorders with which people are most likely to be diagnosed. Other factors, including being a Native American or African American, having low socioeconomic status, being a young adult, and not being married were found to be risk factors for developing a personality disorder (NIH & NIAAA, 2004). Clearly, cultural, ethnic, and social backgrounds should be considered when diagnosing a personality disorder.

In the *DSM-IV-TR*, the personality disorders are grouped into the following three clusters:

1. Cluster A (guarded and eccentric): paranoid, schizoid, and schizotypal personality disorders
2. Cluster B (dramatic, emotional, and unpredictable): antisocial, borderline, histrionic, and narcissistic personality disorders
3. Cluster C (anxious and fearful): avoidant, dependent, and obsessive-compulsive personality disorders

The *DSM-IV-TR* also includes the category of personality disorder not otherwise specified

(NOS). This category encompasses mixed personality disorders. These do not completely fit the criteria for any one disorder but have symptoms of two or more, which in combination meet the criteria for diagnosis of a personality disorder. Personality disorder NOS also includes other personality disorders that are currently under consideration but are not yet viewed as warranting a full-fledged diagnosis (such as depressive personality disorder or passive-aggressive personality disorder).

As is the case with other disorders, caution should be used when diagnosing personality disorders in the presence of a co-occurring mood or substance-related disorder. For a diagnosis of a personality disorder, symptoms must continue to be present after the substance use has been discontinued. The *DSM* also notes that personality traits may not merit the diagnosis of disorder unless they cause "significant functional impairment or distress and are inflexible and maladaptive" (American Psychiatric Association, 2000, p. 689).

Typical Client Characteristics

People with personality disorders tend to come from families in which family breakdown or psychopathology of one or both parents is present (Livesley, 2003). The families usually also failed to model healthy interpersonal and coping skills, so identification with family members perpetuates a pattern of impaired functioning. The form taken by a person's personality disorder often makes sense in light of what the parental messages have been.

Personality disorders tend to be proportionally overrepresented among people who have a history of childhood trauma, emotional abuse, and neglect. Such abuse is also related to later self-harming behaviors. High levels of sexual abuse have also been reported in people with

personality disorders. As many as 70% of people with borderline personality disorder have a history of childhood sexual abuse (Livesley, 2003), compared to 53% of people with other personality disorders (Paris, 2003). A history of sexual abuse also is associated with narcissistic, histrionic, schizotypal, and antisocial personality disorders.

Each personality disorder seems to be strongly associated with a particular defense mechanism. For example, borderline personality disorder is associated with splitting (viewing people as extremely good or extremely bad), whereas paranoid personality disorder is associated with projection. An understanding of their defenses is essential to an understanding of these clients; helping them manage and modify their defenses is usually necessary for successful treatment.

People with personality disorders also usually have dysfunctional and distorted schemas or belief systems, as well as maladaptive coping strategies (Beck et al., 2004), so they have great difficulty successfully managing stressors and life problems. As a result, people with these disorders typically have a long history of disappointments and come to see the world as a hostile environment. Without help, they are rarely able to make the cognitive shifts and develop the skills that would enable them to control dysregulated affect and manage their lives more successfully.

Avoidance is common in people with personality disorders, and self-acceptance is rare. Livesley (2003) notes that these people often "seem at odds with themselves" (p. 87) in an effort to deny or not acknowledge their participation in their own behavior.

Personality, like intelligence, remains relatively stable over time. From the late twenties on, people may "mellow a little with age and become more reliable" (Livesley, 2003, p. 72), but basically their personality has been formed.

Therapists treating personality pathology should begin with the goal of helping people adapt to and better understand their personality traits, develop improved coping skills, and express themselves more effectively, rather than aiming for a complete change in personality.

Assessment

Diagnostic tools can be helpful in identifying personality disorders that sometimes are obscured by other disorders. A number of inventories, including the Millon Clinical Multiaxial Inventory (MCMI), the Minnesota Multiphasic Personality Inventory (MMPI), the Structured Clinical Interview for *DSM-IV* Axis II Personality Disorders (SCID-II; Maffei et al., 1997), and projective tests can all be useful in diagnosing these sometimes overlooked disorders (Millon et al., 2004). Co-occurring Axis I disorders, especially substance-related disorders, should also be assessed in order for treatment to be effective.

Preferred Therapist Characteristics

The establishment of a sound therapeutic alliance is the strongest predictor of successful treatment outcome for people with personality disorders (Meyer & Pilkonis, 2006). Empathy, warmth, compassion, acceptance, respect, and genuineness are the building blocks of the therapeutic alliance. Strong confrontation, punishment, criticism, or other expressions of negative feelings can destroy the fragile therapeutic bond established with a person who has a personality disorder.

Patience is an essential ingredient especially in the early stages of treatment, when the client usually exhibits anxiety or depression and when the groundwork for the therapeutic alliance is being established. Treatment of personality disorders tends to be long term, with progress and the building of trust often very gradual. Not all people with personality disorders are motivated to examine themselves or change. For example, people with paranoid, schizoid, and antisocial personality disorders rarely seek treatment on their own initiative (Meyer & Pilkonis, 2006), and a high proportion of people with personality disorders terminate treatment prematurely. Blocking or sabotaging treatment; fear of change; transference and other reactions to the therapist; cognitive distortions; and overreactions all can act as barriers to effective treatment of a personality disorder.

Apparent treatment resistance often stems from fear of change or from hopelessness, and the therapist should keep those possibilities in mind when the client fails to keep appointments or to complete agreed-upon activities between sessions. The therapist should avoid feeling hurt or angered by these behaviors and should try instead to view them as self-protection on the part of the client.

People with personality disorders tend to have strong transference reactions to their therapists. Some become hostile and resistant; others become needy and dependent. Therapists must monitor and manage any countertransference reactions so that they do not become either overly involved or rejecting toward these clients but instead are appropriately available. Judicious use of limit setting, gentle interpretation, rewards, and modeling also help elicit positive behavior from these clients. Using humor, anecdotes, metaphors, and limited self-disclosure can also help the clients perceive their therapist as genuine and human.

Intervention Strategies

Despite the prevalence of personality disorders in both general and clinical populations, empirical studies on the treatment of these disorders are limited. Personality disorders received little attention in the research literature until the mid-1980s. The personality inventories developed by Millon, along with the *Journal of Personality Disorders*, founded and edited by Millon in 1989, spurred interest in the study of personality disorders. However, most of the recent literature focuses on borderline, antisocial, and schizotypal personality disorders. Little research has been published in the past 35 years on dependent, histrionic, paranoid, or schizoid personality disorders (Boschen & Warner, 2009).

During the 1970s and the 1980s, psychodynamic psychotherapy generally was the preferred approach to treatment. At the end of the last century, the literature focused increasingly on cognitive approaches, as well as on variations of cognitive-behavioral therapy, such as dialectical behavior therapy and schema therapy. In recent years, the release of numerous empirical studies on the effectiveness of psychodynamic psychotherapy has swung the pendulum back toward the middle. With both CBT and psychodynamic approaches empirically supported (Leichsenring & Leibing, 2003), therapists are free to choose from an array of treatment methodologies including newer mentalization-focused and mindfulness-based approaches. A key component of all successful treatment of personality disorders is the therapist's ability to adapt his or her interventions to the client's in-session behavior (Meyer & Pilkonis, 2006). Future research on personality disorders can be expected to take on a dimensional model and to address transdiagnostic traits such as emotion regulation, impulsivity, and avoidance behaviors that may be seen across multiple personality disorders.

In general, therapy for a person with a personality disorder will be multifaceted, with a psychodynamic or cognitive basis, to address the person's core difficulties. Specific interventions are selected to address the client's defenses and individual concerns. The long-standing nature of these disorders, their apparent relationship to family dynamics, and their relatively early origin all suggest an approach that will not only relieve symptoms but also effect change in overall functioning and in the person's view of self and the world.

Beck and associates (2004) report success in treating personality disorders via cognitive therapy. They begin their treatment approach with standard cognitive therapy to elicit and modify dysfunctional automatic thoughts that are contributing to anxiety and depression. Once affective changes begin, the therapist gradually shifts focus from immediate concerns to dysfunctional core schemas that underlie the personality disorder. Guided discovery helps clients see the impact of these core schemas on their lives. Such techniques as deliberate exaggeration, labeling of distortions, decatastrophizing, and reattribution of responsibility for actions and outcomes gradually help people with personality disorders identify and modify their schemas. Concurrent attention is paid to helping people learn coping, communication, decision making, and other important life skills. Behavioral strategies, such as relaxation and role playing, along with exploration of childhood experiences that may have entrenched the schemas, enhance treatment. This kind of integrated treatment, with clear goals and treatment strategies, is especially likely to effect positive change in a personality disorder. Building on Beck's cognitive therapy, Young (1999) has developed schema therapy that helps clients assess, recognize, and change their own internal schemas. Through empathic confrontation and limited reparenting, the therapeutic alliance provides a safe haven in which the client can examine, and change, inappropriate behavior (Rafaeli, Bernstein, & Young, 2011).

Clinicians have been making greater use of control-oriented cognitive strategies in which clients become more mindful. Linehan's dialectical behavior therapy, for example, has been successful in reducing suicidal ideation and self-harm behavior in people with borderline personality disorder (Meyer & Pilkonis, 2006). Emotion-focused therapy, developed by Greenberg (2002), blends Gestalt techniques, psychodrama, and playing the devil's advocate in therapeutic efforts to help clients recognize, regulate, and effectively manage their own emotions.

Behavior therapy has also been used successfully in treating personality disorders, particularly in the initial stages of treatment. Behavior therapy is especially helpful and appealing to people who are reluctant to engage in long-term treatment or who have severely dysfunctional and self-destructive behavioral patterns that require rapid modification. Through behavior therapy, they can learn new social and occupational skills, as well as practical approaches to coping and stress management. Generally, behavior therapy is used to address the Axis I disorders (such as substance-related or mood disorders) and to effect fairly rapid improvement in prominent symptoms, which in turn often increases clients' motivation and confidence in psychotherapy and encourages them to continue treatment, with a focus on underlying personality patterns. Even if these clients do terminate treatment prematurely, at least they are left with positive feelings about their treatment and some initial gains. As a result, they may well return for help if symptoms recur.

New research points to the effectiveness of two specific interventions in the treatment of severe personality disorders. Dialectical behavior therapy (Linehan, 1993) and mentalization-based treatment (MBT; Bateman & Fonagy, 2004, 2007) have been shown to reduce suicide attempts and self-harming behaviors. Transference-focused psychotherapy (Yeomans & Levy, 2002) also shows promise. Clinical trials are currently under way for schema-focused interventions, transference-focused therapy, and other interventions in the treatment of severe personality disorders (Van Luyn, Akhbar, & Livesley, 2007).

A recent meta-analysis on the effectiveness of long-term psychodynamic psychotherapy found greater improvement after longer treatment durations. Leichsenring and Rabung (2008) found greater overall treatment effectiveness after 1 year (50 sessions) of psychodynamic psychotherapy than in patients who had short-term therapy. Paris (1999) found that treatment duration of 1.3 years or 192 sessions were necessary for a 50% reduction in symptoms associated with personality disorders. A 75% reduction was achieved after 216 sessions. He concluded that both lengths of treatment are effective in treating personality disorders.

People with personality disorders typically have deficits in many areas of their lives. Therefore, adjunct services such as career counseling, 12-step programs, and family or couples counseling are often important parts of the treatment package. In severe forms or exacerbations of personality disorders, day treatment, brief hospitalization, or milieu therapy may be indicated, especially for people with borderline or schizotypal personality disorders (Paris, 2003).

Antidepressant medications, mood stabilizers, atypical antipsychotics, and anxiolytics can frequently offer symptom relief. However, medications do not cure personality disorders; they only reduce the severity of their accompanying symptoms, reduce impulsivity, and perhaps facilitate a person's involvement in psychotherapy (Paris, 2003; van Luyn et al., 2007; Zanarini, 2005). Moreover, many people with personality disorders also misuse drugs. Therefore, care must be taken in recommending medication as part of treatment. Empirical data on psychopharmacology for personality disorders has almost exclusively focused on borderline personality disorder. Indeed, one study found that people with borderline personality disorder received, on average, four or five different types of medications (Zanarini, Frankenburg, Hennen, Reich, & Silk, 2004). Such polypharmacy has not been shown to be effective or helpful (Paris, 2003).

Family therapy can be a useful adjunct to individual therapy for a person with a personality disorder. Family members themselves often present disorders that merit attention, and they can also be helped to understand and react helpfully to the client's personality disorder, thereby reducing the secondary gains of the disorder. The client's social and occupational dysfunctions have probably already damaged family relationships, and family therapy can offer the person an opportunity to improve those relationships and develop new ways of relating to family members (Livesley, 2003). The therapist should be careful not to form separate alliances with family members; doing so could jeopardize the client's tenuous trust in the therapeutic process and could be perceived as a rejection.

Group therapy can be another useful adjunct to individual therapy for people with personality disorders. Empirical data suggests that a combination of individual and group therapy can be effective (Livesley, 2003). However, group therapy should generally be initiated in conjunction with individual therapy or only after some progress has been made in individual therapy. These clients' poor social skills, strong mistrust, and dependence needs can turn premature use of group therapy into another disappointing interpersonal experience for them. Once clients are ready for group involvement, the feedback and support they receive from others can provide encouragement for positive change, as well as a safe place for experimenting with new ways of relating both to peers and to authority figures.

Prognosis

The prognosis for effecting major change in a personality disorder seems fair at best because of the deeply ingrained and pervasive nature of these disorders. Nevertheless, the prognosis for reducing symptoms and improving social and occupational functioning is fair to good if clients can be persuaded to remain in and cooperate with treatment. Unfortunately, however, people with personality disorders often are not motivated to change and may leave treatment abruptly and prematurely. Higher-functioning clients and those who are psychologically minded and capable of insight have the best prognosis, but even clients with more severe personality disorders or those who are treatment refractory can still achieve positive, if more gradual, change (Van Luyn et al., 2007).

The process of therapy with personality disorders entails developing a collaborative working alliance and implementing treatment linked to clients' stages of change, with goals ranging from reducing self-harming behaviors to improving maladaptive relationship patterns. The better the therapeutic alliance, the more likely the client will stay and work toward those goals. Now let's turn to a discussion of each of the personality disorders.

PARANOID PERSONALITY DISORDER

The behavioral dynamics of people with paranoid personality disorder contain elements of projection and projective identification. These people believe that others dislike them and treat them badly; consequently, they take a defensive approach to interpersonal relations and frequently protect themselves by treating others badly. When others respond with disapproval and rejection, it becomes a self-fulfilling prophecy, giving people with this personality disorder the responses that they have feared and yet invited.

Description of the Disorder

People with paranoid personality disorder have a persistent suspiciousness and expectation that they will be treated badly by others. According to the *DSM-IV-TR* (American Psychiatric Association, 2000), they manifest at least four of the following patterns:

- Unjustly suspecting others of seeking to harm or take advantage of them.
- Continually questioning the trustworthiness of others.
- Rarely disclosing information about themselves because they believe it will be used against them.
- Interpreting benign comments or behaviors as intended to harm them.
- Being unforgiving and maintaining long-standing grudges.
- Often perceiving themselves, without justification, as under attack.
- Being easily motivated to anger or attack.
- Frequently questioning the faithfulness of their partners.

People with paranoid personality disorder often misinterpret the behavior of others as demeaning or malicious and tend to personalize experiences. As a result of their apprehension about being exploited, criticized, or made to feel helpless, they are constantly on guard. They have little tenderness or sense of humor and can be critical, moralistic, grandiose, insecure, resentful, suspicious, defensive, and jealous. They share little of themselves with others and tend to be rigid and controlling. They are more

interested in things than in people or ideas and have little empathy or understanding of others. These clients have a strong sense of hierarchy and typically appear fiercely independent. They crave power and envy those with more influence and success than they have. Sometimes they achieve a sense of authority by becoming leaders of fringe religious or political groups. Generally, they are free of delusions or hallucinations, but when under stress they may experience brief psychotic episodes.

People with paranoid personality disorder often have concurrent disorders. The most common are other personality disorders (including narcissistic, avoidant, or obsessive-compulsive personality disorders) and anxiety or mood disorders (Millon et al., 2004). Relatives of people with this disorder have an increased incidence of schizophrenia spectrum disorders. Therefore, the symptoms of a paranoid personality disorder actually may be the premorbid phase of another disorder. Beck and associates (2004) report that there may be an underlying genetic component that contributes to the development of paranoid personality disorder.

Approximately 5% of people with personality disorders have paranoid personality disorder, whereas 0.5% to 2.5% of the general population can be diagnosed with this disorder (Sperry, 2003). It is more common among men than among women (Millon et al., 2004).

Typical Client Characteristics

People with paranoid personality disorder "are likely to have grown up in an atmosphere charged with criticism, blame, and hostility, and to have identified with a critical parent" (Sperry, 2003, p. 202). A perfectionistic parent is common, and being the survivor of abuse is not unusual in the histories of people with this disorder.

People with paranoid personality disorder may take pride in what they perceive as their independence and objectivity, and they may view as weak or troubled those who express feelings more easily. They rarely seek treatment on their own and have great difficulty acknowledging a need for help. With little insight into how their behavior contributes to their problems, they tend to externalize blame for their difficulties.

Work and family life may be stressful environments for these people as they typically expect obedience and rigid organization in their family lives and may experience considerable stress when children and partners resist their control. Some can establish a comfortable work or family situation for themselves, as long as they are in charge and do not need to cooperate with others, but that stability may be a tenuous one.

People with this disorder are overly concerned about others' evaluations, and tend to be vigilant in scanning the environment for criticism and malicious intentions of others. They simultaneously believe that they are special and that they are not good enough. They fear being shamed or criticized and spend much time ruminating about their mistreatment by others. To reduce stress and distance themselves from perceived slights, people with paranoid personality disorder tend to isolate themselves, which deprives them of the necessary reality checks that might provide alternative explanations for others' behavior toward them. They tend to avoid intimacy and have considerable difficulty handling stress. They often appear chronically tense due to their constant vigilance (Sperry, 2003). These symptoms are likely to worsen under pressure, failure, or humiliation. Brief psychotic symptoms may even occur in those circumstances.

Preferred Therapist Characteristics

Perhaps the most fundamental goal of therapy for people with paranoid personality disorder is the establishment of trust so that they can become less resistant and more able to engage in therapy. To establish a trusting therapeutic alliance, the therapist should assume a respectful, courteous, and professional stance; be honest though tactful; and not intrude on the client's privacy and independence. Beck and associates (2004) found it helpful to give these clients considerable control over the nature of their treatment, particularly the frequency of their sessions and their between-session tasks. Infrequent sessions, perhaps one every 3 weeks, can reduce the threat of the therapeutic process. These clients have little respect for people who seem weak or inept, however, so therapists need to communicate confidence and knowledge, but without demeaning these clients.

Because people with paranoid personality disorder are often hostile and abrasive, therapists need to monitor their own reactions and resist being intimidated or angered. Limits may need to be set if clients behave in threatening or aggressive ways (Carroll, 2009). Therapists working with these clients should avoid arguing, communicating excessive warmth and concern, and developing therapeutic plans that may evoke suspicion (such as meeting with a client's family when the client is not present). Clients' questionable beliefs should be accepted but not confirmed.

Intervention Strategies

Individual therapy is usually the treatment of choice for people with paranoid personality disorder. Therapy should not emphasize either interpretation or reflection of feelings; both are likely to be threatening. Rather, a behavioral approach that emphasizes the client's rather than the therapist's control and that focuses on problem solving, stress management, and development of assertiveness and other interpersonal skills is most likely to engage the client in the therapeutic process and effect some positive change. People with paranoid personality disorder often appreciate the logic and organization of behavior therapy. They tend to be more trusting of therapists who focus on actions and experiences than of those who focus on inner dynamics and feelings. Reinforcement, modeling, and education can help these clients develop more effective coping mechanisms and social skills and promote a greater sense of self-efficacy, which in turn should help them engage in the next phase of treatment.

Once progress has been made in establishing a collaborative therapeutic relationship and effecting some behavioral change, cognitive therapy can be introduced (Beck et al., 2004). This model, too, offers the appeal of a logical and clear approach. Because people with paranoid personality disorder are prone to overgeneralization, magnifying the negative, and dichotomous thinking, therapy can help these clients consider alternative explanations. This can modify their defensive stance, encourage them to take more responsibility for the impact they have on others, and reduce their anger and hostility. In this stage of treatment, paranoia often evolves into depression, and cognitive approaches can also be used to reduce those symptoms.

To date, little empirical research exists on the effectiveness of treatment for people with paranoid personality disorder (Carroll, 2009). Some clinicians have reported successful use of a psychodynamic or interpersonal approach that emphasizes understanding in the treatment of people with paranoid personality. Beck and colleagues (2004) report promising results with cognitive therapy that helps increase clients' self-efficacy, decrease vigilance and defensiveness, and improve their overall ability to cope with interpersonal problems and concomitant stress. Gentle reality testing can contribute to therapy with these clients. People facing the legal, professional, or relationship consequences of

their behavior may need help to appreciate how important it is for them to modify their behavior and attitudes so as to prevent negative consequences.

Group therapy is rarely indicated for people with paranoid personality disorder. Unless they are in charge, they are acutely uncomfortable in group settings, particularly those that are intimate or confrontational, and they tend to sabotage or flee group therapy.

Although family problems are common for people with paranoid personality disorder, family therapy usually is not indicated until considerable progress has been made in individual therapy. Only when people have some awareness of the impact of their behavior and attitudes on others are they ready to talk about family issues and interact productively with family members.

Transient psychotic symptoms and severe anxiety are sometimes present in these clients. Antianxiety agents and atypical antipsychotic agents can ameliorate those symptoms. Pimozide (Orap) and fluoxetine (Prozac) have also been found useful in reducing paranoid ideation (Sperry, 2003). A referral for medication should be presented cautiously, however, lest people feel insulted, manipulated, or controlled.

Prognosis

Therapy for people with paranoid personality disorder is a long, slow process, but real changes can be made if they can be engaged in the process. An integrative approach to treatment that combines a psychodynamic approach with cognitive-behavioral therapy seems best. Providing cognitive restructuring and behavioral change strategies can successfully help clients cope better. Relapse can be prevented by holding occasional follow-up sessions, rather than having a complete termination. However, people with this disorder often refuse to engage in the therapeutic process, and they frequently terminate therapy prematurely. Even if they do cooperate with therapy and manifest some positive change, treatment is unlikely to result in extensive modification of their pervasive patterns of relating. Therefore, limited goals should be set at the outset of treatment so that both therapist and client have a clear direction and can feel a sense of accomplishment even if treatment is not completed. If treatment continues after the initial goals have been achieved, goals can be revised.

SCHIZOID PERSONALITY DISORDER

Because people with schizoid personality disorder tend to avoid relationships in general, and intimate relationships in particular, they are not likely to seek therapy. Therefore, little research exists on this personality disorder that affects as many as 7.5% of the general population.

Description of the Disorder

According to the *DSM-IV-TR*, the primary feature of schizoid personality disorder is "a pervasive pattern of detachment from social relationships and a restricted range of expression of emotions in interpersonal settings" (American Psychiatric Association, 2000, p. 694). This pattern is evident by early adulthood, and, in all or nearly all contexts, it characterizes the behavior and attitudes of people with this disorder. They tend to prefer solitary activities, shun family and social activities, and are usually perceived as cold and detached. People with schizoid personality disorder are anhedonic and report few if any sources of pleasure. Interest in sexual or interpersonal closeness is minimal or absent.

People with this disorder typically have great difficulty expressing their feelings, may deny having strong emotions, and seem detached and indifferent. When with others, they tend to be guarded and tactless and have a restricted range of emotional response. Most are unaffected by people's reactions to them, although some do acknowledge underlying pain related to their unrewarding social interactions and perceive themselves as social misfits (Beck et al., 2004). Although their reality testing usually is unimpaired, people with schizoid personality disorder often become easily derailed and tangential in their thinking or distracted by irrelevancies (Sperry, 2003).

Such inventories as the Millon Clinical Multiaxial Inventory (MCMI) and the Minnesota Multiphasic Personality Inventory (MMPI) can be helpful in making a diagnosis and in understanding people with schizoid personality disorder. Written responses may be more comfortable for these clients and more informative to therapists than oral responses, especially in the early stages of treatment. Millon and colleagues (2004) suggest that the person's fantasy life could provide rich material for therapy, as any fantasy provides a window into a person's private world of needs and desires. People with schizoid personality disorder should also be assessed for social anxiety.

Schizoid personality disorder is not commonly seen in clinical settings. This disorder seems to be more common among males than among females. However, females with schizoid personality disorder seem to have a higher rate of co-occurring alcohol and drug use disorders than males (Grant et al., 2004).

Typical Client Characteristics

Millon writes that "the schizoid is the personality disorder that lacks a personality" (2004, p. 401). Indeed, from childhood on, people with schizoid personality disorder have few good interpersonal experiences and have the expectation that relationships will be frustrating and disappointing. Early experiences frequently include being subject to bullying, rejection, or abuse (Beck et al., 2004). Rather than expose themselves to what they perceive as more negative experiences, they shun socialization and develop private, isolated lives. Males generally do not date or marry and are not "predisposed to intimate contact" (Sperry, 2003, p. 226). Females may engage in more social and family activities, but they tend to assume a passive role and allow others to make their social decisions. Both men and women with this disorder have poor social skills and few if any close friends. Their capacity for empathy and introspection seems to be severely constricted, and they often view themselves as odd, different, or worthless.

People with schizoid personality disorder have considerable occupational impairment, particularly if their chosen occupations involve interpersonal contact. Some shun employment and continue to live with their parents. Others manage to find stable, secure occupational roles that are congruent with their need for solitude.

In general, people with schizoid personality disorder have a relatively stable existence as long as outside pressures do not intrude. For example, one client with schizoid personality disorder devoted his energy to raising pit bulldogs and collecting poisonous snakes. He had no social life and saw others only for business transactions. He was referred to counseling after his neighbors, feeling endangered by his activities, complained to the police. The client reported contentment with his life; his only concern was his neighbors.

People with this disorder tend to fantasize extensively but almost never lose contact with reality. Their affect is typically flat, and their behavior is lethargic. They tend to be relatively satisfied with their lives, although some engage in considerable intellectualization and denial to justify their lives to themselves and others.

People with schizoid personality disorder typically have been raised in homes that met their physical and educational needs but did not provide emotional interaction, warmth, or social skills (Sperry, 2003). The child may have grown up modeling the parents' aloof, withdrawn style, preferring fantasy or isolation to social interaction. Millon and colleagues (2004) report that a biological predisposition may be seen in infants who are passive and anhedonic. Schizoid personality disorder usually is not accompanied by other prominent disorders, but some people with this disorder exhibit symptoms of depression, anxiety, depersonalization, obsessional thinking, somatic complaints, or brief manic states. This disorder, like the other Cluster A personality disorders (paranoid and schizotypal), may also be a precursor of a psychotic disorder. Coexisting personality disorders may be present, especially schizotypal, antisocial, and avoidant personality disorders.

Preferred Therapist Characteristics

Building trust is a critical ingredient of treatment with people who have schizoid personality disorder, as it is with those who have paranoid personality disorder. People with schizoid personality disorder have little experience in expressing their feelings, engaging in close and collaborative relationships, or trusting others. Confrontation or scrutiny of their emotions generally makes them uncomfortable and may lead to their premature termination of the therapeutic relationship. What they need instead is a corrective emotional experience to decrease their withdrawal and increase their optimism about relationships. Sperry (2003) suggests that an object relations approach to treatment might prove helpful. The therapist needs to take an active and encouraging stance with this type of client and avoid being critical or threatening. A gentle, consistent, patient, accepting, optimistic, available, and supportive therapist is needed to establish a therapeutic alliance. This is likely to be a slow process because, for this client, anxiety is triggered by interpersonal relationships.

People with schizoid personality rarely experience an internal wish to change. They are typically encouraged to seek help by concerned family members or employers who are hoping for a change in these people's ability to relate to others.

Intervention Strategies

Little research exists on therapy for people with schizoid personality disorder, but some cautious generalizations can be made.

Because people with schizoid personality disorder are often ambivalent about therapy, if a supportive therapeutic relationship can be developed, that acceptance by another person may help them to appreciate the value of relationships. Therapists often must first help the client see the benefit of therapy, outlining pros and cons of treatment. Beck and colleagues (2004) suggest that therapist and client collaboratively negotiate a problem list and develop a hierarchy of goals using a Socratic dialogue. Therapists' beliefs must be held in check, as their expression could be construed as criticism by these highly sensitive people, thus reinforcing their core beliefs that relationships are "cruel, unfulfilling, and unwelcoming" (Beck, 2004, p. 147). Those who do attempt therapy are likely to terminate early.

Schema therapy, developed by Young (1999), expands on cognitive therapy to address clients' underlying assumptions and dysfunctional thoughts by using imagery exercises, empathy, limited reparenting, and homework assignments to modify maladaptive

schemas. Used with people diagnosed with schizoid personality disorder, these schemas typically include the perception that life is bland and unfulfilling and that human relationships are not worth the trouble. Clients' fantasies and their apprehension about dependence are other areas that can be productively explored through cognitive therapy. Such inventories as Beck's Dysfunctional Thought Record can facilitate identification and modification of such thoughts, as can guided discovery, which helps people determine their interests and increase their involvement in pleasurable activities. Building on interests that are already present can facilitate clients' involvement in additional activities.

Behavioral techniques can help people with schizoid personality disorder improve their social and communication skills and increase their empathy for others. Therapists should keep in mind, however, that people with schizoid personality disorder generally do not respond well to reinforcement, given their lack of reactivity and the limited importance they attach to interpersonal relationships. They may also resent the intrusive and manipulative aspects of some behavioral approaches. An intellectual approach to behavioral change, such as education to increase assertiveness, self-expression, and social skills, is most likely to succeed. Some clients also respond well to environmental changes that afford them increased but still limited exposure to other people and provide them a natural laboratory for practicing their new skills.

The sequencing of the components of a treatment plan for people with schizoid personality disorder is critical. These clients should not be overwhelmed by a multifaceted treatment strategy, nor should they be pushed into group or family therapy before they are ready. A stable therapeutic alliance should first be established through individual therapy. Only when the person is ready should group or family therapy, assertiveness training, career counseling, or other more active and probably more threatening interventions be introduced.

Group therapy can be helpful to these clients, but therapists must assume a protective stance toward them, especially during the initial stages when they are likely to say little and to appear detached from the group. Intrusive interpretations and forced interactions should be avoided. Other group members must also be carefully selected, to ensure that these clients will not feel pressured or attacked. Sperry (2003) recommends a group that is homogeneous in terms of overall functioning but heterogeneous in terms of personality styles. If accepted by the client, group therapy can provide an educational and affirming socialization experience and offer gentle feedback.

Very few controlled studies have been conducted on pharmacotherapy for the treatment of schizoid personality disorder. In some cases, however, medication to reduce severe anxiety or depression can facilitate therapy (Sperry, 2003). For those with psychotic symptoms, atypical antipsychotic medications such as olanzapine (Zyprexa) or ziprasidone (Geodon) can be helpful.

Prognosis

Schizoid personality disorder can be treated effectively through the use of a combination of treatment approaches and by moving forward slowly. However, premature termination of treatment and failure to benefit or maintain gains from therapy are common (Millon et al., 2004). Many of these clients have established a relatively stable lifestyle and are not motivated to participate in treatment. They may increase their socialization somewhat, especially if required to do so by their employers, but fundamental change is a slow process. Relapse is common for people with schizoid personality

disorder. Without help in identifying the signs of a relapse and without periodic follow-up sessions, people with this disorder have a high likelihood of reverting to their previous isolated behaviors.

SCHIZOTYPAL PERSONALITY DISORDER

Odd, eccentric, and superstitious are adjectives frequently used to describe people with schizotypal personality disorder. Magical thinking is the hallmark symptom of this disorder.

Description of the Disorder

People with schizotypal personality disorder (SPD), like those with paranoid and schizoid personality disorders, have pervasive deficits in interpersonal relations and social skills. They tend to be guarded, suspicious, and hypersensitive. They have few close friends other than first-degree relatives, manifest flat and inappropriate affect, and are uncomfortable and awkward in social situations. In addition, this disorder is characterized by "cognitive or perceptual distortions and eccentricities of behavior" (American Psychiatric Association, 2000, p. 697) that may involve ideas of reference, magical thinking, unusual beliefs or perceptual experiences, prominent superstitions, eccentric actions or grooming, and idiosyncratic speech patterns. People with SPD typically are more dysfunctional and unusual in presentation than are those with paranoid or schizoid personality disorders.

SPD is found in approximately 3% of the general population (Sperry, 2003). Clear information is not available on gender distribution of this disorder, although recent studies indicate that males with SPD tend to have greater dysfunction than females with the disorder, including more drug and alcohol use, fewer friends, and more disability due to odd thinking and beliefs (Dickey et al., 2005). Men are also more likely to have co-occurring paranoid and narcissistic personality disorders. Age and gender seem to be related to the development of schizotypy in the general population (Bora & Arabaci, 2009).

Typical Client Characteristics

People with SPD almost always have significant social and occupational impairment, with as many as 40% having experienced a period of time during which they were unable to work. They usually do not marry or have children but tend to live alone or with their families of origin. Sometimes they become involved with cults or other groups with unusual beliefs.

According to Dickey and colleagues (2005), the most frequently occurring symptoms, reported in more than 78% of people with SPD, are illusions or unusual perceptual experiences, suspiciousness, paranoid ideation, and magical thinking. Their peculiar habits and attitudes generally are evident to those around them and can contribute to their social isolation. People with SPD are often viewed as strange, odd, and eccentric. Their tendency toward isolation perpetuates the cognitive and social slippage that is commonly found in people with this disorder (Sperry, 2003). People with SPD seem to experience more downward drift than those with any other personality disorder and more than would be expected given their usually average to above-average intelligence (Dickey et al., 2005).

SPD seems to have both genetic and environmental components. People with this personality disorder have a higher percentage of first-degree biological relatives with schizophrenia or mood disorders than does the general population (American Psychiatric Association,

2000; Dickey et al., 2005). Research shows that at least some of the dominant symptoms of SPD may be the result of neurological deficits in the frontal lobe, similar to what is seen in schizophrenia (Dickey et al., 2005). The parenting received by people with this disorder is generally consistent but often lacks emotional warmth. Sperry notes that at least one study indicates a genetic predisposition to schizotypy and increased passivity in these clients when they were children, which may have contributed to parental indifference and distance. Experiences of humiliation, abuse, bullying, and rejection are commonly found in the backgrounds of people with SPD, as is discouragement of social involvement (Sperry, 2003).

Age and gender seem to play a role in the development of schizotypal traits. Some traits of schizotypy, mainly psychotic and magical thinking, tend to peak in adolescence and then recede with age, especially in women. Disorganization also seems to recede from adolescence to old age in both genders. Perhaps processes during adolescence may lead to schizotypy or better social adaptation occurs as a result of life experiences. Gender also plays a role in the development of specific schizotypal traits. Men tend to experience more disorganization, and women score higher on social anxiety, magical thinking, and paranoid ideation (Bora & Arabaci, 2009).

Dickey and colleagues (2005) found that more than half of people with SPD have coexisting major depressive disorder, and 25% have anxiety or dysthymia. Transient, stress-related psychotic symptoms also often accompany this disorder. People with SPD tend to somatize and may present vague physical complaints. Suicidal ideation and behavior often accompany this disorder, particularly if a mood disorder or psychotic symptoms are also present. Other personality disorders, including paranoid, avoidant, obsessive-compulsive, and borderline personality disorders, may be present. As is typical of people with schizophrenia spectrum disorders, those with SPD have a high level of suspiciousness, paranoid ideation, and ruminative thought processes that make it difficult for them to establish and maintain social relationships (Dickey et al., 2005). In some cases, SPD is a precursor of schizophrenia.

Preferred Therapist Characteristics

People with SPD, like those with schizoid and paranoid personality disorders, are likely to be resistant to treatment. Building trust is a challenging yet critical ingredient in engaging the person in the therapeutic process. An available, reliable, encouraging, warm, empathic, positive, and nonintrusive stance can help therapists interact effectively with these clients (Sperry, 2003). Because people with SPD tend to ramble and have difficulty making meaningful use of therapy, clinicians will have to be structured and focused and have to teach these clients about psychotherapy. Frequent sessions or telephone calls between sessions can keep clients connected to and involved with treatment. Allowing them to determine the degree of intimacy also can increase their sense of control over and comfort with therapy and can provide a corrective emotional experience.

Several symptoms of SPD, including paranoid ideation and unusual experiences, tend to be treatment resistant, whereas odd behavior and constricted affect were found to be the symptoms most likely to change, according to a 2-year study conducted by McGlashan and others (2005). Therapists sometimes will need to provide clients with basic information and advice on taking care of themselves and dealing with the world. Although some therapists may not be comfortable with this role, it can help clients see the value in therapy.

People with SPD have particular difficulty expressing their feelings and dealing appropriately with interpersonal situations. Therefore, therapists should be prepared for unusual reactions and behaviors on the part of these clients. Therapists will need to manage their own discomfort with the strange and possibly offensive mannerisms of these people, as well as with their lack of motivation for treatment. Therapists should communicate acceptance and support while providing some reality testing and education, keeping in mind that 54 is the average global assessment of functioning rating for people with SPD (Skodol et al., 2002).

On the positive side, these clients are usually willing to talk about themselves and their experiences and do not tend to be manipulative. They generally will be sincere, if guarded and cautious (Sperry, 2003).

Intervention Strategies

The research on treatment of SPD is limited, but treatment usually resembles the treatment for schizoid personality disorder, with the addition of medication. People with SPD are unlikely to seek out treatment on their own. Most people with this disorder seem to accept their lifestyles.

Therapy for people with SPD typically is supportive, lengthy, and slow paced, beginning with supportive interventions and medication and subsequently making gentle use of cognitive and behavioral strategies to promote self-awareness, self-esteem, reality testing, and more socially acceptable behavior. The focus of therapy with these people is likely to be very basic, dealing with personal hygiene and daily activities, seeking to prevent isolation and total dysfunction, and establishing some independence and pleasure in their lives (Sperry, 2003).

Cognitive therapy is helpful to people with SPD and typically focuses on four types of thoughts outlined by Beck and colleagues

(2004): suspicious or paranoid thoughts, ideas of reference, superstitious and magical thoughts, and illusions. Therapists can encourage these clients to determine whether evidence is available for their beliefs. Cognitive therapy can also help them cope more effectively with perceived criticism and with distorted emotional reasoning, which is a common characteristic of people with SPD.

Behavior therapy can improve speech patterns and personal hygiene as well as social skills. Group therapy may also be useful for milder cases of this disorder, but the group members must be carefully chosen, and these clients must be carefully prepared, so that the experience does not prove too threatening.

A growing body of research underscores the effectiveness of combining medication with therapeutic interventions in the treatment of SPD. In five controlled pharmacological trials, atypical antipsychotics such as risperidone (Risperdal) were found to be beneficial in treating psychotic symptoms (Sperry, 2003). Reductions were effected in cognitive disturbance, derealization, ideas of reference, anxiety, depression, social dysfunction, and negative self-image. Anxiolytics can also be useful in reducing the anxiety that often accompanies this disorder. Nevertheless, although medication may reduce the degree of impairment of people with SPD, it does not change basic personality patterns.

Case management is often an important component of treatment for these clients. They sometimes are seen in treatment programs for the chronically mentally ill, where long-term oversight of their functioning can be provided. These clients often benefit from help in locating housing, finding employment that provides support and supervision and is not emotionally stressful, and obtaining needed medication on a regular basis. It is also helpful for them to have a place to turn to in times of crisis.

Prognosis

The prognosis for treatment of people with SPD seems guarded at best. As a schizophrenia spectrum disorder, SPD has a similar genetic predisposition and clinical presentation as schizophrenia. Indeed, symptoms of severe cognitive and functional deficits, psychotic symptoms, social isolation, and downward drift can all be seen in schizophrenia and, to a milder extent, in SPD. Dickey and colleagues (2005) suggest that SPD might better be called schizophrenia II, similar to bipolar II, in which the symptoms resemble those of a bipolar I disorder but are less extreme. Despite the guarded prognosis for significant positive change, however, most people with this disorder do not deteriorate into schizophrenia and do manage to achieve a stable if marginal existence. Realistic goals, focused on improved adaptive functioning and enjoyment of life rather than on personality restructuring, can help both therapist and client view their work as a success.

ANTISOCIAL PERSONALITY DISORDER

Antisocial personality disorder (APD) is the only personality disorder that, by definition, cannot be diagnosed before the age of 18. People with this disorder frequently demonstrate a pervasive pattern of irresponsible behavior that violates and shows disregard for the rights and feelings of others.

Description of the Disorder

In people diagnosed with APD, the symptoms of conduct disorder (see Chapter 2) have persisted beyond the age of 18. This pattern is typified by impulsive and aggressive behavior that is a reaction to social rules and norms. Theft, manipulation, lying, lack of empathy and cruelty to people and animals, vandalism, and fighting are common behaviors. Symptoms of the disorder are likely to be most severe in early adulthood and to diminish spontaneously in midlife.

People with APD are typically unable to sustain employment or monogamous relationships and may lead a "parasitic life" (Millon ct al., 2004, p. 154). They are egocentric, impulsive, reckless, angry, irritable, deceptive, and aggressive. They fail to abide by social and legal guidelines for behavior, are often in financial difficulty, behave irresponsibly as employees and parents, lack empathy, and feel little or no guilt or remorse for their actions. Rather, they justify their behavior, perceiving themselves as superior and infallible, and project blame for their difficulties onto others whom they devalue. People with APD are easily bored and have a high need for excitement, stimulation, and new experiences. They typically enjoy life, although they do not want to bear the consequences of their actions. Despite their professed need for independence, people with APD want to impress others and have difficulty with rejection and delayed gratification. They have faith only in themselves and tend to engage in preemptive aggression, attacking in anticipation of being attacked. They are often shrewd judges of others and can use their verbal and interpersonal skills in manipulative ways. At the same time, they rarely engage in introspection and have little sense of themselves.

People with APD disdain generally accepted values and behaviors, although not all actually engage in criminal behavior. Many find a place for themselves in business, politics, or other settings where a focus on self-interest and accumulation of material goods is rewarded.

Approximately 3% of men and fewer than 1% of women can be diagnosed with this disorder. It has been estimated that as many as 80% of people in prison may have APD (Hiatt & Dishion, 2008).

Typical Client Characteristics

APD tends to run in families and is believed to result from the interplay of genetic predisposition, temperament, stress, and life experiences. In a review of meta-analyses, Ferguson (2010) found that as much as 50% of the variance in APD can be attributed to genetics, with unique experiences responsible for up to 31%, and shared experiences contributing 11%. The brain's paralimbic system is thought to be the area most associated with the development of APD. Specifically, the orbitofrontal cortex which controls impulses and emotional and social decision making appears to be underdeveloped. As a result children do not recognize social cues, are unable to read the emotion underlying a verbal message received from their parents or others, and do not appear to learn from their experiences (Kiehl, 2006; Kiehl & Buckholtz, 2010). These neurological vulnerabilities combine with poor socialization or parenting to create the perfect storm (Hiatt & Dishion, 2008).

People with APD typically grow up in families in which discipline is inconsistent and erratic, sometimes excessively punitive and sometimes lax. These disrupted families often included others who manifested antisocial behavior (Kazdin, 2007). Fathers of people with this disorder typically manifested antisocial and alcoholic behaviors and often left their families or were otherwise unavailable. Mothers characteristically were overburdened (Millon et al., 2004). Unsupportive and defensive communication patterns are common in these families, and many people who are later diagnosed with APD had no childhood models of empathic tenderness. Instead, they learned that they had to look out for themselves and found that violence and aggression could be used to their advantage to intimidate people. They were typically undeterred by punishment; they manifested behavioral problems early on, and engaged in challenging and dangerous activities.

People with APD often have underlying depression and anxiety and more than the other personality disorders, are prone to substance-related disorders and violence (Millon et al., 2004). More than 11% of people with APD have attempted suicide, and 5% complete a suicide attempt (Verona, Patrick, & Joiner, 2001). APD is sometimes accompanied by other personality disorders, notably narcissistic, paranoid, and histrionic personality disorders, as well as by sadistic and negativistic personality patterns (Millon et al., 2004). Occupational and interpersonal dysfunction is almost always present. People with APD have considerable difficulty sustaining warm, intimate relationships and tend to change partners and jobs frequently. Specific traits associated with APD, based on the five-factor model, include increased anger and hostility, impulsiveness, and excitement-seeking. A negative correlation was found between APD and conscientiousness, agreeableness, and warmth (Decuyper, De Pauw, De Fruyt, De Bolle, & De Clercq, 2009).

Preferred Therapist Characteristics

People with APD rarely seek therapy on their own initiative, but often enter treatment because they are court ordered into treatment as a result of breaking the law. Therapy may be a condition of their parole or probation, or they may be treated while incarcerated. The reasons why these clients enter therapy and their motivation to change need to be understood and addressed before treatment can begin (Millon et al., 2004).

Because most people with APD do not initiate or want treatment, developing a therapeutic alliance is not easy. Sperry (2003) suggests that therapists initially empathize and join with the client in his or her hostility, then proceed toward a collaborative relationship. These clients tend to be reluctant to engage in therapy, although some are manipulative and appear superficially cooperative in order to avoid negative consequences. They may afford therapists an initial honeymoon phase, but their opposition to treatment is likely to surface once therapy progresses beyond superficial interactions. These clients typically resent authority figures and may see therapists as part of that group. To reduce the likelihood of being seen in this way, therapists should avoid assuming judgmental and punitive roles, even if they are working in correctional settings. Instead, they should present themselves as specialists and collaborative partners in psychotherapy.

Therapists working with people diagnosed with APD typically encounter a considerable challenge. Once again, the development of trust will be a critical ingredient of successful treatment. Therapists need to be genuine, accepting, and empathic. They also should be self-assured, relaxed, and straightforward and should have a sense of humor.

Directive techniques are often necessary in persuading people with APD to engage in treatment. Beck and colleagues (2004) advise providing these clients with clear explanations of their disorder and setting explicit guidelines and limits for their involvement in therapy. Clear limits in the therapeutic relationship can help prevent clients from becoming hostile and abusive and attempting to engage their therapists in battles; power struggles will only undermine treatment. Therapy should be continued only if clients give some evidence of benefiting from the process.

Therapists who work with people with APD may develop countertransference reactions to their clients that could potentially lead to boundary violations. Disbelief and collusion are common. Therapists are liable to rationalize clients' illegal activities and think clients "aren't that bad" (Sperry, 2003, p. 51) or to succumb to their manipulation. Therapists also may be angered or threatened by the histories of clients with APD, as well as frustrated and discouraged by their lack of progress in treatment. All of these reactions must be monitored and managed for treatment to be effective.

Intervention Strategies

The failure to find an effective treatment for APD has not been due to any lack of research; APD is one of the most studied of the personality disorders. Rather, the discouraging results of outcome research reflect the guarded prognosis for treatment of this disorder.

A history of rejection, underachievement, and an anti-authoritarian bias often leads people with APD to be treatment resistant, rather than treatment seeking (Duggan, 2009). Oftentimes their angry and aggressive behaviors, combined with a violent or criminal background, results in a criminal justice pathway, rather than a mental health treatment approach. When someone with APD does present for treatment, a structured and active approach to therapy is indicated. Although research has yet to identify a treatment approach that has a high degree of effectiveness, a few approaches have achieved at least some improvement in people with APD. A concrete, reality-based approach that addresses anger management, substance use disorders, and provides adjunct treatment seems best (Woo & Keatinge, 2008). Social skills training can also be helpful in regulating behavior, although motivational interviewing may achieve better outcomes than social skills training or anger management with these clients (Sperry, 2003). Motivational interviewing focuses on choice and helps people to consider the options that are available to them. The therapist takes a less authoritative stance and helps clients to recognize that they are in charge of their future and responsible for their own behavior. Milieu and residential approaches, as well as structured group therapy, have achieved some success in strengthening interpersonal skills and prosocial behaviors in people with APD (Sperry, 2003). Therapeutic communities; institutional settings that use token economies; and wilderness programs that involve peer modeling, expectations, and encouragement as well as clear consequences sometimes succeed in breaking through resistance and effecting some change in these clients. For those who are incarcerated, prerelease or halfway programs can also be helpful in facilitating their transition to a more socially acceptable lifestyle.

Residential therapeutic programs established specifically for people who have broken the law typically focus on increasing their responsibility, their trust in themselves and others, and their sense of mastery, while instilling an understanding of the consequences of their behavior. An important benefit of these residential programs is that they remove people from their former environments where their antisocial behavior may have been reinforced by peers. Developing new support systems and a sense of belonging through employment or self-help groups (such as Narcotics Anonymous) can accomplish a similar end.

Individual therapy is an essential ingredient of treatment for people with APD. The first steps in individual therapy include establishing a collaborative therapeutic relationship and setting clear and mutually agreed-on goals. Once those steps have been accomplished, the therapist should set a positive tone, and maintain an optimistic stance (Duggan, 2009).

Behavior, reality, and cognitive therapy can be helpful. Reality therapy can enable people to see the self-destructive nature of their actions, to recognize that their behaviors are not helping them meet their needs, and to make a commitment to change. Behavior therapy can promote positive change by improving problem-solving and decision-making skills, anger management, and impulse control. Beck and associates (2004) recommend cognitive interventions that are designed to promote moral development, abstract thinking, and appreciation for the rights and feelings of others, as well as analysis and modification of dysfunctional thoughts. Millon and colleagues (2004) suggest helping people with APD develop an enlightened self-interest so they can recognize the likely consequences of their actions and determine whether a particular action is in their own best interest. Psychoeducation, often provided in a group format, can be effective at teaching clients self-control and delayed gratification (Duggan, 2009; Sperry, 2003).

Mentalization-based therapy (MBT) and schema therapy hold promise for the treatment of APD. Mentalization-based therapy seeks to provide a safe therapeutic environment in which the person can focus on anxiety-provoking mental states. In people with APD, anxiety-provoking states often occur when self-esteem is threatened. In MBT, treatment alternates between weekly individual sessions and group therapy. Similar to dialectical behavior therapy (DBT), a team of therapists are employed. Therapists actively explore violent acts in the same way suicide and self-harming behaviors are explored in the treatment of borderline personality disorder. Treatment helps clients develop an awareness of their internal mental processes, to recognize when they stop mentalizing and are at risk of acting out, and to begin to respond with alternative behaviors that are consistent with their own goals. MBT has been found to be effective in randomized controlled trials in a partial hospitalization program for people with borderline personality

disorder and is being adapted for use with APD (Bateman & Fonagy, 1999; Bateman & Fonagy, 2008). Contrary to other types of treatment for this population, most mentalizing interventions help the clients feel that the therapist is trying to understand how their internal thought processes have evolved, to consider how the client felt justified in making their poor choices, and to develop better choices consistent with their own self-interest, rather than forcing them to conform to societal values. Clearly, additional operationalization and research on the effectiveness of this approach is needed, but early results seem promising.

Schema therapy integrates cognitive therapy with imagery, empathic confrontation, homework assignments, and limited reparenting (Young, Klosko, & Weishaar, 2003). Maladaptive schemas typically found in people with APD include mistrust (fearing that others will abuse or cheat them), a sense of entitlement, lack of self-control, and the belief that they are defective and will be abandoned by others. Although the focus of treatment is generally on current behavior, people with APD are sometimes less defensive when they are talking about the past, and this may provide a useful bridge to a discussion of current activities. Psychodynamic and insight-oriented therapies are not indicated with these clients, however, even if discussion does focus on past experiences.

An early sign of progress is the emergence of underlying depression (Sperry, 2003). This development can be upsetting to clients and may precipitate a resumption of old patterns of behavior. To encourage clients' persistence in treatment if depression does surface, therapists may need to increase support and empathy. Those whose depression or anxiety are alleviated too quickly, however, may lose motivation to change.

Medication is sometimes combined with therapy in the treatment of people with APD. Lithium, fluoxetine (Prozac), sertraline (Zoloft), and beta-blockers such as propanolol (Inderal) have all demonstrated some effectiveness in helping people control anger and impulsivity (Sperry, 2003). However, in a systematic review of randomized controlled trials, Duggan and colleagues found no convincing evidence for the use of pharmacological interventions in the treatment of APD (Duggan, 2009; Duggan, Huband, Smailagic, Ferriter, & Adams, 2008). If medication is prescribed, it should be prescribed cautiously, because of clients' tendency to misuse drugs and because of their reliance on external rather than internal solutions to problems.

The most effective treatment for APD seems to be prevention. Early intervention in the preschool and elementary school years when the child is first diagnosed with ODD or conduct disorder can have a profound positive effect. Such early interventions have been shown to reduce the conversion rate of childhood conduct disorder to adult APD by as much as 40% to 70% (Duggan, 2009; Woo & Keatinge, 2008). Family therapy can be an especially useful intervention when clients are young, in an effort to reverse familial patterns that are being transmitted. Therapy may also help family members set limits, be consistent, separate from the client, and deal with their own guilt and anger.

Treatment specifically for coexisting substance-related disorders can also be helpful to people with APD and can reduce their motivation to engage in antisocial behavior. One study found that completion of treatment for substance use was the most important factor in reducing postdischarge arrests in people with APD (Messina, Wish, Hoffman, & Nemes, 2002). Even so, many people with APD are resistant to therapy, medication management, or participation in substance treatment programs.

An issue that often arises in the treatment of people diagnosed with APD is the relationship between therapy and punishment, given that many of these clients come into therapy as a consequence of breaking the law. Millon and colleagues (2004) recommend separating therapy and punishment to increase the likelihood of clients' using therapy constructively and not manipulating or deceiving the therapist. At the same time, the threat of punishment can have a powerful coercive effect and can promote initial involvement in therapy. This issue has not been definitively resolved but must be considered by therapists working with people diagnosed as having APD.

Prognosis

The prognosis for treating APD is not good, primarily because of clients' lack of motivation to change (Millon et al., 2004). The presence of co-occurring depression, illicit drug use, alcohol abuse, gambling, or a history of anger and violence make the prognosis even worse. The likelihood of successful treatment is higher with people over the age of 40 who manifest some remorse for their actions, have a history of some attachments, have not been sadistic or violent, are neither very high nor very low in intelligence, and do not create fear in clinicians (Sperry, 2003). Time, according to Sperry, is the greatest healer. As people age, they become less impulsive, and the intensity of antisocial behavior tends to dissipate. Schema therapy also holds hope for the treatment of people with APD. A major randomized controlled trial is currently being undertaken at seven forensic hospitals in the Netherlands. Early findings show promise for the treatment of APD in forensic clients (Rafaeli et al., 2011).

As in the treatment of most of the other personality disorders, realistic and circumscribed goals (such as improvement in prosocial behavior) are likely to lead to a better outcome. Specialized treatment in therapeutic communities and structured programs also seems to help. In most cases, treatment will be long. Sustained treatment aimed at teaching social skills, self-control, and delayed gratification can be helpful in preventing relapse and improving quality of life.

BORDERLINE PERSONALITY DISORDER

More research has been conducted on Borderline Personality Disorder in the last 5 years, than on any other personality disorder. Even so, the evidence-based recommended treatment continues to be psychotherapy, "an intervention long thought to change the *mind* but not necessarily the *brain*" (Oldham, 2009, p. 510).

Description of the Disorder

People with borderline personality disorder (BPD) are characterized primarily by pervasive instability in mood, relationships, behavior, and self-image, as well as by impulsivity (American Psychiatric Association, 2000). This instability affects all or nearly all areas of their lives. The very name of this disorder reflects the precariousness of people with this condition. The name was originally intended to indicate that they were on the border between psychosis and neurosis (Crowell, Beauchaine, & Lenzenweger, 2008). By definition, BPD is characterized by at least five of the following patterns:

- Intense and fluctuating interpersonal relationships

- Self-destructive and impulsive behavior (for example, substance misuse, binge eating, excessive spending, promiscuity)
- Labile moods
- Self-mutilation (usually cutting or burning) or suicidal threats and behavior
- Lack of a stable, internalized sense of self
- Persistent sense of emptiness and boredom
- Frantic efforts to avoid loneliness or abandonment
- Inappropriate anger
- Transient stress-related dissociation or paranoid ideation

The prevalence rate of BPD is approximately 1.6% of the general population 18 years of age or older. An estimated 8% to 11% of people seen in outpatient settings (Koerner & Dimeff, 2007), and as many as 50% of people receiving inpatient psychotherapy, can be diagnosed with this disorder (Sperry, 2003). Seventy-five percent of people with BPD are female (Johnson, Hurley, Benkelfat, Herpertz, & Taber, 2003; Lenzenweger, Lane, Loranger, & Kessler, 2007).

People with BPD can be high functioning or low functioning, depending on several variables, including the degree of occupational and social impairment, co-occurring disorders, and level of insight. Major depressive disorder is the most common co-occurring disorder. Also common are panic disorder with agoraphobia; PTSD; somatoform, dissociative, substance-related, schizoaffective disorders; and other personality disorders (Arntz, van Genderen, & Drost, 2009; Johnson et al., 2003). Sleeping, eating, and grooming habits are often erratic, and people with this disorder almost always experience occupational and social impairment.

Typical Client Characteristics

A history of incest, brutality, early loss, neglect, and other traumas are more common among people with BPD than among people with any other disorder. The majority experience sexual, physical, or emotional abuse, particularly between the ages of 6 and 12 (Arntz et al., 2009). Such early abuse seems to explain the disorganized attachment patterns and negative views of others that are frequently found in people with BPD, as well as the increased incidence of PTSD (Yen et al., 2002). Beck and colleagues (2004) note that it is not the trauma itself that causes BPD, but how the child processes the trauma. Factors such as age, temperament, and other characteristics of the environment at the time of the trauma also contribute to the development of this disorder. Genetic factors account for 30% to 60% of the variance in personality traits (Crowell et al., 2008).

Masterson and Lieberman (2004) note that issues around separation and individuation persist from childhood into adulthood for these clients. People with BPD tend to have little sense of themselves and an external locus of control. They seek to avoid individuation by attaining a symbiotic relationship with another, typically a romantic partner or a therapist. They have considerable difficulty expressing feelings because they often are uncertain of what they are feeling or of how they are expected to be feeling and are fearful of incurring anger and rejection if they make a mistake. They seem to have a sort of false self, built around an effort to please others.

People with BPD seem to have a great deal of underlying anger combined with vengeful impulses. Sometimes these feelings are denied and suppressed lest their expression precipitate abandonment; at other times these feelings are expressed in self-destructive ways that provoke considerable anger in others.

This emotional chaos typically leaves people with BPD in a near-constant state of crisis, which they usually attribute to the actions of other people.

Two forms of behavior are common in people with BPD and need to be distinguished: suicidal intent and self-injuring behavior with no intent to die. More than 75% of people with BPD engage in self-injurious behavior, such as cutting or burning, excessive drinking, high-risk sexual behavior, and suicidal gestures (Oldham, 2006). Paradoxically, people with BPD engage in self-injurious behaviors in an effort to make themselves feel better. Such gestures are generally lacking suicidal intent. As can be expected, these behaviors do sometimes result in death or the need for emergency medical care, but these results are generally unintended. BPD has the highest rate of completed suicide of any of the personality disorders (Arntz et al., 2009). Engaging in self-harm or parasuicidal activities has been estimated to increase the risk of suicidal death by 50% (Gunderson & Ridolfi, 2001).

Impulsive aggression and affective dysregulation are two behaviors typically linked to suicidal and self-injurious behavior in people with BPD, and both seem to have a genetic component (Crowell et al., 2008). Axis I comorbidity is common, and major depressive disorder, substance misuse, and bipolar disorder are positively correlated with feelings of hopelessness and an increased number of suicide attempts (Links & Kola, 2005).

Recent research into the neurological roots of emotion regulation have found dysfunction in the neural circuitry of the emotion regulation centers of the brain that relate to impulsive aggression. Although the details are beyond the scope of this book, a variety of studies have linked reduced serotonin with impulsivity and depressive symptoms, which are commonly found in BPD. A link has also been found between brain chemistry and affective lability, dissociation, and comorbid mood disorders (Coan & Allen, 2008; Johnson et al., 2003).

BPD tends to be particularly severe in late adolescence and early adulthood when emotion dysregulation and self identity are in greatest flux. A disproportionate number of females between the ages of 11 and 21 meet the criteria for BPD, illustrating the difficulty distinguishing between normal adolescent emotional lability and borderline personality disorder (Crowell et al., 2008).

These teens present with multiple problems, multiple self-injuries, and often have families that are invalidating of their emotions or otherwise emotionally dysfunctional. One study reported that 77% of adolescents who were admitted to the emergency room for a suicide attempt failed to attend or complete outpatient treatment (Miller, Rathus, DuBose, Dexter-Mazza, & Goldklang, 2007). Symptoms of BPD gradually improve with age as people with this disorder attain greater stability in their relationships and their vocations. A tendency toward affective instability, strong emotions, and intensity in relationships, however, may be lifelong (American Psychiatric Association, 2000).

Mothers of people with BPD often have mental disorders themselves, most often BPD, a depressive disorder, or psychosis, which causes them to be inconsistent in their parenting and their availability (Sperry, 2003). Fathers are often unavailable or do not interfere in the mother-child bond (Masterson & Lieberman, 2004). Dysfunctional alcohol use is also very prevalent in the families of these clients, as are other substance-related disorders and antisocial personality disorder (American Psychiatric Association, 2000).

Preferred Therapist Characteristics

Therapists who work with people with BPD may find themselves addressing multiple problems simultaneously. Suicide attempts and self-harming behaviors, of course, will take precedence.

Approximately 60% to 70% of people with BPD will attempt suicide, and 10% will succeed (Oldham, 2006). Especially in the early stages of therapy, addressing suicide risk is often the first priority and focus of treatment. The therapist and client should "meet the preoccupation head-on, as a recognized risk and encourage the client to join forces with the therapist to find a better road to travel" (Oldham, 2006, p. 25). For many of these clients, acting out is a defense against boredom and depression and a way of preventing abandonment. Suicidal ideation and behavior may reoccur following a crisis situation and may accompany depression or substance use. Dealing with the underlying problem can reduce the pressure to engage in self-destructive behavior. Clients must be helped to link their actions with their emotions, learn to self-soothe, and find positive ways to reduce disturbing negative affect rather than resort to self-destructive behavior. (For more information on working with suicidal clients, refer to the Appendix at the end of the book.)

Because of the self-destructive and potentially lethal behavior of these clients, any approach to therapy that is used must make an effort to reduce self-harming behaviors and promote more effective functioning and reality testing. Many people with BPD need to be seen several times a week so that stability can be maintained in their lives, suicide can be averted, and the therapeutic alliance can be developed. Therapists need to make clear that they cannot take responsibility for the lives of these clients, and they should not become their rescuers. At the same time, steps must be taken to protect the safety of these clients by providing them with emergency resources, contracting for safety, and developing outside contacts to whom they can turn in times of crisis. Although somewhat dated, therapists may want to refer to the American Psychiatric Association's *Practice Guidelines for the Treatment of Borderline Personality Disorder* (2001) and Guideline Watch (Oldham, 2005) for a treatment framework in which expected roles of the patient and therapist are delineated.

Clients who rate their therapists negatively in the beginning stages of treatment are more likely to terminate therapy prematurely, whereas clients who rate the therapeutic alliance positively are more likely to stay in therapy and to report positive change (Spinhoven, Van Dyck, Giesen-Bloo, Kooiman, & Arntz, 2007). The authors also found that schema-focused therapists were rated higher than transference-focused therapists on factors such as warmth, genuineness, and the creation of a positive therapeutic alliance.

Therapists who work with people with BPD need to maintain a careful balance. Too much attention to these clients can promote dependence or flight, but too little can promote suicidal threats, panic, anger, and failure to develop a therapeutic alliance. Therapists should remain compassionate and nonjudgmental and maintain control in the face of their clients' emotional volatility. Therapists who are active and involved, who provide a stable and safe therapeutic environment seem to fare better. Although therapists should communicate availability, reliability, interest, acceptance, support, genuineness, and empathy to clients with BPD, they must also establish and adhere to clear and consistent limits and guidelines. Extra sessions and supportive telephone calls can be given when they are therapeutically advisable, but they should not be offered as capitulation to clients' manipulations or threats.

Splitting is a common dynamic in the self-images and relationships of people with BPD.

They tend to perceive people in extremes, as either idealized or devalued. The client with BPD typically begins a therapeutic relationship by idealizing the therapist. When the therapist falls short of that ideal, the client then harshly criticizes the therapist, often terminating treatment and moving on to the next idealized therapist.

Noncompliance with treatment is a frequent challenge that therapists face in working with people with BPD. In one study, researchers found that more than 50% terminated treatment prematurely (Crits-Christoph & Barber, 2007). Therapists who recognize the client's underlying struggle with intimacy and fear of abandonment and acknowledge this fear are more likely to help the client see the benefits that treatment has to offer.

These clients are challenging, and tend to elicit the same countertransference reactions among therapists, regardless of which treatment approach the therapist uses. Most therapists report an overwhelmed, disorganized response to these clients with strong negative feelings, resentment, dread, and a wish to avoid them (Betan et al., 2005; Van Luyn, 2007). Therapists will need to deal with their own reactions to these often frustrating and complicated clients and should not be lulled into confidence by positive phases of therapy. Because countertransference reactions can be a useful route to understanding these clients, they should be examined. Inevitably, if therapy is to succeed, therapists will need to find gentle and supportive ways to deal with the resistance and transference. Consultation with colleagues or supervisors is recommended to help therapists maintain their objectivity and equilibrium. Many therapists find it helpful to take a team approach when working with clients with BPD (Norcross & Guy, 2007) or to limit the number of clients with BPD in their caseload (Millon et al., 2004).

Intervention Strategies

A wealth of research in the past 5 years has confirmed the effectiveness of several established psychotherapies and established the effectiveness of several new therapies for the treatment of BPD. Treatments that have demonstrated efficacy in randomized controlled trials include: dialectical behavior therapy, mentalization-based therapy (Leichsenring & Rabung, 2008), transference-focused therapy, schema-focused CBT, supportive psychotherapy, and STEPP group therapy (Gabbard & Horowitz, 2009).

Two modalities, DBT and mentalization-based treatment (MBT), also show promise when applied to treatment-refractory BPD. Such cases in which anger and hostility are severe and are frequently directed toward the therapist are more likely to prevent the development of a therapeutic alliance, which is the foundation on which treatment is based. The inability of clients with BPD to cooperate with therapists often results in early termination, multiple serial therapists, and increased self-harming behaviors (Bateman & Fonagy, 2007). Indeed, one study found that 97% of clients with BPD had previously received treatment from other sources—including an average of 6.1 prior therapists, and 72% had histories of prior hospitalizations (Koerner & Dimeff, 2007). DBT and MBT have been found to provide the structure and support in which a therapeutic alliance can be successful, and progress can be made in such treatment refractory cases (Van Luyn et al., 2007). We turn now to each of the therapies for BPD.

Dialectical Behavior Therapy

Dialectical Behavior Therapy Dialectical behavior therapy (DBT), developed by Linehan and her colleagues (Linehan, 1993), not only has yielded empirical evidence of success in treating people with BPD but also is associated with a reduction in suicidality and self-harming behaviors (Clarkin, Levy, Lenzenweger, & Kernberg, 2007). A manualized version of DBT has been used primarily to treat people with BPD who were chronically suicidal and severely dysfunctional. Generally, DBT is carried out over the course of 12 months. However, several studies indicate that DBT may be equally effective in 6-month treatment programs (Rizvi & Linehan, 2001). In DBT, the therapist takes a dialectical stance, accepting and empathizing with the client's emotional pain while also helping the client develop better coping skills. Goals of DBT are grouped into four key stages: (1) development of commitment to therapy; (2) establishment of stability, connection, and safety; (3) exposure to and emotional processing of the past; and (4) synthesis (increasing self-respect, achieving individual goals). DBT takes a holistic, biopsychosocial perspective, emphasizing the use of persuasive dialogue to promote new understanding and change and incorporating many strategies to help clients improve emotion tolerance and affect regulation (including skills training, use of metaphors, and playing devil's advocate). Clients are asked to make a commitment to a combination of individual and group therapy for at least 6 to 12 months. DBT has been found to be particularly successful in reducing suicidal ideation and self-harming behaviors (Crits-Christoph & Barber, 2007). Improved work and social adjustment have also been reported, as well as reduced anxiety and anger (Linehan, 1993). DBT has also been adapted to treat eating disorders, antisocial personality disorder, and substance use comorbid with BPD (Dimeff & Koerner, 2007; Rizvi & Linehan, 2001).

Schema-Focused CBT

Schema-Focused CBT Cognitive-behavioral therapy has been a long-standing treatment option for people with BPD as they typically harbor many strong and maladaptive core beliefs, such as "I'll be alone forever," "I'm a bad person. I deserve to be punished," and "I must subjugate my wants to the desires of others, or they'll abandon me or attack me" (Beck et al., 2004, p. 200). The strategies of cognitive therapy can result in modification of these dysfunctional thoughts.

Several randomized controlled trails have shown the effectiveness of schema-focused therapy in reducing suicidal actions, decreasing drop-out rates, and improving overall recovery in people with BPD (Farrell, Shaw, & Webber, 2009; Giesen-Bloo, et al., 2006).

Some pathological emotional states of people with BPD can be seen as a regression to similar states in childhood. Young (1999; Young et al., 2003) identified schema modes that are organized patterns of behavior, cognitions, and feelings reflecting these childhood states. These schemas include the abandoned child, the angry/impulsive child, the primitive parent, and the detached protector. Four environmental or familial factors have been identified as contributing to the development of these maladaptive schemas in children who later go on to develop BPD: an unstable or unsafe home environment, overly punitive parents, emotional negation or deprivation, and an environment in which the needs of the child are subjugated to the needs of the parents (Rafaeli et al., 2011).

The person with BPD uses a variety of strategies to avoid feelings and to regulate negative affect, including drugs and alcohol, overeating or excessive sleeping, cutting and other self-harming behaviors, and even attempted suicide. Standard cognitive therapy needs to be adapted to these clients, with initial attention paid to the development of a hierarchy of issues to be addressed. Therapists must first focus on issues of life or death, followed by the development of a collaborative therapeutic relationship. Subsequent attention can then focus on other self-damaging issues and on modifying schemas, reducing dichotomous

thinking, teaching adaptive ways to express emotions, and promoting a sense of self (Beck et al., 2004). Additional guidance on using schema therapy to help clients with BPD can be found in Arntz et al. (2009).

Psychodynamic Psychotherapies For many years, long-term psychodynamic or modified psychoanalytic psychotherapy was viewed as most effective in treating people with borderline personality disorder. New research conducted in the past 5 years now supports this long-held belief. Transference-focused and supportive treatment are both associated with reductions in impulsivity and anger in people with BPD (Clarkin et al., 2007; Leichsenring & Rabung, 2008). Mentalization-based psychotherapy is a newer approach that has also been found effective (Bateman & Fonagy, 2010).

Although all approaches to treating these clients pay some attention to past issues, the primary focus of therapy is usually on the present because, for most of these clients, the present mirrors the past. The therapeutic relationship typically serves as a vehicle to help people work through concerns of separation and individuation and early losses dating back to childhood. Reality testing, rage neutralization, and management of the transference relationship are other important ingredients of psychodynamic therapy with these clients.

Transference-focused therapy. Transference-focused therapy views unintegrated anger as central to borderline pathology and uses the transference interpretation to help clients integrate that anger into a whole object relationship as opposed to splitting off into unrealistic positive or negative objects. Because transference interpretations can have a profound effect on the therapeutic alliance—both positive and negative—transference interpretations are modified when working with clients who have BPD.

Therapists must be discerning. Timing and word choice can be instrumental in the creation of a powerful transference intervention that works, versus one that is perceived by the patient as hurtful and confusing (Gabbard & Horowitz, 2009).

Mentalization-based treatment (MBT). MBT is a psychodynamic therapy rooted in attachment theory with cognitive behavior undertones. MBT is a manualized approach which is delivered over 18 months of weekly individual and group sessions. MBT focuses on internal psychological processes with the goal of helping clients to understand their own and other's mental states, to address faulty thinking about relationship problems which triggers abandonment fears, and to reduce impulsive, self-harming and suicidal behaviors that result. One study found that MBT was better than treatment as usual for people with BPD in a partial hospitalization program over a period of 36 months. Benefits were retained 5 years after treatment ended (Bateman & Fonagy, 2008). MBT is a flexible approach that can be incorporated into other treatments modalities as well.

Supportive therapy. Supportive therapy may be particularly appropriate for people with BPD who are not high functioning. Emphasis is placed on the importance of the therapeutic relationship in bringing about change. Indeed, research has shown that several years of supportive treatment can effect basic personality changes in people with BPD (Sperry, 2003).

Group Therapy The most common form of combined treatment for BPD is group therapy in addition to individual therapy. Homogeneous groups, with co-therapists, seem most likely to be effective. These groups can dilute transference reactions, reduce splitting, provide support and friendship, encourage change of manipulative and dysfunctional behaviors, and model coping skills. One promising adjunctive group treatment

for BPD—Systems Training for Emotional Predictability and Problem Solving (STEPPS)—has demonstrated clinical efficacy in randomized controlled trials (Blum et al., 2008). STEPPS combines cognitive-behavioral techniques, skills training, and a systems perspective in a 20-week manualized outpatient group treatment program. STEPPS has been shown to reduce impulsivity and negative affect, relieve depression, and improve overall functioning. STEPPS was not found to be more effective than treatment as usual for suicide attempts or self-harming behaviors, but STEPPS participants had fewer emergency department visits during treatment and follow-up (Blum et al., 2008).

Schema-focused therapy has also been adapted for treatment in groups. Group work can be more effective than individual therapy for BPD for the following reasons: Group participation more closely mimics the dynamics of the family of origin; more people are available in group therapy to facilitate role plays and therapeutic reenactments; and positive emotions such as respect, emotional validation, and kind communications can help heal the abandoned-child schema (Farrell et al., 2009). These types of comments and opinions are more likely to be accepted when they come from individuals in a group rather than from the therapist (Spinhoven et al., 2007). Schema-focused group therapy has been the focus of several randomized controlled trials. In one RCT, Farrell and colleagues (2009) found that 94% of subjects who participated in schema-focused group therapy no longer met the criteria for borderline personality disorder at the end of treatment.

Medication Symptom-targeted psychopharmacology combined with psychotherapy remains controversial. A meta-analysis of medication for BPD indicated that antidepressant medication was only helpful in the treatment of BPD if it was accompanied by a major depressive episode

(Olabi & Hall, 2010). However, evidence does point to the successful use of mood stabilizers and antipsychotic medications to treat the secondary symptoms of BPD, such as impulsive aggression and affect dysregulation (Olabi & Hall, 2010; Oldham, 2007). Reich (2002) notes that naltrexone (ReVia) has also been found helpful in reducing self-harming behavior. Although benzodiazepines have been used to help calm negative affect, they also reduce inhibitions and actually may lead to additional impulsive behavior; therefore, anxiolytics should probably be avoided in the treatment of BPD. Again, however, medication does not eliminate the basic personality disorder. Any use of medication should be closely monitored, given the high suicide risk of these clients, their frequent noncompliance with treatment, and their fear that improvement may lead to abandonment.

Other Treatment Options Hospitalization may be indicated when clients are experiencing psychotic or suicidal ideation. Typically, hospitalization will be a brief but frequent component of treatment, although crisis intervention and a limited stay in a crisis house can provide safe places for people with BPD.

The literature also supports family therapy as a useful treatment component for many of these clients, especially in conjunction with DBT (Fruzetti, Santisteban, & Hoffman, 2007). In general, the family has played a central role in the development of emotional dysregulation and serves to maintain dysfunctional communication patterns. Couples or family therapy can improve family dynamics and communication and have a positive impact on other troubled family members.

Prognosis

Improvement in BPD tends to run a slow course with many setbacks to be expected along

the way (Van Luyn et al., 2007). Even when progress is made, core conditions of BPD—anger and affect instability—respond more slowly to treatment. Axis I comorbidity is high with these clients, and a more guarded prognosis can be expected as a result. People who are treatment refractory, and those who do not or cannot control suicidal and self-harming behavior, have an elevated risk of death from injury or accident (Oldham, 2006). Combination treatments that address behavior, cognitions, emotion regulation, and also include medication management for symptom relief are more likely to be effective over time in the treatment of this chronic disorder. Symptoms of BPD tend to lessen with age.

HISTRIONIC PERSONALITY DISORDER

Histrionic personality disorder is one of the milder personality disorders. Approximately 9% of those with personality disorders will be diagnosed as histrionic (Millon et al., 2004).

Description of the Disorder

The *DSM-IV-TR* describes histrionic personality disorder as being characterized by "a pervasive pattern of excessive emotionality and attention seeking, beginning by early adulthood and present in a variety of contexts" (American Psychiatric Association, 2000, p. 711). This pattern is characterized by the following features, among others:

- Constant demands for praise or reassurance
- Inappropriate seductiveness
- A need to be the center of attention
- Overemphasis on physical attractiveness

- Exaggerated, shallow, and labile expressions of emotion
- Self-centeredness
- Poor impulse control
- Self-dramatization
- Suggestibility
- A vague, disjointed, general way of speaking

People with this disorder readily become impatient, jealous, manipulative, and volatile. Repression and denial are common defenses. These people also tend to be gullible, to trust others too easily, and to exaggerate the depth of their involvement in their intimate relationships. They usually appear affected and flighty, but their vivacity, imagination, and attractiveness can be engaging. They can also be charming, energetic, and entertaining, especially early in relationships.

People with histrionic personality disorder tend to be other-directed; their moods as well as their feelings about themselves come largely from the reactions they receive from others. They tend to avoid responsibility, feel helpless, and "actively seek out ways that others can be persuaded to take care of them" (Millon et al., 2004, p. 317). Intimate relationships and friendships are both typically impaired. Threats of suicide, although common, are part of these people's exaggerated emotionality and are rarely fatal, but they should nevertheless be taken seriously, as miscalculations can occur and a client may not be rescued as anticipated.

Approximately 2% to 3% of the general population and 10% to 15% of people in clinical settings meet the criteria for this disorder. Torgersen, Kringlen, and Cramer (2001) found the disorder to be diagnosed twice as frequently in women as in men. The *DSM* reports that although histrionic personality disorder is more commonly presented by females than males in clinical settings, the actual gender distribution may not differ greatly in the general population (American Psychiatric Association, 2000).

Histrionic personality disorder is often accompanied by other disorders. A particularly strong connection has been found between histrionic personality disorder and somatoform, depressive, dissociative, anxiety, and substance-related disorders, as well as other personality disorders (Millon et al., 2004). Bipolar and cyclothymic disorders have also been reported in people with histrionic personality disorder (Millon et al., 2004). Histrionic personality disorder shares some traits with paranoid personality disorder. People with histrionic personality disorder are particularly likely to develop paranoid traits under conditions of extreme stress (Paris, 2003).

Typical Client Characteristics

People with histrionic personality disorder typically grew up in families that were dramatic and chaotic but not dangerous (unlike the families of those with BPD). These families frequently have a history of antisocial behavior, other personality disorders, and alcohol-related disorders. They typically provide nurturing only when children are ill and give approval primarily for children's attractiveness, talent, and charm (Sperry, 2003). As children, then, people with this disorder were valued for their external presentation rather than for their inner selves.

Histrionic personality disorder can be viewed in light of attachment theory. These clients often have experienced insufficiency, conflict, and disapproval in their early interactions with their mothers and so have sought attention primarily from their fathers. Consequently, as they mature, these women overemphasize the importance of heterosexual relationships. Their exaggerated emotions, characteristic of the disorder, can be seen as a way to attract, and maintain, attention (Woo & Keatinge, 2008). Males with histrionic personality disorder also experience deprivation from their mothers and may become celibate or engage in compulsive seduction of women.

People with histrionic personality disorder usually are sexually and socially active but may experience sexual difficulties at a higher rate than average (Paris, 2003). They tend to be easily bored; typically, just as they achieve the commitment they seem to be seeking, they shift partners in their quest for the ideal mate. This pattern is exacerbated by the tendency of people with histrionic personality disorder to choose partners who are detached and unemotional and who cannot give them the strong responses they crave. Due to their intrusive and demanding interpersonal style, they may have continued difficulties with relationships across the lifespan, with aging posing a particular challenge to them. People who were overly flirtatious in their youth may need to find another way to be the center of attention as they age (Paris, 2003).

The tendency of people with this disorder to seek out new sources of challenge and stimulation can also interfere with their occupational and social adjustment, and they may have unstable work histories. Their lack of attention to detail and their illogical thinking can also contribute to poor occupational adjustment. If they choose fields that can make accommodations to their unstable temperaments, however, they may be quite successful because they can be driven and energetic in their pursuits.

Preferred Therapist Characteristics

People with histrionic personality disorder tend to be sociable and outgoing and may initially appear to be charming, ingratiating, expressive, and motivated clients, eager to please their therapists. These people do not typically seek therapy voluntarily, and when they do (often after a disappointing end to a relationship), may expect immediate relief from anxiety and depression (Millon et al., 2004, p. 324). Treatment usually begins on a positive note, with the client attempting to charm the therapist, but these clients are externally focused and often want the therapist to retrieve their relationships, fix their problems, or make others (usually a spouse or a partner) change.

As therapy progresses, clients' manipulative and seductive patterns will probably become more evident. They may be annoyed that the therapist has not rescued them, but the secondary gains of therapy—the attention paid by the therapist, and the opportunity to talk about themselves—are often reason enough for them to continue.

Millon and colleagues (2004) report that females with histrionic personality disorders are more likely to seek out male therapists. Their strong need for approval and attention may lead them to seek a romantic relationship with an opposite-sex therapist or to compete with a same-sex therapist.

The therapist must monitor countertransference reactions to these clients, remaining warm, genuine, and accepting yet professional. Clarity and consistency can help build and maintain trust and reduce excessive neediness. The therapist can also make productive therapeutic use of these clients' transference reactions to help clients gain an understanding of how they relate to others and to appreciate the negative impact that their behavior can have.

The therapist should quickly set limits with these clients and must maintain a professional relationship at all times. The clinician should avoid reinforcing dramatic behavior through attention. Millon and colleagues (2004) suggest focusing on process and on the facts of the person's history as a way of setting limits and maintaining appropriate distance. Gentle confrontation also seems to help people with histrionic personality disorder look at the self-destructive nature of their behavior. A detailed agenda, goal setting for each session, and keeping attention focused are necessary, or else the session will be rife with tangential themes and will lack any in-depth problem solving (Millon et al., 2004). Keeping these clients on task will be a challenge because they tend to be distractible and to talk at length in vague, general terms. Their speech may be overly impressionistic; they may resist being introspective, and may avoid tasks that tend to be difficult for them. They are also unable to integrate much of their past, including emotionally upsetting experiences, into their present life, and they have poor reality testing (Millon et al., 2004).

Persuading people with histrionic personality disorder to engage in long-term therapy may be difficult in light of their high need for change, challenge, and stimulation. Such therapeutic strategies as limit setting and confrontation may also make people with histrionic personality disorder feel rejected and unappreciated, and they may become reproachful and demanding, threatening to leave treatment if their needs are not met. Setting a series of clear short-term goals that are meaningful to the client can facilitate extended therapy, as can initiating therapy in an active and engaging fashion and reinforcing even small gains. Empathy should be maintained throughout treatment, as clients who feel that empathy and understanding are slipping away are likely to turn to dramatization for increased effect (Sperry, 2003).

Intervention Strategies

As is the case with most of the other personality disorders, few systematic studies exist on the treatment of histrionic personality disorder (Crits-Christoph & Barber, 2007). Nevertheless, the literature does point to the use of long-

term individual psychodynamic or cognitive-behavioral therapy as the core of treatment. People with histrionic personality disorder need help in thinking more systematically, reducing emotional reactivity, improving reality testing, increasing self-reliance and self-esteem, promoting appropriate expression of feeling, and increasing their awareness of the impact of their behavior on others. Barlow and Durand (2008) recommend therapists help these clients to recognize that their current behavior, while rewarding in the short term, is actually preventing them from achieving long-term success in their interpersonal relationships. Therapy should be systematic and goal-directed, providing an external structure that will help people establish their own sense of identity (Millon et al., 2004).

Sperry (2003) notes that therapists need to set professional boundaries and establish the limits of the relationship early in treatment with these clients because of their tendency to be "dramatic, impulsive, seductive, and manipulative, with potential for suicidal gestures" (p. 141). Treatment failure can easily occur with these clients if the therapist mishandles the erotic transference. The use of counterprojection techniques to remind the client that the therapist is not a transference figure of childhood seems helpful, according to Sperry.

Beck and colleagues (2004) found that people with histrionic personality disorder respond well to cognitive therapy, although modifications have to be made to that treatment approach. A sound therapeutic relationship, meaningful goals, and clear limits have to be established before these clients feel comfortable engaging in cognitive exploration, which is typically antithetical to their usual style. According to Beck and colleagues, therapists who take an active role and make extensive use of collaborative and guided discovery are particularly likely to be successful.

One way to encourage cooperation is to combine structured tools, such as the Dysfunctional Thoughts Record, with more creative activities. Once the therapeutic process is well under way, clients should be encouraged to challenge such basic assumptions as thinking that they are inadequate or must depend on others to survive (Beck et al., 2004). Training people in assertiveness and problem solving, increasing their awareness of others' feelings, and promoting self-awareness have all been helpful and have contributed to reducing impulsivity (Millon et al., 2004). Helping them find new, safer means of stimulation can also be helpful.

Accompanying disorders also should receive attention. Unless depression, anxiety, or somatic symptoms are relieved, these clients may not be able or willing to modify their pervasive dysfunctional patterns.

Group therapy can be very useful in treating people with histrionic personality disorder (Sperry, 2003). That therapeutic experience can provide helpful feedback, enable people to see that their behavior is not getting them the approval and affection they seek, and provide them with an opportunity to try new ways of establishing both casual and close relationships. Group therapy can dilute transference reactions and offer feedback while still providing attention and support to these clients, but they should be carefully screened for group participation to ensure that they do not monopolize the group.

Couples therapy and family therapy often are indicated because defenses of repression and denial can be more effectively treated in those contexts. People with histrionic personality disorder usually have partners with emotional difficulties; obsessive-compulsive patterns are especially common in the partners of women with this disorder (Sperry, 2003). Family therapy can ameliorate the emotional difficulties of both client and partner and can improve their communication and stabilize their relationship.

Medication is sometimes needed for treatment of the symptoms of people with histrionic personality disorder, especially antidepressants for depressive symptoms, including monoamine oxidase inhibitors (MAOIs) to reduce rejection sensitivity, demanding behavior, and somatic complaints in these clients. Naltrexone (ReVia) may also be helpful for those with self-harming behavior (Sperry, 2003). If medication is recommended, considerable caution should be exercised because these clients are prone to suicidal threats and gestures.

Prognosis

People with histrionic personality disorder are likely to benefit from therapy if they can be persuaded to remain in treatment (but persuading them to do so is often a considerable challenge). People with histrionic personality disorder are motivated to make some changes, and their interpersonal skills are good enough to allow them to engage in therapy. Treatment that combines group with individual therapy can be particularly effective.

NARCISSISTIC PERSONALITY DISORDER

Despite their veneer of superiority, many people with narcissistic personality disorder feel extremely vulnerable. Underneath their cool façade is an overwhelming sense of inferiority that must be defended against. Some may erupt with rage, violent behavior, or depression as the result of even the most minor criticism.

Description of the Disorder

Narcissistic personality disorder, according to the *DSM-IV-TR*, is characterized by "a pervasive pattern of grandiosity (in fantasy or behavior), need for admiration, and lack of empathy, beginning by early adulthood and present in a variety of contexts" (American Psychiatric Association, 2000, p. 714). The disorder is characterized by:

- Strong negative reactions to criticism
- Exploitation of others to accomplish one's own goals
- An exaggerated sense of self-importance
- A sense of entitlement
- Constant seeking of attention and praise
- Little appreciation for the feelings of others
- Enviousness, as well as the belief that one inspires envy in others
- Persistent fantasies of high achievement and special endowments, both personally and professionally
- The belief that one can be understood only by special people
- Arrogance and devaluing of others and their accomplishments
- Shallowness and unstable moods

Extensive use of rationalization, denial, and projection are common in people with this disorder (Kernberg, 2000). Most people with narcissistic personality disorder resist looking at their feelings of inferiority and tend to view the cause of their distress as external, failing to see how their own actions and behavior patterns may have contributed. Despite their veneer of superiority, many people with narcissistic personality disorder feel vulnerable and may react even to minor criticisms with depression, violence, or rage.

Research shows a link between narcissism and hostile aggression and bullying behavior. Beck and others (2004) report that violent offenders score high on narcissism. People with narcissistic personality disorder believe they must always appear powerful, in control, and superior to others, concealing their real selves from others lest their fraudulence and failure be discovered. They are frequently troubled by an underlying sense of emptiness.

Narcissistic personality disorder is probably more common among men than among women. This disorder is found in less than 1% of the general population and in 2% to 16% of clinical populations, although the prevalence of narcissistic traits is increasing in the general population (Sperry, 2003). Millon and colleagues (2004) report that narcissism is less prevalent in a collectivist society.

Narcissistic personality disorder is often accompanied by other disorders, including mood disorders, especially hypomania and dysthymic disorder; anorexia nervosa; and substance-related disorders (Beck et al., 2004; Millon et al., 2004). Beck cautions that clinicians should assess for the presence of a delusional disorder, such as erotomanic and grandiose types of that disorder, and also assess to see if the client has decompensated into paranoid delusions as a result of a severe narcissistic injury.

Typical Client Characteristics

Millon and colleagues (2004) note that there are two pathways to the development of narcissistic personality disorder: parental neglect and parental overvaluation in childhood. In the case of neglect, narcissism develops as an attempt to overcompensate for feelings of low self-worth. Lack of empathy and feelings of entitlement often result, and fantasy frequently serves as a substitute for reality. When parents overvalue a child without the child having to work for approval, as frequently occurs with only children, an inflated sense of self-worth develops. As a result, people with narcissistic personality disorder internalize the message that they are superior and deserve special treatment, but also that they will be rejected if they cease to be so exceptional. Shame and humiliation often result when the person with narcissistic personality disorder is confronted with reality.

People with narcissistic personality disorder may become contentious, arrogant, and demanding if they do not receive the treatment they believe they deserve. They tend to have a stunted capacity for intimacy, are often shallow and focused on superficial traits, and seek to control and manipulate others. Thus, their interpersonal relationships typically are impaired. Their quest for the perfect partner to affirm their own perfection can also be extremely damaging. A dissatisfied partner is often the motivation for these clients to seek treatment.

Some people with narcissistic personality disorder manifest occupational impairment. Fear of rejection or humiliation can inhibit their occupational success, as can their poor interpersonal skills, their intolerance of others' successes, and their disregard of rules or the requests of their supervisors. Some, however, driven by their self-absorption and their fantasies of unlimited success, have an impressive occupational history. Their tendency to be self-reliant and to take control of their own lives contributes to their sense of direction.

People with narcissistic personality disorder tend to deteriorate with age; their loss of youthful vitality and good looks may be extremely painful for them. Nevertheless, as Kernberg (2000) observes, the aging process may weaken their grandiose facade and lead them to be more receptive to therapy.

Preferred Therapist Characteristics

People with narcissistic personality disorder typically are quite resistant to treatment. They typically are intolerant of vulnerability or weakness and fear being viewed as inferior (Beck et al., 2004); therefore, they have

difficulty acknowledging that they have any problems or believing that anyone else can help them or understand how uniquely special they are. As in the treatment of most of the other personality disorders, the therapist working with a client who has narcissistic personality disorder needs to communicate acceptance, warmth, genuineness, and understanding in order to engage the client in treatment; any hint of criticism may provoke premature termination.

The therapist should not underestimate the fragility of people with narcissistic personality disorder. These clients may appear powerful, but they must be handled gently. Loss of their defenses can precipitate transient psychotic symptoms and regression.

Although the therapist should not be judgmental, indifference can be as painful to these people as rejection. Therapists might well engage in some cautious sharing of positive reactions to the client, as well as in extensive use of empathy.

People with this disorder tend to be very conscious of authority and are fearful of losing self-determination. These qualities can be used to the therapist's advantage. The therapeutic relationship should be a professional one, with clients accepted as experts on their own concerns and the therapist as the expert on psychotherapy. This collaborative relationship can facilitate clients' acceptance of help and their engagement in a working alliance. Kernberg (2000) emphasizes the importance of giving these clients full credit for any positive changes, to prevent their sabotaging the therapy in order to avoid admitting that another person has helped them.

The therapist should avoid being either seduced by the client's flattery or discouraged by the client's deprecating remarks. Instead, the therapist needs to view these transference reactions as therapeutic material and make use of them. With patience, persistence, and the establishment of clear and appropriate limits, the therapist can sometimes succeed in establishing a positive therapeutic relationship; however, true empathy and rapport may be fleeting (Woo & Keatinge, 2008).

Intervention Strategies

The literature is lacking in controlled outcome studies on treatment of narcissistic personality disorder (Crits-Christoph & Barber, 2007). As with most of the other personality disorders, however, inferences can be drawn about the types of treatment that are most likely to be successful.

Kernberg (2000), Kohut (1971), and others have used a modified psychoanalytic approach with some success to help people with narcissistic personality disorder develop a more accurate sense of reality and make positive personality changes. Kernberg has focused on such basic issues as anger, envy, self-sufficiency, and demands on the self and others, both in reality and in transference. Kohut has used the transference relationship to explore the client's early development as well as the client's wish for a perfect relationship and an ideal self. In an empathic context, both Kernberg and Kohut have explored defenses as well as needs and frustrations.

A psychodynamic approach seems to have a fair chance of succeeding with people who have narcissistic personality disorder and mild dysfunction and who are motivated to engage in therapy. However, this approach probably is not indicated for those who have significant disturbances of affect or impulse control; these clients seem to respond better to expressive, cognitive, and supportive forms of therapy than they do to analytic approaches (Kernberg, 2000).

Beck and colleagues (2004) recommend that cognitive-behavioral treatment begin with the building of a collaborative relationship, an effort to help clients understand how therapy can help them, and the establishment of goals. A focus on behavioral change typically would be the next phase in this kind of treatment. Behavioral interventions that do not require much self-disclosure or discussion of weaknesses are usually more acceptable to these clients than cognitive interventions. Beck suggests using the structured Personality Belief Questionnaire to assess the existence and degree of narcissistic beliefs. The Diagnostic Interview for Narcissism, developed by Gunderson, Ronningstam, and Bodkin (1990), can also be effective.

Building on cognitive-behavioral therapy, Young and colleagues (2003) have developed a detailed treatment model to help people with this disorder recognize, understand, and change early maladaptive schemas. The primary focus of treatment is on the client's intimate relationships and the therapeutic relationship. By reaching the lonely child hidden deep within the client, the therapist helps the client develop tolerance of pain and isolation rather than turning to self-destructive, compulsive, or addictive behaviors (Rafaeli et al., 2011). The therapeutic alliance can be a powerful tool in working with narcissistic clients. Through experiential work, cognitive and educational strategies, use of the here and now of the counseling session, and the modification of behavioral patterns, clients learn to change core schemas related to entitlement, emotional deprivation, and defectiveness.

Significant change in people with narcissistic personality disorder will usually require long-term treatment, but it is difficult to engage people with this disorder in lengthy, intensive treatment because of their limited insight and their extensive rationalization. Therefore, some therapists advocate a model of brief therapy that sets limited goals and focuses on symptoms and current crises rather than on the underlying disorder itself. Treatment that focuses on rapport, cognitive reorientation, reality testing, improvement in communication skills, rehearsal of new behaviors, and application of those behaviors outside the therapeutic setting seems most likely to be effective. Clients with narcissistic personality disorder often have difficulty with loss and failure and may be particularly amenable to therapy focusing on those issues.

Group therapy, consisting exclusively of people diagnosed with narcissistic personality disorder, can be useful to these clients if they are able to tolerate the exposure and negative feedback of the group experience and do not become disruptive (Sperry, 2003). Group therapy can help these clients develop a more realistic sense of themselves, deal with others in less abrasive ways, and stabilize their functioning, but it should always be combined with individual therapy for these clients.

People with narcissistic personality disorder often come into treatment at the urging of an unhappy partner. In such a case, couples therapy may help the partners understand their roles and patterns of interacting and learn more effective ways of communicating with each other. Schema therapy for couples, for example, helps partners understand each other's and their own core needs and schemas, reparent each other, and develop effective communication and coping skills (Young et al., 2003). Related psychoeducation and skills training are then specifically geared to the needs of people with narcissistic personality patterns.

No medication has been found that really modifies narcissistic personality disorder, but medication can treat the symptoms of this disorder in addition to any underlying disorders. SSRIs, for example, have been shown to decrease vulnerability to criticism, impulsivity, and anger in people with narcissistic personality disorders (Sperry, 2003).

Prognosis

People with narcissistic personality disorder are difficult to treat and may require as many as 100 individual sessions (Sperry, 2003). A combination of group and individual or individual and couples therapy can reduce the number of sessions necessary. Nevertheless, despite the challenges presented by these clients, Kernberg (2000) reports a favorable prognosis unless clients have strong features of borderline or antisocial personality disorders. Prognosis is better for those who are higher functioning.

AVOIDANT PERSONALITY DISORDER

People with this disorder typically view themselves as having poor interpersonal skills and as being inferior and unattractive to others. But, unlike people with schizoid personality disorder, those with avoidant personality disorder generally long for companionship and involvement in social activities, but their great anxiety and shyness inhibit their socialization.

Description of the Disorder

The *DSM-IV-TR* describes avoidant personality disorder as characterized by "a pervasive pattern of social inhibition, feelings of inadequacy, and hypersensitivity to negative evaluation that begins by early adulthood and is present in a variety of contexts" (American Psychiatric Association, 2000, p. 718). Typical manifestations of this disorder include emotional fragility, reluctance to become involved in interpersonal contact without guarantees of acceptance, fear of being embarrassed by doing something inappropriate or foolish in public, and avoidance of new and challenging activities that might lead to humiliation.

These people tend to have low self-esteem, to be self-effacing, and to berate themselves for their refusal to take risks in social situations. They fantasize about having a different lifestyle and anguish over their inability to change. Without assistance, however, they typically remain alienated, introverted, mistrustful, and guarded in social situations and avoid them whenever possible. Their need for control and self-protection outweighs their need for companionship.

Males and females are affected by this disorder in approximately equal numbers. About 0.5% to 1% of the general population can be diagnosed with avoidant personality disorder, as can about 10% of people seen in clinical settings. Millon et al. (2004) have found avoidant personality disorder to be one of the more prevalent personality disorders, representing over 10% of those with personality disorders.

Millon notes that "avoidants avoid" unpleasant affect (Millon et al., 2004, p. 205) and are unlikely to disclose the full spectrum of their symptoms. Sperry (2003) has found that people with this disorder have a low tolerance for dysphoria. Thus, when people with this disorder are seen in treatment, another disorder, frequently one involving anxiety and depression, is usually the initial focus. Anxiety disorders, particularly social phobia, seem closely related to avoidant personality disorder, and therapists need to conduct a careful assessment to determine which of these is present. Dissociative disorder, somatoform disorders, and schizophrenia have also been reported in combination with avoidant personality disorder (Millon et al., 2004), as have dependent, borderline, paranoid, schizoid, and schizotypal personality disorders.

Typical Client Characteristics

People with avoidant personality disorder typically come from families that did afford some appropriate nurturing and bonding, but these families were also controlling and critical and very concerned with their children's presenting a positive social image (Sperry, 2003). This combination led these clients to value and desire relationships as children but simultaneously to fear and avoid them, believing that others would inevitably reject them. Even as children, people with avoidant personality disorder were temperamentally shy, had limited social experiences and poor peer relationships, and may have experienced parental rejection. As a result, they had little opportunity to develop social competence and instead restricted their social interactions and became introspective (Sperry, 2003). A preoccupied-fearful attachment style is typically found in people with avoidant personality disorder.

By definition, people with avoidant personality disorder have considerable social impairment, which is typically accompanied by occupational impairment. People with this disorder often have jobs well below their abilities, usually because their fear of risk, rejection, and embarrassment prevents them from seeking promotions, taking an active part in meetings, attending business-related social events, and calling attention to their accomplishments. Sperry (2003) notes that this pattern alone can be diagnostic of avoidant personality disorder.

Females with avoidant personality disorder often have a strongly traditional gender identification. They tend to be passive, insecure, and dependent, and look to others to direct their lives. Although they may have underlying anger about the situation in which they find themselves, they are afraid of the consequences of change.

The life of a person with avoidant personality disorder is unsatisfying and disappointing, even if the person does manage to achieve a comfortable occupational situation. Some people with this disorder marry or develop a few close relationships. Typically, however, their friends tend to be distant, shy, and unstable, providing little help to these clients. Although this disorder tends to improve somewhat with age, the avoidant patterns rarely remit significantly without help. Sperry (2003) notes that people with avoidant personality disorder are prone to decompensate.

Preferred Therapist Characteristics

People with avoidant personality disorder rarely seek treatment specifically for the symptoms of this disorder because that process in itself feels threatening and potentially embarrassing. If they do enter treatment, they often have one foot out the door, testing whether the therapist can be trusted, and may leave at any hint of criticism, disapproval, or embarrassment. In one study, post-treatment follow-up indicated that fully 50% of the participants had dropped out (Roth & Fonagy, 2005).

These people typically are seen in treatment as a result of another disorder (such as agoraphobia or depression), often at the urging of a family member or an employer. Therapists should proceed gradually in light of the apprehension that people with avoidant personality disorder have about treatment and given the fragile equilibrium they have established. Therapists should communicate concern, availability, empathy, acceptance, support, and protection. Building trust may be slow but is integral to the establishment of an effective therapeutic relationship with these clients. Focusing on their strengths, at least initially, can build self-confidence and contribute to the establishment of rapport. Contracting for a specific number of sessions may increase people's commitment to treatment and prevent them from using therapy to avoid confronting real situations.

Over time, therapists can help clients work at increasing tolerance of negative emotions.

Structured social skills training may help guide them in social interactions. Paradoxical intention can also be effective in helping reduce rejection sensitivity (Sperry, 2003). A single woman, for example, who is afraid of being rejected by a man may agree to phone several men and ask them out for coffee. Rejection then becomes part of the goal and reduces the woman's sensitivity.

One advantage that therapists have in working with these clients is that they are in pain, are not happy with themselves, and want to change. They most likely will appreciate the safe environment that the therapist provides. Moreover, these clients generally know how to relate to a select few individuals and have a capacity for introspection. If they can be convinced that therapy can help them and is unlikely to embarrass them, they may have the motivation they need to benefit from treatment and may welcome the opportunity to discuss their concerns.

However, clients with avoidant personality disorder may hesitate to reveal thoughts or experiences that they believe the therapist might criticize or judge, and they may be unwilling to provide direct feedback to the therapist, leaving them at risk for terminating treatment prematurely. Beck and colleagues (2004) suggest that therapists use a feedback form at the end of each session to encourage clients to provide honest assessment of the session. Such forms can help address dissatisfaction, provide a positive model for assertive communication, and help clients give appropriate feedback. Role playing and guided imagery can also help. Therapists may feel frustrated with the apprehensions and slow progress of these clients. Therapists and clients alike will benefit from focusing on progress, no matter how slight. In addition, signs of avoidance can be viewed positively as providing information on impaired behavior and dysfunctional thoughts.

Sperry (2003) has observed two common types of countertransference in therapists working with people who have avoidant personality disorder: overprotectiveness and unrealistic expectations for rapid change. Pacing is important in the treatment of these clients, and therapists should be sure that they are nudging clients forward but not forcing premature confrontation of frightening situations. A gradual shift from general support to selective reinforcement of assertive behavior and positive self-statements can promote progress.

Intervention Strategies

Little empirical research is available to guide treatment of avoidant personality disorder, but guidelines can be drawn from case studies and from research on social phobia. Beck and colleagues (2004) recommend a treatment approach consisting of four stages:

1. Building trust and a positive therapeutic relationship and bringing clients to the point where they are willing to discuss their fear of rejection.
2. Promoting self-awareness and observational skills so that clients become aware of their self-destructive thoughts and behaviors.
3. Using the therapeutic relationship as a "laboratory" (p. 318) to test beliefs and role-play behaviors that clients can implement in the real world.
4. Incorporating mood management techniques to help clients tolerate dysphoria and anxiety.

Behavioral interventions are essential to successful treatment of avoidant personality disorder. Behavior therapy can begin with fairly safe relaxation exercises and then progress to such techniques as training in assertiveness and social skills, modeling, various kinds of role playing and psychodrama, anxiety management, and graduated exposure or desensitization (using a hierarchy of feared situations). Between-session assignments can accelerate behavioral change as long as they do not cause feelings of failure and humiliation. Comparative research on different kinds of behavioral treatments suggests that treatment designed to fit the specific interpersonal problems of the individual is most likely to prove beneficial. For example, clients with problems related to anger and distrust benefited most from graded exposure exercises that required them to approach and talk to other people. Clients with difficulty saying no benefited from both graded exposure and social skills training (Crits-Christoph & Barber, 2007). As with all personality disorders, assessment of individual needs prior to treatment planning is crucial to achieving positive results.

Beck and colleagues (2004) suggest incorporating a focus on cognitions after some behavioral change has been made. Changes in clients' emotions can be used as opportunities to elicit automatic thoughts. Using standard cognitive-behavioral strategies, such as testing automatic thoughts and assumptions, can help these clients become aware of and change negative self-talk and help them overcome cognitive and emotional avoidance. Using prediction logs to point out any discrepancies between expectations and reality, positive-experience logs, and lists of evidence for and against automatic thoughts (such as "If people really knew me, they would reject me," p. 318) can promote changes in self-critical cognitions.

Because people with avoidant personality disorder tend to avoid negative emotions and thoughts, interventions should include psychoeducation on the processes of exposure and desensitization, and encouragement for clients to tolerate and become more comfortable with negative feelings. The addition of psycho-dynamic therapy to the treatment plan can promote further gains and help people address issues related to their harsh superegos, underlying shame, and projection of unrealistic self-expectations onto others (Millon et al., 2004). Interpretations should be made with caution, however, because these clients' poor self-concepts and hypersensitivity make them easily hurt by their therapists. Beck and colleagues (2004) suggest that patients rate their discomfort with feedback from their therapists on a scale of 0 to 100 to ensure that the level is perceived as tolerable.

Schema-focused cognitive therapy has also proven effective in working with people with avoidant personality disorder. One study found positive outcomes at the end of treatment that were sustained at 1-year follow-up (Crits-Christoph & Barber, 2007). As mentioned earlier, schema therapy incorporates cognitive, experiential, and behavioral interventions, as well as the use of the therapeutic relationship itself, to help clients identify and change maladaptive schemas. Schemas frequently associated with avoidant personality disorder include defectiveness, self-sacrifice, social isolation, and approval seeking. Through the use of imagery exercises, empathic confrontation, homework assignments, and limited reparenting, schema therapy helps people change (Beck et al., 2004; Rafaeli et al., 2011).

As people with avoidant personality disorder improve, group therapy can be an important addition to treatment. It can help clients learn and practice new social skills in a safe context, receive feedback and encouragement, and increase their comfort with others. One limited study of 17 people in a group behavioral treatment program found that systematic desensitization, behavioral rehearsal, and self-image work conducted in a 4-day intensive group setting yielded positive changes that were sustained at 1-year follow-up (Crits-Christoph & Barber, 2007). Gains were made primarily in reducing the participants' fear of negative evaluation. Nevertheless, people with avoidant personality disorder should not be placed in group therapy prematurely. Inappropriate placement in a therapy group can be very threatening and can lead these clients to terminate treatment abruptly.

Family therapy can be useful, too, if clients are actively involved with family members. The families of people with avoidant personality disorder typically either try to be helpful by protecting these clients or try to effect change by insisting on the clients' greater involvement with others. Beck and colleagues (2004) note that combining couples therapy with social skills training can help decrease social anxiety and encourage people who tend to "hide in the margins of relationships" (p. 320) to break out of patterns that perpetuate avoidant behavior and, instead, to improve and increase their social interactions. These people also often have partner relationships that are characterized by interpersonal distance, and family therapy can modify that pattern, facilitating the establishment of interactions that are more rewarding to both partners.

Medication usually is not needed in the treatment of avoidant personality disorder, and people with this disorder seem uncomfortable with the idea of taking medication (probably because they fear loss of control). These clients also benefit from taking credit for positive changes rather than attributing them to medication. Nevertheless, sometimes medications that have been helpful in the treatment of people with social phobia—such as the SSRIs paroxetine (Paxil) and sertraline (Zoloft), as well as benzodiazepines—can also reduce anxiety, shyness, and sensitivity to rejection in people with avoidant personality disorder.

According to Beck and colleagues (2004), relapse prevention is an important element of treatment for these clients because their avoidant behavior often returns after therapy. Helping clients predict difficulties that may arise after termination and developing a plan to help them cope effectively with those difficulties can be an important part of the termination process. Relapse prevention can include infrequent but ongoing follow-up sessions and may include the agreement that the client will continue using assertive behaviors and pursuing new friendships and challenging tasks. Clients should be instructed to pay continuing attention to situations they are avoiding and to the thoughts underlying such behavior so that they can effectively use what they have learned through therapy after they have completed their treatment.

Prognosis

As with most of the other personality disorders, prognosis for avoidant personality disorder is not very positive and depends on the setting of realistic goals and on clients' finding interpersonal and occupational environments that meet their needs. Most people with avoidant personality disorder can make meaningful changes as long as they are willing to invest in therapy, but they probably will always tend to have self-doubts, as well as some discomfort in new interpersonal situations.

DEPENDENT PERSONALITY DISORDER

Dependent personality disorder is the most commonly diagnosed personality disorder, found in approximately 14% of those with personality disorders and at least 2.5% of the general population (Millon et al., 2004; Sperry,

2003). People with dependent personality disorder are frequently seen in therapy, and unless care is taken, may become dependent on their therapists.

Description of the Disorder

Dependent personality disorder, according to the *DSM-IV-TR*, is characterized by "a pervasive and excessive need to be taken care of that leads to submissive and clinging behavior and fears of separation" (American Psychiatric Association, 2000, p. 721). People with this disorder typically have great difficulty making decisions independently and without reassurance. They look to others to make major decisions for them, and they avoid disagreeing with others lest they be rejected. They feel uncomfortable, frightened, and helpless when they are alone and when they are required to take initiative. They go out of their way to be helpful in order to be liked, are hypersensitive to criticism and disapproval, fear abandonment, and, if a close relationship ends, feel devastated and driven to quickly find another relationship that provides care and nurturance.

People with dependent personality disorder have low self-esteem, low self-confidence, and a high need for reassurance. They believe that they have little to offer and so must assume a secondary, even subservient, position with respect to others in order to be accepted. They tend to be inordinately tolerant of destructive relationships and unreasonable requests. They typically are other directed, and their gratifications and disappointments hinge on the reactions they receive from others. At the same time, they are egocentric in that they are pleasing others to gain appreciation. They tend to think in dichotomous ways, believe in absolutes, and catastrophize (Millon et al., 2004; Sperry, 2003).

People with dependent personality disorder are frequently seen in treatment. This disorder seems to be more commonly diagnosed among females than among males, but this apparent pattern has raised the question of whether some women who embrace traditional female roles are being discriminated against by being inappropriately diagnosed as having dependent personality disorder. Gender, age, and cultural factors should be taken into account before this diagnosis is made.

The seeds of dependent personality disorder are often seen in an early history of separation anxiety disorder or chronic illness. People with dependent personality disorder also have a predisposition to depression. The two disorders share similar traits, such as hopelessness, helplessness, lack of initiative, and difficulty making decisions (Beck et al., 2004). Other disorders, such as anxiety disorders, somatoform disorders, substance use disorders, eating disorders, and other personality disorders, are also frequently diagnosed along with dependent personality disorder (Beck et al., 2004; Millon et al., 2004; Sperry, 2003). Symptoms are especially likely to emerge or worsen after a loss or an anticipated abandonment.

Typical Client Characteristics

Not surprisingly, many people with dependent personality disorder report a history of having been overprotected. As infants, they were characterized as low in energy, sad, and withdrawn (Sperry, 2003). They typically were pampered as children and were expected to behave perfectly and to maintain strong family ties and loyalties; autonomy was discouraged (Millon et al., 2004). Research shows that the families of these children ranked low on expressiveness and ranked high on need to control. Sperry (2003) found that as children, people with dependent personality disorder were filled with self-doubt, avoided competitive activities, and had peer relationships that left them feeling awkward, unattractive, and incompetent.

People with dependent personality disorder tend to have a small number of significant others on whom they are dependent and who seem to accept their passive and submissive attitudes. Sperry (2003) notes that they cling to significant others even if they are not happy with the relationships, because they prefer unsatisfying relationships to being alone.

People with this disorder may function satisfactorily in occupations that are consistent with their need to be told what to do and to receive approval. They have difficulty with tasks that require independent action and decisions, however, and may appear fragile, indecisive, placating, and more immature and less competent than others. These traits reinforce these people's sense of inadequacy and weakness, leading them to perpetuate the pattern by turning to those around them for help and support (Millon et al., 2004).

Even when these people's lives seem to be going well, they experience little happiness and seem to have a pervasive underlying pessimistic and dysphoric mood. They typically appear rigid, judgmental, and moralistic, especially under stress. In crisis, despondency increases and suicidal ideation may surface.

Preferred Therapist Characteristics

People with dependent personality disorder may seek therapy voluntarily after an experienced or threatened loss of a relationship (particularly through bereavement or divorce), or they may seek therapy at the suggestion of a partner, another relative, or an employer. These clients also may ask for help with secondary symptoms, such as depression and substance use (Millon et al., 2004). They typically are apprehensive about therapy but want help in averting any threatened loss. Nevertheless, they are unlikely to have much initial interest in becoming more assertive and independent. They tend to be passive clients, waiting for their therapists to ask them questions or give direction to the sessions. They tend to view the therapist as someone else on whom to depend—a magic helper—and probably will work hard to please the therapist rather than themselves.

The challenge for the therapist is to use these dynamics constructively. The client's wish to please may be used to develop rapport and encourage increased independence. Changes made only to please the therapist are not likely to persist outside the sessions, however, and do not reflect internal change.

In working with a person who has a dependent personality disorder, the therapist should probably begin in a directive and structured way, to give focus to the sessions. In order to establish rapport, the therapist will also need to communicate a great deal of support, acceptance, and empathy and should guard against appearing critical. Some initial dependence on the part of the client should be allowed as part of the rapport-building process. With the development of a therapeutic alliance, however, the therapist should gradually assume less responsibility and encourage the client to take more control of the sessions. The therapist should continue to convey empathy, appreciation, and optimism, but should also ask clients to make a commitment to working on their own concerns. The therapist should not give the client feedback on dependence needs, however, or offer interpretations of the transference until less threatening approaches have effected some improvement. The overall goal of treatment will be to promote the client's self-reliance, self-expression, and autonomy in a safe context and then facilitate the transfer of those experiences to settings outside the therapy room. Termination is likely to be particularly difficult, and the therapist will need to be cautious lest the client feel abandoned. Beck and colleagues (2004) recommend tapering off sessions whenever possible and offering

continuing booster sessions as a way of easing into termination.

More than any other client, those with dependent personality disorder tend to develop a romantic attachment to the therapist (Beck et al., 2004). The therapist should set clear limits on the relationship with the client, avoid any physical contact, and explain that such romantic feelings are not unusual in therapeutic relationships but that this relationship will remain a professional one.

Strong countertransference reactions to these clients are common (Beck et al., 2004; Livesley, 2003; Sperry, 2003). The therapist may find this type of client frustrating and annoying or may want to protect the client from mistreatment. The therapist needs to manage these feelings and be sure that these feelings do not damage the therapeutic relationship.

Intervention Strategies

Both long-term and short-term psychodynamic approaches have demonstrated effectiveness with people who have dependent personality disorder (Sperry, 2003). Psychodynamic approaches involve allowing the emergence of a dependent transference that is then dealt with in growth-promoting ways. In addition, encouragement and support are used to promote autonomy and improved communication and problem solving. These interventions can help improve clients' self-esteem, increase their sense of autonomy and individuation, teach them to manage their own lives and to ask for help and support without being manipulative, and relieve their fears of harming others or being devastated by rejection. Short-term psychodynamic approaches typically involve weekly therapy for three to five months. These approaches are most likely to succeed when the client presents a clear and circumscribed focal conflict or issue, can rapidly form a therapeutic alliance, and is unlikely to act out or regress (Sperry, 2003). A psychodynamic approach requires both commitment to therapy and introspection and will not be right for everyone with a dependent personality disorder; for example, it would not be indicated for people with considerable separation anxiety and low ego strength.

Cognitive-behavioral therapy has also been used effectively to ameliorate some of the symptoms of dependent personality disorder (Beck et al., 2004; Sperry, 2003). The treatment is similar to that recommended for avoidant personality disorder. It usually includes relaxation and desensitization to help the client handle challenging interpersonal situations, and provides training in assertiveness and communication skills to help the client identify and express feelings and wants in more functional ways. Standard behavioral techniques, such as modeling, reinforcement, and rehearsal, can all contribute to the client's improvement. Homework assignments should be practiced in sessions initially, to reduce the fear of failure. Properly handled, between-session tasks are likely to be completed because these clients typically follow directions and want to please.

Cognitive therapy is generally used to treat dependent personality disorder only after a therapeutic relationship has been formed and some gains have been made through supportive and behavioral interventions. Cognitive therapy can challenge those dichotomous and dysfunctional beliefs that limit clients' autonomy and impair their self-esteem. It can be empowering and reinforcing for clients to gather evidence of their competence and learn to use coping and problem-solving skills. As clients gain experience in these and other skills (such as self-monitoring, accurate self-evaluation, and reinforcement), they can assume greater responsibility for their sessions.

Practical issues like housing and employment sometimes require attention because many people with dependent personality disorder seek therapy after the end of a marriage or long relationship. Helping them successfully reestablish themselves can promote positive behavioral changes, and the tasks involved in their getting reestablished can serve as vehicles for applying what they have learned in therapy.

Family and group therapy are often indicated for these clients. Those treatment settings can afford them the opportunity to try out new ways of expressing themselves and relating to others while receiving support and encouragement along the way. Group therapy has been found to reduce the number of crisis visits and the amount of medication used by these clients (Piper & Ogrondniczuk, 2005). Family therapy may be difficult if the client has a resistant partner, but the family's collaboration can both facilitate progress and improve familial relationships. Therapeutic groups need to be chosen carefully for these clients so as not to overwhelm and threaten them or expose them to undue pressure to leave a harmful relationship. At the same time, shifting a client from individual to group treatment can reduce transference and facilitate termination.

Schema therapy, as mentioned earlier, can help people develop new core cognitions. Those with dependent personality disorder can learn to overcome their approval-seeking dependent pattern, as well as some of their self-doubts.

People with dependent personality disorder sometimes request medication. These clients also sometimes misuse drugs, and the belief that they need medication can detract from their growing sense of competence. Although some medications can reduce dysregulated behavior, depression, and anxiety, Sperry (2003) notes that a similar effect can be achieved through social skills training. He suggests that the building of social skills target five specific areas: cognition, emotional containment and regulation, perceptions, physiology (through meditation and relaxation), and behavior (through assertiveness and communication skills).

Prognosis

Treatment of this disorder has a relatively good prognosis. People with dependent personality disorder are trusting. They can form relationships and make commitments. They want to please, and they can ask for help. All these attributes lead to a somewhat better prognosis and a shorter and more rewarding course of therapy than is found in treating most of the other personality disorders (Sperry, 2006).

OBSESSIVE-COMPULSIVE PERSONALITY DISORDER

This disorder differs markedly from the similarly named obsessive-compulsive disorder (OCD), which is an anxiety disorder. Obsessive-compulsive personality disorder is a pervasive and ego-syntonic lifestyle, whereas OCD is typically uncomfortable and characterized by specific obsessions and compulsions.

Description of the Disorder

Perfectionism and inflexibility characterize obsessive-compulsive personality disorder (OCPD). The following manifestations are typical of this pervasive pattern (American Psychiatric Association, 2000):

- Impaired performance on tasks and activities because of preoccupation with details, rules, order, duties, and perfection.
- A strong need to control others.
- Avoidance of delegating tasks for fear that they will not be done correctly.

- Overinvolvement in work, accompanied by minimal attention to leisure and social activities.
- Indecisiveness.
- Rigid moral and ethical beliefs.
- Restricted expression of emotion.
- Reluctance to give to others without the promise of personal gain.
- Harsh self-criticism.
- Difficulty discarding objects that no longer have value.

Although people with OCPD seem indifferent to the feelings of others, they are sensitive to slights themselves and often overreact to real or imagined insults. These clients tend to be well defended, typically using rules to insulate themselves from their emotions and requiring others to conform to their rules as well. In fact, these clients may become so overly involved with rules that they become rigid and perfectionistic, although they can be quite accomplished and conscientious (Millon et al., 2004).

Although most people with OCPD do not experience specific unwanted and intrusive obsessions or compulsions, research has found that as many as 44% of those with OCD also meet the criteria for OCPD (Beck et al., 2004).

OCPD is approximately twice as common among males as females, although many of the traits of this disorder, such as perfectionism and control, are also likely to be found in women who have eating disorders, particularly anorexia nervosa. This disorder is present in approximately 1% of the general population and in 3% to 10% of people seen at mental health centers.

Anxiety and depression are frequent accompaniments of OCPD (Millon et al., 2004). In people with this disorder, depression often follows a perceived loss or failure and is particularly common in later life (Beck et al., 2004). People with this disorder often seek treatment for psychosomatic disorders or sexual dysfunctions, rather than for rigid or perfectionistic behaviors.

Typical Client Characteristics

People diagnosed with OCPD typically experienced strict and punitive parenting that was designed to ensure that they did not cause trouble (Sperry, 2003). The home environments of people with this disorder have usually been rigid, emphasizing control (Beck et al., 2004). Not surprisingly, parents' punitive and authoritarian behavior may be a reflection of their own OCPD. OCPD is more common among first-degree relatives of those with the same disorder than it is in the general population.

People with this disorder almost inevitably have interpersonal and social difficulties. A spouse may insist on couples therapy to help resolve lack of emotional availability, workaholic behavior, and lack of time spent with the family (Beck et al., 2004). People with OCPD tend to be cold, mistrustful, demanding, and uninteresting, and to put little time or effort into building relationships and communicating feelings. They are typically angry and competitive toward others, have difficulty expressing emotions or affection, and are most comfortable in the intellectual realm. Their lives tend to be joyless and focused on work and obligations.

Their occupational development may or may not be impaired, and they typically have greater occupational success than people with other personality disorders because they are tireless and dedicated workers (Millon et al., 2004). Nevertheless, people with OCPD have difficulty delegating, collaborating, and supervising. They tend to be self-righteous and domineering, and they usually have poor relationships with coworkers, whom they tend to view as incompetent and irresponsible. People with OCPD also tend to have difficulty bringing projects to closure because of their indecisiveness, attention to minutia, and perfectionism, and this pattern may cause them to miss deadlines and have work-related difficulties.

Preferred Therapist Characteristics

People with OCPD tend to be difficult clients. They have trouble giving up control and accepting help from others, and they have little facility with insight and self-expression. They often focus on external events and physical rather than psychological complaints in treatment. New situations make them anxious, and they are likely to become even more obstinate and resistant in therapy than they usually are (Millon et al., 2004). If they can become engaged in conversation, they tend to complain bitterly about others' incompetence and how unappreciated they feel. Their interest is in changing others rather than in changing themselves, and they may attack therapists who suggest that they need to make changes. They also may feel competitive with their therapists and may have an investment in sabotaging therapy or proving their therapists incompetent.

Establishing rapport can be difficult with clients who have OCPD, due to their rigidity, discomfort with emotion, and denial of the importance of relationships. Beck notes that therapy with a person with OCPD is likely to be businesslike and problem-focused, with little discussion of emotions. Countertransference issues can revolve around the need for control, and therapists should be aware of their own compulsive traits so that they do not interfere with therapy or result in a power struggle with the client (Beck et al., 2004).

Involving people with this disorder in a productive therapeutic relationship clearly presents a considerable challenge. These clients are respectful of authority, however, as well as persevering, and they usually comply with rules and directions (although they may feel inwardly defiant). Therapists may initially be able to use the authority of their education and position to elicit a short-term commitment to therapy from these clients.

Therapists should be sure not to engage in power struggles and arguments with these clients. Other ways for therapists to earn the admiration of these people and enable them to accept help are to treat them in a respectful and professional way; to refrain from violating their defenses and their need for privacy; to collaborate with them on therapeutic decisions; and to be prompt, organized, and efficient. Too much attention to emotion can be upsetting to these clients, but acceptance, support, and empathy can help convince them that their therapists are not their enemies.

Intervention Strategies

Little clear research exists on effective treatment of OCPD, although multiple studies support the use of cognitive and behavioral interventions with this disorder (Beck et al., 2004). Even though long-term psychodynamic or modified psychoanalytic therapy may be ideal for people with this disorder, it is difficult to involve them in therapy that is extended, intensive, and introspective. Emotion is equated with being out of control; thus most people with OCPD will intellectualize, somaticize, or deny affect (Millon et al., 2004). Therefore, more present- and action-oriented approaches, consistent with these clients' limited insight and intolerance of yielding control, will often be used to help them establish more realistic expectations for themselves and others.

Cognitive-behavioral therapy is likely to be well received by people with OCPD because that approach is structured, problem-centered, and present-oriented, requiring only limited analysis and expression of emotions. Behavior therapy can be useful in reducing some of the dysfunctional actions of these clients. It can also increase their ability to plan and make decisions, their involvement in leisure and social activities, and their facility in communicating their feelings and reactions positively and assertively. Having a mutually agreed-on list of prioritized goals can keep these clients working productively and can minimize complaining and oppositional tactics. Modeling humor and spontaneity in controlled ways can teach these clients new ways of behaving. Because of their increased anxiety and psychosomatic symptoms, relaxation techniques for stress management can also contribute to the improvement of OCPD, as can thought stopping, social skills training, desensitization, and response prevention.

Beck and colleagues (2004) report success in using a modified version of cognitive therapy with these clients. In this approach, behavioral experiments rather than direct disputation were used to change such characteristic automatic thoughts as "I must avoid mistakes to be worthwhile" (p. 339). Inventories like the weekly activity schedule and the Dysfunctional Thought Record increased structure and, correspondingly, clients' cooperation.

People with OCPD typically are apprehensive about participating in group and family therapy because of their reluctance to disclose their feelings to others and their fear of humiliation. If their commitment to individual therapy can be sustained long enough for them to make some positive changes, however, they may later be able to make productive use of group or family therapy. Those approaches can offer them feedback, as well as the opportunity to learn and experiment with new interpersonal behaviors and to improve relationships. Nevertheless, therapists should be sure that these clients do not monopolize group or family sessions and are ready to listen to others.

Millon and colleagues (2004) note that people with OCPD tend to marry people who have dependent or histrionic personalities—people whose neediness meshes nicely with the need to control on the part of the person with OCPD. Couples therapy can help improve these relationships, resolve sexual issues, and establish rules for handling trouble spots.

Medication generally is not necessary for treatment of people with OCPD, but some medications have demonstrated effectiveness in treating obsessive-compulsive disorder and may be beneficial in the treatment of OCPD as well (Sperry, 2003). The 5-HT antidepressants—fluoxetine (Prozac), sertraline (Zoloft), paroxetine (Paxil), citalopram (Celexa), and escitalopram (Lexapro)—seem to work directly on the brain's 5-HT neurons to reduce symptoms of OCD (Preston, O'Neal, & Talaga, 2010). Medication is also indicated for relief of severe anxiety and depression accompanying OCPD.

Relapse prevention can be helpful to people with OCPD, just as it can be to people with most of the other personality disorders. Beck and colleagues (2004) suggest teaching people to monitor their own progress and scheduling periodic booster sessions.

Prognosis

Without treatment, OCPD usually is relatively stable over time, neither improving nor worsening. Many case studies report improvement, if not major personality changes, through therapy. As is the case with most of the other personality disorders, a small number of these clients probably make major changes as a result of therapy. A larger number make some important behavioral and attitudinal changes, and another large number either leave therapy prematurely or remain resistant to help. Overall, then, the prognosis is probably only fair for treatment of OCPD.

PERSONALITY DISORDERS NOT OTHERWISE SPECIFIED

The *DSM-IV-TR* includes an NOS (not otherwise specified) category at the end of its section on personality disorders. This category is used by clinicians when the manifestations of a personality disorder are mixed and straddle more than one disorder, not fully meeting the criteria for a specific disorder, or when the clinician determines that a personality disorder included in the *DSM*'s Appendix B (Criteria Sets and Axes Provided for Further Study) is appropriate.

As with other personality disorders, the criteria specify that these disorders must be pervasive and cause significant difficulties in relationships, behavior, and educational or work settings. Johnson and others (2005) discovered that adolescents diagnosed with personality disorder NOS were just as likely to have difficulties in these areas of life and to have co-occurring Axis I disorders as adolescents diagnosed with Cluster A, B, or C personality disorders.

Appendix B also includes two personality disorders that were included in the *DSM-IV* despite considerable overlap with other disorders: passive-aggressive (negativistic) personality disorder and depressive personality disorder.

Passive-aggressive personality disorder was removed from the *DSM-III*, but continues to be a useful clinical construct that deserves consideration in assessment of psychopathology (Hopwood, Morey, Markowitz, Pinto, Skodol, et al., 2009). The main feature of passive-aggressive personality disorder is "a pervasive pattern of negativistic attitudes and passive resistance to demands for adequate performance in social and occupational situations" (American Psychiatric Association, 2000, p. 789). It is frequently related to substance use disorders, suicidal behavior, and borderline and antisocial personality disorders.

Depressive personality disorder is a "pervasive pattern of depressive cognitions and behaviors that begins by early adulthood" (p. 788) and includes worried, negative, and unhappy thoughts; low self-esteem; self-criticism; and feelings of unworthiness that permeate the person's cognitions and become a way of life. The disorder is not better accounted for by a major depressive episode or dysthymic disorder. In their investigation of dysthymic disorder and depressive personality disorder, Sprock and Fredendall (2008) found considerable overlap and comorbidity between the two disorders as currently defined. Future editions of the *DSM* will, no doubt, clarify these issues.

Treatment recommendations for the other types of personality disorders provide the basis for determining the treatment of personality disorder NOS, especially when a mixed type includes features of more than one personality disorder. Treatment should be adapted to meet the needs of the particular client.

TREATMENT RECOMMENDATIONS: CLIENT MAP

Recommendations on treating personality disorders are summarized here, according to the framework of the Client Map.

CLIENT MAP

Diagnosis

Personality disorders (paranoid, schizoid, schizotypal, antisocial, borderline, histrionic, narcissistic, avoidant, dependent, and obsessive-compulsive)

Objectives of Treatment

Immediate: Create a therapeutic alliance

Short- to medium-term objectives: improve social and occupational functioning, communication skills, self-esteem, empathy, and coping mechanisms; develop appropriate sense of responsibility; reduce any accompanying depression or anxiety

Long-term objectives: modify underlying dysfunctional personality patterns

Assessments

Broad-based personality inventory (for example, the Millon Clinical Multiaxial Inventory)

Measures of specific symptoms (for example, substance use, depression, anxiety)

Clinician Characteristics

Consistent

Able to set limits

Able to communicate acceptance and empathy in the face of resistance, hostility, or dependence

Good ability to manage transference and countertransference reactions

Patient and comfortable with slow progress

Location

Usually outpatient setting

Emergency and inpatient settings, as necessary, to deal with suicidal ideation or regression

Interventions to Be Used

Motivational interviewing with resistant or court-ordered clients

Psychodynamic (to modify dysfunctional personality)

Behavioral and cognitive (to effect change in coping skills and relationships and to address presenting problems)

Schema-focused therapy

Dialectical behavior therapy and mentalization-focused therapy for borderline and antisocial personality

Crisis management, as needed

Emphasis of Treatment

Strong emphasis on establishing a therapeutic relationship with attention paid to ruptures to the alliance

Emphasis balanced between supportive and exploratory elements

Simultaneous emphasis on fostering client's responsibility

Attention to both past and present concerns

Numbers

Individual therapy usually primary, combined later with family or couples therapy

Group therapy often very useful in combination with individual therapy after client is able to tolerate group without becoming frightened or destructive

Timing

Usually long-term, but with development of short-term goals to discourage premature termination

Gradual but steady pace

More than one session per week possible, especially when client is in crisis

Long-term follow-up to address possibility of relapse

Medications Needed

Not effective in modifying basic personality disorder

May sometimes help alleviate depression, anxiety, or psychotic symptoms

Should be used with caution in light of client's tendency to misuse substances or attempt suicide

Adjunct Services

Possibly self-help groups, such as Alcoholics Anonymous, Narcotics Anonymous, social groups

Career counseling

Assertiveness training

Prognosis

Usually fair, but variable

Can be good for short-term behavioral changes

Fair for underlying personality changes

CLIENT MAP OF EMILY L.

This chapter opened with a description of Emily L., a 25-year-old woman who was seen for therapy after a suicide attempt. Emily's background included emotional and physical abuse and loss of both biological parents. She presented a long history of depression, maladaptive substance use, and instability in relationships and employment. Emily was a challenging client because of her multiple symptoms, her previous unsuccessful treatments, her suicidal behavior, her limited sense of self, and her lack of support systems. She initially idealized her therapists, made excessive demands on them, and then left treatment when they failed to meet her demands. Her principal diagnosis was borderline personality disorder. The following Client Map presents recommendations for treating Emily.

Diagnosis

Axis I: 296.33 Major depressive disorder, recurrent, severe 300.4 Dysthymic disorder, severe 305.00 Alcohol abuse, moderate 312.39 Trichotillomania, moderate

Axis II: 301.83 Borderline personality disorder (principal diagnosis)

Axis III: 278.0 Obesity

Axis IV: Marital conflict and abuse; history of childhood sexual, emotional, and physical abuse

Axis V: Global assessment of functioning (GAF scale): current GAF = 25

Objectives of Treatment

Reduction of depression and suicidal ideation

Improvement of coping skills (stress management, verbal self-expression, assertiveness)

Abstinence from alcohol

Reduction of hair pulling

Improved support systems and safety

Establishment of rewarding and realistic goals and direction

Increased stability and sense of competence

Improved and expanded relationships

Modification of self-destructive personality patterns and behaviors, especially suicidal ideation

Working through history of abuse

Assessments

Millon Clinical Multiaxial Inventory

Michigan Alcoholism Screening Test

Beck Depression Inventory

Medical examination

Clinician Characteristics

Stable

Accepting and supportive

Able to set and maintain clear limits

Able to manage transference and countertransference reactions

Location of Treatment

Outpatient setting

Inpatient and day treatment settings as needed

Interventions to Be Used

Supportive and behavioral therapy at first (to build a therapeutic relationship and enable client to see that therapy could be useful)

Contracts specifying alternative coping behaviors (to prevent suicidal behavior and reduce alcohol consumption)

Development of a safety plan (to protect client from abuse by her husband)

Rewarding activities and between-session tasks (to promote motivation, begin to build feelings of competence, and reduce depression)

Later integration of cognitive, DBT, and psychodynamic approaches (to help client deal with past losses and profound feelings of hopelessness, emptiness, and worthlessness)

Emphasis of Treatment

Supportive and structured emphasis (but promoting client's responsibility)

Initial emphasis on the present and on behavior

Later emphasis on past issues and underlying dysfunction and dynamics

Numbers

Primarily individual therapy at first

Subsequent marital therapy (to help client and her husband improve their relationship and eliminate abuse)

Group therapy (after amelioration of client's immediate difficulties, and with client's growing ability to partici-pate effectively and benefit from feedback, support, and opportunities for socialization and practice of interpersonal skills)

Timing

Long-term (if client willing)

Steady pace, with communication of clear expectations

Medications Needed

Antidepressant medication probably useful, but with careful monitoring in light of client's suicidal ideation

Adjunct Services

Alcoholics Anonymous

Nutritional counseling

Exercise and weight-control programs

Education about alcohol use, stress management, assertiveness, and job seeking

Prognosis

Fair at best, in light of client's history of treatment failures

RECOMMENDED READING

Arntz, A., van Genderen, H., & Drost, J. (2009). *Schema therapy for borderline personality disorder*. Malden, MA: Wiley.

Bateman, A., & Fonagy, P. (2004). *Psychotherapy for border-line personality disorder: Mentalization-based treatment*. New York, NY: Oxford University Press.

Beck, A. T., Freeman, A., Davis, D. D., & Associates. (2004). *Cognitive therapy of personality disorders* (2nd ed.). New York, NY: Guilford Press.

Caligor, E., Kernberg, O. F., & Clarkin, J. F. (2007). *Hand-book of dynamic psychotherapy for higher level personality pa-thology*. Arlington, VA: American Psychiatric Publishing.

Dimeff, L. A., & Koerner, K. (Eds.). (2007). *Dialectical be-havior therapy in clinical practice: Application across disorders and settings*. New York, NY: Guilford Press.

Oldham, J. M., Skodol, A. E., & Bender, D. S. (2005). *The American Psychiatric Publishing Textbook on Personality Dis-orders*. Arlington, VA: American Psychiatric Publishing.

Rafaeli, E., Bernstein, D. P., & Young, J. (2011). *Schema therapy: Distinctive features*. New York, NY: Routledge.

Sperry, L. (2006). *Cognitive behavior therapy of DSM-IV-TR personality disorders: Highly effective interventions for the most common personality disorders* (2nd ed.). New York, NY: Routledge.

Young, J. E., Klosko, J. S., & Weishaar, M. (2003). *Schema therapy: A practitioner's guide*. New York, NY: Guilford Press.

9 Disorders Involving Impairment in Awareness of Reality

Psychotic and Dissociative Disorders

Victor J., a 22-year-old college senior, was brought to the psychologist in the college counseling center by his roommate, Arnold, who expressed great concern about Victor's thoughts and behaviors. Several months earlier, Victor had spent the winter break in New York City with Arnold and his divorced mother, Vanessa. During that time, Vanessa, a well-known writer of romance novels, had gone out of her way to entertain Victor. She took Victor and Arnold out to dinner and to the theater, introduced them to her friends, and took them shopping.

Upon returning to college, Victor told Arnold that Vanessa and he were in love and would marry in the spring, after graduation. He began writing impassioned letters to Vanessa, calling her frequently, and spending most of his free time reading her novels.

At first Vanessa was amused; she teased Victor about his interest in "an older woman." The teasing only prompted more passionate and graphic letters, however. Vanessa tried repeatedly to let Victor know that she was not romantically interested in him, but even when she returned his letters unopened, he continued his avowals of love. He told Arnold that his mother was concealing her real feelings because she did not want to upset her son.

The week before Victor was brought for counseling, he had borrowed money and traveled to New York, where he went to Vanessa's office. When she told him she was busy and did not want to see him, he refused to leave for several hours and reappeared at her office for the next few days. Vanessa believed that Victor had taken some notes from her desk and had rummaged through her files and her wastebasket.

Victor had dated little in college and generally seemed uncomfortable around women his own age. He had grown up in a lower-middle-class family. His father owned an automobile repair business and had been opposed to Victor's attending college. He expected Victor to join him in the business after graduation. Although Victor's grades had declined somewhat, he was passing all his courses and was due to graduate in 2 months. Interviews with Victor indicated that he was experiencing delusional disorder, erotomanic type, a mental disorder that involves loss of contact with reality.

OVERVIEW OF PSYCHOTIC AND DISSOCIATIVE DISORDERS

This chapter considers a diverse array of disorders that are characterized by impairment in awareness of reality. The psychotic and dissociative disorders include schizophrenia, schizoaffective disorder, delusional disorder, as well as dissociative disorders. These disorders significantly impact people's lives.

Description of the Disorders

Each of the psychotic and dissociative disorders differ considerably in terms of origin, duration, treatment, and prognosis. What connects them is similarity in their symptoms: These disorders typically involve a distortion or impairment in memory, awareness of reality, or both. Most of these disorders produce marked dysfunction in at least one area of life. People with these disorders are often unable to present a clear picture of their symptoms. Therefore, these disorders can challenge the diagnostician and are sometimes misdiagnosed as cognitive, mood, or substance-induced disorders. Misdiagnosis is unfortunate, of course, because it can lead to inappropriate treatment.

Psychotic Disorders The *DSM-IV-TR* (American Psychiatric Association, 2000) lists the following six psychotic disorders:

1. Schizophrenia
2. Brief psychotic disorder
3. Schizophreniform disorder
4. Delusional disorder
5. Schizoaffective disorder
6. Shared psychotic disorder

Each of the psychotic disorders is considered a separate entity in the *DSM*. However, a growing body of research indicates that these disorders share a similar genetic basis and transmission process and are part of a spectrum of disorders.

The length and number of psychotic episodes has been linked to the development of permanent cognitive dysfunction as well as to dementia later in life (Post, 2010; Power, 2010). Early diagnosis and treatment of psychosis can shorten the duration of the episode, minimize family and work-related dysfunction, and reduce the number of lifetime hospitalizations. Detection and intervention, in the first three to five years following onset of a psychotic episode, also reduces the risk of suicide and has a crucial impact on later biological, psychological, and social outcomes. Although not included in the *DSM-IV-TR*, a subsyndromal diagnosis of attenuated psychosis syndrome may be an indicator that a person is at risk for developing psychosis. Criteria might include one of the following symptoms: delusions, hallucinations, or disorganized speech, but with reality testing intact and without meeting the criteria for any of the psychotic disorders. The advantages of such a diagnosis would include early treatment and possible prevention. But any potential negative effects of early diagnosis or of false positives must also be taken into account. For a complete discussion of this important topic, readers are referred to the writings of Carpenter (2009), Heckers (2009), and Woods and colleagues (2009).

The National Institute for Clinical Excellence (NICE) has established guidelines that emphasize recovery, pharmacological treatment, social skills training, and family participation in the treatment of psychotic disorders (NICE, 2009). The literature on recovery reinforces these guidelines (French, 2010).

Schizophrenia, delusional disorder, and schizoaffective disorder are considered in detail in later sections of this chapter. Brief psychotic disorder and schizophreniform disorder are described and discussed together. Shared psychotic disorder, which involves one or more people adopting the psychotic beliefs of another person, is not discussed here because it is rarely presented in clinical settings and because the dominant member of the dyad or group usually meets the criteria for a diagnosis of schizophrenia.

Dissociative Disorders The dissociative disorders present a different picture from that of the psychotic disorders, although they too involve symptoms related to awareness of reality, memory, consciousness, perceptions, and personality integration. In the past 20 years, the study of dissociation has flourished, partially as a result of research connecting dissociation and traumatic life events. Cardena describes dissociation as a process of compartmentalization and alteration of consciousness. Examples of compartmentalization include amnesia and the development of discrete identities as occurs in dissociative identity disorder. In alterations of consciousness, the person or the environment is experienced as unreal or detached, as in the case of depersonalization. Various psychological functions can be dissociated, including emotions, physical sensations, memory, identity, and the sense of self or the environment (Cardena & Weiner, 2004).

Not all dissociative experiences are pathological. Examples of benign episodes of dissociation are the hypnotic states or momentary lapses in awareness that may occur, for example, when people are driving familiar routes. Dissociative episodes are maladaptive only when they become chronic, recurrent, and uncontrollable and when they are severe enough to cause distress or impairment in functioning.

Dissociative disorders seem to be increasing, perhaps in relation to traumatic, conflicted, or highly stressful life experiences, which also seem to be on the rise. Or perhaps the development of valid and reliable assessment tools and the increasing acceptance of the relationship between trauma and acute and chronic dissociative symptoms have resulted in improved diagnosis of these disorders.

Some dissociative disorders begin and end suddenly, although recurrent episodes are common. They tend to make their initial appearance in childhood or adolescence. Between 80% and 90% of abused infants show a type of attachment behavior that resembles dissociation and that is predictive of later development of dissociation (Thomas, 2003). In fact, the majority of people who develop dissociative identity disorder have experienced incest, rape, or physical abuse during childhood.

The *DSM-IV-TR* defines four types of dissociative disorders, in addition to dissociative disorder not otherwise specified:

1. Dissociative identity disorder
2. Dissociative fugue
3. Dissociative amnesia
4. Depersonalization disorder

Dissociative fugue and dissociative amnesia involve a person's temporarily forgetting important components of his or her life, to a more extensive or more extreme degree than would be due to ordinary forgetfulness. By definition, neither disorder is caused by substances or by a general medical condition. Both tend to occur suddenly at times of trauma or unusual stress, are typically of brief duration, and usually remit without recurrence. Both disorders are rare but increase during such circumstances as natural disasters, accidents, or warfare.

Typical Client Characteristics

Just as the disorders in this chapter vary considerably, so do the people who develop them. The premorbid functioning of people with psychotic and dissociative disorders varies widely. Some have poor prior adjustment; others previously manifested positive social skills and sound coping mechanisms.

Disturbed family relationships are especially common, and a direct relationship has been found between disordered attachment between parent and child and the later development of dissociative disorders (Cardena & Weiner, 2004). Often, a history of emotional neglect and abuse precedes the development of a dissociative disorder, or a personality disorder, which has a high incidence of comorbidity (Sierra, 2009). The disorders discussed in this chapter also differ in terms of their development. Some people experience gradual deterioration, whereas others suffer a rapid alteration in consciousness or loss of contact with reality in response to an immediate stressor.

People with dissociative or psychotic disorders typically are aware that something is wrong but may not understand what is happening, may conceal their symptoms for fear of being harmed or hospitalized, and may not be receptive to help that is offered. While their symptoms are present, their social and occupational adjustment is almost invariably affected, although the degree of disturbance ranges from mild and circumscribed to severe and pervasive, according to the particular disorder and its manifestation.

Assessment

Diagnosis of any disorder reflected by impaired memory should involve neurological, medical, and psychiatric evaluations. Because many general medical conditions, as well as substance use, can cause memory impairment, those causes should be ruled out before a diagnosis of a dissociative disorder is made. Clouded consciousness and disorientation, particularly in a person past middle age, suggest that a cognitive disorder or a medical condition rather than a dissociative disorder may be present.

Because symptoms of these disorders may be difficult to describe and clients often speak metaphorically, clinicians should use rating scales and a more structured interview style when assessing a person for a possible dissociative disorder, The Cambridge Depersonalization Scale (Sierra & Berrios, 2000; Sierra, 2009) contains 29 items that rate people on four distinct dimensions: derealization, emotional numbing, anomalous body experiences, and problems in subjective recall (Sierra, Baker, Medford, & David, 2005). The Structured Clinical Interview for Depersonalization and Derealization Spectrum (SCI-DER; Mula et al., 2008) is a new scale that focuses on symptoms of dissociation. The SCI-DER seems promising for assessing dissociative disorders, but more research is needed.

Assessing for comorbidity can also be difficult as many of the symptoms of dissociative and psychotic disorders are also symptoms of mood, anxiety, personality, and substance use disorders. These other disorders may also be comorbid with a dissociative or psychotic disorder. Psychosis, for example, is often found in atypical depression, bipolar disorder, and substance abuse and dependence (Sierra, 2009).

Preferred Therapist Characteristics

With the exception of dissociative identity disorder and depersonalization disorder, treatment of these disorders generally requires medical as well as psychological intervention. As a result, psychologists, counselors, and other nonmedical mental health professionals often collaborate with physicians and social service professionals to treat clients with all the disorders described in this chapter.

Medication compliance and management is frequently a goal of treatment, especially when psychosis is present. Therapists will also need to employ a variety of approaches, often including long-term intensive psychodynamic psychotherapy, hypnotherapy, and cognitive-behavioral therapy. They will need to be comfortable dealing with people who typically do not present a clear and coherent picture of their symptoms or history and who may be reluctant clients. They also need to be able to deal with chronic mental disorders, as well as those that respond rapidly to treatment.

Concern for the client's safety should be the overriding concern of therapists working with people exhibiting dissociative or psychotic symptoms. Sensitivity, previous clinical experience with people who have been abused, and an ability to proceed at the client's pace rather than exerting their own influence are all necessary attributes of therapists who work with survivors of trauma and abuse, many of whom experience dissociative disorders. Thomas (2003) reports that the first stage of treatment for clients who have been injured by their caregivers is the development of a sense of safety, along with reassurance that therapists will not use their position of power to do harm. Creation of a therapeutic alliance will revolve around the client's need for safety. Interventions addressing traumatic memories are generally saved for later in treatment when the client is better able to tolerate intense emotions.

Intervention Strategies

The nature of the treatment indicated for the disorders discussed in this chapter varies greatly with respect to duration and approach to treatment. Specifics are provided in the sections on the individual disorders.

Prognosis

Prognosis for these disorders is uncertain but bears some relationship to duration. Those disorders that are of shorter duration, such as brief psychotic disorder and dissociative amnesia, typically respond well to relatively brief treatment. Those of longer duration, especially those of insidious onset, such as schizophrenia and dissociative identity disorder, have a less favorable prognosis and usually require long-term treatment.

PSYCHOTIC DISORDERS

Psychotic disorders include schizophrenia, brief psychotic disorder, schizophrenoform disorder, delusional disorder, schizoaffective disorder, and shared psychotic disorder, which is rarely encountered in clinical settings.

Schizophrenia

Description of the Disorder Schizophrenia is by definition a relatively long-standing and pervasive disorder. The *DSM-IV-TR* lists the following symptoms as characteristic of this disorder:

- Bizarre delusions (disturbances in thoughts and logic)
- Hallucinations, usually auditory and commanding or threatening (disturbances in sensory experiences)
- Disorganized speech and behavior
- Flat or very inappropriate affect
- Markedly impaired social and occupational functioning
- A confused sense of self
- Limited insight
- Dependence conflicts
- Loose associations
- Concrete thinking
- Physical awkwardness
- Psychomotor disturbances (for example, catatonic symptoms)
- Dysphoric mood

Schizophrenia typically involves a prodromal (initial) phase, when functioning declines and symptoms begin; an active phase, when so-called positive symptoms such as delusions, hallucinations, and incoherence typically are present; and a residual phase, in which severe symptoms have abated but signs of the disorder are still evident. These signs include such symptoms as flattened affect, restricted thought and speech patterns, and lack of goals or motivation, which have been referred to as the negative symptoms of psychosis. To warrant a diagnosis of schizophrenia, the course of the disorder must be at least six months in duration, including at least one month of the positive symptoms (unless it can be assumed that those symptoms would have persisted for that length of time had treatment not been provided).

The *DSM-IV-TR* describes three major types of schizophrenia. The paranoid type seems to be the most common type in the United States. It typically is characterized by systematized delusions and hallucinations that are related to a theme of grandiosity and persecution. Anger, suspiciousness, and hostility are usually also present (Pratt & Mueser, 2002). Schizophrenia, paranoid type, tends to involve less evidence of incoherence, disorganization, catatonia, and inappropriate affect, as well as a later onset and a better prognosis, than the other types of schizophrenia. The disorganized type, formerly known as the hebephrenic type, is associated with poor previous functioning, an early and insidious onset, extreme impairment, confusion and disorganization in speech and behavior, and flat or inappropriate affect. The catatonic type is uncommon in the United States. It is characterized by some form of catatonia (stupor, rigidity, excitement, or posturing) and by negativity and repetitive imitation of others' words and gestures.

Undifferentiated and residual types of schizophrenia also are included in the *DSM-IV-TR*. The undifferentiated type includes a mix of the positive symptoms of schizophrenia but does not meet the criteria for any one of the three types just described. The residual type either follows a full-blown episode of schizophrenia and reflects only the negative symptoms of the disorder or is a circumscribed presentation of at least two positive symptoms.

Schizophrenia usually begins in early adulthood and starts three to four years earlier in males than in females (Evans et al., 2005). Fifty percent of initial episodes of this disorder occur between the ages of 15 and 25, with 80% occurring between 15 and 35 (Marshall et al., 2005). Onset is rare after the age of 50 or before adolescence. Schizophrenia has a prevalence of approximately 1% (Pratt & Mueser, 2002). Incidence of this disorder is approximately equal in both genders and across cultures and religions (Jablensky, 1999), although some research has shown a higher rate of psychosis and schizophrenia among first-generation immigrants (Singh & Kunar, 2010). Because this increase disappears in the second generation, researchers believe that stress or adversity may be related to the development of a psychotic disorder.

Early (prodromal) symptoms may include magical thinking, illusions, social withdrawal, mood disorders, lack of motivation, cognitive deficits (lack of concentration), and obsessive behaviors (Pratt & Mueser, 2002). These symptoms may be present for years before overt symptoms of psychosis develop. In fact, Evans et al. (2005) report the average duration of psychotic symptoms before diagnosis and treatment is 1 year, and 3 years if earlier, prodromal symptoms are added. Even so, most people will recover from this first episode.

Symptoms of psychosis are delineated as either positive or negative based on comparison to their intensity of occurrence in the average person. Thus, positive symptoms (such as delusions, and auditory and visual hallucinations) involve thoughts and perceptions beyond what most people experience, whereas negative symptoms (such as blunted affect, restricted speech, and lack of motivation) are less (of emotion, communication, and drive) than most people experience. In general, negative symptoms occur before positive ones and may linger after positive symptoms have been eliminated (Evans et al., 2005).

Research on the causes of schizophrenia has implicated heredity, environmental factors, and neurological dysfunction. Positron emission tomography (PET) has demonstrated differences between brains of people diagnosed with schizophrenia and those without the disorder. Abnormal dopamine activity has been documented in people with schizophrenia. A high incidence of eye-movement dysfunction and immunological abnormalities has also been noted in people with this disorder. People with schizophrenia are unusually likely to have experienced stressful events in the 3 weeks prior to onset of the disorder. This and the increase in dopamine activity have led to the stress–diathesis model for the disorder's onset, whereby biological (physical) and psychological (emotional) stress combine to activate a neurological predisposition toward the disorder.

Schizophrenia tends to run in families; first-degree relatives have a risk of developing schizophrenia that is 12 times greater than the general population (Evans et al., 2005). Despite the increased risk, nearly 60% of people with schizophrenia do not have a first-degree relative with the disorder, and fewer than 35% of the children born to parents diagnosed with schizophrenia eventually develop the disorder (Mjellem & Kringlen, 2001). Clearly, factors other than genetics are at play.

New research in molecular genetics indicates that rather than a single gene, many genes may work together to create susceptibility to the symptoms that make up disorders on the schizophrenia spectrum. Studies found that people with a family history of schizophrenia were at risk of developing not only schizophrenia but also the schizotypal traits of magical thinking, unusual perceptions, and unusual speech that are frequently associated with the positive symptoms of schizophrenia, in addition to the schizoid traits of paranoia and isolation consistent with negative symptoms (Freudenreich, 2008). This genetic liability toward schizophrenia may result in the development of a Cluster A personality disorder (schizotypal, schizoid, paranoid) or avoidant personality disorder (Tienari et al., 2003). These personality disorders sometimes precede the onset of schizophrenia (American Psychiatric Association, 2000). What causes one person to develop traits, another to develop a personality disorder, and yet another to develop schizophrenia is the subject of many ongoing studies.

Genetics, of course, is not the entire story, as twin studies show the concordance rate for schizophrenia in identical twins to be only 50%. Therefore, environmental factors both prenatal and perinatal, have been found to influence the development of the disorder. Being born in an urban setting or in the winter months, low socioeconomic status, low birth weight, smaller head circumference, and other risk factors have been found to be correlated with schizophrenia (Lewis & Levitt, 2002).

Trauma seems to play an important role in the development of psychotic disorders. More than two thirds of people hospitalized for a psychotic disorder experienced at least one trauma prior to the event; half were exposed to life-threatening traumas; almost one third had been the victims of childhood trauma. A direct link connects childhood trauma (emotional, physical, psychological, and sexual abuse before the age of 16) to the likelihood of developing positive symptoms of psychosis as an adult (Spauwen, Krabbendam, Lieb, Wittchen, & van Ohs, 2006). As discussed in the section on PTSD (Chapter 5), cumulative trauma damages personality structures and basic capacities to feel, trust, and relate to others. The greater the trauma, dose for dose, the greater the amount of damage.

New research indicates that as many as 33% of people who develop psychotic symptoms (command hallucinations, ideas of reference, or paranoia) may develop PTSD as a result of experiencing these symptoms. Some aspects of hospitalization for psychosis (e.g., involuntary admission, restraint, seclusion) can be traumatizing for the people experiencing them (Bernard, Jackson, & Patterson, 2010). The number of hospital admissions, types of admission (whether voluntary or involuntary), and experiences while admitted can all play a role.

Typical Client Characteristics Prior adjustment often reflects precursors of the disorder. People with schizophrenia tend to have been socially awkward and isolated, passive, mildly eccentric, impulsive, uncomfortable with competition, and absorbed with fantasy. In adolescence, these symptoms may have led to social isolation, poor social skills, or to use of drugs and alcohol as a means to alleviate social anxiety and to develop a network of peers who were more accepting of such eccentricities (Laudet, Magura, Vogel, & Knight, 2004). Recent research shows that certain drugs (cannabis, amphetamines, and cocaine) may actually promote the onset of psychotic symptoms in vulnerable individuals. Especially when used early in life, cannabis use increases the risk of developing schizophrenic symptoms (Wilson, 2010). Cannabis use also portends a poorer prognosis for people who have an established vulnerability to psychosis.

The lifetime prevalence of substance use disorders in people with schizophrenia is high, although actual figures vary from study to study. Sensitivity to the psychoactive effects of substances tends to be greater in people with schizophrenia than in other people. Substance use is also more frequent in part because some substances, such as alcohol, apparently reduce the psychotic, neurological, and affective symptoms of schizophrenia. Most people with schizophrenia smoke cigarettes, as many as 50% meet the criteria for an alcohol use disorder, and the incidence of cannabis use is higher than in the general population (Barnett et al., 2007; Goswami, Mattoo, Basu, & Singh, 2004).

Such dual diagnosis has important clinical implications and is associated with relapse and increased hospitalizations. Other negative effects of the dual diagnosis of schizophrenia and substance use include depression, suicidal ideation, medication noncompliance, financial and legal problems, violence, victimization, increased risk of developing infectious diseases (for example, HIV, hepatitis A and B), and homelessness and housing instability (Laudet et al., 2004; Pratt & Mueser, 2002).

In addition to substance use disorders, people with schizophrenia typically have co-occurring mental disorders, especially depression and posttraumatic stress disorder (PTSD). PTSD, which co-occurs in 29% to 43% of people who have schizophrenia, has been shown to exacerbate symptoms of the disorder, so detection and effective treatment of trauma-related symptoms may help improve treatment outcomes for schizophrenia.

An unstable employment history is common for people with a history of schizophrenia. Holding a job may be particularly challenging for people who are experiencing cognitive impairment. Overall, deficits in the frontal lobe related to executive function cause significant problems that negatively impact the ability to cope with day-to-day stress or social interactions. Recovery may not necessarily result in the ability to live independently or to hold a job, especially for those who are dually diagnosed with both schizophrenia and substance use problems (Laudet et al., 2004).

Studies have shown that more than 55% of people with schizophrenia do not follow treatment recommendations or take medication as prescribed (Pratt & Mueser, 2002). Medication noncompliance is associated with elevated symptom levels, impairments in executive function, and increased rates of relapse and rehospitalization. Most people with schizophrenia also have significant medical illnesses, and as many as 45% report poor sleep quality is a frequent problem (Ritsner & Gibel, 2007).

Suicidal ideation is common; about half of those with this disorder make suicide attempts, and, for 10% to 13% of that group, the attempts result in death (Ritsner & Awad, 2007). In this population, most suicide attempts occur within the first five years following the initial diagnosis (Power, 2010). Depression, usually most severe immediately after a psychotic episode, has a strong association with suicide risk in people with schizophrenia (Pratt & Mueser, 2002). Interested readers are referred to the Appendix for a complete discussion of suicide assessment and prevention.

In recent years, attention has turned to community fears about the possibility of violence among people with schizophrenia. Several recent empirical studies have looked at the connection between symptoms of psychosis and violence, with mixed results. Whereas some studies found that manic symptoms, delusions, paranoia, and impaired overall functioning are correlated with homicidal ideation and intent, 11 other studies found that delusions, especially those of a grandiose nature, can have an ameliorating effect on both violent behavior and suicidal ideation (Grunebaum et al., 2001). One study, the Clinical Antipsychotic Trials of Intervention Effectiveness (CATIE) indicated a 6-month prevalence rate of any act of violence among the 1,500 people sampled was 19.1%. Serious acts of violence, such as assault, threat or use of a lethal weapon, or sexual assault were much less common (3.6%) (Swanson et al., 2006).

Delusional motivation for violence is rare; violence is more likely to be associated with anger and impulsivity, rather than delusions. Psychotic and depressive symptoms, childhood history of conduct problems and victimization, persistent aggressive behavior, antisocial personality disorder, and drug use are all linked to increased risk of violence in people with schizophrenia (Freudenreich, 2008; Nolan, Volavka, Mohr, & Czobor, 1999; Schwartz, Reynolds, Austin, & Petersen, 2003; Swanson et al., 2006).

Schwartz and colleagues (2003) recommend that therapists working with male clients with schizophrenia assess clients' overall homicidal ideation and intent and carefully evaluate symptoms of mania, substance use, and active psychotic symptoms. Impairment in reality testing, judgment, communication, and other areas of cognitive functioning may also contribute to violent behavior. Some evidence indicates that violence may be associated with more severe neurological impairments, hostility, suspiciousness, and decompensating behaviors which make clients more volatile, paranoid, impulsive, and dangerous (Freudenreich, 2008).

Assessment Early assessment and treatment of psychotic symptoms are necessary for the reduction and prevention of more severe symptoms. Some assessment tools can help to identify subdiagnostic hallucinations and delusions, in other words, symptoms that do not yet meet the full criteria for psychosis. The Positive and Negative Syndromes Scale (PANSS; Kay, Fiszbein, & Opler, 1987), and the Structured Interview for Psychotic Symptoms (SIPS; Miller et al., 1999) can help identify at-risk mental states (French, 2010).

Flexibility and creativity are needed because clients with psychotic symptoms often have difficulty reporting their symptoms and previous history in an accurate or clear manner. An initial assessment may include a combination of interviews with the client, a parent, and a trusted friend. Assessment of positive and negative symptoms, global assessment of functioning, and assessment for co-occurring disorders are important. Equally important is assessment of life domains that may be contributing to negative functioning, such as medication noncompliance, difficulties in occupational performance, and instability of housing and family environment.

Levels of anxiety and depression should also be monitored frequently throughout the course of treatment. The Beck Depression Inventory (BDI; Beck, Steer, & Brown, 1996) and the Beck Anxiety Inventory (BAI; Beck & Steer, 1990) are useful for this purpose. Both are empirically validated and easy to administer, score, and interpret. Due to the frequency with which substance misuse and PTSD co-occur in people with schizophrenia, assessing for both concerns and integrating the results into the treatment plan is also important.

Preferred Therapist Characteristics Above all, therapists who work with clients with schizophrenia must be able to convey respect toward the client, and an optimistic attitude toward recovery. Recovery from any adversity involves a psychosocial process of developing hope, learning to manage adversity realistically, and being able to move on with life (Drake & Mueser, 2002; French, 2010). The quality of the relationship among the treatment team of physicians, therapists, and family can also be an important determinant of treatment outcome.

A therapeutic alliance based on compassionate care that reduces anxiety and enhances treatment compliance seems to be integral to recovery. Therapists working with people with schizophrenia should be available, consistent, patient, and straightforward. Warmth, reassurance, optimism, empathy, genuineness,

stability, support, and acceptance on the part of the therapist are all important in forming a positive and trusting working relationship with people diagnosed as having schizophrenia, many of whom are suspicious, guarded, and withdrawn. Limits also need to be established for the protection of these clients and their therapists. Simply sitting with a distraught client, taking a walk, discussing neutral topics of interest (such as a movie), or providing practical assistance can promote a therapeutic alliance that offers support and comfort.

Another important focus of treatment is helping the client regain contact with reality. Delusional beliefs are best approached with a combination of curiosity and confusion. Therapists should avoid confrontation, while also not supporting the client's delusional system (Freudenreich, 2008). Part of the therapist's role can be to teach the person with schizophrenia to recognize delusions and hallucinations for what they are—tricks of the mind. This kind of perspective avoids the need to debate the veracity of clients' experiences and can increase understanding and appropriate discussion of the phenomena. As mentioned earlier, helping clients with delusions to recognize when they are guilty of confirmation bias can be helpful in improving cognitive processing. Arguing with or interrogating these clients about their delusions or hallucinations is likely to be nonproductive and harmful to the therapeutic relationship.

The overarching goal of therapy is to enable clients with schizophrenia to function effectively with their lives. Therapists must find a balance between overwhelming and under supporting these vulnerable clients. Too much closeness can lead to regression, but too much distance can result in alienation. Therapists should be aware of and understand barriers to recovery, and recognize and reinforce client's efforts at self-efficacy, improved coping, and attempts at socialization.

Intervention Strategies   Treatment for schizophrenia usually entails a combination of medication and psychosocial interventions that target both the acute psychotic phase of the disorder and the debilitating residual symptoms. Hospitalization is often required, particularly during the active phase of the disorder if the person becomes floridly psychotic, suicidal, or refuses to eat or drink. The average hospital stay for these clients has declined in length, largely due to pressure from managed care and insurance companies, and is now measured in days rather than weeks. This can pose problems for people with schizophrenia and their families, as many people are being released before they have become stabilized on their medications (Torrey, 2006).

Day treatment centers, partial hospitalization, and halfway houses can be helpful once recovery has begun and acute symptoms have subsided. These transitional settings can promote socialization, ease people's return to independent living, and, as necessary, provide long-term maintenance. Use of these treatment facilities is increasing as the length of hospital stays is decreasing.

Medication.   Medication is almost always a component of treatment and is beneficial to most but not all who are diagnosed with schizophrenia. Neuroleptic drugs can effectively alleviate symptoms, particularly the positive symptoms of psychosis (delusions and hallucinations). Medication is less effective in treating the negative symptoms (blunted affect, depression, social withdrawal). Large numbers of clinical trials have demonstrated the effectiveness of such atypical antipsychotics as risperidone (Risperdal), olanzapine (Zyprexa), and clozapine (Clozaril) in the treatment of schizophrenia (Bradford, Stroup, & Lieberman, 2002). These newer medications have been found to be as effective as the older antipsychotic medications like chlorpromazine

(Thorazine) and haloperidol (Haldol), to have a reduced side-effect profile, and to have a lower risk of causing extrapyramidal symptoms such as tardive dyskinesia. However, recent reports have linked several of the atypical antipsychotics to weight gain and increased risk of diabetes. Careful monitoring of blood glucose levels may prevent diabetes and reduce associated illnesses in people with increased risk (Mahgerefteh, Pierre, & Wirshing, 2006).

Medication is important as well in reducing the risk of relapse. Most people treated for schizophrenia need continued medication after their symptoms have been alleviated. Controlled clinical trials indicate that 1-year posttreatment, 30% of people with schizophrenia will have relapsed while on medication. Those who discontinue medication have relapse rates of 65% to 75% within one year (Bradford et al., 2002; Harkavy-Friedman, 2006).

Medication compliance is a particular problem for people with schizophrenia, and compliance rates have been reported to be as low as 50%. Rehospitalizations, increased suicidality, and premature death may result from medication noncompliance (Harkavy-Friedman, 2006). Medication compliance therapy, including discussion of medication side effects, can be an important part of treatment for people with severe mental illness (Wirshing & Buckley, 2003). Reasons why people with schizophrenia do not take their medication include unwanted side effects of the medication, negative attitudes toward medication, a desire to experience mania or grandiose delusions, apprehension about developing extrapyramidal symptoms such as tardive dyskinesia, and, for those who have paranoid schizophrenia, fear that others are trying to control them through their medication. Providing clients with education about their mental and physical health, discussing and encouraging medication compliance, and educating family members about strategies to help deal with noncompliance issues can help promote treatment compliance as well as provide support, socialization, and practical help (Pratt & Mueser, 2002; Wirshing & Buckley, 2003). Many of the antipsychotic medications are available in long-acting, injectable forms, which can help people adhere to their medication regime (West et al., 2008). For others, electroconvulsive therapy (ECT) can also be an effective alternative to medication.

Psychosocial interventions. The American Psychiatric Association's *Practice Guideline for the Treatment of Patients with Schizophrenia* (2004b) recommends combining psychosocial interventions with medication management for the treatment of schizophrenia. After the person with schizophrenia has become stabilized on medications, psychosocial interventions can begin. Treatments that incorporate behavioral and cognitive-behavioral therapy, social skills training, family education and participation, and substance use treatment (if indicated), and that encourage medication compliance as part of a multifaceted approach, have been found most effective in the treatment of schizophrenia (Bradford et al., 2002; Evans et al., 2005; Mahgerefteh et al., 2006; Pratt & Mueser, 2002; Tarrier, 2008).

Behavior therapy. Behavior therapy is the primary approach to psychotherapy for people with schizophrenia. This approach typically focuses on providing the information and skills necessary for people to reduce bizarre and destructive behavior and improve functioning. Development of practical life skills can also be beneficial in facilitating people's resocialization and their adjustment to living with their families or on their own after a period of hospitalization. Adjustment can be facilitated by training in useful occupational skills and by increased involvement in recreational activities. Behavior therapy can be provided via inpatient or outpatient treatment in individual or group formats.

Hospitals and day treatment centers sometimes use behavioral models, such as milieu therapy or token economies, to reinforce desirable behaviors.

Skills training. Pratt and Mueser (2002) conducted a meta-analysis of skills training programs and found that the number of weeks of training was positively correlated with size of treatment effect. Skills training programs that take place at least twice a week for a minimum of six months have been found to be most effective in helping people diagnosed with schizophrenia. Although often conducted in groups, such training could also include an individual focus. The group provides a safe setting in which to identify and practice skills without fear of negative consequences.

UCLA's Clinical Research Center for Schizophrenia and Psychiatric Rehabilitation has created several skills-training modules that have been empirically validated and proven effective in improving social and independent living skills in people with schizophrenia. Module topics include:

- Symptom self-management
- Recreation and leisure activities
- Medication self-management
- Community reentry
- Job search
- Basic conversation skills
- Friendship and dating

The UCLA modules include didactic instruction, role plays, problem solving, homework, and in vivo behavioral rehearsal.

Cognitive-behavioral therapy. CBT has also received support in the treatment of schizophrenia as an adjunct to medication and social skills training (Newton & Cotes, 2010; Tarrier, 2008; Turkington, Dudley, Warman, & Beck, 2004). To date, some limited evidence has shown that CBT reduces relapse and hospital readmission rates (Tarrier, 2008), but the main goal of CBT is to reduce the stress and functional impairment caused by psychotic symptoms (Newton & Cotes, 2010).

Social support was found to be as effective as CBT in terms of symptom improvement (Milne, Wharton, James, & Turkington, 2006). This was found to be especially true in first episode psychosis for those under the age of 21 who may be more vulnerable, and less able to engage in more structured therapy (Newton & Cotes, 2010). Adapted CBT used in vocational rehabilitation has been found to reduce self-stigma associated with having a severe mental illness, and cognitive enhancement therapy has been found to help people with delusional thinking (Lysaker, 2008; Wright, Turkington, Kingdon, & Basco, 2009).

Several published meta-analyses of CBT for psychosis (CBTp) used in conjunction with antipsychotic medication and case management have shown CBTp to be effective in treating positive symptoms of schizophrenia and other psychotic disorders (Tarrier, 2008). Although the effect size was modest, the outcome is important because as many as 25% of people with schizophrenia who are treated with antipsychotic medications continue to have hallucinations and delusions.

Identifying and treating each phase of the disorder as it occurs seems to improve prognosis. So, the aim of CBT interventions in the prodromal, acute, partial remission, remission, and relapse stages are each designed to focus on a different goal such as preventing full-blown psychosis in the prodromal phase, or symptom reduction and self-esteem enhancement during the phase of partial remission. A study by Tarrier and Wykes (2004) found that CBTp that focused on relapse prevention achieved a 21% success rate.

Psychodynamic approaches. Psychodynamic psychotherapy has not received much support in the treatment of schizophrenia. In fact, the emotional intensity of that approach may even be harmful. For example, one study found that persons living alone who received such therapy actually had elevated relapse rates (Evans et al., 2005).

Family education and counseling. Education and counseling for the family are a particularly important component of treatment for schizophrenia and have been found to increase medication compliance and reduce relapse rates by as much as 25% (Glynn, Cohen, Dixon, & Niv, 2006). For some families the trauma and shock of having a family member become delusional or experience hallucinations are so great that they experience denial that anything is wrong. Others become angry or grieve the loss of the person they may have become. Family members with both types of experiences could benefit from understanding the nature of this disorder.

In addition, what has been called high expressed emotion (high EE) in the families of people with schizophrenia can contribute to stress and possibly provoke a reemergence of acute symptoms. Family training that focuses on reducing critical comments, emotional overinvolvement, and hostility toward the person with schizophrenia has been shown to produce beneficial effects on the course of the disorder (Evans et al., 2005). Relapse rates for schizophrenia are lower when family members participate in family treatment; medication compliance increases; high EE is reduced; and family members learn communication skills, problem solving, and coping skills (Mino, Shimodera, Inoue, Fujita, & Fukuzawa, 2007).

Clearly, family support and education are important components of the effective treatment of this chronic disorder. Burbach, Fadden, and Smith (2010) note that timing of family interventions can be important. Families may benefit from different types of help at different phases (i.e., symptom explanation during the prodromal phase, help with grief and loss during the acceptance phase, and relapse prevention during the recovery phase).

Integrated dual diagnosis treatment. Because the co-occurrence of schizophrenia and substance use is so high, integrated treatments in which the same clinical team addresses both disorders simultaneously have become the prevalent therapeutic model for people who are dually diagnosed with these two disorders. Recent studies support the effectiveness of this approach (Drake & Mueser, 2002; Laudet et al., 2004). Successful interventions for dual diagnosis generally take a long-term perspective and involve intensive case management that focuses on substance use counseling, motivational interventions, social support, staged interventions, regular drug screens, and a family counseling component, as well as attention to other needs such as employment, housing, and physical health. Unlike 12-step programs, most dual diagnosis programs follow a harm-reduction model that anticipates and plans for relapse as part of the recovery process (Mahgerefteh et al., 2006).

Integrated treatments generally take a cautious approach to prescription medication. This includes recognizing signs and symptoms of withdrawal and drug use, and avoiding medication with a high likelihood of addiction (for example, benzodiazepines), while ensuring that psychotic symptoms are adequately treated and drug and alcohol cravings and urges are discussed and addressed. Medication compliance should also be carefully monitored, as many people who are actively using substances discontinue medication to avoid drug interactions (Pratt & Mueser, 2002).

Group therapy. Group therapy can be helpful in providing information, promoting appropriate use of medication, improving skills (such as communication, problem solving, and socialization), encouraging constructive activities, facilitating reality testing, and providing support and encouragement that fosters resilience (Evans et al., 2005). Social skills training programs, vocational rehabilitation programs, and clubhouses can offer camaraderie as well as valuable resources to help people with dual diagnoses develop friendships and obtain employment and housing assistance.

Long-term management and relapse prevention. Long-term management of this disorder requires vigilance with regard to symptom exacerbation, substance use, and relapse (Bradford et al., 2002). Depression, anxiety, and substance use often co-occur with schizophrenia and need to be addressed to reduce suicide risk, improve self-esteem, and increase functioning.

Self-stigma about mental illness impacts whether awareness of their illness leads to quality of life improvements or results in reduced functioning. When people with schizophrenia become protagonists in their own lives and begin to develop realistic appraisals of themselves with awareness of their own strengths and weaknesses, they are better able to manage their disorder. People with schizophrenia who experience greater self-stigma about their disorder tend to have less insight and reduced functioning overall (Lysaker, 2008).

Protective factors that foster resilience and reduce the likelihood of relapse include perceived social support, self-esteem and self-efficacy; traits of novelty seeking, extroversion and agreeableness; and being task-oriented (Ritsner & Gibel, 2007).

Relapse rarely occurs without advance warning. Prodromal symptoms can last for days or weeks and include nonpsychotic symptoms such as dysphoria, irritability, changes in mood, sleep disturbances, anxiety, and magical thinking or paranoia. During this time, the person may become more withdrawn, socially isolating, or appear preoccupied. Bizarre symptoms or talking strangely may occur. Since early intervention can help ward off a complete psychotic break, helping the client to recognize his or her own particular early warning signs can be instrumental in reducing the severity of the episode (Tarrier, 2008).

Stress (including trauma; exposure to hostile environments; and instability in family, housing, occupational, or other domains) can precipitate relapses and contribute to impairment in other life functions. Coping resources and the ability to obtain social support can minimize the effects of stress and decrease the need for acute care. Thus, interventions that increase resilience and help clients develop stable goals, improve self-esteem, increase insight and positive affect can improve outcomes in people with schizophrenia.

Continued case management that includes occupational therapy, supported employment, housing assistance, and assertive community treatment programs are an important part of rehabilitation efforts for people with schizophrenia. Community treatment programs reduce the time that people with schizophrenia spend in hospitals and bridge the gap between in-patient hospitalization and independent living (Mahgerefteh et al., 2006).

Extended contact with helping professionals, often via treatment programs for the chronically mentally ill, also contributes to long-term reduction in relapse rates (Roth & Fonagy, 2005). The Family-to-Family education program, developed by the National Alliance for the Mentally Ill (NAMI), involves a highly structured 12-week program that increases education and knowledge about the disorder, improves coping strategies, empowers families to take an active role, and reduces stress and family anxiety (Evans et al., 2005). NAMI can be useful to families and people with schizophrenia and other severe mental illnesses (www.nami.org).

Prognosis　A return to full and healthy functioning after an episode of schizophrenia is unusual. Approximately 50% of people hospitalized with this disorder are hospitalized again within two years of an initial episode. Although the acute symptoms may be controlled with medication, people are frequently left with psychotic depression, which involves feeling apathetic, socially uncomfortable, depressed, and uneasy in handling emotions. Unfortunately, those who relapse within five years have a 78% chance of a second relapse. The risk of personality deterioration increases greatly after the second relapse and worsens with each successive episode, as does the risk of another relapse. The prognosis is particularly poor if the disorder begins with a gradual deterioration that has extended over many years, if the person is dually diagnosed with a drug or alcohol problem in addition to schizophrenia, or if the person with schizophrenia has extensive exposure to high expressed emotion within their family.

The following factors are some of those associated with a more positive prognosis for the treatment of schizophrenia (and for schizophreniform disorder, discussed later):

- *Premorbid factors.* Positive premorbid functioning, especially in social areas; positive work history; intelligence that is average or higher; good neurocognitive functioning; being married or having a stable partner relationship.
- *Factors related to characteristics of the disorder.* Abrupt onset, particularly when there is an identifiable precipitant; midlife onset; symptoms of confusion and perplexity; depression; absence of flattened affect, psychotic assaultiveness, or schizoid personality disorder.

- *Family and environmental factors.* Absence of a family history of schizophrenia; family history of depression and mania; positive and supportive environment to which client will return; family involvement in therapy.

A positive prognosis also is associated with early, continual intervention; compliance with recommended medication and aftercare; lack of substance use; an adequate financial and living situation; having social and recreational activities, and adequate subjective well-being (Kopelowicz, Liberman, & Zarate, 2007; Lambert et al., 2006).

In addition to relapses and residual symptoms, people with schizophrenia often must cope with extrapyramidal symptoms that are the severe and sometimes permanent side effects of neuroleptic antipsychotic medication. Tardive dyskinesia, characterized by involuntary smacking and sucking movements of the lips and tongue, results from long-term use of antipsychotic medications. This gives people an unusual appearance and can interfere with their social and occupational adjustment.

Unfortunately, there are cases in which the client does not improve despite medication management and concerted efforts on the part of physicians, therapists, and family members. But as more research becomes available and new treatment options are developed, the number of treatment refractory cases is diminishing.

Brief Psychotic Disorder and Schizophreniform Disorder

Brief psychotic disorder and schizophreniform disorder share many of the symptoms of schizophrenia but differ in conditions of onset and duration. Both disorders may resolve themselves after a short period of time, or may be precursors to the later diagnosis of

schizophrenia. Following a description of brief psychotic disorder and schizophrenoform disorder, client and clinician characteristics, treatment interventions, and prognosis will be discussed together.

Brief psychotic disorder may resemble schizophrenia, as well as delusional disorder (discussed later). According to the *DSM-IV-TR*, the essential feature of brief psychotic disorder is "the sudden onset of at least one of the following positive psychotic symptoms: delusions, hallucinations, disorganized speech . . . , or grossly disorganized or catatonic behavior" (American Psychiatric Association, 2000, p. 329). This disorder lasts at least one day but less than one month, and the person eventually has a full return to premorbid levels of functioning.

Three subtypes of this disorder are described in the *DSM-IV-TR*. In the type described as with marked stressor(s), the onset of symptoms is preceded by an identifiable and prominent stressor (for example, natural disasters, rape, or combat experience) and typically is accompanied by extreme and rapid emotional shifts and a strong feeling of confusion. Multiple concurrent stressors are particularly likely to precipitate this disorder. The second type, with postpartum onset, begins within four weeks of giving birth. The disorder typically is characterized by depression and thoughts of suicide or infanticide. Due to the unpredictability of such clients, the baby is usually separated from the mother until she improves. In most cases, a mood disorder is ultimately diagnosed, although a small minority will be diagnosed as having schizophrenia (Torrey, 2006). The third type, without marked stressor(s), does not fit either of the other two patterns.

Unlike schizophrenia, brief psychotic disorder usually is not preceded by evidence of prodromal symptoms. This relatively uncommon disorder may begin in adolescence but is more likely to begin in the late twenties or early thirties. Symptoms of brief psychotic disorder must include at least one psychotic symptom and may include emotional volatility, bizarre behavior, paranoia, screaming, or catatonia. Lack of memory of the event may also be present. Delirium, drug-induced psychosis, and acute stress disorder must be ruled out (Sadock, 2007).

Schizophreniform disorder is usually characterized by symptoms that may be indistinguishable from the most prominent symptoms of schizophrenia. These include impaired reality testing, extremely inappropriate behavior, bizarre delusions and hallucinations, incoherence, and catatonia. Schizophreniform disorder is more like schizophrenia than brief psychotic disorder is, in that it may include a prodromal phase, does not usually have an identifiable precipitant, and includes passive as well as active features of schizophrenia. Agitation and high anxiety are common in schizophreniform disorder, but flat affect is unusual. Unlike schizophrenia, impaired social or occupational functioning is not an essential feature of the disorder but often will be present.

Schizophreniform disorder is distinguished from schizophrenia primarily in terms of duration. Schizophreniform disorder, by definition, has a duration of at least one month but less than six months (including prodromal, active, and residual phases). As mentioned earlier, brief psychotic disorder and schizophreniform disorder fall on the schizophrenia spectrum and share common abnormalities in brain functioning with schizophrenia. Brief psychotic disorder has the best prognosis and schizophrenia the worst. Schizophreniform disorder may be viewed as a bridge between these two disorders on the continuum. Approximately one third of those diagnosed with schizophreniform disorder will recover within six months. Of the

remaining two thirds, most will subsequently be diagnosed with schizophrenia or schizoaffective disorder (American Psychiatric Association, 2000).

If diagnosis of either brief psychotic disorder or schizophreniform disorder is made before recovery, the diagnosis is viewed as provisional and as subject to change if the disorder lasts longer than anticipated. Thus, both disorders are sometimes actually the early stages of schizophrenia.

Typical Client Characteristics Like schizophrenia, both brief psychotic disorder and schizophreniform disorder occur equally in men and women and are more common in people who have had preexisting emotional disorders, particularly personality disorders typified by emotional instability, suspiciousness, and impaired socialization. Depression and suicidal ideation also often coexist with or follow both brief psychotic disorder and schizophreniform disorder. The immediate aftermath of a severe psychotic episode is the most common time for these symptoms to emerge.

As mentioned earlier, substance use has been found to play a role in the development of psychosis, and brief psychotic episodes often occur after amphetamine, cocaine, or cannabis use. A history of traumatic incidents across the life span and recent stressful events can also contribute to the development of psychosis. For example, higher than expected rates of psychosis have been found in people who had recently immigrated from another country (Dealberto, 2010). Therapists should also assess for other medical conditions, substance use, time of symptom onset, course, premorbid functioning, and family history.

Preferred Therapist Characteristics People diagnosed with brief psychotic disorder or schizophreniform disorder typically benefit from supportive, safe, and structured therapeutic relationships that avoid casting them in a negative light. Acceptance, respect, genuineness, and empathy can be instrumental in helping people come to terms with the events that have triggered their disorders and in restoring their awareness of reality. Modeling by therapists and identification with therapists can increase clients' use of effective coping mechanisms, as well as their efforts to take control of their lives.

Intervention Strategies Initial treatments of brief psychotic disorder and schizophreniform disorder have many similarities to the treatment of schizophrenia. People with these disorders may be so severely incapacitated, aggressive, or disoriented and out of touch with reality that hospitalization and medication are required to protect them, calm them down, and alleviate acute symptoms. People diagnosed with schizophreniform disorder have been found to respond faster to antipsychotic medication than people with schizophrenia; 75% respond within eight days (Sadock, 2007). Brief treatment strategies with clear goals seem best and long-term medication or extended inpatient treatment are unusual, unless a comorbid mental disorder is present. ECT has been found helpful in the treatment of brief reactive psychosis, but is generally reserved for medication-resistant cases of schizophreniform disorder.

Once the psychotic symptoms have subsided, the focus of treatment usually will shift quickly, with psychotherapy rather than medication being the primary ingredient of treatment. In this second phase of treatment, attention should be paid to the nature of any precipitants (including drugs or alcohol), and interventions should be used to help people address stressors that may have preceded symptoms. People with these disorders often are in crisis, so a crisis-intervention approach to

therapy can provide useful direction. According to that model, people are assisted in taking a realistic look at their circumstances, becoming aware of and expressing their feelings and reactions, identifying and mobilizing the coping mechanisms that they have used effectively in the past, and applying them to the current circumstances. Specific additional interventions are determined by the nature of the precipitant, but those interventions generally are short term and symptom focused, emphasizing cognitive, behavioral, and supportive approaches rather than long-term exploratory ones.

Group and family treatment also may help clients and their families deal with the aftermath of these disorders, as well as promote effective resolution of any precipitants and restore positive social and occupational functioning. Strong family support has been linked with reduced stress, increased medication compliance, and better treatment outcomes. As with schizophrenia, high expressed emotion increases stress levels and is likely to increase the possibility of relapse. Encouraging people to draw on support systems, decrease social isolation, and improve interpersonal relatedness is consistently endorsed as effective in facilitating recovery, crisis resolution, and abatement of residual symptoms (Davidson, O'Connell, Tondora, Lawless, & Evans, 2005; Shahar et al., 2004).

Prognosis People who are diagnosed with brief psychotic disorder or schizophreniform disorder and whose disorders seem to be related to a severely stressful life event have a good prognosis. Although psychotic episodes may vary in duration and symptoms, brief psychotic disorder frequently remits within a few weeks. Even if a precipitant cannot be identified, psychotic disorders that are brief in nature have a better prognosis than those that are lengthy or recurrent. Clarke and colleagues (2006) found that 4 years after an initial episode of psychosis, those who had the shortest length of time before treatment began had the best functional and symptomatic outcomes.

The prognosis for a brief psychotic disorder that does not progress to another disorder is by definition excellent. Symptoms of such a disorder typically remit quickly. Nevertheless, the active phase may be followed by temporary symptoms of depression, confusion, and anxiety as clients deal with the stressors that precipitated the disorder and with the experience of having had their functioning severely impaired. Clients often feel embarrassed and stigmatized at having had psychotic symptoms and fear a recurrence and its accompanying loss of control.

According to the *DSM-IV-TR*, features associated with a positive prognosis for recovery from schizophreniform disorder are a brief prodromal period (four weeks or less), confusion and perplexity during the active phase of the disorder, better insight into the illness, good previous functioning, and affect that is depressed rather than flat or blunted.

However, those who have had a psychotic episode are more likely to experience a wide range of biological, social, and environmental influences that contribute to the development of psychosis. Those who have had a psychotic episode, even one of brief duration, are 50% more likely to experience another (French, et al., 2010). Early diagnosis and early treatment with medication, supportive therapy, and patient and family education are crucial to promoting recovery.

Delusional Disorder

People with a delusional disorder are frequently misdiagnosed, or not diagnosed at all, since their symptoms are related to faulty cognitions, rather than bizarre behaviors or perceptions. Unless the delusional person becomes aggressive or litigious, they may not be referred for treatment.

Description of the Disorder Delusional disorder typically is less pervasive and disabling than schizophreniform disorder or schizophrenia, but may have some similar symptoms. According to the *DSM-IV-TR*, a delusional disorder is characterized by the presence of nonbizarre (possible or believable) delusions of at least one-month duration. The delusions typically are circumscribed, and the person's overall behavior, apart from the delusions, usually does not seem odd or severely impaired. This is a disorder of thoughts rather than of perceptual experiences. Hallucinations are absent or minimal. A history of schizophrenia rules out the diagnosis of this disorder.

The type of delusional disorder experienced by a person should be specified when this diagnosis is made. The *DSM* identifies the following five types of delusional disorders, in addition to mixed and unspecified types:

1. *Erotomanic type.* Unrealistic beliefs about a romantic relationship, often with a stranger or a person in a higher position, and sometimes associated with stalking behavior.

2. *Grandiose type.* Typically, the inaccurate belief that one has a special talent or has made an important discovery.

3. *Jealous type.* Unfounded belief that one's partner is unfaithful.

4. *Persecutory type.* The most common type of delusional disorder, involving the incorrect belief that others are seeking to harm one, and sometimes associated with violent retaliation or lawsuits based on perceived wrongs.

5. *Somatic type.* Intense, unrealistic beliefs focused on the body, such as being certain that one has a serious disease.

The onset of a delusional disorder typically occurs in middle or late adulthood and may be acute, chronic, or recurrent. Delusional disorder is rare, occurring in approximately 0.03% of the population. It occurs with approximately equal frequency in both genders, but the jealous type is more common in men (American Psychiatric Association, 2000). Women who develop delusional disorder are more likely to be widows, and men are more likely to be single. Men tend to develop worse symptoms and functioning and are more likely to have substance use disorders or schizoid or schizotypal personality disorder prior to the diagnosis (de Portugal et al., 2010).

Typical Client Characteristics People with delusional disorder typically demonstrate satisfactory premorbid functioning, although they tend to be excessively sensitive, below average in intelligence and insight, and prone to underachievement. People who are recent immigrants and who come from lower socioeconomic backgrounds are more likely to develop a delusional disorder, as are people who are isolated.

Delusional disorder is often preceded by a period of stress and by an experience that evokes strong feelings of insecurity, distrust, and self-doubt—for example, job loss or divorce. The delusion sometimes is a defense mechanism, particularly one involving denial, projection, or re-action formation, and provides the person a way to preserve self-esteem and be protected from feelings of rejection, inadequacy, or guilt. The delusions may occur as a psychological compensation for the disappointments of life. Ideas of reference (the idea that random events have special meaning) are common in this disorder, as is magical thinking.

It is estimated that 20% to 30% of people regularly have paranoid thoughts, and 10% of those people will hold onto delusions despite reality to the contrary (Freeman & Garety, 2009). Most do not interfere with daily or occupational functioning. A genetic basis for this

disorder has not been well established, although first-degree relatives are more likely to have avoidant or paranoid personality disorders (American Psychiatric Association, 2000). People with delusional disorder may appear to be relatively unimpaired when they are not discussing their delusions, and daily functioning may not be interrupted. However, those with severe forms of the disorder may act on their delusions and have severe impairments in interpersonal relationships and occupational functioning. Delusions involving guilt are associated with more severe suicidal ideation, yet delusions in isolation do not constitute an independent risk factor for current suicidal ideation or past suicide attempts (Grunebaum et al., 2001). In fact, grandiose delusions were found to provide a protective factor.

People with delusional disorder tend to be low in self-esteem, isolated, easily frustrated, mistrustful, and fearful of intimacy. Irritability and a dysphoric mood are common in people with delusional disorder, although moods vary according to the nature of the delusions to which they are linked. For many people with delusional disorder, the world is a hostile and unfriendly place and they often feel taken advantage of, and tend to overreact to criticism. People with delusional disorder tend to be defensive and argumentative, particularly with authority figures. They typically project blame for their own failures and shortcomings onto others, sometimes have ideas of reference, and may be perceived as hostile, suspicious, and excessively critical of themselves and others. Their social and sexual adjustment is often flawed, although their occupational adjustment may be satisfactory. Litigious and aggressive behavior may be manifested in response to delusions, and people with this disorder may affiliate with a like-minded group. For example, a man with conspiratorial delusions about the government may join a political group that shares his beliefs (Woo

& Keatinge, 2008). Grandiose delusions may include success and achievement; paranoid delusions may involve hypervigilence and fear (Munro, 2008); jealous delusions may result from the fear of losing the affections of another person.

Most people with delusional disorders share several faulty cognitions including a bias toward jumping to conclusions, making premature decisions, and attributional bias—blaming others rather than themselves. They often have confirmation bias, seeking evidence that supports their conclusions rather than those that refute them.

Preferred Therapist Characteristics Therapists should deal gently with people with delusional disorder, respecting their need for privacy and not arguing with them about their delusional beliefs. Instead, therapists should be supportive, accepting, empathic, fair, and professional, serving as positive role models in an effort to engage these people in treatment and encourage more effective coping methods.

Therapists should discuss the delusions enough to understand their nature and possible functions but should not participate in clients' delusional belief systems. Kantor (2004) recommends that therapists provide affirmation and support when working with delusional clients. Rather than challenging clients' beliefs, therapists can provide alternative explanations and invite client curiosity in validating a hypothesis. In this manner, correcting errors in cognition can be done indirectly, by providing alternative positive interpretations. If clients demand to know whether therapists believe their delusions, therapists can respond, "I don't know, but I know it is very important to you and is having a great impact on your life." The therapeutic focus, then, should be on the immediate precursors and consequences of the delusions and on the personality traits that may

have contributed to the development of the delusions rather than on the unrealistic beliefs themselves.

Conditions of the therapeutic relationship are particularly important in treating people with delusional disorder. Without a positive relationship, therapy is not likely to take place, but with a positive relationship, much can be accomplished.

Intervention Strategies People with delusional disorder rarely seek treatment of their own volition and typically function well enough to avoid involuntary treatment. As a result, they rarely are seen in treatment, and little research is available on the effective treatment of this disorder. Some inferences can be drawn from the literature, however.

Although 1% to 4% of people admitted to psychiatric hospitals have delusional disorder (Preston, O'Neal, & Talaga, 2010), most people with a delusional disorder can be treated with medication on an outpatient basis. The suspiciousness that is typical of people with delusional disorder may lead them to refuse medication or fail to comply with prescribed treatments, and to mistrust those who recommend medication. Nevertheless, in a review of 224 cases of delusional disorder from 1994 to 2004, 50% had a positive response to antipsychotic medication (Manschrek & Khan, 2006). Medications that have shown some effectiveness include pimozide (Orap) and such atypical antipsychotics as risperidone (Risperdal), olanzapine (Zyprexa), and ziprasidone (Geodon). Medication is most likely to be effective in the treatment of somatic delusions and in cases where there has been an apparent precipitant and early diagnosis. Co-occurring mood or anxiety disorders should also be treated with appropriate medication. Delayed treatment of psychosis can result in poorer treatment response and incomplete resolution of delusional thoughts (Preston et al., 2010).

Establishment of a supportive therapeutic relationship is essential to reduce fear and facilitate adherence to treatment. Psychoeducation and social skills training are important to help minimize isolation and stress. CBT may be helpful in the treatment of delusional disorder but no randomized controlled trials have yet been published and research on its effectiveness is "mixed and modest" (Garety, Bentall, & Freeman, 2008, p. 329). Therapists who use CBT with their clients with delusions should focus on modifying core beliefs and schemas, helping clients replace negative thoughts with positive alternatives, and teaching empathy. Reality testing should be done gently without blaming, confrontation, or engaging in a power struggle with the client (Kantor, 2004). Encouraging independence and the expression of feelings also can be helpful. An emphasis on clients' strengths, positive behaviors, and improvements can contribute to client resilience.

Clients' motivation for treatment can be increased with an initial focus on distressing secondary symptoms (such as insomnia or occupational concerns) rather than on delusions, their precipitants, and their consequences. Some attention should also be paid to the delusions themselves because they typically serve a symbolic function that, if understood, could facilitate treatment. For example, the therapist who understands that a narcissistic grandiose delusion is behind a client's belief that the CIA is watching her will not dispel the delusion by confronting the client with reality, but rather encourage the client to satisfy her need for positive reinforcement and attention via realistic and growth-promoting goals and plans, rather than fantasy (Kantor, 2004).

As people begin to improve, depression and anxiety that were masked by delusional symptoms may emerge. Therapists and clients alike should be prepared for this development and should view it as a sign of progress. If depression and anxiety do emerge, the focus of treatment should be shifted to amelioration of these affective symptoms.

Family therapy is often an important ingredient of treatment. Because these clients continue to function relatively well, family members may not understand that the clients are experiencing a mental disorder. Particularly if family members have been cast in an unfavorable light by a delusional belief system, they may feel angry and unsympathetic and may benefit from help in understanding the nature of the disorder. Reducing any family-related stress and conflict that are contributing to the delusional disorder can also help alleviate symptoms. Nevertheless, family therapy should be undertaken only with clients' permission, and clients should be reassured that family sessions will be discussed with them if they are not present at family meetings.

Although people diagnosed with delusional disorder often need to improve their social skills and relationships, they typically do not derive much benefit from group therapy. They tend to use their delusions to protect themselves from the group and wind up alienating other group members.

Prognosis   Although delusional disorder has a somewhat better prognosis than schizophrenia and does not have the same pervasive impact on functioning as that disorder does, the prognosis for treatment of delusional disorder is uncertain. Some people recover quickly—particularly women; people with good premorbid functioning; and those for whom the disorder has had a rapid onset, brief duration, and an apparent precipitant. For others, however, the disorder has a chronic course, and these people may experience alternating periods of remission and relapse over many years. Still others go on to develop schizophrenia. Those with delusional disorder of the persecutory, somatic, and erotomanic types seem to have better prospects for recovery than those with delusional disorder of the grandiose and jealous types (Kantor, 2004).

Schizoaffective Disorder

Schizoaffective disorder is one of the most complicated diagnoses listed in the *DSM-IV-TR*. Important new research has helped to clarify the symptoms that distinguish schizoaffective disorder from either schizophrenia or bipolar disorders.

Description of the Disorder Schizoaffective disorder, by definition, meets the criteria for a significant mood disorder (either major depressive disorder or bipolar I or II disorder) as well as for the active phase of schizophrenia. The disorder includes at least two weeks of delusions or hallucinations that are not accompanied by prominent mood symptoms, although depression or mania is present throughout most of the course of the disorder. Minimum duration for this disorder is one month. Some view schizoaffective disorder as two discrete disorders—schizophrenia and a mood disorder—or as an atypical form of mania or depression; others believe it belongs on a spectrum of psychotic mood disorders, with schizophrenia being the most chronic and bipolar and unipolar depression representing the least severe end of the spectrum. On this continuum schizoaffective disorder is viewed as the bridge between the mood disorders and schizophrenia. Some current data supports the dichotomy hypothesis and other data link the two disorders (Lake, 2010).

Less than 1% of the population is diagnosed as having this disorder, which is less common than schizophrenia and much less common than mood disorders, although the lifetime prevalence rate has not been determined due to a "lack of reliable diagnostic criteria" (Aires, 2010, p. 98). Indeed, inter-rater reliability is low for schizoaffective disorder, and many other disorders such as depression with psychosis and the negative symptoms of schizophrenia can look very much like schizoaffective disorder.

Disorders observed to precede or accompany schizoaffective disorder include substance-related disorders and schizoid, schizotypal, paranoid, and borderline personality disorders. Other disorders may develop later (American Psychiatric Association, 2000).

Typical Client Characteristics Two types of schizoaffective disorder have been identified. The bipolar type of schizoaffective disorder most often appears in early adulthood; the depressive type usually begins later. The age of onset of schizoaffective disorder is later for women than for men, with women particularly likely to manifest the depressive type. This disorder is more prevalent among women and among those with first-degree relatives who have been diagnosed as having schizophrenia or a major mood disorder (American Psychiatric Association, 2000). Men with this disorder frequently exhibit antisocial personality traits and flat affect (Sadock, 2007).

In general, the demographic backgrounds and premorbid patterns of adjustment for those with schizoaffective disorder are more like the backgrounds and patterns of people with major depressive disorder than like those of people with schizophrenia or a bipolar disorder. Due to frontal lobe cognitive dysfunction, social and occupational impairment typically accompany schizoaffective disorder. Even after achieving remission from the positive and negative symptoms of schizoaffective disorder, only one-quarter of the people in a 4-year longitudinal study achieved sustained social and occupational recovery (Robinson, Woerner, McMeniman, Mendelowitz, & Bilder, 2004). Many people with schizoaffective disorder perceive themselves as diminished in relation to their former level of functioning. According to Lysaker and others, self-stigma in combination with poor insight can lead to decreased functioning and a reduced quality of life. Across the schizophrenia spectrum, quality of life impairment syndrome is associated with decreased life satisfaction, increased stress and depression, and more suicidal ideation (Lysaker, Roe, & Yanos, 2007; Ritsner & Gibel, 2007). Poor quality of life is associated with suicidal ideation, and at least 10% of people affected by this disorder commit suicide.

Little clear information is available about the causes of schizoaffective disorder, although the disorder sometimes appears in relatively healthy people after a stressful precipitant; in these cases, onset is usually sudden and is accompanied by marked turmoil and confusion. Although less severe than in schizophrenia, poor insight is also common and must be addressed if treatment is to be successful.

Preferred Therapist Characteristics

Therapist variables discussed in the section on schizophrenia probably also are applicable to schizoaffective disorder. Therapists should provide support, structure, reality testing, empathy, acceptance, and reassurance to allay the resistance and suspiciousness that often accompany psychotic symptoms. Establishing realistic goals and avoiding situations that lead clients to feel demoralized and to blame themselves are important. People with schizoaffective disorder often experience a period of prolonged psychosis following a depressed or manic episode, so therapists must be able to work with them to restore their previous level of functioning.

Intervention Strategies

Research on evidence-based treatments specific to schizoaffective disorder is lacking, in part due to the heterogeneity of populations used in research studies (Maj, Pinozzi, Formicola, Bartoli, & Bucci, 2010). In many cases, people with schizoaffective disorder and people with schizophrenia have been combined in the same studies, resulting in distorted outcomes. Because schizoaffective disorder has features of both a psychotic disorder and a mood disorder, treatment should focus on affective as well as psychotic symptoms and must be individualized. In general, psychotherapy and appropriate medication are the treatments of choice. It seems prudent to base treatment initially on the most prominent symptoms.

Psychotherapy for people diagnosed with schizoaffective disorder usually resembles approaches used to treat schizophrenia. Because people with schizoaffective disorder are likely to lack insight, psychoeducation about the disorder and medication management should be an important component of early treatment with clients.

Psychotherapy for people with schizoaffective disorder needs to be concrete and supportive, with a focus on developing goals, building social skills, and providing occupational training to stabilize and improve quality of life (Ritsner & Gibel, 2007). As in all severe mental illnesses, family support is associated with improved outcomes, therefore family-focused therapy should be implemented to increase family members' understanding of the disorder, improve the family environment, and reduce high expressed emotion (Miklowitz, 2004). Group therapy is generally contraindicated for people with schizoaffective disorder, due to their discomfort in social situations and the frequent occurrence of paranoia.

Medication is almost always necessary to reduce both psychotic and affective symptoms, and a referral for medical evaluation should be made for people with schizoaffective disorder. Determining the appropriate drugs can be challenging, however, because multiple medications may be needed and because the side effects of a medication designed to ameliorate one facet of this disorder may exacerbate symptoms involved in another facet. Therefore, a trial-and-error approach is often necessary in determining the best combination of medications for this disorder. Volavka and colleagues (2002) conducted a 14-week double-blind medication trial in which clozapine (Clozaril), rispiridone (Risperdal), and olanzapine (Zyprexa) were shown to be more effective than haloperidol (Haldol) in the reduction of positive and negative symptoms associated with schizoaffective disorder. Maintenance on clozapine (Clozaril) has also yielded positive results; 65% of clients in one study had no further hospitalizations or mood episodes (Zarate, Tohen, Banov, & Weiss, 1995). Lithium, antidepressants, atypical antipsychotics, and neuroleptics all have been found useful in treating some cases of schizoaffective disorder (Robinson et al., 2004). Lithium has been particularly helpful in the maintenance of people with the bipolar type of this disorder. Blood chemistry needs to be monitored regularly, as the side effects of lithium and antipsychotic medications can be severe. Electroconvulsive therapy is an option for people who do not have a good response to medication. More than 100,000 people each year receive ECT for mood and thought disorders including schizoaffective disorder (Mankad, Beyer, Weiner, & Krystal, 2010).

Medication treatment for schizoaffective disorder must address the acute and maintenance phases and address immediate, short-term, and long-term goals (Patel & Deligiannidis, 2010). Many people diagnosed as having schizoaffective disorder require some period of hospitalization in addition to medication during the acute phase. Extensive treatment after hospitalization is often needed for people with severe forms of the disorder, especially until they are stabilized on medication. Family and social support, a stable schedule and routine, psychotherapy, regular exercise, and a healthy diet can all help maintain treatment gains.

Prognosis Ten-year outcome studies confirm a more promising prognosis for schizoaffective disorder than for schizophrenia (Harrow, Grossman, Herbener, & Davies, 2000; Robinson et al., 2004). Some people with schizoaffective disorder achieve good interepisodic recovery, whereas others may remain chronically impaired. Mood-incongruent psychotic features are associated with a poor prognosis, as are impaired premorbid functioning, early onset, unremitting course, a family history of schizophrenia, and a predominance of psychotic symptoms. Relapse is common, however, if medication is discontinued. Such organizations as the National Alliance for Research on Schizophrenia and Depression and the National Alliance for the Mentally Ill (www.nami.org) offer additional information as well as family education.

DISSOCIATIVE DISORDERS

Dissociative disorders share a common element: an inability to integrate memories and experiences into awareness. Being unaware of or unable to recall important incidents is a major symptom in the diagnosis of dissociative fugue, dissociative amnesia, depersonalization disorder, and dissociative identity disorder (formerly called multiple personality disorder).

Dissociative Identity Disorder

The dissociative disorder that seems to receive the most attention in books and movies is dissociative identity disorder (DID). According to the *DSM-IV-TR,* "The essential feature of dissociative identity disorder is the presence of two or more distinct identities" that repeatedly assume control of the person's behavior (American Psychiatric Association, 2000, p. 526).

Description of the Disorder People with dissociative identity disorder cannot integrate aspects of their identity, memory, and awareness and often are unable to recall important personal information. Dissociative identity disorder continues to be a controversial diagnosis, with some researchers considering the *DSM-IV* to focus too much attention on alter identities rather than considering DID as a structural dissociation of the personality (Dell, 2006; Gillig, 2009; van der Hart, Nijenjuis, Steele, & Brown, 2004). Regardless of how DID is conceptualized, dramatic cases in which as many as 100 distinct identities alternate in some way to control a person's identity have been reported, although half of cases report 10 or fewer (American Psychiatric Association, 2000). Each identity may claim to have a different history, self-image, gender, name, and other personal features. The three most common roles for identities are inadequate or confused protectors, terrified children, and persecutors who violently act out (Ellason & Ross, 1997; Thomas, 2003). Along with the alter identities, pervasive symptoms of DID include the inability to recall important personal information, headaches, erratic behavior, PTSD, and other types of memory loss or fugue symptoms (American Psychiatric Association, 2000).

Prevalence rates are unclear, but incidence of DID ranges from 0.01% to 1% of the general population (Maldonado, Butler, & Spiegel, 2002) and rises to 5% to 20.7% among psychiatric inpatients (Brand et al., 2009). The disorder has been identified across all major racial groups, socioeconomic classes, and cultures. Treatment usually is sought by a primary or host identity or at the urging of family members.

Onset of DID usually is in childhood, after a severe trauma or accompanying negative and abusive experiences in a context involving few support systems. Indeed, more than 90% of people diagnosed with DID report histories of childhood abuse, neglect, or highly disorganized parental approaches that resulted in disorganized attachment (Blizzard, 1997, 2003; Maldonado

et al., 2002; Thomas, 2003). Females are far more likely to be diagnosed with this disorder than are males, although some believe that men with this disorder are more likely to be in prisons than in mental health settings. Although the disorder begins in early childhood, the average age at diagnosis is 29 to 35 years old. Because of the long-standing and deeply ingrained nature of this disorder, the limited awareness that people with DID have of their condition, and their tendency to conceal their symptoms, this disorder can be mistaken for other dissociative disorders, personality disorders, or psychotic disorders. Diagnosis is also difficult because psychological assessments and physiological tests (such as EEGs, galvanic skin response, and cerebral blood flow) have yielded ambiguous results (D. Sue, Sue, & Sue, 2006). Few people with DID present their symptoms openly at initial treatment. Consequently, people often spend years in the mental health system before an accurate diagnosis is made. The average time from the appearance of symptoms to an accurate diagnosis is six years, with most people being diagnosed with three to four other disorders prior to receiving a diagnosis of DID (Brand, Armstrong, & Lowenstein, 2006).

Rifkin and colleagues developed a methodology for diagnosing DID that they believe approaches "the gold standard of diagnosis" (Rifkin, Ghisalbert, Dimatou, Jin, & Sethi, 1998, p. 845). Using a random sampling of 100 women in a teaching hospital setting, one of two clinicians first interviewed each patient using the Structured Clinical Interview for *DSM-IV* Dissociative Disorders (SCID-D) as an interview guide. Those who tested positive for DID were then interviewed by a second clinician, also using the structured interview technique. Rifkin and colleagues identified a 1% occurrence rate of DID among female psychiatric inpatients. The authors report that their results are lower than other studies of psychiatric inpatients, but that their method is superior to the use of self-report measures or fixed questionnaires such as the Dissociative Disorder Interest Scale (DDIS) and the Dissociative Experiences Scale (DES; Bernstein & Putnam, 1986). The methodology may also have implications for outpatient assessment. Clearly, further research is needed on the assessment of DID.

Typical Client Characteristics Typically, people with DID have significant memory gaps and a distinct manner of speaking that includes vagueness in their language, use of the third person when referring to themselves, and abrupt changes in tone (Brand et al., 2009). They are more likely to be introspective, self-reflective, above average in intelligence, and experience "traumatic flooding," or frequent intrusions of traumatic material (Scroppo, Drob, Weinberger, & Eagle, 1998).

People with DID are often diagnosed with schizophrenia or borderline personality disorder. A distinguishing characteristic between the disorders is that people with DID elaborate on and imaginatively alter their experiences whereas people with borderline personality disorder reduce experience and respond affectively. People with DID are also more socially focused than people who have disorders on the schizophrenia spectrum (Brand et al., 2009).

The degree of impairment of people with DID varies widely. Symptoms that frequently accompany this disorder include substance misuse, self-mutilation, suicidal and aggressive impulses, eating and sexual difficulties, sleeping problems, time lapses, disorientation, phobias, hallucinatory experiences, feelings of being influenced or changed, and mood swings (Ellason & Ross, 1997; Ford & Courtois, 2009). People with DID are more likely to have imaginative thoughts, a greater openness to altered states of consciousness, a highly unconventional view of reality, and difficulty integrating

information and new learning into their lives. They also score higher on traits of self-transcendence and self-directedness (Maldonado et al., 2002). A history of somatic symptoms is common, especially migraine headaches and intestinal disturbances.

Typically, people with DID have at least two additional mental disorders, with depression being the most common, and PTSD, substance use disorder, and personality disorders (especially borderline personality disorder) being particularly frequent (Ellason & Ross, 1997). Researchers have linked all types of trauma in the developmental years (emotional abuse, neglect, confinement, maternal dysfunction, traumatic and stressful life events, physical and sexual abuse) with increased levels of dissociative symptoms. Severity of symptoms appears to be correlated with age of onset; more severe symptoms are associated with an earlier onset (Maldonado et al., 2002). Twin studies suggest that genetics might also influence the development of dissociative identity disorder.

Preferred Therapist Characteristics People with dissociative disorders typically are coping with considerable stress and anxiety. They may be confused and frightened by their disorder and fear that they are going insane. They need a warm, supportive therapeutic relationship that provides them clear information on the nature, course, and treatment of their disorder and reassures them that deterioration is unlikely and that the prognosis for improvement is good.

More than any other diagnosis, the importance of a strong therapeutic relationship is critical for people with DID, who usually have been abused and violated by their caregivers, making trust and self-disclosure difficult. Therapists should present a safe environment by demonstrating a supportive nature, personal and professional reliability, and exposure to consistent therapeutic interactions (Steele & van der Hart, 2009).

Reality testing is an important area of intervention because people with DID are prone to misperceiving reality. Attempts to obtain succinct answers from a dissociative client can be difficult. It is not unusual for them to be confused about the facts, vague, or forgetful.

Clients' reports of their abuse can be particularly troubling to therapists. Countertransference may occur in which therapists become enraged with those who abused their clients, and want to care for and rescue the clients. This reaction is understandable, but it is, of course, countertherapeutic and can detract from clients' growing self-confidence. At the same time, however, complete therapist neutrality also is undesirable; this can give clients the message that others will sit passively while they are hurt. Rather, therapists should model appropriate parenting to a client who has lacked appropriate parenting in his or her life (Thomas, 2003). Therapists should strive to instill realistic hope and promote clients' active participation in recovery, but should at the same time protect them from moving too quickly or triggering an avoidant response.

Intervention Strategies Treatment of DID typically is a long, slow, challenging process that requires years of therapy and a skillful therapist. General psychotherapy that is not geared to the special needs of this disorder is unlikely to promote improvement. However, controlled studies and comprehensive research on DID are rare. Empirical research about the most effective treatment outcomes is lacking, although numerous case histories are available. One study reports therapists treating clients with dissociative disorders rated individual psychotherapy as most effective, followed by (or concurrent with) antidepressant and anxiolytic medication, and expressive therapies (Brand et al., 2009). Treatment that

helps clients identify and reduce the use of dissociation seems promising (ISSD, 2005).

Treatment modalities for DID are frequently based on the research on severe trauma and PTSD. Dividing therapy into a three-step process can be helpful. The first step is the development of a therapeutic alliance and creating a safe environment for the client. Once a client feels safe, the second step naturally unfolds as the person reveals his or her trauma experience. In the third step, the therapist works to repair the damage and encourages the client to expand social connections. As in all trauma work, the process must be seamless, with no disconnect between the therapeutic alliance and interventions (Ford & Courtois, 2009). Any therapeutic breaks must be addressed by the therapist in a direct and nondefensive manner.

Treatment that focuses on uncovering and working through traumatic memories is important in helping people recover from DID. The early age at which the traumas occurred, the fear induced by the traumatic experiences, and neural changes during stress can all interfere with recall and accuracy of memories. Thus, hypnosis is one of the most frequently used techniques in the treatment of DID (Maldonado et al., 2002). An important goal of treatment is to help clients integrate the various aspects of their personality into one identity that can function well (Butcher et al., 2006), but this process must be carefully paced to avoid retraumatization.

Adjunct modes of treatment can be helpful to people with DID. Homogeneous group therapy with a present-oriented focus can be particularly beneficial in helping people with DID understand themselves better and participate with other people in a social context. Group interaction, compassion, tolerance, patience, and sharing can all be experienced firsthand (Maldonado et al., 2002). Expressive therapy can facilitate awareness of emotions, development of insight, and recall of past experiences. Family therapy, focused on the current family, can promote understanding and improve relationships, although therapy with a family of origin that was abusive is generally contraindicated.

No controlled studies were located on the use of cognitive-behavioral therapy in the treatment of DID. However, as in the treatment of PTSD, cognitive-behavioral therapy can be used to develop coping skills and to help people control dissociation use or overcome dissociative events (Maldonado et al., 2002).

Medication is not effective in treating the core symptoms of DID, and yet it is not uncommon for people with dissociative disorders to be prescribed multiple medications (Brand et al., 2009). Medication used in the treatment of symptoms such as depression has met with mixed reviews; a randomized controlled study of people with DID indicated no difference between treatment with the SSRI fluoxetine (Prozac) versus a placebo (Simeon, Guralnik, Schmeidler, & Knutelska, 2004).

Prognosis Despite the severity of DID, Ellason and Ross (1997) found that 54 out of 135 people with DID treated in a specialized inpatient unit had improved dramatically at 2-year follow-up. Improvement was measured in terms of reducing depression, psychosis, and borderline symptoms. Another follow-up study of 25 people was less successful. However, both studies reinforce the need for lengthy treatment, as well as a less optimistic prognosis associated with DID that began early in life.

Dissociative Fugue, Dissociative Amnesia, and Depersonalization Disorder

Dissociative fugue, dissociative amnesia, and depersonalization disorder tend to receive much less attention than DID, but are far more frequently diagnosed. For example, most people have experienced the symptoms of depersonalization at some point in their lives.

Description of the Disorders All three of these disorders share the common feature of dissociation. The disorders can be distinguished by onset, length of symptoms, and degree of impairment.

Dissociative Fugue. Dissociative fugue (and dissociative amnesia, discussed in the next section) involves temporary forgetting of important components of a person's life. The forgetting is more extensive or extreme than would be experienced with ordinary forgetfulness, and often reflects a desire to withdraw from painful emotional experiences, such as severe assault or rape, or natural disasters. According to Maldonado and colleagues (2002), the most common stressors that trigger fugue states are marital discord, financial and occupational difficulties, and war-related situations. Dissociative fugue (as well as dissociative amnesia) is not caused by substances or a general medical condition.

People with disassociative fugue do not exhibit signs of being ill such as changes in appearance or odd behavior. They are more likely to develop sudden confusion about their identity and tend to wander away from work or home, even traveling to other places. Some people stay away for hours or even months, in this confused state. In a small percentage of cases, a new identity develops, typically that of a more energetic, outgoing, and adventurous personality. Awareness of the old personality and of the amnesia usually is absent.

The behaviors of people with dissociative fugue generally are unremarkable, although their memory loss may cause others to pay attention to them and try to help them. Such states may manifest a part of the self that is not commonly seen in everyday life (Steele & van der Hart, 2009). When the fugue state is gone (usually suddenly and spontaneously), people with this disorder typically are confused by what has happened to them, may have amnesia for troubling past events, and cannot recall the details of the fugue state. People with dissociative fugue may experience depression, remorse, anger, and suicidal impulses during the postfugue period and may need to repair the social and occupational consequences of their absence. Dissociative fugue has been associated with alcohol misuse, mood disorders, and personality disorders.

Dissociative amnesia. Dissociative amnesia involves partial amnesia or forgetting of important personal information, such as the names and identities of significant family members, one's place of employment, or events during a circumscribed period of time. The *DSM-IV-TR* describes five types of amnesia that can characterize this disorder:

1. Localized amnesia, focused on events during a limited period.
2. Selective amnesia, involving recall of some but not all events during a certain period.
3. Generalized amnesia, or inability to recall one's entire life.
4. Continuous amnesia, which involves the inability to recall events up to a specific point.
5. Systematized amnesia, or failure to recall certain categories of events or information.

The first two represent the most common types of this disorder. This diagnosis has been used for some people who report having recovered memories of traumatic childhood experiences.

Like those who have experienced dissociative fugue, people with dissociative amnesia sometimes report a broad range of symptoms after memory has been regained, including depression, aggressive and suicidal impulses, impaired functioning, sexual dysfunction, self-mutilation, trance states, and Ganser's syndrome (presenting approximate answers to questions) (American Psychiatric Association, 2000).

Dissociative amnesia, like dissociative fugue, tends to occur suddenly at times of traumatic events or unusual stress, is typically of brief duration, and may remit without recurrence. For example, after the September 11 attacks on the World Trade Center, several people who had been reported missing were later found alive, but had apparently developed dissociative amnesia (Tucker, 2002). Dissociative amnesia has been reported following robbery, torture, physical abuse, and combat trauma (Steele & van der Hart, 2009). After such an overwhelming trauma, a person may experience fragmentation or a polarization of their sense of self and may dissociate from affect or painful memories. These symptoms may buffer the full impact of the traumatic experience. However, even though people cannot recall these memories, the memories continue to influence them.

Depersonalization disorder. The *DSM-IV-TR* describes depersonalization disorder as characterized by "a feeling of detachment and estrangement from one's self" (American Psychiatric Association, 2000, p. 530). People with this disorder report feeling like robots, feeling as if they were in a dream or a movie, or feeling as though they are outside their bodies, observing themselves. Despite these unusual sensations, delusions and hallucinations are not present, and reality testing is intact. Nevertheless, the symptoms are severe and persistent enough to cause considerable distress or impairment. Symptoms of depression, anxiety, and somatic distress often accompany this disorder, and people sometimes believe that these symptoms are signs that they are crazy.

Nearly 50% of people have experienced some form of depersonalization, albeit in a brief, single episode (Maldonado et al., 2002). The symptom of depersonalization is fairly common in mental disorders and the diagnosis of the disorder should be given only when symptoms are severe and cause impairment in functioning as well as marked distress.

Onset of depersonalization disorder tends to be rapid, usually is associated with severe stress or trauma, and can occur at any age including the childhood years, although its onset is most common between the ages of 15 and 30. This disorder may be brief or chronic, persistent or episodic. As with all the dissociative disorders, it is more common among females than among males.

Typical Client Characteristics   Depersonalization disorder is particularly common among adolescents. It also seems more prevalent among people with substance-related, anxiety, and somatization disorders. Other co-occurring disorders may include depression, and avoidant, borderline, and obsessive-compulsive personality disorders (Maldonado et al., 2002). Cultural variables should be considered when diagnosing dissociative disorders; culturally sanctioned trance experiences should not be mistaken for depersonalization disorder.

The types of symptoms commonly found in people with depersonalization disorder can be divided into two clusters. The first cluster consists of visual derealization, altered body experiences, emotional numbing, and subjective feelings of memory loss. The second cluster includes heightened self-observation, altered experiences of time, and being unable to entertain thoughts or visualizations (Simeon & Abugel, 2006). People who are experiencing depersonalization generally do not function well at work or in school, and report they spend an inordinate amount of time trying to make up for their spaciness and their distorted sense of self.

Research on the characteristics of people who experience dissociative fugue or amnesia is limited, but the disorders seem to be more prevalent among people who are highly suggestible, who are easily hypnotized, and who also report symptoms of depression and anxiety (American Psychiatric Association, 2000). Both disorders

are rare but increase under circumstances of natural disaster, accidents, or warfare.

Preferred Therapist Characteristics   For many people with dissociative fugue, dissociative amnesia, or depersonalization disorder, a therapeutic relationship based on safety and support is sufficient to promote spontaneous remission. Therefore, therapists working with these clients need to be warm, supportive, consistent, and straightforward. They should be able to establish a stress-free relationship in which their clients can sort through disturbing memories in a psychologically and physically safe environment.

Intervention Strategies   A calm, congruent, empathic, and genuine approach is essential when working with people with depersonalization and dissociative disorders. Therapists should speak in a clear, precise, and unambiguous manner. They must also be certain to attend to their clients' non-verbal responses and to address any ruptures in the therapeutic alliance as they occur (Steele & van der Hart, 2009).

Dissociative fugue and dissociative amnesia. The treatments for dissociative fugue and dissociative amnesia are quite similar (Maldonado et al., 2002). Typically, the first step is to build a positive therapeutic relationship while helping people achieve a safe and stable life situation. Once those goals have been accomplished, the second step is to help people regain any memories that may not yet have been recovered and deal with the traumas or stressors that may have precipitated memory loss or flight. The third step in treatment is to help people integrate their upsetting experiences into their lives, reorder and move on with their lives, and develop coping skills that seem likely to help them manage future stressors more successfully.

Although this process sounds straightforward, people may find it challenging to come to terms with traumatic experiences and their consequences (such as flashbacks and withdrawal), as well as to deal with the feelings (such as shame, self-blame, rage, fear, and hopelessness) that often result not just from traumas but also from having had a dissociative disorder. Careful pacing, grounding, and considerable support are needed to control people's exposure to upsetting material, as well as to help some of these clients recognize and accept their inability to fully process their traumatic experiences. Dissociative disorders often function as defense mechanisms and should not be stripped away before people have developed other ways of taking care of themselves. Maintaining control and a sense of self is usually important to people with dissociative disorders, and that need should be respected.

Many types of interventions can contribute to treatment. In dissociative fugue and dissociative amnesia, hypnosis can facilitate the controlled uncovering of memories, as well as the working through and integration of those memories (Ellason & Ross, 1997; Maldonado et al., 2002). Medication, including barbiturates and benzodiazepines, can also be helpful in restoring lost memories and reducing anxiety. Expressive-supportive psychodynamic psychotherapy, encouraging exploration, coping, the building of confidence, and the expression of feelings can also help reduce anxiety. Once memory has been regained, psychotherapy can be useful in helping people deal with the precipitants of their amnesia. Other interventions, such as family therapy, free association, environmental change, cognitive therapy, and behavior therapy, also can help ameliorate dissociative fugue and dissociative amnesia and can help people cope with stress-related precipitants. Group therapy, particularly with others who have survived similar traumatic experiences, can be helpful as long as caution is exercised in pacing and in establishing safety (Ellason & Ross, 1997).

Depersonalization Disorder   The overall goal of treatment for depersonalization disorder is to help people regain their sense of reality and develop a feeling of personality integration. A first step toward this goal is to provide education on the nature of depersonalization disorder. Clarifying and normalizing the symptoms of this disorder can often be very therapeutic and can reduce fear about the meaning of the symptoms. The choice of subsequent interventions depends primarily on other disorders and experiences that are associated with the depersonalization. Effective treatment for depersonalization disorder should include assessment and treatment of co-occurring conditions (Maldonado et al., 2002).

Although the most effective treatment for depersonalization disorder has yet to be identified, many forms of treatment have been used successfully with this disorder, including cognitive-behavioral therapy with mindfulness, acceptance and commitment therapy, behavior therapy, hypnosis, group and family therapy, and SSRIs and anxiolytics to treat symptoms of depression and anxiety (Jimenez-Genchi, 2004; Maldonado et al., 2002). Case reports indicate these interventions have helped some clients and been ineffective with others. Few data-based studies are available to provide general guidance for treatment of this disorder partly because people usually do not seek treatment for its symptoms. Consequently, therapists should determine as accurately as possible what symptoms and past experiences need attention and what treatment approaches are most likely to have a positive impact on those associated difficulties. Finally, improvement of coping skills, life and stress management, and integration of self and experiences almost always are indicated as part of treatment for these clients.

Prognosis   The prognosis is excellent for a rapid and complete recovery from initial episodes of dissociative fugue and dissociative amnesia, particularly if they are linked to specific precipitants (Spiegel, 1996). Recovery is often spontaneous, although it can be facilitated by treatment, but recurrences are common.

Treatment for depersonalization disorder has been shown to improve prognosis, although more research is necessary (Hunter, Baker, Phillips, Sierra, & David, 2005; Simeon et al., 2004). Symptoms may be fairly stable or may wax and wane in response to stressors.

TREATMENT RECOMMENDATIONS: CLIENT MAP

Treatment recommendations for disorders involving impairment in awareness of reality are summarized here according to the Client Map format. Because these disorders do vary widely, readers are also encouraged to review the preceding sections on the specific disorders.

CLIENT MAP

Diagnosis

Disorders involving impairment in awareness of reality (schizophrenia, brief psychotic disorder, schizophreniform disorder, delusional disorder, schizoaffective disorder, dissociative identity disorder, dissociative fugue, dissociative amnesia, depersonalization disorder)

Objectives of Treatment

Establish a safe, supportive environment in which therapy can be most effective

As possible, reduce or eliminate prominent symptoms

Restore client's awareness of reality

Maximize client's coping abilities and emotional and behavioral adjustment to the disorder

Help client deal with any precipitating stressors or traumatic experiences

If needed, improve social and occupational functioning

Prevent relapse

Enable family members to develop understanding of the disorder, deal with their own related needs and feelings, and learn how to help the family member

Assessments

Usually medical, neurological, or psychological evaluations, or all three

Inventories of specific symptoms (non-suicidal self-injury, suicidal ideation, dissociation, substance use, stress, depression), to clarify diagnosis and provide useful information on level of functioning and secondary symptoms

Clinician Characteristics

Able to communicate caring, consistency, and optimism

Able to establish a trusting and sometimes long-term therapeutic relationship

Knowledgeable about usual nature and course of disorder

Able to manage countertransference reactions, especially with clients who have experienced abuse or other traumatic experiences

Able to collaborate with medical personnel, family and individual psychotherapists, and rehabilitation counselors

Able to provide support and, as necessary, long-term treatment to client and family

Location of Treatment

For psychotic disorders, often inpatient setting initially, with later outpatient setting (sometimes day treatment)

For dissociative disorders, usually outpatient setting, with hospitalization as necessary if client is in crisis or overwhelmed by traumatic memories

Interventions to Be Used

Supportive psychotherapy to maintain stabilization

Family therapy, to promote family members' understanding, improve clients' compliance with medication, and support client adjustment

Education on the disorder

Medication (especially for the psychotic disorders)

Behavior therapy, to promote development of coping mechanisms and stress management

Hypnotherapy, psychodynamic psychotherapy, and cognitive therapy as indicated for specific disorders

Emphasis of Treatment

Variable according to nature of disorder (for example, focus on behavior and symptom alleviation for psychotic disorders; focus on exploration of background and dynamics of disorder for dissociative identity disorder)

Emphasis on supportiveness and structure typical

Numbers

Primarily individual treatment

Family therapy also useful

Group therapy only in specialized forms (milieu therapy for schizophrenia; homogeneous group therapy for people who experienced abuse and who are diagnosed with dissociative identity disorder)

Timing

Long term, with some exceptions, including brief psychotic disorder and dissociative amnesia

Sometimes several sessions per week

Medications Needed

Almost always indicated for psychotic disorders

Sometimes indicated for dissociative disorders

Should be monitored carefully to minimize side effects and prevent misuse or suicide

Adjunct Services

Rehabilitation counseling

Social skills training and development of activities

Respite care for families

Prognosis

Variable, depending on the disorder (for example, excellent for brief psychotic disorder, good for dissociative amnesia and dissociative identity disorder, fair for schizophrenia)

CLIENT MAP OF VICTOR J.

This chapter began with a description of Victor J., a 22-year-old college senior who believed that his roommate's mother was in love with him. Victor's poor coping and social skills, his apprehension about graduating from college, and his apparent wish to escape from his family environment all probably contributed to the development of his delusional disorder. Treatment focused on helping him address and alleviate his stressors and improve his coping skills had a rapid effect on Victor's symptoms. His delusional beliefs began to fade in intensity and quickly ceased to become a dominant theme. Victor was then able to invest energy in completing his college studies and seeking employment. Victor made many positive changes within about six months, and his medication was stopped, although he was expected to need continued psychotherapy after the initial interventions. The following Client Map outlines the treatment recommended for Victor.

Diagnosis

Axis I: 297.1 Delusional disorder, erotomanic type, moderate
Axis II: Avoidant personality traits
Axis III: No medical problems reported
Axis IV: Impending college graduation, conflict with family
Axis V: Global assessment of functioning (GAF Scale): current GAF = 52

Objectives of Treatment

Eliminate delusional symptoms
Improve social and relationship skills
Improve communication skills
Establish realistic and rewarding postgraduation plans
Improve socialization, leisure activities, coping mechanisms, support systems, self-confidence, and self-reliance
Facilitate exploration, understanding, and resolution of family issues

Assessments

Referral for medical and neurological tests, to rule out the possibility of a cognitive disorder

Clinician Characteristics

Supportive and patient
Empathic
Skilled at reducing resistance and restoring contact with reality
Preferably male, to serve as a role model for client
Knowledgeable about family dynamics

Location of Treatment

Outpatient setting

Interventions to Be Used

Education about symptoms, communication skills, development of alternative solutions to problems, and effective decision making
Individual therapy combining supportive, cognitive, and behavioral elements
Emphasis on development of strong therapeutic alliance
Behavior therapy, especially to build up client's coping mechanisms
Training in stress management
Assistance in developing plans for after graduation
Validation of client's feelings, but with minimum discussion of client's delusional beliefs

Emphasis of Treatment

Emphasis on structure
Relatively directive emphasis, with supportiveness and orientation to the present also important
Focus on behavioral and affective elements, in holistic context

Numbers

Individual therapy, perhaps followed by group therapy with sufficient abatement of symptoms to permit client to benefit from group feedback and opportunity to practice communication skills

Timing

Gentle yet steady pace, to quickly develop client's commitment to treatment and reduce symptoms
Moderate duration

Medications Needed

Medication prescribed as short-term aid to reducing client's thought disorder and anxiety and facilitating his involvement in therapy

Adjunct Services

Cycling group (to promote client's present enjoyment of biking and facilitate his involvement in a nondemanding, rewarding activity likely to offer increased contact with other young people but unlikely to create discomfort or embarrassment)

Prognosis

Excellent, with combination of medication and psychotherapy
Extended follow-up psychotherapy anticipated

RECOMMENDED READING

Bellack, A. S., Mueser, K. T., Gingerich, S., & Agresta, J. (2004). *Social skills training for schizophrenia: A step-by-step guide* (2nd ed.). New York, NY: Guilford Press.

French, P., Smith, J., Shiers, D., Reed, M., & Rayne, M. (Eds.). (2010). *Promoting recovery in early psychosis.* Oxford, United Kingdom: Wiley-Blackwell.

Graham, H. L., Copello, A., Birchwood, M. J., & Mueser, K. T. (Eds.). (2003). *Substance misuse in psychosis: Approaches to treatment and service delivery.* Hoboken, NJ: Wiley.

International Society for the Study of Dissociation. (2005). Guidelines for treating dissociative identity disorder in adults. *Journal of Trauma and Dissociation, 6,* 69–149.

Murray, W. H. (2006). *Schizoaffective disorder: New research.* Hauppage, NY: Nova Science.

Sierra, M. (2009). *Depersonalization: A new look at a neglected syndrome.* New York, NY: Cambridge University Press.

Thomas, P. M. (2003). Protection, dissociation, and internal roles: Modeling and treating the effects of child abuse. *Review of General Psychology, 7,* 364–380.

Torrey, E. F. (2006). *Surviving schizophrenia: A manual for families, patients, and providers* (5th ed.). New York, NY: HarperCollins.

van der Hart, O., Nijenhuis, E. R. S., & Steele, K. (2006). *The haunted self: Structural dissociation and the treatment of chronic traumatization.* New York, NY: Norton.

10 The Future of Diagnosis and Treatment Planning

This, the fourth edition of *Selecting Effective Treatments,* provides a pathway for treatment of mental disorders based on the most recent evidence-based research, while at the same time recognizing that the diagnosis and treatment of mental disorders are part of a dynamic and evolving field. The highly anticipated publication of the fifth edition of the *Diagnostic and Statistical Manual* in the next few years will provide new diagnoses and improvements and clarifications to many of the current mental disorders. And new and exciting research is currently under way that will inspire innovative theories and practices in the future.

The biological, psychological, and social development of a human being is complex. The next decades will reveal more about how these biopsychosocial influences interact to shape the individual person. More will be learned about the neurobiological underpinnings of behavior and the importance of prenatal and early life influences and trauma on the person across the life span. The constantly changing society in which we live also impacts on human behavior—the worldwide economic downturn, military involvements in Iraq and Afghanistan, natural disasters, terrorism, the Internet and social media, to name just a few. How could these influences not shape and inform our understanding of diagnosis and treatment in fundamentally new and interesting ways?

In an attempt to look at the future of our field, this chapter provides a brief glimpse into what clinicians can expect in the coming years, based on the research and changes that are currently under way.

NEW UNDERSTANDING OF DIAGNOSIS

Rapid advances in our understanding of the brain and how it functions have improved diagnostic accuracy and enhanced treatment options. At the same time, advances in molecular genetics are changing the way we conceptualize disorders. The more we learn about the complex interplay of biological, psychological, and environmental events, the sooner we can assess, and some day even prevent, the development of these disorders. New research in these areas will change the way we look at diagnosis. Of course, the forthcoming publication of the fifth edition of the *Diagnostic and Statistical Manual (DSM-5)* will fine-tune diagnostic criteria for many of the disorders, propose new diagnoses, and perhaps even eliminate a few.

Neurobiology

As we learn more about the physiological and biochemical processes of the brain, and the use of neuroimaging, computerized axial tomography (CAT), positron emission tomography (PET), magnetic resonance imaging (MRI), and functional MRI (fMRI) provide increasing diagnostic accuracy for a variety of disorders, such as dementia, mood disorders, and schizophrenia (Phillips, 2009). In the future, the refinement of these and even newer tests, taken together with clinical assessments of a person's behavior, thoughts, and emotions, will provide better diagnostic accuracy for a wide range of mental disorders. EEGs may even be used to document treatment effectiveness someday.

Along with our increased knowledge of neurological influences on behavior comes a realization that many brain conditions can be reduced or prevented with earlier assessment and intervention. The greatest impact of early interventions is on our children.

Currently, one in five children meets the diagnostic criteria for a mental disorder. Fifty percent of adult disorders were first manifested in childhood (Hunsley & Mash, 2010; Mash & Barkley, 2010). Consistent with a growing focus on earlier childhood assessment and treatment, comes a renewed focus on the interactions between parent and child and increasing awareness of the need to take a prevention-oriented approach for high-risk populations (families with a history of substance abuse or mental illness, single parent households, those who live in poverty, first-generation immigrants, and those with a history of trauma from war, suicide, violence, accidents, or natural disasters).

A fascinating area of growth in the coming years will be the field of perinatal psychiatry. This emerging specialty area focuses on the mental health of infants and parents in the pre- and postnatal periods, aimed at early intervention, prevention, and treatment (Gelso, 2010). Research on the interactions between the mother and infant, maternal psychopathology, infant psychopathology, or a combination of all three is expected to result in the development of an increasing number of early interventions for disorders such as postpartum depression, bipolar disorder, schizophrenia, and autism spectrum disorders.

Molecular Genetics and Spectrum Disorders

As we become better able to distinguish between biological causes and psychosocial causes of disorders, treatments will become more specific, and prevention will become more focused. This does not mean that a pharmacological or medical approach will be found for every disorder, but rather that research will be better able to determine which psychotherapy treatments, in combination with which medications (if appropriate), are best suited to a particular mental disorder. We need to study and treat both the psychosocial and the biological elements of mental disorders. This is evident in schizophrenia, for example, which has a genetic component, as evidenced by twin studies that show a nearly 50% concordance rate among identical twins. Yet the concordance rate is *only* 50%, indicating that something more than genetics influences the development of this disorder.

Family, twin, and adoption studies can go only so far. Research in the area of molecular genetics is leading to the identification of multiple contributing genes that work together to create an underlying susceptibility to a particular disorder. For example, rather than one gene responsible for the development of schizophrenia, multiple genes have been identified that each contribute a degree of pathology. How these genes function and are influenced by environmental and other factors can determine whether the person develops schizophrenia, experiences a milder version of the disorder such as schizotypal personality disorder, or has no disorder at all. Current research suggests a spectrum of psychotic disorders that lie on a continuum and include multiple biopsychosocial variables that contribute to the development of symptoms.

The spectrum disorder concept is being considered for other disorders as well. Some proposed spectra include bipolar spectrum disorders (ranging from cyclothymia to bipolar I disorder); an autism spectrum; and several anxiety spectrum disorders, including a PTSD spectrum, an OCD spectrum, and a panic disorder spectrum. Our understanding of spectrum disorders is still evolving, so there are no hard-and-fast boundaries. The concept challenges the currently accepted system of categorical diagnoses that serves as the basis of the *DSM* and the *ICD-10* manuals. Look to the future of psychiatric genetics to provide insight into the susceptibility of families to inherit certain conditions and their accompanying symptoms.

Anticipated Publication of DSM-5

The *Diagnostic and Statistical Manual of Mental Disorders* is an evolving and complex document. Work by the American Psychiatric Association committees and work groups on the development of the *DSM-5* has been under way for more than a decade. Clinical experience commonly provides the basis for scientific research and often leads to changes in treatments even before they are scientifically validated.

Considerable research and discussion informs decisions about the addition of new disorders to the *DSM*. Several that are under consideration include nonsubstance-related addictions such as pathological gambling and sexual addiction. Behaviors associated with clinical diagnoses, such as psychosis, self-harm, and suicidal ideation, are being looked at in efforts to provide more

information and clarity in assessment with the hopes of earlier interventions and prevention. Other diagnoses worthy of discussion include executive system dysfunction, which refers to the functioning of the brain's frontal lobe, where executive functions are located, and emotion regulation disorder.

Perhaps the biggest changes in the *DSM-5* may relate to Axis II personality disorders. Current proposals on the *DSM-5* Web site (www.dsm5.org) call for the creation of a hybrid dimensional-categorical approach based on the popular five-factor model of personality. Five main personality types would exist: borderline, antisocial/psychopathic, avoidant, obsessive-compulsive, and schizotypal types. Clinicians might choose the type that fits best, and then focus on possible trait domains (for example, negative emotionality, introversion, antagonism, disinhibition, compulsivity, and schizotpy).

Following are some of the other changes potentially being considered for the *DSM-5* (APA, 2010):

- Diagnostic changes to posttraumatic stress disorder that reflect new research and insights into the causes and development of PTSD.

- Gender identity disorder (GID) is one of the most controversial diagnoses in the *DSM*. Just as homosexuality was determined not to be a mental disorder and was therefore removed from the third edition of the *DSM*, uncertainty also surrounds the diagnosis of GID. Whether GID is considered to be a physical disorder, a mental disorder, or a normal variation of human behavior will impact its inclusion (or revision as gender dysphoria) in the *DSM-5*.

- Changes in the mood disorders criteria could provide better clarification between bipolar and unipolar depression. The grief exclusion criterion is also being considered for deletion from the criteria for major depression. Work groups are considering improvements in the assessment and prediction of the development of psychosis.

- The classifications of substance abuse and dependence will likely be reclassified as addiction and related disorders, and a behavioral addiction category may be developed. The first behavioral addiction will be pathological gambling (which currently exists in the *DSM-IV-TR*, but is being recategorized). A second behavioral addiction, Internet addiction, is also being considered, but may fit more appropriately in the appendix until additional research is available.

- A new sexual disorder diagnostic category is under consideration. Hypersexual disorder refers to people who engage in sexual fantasies, urges, and behavior in an attempt to relieve anxiety, depression, or stress and are unable to control those urges.

- Multiple changes are expected to be made in the disorders first diagnosed in infancy and early childhood. Asperger's disorder is expected to be incorporated into the broader category of autism spectrum disorders; the criteria for reactive attachment disorder is expected to be revised; newer disorders such as temper dysregulation disorder, late language emergence, and nonsuicidal self-injury are also being considered at this time.

- Binge eating disorder (included in the *DSM-IV-TR* under eating disorder-NOS), is expected to be recognized as an eating disorder in its own right. Several changes are also expected to be made to the criteria for anorexia

nervosa and bulimia nervosa. Eating disorder-NOS may be retitled as feeding and eating conditions not elsewhere classified and may include pica, atypical anorexia, purging disorder, and other eating problems that do not meet the full criteria of an eating disorder.

- Obsessive-compulsive disorder may be reclassified as an anxiety and obsessive-compulsive spectrum disorder. Hoarding, skin picking, and olfactory reference syndrome may be added as new disorders, or listed in an appendix for further research. Insight specifiers (good, fair, poor, or absent) may be added for some of the anxiety disorders.

Other reclassifications, changes in diagnostic criteria, word clarifications, and more are anticipated with the publication of the *DSM-5*. A more developmental approach is also being considered in recognition that most adult disorders began in childhood. The overall goal is to improve the reliability of diagnosis and increase the publication's clinical utility.

Revision of the *DSM* is a huge undertaking. Proposed revisions have been drafted and reviewed, field trials have been held, and a healthy discourse continues online and in professional journals. The public comment period and second round of field trials will come to an end, and the committees and work groups will set about the task of writing and editing the final version of the *DSM-5*. If everything goes according to the revised timeline developed by the American Psychiatric Association, the *DSM-5* is expected to be published in May 2013.

CHANGES IN TREATMENT

Just as diagnoses evolve, approaches to treatment grow and change, too. Following are several trends worth watching. We begin with new, evidence-based support for the therapeutic alliance, our constant rudder in a sea of change.

The Therapeutic Alliance

The future is likely to bring an alliance-building focus in education and training, in treatment interventions, and in research. As discussed in Chapter 1, more than 20 meta-analytic reviews have documented that the alliance between the therapist and the client is crucial to successful treatment outcomes, regardless of treatment modality or diagnosis. Stated another way, without the development of a good working relationship between the therapist and the client, treatment stands little chance of being effective.

Binder and Henry recommend training programs that teach students to "reflect in action" (p. 300). That is to recognize any negative processes within the therapy session and to monitor their own reactions to it. Look for counselor skills training programs that focus on developing positive interpersonal relationships, that address issues of transference and countertransference in the here and now, and that help students identify and address client mistrust, hostility, dissatisfaction, and lack of engagement in therapy (Binder & Henry, 2010). Perhaps skills training programs will involve a computer-generated interactive process that allows trainees to experience and react to vignettes in vivo.

Clients will be well-served by therapists who are able to maintain the alliance over the course of therapy, and address and repair any potential ruptures that occur. Although having a theoretical orientation is important, and having a variety of effective techniques and strategies at our disposal is wise, attending to these interpersonal issues are more important than just learning a few techniques that can help build the alliance. Most therapists, whether new to the field or seasoned professionals, could benefit from training to enhance their interpersonal skills, repair ruptures in the relationship, and reduce early terminations (Crits-Cristoph, Crits-Cristoph, & Gibbons, 2010).

In the future, treatment manuals, books on evidence-based practice, and computer-assisted counseling will also be mindful of the therapy relationship and include suggestions for adapting, tailoring, or fine-tuning it into a powerful alliance that portends success. Future alliance research will more narrowly focus on measures to improve retention rates, enhance client functioning, solidify interactions, and otherwise help clients to succeed (Norcross & Lambert, 2011).

Accountability and Evidence-Based Treatment

Managed care requirements for evidence-based treatment (EBT) are expected to increase over the coming years, and some experts predict that at some point in the future *only* evidence-based practices will be reimbursed by managed care organizations (Yalom, 2009). EBP will determine how psychotherapy is conducted and what is reimbursed (Norcross, Hogan, & Koocher, 2008). Already many federal, military, and state funding agencies are beginning to provide reimbursement only for empirically supported treatments (Levant & Hassan, 2008). As third-party payers increasingly follow the medical model, clinicians will be required to document that their interventions are medically necessary and evidence-based (Thomason, 2010). Of course, non-EBP therapies are expected to continue, but probably will not be eligible for third-party reimbursement.

Manualized treatment, clinical guidelines, goal setting and assessment, case tracking, and paperwork are all important elements of efforts to provide cost-effective, empirically based treatments. Therapists are currently required by managed care organizations (MCOs) to be able to document progress for each client. They accomplish this through assessments, treatment plans, and progress notes. The current focus on accountability in the health-care system is giving rise to the need to demonstrate that interventions have positive outcomes and improve patient care. Therapists increasingly research their own work and provide evidence of their personal effectiveness with a caseload of clients as part of continuing efforts to improve treatment outcomes.

Occasional treatment failures or setbacks are inevitable, but therapists can take steps to maximize the likelihood of a successful treatment alliance. Misdiagnosis is only one possible reason for a treatment failure. Others include lack of expertise on the part of the therapist, inappropriate choice of treatment, a challenging client, or a treatment-resistant disorder. Based on empirical research, the American Psychological Association has developed a list of 18 empirically supported or evidence-based practices and will be creating clinical treatment guidelines for each methodology in the coming years.

Following evidence-based treatment recommendations, while not guaranteed to be successful, can certainly provide a roadmap to follow. Consulting with other mental health practitioners is another important step. Therapists should not hesitate to refer clients for evaluation by someone from a related discipline (perhaps a neurologist or a psychiatrist) to confirm or clarify a diagnosis. Discussion of a case with colleagues also can be useful in gaining ideas for diagnosis and treatment. Frequent evaluation of the progress attained in meeting the goals established in a Client Map is imperative in monitoring a treatment's effectiveness. As indicated in Chapter 1, people typically manifest progress fairly early in therapy; if even slight progress is not made in the first few months of treatment, reevaluation and modification of the goals, the treatment plan, or the therapist-client interaction probably are needed. In addition,

keeping up to date with the research on treatment effectiveness can enhance therapists' ability to provide effective treatment.

Transdiagnostic Treatment Modalities

Treatment modalities continuously evolve based on comparative effectiveness research that determines what treatment works with a particular client and in what situation. In the absence of any one treatment intervention to successfully address all client needs, there has been a growing recognition that targeting the common functional relationships that occur across disorders may have a number of important benefits compared to diagnosis-specific approaches. Transdiagnostic treatment appears to have a high potential for providing effective and practical treatment above and beyond diagnosis-specific interventions, especially in treatment-resistant and complicated or overlapping symptomatology.

Transdiagnostic approaches to treatment focus on specific symptom relief as part of the overall treatment plan. For example, emotion dysregulation, a symptom found in many disorders, has been effectively treated with dialectical behavior therapy (DBT) in the treatment of borderline personality disorder. The techniques of DBT (structured social skills training, mindfulness, acceptance and commitment to change, to name a few) have been found to be effective in decreasing self-harm and suicidal behaviors. As a result, DBT is now being used to treat emotion dysregulation across a wide array of disorders including bipolar disorders, major depressive disorder, and other mood disorders. Similarly, impulsivity, a primary symptom of ADHD, alcohol and substance abuse, gambling, and some personality disorders, has become the focus of adjunctive group therapy to provide symptom relief to people regardless of their overall diagnosis. Initial results also indicate this may contribute to the overall success rate of treatment.

The future will bring more of these trans-diagnostic, or unified, treatment protocols, which target common maintaining factors found in multiple disorders or mixed diagnostic groups. Even though transdiagnostic treatment is still in its infancy, a review of outcome studies to date has found it to be affiliated with improvements in symptoms, improvements in co-occurring disorders, better outcomes than wait-list controls, increased satisfaction with the therapeutic alliance, and a high degree of client satisfaction and group cohesion (McEvoy, Nathan, & Norton, 2009). As we have seen in previous chapters, transdiagnostic approaches are being created to treat the symptoms of eating disorders, anger management, emotion regulation, couples communication, impulsivity, anxiety, and depression, among others (Allen et al., 2008; Ehrenreich-May & Bilek, 2011; Fairburn et al., 2008; Hayes, Strosahl, & Wilson, 2005).

Additional research will help to determine what common factors within individuals serve to maintain emotional disorders and which treatments can be unified. There is no doubt that the future will provide additional applications of this exciting methodology and provide an important contribution to existing literature.

Medication

As we gain more knowledge of the brain and its chemistry, medication will continue to play an important role in the treatment of mental disorders. This is not to say that medication will eliminate psychotherapy; on the contrary, medication and psychotherapy will continue to work together synergistically for increased effectiveness in the treatment of many disorders. Just as medications for schizophrenia, the bipolar disorders, autism, and ADHD are more effective when combined with a psychotherapeutic component, so, too, will most future interventions

benefit when physicians and mental health therapists work together.

However, research shows that a large number of people do not follow through on medication recommendations or they stop taking medication prematurely. Regular psychotherapy can help; through education, stress reduction, support, and the power of the therapeutic alliance. Clinicians can encourage their clients to follow both medical and nonmedical treatment recommendations. Even when therapy appears to be more powerful than medication, the initial use of medication often can increase people's ability to benefit from therapy. An example of this is the combined use of medication and cognitive-behavioral therapy in the treatment of some anxiety disorders.

Exciting new medications are being reviewed for treatment of substance use disorders, impulse-control disorders, insomnia, eating disorders, and dementia. More than 30 new medications are under review for schizophrenia alone. Vaccines for nicotine addiction and alcohol abuse are also being considered. The use of newer medications with fewer side effects will also enhance the impact of therapy.

Polypharmacy and medicinal cocktails that combine three, four, or five different medications individualized to obtain the desired effect have become common. The use of multiple medications is sometimes used to augment the effect of a medication or as an adjunct to decrease the side effects of another medication. The use of multiple medications has become common practice in psychiatric hospitals, as well as with people who have more than one diagnosis, and in the elderly population. Alarmingly, the practice of polypharmacy has also increased significantly in the past decade in the pediatric and adolescent population, even though little research is available on the effect of multiple psychotropic medications on children (Comer, Olfson, & Mojtabai, 2010).

The increasing practice of polypharmacy can have serious negative consequences including unwanted drug interactions, increased cost, a complex drug regimen that makes compliance difficult, and an increase in the risk of adverse medication-related events. Therapists who work with clients in need of polypharmacy should maintain close contact with the prescribing physician and monitor any adverse symptoms or reactions.

New Treatment Delivery Methods

Telephones have been used for therapy for 35 years, but it has only been in the past 20 years that mobile phones have become a personal necessity and in many countries actually outnumber landlines. Numerous clinical interventions involving mobile phones have become commonplace such as telephone counseling, relaxation applications, and medication and appointment reminders. Text messaging has helped college students lose weight, quit smoking, and manage exam stress (Preziosa, Grassi, Gaggioli, & Riva, 2009). Mindfulness and breathing apps are being downloaded to PDAs as instant relaxation cues. Although little research is available on the successfulness of these aids, the possibilities seem endless for helping people maintain their motivation, monitor their behavior, and improve compliance with treatment, and feel better.

Online testing, computer-based therapist referrals, and videotherapy as an adjunct to therapy are also fairly common elements of present-day therapy and attest to the power and convenience of the Internet in the treatment of mental health disorders. Most therapists use e-mail as a medium for scheduling appointments and responding to short requests for information. No empirical research has been conducted on the efficacy of using e-mail for clinical interventions, and the use of e-mail

poses additional questions of security; confidentiality; record keeping; and other clinical, legal, and ethical issues.

Whether using e-mail, Skype, videoconferencing, or other electronic media, therapists should ensure that in all electronic communication with, for, and about clients, confidentiality is at the forefront.

Internet-Based Delivery Methods The manner in which psychotherapy can be delivered is changing, but not as rapidly as the technology. Computerized self-help via online support groups, e-mail, blogs, or chats; health education sites and YouTube videos; virtual reality; Internet counseling; and videoconferenced psychotherapy all are in their infancy. As the Internet has grown into one of the leading providers of health-care information, special forums have sprouted to meet the educational needs of people with specific disorders. Such forums can provide the latest research on empirically supported treatments and can direct interested parties to online communities that offer support and other information for participants. At the same time, Internet sites can provide erroneous and even destructive information. For example, sites exist for people with anorexia nervosa and bulimia nervosa in which participants share ways to lose weight and conceal their weight loss. Therapists should be careful to check out any sites they recommend and inquire about the specifics of sites that are frequently used by their clients.

Social Media The recent explosion of social networking sites (Facebook, Twitter, YouTube, LinkedIn, and others), as well as the ability to obtain instantaneous information with the click of a search engine, raises additional ethical issues for clinicians who choose to participate in social networking sites themselves. To date, no ethical guidelines have been developed by professional counseling organizations such as the APA or ACA that would clarify therapists' online behavior. It seems prudent, however, for therapists to be mindful of their professional role, weigh the benefits and harms that could result, and be aware of ethical and agency rules regarding interactions with clients. When writing on blogs, Twitter, Faccbook, or other social media, clinicians should consider what they are disclosing and the impact it may have on their clinical work.

E-Therapy Cybercounseling or e-therapy has become increasingly popular and a small number of studies attest to its positive potential (Marks, Cavanagh, & Gega, 2007; Ruskin et al., 2004). Online counseling is being provided via e-mail, bulletin boards, chat rooms, interactive video, and Internet hookups such as Skype. Although many therapists express guarded concern about participating in cybercounseling, videocounseling may actually increase a client's sense of control and satisfaction with therapy (Simpson, 2009). Most counselors seem willing to use e-therapy as an adjunct to face-to-face counseling, with those who have more experience with the technology rating it more successfully (Coyle, Doherty, Sharry, & Matthews, 2007).

A growing number of studies indicate technology-assisted counseling can be clinically effective and acceptable to clients (Simpson, 2009). It is often a necessary intervention, enabling counselors and clients to communicate across distances, when circumstances warrant. The benefits of technology include being able to reach a diverse group of people who would otherwise not be reached, in such settings as forensic and corrections centers and in such locations as rural areas where long distances separate clinicians from their clients. Especially for people for whom transportation or face-to-face meetings present a problem (including people who are elderly, impoverished, hearing impaired, disabled, or reluctant to attend therapy because of anxiety or embarrassment),

technology can provide access to therapy they would otherwise never have received (Rees & Stone, 2005). One study showed the working alliance was comparable to face-to-face counseling, and clients positively evaluated the experience and reported improvement and satisfaction (Barak & Bloch, 2006). In a randomized controlled study of veterans who had depression and received videocounseling, no difference was found between face-to-face and videolink counseling. Equivalent improvement scores (and drop-out rates) were reported (Wootten, Yellowlees, & McLaren, 2003). Future research should address outcomes, cost-effectiveness, and factors that contribute to nonadherence. Many believe that e-therapy should be an adjunct to clinical care and not a replacement.

Many researchers have compared videoconferencing to face-to-face therapy (Glueckauf et al., 2002; Schopp, Johnstone, & Merrell, 2000; Simpson, 2009). In all these studies, no difference was found in the therapeutic alliance or outcomes. Rees and Stone (2005) conclude that the therapeutic alliance is not compromised by the use of videoconferencing for psychotherapy, but that psychologists rated the alliance more negatively, perhaps because of a negative bias against videoconferencing or possibly because it poses a different and unfamiliar way of working with clients. Therapists are trained to observe both verbal and nonverbal cues during therapy sessions. Rees and Stone suggest that additional published effectiveness research and training of therapists in alternative delivery methods could increase their usage.

The use of videoconferencing technology in the delivery of clinical supervision has also become increasingly popular. In several studies, supervisors preferred face-to-face supervision, but videoconferencing was viewed as a cost-effective and appropriate tool, especially when discussing unpleasant or difficult topics (Simpson, 2009).

Virtual Reality Virtual reality has found a partner in the delivery of exposure therapy for the treatment of PTSD, specific phobias, and trauma-related injuries. Videotaped images or computer-generated graphics can provide the anxious client with increased exposure to the feared object. Specific phobias, such as dental phobias and fear of flying, spiders, and heights, have all been successfully treated (D. Sue, Sue, & Sue, 2006).

Developing Internet Interventions Nearly 85% of Internet users seek health-care information online (Taylor, Jobson, Winzelberg, & Abascal, 2002). People benefit from increased social support, positive role models, improved empowerment, professional support, and advocacy online just as they would in face-to-face groups. Initial research also indicates that the use of online services may actually help reduce client inhibitions about therapy (Cook & Doyle, 2002). Therapists who decide to offer their services online should not only be technologically savvy, but must educate themselves about use of the medium. Ritterband and colleagues (2003) briefly outline important steps involved in developing Internet interventions, reminding therapists that "[a]n effective face-to-face intervention is the gold standard by which an Internet intervention will ultimately be compared" (p. 530). They suggest that therapists use caution when creating such interventions and keep in mind the appropriateness of the disorder for Internet treatment; the effectiveness of Internet treatment; legal and ethical issues such as privacy, confidentiality, and credentialing; and client accessibility to the Internet, hardware issues, and other considerations. Finally, any such program must first be tested to determine feasibility, usability, and effectiveness. A list of Internet interventions is beyond the scope of this book, but interventions currently in use run the gamet from support systems for people with life-threatening illnesses to the treatment of childhood encopresis.

The future promises even more technologies and applications for behavioral health service providers. Adolescents are frequent media users and their technological skills can be a resource to help reduce stigma associated with treatment for mental disorders. Ritterband and others (2003) suggest that if the use of interactive video and colorful graphics makes treatment more fun for young people, it is more likely to be used. Clearly, Internet technologies serve a useful purpose as adjunct treatments for a variety of disorders and can be expected to increase over the coming years. Training and supervision in the use of technology for therapeutic purposes may be a good idea to increase therapist confidence and competency. Both the American Counseling Association (ACA) and the National Board for Certified Counselors (NBCC) have developed ethical guidelines for the use of cybercounseling, which are available on their websites (www.counseling.org/ethics and www.nbcc.org).

SOCIAL AND CULTURAL INFLUENCES

Some social and cultural factors have a more immediate impact, while others, such as the Healthcare and Education Reconciliation Act of 2010 signed into law by President Barack Obama, will not be fully operational for several years. Following are some of the changes occurring around us that influence the future of diagnosis and treatment planning.

Spirituality and Religion

Since the beginning of the millennium there has been a growing trend among Americans to instill more meaning into their daily lives. The virtues of gratitude, forgiveness, acceptance, mindfulness, optimism, and resilience have become household words, partially as a result of the Internet, books and periodicals, satellite radio, and, yes, even the Oprah Winfrey Network.

Increased integration of spirituality and religion into clinical practice is likely to occur as more clients want and expect this as part of holistic treatment. Therapists who are willing to address spiritual issues in session send a message that they recognize and are interested in treating the whole person. Such respect for the individual is likely to improve the alliance and increase the success of interventions as a result. Spirituality and religion, always a part of pastoral counseling programs, are now being mainstreamed into the clinical training programs in many graduate schools, because, as Sperry (2001) and Walsh (2009) note:

- Spirituality is an important part of individual and family values and concerns.
- It is consistent with an increased focus on positive psychology.
- New research reveals the positive effects of forgiveness, meditation, and spirituality on mental and physical health.
- It is part of diversity and providing culturally competent psychotherapy. Clinicians are looking for more meaning in their own lives.

There are many situations in which spirituality naturally enters into the counseling process—when discussing grief and loss, at times of crisis, when trying to make sense of life transitions, when making a concerted effort to instill meaning in life, and of course, when working with end of life issues. Therapists are honored in those moments to share that connection.

Therapists who ask about a client's spiritual history are acknowledging their clients' spiritual lives and accepting them as a whole person. Spirituality and religion may promote better

mental health, foster resilience, and provide positive coping skills. The American Medical Association suggests physicians conduct the following simple assessment when working with terminally ill patients.

- Is religion or spirituality important to you?
- Has faith been important to you at specific times in your life?
- Do you talk to someone about religious matters?
- Would you like to explore religion or spirituality with someone?

Being a spiritually attuned psychotherapist does not mean becoming an expert on religion. It does mean being open and responsive to client's spiritual concerns when they arise—from the initial intake assessment through the termination process. Readers interested in more information on this topic are referred to resources at the end of this chapter.

Multicultural Influences

The future will bring the advancement of psychotherapy around the globe with a corresponding increase in the need for multicultural competency. Hundreds of different cultures are represented in the United States alone, and thousands of cultures exist globally. In the future, more culturally sensitive counseling will be available that respects the cultural components of diagnosis and treatment of the client.

Cultural competency is expected of today's clinicians. Most have been trained with a greater sensitivity to and awareness of diversity, including an expanded definition that includes not only ethnic and cultural backgrounds but abilities, age, gender, religious and spiritual preferences, socioeconomic status, sexual orientation, and other variables. Awareness of the impact of gender and cultural background on personality and emotional health and pathology has also led to the inclusion in the *DSM-IV-TR* and other professional texts of extensive narrative material on the relationship of those variables to many of the diagnoses. (For example, particular caution must be exercised in the diagnosis of disorders like dependent personality disorder that are found much more in one gender or cultural group than in others.) The inclusion of this narrative material is indicative of an effort to help clinicians distinguish patterns reflecting cultural influences from those reflecting pathology and, when appropriate, recognize cultural differences in pathology.

Historical Influences

Historical change is another force that shapes our understanding of the diagnosis and treatment of mental disorders. The wars in Iraq and Afghanistan, a worldwide recession, increased focus on terrorism, and devastation from natural disasters leave survivors reeling from the effects of destruction on an unimaginable scale. A growing interest in the effect of trauma and stress on mental, physical, and spiritual well-being and increased interest in PTSD and brain-related disorders have resulted. Many techniques that were once considered alternative (such as meditation, relaxation, and mindfulness-based training) are now considered mainstream as randomized controlled trials back up their effectiveness with specific clients and conditions. The impact that historical change will have on future diagnosis and treatment planning, although difficult to predict, is certain to be considerable.

Political, Legislative, and Economic Influences

It is also difficult to predict the impact of political, legislative, and economic change on the funding of programs and on attitudes toward

mental illness, but these kinds of changes are just as important and just as inevitable as historical change. For example, during the Kennedy-Johnson era, funds were made available to develop a nationwide network of community mental health centers. In more recent years, we have seen a decrease in funding for these programs, and this decrease has contributed to a growing number of chronically mentally ill people being released into the community without sufficient support or follow-up care.

Rapid growth of health maintenance organizations, preferred provider organizations, and employee assistance programs, which are concerned with cost containment, have further contributed to the emphasis on brief treatment of mental disorders. Some third-party payers offer clients little choice of treatment provider, and pay little attention to the need for extended treatment for amelioration and prevention of certain mental disorders. Therefore, some people make the choice either to pay large bills themselves for psychotherapy or not receive the treatment they need.

Legislation has also contributed to a shift in who provides mental health services. For example, the number of psychiatrists has been declining, and the number of doctoral-level psychologists has not grown rapidly; at the same time, the number of mental health counselors and social workers has increased considerably, and legislation has both reflected and facilitated these trends. Moreover, current federal legislation mandates third-party payers to provide equity in annual and lifetime limits of payment for treatment of mental and physical disorders. Legislation to provide true parity in copayments, deductibles, and number of visits between mental health and other medical benefits (known as the Paul Wellstone and Pete Domenici Mental Health Parity and Addiction Act of 2008) took effect in October 2009. The bill's passage should make psychotherapy increasingly available to the

150 million Americans who have private and public health insurance. The full impact of the new national health insurance plan (the Healthcare and Education Reconciliation Act of 2010) signed into law in 2010 will not be realized for several years.

Managed care continues to be a fact of life for clinicians, with the focus maintained on cost-effective and efficient treatment. At the same time, MCOs are also becoming more user friendly, with much of the documentation, including billing, being conducted online.

The future of diagnosis and treatment clearly will be affected by many factors and will continue to evolve through research and practice as well as through clinical, biological, social, historical, legal, political, and economic learning and change. One hopes that most of this change will lead to more accurate diagnosis and more effective treatment. We have already learned a great deal, but the field of psychotherapy is in its late adolescence at best; this book alone probably covers more options for treatment than could be explored in all the doctoral dissertations and research projects that will be conducted in the next decade.

The rapid and often unpredictable changes in the field are both exciting and disconcerting. The challenge to mental health therapists is to stay aware of change, incorporate it wisely and selectively into their own therapeutic practices, and promote positive change in their professions. In so doing, they will be able to maximize the rewards that they receive from the practice of their profession and the benefits that psychotherapy can bring to their clients.

RECOMMENDED READING

Anthony, K., & Nagel, D. M. (2010). *Therapy online: A practical guide*. London, England: Sage.

Aten, J. D., & Leach, M. M. (2008). *Spirituality and the therapeutic process: A comprehensive resource from intake to termination*. Arlington, VA: American Psychological Association.

Barlow, D. H. (Ed.). (2007). *Clinical handbook of psychological disorders* (4th ed.). New York, NY: Guilford Press.

Barlow, D. H., Ellard, K. K., Fairholme, C. P., Farchione, T. J., Boisseau, C. L., Ehrenreich-May, J. T., & Allen, L. B. (2010). *Unified protocol for transdiagnostic treatment of emotional disorders: Workbook (unified transdiagnostic treatments that work)*. New York, NY: Oxford University Press.

Cashwell, C. S., & Young, J. S. (Eds.). (2005). *Integrating spirituality and religion into counseling: A guide to competent practice*. Alexandria, VA: American Counseling Association.

Fisher, J. E., & O'Donohue, W. T. (Eds.). (2010). *Practitioner's guide to evidence-based psychotherapy*. New York, NY: Springer.

Gold, J. M. (2010). *Counseling and spirituality: Integrating spiritual and clinical orientations*. Princeton, NC: Merrill.

Levant, R. F. (2005). *Report of the 2005 presidential task force on evidence-based practice*. Washington, DC: American Psychological Association.

Matsumoto, D. (Ed.). (2010). *Handbook of intercultural communication*. Washington, DC: American Psychological Association.

Morgan, O. J. (2006). *Counseling and spirituality: Views from the profession*. Boston, MA: Houghton Mifflin.

Norcross, J. C., Hogan, T. P., & Koocher, G. P. (2008). *Clinician's guide to evidence-based practice*. New York, NY: Oxford University Press.

Seligman, L. (2004). *Diagnosis and treatment planning in counseling* (3rd ed.). New York, NY: Kluwer/Plenum.

Walsh, F. (2009). *Spiritual resources in family therapy* (2nd ed.). New York, NY: Guilford Press.

Weisz, J. R., & Kazdin, A. E. (Eds.). (2010). *Evidence-based psychotherapies for children and adolescents* (2nd ed.). New York, NY: Guilford Press.

Wiederhold, B. K., Riva, G., & Kim, S. I. (2010). *Annual review of cybertherapy and telemedicine*. Fairfax, VA: IOS Press.

DSM-5 Update to *Selecting Effective Treatments,* Fourth Edition

HOW TO USE THIS CHAPTER

If you are reading these words, it is most likely with the goal of being able to link the diagnosis of mental disorders with the best evidence-based treatment practices available. The publication of the fifth edition of the *Diagnostic and Statistical Manual of Mental Disorders* (*DSM-5*) in May 2013 changed the diagnostic criteria for many disorders; created some new disorders (e.g., hoarding, binge eating disorder, skin excoriation); and removed a few disorders completely. It's not surprising if clinicians are confused!

The goal of this additional chapter to the fourth edition of *Selecting Effective Treatments* (*SET-4*) is to highlight these changes, no matter how small, in a logical and systematic manner so that readers can easily make the transition from *DSM-IV* to the new *DSM-5*.

For each diagnosis, the reader will be alerted to any changes from *DSM-IV* to *DSM-5*, given information on the implications of these changes for diagnosis and assessment, and be advised as to how these changes may affect treatment. When additional information is necessary for further clarification, the specific pages in *SET-4* or in *DSM-5* will be provided so that you can find the exact information you need to make an accurate diagnosis and informed treatment decision. This process won't be easy; after all, there are a lot of

changes in *DSM-5*! But by following this systematic process, readers will feel competent that their diagnostic skills are accurate as well as consistent with the new *DSM-5* changes—benefiting their clients and ensuring that they receive the care they deserve. Now, let's get started.

INTRODUCTION TO *DSM-5*

Over the past 60 years, the *Diagnostic and Statistical Manual of Mental Disorders* (*DSM*) published by the American Psychiatric Association (APA) has become the standard reference for mental health professionals in the United States. With the publication of the fifth edition earlier this year, *DSM-5* has become more consistent with the International Classification of Diseases (ICD, the coding system used in the United States) put out by the World Health Organization (WHO).

DSM-5 incorporates years of research about the brain, human behavior, and genetics. Thousands of experts participated in more than 160 task forces, work groups, and study groups over a 12-year period to research, measure, and conduct field trials of diagnostic criteria for the mental health disorders. In December 2012, the Board of Trustees of the American Psychiatric Association approved the final changes that now constitute *DSM-5*.

All of the additions or substantive changes to *DSM-5* were supported by research and planned with the intent to improve diagnosis and treatment, and to be able to be incorporated into routine clinical practice. According to APA, all changes were "intended to more clearly and accurately define the criteria for that mental disorder. Doing so helps to ensure that the diagnosis is accurate as well as consistent from one clinician to another—benefiting patients and the care they receive" (APA, 2013b).

These and other enhancements to *DSM-5*, such as changes in the organizational structure, use of dimensional measures, and consistency with ICD codes are planned to increase the manual's clinical utility and enhance its value for clinicians and researchers alike.

To help clinicians conceptualize and diagnose disorders, *DSM-5* is divided into three sections:

> Section I provides a basic introduction on how to use the new manual and how to diagnose using a non-axial system, and a new definition of a mental disorder as a syndrome that causes clinically significant problems with cognitions, emotion regulation, or behavior that results in dysfunctional mental functioning and is "associated with significant distress or disability in social, occupational, or other important activities" (APA, 2013a, p. 20).
>
> Section II provides 20 classifications of disorders that focus on diagnostic criteria and codes.
>
> Section III, Emerging Measures and Models, includes assessment measures, cultural formulation, an alternative model for personality disorders, and conditions for further study.

The Appendix of *DSM-5* includes highlights of the changes made from *DSM-IV* to *DSM-5*, glossaries of terms and cultural concepts of distress, and ICD-9 and ICD-10 codes.

We turn now to a more detailed look at several important changes in *DSM-5* that will impact how clinicians conceptualize the diagnosis of mental disorders: the elimination of the multiaxial system of diagnosis, the adoption of a dimensional approach to diagnosis, developmental and lifespan considerations, and the expansion of gender-related and cultural considerations.

Using a Non-Axial System

The multi-axial system has been replaced in *DSM-5* with a non-axial system that combines Axis I, Axis II, and Axis III into one diagnosis with all mental and other medical diagnoses listed together. The principal diagnosis is listed first.

In keeping with the established World Health Organization guidelines, other conditions that may be the focus of clinical attention will continue to be listed separately from the diagnosis to highlight relevant factors that affect the client's diagnosis, prognosis, or treatment, or if they best represent the client's presenting problem. This list of psychosocial and environmental problems has been expanded in *DSM-5* with additional V codes (from ICD-9) and Z codes (from ICD-10) developed by the World Health Organization as part of the International Classification of Diseases.

The Global Assessment of Functioning scale (Axis V) has also been eliminated. In its place, WHO's Disability Assessment Schedule (WHODAS) is included as a measurement of functioning in *DSM-5*'s Section III. Additional assessment measures are included in the print version of *DSM-5* and online at http://www.psychiatry.org/dsm5

DSM-5 reassures us that a multi-axial system is not required to make a diagnosis of a mental disorder, although that system has been adopted by many insurance companies and governmental agencies. The elimination of the multi-axial system brings *DSM-5* more closely in line with the World Health Organization's system of diagnosis, which separates a person's diagnosis from his or her functional status.

Dimensional Approach to Diagnosis

DSM-5 takes a more dimensional approach to diagnosis. This attitude is demonstrated in the adoption of the spectrum approach, through re-classification of disorders into internalizing and externalizing clusters, and with the increased consistency with the ICD system.

- *The spectrum approach.* In many instances, separate disorders are not really separate at all, but are actually related conditions on a continuum of behavior, with some conditions reflecting mild symptoms, while other conditions are much more severe. Consider, for example, bipolar disorders as a spectrum. Individuals can present with a range of symptoms from mild (cyclothymia), to moderate (bipolar II), or more severe (bipolar I). *DSM-5* adopts the spectrum concept for many disorders, including substance abuse, autism, and schizophrenia. Using a spectrum approach allows clinicians to consider disorders on a continuum of severity.

- *Internalizing versus externalizing clusters.* Disorders have also been reclassified into clusters of disorders based on internalizing and externalizing factors. Internalizing disorders are those in which anxiety, depression, and somatic symptoms are prevalent. Externalizing disorders have more disturbances of conduct, impulse control, and substance use.

- *Increased consistency with ICD.* Another consideration relative to reclassification of disorders in *DSM-5* was the desire to be more in line with the ICD system. For consistency in diagnosis, coding, and future research, the two organizations are moving toward a single international classification of disorders. Because they are still in use at the time of *DSM-5's* publication, it includes codes for both ICD-9 and ICD-10.

A Developmental and Lifespan Approach

When possible, the *DSM-5* chapters have been organized in keeping with a developmental focus across the lifespan. Classification ranges from the two bookends of neurodevelopmental disorders (conditions that develop early in life such as autism) to the last chapter on neurocognitive disorders that develop later in life (e.g., Alzheimer's). The chapters in between commonly manifest in adolescence and young adulthood. These disorders are then arranged according to internalizing disorders, externalizing disorders, and other disorders.

This developmental and lifespan approach is also seen within chapters, as well. As mentioned earlier, disorders that were first diagnosed in childhood are now incorporated into the overall discussion for anxiety, depressive, bipolar, and trauma-related disorders; schizophrenia; and eating disorders. As part of the lifespan developmental focus of *DSM-5*, each disorder, when appropriate, includes diagnostic criteria and specifiers that relate to childhood onset for the specific disorder.

Two new disorders included in *DSM-5* provide an important developmental bridge between the early recognition of symptoms in childhood and the diagnosis of a full-blown disorder later in life. Disruptive mood dysregulation disorder (which will be discussed later when we cover the *DSM-5* chapter on depressive disorders) focuses on the occurrence between the ages of 6 and 17 of extreme emotional dysregulation without assuming that a diagnosis of more severe magnitude will occur in adulthood. Clinicians should also be aware of attenuated psychosis syndrome, which is included in Section III, Emerging Measures and Models, as it pertains to subsyndromal symptoms of psychosis that may begin in childhood, and might be a precursor to a full-blown psychotic disorder.

Other disorders currently being studied for further consideration also may have taken root in childhood and adolescence. Internet gaming disorder, nonsuicidal self-injury, and suicidal behavior disorder are all associated, to some degree, with onset in adolescence. Clinicians who work with young people will want to refer to the relevant sections of *DSM-5* for additional information on these emerging disorders.

More Cultural and Gender Considerations in DSM-5

A welcome enhancement to *DSM-5* is the inclusion of additional gender differences and cultural considerations where appropriate throughout the text when symptoms may be informed by a client's gender, culture, race, ethnicity, religion, or geographical origin. Some of the diagnostic criteria have been made more gender sensitive and culturally sensitive, with variations in presentation provided. For example, social anxiety disorder now incorporates the fear of offending others, which may be manifested in some Asian cultures that emphasize the importance of not harming others. More cultural definitions, examples, and explanations are provided in the Appendix to help clinicians understand how clients from various cultures think and talk about psychological problems. And a comprehensive

cultural formulation interview guides clinicians through person-centered assessments that focus on background in terms of culture, race, ethnicity, religion, or geographical origin. All of the gender-related information and cultural concepts included in *DSM*-5 have been written and reviewed with the intent of improving diagnosis and treatment (APA, 2013a).

It is beyond the scope of this introduction to include a complete assessment of the evolution of the *Diagnostic and Statistical Manual of Mental Disorders*. Interested readers will find such history in the introductory pages of *DSM-5*. The takeaway message clinicians need to know to conduct a diagnosis in a non-axial system is the same guidance they have used in a multi-axial system—a comprehensive clinical assessment must include a complete bio-psychosocial assessment of factors that have contributed to, and that continue to sustain, the mental disorder. After all, the ultimate goal is to conduct an accurate diagnosis so that the appropriate evidence-based treatment can begin. This is also the goal of this book.

Organization of This Chapter

To begin, it was necessary to adopt the new *DSM-5* developmental structure for mental disorders, which reclassifies disorders into 20 chapters based on their relatedness to each other and their similarities in characteristics. As a result, disorders first diagnosed in childhood are no longer a separate chapter, having grown up, so to speak, and been dispersed into the larger family of disorders. For example, childhood trauma has been relocated to a new chapter on trauma and related disorders, autism spectrum disorder is found in the neurodevelopmental chapter, and oppositional defiant disorder (ODD) and conduct disorder form the basis for a new chapter, Disruptive, Impulse Control, and Conduct Disorders.

Some familiar disorders have been subsumed into other chapters or eliminated completely. Asperger's disorder, for example, has been subsumed into the broader diagnosis of autism spectrum disorders. Adjustment disorder has been reclassified as a trauma- or stressor-related disorder. Meanwhile, some disorders have merely changed names. Hypochondriasis, for instance, has been relabeled as "health illness anxiety." These and many other changes will be discussed in this chapter.

For ease of use, this additional chapter to *SET-4* follows the same classification of disorders as *DSM-5*, and, when applicable, notes the name changes in parentheses. Following are the 20 chapters on diagnostic criteria in *DSM-5*:

- Neurodevelopmental Disorders
- Schizophrenia Spectrum and Other Psychotic Disorders
- Bipolar and Related Disorders
- Depressive Disorders
- Anxiety Disorders
- Obsessive-Compulsive and Related Disorders
- Trauma- and Stressor-Related Disorders
- Dissociative Disorders
- Somatic Symptom and Related Disorders
- Feeding and Eating Disorders
- Elimination Disorders
- Sleep-Wake Disorders
- Sexual Dysfunctions
- Gender Dysphoria
- Disruptive, Impulse-Control, and Conduct Disorders
- Substance-Related and Addictive Disorders
- Neurocognitive Disorders
- Personality Disorders
- Medication-Induced Movement Disorders and Other Adverse Effects of Medication
- Other Conditions That May Be a Focus of Clinical Attention

We now turn to a more in-depth discussion of the 20 chapters at the heart of the *DSM-5*. We focus specifically on what has changed from *DSM-IV*, what this means for diagnosis, and the implications of these changes on the selection of effective, evidence-based treatments.

NEURODEVELOPMENTAL DISORDERS

DSM-5 replaces the chapter on disorders first diagnosed in infancy, childhood, or adolescence with a new chapter, Neurodevelopmental Disorders. These are a group of disorders that first appear in the early developmental period—generally before a child first starts school. The resulting deficits cause difficulties in personal, social, and academic functioning. Some disorders are discrete (e.g., specific learning disorder), and some disorders involve global deficits or delays (e.g., autism spectrum disorder). A few new disorders have been added to the Neurodevelopmental Disorders chapter, and some changes have been made to existing conditions.

The following list encompasses all of the neurodevelopmental disorders in *DSM-5*. Disorders that in the past would also have been first diagnosed in childhood (e.g., elimination disorders, reactive attachment disorder, feeding disorders of childhood) have been relocated to relevant chapters.

Intellectual Disabilities
- Intellectual Disability (Intellectual Developmental Disorder)
- Global Developmental Delay
- Unspecified Intellectual Disability

Communication Disorders
- Language Disorder
- Childhood-Onset Fluency Disorder (Stuttering)

- Social (Pragmatic) Communication Disorder
- Unspecified Communication Disorder

Autism Spectrum Disorder

Attention-Deficit/Hyperactivity Disorder (ADHD)

Other Specified Attention-Deficit/Hyperactivity Disorder (ADHD)

Unspecified Attention-Deficit/Hyperactivity Disorder (ADHD)

Specific Learning Disorder

Motor Disorders

- Developmental Coordination Disorder
- Stereotypic Movement Disorder
- Tic Disorders
- Other Specified Tic Disorder
- Unspecified Tic Disorder

Other Neurodevelopmental Disorder

Unspecified Neurodevelopmental Disorder

We turn now to a more detailed look at each of the neurodevelopmental disorders, focusing on changes relevant to *SET-4*.

Intellectual Disability (Formerly Mental Retardation)

Mental retardation has been renamed intellectual development disorder (IDD) in *DSM-5* to reflect changes in U.S. federal law (Public Law 111–256), which replaced the term *mental retardation* with *intellectual disability*. The criteria for IDD has changed, and people with IDD are no longer categorized solely on the basis of IQ, although IQ must be at least two standard deviations from the mean (70 or less).

IDD is characterized by deficits in cognitive abilities (e.g., problem solving, planning, reasoning, judgment) and adaptive functioning. Diagnostic criteria emphasize the importance of assessing both cognitive abilities and adaptive functioning. The severity level (mild, moderate, severe, or profound) of the intellectual disability will be determined by the person's ability to meet developmental and sociocultural standards for independence and social responsibility, not by the IQ score. A table listing IDD severity levels (mild, moderate, severe, or profound) across three different domains (conceptual, social, and practical) is included on pages 34–36 of *DSM-5*.

A great deal of comorbidity exists among the neurodevelopmental disorders. For example, children born with neurobehavioral disorder due to prenatal alcohol exposure (ND-PAE; formerly fetal alcohol syndrome) often develop mild intellectual developmental disorders (see *SET-4*, p. 51).

Global developmental delay is diagnosed if the severity level cannot be accurately determined. This diagnosis is restricted to children under the age of 5. If the degree of intellectual disability cannot be determined, unspecified intellectual disability would be the diagnosis.

In general, treatment strategies for IDD that take a developmental approach are most likely to be successful. Individualized treatment plans should involve the family, begin at an early age, and continue into adulthood. Refer to pages 49–52 of *SET-4* for specific information on assessment and treatment strategies for IDD.

Communication Disorders

The criteria remain the same for the communication disorders in *DSM-5*, with the exception of language disorder, which combines expressive and mixed-expressive language disorders from *DSM-IV* into one disorder, and the addition of social (pragmatic) communication disorder, which is discussed next. Overall, *DSM-5* includes the following communication disorders:

- language
- speech sound disorder (formerly phonological disorder)

- childhood onset fluency disorder (stuttering)
- social (pragmatic) communication disorder
- unspecified communication disorder

Social (pragmatic) communication disorder is a new condition. Children diagnosed with this disorder have deficits in the social use of verbal and nonverbal communication, including the following:

- using communication appropriately for social purposes
- matching communication to the needs of the situation (e.g., speaking differently in a library than at home)
- understanding rules for conversing (e.g., using nonverbal signals to regulate interaction)
- difficulty making inferences if something is not stated explicitly

If restricted repetitive behaviors, interests, and activities (RRBs) are present, then social communication disorder cannot be diagnosed. Some children diagnosed with pervasive developmental disorder not otherwise specified (PDD-NOS) under *DSM-IV* may now meet the criteria for social communication disorder in *DSM-5*.

Autism Spectrum Disorder

With the publication of *DSM-5* comes the integration of four disorders into the broad category of Autism Spectrum Disorder. Autistic disorder, Asperger's disorder, childhood disintegrative disorder, and PDD-NOS have been combined into a single category in recognition of the fact that reliability of distinguishing between these groups had been poor and there is no research to support maintaining them as separate and distinct disorders. The following new diagnostic criteria are intended to improve reliability and decrease complexity of diagnosis (e.g., *DSM-5* has 11 different ways to meet the diagnostic criteria, whereas *DSM-IV* reportedly allowed 2,027 diagnostic possibilities).

The new diagnostic criteria for autism spectrum disorder are characterized by the presence of the following:

- Deficits in social communication and interaction in multiple domains, including:
  - deficits in social interactions (e.g., lack of reciprocity in conversation)
  - problems with nonverbal communication skills (e.g., lack of eye contact, body language)
  - difficulty understanding relationships (e.g., creating, maintaining, and understanding nuances in behavior)
- Restricted repetitive behaviors, interests, and activities (RRBs) such as:
  - repetitive motor movement (head banging, flapping, or rocking)
  - ritualized behavior (verbal or nonverbal)
  - unusually strong interests in unusual objects or perseveration
  - heightened sensitivity to sensory stimulation (wind, pain, sound, smell, touch)

Severity level for autism spectrum disorder is determined along a continuum, on the basis of degree of impairment for social communication impairments and RRBs separately, according to the following degree:

- Level 1 (requiring support)
- Level 2 (requiring substantial support)
- Level 3 (requiring very substantial support)

Under this new dimensional approach to diagnosis, some people on the autism spectrum show mild symptoms, while others have much more severe symptoms (indicated by documentation of Level 3). Interested readers should refer to *DSM-5* for a matrix of severity for autism spectrum disorder (APA, 2013a, p. 52).

A Note About Asperger's

The *DSM-5* Childhood and Adolescent Disorders Work Group recommended the use of dimensions of severity instead of a separate diagnosis for Asperger's disorder. Subsuming Asperger's disorder into the overall autism spectrum has been one of the most, if not *the* most, controversial change in *DSM-5*. According to the American Psychiatric Association, the decision was made after considerable research on diagnostic criteria, outcomes, course, etiology, neurocognitive profile, and treatment, among others. Concerns raised by this change include the possibility of increased stigma as people with Asperger's are conceptualized as being on the autism spectrum. Conversely, increased services may now be available to meet the needs of children and adults who in the past may have been denied services because they did not meet the diagnostic criteria set down in *DSM-IV*. The complete impact of the change to a dimensional assessment approach based on verbal language abilities, social interaction, intelligence, and independent living capacity may prove to be a positive change, particularly for children. It seems possible that adults who were previously diagnosed with Asperger's may not benefit as much, although the *DSM-5* also clearly states that "Individuals with a well-established *DSM-IV* diagnosis of autistic disorder, Asperger's disorder, or pervasive developmental disorder not otherwise specified should be given the diagnosis of autism spectrum disorder" (APA, 2013a, p. 51) (*DSM-5* Childhood and Adolescent Disorders Work Group, 2010; Frazier et al., 2012; Mao & Yen, 2010).

Differential diagnosis for autism spectrum disorder rules out Rett syndrome, which may share some of the same symptoms as autism spectrum disorder, but not all. If RRBs are absent, social communication disorder would be diagnosed rather than autism spectrum disorder. This discussion of criteria for autism spectrum disorder replaces the discussion of pervasive developmental disorders found on pages 55–64 of *SET-4*. Preferred therapist characteristics, intervention strategies, and overall treatment recommendations remain largely the same.

Attention-Deficit/Hyperactivity Disorder (ADHD)

The diagnostic criteria for ADHD in *DSM-5* remain largely the same as in *DSM-IV-TR*. Eighteen symptoms are provided, along with the requirement that at least six symptoms in one domain must be observed for diagnosis. A change in the *DSM-5* diagnostic criteria for ADHD allows the disorder to be diagnosed at any point across the lifespan, in adults as well as children. Twenty years of research indicates that many adults have the symptoms of ADHD even though they were not diagnosed in childhood. To diagnose older adolescents and adults, the requirement for onset of symptoms prior to the age of 7 has been loosened to require that five impulsive, inattentive, or hyperactive symptoms were present before the age of 12 (APA, 2013a). Other changes in the *DSM-5* section on ADHD include the provision of adult examples and the requirement that several symptoms must be found in each setting. Other changes include:

- ADHD subtypes are now referred to as specifiers.
- A co-occurring diagnosis with autism spectrum disorder is now allowed.
- The cutoff for symptoms for adult diagnosis of ADHD is set at five symptoms rather than the six symptoms required for a younger person.

The prevalence of ADHD in adults is 4.4%. A recent longitudinal study published in the journal *Pediatrics* found that 30% of adults who were diagnosed with ADHD as children continued to have the disorder at the age of 27. In addition, the suicide rate for adults who had childhood ADHD was 5 times higher than for adults who did not have childhood ADHD (Barbaresi et al., 2013).

Assessment and treatment options for adult ADHD include cognitive therapy and coaching in time-management and life skills. Adults also benefit from finding ways to work around specific problems they face—for example, creating a place for keys for those who lose keys, or setting out clothes the night before if being late to work is an issue. Cognitive behavior therapy (CBT) should always be recommended before resorting to medication management. Research indicates that CBT in conjunction with medication is more effective than stimulant medication alone for the treatment of ADHD in adults (Montano, 2004). Mindfulness-based cognitive therapy has also been found to be helpful. Assessment and treatment options for childhood ADHD remain the same as outlined on pages 64–72 of *SET-4*—mainly a multimodal treatment strategy that combines parent training with individual counseling for the child, along with medication management if needed.

Specific Learning Disorder

DSM-5 broadens the *DSM-IV* criteria to embrace distinct disorders that impede the acquisition of one or more of the following academic skills: oral language, reading, written language, or mathematics. For each disorder, the severity level of mild, moderate, or severe must be specified.

Motor Disorders

Developmental coordination disorder, stereotypic movement disorder, and tic disorders have been subsumed under the broader category of Motor Disorders in *DSM-5*. Coded specifiers for each type of disorder are included along with diagnostic criteria, prevalence rates, and differential diagnosis. The tic criteria have been standardized across all of the disorders in Chapter 1. Stereotypic movement disorder has been more clearly differentiated from body-focused repetitive behavior disorders that are listed in the *DSM-5* chapter on obsessive-compulsive disorder.

We now move from the neurodevelopmental disorders to a new chapter in *DSM-5*, Schizophrenia Spectrum and Other Psychotic Disorders.

SCHIZOPHRENIA SPECTRUM AND OTHER PSYCHOTIC DISORDERS

DSM-5 takes a spectrum approach to schizophrenia and other psychotic disorders, with all of the disorders being defined by the presence of the following five domains: (1) delusions, (2) hallucinations, (3) disorganized thinking (or speech), (4) disorganized or abnormal motor behavior, and (5) negative symptoms. Persons are diagnosed on the spectrum according to the number and degree of deficits, ranging from schizotypal personality disorder, a relatively mild personality disorder, to schizophrenia, in which hallucinations and delusions are prominent. The presence or absence of mood symptoms along with psychosis has prognostic value and can be used to guide treatment.

The relocation of these disorders near the beginning of the *DSM-5* indicates the strong relationships with neurocognitive disorders, and the likelihood of a strong genetic link among the psychotic disorders (see Chapter 9, Disorders Involving Impairment in Awareness of Reality, on page 403 of *SET-4*). Readers need to be aware of some small changes that impact the diagnosis of psychotic disorders in the schizo-phrenia spectrum, although treatment recom-mendations remain the same as detailed on pages 413–417 of *SET-4*.

The following list provides an outline for the new *DSM-5* chapter on Schizophrenia Spectrum and Other Psychotic Disorders. A detailed explanation of changes and the implications for assessment, diagnosis, and treatment follows.

- schizotypal (personality) disorder
- delusional disorder
- brief psychotic disorder
- schizophreniform disorder
- schizophrenia
- schizoaffective disorder
- substance/medication-induced psychotic disorder
- psychotic disorder due to another medical condition
- catatonia associated with another mental disorder
- catatonic disorder due to another medical condition
- unspecified catatonia
- other specified schizophrenia spectrum and other psychotic disorder
- unspecified schizophrenia spectrum and other psychotic disorder

Schizotypal (Personality) Disorder

Considered to be on the mild side of the schizo-phrenia spectrum, schizotypal personality dis-order is listed in this chapter in *DSM-5*, although the criteria and text remain in the chapter on personality disorders. No changes have been made to schizotypal personality dis-order from *DSM-IV*.

Delusional Disorder

A hallmark of this disorder is the lack of impair-ment in areas of functioning. Indeed, persons with delusional disorder may appear to be quite normal in appearance and behavior, until they begin to discuss their delusional ideas. In *DSM-5*, "with bizarre content" is now a course specifier, and the requirement that delusions must be non-bizarre has been lifted (refer to page 421 of *SET-4* for a refresher on bizarre and non-bizarre delusions). Differential diagnosis is aided by new exclusion criteria that state that symptoms must not be better explained by con-ditions such as obsessive-compulsive disorder or body dysmorphic disorder with absent insight/delusional beliefs (APA, 2013a). Shared delu-sional disorder (pas de deux) has been eliminated from *DSM-5*. If the diagnosis meets the criteria for delusional disorder, then that diagnosis is made. If the criteria for delusional disorder are not met but shared beliefs are present, the diag-nosis would be: other specified schizophrenia spectrum and other psychotic disorder.

Brief Psychotic Disorder and Schizophreniform Disorder

Sudden onset of psychotic symptoms with re-turn to normal within a month is considered to be a brief psychotic disorder. If the disorder con-tinues for 1 month or longer, it is diagnosed as schizophreniform disorder. Both disorders share the same diagnostic criteria as schizophrenia and generally differ only in terms of duration.

Schizophrenia

Two major changes have been made in the criteria for the diagnosis of schizophrenia. The first is the elimination of two symptoms in Cri-terion A that were found to have poor reliability and nonspecificity (e.g., bizarre delusions and Schneiderian first-rank auditory hallucinations). Instead, *DSM-5* now requires two Criterion A symptoms to be present for the diagnosis of schizophrenia. In addition, the person must have at least one of the following core positive symptoms: delusions, hallucinations, or disorganized speech.

The subtypes of schizophrenia have also been removed. It is no longer necessary to distinguish among the paranoid, disorganized, undifferentiated and residual, or catatonic types. These distinctions were found to be lacking in diagnostic stability, reliability, and validity, and were not predictive of treatment response or longitudinal course. Instead, *DSM-5* offers a dimensional approach to schizophrenia and the psychotic disorders that allows clinicians to rate severity of core symptoms and discern client behavior on a spectrum. Although catatonia was removed as a subtype of schizophrenia, it remains as a specifier.

A Note About Attenuated Psychosis Syndrome

It is a well-known fact that early diagnosis and treatment of symptoms of psychosis improve long-term prognosis. However, the benefits must be balanced with consideration of any possible negative effects of early treatment such as stigma or overprescription of antipsychotics. *DSM-5* Section III subsection Conditions for Further Study includes conditions that with further research may become full-blown disorders in future updates of *DSM-5*. One of the proposed criteria sets provides symptoms and diagnostic features of attenuated psychosis, which usually first appears in adolescents and young adults. Suggestions for assessment are provided on page 411 of *SET-4*.

Schizoaffective Disorder

This disorder has long been considered to be a bridge between a bipolar or mood disorder and schizophrenia, with people having symptoms of depression or mania as well as psychotic symptoms. These symptoms may occur concurrently or at different points in the duration of the disorder. *DSM-5* now looks at schizoaffective disorder longitudinally, across the course and duration of the disorder, and clarifies that a mood disorder must remain for "most of the time" after Criterion A has been met. This new criterion in *DSM-5* should improve the clinician's ability to make an accurate differential diagnosis that rules out schizophrenia or a bipolar or depressive disorder. Refer to page 425 of *SET-4* for more details on diagnosis and treatment of schizoaffective disorder.

Catatonia

While no longer a subtype of schizophrenia, *DSM-5* allows for catatonia to be included as a specifier for any psychotic, bipolar, or depressive disorder; as a separate diagnosis in the context of another medical condition; or as another unspecified disorder. The criteria remain the same as in *DSM-IV*; a major difference in *DSM-5* is that all contexts require the presence of three catatonic symptoms out of a total of 12 possible symptoms (e.g., waxy flexibility, negativism, posturing, mimicking others' speech or movements, lack of response, agitation, grimacing, repetitive movements, catalepsy, stupor).

BIPOLAR AND RELATED DISORDERS

The diagnosis and treatment of mood disorders has been refined in *DSM-5* by dividing the mood disorders into two distinct chapters: a chapter on bipolar and related disorders (bipolar I and II, cyclothymic disorder, and four new disorders), and a chapter on depressive disorders. Disruptive mood dysregulation disorder (DMDD) is a new diagnosis for children under the age of 18 who present with extreme emotional and behavioral dysregulation. While DMDD may fit the symptoms of either a bipolar disorder or a depressive disorder, its description is included in the chapter on depressive disorders to be discussed later.

Bipolar I, Bipolar II, and Cyclothymia

DSM-5 includes 6 pages of course specifiers for bipolar and related disorders. Many specifiers are the same as in *DSM-IV* (e.g., "with rapid cycling," "with seasonal pattern"). New specifiers have been made in the bipolar disorders in *DSM-5* to facilitate earlier and more accurate diagnosis. Diagnosis of mania has been enhanced with the inclusion of changes in "activity and energy level," not just changes in mood. A new specifier, "with mixed features," replaces the mixed episode criterion that was found in *DSM-IV*. The specifier can be applied to episodes of depression (in either major depressive disorder [MDD] or bipolar disorders) when features of mania or hypomania are present, or to hypomania or mania when depressive features are present. The distinction is that the "mixed episode" specifier in *DSM-IV* required the person to meet the full criteria for both mania and a major depressive episode concurrently. That is no longer the case.

Other Bipolar Disorders

There are many variations of bipolar disorder, in addition to bipolar I, bipolar II, and cyclothymia. Bipolar disorder NOS was a frequently used diagnosis in *DSM-IV* that has been replaced with the following four diagnoses to specify the appropriate type of bipolar disorder that is being presented. Readers are reminded that in children, a diagnosis of disruptive mood dysregulation disorder (which will be discussed later) will generally be more appropriate than the diagnosis of bipolar disorder.

1. substance/medication-induced bipolar and related disorder
2. bipolar and related disorder due to another medical condition

3. other specified bipolar and related disorder
4. unspecified bipolar and related disorder

Substance/medication-induced bipolar and related disorder would be the appropriate diagnosis if there is evidence that the symptoms of bipolar disorder occurred during or soon after substance intoxication or withdrawal, or after the exposure to a medication that is known to produce the symptoms of bipolar disorder. In such situations, the substance ingested would be listed along with a specifier indicating whether onset was during intoxication or during withdrawal.

Bipolar and related disorder due to another medical condition would be the appropriate diagnosis if the manic, hypomanic, or mixed symptoms occur as a direct pathophysiological result of another medical condition. The medical conditions most commonly associated with the development of a bipolar disorder are Cushing's disease, hyperthyroidism, lupus, multiple sclerosis, stroke, and traumatic brain injury (APA, 2013a).

Other specified bipolar and related disorder can be diagnosed in the following four distinct ways: (1) persons with a history of a major depressive disorder who now meet all but the duration criterion for hypomania (i.e., at least 4 consecutive days); (2) persons who meet the duration criterion but have too few symptoms of hypomania to meet the overall criteria for bipolar II; (3) the presence of a hypomanic episode without any history of major depressive disorder (MDD); and (4) short-duration cyclothymia (less than 24 months) in which hypomania and depressive symptoms are present for most days but do not meet the full criteria for MDD, mania, hypomania, or a psychotic disorder. (The duration criterion is reduced to less than 12 months for children and adolescents.) In the presence of this constellation of symptoms, other specified bipolar and related disorder would be the diagnosis.

"Unspecified bipolar and related disorder" refers to the presentation of symptoms of a bipolar disorder that do meet the full criteria, but in which distress in social, occupational, or other areas of functioning is present. Insufficient information may be available or the clinician may choose not to specify the reason the criteria were not met.

Anxious Distress Specifier

Anxious distress is a new specifier to be considered in all mood disorders, including bipolar and related disorders. "Anxious distress" refers to persons exhibiting anxiety symptoms above and beyond the diagnostic criteria for a mood disorder (bipolar or depressive). Following is a description of the anxious distress specifier that is applicable to bipolar disorders and depressive disorders.

To qualify for the anxious distress specifier, a minimum of two of the following symptoms must be present most days during the current or most recent period of mania, hypomania, or depression (APA, 2013a).

- tension or feeling wound up
- restlessness
- inability to concentrate
- dread of something terrible happening
- fear of losing control

Severity levels—mild (two symptoms), moderate (three symptoms), moderate to severe (four or five symptoms), or severe (four or five symptoms with motor agitation)—should be assessed for anxious distress.

A great deal of research indicates that the presence of anxiety in conjunction with depression can be destabilizing and may potentially increase the risk of suicidality, longer duration of illness, or lack of response to treatment. Thus, the anxious distress specifier must be accurately assessed, along with additional assessment of suicidal risk factors, including potential plans, thoughts, or history, in persons who exhibit moderate to severe levels of anxious distress. Relevant intervention strategies for the treatment of bipolar disorders can be found on pages 176–181 of *SET-4*. Assessment of suicidal risk can be facilitated with the information contained in the Appendix of *SET-4* (pages 453–460). Suicide assessment should also be kept in mind when making a diagnosis of major depressive disorder, to which we now turn.

DEPRESSIVE DISORDERS

The *DSM-5* chapter on depressive disorders includes two new disorders: (1) premenstrual dysphoric disorder (previously in the Appendix of *DSM-IV*), and (2) disruptive mood dysregulation disorder (DMDD), which is specific to children who present with extreme irritability and emotional dysregulation. Depression is conceptualized in a new way. Dysthymia has been combined with chronic major depressive disorder and is now referred to as "persistent depressive disorder." Also new in *DSM-5* is the elimination of the bereavement exclusion criterion from the diagnosis of major depressive disorder. Following is a list of depressive disorders, followed by a more detailed explanation of specific changes from *DSM-IV* to *DSM-5*.

- Disruptive Mood Dysregulation Disorder
- Major Depressive Disorder
- Persistent Depressive Disorder (Dysthymia)
- Premenstrual Dysphoric Disorder
- Substance/Medication-Induced Depressive Disorder

- Depressive Disorder Due to Another Medical Condition
- Other Specified Depressive Disorder
- Unspecified Depressive Disorder

Disruptive Mood Dysregulation Disorder

Persistent irritability disproportionate to the situation and unrelenting over a 12-month period is the hallmark of disruptive mood dysregulation disorder, a new *DSM-5* disorder that affects children over the age of 6.

The intent of this disorder is to distinguish children with the milder DMDD from the diagnosis of bipolar disorder, childhood onset. Overall, research does not indicate that the preponderance of children diagnosed and treated for bipolar disorder actually go on to develop bipolar disorder as adults. In fact, longitudinal studies indicate that the majority of children treated for symptoms of intense irritability and disruptive behavior actually develop unipolar depression or anxiety disorders as young adults. In effect, bipolar disorder occurs in less than 1% of children before the onset of puberty. Since little research is available on the long-term effects of psychotropic medications on young brains that are not fully developed, the intent of this disorder diagnosis is to reduce the number of such prescriptions that are given to young children. For a complete discussion of both sides of the controversy surrounding the diagnosis of bipolar disorder in children, refer to Leibenluft 2011 and Washburn, West, and Heil 2011.

Symptoms of DMDD include:

- Severe chronic temper outbursts, verbal aggression, or emotional storms occur that are out of proportion to the situation.
- The outbursts occur an average of three or more times per week.
- They occur for a period of 12 or more months.

- Persistent irritability does not remit when stressors go away, or between episodes, and is observable by others (e.g., friends, family, teachers).
- Irritability is observed in at least two out of three settings (home, school, with peers) and is severe in at least one of these locations.
- The diagnosis cannot be made prior to the age of 6, nor after the age of 18.
- Historical assessment finds that these symptoms were present prior to the age of 10.
- There has been no prior diagnosis of a mania or euphoric mood lasting longer than 1 day.
- The behaviors do not occur as a result of a major depressive or other disorder such as anxiety, persistent depressive disorder, or posttraumatic stress disorder (PTSD).
- The disorder is not better accounted for by a substance or a medical or neurological condition.

DMDD is a severe disorder. Approximately 50% of children who present with these symptoms will continue to have chronic irritability 1 year later. The behavior is extreme enough to cause disruption in peer and family relationships, difficulties in school, and problems maintaining relationships. Dangerous behaviors such as aggression, suicide attempts, and self-harming are common, as is hospitalization. The presence of co-occurring disorders is also high, so careful assessment is necessary to distinguish DMDD from childhood onset of bipolar disorder, oppositional defiant disorder (ODD), ADHD, and intermittent explosive disorder. Oppositional defiant disorder is most frequently comorbid with DMDD. Intermittent explosive disorder, which has a duration of 3 months with remittance between episodes, should not be diagnosed concurrently with DMDD, which has a 12-month minimum duration and remains persistent over the 12-month period.

The behavior must also be inconsistent with the child's age and developmental level and cannot be better explained by autism spectrum disorder, PTSD, or pervasive developmental disabilities. If the child has already been diagnosed with bipolar disorder, intermittent explosive disorder, or oppositional defiant disorder, a diagnosis of DMDD would not be appropriate (APA, 2013a).

Major Depressive Disorder

With two exceptions, the diagnosis and treatment of the classic major depressive disorder remain the same as described on pages 156–165 of *SET-4*. The exceptions are the addition of the "with mixed features" specifier (as previously described in the chapter on bipolar disorders) and the elimination of the bereavement exclusion, which we address next.

The Bereavement Exclusion A major change in the diagnosis of major depressive disorder is the removal of the bereavement exclusion, which prevented a person who was grieving from being diagnosed with major depressive disorder in the first 2 months following the death of a loved one. Under the old *DSM-IV* criteria, a person would have been considered to be grieving rather than depressed. APA research teams discovered, however, that persons who had experienced a major depressive episode prior to a major loss were far more likely to have a recurrent depressive episode after a loss, and the bereavement exclusion was preventing them from being accurately diagnosed and receiving the appropriate care. Second, removal of the bereavement exclusion is an acknowledgment of the fact that grief does not end after only 2 months. Grief is a far more complicated

process that must take into account multiple factors, including relationship, age, and cause of death. Grieving the loss of a spouse after 50 years of marriage, for example, may never be resolved, and certainly not within the 2-month period of time allotted for grief.

DSM-5 includes a comprehensive footnote (APA, 2013a, p. 161) to clarify the purpose of the bereavement exclusion and to help clinicians distinguish between symptoms of grief and loss and the presence of a major depressive episode (MDE), while also understanding that both may be present. When grief occurs in conjunction with an MDE, symptoms may be more severe and poorer outcomes may result, including increased risk for suicidality and risk of developing persistent complex bereavement disorder, a condition for further study that can be found in *DSM-5* Section III.

New Specifiers As described earlier in the bipolar disorders section, an "anxious distress" specifier has been added in *DSM-5* for all depressive disorders, and the specifier "with mixed features" allows for the possibility of manic features in a person diagnosed with unipolar depression.

Persistent Depressive Disorder (Dysthymia)

Dysthymic disorder, which appeared in *DSM-IV*, has been combined with chronic major depressive disorder to create this broader category of persistent depressive disorder (PDD). The hallmark of this disorder is a depressed mood that lasts most of the day, for most days, over a 2-year period (1 year for children and adolescents). The chronicity of this disorder can be identified through the use of course specifiers that are similar to those for major depressive disorder. Risk factors for childhood onset of PDD include parental loss or separation. The early onset specifier is given if the disorder is diagnosed prior to the age of 21.

Premenstrual Dysphoric Disorder

It has been estimated that 75% of women experience minor symptoms premenstrually, with 20% to 30% experiencing premenstrual disorder. Only 2% to 10% of women, however, are expected to meet the criteria for the more severe premenstrual dysphoric disorder (PMDD) associated with clinically significant distress. The criteria for PMDD are substantially the same as they appeared in the Appendix to *DSM-IV*, requiring 5 of the following 11 symptoms to be necessary for diagnosis:

1. feelings of hopelessness, sadness, or low self-esteem
2. feeling tense or anxious
3. emotional lability that includes tearfulness
4. irritability, often accompanied by increased interpersonal conflict
5. difficulty concentrating
6. tiredness, lethargy, or lack of energy
7. changes in appetite, cravings, or binge eating
8. decreased interest in activities
9. sleep disturbances—oversleeping or insomnia
10. feelings of being overwhelmed
11. headaches, bloating, breast tenderness or other physical symptoms

The symptoms must be present most months in the previous 12-month period, appearing in the week prior to the onset of menses, and receding after menses begins. Symptoms may be as severe as major depressive disorder, although lasting for less than a week. The symptoms must cause marked disruption in social or occupational functioning during the affected week.

Assessment of PMDD begins by charting symptoms for a 2-month period to confirm the presence of a cyclical pattern. The chart should be maintained daily, and may include self-report and/or input from a person who lives with the woman.

PMDD must be distinguished from mental disorders made worse premenstrually. The symptoms cannot be a result of medication or substance use, nor an exacerbation of a current medical condition (e.g., hyperthyroidism). If oral contraceptives are used, PMDD cannot be diagnosed unless symptoms continue and are as severe when contraceptives are removed. Most cases of PMDD worsen with age and then subside with the onset of menopause (APA, 2013a).

Treatment for PMDD focuses on controlling or minimizing symptoms. Women should not suffer because of fears about stigma. Antidepressants and anxiolytics administered during the period between ovulation and onset of menses have been shown to reduce emotionality and other symptoms. Selective serotonin reuptake inhibitors (SSRIs) are considered to be the first line of treatment for PMDD (Cunningham et al., 2009). The most studied treatments have been the use of birth control pills to suppress ovulation and level out hormones over time. Vitamins and supplements such as vitamin B6, calcium, and magnesium have been shown to help in some studies, but more research is necessary. Other treatments include herbal remedies (to reduce irritability, mood swings, and headaches; aerobic exercise to improve mood and energy; lifestyle changes such as relaxation; and cognitive therapy to help reduce stress (Pearlstein & Steiner, 2008).

Substance/Medication-Induced Depressive Disorder

The use of alcohol or illicit drugs can result in development of depression while using the substance or during the withdrawal period. Similarly, many medications prescribed to treat physical and psychological conditions, including antidepressants, may also have the untoward side effect of causing depression (APA, 2013a). Antidepressants are generally considered safe; however, the suicide risk for young adults ages 18 to 24 who begin taking antidepressants was large enough for the Food and Drug Administration (FDA) to issue a black-box warning to advocate careful monitoring of clients in this age group for treatment-emergent suicidal ideation (Friedman & Leon, 2007; Seligman & Reichenberg, 2012).

Depressive Disorder Due to Another Medical Condition

Stroke, Parkinson's disease, Huntington's disease, lupus, and Cushing's disease are all illnesses that have been linked with depression. Some symptoms may be episodic and may go away after the medical disorder is treated. There is also a clear connection between some severe medical disorders and suicide, especially in the weeks following the initial diagnosis.

Other Specified Depressive Disorder

When criteria for a specific depressive disorder are not completely met, one of the following designations can be considered: recurrent brief depression (does not meet duration criterion), short-duration depressive episode (in situations without a prior history of mood disorder), and depressive episode with insufficient symptoms (depressed affect and at least one other symptom).

Unspecified Depressive Disorder

This diagnosis is given when depression is present and causes significant problems in social, occupational, or other important areas of functioning, but does not meet the full criteria for any of the depressive disorders listed earlier, and the clinician does not wish to specify or does not have enough information to give a more specific diagnosis.

Additional Specifiers for Depressive Disorders

DSM-5 maintains all of the specifiers for depressive disorder that were found in *DSM-IV* (e.g., "with melancholic features," "with atypical features," "with psychotic features," "with catatonia," "with paripartum onset," "with seasonal pattern," "in partial remission versus in full remission," and specifiers of severity. As mentioned earlier in the discussion of bipolar disorders, *DSM-5* also adds an "anxious distress" specifier to all mood disorders, along with an assessment of current severity level.

ANXIETY DISORDERS

Many reclassifications have affected the *DSM-IV* chapter on anxiety disorders. As mentioned earlier, in keeping with the developmental lifespan approach of *DSM-5*, several disorders previously located in the children's section of *DSM-IV* (e.g., separation anxiety disorder and selective mutism) have been reclassified as anxiety disorders, although the criteria remain much the same. Some disorders previously considered to be anxiety disorders (e.g., acute stress disorder and posttraumatic stress disorders) have been moved to a new chapter, Trauma- and Stressor-Related Disorders, reflecting the closeness of the relationships among them.

Minimal changes have been made to the criteria for the diagnosis of anxiety disorders, with the exception of separate criteria for agoraphobia and panic disorder, and the addition of a "performance only" specifier for social anxiety disorder. To summarize, the *DSM-5* chapter related to anxiety disorders now includes the following disorders:

- separation anxiety disorder
- selective mutism
- specific phobia
- social anxiety disorder (formerly social phobia)
- panic disorder
- panic attack
- agoraphobia
- generalized anxiety disorder
- substance/medication–induced anxiety disorder
- anxiety disorder due to another medical condition
- other specified anxiety disorder
- unspecified anxiety disorder

Assessment, preferred therapist characteristics, and treatment strategies for the anxiety disorders remain the same as outlined in *SET-4*. The criteria for agoraphobia, specific phobia, and social anxiety disorder no longer require that the person recognize that the anxiety is unreasonable or excessive. Instead, and after accounting for cultural context, the anxiety must be out of proportion to the actual danger or threat imposed by the situation. The requirement of a 6-month duration is now extended to all ages in *DSM-5*, with the intent of reducing the overdiagnosis of short-lived fears or anxieties. We turn now to highlights of the changes included in this chapter.

Separation Anxiety and Selective Mutism

Separation anxiety disorder and selective mutism have been reclassified in *DSM-5* as anxiety disorders. The criteria for these two distinct disorders remain the same; the only difference is their relocation to this chapter from the *DSM-IV*

category of disorders that are first diagnosed in childhood and adolescence.

Specific Phobia

The core criteria of specific phobias remain largely unchanged, with the addition of the broadbrush criteria change for all anxiety disorders (minimum 6-month duration and the deletion of the requirement that the person must recognize that the anxiety is excessive). The specific types of phobias (see pg. 210 of *SET-4*) are now considered to be specifiers.

Social Anxiety Disorder

This was previously referred to as "social phobia." The criteria for *DSM-5* social anxiety disorder remain largely the same, with the adoption of the following changes:

Minimum duration of 6 months applies to all ages.

The requirement that the person recognize that the fear or anxiety is excessive has been dropped.

The "generalized" specifier has been replaced with a "performance only" specifier, in recognition of a distinct subset of social anxiety disorder that relates specifically to people whose anxiety response is specific to public speaking or performing in front of an audience. Age of onset and etiology appear to be different for the "performance only" specifier, which has implications for assessment and treatment recommendations as well.

Panic Disorder

The occurrence of panic disorder and that of agoraphobia have been separated in *DSM-5*. Previous options for diagnosis were panic disorder without agoraphobia, panic disorder with agoraphobia, and agoraphobia without history of panic disorder. *DSM-5* has replaced this with two distinct disorders: (1) panic disorder and (2) agoraphobia. Persons with both panic disorder and agoraphobia would now receive two diagnoses, in recognition of the fact that many people with agoraphobia do not experience symptoms of panic. The diagnostic criteria for agoraphobia now require two or more agoraphobic situations prior to diagnosis, as well as the changes noted earlier (the anxiety must be of a minimum 6 months' duration, and be determined by the clinician to be excessive).

The essential features of panic disorder (discussed on pages 197–202 of *SET-4*) remain largely the same, although type descriptions of situationally bound (in anticipation of a specific trigger), situationally predisposed (usually associated with a specific trigger), and unexpected/uncued (unrelated to any obvious trigger) have been simplified into two type descriptions: unexpected and expected. Recurrent panic attacks that occur in conjunction with thunderstorms, for example, would be referred to as "expected."

The feelings of panic are caused by fear and stress, and commonly co-occur in other *DSM-5* disorders as well. Thus panic attacks can serve as a diagnostic indicator of severity, course, and prognosis across a variety of disorders, and can be listed as a specifier for any *DSM-5* disorder.

Agoraphobia

Agoraphobia has been unlinked from panic disorder and is now a separate diagnosis under *DSM-5*. The criteria for agoraphobia include fear and anxiety of being in public (closed spaces, public transportation), fear of being unable to escape, avoidance of such situations, or requiring a companion. The fear must be persistent (lasting 6 months or more), must be out of proportion to the danger that is present, and cannot be accounted for by another psychological or medical disorder. If both panic and agoraphobia are present, both would be listed.

OBSESSIVE-COMPULSIVE AND RELATED DISORDERS

Obsessive-compulsive disorder (OCD) has become the 10th leading cause of disability in the developed countries. It seems fitting that this debilitating and chronic disorder is the focus of its own chapter in *DSM-5*. In keeping with the reorganization of *DSM-5* to locate related disorders in the same chapter, body dysmorphic disorder (no longer considered to be a somatoform disorder) and trichotillomania (hair-pulling disorder) have also been moved to this chapter. Two new disorders have been added—hoarding disorder and excoriation/skin-picking disorder—and will be discussed at length here. Medication-induced obsessive-compulsive disorder and obsessive-compulsive and related disorder due to another medical condition are also included here.

Following the list of disorders comprising the new *DSM-5* chapter Obsessive-Compulsive and Related Disorders, diagnostic criteria, specifiers, and other details are provided for information that was not included in *DSM-IV*.

- obsessive-compulsive disorder
- body dysmorphic disorder
- hoarding disorder
- trichotillomania (hair-pulling disorder)
- excoriation (skin-picking) disorder
- substance/medication-induced obsessive-compulsive and related disorder
- obsessive-compulsive and related disorder due to another medical condition
- other specified obsessive-compulsive and related disorder
- unspecified obsessive-compulsive and related disorder

Obsessive-Compulsive Disorder (OCD)

Obsessive-compulsive disorder has been relocated from the anxiety disorders chapter to this new chapter in *DSM-5*. With the exception of a few new specifiers for OCD, the bulk of the criteria remain the same (refer to pages 216–221 in *SET-4*). The specifier "with poor insight" has been expanded in *DSM-5* to provide a range: good/fair insight, poor insight, or absent insight/delusional. The insight specifier should help improve differential diagnosis. For example, OCD absent insight/delusional should not be confused with a schizophrenia spectrum or other psychotic disorder. A tic-related specifier has also been added in recognition of the growing acknowledgment of the relationship between tic disorder and the development of OCD.

Body Dysmorphic Disorder

This disorder was previously considered to be one of the somatoform disorders, and is now more appropriately listed in the OCD family. Most of the criteria remain the same (refer to page 333 in *SET-4*), with the addition of a new criterion to describe repetitive thoughts or behaviors related to preoccupation with perceived defects or flaws in physical appearance. Insight specifiers (fair, poor, absent insight/delusional) have also been added. For example, a person lacking insight who completely believes that the perceived defect or appearance flaw is abnormal or disgusting would be diagnosed with body dysmorphic disorder, absent insight/delusional, instead of the former diagnosis under *DSM-IV* of delusional disorder, somatic type. Treatment strategies remain the same (e.g., habit reversal and exposure and response prevention training, CBT for milder disorders, and combination therapy with SSRIs for people who present with more severe or delusional symptoms).

Hoarding Disorder

Hoarding behavior, previously a symptom of obsessive-compulsive personality disorder in *DSM-IV*, is now considered to be a discrete disorder grounded on research-based evidence of its diagnostic validity and clinical utility (APA, 2013a). This disorder may have distinctive neurobiological correlates and is frequently associated with symptoms such as the accumulation of items and clutter that prevent the normal use of a space (for example, using the shower as a place to store boxes of clothing). The symptoms must cause significant distress or impairment in areas of functioning, and may or may not be associated with excessive acquisition. Insight specifiers (good/fair, poor, or absent insight/delusional) have been determined for hoarding disorder in an effort to improve differential diagnosis and distinguish people who hoard and lack insight from those who may have a schizophrenia spectrum or other psychotic disorder that results in accumulation of objects because of delusional beliefs.

Hoarding disorder is new to *DSM-5*. The criteria for diagnosis of this new disorder include the following:

- The person has long-standing problems with discarding (including selling, recycling, throwing away, or donating) possessions, even those that have no actual value.
- Saving items is intentional, and feelings of distress (e.g., anxiety, fear of losing important information, loss of emotional attachment to items, fear that the item will be needed later) arise at the thought of discarding the items.
- The large volume of clutter interferes with the use of "active living areas" for the purpose for which they were intended (e.g., dining room table so cluttered with papers and books that it hasn't been used for dining in months).
- Distress or impairment in social, occupational, or other important areas of functioning must be present. For

example, relationships may end because the person does not allow others inside the house because moving from room to room through piles of detritus would be untenable.

- The symptoms of hoarding must not be caused by the presence of a medical condition (e.g., brain injury).
- The disorder is not the result of a separate mental disorder (OCD, MDD, autism spectrum disorder, or others).

Specifiers for hoarding disorder include:

- *With excessive acquisition*—Approximately 80% to 90% of people who meet the criteria for this disorder will also display excessive acquisition in addition to difficulty discarding items. Excessive acquisition is defined in *DSM-5* as excessive buying, acquiring items for free (or less commonly stealing), acquiring items for which there is no space, or acquiring items that are not needed. Distress may be experienced if the person is inhibited from acquiring possessions.
- *With or without insight*—Level of insight (good or fair, poor, or absent insight/ delusional) must be specified. Good or fair insight assumes the person is aware that the hoarding behavior is excessive and causes problems. Poor insight is specified if the person mostly believes that hoarding-related behavior is not a problem, despite evidence to the contrary. Absent insight/delusional beliefs would be indicated if the person is convinced the beliefs or behaviors are not a problem.

Hoarding behavior has become increasingly common, affecting 2% to 6% of the population in the United States and Europe. The disorder is nearly three times more likely to occur in adults age 55 or older than in younger adults. Hoarding can be distinguished from "collecting," which is organized and intentional and does not result in clutter, distress, or impairment seen in hoarding disorder. Clutter, a requirement of Criterion C, is defined as: "a large group of usually unrelated or marginally related objects piled together in a disorganized fashion in spaces designed for other purposes" (APA, 2013a, p. 248). Criterion C also emphasizes that the clutter must be present in the active living areas of the home, and not just garages, sheds, basements, or other areas designed for storage. If the lack of clutter is the result of third-party intervention (professionals, family, or authorities), the person is still considered to have a hoarding disorder.

Approximately 50% of persons who develop hoarding disorder have a first-degree relative who hoards. Indecisiveness is a common trait, and many report that a traumatic or stressful event (such as the death of a loved one) precipitated the development of the disorder. As many as 75% of persons with hoarding disorder have a comorbid mood or anxiety disorder. Only 20% also qualify for a diagnosis of OCD. Hoarding behavior that is the result of a brain injury or neurodevelopmental disorder, or with gradual onset following the diagnosis of a neurocognitive disorder (e.g., Alzheimer's), would not be diagnosed as hoarding disorder.

Cognitive behavior therapy that focuses on exposure and response-prevention therapy (ERT) appears to be the best treatment for hoarding disorder, although many people refuse to participate. ERT is described on pages 219–220 of *SET-4*. Also helpful are cognitive therapy that helps people who hoard to challenge their faulty beliefs (e.g., that the possessions are valuable, that they need the items) and family involvement in treatment. The use of visualization to imagine success, mindfulness to help reduce negative psychological states, and photographs to measure progress can also be helpful. For a complete discussion of the use of exposure and response-prevention therapy for the treatment of hoarding disorder, refer to Seligman and Reichenberg, 2013.

Trichotillomania (Hair-Pulling Disorder)

The only changes from *DSM-IV* are the parenthetical inclusion of the words *hair-pulling disorder* to the name, and its relocation from the behavior and impulse control disorders to the chapter on obsessive-compulsive disorders. The criteria for this disorder have not changed from *DSM-IV* (refer to page 303 in *SET-4*).

Excoriation (Skin-Picking) Disorder

Recurrent skin-picking, most commonly on arms, face, and hands, is the focus of a new disorder in *DSM-5*. Excoriation affects 1.4% of the population, and is more common in persons with obsessive-compulsive disorder and their first-degree family members. This disorder is highly gender specific, with females constituting 75% of the people affected. While onset may occur at any age, most frequently it coincides with the onset of puberty, and may begin with a dermatological condition such as acne; it may increase in time spent, and may involve rituals. Specific criteria for excoriation (skin-picking) disorder are:

- There is recurrent skin picking that results in lesions.
- Repeated attempts to stop skin picking must have been made.
- Distress or impairment in social, occupational, or other important areas of functioning must be present. Distress may also include embarrassment, shame, and other emotions that result from the skin picking.

- The symptoms of skin picking must not be caused by the use of a drug or as the result of a medical condition.
- The disorder is not better accounted for by a separate mental disorder (e.g., delusions or hallucinations that lead the person to pick the skin during a psychotic episode), or associated with attempts at self-harm or suicide.

This disorder is highly comorbid with OCD, trichotillomania, and major depressive disorder. It may also coincide with other specified obsessive-compulsive and related disorders such as body-focused repetitive behavior disorders (nail-biting, lip-chewing), which should also be considered.

Substance/Medication-Induced Obsessive-Compulsive and Related Disorder and Obsessive-Compulsive and Related Disorder Due to Another Medical Condition

Both of these disorders were added to this chapter on OCD in recognition of the fact that many anxiety disorders listed in *DSM-IV* included the specifier "with obsessive-compulsive symptoms." In other words, this disorder reflects the reality that some medications, substances, or medical conditions can induce symptoms similar to obsessive-compulsive and related disorders. If obsessive-compulsive and related disorder due to another medical condition is diagnosed, specify if it is with OCD-like symptoms, with appearance preoccupations, with hoarding symptoms, with hair-pulling symptoms, or with skin-picking symptoms.

Other Specified and Unspecified Obsessive-Compulsive and Related Disorders

These two categories apply to symptoms that are similar to OCD but do not meet the full criteria.

Examples provided in *DSM-5* include, but are not limited to, the following:

- Body-dysmorphic-like disorder with actual flaws: A preoccupation with real flaws in physical appearance becomes obsessive and interferes with daily functioning.
- Body-dysmorphic-like disorder without repetitive behaviors: This is self-explanatory.
- Body-focused repetitive behaviors (nail-biting, lip-biting, self-pinching, cheek-chewing): These have resulted in failed attempts to extinguish or reduce the behaviors.
- Nondelusional obsessional jealousy that involves a preoccupation with thoughts that one's partner is involved in infidelity. These beliefs may lead to the performance of repetitive behaviors (checking, calling, etc.) that cause clinically significant distress and disrupt the person's life.
- *Koro*: This is an intense anxiety that the penis will recede into the body (in females the belief is about the vulva or nipples).
- *Shubo-kyofu*: This is an intense fear of having a deformity (similar to body dysmorphic disorder).
- *Jikoshu-kyofu* (olfactory reference syndrome): This is an intense fear of having a foul body odor.

Unspecified Obsessive-Compulsive and Related Disorder

This diagnosis is used in situations in which the symptoms do not meet all of the criteria of an obsessive-compulsive or related disorder and the clinician does not have sufficient information to make a more specific diagnosis.

TRAUMA- AND STRESSOR-RELATED DISORDERS

As noted earlier, this new chapter in *DSM-5* combines childhood diagnosis of reactive attachment disorder with the adjustment disorders, acute stress disorder, PTSD, and others into one chapter focused on disorders in which a stressful or traumatic life event has precipitated the onset of symptoms. Exposure to stress or trauma can result in a wide range of symptoms depending on age, previous exposure to trauma, temperament, and environmental factors. Internalizing symptoms (i.e., anxiety), externalizing symptoms (anger, aggression), or a mixture of both are possible. The heterogeneous disorders included in this chapter are the following:

- reactive attachment disorder (RAD)
- disinhibited social engagement disorder
- posttraumatic stress disorder
- acute stress disorder
- adjustment disorders
- other specified trauma- and stressor-related disorder
- unspecified trauma- and stressor-related disorder

We now turn to a discussion of each of the trauma- and stressor-related disorders with respect to any variance with *DSM-IV* and the fourth edition of *Selecting Effective Treatments*. One major change in *DSM-5* is the division of the two subtypes of reactive attachment disorder (inhibited versus disinhibited) into two distinct disorders that share the same etiology and prerequisite of social neglect (e.g., the absence of adequate caregiving). The neglect must occur before the age of 5 and limit the child's ability to form appropriate attachments. The distinction between the two disorders involves externalizing versus internalizing behavior and has implications across the lifespan.

Reactive Attachment Disorder (RAD)

The *DSM-5* criteria for RAD are the same as those in *DSM-IV-TR*, except, of course, the disinhibited subtype is no longer applied since it has become a distinct disorder. The information on diagnosis and treatment of RAD (found on pages 103–106 of *SET-4*) remains accurate and relevant. The child manifests symptoms of emotional withdrawal or inhibition toward caregivers, has limited positive affect, and rarely seeks or responds to comfort when distressed.

Disinhibited Social Engagement Disorder

The criteria for this new *DSM-5* disorder are similar to those for RAD in that the child must be at least 9 months old, the child has experienced social neglect or changes in caregivers to the point that appropriate attachments have not been formed, and the disorder is specified as persistent if it has been present for more than 12 months. In addition, to meet the criteria for this new disorder requires indiscriminate sociability with unfamiliar adults, manifested by at least two of the following:

- reduced hesitancy in approaching and interacting with unfamiliar adults
- being overly familiar with strangers (that is inconsistent with age-appropriate behavior or culture)
- lack of concern about checking back with an adult caregiver, or wandering away without supervision
- willingness to go off with an unfamiliar adult with little or no hesitation

Because social impulsivity is also a feature of ADHD, care should be taken to differentiate between the two disorders. Disinhibited social engagement disorder can also be comorbid with cognitive and language delays, stereotypies, and other conditions associated with neglect.

However, symptoms of the disorder may persist long after the conditions of neglect have been eliminated, and children with this disorder may show no signs of disordered attachment (APA, 2013a).

Disinhibited social engagement disorder impairs a child's ability to interact in a culturally appropriate manner that is consistent with age-appropriate social boundaries. This may impact the child's relationships with adults and peers throughout his or her lifetime.

Assessment of attachment behavior should be part of a comprehensive bio-psychosocial assessment. The development of this new disorder has implications for addressing the impact of relationships on the development, maintenance, and recovery of mental disorders. Prior to *DSM-5*, relational disorders were generally acknowledged as V codes (e.g., parent–child relational problems, upbringing away from parents, problems related to primary support group) and did not qualify for a diagnosis of a mental condition. Expanding attachment–related disorders into reactive attachment disorder and disinhibited social engagement disorder, and applying the diagnostic criteria across the lifespan, allows for consideration of the importance of relational processes in the development of mental disorders.

Before treatment can begin, serious neglect must first be assessed and environmental changes made to ensure adequate caregiving. Therapist characteristics and intervention strategies as outlined for RAD (see page 105 of *SET-4*) are also appropriate for the treatment of this disorder, which may persist through adolescence. Future research is expected to shed light on adolescent and adult manifestations of this disorder, which have not yet been determined.

Posttraumatic Stress Disorder

As mentioned earlier, significant changes have been made in the classification and conceptualization of posttraumatic stress disorder (PTSD), including reclassification as a trauma- and stressor-related disorder. Many of the diagnostic criteria remain the same as in *DSM-IV*, but a significant number of alterations have been made. The criteria alone now fill nearly four pages of *DSM-5*, and include separate criteria for children 6 years and younger. Readers should refer to *DSM-5* for a complete list of criteria for PTSD. Highlights of the changes between *DSM-IV* and *DSM-5* include the following.

Criterion A is more explicit about what type of stressor qualifies as a traumatic event (e.g., sexual assault, actual or threatened death, serious injury), and requires discussion of whether the traumatic event (or events) was experienced directly, witnessed, experienced indirectly, or the result of repeated exposure to details of traumatic events.

Criterion A2 from *DSM-IV* has been eliminated. As a result, it is no longer a requirement that a person must have intense fear, helplessness, or horror in reaction to the stressor.

The three symptom clusters in *DSM-IV* have been divided into four symptom clusters in *DSM-5* with the addition of a behavioral symptom criterion:

1. intrusion symptoms (e.g., intrusive memories, distressing dreams, dissociative reactions or flashbacks, intense distress, and physiological response to triggers)
2. persistent avoidance of memories, thoughts, or feelings surrounding the traumatic event, or avoidance of external reminders (e.g., people, places)
3. persistent negative alterations in cognitions and mood (numbing, cognitive distortions, detachment)
4. hypervigilance or heightened arousal (e.g., aggression, angry outbursts, sleep disturbances, problems with concentration, reckless or self-destructive behavior)

In addition to revisions to clarify symptom expression, three new symptoms were added to the criteria:

1. persistent and distorted cognitions that lead the person to blame self or others
2. persistent negative emotional state (e.g., fear, horror, anger, guilt, shame)
3. reckless or self-destructive behavior

PTSD is now developmentally sensitive, in that diagnostic thresholds have been lowered for children over the age of 6, and separate criteria are provided for children 6 years of age and younger. Longitudinal studies indicate PTSD in childhood can persist into adulthood. Early childhood trauma can create a biological vulnerability to other neurodevelopmental, learning, and externalizing disorders. Trauma experienced in midchildhood or adolescence can lead to disorders of self-regulation, including eating disorders, substance use disorders, nonsuicidal self-injury, and criminal behavior. Early assessment and intervention, adapted to the child's developmental level, can reduce symptoms of PTSD in children.

DSM-5 includes the following specifiers for PTSD:

- with dissociative symptoms (e.g., depersonalization or derealization), and
- with delayed expression (in which full diagnostic criteria are not met until 6 months after the event)

The implications of these changes are legion. Assessment measures for PTSD are being revised to reflect changes in symptoms and criteria for diagnosis. Developmentally appropriate criteria are now available to diagnose childhood onset. This should result in earlier treatment and reduced pathology across the lifespan. More research is being conducted on pretraumatic factors (temperament, environment, and genetic and physiological factors) that lead to the development of PTSD. It is hoped that earlier detection and treatment will reduce the likelihood of developing one of the many comorbid disorders that people with PTSD are 80% more likely to acquire (e.g., substance use disorders; anxiety, depressive, and bipolar disorders; and, in children, oppositional defiant disorder and separation anxiety disorder).

Acute Stress Disorder

Changes in criteria for acute stress disorder are the same as those listed earlier for PTSD (i.e., directly experiencing the traumatic event is no longer required, nor is an intense fear or horror as a reaction to the traumatic event; some symptoms have been clarified, and new symptoms have been added). Persons who report 9 out of 14 symptoms in the five categories of intrusion, negative mood, dissociation, avoidance, and arousal could be diagnosed with acute stress disorder. Symptoms must begin within 3 days and last up to a month for the diagnosis to be made. Symptoms that persist longer than 1 month and meet the criteria for PTSD would be diagnosed as PTSD.

Adjustment Disorders

Adjustment disorders have been reconceptualized as stress-response syndromes that occur after exposure to a significant life stressor (e.g., job loss, divorce, relationship problems). As such, they are quite common, affecting as many as 5% to 20% of outpatients and nearly 50% of psychiatric inpatients. By definition, the stressor must have occurred within 3 months of symptom onset, and resolve within 6 months of the stressor

having ended. The subtypes (i.e., disturbances of mood, anxiety, or conduct) remain the same in *DSM-5*. Many diagnoses of medical disorders are comorbid with adjustment disorders. Personality disorders, major depressive disorder, and PTSD should be ruled out. Cultural considerations should be taken into account, and clinicians should make the diagnosis of adjustment disorder only when the response to stress is greater than what would normally be expected.

With the acknowledgment that adjustment disorders are now considered to be trauma- and stressor-related disorders, the criteria remain the same as in *DSM-IV*. The description of the disorder, its assessment, and its treatment remain the same (see pages 128–136 of *SET-4*).

Other Specified Trauma- and Stressor-Related Disorder

This category is used to diagnose other trauma- or stressor-related disorders that do not meet the criteria for one of the main disorders in this section. The clinician then specifies the cause of the stressor (e.g., adjustment-like disorders with prolonged duration of more than 6 months without prolonged duration of stressor).

Unspecified Trauma- and Stressor-Related Disorder

This category includes subclinical diagnosis of a trauma- or stressor-related disorder in which the clinician chooses not to provide the reason why the criteria were not met and does not have enough information to make a specific diagnosis.

DISSOCIATIVE DISORDERS

Several changes have been made in *DSM-5* that impact the diagnosis of disorders involving impairment in awareness of reality. The four distinct dissociative disorders found in *DSM-IV* have been merged into three disorders in DSM-5. (Dissociative fugue is no longer considered to be a separate condition, but has been added as a specifier to dissociative amnesia).

1. dissociative identity disorder (DID)
2. dissociative amnesia
3. depersonalization/derealization disorder

The overall prevalence for dissociative disorders is unknown. *DSM-5* reminds us that trance and possession phenomena are dissociative states that reflect commonly accepted ways of expressing distress in some cultures. Apart from the criteria changes described next, the descriptions of dissociative disorders in *DSM-5* remain largely unchanged.

Criterion A for dissociative identity disorder now specifies that transitions in identity may be observable by others as well as self-reported. Criterion A has also been expanded to include "certain possession-form phenomena and functional neurological symptoms to account for more diverse presentations of the disorder," although the majority of possession states are considered to be a normal part of spiritual practice and do not meet the criteria for DID. Criterion B allows for recurrent gaps in recall of everyday events and not just for traumatic experiences.

Dissociative fugue is a rare condition. In *DSM-5* it is now a subtype of dissociative amnesia.

Other specified dissociative disorders include chronic syndromes of mixed dissociative symptoms; identity disturbances as a result of brainwashing, torture, or thought reform; acute dissociative reaction to stressful events (lasting less than 1 month); and dissociative trance (which is not associated with a cultural or religious practice). Since 95 % of people with this disorder experience symptoms prior to the age of 25, *DSM-5* recommends referral of

patients over the age of 40 for underlying medical evaluation. Stress, immature defenses including denial of reality, projection, or idealization can contribute to this disorder, as can depression, anxiety, and illicit drug use, which must be ruled out.

SOMATIC SYMPTOM AND RELATED DISORDERS

This new chapter in *DSM-5* identifies disorders characterized by thoughts, feelings, and behaviors related to somatic symptoms (previously referred to in *DSM-IV* as somatoform disorders). Several disorders have been eliminated, some have been renamed. and others have been clarified. Some disorders may involve an unsubstantiated belief about a person's illness or the illness of another (as in factitious disorder), some may result from medically unexplained symptoms (as in functional neurological symptom disorder), and some may adversely affect an already known medical condition (such as anxiety aggravating asthma, or poor adherence to treatment). One of the biggest changes in this section is the removal of unexplained symptoms as a key feature of somatic disorders. For example, persons diagnosed under the new *DSM-5* guidelines with somatic symptom disorder may or may not have a diagnosed medical condition. The key feature of each somatic disorder is an excessive response—marked thoughts, feelings, and behaviors in excess of what would be expected—related to somatic symptoms.

Somatic Symptom Disorder

Unlike *DSM-IV's* somatization disorder, somatic symptom disorder in *DSM-5* does not require specific physical or sexual symptoms, occurence before 30 years of age, or the presence of pain. Rather, somatic symptom disorder criterion A requires a minimum of one somatic symptom that results in significant disruption of everyday life. Criterion B requires actions, thoughts, or feelings about the symptoms that are either: excessive in the amount of time devoted to them, out of proportion to the degree of seriousness, or include a high level of anxiety. Criterion C requires being symptomatic for a minimum of 6 months.

"With predominant pain," is now a specifier to somatic symptom disorder. This would have been diagnosed as pain disorder in *DSM-IV*. Other specifiers include "persistent" if symptoms have been of long duration, are particularly severe, or cause marked impairment. Severity levels (mild, moderate, and severe) should also be specified.

Illness Anxiety Disorder

Hypochondriasis has been reconceptualized in *DSM-5*. Anxiety and preoccupied thoughts of having or acquiring a serious illness must be present for a minimum of 6 months, with minimal or no somatic symptoms. If somatic symptoms are significant, the diagnosis of somatic symptom disorder would be more appropriate. *DSM-5* notes that nearly 75% of people who would have been diagnosed with hypochondriasis under *DSM-IV*, will now be diagnosed with somatic symptom disorder. The other 25% will more appropriately be diagnosed with illness anxiety disorder.

Conversion Disorder (Functional Neurological Symptom Disorder)

This rare disorder has been renamed functional neurological symptom disorder. A new criterion B requires clinical evidence that symptoms are incompatible with any known neurological or medical condition.

Symptom type specifiers have also been added to help clarify functional neurological symptom disorder:

- symptoms (e.g., with weakness or paralysis, with seizures, with mixed symptoms)
- episode severity (acute or persistent)
- with or without psychological stressor (specify stressor, if appropriate)

According to *DSM-5*, clinical findings must show evidence of incompatibility with neurological disease. Signs of inconsistency between exams, or exam results that are inconsistent when tested another way, would be sufficient. The overall clinical picture is important in making this diagnosis.

Psychological Factors Affecting Other Medical Conditions

Psychological factors such as stress, denial of symptoms, or anxiety can adversely affect many medical conditions, including asthma, migraine, fibromyalgia, diabetes, and heart disease. This disorder has been repositioned in the Somatic Symptom and Related Disorders chapter in *DSM-5*. It was previously listed in *DSM-IV* as another condition that may be a focus of clinical attention. The prevalence rate of this disorder is unclear, but it may occur at any time across the lifespan.

The diagnostic criteria require the presence of a medical condition (other than a mental disorder) that affects the person in one of the following ways:

- The psychological factors have affected the medical condition in an adverse way (e.g., delayed recovery).
- The psychological factors interfere with treatment for a medical condition (e.g., poor adherence to treatment protocol).

- The psychological factors create additional health risks.
- The psychological factors influence or exacerbate the underlying medical problem and result in the need for medical attention.

The symptoms must not be better explained by another mental disorder such as PTSD or panic disorder. Severity is specified by one of the following: mild (increases medical risk; moderate (aggravates underlying condition); severe (results in need for hospitalization); or extreme (severe, life-threatening risk).

Differential diagnosis requires distinguishing this disorder from psychological disorders that occur following diagnosis of a medical condition, which is more appropriately diagnosed as one of the adjustment disorders (as a response to an identifiable stressor). Somatic symptom disorder and illness anxiety disorder should also be ruled out.

Factitious Disorder

Factitious disorder has been moved to this chapter because somatic symptoms are predominant. Criteria that distinguished whether falsified symptoms were of medical or psychological origin have been removed from this disorder. Factitious disorder by proxy has been renamed factitious disorder imposed on another. Although rare, these disorders are most likely to be seen in medical settings, where they are estimated to affect about 1% of patients.

Other Specified Somatic Symptom and Related Disorder

This category includes symptoms that cause clinically significant distress but do not meet the criteria for any of the other somatic disorders. Included are symptoms of short duration (less than 6 months), brief illness anxiety (less than 6 months), illness anxiety disorder without excessive health-related behaviors, or pseudocyesis (false belief of being pregnant).

FEEDING AND EATING DISORDERS

This new chapter in *DSM-5* incorporates several disorders that were first diagnosed in infancy, childhood, or adolescence, including pica and restrictive eating. The eating disorders (anorexia nervosa and bulimia nervosa) have been moved here, and binge eating disorder (which was previously in the Appendix of *DSM-IV*) is now included as a distinct disorder. Finally, preliminary diagnostic criteria are included for other specified feeding or eating disorder and unspecified feeding or eating disorder. More information on each of these disorders is given next. All of the feeding and eating disorders are exclusive, with the exception of pica, which may be diagnosed in the presence of another feeding or eating disorder (APA, 2013a).

Pica and Rumination Disorder

Pica and rumination disorder are two distinct disorders from the *DSM-IV* chapter on disorders usually first diagnosed in childhood. Although they have been moved to the Feeding and Eating Disorders chapter, the diagnostic criteria for these disorders remain basically the same in *DSM-5*.

Avoidant/Restrictive Food Intake Disorder (Formerly Feeding Disorder of Infancy or Early Childhood)

The criteria have been significantly expanded for this disorder. Food avoidance, restricted nutritional intake, or lack of interest in eating is most common in infancy or early childhood but may persist throughout adulthood. This disorder can be diagnosed at any age for those who meet Criterion A, and if the condition is not better explained by the presence of an eating disorder, another medical condition, a co-occurring mental disorder, a culturally sanctioned practice (e.g., religious fasting), or a lack of available food.

For Criterion A to be met, the persons must have an eating disturbance that causes them to fail to consume adequate nutrition for their energy needs and they must exhibit one or more of the following:

- There has been a significant weight loss or a failure to gain age-appropriate weight if an infant or child.
- There is a notable nutrition deficiency.
- Oral supplements or enteral feeding has become necessary to maintain adequate nutritional intake (for example, children with failure to thrive, adults who require tube feeding in the absence of a medical condition).
- The condition causes significant interference with psychosocial functioning.

In some situations, food avoidance or restriction may be the result of heightened sensitivity to smells, texture, or taste. Food avoidance may also occur after an unpleasant experience (e.g., vomiting or choking on food). Developmentally normal restriction of food, as in toddlers who are picky eaters or elderly adults who have reduced food intake, would not meet the criteria for this disorder. The disorders that co-occur most frequently with avoidant/restrictive food intake disorder are neurodevelopmental disorders (such as autism spectrum, ADHD, and intellectual disability); anxiety; and OCD.

Anorexia Nervosa and Bulimia Nervosa

Anorexia nervosa and bulimia nervosa are two distinct disorders from the *DSM-IV* chapter on eating disorders. The diagnostic criteria for these disorders remain basically the same in *DSM-5*. Additional information on the diagnosis, assessment, and treatment of anorexia or bulimia can be found on pages 274–285 of *SET-4*.

Binge Eating Disorder (BED)

Binge eating is now a full-fledged disorder in *DSM-5*, and its diagnostic criteria remain largely the same as listed in the Appendix of *DSM-IV* (refer to pages 274–285 of *SET-4*), except the criteria have been changed to require an average of one episode weekly over a 3-month period. In other words, binge eating disorder is described as recurrent occasions of eating, in a discrete period of time, an amount of food that is substantially larger than most people would consume under the same circumstances, and a feeling of lack of control over eating during the episode. Episodes of binge eating include at least three of the following:

- eating much faster than usual
- eating until physically uncomfortable
- eating large amounts even when not hungry
- embarrassment over the amount of food that is eaten and therefore eating alone
- feelings of disgust, depression, or guilt after the episode of overeating

To qualify as binge eating disorder, the binge eating occurs on average at least once a week for 3 months and is accompanied by marked distress (e.g., negative affect, guilt, shame, and disgust). Binge eating is not accompanied by the use of compensatory behaviors such as overexercise, purging, or fasting, and is not better accounted for by a diagnosis of anorexia nervosa or bulimia nervosa.

The following course specifiers for binge eating disorder should be noted:

- in full or partial remission
- severity level, ranging from mild (one to three binge-eating episodes) to moderate (four to seven episodes), severe (8 to 13 episodes), or extreme (14 or more episodes) per week

All eating disorders are physically damaging and potentially life-threatening, so a complete assessment should include a referral for a physical exam, as well as obtaining a history of the client's dieting and weight loss across the lifespan. Any compensatory activities (e.g., laxative abuse, purging) should also be monitored.

Treatment for binge eating disorder is similar to treatment for bulimia nervosa, specifically CBT, dialectical behavior therapy (DBT), interpersonal therapy (IPT), and mindfulness-based cognitive therapy. To date, CBT and IPT exhibit the most empirical support in randomized controlled trials (Alexander, Goldschmidt, & Le Grange, 2013). But DBT, self-help programs, and training in mindfulness have also shown promise. Because a large number of people with BED have experienced trauma or physical abuse in childhood, treatment using eye movement desensitization and reprocessing may also be appropriate.

Other Specified Feeding or Eating Disorder (Formerly Eating Disorder NOS in DSM-IV)

This category is appropriate for use in the following five situations:

1. The client does not meet the full criteria for bulimia nervosa.
2. The client does not meet the full criteria for binge eating disorder.
3. The behavior is solely a purging disorder in the absence of overeating.
4. The criteria for anorexia are met, but the client's weight remains within the normal range (atypical anorexia).

5. There is a diagnosis of night eating syndrome in which the person has recurrent episodes of eating at night, eating after awakening from sleep, or consuming large amounts of food after the regular dinnertime.

Unspecified Feeding or Eating Disorder

This category can be used when symptoms of an eating disorder are present and severe enough to cause distress or impairment in one or more areas of functioning, but the criteria for a specific feeding or eating disorder are not met, or there is not enough information available to make a more definitive diagnosis.

ELIMINATION DISORDERS

Encopresis and enuresis have been moved from the *DSM-IV* section on mental disorders first diagnosed in childhood, to a new chapter on elimination disorders in *DSM-5*. No significant changes have been made to the criteria for these disorders in *DSM-5*. The criteria, assessment, and interventions for treatment remain the same as those found on pages 91–96 of *SET-4*.

SLEEP-WAKE DISORDERS

In *DSM-5*, a new chapter has been created specifically for sleep-wake disorders, which contains the same primary subgroups of sleep disorders as *DSM-IV*. With minor exceptions, the descriptions, client characteristics, assessments, and intervention strategies found on pages 308–315 of *SET-4* remain the same for the major subgroupings of Sleep-Wake Disorders:

- insomnia disorder (formerly primary insomnia)
- hypersomnolence disorder

- narcolepsy
- breathing-related sleep disorders
- circadian rhythm sleep-wake disorders
- parasomnias

It bears noting that the field of sleep disorders has grown exponentially since the publication of *DSM-IV* and biological validators for diagnosis are now used in *DSM-5*. Scientific studies, including polysomnography, are often helpful in determining diagnosis for many of the Sleep-Wake Disorders, including narcolepsy, restless legs syndrome, and breathing-related sleep disorder.

Although sleep disorders related to another mental disorder and sleep disorders due to a general medical condition have been removed from *DSM-5*, many sections have been expanded to reflect the current level of knowledge now available on the subject. For example, breathing-related sleep disorders have been divided into three distinct disorders—obstructive sleep apnea, central sleep apnea, and sleep-related hypoventilation. Rapid-eye movement sleep behavior disorder and restless legs syndrome (formerly Sleep Disorders NOS) have become independent disorders. Also, pediatric and developmental criteria are now integrated into the text where appropriate.

SEXUAL DYSFUNCTIONS

The following disorders constitute the new *DSM-5* chapter on sexual dysfunctions:

- delayed ejaculation
- erectile disorder
- female orgasmic disorder
- female sexual interest/arousal disorder
- genito-pelvic pain/penetration disorder
- male hypoactive sexual desire disorder
- premature (early) ejaculation

- substance/medication-induced sexual dysfunction
- other specified sexual dysfunction
- unspecified sexual dysfunction

The bulk of the information found on pages 285–292 of *SET-4* remains accurate, with the addition of the following enhancements to *DSM-5*:

- Female sexual desire and arousal disorders have been combined into one disorder (female sexual interest/arousal disorder).
- Sexual aversion disorder has been removed due to a lack of supporting research.
- All sexual dysfunctions now require a minimum duration of 6 months, with the exception of substance/medication-induced sexual dysfunction.
- More precise criteria are set for degree of severity.
- All sexual dysfunctions can be divided into two subtypes: (1) lifelong versus acquired and (2) generalized versus situational. Lifelong refers to problems that have been present since the first sexual experience, and acquired relates to disorders that occur after a relatively healthy period of sexual experience. Generalized subtype refers to sexual problems that are not related to specific experiences, situations, or partners; situational subtype refers to those problems that occur only in conjunction with specific contexts.
- Genito-pelvic pain/penetration disorder has been added as a new disorder that combines vaginismus and dyspareunia, which were previously comorbid disorders that were difficult to distinguish under *DSM-IV*.

DSM-5 also includes information on associated factors that may correlate with sexual dysfunctions, including medical factors, partner factors, relationship factors, individual vulnerability factors, and cultural or religious factors. If severe relationship distress or another stressor seems a more appropriate explanation of the symptoms of sexual difficulties, then the appropriate V or Z code for the relationship problem or stressor should be used instead of the sexual dysfunction.

GENDER DYSPHORIA (FORMERLY GENDER IDENTITY DISORDER)

Gender identity disorder (GID) as defined in *DSM-IV-TR* was a controversial diagnosis, and the term was considered to be pejorative by people whose gender at birth was contrary to the gender they later identified with. *DSM-5* has changed important criteria and renamed the disorder "gender dysphoria."

As with all other disorders listed in *DSM-5*, a critical element of determining the presence of a disorder is the presence of clinically significant distress associated with the condition. In other words, doubts about one's gender or gender nonconformity do not constitute a mental disorder. Rather, clinically significant distress or impairment in social, occupational, or other important areas of functioning must be present (APA, 2013a). *DSM-5* contains separate sets of criteria for children, adolescents, and adults, and reconceptualizes the phenomenon as gender incongruence rather than identification with the gender other than the one born with.

Specific criteria for gender dysphoria include:

- There must be a marked difference between the person's expressed gender and the gender others would assign him or her.

- These feelings must be present for at least 6 months.
- In children, the desire to be another gender must be present and must be verbalized.
- Clinically significant distress or impairment in social, occupational, or other important areas of functioning must be experienced.

A new specifier has been added to identify clients who have undergone medical treatment in support of the new gender assignment.

The typical client characteristics for this disorder remain the same as those outlined on page 296 of *SET-4*. Readers are reminded that gender identity is a fluid concept that encompasses feelings about the body, social roles, gender identification, and sexuality. The therapist's comfort level and attitudes can affect the client's disclosure of sexual topics. Treatment can be complicated, especially if clients are considering gender reassignment surgery. Therapists who are not comfortable or who lack experience working with transgendered people should refer clients to a qualified therapist who has experience working with gender dysphoria.

DISRUPTIVE, IMPULSE CONTROL, AND CONDUCT DISORDERS

Lack of emotional and behavioral self-control is the hallmark of the behaviors in this new chapter in *DSM-5*. The two disruptive behavior disorders of childhood (oppositional defiant disorder and conduct disorder) have been subsumed into this new chapter. Following is a complete list of disruptive, impulse control, and conduct disorders:

- oppositional defiant disorder
- intermittent explosive disorder

- conduct disorder
- antisocial personality disorder
- pyromania
- kleptomania
- other specified disruptive and impulse control disorder
- unspecified impulse control disorder

Because it is thought to be on a continuum with oppositional defiant disorder (ODD) and conduct disorder, antisocial personality disorder is included both here and in the chapter on personality disorders. For the most part, the criteria, assessments, and treatments listed for these disorders remain the same as described on pages 299–302 of *SET-4*, with the following changes.

Oppositional Defiant Disorder

This disorder is characterized by three types of symptoms:

1. angry/irritable mood
2. argumentative/defiant behavior
3. vindictiveness (being spiteful at least twice in the most recent 6-month period)

High levels of emotional reactivity and frustration intolerance continue to form the basis of this disorder.

Intermittent Explosive Disorder

Physical aggression is no longer a requirement of intermittent explosive disorder (IED). Nondestructive and noninjurious physical aggression and verbal aggression are now sufficient to diagnose this condition, which also includes a minimum age of 6 (or equivalent developmental level) for diagnosis. Enhanced criteria delineate the frequency and nature of the outbursts (i.e.,

impulsive and/or anger based) and, as with all disorders, symptoms must cause personal distress, create difficulties in relationships or employment, or result in legal or financial problems. The impulsive rather than premeditated nature of the outbursts delineates IED from conduct disorder.

Conduct Disorder

Exclusionary criteria for conduct disorder have been removed from *DSM-5* and a new specifier, "with limited prosocial emotions," has been added. This has also been referred to in the literature as the "callous and unemotional" specifier, and is indicated only if the person meets two or more of the following characteristics in multiple relationships and settings over a minimum of a 12-month period:

- Lack of remorse or guilt—is not remorseful or concerned about the person being hurt.
- Callousness—lacks empathy, is unconcerned about the feelings of others, is concerned only with the effects on himself or herself, is cold or uncaring about others.
- Lack of concern about performance—is unconcerned about school or work performance, does not put forth efforts, blames others for poor performance.
- Shallow or deficient affect—does not express feelings or emotions to others except in shallow, self-serving ways (e.g., manipulative emotions, emotions that contradict behavior).

Age of onset for conduct disorder can be specified as childhood onset (before the age of 10), adolescent onset (after the age of 10), or unspecified onset (age of onset unknown).

Level of severity is specified as

- mild—few conduct problems in excess of those needed to diagnose,
- moderate—between mild and severe, or
- severe—many symptoms in excess of the number required to diagnose, or severe harm has been caused to others (e.g., rape, use of a weapon, physical cruelty).

According to *DSM-5*, the context in which conduct disorders occur should be considered (e.g., war zones, high-crime areas). Gender also plays a role, with males tending to exert both physical and relational aggression, whereas females tend to exhibit more relational aggression and lying. In general, impulsive and oppositional behavior tends to increase during the preschool years and adolescence. Care must be taken to ensure that the frequency and intensity of the symptoms are beyond what is normative for the child's age and stage of development.

ADHD is commonly comorbid with all of the disruptive, impulse control, and conduct disorders, and its co-occurrence is associated with more severe outcomes. It would seem that ADHD belongs in this chapter, as it is conceptualized as being on a continuum with ODD, conduct disorder, and antisocial personality disorder. However, because of the large body of research supporting the neurological underpinnings of ADHD, it is located in the Neurodevelopmental Disorders chapter of *DSM-5*.

Pyromania

The diagnostic criteria and treatment interventions for this rare disorder (affecting less than 1% of the population) remain the same as those listed in *DSM-IV*. Refer to page 301 of *SET-4* for additional details.

Kleptomania

This disorder is also rare, affecting 0.3% to 0.6% of the population, of whom 75% of those affected are female. No changes have been made to the *DSM-IV* criteria for kleptomania, and the information found on page 301 of *SET-4* remains relevant.

Other Specified Disruptive, Impulse Control, and Conduct Disorder

This diagnosis is given in situations in which the clinician can specify why criteria for a specific disorder was not met. For example, the outbursts do not meet the frequency level required.

Unspecified Disruptive, Impulse Control, and Conduct Disorder

This is the preferred diagnosis when the clinician does not wish to specify the reason why criteria are not met, or, as in the case of an emergency room presentation, adequate information is not available to make a specific diagnosis.

SUBSTANCE-RELATED AND ADDICTIVE DISORDERS

Many changes have been made to the Substance-Related and Addictive Disorders chapter of *DSM-5*. The inclusion of gambling disorder is noteworthy, as it is the first behavioral disorder to be included in this section. Other significant changes include the merging of substance abuse and dependence into one substance use disorder, and the addition of cannabis withdrawal and caffeine withdrawal as new disorders.

Substance-Related Disorders

In an effort to streamline the diagnosis of substance use disorders, *DSM-5* combines the categories of substance abuse and substance dependence into one all-encompassing disorder, substance use disorder, for which two criteria are necessary for diagnosis (*DSM-IV* required the endorsement of only one item). The new diagnosis of substance use disorder adopts the spectrum approach, with degree of severity being qualified as "mild," "moderate," or "severe." The clinical implications of these, and other changes to this section of *DSM-5*, include the following:

- Clinicians will have one disorder to treat, which will reduce confusion and eliminate the need to distinguish between two criteria sets—one for abuse and a separate set for dependence.
- The new requirement that two symptoms instead of one must be endorsed for diagnosis recognizes that substance use disorders are a pattern of behavior, rather than just one problem area.
- Diagnostic criteria have been combined and strengthened into a list of 11 symptoms.
- A craving criterion (or a strong desire or urge to use the substance) has been added to *DSM-5*, bringing it closer to alignment with ICD-9, published by the World Health Organization.
- The diagnosis of polysubstance dependence has been removed. When more than one substance use disorder is diagnosed, each should be recorded individually.
- Severity of the substance use disorder is now based on the number of symptoms that are met. For example, if the client endorses two or three symptoms, the diagnosis is "mild substance use disorder"; having four or five symptoms is considered "moderate"; and six or more is "severe."
- The previous symptom of substance-related legal problems has been dropped

from *DSM-5*. While arrests for driving under the influence (DUI) are a major reason people seek treatment for substance use disorders, it was not found to be predictive of dysfunction or indicative of level of severity. Also removed is the specifier "with or without physiological dependence."

- New specifiers have been added for "in a controlled environment" and "on maintenance therapy," as the case may be.
- "Early remission" from a substance use disorder is defined in *DSM-5* as having 3 to 12 months elapse without meeting any criteria (except craving) for the disorder. "Sustained remission" is specified if 12 months or more have passed without meeting any criteria except craving or a strong desire or urge to use the substance.

The following 10 separate classes of drugs considered in *DSM-IV-TR* remain the same in *DSM-5*:

1. alcohol
2. caffeine
3. cannabis
4. hallucinogens
5. inhalants
6. opioids
7. sedatives, hypnotics, and anxiolytics
8. stimulants
9. tobacco
10. other (or unknown) substances.

A distinction is made between substance use disorders and substance-induced disorders. Substance-induced disorders are

- intoxication,
- withdrawal, and

- other substance/medication-induced mental disorders (e.g., substance-induced psychosis, substance-induced depressive disorder).

DSM-5 provides an overview of this information as well as recording and coding procedures for each disorder. Readers who work with clients with substance use disorders should carefully read the relevant substance-related disorder section in *DSM-5* for diagnostic criteria, course specifiers, and recording procedures. For example, Criterion A of alcohol use disorder specifies a pattern of use leading to impairment or distress with the new requirement of at least 2 of the following 11 symptoms being met in a 12-month period:

1. drinking more than intended, or for longer than intended
2. efforts to control or cut back on drinking having been unsuccessful
3. large amounts of time spent obtaining, using, or recovering from alcohol
4. cravings (the presence of a strong desire to drink)
5. recurrent use resulting in problems at work, home, or school
6. continued use despite recurrent social or interpersonal problems resulting from drinking
7. curtailing important activities in favor of alcohol use
8. alcohol use despite potentially hazardous outcomes (drinking and driving, for example)
9. continued alcohol use despite knowledge that alcohol use is causing or exacerbating a persistent physical or psychological problem
10. tolerance or a need for increased amounts of alcohol
11. withdrawal symptoms

If the person indicates the presence of two or more symptoms, an alcohol use disorder would be diagnosed. The clinician then specifies if in early or sustained remission and if in a controlled environment. Coding would be based on current level of severity:

- mild: presence of two or three symptoms
- moderate: presence of four or five symptoms
- severe: presence of six or more symptoms.

Caffeine Withdrawal

Also new to *DSM-5*, caffeine withdrawal has been added as a viable disorder, with four sets of criteria: prolonged daily use, and abruptly stopping caffeine use followed within 24 hours by at least three of the following symptoms: headache, fatigue, bad mood or irritability, lack of concentration, and flu-like symptoms. These symptoms cause significant distress and are not better accounted for by another medical condition or mental disorder.

Cannabis Withdrawal

Unlike cannabis use and cannabis intoxication, which were listed in *DSM-IV*, cannabis withdrawal is new to *DSM-5*. Cannabis withdrawal occurs after a heavy or prolonged period of time in which cannabis was used most days for several months. Symptoms occur within 7 days, and must include three or more of the symptoms of irritability, anxiety, difficulty sleeping, reduced appetite, depressed mood, restlessness, and at least one physical symptom (e.g., headache, sweating). *DSM-5* includes a coding note that cannabis withdrawal can occur only in conjunction with a moderate or severe cannabis use disorder.

Gambling Disorder

Only one non-substance-related disorder, gambling, is included in the Substance-Related and Addictive Disorders chapter of *DSM-5*, although the criteria remain the same as in *DSM-IV* (see pages 302–303 in *SET-4*). The rationale for moving a behavioral disorder to this section of *DSM-5* includes scientific evidence indicating that gambling activates areas of the brain similar to the brain's reward systems that are activated by substances. Other repetitive behaviors that could lead people to difficulties if not controlled (such as shopping, gaming, and sex) do not have sufficient peer-reviewed research to be labeled as mental disorders. Of these three, Internet gaming disorder is the only one that is included in *DSM-5*'s Section III subsection Conditions for Further Study. By moving gambling disorder into the Substance-Related and Addictive Disorders chapter of *DSM-5*, the implication is made that additional behavioral syndromes will be recognized as mental disorders at a future date.

Some professionals have heralded the *DSM-5* changes in substance use disorder as "a good start," while also wishing the American Psychiatric Association had included quantitative data based on the correlation between frequency and quantity of substance use and increased risk of disease and death (Lembke, Bradley, Henderson, Moos, & Harris, 2011). Such information is currently available, although lacking in *DSM-5*, which Lembke 2013 notes may be due, in part, to the difficulty of quantifying substances such as marijuana, heroin, or prescription drugs into standard units. It is much easier to quantify standard units of alcohol.

Although not necessary for determining a *DSM-5* diagnosis, clinicians should continue to assess quantity of use and motivation to change so they can prepare appropriate treatment plans, recognizing that clients with substance use disorders may deny, obscure, or underreport their symptoms. A tendency to minimize or normalize substance-related problems is inherent in substance use disorders. Clinicians must address any ambivalence or lack of motivation to change early on in the assessment process if treatment is to be successful with this population. General suggestions for assessment, intervention, and treatment of all substance use disorders as found on pages 241–247 (all substance use disorders), 253–258 (alcohol), 270–273 (drug-related disorders), and 305–308 (gambling) of *SET-4* remain the same.

NEUROCOGNITIVE DISORDERS

These disorders (referred to as "Delirium, Dementia, Amnestic, and Other Cognitive Disorders" on pages 339–343 of *SET-4*) have been moved in *DSM-5* to the chapter on Neurocognitive Disorders (NCD). Dementia is now subsumed under major neurocognitive disorder, although it can also be listed as a symptom in the subtypes, where it is frequently found to occur.

Mild neurocognitive disorder is a new disorder in *DSM-5* that permits the identification of less severe symptoms of cognitive impairment. It is intended to distinguish between mild and severe cognitive impairment with the intention of providing earlier treatment for a slower progression of the neurocognitive disorder.

The criteria for neurocognitive disorders are based on defined cognitive domains that are provided in *DSM-5* Table 1 (APA, 2013a, p. 593–595). Although cognitive deficits may also be present in other mental disorders, including schizophrenia, only disorders whose main features are cognitive are considered in the NCD category. These disorders are not present at birth, and when they occur they represent a decline from previous levels of functioning. Unlike any of the other disorders included in

DSM-5, diagnosis of the pathology and often the etiology of neurocognitive disorders can frequently be determined.

More substantive changes to the Neurocognitive Disorders (NCD) chapter include distinctions among the following specifiers:

- due to Alzheimer's disease
- frontotemporal degeneration
- with Lewy bodies
- vascular neurocognitive disorder
- due to traumatic brain injury
- substance/medication-induced
- due to HIV infection
- due to prion disease
- due to Parkinson's disease
- due to Huntington's disease
- due to another medical condition
- due to multiple etiologies

Clients presenting with symptoms of dementia or other cognitive impairments should first be referred to a physician for a complete medical and neurological assessment. Therapists working with this population usually work closely with the medical community to develop assessment and treatment plans.

PERSONALITY DISORDERS

Despite many years of research and an exploration of a radical revision to the diagnosis of personality disorders, in the end the American Psychiatric Association Board of Trustees voted not to implement structural change to the personality disorders section at this time. Therefore, the categorical model of personality disorders as listed and described in *SET-4* remains unchanged, and the criteria for all 10 personality disorders described on pages 347–401 of *SET-4* remain the same. (Note: An alternative *DSM-5* Model for Personality

Disorders is included in *DSM-5*'s Section III: Emerging Methods and Models for additional study and research.)

PARAPHILIC DISORDERS

The paraphilias described on pages 292–296 of *SET-4* retain the same criteria, assessments, and treatment interventions in *DSM-5*. However, the name has been changed to paraphilic disorders to underscore that while having a paraphilia is necessary for the diagnosis of paraphilic disorder, it is not enough to warrant diagnosis of a mental disorder. In other words, the paraphilia must also cause distress or impairment to the individual, or the fulfillment of the paraphilia must involve personal harm, or risk of harm, to others in order to meet the criteria of a paraphilic disorder (APA, 2013a).

The following course specifiers have been added to the diagnostic criteria for all paraphilic disorders:

- in a controlled environment (specifically living in an institution or other setting in which the behavior is restricted)
- in full remission (which is defined as: "The individual has not acted on the urges with a nonconsenting person, and there has been no distress or impairment in social, occupational, or other areas of functioning, for at least 5 years while in an uncontrolled environment.") (APA, 2013a, p. 687)

To make a diagnosis of paraphilic disorder, persons must now satisfy both Criterion A and Criterion B. Those who satisfy Criterion A but not B would be said to have a paraphilia, not a paraphilic disorder.

OTHER CONDITIONS THAT MAY BE A FOCUS OF CLINICAL ATTENTION

Other conditions that may affect the diagnosis and treatment of mental disorders are also included in *DSM-5*. While these conditions are not mental disorders, they may be coded if they are the reason for the current visit or if they help to explain the need for testing or treatment, or otherwise impact the patient's care.

Following is a select list of conditions from ICD-9 (V codes) and ICD-10 (Z codes). The complete list of conditions can be found on page 715 of the *DSM-5*.

- problems related to family (e.g., sibling relational problem, upbringing away from parents, parental relationship distress)
- problems related to primary support group (e.g., relationship distress with spouse, disruption of family by separation or divorce, high expressed emotion level within family)
- uncomplicated bereavement (i.e., normal grieving as reaction to the death of a loved one)
- suspected or confirmed child maltreatment or neglect (physical abuse, sexual abuse, neglect, psychological abuse)
- adult maltreatment and neglect (partner violence, sexual violence, psychological abuse or neglect)
- educational, occupational, housing, or legal problems
- financial problems (lack of food, low income, severe poverty, insufficient means)
- phase of life problem
- legal problems
- problems related to living alone
- acculturation difficulty

- religious or spiritual problem
- problems related to unwanted pregnancy
- victim of torture or terrorism
- exposure to disaster or war
- history of self-harm
- history of military deployment
- problems related to lifestyle (poor hygiene, inappropriate diet, high-risk sexual behavior)
- nonadherence to medical treatment
- malingering
- wandering associated with a medical disorder
- borderline intellectual functioning

While not themselves mental disorders, these conditions provide a background and help clinicians understand some of the underlying circumstances the person may be facing that may impact treatment now and into the future.

SECTION III: EMERGING MEASURES AND MODELS

Section III of *DSM-5* provides tools that can help facilitate diagnosis of the conditions listed in Section II, as well as criteria sets for conditions that require additional research. While some measures and scales are included in *DSM-5*, such as a hand-scored simple version of the World Health Organization Disability Assessment Schedule (WHODAS 2.0), the APA recommends that clinicians link into the eHRS (electronic health records) for more complex assessments of symptoms (APA, 2013a, p. 745). WHODAS 2.0 can be used as an assessment scale, and may also be used at regular intervals to track progress.

The diagnostic tools include

- assessment and cross-cutting symptom measures by age,

- clinician-rated dimensions of severity for psychotic symptoms,
- World Health Organization's Disability Assessment Schedule (WHODAS 2.0),
- suggested cultural formulation interviews that increase awareness of how cultural context can influence presentation of mental illness and subsequently influence diagnoses, and
- an alternative model for diagnosing personality disorders.

The alternative *DSM-5* model for diagnosing personality disorders is intended to be easier and more intuitive for clinicians to use. The alternative model of personality disorders retains the most useful aspects of the categorical system and also retains six personality disorders: antisocial, avoidant, borderline, narcissistic, obsessive-compulsive, and schizotypal. Another category called personality disorder—trait specified (PD-TS) was created for persons who meet the general criteria for a personality disorder but do not have one of the previously specified disorders. PD-TS would replace the PD-NOS category from *DSM-IV-TR.*

The 20-page description of the new methodology is too extensive to be included here. Clinicians who would like to explore how the alternative model could enhance their diagnosis of personality disorders, or learn how it can be used to assess personality functioning and traits in the absence of a personality disorder, can find the full version of the alternative model on pages 761–781 of *DSM-5.*

Section III also includes material on disorders that are proposed for future research, similar to the Appendix material in *DSM-IV-TR.* The inclusion in *DSM-5* of these conditions for further study is based on extensive research. The following criteria sets, while not found to have sufficient evidence to warrant their inclusion as official diagnoses at this time, are no exception.

Accordingly, the specific items, thresholds, and durations for each of the eight conditions for further study were determined by consensus of the experts, based on literature review, data re-analysis, and field trial results (APA, 2013a, p. 783).

Some disorders (e.g., binge eating disorder) have been moved from the Appendix of *DSM-IV-TR* into Section II based on the preponderance of research. Similarly, categories and conditions that appeared in the Appendix to *DSM-IV* have been removed after additional research failed to produce enough evidence to warrant their inclusion as individual disorders.

The following conditions for further study are not intended for clinical use, but rather to encourage future research. The eight proposed disorders are

1. attenuated psychosis syndrome,
2. depressive episodes with short-duration hypomania,
3. persistent complex bereavement disorder,
4. caffeine use disorder,
5. Internet gaming disorder,
6. neurobehavioral disorder due to prenatal alcohol exposure (ND-PAE),
7. nonsuicidal self-injury (NSSI), and
8. suicidal behavior disorder.

Attenuated Psychosis Syndrome

Magical thinking, perceptual distortions, and difficulty with frontal lobe functions (e.g., lack of concentration, disorganization, cognitive dysfunction) are hallmarks of attenuated psychosis. Based on current studies, only one third of people with a first diagnosis of psychosis go on to develop a full-blown psychotic disorder. Thus, the inclusion of attenuated psychosis syndrome in Section III of *DSM-5* makes sense. Of those who seek help, it is estimated that 18% will meet the criteria for a psychotic disorder in the coming year; 32% will meet the criteria within 3 years; and others may develop depression or bipolar disorder with psychotic features, although the development of a schizophrenia spectrum disorder is more common.

Depressive Episodes With Short-Duration Hypomania

The proposed criteria for this condition for further study include a lifetime experience of at least one major depressive episode with at least two hypomanic periods of at least 2 but less than 4 consecutive days. If the hypomanic symptoms last 4 days or more, the diagnosis would become bipolar II; if psychosis is present, it is by definition mania, and the diagnosis would be bipolar I.

If the hypomanic features appear concurrently with a major depressive episode, the diagnosis would be major depressive disorder with mixed features. All of these disorders can be differentiated from cyclothymic disorder because of the occurrence of at least one major depressive episode.

The prevalence rate of short-duration hypomania is unknown, but it may be more common in females who present with features of atypical depression. A family history of mania may be found, as well as a higher rate of suicide attempts than in healthy individuals. Substance use disorder, particularly alcohol use disorder, is commonly comorbid, as are anxiety disorders.

Persistent Complex Bereavement Disorder

Following the death of a loved one, a person may experience one or more of the following symptoms: yearning or longing for the deceased, intense sorrow, preoccupation with the deceased, or preoccupation with the circumstances surrounding his or her death. If the symptoms persist on most days for at least a 12-month period (6 months in the case of a child), and if the

person experiences reactive distress to the death (e.g., disbelief, anger, avoidance) or social/identity disruption (expressed desire to die, isolation, confusion about life role, lack of interest in activities that once provided pleasure), the diagnosis may be persistent complex bereavement disorder. Specify if bereavement is due to traumatic circumstances such as homicide or suicide.

Caffeine Use Disorder

Caffeine is the only substance-related disorder that does not have a use disorder described in *DSM-5*, although caffeine tolerance and withdrawal are included. Caffeine use disorder, as included in Section III, is proposed for further study and includes a pattern of caffeine use and failure to control use despite negative consequences such as heart, stomach, and urinary problems; symptoms of anxiety, depression, insomnia, and irritability; and difficulty concentrating (APA, 2013a). A distinction must be made between nonproblematic and problematic use of caffeine, given the high numbers of caffeine users in the general population.

Internet Gaming Disorder

This proposed disorder is based on more than 17 years of research, which indicates that Internet gaming has many of the basic hallmarks of an addiction (e.g., preoccupation with use, withdrawal symptoms, tolerance, loss of interest in other pursuits, unsuccessful attempts to quit, and usage to escape unpleasant feelings). People with Internet gaming disorder have been found to exhibit changes in the frontal lobe of the brain that controls attention, executive function, and emotion processing; some of the changes are comparable to the brains of people addicted to heroin and cocaine. Many recent studies point to the possibility of a genetic link in Internet addiction, as well as the possibility of changes in how the brain's dopamine system functions.

Internet gaming disorder may be associated with major depressive disorder, ADHD, and OCD. In the case of online gambling, a diagnosis of gambling disorder must be ruled out.

Effective treatment for Internet gaming disorder would be similar to treatment for other addictions. Mindfulness-based strategies can help people recognize triggers to addictive behavior and find substitutes for the behavior. Cognitive behavior therapy can be effective in helping people change maladaptive cognitions that encourage pathological Internet usage (e.g., online sex, gambling).

Neurobehavioral Disorder Due to Prenatal Alcohol Exposure (ND-PAE)

Prenatal alcohol exposure has been shown to have a teratogenic effect on the central nervous system of the developing fetus. Proposed criteria for this disorder, which is estimated to affect 2% to 5% of the population prenatally, include

- impaired neurocognitive functioning (e.g., IQ below 70, impaired executive functioning, impaired learning and memory);
- impaired self-regulation (e.g., mood lability, frequent outbursts, impaired impulse control); and
- impairment in adaptive functioning (e.g., communication deficit, difficulty reading social cues, delayed ability to manage daily schedule).

Onset of ND-PAE must occur in childhood and must not be the result of postnatal use of substances. Research indicates that children with ND-PAE have more difficulties in school, poor employment records, legal trouble, and dependent living arrangements. Their risk of suicide is also higher, especially in late adolescence and early adulthood.

Nonsuicidal Self-Injury (NSSI)

Nonsuicidal self-injury is a maladaptive coping strategy that is frequently used to reduce emotional pain. NSSI is often, but not always, related to an increased risk of suicide. In *DSM-IV-TR*, self-injury was listed as a symptom of borderline personality disorder, which was the only category in which cutting or other self-harming behaviors appeared. Given a 12% to 23% prevalence rate of NSSI among nonclinical adolescent populations, clearly many teens who do not meet the criteria for borderline personality disorder are also in need of help, and some are at increased risk of accidental death from NSSI or as a result of later suicide attempts (Plener & Fegert, 2012; Washburn et al., 2012). Longitudinal studies have found a decline in rates of NSSI in adulthood, resulting in a larger focus on adolescents to help curb this very dangerous yet highly treatable condition.

Rates of NSSI appear to increase following media exposure and exposure to self-injurious practices shared on the Internet. Clinicians are advised to assess their adolescent clients' online behavior (Washburn et al., 2012).

Current research is available about successful treatment for NSSI, although no treatment has been designed specifically for use with the high-risk adolescent population. Therapeutic approaches to treating NSSI are similar to those used to treat self-harming behaviors in people with borderline personality disorder. Specifically, dialectical behavior therapy, schema-focused CBT, and mentalization-based treatment (MBT) modalities have been found to decrease suicidality and nonsuicidal self-harming behaviors. Physical activity and participation in organized sports have been found to be protective against NSSI behaviors in adolescence. Because of the alarming increase in the incidence of NSSI, research is currently underway to explore the effect of short-term problem-solving behavior and transdiagnostic treatment approaches. The Appendix in *SET-4* provides a more in-depth discussion of treatment modalities for NSSI. Clearly the positioning of NSSI in Section III of *DSM-5* is a strong message that more research is needed on this important disorder, which can sometimes have lethal outcomes.

Suicidal Behavior Disorder

Suicide is a leading cause of death worldwide. As many as 25% to 35% of persons who make one suicide attempt will make another. The risk of suicide increases with the co-occurrence of many of the mental disorders included in this book, including depression and bipolar disorders, disorders on the schizophrenia spectrum, anxiety and trauma-related disorders, eating disorders, and adjustment disorders. The inclusion of suicidal behavior disorder as a condition for further study in *DSM-5* and the addition of suicide risk factors to applicable disorders are part of an ongoing recognition that despite efforts to reduce the number of people who take their own lives each year, the suicide rate has remained steady, at 10 to 13 suicides per 100,000 people, for more than 70 years. Tools for risk assessment and prevention may be available from the *DSM-5* website (http://www.dsm5 .org), or by turning to pages 453–460 of *SET-4*.

Proposed criteria for suicidal behavior disorder include a suicide attempt within the past 24 months that was self-initiated, was expected to lead to death, did not meet the criteria for nonsuicidal self-injury (which was described earlier), did not occur in a state of delirium or confusion, and was not undertaken solely for a political or religious objective. The diagnosis does not apply to suicidal ideation or preparatory acts in the absence of an attempt. Specify if "current" (not more than 12 months have elapsed since the last suicide attempt) or "in early

remission" (12 to 24 months since the last attempt).

Suicidal behavior is difficult to predict. One study found that as many as 76% of people who completed suicide while inpatients in a psychiatric hospital had denied any suicidal ideation in the week preceding their deaths (Busch, Fawcett, & Jacobs, 2003). Other research confirms that neither psychiatrists nor the patients themselves were able to predict future suicide (Nock, Hwang, Sampson, & Kessler, 2010). Current research is underway to determine other methods of identifying people who are at high risk of suicide (Tingley, 2013).

THE FUTURE OF DIAGNOSIS AND TREATMENT PLANNING

We come now to the end of our *DSM-5* update to the fourth edition of *Selecting Effective Treatments*. The text closes with a chapter on the future of diagnosis. Many anticipated changes (e.g., the movement toward diagnosing disorders on a spectrum, the publication of *DSM-5*, and increased research on the neurobiological underpinnings of disorders) have all come to fruition in the past few years, along with many changes in treatment (e.g., accountability and requirements for evidence-based practice, new treatment delivery methods through the Internet, social media, and e-therapy).

Transdiagnostic treatment approaches that address similar symptoms across a variety of conditions continue to gain in popularity as a cost-effective way to target specific behaviors and provide symptom relief (refer to page 444 of *SET-4*). Treatment that can address a major symptom—suicidal thinking, for example—regardless of whether the person is old or young, has depression or ADHD, uses substances or is anorexic, can be effective in reducing suicidal behaviors and decreasing suicide overall. Similarly, addressing anger and irritability as a symptom can help persons with mood disorders, anxiety, conduct disorders, and some personality disorders learn to make more self-informed choices. Initial research indicates that adjunctive group therapy can be helpful in providing symptom relief across diagnoses.

We are happy to see the addition of cultural formularies, interviews, and a glossary to the fifth edition of the *DSM.* Future changes will no doubt accompany the introduction of ICD-11 in addition to keeping pace with developments in science, research, and medicine. It is hoped that as new information and research become available there will be timely updates to the *Diagnostic and Statistical Manual of Mental Disorders* that allow practitioners to provide the most current diagnoses and treatments available.

APPENDIX

Suicide Assessment and Prevention

Suicide ranks as the 11th leading cause of death for adults, and the third leading cause of death for adolescents. More than 30,000 Americans die each year by suicide; nearly half of them were in treatment for a mental disorder at the time. Working with suicidal clients can be a challenging experience, but if therapists know the warning signs and risk factors, know how to conduct an accurate lethality risk assessment, and recommend appropriate interventions, working with this population can be rewarding as well.

OVERVIEW OF SUICIDE

- Each year, 125,000 people age 10 to 24 are taken to the emergency room because of a suicide attempt.
- One quarter of counselors have lost a client to suicide (Rogers & Oney, 2005).
- 72% of people who have a suicidal plan actually make an attempt (Kessler, Borges, & Wallers, 1999).
- Between 40% and 60% of people who die by suicide are intoxicated at the time of death (U.S. Dept. of Health and Human Services, 2001).
- Between 12 and 25 suicidal attempts are estimated to occur for every suicidal death.

A wide range of mental disorders increase the odds of experiencing suicide ideation, particularly anxiety and mood disorders, Cluster B personality disorders, substance use disorders, and behavioral and conduct disorders.

However, only those disorders that are characterized by anxiety and poor impulse control are predictive of which people with suicidal ideation will tend to act on those thoughts (Nock & Kessler, 2007).

According to Wilhelm (2006), rates of completed suicide increase when people have any of the following:

- Melancholic or psychotic depression
- Chronic medical illness
- Personality disorders
- A co-occurring substance use disorder
- Little social support
- Access to a gun

However, the strongest predictor of suicide attempts in developed countries are mood disorders. Depression is "the greatest predictor" of suicide (Carrier & Ennis, 2004, p. 97) and has been implicated in as many as 85% of suicidal deaths (Haley, 2004). Suicide, like depression, seems to have a genetic or familial component: More than 11% of those who attempt suicide have a family member who has attempted or completed suicide (Maris, 2002), although no one knows if the link is genetic, the result of modeled behavior, or a combination of the two. People who have been exposed to suicide in their families are 8 times more likely to complete suicide themselves (Colt, 2006). Family dysfunction, mental illness, the death of a parent, and other variables contribute. People suffering from depression may be in such severe emotional pain that they feel as if their symptoms will never end, and suicide may seem to be the only escape.

The following are some other secondary symptoms common in depression:

- *Emotional symptoms:* anxiety, anger and hostility, irritability and agitation, social and marital distress.
- *Behavioral symptoms:* crying, neglect of appearance, withdrawal, dependence, lethargy, reduced activity, poor social skills, psychomotor retardation, or agitation.
- *Attitudinal symptoms:* pessimism, helplessness, thoughts of death or suicide, low self-esteem, guilt.
- *Cognitive symptoms:* reduced concentration, indecisiveness, distorted thinking.
- *Physiological symptoms:* sleep disturbances, loss of appetite, decreased sexual interest, gastrointestinal and menstrual difficulties, muscle pains, headaches.

Depressed clients should always be asked about suicidal thinking. If suicidal ideation is present, information should be gathered about any plans that have been formulated, as well as about the availability of means. Because those who have a plan are far more likely to attempt suicide than those whose plans are vague or are planned to occur sometime in the future, having a plan is considered to be a high risk for suicide—particularly if the person has the means to carry out a plan. In such cases, consideration must be given to eliminating the means, or otherwise foiling the attempt by contacting family members or friends, increasing the frequency of sessions and offering between-session telephone contact, or, if all else is rejected by the client, hospitalization to ensure the client's safety.

Although much research is available on risk factors and warning signs for suicide, nothing has yet been developed that can predict who will and who will not make a suicide attempt. A recent survey of psychiatrists and their patients found that psychiatrists accurately predicted suicidal behavior in less than 15% of cases, and the clients correctly predicted their own future suicides less than 20% of the time (Nock, Hwang, Sampson, & Kessler, 2010). Not surprisingly, one study of people who had survived fairly lethal suicide attempts found that nearly 25% had made the decision to end their lives just 5 minutes prior to making the attempt (Colt, 2006).

For therapists, then, knowing the risk factors and warning signs for suicide is just the first step in a process of determining when and how to intervene.

In addition to depression, some of the risk factors that are correlated with increased suicide risk follow. Readers are reminded that not all risk factors will be present, and that people with multiple risk factors may not be suicidal. Risk factors are not causative.

- A prior history of suicide attempts is the biggest risk factor for future completed suicide.
- Four out of five suicidal deaths are male.
- Suicide occurs more frequently in the months immediately following release from a psychiatric hospital.
- Five percent of suicides occur while inside a psychiatric facility.
- Most suicide is associated with a current depressive or mixed episode.

- White women between the ages of 50 and 54 are the fastest growing demographic group for suicide.
- Co-occurring anxiety disorders, such as panic disorder and PTSD, increase risk. In 2010, 1 in 5 people who died by suicide were veterans.
- Men generally use more lethal means (firearms, ropes), while women are more likely to use prescription drugs.
- Women make more than 3 times as many attempts as men, but have a lower completion rate.

Anxiety and poor impulse control tend to predict the transition from suicidal ideation to actual suicide attempts (Nock & Kessler, 2007). People with borderline personality disorder account for 9% to 33% of all suicides. Traits of emotional dysregulation, anxiety, and anger most likely contribute (Pompili et al., 2005). A history of trauma (including physical or sexual abuse), destructive and impulsive behavior, and prior suicide attempts also increase the risk.

As noted earlier, the prominence of suicidal behavior has been well established in the major psychiatric disorders such as bipolar disorder and schizophrenia. Suicidal behaviors are equally as prominent in people with adjustment disorders. Although the research is limited, as many as one-quarter of people with adjustment disorders, regardless of age or gender, report suicidal thoughts or behaviors (Pelkonen et al., 2005). This is particularly true in those with a previous history of mental health treatment, severe psychosocial impairment, dysphoric mood, and agitation.

Being aware of the risk factors is a good first step toward assessing suicidality, but it is not enough. The majority of people who make a suicide attempt give verbal or written messages of their intentions beforehand. Warning signs can include any of the following:

- Giving away prized possessions
- Talking about not being around
- Verbal statements or written notes of suicide plans
- Preoccupation with death or other behaviors indicating the end is near (Brent et al., 1999; Cavanagh, Carson, Sharpe, & Lawrie, 2003; Nock, Hwang, Sampson, & Kessler, 2010)

Suicidal behavior is not limited to adults. A national survey of high school students found that 17% had seriously considered suicide in the past 12 months, 13% had a plan, and 8% had made an attempt (CDC, 2007). Desperation, according to Colt (2006), is the affective state most linked to adolescents who are suicidal. Many young people have had few incidents of loss, failure, or depression in their short lifetimes, and have not developed the callouses necessary to protect themselves. With an external locus of control—looking to others for their self-worth, and especially if there is low self-esteem, adolescents are likely to believe that their self-worth is created by their relationship, and when that relationship fails, their self-worth plummets.

The greatest risk for suicide is found in American Indian, Alaskan native, and GLBT and questioning youth. Although the actual number of adolescents who die by suicide each year is relatively low (approximately 2,000 in the United States), even one suicidal death is too many, and could have been prevented.

It bears repeating that suicide is never the result of just one stressor. Rather a psychological vulnerability to stress, and a complex interaction of other psychosocial problems, combine to load the gun. After that, it takes little to pull the trigger. The stressor is not the cause of suicide, rather it is the vulnerability to stress in general, combined with a history of problems, that cause problems to aggregate into a perfect storm.

THERAPIST CHARACTERISTICS

Many therapists have limited expertise, education, or experience with clients who have reached such depths of despair. A recent poll found that 13% of the general population admit to having had thoughts about ending their own lives. Based on that statistic, therapists can expect a minimum of 1 out of every 10 clients they see to have had suicidal ideation (Rogers & Oney, 2005).

Therapists must overcome their own anxiety and keep in mind that their best tool is themselves. When a new client presents with suicidal ideation, the therapist begins by establishing rapport and quickly building a therapeutic alliance, while simultaneously conducting a psychosocial and lethality assessment. By using strong empathy skills and expressing genuine respect for the client and concern for his or her distress, the therapist joins with the client to assess where they are and confers reassurance that they are in a safe place, that help is available, and that there is hope.

The use of empathy and reflective listening reassures the client, and keeps the focus on the client and in the moment—it is the only countertransference reaction that is helpful and not harmful with a suicidal client (Clark, 2010). Therapists should always keep in mind that any discomfort they are feeling is secondary to the pain being expressed by the client. By maintaining a caring, empathic, and nurturing environment, using a mental checklist rather than a printed assessment instrument, and remembering the risk factors and warning signs of suicide, the therapist can proceed gently down the assessment path while simultaneously creating a powerful therapeutic alliance.

The American Association of Suicidology developed the acronym "Is Path Warm?" to assist in remembering the warning signs of suicide:

I = Ideation

S = Substance abuse and alcohol consumption, which reduces inhibitions and increases the risk

P = Purposelessness. Has the person lost hope, meaning, and purpose in life?

A = Anxiety, especially agitated anxiety, mixed depressive/manic states, and changes in sleep patterns can precede suicide attempts

T = Trapped. Does the person feel that there is no way out of their current situation? Do they feel trapped?

H = Hopelessness, even more than depression, is affiliated with suicidal risk. People with suicidal ideation often develop tunnel vision and cannot see outside of the bleak tunnel to envision a positive future. Walking alongside them and helping them to put one foot in front of the other until they can turn a corner in the tunnel and see the light in front of them may be necessary.

W = Withdrawal from family, friends, and activities that previously gave them pleasure. Low self-esteem, worthlessness, shame, and guilt can all precipitate isolating behavior and an inability to participate in family or group activities.

A = Anger, revenge, erratic behavior that serves to harm themselves or others may be observed.

R = Reckless or impulsive behaviors, including high-risk behaviors or lack of concern for safety, destructive relationships, emotion dysregulation, and bullying, particularly in young people, can all be signs of potential future suicidal behaviors.

M = Mood changes that include dramatic changes in behavior, mood, or personality. As with most mood disorders, changes in sleep or appetite, changes in concern about physical appearance or self-care, difficulty concentrating, pressured speech or retarded movements are all signs to be aware of.

By asking open-ended questions, expressing empathy, and genuine concern, the therapist supports the client while he or she describes the problem and any major concerns that have contributed to it. Is this the last straw? Have they moved out of a violent situation? Do they have no place else to go? By allowing the person to vent, the therapist's office becomes a safe haven for the expression of feelings, no matter how desperate, destructive, or painful they might be. Each statement is responded to with nonjudgmental reflections that encourage the person to say more and to go deeper into his or her feelings and emotions. As the person continues to define the problem, the therapist is making a mental note of any red flags of suicidal risk and lethality and beginning to identify possible areas of strength and coping that may be drawn upon to generate ideas toward an action plan.

Only after the full picture has emerged, after the client has begun to feel validated and understood, and a trusting alliance has been formed, can the therapist safely move toward exploration of problem solving and begin to identify coping mechanisms and potential solutions to the problem. Collaboratively, the client and therapist develop an action plan for the crisis at hand and establish an agreement and follow-up strategies. At this point, the crisis may be resolved enough that the therapist is no longer fearful for the person's safety. If not, and if concerns continue about the client's safety in the coming hours and days, therapists should seek voluntary hospitalization rather than a no-suicide contract. There is little empirical support for the use of a no-suicide contract, and research indicates that it is only as good as the quality of the therapeutic alliance.

ASSESSMENT

One study found that more than half of all therapists who lost a client to suicide failed to recognize suicidal risk factors (Hendin et al., 2001), which may include any or all of the following:

1. Precipitating event (real or perceived loss).
2. Guilt or other affective state related to the loss (abandonment, anger).
3. Behavioral patterns that point toward suicidal intent (impulsivity, reckless driving, substance use, or other self-defeating, or self-harming behaviors).

Much has been written about recognizing the difference between suicidal gestures and suicidal intent. In the moment, all suicidal ideation, gestures, threats, and plans must be taken seriously. Many suicidal acts labeled as gestures (such as cutting or other self-harming behaviors) may, whether intentionally or by accident, result in death. And many people who have made a cry for help with a suicidal gesture that was not taken seriously, have felt the need to make more lethal attempts in an effort to get help. Therefore, all discussion of suicide must be taken seriously, addressed with empathy and nonjudgmental concern, and assessed to determine risk.

The most powerful tool to help the client in crisis is empathy (Rogers & Oney, 2005). Therapists should be congruent, and use the anxiety, alarm, or distress they genuinely feel to express concern for the client and his or her well-being, conduct a thorough assessment of suicidal ideation, and implement a treatment plan that is appropriate to the level of risk determined.

When to Assess

Assessment of suicidal risk should always be conducted in the initial intake session, in later sessions in which the client is depressed or experiencing a crisis or loss, and on an ongoing basis for those who may be at highest risk and who have a prior history of suicide attempts.

Most people with suicidal ideation are ambivalent. They don't want to die; but they desperately want the emotional pain to end. People who cannot see alternatives, who develop cognitive symptoms of constricted thinking, or who have psychotic symptoms or dementia are at increased risk.

How to Assess

As previously mentioned, empathy is the first intervention that should be used with suicidal clients. A person-centered approach to crisis counseling, based on the theories of Carl Rogers, keeps the focus on the client's feelings and reduces the therapist's fears and anxieties about how to handle the situation.

More than two dozen suicide assessment instruments are available, but therapists are warned that the use of such black-and-white instruments with people who are suicidal has been shown to impede the establishment of a positive therapeutic alliance—a fundamental tool in reducing suicidal intent. Clients who were suicidal were found to prefer more frequent sessions with counselors, 24-hour counselor availability, a detailed emergency plan written on an index card they could put in their wallets, and more interaction in sessions on the part of the counselor. No-suicide contracts and assessment forms were found to be least helpful (Bartlett, 2006).

Using an assessment form, rather than asking questions face-to-face, prevents the therapist from developing a connection, and following up on important information

necessary to understanding the depth of the client's feelings. In the initial assessment, feeling that one has been heard, and connecting with an empathic human being may be the only treatment that can make a difference. Rather than relying on assessment forms and questionnaires, therapists should be well aware of risk factors, epidemiological data, and warning signs that the client shares, so that appropriate open-ended questions can be asked.

To assess lethality, therapists should ask if there is a plan; if there is a plan, what are the means? Does the client have access to the means? Will the plan be carried out now or some time in the future? Is the plan specific and current? Or is it vague? Not surprisingly, the risk of death is greater if the plan includes more lethal means such as a gun or a rope, or if there is less likelihood of intervention.

Protective factors should also be assessed. Protective factors are traits and characteristics that are associated with decreased risk of suicide across the lifespan. Religion or spirituality, cohesive family life, problem-solving skills or a positive attitude, even a pet, can all be reasons to stay connected to this world. Assessing for both risk factors and protective factors helps the therapist to look at the whole picture and develop a comprehensive assessment of risk.

Levels of risk can range from none, to mild, moderate, or severe. Based on assessed risk, the therapist will then select the level of intervention that is appropriate (Kanel, 2007). The following list of risk factors are merely a guide. All suicidal clients must be assessed individually, by a culturally competent therapist (Bartlett & Daughhetee, 2010; Granello, 2010).

Low Risk   Low risk can be inferred if no suicide plan has been developed, or if it is vague or unrealistic; if the person lives with others and the probability of intervention is high; and if the problem is acute, with a precipitant that is likely to resolve itself. The person at low risk is clear about their desire to live, and no alcohol is involved.

Moderate Risk This is the level of risk most frequently seen in the therapist's office. A plan has been developed that is hours or days in the future; the person has the means as well as the ability to carry out the plan; no alcohol is involved, and the probability of intervention is low to moderate.

High Risk The suicide plan is specific, the method is highly lethal, and the person can describe when and how they will carry out their plan. Stressors are acute, and the person cannot see a resolution or alternative to the problem. The person is isolated, is under the influence of drugs or alcohol, and does not express any ambivalence.

Not all risk factors are found in clients who attempt suicide, and not all clients with risk factors will attempt suicide. As mentioned earlier, neither psychiatrists nor suicidal clients themselves were effective at predicting future suicide attempts (Nock et al., 2010). Knowing the risk factors, however, can help clinicians to become more aware of who might attempt suicide and provide appropriate interventions as a result.

INTERVENTION

Three options are available for intervention with suicidal clients: immediate hospitalization, referral to a partial hospitalization program, and outpatient psychotherapy. Clearly, some of the clients who present with suicidal ideation will warrant immediate referral for hospitalization to keep them safe and protect them from self-harm. But many will not, and the therapist

must be competent and thorough during the assessment process in order to make a solid determination. If it is determined that the person poses a risk of self-harm, they must not be left alone. Arrangements should be made to contact relatives, a friend, or an ambulance to transport the person to the hospital. It is generally not a good idea for the therapist in private practice, or working with an agency, to transport the person to the hospital. Once admitted, the client will be under the care of the hospital staff, and will undergo a psychiatric evaluation. The therapist may be called on to provide documentation, and background information, but most likely will not be in contact with the client until he or she is discharged from the hospital.

Some states allow therapists and counselors to admit clients to partial hospitalization programs (PHP), other states require a physician's referral. A PHP (also known as a day-treatment program) is an outpatient program that may take place at a hospital or other location. Psychoeducation, individual and group counseling, and medication management are provided in an intensive, outpatient setting. The program generally runs several hours a day, 5 days a week, over the course of several weeks or months.

In most cases, outpatient psychotherapy can be effective in the treatment of suicidal ideation. Empathy fosters collaboration and provides an intervention to adhere to in a crisis. Following the development of an empathic alliance, and the creation of goals and a plan to weather the crisis, therapists may choose to implement cognitive behavioral therapy to focus on narrow thoughts and faulty cognitions.

For clients who are determined to be at lower levels of risk, a safety plan can be developed. Unlike safety contracts—documents in which clients agree not to kill themselves—a safety plan is a collaboration between therapist and client that spells out what the client will do if he or she no longer feels safe, and before any suicidal activity takes place. Most safety plans include at least three or four trusted people, including the therapist, who the client agrees to call if they begin to feel suicidal. Depending on the need, outpatient therapy is usually increased to two or more times a week until the crisis has passed, and any free time is planned so that the client will not be alone for extended periods of time.

Therapists should remember that the use of assessment forms, no-suicide contracts, and hospitalization as a first resort, serve to sever connections between the therapist and client and are frequently the result of the therapist's own discomfort in working with suicidal clients.

After every intervention with a suicidal client, therapists should be sure to document the actions that they took, and why they took them. Therapists should also seek supervision, debrief with a fellow therapist, and practice appropriate self-care. Always be sure to follow up with the client after referral for hospitalization or PHP programs, and whenever there has been a particularly difficult session (W. Hankammer, Snyder, & Hankammer, 2006).

PROGNOSIS

People who are experiencing a brief, time-limited crisis, who have good support systems and a lack of co-occurring mental disorders or family history of suicide or mental illness, are likely to fare best. For many, the current crisis will pass, and they may never experience another suicidal episode. The crisis may have resulted in their reaching out to friends and family, strengthening their resources, and developing resilience.

For others, however, particularly those with co-occurring mood disorders, OCD, or schizophrenia; those who have chronic stressors; those who have experienced trauma or abuse; and those who have a history of reckless behavior, explosive anger, alcohol use, or obsessive preoccupation with suicidal thoughts, prognosis may not be as good.

Unfortunately, despite all that we know about risk factors for suicide, effectively predicting who is at greatest risk, and developing prevention strategies continues to be elusive.

RESOURCES

Nationally, the American Association of Suicidology offers conferences, workshops, continuing education, journals, books, and other resources. Contact local suicide prevention programs and crisis hotlines for training options locally.

Colt, G. H. (2006). *November of the soul: The enigma of suicide*. New York, NY: Scribner.

Granello, D. H., & Granello, P. F. (2007). *Suicide: An essential guide for helping professionals and educators*. Boston, MA: Pearson.

Jackson-Cherry, L. R., & Erford, B. T. (2010). *Crisis intervention and prevention*. Upper Saddle River, NJ: Pearson.

Kanel, K. (2007). *A guide to crisis intervention* (3rd ed.). Belmont, CA: Thomson.

LivingWorks. (2010). *Applied Suicide Intervention Skills Training (ASIST) handbook*. Fayetteville, NC: Author. Available at: www.livingworks.net

References

Aardema, F., & Wu, K. D. (2011). Imaginative, dissociative, and schizotypal processes in obsessive-compulsive symptoms. *Journal of Clinical Psychology*, *67*, 74–81.

Abbass, A., Kisely, S., & Kroenke, K. (2009). Short-term psychodynamic psychotherapy for somatic disorders: Systematic review and meta-analysis of clinical trials. *Psychotherapy and Psychosomatics*, *78*, 265–274.

Abraham, A. J., & Roman, P. (2010). Early adoption of injectable naltrexone for alcohol-use disorders: Findings in the private-treatment sector. *Journal of Studies on Alcohol and Drugs*, *7*, 460–466.

Abramowitz, J. S. (1997). Effectiveness of psychological and pharmacological treatments for obsessive compulsive disorder: A quantitative review. *Journal of Consulting and Clinical Psychology*, *65*, 44–52.

Achenbach, T. (1991). *Manual for the child behavior checklist*. Burlington: University of Vermont, Department of Psychiatry.

Achenbach, T. M., & Rescorla, L. A. (2001). *Manual for the ASEBA school-age forms and profiles*. Burlington, VT: University of Vermont, Research Center for Children, Youth, and Families.

Adams, A. N., Adams, A. N., & Miltenberger, R. G. (2008). Habit reversal training. In W. T. O'Donohue & J. E. Fisher (Eds.), *Cognitive behavior therapy: Applying empirically supported techniques in your practice* (2nd ed., pp. 245–252). Hoboken, NJ: Wiley.

Adams, L., Gouvousis, A., VanLue, M., & Waldron, C. (2004). Social story intervention: Improving communication skills in a child with autism spectrum disorder. *Focus on Autism and Other Developmental Disabilities*, *19*, 87–94.

Adamson, S. J., Heather, N., Morton, V., & Raistrick, D. (2010). Initial preference for drinking goal in the treatment of alcohol problems: II. Treatment outcomes. *Alcohol and Alcoholism*, *45*, 136–142.

Adamson, S. J., Sellman, J. D., & Frampton, C. M. A. (2009). Patient predictors of alcohol treatment outcome: A systematic review. *Journal of Susbstance Abuse Treatment*, *36*, 75–86.

Adan, R. A. H., & Kaye, W. H. (2011). *Behavioral neurobiology of eating disorders*. New York, NY: Springer.

Adler-Tapia, R., & Settle, C. (2009a). Healing the origins of trauma: An introduction to EMDR in treatment with children and adolescents. In A. Rubin & D. W. Springer (Eds.), *Treatment of traumatized adults and children: Clinician's guide to evidence-based practice* (pp. 349–418). Hoboken, NJ: Wiley.

Adler-Tapia, R. L., & Settle, C. S. (2009b). EMDR psychotherapy with children. In A. Rubin & D. W. Springer (Eds.), *Treatment of traumatized adults and children: Clinician's guide to evidence based practice*. Hoboken, NJ: Wiley.

Agency for Healthcare Research and Quality. (2006). *Management of eating disorders*. AHRQ Publication No. 06-E010. Research Triangle Park, NC: RTI-UNC Evidence-Based Practice Center.

Agosti, V., & Stewart, J. W. (2001). Atypical and non-atypical subtypes of depression: Comparison of social functioning, symptoms, course of illness, comorbidity, and demographic features. *Journal of Affective Disorders*, *65*, 75–79.

Agras, W. S., Hammer, L., & McNicholas, F. (1999). A prospective study of the influence of eating-disordered mothers on their children. *International Journal of Eating Disorders*, *25*, 327–334.

Ahn, H., & Wampold, B. E. (2001). Where oh where are the specific ingredients? A meta-analysis of component studies in counseling and psychotherapy. *Journal of Counseling Psychology*, *48*, 251–257.

Ainsworth, M. D. S., Blehar, M. S., Waters, E., & Wall, S. (1978). *Patterns of attachment: A psychological study of the strange situation.* Mahwah, NJ: Erlbaum.

Aires, D. J. (2010). Schizophrenia and schizoaffective are psychotic mood disorders, *Psychiatric Annals, 40,* 98–102.

Akechi, T., Okuyama, T., Sugawara, Y., Nakano, T., Shima, Y., & Uchitomi, Y. (2004). Major depression, adjustment disorders, and post-traumatic stress disorder in terminally ill cancer patients: Associated and predictive factors. *Journal of Clinical Oncology, 22,* 1957–1965.

Akiskal, H. (2005). Searching for behavioral indicators of bipolar II in patients presenting with major depressive episodes: The red sign, the rule of three and other biographic signs of temperamental extravagance, activation and hypomania, *Journal of Affective Disorders, 84,* 279–290.

Akiskal, H., & Benazzi, F. (2006). Does the FDA proposed list of possible correlates of suicidality associated with antidepressants apply to an adult private practice population? *Journal of Affective Disorders, 94,* 105–110.

Albano, A. M., Chorpita, B. F., & Barlow, D. H. (2003). Childhood anxiety disorders. In E. J. Mash & R. A. Barkley (Eds.), *Child psychopathology* (2nd ed., pp. 279–329). New York, NY: Guilford Press.

Alexander, J. F., & Parsons, V. B. (1982). *Functional family therapy: Principles and procedures.* Carmel, CA: Brooks-Cole.

Alexander, J., Goldschmidt, A. B., & Le Grange, D. (2013). *A clinician's guide to binge eating disorder.* New York, NY: Routledge.

Allen, A., & Hollander, E. (2006). Sexual compulsions. In E. Hollander & D. J. Stein (Eds.), *Clinical manual of impulse-control disorders* (pp. 87–114). Arlington, VA: American Psychiatric Publishing.

Allen, L. B., McHugh, R. K., & Barlow, D. H. (2008). Emotional disorders: A unified protocol. In D. H. Barlow (Ed.), *Clinical handbook of psychological disorders: A step-by-step treatment manual* (4th ed., pp. 216–249). New York, NY: Guilford Press.

Allen, L. A., Woolfolk, R. L., Escobar, J. I., Gara, M. A., & Harner, R. M. (2006). Cognitive-behavioral therapy for somatization disorder: A randomized controlled trial. *Archives of Internal Medicine, 166,* 1512–1518.

Althof, S. E. (2007). Treatment of rapid ejaculation: Psychotherapy, pharmacotherapy, and combined therapy. In S. R. Leiblum (Ed.), *Principles and practice of sex therapy* (4th ed., pp. 212–240). New York, NY: Guilford Press.

Altman, E. (2004). Differential diagnosis and assessment of adult bipolar disorder. In S. L. Johnson & R. L. Leahy (Eds.), *Psychological treatment of bipolar disorder* (pp. 35–57). New York, NY: Guilford Press.

American Academy of Child and Adolescent Psychiatry. (2003). *Policy statement: Coercive interventions for reactive attachment disorder.* Washington, DC: Author.

American Academy of Child and Adolescent Psychiatry. (2005). *Practice parameter for the assessment and treatment of children and adolescents with reactive attachment disorders in infancy and childhood.* Available: www.aacap.org

American Academy of Child and Adolescent Psychiatry. (2007a). AACAP official action: Practice parameter for the assessment and treatment of children and adolescents with attention deficit/hyperactivity disorder. *Journal of the American Academy of Child & Adolescent Psychiatry, 46,* 894–921.

American Academy of Child and Adolescent Psychiatry. (2007b). AACAP official action: Practice parameter for the assessment and treatment of children and adolescents with bipolar disorder. *Journal of the American Academy of Child & Adolescent Psychiatry, 46,* 107–125.

American Academy of Child and Adolescent Psychiatry. (2007c). AACAP official action: Practice parameter for the assessment and treatment of children and adolescents with depressive disorders. *Journal of the American Academy of Child & Adolescent Psychiatry, 46,* 1503–1526.

American Academy of Child and Adolescent Psychiatry. (2007d). AACAP official action: Practice parameter for the assessment and treatment of children and adolescents with oppositional defiant disorder. *Journal of the American Academy of Child & Adolescent Psychiatry, 46,* 127–141.

American Academy of Pediatrics. (2001). *Clinical practice guidelines: Treatment of the school-aged child with attention-deficit/hyperactivity disorder.* American Academy of Pediatrics. [Online.] Available: www.aappolicy.aappublications.org

American Association on Mental Retardation. (2002). *Mental retardation: Definition, classification, and systems of support* (10th ed.). Washington, DC: Author.

American Association of Suicidology. (2006). *Assessing and managing suicide risk.* Washington, DC: Author.

American Cancer Society. (2006). Help with physical addiction: Nicotine replacement therapy and other medicines. In *Guide to quitting smoking*. Available: www.cancer.org

American Foundation for Suicide Prevention. (2005). *Guidelines for reporting on suicide*. Downloaded from www.afsp.org/education/printrecommendations.htm

American Psychiatric Association. (2000). *Diagnostic and statistical manual of mental disorders* (4th ed., text rev.). Washington, DC: Author.

American Psychiatric Association. (2001). *Practice guidelines for the treatment of borderline personality disorder*. Washington, DC: Author.

American Psychiatric Association. (2002). *Position statement: Reactive attachment disorder*. Washington, DC: Author.

American Psychiatric Association. (2004a). *Practice guideline for the treatment of patients with bipolar disorder* (2nd ed.). Washington, DC: Author.

American Psychiatric Association. (2004b). *Practice guideline for the treatment of patients with schizophrenia*. Washington, DC: Author.

American Psychiatric Association. (2010). *Reformulation of personality disorders in DSM-5*. American Psychiatric Association. Available: www.dsm5.org/ProposedRevisions/Pages/PersonalityandPersonalityDisorders.aspx

American Psychiatric Association (2013a). *Diagnostic and statistical manual of mental disorders* (5th ed.). Washington, DC: American Psychiatric Publishing.

American Psychiatric Association. (2013b). Making a case for new disorders. Downloaded May 15, 2013, from http://www.dsm-5-making-a-case-for-new-disorders.pdf

American Psychiatric Association and American Academy of Child and Adolescent Psychiatry (2010). *The use of medication in treating childhood and adolescent depression: Information for patients and families*. Washington, DC: Author.

American Psychological Association Task Force on Evidence-Based Practice for Children and Adolescents. (2008). *Disseminating evidence-based practice for children and adoelscents: A systems approach to enhancing care*. Washington, DC: American Psychological Association.

American Psychological Association. (2005). *Policy statement on evidence-based practice in psychology*. Retrieved from www2.apa.org/practice/abpstatement.pdf

Anastopoulos, A. D., & Farley, S. E. (2003). A cognitive-behavioral training program for parents of children with attention-deficit/hyperactivity disorder. In A. E. Kazdin & J. R. Weisz (Eds.), *Evidence-based psychotherapies for children and adolescents* (pp. 187–203). New York, NY: Guilford Press.

Anda, R. F., Felitti, V. J., Bremner, J. D., Walker, J. D., Whitfield, C., Perry, B. D., . . . Giles, W. H. (2006). The enduring effects of abuse and related experiences in childhood: A convergence of evidence from neurobiology and epidemiology. *European Archives of Psychiatry and Clinical Neuroscience, 256,* 174–186.

Anderson, C., & Bulik, C. (2003). Gender differences in compensatory behaviors, weight and shape salience, and drive for thinness. *Eating Behaviors, 5,* 1–11.

Anderson, E. M., & Lambert, M. J. (2001). A survival analysis of clinically significant change in outpatient psychotherapy. *Journal of Clinical Psychology, 57,* 875–888.

Anderson, T., Ogles, B. M., Patterson, C. L., Lambert, M. J., Vermeersch, D. A. (2009). Therapist effects: Facilitative interpersonal skills as a predictor of therapist success. *Journal of Clinical Psychology, 65,* 755–768.

Andrews, T. (2005). Commentary on Riva, G., Virtual reality in psychotherapy: Review. *CyberPsychology & Behavior, 8,* 231–232.

Angst, J., Adolfsson, R., Benazzi, F., Gamma, A., Hantouche, E., Meyer, T. D., . . . Scott, J. (2005). The HCL-32: Towards a self-assessment tool for hypomanic symptoms in outpatients. *Journal of Affective Disorders, 88,* 217–233.

Anthony, K., & Nagel, D. M. (2010). *Therapy online: A practical guide*. London, England: Sage.

Anton, R. F., O'Malley, S. S., Ciraulo, D. A., Cisler, R. A., Couper, D., Donovan, D. M., . . . COMBINE Study Research Group. (2006). Combined pharmacotherapies and behavioral interventions for alcohol dependence: The COMBINE Study: A randomized controlled trial. *Journal of the American Medical Association, 295,* 2003–2017.

Antony, M. M., & Barlow, D. H. (Eds.). (2010). *Handbook of assessment and treatment planning for psychological disorders,* 2nd ed. New York, NY: Guilford Press.

Antony, M. M., & Barlow, D. H. (2002). Specific phobias. In D. H. Barlow (Ed.), *Anxiety and its disorders* (pp. 380–417). New York, NY: Guilford Press.

Antony, M. M., Orsillo, S. M., & Roemer, L. (Eds.). (2001). *Practitioner's guide to empirically based measures of anxiety*. New York, NY: Kluwer Academic/Plenum.

Arehart-Treichel, J. (2009, May 15). Economic crisis taking toll on American Mental Health. *Psychiatric News, 44,* 4–12.

Arfken, C. L., Kubiak, S. P., & Farrag, M. (2009). Acculturation and polysubstance abuse in Arab-American treatment clients. *Transcultural Psychiatry*, *46*, 608–622.

Armstrong, J., Carlson, E. B., & Putnam, F. (1997). *Adolescent Dissociative Experiences Scale-II (A-DES)*. Retrieved from www.energyhealing.net/pdf_files/ades.pdf

Arnkoff, D. B., Glass, C. R., & Shapiro, S. J. (2002). Clients' expectations and preferences. In J. C. Norcross (Ed.), *Psychotherapy relationships that work: Therapist contributions and responsiveness to patients* (pp. 335–356). New York, NY: Oxford University Press.

Arntz, A., van Genderen, H., & Drost, J. (2009). *Schema therapy for borderline personality disorder*. Malden, MA: Wiley.

Asarnow, R. F., & Kernan, C. L. (2008). Childhood schizophrenia. In T. P. Beauchaine & S. P. Hinshaw (Eds.), *Child and adolescent psychopathology* (pp. 614–642). Hoboken, NJ: Wiley.

Aschenbrand, S. G., Kendall, P. C., Webb, A., Safford, S. M., & Flannery-Schroeder, E. (2003). Is childhood separation anxiety disorder a predictor of adult panic disorder and agoraphobia? A seven-year longitudinal study. *Journal of the American Academy of Child and Adolescent Psychiatry*, *42*, 1478–1485.

Ashton, A. K. (2007). The new sexual pharmacology: A guide for the clinician. In S. R. Leiblum (Ed.), *Principles and practice of sex therapy* (4th ed., pp. 509–542). New York, NY: Guilford Press.

Aten, J. D., & Leach, M. M. (2008). *Spirituality and the therapeutic process: A comprehensive resource from intake to termination*. Arlington, VA: American Psychological Association.

Aubry, J., Ferrero, F., & Schaad, N. (2007). *Pharmacotherapy of bipolar disorders*. Hoboken, NJ: Wiley.

Azar, S. T., & Wolfe, D. A. (2006). Child physical abuse and neglect. In E. J. Mash & R. A. Barkley (Eds.), *Treatment of childhood disorders* (3rd ed., pp. 595–646). New York, NY: Guilford Press.

Azrin, N. H., Sneed, T. J., & Foxx, R. M. (1973). Dry bed: A rapid method of eliminating bedwetting (enuresis) of the retarded. *Behaviour Research and Therapy*, *11*, 427–434.

Bachelor, A., & Horvath, A. (2010). The therapeutic relationship. In B. L. Duncan, S. D. Miller, B. E. Wampold, & M. A. Hubble (Eds.), *The heart and soul of change: Delivering what works in therapy* (2nd ed., pp. 133–178). Washington, DC: American Psychological Association.

Bader, P., McDonald, P., & Selby, P. (2009). An algorithm for tailoring pharmacotherapy for smoking cessation: Results from a Delphi panel of international experts. *Tobacco Control*, *18*, 34–42.

Bagenholm, A., & Gillberg, C. (1991). Psychosocial effects on siblings of children with autism and mental retardation: A population-based study. *Journal of Mental Deficiency Research*, *35*, 291–307.

Baggerly, J. N. (2010). Evidence-based standards and tips for play therapy researchers. In. J. N. Baggerly, D. C. Ray, & S. C. Bratton (Eds.), *Child-centered play therapy research: The evidence base for effective practice* (pp. 467–480). Hoboken, NJ: Wiley.

Baggerly, J. N., Ray, D. C., & Bratton, S. C. (Eds.). (2010). *Child-centered play therapy research: The evidence base for effective practice*. Hoboken, NJ: Wiley.

Bagheri, M. M., Kerbeshian, J., & Burd, L. (1999). Recognition and management of Tourette's syndrome and tic disorders. *American Family Physician*, *59*, 2263–2272.

Bailine, S., Fink, M., Knapp, R., Petrides, G., Hussain, M. M., Rasmussen, K., . . . Kellner, C. H. (2010). Electroconvulsive therapy is equally effective in unipolar and bipolar depression. *Acta Psychiatrica Scandinavica*, *121*, 431–436.

Baird, G., Charman, T., Cox, A., Baron-Cohen, S., Swettenham, J., Wheelwright, S., & Drew, A. (2001). Screening and surveillance for autism and pervasive developmental disorders. *Archives of Disease in Childhood*, *84*, 468–475.

Baker, S. L., Patterson, M. D., & Barlow, D. H. (2002). Panic disorder and agoraphobia. In M. M. Antony & D. H. Barlow (Eds.), *Handbook of assessment and treatment planning for psychological disorders* (pp. 67–112). New York, NY: Guilford Press.

Balázs, J., Benazzi, F., Rihmer, Z., Rihmer, A., Akiskal, K. K., & Akiskal, H. S. (2006). The close link between suicide attempts and mixed (bipolar) depression: Implications for suicide prevention. *Journal of Affective Disorders*, *91*, 133–138.

Baldessarini, R. J., & Tondo, L. (2003). Suicide risk and treatments for patients with bipolar disorder. *Journal of the American Medical Association*, *290*, 1517–1519.

Banham, L., & Gilbody, S. (2010). Smoking cessation in severe mental illness: What works? *Addiction*, *105*, 1176–1189.

Barak, A., & Bloch, N. (2006). Factors related to perceived helpfulness in supporting highly distressed individuals through an online support chat. *CyberPsychology & Behavior*, *9*, 60–68.

Barbaree, H. E., & Marshall, W. E. (1985). Anxiety based disorders. In M. Hersen & S. M. Turner (Eds.), *Diagnostic interviewing* (pp. 55–77). New York, NY: Plenum.

Barbaresi, W. J., Colligan, R. C., Weaver, A. L., Voigt, R. G., Killian, J. M., & Katusic, S. K. (2013). Mortality, ADHD, and psychosocial adversity in adults with childhood ADHD: A prospective study. *Pediatrics*, *131*, 637–644.

Barber, J. P., Connolly, M. B., Crits-Christoph, P., Gladys, L., & Siqueland, L. (2000). Alliance predicts patients' outcome beyond in-treatment change in symptoms. *Journal of Consulting and Clinical Psychology*, *68*, 1027–1032.

Barbour, K. A., Edenfield, T. M., & Blumenthal, J. A. (2007). Exercise as a treatment for depression and other psychiatric disorders: A review. *Journal of Cardiopulmonary Rehabilitation and Prevention*, *27*, 359–367.

Barkley, R. A. (2006). *Attention-deficit hyperactivity disorder: A handbook for diagnosis and treatment* (3rd ed.). New York, NY: Guilford Press.

Barkley, R. A., & Murphy, K. R. (2006). *Attention deficit hyperactivity disorder: A clinical workbook* (3rd ed.). New York, NY: Guilford Press.

Barlow, D. H. (2002). *Anxiety and its disorders: The nature and treatment of anxiety and panic* (2nd ed.). New York, NY: Guilford Press.

Barlow, D. H. (Ed.). (2007). *Clinical handbook of psychological disorders: A step-by-step treatment manual* (4th ed.). New York, NY: Guilford Press.

Barlow, D. H., Allen, L. B., & Basden, S. L. (2007). Psychosocial treatments for panic disorders, phobias, and generalized anxiety disorder. In P. E. Nathan & J. M. Gorman (Eds.), *A guide to treatments that work* (3rd ed., pp. 351–394). New York, NY: Oxford University Press.

Barlow, D. H., Craske, M. G., Cerny, J. A., & Klosko, J. S. (1989). Behavioral treatment of panic disorder. *Behavior Therapy*, *20*, 261–282.

Barlow, D. H., & Durand, V. M. (2008). *Abnormal psychology: An integrative approach* (2nd ed.). Pacific Grove, CA: Brooks/Cole.

Barlow, D. H., Ellard, K. K., Fairholme, C. P., Farchione, T. J., Boisseau, C. L., Ehrenreich-May, J. T., & Allen, L. B. (2010). *Unified protocol for transdiagnostic treatment of emotional disorders: Workbook (Unified Transdiagnostic Treatments that Work)*. New York, NY: Oxford University Press.

Barnett, J. H., & Smoller, J. W. (2009). The genetics of bipolar disorder. *Neuroscience, 164*, 331–343.

Barnett, J. H., Werners, U., Secher, S. M., Hill, K. E., Brazil, R., Masson, K., . . . Johns, P. B. (2007). Substance use in a population-based clinical sample of people with first-episode psychosis. *British Journal of Psychiatry*, *190*, 515–520.

Baron-Cohen, S., Allen, J., & Gillberg, C. (1992). Can autism be detected at 18 months? The needle, the haystack, and the CHAT. *British Journal of Psychiatry*, *161*, 839–843.

Barrett, P. B., Duffy, A. L., Dadds, M. R., & Rapee, R. M. (2001). Cognitive-behavioral treatment of anxiety disorders in children: Long-term (6-year) follow-up. *Journal of Consulting and Clinical Psychology*, *69*, 135–141.

Barrett, P. M., & Shortt, A. L. (2003). Parental involvement in the treatment of anxious children. In A. E. Kazdin & J. R. Weisz (Eds.), *Evidence-based psychotherapies for children and adolescents* (pp. 101–119). New York, NY: Guilford Press.

Barsky, A., Orav, E. J., & Bates, D. W. (2005). Somatization increases medical utilization and costs independent of psychiatric and medical comorbidity. *Archives of General Psychiatry*, *62*, 903–910.

Bartlett, M. L. (2006). The efficacy of a no-suicide contracts with clients in counseling on an outpatient basis. *Dissertation Abstracts International*, 67, 3438, 06B UMI No. 3225247

Bartlett, M. L., & Daughhetee, C. (2010). Risk assessment. In B. Erford & L. Jackson-Cherry (Eds.), *Crisis: Intervention and prevention*. Upper Saddle River, NJ: Pearson.

Bartley, M., & Ferrie, J. (2010). Do we need to worry about the health risk of unemployment? *Journal of Epidemiology and Community Mental Health*, *64*, 5–6.

Basson, R. (2007). Sexual desire/arousal disorders in women. In S. R. Leiblum (Ed.), *Principles and practice of sex therapy* (4th ed., pp. 25–53). New York, NY: Guilford Press.

Bateman, A., & Fonagy, P. (1999). Effectiveness of partial hospitalization in the treatment of borderline personality disorder: A randomized controlled trial. *American Journal of Psychiatry*, *156*, 1563–1569.

Bateman, A., & Fonagy, P. (2004). *Psychotherapy for borderline personality disorder: Mentalization-based treatment*. New York, NY: Oxford University Press.

Bateman, A., & Fonagy, P. (2007). Borderline personality disorder, day hospitalization, and mentalization, In J. V. Van Luyn, S. Akhtar, & W. Livesley (Eds.), *Severe personality disorders* (pp. 118–136). Cambridge, UK: Cambridge University Press.

Bateman, A., & Fonagy, P. (2008). Comorbid antisocial and borderline personality disorders: Mentalization-based treatment. *Journal of Clinical Psychology: In Session, 64,* 181–194.

Bateman, A., & Fonagy, P. (2010). Randomized controlled trial of outpatient mentalization-based treatment versus structured clinical management for borderline personality disorder. *Focus, 8,* 55–65.

Beauchaine, T. P., & Hinshaw, S. P. (Eds.). (2008). *Child and adolescent psychopathology.* Hoboken, NJ: John Wiley & Sons.

Bebko, J. M., Weiss, J. A., Demark, J. L., & Gomez, P. (2006). Discrimination of temporal synchrony in intermodal events by children with autism and children with developmental disabilities without autism. *Journal of Child Psychology and Psychiatry, 47,* 88–98.

Beck, A. T., & Emery, G. (1985). *Anxiety disorders and phobias.* New York, NY: Basic Books.

Beck, A. T., Freeman, A., Davis, D. D., & Associates. (2004). *Cognitive therapy of personality disorders* (2nd ed.). New York, NY: Guilford Press.

Beck, A. T., Rush, A. J., Shaw, B. F., & Emery, G. (1979). *Cognitive therapy of depression.* New York, NY: Guilford Press.

Beck, A. T., & Steer, R. A. (1990). *Manual for the Beck Anxiety Inventory.* San Antonio, TX: Psychological Corporation.

Beck, A. T., Steer, R. A., & Brown, G. K. (1996). *Beck Depression Inventory* (2nd ed. manual). San Antonio, TX: Psychological Corporation.

Beck, J. (2005). *Cognitive therapy for challenging problems.* New York, NY: Guilford Press.

Beck, M., Friedlander, M. L., & Escudero, V. (2006). Three perspectives on clients' experiences of the therapeutic alliance: A discovery-oriented investigation. *Journal of Marital and Family Therapy, 32,* 355–368.

Becker, K. D., Stuewig, J., Herrera, V. M., & McCloskey, L. A. (2004). A study of firesetting and animal cruelty in children: Family influences and adolescent outcomes. *Journal of the American Academy of Child and Adolescent Psychiatry, 43,* 905–912.

Beers, S. R., & DeBellis, M. D. (2002). Neuropsychological function in children with maltreatment-related posttraumatic stress disorder. *Journal of Psychiatry, 159,* 483–486.

Begley, M., & Quayle, E. (2007). The lived experience of adults bereaved by suicide: A phenomenological study. *Crisis, 28,* 26–34.

Bellack, A., & Mueser, K. T. (1993). Psychosocial treatment for schizophrenia. *Schizophrenia Bulletin, 19,* 317–336.

Bellack, A., Mueser, K. T., Gingerich, S., & Agresta, J. (2004). *Social skills training for schizophrenia* (2nd ed.). New York, NY: Guilford Press.

Benazon, N. R., & Coyne, J. C. (2000). Living with a depressed spouse. *Journal of Family Psychology, 14,* 71–79.

Bender, K., Springer, D. W., & Kim, J. S. (2006). Treatment effectiveness with dually diagnosed adolescents: A systematic review. *Brief Treatment and Crisis Intervention, 6,* 177–205.

Benton, T. D., & Lynch, J. (2006, July 13). Adjustment disorders. *EMedicine.* Available: www.emedicine.com/Med/topic3348.htm

Berardelli, A., Curr, A., Fabbrini, G., Gillio, F., & Manfredi, M. (2003). Pathophysiology of tics and Tourette's syndrome. *Journal of Neurology, 250,* 781–787.

Bergman, R. L., Piacentini, J., & McCracken, J. T. (2002). Prevalence and description of selective mutism in a school-based sample. *Journal of the American Academy of Child and Adolescent Psychiatry, 41,* 938–946.

Berman, J. S., & Norton, N. C. (1985). Does professional training make a therapist more effective? *Psychological Bulletin, 98,* 401–407.

Bernal, M., Haro, J. M., Bernert, S., Brugha, T., de Graff, R., Bruffaerts, R., . . . ESEMED/MHEDEA Investigators. (2007). Risk factors for suicidality in Europe: Results from the ESEMED study. *Journal of Affective Disorders, 101,* 27–34.

Bernard, M., Jackson, C., & Patterson, P. (2010). Trauma and first episode psychosis. In P. French, J. Smith, D. Shiers, M. Reed, & M. Rayne (Eds.), *Promoting recovery in first psychosis: A practice manual.* Oxford, United Kingdom: Wiley-Blackwell.

Bernstein, D. P., Fink, L., Handlesman, L., Foote, J., Lovejoy, M., Wenzel, K., . . . Ruggiero, J. (1994). Initial reliability and validity of a new retrospective measure of child abuse and neglect. *American Journal of Psychiatry, 151,* 1132–1136.

Bernstein, E. B., & Putnam, F. W. (1986). Development, reliability, and validity of a dissociation scale. *Journal of Nervous and Mental Disease, 174,* 727–735.

Berstein, D. A., Borkovec, T. D., & Hazlett-Stephens, H. (2000). *New directions in progressive relaxation training: A guide for helping professionals.* Westport, CT: Praeger.

Betan, E., Heim, A. K., Zittel-Conklin, C., & Westen, D. (2005). Countertransference phenomena and personality pathology in a clinical practice: An empirical investigation. *American Journal of Psychiatry, 162,* 890–898.

Beutler, L. E., & Consoli, A. J. (1993). Matching the therapist's interpersonal stance to clients' characteristics: Contributions from systematic eclectic psychotherapy. *Psychotherapy, 30*, 417–422.

Beutler, L. E., Crago, M., & Arizmendi, T. G. (1986). Therapist variables to psychotherapy process. In S. L. Garfield & A. E. Bergin (Eds.), *Handbook of psychotherapy and behavior change* (3rd ed., pp. 257–310). New York, NY: Wiley.

Biederman, J., Mick, E., Faraone, S. V., & Wozniak, J. (2004). Pediatric bipolar disorder or disruptive behavior disorder? *Primary Psychiatry, 11*, 36–41.

Bienvenu, O. J., Samuels, J. F., Riddle, M. A., Hoehn-Saric, R., Liang, K. Y., Cullen, B. A. M., . . . Nestadt, G. (2000). The relationship of obsessive-compulsive disorder to possible spectrum disorders: Results from a family study. *Biological Psychiatry, 48*, 287–293.

Binder, J. L., & Henry, W. P. (2010). Developing skills in managing negative process. In J. C. Muran & J. P. Barber (Eds.), *The therapeutic alliance: An evidence-based guide to practice* (pp. 285–303). New York, NY: Guilford Press.

Birch, L. L., Fisher, J. O., & Davison, K. K. (2003). Learning to overeat: Maternal use of restrictive feeding practices promotes girls' eating in the absence of hunger. *American Journal of Clinical Nutrition, 78*, 215–220.

Birmaher, B., Axelson, D., Strober, M., Gill, M. K., Chiapetta, L., Ryan, N., . . . Keller, M. (2006). Clinical course of children and adolescents with bipolar spectrum disorders. *Archives of General Psychiatry, 63*, 175–183.

Birmaher B., & Brent D. (2007). AACAP Work Group on Quality Issues. Practice parameter for the assessment and treatment of children and adolescents with depressive disorders. Washington (DC): American Academy of Child and Adolescent Psychiatry.

Birmaher, B., & Brent, D. A. (2010). Depression/dysthymia. In M. Dulcan (Ed), *Textbook of Child & Adolescent Psychiatry*. Arlington, VA: American Psychiatric Publishing.

Bitran, S., Morissette, S., Spiegel, D., & Barlow, D.H. (2008). A pilot study of sensation focused intensive treatment for panic disorder with moderate to severe agoraphobia: Preliminary outcome and benchmarking data. *Behavior Modification, 32*, 196–214.

Black, B., & Uhde, T. W. (1995). Psychiatric characteristics of children with selective mutism: A pilot study. *Journal of American Academy of Child and Adolescent Psychiatry, 34*, 847–856.

Black, S. E., Doody, R., Li, H., McRae, T., Jambor, M. K., Xu, Y., . . . Richardson, S. (2007). Donepezel improves cognitive and global functioning in patients with severe Alzheimer disease. *Neurology, 69*, 459–469.

Blader, J. C., & Carlson, G. A. (2007). Increased rates of bipolar disorder diagnoses among U. S. child, adolescent, and adult inpatients, 1996–2004. *Biological Psychiatry, 62*, 107–114.

Blake, D. D., Weathers, F., Nagy, L. M., Kaloupek, D. G., Klauminzer, G., & Charney, D. S. (1990). A clinician rating scale for assessing current and lifetime PTSD: The CAPS-1. *Behavior Therapist, 13*, 187–188.

Blakely, T. A., Collings, S. C. D., & Atkinson, J. (2003). Unemployment and suicide. Evidence for a causal relationship? *Journal of Epidemiology of Community Mental Health, 165*, 594–600.

Blanchard, E. B., Jones-Alexander, J., Buckley, T. C., & Forneris, C. A. (1996). Psychometric properties of the PTSD checklist. *Behaviour Research and Therapy, 34*, 669–673.

Blanco, C., Grant, J., Petry, N. M., Simpson, H. B., Alegria, A., Liu, S., & Hasin, D. (2008). Prevalence and correlates of shoplifting in the United States: Results from the national epidemiologic survey on alcohol and related conditions (NESARC). *American Journal of Psychiatry, 165*, 905–913.

Bleiberg, E., & Markowitz, J. C. (2008). Interpersonal psychotherapy for depression. In D. H. Barlow (Ed.), *Clinical handbook of psychological disorders: A step-by-step treatment manual* (4th ed., pp. 306–327). New York, NY: Guilford Press.

Blissett, J., Meyer, C., & Haycraft, E. (2007). Maternal mental health and child feeding problems in a non-clinical group. *Eating Behaviors, 8*, 311–318.

Blizzard, R. (1997). The origins of dissociative identity disorder from an object relations and attachment theory perspective. *Dissociation, 10*, 223–229.

Blizzard, R. (2003). Disorganized attachment, development of dissociated self states, and a relational approach to treatment. *Journal of Trauma and Dissociation, 4*, 27–50.

Bloom, B. (2002). Brief intervention for anxiety disorders: Clinical outcome studies. *Brief Treatment and Crisis Intervention, 2*, 325–329.

Blum, N., St. John, D., Pfohl, B., Stuart, S., McCormick, B., Allen, J., . . . Black, D. W. (2008). Systems training for emotional predictability and problem solving (STEPPS) for outpatients with borderline personality disorder: A randomized controlled trial and 1-year follow-up. *American Journal of Psychiatry, 165*, 468–478.

Blume, A. W., & Marlatt, G. A. (2008). Harm reduction. In W. T. O'Donohue and J. E. Fisher (Eds.), *Cognitive behavior therapy: Applying empirically supported techniques in your practice* (2nd ed., pp. 253–259). Hoboken, NJ: Wiley.

Blume, A. W., Morera, O. F., & de la Cruz, B. G. (2007). Assessment of addictive behaviors in ethnic-minority cultures. In D. M. Donovan & G. A. Marlatt (Eds.), *Assessment of addictive behaviors* (2nd ed., pp. 49–70). New York, NY: Guilford Press.

Blumenthal, J. A., Babyak, M. A., Doraiswamy, P. M., Watkins, L., Hoffman, B. M., Barbour, K. A., . . . Sherwood, A. (2007). Exercise and pharmacotherapy in the treatment of major depressive disorder. *Psychosomatic Medicine, 69*, 587–596.

Bohart, A., & Tallman, K. (1999). *How clients make therapy work: The process of active self-healing*. Washington, DC: American Psychological Association.

Bolles, R. N. (2006). *What color is your parachute? A practical manual for job hunters and career changers* (Rev. ed.). Berkeley, CA: Ten Speed Press.

Bond, M. R. (2006). Psychiatric disorders and pain. In S. B. McMahon & M. Kottzenburg (Eds.), *Wall and Melzack's textbook of pain* (5th ed., pp. 259–266). Philadelphia, PA: Elsevier Churchill Livingstone.

Bonnet, M. H., & Arand, D. L. (2008). Chronic insomnia. In S. R. Pandi-Perumal, J. C. Verster, J. M. Monti, M. Lader, & S. Z. Langer (Eds.), *Sleep disorders: Diagnostics and therapeutics* (pp. 80–89). New York, NY: Informa Healthcare.

Bora, E., & Arabaci, L. B. (2009). Effect of age and gender on schizotypal personality traits in the normal population. *Psychiatry and Clinical Neurosciences, 63*, 663–669.

Bordin, E. S. (1979). The generalizability of the psychoanalytic concept of the working alliance. *Psychotherapy, 16*, 252–260.

Borkovec, T. D., & Ruscio, A. M. (2001). Psychotherapy for generalized anxiety disorder. *Journal of Clinical Psychiatry, 62*, 37–42.

Boschen, M. J., & Warner, J. C. (2009). Publication trends in individual DSM personality disorders: 1971–2015. *Australian Psychologist, 44*, 136–142.

Boss, P. (2006). *Loss, trauma, and resilience: Therapeutic work with ambiguous loss*. New York, NY: Norton.

Bourne, E. J. (2005). *The anxiety and phobia workbook* (4th ed.). New York, NY: Harbinger.

Bowen, S., Chawla, N., & Marlatt, G. A. (2010). *Mindfulness-based relapse prevention for addictive behaviors: A clinician's guide*. New York, NY: Guilford Press.

Bowen, S., & Marlatt, A. (2009). Surfing the urge: Brief mindfulness-based intervention for college student smokers. *Psychology of Addictive Behaviors, 23*, 666–671.

Bowlby, J. (1969/1982). *Attachment and loss: Vol. 1. Attachment*. New York: Basic Books. (Original work published 1969)

Bowman, D., Scogin, F., Floyd, M., & McKendree-Smith, N. (2001). Psychotherapy length of stay and outcome: A meta-analysis of the effect of therapist sex. *Psychotherapy, 38*, 142–148.

Bozarth, J. D., Zimring, F. M., & Tausch, R. (2001). Client-centered therapy: The evolution of a revolution. In D. J. Cain & J. Seeman (Eds.), *Handbook of research and practice in humanistic psychotherapy* (pp. 147–188). Washington, DC: American Psychological Association.

Brach, T. (2004). *Radical acceptance: Embracing your life with the heart of a Buddha*. New York, NY: Bantam Dell.

Bradford, D., Stroup, S., & Lieberman, J. (2002). Pharmacological treatments for schizophrenia. In P. E. Nathan & J. M. Gorman (Eds.), *A guide to treatments that work* (2nd ed., pp. 169–200). New York, NY: Oxford University Press.

Brand, B. L., Armstrong, J. G., Loewenstein, R. J. (2006). Psychological assessment of patients with dissociative identity disorder. *Psychiatric Clinics of North America, 29*, 145–168.

Brand, B., Lanins, R., McNary, S., Classen, C., Loewenstein, R., Pain, C., & Putnam, F. (2009). A naturalistic study of dissociative identity disorder and dissociative disorder not otherwise specified patients treated by community clinicians, *Psychological Trauma: Theory, Research, Practice, and Policy, 1*, 153–171.

Brand, B. L., Armstrong, J. G., Loewenstein, R. J., & McNary, S.W. (2009). Personality differences on the Rorschach of dissociative identity disorder, borderline personality disorder, and psychotic inpatients. *Psychological Trauma: Theory, Research, Practice, and Policy, 1*(3), 188–205.

Brand, J. E., Levy, B. R., & Gallo, W. T. (2008). Effects of layoffs and plant closings on depression among older workers. *Research on Aging, 30*, 701–721.

Bratton, S., Landreth, G., Kellam, T., & Blackard, S. (2006). *Child-parent relationship therapy (CPRT) treatment manual: A 10-session filial therapy model for training parents*. New York, NY: Taylor & Francis.

Bratton, S., Ray, D., Rhine, T., & Jones, L. (2005). The efficacy of play therapy with children: A meta-analytic review of the outcome research. *Professional Psychology: Research and Practice, 36*, 376–390.

Brent, D. A., Baugher, M., Bridge, J., Chen, T., & Chiappetta, L. (1999). Age- and sex-related risk factors for adolescent suicide. *Journal of the American Academy of Child and Adolescent Psychiatry, 38*, 1497–1505.

Brewer, J. A., Bowen, S., Smith, J. T., Marlatt, G. A., & Potenza, M. N. (2010). Mindfulness-based treatments for co-occurring depression and substance use disorders: What can we learn from the brain? *Addiction, 105*, 1698–1706.

Bridge, J. A., Iyengar, S., Salary, C. B., Barbe, R. P., Birmaher, B., Pincus, H. A., . . . Brent, D. A. (2007). Clinical response and risk for reported suicidal ideation and suicide attempts in pediatric antidepressant treatment: A meta-analysis of randomized controlled trials. *Journal of the American Medical Association, 297*, 1683–1696.

Bridges, W. (2001). *The way of transition: Embracing life's most difficult moments.* Cambridge, MA: Perseus.

Briere, J. (2005). *Trauma symptom checklist for young children: Professional manual.* Lutz, FL: Psychological Assessment Resources.

Brinkmeyer, M. Y., & Eyberg, S. M. (2003). Parent-child interaction therapy for oppositional children. In A. E. Kazdin & J. R. Weisz (Eds.), *Evidence-based psychotherapies for children and adolescents* (pp. 204–223). New York, NY: Guilford Press.

Brooks-Gunn, J., Klebanov, P. K., Smith, J., Duncan, G. J., & Lee, K. (2003). The black-white test score gap in young children: Contributions of test and family characteristics. *Applied Development Science, 7*, 239–252.

Brotto, L. A., Krychman, M., & Jacobson, P. (2008). Eastern approaches for enhancing women's sexuality: Mindfulness, acupuncture, and yoga. *Journal of Sexual Medicine, 5*, 2741–2748.

Brown, T. A., Di Nardo, P. A., & Barlow, D. H. (1994). *Anxiety Disorders Interview Schedule for DSM-IV (ADIS-IV).* San Antonio, TX: Psychological Corporation Graywind.

Brown, T. A., O'Leary, T. A., & Barlow, D. H. (1993). Generalized anxiety disorder. In D. H. Barlow (Ed.), *Clinical handbook of psychological disorders* (2nd ed., pp. 137–188). New York, NY: Guilford Press.

Bryant, R. A., & Harvey, A. G. (2000). *Acute stress disorder: A handbook of theory, assessment, and treatment.* Washington, DC: American Psychological Association.

Buchsbaum, D. G., Buchanan, R. G., Centor, R. M., Schnoll, S. H., & Lawton, M. J. (1991). Screening for alcohol abuse using CAGE scores and likelihood ratios. *Annals of Internal Medicine, 115*, 774–777.

Budman, S. H. (1981). *Forms of brief therapy.* New York, NY: Guilford Press.

Bulik, C. M., Sullivan, P. F., Tozzi, F., Furberg, H., Lichtenstein, P., & Pedersen, N. L. (2006). Prevalence, heritability, and prospective risk factors for anorexia nervosa. *Archives of General Psychiatry, 63*, 305–312.

Burbach, F. R., Fadden, G., & Smith, J. (2010). Family interventions for first episode psychosis. In P. French, J. Smith, D. Shiers, M. Reed, & M. Rayne (Eds.), *Promoting recovery in early psychosis* (pp. 210–225). Oxford, United Kingdom: Wiley-Blackwell.

Burgard, S., Brand, J., & House, J. S. (2007). Toward a better estimation of the effect of job loss on health. *Journal of Health and Social Behavior, 48*, 369–384.

Burke, B. L., Arkowitz, H., & Menchola, M. (2003). The efficacy of motivational interviewing: A meta-analysis of controlled clinical trials. *Journal of Consulting and Clinical Psychology, 71*, 843–861.

Burlingame, G. M., Fuhriman, A., & Mosier, J. (2003). The differential effectiveness of group psychotherapy: A meta-analytic perspective. *Group Dynamics: Theory, Research, and Practice, 7*, 3–12.

Busch, K. A., Fawcett, J., & Jacobs, D. G. (2003). Clinical correlates of inpatient suicide. *Journal of Clinical Psychiatry, 64*(1), 14–19.

Butcher, J. N., Mineka, S., & Hooley, J. M. (2006). *Abnormal psychology* (13th ed.). Boston, MA: Pearson Education.

Butler, A. C., Chapman, J. E., Forman, E. M., & Beck, A. T. (2006). The empirical status of cognitive-behavioral therapy: A review of meta-analyses. *Clinical Psychology Review, 26*, 17–31.

Cain, D. J., & Seeman, J. (Eds.). (2001). *Humanistic psychotherapies: Handbook of research and practice.* Washington, DC: American Psychological Association.

Caligor, E., Kernberg, O. F., & Clarkin, J. F. (2007). *Handbook of dynamic psychotherapy for higher level personality pathology.* Arlington, VA: American Psychiatric Publishing.

Camacho, A., & Akiskal, H. S. (2005). Proposal for a bipolar-stimulant spectrum: Temperament, diagnostic validation and therapeutic outcomes with mood stabilizers. *Journal of Affective Disorders, 85*, 217–230.

Campbell, L. A., & Brown, T. A. (2002). Generalized anxiety disorder. In M. M. Antony & D. H. Barlow (Eds.), *Handbook of assessment and treatment planning for psychological disorders* (pp. 147–181). New York, NY: Guilford Press.

Canton, C. L. M., Hasin, D. S., Shrout, P. E., Drake, R. E., Dominguez, B., First, M. B., . . . Schanzer, B. (2007). Stability of early-phase primary psychotic disorders with concurrent substance use and substance-induced psychosis. *British Journal of Psychiatry, 190*, 105–111.

Cantwell, D. P. (1996). Attention deficit disorder: A review of the past 10 years. *Journal of the American Academy of Child and Adolescent Psychiatry, 35*, 978–987.

Cardena, E., & Weiner, L. A. (2004). Evaluation of dissociation throughout the lifespan. *Psychotherapy, 41*, 496–508.

Carlson, G. A. (1998). Mania and ADHD: Comorbidity or confusion. *Journal of Affective Disorders, 51*, 177–187.

Carlstedt, R. A. (2011). Conceptual, methodological and practical foundations of integrative evidence-based clinical research, diagnostics, and interventions. In R. A. Carlstedt (Ed.), *Handbook of integrative clinical psychology, psychiatry, and behavioral medicine: Perspectives, practice, and research* (pp. 1–16). New York, NY: Springer.

Carmody, J., Baer, R. A., Lykins, E.L.B., & Olendzki, N. (2009). An empirical study of the mechanisms of mindfulness in a mindfulness-based stress reduction program. *Journal of Clinical Psychology, 65*, 613–626.

Carpenter, W. T. (2009). Anticipating DSM-V: Should psychosis risk become a diagnostic class? *Schizophrenia Bulletin, 35*, 841–843.

Carr, A. (2009). The effectiveness of family therapy and systemic interventions for child-focused problems. *Journal of Family Therapy, 31*, 3–45.

Carrier, J. W., & Ennis, K. (2004). Depression and suicide. In D. Capuzzi (Ed.), *Suicide across the lifespan* (pp. 39–62). Alexandria, VA: American Counseling Association.

Carroll, A. (2009). Are you looking at me? Understanding and managing paranoid personality disorder. *Advances in Psychiatric Treatment, 15*, 40–48.

Carroll, K. M., & Ball, S. A. (2007). Assessment of cocaine abuse and dependence. In D. M. Donovan & G. A. Marlatt (Eds.), *Assessment of addictive behaviors* (2nd ed., pp. 155–184). New York, NY: Guilford Press.

Carroll, R. A. (2007). Gender dysphoria and transgender experiences. In S. R. Leiblum (Ed.), *Principles and practice of sex therapy* (4th ed., pp. 477–508). New York, NY: Guilford Press.

Casey, P. (2009). Adjustment disorder: Epidemiology, diagnosis and treatment. *CNS Drugs, 23*, 927–938.

Cashwell, C. S., & Young, J. S. (Eds.). (2005). *Integrating spirituality and religion into counseling: A guide to competent practice*. Alexandria, VA: American Counseling.

Castellini, G., Mannucci, E., Mazzei, C., Lo Sauro, C., Faravelli, C., Rotella, C. M., . . . Ricca, V. (2010). Sexual function in obese women with and without binge eating disorder. *Journal of Sexual Medicine, 7*, 3969–3978.

Caton, C. L. M., Hasin, D. S., Shrout, P. E., Drake, R. E., Dominguez, B., First, M. B., . . . Schanzer, B. (2007). Stability of early-phase primary psychotic disorders with concurrent substance use and substance-induced psychosis. *British Journal of Psychiatry, 190*, 105–111.

Cavanagh, J. T. O., Carson, A. J., Sharpe, M. & Lawrie, S. M. (2003). Psychological autopsy studies of suicide: a systematic review. *Psychological Medicine, 33*, 395–405.

Centers for Disease Control and Prevention. (2003). *Web-based injury statistics query and reporting system (WISQARS)*. National Center for Injury Prevention and Control. Available: www.cdc.gov/ncipc/wisqars

Centers for Disease Control and Prevention. (2007). Prevalence of autism spectrum disorders. *Morbidity and Mortality Weekly Report, 56*, 1–11.

Centers for Disease Control and Prevention. (2007). *Suicide facts at a glance*. Retrieved from www.cdc/gov

Chamberlain, L. L., & Jew, C. L. (2005). Assessment and diagnosis. In P. Stevens & R. L. Smith (Eds.), *Substance abuse counseling: Theory and practice* (3rd ed., pp. 123–158). Upper Saddle River, NJ: Pearson.

Chamberlain, P., & Smith, D. K. (2003). Antisocial behavior in children and adolescents. In A. E. Kazdin & J. R. Weisz (Eds.), *Evidence-based psychotherapies for children and adolescents* (pp. 282–300). New York, NY: Guilford Press.

Chambers, W. J., Puig-Antich, J., Hirsch, M., Paez, B., Ambrosini, P. J., Tabrizi, M. A., & Davies, M. (1985). The assessment of affective disorders in children and adolescents by semi-structured interview: Test-retest reliability of the Schedule for Affective Disorders and Schizophrenia for School-age Children, Present Episode Version. *Archives of General Psychiatry, 42*, 696–702.

Chambless, D. L., Caputo, G., Bright, P., & Gallagher, R. (1984). Assessment of fear in agoraphobics: The body sensations questionnaire and the agoraphobic cognition questionnaire. *Journal of Consulting and Clinical Psychology, 52*, 1090–1097.

Chambless, D. L., Caputo, G., Gracely, S., Jasin, E., & Williams, C. (1985). The Mobility Inventory for Agoraphobia. *Behaviour Research and Therapy, 23*, 35–44.

Chemtob, C. M., Nakashima, J., & Carlson, J. G. (2002). Brief treatment for elementary school children with disaster-related posttraumatic stress disorder: A pilot study. *Journal of Clinical Psychology, 58,* 99–112.

Cherpitel, C. J. (2000). A brief screening instrument for problem drinking in the emergency room: The RA P S4. *Journal of Studies on Alcohol, 61,* 447–449.

Chorpita, B. F., Becker, K. D., & Daleiden, E. L. (2007). Understanding the common elements of evidence-based practice: Misconceptions and clinical examples. *Journal of the American Academy of Child and Adolescent Psychiatry, 46,* 647–652.

Christensen, A., Wheeler, J. G., & Jacobson, N. S. (2008). Couple distress. In D. H. Barlow (Ed.), *Clinical handbook of psychological disorders: A step-by-step treatment manual* (4th ed., pp. 662–689). New York, NY: Guilford Press.

Christenson, G. A., Mackenzie, T. B., & Mitchell, J. E. (1991). Characteristics of 60 adult chronic hair pullers. *American Journal of Psychiatry, 148,* 365–370.

Cimbora, D. M., & McIntosh, D. N. (2003). Emotional responses to antisocial acts in adolescent males with conduct disorder: A link to affective morality. *Journal of Clinical Child and Adolescent Psychology, 32,* 296–301.

Clark, A. J. (2010). Empathy: An integral model in the counseling process. *Journal of Counseling and Development, 88,* 348–356.

Clarke, G., DeBar, L., Ludman, E., Asarnow, J., & Jaycox, L. (2002). *Steady Project intervention manual: Collaborative care, cognitive-behavioral program for depressed youth in a primary care setting.* Available: www.kpchr.org /public/acwd/acwd.html.

Clarke, M., Whitty, P., Browne, S., McTigue, O., Kamali, M., Gervin, M., . . . O'Callaghan, E. (2006). Untreated illness and outcome of psychosis. *British Journal of Psychiatry, 189,* 235–240.

Clarkin, J. F., Frances, A. J., & Perry, S. (1992). Differential therapeutics: Macro and micro levels of treatment planning. In J. C. Norcross & M. R. Goldfried (Eds.), *Handbook of psychotherapy integration* (pp. 463–502). New York, NY: Basic Books.

Clarkin, J. F., Levy, K. N., Lenzenweger, M. F., & Kernberg, O. F. (2007). Evaluating three treatments for borderline personality disorder: A multiwave study. *American Journal of Psychiatry, 164,* 922–928.

Coan, J. A., & Allen, J. J. B. (2008). Affective style and risk for psychopathology. In T. P. Beauchaine & S. P. Hinshaw (Eds.), *Child and adolescent psychopathology* (pp. 234–264). Hoboken, NJ: Wiley.

Coccaro, E. F., & Danehy, M. (2006). Intermittent explosive disorder. In E. Hollander & D. J. Stein (Eds.), *Clinical manual of impulse-control disorders* (pp. 19–38). Arlington, VA: American Psychiatric Publishing.

Coccaro, E. F., Harvey, P. D., Kupsaw-Lawrence, E., Herbert, J. L., & Bernstein, D. P. (1991). Development of neuropharmacologically based behavioral assessments of impulsive aggression. *Journal of Neuropsychiatry, 3,* S44–S51.

Coccaro, E. F., Posternak, M. A., & Zimmerman, M. (2005). Prevalence and features of intermittent explosive disorder in a clinical setting. *Journal of Clinical Psychiatry, 66,* 1221–1227.

Cohan, S. L., Chavira, D. A., & Stein, M. B. (2006). Practitioner review: Psychosocial interventions for children with selective mutism: A critical evaluation of the literature from 1990–2005. *Journal of Child Psychology and Psychiatry, 47,* 1085–1097.

Cohen, J. A., Deblinger, E., Mannarino, A. P., & Steer, R. (2004). A multi-site, randomized, controlled trial for children with sex-abuse related PTSD symptoms. *Journal of the American Academy of Child and Adolescent Psychiatry, 42,* 393–402.

Cohen, J. A., Mannarino, A. P., & Deblinger, E. (2006). *Treating trauma and traumatic grief in children and adolescents.* New York, NY: Guilford Press.

Coleman, H. K. L., Wampold, B. E., & Casali, S. L. (1995). Ethnic minorities' ratings of ethnically similar and European American counselors: A meta-analysis. *Journal of Counseling Psychology, 42,* 55–64.

Coleman, M. C., & Webber, J. (2002). *Emotional and behavioral disorders: Theory and practice.* Boston, MA: Allyn & Bacon.

Colom, F., Vieta, E., Sánchez-Moreno, J., Martínez-Arán, A., Reinares, M., Goikolea J. M., & Scott, J. (2005). Stabilizing the stabilizer: Group psychoeducation enhances the stability of serum lithium levels. *Bipolar Disorders, 7,* 32–36.

Colt, G. H. (2006). *November of the soul: The enigma of suicide.* New York, NY: Scribner.

Colvin, L., Fyfe, S., Leonard, S., Schiavello, T., Ellaway, C., de Klerk, N., . . . Leonard, H. (2003). Describing the phenotype in Rett syndrome using a population database. *Archives of Disease in Childhood, 88,* 38–43.

Comer, J. S., Olfson, M., & Mojtabai, R. (2010). National trends in child and adolescent psychotropic polypharmacy in office-based practice, 1996–2007. *Journal of the American Academy of Child and Adolescent Psychiatry, 49,* 1001–1010.

Committee on Treatment of Posttraumatic Stress Disorder (2008). *Treatment of posttraumatic stress disorder: An assessment of the evidence.* Institute of Medicine of the National Academies. Washington, DC: National Academies Press.

Compton, W. M., Grant, B. F., Colliver, J. D., Glantz, M. D., & Stinson, F. S. (2004). Prevalence of marijuana use disorders in the United States: 1991–1992 and 2001–2002. *Journal of the American Medical Association, 291,* 2114–2121.

Conners, C. K. (1997). *Conners' Rating Scale—Revised manual.* North Tonawanda, NY: Mental Health Systems.

Connors, G. J., Walitzer, K. S., & Dermen, K. H. (2002). Preparing clients for alcoholism treatment: Effects on treatment participation and outcomes. *Journal of Consulting and Clinical Psychology, 70,* 1161–1169.

Constantino, M. J., Arnow, B. A., Blasey, C., & Agras, W. S. (2005). The association between patient characteristics and the therapeutic alliance in cognitive-behavioral and interpersonal therapy for bulimia nervosa. *Journal of Consulting and Clinical Psychology, 73,* 203–211.

Cook, A., Blaustein, M., Spinazzola, J., & van der Kolk, B. (Eds.). (2003). *Complex trauma in children and adolescents.* White paper from the National Child Trauma Stress Network. U. S. Department of Health and Human Services.

Cook, J. E., & Doyle, C. (2002). Working alliance in on-line therapy as compared to face-to-face therapy: Preliminary results. *CyberPsychology & Behavior, 5,* 95–105.

Coryell, W. H. (2002). Maintenance therapies in bipolar affective disorder. In L. N. Yatham, V. Kusumakar, & S. P. Kutcher (Eds.), *Bipolar disorder: A clinician's guide to biological treatments* (pp. 59–84). Philadelphia, PA: Brunner-Routledge.

Costin, C. (2007). *The eating disorder sourcebook: A comprehensive guide to the causes, treatments, and prevention of eating disorders,* (3rd ed.). New York, NY: McGraw Hill.

Cottone, J., Drucker, P., & Javier, R. A. (2003). Gender differences in psychotherapy dyads: Changes in psychological symptoms and responsiveness to treatment during three months of therapy. *Psychotherapy, 40,* 297–308.

Courtois, C. A., & Ford, J. D. (2009). *Treating complex traumatic stress disorders: An evidence-based guide.* New York, NY: Guilford Press.

Cowan, P. A., Cohn, D. A., Cowan, C. P., & Pearson, J. L. (1996). Parents' attachment histories and children's externalizing and internalizing behaviors: Exploring family systems models of linkage. *Journal of Consulting and Clinical Psychology, 64,* 53–64.

Cox, D. J., Ritterband, L. M., Quillian, W., Kovatchev, B., Morris, J., Sutphen, J., & Borowitz, S. (2003). Assessment of behavioral mechanisms maintaining encopresis: Virginia Encopresis-Constipation Apperception Test. *Journal of Pediatric Psychology, 28,* 375–382.

Cox, D. J., Sutphen, J., Borowitz, S., Kovatchev, B., & Ling, W. (1998). Contribution of behavior therapy and biofeedback to laxative therapy in the treatment of pediatric encopresis. *Annals of Behavioral Medicine, 20,* 70–76.

Coyle, D., Doherty, G., Sharry, J., & Matthews, M. (2007). Computers in talk-based mental health interventions. *Interacting with Computers, 19,* 545–562.

Coyne, J. C. (1976). Depression and the response of others. *Journal of Abnormal Psychology, 85,* 186–193.

Craighead, L. W. (2002). Obesity and eating disorders. In M. M. Antony & D. H. Barlow (Eds.), *Handbook of assessment and treatment planning for psychological disorders* (pp. 300–340). New York, NY: Guilford Press.

Craighead, W. E., Sheets, E. S., Brosse, A. L., & Ilardi, S. S. (2007). Psychosocial treatments for major depressive disorder. In P. E. Nathan & J. M. Gorman (Eds.), *A guide to treatments that work* (3rd ed., pp. 289–308). New York, NY: Oxford University Press.

Craske, M. G., Antony, M. M., & Barlow, D. H. (2006). *Mastering your fears and phobias: Therapist guide* (2nd ed.). New York, NY: Oxford University Press.

Craske, M. G., & Barlow, D. H. (2006). *Mastery of your anxiety and panic: Client workbook for anxiety and panic* (4th ed.). New York, NY: Oxford University Press.

Craske, M. G., & Barlow, D. H. (2008). Panic disorder and agoraphobia. In D. H. Barlow (Ed.), *Clinical handbook of psychological disorders* (4th ed., pp. 1–64). New York, NY: Guilford Press.

Craven, M., & Bland, R. (2006). Better practices in collaborative mental health care: An analysis of the evidence base. *Canadian Journal of Psychiatry, 51*(Suppl. 1), 7S–72S.

Crits-Christoph, P., & Barber, J. P. (2007). Psychological treatments for personality disorders. In P. E. Nathan & J. M. Gorman (Eds.), *A guide to treatments that work* (3rd ed., pp. 641–658). New York, NY: Oxford University Press.

Crits-Christoph, P., Crits-Christoph, K., & Gibbons, M.B.C. (2010). Training in alliance-fostering techniques. In J. C. Muran & J. P. Barber (Eds.), *The* therapeutic alliance: An evidence-based guide to practice (pp. 304–319). New York, NY: Guilford Press.

Crosson-Tower, C. (2005). *Understanding child abuse and neglect* (6th ed.). Boston, MA: Allyn & Bacon.

Crowell, S. E., Beauchaine, T. P., & Lenzenweger, M. F. (2008). The development of borderline personality disorder and self-injurious behavior. In T. P. Beauchaine & S. P. Hinshaw (Eds.), *Child and adolescent psychopathology* (pp. 510–539). Hoboken, NJ: John Wiley & Sons.

Cuddy-Casey, M. (1997). A case study using a child-centered play therapy approach to treat enuresis and encopresis. *Elementary School Guidance and Counseling, 31*, 220–223.

Cujé, B. B. (2010). *Become the person you were meant to be: The choice cube method, step-by-step to choice and change.* Arlington, VA: Booksurge.

Cunningham, J., Yonkers, K. A., O'Brien, S., & Eriksson, E. (2009). Update on research and treatment of premenstrual dysphoric disorder. *Harvard Review of Psychiatry, 17*, 120–137.

Cusick, L. (2005). Widening the harm reduction agenda: From drug use to sex work. *International Journal of Drug Policy, 17*, 3–11.

Dalai Lama, & Cutler, H. C. (1998). *The art of happiness: A handbook for living.* New York, NY: Riverhead Books.

Davidson, L., O'Connell, M. J., Tondora, J., Lawless, M., & Evans, A. C. (2005). Recovery in serious mental illness: A new wine or just a new bottle? *Professional Psychology: Research and Practice, 36*, 480–487.

Davis, J. L., Newman, E., & Pruiksma, K. E. (2009). *Cognitive behavioral treatment of traumatized adults.* In A. Rubin and D. W. Springer (Eds.), *Treatment of traumatized adults and children: Clinician's guide to evidence-based practice* (pp. 103–178). Hoboken, NJ: Wiley.

Dawson, D. A., Grant, B. F., Stinson, F. S., Chou, P. S., Huang, B., & Ruan, W. J. (2005). Recovery from DSM-IV alcohol dependence: United States, 2001–2002. *Addiction, 100*, 281–292.

Dawson, G., & Faja, S. (2008). Autism spectrum disorders: A developmental perspective. In T. P. Beauchaine & S. P. Hinshaw (Eds.), *Child and adolescent psychopathology* (pp. 575–613). Hoboken, NJ: Wiley.

Dawson, G., & Osterling, J. (1997). Early intervention in autism: Effectiveness and common elements of current approaches. In M. J. Guralnick (Ed.), *The effectiveness of early intervention: Second generation research* (pp. 307–326). Baltimore, MD: Brookes.

Dealberto, M. J. (2010). Ethnic origin and increased risk for schizophrenia in immigrants to recent and traditional countries of immigration. *Acta Psychiatry Scandinavia, 121*, 325–339.

Deckersbach, T., Rauch, S., Bulhmann, U., & Wilhelm, S. (2006). Habit reversal versus supportive psychotherapy in Tourette's disorder: A randomized controlled trial and predictors of treatment response. *Behaviour Research and Therapy, 44*, 1079–1090.

Decuyper, M., De Pauw, S., De Fruyt, F., De Bolle, M., & De Clercq, B. (2009). A meta-analysis of psychopathy, antisocial personality disorder, and FFM associations. *European Journal of Personality, 23*, 531–565.

Deffenbacher, J. L., Filetti, L. B., Lynch, R. S., Dahlen, E. R., & Oetting, E. R. (2002). Cognitive-behavioral treatment of high anger drivers. *Behaviour Research and Therapy, 40*, 895–910.

Delgado, P. L., & Gelenberg, A. J. (2001). Antidepressant and antimanic medication. In G. O. Gabbard (Ed.), *Treatments of psychiatric disorders* (pp. 1137–1179). Washington, DC: American Psychiatric Press.

Dell, P. F. (2006). A new model of dissociative identity disorder. *Psychiatric Clinics of North America, 29*, 1–26.

della Cava, M. R. (2006, February 27). When sleep is just a dream. *USA Today, A–1.*

DeLong, R. (1994). Children with autism spectrum disorder and history of affective disorder. *Developmental Medicine and Child Neurology, 36*, 674–688.

de Portugal, E., Gonzalez, N., Miriam, V., Haro, J. M., Usal, J., & Cervilla, J. A. (2010). Gender differences in delusional disorder: Evidence from an outpatient sample, *Psychiatry Research, 177*, 235–239.

DeRogatis, L. R. (1997). The DeRogatis Interview for Sexual Functioning: An introductory report. *Journal of Sex and Marital Therapy, 23*, 291–304.

DeRogatis, L. R., & Burnett, A. L. (2008). The epidemiology of sexual dysfunctions. *Journal of Sexual Medicine, 5*, 289–300.

de Shazer, S. (1991). *Putting difference to work.* New York, NY: Norton.

Dickey, C. C., McCarley, R. W., Niznikiewicz, M. A., Voglmaier, M. M., Seidman, L. J., Kim, S., & Shenton, M. E. (2005). Clinical, cognitive, and social characteristics of a sample of neuroleptic-naïve persons with schizotypal personality disorder. *Schizophrenia Research, 78*, 297–308.

DiClemente, C. C. (2003). *Addictions and change: How addictions develop and addicted people recover.* New York, NY: Guilford Press.

Diener, M. J., Hilsenroth, M. J., & Weinberger, J. (2007). Therapist affect, focus and patient outcomes in psychodynamic psychotherapy: A meta-analysis. *American Journal of Psychiatry, 164,* 936–941.

Dimeff, L., & Koerner, K. (Eds.). (2007). *Dialectical behavior therapy in clinical practice: Applications across disorders and settings.* New York, NY: Guilford Press.

Dimidjian, S., Hollon, S. D., Dobson, K. S., Schmaling, K. B., Kohlenberg, R. J., Addis, M. E., . . . Jacobson, N. S. (2006). Randomized trial of behavioral activation, cognitive therapy, and medication in the acute treatment of adults with major depression. *Journal of Consulting and Clinical Psychology, 74,* 658–670.

Dimidjian, S., & Linehan, M. M. (2008). Mindfulness practice. In W. T. O'Donohue & J. E. Fisher (Eds.), *Cognitive behavior therapy: Applying empirically supported techniques in your practice* (2nd ed., pp. 327–336). Hoboken, NJ: Wiley.

Dimidjian, S., Martell, C. R., Addis, M. E., & Herman-Dunn, R. (2008). Behavioral activation for depression. In D. H. Barlow (Ed.), *Clinical handbook of psychological disorders: A step-by-step treatment manual.* New York, NY: Guilford Press.

DiNardo, P., Brown, T. A., & Barlow, D. H. (1994). *The anxiety disorder schedule for DSM-IV: Lifetime version* (ADIS-IV-L). San Antonio, TX: Psychological Corporation.

Dishion, T. J., & Andrews, D. W. (1995). Preventing escalation in problem behaviors with high-risk young adolescents: Immediate and 1-year outcomes. *Journal of Consulting and Clinical Psychology, 63,* 538–548.

Dishion, T. J., McCord, J., & Poulin, F. (1999). When interventions harm: Peer groups and problem behavior. *American Psychologist, 54,* 755–764.

Dobson, K. S., Hollon, S. D., Dimidjian, S., Schmaling, K. B., Kohlenberg, R. J., Gallop, R. J., . . . Jacobson, N. S. (2008). Randomized trial of behavioral activation, cognitive therapy, and antidepressant medication in the prevention of relapse and recurrence in major depression. *Journal of Consulting and Clinical Psychology, 76,* 468–477.

Donohue, B., Allen, D. N., & LaPota, H. B. (2009). Family behavior therapy for substance abuse and associated problems. In D. W. Springer and A. Rubin (Eds.), *Substance abuse treatment for youth and adults* (pp. 205–258). Hoboken, NJ: Wiley.

Donovan, D. M. (2007). Assessment of addictive behaviors for relapse prevention. In D. M. Donovan & G. A. Marlatt (Eds.), *Assessment of addictive behaviors* (2nd ed., pp. 1–48). New York, NY: Guilford Press.

Donovan, D. M., Anton, R. F., Miller, W. R., Longabaugh, R., Hosking, J. D., & Youngblood, M. (2008). Combined pharmacotherapies and behavioral interventions for alcohol dependence (The COMBINE Study): Examination of posttreatment drinking outcomes. *Journal of Studies on Alcohol and Drugs, 69,* 5–13.

Donovan, D. M., & Marlatt, G. A. (Eds.). (2008). *Assessment of addictive behaviors* (2nd ed.). New York, NY: Guilford Press.

Doyle, A. E., Biederman, J., Seidman, L. J., Rske-Nielsen, J. J., & Faraone, S. V. (2005). Neuropsychological functioning in relatives of girls with and without ADHD. *Psychological Medicine, 35,* 1121–1132.

Dozois, D. J. A., & Dobson, K. S. (2002). Depression. In M. M. Antony & D. H. Barlow (Eds.), *Handbook of assessment and treatment planning for psychological disorders* (pp. 259–299). New York, NY: Guilford Press.

Drake, R. E., Essock, S. M., Shaner, A., Carey, K. B., Minkoff, K., Kola, L., . . . Rickards, L. (2001). Evidence-based practices: Implementing dual diagnosis services for clients with severe mental illness. *Psychiatric Services, 52,* 469–476.

Drake, R. E., & Mueser, K. T. (2002). Co-occurring alcohol use disorder and schizophrenia. *Alcohol: Research & Health, 26,* 99–102.

Drgon, T., Montoya, I., Johnson, C., Liu, Q. R., Walther, D., Hamer, D., & Uhl, G. R. (2009). Genome-wide association for nicotine dependence and smoking cessation success in NIH research volunteers. *Molecular Medicine, 15,* 21–27.

Driessen, E., & Hollon, S. D. (2010). Cognitive behavioral therapy for mood disorders: Efficacy, moderators and mediators. *Psychiatric Clinics of North America, 33,* 537–555.

Druss, B. G., Hwang, I., Petukhova, M., Sampson, N. A., Wang, P. S., & Kessler, R. C. (2009). Impairment in role functioning in mental and chronic medical disorders in the United States: Results from the National Comorbidity Survey Replication. *Molecular Psychiatry, 14,* 728–737.

DSM-5 Childhood and Adolescent Disorders Work Group (2010). *Asperger's disorder proposed revisions: Disorders usually first diagnosed in infancy, childhood, or adolescence,* DSM-5 development. Arlington, VA: American Psychiatric Association. http://www .dsm5.org/ProposedRevisions/Pages/proposed revision.aspx?rid=97#

Duggan, C. (2009). A treatment guideline for people with antisocial personality disorder: Overcoming attitudinal barriers and evidential limitations. *Criminal Behaviour and Mental Health, 19*, 219–223.

Duggan, C., Huband, N., Smailagic, N., Ferriter, M., & Adams, C. (2008). The use of pharmacological treatments for people with personality disorder: A systematic review of randomized controlled trials. *Personality and Mental Health, 2*, 119–170.

Duke, D. C., Keeley, M. L., Geffken, G. R., & Storch, E. A. (2010). Trichotillomania: A current review. *Clinical Psychology Review, 30*, 181–193.

Dulcan, M. K. (2009). *Dulcan's textbook of child and adolescent psychiatry.* Washington, DC: American Psychiatric Publishing.

Duncan, B., Miller, S., Wampold, B., & Hubble, M. (Eds.). (2010). *The heart and soul of change: Delivering what works in therapy* (2nd ed.). Washington, DC: American Psychological Association.

Dunn, M. A. (2005). *S. O. S. Social Skills in Our Schools: A social skills program for children with pervasive developmental disorders, including high-functioning autism and Asperger syndrome, and their typical peers.* Overland Park, KS: Autism Asperger Publishing Co.

Dunn, R., & Honigsfeld, A. (2009). *Differentiating instruction for at risk students: What to do and how to do it.* Lanham, MD: Rowman & Littlefield Education.

Durlak, J. A., Fuhrman, T., & Lampman, C. (1991). Effectiveness of cognitive-behavior therapy for maladapting children: A meta-analysis. *Psychological Bulletin, 110*, 204–214.

Dutra, L., Stathopoulou, G., Basden, S. L., Leyro, T. M., Powers, M. B., & Otto, M. W. (2008). A meta-analytic review of psychosocial interventions for substance use disorders. *American Journal of Psychiatry, 165*, 179–187.

DuVal, S. (2005). Six-year-old Thomas diagnosed with pediatric onset bipolar: A case study. *Journal of Child and Adolescent Psychiatric Nursing, 18*, 38–42.

Eaves, L. C., & Ho, H. H. (2004). The very early identification of autism: Outcome to age 4½–5. *Journal of Autism and Developmental Disorders, 34*, 367–378.

Eells, T. D., Lombart, K. G., Kendjelic, E. M., Turner, L. C., & Lucas, C. P. (2005). The quality of psychotherapy case formulations: A comparison of expert, experienced, and novice cognitive-behavioral and psychodynamic therapists. *Journal of Consulting and Clinical Psychology, 73*, 579–589.

Egan, S. K., & Perry, D. G. (2001). Gender identity: A multidimensional analysis with implications for psychosocial adjustment. *Developmental Psychology, 37*, 451–463.

Ehlers, S., Gillberg, C., & Wing, L. (1999). A screening questionnaire for Asperger syndrome and other high-functioning autism spectrum disorders in school age children. *Journal of Autism and Developmental Disorders, 29*, 129–141.

Ehrenreich-May, J., & Bilek, E. L. (2011). The development of a transdiagnostic, cognitive behavioral group intervention for childhood anxiety disorders and co-occurring depression symptoms. *Cognitive and Behavioral Practice.*

Eifert, G. H., & Forsyth, J. P. (2005). *Acceptance and commitment therapy for anxiety disorders.* Oakland, CA: New Harbinger.

Eisendrath, S. J. (2001). Factitious disorders and malingering. In G. O. Gabbard (Ed.), *Treatments of psychiatric disorders* (3rd ed., pp. 1825–1844). Washington, DC: American Psychiatric Press.

Elkind, D. (2007). *The power of play: How spontaneous imaginative activities lead to happier, healthier children.* Cambridge, MA: Da Capo Press.

Ellason, J. W., & Ross, C. A. (1997). Two-year follow-up of inpatients with dissociative disorder. *American Journal of Psychiatry, 154*, 832–839.

Elliott, E. J. (2002). Juvenile justice diversion and intervention. In D. Kolko (Ed.), *Handbook on firesetting in children and youth* (pp. 383–394). San Diego, CA: Academic Press.

Elliott, R. (1995). Therapy process research and clinical practice: Practical strategies. In M. Aveline & D. A. Shapiro (Eds.), *Research foundations for psychotherapy practice* (pp. 49–72). Chichester, England: Wiley.

Elliott, R. (2001). Research on the effectiveness of humanistic therapies: A meta-analysis. In D. J. Cain & J. Seeman (Eds.), *Handbook of research and practice in humanistic psychotherapy* (pp. 57–82). Washington, DC: American Psychological Association.

Ellis, A., & Tafrate, R. C. (1997). *When AA doesn't work for you: Rational steps to quitting alcohol.* Fort Lee, NJ: Barricade.

Eng, M. Y., Luczak, T. E., & Wall, S. L. (2007). ALDH2, ADH1B, and ADH1C genotypes in Asians: A literature review. *Alcohol Research and Health, 30*, 23–27.

Epp, A. M., Dobson, K. S., & Cottraux, J. (2009). Applications of individual cognitive-behavioral therapy to specific disorders: Efficacy and indications. In G. O. Gabbard (Ed.). *Textbook of psychotherapeutic treatments* (pp. 239–262). Arlington, VA: American Psychiatric Publishing.

Epstein, E. E., & McCrady, B. S. (2009). *A cognitive behavioral treatment program for overcoming alcohol problems: Therapists' guide.* New York, NY: Oxford University Press.

Escobar, J. I. (2004). Transcultural aspects of dissociative and somatoform disorders. *Psychiatric Times, 21,* 5.

Escudero, V., Heatherington, L., & Friedlander, M. L. (2010). Therapeutic alliances and alliance building in family therapy. In J. C. Muran & J. P. Barber (Eds.), *The therapeutic alliance: An evidence-based guide to practice* (pp. 240–262). New York: Guilford Press.

Evans, D. L., Foa, E. B., Gur, R. E., Hendin, H., O'Brien, C. P., Seligman, M. E. P., & Walsh, B. T. (2005). *Treating and preventing adolescent mental health disorders.* New York, NY: Oxford University Press.

Eyberg, S. M., & Pinkus, D. (1999). *The Eyberg Child Behavior Inventory and Sutter-Eyberg Student Behavior Inventory: Professional manual.* Lutz, FL: Psychological Assessment Resources.

Fairburn, C. G. (2007). *Cognitive behavior therapy and eating disorders.* New York, NY: Guilford Press.

Fairburn, C. G., & Cooper, Z. (1993). The Eating Disorders Examination (12th ed.). In C. G. Fairburn & G. T. Wilson (Eds.), *Binge eating: Nature, assessment, and treatment* (pp. 317–360). New York, NY: Guilford Press.

Fairburn, C. G., Cooper, Z., Doll, H. A., Norman, P., & O'Connor, M. (2000). The natural course of bulimia nervosa and binge eating disorder in young women. *Archives of General Psychiatry, 57,* 659–665.

Fairburn, C. G., Cooper, Z., Doll, H. A., O'Connor, M. E., Bohn, K., Hawker, D. M., Wales, J. A., & Palmer, R. L. (2009). Transdiagnostic cognitive-behavioral therapy for patients with eating disorders: A two-site trial with 60-week follow-up. *American Journal of Psychiatry, 166,* 311–319.

Fairburn, C. G., Cooper, Z., Shafran, R., & Wilson, G. T. (2008). Eating disorders: Transdiagnostic protocol. In D. H. Barlow (Ed.), *Clinical handbook of psychological disorders: A step-by-step treatment manual* (4th ed., pp. 578–614). New York, NY: Guilford Press.

Fairburn, C. G., & Harrison, P. J. (2003). Eating disorders. *Lancet, 361,* 407–416.

Fallon, B. A., & Feinstein, S. (2001). Hypochondriasis. In K. A. Phillips (Ed.), *Somatoform and factitious disorders* (pp. 27–60). Washington, DC: American Psychiatric Association.

Faraone, S. V., & Biederman, J. (2005). What is the prevalence of adult ADHD? Results of a population screen of 966 adults. *Journal of Attention Disorders, 9,* 384–391.

Farrell, J. M., Shaw, I. A., & Webber, M. A. (2009). A schema-focused approach to group psychotherapy for outpatients with borderline personality disorder: A randomized controlled trial. *Journal of Behavior Therapy and Experimental Psychiatry, 40,* 317–328.

Fawzy, F. I., Fawzy, N. W., Hyun, C. S., Elashoff, R., Guthrie, D., Fahey, J. L., & Morton, D. L. (1993). Malignant melanoma. *Archives of General Psychiatry, 50,* 681–689.

Feder, B. J. (2006, September 10). Battle lines in treating depression. *New York Times,* p. 21.

Feldman, M. D., Hamilton, J. C., & Deemer, H. N. (2001). Factitious disorder. In K. A. Phillips (Ed.), *Somatoform and factitious disorders* (pp. 129–159). Washington, DC: American Psychiatric Publishing.

Fenster, A. (1993). Reflections on using group therapy as a treatment modality—why, how, for whom and when: A guide to clinicians, supervisors and instructors. *Group, 17,* 84–101.

Ferguson, C. J. (2010). Genetic contributions to antisocial personality and behavior: A meta-analytic review from an evolutionary perspective. *Journal of Social Psychology, 150,* 160–180.

Fergusson, D., Poulton, R., & Smith, P., & Boden, J. M. (2006). Cannabis and psychosis. *British Medical Journal, 332,* 172–176.

Ferguson, K. E., & Sgambati, R. E. (2008). Relaxation. In W. T. O'Donohue & J. E. Fisher (Eds.), *Cognitive behavior therapy: Applying empirically supported techniques in your practice* (2nd ed., pp. 434–444). Hoboken, NJ: Wiley.

Field, L. F., & Seligman, L. (2004). Mood disorders in children and adolescents. In R. R. Erk (Ed.), *Counseling treatment for children and adolescents with DSM-IV-TR disorders* (pp. 239–272). Upper Saddle River, NJ: Pearson.

Findling, R., McNamara, N. K., Youngstrom, E. A., et al. (2005). Young Mania Rating Scale. *Double-Blind 18-Month Trial of Lithium versus Divalproex Maintenance Treatment in Pediatric Bipolar Disorder, 44,* 409–417.

Finney, J. W., Wilbourne, P. L., & Moos, R. H. (2007). Psychosocial treatments for substance use disorders. In P. E. Nathan & J. M. Gorman (Eds.), *A guide to treatments that work* (3rd ed., pp. 179–202). New York, NY: Oxford University Press.

Fiore, F. C., Jaen, C. R., Baker, B., Bailey, W. C., Benowitz, N. L., & Curry, S. J. (2008). *Treating tobacco use and dependence: 2008 update. Clinical practice guideline.*

Rockville, MD: U.S. Department of Health and Human Services Public Health Service. Retrieved from www.ahrq.gov/clinic/tobacco/tobaqrg.htm

First, M. B., Spitzer, R. L., Gibbon, M., & Williams, J. B. W. (2002). *Structured Clinical Interview for DSM-IV Axis I Disorders, Patient version (SCID-I/P)*. New York, NY: Biometrics Research.

Fischer, S., Smith, G. T., & Anderson, K. G. (2003). Clarifying the role of impulsivity in bulimia nervosa. *International Journal of Eating Disorders, 3*, 406–411.

Fisher, J. E., & O'Donohue, W. T. (Eds.). (2010). *Practitioner's guide to evidence-based psychotherapy*. New York, NY: Springer.

Flessner, C. A., Penzel, F., Trichotillomania Learning Center-Scientific Advisory Board, & Keuthen, N. J. (2010). Current treatment practices for children and adults with trichotillomania: Consensus among experts. *Cognitive and Behavioral Practice, 17*, 290–300.

Flory, K., Milich, R., Lynam, D. R., Leukefeld, C., & Clayton, R. (2003). Relation between childhood disruptive behavior disorders and substance use and dependence symptoms in young adulthood: Individuals with symptoms of attention-deficit/hyperactivity disorder and conduct disorder are uniquely at risk. *Psychology of Addictive Behaviors, 17*, 151–158.

Foa, E. B., Davidson, J., & Rothbaum, B. O. (1995). Posttraumatic stress disorder. In G. O. Gabbard (Ed.), *Treatments of psychiatric disorders* (pp. 1499–1520). Washington, DC: American Psychiatric Press.

Foa, E. B., Ehlers, A., Clark, D. M., Tolin, D. F., & Orsillo, S. M. (1999). Post-traumatic Cognitions Inventory (PTCI): Development and validation. *Psychological Assessment, 11*, 303–314.

Foa, E. B., Huppert, J. D., Leiberg, S., Langner, R., Kichic, R., Hajcak, G., & Salkovskis, P. M. (2002). The Obsessive-compulsive Inventory: Development and validation of a short version. *Psychological Assessment, 14*, 485–496.

Foa, E., Keane, T., Friedman, M., & Cohen, J. A. (2009). *Effective treatments for PTSD: Practice guidelines from the International Society for Traumatic Stress Studies*. New York, NY: Guilford Press.

Forchetti, C. M. (2005). Treating patients with moderate to severe Alzheimer's disease. *The Primary Care Companion to the Journal of Clinical Psychiatry, 7*, 155–161.

Ford, J. D., & Courtois, C. A. (2009). Defining and understanding complex trauma and complex traumatic stress disorders. In C.A. Courtois & J. D. Ford (Eds.),

Treating complex traumatic stress disorders: An evidence-based guide (pp. 13–30). New York, NY: Guilford Press.

Forman, E. M., Herbert, J. D., Moitra, E., Yeomans, P. D., & Geller, P. A. (2007). A randomized controlled effectiveness trail of acceptance and commitment therapy and cognitive therapy for anxiety and depression. *Behavior Modification, 31*, 772–799.

Forsyth, J. P., Fuse, T., & Acheson, D. T. (2008). Interoceptive exposure for panic disorder. In W. T. O'Donohue & J. E. Fisher (Eds.), *Cognitive behavior therapy: Applying empirically supported techniques to your practice* (pp. 296–308). Hoboken, NJ: Wiley.

Forty, L., Kelly, M., Jones, L., Jones, I., Barnes, E., Caesar, S., . . . Smith, D. (2010). Reducing the Hypomania Checklist (HCL-32) to a 16-item version. *Journal of Affective Disorders, 124*, 351–356.

Frank, E. (2005). *Treating bipolar disorder: A clinician's guide to interpersonal and social rhythm therapy*. New York, NY: Guilford Press.

Frank, E., Kupfer, D. J., Thase, M. E., Mallinger, A. G., Swartz, H. A., Fagiolini, A. M., . . . Monk, T. (2005). Two-year outcomes for interpersonal and social rhythm therapy in individuals with bipolar I disorder. *Archives of General Psychiatry, 62*, 996–1004.

Frank, E., & Swartz, H. A. (2004). Interpersonal and social rhythm therapy. In S. L. Johnson & R. L. Leahy (Eds.), *Psychological treatment of bipolar disorder* (pp. 162–183). New York, NY: Guilford Press.

Frank, J. D., & Frank, J. B. (1991). *Persuasion and healing: A comparative study of psychotherapy* (3rd ed.). Baltimore, MD: Johns Hopkins University Press.

Franklin, G. A., Pucci, P. S., Arbabi, S., Brandt, M., Wahl, W. L., & Taheri, P. A. (2002). Decreased juvenile arson and firesetting recidivism after implementation of a multidisciplinary prevention program. *Journal of Trauma-Injury Infection and Critical Care, 53*, 260–266.

Franklin, M. E., & Foa, E. B. (2007). Cognitive behavioral treatments for obsessive compulsive disorder. In P. E. Nathan & J. M. Gorman (Eds.), *A guide to treatments that work* (2nd ed., pp. 367–386). New York, NY: Oxford University Press.

Franklin, M. E., & Foa, E. B. (2008). Obsessive compulsive disorder. In. D. H. Barlow (Ed.), *Clinical handbook of psychological disorders: A step-by-step treatment manual* (4th ed., pp. 164–215). New York, NY: Guilford Press.

Franklin, M. E., Ledley, D. A., & Foa, E. B. (2008). Response prevention. In W. T. O'Donohue and J. E.

Fisher (Eds.), *Cognitive behavior therapy: Applying empirically supported techniques in your practice* (2nd ed., pp. 445–451). Hoboken, NJ: Wiley.

Franklin, M. E., Tolin, D. F., & Diefenbach, G. J. (2006). Trichotillomania. In E. Hollander & D. J. Stein (Eds.), *Clinical manual of impulse-control disorders* (pp. 149–174). Arlington, VA: American Psychiatric Publishing.

Frazier, T. W., Youngstrom, E. A., Speer, L., Embacher, R., Law, P., Constantino, J., . . . Eng, C. (2012). Validation of proposed *DSM-5* criteria for Autism Spectrum Disorder. *Journal of the American Association of Child and Adolescent Psychiatry, 51,* 28–40.

Freeman, D., & Garety, P. A. (2009). Delusions. In J. E. Fisher & W. T. O'Donohue (Eds.), *Practitioner's guide to evidence-based psychotherapy* (pp. 205–213). New York, NY: Springer.

French, P. (2010). Early detection and treatment opportunities for people at high risk of developing psychosis. In P. French, J. Smith, D. Shiers, M. Reed, & M. Rayne (Eds.), *Promoting recovery in early psychosis* (pp. 93–108). Oxford, United Kingdom: Wiley-Blackwell.

French, P., Smith, J., Shiers, D., Reed, M., & Rayne, M. (Eds.). (2010). *Promoting recovery in early psychosis.* Oxford, United Kingdom: Wiley-Blackwell.

Freudenreich, O. (2008). *Psychotic disorders: A practical guide.* Philadelphia, PA: Lippincott Williams & Wilkins.

Friedman, R. A., & Leon, A. C. (2007). Expanding the black box—Depression, antidepressants, and the risk of suicide. *New England Journal of Medicine, 356,* 2343–2346.

Fröhlich, C., Jacobi, F., & Wittchen, H. U. (2006). *DSM-IV* pain disorder in the general population: An exploration of the structure and threshold of medically unexplained pain symptoms. *European Archives of Psychiatry and Clinical Neuroscience, 256,* 187–196.

Fruzzetti, A. E., Santisteban, D. A., & Hoffman, P. D. (2007). Dialectical behavior therapy with families. In L. A. Dimeff & K. Koerner (Eds.), *Dialectical behavior therapy in clinical practice: Applications across disorders and settings* (pp. 222–244). New York, NY: Guilford Press.

Gabbard, G. O., & Horowitz, M. J. (2009). Insight, transference interpretation, and therapeutic change in the dynamic psychotherapy of borderline personality disorder. *American Journal of Psychiatry, 166,* 517–521.

Gallo, D. P. (2010). *Diagnosing autism spectrum disorders: A lifespan perspective.* West Sussex, United Kingdom: Wiley-Blackwell.

Garb, H. N. (1998). Clinical judgment. In H. N. Garb (Ed.), *Studying the clinician: Judgment research and psychological assessment* (pp. 173–206). Washington, DC: American Psychological Association.

Garety, P., Bentall, R. P., & Freeman, D. (2008). Research evidence of the effectiveness of cognitive behavioural therapy for persecutory delusions: More work is needed. In D. Freeman & R. Bentall (Eds.), *Persecutory delusions: Assessment, theory and practice* (pp. 329–350). London, England: Oxford University Press.

Garfield, S. L. (1986). Research on client variables in psychotherapy. In S. L. Garfield & A. E. Bergin (Eds.), *Handbook of psychotherapy and behavior change* (3rd ed., pp. 213–256). Hoboken, NJ: Wiley.

Garno, J. L., Goldberg, J. F., & Ramirez, P. M., & Ritzler, B. A. (2005). Impact of childhood abuse on the clinical course of bipolar disorder. *British Journal of Psychiatry, 186,* 121–125.

Garrett, J., Landau-Stanton, J., Stanton, M. D., Stellato-Kabat, J., & Stellato-Kabat, D. (1997). ARISE: A method for engaging reluctant alcohol- and drug-dependent individuals in treatment. *Journal of Substance Abuse Treatment, 14,* 235–248.

Gaub, M., & Carlson, C. (1997). Gender differences in ADHD: A meta-analysis and critical review. *Journal of the American Academy of Child and Adolescent Psychiatry, 36,* 1036–1045.

Geary, D. C. (2003). Learning disabilities in arithmetic: Problem-solving differences and cognitive deficits. In H. L. Swanson, K. R. Harris, & S. Graham (Eds.), *Handbook of learning disabilities* (pp. 199–212). New York, NY: Guilford Press.

Geller, B., & Luby, J. (1997). Child and adolescent bipolar disorder: A review of the past 10 years. *Journal of the American Academy of Child and Adolescent Psychiatry, 36,* 1168–1176.

Geller, J., Brown, K. E., Zaitsoff, S. L., Goodrich, S., & Hastings, F. (2003). Collaborative versus directive interventions in the treatment of eating disorders: Implications for care providers. *Professional Psychology: Research and Practice, 34,* 406–413.

Gelso, C. J. (2010). *The real relationship in psychotherapy: The hidden foundation of change.* Washington, DC: American Psychological Association.

Gendlin, E. T. (1996). *Focusing-oriented psychotherapy: A manual of the experiential method.* New York, NY: Guilford Press.

George, C., Kaplan, N., & Main, M. (1984). *Adult Attachment Interview.* Unpublished manuscript, University of California at Berkeley.

Gerardi, M., Rothbaum, B. O., Ressler, K., Heekin, M., & Rizzo, A. (2008). Virtual reality exposure therapy using a virtual Iraq: Case report. *Journal of Traumatic Stress, 21,* 209–213.

Giesen-Bloo, J., Van Dyck, R., Spinhoven, P., Van Tilburg, W., Dirksen, C., Van Asselt, T., . . . Arntz, A. (2006). Outpatient psychotherapy for borderline personality disorder: A randomized trial of schema-focused therapy vs. transference-focused therapy. *Archives of General Psychiatry, 63,* 649–658.

Gilliam, J. E. (2001) *Gilliam Asperger's Scale Examiner's Manual.* Austin, TX: Pro-Ed.

Gillies, L. A. (2001). Interpersonal psychotherapy for depression and other disorders. In D. H. Barlow (Ed.), *Clinical handbook of psychological disorders* (3rd ed., pp. 309–331). New York, NY: Guilford Press.

Gillig, P. M. (2009). Dissociative identity disorder: A controversial diagnosis. *Psychiatry, 6,* 24–29.

Girgus, J. S., & Nolen-Hoeksema, S. (2006). Cognition and depression. In C.L.M., Keyes & S. H. Goodman (Eds.), *Women and depression* (pp. 147–175). New York, NY: Cambridge University Press.

Glasser, W. (1990). *The control theory and reality therapy workbook.* Canoga Park, CA: Institute for Reality Therapy.

Glazener, C., Evans, J., & Paro, R. (2003). Alarm interventions for nocturnal enuresis in children. *Cochrane Database of Systematic Reviews, 2,* CD002911.

Glezer, A., Byatt, N., Cook, R., & Rothschild, A. J. (2009). Polypharmacy prevalence rates in the treatment of unipolar depression in an outpatient clinic. *Journal of Affective Disorders, 117,* 18–23.

Gloaguen, V., Cottraux, J., Cucherat, M., & Blackburn, I. M. (1998). A meta-analysis of the effects of cognitive therapy in depressed patients. *Journal of Affective Disorders, 49,* 59–72.

Glueckauf, R. L., Fritz, S. P., Eckland, J., Eric, P., Liss, H. J., & Dages, P. (2002). Videoconferencing-based counseling for rural teenagers with epilepsy: Phase I findings. *Rehabilitation Psychology, 47,* 49–72.

Glynn, S. M., Cohen, A. N., Dixon, L. B., & Niv, N. (2006). The potential impact of the recovery movement on family interventions for schizophrenia: Opportunities and obstacles. *Schizophrenia Bulletin, 32,* 451–463.

Godfrin, K. A., & van Heeringen, C. (2010). The effects of mindfulness-based cognitive therapy on recurrence of depressive episodes, mental health and quality of life: A randomized controlled study. *Behaviour Research and Therapy, 48,* 738–746.

Godley, S. H., Smith, J. E., Meyers, R. J., & Godley, M. D. (2009). Adolescent Community Enforcement Approach (A-CRA). In D. W. Springer and A. Rubin (Eds.), *Substance abuse treatment for youth and adults: Clinician's guide to evidence-based practice* (pp. 109–201). Hoboken, NJ: Wiley.

Gold, J. M. (2010). *Counseling and spirituality: Integrating spiritual and clinical orientations.* Princeton, NC: Merrill.

Golden, R. N., Gaynes, B. N., Ekstrom, R. D., Hamer, R. M., Jacobsen, F. M., Suppes, T., . . . Nemeroff, C. B. (2005). The efficacy of light therapy in the treatment of mood disorders: A review and meta-analysis of the evidence. *American Journal of Psychiatry, 162,* 656–662.

Goldfried, M. R., Greenberg, L. S., & Marmar, C. R. (1990). Individual psychotherapy: Process and outcome. *Annual Review of Psychology, 41,* 659–688.

Goldman, L. S., Genel, M., Bezman, R. J., & Slanetz, P. J. (1998). Diagnosis and treatment of attention-deficit/hyperactivity disorder in children and adolescents. *Journal of the American Medical Association, 279,* 1100–1107.

Goldstein, A. J., de Beurs, E., Chambless, D. L., & Wilson, K. A. (2000). EMDR for panic disorder with agoraphobia: Comparison with waiting list and credible attention-placebo control conditions. *Journal of Consulting and Clinical Psychology, 68,* 947–956.

Goldstein, B. I., & Levitt, A. J. (2006). Further evidence for a developmental subtype of bipolar disorder defined by age at onset: Results from the National Epidemiologic Survey on Alcohol and Related Conditions. *American Journal of Psychiatry, 163,* 1833–1636.

Goldstein, T. R., Axelson, D., Birmaher, B., & Brent, D. A. (2007). Dialectical behavior therapy for adolescents with bipolar disorder: A 1-year open trial. *Journal of the American Academy of Child and Adolescent Psychiatry, 46,* 820–830.

Goldstein, T. R., Birmaher, B., Axelson, D., Ryan, N. D., Strober, M. A., Gill, M. K., . . . Keller, M. (2005). History of suicide attempts in pediatric bipolar disorder: Factors associated with increased risk. *Bipolar Disorders, 7,* 525–535.

Goleman, D. (Ed.). (2003). *Destructive emotions.* New York, NY: Bantam Books.

Golier, J. A., Legge, J., & Yehuda, R. (2007). Pharmacological treatments for posttraumatic stress disorder. In P. E. Nathan & J. M. Gorman (Eds.), *A guide to treatments that work* (3rd ed., pp. 475–512). New York, NY: Oxford University Press.

Gooding, P., & Tarrier, N. (2009). A systematic review and meta-analysis of cognitive-behavioural interventions to reduce problem gambling: Hedging our bets? *Behaviour Research and Therapy, 47*, 592–607.

Goodman, S. H., & Tully, E. (2006). Depression in women who are mothers: An integrative model of risk for the development of psychopathology in their sons and daughters. In C. L. M. Keyes & S. H. Goodman (Eds.), *Women and depression* (pp. 241–282). New York, NY: Cambridge University Press.

Goodwin, R. D., Faravelli, C., Rosi, S., Cosci, F., Truglia, E., deGraff, R., & Wittchen, H. U. (2005). The epidemiology of panic disorder and agoraphobia in Europe. *European Neuropsychopharmacology, 15*, 435–443.

Goodyer, I., Dubicka, B., Wilkinson, P., Kelvin, R., Roberts, C., Byford, S., . . . Harrington, R. (2007). Selective serotonin reuptake inhibitors (SSRIs) and routine specialist care with and without cognitive behavior therapy in adolescents with major depression: Randomized controlled trial. *British Medical Journal, 335*, 142.

Gosselin, P., Ladouceur, R., Morin, C. M., Dugas, M. J., & Baillargeon, L. (2004). Discontinuation among adults with GAD: A randomized trial of cognitive-behavioral therapy. *Journal of Consulting and Clinical Psychology, 74*, 908–919.

Goswami, S., Mattoo, S. K., Basu, D., & Singh, G. (2004). Substance-abusing schizophrenics: Do they self medicate? *American Journal of Addictions, 13*, 139–150.

Gottdiener, W. H. (2006). Individual psychodynamic psychotherapy of schizophrenia: Empirical evidence for the practicing clinician. *Psychoanalytic Psychology, 23*, 583–589.

Gottman, J. M., Coan, J., Carrere, S., & Swanson, C. (1998). Predicting marital happiness and stability from newlywed interactions. *Journal of Marriage and the Family, 60*, 5–22.

Gottman, J. M., & Silver, N. (2000). *The seven principles for making marriage work*. New York, NY: Three Rivers Press.

Graham, H. L., Copello, A., Birchwood, M. J., & Mueser, K. T. (Eds.). (2003). *Substance misuse in psychosis: Approaches to treatment and service delivery*. Hoboken, NJ: Wiley.

Granello, D. (2010). The process of suicide risk assessment: Twelve core principles, *Journal of Counseling & Development, 88*, 363–370.

Granello, D. H., & Granello, P. F. (2007). *Suicide: An essential guide for helping professionals and educators*. Boston, MA: Pearson Education.

Grant, B. F., Hasin, D. S., Stinson, F. S., Dawson, D. A., Chou, S. P., Ruan, W. J., & Pickering, R. P. (2004). Prevalence, correlates, and disability of personality disorders in the U.S.: Results from the National Epidemiologic Survey on Alcohol and Related Conditions. *Journal of Clinical Psychiatry, 65*, 948–958.

Grant, B. F., & Odlaug, B. L. (2008). Kleptomania: Clinical characteristics and treatment. *Rev Bras Psychiatrica, 30* (Supp.), S11–S15.

Grant, J. E. (2006). Kleptomania. In E. Hollander & D. J. Stein (Eds.), *Clinical manual of impulse-control disorders* (pp. 175–202). Arlington, VA: American Psychiatric Publishing.

Grant, J. E., & Kim, S. W. (2002). Clinical characteristics and associated psychopathology of 22 patients with kleptomania. *Comprehensive Psychiatry, 43*, 378–384.

Grant, J. E., & Portenza, M. N. (2007). *Young adult mental health*. New York, NY: Oxford University Press.

Grant, B., Stinson, F., Hasin, D., Dawson, D., Chou, P., Ruan, J., & Huang, B. (2005). Prevalence, Correlates and comorbidity of bipolar I disorder and axis I and II disorders: Results from the National Epidemiologic Survey on Alcohol and Related Conditions. *Journal of Clinical Psychiatry, 62*, 137–145.

Green, J., & Goldwyn, R. (2002). Attachment disorganization and psychopathology: New findings in attachment research and their potential implication for developmental psychopathology in childhood. *Journal of Child Psychology and Psychiatry, 43*, 835–846.

Green, R. (1987). *The sissy boy syndrome and the development of homosexuality*. New Haven, CT: Yale University Press.

Greenberg, L. S. (2002). *Emotion-focused therapy: Coaching clients to work through their feelings*. Washington, DC: American Psychological Association.

Greenberg, L. S., Elliott, R., & Lietaer, G. (1994). Research on humanistic and experiential psychotherapies. In A. E. Bergin & S. L. Garfield (Eds.), *Handbook of psychotherapy and behavior change* (4th ed., pp. 509–539). Hoboken, NJ: Wiley.

Greenberg, L. S., & Johnson, S. M. (1988). *Emotionally focused therapy for couples*. New York, NY: Guilford Press.

Greenberg, L. S., & Watson, J. C. (2000). Alliance ruptures and repairs in experiential therapy. *Journal of Clinical Psychology, 56*, 175–186.

Greenberg, L. S., & Watson, J. C. (2005). *Emotion focused therapy for depression*. Washington, DC: American Psychological Association.

Greenberg, L. S., Watson, J. C., Elliott, R., & Bohart, A. (2001). Empathy. *Psychotherapy, 38,* 380–384.

Greenberg, M. T., Lengua, L. J., Coie, J., Pinderhughes, E., & Conduct Problems Prevention Research Group. (1999). Predicting developmental outcomes at school entry using a multiple-risk model: Four American communities. *Developmental Psychology, 35,* 403–417.

Greenberg, W. M., Rosenfeld, D. N., & Ortega, E. A. (1995). Adjustment disorder as an admission diagnosis. *American Journal of Psychiatry, 152,* 459–461.

Greenhill, L. L., & Ford, R. E. (2002). Childhood attention-deficit hyperactivity disorder: Pharmacological treatments. In P. E. Nathan & J. M. Gorman (Eds.), *A guide to treatments that work* (2nd ed., pp. 25–56). New York, NY: Oxford University Press.

Greenspan, M., & Kulish, N. M. (1985). Factors in premature termination in long-term psychotherapy. *Psychotherapy, 22,* 75–82.

Grieger, T. A., Cozza, S. J., Ursano, R. J., Hoge, C., Martinez, P. E., Engel, C. C., & Wain, H. J. (2006). Posttraumatic stress disorder and depression in battle-injured soldiers. *American Journal of Psychiatry, 163,* 1777–1783.

Grieger, T. A., Fullerton, C. S., & Ursano, R. J. (2003). Posttraumatic stress disorder, alcohol use, and perceived safety after the terrorist attack on the Pentagon. *Psychiatric Services, 54,* 1380–1382.

Grilo, C. M., & Mitchell, J. E. (2009). *The treatment of eating disorders: A clinical handbook.* New York, NY: Guilford Press.

Grilo, C. M., Sinha, R., & O'Malley, S. S. (2002). *Eating disorders and alcohol use disorders: Research update.* Washington, DC: U.S. Government Printing Office.

Gruber, J., & Persons, J. B. (2010). Unquiet treatment: Handling treatment refusal in bipolar disorder. *Journal of Cognitive Psychotherapy: An International Quarterly, 24,* 16–25.

Grunebaum, M. F., Oquendo, M. A., Harkavy-Friedman, J. M., Ellis, S., Li, S., Haas, G. L., . . . Mann, J. J. (2001). Delusions and suicidality. *American Journal of Psychiatry, 158,* 742–747.

Guerney, B. G., Jr. (1977). *Relationship enhancement: Skill training programs for therapy, problem prevention and enrichment.* San Francisco, CA: Jossey-Bass.

Guerney, B. G., Jr. (1994). The role of emotion in relationship enhancement marital/family therapy. In S. Johnson & L. Greenberg (Eds.), *The heart of the matter: Perspectives on emotion in marital therapy* (pp. 124–150). New York, NY: Brunner/Mazel.

Gunderson, J. G., & Ridolfi, M. E. (2001). Borderline personality disorder: Suicidality and self-mutilation. *Annals of the New York Academy of Sciences, 932,* 61–77.

Gunderson, J. G., Ronningstam, E., & Bodkin, A. (1990). The diagnostic interview for narcissistic patients. *Archives of General Psychiatry, 47,* 676–680.

Gustafson, D. H., Shaw, B. R., Isham, A., Baker, T., Boyle, M. G., & Levy, M. (2010). Explicating an evidence-based, theoretically informed, mobile technology-based system to improve outcomes for people in recovery for alcohol dependence. *Substance Use & Misuse, 46,* 96–111.

Hagopian, L. P., & Boelter, E. W. (2005). *Applied behavioral analysis: Overview and summary of scientific support.* Baltimore: Kennedy Krieger Institute and Johns Hopkins University School of Medicine. Available: www.kennedykrieger.org

Haley, M. (2004). Risk and protective factors. In D. Capuzzi (Ed.), *Suicide across the lifespan* (pp. 95–138). Alexandria, VA: American Counseling Association.

Hall, S. E. K., & Geher, G. (2003). Behavioral and personality characteristics of children with reactive attachment disorder. *Journal of Psychology, 137,* 145–162.

Hallowell, E. M., & Ratey, J. J. (1994). *Driven to distraction.* New York, NY: Pantheon Books.

Hambley, J., Arbour, S., & Sivagnanasundaram, L. (2010). Comparing outcomes for alcohol and drug abuse clients: A 6-month follow-up of clients who completed a residential treatment program. *Journal of Substance Use, 15,* 184–200.

Handen, B. L., & Gilchrist, R. H. (2006). Mental retardation. In E. J. Mash & R. A. Barkley (Eds.), *Treatment of childhood disorders* (3rd ed., pp. 411–454). New York, NY: Guilford Press.

Handleman, J., & Harris, S. L. (Eds.). (2001). *Preschool education programs for children with autism.* Austin, TX: Pro-Ed.

Hankammer, W., Snyder, B., & Hankammer, C. C. (2006). Empathy as the primary means in suicide assessment. *Journal for the Professional Counselor, 21,* 5–19.

Hanna, F., & Hunt, W. P. (1999). Techniques for psychotherapy with defiant, aggressive adolescents. *Psychotherapy, 36,* 1.

Hansen, N. B., & Lambert, M. J. (2003). An evaluation of the dose-response relationship in naturalistic treatment settings using survival analysis. *Mental Health Services Research, 5,* 1–12.

Hansen, R. E., & Spratt, E. G. (2002). Reactive attachment disorder: What we know about the disorder and implications for treatment. *Child Maltreatment, 5,* 137–145.

Harbin, G. L., McWilliam, R. A., & Gallagher, J. J. (2000). Services for young children with disabilities and their families. In J. P. Shonkoff & S. J. Meisels (Eds.), *Handbook of early childhood intervention* (2nd ed., pp. 387–415). New York, NY: Cambridge University Press.

Hardesty, V. A., & Gayton, W. F. (2002). The problem of children and fire: An historical perspective. In D. Kolko (Ed.), *Handbook on firesetting in children and youth* (pp. 1–13). San Diego, CA: Academic Press.

Harkavy-Friedman, J. M. (2006). Can early detection of psychosis prevent suicidal behavior? *American Journal of Psychiatry, 163,* 768–770.

Harris, S. L., Handleman, J. S., & Jennett, H. K. (2005). Models of educational intervention for students with autism: Home, center, and school-based programming. In F. R. Volkmar, R. Paul, A. Klin, & D. Cohen (Eds.), *Handbook of autism and pervasive developmental disorders* (3rd ed., pp. 1043–1054). Hoboken, NJ: Wiley.

Harrow, M., Grossman, L. S., Herbener, E. S., & Davies, E. W. (2000). Ten-year outcome: Patients with schizoaffective disorders, schizophrenia, affective disorders and mood-incongruent psychotic symptoms. *British Journal of Psychiatry, 177,* 421–426.

Hart, A., & Thomas, H. (2000). Controversial attachments: The indirect treatment of fostered and adopted children via parent therapy. *Attachment and Human Development, 2,* 306–327.

Hart, E. L., Lahey, B. B., Loeber, R., & Hanson, K. S. (1994). Criterion validity of informants in the diagnosis of disruptive behavior disorders in children: A preliminary study. *Journal of Consulting and Clinical Psychology, 62,* 410–414.

Hartley-McAndrew, M., & Weinstock, A. (2010, April). Autism Spectrum Disorder: Correlation between aberrant behaviors, EEG abnormalities, and seizures. *Neurology International,* North America, 2. Retrieved from www.pagepress.org/journals/index.php/ni/article/view/ni.2010.e10/2096

Haskett, M. E., Nears, K., Ward, C. S., & McPherson, A. V. (2006). Diversity in adjustment of maltreated children: Factors associated with resilient functioning. *Clinical Psychology Review, 26,* 796–812.

Hatchett, G. T. (2010). Differential diagnosis of borderline personality disorder from bipolar disorder. *Journal of Mental Health Counseling, 32,* 189–217.

Havens, L. L., & Ghaemi, S. N. (2005). Existential despair and bipolar disorder: The therapeutic alliance as a mood stabilizer. *American Journal of Psychotherapy, 5,* 137–147.

Hayes, J. A., Gelso, C. J., & Hummel, A. M. (2011). Managing countertransference. In J. C. Norcross (Ed.), *Psychotherapy relationships that work: Evidence-based responsiveness* (2nd ed.). New York, NY: Oxford University Press.

Hayes, S. C., & Strosahl, K. D. (2010). *A practical guide to acceptance and commitment therapy.* New York, NY: Springer Press.

Hayes, S. C., Strosahl, K. D., & Wilson, K. G. (2005). *Acceptance and commitment therapy: A unified model of behavior change* (2nd ed.). New York, NY: Guilford Press.

HBIGDA. (2001). *Harry Benjamin International Gender Dysphoria Association's Standards of Care for Gender Identity Disorders,* 6th Version. Available: http://wpath.org-documents-socv6.pdf.

Head, L. S., & Gross, A. M. (2008). Systematic desensitization. In W. T. O'Donohue and J. E. Fisher (Eds.), *Cognitive behavior therapy: Applying empirically supported techniques in your practice* (2nd ed., pp. 542–549). Hoboken, NJ: Wiley.

Heather, N., Adamson, S. J., Raistrick, D., & Slegg, G. P. (2010). Initial preference for drinking goal in the treatment of alcohol problems: I. Baseline differences between abstinence and non-abstinence groups. *Alcohol and Alcoholism, 45*(2), 128–135.

Heckers, S. (2009). Who is at risk for a psychotic disorder? *Schizophrenia Bulletin, 35,* 847–850.

Hedges, D. W., Woon, F. L., & Hoopes, S. P. (2009). Caffeine-induced psychosis: A case report. *CNS Spectrums, 14,* 127–129.

Heimberg, R. G., & Becker, R. E. (2002). *The nature and treatment of social fears and phobias.* New York, NY: Guilford Press.

Heimberg, R. G., Liebowitz, M. R., Hope, D. A., Schneier, F. R., Holt, C. S., Welkowitz, L. A., . . . Klein, D. F. (1998). Cognitive behavioral group therapy vs. phenelzine therapy for social phobia. *Archives of General Psychiatry, 55,* 1133–1141.

Hendin, H., Maltberger, J., Lipschitz, A., Haas, A., & Kyle, J. (2001). Recognizing and responding to a suicide crisis. *Suicide and life threatening behaviour, 31,* 115–128.

Henggeler, S. W., & Schaeffer, C. (2010). Treating serious antisocial behavior using multisystemic therapy. In J. R. Weisz & A. E. Kazdin (Eds.), *Evidence-based psychotherapies for children and adolescents* (2nd ed., pp. 259–276). New York, NY: Guilford Press.

Herbert, J. D., Forman, E. M., & England, E. L. (2008). Pyschological acceptance. In W. T. O'Donohue and J. E. Fisher (Eds), *Cognitive behavior therapy: Applying empirically supported techniques in your practice* (2nd ed., pp. 4–16). Hoboken, NJ: Wiley.

Hersoug, A. G., Hoglend, P., Havik, O., von der Lippe, A., & Monsen, J. (2009). Therapist characteristics influencing the quality of alliance in long-term psychotherapy. *Clinical Psychology and Psychotherapy, 216,* 100–110.

Hess, R. S., & Street, E. M. (1991). The effect of acculturation on the relationship of counselor ethnicity and client ratings. *Journal of Counseling Psychology, 38,* 71–75.

Hester, R. K., Delaney, H. D., & Campbell, W. (2011). ModerateDrinking.com and Moderation Management: Outcomes of a randomized clinical trial with non-dependent problem drinkers. *Journal of Consulting and Clinical Psychology, 79,* 215–224.

Hester, R. K., & Miller, W. R. (Eds.) (2003). *Handbook of alcoholism treatment approaches: Effective alternatives* (3rd ed.). Boston, MA: Allyn & Bacon.

Hiatt, K. D., & Dishion, T. J. (2008). Antisocial personality development. In T. P. Beauchaine & S. P. Hinshaw (Eds.), *Child and adolescent psychopathology* (pp. 370–404). Hoboken, NJ: Wiley.

Hinshaw, S., Klein, R., & Abikoff, H. (2007). Childhood attention-deficit hyperactivity disorder: Nonpharmacological treatments and their combination with medication. In P. Nathan & J. Gorman (Eds.), *A Guide to Treatments that Work* (3rd ed., pp. 3–28). New York, NY: Oxford University Press.

Hinshaw, S. P., & Lee, S. S. (2003). Conduct and oppositional defiant disorders. In E. J. Mash & R. A. Barkley (Eds.), *Child psychopathology* (2nd ed., pp. 144–198). New York, NY: Guilford Press.

Hoch, A. L. (2009). Trauma-focused cognitive behavioral therapy for children. In A. Rubin & D. W. Springer (Eds.), *Treatment of traumatized adults and children: Clinician's guide to evidence-based practice* (pp. 179–253). Hoboken, NJ: Wiley.

Hoek, H. W., van Harten, P. N., Hermans, K., Katzman, M. A., Matroos, G. F., & Susser, E. S. (2005). The incidence of anorexia nervosa on Curacao. *American Journal of Psychiatry, 162,* 748–752.

Hofmann, S. G., & Barlow, D. H. (2002). Social phobia (social anxiety disorder). In D. H. Barlow (Ed.), *Anxiety and its disorders* (pp. 454–476). New York, NY: Guilford Press.

Hoge, C. W., Castro, C. A., Messer, S. C., McGurk, D., Cotting, D. I., & Koffman, R. L. (2004). Combat duty in Iraq and Afghanistan, mental health problems, and barriers to care. *New England Journal of Medicine, 351,* 13–22.

Holder-Perkins, V., & Wise, T. N. (2001). Somatization disorder. In K. A. Phillips (Ed.), *Somatoform and factitious disorders* (pp. 1–21). Washington, DC: American Psychiatric Association.

Hollander, E., Baker, B. R., Kahn, J., & Stein, D. J. (2006). Conceptualizing and assessing impulse-control disorders. In E. Hollander & D. J. Stein (Eds.), *Clinical manual of impulse-control disorders* (pp. 1–18). Arlington, VA: American Psychiatric Publishing.

Hollander, E., & Stein, D. J. (Eds.). (2006). *Clinical manual of impulse-control disorders.* Arlington, VA: American Psychiatric Publishing.

Hollon, S. D. (2000). Cognitive therapy. In A. E. Kazdin (Ed.), *Encyclopedia of psychology* (Vol. 2, pp. 169–172). Washington, DC, and New York: American Psychological Association/Oxford University Press.

Hollon, S. D., & Beck, A. T. (2004). Cognitive and cognitive behavioral therapies. In M. J. Lambert (Ed.), *Bergin and Garfield's handbook of psychotherapy and behavior change* (pp. 447–492). Hoboken, NJ: Wiley.

Hollon, S. D., Stewart, M. O., & Strunk, D. R. (2006). Enduring effects for cognitive behavioral therapy in the treatment of depression and anxiety. *Annual Review of Psychology, 57,* 285–315.

Hommer, D., Momenan, R., Kaiser, E., & Rawlings, R. (2001). Evidence for a gender-related effect of alcoholism on brain volumes. *American Journal of Psychiatry, 158,* 198–204.

Hopwood, C. J., Morey, L. C., Markowitz, J. C., Pinto, A., Skodol. A. E., Gunderson, J. . . . Sanislow, C. A. (2009). The construct validity of passive-aggressive personality disorder. *Psychiatry: Interpersonal and Biological Processes, 72,* 256–267.

Horvath, A. O., & Laborsky, L. (1993). The role of the therapeutic alliance in psychotherapy. *Journal of Consulting and Clinical Psychology, 61,* 561–573.

Horvath, A. O., Symonds, D., & Tapia, L. (2010). Therapeutic alliances in couples therapy: The web of relationships. In J. C. Muran & J. P. Barber (Eds.), *The therapeutic alliance: An evidence-based guide to practice* (pp. 210–239). New York, NY: Guilford Press.

Houts, A. C. (2010). Behavioral treatment for enuresis. In J. R. Weisz & A. E. Kazdin (Eds.), *Evidence-based psychotherapies for children and adolescents* (2nd ed., pp. 359–374). New York, NY: Guilford Press.

Hu, G., Wilcox, H. C., Wissow, L., & Baker, S. P. (2008). Mid-life suicide: An increasing problem in U. S. Whites: 1999–2005. *American Journal of Preventive Medicine*, *35*, 589–593.

Hudson, J. I., Hiripi, E., Pope, H. G., & Kessler, R. C. (2007). The prevalence and correlates of eating disorders in the National Comorbidity Survey Replication. *Biological Psychiatry*, *61*, 348–358.

Hudson, J. L., & Rapee, R. M. (2001). Parent-child interactions and the anxiety disorders: An observational analysis. *Behaviour Research and Therapy*, *39*, 1411–1427.

Huey, S. J., & Polo, A. J. (2008). Evidence-based psychosocial treatments for ethnic minority youth. *Journal of Clinical Child and Adolescent Psychology*, *37*, 262–301.

Hughes, J. (2008). An algorithm for choosing among smoking cessation treatments. *Journal of Substance Abuse Treatments*, *34*, 426–432.

Hung, Y., & Huang, T. (2006). Lorazepam and diazepam rapidly relieve catatonic features in major depression. *Clinical Neuropharmacology*, *29*, 144–147.

Hunsley, J., Crabb, R., & Mash, E. J. (2004). Evidence-based clinical assessment. *Clinical Psychologist*, *57*, 25–32.

Hunsley, J., & Mash, E. J. (2010). Role of assessment in evidence-based practice. In M. M. Antony & D. H. Barlow (Eds.), *Handbook of assessment and treatment planning for psychological disorders* (2nd ed, pp. 3–22). New York, NY: Guilford Press.

Hunt, J. I., Dyl, J., Armstrong, L., Litvin, E., Sheeran, T., & Spirito, A. (2005). Frequency of manic symptoms and bipolar disorder in psychiatrically hospitalized adolescents using the K-SADS mania rating scale. *Journal of Child and Adolescent Psychopharmacology*, *15*, 918–930.

Hunter, E. C., Baker, D., Phillips, M. L., Sierra, M., & David, A. S. (2005). Cognitive-behaviour therapy for depersonalisation disorder: An open study. *Behaviour Research and Therapy*, *43*, 1121–1130.

Imel, Z. E., Malterer, M. B., McKay, K. M., & Wampold, B. E. (2008). A meta-analysis of psychotherapy and medication in unipolar depression and dysthymia. *Journal of Affective Disorders*, *110*, 197–206.

Institute of Medicine. (2008). *Treatment of posttraumatic stress disorder: An assessment of the evidence*. Washington, DC: Author.

International Society for the Study of Dissociation. (2005). Guidelines for treating dissociative identity disorder in adults. *Journal of Trauma and Dissociation*, *6*, 69–149.

Jaberghaderi, N., Greenwald, R., Rubin, A., Dolatabadim, S., & Zand, S. O. (2004). A comparison of CBT and EMDR for sexually abused Iranian girls. *Clinical Psychology and Psychotherapy*, *11*, 358–368.

Jablensky, A. (1999). Schizophrenia: Epidemiology. *Current Opinion in Psychiatry*, *12*, 19–28.

Jackson-Cherry, L. R., & Erford, B. T. (2010). *Crisis intervention and prevention*. New York, NY: Pearson.

Jacobi, C., Hayward, C., de Zwaan, M., Kraemer, H. C., & Agras, W. S. (2004). Coming to terms with risk factors for eating disorders: Application of risk terminology and suggestions for a general taxonomy. *Psychological Bulletin*, *130*, 19–65.

Jacobs, B., Green, J., Kroll, L., Tobias, C., Dunn, G., & Briskman, J. (2009). The effect of in-patient care on measured health needs of children and adolescents. *Journal of Child Psychology and Psychiatry*, *50*, 1273–1281.

Jacobs, D. F. (1988). Evidence for a common dissociative like reaction among addicts. *Journal of Gambling Behavior*, *4*, 27–37.

Jaffe, W. B., & D'Zurilla, T. J. (2003). Adolescent problem-solving, parent problem-solving, and externalizing behavior in adolescents. *Behavior Therapy*, *34*, 295–311.

Jakupcak, M., Cook, J., Imel, Z., Fontana, A., Rosenheck, R., & McFall, M. (2009). Posttraumatic stress disorder as a risk factor for suicidal ideation in Iraq and Afghanistan War veterans. *Journal of Traumatic Stress*, *22*, 303–306.

Janicak, P. G., O'Reardon, J. P., Sampson, S. M. Husain, M. M., Lisanby, S. H., Rado, J. . . . Demitrack, M. A. (2008). Transcranial magnetic stimulation (TMS) in the treatment of major depression: A comprehensive summary of safety experience from acute exposure, extended exposure and during reintroduction treatment. *Journal of Clinical Psychiatry*, *69*, 222–232.

Jankovic, J. (2001). Tourette's syndrome. *New England Journal of Medicine*, *345*, 1184–1192.

Jefferson, J. W. (2003). Bipolar disorders: A brief guide to diagnosis and treatment. *Focus*, *1*, 7–14.

Jeffres, M. J. (2004). The efficacy of EMDR with traumatized children. *Dissertation Abstracts International: Section B: The Sciences and Engineering*, *64*(8-B), 4042.

Jessor, R., Donovan, J. E., & Costa, F. M. (1991). *Beyond adolescence: Problem behavior and young adult development*. New York, NY: Cambridge University Press.

Jimenez-Genchi, A. M. (2004). Repetitive transcranial magnetic stimulation improves depersonalization: A case report. *CNS Spectrums*, 375–376.

Johnson, C. R. (2002). Mental retardation. In M. Hersen (Ed.), *Clinical behavior therapy: Adults and children* (pp. 420–433). Hoboken, NJ: Wiley.

Johnson, J. G., Cohen, P., Kotler, L., Kasen, S., & Brook, J. S. (2002). Psychiatric disorders associated with risk for the development of eating disorders during adolescence and early adulthood. *Journal of Consulting and Clinical Psychology, 70*, 1119–1128.

Johnson, J. G., First, M. B., Cohen, P., Skodol, A. E., Kasen, S., & Brook, J. S. (2005). Adverse outcomes associated with personality disorder not otherwise specified in a community sample. *American Journal of Psychiatry, 162*, 1926–1932.

Johnson, J. H., Rasbury, W. C., & Siegel, L. J. (1997). *Approaches to child treatment: Introduction to theory, research, and practice* (2nd ed.). Boston, MA: Allyn & Bacon.

Johnson, P. A., Hurley, R. A., Benkelfat, C., Herpertz, S. C., & Taber, K. H. (2003). Understanding emotion regulation in borderline personality disorder: Contributions of neuroimaging. *Journal of Neuropsychiatry and Clinical Neuroscience, 15*, 397–402.

Johnson, S. (2004). *The practice of emotionally focused couple therapy: Creating connection* (2nd ed.). Philadelphia, PA: Brunner-Routledge.

Johnson, S. L. (2004). Defining bipolar disorder. In S. L. Johnson & R. L. Leahy (Eds.), *Psychological treatment of bipolar disorder* (pp. 3–16). New York, NY: Guilford Press.

Johnson, S. L., & Fristad, M. (2008). Bipolar disorders across the lifespan. *Journal of Clinical Psychology, 64*, 365–367.

Johnson, S. L., & Fulford, D. (2008) Development of the treatment attitudes questionnaire in bipolar disorder. *Journal of Clinical Psychology, 64*, 466–481.

Johnson, V. E. (1986). *Intervention: How to help someone who doesn't want help. A step-by-step guide for families and friends of chemically dependent persons.* Minneapolis, MN: Johnson Institute.

Johnston, L. D., O'Malley, P. M., Bachman, J. G., & Schulenberg, J. E. (2011). *Monitoring the Future national results on adolescent drug use: Overview of key findings, 2010.* Ann Arbor: Institute for Social Research, The University of Michigan.

Johnston, L. D., O'Malley, P. M., Bachman, J. G., & Schulenberg, J. E. (2010). *Monitoring the Future national survey results on drug use, 1975-2009, Volume II: College students*

and adults ages 19–50 (NIH Publication No. 10-7585). Bethesda, MD: National Institute on Drug Abuse.

Joiner, T. E., Jr. (2000). Depression's vicious scree: Self-propagating and erosive processes in depression chronicity. *Clinical Psychology: Science and Practice, 7*, 203–218.

Joinson, C., Heron, J., Butler, U., von Gontard, A., & Avon Longitudinal Study of Parents and Children Study Team. (2006). Psychological differences between children with and without soiling problems. *Pediatrics, 117*, 1575–1584.

Jones, R. T., Fletcher, K., & Ribb, D. R. (2002). *Child's Reaction to Traumatic Events Scale-Revised (CRTES-R).* Blacksburg, VA: Virginia Technological University.

Jones, S. (2004). Psychotherapy of bipolar disorder: A review. *Journal of Affective Disorders, 80*, 101–114.

Jones, S. H. (2001). Circadian rhythms, multilevel models of emotion and bipolar disorder: An initial step towards integration? *Clinical Psychology Review, 21*, 1193–1209.

Judd, L., Akiskal, H., Schettler, P., Coryell, W., Endicott, J., Maser, J. D., . . . Keller, M. B. (2003). A prospective investigation of the natural history of the long-term weekly symptomatic status of bipolar II disorder, *Archives of General Psychiatry, 60*, 261–269.

Kabat-Zinn, J. (1990). *Full catastrophe living: Using the wisdom of your body and mind to face stress, pain, and illness.* New York, NY: Dell.

Kabat-Zinn, J. (2003). Mindfulness-based interventions in context: Past, present, and future. *Clinical Psychology Science and Practice, 10*, 144–156.

Kabat-Zinn, J., Chapman, A., & Salmon, P. (1997). The relationship of cognitive and somatic components of anxiety to patient preference for alternative relaxation techniques. *Mind/Body Medicine, 2*, 101–109.

Kabot, S., Masi, W., & Segal, M. (2003). Advances in the diagnosis and treatment of autism spectrum disorders. *Professional Psychology: Research and Practice, 34*, 26–33.

Kadesjo, B., & Gillberg, C. (2000). Tourette's disorder: Epidemiology and comorbidity in primary school children. *Journal of the American Academy of Child and Adolescent Psychiatry, 39*, 548–555.

Kafka, M. P. (2007). Paraphilia-related disorders: The evaluation and treatment of non-paraphilic hypersexuality. In S. R. Leiblum (Ed.), *Principles and practice of sex therapy* (4th ed., pp. 442–476). New York, NY: Guilford Press.

Kafka, M. P., & Hennen, J. (2002). A DSM-IV Axis I comorbidity study of males (n = 120) with paraphilias and paraphilia-related disorders. *Sexual Abuse: A Journal of Research and Treatment, 14*, 349–366.

Kahng, S., Iwata, B. A., & Lewin, A. B. (2002). Behavioral treatment of self-injury, 1964–2000. *American Journal on Mental Retardation, 107*, 212–221.

Kamphaus, R. W. (2000). Learning disabilities. In A. E. Kazdin (Ed.), *Encyclopedia of psychology*. Washington, DC and New York: American Psychological Association/Oxford University Press.

Kanel, K. (2007). *A guide to crisis intervention* (3rd ed.). Belmont, CA: Thomson.

Kantor, M. (2004). *Understanding paranoia*. Westport, CT: Praeger.

Kaplan, H. S. (1995). *The sexual desire disorders: Dysfunctional regulation of sexual motivation*. New York, NY: Routledge.

Karel, M. J., Ogland-Hand, S., & Gatz, M. (2002). *Assessing and treating late-life depression*. New York, NY: Basic Books.

Kaslow, N. J., & Thompson, M. P. (1998). Applying the criteria for empirically supported treatments to studies of psychosocial interventions for child and adolescent depression. *Journal of Clinical Child Psychology, 27*, 146–155.

Kay, S. R., Fiszbein, A., & Opler, L. A. (1987). The Positive and Negative Syndrome Scale (PANSS) for schizophrenia. *Schizophrenia Bulletin, 13*, 261–276.

Kaye, W. H., Frank, G. K., Bailer, U. F., Henry, S. E., Meltzer, C. C., Price, J. C., . . . Wagner, A. (2005). Serotonin alterations in anorexia and bulimia nervosa: New insights from imaging studies. *Physiological Behavior, 85*, 73–81.

Kazdin, A. E. (1993). Psychotherapy for children and adolescents: Current progress and future research directions. *American Psychologist, 48*, 644–657.

Kazdin, A. E. (1997). Psychosocial treatments for conduct disorder in children. *Journal of Child Psychology and Psychiatry and Allied Professions, 38*, 161–178.

Kazdin, A. E. (2000). *Psychotherapy for children and adolescents: Directions for research and practice*. New York, NY: Oxford University Press.

Kazdin, A. E. (2003). Problem-solving skills training and parent management training for conduct disorder. In A. E. Kazdin & J. R. Weisz (Eds.), *Evidence-based psychotherapies for children and adolescents* (pp. 241–262). New York, NY: Guilford Press.

Kazdin, A. E. (2007). Psychosocial treatments for conduct disorder in children and adolescents. In P. E. Nathan & J. M. Gorman (Eds.), *A guide to treatments that work* (3rd ed., pp. 71–104). New York, NY: Oxford University Press.

Kazdin, A. E. (2008). Evidence-based treatment and practice: New opportunities to bridge clinical research and practice, enhance the knowledge base, and improve patient care. *American Psychologist, 63*, 146–159.

Kazdin, A. E. (2010). PSST and PMT for oppositional defiant disorder and conduct disorder. In J. Weisz & A. Kazdin (Eds.), *Evidence-based psychotherapies for children and adolescents* (2nd ed., pp. 211–226). New York, NY: Guilford Press.

Keane, T. M., & Barlow, D. H. (2002). Posttraumatic stress disorder. In D. H. Barlow (Ed.), *Anxiety and its disorders* (pp. 418–453). New York, NY: Guilford Press.

Keel, P. K., & Striegel-Moore, R. H. (2009). The validity and clinical utility of purging disorder. *International Journal of Eating Disorders, 8*, 706–719.

Keitner, G. I., Garlow, S. J., Ryan, C. E., Ninan, P. T., Solomon, D. A., Nemeroff, C. B., & Keller, M. B. (2009). A randomized, placebo-controlled trial of risperidone augmentation for patients with difficult-to-treat unipolar, non-psychotic major depression. *Journal of Psychiatric Research, 43*, 205–214.

Kendall, P. C., Aschenbrand, S. G., & Hudson, S. G. (2003). Child-focused treatment of anxiety. In A. E. Kazdin & J. R. Weisz (Eds.), *Evidence-based psychotherapies for children and adolescents* (pp. 81–100). New York, NY: Guilford Press.

Kennedy, S. H., Welsh, B. R., Fulton, K., Soczynska, J. K., McIntyre, R. S., O'Donovan, C., . . . Martin, N. (2010). Frequency and correlates of gambling problems in outpatients with major depressive disorder and bipolar disorder. *Canadian Journal of Psychiatry, 55*, 568–576.

Kernberg, O. (2000). *Borderline conditions and pathological narcissism*. New York, NY: Jason Aronson.

Kessler, R. C. (2006a). The epidemiology of depression among women. In C.L.M. Keyes & S. H. Goodman (Eds.), *Women and depression* (pp. 22–40). New York, NY: Cambridge University Press.

Kessler, R. C. (2006b). The prevalence and correlates of adult ADHD in the United States: Results from the national comorbidity survey replication. *American Journal of Psychiatry, 163*, 716–723.

Kessler, R. C., Adler, L., Ames, M., Demler, O., Faraone, S. V., Hiripi, E., . . . Walters, E. E. (2005). The World Health Organization Adult ADHD Self-Report Scale

(ASRS): A short screening scale for use in the general population. *Psychological Medicine, 35*, 245–256.

Kessler, R. C., Berglund, P., Demler, O., Jin, R., Merikangas, K., & Walters, E. E. (2005). Lifetime prevalence and age of onset distributions of DSM-IV disorders in the National Comorbidity Survey Replication. *Archives of General Psychiatry, 62*, 593–602.

Kessler, R. C., Borges, G., & Walters, E. E. (1999). Prevalence of and risk factors for lifetime suicide attempts in the National Comorbidity Survey, *Archives of General Psychiatry, 56*, 617–626.

Kessler, R. C., Chiu, W. T., Demler, O., & Walters, E. E. (2005). Prevalence, severity, and comorbidity of 12-month DSM-IV disorders in the National Comorbidity Survey Replication. *Archives of General Psychiatry, 62*, 617–627.

Kessler R. C., Hwang I., LaBrie R., Petukhova M., Sampson N. A., Winters K. C., & Shaffer, H. J. (2008). DSM-IV pathological gambling in the National Comorbidity Survey Replication. *Psychological Medicine, 38*, 1351–1360.

Kessler, R. C., Stang, P., Wittchen, H. U., Stein, M., & Walters, E. E. (1999). Lifetime co-morbidities between social phobia and mood disorders in the U.S. National Co-morbidity Survey. *Psychological Medicine, 29*, 555–567.

Keyes, C. L. M., & Goodman, S. H. (Eds.). (2006). *Women and depression.* New York, NY: Cambridge University Press.

Kho, K. H., van Vresswijk, M. F., Simpson, S., & Zwinderman, A. H. (2003). A meta-analysis of electroconvulsive therapy efficacy in depression. *Journal of ECT, 19*, 139–147.

Kiehl, K. A. (2006). A cognitive neuroscience perspective on psychopathy: Evidence for paralimbic system dysfunction. *Psychiatry Research, 142*, 107–128.

Kiehl, K. A., & Buckholtz, J. W. (2010). Inside the mind of a psychopath. *Scientific American Mind, 21*, 22–29.

Kilpatrick, D. G., Ruggiero, K. J., Acierno, R., Saunders, B. E., Resnick, H. S., & Best, C. L. (2003). Violence and risk of PTSD, major depressive disorder, substance abuse/dependence, and comorbidity. Results from the national survey of adolescents. *Journal of Consulting and Clinical Psychology, 71*, 692–700.

King, M. P., & Tucker, J. A. (2000). Behavior change patterns and strategies distinguishing moderation drinking and abstinence during the natural resolution of alcohol problems without treatment. *Psychology of Addictive Behaviors, 14*, 48–55.

Kingsberg, S. A. (2002). The impact of aging on sexual function in women and their partners. *Archives of Sexual Behavior, 31*, 421–437.

Kingsberg, S. A. (2004). Just ask! Talking to patients about sexual function. *Sexuality, Reproduction & Menopause, 2*, 199–203.

Kingsberg, S. A., Simon, J. A., & Goldstein, I. (2008). The current outlook for testosterone in the management of hypoactive sexual desire disorder in postmenopausal women. *Journal of Sexual Medicine, 5* (Suppl. 4), 177–178.

Klerman, G. L., Weissman, M. M., Rounsaville, B. J., & Chevron, E. S. (1984). *Interpersonal psychotherapy of depression.* New York, NY: Basic Books.

Klorman, R., Hastings, J. E., Weerts, T. C., Melamed, B. G., & Lang, P. J. (1974). Psychometric descriptions of some specific-fear questionnaires. *Behavior Therapy, 5*, 401–409.

Kluger, J. (2003, September). Real men get the blues. *Time*, pp. 48–49.

Knaevelsrud, C., & Maercker, A. (2007). Internet-based treatment for PTSD reduces distress and facilitates the development of a strong therapeutic alliance: A randomized controlled clinical trial. *BMC Psychiatry, 7*, 13.

Koegel, L. K. (2000). Interventions to facilitate communication in autism. *Journal of Autism and Developmental Disorders, 30*, 383–391.

Koegel, R. L., Camarata, S., Koegel, L. K., Ben-Tall, A., & Smith, A. E. (2008). Increasing speech intelligibility in children with autism. *Journal of Autism and Developmental Disorders, 28*, 241–251.

Koegel, R. L., Koegel, L. K., Vernon, T. W., & Brookman-Frazee, L. I. (2010). Empirically supported pivotal response treatment for children with autism spectrum disorders. In J. R. Weisz & A. E. Kazdin (Eds.), *Evidence-based psychotherapies for children and adolescents* (2nd ed., pp. 327–343). New York, NY: Guilford Press.

Koerner, K., & Dimeff, L. A. (2007). Overview of dialectical behavior therapy. In L. A. Dimeff & K. Koerner (Eds.), *Dialectical behavior therapy: Applications across disorders and settings* (pp. 1–18). New York, NY: Guilford Press.

Koerner, K., & Linehan, M. M. (2008). Validation principles and strategies. In W. T. O'Donohue and J. E. Fisher (Eds.), *Cognitive behavior therapy: Applying empirically supported techniques in your practice* (2nd ed., pp. 576–582). Hoboken, NJ: Wiley.

Kohut, H. (1971). *The analysis of self.* Madison, CT: International Universities Press.

Kopelowicz, A., Liberman, R. P., & Zarate, R. (2007). Psychosocial treatments for schizophrenia. In P. E. Nathan & J. M. Gorman (Eds.), *A guide to treatments that work* (3rd ed., pp. 203–242). New York, NY: Oxford University Press.

Korszun, A., Altemus, M., & Young, E. A. (2006). The biological underpinnings of depression. In C. L. M. Keyes & S. H. Goodman (Eds.), *Women and depression* (pp. 41–61). New York, NY: Cambridge University Press.

Kotler, L. A., Cohen, P., Davies, M., Pine, D. S., & Walsh, B. T. (2001). Longitudinal relationships between childhood, adolescent, and adult eating disorders. *Journal of the American Academy of Child and Adolescent Psychiatry, 40,* 1434, 1440.

Kovacs, M. (1983). *Children's Depression Inventory (CDI).* Pittsburgh, PA: University of Pittsburgh School of Medicine.

Kozlowska, K., Foley, S., & Crittenden, P. (2006). Factitious illness by proxy: Understanding underlying psychological processes and motivations. *Australian and New Zealand Journal of Family Therapy, 27,* 92–104.

Kramer, U., Despland, J., Michel, L., Drapeau, M., & de Roten, Y. (2010). Change in defense mechanisms and coping over the course of short-term dynamic psychotherapy for adjustment disorder. *Journal of Clinical Psychology, 66,* 1232–1241.

Kranzler, H. R. (2006). Evidence-based treatments for alcohol dependence: New results and new questions. *Journal of the American Medical Association, 295,* 2075–2076.

Krautter, T., & Lock, J. (2004). Treatment of adolescent anorexia nervosa using manualized family-based treatment. *Clinical Case Studies, 3,* 107–123.

Kristensen, H. (2000). Selective mutism and comorbidity with developmental disorder/delay, anxiety disorder, and elimination disorder. *Journal of American Academy of Child and Adolescent Psychiatry, 39,* 249–256.

Kristensen, H., & Torgersen, S. (2001). MCMI-II personality traits and symptom traits in parents of children with selective mutism: A case-control study. *Journal of Abnormal Psychology, 110,* 4.

Kroenke, K. (2007). Efficacy of treatment for somatoform disorders: A review of randomized controlled trials. *Psychosomatic Medicine, 69,* 881–888.

Kronenberger, W. G., & Meyer, R. G. (2001). *The child clinician's handbook* (2nd ed.). Boston, MA: Allyn & Bacon.

Kroutil, L. A., Van Brunt, D. L., Herman-Stahl, M. A., Heller, D. C., Bray, R. M., & Penne, M. A. (2006). Nonmedical use of prescription stimulants in the United States. *Drug and Alcohol Dependence, 84,* 135–143.

Krupnick, J. L., Sotsky, S. M., Elkin, I., Simmens, S., Moyer, J., Watkins, J., & Pilkonis, P. A. (1996). The role of the therapeutic alliance in psychotherapy and pharmacotherapy outcome: Findings in the National Institute of Mental Health treatment of depression collaborative research program. *Journal of Consulting and Clinical Psychology, 64,* 532–539.

Kübler-Ross, E. (1997). *Living with death and dying.* New York, NY: Scribner.

Kübler-Ross, E., & Kessler, D. (2001). *Life lessons.* New York, NY: Scribner.

Kübler-Ross, E., & Kessler, D. (2005). *On grief and grieving.* New York, NY: Scribner.

Kuhn, B. R., Marcus, B. A., & Pitner, S. L. (1999). Treatment guidelines for primary nonretentive encopresis and stool toileting refusal. *American Family Physician, 59,* 2171–2178.

Kushida, C. A., Littner, M. R., Morgenthaler, T., Alessi, C. A., Bailey, D., Coleman, J., . . . Wise, M. (2005). Practice parameters for the indications for polysomnography and related procedures: An update for 2005. *Sleep, 28,* 499–521.

Kushner, H. S. (2004). *When bad things happen to good people.* New York, NY: Anchor Books.

Ladouceur, R., Lachance, S., & Fournier P. (2009). Is control a viable goal in the treatment of pathological gambling? *Behavior Research and Therapy, 47,* 189–197.

Ladd, G. T., & Petry, N. M. (2003). A comparison of pathological gamblers with and without substance abuse treatment histories. *Experimental and Clinical Psychopharmacology, 11,* 202–209.

Lahey, B. B. (2008). Oppositional defiant disorder, conduct disorder, and juvenile delinquency. In T. P. Beauchaine & S. P. Hinshaw (Eds.), *Child and adolescent psychopathology* (pp. 335–369). Hoboken, NJ: Wiley.

Lake, C. R. (2010). Schizophrenia and bipolar disorder: No dichotomy, a continuum, or one disease? *Psychiatric Annals, 40,* 72–75.

Lam, D. H., Watkins E. R., Hayward P., Bright, J., Wright, K., Kerr, N., . . . Sham, P. (2003). A randomized controlled study of cognitive therapy for relapse prevention for bipolar affective disorder: Outcome of the first year. *Archives of General Psychiatry, 60,* 145–152.

Lambert, M. J. (1982). *The effects of psychotherapy.* New York, NY: Human Sciences Press.

Lambert, M. J. (2010). Yes, it is time for clinicians to routinely monitor treatment outcome. In B. L. Duncan, S. D. Miller, B. E. Wampold, & M. A. Hubble (Eds.), *The heart and soul of change: Delivering what works in therapy* (2nd ed., pp. 133–178). Washington, DC: American Psychological Association.

Lambert, M. J., & Anderson, E. M. (1996). Assessment for the time-limited psychotherapies. *American Psychiatric Press Review of Psychiatry, 15,* 23–42.

Lambert, M. J., & Barley, D. E. (2001). Research summary on the therapeutic relationship and psychotherapy outcome. *Psychotherapy, 38,* 357–361.

Lambert, M. J., & Bergin, A. E. (1994). The effectiveness of psychotherapy. In A. E. Bergin & S. L. Garfield (Eds.), *Handbook of psychotherapy and behavior change* (4th ed., pp. 143–189). Hoboken, NJ: Wiley.

Lambert, M. J., & Cattani-Thompson, K. (1996). Current findings regarding the effectiveness of counseling: Implications for practice. *Journal of Counseling and Development, 74,* 601–608.

Lambert, M. J., & Ogles, B. M. (2004). The efficacy and effectiveness of psychotherapy. In M. J. Lambert (Ed.), *Bergin and Garfield's handbook of psychotherapy and behavior change* (pp. 139–193). Hoboken, NJ: Wiley.

Lambert, M., Schimmelmann, B. G., Nabor, D., Schacht, A., Karow, A., Wagner, T., & Czekalla, J. (2006). Prediction of remission as a combination of symptomatic and functional remission and adequate subjective well-being in 2960 patients with schizophrenia. *Journal of Clinical Psychiatry, 67,* 1690–1697.

Landreth, G. I., & Bratten, S. (2006). *Child-parent relationship therapy: A 10-session filial therapy model.* New York, NY: Routledge.

Langer, S. J., & Martin, J. I. (2004). How dresses can make you mentally ill: Examining gender identity disorder in children. *Child & Adolescent Social Work Journal, 21,* 5–23.

Lariviere, N., Desrosiers, J., Tousignant, M., & Boyer, R. (2010). Who benefits the most from psychiatric day hospitals: A comparison of three clinical groups. *Journal of Psychiatric Practice, 16,* 93–102.

LaSasso, C. (2008). Eating, sleep, sexual, and gender identity disorders. In S. M. Woo & C. Keatinge (Eds.), *Diagnosis and treatment of mental disorders across the lifespan* (pp. 745–800). Hoboken, NJ: Wiley.

Laudet, A. B., Magura, S., Vogel, H. S., & Knight, E. L. (2004). Perceived reasons for substance misuse among persons with a psychiatric disorder. *American Journal of Orthopsychiatry, 74,* 365–375.

Lauman, E. O., Paik, A., & Rosen, R. C. (1999). Sexual dysfunction in the United States: Prevalence and predictors. *Journal of the American Medical Association, 281,* 537–544.

Laws, D. R., & O'Donohue, W. T. (Eds.). (2008). Sexual deviance: *Theory, assessment, and treatment* (2nd ed.). New York, NY: Guilford Press.

Leahy, R. L. (2004). Cognitive therapy. In S. L. Johnson & R. L. Leahy (Eds.), *Psychological treatment of bipolar disorder* (pp. 139–161). New York, NY: Guilford Press.

Leckman, J. F. (2002). Tourette's syndrome. *Lancet, 360,* 1577–1586.

Leckman, J. F., & Cohen, D. J. (1994). Tic disorders. In M. Rutter, E. Taylor, & L. Hersov (Eds.), *Child and adolescent psychiatry: Modern approaches* (pp. 455–466). Cambridge, MA: Blackwell.

Leckman, J. F., Zhang, H., Vitale, A., Lahnin, F., Lynch, K., Bondi, C., . . . Peterson, B. (1998). Course of tic severity in Tourette syndrome: The first two decades. *Pediatrics, 102,* 14–19.

Ledgerwood, D. M., Steinberg, M. A., Wu, R., & Potenza, M. N. (2005). Self-reported gambling-related suicidality among gambling helpline callers. *Psychology of Addictive Behaviors, 19,* 175–183.

LeFoll, B. L., & George, T. P. (2007). Treatment of tobacco dependence: Integrating recent progress into practice. *Canadian Medical Association Journal, 177,* 1373–1400.

Leibenluft, E., Charney, D. S., Towbin, K. E., Bhangoo, R. K., & Pine, D. S. (2003). Defining clinical phenotypes of juvenile mania. *American Journal of Psychiatry, 160,* 430–437.

Leibenluft, E. (2011). Severe mood dysregulation, irritability, and the diagnostic boundaries of bipolar disorder in youth. *American Journal of Psychiatry, 168,* 129–142.

Leiblum, S. R. (2007). *Principles and practice of sex therapy* (4th ed.). New York, NY: Guilford Press.

Leichsenring, F. (2005). Are psychodynamic and psychoanalytic therapies effective? *International Journal of Psychoanalysis, 86,* 841–868.

Leichsenring, F. (2009). Psychodynamic psychotherapy: A review of efficacy and effectiveness studies. In R. A. Levy, & J. S. Ablon (Eds.), *Handbook of evidence-based psychodynamic psychotherapy: Bridging the gap between science and practice* (pp. 3–27). Totowa, NJ: Humana Press.

Leichsenring, F., & Leibing, E. (2003). The effectiveness of psychodynamic therapy and cognitive behavior therapy in the treatment of personality disorders: A meta-analysis. *American Journal of Psychiatry, 160,* 1223–1232.

Leichsenring, F., & Rabung, S. (2008). Effectiveness of long-term psychodynamic psychotherapy: A meta-analysis. *Journal of the American Medical Association, 300,* 1551–1565.

Lejoyeux, M., McLoughlin, M., & Ades, J. (2006). Pyromania. In E. Hollander & D. J. Stein (Eds.), *Clinical manual of impulse-control disorders* (pp. 229–250). Arlington, VA: American Psychiatric Publishing.

Lembke, A., Bradley, K. A., Henderson, P., Moos, R., & Harris, A. H. (2011). What the future holds. *Journal of General Internal Medicine, 26,* 777–782.

Lembke, A. (2013, May 9). "When it comes to addiction, the *DSM-5* gets it right, but . . . " NY: Pacific Standard. Downloaded May 13, 2013, from http://www.psmag.com/health/when-it-comes-to-addiction-the-dsm-5-gets-it-right-but-572

Lengacher, C. A., Johnson-Mallard, V., Post-White, J., Moscoso, M. S., Jacobsen, P. B., Klein, T. W., . . . Kip, K. E. (2009). Randomized controlled trial of mindfulness-based stress reduction (MBSR) for survivors of breast cancer. *Psycho-Oncology, 18,* 1261–1272.

Lenzenweger, M. F., Lane, M. C., Loranger, A. W., & Kessler, R. C. (2007). *DSM-IV* personality disorders in the National Comorbidity Survey Replication. *Biological Psychiatry, 62,* 553–564.

Levant, R. F. (2005). *Report of the 2005 presidential task force on evidence-based practice.* Washington, DC: American Psychological Association.

Levant, R. F., & Hassan, N. T. (2008). Evidence-based practice in psychology. *Professional Psychology: Research and Practice, 39,* 658–662.

Levensky, E. R., Kersh, B. C., Cavasos, L. L., & Brooks, J. A. (2008). Motivational interviewing. In W. T. O'Donohue & J. E. Fisher (Eds.), *Cognitive behavior therapy: Applying empirically supported techniques in your practice* (2nd ed., pp. 357–366). Hoboken, NJ: Wiley.

Levin, A. V., & Sheriden, M. S. (1995). *Munchausen syndrome by proxy: Issues in diagnosis and treatment.* New York, NY: Lexington.

Levin, F. R., & Hennessy, G. (2004). Bipolar disorder and substance abuse. *Biological Psychiatry, 56,* 738–748.

Levis, D. J. (2008). The prolonged CS exposure techniques of implosive (flooding) therapy. In W. T. O'Donohue & J. E. Fisher (Eds.), *Cognitive behavior therapy: Applying empirically supported techniques in your practice* (2nd ed., pp. 272–282). Hoboken, NJ: Wiley.

Levy, K. N., Meehan, K. B., Kelly, K. M., Reynoso, J. S., Weber, M., Clarkin, J. F., & Kernberg, O. F. (2006). Change in attachment patterns and reflective function in a randomized control trial of transference focused psychotherapy for borderline personality disorder. *Journal of Consulting and Clinical Psychology, 74,* 1027–1040.

Lewinsohn, P. M., Seeley, J. R., & Klein, D. N. (2003). Bipolar disorder in adolescence. *Acta Psychiatrica Scandinavica, 108* (Suppl. 418), 47–50.

Lewis, D. A., & Levitt, P. (2002). Schizophrenia as a disorder of neurodevelopment. *Annual Review of Neuroscience, 25,* 409–432.

Lieber, C. S. (2000). Ethnic and gender differences in ethanol metabolism. *Alcoholism: Clinical & Experimental Research, 24,* 417–418.

Lieberman, A. F., Silverman, R., & Pawl, J. (2000). Infant-parent psychotherapy. In C. H. Zeanah (Ed.), *Handbook of infant mental health* (2nd ed.). New York, NY: Guilford Press.

Lighthall, A. (2010). The rules of engagement. *Psychotherapy Networker, 34,* 43–45.

Lilenfeld, L. R., Kaye, W. H., Greeno, C. G., Merikangas, K. R., Plotnicov, K., Pollice, . . . Nagy, L. (1997). Psychiatric disorders in women with bulimia nervosa and their first-degree relatives: Effects of comorbid substance dependence. *International Journal of Eating Disorders, 22,* 255–264.

Lilienfeld, S. O., Lynn, S. J., & Lohr, J. M. (2003). Science and pseudoscience in clinical psychology: Initial thoughts reflections, and considerations. In. S. O. Lilienfeld, S. J. Lynn, & J. M. Lohr (Eds.), *Science and pseudoscience in clinical psychology* (pp. 1–14). New York, NY: Guilford Press.

Lindau, S. T., & Gavrilova, N. (2010). Sexual activity in middle to later life. *British Medical Journal, 340,* 850.

Lindau, S. T., Schumm, L. P., Laumann, E. O., Levinson, W., O'Muircheartaigh, C. A., & Waite, L. J. (2007). A study of sexuality and health among older adults in the United States. *New England Journal of Medicine, 357,* 762–774.

Lindberg, N., Holi, M. M., Tani, P., & Virkkunen, M. (2005). Looking for pyromania: Characteristics of a consecutive sample of Finnish male criminals with histories of recidivist fire-setting between 1973 and 1993. *BMC Psychiatry, 5,* 1–5.

Linehan, M. (1993). *Cognitive-behavioral treatment of borderline personality disorder.* New York, NY: Guilford Press.

Linehan, M. M., & Dexter-Mazza, E. T. (2008). Dialectical behavior therapy for borderline personality disorder. In D. H. Barlow (Ed.), *Clinical handbook of psychological disorders: A step-by-step treatment manual* (4th ed., pp. 365–420). New York, NY: Guilford Press.

Linehan, M. M., Comtois, K. A., Murray, A. M., Brown, M. Z., Gallop, R. L., Heard, H. L., . . . Behavioral Research and Therapy Clinics. (2006). Two-year randomized trial and follow-up of dialectical behavior therapy vs. treatment-by-experts for suicidal behaviors and borderline personality disorder. *Archives of General Psychiatry, 63,* 757–766.

Links, P. S., & Kola, N. (2005). Assessing and managing suicide risk. In J. M. Oldham, A. E. Skodol, & D. S. Bender (Eds.), *The American Psychiatric Publishing textbook of personality disorders* (pp. 449–462). Washington, DC: American Psychiatric Association.

Linscheid, T. R. (1992). Eating problems in children. In C. E. Walker & M. C. Roberts (Eds.), *Handbook of clinical child psychology* (pp. 451–473). Hoboken, NJ: Wiley.

Littrell, J. M., Malia, J. A., & Vanderwood, J. (1995). Single session brief counseling in a high school. *Journal of Counseling and Development, 73,* 451–458.

Litz, B. T., Miller, M. W., Ruef, A. M., & McTeague, L. M. (2002). Exposure to trauma in adults. In M. M. Antony & D. H. Barlow (Eds.), *Handbook of assessment and treatment planning for psychological disorders* (pp. 215–258). New York, NY: Guilford Press.

Livesley, W. J. (2003). *Practical management of personality disorders.* New York, NY: Guilford Press.

Livesley, W. J. (2007). A framework for inte grating dimensional and categorical classifications of personality disorder. *Journal of Personality Disorders, 21,* 199–224.

Livingston, R. (1991). Anxiety disorders. In M. Lewis (Ed.), *Child and adolescent psychiatry: A comprehensive textbook* (pp. 673–685). Baltimore, MD: Williams & Wilkins.

LivingWorks. (2010). *Applied Suicide Intervention Skills Training (ASIST) handbook.* Fayetteville, NC: Author. Available: www.livingworks.net

Lloyd, A. (2008). Urge surfing. In W. T. O'Donohue & J. E. Fisher (Eds.), *Cognitive behavior therapy: Applying empirically supported techniques in your practice* (2nd ed., pp. 571–575). Hoboken, NJ: Wiley.

Lochman, J. E., Barry, T. D., & Pardini, D. A. (2003). Anger control for aggressive youth. In A. E. Kazdin & J. R. Weisz (Eds.), *Evidence-based psychotherapies for children and adolescents* (pp. 263–281). New York, NY: Guilford Press.

Lochman, J. E., Boxmeyer, C., Powell, N., Qu, L., Wells, K., & Windle, M. (2009). Dissemination of the Coping Power program: Importance of intensity of counselor training. *Journal of Consulting and Clinical Psychology, 77,* 397–409.

Lochman, J. E., Boxmeyer, C. I., Powell, N. P., Barry, T. D., & Pardini, D. A. (2010). Anger control for aggressive youth. In J. Weisz & A. Kazdin (Eds.), *Evidence-based psychotherapies for children and adolescents* (2nd ed., pp. 227–242). New York, NY: Guilford Press.

Lord, C., Rutter, M., & Couteur, A. (1994). Autism Diagnostic Interview-Revised: A revised version of a diagnostic interview for caretakers of individuals with possible pervasive developmental disorders. *Journal of Autism and Developmental Disorders, 24,* 659–685.

Lovaas, O. I., & Smith, T. (2003). Early and intensive behavioral intervention in autism. In A. E. Kazdin & J. R. Weisz (Eds.), *Evidence-based psychotherapies for children and adolescents* (pp. 325–340). New York, NY: Guilford Press.

Love, A., James, D., & Willner, P. (1998). Desires for Alcohol Questionnaire (DAQ); A comparison of two alcohol craving questionnaires. *Addiction, 93,* 1091–1102.

Luborsky, L., Diguer, L., Cacciola, J., Barbar, J. P., Moras, K., Schmidt, K., & De Rubeis, R. J. (1996). Factors in outcomes of short-term dynamic psychotherapy for chronic depression versus nonchronic depression. *Journal of Psychotherapy Practice and Research, 5,* 152–159.

Luby, J. L. (2009). Early childhood depression. *American Journal of Psychiatry, 166,* 974–979.

Luby, J. L., & Belden, A. (2006). Defining and validating bipolar disorder in the preschool period. *Development and Psychopathology, 18,* 971–988.

Luby, J. L., Belden, A. C., & Tandon, M. (2010). Bipolar disorder in the preschool period: Development and differential diagnosis. In D. J. Miklowitz & Dante Cicchetti (Eds.), *Understanding bipolar disorder: A developmental psychopathology perspective* (pp. 108–133). New York, NY: Guilford Press.

Luce, K. H., Winzelberg, A. J., Zabinski, M. F., & Osborne, M. I. (2003). Internet-delivered psychological interventions for body image dissatisfaction and disordered eating. *Psychotherapy, 40,* 148–154.

Lyon, C., & Schnall, J. (2005). What is the best treatment for nocturnal enuresis in children? *Journal of Family Practice, 54,* 905–909.

Lyon, G. R., Fletcher, J. M., Fuchs, L. S., & Chhabra, V. (2006). Learning disabilities. In E. J. Mash & R. A. Barkley (Eds.), *Treatment of childhood disorders* (3rd ed., pp. 512–594). New York, NY: Guilford Press.

Lyons-Ruth, K., Zeanah, C. H., & Benoit, D. (1996). Disorder and risk for disorder during infancy and toddlerhood. In E. J. Mash & R. A. Barkley (Eds.), *Child psychopathology* (pp. 457–491). New York, NY: Guilford Press.

Lysaker, J. T. (2008). *Schizophrenia and the fate of the self.* New York, NY: Oxford University Press.

Lysaker, P. H., Roe, D., & Yanos, P. T. (2007). Toward understanding the insight paradox: Internalized stigma moderates the association between insight and social functioning, hope, and self-esteem among people with schizophrenia spectrum disorders. *Schizophrenia Bulletin, 33,* 192–199.

Ma, S. H., & Teasdale, J. D. (2004). Mindfulness-based cognitive therapy for depression: Replication and exploration of differential relapse prevention effects. *Journal of Consulting and Clinical Psychology, 72,* 31–40.

MacKay, S., Paglia-Boak, A., Henderson, J., Marton, P., & Adlaf, E. (2009). Epidemiology of firesetting adolescents: Mental health and substance use correlates. *Journal of Child Psychology and Psychiatry, 50,* 1282–1290.

Mackenzie, M. J., Carlson, L. E., Munoz, M., & Speca, M. (2007). A qualitative study of self-perceived effects of Mindfulness-based Stress Reduction (MBSR) in a psychosocial oncology setting. *Stress and Health: Journal of the International Society for the Investigation of Stress, 23,* 59–69.

Mackinaw-Koons, B., & Fristad, M. A. (2004). Children with bipolar disorder: How to break down barriers and work effectively together. *Professional Psychology: Research and Practice, 35,* 481–484.

Maestro, S., Muratori, F., Cavallaro, M. C., Pei, F., Stern, D., Golse, B., & Palacio-Espasa, F. (2002). Attentional skills during the first 6 months of age in autism spectrum disorder. *Journal of the American Academy of Child and Adolescent Psychiatry, 41,* 1239–1245.

Maffei, C., Fossati, A., Agostoni, I., Barraco, A., Bagnato, M., Deborah, D., . . . Petrachi, M. (1997). Interrater reliability and internal consistency of the Structured Clinical Interview of DSM-IV Axis II personality disorders (SCID-II) version 2.0. *Journal of Personality Disorders, 11,* 279–284.

Magill, M., & Ray, L. A. (2009). Cognitive-behavioral treatment with adult alcohol and illicit drug users: A meta-analysis of randomized controlled trials. *Journal of Studies on Alcohol and Drugs, 70,* 516–527.

Magnavita, J. J. (2010). *Evidence-based treatment of personality dysfunction; Principles, methods, and processes.* Arlington, VA: American Psychological Association.

Maguen, S., Lucenko, B. A., Reger, M. A., Gahm, G. A., Litz, B. T., Seal, K. H., . . . Marmar, C. R. (2010). The impact of reported direct and indirect killing on mental health symptoms in Iraq war veterans. *Journal of Traumatic Stress, 23,* 86–90.

Mahgerefteh, S., Pierre, J. M., & Wirshing, D. A. (2006). Treatment challenges in schizophrenia: A multifaceted approach to relapse prevention. *Psychiatric Times, 23.* Available: www.psychiatrictimes.com/article

Mahowald, M. W., & Schenck, C. H. (2005). Insights from studying human sleep disorders. *Nature, 437,* 1279–1285.

Maina, G., Rosso, G., & Bogetto, F. (2009). Brief dynamic therapy combined with pharmacotherapy in the treatment of major depressive disorder: Long-term results. *Journal of Affective Disorders, 114,* 200–207.

Maina, G., Salvi, V., Rosso, G., & Bogetto, F. (2010). Cyclothymic temperament and a major depressive disorder: A study on Italian patients, *Journal of Affective Disorders, 121,* 199–203.

Maine, M., Davis, W. N., & Shure, J. (Eds.). (2008). *Effective clinical practice in the treatment of eating disorders: The heart of the matter.* New York, NY: Routledge.

Maine, M., McGilley, B. H., & Bunnell, D. (Eds.). (2010). *Treatment of eating disorders: Bridging the research-practice gap.* Burlington, MA: Elsevier.

Maj, M., Pinozzi, R., Formicola, A. M., Bartoli, L., & Bucci, P. (2010). Reliability and validity of the DSM-IV diagnostic category of schizoaffective disorder: Preliminary data. *Journal of Affective Disorders, 57,* 95–98.

Maldonado, J. R., Butler, L. D., & Spiegel, D. (2002). Treatments for dissociative disorders. In P. E. Nathan & J. M. Gorman (Eds.), *A guide to treatments that work* (2nd ed., pp. 463–496). New York, NY: Oxford University Press.

Maldonado, J. R., & Spiegel, D. (2001). Conversion disorder. In K. A. Phillips (Ed.), *Somatoform and factitious disorders* (pp. 95–121). Washington, DC: American Psychiatric Association.

Maletzky, B. M. (2002). The paraphilias: Research and treatment. In P. E. Nathan & J. M. Gorman (Eds.), *A guide to treatments that work* (2nd ed., pp. 525–558). New York, NY: Oxford University Press.

Malik, M. L., Beutler, L. E., Alimohamed, S., Gallagher-Thompson, D., & Thompson, L. (2003). Are all cognitive therapies alike? A comparison of cognitive and noncognitive therapy process and implications for the application of empirically supported treatments. *Journal of Counseling and Clinical Psychology, 71*, 150–158.

Mankad, M. V., Beyer, J. L., Weiner, R. D., & Krystal, A. (2010). *Clinical manual of electroconvulsive therapy.* Arlington, VA: American Psychiatric Publishing.

Manos, R. C., Kanter, J. W., & Busch, A. M. (2010). A critical review of assessment strategies to measure the behavioral activation model of depression. *Clinical Psychology Review, 30*, 547–561.

Manschreck, T. C., & Khan, N. L. (2006). Recent advances in the treatment of delusional disorder. *Canadian Journal of Psychiatry, 1*, 114–119.

Mansell, W. (2007). An integrative formulation-based cognitive treatment of bipolar disorders: Application and illustration. *Journal of Clinical Psychology: In Session, 63*, 447–461.

Mao, A. R., & Yen, J. (2010). Review of proposed changes in child and adolescent psychiatry diagnostic criteria for *DSM-Version 5. Child & Adolescent Psychopharmacology News, 15* (3), 1–8.

Marchi, M., & Cohen, P. (1990). Early childhood eating behaviors and adolescent eating disorders. *Journal of the American Academy of Child and Adolescent Psychiatry, 29*, 112–117.

Marecek, J. (2006). Social suffering, gender, and women's depression. In C.L.M. Keyes & S. H. Goodman (Eds.), *Women and depression* (pp. 283–308). New York, NY: Cambridge University Press.

Margulies, S. (2001). *Getting divorced without ruining your life.* New York, NY: Fireside.

Maris, R. W. (2002). Suicide. *Lancet, 360*, 319–326.

Marks, I. M., Cavanagh, K., & Gega, L. (2007). *Hands-on help: Computer-aided psychotherapy.* London, England: Psychology Press.

Markway, B., & Markway, G. (2003). *Painfully shy: How to overcome social anxiety and reclaim your life.* New York, NY: St. Martin's Griffin.

Marlatt, G. A. (Ed.). (1998). *Harm reduction: Pragmatic strategies for managing high-risk behaviors.* New York, NY: Guilford Press.

Marlatt, G. A., & Gordon, J. R. (Eds.). (1985). *Relapse prevention: Maintenance strategies in the treatment of addictive behaviors.* New York, NY: Guilford Press.

Marlatt, G. A., & Witkiewitz, K. (2007). Relapse prevention for alcohol and drug problems. In G. A. Marlatt & D. M. Donovan (Eds.), *Relapse prevention:*

Maintenance strategies in the treatment of addictive behaviors (2nd ed., pp. 1–44). New York, NY: Guilford Press.

Marnach, M. L., & Casey, P. M. (2008). Understanding women's sexual health: A case-based approach. *Mayo Clinic Proceedings, 83*, 1382–1387.

Marshall, M., Lewis, S., Lockwood, A., Drake, R., Jones, P., & Croudace, T. (2005). Association between duration of untreated psychosis and outcome in cohorts of first-episode patients: A systematic review. *Archives of General Psychiatry, 62*, 975–983.

Marshall, W. L., Fernandez, Y. M., & Serran, G. A. (Eds.). (2006). *Sexual offender treatment: Controversial issues.* Chichester, United Kingdom: Wiley.

Martell, C. R., Dimidjian, S., & Herman-Dunn, R. (2010). *Behavioral activation for depression: A clinician's guide.* New York, NY: Guilford Press.

Martin, D. J., Garske, J. P., & Davis, M. K. (2000). Relation of the therapeutic alliance with outcome and other variables: A meta-analytic review. *Journal of Counseling and Clinical Psychology, 68*, 438–450.

Mash, E. J. (2006). Treatment of child and family disturbance: A cognitive-behavioral systems perspective. In E. J. Mash & R. A. Barkley (Eds.), *Treatment of childhood disorders* (3rd ed., pp. 3–62). New York, NY: Guilford Press.

Mash, E. J., & Barkley, R. A. (Eds.). (2006). *Treatment of childhood disorders* (3rd ed.). New York, NY: Guilford Press.

Mash, E. J., & Barkley, R. A. (Eds.). (2010). *Assessment of childhood disorders* (4th ed.). New York, NY: Guilford Press.

Mash, E. J., & Wolfe, D. A. (2010). *Abnormal child psychology* (4th ed.). Belmont, CA: Wadsworth.

Masters, W. H., & Johnson, V. E. (1970). *Human sexual inadequacy.* Boston, MA: Little, Brown.

Masterson, J. F., & Lieberman, A. R. (Eds.). (2004). *A therapist's guide to the personality disorders: The Masterson approach.* Phoenix, AZ: Zeig Tucker & Theisen.

Mathers, B., Degenhardt, L., Phillips, B., Wiessing, L., Hickman, M., Strathdee, S. A., . . . Mattick, R. P. (2008). Global epidemiology of injecting drug use and HIV among people who inject drugs: A systematic review. *Lancet, 372*, 1733–1745.

Matsumoto, D. (Ed.) (2010). *Handbook of intercultural communication.* Washington, DC: American Psychological Association.

Matta, J., Thompson, R. J., & Gotlib, I. H. (2010). BDNF genotype moderates the relation between physical activity and depressive symptoms. *Health Psychology, 29*, 130–135.

Mattick, R. P., & Clarke, J. C. (1998). Development and validation of measures of social phobia scrutiny fear and social interaction anxiety. *Behaviour Research and Therapy, 36,* 455–470.

Matza, L. S., Revicki, D. A., Davidson, J. R., & Stewart, J. W. (2003). Depression with atypical features in the national comorbidity survey. *Archives of General Psychiatry, 60,* 817–826.

Maurice, C., Green, G., & Foxx, R. M. (1996). *Making a difference: Behavioral interventions for autism.* Austin, TX: Pro-Ed.

Mayes, S. D., & Calhoun, S. L. (2004). Influence of IQ and age in childhood autism: Lack of support for *DSM-IV* Asperger's disorder. *Journal of Developmental and Physical Disabilities, 16,* 257–272.

Mayfield, D., McLeod, G., & Hall, P. (1974). The CAGE questionnaire: Validation of a new alcoholism instrument. *American Journal of Psychiatry, 131,* 1121–1123.

Maxwell, J. C. (2005). Party drugs: Properties, prevalence, patterns, and problems. *Substance Use & Misuse, 40,* 9–10.

Mazzucchelli, T., Kane, R., & Rees, C. (2009). Behavioral activation treatments for depression in adults: A meta-analysis and review. *Clinical Psychology Scientific Practice, 16,* 383–411.

McAweeney, M., Rogers, N. L., Huddleston, C., Moore, D., & Gentile, J. P. (2010). Symptom prevalence of ADHD in a community residential substance abuse treatment program. *Journal of Attention Disorders, 13,* 601–608.

McCabe, M. P. (1998). Sexual Function Scale: History and current factors. In C. Davis, W. Yarber, R. Bauseman, G. E., Schreer, S. Davis, & G. Schreer (Eds.), *Handbook of sexuality-related measures* (p. 275). Thousand Oaks, CA: Sage.

McCabe, M. P. (2005). The role of performance anxiety in the development and maintenance of sexual dysfunction in men and women. *International Journal of Stress Management, 12,* 379–388.

McCabe, R. E., & Antony, M. M. (2002). Specific and social phobia. In M. M. Antony & D. H. Barlow (Eds.), *Handbook of assessment and treatment planning for psychological disorders* (pp. 113–146). New York, NY: Guilford Press.

McCabe, S. E., West, B. T., Morales, M., Cranford, J. A., & Boyd, C. J. (2007). Does early onset of nonmedical use of prescription drugs predict subsequent prescription drug abuse and dependence? Results from a national study. *Addiction, 102,* 1920–1930.

McConnaughy, E. A., Prochaska, J. O., & Velicer, W. F. (1983). Stages of change in psychotherapy: Measurement and sample profiles. *Psychotherapy, 20,* 368–375.

McConnaughy, R. (2005). Asperger syndrome: Living outside the bell curve. *Journal of the Medical Library Association, 93,* 139–140.

McCrady, B. S. (2006). Family and other close relationships. In W. R. Miller & K. M. Carroll (Eds.), *Rethinking substance abuse* (pp. 166–181). New York, NY: Guilford Press.

McDonough, S. (2000). Interaction guidance: An approach for difficult-to-engage families. In C. H. Zeanah (Ed.), *Handbook of infant mental health* (pp. 485–493). New York, NY: Guilford Press.

McElroy, S. L., & Kotwal, R. (2006). Binge eating. In E. Hollander & D. J. Stein (Eds.), *Clinical manual of impulse-control disorders* (pp. 115–148). Arlington, VA: American Psychiatric Publishing.

McElroy, S. L., Soutullo, C. A., Beckman, D. A., Taylor, P., Jr., & Keck, P. E. Jr. (1998). *DSM-IV-TR* intermittent explosive disorder: A report of 27 cases. *Journal of Clinical Psychiatry, 59,* 203–210.

McEvoy, P. M., Nathan, P., & Norton, P. J. (2009). Efficacy of transdiagnostic treatments: A review of published outcome studies and future research directions. *Journal of Cognitive Psychotherapy, 23,* 20–33.

McGilley, B. H., & Szablewski, J. K. (2010). Recipe for recovery: Necessary ingredients for the client's and clinician's success. In M. Maine, B. H. McGilley, & D. Bunnell D., (Eds.). *Treatment of eating disorders: Bridging the research-practice gap* (pp. 197–215). Burlington, MA: Elsevier.

McGlashan, T. H., Grilo, C. M., Sanislow, C. A., Ralevski, E., Morey, L. C., Gunderson, J. G., . . . Pagano, M. (2005). Two-year prevalence and stability of individual DSM-IV criteria for schizotypal, borderline, avoidant, and obsessive-compulsive personality disorders: Toward a hybrid model of Axis II disorders. *American Journal of Psychiatry, 162,* 883–889.

McGoldrick, M., Giordano, J., & Garcia-Preto, N. (Eds.). (2005). *Ethnicity and family therapy* (3rd ed.). New York, NY: Guilford Press.

McGrath, J., Welham, J., Scott, J., Varghese, D., Degenhardt, L., Hayatbakhsh, M. R., . . . Najman, J. M. (2010). Association between cannabis use and psychosis-related outcomes using sibling pair analysis in a cohort of young adults. *Archives of General Psychiatry,* 440–447.

McGrath, M., Mellon, M., & Murphy, L. (2000). Empirically supported treatments in paediatric psychology: Constipation and encopresis. *Journal of Paediatric Psychology, 25*, 115–154.

McHolm, A. E., Cunningham, C. E., & Vanier, M. K. (2005). *Helping your child with selective mutism: Practical steps to overcome a fear of speaking*. Oakland, CA: New Harbinger.

McIntyre, J. R. (2004). Family treatment of substance abuse. In S.L.A. Straussner (Ed.), *Clinical work with substance-abusing clients* (2nd ed., pp. 237–263). New York, NY: Guilford Press.

McKenry, P. C., & Price, S. J. (Eds.). (2005). *Families and change: Coping with stressful events and transitions* (3rd ed.). Thousand Oaks, CA: Sage.

McLellan, J., Kowatch, R., & Findling, R. L. (2007). Practice parameter for the assessment and treatment of children and adolescents with bipolar disorder. *Journal of the American Academy of Child and Adolescent Psychiatry, 46*, 107–125.

McLellan, T. A., Kushner, H., Metzger, D., Peters, R., Smith, I., Grissom, G., . . . Argeriou, M. (1992). The fifth edition of the Addiction Severity Index. *Journal of Substance Abuse Treatment, 9*, 199–213.

McMahon, R. J., Wells, K. C., & Kotler, J. S. (2006). Conduct problems. In E. J. Mash & R. A. Barkley (Eds.), *Treatment of childhood disorders* (3rd ed., pp. 137–270). New York, NY: Guilford Press.

Medda, P., Perugi, G., Zanello, S., Ciufa, M., & Cassano, G. B. (2009). Response to ECT in bipolar I, bipolar II, and unipolar depression. *Journal of Affective Disorders, 118*, 55–59.

Meichenbaum, D. H. (2008). Stress inoculation training. In W. T. O'Donohue & J. E. Fisher (Eds.), *Cognitive behavior therapy: Applying empirically supported techniques in your practice* (2nd ed., pp. 529–532). Hoboken, NJ: Wiley.

Meichenbaum, D. H., & Deffenbacher, J. L. (1988). Stress inoculation training. *Counseling Psychologist, 16*, 69–90.

Memon, S. A., Mandhan, P., Qureshi, J. N., & Shairani, A. J. (2003). Recurrent Rapunzel syndrome: A case report. *Medical Science Monitor, 9*, 92–94.

Mercer, V. E. (2008). Stress management intervention. In W. T. O'Donohue and J. E. Fisher (Eds.), *Cognitive behavior therapy: Applying empirically supported techniques in your practice* (2nd ed., pp. 533–541). Hoboken, NJ: Wiley.

Messer, S. B. (2001). What makes brief psychodynamic therapy time efficient. *Clinical Psychology: Science and Practice, 8*, 5–22.

Messer, S. B., & Kaplan, A. H. (2004). Outcomes and factors related to efficacy in brief psychodynamic therapy. In D. P. Charman (Ed.), *Core processes in brief psychodynamic psychotherapy: Advancing effective practice* (pp. 103–118); Mahwah, NJ: Lawrence Erlbaum Associates.

Messer, S. B., & Warren, C. S. (1995). *Models of brief psychodynamic therapy: A comparative approach*. New York, NY: Guilford Press.

Messer, S. B., & Wolitsky, D. L. (2010). A psychodynamic perspective on the therapeutic alliance: Theory, research, and practice. In J. C. Muran & J. P. Barber (Eds.), *The therapeutic alliance: An evidence-based guide to practice* (pp. 97–122). New York, NY: Guilford Press.

Messina, N., Wish, E., Hoffman, J., & Nemes, S. (2002). Antisocial personality disorder and TC treatment outcomes. *American Journal of Drug and Alcohol Abuse, 28*, 197–212.

Messman, T. L., & Long, P. J. (1996). Child sexual abuse and its relationship to revictimization in adult women: A review. *Clinical Psychology Review, 16*, 397–420.

Meyer, B., & Pilkonis, P. A. (2006). Developing treatments that bridge personality and psychopathology. In R. F. Krueger & J. L. Tackett (Eds.), *Personality and psychopathology* (pp. 262–291). New York, NY: Guilford Press.

Meyer, B., Pilkonis, P. A., Krupnick, J. L., Egan, M. K., Simmens, S. J., & Sotsky, S. M. (2002). Treatment expectancies, patient alliance, and outcome: Further analyses from the National Institute of Mental Health treatment of depression collaborative research program. *Journal of Counseling and Clinical Psychology, 70*, 1051–1055.

Meyer, R. G. (1983). *California Psychological Inventory*. Palo Alto, CA: Consulting Psychologists Press.

Meyer, R. G., & Deitsch, S. E. (1996). *The clinician's handbook* (2nd ed.). Boston, MA: Allyn & Bacon.

Meyer, T. J., & Mark, M. M. (1995). Effects of psychosocial interventions with adult cancer patients: A meta-analysis of randomized experiments. *Health Psychology, 14*, 101–108.

Meyer, T. J., Miller, M. L., Metzger, R. L., & Borkovec, T. D. (1990). Development and validation of the Penn State Worry Questionnaire. *Behaviour Research and Therapy, 28*, 487–495.

Miklowitz, D. J. (2004). Family therapy. In S. L. Johnson & R. L. Leahy (Eds.), *Psychological treatment of bipolar disorder* (pp. 184–202). New York, NY: Guilford Press.

Miklowitz, D. J. (2006a). An update on the role of psychotherapy in the management of bipolar disorder. *Current Psychiatry Reports, 8*, 498–503.

Miklowitz, D. J. (2006b). Psychosocial interventions in bipolar disorders: Rationale and effectiveness. In H. S. Akiskal and M. Tohen (Eds.), *Bipolar psychopharmacotherapy: Caring for the patient* (pp. 313–332). Hoboken, NJ: Wiley.

Miklowitz, D. J. (2008a). Bipolar disorder. In D. H. Barlow (Ed.), *Clinical handbook of psychological disorders: A step-by-step treatment manual* (4th ed., pp. 421–462). New York, NY: Guilford Press.

Miklowitz, D. J. (2008b). *Bipolar disorder: A family focused treatment approach* (2nd ed.). New York, NY: Guilford Press.

Miklowitz, D. J. (2011). *The bipolar survival guide* (2nd ed.). New York, NY: Guilford Press.

Miklowitz, D. J., Biuckians, A., & Richards, J. D. (2006). Early onset bipolar disorder: A family treatment perspective. *Development and Psychopathology, 18*, 1247–1265.

Miklowitz, D. J., & Cicchetti, D. (Eds.). (2010). *Understanding bipolar disorder: A developmental psychopathology perspective*. New York, NY: Guilford Press.

Miklowitz, D. J., & Craighead, W. E. (2007). Psychosocial treatments for bipolar disorder. In P. E. Nathan & J. M. Gorman (Eds.), *A guide to treatments that work* (3rd ed., pp. 309–322). New York, NY: Oxford University Press.

Miklowitz, D. J., & Goldstein, M. J. (1997). *Bipolar disorder: A family-focused treatment approach*. New York, NY: Guilford Press.

Miklowitz, D. J., Otto, M. W., Frank, E., Reilly-Harrington, N. A., Kogan, J. N., Sachs, G. S., . . . Wisniewski, S. R. (2007). Intensive psychosocial intervention enhances functioning in patients with bipolar depression: Results from a 9-month randomized controlled trial. *American Journal of Psychiatry, 164*, 1340–1347.

Miller, A. L., Rathus, J. H., DuBose, A. P., Dexter-Mazza, E. T., & Goldklang, A. R. (2007). Dialectical behavior therapy for adolescents. In L. A. Dimeff & K. Koerner (Eds.), *Dialectical behavior therapy in clinical practice: Applications across disorders and settings* (pp. 245–297). New York, NY: Guilford Press.

Miller, E. T., Neal, D. J., Roberts, L. J., Baer, J. S., Cressler, S. O., Metrik, J., & Marlatt, G. A. (2002). Test-retest reliability of alcohol measures: Is there a difference between Internet-based assessment and traditional methods? *Psychology of Addictive Behaviors, 16*, 56–63.

Miller, J. J., Fletcher, K., & Kabat-Zinn, J. (1995). Three-year follow-up and clinical implications of a mindfulness-based stress reduction intervention in the treatment of anxiety disorders. *General Hospital Psychiatry, 17*, 192–200.

Miller, R. S., Johnson, J. A., & Johnson, J. K. (1991). Assessing the prevalence of unwanted childhood sexual experiences. *Journal of Psychology and Human Sexuality, 4*, 43–54.

Miller, T. J., McGlashan, T. H., Woods, S. W., Stein, K., Driesen, N., Corcoran, C. M., . . . & Davidson, L. (1999). Symptom assessment in schizophrenic prodromal states. *Psychiatric Quarterly, 70*, 273–287.

Miller, W. R., & Carroll, K. M. (2006). Drawing the sciences together: Ten principles, ten recommendations. In. W. R. Miller & K. M. Carroll (Eds.), *Rethinking substance abuse* (pp. 293–311). New York, NY: Guilford Press.

Miller, W. R., & Harris, R. (2000). A simple scale for Gorski's warning signs for relapse. *Journal of Studies on Alcohol, 61*, 759–765.

Miller, W. R., & Rollnick, S. (2002). *Motivational interviewing: Preparing people to change addictive behavior*. New York, NY: Guilford Press.

Miller, W. R., & Tonigan, J. S. (1996). Assessing drinkers' motivation for change: The stages of change readiness and treatment eagerness scale (SOCRATES). *Psychology of Addictive Behaviors, 10*, 81–89.

Millon, T., & Grossman, S. (2007). *Resolving difficult clinical syndromes: A personalized psychotherapy approach*. Hoboken, NJ: Wiley.

Millon, T., Grossman, S., Millon, C., Meagher, S., & Ramnath, R. (2004). *Personality disorders in modern life* (2nd ed.). Hoboken, NJ: Wiley.

Milne, D., Wharton, S., James, I., & Turkington, D. (2006). Befriending versus CBT for schizophrenia: A convergent and divergent fidelity check. *Behavioural and Cognitive Psychotherapy, 34*, 25–30.

Milrod, B., Leon, A. C., Busch, F., Rudden, M., Schwalberg, M., Clarkin, J., & Shear, M. K., (2007). A randomized control trial of psychoanalytic psychotherapy for panic disorder. *American Journal of Psychiatry, 164*, 265–272.

Mino, Y., Shimodera, S., Inoue, S., Fujita, H., & Fukuzawa, K. (2007). Medical cost analysis of family psychoeducation for schizophrenia. *Psychiatry and Clinical Neurosciences, 61*, 20–24.

Mitchell, J. E., Agras, S., & Wonderlich, S. (2007). Treatment of bulimia nervosa. Where are we and where are we going? *International Journal of Eating Disorders, 40,* 95–101.

Mittelman, M. S., Roth, D. L., Coon, D. W., & Haley, W. E. (2004). Sustained benefit of supportive intervention for depressive symptoms in the caregivers of patients with Alzheimer's disease. *American Journal of Psychiatry, 161,* 850–856.

Mjellem, N., & Kringlen, E. (2001). Schizophrenia. A review, with emphasis on the neurodevelopmental hypothesis. *Nordic Journal of Psychiatry, 55,* 301–309.

Montano, B. (2004). Diagnosis and treatment of ADHD in adults in primary care. *Journal of Clinical Psychiatry, 65* (Suppl. 3), 18–21.

Moore, T. H., Zammit, S., Lingford-Hughes, A., Barnes, T. R., Jones, P. B., Burke, M., & Lewis, G. (2007). Cannabis use and risk of psychotic or affective mental health outcomes: A systematic review. *Lancet, 370,* 319–328.

Moreno, C., Jaje, G., Blanco, C., Jiang, H., Schmidt, A. B., & Olfson, M. (2007). National trends in the outpatient diagnosis and treatment of bipolar disorder in youth. *Archives of General Psychiatry, 64,* 1032–1039.

Morgan, O. J. (2006). *Counseling and spirituality: Views from the profession.* Boston, MA: Houghton Mifflin.

Morin, C. M. (1993). *Insomnia. Psychological assessment and management.* New York, NY: Guilford Press.

Morin, C. M., & Espie, C. A. (2003). *Insomnia: A clinician's guide to assessment and treatment.* New York, NY: Springer.

Morris, T. L., & March, J. S. (2004). *Anxiety disorders in children and adolescents* (2nd ed.). New York, NY: Guilford Press.

Moul, D. E., Morin, C. M., Buysse, D. J., Reynolds, C. F., & Kupfer, D. J. (2007). Effective treatments for insomnia and restless leg syndrome. In P. E. Nathan & J. M. Gorman (Eds.), *A guide to treatments that work* (3rd ed., pp. 611–640). New York, NY: Oxford University Press.

MTA Cooperative Group. (1999). A 14-month randomized clinical trial of treatment strategies for attention-deficit/hyperactivity disorder. *Archives of General Psychiatry, 56,* 1073–1086.

MTA Cooperative Group. (2004). National Institute of Mental Health Multimodal Treatment Study of ADHD follow-up: 24-month outcomes of treatment strategies for attention-deficit/hyperactivity disorder. *Pediatrics, 113,* 754–761.

Mueser, K. T., Drake, R. E., Turner, W., & McGovern, M. (2006). Comorbid substance use disorders and psychiatric disorders. In W. R. Miller & K. M. Carroll (Eds.), *Rethinking substance abuse* (pp. 115–133). New York, NY: Guilford Press.

Mufson, L., Dorta, K. P., Moreau, D., & Weissman, M. M. (2004). *Interpersonal psychotherapy for depressed adolescents* (2nd ed.). New York, NY: Guilford Press.

Mula, M., Pini, S., Calugi, S., Preve, M., Masini, M., Giovannini, I., . . . Cassano, G. B. (2008). Validity and reliability of the Structured Clinical Interview for Depersonalization-Derealization Spectrum (SCI-DER). *Neuropsychiatric Disease and Treatment, 4,* 977–998.

Munro, A. (2008). Aspects of persecutory delusions in the setting of delusional disorder. In D. Freeman & R. Bentall (Eds.), *Persecutory delusions: Assessment, theory and practice* (pp. 105–120). London, England: Oxford University Press.

Muran, J. C., & Barber, J. P. (2010). *The therapeutic alliance: An evidence-based guide to practice.* New York, NY: Guilford Press.

Muran, J. C., Safran, J. D., & Eubanks-Carter, C. (2010). Developing therapist abilities to negotiate alliance ruptures. In J. C. Muran & J. P. Barber (Eds.), *The therapeutic alliance: An evidence-based guide to practice* (pp. 320–340). New York, NY: Guilford.

Murphy, C. M., & Maiuro, R. D. (Eds.). (2009). *Stages of change in intimate partner violence.* New York, NY: Springer.

Murray, C. E., & Johnston, C. (2006). Parenting in mothers with and without attention-deficit/hyperactivity disorder. *Journal of Abnormal Psychology, 115,* 52–61.

Murray, C. I. L., & Lopez, A. D. (Eds.) (1996). *The global burden of disease and injury series: Vol. I: A comprehensive assessment of mortality and disability from disease, injuries, and risk factors in 1990 and projected to 2020.* Cambridge, MA: Harvard University Press.

Murray, W. H. (2006). *Schizoaffective disorder: New research.* Hauppage, NY: Nova Science.

Mutschler, J., Buhler, M., Grosshans, M., Diehl, A., Mann, K., & Kiefer, F. (2010). Disulfiram, an option for the treatment of pathological gambling? *Alcohol and Alcoholism, 45,* 214–216.

Myers, I. B., & McCauley, M. H. (1985). *A guide to the development and use of the Myers-Briggs Type Indicator.* Palo Alto, CA: Consulting Psychologists Press.

Myles, B. S., Bock, S. J., & Simpson, R. L. (2001). *Asperger's Symptom Diagnosis Scale.* Austin, TX: Pro-Ed.

Nagata, R., Kawarada, Y., Kirike, N., & Iketani, T. (2000). Multi-impulsivity of Japanese patients with eating disorders: Primary and secondary impulsivity. *Psychiatry Research, 94,* 239–250.

Najavits, L. M. (2007). Psychosocial treatments for posttraumatic stress disorder. In P. E. Nathan & J. M. Gorman (Eds.), *A guide to treatments that work* (3rd ed., pp. 513–530). New York, NY: Oxford University Press.

Najavits, L. M. (2009). Seeking safety: An implementation guide. In D. W. Springer & A. Rubin (Eds.), *Substance abuse treatment for youth and adults: Clinicians guide to evidence-based practice* (pp. 311–347). Hoboken, NJ: Wiley.

Nappi, R. E., & Lachowsky, M. (2009). Menopause and sexuality: Prevalence of symptoms and impact on quality of life. *Maturitas, 63,* 138–141.

Nathan, P. E., & Gorman, J. M. (2002). *A guide to treatments that work* (2nd ed.). New York, NY: Oxford University Press.

Nathan, P. E., & Gorman, J. M. (2007). *A guide to treatments that work* (3rd ed.). New York, NY: Oxford University Press.

National Board for Certified Counselors and Center for Credentialing and Education. (n.d.). *The practice of Internet counseling.* Retrieved from www.nbcc.org/webethics2

National Center for Health Statistics. (2003). *Health United States 2003 with chartbook on trends in the health of Americans.* Hyattsville, MD: Author.

National Child Traumatic Stress Network. (n.d.). Retrieved from www.nctsnet.org/resources/topics/treatments-that-work/promising-practices

National Health Interview Survey. (2008). *National Center for Health Statistics. Centers for Disease Control and Prevention.* Atlanta, GA: CDC.

National Highway Traffic Safety Administration. (2003). *Findings: National Survey of Distracted and Drowsy Driving,* Vol. 1. Washington, DC: Author.

National Institute for Clinical Effectiveness (NICE). (2009). *NICE Clinical Guideline 82: Core interventions in the treatment and management of schizophrenia in primary and secondary care.* London, England: NICE.

National Institute on Drug Abuse. (2004). *NIDA infofacts: Marijuana.* Available: www.drugabuse.gov/infofacts/marijuana.html

National Institute on Drug Abuse. (2009). *A cognitive behavioral approach: Treating cocaine addiction.* Available: www.drugabuse.gov/txmanuals/cbt/cbt4.html

National Institute of Mental Health. (2002). *Child and adolescent bipolar disorder: An update from the National Institute of Mental Health.* Bethesda, MD: Author.

National Institute of Mental Health. (2004). *Autism spectrum disorders (pervasive developmental disorders).* Available: www.nimh.nih.gov/publicat/autism.cfm

National Institute of Mental Health. (2005). *Mental illness exacts heavy toll, beginning in youth.* Available: www.nimh.nih.gov/press/mentalhealthstats.cfm

National Institutes of Health and the National Institute on Alcohol Abuse and Alcoholism (2004). *2001–2002 National Epidemiologic Survey on Alcohol and Related Conditions.* Washington, DC: National Institutes of Health.

National Research Council, Committee on Educational Interventions for Children with Autism, Division of Behavioral and Social Sciences and Education. (2001). *Educating children with autism.* Washington, DC: National Academy Press.

National Wellness Institute. (1983). *Lifestyle assessment questionnaire* (2nd ed.). Stevens Point: University of Wisconsin-Stevens Point Institute for Lifestyle Improvement.

Nemeroff, C. B., & Schatzberg, A. F. (2007). Pharmacological treatments for unipolar depression. In P. E. Nathan & J. M. Gorman (Eds.), *A guide to treatments that work* (3rd ed., pp. 271–288). New York, NY: Oxford University Press.

Neria, Y., Bromet, E. J., Carlson, G. A., & Naz, B. (2005). Assaultive trauma and illness course in childhood bipolar disorder: Findings from the Suffolk County mental health project. *Acta Psychiatrica Scandinavica, 111,* 380–383.

New Freedom Commission on Mental Health. (2003). *Achieving the Promise: Transforming Mental Health Care in America. Executive Summary.* DHHS Pub. No. SMA- 03-3831. Rockville, MD.

Newsom, C., & Hovanitz, C. A. (2006). Autistic spectrum disorders. In E. J. Mash & R. A. Barkley (Eds.), *Treatment of childhood disorders* (3rd ed., pp. 455–511). New York, NY: Guilford Press.

Newton, E., & Cotes, E. (2010). Cognitive behavioral interventions in early intervention services. In P. French, J. Smith, D. Shiers, M. Reed, & M. Rayne (Eds.), *Promoting recovery in early psychosis* (pp. 54–65). Oxford, United Kingdom: Wiley-Blackwell.

Neziroglu, F., & Khemlani-Patel, S. (2002). A review of cognitive and behavior treatment of body dysmorphic disorder. *CNS Spectrums, 7,* 464–471.

Nezu, A. M., Nezu, C. M., & McMurran, M. (2008). Problem-solving therapy. In W. T. O'Donohue and J. E. Fisher (Eds.), *Cognitive behavior therapy: Applying empirically supported techniques in your practice* (2nd ed., pp. 402–407). Hoboken, NJ: Wiley.

Nickel, R., Ademmer, K., & Egle, U. T. (2010). Manualized psychodynamic-interactional group therapy for the treatment of somatoform pain disorders. *Bulletin of the Meninger Clinic, 24,* 219–237.

Nickel, R., & Egle, U. T. (2006). Psychological defense styles, childhood adversities and psychopathology in adulthood. *Child Abuse & Neglect, 30,* 157–170.

NIDA. *A cognitive behavioral approach: Treating cocaine addiction.* Available: www.drugabuse.gov/txmanuals/cbt/cbt4.html

Nielsen, S. L., Lambert, M. J., Smart, D. W., Okiishi, J., Isakson, R. L., Pedersen, T., & Nielsen, D. L. (2011). The implementation of empirically supported psychotherapy: Practice foundations. In R. A. Carlstedt (Ed.) *Handbook of integrative clinical psychology, psychiatry, and behavioral medicine: Perspectives, practice, and research* (pp. 59–79). New York, NY: Springer.

Nigg, J., & Nikolas, M. (2008). Attention-deficit/Hyperactivity disorder. In T. P. Beauchaine & S. P. Hinshaw (Eds.), *Child and adolescent psychopathology* (pp. 301–334). Hoboken, NJ: Wiley.

Nock, M. K., Hwang, I., Sampson, N. A., & Kessler, R. C. (2010). Mental disorders, comorbidity and suicidal behavior: Results from the National Comorbidity Survey Replication. *Molecular Psychiatry, 15,* 868–876.

Nock, M. K., & Kessler, R. C. (2007). Prevalence of and risk factors for suicide attempts versus suicide gestures: Analysis of the National Comorbidity Survey. *Journal of Abnormal Psychology, 115,* 616–623.

Nolan, K. A., Volavka, J., Mohr, P., & Czobor, P. (1999). Psychopathy and violent behavior among patients with schizophrenia or schizoaffective disorder. *Psychiatric Services, 50,* 787–792.

Noordsy, D. L., McQuade, D. V., & Mueser, K. T. (2003). Assessment considerations. In H. L. Graham, A. Copello, M. J. Birchwood, & K. T. Mueser (Eds.), *Substance misuse in psychosis: Approaches to treatment and service delivery* (pp. 159–180). Chichester, England: Wiley.

Norcross, J. C. (Ed.). (2011). *Psychotherapy relationships that work: Evidence-based responsiveness* (2nd ed.). New York, NY: Oxford University Press.

Norcross, J. C. (2010). The therapeutic relationship. In B. Duncan, S. Miller, B. Wampold, & M. Hubble (Eds.), *The heart and soul of change: Delivering what works in therapy* (2nd ed.). Washington, DC: American Psychological Association.

Norcross, J. C., & Drewes, A. A. (2009). Self-care for child therapists. Leaving it at the office. In A. A. Drewes (Ed.), *Blending play therapy with cognitive behavioral therapy: Evidence-based and other effective treatments and techniques* (pp. 473–493). Hoboken, NJ: Wiley.

Norcross, J. C., & Guy, J. D. (2007). *Leaving it at the office: A guide to psychotherapist self-care.* New York, NY: Guilford Press.

Norcross, J. C., Hogan, T. P., & Koocher, G. P. (2008). *Clinician's guide to evidence-based practice.* New York, NY: Oxford University Press.

Norcross, J. C., Koocher, G. P., & Garofalo, A. (2006). Discredited psychological treatments and practice: A Delphi Poll. *Professional Psychology: Research and Practice, 37,* 515–522.

Norcross, J. C., & Lambert, M. J. (2011). Evidence-based therapy relationships. In J. C. Norcross (Ed.). *Psychotherapy relationships that work: Evidence-based responsiveness* (2nd ed.). New York, NY: Oxford University Press.

Norcross, J. C., & Wampold, B. E. (2011). Evidence-based therapy relationships: Research conclusions and clinical practices. In J. C. Norcross (Ed.), *Psychotherapy relationships that work: Evidence-based responsiveness* (2nd ed., pp. 423–430). New York, NY: Oxford University Press.

Nowell, P. D., Buysse, D. J., Morin, C., Reynolds, C. F., & Kupfer, D. J. (2002). Effective treatments for selected sleep disorders. In P. E. Nathan & J. M. Gorman (Eds.), *A guide to treatments that work* (2nd ed., pp. 593–609). New York, NY: Oxford University Press.

Oakley, L. D. (2005). Neurobiology of nonpsychotic illnesses. In L. C. Copstead & J. L. Banasik (Eds.), *Pathophysiology: Biological and behavioral perspectives* (3rd ed., pp. 1192–1209). St. Louis, MO: Elsevier Saunders.

O'Brien, C. P., & McKay, J. (2007). Pharmacological treatments for substance use disorders. In P. E. Nathan & J. M. Gorman (Eds.), *A guide to treatments that work* (2nd ed., pp. 145–178). New York, NY: Oxford University Press.

Ockert, D., Baier, A. R., & Coons, E. E. (2004). Treatment of stimulant dependence. In S. L. A. Straussner (Ed.), *Clinical work with substance-abusing clients* (2nd ed., pp. 209–234). New York, NY: Guilford Press.

O'Donohue, W. T., & Fisher, J. E. (Eds.). (2008). *Cognitive behavior therapy: Applying empirically supported techniques in your practice* (2nd ed.). Hoboken, NJ: Wiley.

Ohayon, M. M., Guilleminault, C., Paiva, T., Priest, R. G., Rapoport, D. M., Sagales, T., . . . Zulley, J. (1997). An international study on sleep disorders in the general population: Methodological aspects of the use of the Sleep-EVAL system. *Sleep, 12,* 1086–1092.

Ohayon, M. M., & Okun, M. L. (2006). Occurrence of sleep disorders in the families of narcoleptic patients. *Neurology, 67,* 703–705.

Ohayon, M. M., & Schatzberg, A. F. (2002). Prevalence of depressive episodes with psychotic features in the general population. *American Journal of Psychiatry, 159,* 1855–1861.

Okamura, H., Watanabe, T., Narabayashi, M., Katsumata, N., Ando, M., & Adachi, I. (2002). Psychological distress following first recurrence of disease in patients with breast cancer: Prevalence and risk factors. *Breast Cancer Research and Treatment, 61,* 131–137.

Olabi, B., & Hall, J. (2010). Review: Borderline personality disorder: Current drug treatments and future prospects. *Therapeutic Advances in Chronic Disease, 1,* 59–66.

Oldham, J. M. (2005). *Guideline watch for the practice guideline for the treatment of patients with borderline personality disorder.* Arlington, VA: American Psychiatric Association. Available: www.psych.org/psych_pract/treatg/pg/prac_guide.cfm

Oldham, J. M. (2006). Borderline personality disorder and suicidality. *American Journal of Psychiatry, 163,* 20–26.

Oldham, J. M. (2007). Psychodynamic psychotherapy for personality disorders. *American Journal of Psychiatry, 164,* 1465–1467.

Oldham, J. M. (2009). Borderline personality disorder comes of age. *American Journal of Psychiatry, 166,* 509–511.

Oldham, J. M., Skodol, A. E., & Bender, D. S. (2005). *The American Psychiatric Publishing textbook on personality disorders.* Arlington, VA: American Psychiatric Publishing.

Olfson, M., Marcus, S. C., Tedeschi, M., & Wan, G. J. (2006). Continuity of antidepressant treatment for adults with depression in the United States. *American Journal of Psychiatry, 163,* 101–108.

Oltmanns, T. F., & Emery, R. E. (2007). *Abnormal psychology* (5th ed.). Upper Saddle River, NJ: Pearson.

Orlinsky, D. E., Grawe, K., & Parks, B. K. (1994). Process and outcome in psychotherapy. In A. E. Bergin & S. L. Garfield (Eds.), *Handbook of psychotherapy and behavior change* (4th ed., pp. 270–376). Hoboken, NJ: Wiley.

Orlinsky, D. E., & Howard, K. I. (1986). Process and outcome in psychotherapy. In S. L. Garfield & A. E. Bergin (Eds.), *Handbook of psychotherapy and behavior change* (3rd ed., pp. 311–381). Hoboken, NJ: Wiley.

Orth, M., Kirby, R., Richardson, M. P., Snijders, A. H., Rothwell, J. C., Trimble, M. R., Robertson, M. M., & Munchau, A. (2004). Subthreshold rTMS over premotor cortex has no effect on tics in patients with Gilles de la Tourette syndrome. *Clinical Neurophysiology, 116,* 764–768.

Öst, L. (1996). One-session group treatment of spider phobia. *Behaviour Research and Therapy, 34,* 707–715.

Öst, L. (2008). Efficacy of the third wave of behavior therapies. *Behaviour Research and Therapy, 46,* 296–321.

Pace, G. M., & Toyer, E. A. (2000). The effects of a vitamin supplement on the pica of a child with severe mental retardation. *Journal of Applied Behavior Analysis, 33,* 619–622.

Pallanti, S., Rossi, N. B., & Hollander, E. (2006). Pathological gambling. In E. Hollander & D. J. Stein (Eds.), *Clinical manual of impulse-control disorders* (pp. 251–289). Arlington, VA: American Psychiatric Publishing.

Pandi-Perumal, S. R., Verster, J. C., Monti, J. M., Lader, M., & Langer, S. Z. (Eds.). (2008). *Sleep disorders: Diagnostics and therapeutics.* New York, NY: Informa Healthcare.

Paniagua, F. A. (2001). *Diagnosis in a multicultural context: A casebook for mental health professionals.* Thousand Oaks, CA: Sage.

Pantalon, M., & Motta, R. W. (1998). Effectiveness of anxiety management training in the treatment of posttraumatic stress disorder: A preliminary report. *Journal of Behavioral Therapy and Experiential Psychiatry, 29,* 21–29.

Pape, P. A. (2004). Assessment and intervention with alcohol- and drug-abusing women. In S. L. A. Straussner (Ed.), *Clinical work with substance-abusing clients* (2nd ed., pp. 347–369). New York, NY: Guilford Press.

Parikh, S. V., LeBlanc, S. R., & Ovanessian, M. M. (2010). Advancing bipolar disorder: Key lessons from the Systematic Treatment Enhancement Program for

Bipolar Disorder (STEP-BD). *Canadian Journal of Psychiatry*, *55*, 136–143.

Paris, J. (1999). Borderline personality disorder. In T. Millon, P. H. Blaney, & R. D. Davis (Eds.), *Oxford textbook of psychopathology* (pp. 628–652). New York, NY: Oxford University Press.

Paris, J. (2003). *Personality disorders over time: Precursors, course, and outcome*. Arlington, VA: American Psychiatric Publishing.

Paris, J. (2007). The nature of borderline personality disorder: Multiple dimensions, multiple symptoms, but one category. *Journal of Personality Disorders 21*, 457–473.

Parrish, D. E. (2009). Cognitive behavioral coping skills therapy for adults. In D. W. Springer & A. Rubin (Eds.), *Substance abuse treatment for youth and adults: Clinician's guide to evidence-based practice* (pp. 259–310). Hoboken, NJ: Wiley.

Pastor, P. N., & Reuben, C. A. (2008). Diagnosed attention deficit hyperactivity disorder and learning disability: United States, 2004–2006. National Center for Health Statistics. *Vital Health Statistics*, *20*, 237.

Patel, J. K., & Deligiannidis, K. M. (2010). Schizophrenia and schizoaffective disorder. In A. J. Rothschild (Ed.), *Antipsychotic Medications* (pp. 5–43). Washington, DC: American Psychiatric Publishing.

Patterson, G. R. (1982). *A social learning approach to family intervention*. Eugene, OR: Castalia.

Paula, S. T. (2009). Play therapy techniques for affect regulation. In A. A. Drewes (Ed.), *Blending play therapy with cognitive behavioral therapy: Evidence based and other effective treatments and techniques* (pp. 353–372). Hoboken, NJ: Wiley.

Pavuluri, M. N., Birmaher, B., & Naylor, M. W. (2005). Pediatric bipolar disorder: A review of the past 10 years. *Journal of the American Academy of Child and Adolescent Psychiatry*, *44*, 231–235.

Pavuluri, M. N., Graczyk, P. A., Henry, D. B., Carbray, J. A., Heidenreich, J., & Miklowitz, D. J. (2004). Child- and family-focused cognitive-behavioral therapy for pediatric bipolar disorder. *Journal of the American Academy of Child and Adolescent Psychiatry*, *43*, 528–537.

Paxon, J. E. (1995). Relapse prevention for individuals with developmental disability. *Journal of Psychoactive Drugs*, *27*, 167–172.

PDM Task Force. (2006). *Psychodynamic diagnostic manual*. Silver Spring, MD: Alliance of Psychodynamic Organizations.

Pearlstein, T., & Steiner, M. (2008). Premenstrual dysphoric disorder: Burden of illness and treatment update. *Journal of Psychiatry and Neuroscience*, *33*, 299–301.

Pelkonen, M., Marttunen, M., Henriksson, M., & Lönnqvist, J. (2005). Suicidality in adjustment disorder, clinical characteristics of adolescent outpatients. *European Child and Adolescent Psychiatry*, *14*, 174–180.

Penland, H. R., Weder, N., & Tampi, R. R. (2005). The catatonic dilemma expanded. *Annals of General Psychiatry*, *5*, 14.

Penninx, B. W. J. H. (2006). Women's aging and depression. In C. L. M. Keyes & S. H. Goodman (Eds.), *Women and depression* (pp. 129–146). New York, NY: Cambridge University Press.

Penza, K. M., Heim, C., & Nemeroff, C. B. (2006). Trauma and depression. In C. L. M. Keyes & S. H. Goodman (Eds.), *Women and depression* (pp. 360–381). New York, NY: Cambridge University Press.

Perlis, R. H., Ostacher, M. J., Patel, J. K., Marangell, L. B., Zhang, H., Wisniewski, S. R., . . . Thase, M. E. (2006). Predictors of recurrence in bipolar disorder: Primary outcomes from the Systematic Treatment Enhancement Program for Bipolar Disorder (STEP-BD). *American Journal of Psychiatry*, *163*, 217–224.

Perls, F. (1969). *Gestalt therapy verbatim*. Lafayette, CA: Real People Press.

Perry, B. D. (2008). Child maltreatment: A neurodevelopmental perspective on the role of trauma and neglect in psychopathology. In T. P. Beauchaine & S. P. Hinshaw (Eds.), *Child and adolescent psychopathology* (pp. 93–128). Hoboken, NJ: Wiley.

Perugi, G., Ghaemi, S. N., & Akiskal, H. (2006). Diagnostic and clinical management approaches to bipolar depression, bipolar II, and their co-morbidities. In H. Akiskal & M. Tohen (Eds.), *Pscyhopharmacotherapy*. (pp. 193–234). West Sussex, England: Wiley.

Peterson, L., Reach, K., & Grube, S. (2003). Health-related disorders. In E. J. Mash & R. A. Barkley (Eds.), *Child psychopathology* (2nd ed., pp. 716–749). New York, NY: Guilford Press.

Petry, N. M. (2000). Psychiatric symptoms in problem gambling and non-problem gambling substance abusers. *American Journal of Addictions*, *9*, 163–171.

Pettit, J. W., & Joiner, T. E. (2006). *Chronic depression*. Washington, DC: American Psychological Association.

Philip, N., Carpenter, L., Tyrka, A., & Price, L. (2009). Augmentation of antidepressants with atypical antipsychotics: A review of the current literature. *Journal of Psychiatric Practice*, *14*, 34–44.

Phillips, K. A. (2001). Body dysmorphic disorder. In K. A. Phillips (Ed.), *Somatoform and factitious disorders* (pp. 67–88). Washington, DC: American Psychiatric Association.

Phillips, K. A. (2009). *Understanding body dysmorphic disorder.* New York, NY: Oxford University Press.

Phillips, M. L. (2009). The emerging role of neuroimaging in psychiatry. *American Journal of Psychiatry*, *164*, 697–699.

Piacentini, J., & Chang, S. (2005). Habit reversal training for tic disorders in children and adolescents. *Behavior Modification*, *29*, 803–822.

Piper, W. E., & Ogrodniczuk, J. S. (2005). Group treatment. In J. M. Oldham, A. E. Skodol, & D. S. Bender (Eds.), *Textbook of personality disorders* (pp. 347–373). Washington, DC: American Psychiatric Publishing.

Pitschel-Walz, G., Leucht, S., Bauml, J., Kissling, W., & Engel, R. R. (2001). The effects of family interventions on relapse and rehospitalization in schizophrenia: A meta-analysis. *Schizophrenia Bulletin*, *27*, 73–92.

Plener, P. L., & Fegert, J. J. (2012). Non-suicidal self-injury: State of the art perspective of a proposed new syndrome for DSM V [sic]. *Child and Adolescent Psychiatry and Mental Health*, *6*, 9.

Pliszka, S. R., Carlson, C. L., & Swanson, J. M. (2001). *ADHD with comorbid disorders: Clinical assessment and management.* New York, NY: Guilford Press.

Podell, J. L., Martin, E. D., & Kendall, P. C. (2008). Incorporating play within a manual-based treatment for children and adolescents with anxiety disorders. In A. Drewes (Ed.), *Blending play therapy with cognitive behavioral therapy: Evidence-based and other effective treatments and techniques* (pp. 165–178). New York, NY: Wiley.

Podell, J. L., Mychailyszyn, M., Edmunds, J., Puleo, C. M., & Kendall, P. C. (2010). The Coping Cat Program for anxious youth: The FEAR plan comes to life. *Cognitive and Behavioral Practice*, *17*, 132–141.

Polanczyk, G., de Lima, M. S., Horta, B. L., Biederman, J., & Rohde, L. A. (2007). The worldwide prevalence of ADHD: A systematic review and metaregression analysis. *American Journal of Psychiatry*, *164*, 942–948.

Polanczyk, G., & Rohde, L. A. (2007). Epidemiology of attention-deficit/hyperactivity disorder across the lifespan. *Current Opinion in Psychiatry*, *20*, 386–392.

Poleshuck, E. L., Gamble, S. A., Cort, N., Cerrito, B., Rosario-McCabe, L. A., Hoffman-King, D., & Giles, D. E. (2010). Interpersonal psychotherapy for co-occurring depression and chronic pain. *Professional Psychology: Research and Practice*, *41*, 312–318.

Polyakova, I., Knobler, H. Y., Ambrumova, A., & Lerner, V. (1998). Characteristics of suicidal attempts in major depression versus adjustment reactions. *Journal of Affective Disorders*, *47*, 174–180.

Pompili, M., Girardi, P., Roberto, A., & Tatarelli, R. (2005). Suicide in borderline personality disorder: A meta-analysis. *Nordic Journal of Psychiatry*, *51*, 319–324.

Popper, C. W., & Gherardi, P. C. (1996). Anxiety disorders. In J. M. Wiener (Ed.), *Diagnosis and psychopharmacology of childhood and adolescent disorders* (2nd ed., pp. 294–348). Hoboken, NJ: Wiley.

Porta, M., Sevelto, D., Sassi, M., Brambilla, A., Defendi, S., Priori, A., & Robertson, M. (2009). Issues related to deep brain stimulation for treatment refractory Tourette's syndrome. *European Neurology*, *62*, 264–273.

Portzky, G., Audenaert, K., & van Heeringen, K. (2005). Adjustment disorder and the course of the suicidal process in adolescents. *Journal of Affective Disorders*, *87*, 265–270.

Post, R. M. (2010). Overlaps between schizophrenia and bipolar disorder. *Psychiatric Annals*, *40*, 106–112.

Power, P. (2010). Suicide prevention in early psychosis. In P. French, J. Smith, D. Shiers, M. Reed, & M. Rayne (Eds.), *Promoting recovery in early psychosis* (pp. 180–190). Oxford, United Kingdom: Wiley-Blackwell.

Powers, M. B., Zum Vörde Sive Vörding, M. B., & Emmelkamp, P. M. G. (2010). Acceptance and commitment therapy: A meta-analytic review. *Psychotherapy and Psychosomatics*, *78*, 73–80.

Pratt, S. I., & Mueser, K. T. (2002). Schizophrenia. In M. M. Antony & D. H. Barlow (Eds.), *Handbook of assessment and treatment planning for psychological disorders* (pp. 375–414). New York, NY: Guilford Press.

Preston, J. D., O'Neal, J. H., & Talaga, M. C. (2010). *Handbook of clinical psychopharmacology for therapists* (6th ed.). Oakland, CA: New Harbinger.

Preziosa, A., Grassi, A., Gaggioli, A., & Riva, G. (2009). Therapeutic applications of the mobile phone. *British Journal of Guidance & Counselling*, *37*, 313–325.

Price, D. (2006). Do hypnotic analgesic interventions contain placebo effects? *Pain*, *124*, 238–239.

Price, P. (2004). *The cyclothymia workbook.* Oakland, CA: Prentice Hall.

Principe, J. M., Marci, C. D., & Glick, D. M. (2006). The relationship among patient contemplation, early alliance, and continuation in psychotherapy. *Psychotherapy, 43*, 238–243.

Prochaska, J. O., & Norcross, J. C. (2010). *Systems of psychotherapy: A transtheoretical analysis* (7th ed.). Pacific Grove, CA: Brooks/Cole.

Project MATCH Research Group. (1998). Matching alcoholism treatments to client heterogeneity: Project MATCH three-year drinking outcomes. *Alcoholism: Clinical and Experimental Research, 22*, 1300–1311.

Pujois, Y., Meston, C. M., & Seal, B. N. (2010). The association between sexual satisfaction and body image in women. *Journal of Sexual Medicine, 7*, 905–916.

Quinn, B. (2007). *Bipolar disorder*. Hoboken, NJ: Wiley.

Quinn, W. H., Dotson, D., & Jordan, K. (1997). Dimensions of the therapeutic alliance and their associations with outcome in family therapy. *Psychotherapy Research, 7*, 429–438.

Radoo, B. M., & Kutscher, E. C. (2009). Visual hallucinations associated with varenicline: A case report. *Journal of Medical Case Reports, 3*, 7560.

Rafaeli, E., Bernstein, D. P., & Young, J. (2011). *Schema therapy: Distinctive features*. New York, NY: Routledge.

Rand, D. C., & Feldman, M. D. (2001). An exploratory model for Munchausen by proxy abuse. *International Journal of Psychiatry in Medicine, 31*, 113–126.

Randolph, E. M. (1996). *Randolph Attachment Disorder Questionnaire*. Evergreen, CO: Institute for Attachment.

Rapoport, J. L., & Ismond, D. R. (1996). *DSM-IV training guide for diagnosis of childhood disorders*. New York: Brunner/Mazel.

Rapport, M. D., & Moffitt, C. (2002). Attention deficit/hyperactivity disorder and methylphenidate. A review of height/weight, cardiovascular, and somatic complaint side effects. *Clinical Psychology Review, 22*, 1107–1131.

Rauch, S.A.M., Defever, E., Favorite, T., Duroe, A., Garrity, C., Martis, B., & Liberzon, I. (2009). Prolonged exposure for PTSD in a Veterans Health Administration PTSD clinic. *Journal of Traumatic Stress, 22*, 60–64.

Rawson, R. A., Sodano, R., & Hillhouse, M. (2007). Assessment of amphetamine use disorders. In D. M. Donovan & G. A. Marlatt (Eds.), *Assessment of addictive behaviors* (2nd ed., pp. 185–214). New York, NY: Guilford Press.

Ray, D. C. (2006). Evidence-based play therapy. In C. Schaefer & H. Kaduson (Eds.), *Contemporary play therapy* (pp. 136–157). New York, NY: Guilford Press.

Read, J., van Ohs, J., Morrison, A. P., & Ross, C. A. (2005). Childhood trauma, psychosis, and schizophrenia: A literature review with theoretical and clinical implications. *Acta Psychiatrica Scandinavia, 112*, 330–350.

Rees, C. S., & Stone, S. (2005). Therapeutic alliance in face-to-face versus videoconference psychotherapy. *Professional Psychology: Research and Practice, 36*, 649–653.

Regeer, E. J., Ten Have, M., Rosso, M. L., Hakkaart-Van Roijen, L., Vollebergh, W., & Nolen, W.A. (2004). Prevalence of bipolar disorder in the general population: A reappraisal study of the Netherlands Mental Health Survey and Incidence Study. *Acta Psychiatrica Scandinavica, 110*, 374–382.

Reich, J. (2002). Drug treatment of personality disorder traits. *Psychiatric Annals, 32*, 590–600.

Reichenberg, L. W. (2010). Grief and loss. In L. R. Jackson-Cherry & B. T. Erford (Eds.), *Crisis intervention and prevention* (pp. 73–102). New York, NY: Pearson.

Reichow, B., & Wolery, M. (2009). Comprehensive syntheses of early intensive behavioral interventions for young children with autism based on the UCLA Young Autism Project model. *Journal of Autism and Development Disorders, 39*, 23–41.

Reid, T. R. (2005, January). Caffeine. *National Geographic* (pp. 2–33).

Reinecke, M., Ryan, N., & DuBois, D. (1998). Cognitive therapy of depression in adolescence: A review and meta-analysis. *Journal of the American Academy of Child and Adolescent Psychiatry, 37*, 26–34.

Reisberg, B., Doody, R., Stoffler, A., Schmitt, F., Ferris, S., & Mobius, H. J. (2003). Memantine in moderate-to-severe Alzheimer's disease. *New England Journal of Medicine, 348*, 1333–1341.

Resick, P. A., & Calhoun, K. S. (2001). Posttraumatic stress disorder. In D. H. Barlow (Ed.), *Clinical handbook of psychological disorders: A step-by-step treatment manual* (3rd ed., pp. 60–113). New York, NY: Guilford Press.

Resick, P. A., Monson, C. M., & Rizvi, S. L. (2008). Posttraumatic stress disorder. In D. H. Barlow (Ed.), *Clinical handbook of psychological disorders: A step-by-step treatment manual* (4th ed., pp. 65–122). New York, NY: Guilford Press.

Resick, P. A., Schnicke, M. K., & Markway, B. G. (1991). *The relation between cognitive content and PTSD*. Paper presented at the 25th Annual Convention of the Association for the Advancement of Behavioral Therapy; New York, NY.

Resnick, H., Galea, S., Kilpatrick, D., & Vlahov, D. (2004). Research on trauma and PTSD in the aftermath of 9/11. *PTSD Research Quarterly, 15*, 1–4.

Rettew, D. C. (2000). Avoidant personality disorder, generalized social phobia, and shyness: Putting the personality back into personality disorders. *Harvard Review of Psychiatry, 6*, 283–297.

Rey, J. M., Walter, G., & Soutullo, C.A. (2007). Oppositional defiant and conduct disorders. In A. Martin & F. R. Volkmar (Eds.), *Lewis's child and adolescent psychiatry: A comprehensive textbook* (4th ed., pp. 454–466). Philadelphia, PA: Lippincott Williams & Wilkins.

Reynolds, C. R., & Kamphaus, R. W. (2002). *Behavior assessment system for children*. Circle Pines, MN: American Guidance Service.

Reynolds, C. R., & Richmond, B. O. (1985). *Revised children's manifest anxiety scale*. Los Angeles, CA: Western Psychological Services.

Rhebergen, D., Beekman, A.T.F., de Graaf, R., Nolen, W. A., Spijker, J., Hoogendijk, W. J., & Penninx, B. (2010). Trajectories of recovery of social and physical functioning in major depression, dysthymic disorder, and double depression: A 3-year follow-up. *Journal of Affective Disorders, 124*, 148–156.

Rhee, S. H., & Waldman, I. D. (2002). Genetic and environmental influences on antisocial behavior: A meta-analysis of twin and adoption studies. *Psychological Bulletin, 128*, 490–529.

Richters, M., & Volkmar, F. (1994). Reactive attachment disorder of infancy or early childhood. *Journal of the American Academy of Child and Adolescent Psychiatry, 33*, 328–332.

Rifkin, A., Ghisalbert, D., Dimatou, S., Jin, C., & Sethi, M. (1998). Dissociative identity disorder in psychiatric inpatients. *American Journal of Psychiatry, 155*, 844–845.

Rimondini, M., Del Piccolo, L., Goss, C., Mazzi, M., Paccaloni, M., & Zimmermann, C. (2010). The evaluation of training in patient-centered interviewing skills for psychiatric residents. *Psychological Medicine, 40*, 467–476.

Ritchie, E. C., & Huff, T. G. (1999). Psychiatric aspects of arsonists. *Journal of Forensic Science, 44*, 733–740.

Ritsner, M. S., & Awad, A. G. (2007). *Quality of life impairment in schizophrenia, mood and anxiety disorders: New perspectives on research and treatment*. Dordrecht, The Netherlands: Springer.

Ritsner, M. S., & Gibel, A. (2007). Quality of life impairment syndrome in schizophrenia. In M. S. Ritsner & A. G. Awad (Eds.), *Quality of life impairment in schizophrenia, mood and anxiety disorders: New perspectives on research and treatment* (pp. 173–226). Dordrecht, The Netherlands: Springer.

Ritterband, L. M., Cox, D. J., Kovatchev, B., McKnight, L., Walker, L. S., Patel, K., . . . Sutphen, J. (2003). An Internet intervention as adjunctive therapy for pediatric encopresis. *Journal of Counseling and Clinical Psychology, 71*, 910–917.

Riva, G. (2009). Virtual reality: An experiential tool for clinical psychology. *British Journal of Guidance & Counselling, 37*, 337–345.

Rivas-Vazquez, R. A., Rice, J., & Kalman, D. (2003). Pharmacotherapy of obesity and eating disorders. *Professional Psychology: Research and Practice, 34*, 562–566.

Rizvi, S. L., & Linehan, M. M. (2001). Dialectical behavior therapy for personality disorders. *Current Psychiatry Reports, 3*, 64–69.

Rizvi, S., & Zaretsky, A. E. (2007). Psychotherapy through the phases of bipolar disorder: Evidence for general efficacy and differential effects. *Journal of Clinical Psychology: In Session, 63*, 491–506.

Robbins, M. S., Turner, C. W., & Alexander, J. F. (2003). Alliance and dropout in family therapy for adolescents with behavior problems: Individual and systemic effects. *Journal of Family Psychology, 17*, 534–544.

Roberts, A. R. (2002). Assessment, crisis intervention, and trauma treatment: The integrative ACT intervention model. *Brief Treatment and Crisis Intervention, 2*, 1–21.

Roberts-Harewood, M., & Davies, S. C. (2001). Pica in sickle cell disease: She ate the headboard. *Archives of Disease in Childhood, 85*, 510.

Robins, C. J., Ivanoff, A. M., & Linehan, M. M. (2001). Dialectical behavior therapy. In W. J. Livesley (Ed.), *Handbook of personality disorders* (pp. 437–459). New York, NY: Guilford Press.

Robinson, D. G., Woerner, M. G., McMeniman, M., Mendelowitz, A., & Bilder, R. M. (2004). Symptomatic and functional recovery from a first episode of schizophrenia or schizoaffective disorder. *American Journal of Psychiatry, 161*, 473–479.

Robinson, J. R. (2002). Attachment problems and disorders in infants and young children: Identification, assessment and intervention. *Infants and Young Children, 14*, 6–18.

Rockland, L. H. (2003). *Supportive therapy: A psychodynamic approach*. New York, NY: Basic Books.

Rodebaugh, T. L., Holaway, R. M., & Heimberg, R. G. (2004). The treatment of social anxiety disorder. *Clinical Psychology Review, 24*, 883–908.

Roemer, L., Orsillo, S. M., & Barlow, D. H. (2002). Generalized anxiety disorder. In D. H. Barlow (Ed.), *Anxiety and its disorders* (pp. 477–515). New York, NY: Guilford Press.

Roemer, L., Orsillo, S. M., & Salters-Pedneault, K. (2008). Efficacy of an acceptance-based behavior therapy for generalized anxiety disorder: Evaluation in a randomized controlled trial. *Journal of Consulting and Clinical Psychology, 76*, 1083–1089.

Rogers, C. (1957). The necessary and sufficient conditions of therapeutic personality change. *Journal of Consulting Psychology, 21*, 95–103.

Rogers, C. (1965). *Client-centered therapy: Its current practice, implications, and theory.* Boston, MA: Houghton Mifflin. (Original work published 1951)

Rogers, C. (1967). The conditions of change through a client-centered viewpoint. In B. Berenson & R. Carkhuff (Eds.), *Sources of gain in counseling and psychotherapy.* New York, NY: Holt, Rinehart, & Winston.

Rogers, C. (1980). *A way of being.* Boston, MA: Houghton Mifflin.

Rogers, J. R., & Oney, K. M. (2005). Clinical use of suicide assessment scales: Enhancing reliability and validity through the therapeutic relationship. In R. I. Yufit & D. Lester (Eds.), *Assessment, treatment, and prevention of suicidal behavior* (pp. 7–27). Hoboken, NJ: Wiley.

Rogers, R., Kropp, P. R., Bagby, R. M., & Dickens, S. E. (1992). Faking specific disorders: A study of the structured interview of reported symptoms (SIRS). *Journal of Clinical Psychology, 48*, 643–648.

Rollnick, S., Heather, N., Gold, R., & Hall, W. (1992). Development of a brief readiness to change questionnaire for use in brief, opportunistic interventions among excessive drinkers. *British Journal of Addictions, 87*, 743–754.

Rollnick, S., Miller, W. R., & Butler, C. C. (2008). *Motivational interviewing in health care: Helping patients change behavior.* New York, NY: Guilford Press.

Rosen, R. C., Brown, C., Heiman, I., Leiblum, S., Meston, C., Shabsigh, R., . . . Agostino, R. D. (2000). The Female Sexual Function Index (FSFI): A multidimensional self-report instrument for the assessment of female sexual function. *Journal of Sex and Marital Therapy, 26*, 191–208.

Rosen, R. C., Cappelleri, J. C., & Gendrano, N. (2002). The International Index of Erectile Function (IIEF): A state-of-the-science review. *International Journal of Impotence Research, 14*, 226–244.

Rosenbaum, T. (2007). Physical therapy management and treatment of sexual pain disorders. In S. R. Leiblum (Ed.), *Principles and practice of sex therapy* (4th ed., pp. 212–240). New York, NY: Guilford Press.

Rosenthal, N. E. (2006). *Winter blues: Everything you need to know to beat seasonal affective disorder* (2nd ed.). New York, NY: Guilford Press.

Rosenvinge, J. H., Martinussen, M., & Ostensen, E. (2000). The comorbidity of eating disorders and personality disorders: A meta-analytic review of studies published between 1983 and 1998. *Eating and Weight Disorders, 5*, 52–61.

Rosenzweig, S. (1936). Some implicit common factors in diverse methods of psychotherapy. *American Journal of Orthopsychiatry, 6*, 412–415.

Ross, E. C. (Ed.). (2001). *Managed behavioral health care handbook.* Gaithersburg, MD: Aspen.

Rotgers, F. (2008). Moderate drinking training for problem drinkers. In W. T. O'Donohue & J. E. Fisher (Eds.), *Cognitive behavior therapy: Applying empirically supported techniques in your practice* (2nd ed., pp. 337–341). Hoboken, NJ: Wiley.

Roth, A., & Fonagy, P. (2005). *What works for whom? A critical review of psychotherapy research* (2nd ed.). New York, NY: Guilford Press.

Rothbaum, B. O. (2005). Commentary on Riva, G., Virtual reality in psychotherapy: Review. *Cyber Psychology & Behavior, 8*, 239–240.

Rowa, K., & Antony, M. M. (2005). Psychological treatments for social phobia. *Canadian Journal of Psychiatry, 50*, 308–315.

Roy-Byrne, P. P., & Cowley, D. S. (2007). Pharmacological treatments for panic disorder, generalized anxiety disorder, specific phobia, and social anxiety disorder. In P. E. Nathan & J. M. Gorman (Eds.), *A guide to treatments that work* (3rd ed., p. 420). New York, NY: Oxford University Press.

Rubin, A. (2009). Introduction: Evidence-based practice and empirically supported interventions for trauma. In A. Rubin & D. W. Springer (Eds.), *Treatment of traumatized adults and children: Clinician's guide to evidence-based practice* (pp. 3–28). Hoboken, NJ: Wiley.

Rubin, A., & Springer, D. W. (Eds). (2009). *Treatment of traumatized adults and children: Clinician's guide to evidence-based practice.* Hoboken, NJ: Wiley.

Rudel, A., Hubert, C., Juckel, G., & Edel, M. A. (2009). Combination of dialectical behavioral therapy (DBT) and duloxetine in kleptomania. *Psychiatrische Praxis, 36*, 293–296.

Ruff, S., McComb, J. L., Coker, C. J., & Sprenkle, D. H. (2010). Behavioral couples therapy for the treatment of substance abuse: A substantive and methodological review of O'Farrell, Fals-Stewart, and colleagues' program of research. *Family Process*, *49*, 439–456.

Ruskin, P. E., Silver-Aylaian, M., Kling, M. A., Reed, S. A., Bradham, D. D., Hebel, J. . . . Hauser, P. (2004). Treatment outcomes in depression: Comparison of remote treatment through telepsychiatry to in-person treatment. *American Journal of Psychiatry, 161*, 1471–1477.

Sachs, G. S. (2004). *Managing bipolar affective disorder.* London, England: Science Press.

Sachs, G. S. (2008). Psychosocial interventions as adjunctive therapy for bipolar disorder, *Journal of Psychiatric Practice, Suppl 2*, 39–44.

Sachse, R., & Elliott, R. (2001). Process-outcome research on humanistic therapy variables. In D. J. Cain & J. Seeman (Eds.), *Humanistic psychotherapies: Handbook of research and practice* (pp. 83–115). Washington, DC: American Psychological Association.

Sadock, V. (2007). *Kaplan and Sadock's synopsis of psychiatry: Behavioral sciences/clinical psychiatry* (10th ed.). Philadelphia, PA: Lippincott Williams, & Wilkins.

Safer, D. L., Robinson, A. H., & Jo, B. (2010). Outcome from a randomized controlled trail of group therapy for binge eating disorder: Comparing dialectical behavior therapy adapted for binge eating to an active comparison group therapy. *Behavior Therapy, 41*, 106–120.

Safran, J. D., Muran, C., & Eubanks-Carter, C. (2011). Repairing alliance ruptures. In J. C. Norcross (Ed.), *Psychotherapy relationships that work: Evidence-based responsiveness* (2nd ed.). New York, NY: Oxford University Press.

Sagar, A. (2005). Long term health risks due to impaired nutrition in women with a past history of bulimia nervosa. *Nutrition Noteworthy, 7*, Article 8. Available: http://repositories.cdlib.org/uclabiolchem/nutrition noteworthy/vol7/iss1/art8

Sakkas, P. (2003). Induction of mania by rTMS: Report of two cases. *European Psychiatry, 18*, 196–198.

Saladin, M. E., & Santa Ana, E. J. (2004). Controlled drinking: More than just a controversy. *Current Opinions in Psychiatry, 17*, 175–187.

Sampson, M., Stephens, N. S., & Velasquez, M. M. (2009). Motivational interviewing. In D. W. Springer & A. Rubin (Eds.), *Substance abuse treatment for youth and adults: Clinician's guide to evidence-based practice* (pp. 3–56). Hoboken, NJ: Wiley.

Sanchez-Craig, M., Wilkinson, D. A., & Davila, R. (1995). Empirically based guidelines for moderate drinking: 1-year results from three studies with problem drinkers. *American Journal of Public Health, 85*, 823–828.

Sarokoff, R. A., Taylor, B. A., & Poulson, C. L. (2001). Teaching children with autism to engage in conversational exchanges: Script fading with embedded textual stimuli. *Journal of Applied Behavior Analysis, 24*, 81–84.

Saudino, K. J., Ronald, A., & Plomin, R. (2005). The etiology of behavior problems in 7-year-old twins: Substantial genetic influence and negligible shared environmental influence for parent ratings and ratings by same and different teachers. *Journal of Abnormal Child Psychology, 33*, 113–130.

Saul, S. (2007, March 15). FDA issues warning on sleeping pills. *New York Times,* B-1.

Saunders, J. B., Aasland, O. G., Babor, T. F., DeLaFuente, J. R., & Grant, M. (1993). Development of the Alcohol Use Disorders Identification Test (AUDIT): WHO collaborative project on early detection of persons with harmful alcohol consumption. *Addiction, 88*, 296–303.

Savard, J., & Morin, C. M. (2002). Insomnia. In M. M. Antony & D. H. Barlow (Eds.), *Handbook of assessment and treatment planning for psychological disorders* (pp. 523–555). New York, NY: Guilford Press.

Saxena, S., & Sharan, P. (2006). Services and treatment for depression: International perspectives and implications for a gender-sensitive approach. In C.L.M. Keyes & S. H. Goodman (Eds.), *Women and depression* (pp. 417–449). New York, NY: Cambridge University Press.

Schatzberg, A. F. (2005). Recent studies in the biology and treatment of depression. *Focus, 3*, 14–24.

Schiffman, J., Becker, K. D., & Daleiden, E. L. (2006). Evidence-based services in a statewide public mental health system: Do the services fit the problems? *Journal of Clinical Child and Adolescent Psychology, 35*, 13–19.

Schnyder, U. (2009). Future perspectives in psychotherapy. *European Archives of Psychiatry and Clinical Neuroscience, 259* (Suppl. 2), 123–128.

Schopler, E., Reichler, R. J., De Vellis, R. F., & Daly, K. (1991). *Childhood autism rating scale.* Los Angeles, CA: Western Psychological Services.

Schopp, L., Johnstone, B., & Merrell, D. (2000). Telehealth and neuropsychological assessment: New opportunities for psychologists. *Professional Psychology: Research and Practice, 31*, 179–183.

Schramm, E., Hohagen, F., Grasshoff, U., Riemann, D., Hajak, G., Weess, H. G., & Berger, M. (1993). Test-retest reliability and validity of the Structured Interview for Sleep Disorders according to *DSM-III-R*. *American Journal of Psychiatry, 150*, 867–872.

Schreier, H. (2002). Munchausen by proxy defined. *Pediatrics, 110*, 985–988.

Schreier, H. (2004). Munchausen by proxy. *Current Problems in Pediatric and Adolescent Health Care, 34*, 126–143.

Schuckit, M. A. (2010). *Drug and alcohol abuse: A clinical guide to diagnosis and treatment* (6th ed.). New York, NY: Springer.

Schwartz, R. C., Reynolds, C. A., Austin, J. F., & Petersen, S. (2003). Homicidality in schizophrenia: A replication study. *American Journal of Orthopsychiatry, 73*, 74–77.

Schwartz, R. H., & Shipon-Blum, E. (2005). Shy child? Don't overlook selective mutism. *Contemporary Pediatrics, 22*, 30–34.

Scott, J., Paykel, E., Morriss, R., Bentall, R., Kinderman, P., Johnson, T., . . . Hayhurst, H. (2006). Cognitive behavioural therapy for severe and recurrent bipolar disorders: Randomised controlled trial. *British Journal of Psychiatry, 189*, 515–519.

Scott, W. D., & Cervone, D. (2008). Self-efficacy interventions: Guided mastery therapy. In W. T. O'Donohue & J. E. Fisher (Eds), *Cognitive behavior therapy: Applying empirically supported techniques in your practice* (2nd ed., pp. 390–395). Hoboken, NJ: Wiley.

Scroppo, J. C., Drob, S. L., Weinberger, J. L., & Eagle, P. (1998). Identifying dissociative identity disorder: A self-report and projective study. *Journal of Abnormal Psychology, 107*, 272–284.

Seal, K. H., Metzler, T. J., Gima, K. S., Bertenthal, D., Maguen, S., & Marmar, C. R. (2009). Trends and risk factors for mental health diagnoses among Iraq and Afghanistan Veterans using Department of Veterans Affairs Health Care, 2002–2008. *American Journal of Public Health, 99*, 1651–1658.

Sedlak, A. J., & Broadhurst, D. D. (1996). *Third national incidence study of child abuse and neglect*. Washington, DC: U.S. Government Printing Office.

Segal, N. L. (2006). Two monozygotic twin pairs discordant for female-to male transsexualism. *Archives of Sexual Behavior, 35*, 347–358.

Segal, Z. V., Williams, J. M., & Teasdale, J. D. (2002). *Mindfulness-based cognitive therapy for depression: A new approach to preventing relapse*. New York, NY: Guilford Press.

Segraves, T., & Althof, S. (2002). Psychotherapy and pharmacotherapy for sexual dysfunctions. In P. E. Nathan & J. M. Gorman (Eds.), *A guide to treatments that work* (2nd ed., pp. 497–524). New York, NY: Oxford University Press.

Selby, P. (2007). Smoking cessation. In J. Gray (Ed.), *Therapeutic choices* (5th ed.), Ottawa, Ontario: Canadian Pharmacist Association.

Selby, P., Voci, S. C., Zawertailo, L. A., George, T. P., & Brands, B. (2010). Individualized smoking cessation treatment in an outpatient setting: Predictors of outcome in a sample with psychiatric and addictions co-morbidity. *Addictive Behaviors, 35*, 811–817.

Seligman, L. (1994). *Developmental career counseling and assessment*. Thousand Oaks, CA: Sage.

Seligman, L. (1998). *Promoting a fighting spirit: Psychotherapy for cancer patients, survivors, and their families*. San Francisco, CA: Jossey-Bass.

Seligman, L. (2004). *Diagnosis and treatment planning in counseling* (3rd ed.). New York, NY: Kluwer/Plenum.

Seligman, L., & Hardenburg, S. A. (2000). Assessment and treatment of paraphilias. *Journal of Counseling and Development, 78*, 107–113.

Seligman, L., & Moore, B. M. (1995). Diagnosis of mood disorders. *Journal of Counseling and Development, 74*, 65–69.

Seligman, L., & Reichenberg, L. W. (2010). *Theories of counseling and psychotherapy: Systems, strategies, and skills* (3rd ed.). New York, NY: Pearson.

Seligman, L., & Reichenberg, L. W. (2012). *Selecting effective treatments: A comprehensive, systematic guide to treating mental disorders* (4th ed.). Hoboken, NJ: Wiley.

Seligman, L., & Reichenberg, L. W. (2013). *Theories of counseling and psychotherapy: Systems, strategies and skills* (4th ed.). New York, NY: Pearson.

Seligman, M. E. P. (1990). *Learned optimism*. New York, NY: Pocket Books.

Seligman, M. E. P. (1995). The effectiveness of psychotherapy. *American Psychologist, 50*, 965–974.

Seligman, M. E. P., Steen, T. A., Park, N., & Peterson, C. (2005). Positive psychology progress: Empirical validation of interventions. *American Psychologist, 60*, 410–421.

Selzer, M. L. (1971). The Michigan Alcoholism Screening Test: The quest for a new diagnostic instrument. *American Journal of Psychiatry, 127*, 1653–1658.

Severtson, S. G., von Thomsen, S., Hedden, S. L., & Latimer, W. (2010). The association between executive functioning and motivation to enter treatment among regular users of heroin and/or cocaine in Baltimore, MD. *Addictive Behavior, 35*, 717–720.

Sewell, R. A., & Petrakis, I. L. (2011). Does gamma-hydroxybutyrate (GHB) have a role in the treatment of alcoholism? *Alcohol and Alcoholism*, *46*, 1–2.

Shaffer, D., & Craft, L. (1999). Methods of adolescent suicide prevention. *Journal of Clinical Psychiatry*, *60*, 70–74.

Shahar, G., Trower, P., Iqbal, Z., Birchwood, M., Davidson, L., & Chadwick, P. (2004). The person in recovery from acute and severe psychosis: The role of dependency, self-criticism, and efficacy. *American Journal of Orthopsychiatry*, *74*, 480–488.

Shapiro, F. (1989). Efficacy of the eye movement desensitization procedure in the treatment of traumatic memories. *Journal of Traumatic Stress*, *2*, 199–223.

Sharpless, B. A., Muran, J. C., & Barber, J. P. (2010). CODA: Recommendations for practice and training. In J. C. Muran & J. P. Barber (Eds.), *The therapeutic alliance: An evidence-based guide to practice* (pp. 341–354). New York, NY: Guilford Press.

Shaw, R., Dayal, S., Hartman, J. K., & DeMaso, D. (2008). Factitious disorder by proxy: Pediatric condition falsification. *Harvard Review of Psychiatry*, *16*, 215–224.

Shear, K., Jin, R., Ruscio, A. M., Walters, E. E., & Kessler, R. C. (2006). Prevalence and correlates of estimated DSM-IV child and adult separation anxiety disorder in the National Comorbidity Survey Replication, *American Journal of Psychiatry*, *163*, 1074–1083.

Shedler, J. (2010). The efficacy of psychodynamic psychotherapy. *American Psychologist*, *65*, 98–109.

Shen, Y. J. (2010). Effects of postearthquake group play therapy with Chinese children. In J. N. Baggerly, D. C. Ray, & S. C. Bratton (Eds.), *Child centered play therapy research: The evidence base for effective practice* (pp. 85–104). Hoboken, NJ: Wiley.

Sheperis, C. J., Doggett, R. A., Hoda, N. E., Blanchard, T., Renfro-Michel, E. L., Holdiness, S. H., & Schlagheck, R. (2003). The development of an assessment protocol for reactive attachment disorder. *Journal of Mental Health Counseling*, *25*, 291–310.

Sheperis, C. J., Renfro-Michel, E. L., & Doggett, R. A. (2003). In-home treatment of reactive attachment disorder in a therapeutic foster care system: A case example. *Journal of Mental Health Counseling*, *25*, 76–89.

Sheridan, M. S. (2003). The deceit continues: An updated literature review of Munchausen syndrome by proxy. *Child Abuse & Neglect*, *27*, 431–451.

Siegel, B. (1999). *Pervasive Developmental Disorder Screening Test II*. San Francisco: University of San Francisco, Langley Porter Psychiatric Institute, Pervasive Developmental Disorder Laboratory and Clinic.

Sierra, M. (2009). *Depersonalization: A new look at a neglected syndrome*. New York, NY: Cambridge University Press.

Sierra, M., Baker, D., Medford, N., & David, A. S. (2005). Unpacking the depersonalization syndrome: An exploratory factor analysis on the Cambridge Depersonalization Scale. *Psychological Medicine*, *35*, 1523–1532.

Sierra, M., & Berrios, G. E. (2000). The Cambridge Depersonalization Scale: A new instrument for the measurement of depersonalization. *Psychiatry Research*, *93*, 153–164.

Sills, T., Wunderlich, G., Pyke, R., Segraves, R. T., Leiblum, S., Clayton, A., . . . Evans, K. (2005). The sexual interest and desire inventory-female (SIDI-F): Item response analyses of data from women diagnosed with hypoactive sexual desire disorder. *Journal of Sexual Medicine*, *2*, 801–818.

Silver, L. B. (2006). *The misunderstood child: Understanding and coping with your child's learning disabilities* (4th ed.). New York, NY: Three Rivers Press.

Silverman, W. K., & Rabian, B. (1999). Rating scales for anxiety and mood disorders. In D. Shaffer, C. P. Lucas, and J. E. Richters (Eds.), *Diagnostic assessment in child and adolescent psychopathology* (pp. 127–166). New York, NY: Guilford Press.

Simeon, D., & Abugel, J. (2006). *Feeling unreal: Depersonalization disorder and the loss of self*. New York, NY: Oxford University Press.

Simeon, D., Guralnik, O., Schmeidler, J., & Knutelska, M. (2004). Fluoxetine therapy in depersonalisation disorder: Randomised controlled trial. *British Journal of Psychiatry*, *185*, 31–36.

Simon, G. E. (2002). Management of somatoform and factitious disorders. In P. E. Nathan & J. M. Gorman (Eds.), *A guide to treatments that work* (2nd ed., pp. 447–461). New York, NY: Oxford University Press.

Simon, W. (2009). Follow-up psychotherapy outcome of patients with dependent, avoidant and obsessive-compulsive personality disorders: A meta-analytic review. *International Journal of Psychiatry in Clinical Practice*, *13*, 153–165.

Simpson, S. (2009). Psychotherapy via videoconferencing: A review. *British Journal of Guidance & Counselling*, *37*, 271–286.

Singh, S. P., & Kunar, S. S. (2010). Cultural diversity in early psychosis. In P. French, J. Smith, D. Shiers, M. Reed, & M. Rayne (Eds.), *Promoting recovery in early psychosis* (pp. 66–72). Oxford, United Kingdom: Wiley-Blackwell.

Sinha, R., & Rush, A. J. (2006). Treatment and prevention of depression in women. In C. M. Mazure & G. P. Keita (Eds.), *Understanding depression in women: Applying empirical research to practice and policy* (pp. 45–70). Washington, DC: American Psychological Association.

Skeppar, P., & Adolfsson, R. (2006). Bipolar II and the bipolar spectrum. *Nordic Journal of Psychiatry, 60,* 7–22.

Skodol, A. E., Gunderson, J. G., McGlashan, T. H., Dyck, I. R., Stout, R. L., Bender, D. S., . . . Oldham, J. M. (2002). Functional impairment in patients with schizotypal, borderline, avoidant or obsessive-compulsive personality disorder. *American Journal of Psychiatry, 159,* 276–283.

Sledge, W. H., Tebes, J., Rakfeldt, J., Davidson, L., Lyons, L., & Druss, B. (1996). Day hospital/crisis respite care versus inpatient care: Part I: Clinical outcomes. *Journal of Psychiatry, 153,* 1065–1073.

Slutske, W. S., Piasecki, T. M., Blaszczynski, A., & Martin, N. G. (2010). Pathological gambling recovery in the absence of abstinence. *Addiction, 105,* 2169–2175.

Smith, B. H., Barkley, R. A., & Shapiro, C. J. (2006). Attention-deficit/hyperactivity disorder. In E. J. Mash & R. A. Barkley (Eds.), *Treatment of childhood disorders* (3rd ed., pp. 65–136). New York, NY: Guilford Press.

Smith, E. J. (2006). The strength-based counseling model. *Counseling Psychologist, 34,* 134–144.

Smith, M. L., Glass, G. V., & Miller, T. J. (1980). *The benefits of psychotherapy.* Baltimore, MD: Johns Hopkins University Press.

Smith, R. L., & Capps, F. (2005). The major substances of abuse and the body. In P. Stevens & R. L. Smith (Eds.), *Substance abuse counseling: Theory and practice* (3rd ed., pp. 36–85). Upper Saddle River, NJ: Pearson Education.

Smith, T. (2010). Early and intensive behavioral intervention in autism. In J. R. Weisz & A. E. Kazdin (Eds.), *Evidence-based psychotherapies for children and adolescents* (2nd ed., pp. 312–326). New York, NY: Guilford Press.

Smith-Myles, B., & Simpson, R. L. (2002). Asperger syndrome: An overview of characteristics. *Focus on Autism and Other Developmental Disabilities, 17,* 132–137.

Somerset, W., Newport, D. J., Ragan, K., & Stowe, Z. N. (2006). Depressive disorders in women: From menarche to beyond the menopause. In C.L.M. Keyes &

S. H. Goodman (Eds.), *Women and depression* (pp. 62–88). New York, NY: Cambridge University Press.

Spauwen, J., Krabbendam, L., Lieb, R., Wittchen, H., & van Ohs, J. (2006). Impact of psychological trauma on the development of psychotic symptoms: Relationship with psychosis proneness. *British Journal of Psychiatry, 188,* 527–533.

Spector, I. P., Carey, M. P., & Steinberg, L. (1996). The Sexual Desire Inventory: Development, factor structure, and evidence of reliability. *Journal of Sex and Marital Therapy, 22,* 175–190.

Speltz, M. L., McClellan, J., DeKlyen, M., & Jones, K. (1999). Preschool boys with ODD: Clinical presentation and diagnostic change. *Journal of the American Academy of Child and Adolescent Psychiatry, 38,* 838–845.

Spence, S. H. (1997). Structure of anxiety symptoms among children: A confirmatory factor-analytic study. *Journal of Abnormal Psychology, 106,* 280–297.

Spence, S. H. (1998). A measure of anxiety symptoms among children. *Behavior Research and Therapy, 36,* 545–566.

Spence, S. H., Barrett, P. M., & Turner, C. M. (2003). Psychometric properties of the Spence Children's Anxiety Scale (SCAS) with young adolescents. *Anxiety Disorders, 17,* 605–625.

Sperry, L. (2001). *Spirituality in clinical practice: Incorporating the spiritual dimension in psychotherapy and counseling.* New York, NY: Routledge.

Sperry, L. (2003). *Handbook of diagnosis and treatment of DSM-IV-TR personality disorders* (2nd ed.). Philadelphia, PA: Brunner-Routledge.

Sperry, L. (2006). *Cognitive behavior therapy of DSM-IV-TR personality disorders: Highly effective interventions for the most common personality disorders* (2nd ed.). New York, NY: Routledge.

Spiegel, B. R., & Fewell, C. H. (2004). Twelve-step programs as a treatment modality. In S. L. A. Straussner (Ed.), *Clinical work with substance-abusing clients* (2nd ed., pp. 125–145). New York, NY: Guilford Press.

Spiegel, D. (1996). Dissociative disorders. In R. E. Hales & S. C. Yudofsky (Eds.), *The American Psychiatric Press synopsis of psychiatry* (pp. 583–604). Washington, DC: American Psychiatric Press.

Spinhoven, P., Van Dyck, R., Giesen-Bloo, J., Kooiman, K., & Arntz, A. (2007). The therapeutic alliance in schema-focused therapy and transference-focused psychotherapy for borderline personality disorder.

Journal of Consulting and Clinical Psychology, 75, 104–115.

Springer, D. W. (2009). Research providing the evidence base for interventions in this book. In D. W. Springer & A. Rubin (Eds.), *Substance abuse treatment for youth and adults* (pp. 353–362). Hoboken, NJ: Wiley.

Springer, D. W., McNeece, C. A., & Arnold, E. M. (2003). *Substance abuse treatment for criminal offenders: An evidence-based guide for practitioners.* Washington, DC: American Psychological Association.

Springer, D. W., & Rubin, A. (Eds.). (2009). *Substance abuse treatment for adolescents and adults: Clinician's guide to evidence-based practice.* Hoboken, NJ: Wiley.

Sprock, J., & Fredendall, L. (2008). Comparison of prototypic cases of depressive personality disorder and dysthymic disorder. *Journal of Clinical Psychology, 64,* 1293–1317.

Stahl, B., & Goldstein, E. (2010). *Mindfulness based stress reduction workbook.* Oakland, CA: New Harbinger.

Stasiewicz, P. R., Herrman, D., Nochajski, T. H., & Dermen, K. H. (2006). Motivational interviewing: Engaging highly resistant clients in treatment. *Counselor, 7,* 26–32.

Steele, K., & van der Hart, O. (2009). Treating dissociation. In C. A. Courtois and J. D. Ford (Eds.), *Treating complex traumatic stress disorders: An evidence-based guide* (pp. 145–165). New York, NY: Guilford Press.

Stein, D. J., Harvey, B., Seedat, S., & Hollander, E. (2006). Treatment of impulse-control disorders. In E. Hollander & D. J. Stein (Eds.), *Clinical manual of impulse-control disorders* (pp. 309–325). Arlington, VA: American Psychiatric Publishing.

Steketee, G., & Barlow, D. H. (2002). Obsessive-compulsive disorder. In D. H. Barlow (Ed.), *Anxiety and its disorders* (pp. 516–550). New York, NY: Guilford Press.

Steketee, G., & Frost, R. (2004). Compulsive hoarding: Current status of research. *Clinical Psychology Review, 23,* 905–927.

Steketee, G., Frost, R., & Bogart, K. (1996). The Yale-Brown Obsessive Compulsive Scale: Interview versus self-report. *Behaviour Research and Therapy, 34,* 675–684.

Steketee, G., & Pigott, T. A. (2006). *Obsessive compulsive disorder: The latest assessment and treatment strategy* (3rd ed.). Kansas City, MO: Compact Clinicals.

Stemberger, R. M. T., Thomas, A. M., Mansueto, C. S., & Carter, J. G. (2003). Personal toll of trichotillomania: Behavioral and interpersonal sequelae. *Journal of Anxiety Disorders, 14,* 97–104.

Stephens, R. S., Roffman, R. A., & Curtain, L. (2000). Comparison of extended versus brief treatments for marijuana use. *Journal of Consulting and Clinical Psychology, 68,* 898–908.

Stephenson, K. R., & Meston, C. M. (2010). When are sexual difficulties distressing for women? The selective protective value of intimate relationships. *Journal of Sexual Medicine, 7,* 3683–3694.

Sterling, R. C., Gottheil, E., Weinstein, S. P., & Serota, R. (1998). Therapist/patient race and sex matching. *Addiction, 93,* 1043–1050.

Stevens, P., & Smith, R. L. (2005). *Substance abuse counseling: Theory and practice* (3rd ed.). Upper Saddle River, NJ: Pearson.

Stewart, R. E., & Chambless, D. L. (2009). Cognitive-behavioral therapy for adult anxiety disorders in clinical practice: A meta-analysis of effectiveness studies. *Journal of Consulting and Clinical Psychology, 77,* 595–606.

Stice, E., & Bulik, C. M. (2008). Eating disorders. In T. P. Beauchaine & S. P. Hinshaw (Eds.), *Child and adolescent psychopathology* (pp. 643–669). Hoboken, NJ: Wiley.

Stice, E., Burton, E., & Shaw, H. (2004). Prospective relations between bulimic pathology, depression, and substance abuse: Unpacking comorbidity in adolescent girls. *Journal of Consulting and Clinical Psychology, 72,* 62–71.

Stinchfield, R., & Winters, K. C. (2001). Outcome of Minnesota's gambling treatment programs. *Journal of Gambling Studies, 17,* 217–245.

Stirling, J. (2007). Beyond Munchausen Syndrome by Proxy: Identification and treatment of child abuse in a medical setting. *Pediatrics, 119,* 1026–1030.

Stoeter, P., Bauermann, T., Nickel, R., Corluka, L., Gawehn, J., Vucurevic, G., . . . Egle, U. T. (2007). Cerebral activation in patients with somatoform pain disorder exposed to pain and stress: An fMRI study. *Neuroimage, 36,* 418–430.

Stolbach, B. C. (1997). The Children's Dissociative Experiences Scale and Posttraumatic Symptom Inventory: Rationale, development, and validation of a self-report measure. *Dissertation Abstracts International, 58* (03), 1548B.

Stone, W. L., Coonrod, E. E., Turner, L. M., & Pozdol, S. L. (2004). Psychometric properties of the STAT for early autism screening. *Behavioral Science, 34,* 691–701.

Storch, E. A., Murphy, T. K., Geffken, G. R., Sajid, M., Allen, P., Roberti, J. W., & Goodman, W. K. (2005). Reliability and validity of the Yale Global

Tic Severity Scale. *Psychological Assessment, 17,* 486–491.

Strain, J. J., Klipstein, K. G., & Newcorn, J. H. (2011). Adjustment disorders. In R. E. Hales, S. C. Yudofsky, & G. O. Gabbard (Eds.), *Essentials of psychiatry* (3rd ed., pp. 255–270). Arlington, VA: American Psychiatric Publishing.

Strauss, J. L., & Johnson, S. L. (2006). Treatment alliance predicts improved treatment attitudes and decreased manic symptoms in bipolar disorder. *Psychiatry Research, 145,* 215–223.

Stricker, G., & Gold, J. (Eds.). (2006). *A casebook of psychotherapy integration.* Washington, DC: American Psychological Association.

Striegel-Moore, R. H., Dohm, F. A., Kraemer, H. C., Taylor, C. B., Daniels, S., Crawford, P. B, & Schreiber, G. B. (2003). Eating disorders in white and black women. *American Journal of Psychiatry, 160,* 1326–1331.

Strub, R. L., & Black, F. W. (2000). *The mental status examination in neurology* (4th ed.). Philadelphia, PA: Davis.

Stuart, S., & Noyes, R. (1999). Attachment and interpersonal communication in somatization. *Psychosomatics, 40,* 34–43.

Sturmey, P. (2009). Behavior activation is an evidence-based treatment for depression. *Behavior Modification, 33,* 818–829.

Substance Abuse and Mental Health Services Administration. (2003). *Results from the 2002 National Survey on Drug Use and Health: National findings.* NHSDA Series H-22 (DHHS Pub. No. SMA 03-3836). Rockville, MD: Author. Available: www.oas.samhsa.gov/nhsda/2k2nsduh/Results/2k2Results.htm

Substance Abuse and Mental Health Services Administration. (2006). *Results from the 2005 National Survey on Drug Use and Health: National findings.* NSDUH Series H-30 (DHHS Pub. No. SMA 06-4194). Rockville, MD: Author.

Substance Abuse and Mental Health Services Administration. (2010). *Results from the 2009 National Survey on Drug Use and Health: Volume I. Summary of National Findings* (Office of Applied Studies, NSDUH Series H-38A, HHS Publication No. SMA 10-4586). Rockville, MD: Author. Available: www.oas.samhsa.gov

Sue, D., Sue, D. W., & Sue, S. (2006). *Understanding abnormal behavior* (8th ed.). Boston, MA: Houghton Mifflin.

Sue, D. W., Ivey, A. E., & Pedersen, P. B. (1996). *A theory of multicultural counseling and psychotherapy.* Pacific Grove, CA: Brooks/Cole.

Sullivan, E. V., Fama, R., Rosenbloom, M. J., & Pfefferbaum, A. (2002). A profile of neuropsychological deficits in alcoholic women. *Neuropsychology, 16,* 74–83.

Swanson, J. W., Swartz, M. S., Van Dorn, R. A., Elbogen, E. B., Wagner, H. R., Rosenheck, R. A., . . . Lieberman, J. A. (2006). A national study of violent behavior in persons with schizophrenia. *Archives of General Psychiatry, 63,* 490–499.

Swartz, C. M. (2010). Psychotic depression or schizophrenia. *Psychiatric Annals, 40,* 92–97.

Syad, T. (2003). Safety and efficacy of the nicotine patch and gum for the treatment of adolescent tobacco addiction. *Journal of Pediatrics, 147,* 406–407.

Szklo-Coxe, M., Young, T., Finn, L., & Mignot, E. (2007). Depression: Relationships to sleep paralysis and other sleep disturbances in a community sample. *Journal of Sleep Research, 16,* 297–312.

Szklo-Coxe, M., Young, T., Peppard, P. E., Finn, L. A., & Benca, R. M. (2010). Prospective associations of insomnia markers and symptoms with depression. *American Journal of Epidemiology, 171,* 709–720.

Tanielian, T., & Jaycox, L. H. (Eds.). (2008). *Invisible wounds of war: Psychological and cognitive injuries, their consequences, and services to assist recovery.* Santa Monica, CA: Rand Corporation.

Tarrier, N. (2008). Schizophrenia and other psychotic disorders. In D. H. Barlow (Ed.), *Clinical handbook of psychological disorders: A step-by-step treatment manual* (4th ed., pp. 463–491). New York, NY: Guilford Press.

Tarrier, N., & Wykes, T. (2004) Is there evidence that cognitive behaviour therapy is an effective treatment for schizophrenia? A cautious or cautionary tale? *Behaviour Research and Therapy, 42,* 1377–1401.

Tarter, R. E., Sambrano, S., & Dunn, M. G. (2002). Predictor variables by developmental stages: A Center for Substance Abuse Prevention multisite study. *Psychology of Addictive Behaviors, 16,* S3–S10.

Task Force on Promotion and Dissemination of Psychological Procedures. (1995). Training in and dissemination of empirically validated psychological treatments: Report and recommendations. *Clinical Psychologist, 48,* 2–23.

Tatarsky, A., & Marlatt, G. A. (2010). State of the art in harm reduction psychotherapy: An emerging treatment for substance misuse. *Journal of Clinical Psychology: In Session, 66,* 117–122.

Taylor, C. B., Jobson, K., Winzelberg, A., & Abascal, L. (2002). The use of the internet to provide evidence-based integrated treatment programs for mental health. *Psychiatric Annals, 21,* 671–677.

Taylor, J. Y., Caldwell, C. H., Baser, R. E., Faison, N., & Jackson, J. S. (2007). Prevalence of eating disorders among blacks in the National Survey of American Life. *International Journal of Eating Disorders, 40*(Suppl.), 510–514.

Taylor, S., Thordarson, D. S., & Sochting, I. (2002). Obsessive-compulsive disorder. In M. M. Antony & D. H. Barlow (Eds.), *Handbook of assessment and treatment planning for psychological disorders* (pp. 182–214). New York, NY: Guilford Press.

Teasdale, J., Williams, J., Soulsby, J. M., Segal, Z. V., Ridgeway, V. A., & Lau, M. A. (2000). Prevention of relapse/recurrence in major depression by mindfulness-based cognitive therapy. *Journal of Consulting and Clinical Psychology, 68,* 615–623.

Teng, E. J., Woods, D. W., & Twohig, M. P. (2006). Habit reversal as a treatment for chronic skin-picking. *Behavior Modification, 30,* 411–422.

ter Kuile, M. M., Weijenborg, P. T. M., Beekman, A., Bulte, I., & Melles, R. (2009). Therapist-aided exposure for women with lifelong vaginismus: A replicated single-case design. *Journal of Consulting and Clinical Psychology, 77,* 149–159.

Teyber, E., & McClure, F. H. (2011). *Interpersonal process in therapy: An integrative model,* 6th ed. Belmont, CA: Brooks/Cole.

Thiedke, C. C. (2003). Nocturnal enuresis. *American Family Physician, 67,* 1499–1506.

Thomas, J. L., Wilk, J. E., Riviere, L. A., McGurk, D., Castro, C. A. & Hoge, C. W. (2010). Prevalence of mental health problems and functional impairment among active component and National Guard soldiers 3 and 12 months following combat in Iraq. *Archives of General Psychiatry, 67,* 614–623.

Thomas, P. M. (2003). Protection, dissociation, and internal roles: Modeling and treating the effects of child abuse. *Review of General Psychology, 7,* 364–380.

Thomason, T. C. (2010). The trend toward evidence-based practice and the future of psychotherapy. *American Journal of Psychotherapy, 64,* 29–38.

Thompson, C. L., Rudolph, L. B., & Henderson, D. A. (2003). *Counseling children* (6th ed.). Belmont, CA: Wadsworth.

Thompson, V. L., Bazile, A., & Akbar, M. (2004). African American perceptions of psychotherapy and psychotherapists. *Professional Psychology: Research and Practice, 35,* 19–26.

Tienari, P., Wynne, L. C., Laksy, K., Moring, J., Nieminen, P., Sorri, A., . . . Wahlberg, K. (2003). Genetic boundaries of the schizophrenia spectrum: Evidence from the Finnish adoptive family study of schizophrenia. *American Journal of Psychiatry, 160,* 1587–1594.

Tingley, K. (2013, June 30). I'm not okay: Uncovering the self-destructive impulse that many people hide even from themselves. *New York Times Magazine, 23–27,* 46–47.

Torgersen, S., Kringlen, E., & Cramer, V. (2001). The prevalence of personality disorders in a community sample. *Archives of General Psychiatry, 58,* 590–596.

Torrey, E. F. (2006). *Surviving schizophrenia: A manual for families, patients, and providers* (5th ed.). New York, NY: HarperCollins.

Totterdell, P., & Kellett, S. (2008). Restructuring mood in cyclothymia using cognitive behavioral therapy: An intensive time-sampling study. *Journal of Clinical Psychology, 64,* 501–518.

Towbin, K. E., & Cohen, D. J. (1996). Tic disorders. In J. M. Wiener (Ed.), *Diagnosis and psychopharmacology of childhood and adolescent disorders* (2nd ed., pp. 349–369). New York, NY: Wiley.

Trafford, A. (1992). *Crazy time: Surviving divorce and building a new life* (Rev. ed.). New York, NY: HarperCollins.

Tsatsanis, K. D., Foley, C., & Donehower, C. (2004). Contemporary outcome research and programming guidelines for Asperger's syndrome and high-functioning autism. *Topics in Language Disorders, 24,* 249–259.

Tucker, E. (2002, August 28). Two men missing since 9/11 found alive in hospitals. *Houston Chronicle,* p. A–15.

Tucker, J. A., Vuchinich, R. E., & Murphy, J. G. (2002). Substance use disorders. In M. M. Antony & D. H. Barlow (Eds.), *Handbook of assessment and treatment planning for psychological disorders* (pp. 415–451). New York, NY: Guilford Press.

Turk, C. L., Heimberg, R. G., & Magee, L. (2008). Social anxiety disorder. In D. H. Barlow (Ed.), *Clinical handbook of psychological disorders* (4th ed., pp. 123–167). New York, NY: Guilford Press.

Turkington, D., Dudley, R., Warman, D. M., & Beck, A. T. (2004) Cognitive behavioral therapy for schizophrenia: A review. *Journal of Psychiatric Practice, 10,* 5–16.

Twohig, M. P., Hayes, S. C., Plumb, J. C., Pruitt, L. D., Colins, A. B., Hazlett-Stevens, H., & Woidneck, M. R. (2010). A randomized clinical trial of acceptance and commitment therapy versus progressive relaxation training for obsessive-compulsive disorder. *Journal of Consulting and Clinical Psychology, 78,* 705–716.

Tyndall-Linn, A. (2010). Intensive sibling group play therapy with child witnesses of domestic violence. In J. N. Baggerly, D. C. Ray, & S. C. Bratton (Eds.), *Child centered play therapy research: The evidence base for effective practice.* Hoboken, NJ: Wiley.

United Nations. (2010). *World drug report, 2010.* New York, NY: United Nations Publications. Vienna, Austria: United Nations Office on Drugs and Crime.

U.S. Department of Health and Human Services. (2006). *Child maltreatment, 2004.* Available: www.acf.hhs.gov/programs/cb/pubs/cm04/index.htm

U.S. Department of Health and Human Services, Office of Inspector General. (2000). *Mandatory managed care: Changes in Medicaid mental health services.* Washington, DC: U.S. Department of Health and Human Services.

U.S. Department of Health and Human Services, Public Health Service. (2001). National strategy for suicide prevention: Goals and objectives for action (DHHS Publication No. SMA 01-3517). Rockville, MD. Available: www.mentalhealth.samhsa.gov/suicideprevention/strategy.asp

U.S. Public Health Service. (2008). *Agency for Healthcare Research and Quality. Treating tobacco use and dependence: Quick reference guide for clinicians.* Rockville, MD: Author. Available: www.ahrq.gov/clinic/tobacco/tobaqrg.htm

U.S. Suicide rate increasing: Largest increase seen in middle-aged white women. *ScienceDaily.* Retrieved from www.sciencedaily.com/releases/2008/

Üstün, T. B., Ayuso-Mateos, J. L., Chatterji, S., Mathers, C., & Murray, C.J.L. (2004). Global burden of depressive disorders in the year 2000, *The British Journal of Psychiatry, 184,* 386–392.

van der Hart, O., Nijenhuis, E., Steele, K., & Brown, D. (2004). Trauma-related dissociation: Conceptual clarity lost and found. *Australian and New Zealand Journal of Psychiatry, 38,* 906–914.

van der Hart, O., Nijenhuis, E.R.S., & Steele, K. (2006). *The haunted self: Structural dissociation and the treatment of chronic traumatization.* New York, NY: Norton.

van der Klink, J. J., & van Dijk, F. J. (2003). Dutch practice guidelines for managing adjustment disorders in occupational and primary health care. *Scandinavian Journal of Work and Environmental Health, 29,* 478–487.

van der Kolk, B. A., Spinazzola, J., Blaustein, M. E., Hopper, J. W., Hopper, E. K., Korn, D. L., & Simpson, W. B. (2007). A randomized clinical trial of eye movement desensitization and reprocessing (EMDR), fluoxetine, and pill placebo in the treatment of posttraumatic stress disorder: Treatment effects and long-term maintenance. *Journal of Clinical Psychiatry, 68,* 37–46.

van Dijk, S. (2011). *Don't let your emotions run your life for teens: Dialectical behavior therapy skills for helping teens manage mood swings, control angry outbursts, and get along with others.* Oakland, CA: New Harbinger Books.

van Luyn, J. V., Akhtar, S., & Livesley, W. J. (2007). *Severe personality disorders.* Cambridge, UK: Cambridge University Press.

Veale, D., & Neziroglu, F. (2010). *Body dysmorphic disorder: A treatment manual.* Hoboken, NJ: Wiley.

Verona, E., Patrick, C. J., & Joiner, T. E. (2001). Psychopathy, antisocial personality, and suicide risk. *Journal of Abnormal Psychology, 110,* 462–470.

Viorst, J. (1998). *Necessary losses.* New York, NY: Free Press.

Visser, S. (2010). *Morbidity and Mortality Weekly Report.* Child development studies team, National Center on Birth Defects and Developmental Disabilities, U.S. Centers for Disease Control.

Volavka, J., Czobor, P., Sheitman, B., Lindenmayer, P., Citrome, L., McEvoy, J., . . . Lieberman, J. (2002). Clozapine, olanzapine, risperidone, and haloperidol in treatment-resistant patients with schizophrenia and schizoaffective disorder. *American Journal of Psychiatry, 159,* 255–262.

Wadhwa, P. D., Glynn, L., Hobel, C. J., Garite, T. J., Porto, M., Chicz-DeMet, A., . . . Sandman, C. A. (2002). Behavioral perinatology: Biobehavioral processes in human fetal development. *Regulatory Peptides, 108,* 149–157.

Wagner, B., Knaevelsrud, C., & Maercker, A. (2007). Internet-based treatment for PTSD reduces distress and facilitates the development of a strong therapeutic alliance. *Cognitive Behavior Therapy, 36,* 156–161.

Wagner, E. F., & Austin, A. M. (2009). Problem solving and social skills training. In D. W. Springer & A. Rubin (Eds.), *Substance abuse treatment for youth and adults* (pp. 57–108). Hoboken, NJ: Wiley.

Wallerstein, R. S. (1986). *Forty-two lives in treatment.* New York, NY: Guilford Press.

Walser, R. D., & Westrup, D. (2008). *Acceptance and commitment therapy for the treatment of post-traumatic stress disorder and trauma-related problems.* Oakland, CA: New Harbinger Books.

Walsh, F. (2009). *Spiritual resources in family therapy* (2nd ed.). New York, NY: Guilford Press.

Walsh, R. (2000). Asian psychotherapies. In R. Corsini & D. Wedding (Eds.), *Current psychotherapies* (6th ed., pp. 407–444). Itsaca, IL: Peacock.

Walsh, R., & Shapiro, S. L. (2006). The meeting of meditative disciplines and western psychology: A mutually enriching dialogue. *American Psychologist, 61*, 227–239.

Wampold, B. E. (2001). *The great psychotherapy debate: Models, methods, and findings.* Mahwah, NJ: Lawrence Erlbaum Associates.

Wampold, B. E., & Brown, G. S. (2005). Estimating variability in outcomes attributable to therapists: A naturalistic study of outcomes in managed care. *Journal of Consulting and Clinical Psychology, 73*, 914–923.

Wang, P. S., Berglund, P., Olfson, M., Pincus, H. A., Wells, K. B., & Kessler, R. C. (2005). Failure and delay in initial treatment contact after first onset of mental disorders in the National Comorbidity Survey Replication. *Archives of General Psychiatry, 62*, 603–613.

Washburn, J. J., Richardt, S. L., Styer, D. M., Gebhardt, M., Juzwin, K. R., Yourek, A., & Aldridge, D. (2012). Psychotherapeutic approaches to non-suicidal self-injury in adolescents. *Child and Adolescent Psychiatry and Mental Health, 6.*

Washburn, J. J., West, A. E., & Heil, J. A. (2011). Treatment of pediatric bipolar disorder: A review. *Minerva Psichiatrica, 52*, 21–33.

Watson, H. J., Anderson, R. A., & Rees, C. S. (2010). Evidence-based clinical management of obsessive compulsive disorder. In R. A. Carlstedt (Ed.), *Handbook of integrative clinical psychology, psychiatry, and behavioral medicine: Perspectives, practice, & research* (pp. 411–442). New York, NY: Springer.

Weber, M. K., Floyd, R. L., Riley, E. P., & Snider, D. E. (2002). National task force on fetal alcohol syndrome and fetal alcohol effect: Defining the national agenda for fetal alcohol syndrome and other prenatal alcohol-related effects. *Morbidity and Mortality Weekly Report Recommendations and Reports, 51*(RR-14), 9–12.

Webster-Stratton, C. H., & Reid, M. J. (2010). The incredible years parents, teachers and children training series: A multifaceted treatment approach for young children with conduct problems. In J. Weisz & A. Kazdin (Eds.), *Evidence-based psychotherapies for children and adolescents* (2nd ed., pp. 194–210). New York, NY: Guilford Press.

Webster-Stratton, C. H., Reid, M. J., & Murrihy, R. C. (2010). The incredible years program for children

from infancy to pre-adolescence: Prevention and treatment of behavior problems. In A. D. Kidman & T. H. Ollendick (Eds.), *Clinical handbook of assessing and treating conduct problems in youth* (pp. 117–138). New York, NY: Springer.

Wechsler, D. (2001). *Wechsler Individual Achievement Test* (2nd ed.). San Antonio, TX: Psychological Corporation.

Weinstock, L. M., & Whisman, M. A. (2004). The self-verification model of depression and interpersonal rejection in heterosexual dating relationships. *Journal of Social and Clinical Psychology, 23*, 240–259.

Weissman, M. M., Markowitz, J. C., & Klerman, G. L. (2000). *Comprehensive guide to interpersonal psychotherapy.* New York, NY: Basic Books.

Weisz, J. R., & Hawley, K. M. (2002). Developmental factors in the treatment of adolescents. *Journal of Consulting and Clinical Psychology, 70*, 21–43.

Weisz, J. R., & Kazdin, A. E. (Eds.). (2010). *Evidence-based psychotherapies for children and adolescents* (2nd ed.). New York, NY: Guilford Press.

Weisz, J. R., Weiss, B., Han, S. S., Granger, D. A., & Morton, T. (1995). Effects of psychotherapy with children and adolescents revisited: A meta-analysis of treatment outcome studies. *Psychological Bulletin, 117*, 450–468.

Weller, E. B., Danielyan, A. K., & Weller, R. A. (2004). Somatic treatment of bipolar disorder in children and adolescents. *Psychiatric Clinics of North America, 27*, 155–178.

Wells, A. (2009). *Metacognitive therapy for anxiety and depression,* New York, NY: Guilford Press.

West, J. C., Marcus, K. C., Wilk, J., Countis, L., Regier, D. A., & Olfson, M. (2008). Use of depot antipsychotic medications for medication nonadherence in schizophrenia. *Schizophrenia Bulletin, 34*, 995–1001.

Whisman, M. A., Weinstock, L. M., & Tolejko, N. (2006). Marriage and depression. In C. L. M. Keyes & S. H. Goodman (Eds.), *Women and depression* (pp. 219–240). New York, NY: Cambridge University Press.

White, J., & Wynne, L. S. (2009). Kinder training: An Adlerian-based model to enhance teacher-student relationships. In A. A. Drewes (Ed.), *Blending play therapy with cognitive behavioral therapy: Evidence-based and other effective treatments and techniques* (pp. 281–296). Hoboken, NJ: Wiley.

White, K. S., & Barlow, D. H. (2002). Panic disorder and agoraphobia. In D. H. Barlow (Ed.), *Anxiety and its disorders* (pp. 328–379). New York, NY: Guilford Press.

White, L. A., Fisher, W. A., Byrne, D., & Kingma, R. (1977, October). *Development and validation of a measure of effective orientation to erotic stimuli: The Sexual Opinion Survey.* Paper presented at the meeting of the Midwestern Psychological Association, Chicago.

White, S. W., Koenig, K., & Scahill, L. (2007). Social skills development in children with autism spectrum disorders: A review of the intervention research. *Journal of Autism and Developmental Disorders, 37,* 1858–1868.

Widiger, T. A., Mullins-Sweatt, S., & Anderson, K. G. (2006). Personality and depression in women. In C. L. M. Keyes & S. H. Goodman (Eds.), *Women and depression* (pp. 176-198). New York, NY: Cambridge University Press.

Wiederhold, B. K., Riva, G., & Kim, S. I. (2010). *Annual review of cybertherapy and telemedicine.* Fairfax, VA: IOS Press.

Wiegel, M., Wincze, J. P., & Barlow, D. H. (2002). Sexual dysfunction. In M. M. Antony & D. H. Barlow (Eds.), *Handbook of assessment and treatment planning for psychological disorders* (pp. 481–522). New York, NY: Guilford Press.

Wiking, E., Johansson, S., & Sundquist, J. (2004). Ethnicity, acculturation, and self-reported health. A population based study among immigrants from Poland, Turkey, and Iran in Sweden. *Journal of Epidemiology of Community Health, 58,* 574–582.

Wilcox, H. C., Conner, K., & Caine, E. (2004). Risk for suicide associated with drug use disorders: An empirical review. *Drug and Alcohol Dependence, 76S,* S11–S19.

Wildes, M. D., & Marcus, J. E. (2009). Obesity: Is it a mental disorder? *International Journal of Eating Disorders, 42,* 739–753.

Wilens, T. E., & Upadhyaya, H. P. (2007). Impact of substance use disorder on ADHD and its treatment. *Journal of Clinical Psychiatry, 68,* e20.

Wilhelm, K. (2006). Depression: From nosology to global burden. In C.L.M. Keyes & S. H. Goodman (Eds.), *Women and depression* (pp. 3–21). New York, NY: Cambridge University Press.

Williams, J. W., Barrett, J., & Oxman, T. (2000). Treatment of dysthymia and minor depression in primary care: A randomized controlled trial in older adults. *Journal of the American Medical Association, 284,* 1519–1526.

Williams, M., Teasdale, J., Segal, Z., & Kabat-Zinn, J. (2007). *The mindful way through depression.* New York, NY: Guilford Press.

Williams, S. H. (2005). Medications for treating alcohol dependence. *American Family Physician, 72,* 1775–1780.

Wilson, G. T., & Fairburn, C. G. (2007). Treatments for eating disorders. In P. E. Nathan & J. M. Gorman (Eds.), *A guide to treatments that work* (2nd ed., pp. 579–611). New York, NY: Oxford University Press.

Wilson, G. T., Grilo, C. M., & Vitousek, K. M. (2007). Psychological treatment of eating disorders. *American Psychologist, 62,* 199–216.

Wilson, I. (2010). Substance misuse in first-episode psychosis. In P. French, J. Smith, D. Shiers, M. Reed, & M. Rayne (Eds.), *Promoting recovery in early psychosis* (pp. 147–156). Oxford, United Kingdom: Wiley-Blackwell.

Wilson, K., Mills, E., Ross, C., McGowan, J., & Jadad, A. (2003). Association of autistic spectrum disorder and the measles, mumps and rubella vaccine: A systematic review of current epidemiological evidence. *Archives of Pediatric and Adolescent Medicine, 157,* 628–634.

Wilson, S. L. (2001). Attachment disorders: Review and current status. *Journal of Psychology, 135,* 37–51.

Wincze, J. P., Bach, A. K., & Barlow, D. H. (2008). Sexual dysfunction. In D. H. Barlow (Ed.), *Clinical handbook of psychological disorders: A step-by-step manual* (4th ed., pp. 615–661). New York, NY: Guilford Press.

Wincze, J. P., & Carey, M. P. (2001). *Sexual dysfunction: A guide for assessment and treatment.* New York, NY: Guilford Press.

Winston, A. P., Hardrick, E., & Jaberi, N. (2005). Neuropsychiatric effects of caffeine. *Advances in Psychiatric Treatment, 11,* 432–439.

Wintersteen, M. B., Mensinger, J. L., & Diamond, G. S. (2005). Do gender and racial differences between patient and therapist affect therapeutic alliance and treatment retention in adolescents? *Professional Psychology: Research and Practice, 36,* 400–408.

Wirshing, D. A., & Buckley, P. (2003, May). Schizophrenia treatment challenges. *Psychiatric Times, 20.* Available: www.psychiatrictimes.com/p030540.html

Witkiewitz, K., & Marlatt, G. A. (2004). Relapse prevention for alcohol and drug problems: That was Zen, this is Tao. *American Psychologist, 59,* 224–235.

Wolpe, J. (1958). *Psychotherapy by reciprocal inhibition.* Palo Alto, CA: Stanford University Press.

Wong, E. C., Kim, B. S., Zane, N. W. S., Kim, I. J., & Huang, J. S. (2003). Examining culturally based variables associated with ethnicity: Influences on credibility perceptions of empirically supported interventions. *Cultural Diversity and Ethnic Minority Psychology, 9,* 88–96.

Woo, S. M., & Keatinge, C. (2008). *Diagnosis and treatment of mental disorders across the lifespan.* Hoboken, NJ: Wiley.

Woodcock, R. W., & Johnson, M. B. (2001). *Woodcock-Johnson-III tests of achievement.* New York, NY: Riverside.

Woods, D. W., Wetterneck, C. T., & Flessner, C. A. (2006). A controlled evaluation of acceptance and commitment therapy plus habit reversal for trichotillomania. *Behaviour Research and Therapy, 44,* 639–656.

Woods, S. W., Addington, J., Cadenhead, K. S., Cannon, T. D., Cornblatt, B. A., Heinssen, R., . . . McGlashan, T. H. (2009). Validity of the prodromal risk syndrome for first psychosis: Findings from the North American Prodrome Longitudinal Study. *Schizophrenia Bulletin, 35,* 894–908.

Woodside, D. B. (2004). Assessing and treating men with eating disorders. *Psychiatric Times, 11,* 989–990.

Woodside, D. B., Garfinkel, P. E., Lin, E., Goering, P., Kaplan, A. S., Goldbloom, D. S., & Kennedy, S. H. (2001). Comparisons of men with full or partial eating disorders, men without eating disorders, and women with eating disorders in the community. *American Journal of Psychiatry, 158,* 570–574.

Woolfolk, R. L., & Allen, L. A. (2007). *Treating somatization: A cognitive behavioral approach.* New York, NY: Guilford Press.

Wootten, R., Yellowlees, P. M., & McLaren, P. (2003). *Telepsychiatry and e-mental health.* Glasgow: Bell and Bain.

World Federation of Societies of Biological Psychiatry (WFSBP). (2007). Pharmacotherapy of bipolar disorders. Task Force on Treatment Guidelines for Bipolar Disorders. *World Journal of Biological Psychiatry, 8,* 212–244.

World Health Organization (2005). *ICD-10 classification of mental and behavioural disorders.* Geneva, Switzerland: World Health Organization.

Wright, J., Turkington, D., Kingdon, D. G., & Basco, M. R. (2009). *Cognitive-behavior therapy for severe mental illness: An illustrated guide.* Washington, DC: American Psychiatric Publishing.

Wu, L. T., Parrott, A. C., Ringwalt, C. L., Patkar, A. A., Mannelli, P., & Blazer, D. G. (2009). The high prevalence of substance use disorders among recent MDMA users compared with other drug users: Implications for intervention. *Addictive Behaviors, 34,* 654–661.

Wu, L. T., Pilowsky, D. J., & Schlenger, W. E. (2004). Inhalant abuse and dependence among adolescents in the United States. *Journal of American Academy of Child and Adolescent Psychiatry, 43,* 1206–1214.

Yager, J. (2001). E-mail as a therapeutic adjunct in the outpatient treatment of anorexia nervosa: Illustrative case material and discussion of the issues. *International Journal of Eating Disorders, 29,* 125–138.

Yalom, I. D. (1995). *The theory and practice of group psychotherapy* (4th ed.). New York, NY: Basic Books.

Yalom, V. (2009). *Featured interview with Nick Cummings, Ph.D.* Retrieved from www.psychotherapy.net/interview/Nick_Cummings

Yang, C., & Ebben, M. R. (2008). Behavioral therapy, sleep hygiene, and psychotherapy. In S. R. Pandi-Perumal, J. C. Verster, J. M. Monti, M. Lader, & S. Z. Langer (Eds.), *Sleep disorders: Diagnostics and therapeutics* (pp. 115–123). New York, NY: Informa Healthcare.

Yanovski, S. Z. (1993). Binge eating disorder: Current knowledge and future directions. *Obesity Research, 1,* 306–324.

Yatham, L. N., & Kusumakar, V. (2002). Anticonvulsants in treatment of bipolar disorder: A review of efficacy. In L. N. Yatham, V. Kusumakar, & S. P. Kutcher (Eds.), *Bipolar disorder: A clinician's guide to biological treatments* (pp. 201–240). Philadelphia, PA: Brunner-Routledge.

Yatham, L. N., Kusumakar, V., & Kutcher, S. P. (2002). Treatment of bipolar depression. In L. N. Yatham, V. Kusumakar, & S. P. Kutcher (Eds.), *Bipolar disorder: A clinician's guide to biological treatments* (pp. 17–32). Philadelphia, PA: Brunner-Routledge.

Yell, M. L. (2011). *The law and special education.* Oakland, CA: Prentice Hall.

Yeomans, F. E., & Levy, K. N. (2002). An object relations perspective on borderline personality disorder. *Acta Neuropsychiatrica, 14,* 76–80.

Yen, S., Shea, M. T., Battle, C., Johnson, D. M., Zlotnick, C., Dolan-Sewell, R., . . . McGlashan, T. H. (2002). Traumatic exposure and posttraumatic stress disorder in borderline, schizotypal, avoidant, and obsessive-compulsive personality disorders: Findings from the collaborative longitudinal personality disorders study. *Journal of Nervous and Mental Disease, 190,* 510–518.

Young, J. E. (1999). *Cognitive therapy for personality disorders: A schema-focused approach* (3rd ed.). Sarasota, FL: Professional Resource Press.

Young, J. E., Klosko, J. S., & Weishaar, M. (2003). *Schema therapy: A practitioner's guide.* New York, NY: Guilford Press.

Young, J. E., Rygh, J. L., Weinberger, A. D., & Beck, A. T. (2008). Cognitive therapy for depression. In D. H. Barlow (Ed.), *Clinical handbook of psychological disorders: A step-by-step treatment manual* (4th ed., pp. 250–305). New York, NY: Guilford Press.

Youngstrom, E. A., Birmaher, B., & Findling, R. L. (2008). Pediatric bipolar disorder: Validity, phenomenology, and recommendations for diagnosis. *Bipolar Disorders, 10,* 194–214.

Zaghrout-Hodali, M., Alissa, F., & Dodgson, P. (2008). Building resilience and dismantling fear: EMDR group protocol with children in an area of ongoing trauma. *Journal of EMDR Practice & Research, 2,* 106–113.

Zahedi, S., Kamath, J., & Winokur, A. (2008). Interrelationships between sleep, depression, and antidepressant drugs. In S. R. Pandi-Perumal, J. C. Verster, J. M. Monti, M. Lader, & S. Z. Langer (Eds.), *Sleep disorders: Diagnostics and therapeutics* (pp. 427–442). New York, NY: Informa Healthcare.

Zanarini, M. C. (2005). *Borderline personality disorder.* New York, NY: Informa Healthcare.

Zanarini, M. C., Frankenburg, F. R., Hennen, J., Reich, B., & Silk, K. R. (2004). Axis I comorbidity in patients with borderline personality disorder: 6-year follow-up and prediction of time to remission. *American Journal of Psychiatry, 161,* 2108–2114.

Zarate, C. A., & Tohen, M. F. (2002). Bipolar disorder and comorbid Axis I disorders: Diagnosis and management. In L. N. Yatham, V. Kusumakar, & S. P. Kutcher (Eds.), *Bipolar disorder: A clinician's guide to biological treatments* (pp. 115–138). Philadelphia, PA: Brunner-Routledge.

Zarate, C. A., Tohen, M. F., Banov, M. D., & Weiss, M. K. (1995). Is clozapine a mood stabilizer? *Journal of Clinical Psychiatry, 56,* 108–112.

Zayfert, C., & Becker, C. B. (2007). *Cognitive behavioral therapy for PTSD: A case formulation approach.* New York, NY: Guilford Press.

Zeanah, C. H. (Ed.). (2009). *Handbook of infant mental health* (3rd ed.). New York, NY: Guilford Press.

Zeanah, C. H., & Boris, N. W. (2000). Disturbances and disorders of attachment in early childhood. In C. H. Zeanah (Ed.), *Handbook of infant mental health* (2nd ed., pp. 353–368). New York, NY: Guilford Press.

Zeanah, C. H., & Emde, R. N. (1994). Attachment disorders in infancy and childhood. In M. Rutter, E. Taylor, & L. Hersov (Eds.), *Child and adolescent psychiatry: Modern approaches* (pp. 490–504). Cambridge, MA: Blackwell.

Zeanah, C. H., Scheeringa, M. S., Boris, N. W., Heller, S. S., Smyke, A. T., & Trapani, J. (2004). Reactive attachment disorder in maltreated toddlers. *Child Abuse & Neglect, 28,* 877–888.

Zerbe, K. (2008). *Integrated treatment of eating disorders: Beyond the body betrayed.* New York, NY: Norton.

Zisser, A., & Eyberg, S. M. (2010). *Treating oppositional behavior in adolescents using parent-child interaction therapy.* In J. Weisz & A. Kazdin (Eds.), Evidence-based psychotherapies for children and adolescents (2nd ed., pp. 179–193.) New York, NY: Guilford Press.

Zoellner, L. A., Abramowitz, J. S., Moore, S. A., & Slagle, D. M. (2008). Flooding. In W. T. O'Donohue and J. E. Fisher (Eds.), *Cognitive behavior therapy: Applying empirically supported techniques to your practice* (pp. 202–211). Hoboken, NJ: Wiley.

Zuroff, D. C., Kelly, A. C., Leybman, M. J., Blatt, S. J., & Wampold, B. E. (2010). Between-therapist and within-therapist differences in the quality of the therapeutic relationship: Effects on maladjustment and self-critical perfectionism. *Journal of Clinical Psychology, 66,* 681–697.

About the Authors

Linda Seligman received her A.B. degree from Brandeis University, her M.A. degree in guidance and counseling from Teachers College of Columbia University, and her Ph.D. degree in counseling psychology from Columbia University. She was an author, researcher, educator, and practicing psychologist and counselor. All those roles are reflected in the research, discussion, and examples presented in this book.

Seligman was *professor emeritus* at George Mason University, where she was director of the doctoral program in education and in charge of the Community Agency Counseling Program. She also taught at Johns Hopkins, Walden University, and Marymount University. Her many publications include such books as: *Assessment in Developmental Career Counseling, Diagnosis and Treatment Planning in Counseling, Developmental Career Counseling and Assessment, Promoting a Fighting Spirit: Psychotherapy for Cancer Patients, Survivors, and Their Families, Fundamental Skills for Mental Health Professionals, Conceptual Skills for Mental Health Professionals*, and previous editions of this book. She has also published more than eighty book chapters and professional articles.

Seligman was a past president of the Virginia Mental Health Counselors Association and editor of the *Journal of Mental Health Counseling.* She had also served on the editorial boards of the *Journal of Counseling and Development* and the *Virginia Counselors Journal.* She was selected as a Distinguished Professor by George Mason University and, in 1990, was named Researcher of the Year by the American Mental Health Counselors Association, which presented her with the Counselor of the Year Award in 2008.

Lourie W. Reichenberg is licensed as a professional counselor in Virginia, and is certification-eligble in process experiential/emotion focused therapy for couples. She received her B.A. degree in psychology from Michigan State University and her M.A. degree in counseling psychology from Marymount University. She is in private practice in Falls Church, Virginia. Her practice includes people with a broad range of concerns and mental disorders, notably adjustment, mood, and anxiety disorders. Reichenberg has a particular interest in working with people who have lost family members to suicide, people in crisis, and as a part of the treatment team for people with bipolar disorder.

She is the co-author, with Linda Seligman, of *Theories of Counseling and Psychotherapy: Systems, Strategies, and Skills,* and the previous edition of this book. Her chapter on "Grief and Loss" appeared in the textbook *Crisis Intervention and Prevention* and she has edited more than 30 books and monographs on mental health and human resource related topics. In addition to individual and couples counseling, she also provides workshops and educational programs to community governmental and mental health agencies on assessing and preventing suicide risk, and working with families of people with bipolar disorder. She also offers training and supervision to people seeking licensure as counselors, as well as to practicing clinicians, at her private practice in Northern Virginia.

Author Index

Chavira, D. A., 102
Chawla, N., 244, 318
Chemtob, C. M., 120
Chen, T., 455
Cherpitel, C. J., 252
Chevron, E. S., 160
Chhabra, V., 53, 54
Chiapetta, L., 115
Chiappetta, L., 455
Chicz-DeMet, A., 153
Chiu, W. T., 173, 192, 214
Chorpita, B. F., 10, 97, 98
Chou, P., 181
Chou, P. S., 256
Christensen, A., 32
Christenson, G. A., 304
Cicchetti, D., 112, 113, 115, 124
Cimbora, D. M., 79
Ciraulo, D. A., 255, 258
Cisler, R. A., 255, 258
Citrome, L., 427
Ciufa, M., 163
Clark, A. J., 456
Clark, D. M., 225
Clarke, G., 110
Clarke, J. C., 215
Clarke, M., 420
Clarkin, J. F., 20, 31, 374, 375, 401
Clarkin, J., 20
Classen, C., 428, 429, 430
Clayton, A., 288
Clayton, R., 250
Coan, J., 23
Coan, J. A., 372
Coccaro, E. F., 242, 300
Cohan, S. L., 102
Cohen, A. N., 415
Cohen, D. J., 87, 89
Cohen, J. A., 120, 226
Cohen, P., 87, 275, 279, 397
Cohn, D. A., 106
Coie, J., 76
Coker, C. J., 32
Coleman, H. K. L., 16
Coleman, J., 312, 313
Coleman, M. C., 98
Colins, A. B., 220
Collings, S. C. D., 131
Colliver, J. D., 262
Colom, F., 180
Colt, G. H., 454, 455, 460
Colvin, L., 58
COMBINE Study Research Group, 255, 258
Comer, J. S., 445
Compton, W. M., 262
Comtois, K. A., 135
Conduct Problems Prevention Research Group, 76
Conner, K., 181
Conners, C. K., 44, 68, 78
Connolly, M. B., 3
Connors, G. J., 24
Consoli, A. J., 10

Constantino, M. J., 280
Cook, A., 119
Cook, J., 222
Cook, J. E., 448
Cook, R., 162
Coon, D. W., 346
Coonrod, E. E., 60
Coons, E. E., 261
Cooper, Z., 279, 281, 282, 283, 284, 445
Copello, A., 438
Corcoran, C. M., 411
Corluka, L., 325
Cornblatt, B. A., 404
Cort, N., 330
Coryell, W., 170, 172
Coryell, W. H., 173, 182
Cosci, F., 199
Costa, F. M., 260
Costin, C., 274, 275, 277, 280, 283
Cotes, E., 414, 415
Cotting, D. I., 224
Cottone, J., 16
Cottraux, J., 22, 160
Countis, L., 414
Couper, D., 255, 258
Courtois, C. A., 3, 429, 430
Couteur, A., 60
Cowan, C. P., 106
Cowan, P. A., 106
Cowley, D. S., 198, 201, 202, 230, 234
Cox, A., 55, 56, 60, 61, 64
Cox, D. J., 91, 92, 448
Coyle, D., 447
Coyne, J. C., 152, 154
Cozza, S. J., 224
Crabb, R., 243
Craft, L., 41
Crago, M., 17
Craighead, L. W., 276, 277, 279, 281
Craighead, W. E., 32, 156, 159, 160, 164, 167, 173, 175
Cramer, V., 378
Cranford, J. A., 268
Craske, M. G., 196, 198, 200, 201, 237
Craven, M., 321
Crawford, P. B, 275
Cressler, S. O., 252
Crits-Christoph, K., 3, 443
Crits-Christoph, P., 349, 373, 374, 380, 384, 388, 389, 443
Crittenden, P., 337
Crosson-Tower, C., 147
Croudace, T., 408
Crowell, S. E., 370, 371, 372
Cucherat, M., 160
Cuddy-Casey, M., 93
Cujé, B. B., 140, 147
Cullen, B. A. M., 304
Cunningham, C. E., 102
Cunningham, J., 468
Curr, A., 88
Curtain, L., 263
Cusick, L., 244
Cutler, H. C., 147, 420

Subject Index